Your Office

Microsoft® Excel 2016
Comprehensive

Amy Kinser

JACOBSON | KINSER | MORIARITY

PEARSON

Boston   Columbus   Indianapolis   New York   San Francisco

Amsterdam   Cape Town   Dubai   London   Madrid   Milan   Munich   Paris   Montréal   Toronto

Delhi   Mexico City   São Paulo   Sydney   Hong Kong   Seoul   Singapore   Taipei   Tokyo

Editorial Director: Andrew Gilfillan
Senior Editor: Samantha McAfee Lewis
Team Lead, Project Management: Laura Burgess
Project Manager: Anne Garcia
Program Manager: Emily Biberger
Development Editor: Vonda Keator
Editorial Assistant: Michael Campbell
Director of Product Marketing: Maggie Waples
Director of Field Marketing: Leigh Ann Sims
Product Marketing Manager: Kaylee Carlson
Field Marketing Managers: Joanna Sabella & Molly Schmidt
Marketing Assistant: Kelli Fisher

Senior Operations Specialist: Maura Zaldivar-Garcia
Senior Art Director: Diane Ernsberger
Manager, Permissions: Karen Sanatar
Interior and Cover Design: Studio Montage
Cover Photo: Courtesy of Shutterstock® Images
Associate Director of Design: Blair Brown
Product Strategy Manager: Eric Hakanson
Vice President, Product Strategy: Jason Fournier
Digital Product Manager: Zachary Alexander
Media Project Manager, Production: John Cassar
Full-Service Project Management: Cenveo Publisher Services
Composition: Cenveo Publisher Services

Credits and acknowledgments borrowed from other sources and reproduced, with permission, in this textbook appear on appropriate page within text.

Microsoft and/or its respective suppliers make no representations about the suitability of the information contained in the documents and related graphics published as part of the services for any purpose. All such documents and related graphics are provided "as is" without warranty of any kind. Microsoft and/or its respective suppliers hereby disclaim all warranties and conditions with regard to this information, including all warranties and conditions of merchantability, whether express, implied or statutory, fitness for a particular purpose, title and non-infringement. In no event shall Microsoft and/or its respective suppliers be liable for any special, indirect or consequential damages or any damages whatsoever resulting from loss of use, data or profits, whether in an action of contract, negligence or other tortious action, arising out of or in connection with the use or performance of information available from the services.

The documents and related graphics contained herein could include technical inaccuracies or typographical errors. Changes are periodically added to the information herein. Microsoft and/or its respective suppliers may make improvements and/or changes in the product(s) and/or the program(s) described herein at any time.

Microsoft® and Windows® are registered trademarks of the Microsoft Corporation in the U.S.A. and other countries. This book is not sponsored or endorsed by or affiliated with the Microsoft Corporation.

Pearson Education Ltd., London
Pearson Education Singapore, Pte. Ltd
Pearson Education, Canada, Inc.
Pearson Education—Japan
Pearson Education Australia PTY, Limited

Pearson Education North Asia Ltd., Hong Kong
Pearson Educación de Mexico, S.A. de C.V.
Pearson Education Malaysia, Pte. Ltd.

Library of Congress Cataloging-in-Publication Data available upon request

5   17
ISBN-10: 0-13-447956-4
ISBN-13: 978-0-13-447956-9

Dedications

I dedicate this series to my Kinser Boyz for their unwavering love, support, and patience; to my parents and sister for their love; to my students for inspiring me; to Sam for believing in me; and to the instructors I hope this series will inspire!

Amy S. Kinser

I dedicate this book to the three most imaginative, exciting, and encouraging pages in my book of life; Paige, Emma, and Jerra!

Kristyn A. Jacobson

For my wife, Amy, and our two boys, Matt and Aidan. I cannot thank them enough for their support, love, and endless inspiration.

J. Eric Kinser

I dedicate this book to my beautiful and amazing wife, April. Without her support and understanding, this would not have been possible. Also, to my wonderful son, Patton, whose strength to overcome so many obstacles in his life, inspires me to continue to do my best work.

Brant Moriarity

About the Authors

Amy S. Kinser, Esq., Series Editor

Amy holds a B.A. degree in Chemistry with a Business minor from Indiana University, and a J.D. from the Maurer School of Law, also at Indiana University. After working as an environmental chemist, starting her own technology consulting company, and practicing intellectual property law, she has spent the past 15 years teaching technology at the Kelley School of Business in Bloomington, Indiana. Currently, she serves as the Director of Computer Skills and Senior Lecturer at the Kelley School of Business at Indiana University. She also loves spending time with her two sons, Aidan and J. Matthew, and her husband J. Eric.

Kristyn A. Jacobson

Kristyn holds an M.S. in Education from the University of Wisconsin-La Crosse and a B.S. in Business Education from the University of Wisconsin-Eau Claire. She has been a faculty member and department chair of the Business Technology department at Madison College in Madison, Wisconsin for over 14 years. She also serves as the curriculum coordinator for Microsoft Excel beginning, intermediate, and advanced level courses for the college. As well as teaching, Kristyn provides training to businesses on the Microsoft Office Suite including MS Project, project management, customer service, personal productivity, and time management. Prior to teaching at Madison College, she taught at a business college in Des Moines, Iowa where she helped implement their online learning program while also teaching traditional business courses.

J. Eric Kinser

Eric Kinser received his B.S. degree in Biology from Indiana University and his M.S. in Counseling and Education from the Indiana School of Education. He has worked in the medical field and in higher education as a technology and decision support specialist. He is currently a senior lecturer in the Operations and Decision Technology Department at the Kelley School of Business at Indiana University. When not teaching he enjoys experimenting with new technologies, traveling, and hiking with his family.

Brant Moriarity

Brant P. Moriarity earned a B.A. in Religious Studies/Philosophy and a M.S. in Information Systems at Indiana University. He is a Senior Lecturer at the Indiana University's Kelley School of Business where he teaches topics such as data management and analysis, as well as the strategic use of Information Systems in business. He is also the founder of Beats Per Minute Technologies, LLC, bringing the benefits of business analytics to small businesses and non-profit organizations.

Brief Contents

Contents

Contents   ix

EXCEL BUSINESS UNIT 7   687

Acknowledgments

The *Your Office* team would like to thank the following reviewers who have invested time and energy to help shape this series from the very beginning, providing us with invaluable feedback through their comments, suggestions, and constructive criticism.

We'd like to thank all of our conscientious reviewers, including those who contributed to our previous editions:

Sven Aelterman
Troy University

Nitin Aggarwal
San Jose State University

Heather Albinger
Waukesha County Technical College

Angel Alexander
Piedmont Technical College

Melody Alexander
Ball State University

Karen Allen
Community College of Rhode Island

Maureen Allen
Elon University

Wilma Andrews
Virginia Commonwealth University

Mazhar Anik
Owens Community College

David Antol
Harford Community College

Kirk Atkinson
Western Kentucky University

Barbara Baker
Indiana Wesleyan University

Kristi Berg
Minot State University

Kavuri Bharath
Old Dominion University

Ann Blackman
Parkland College

Jeanann Boyce
Montgomery College

Lynn Brooks
Tyler Junior College

Cheryl Brown
Delgado Community College West Bank Campus

Bonnie Buchanan
Central Ohio Technical College

Peggy Burrus
Red Rocks Community College

Richard Cacace
Pensacola State College

Margo Chaney
Carroll Community College

Shanan Chappell
College of the Albemarle, North Carolina

Kuan-Chou Chen
Purdue University, Calumet

David Childress
Ashland Community and Technical College

Keh-Wen Chuang
Purdue University North Central

Suzanne Clayton
Drake University

Amy Clubb
Portland Community College

Bruce Collins
Davenport University

Linda Collins
Mesa Community College

Margaret Cooksey
Tallahassee Community College

Charmayne Cullom
University of Northern Colorado

Christy Culver
Marion Technical College

Juliana Cypert
Tarrant County College

Harold Davis
Southeastern Louisiana University

Jeff Davis
Jamestown Community College

Jennifer Day
Sinclair Community College

Anna Degtyareva
Mt. San Antonio College

Beth Deinert
Southeast Community College

Kathleen DeNisco
Erie Community College

Donald Dershem
Mountain View College

Sallie Dodson
Radford University

Joseph F. Domagala
Duquesne University

Bambi Edwards
Craven Community College

Elaine Emanuel
Mt. San Antonio College

Diane Endres
Ancilla College

Nancy Evans
Indiana University, Purdue University, Indianapolis

Christa Fairman
Arizona Western College

Marni Ferner
University of North Carolina, Wilmington

Paula Fisher
Central New Mexico Community College

Linda Fried
University of Colorado, Denver

Diana Friedman
Riverside Community College

Susan Fry
Boise State University

Virginia Fullwood
Texas A&M University, Commerce

Janos Fustos
Metropolitan State College of Denver

John Fyfe
University of Illinois at Chicago

Saiid Ganjalizadeh
The Catholic University of America

Randolph Garvin
Tyler Junior College

Diane Glowacki
Tarrant County College

Jerome Gonnella
Northern Kentucky University

Lorie Goodgine
Tennessee Technology Center in Paris

Connie Grimes
Morehead State University

Debbie Gross
Ohio State University

Babita Gupta
California State University, Monterey Bay

Lewis Hall
Riverside City College

Jane Hammer
Valley City State University

Marie Hartlein
Montgomery County Community College

Darren Hayes
Pace University

Paul Hayes
Eastern New Mexico University

Mary Hedberg
Johnson County Community College

Lynda Henrie
LDS Business College

Deedee Herrera
Dodge City Community College

Marilyn Hibbert
Salt Lake Community College

Jan Hime
University of Nebraska, Lincoln

Cheryl Hinds
Norfolk State University

Mary Kay Hinkson
Fox Valley Technical College

Margaret Hohly
Cerritos College

Brian Holbert
Spring Hill College

Susan Holland
Southeast Community College

Anita Hollander
University of Tennessee, Knoxville

Emily Holliday
Campbell University

Stacy Hollins
St. Louis Community College Florissant Valley

Mike Horn
State University of New York, Geneseo

Christie Hovey
Lincoln Land Community College

Margaret Hvatum
St. Louis Community College Meramec

Jean Insinga
Middlesex Community College

Kristyn Jacobson
Madison College

Jon (Sean) Jasperson
Texas A&M University

Glen Jenewein
Kaplan University

Gina Jerry
Santa Monica College

Dana Johnson
North Dakota State University

Mary Johnson
Mt. San Antonio College

Linda Johnsonius
Murray State University

Carla Jones
Middle Tennessee State University

Susan Jones
Utah State University

Nenad Jukic
Loyola University, Chicago

Sali Kaceli
Philadelphia Biblical University

Sue Kanda
Baker College of Auburn Hills

Robert Kansa
Macomb Community College

Susumu Kasai
Salt Lake Community College

Linda Kavanaugh
Robert Morris University

Debby Keen
University of Kentucky

Mike Kelly
Community College of Rhode Island

Melody Kiang
California State University, Long Beach

Lori Kielty
College of Central Florida

Richard Kirk
Pensacola State College

Dawn Konicek
Blackhawk Tech

John Kucharczuk
Centennial College

David Largent
Ball State University

Frank Lee
Fairmont State University

Luis Leon
The University of Tennessee at Chattanooga

Freda Leonard
Delgado Community College

Julie Lewis
Baker College, Allen Park

Suhong Li
Bryant Unversity

Renee Lightner
Florida State College

John Lombardi
South University

Rhonda Lucas
Spring Hill College

Adriana Lumpkin
Midland College

Lynne Lyon
Durham College

Nicole Lytle
California State University, San Bernardino

Donna Madsen
Kirkwood Community College

Susan Maggio
Community College of Baltimore County

Michelle Mallon
Ohio State University

Kim Manning
Tallahassee Community College

Paul Martin
Harrisburg Area Community College

Cheryl Martucci
Diablo Valley College

Sebena Masline
Florida State College of Jacksonville

Sherry Massoni
Harford Community College

Lee McClain
Western Washington University

Sandra McCormack
Monroe Community College

Sue McCrory
Missouri State University

Barbara Miller
University of Notre Dame

Johnette Moody
Arkansas Tech University

Michael O. Moorman
Saint Leo University

Kathleen Morris
University of Alabama

Alysse Morton
Westminster College

Elobaid Muna
University of Maryland Eastern Shore

Jackie Myers
Sinclair Community College

Russell Myers
El Paso Community College

Bernie Negrete
Cerritos College

Melissa Nemeth
Indiana University, Purdue University, Indianapolis

Jennifer Nightingale
Duquesne University

Kathie O'Brien
North Idaho College

Michael Ogawa
University of Hawaii

Janet Olfert
North Dakota State University

Rene Pack
Arizona Western College

Patsy Parker
Southwest Oklahoma State Unversity

Laurie Patterson
University of North Carolina, Wilmington

Alicia Pearlman
Baker College

Diane Perreault
Sierra College and California State University, Sacramento

Theresa Phinney
Texas A&M University

Vickie Pickett
Midland College

Marcia Polanis
Forsyth Technical Community College

Rose Pollard
Southeast Community College

Stephen Pomeroy
Norwich University

Leonard Presby
William Paterson University

Donna Reavis
Delta Career Education

Eris Reddoch
Pensacola State College

James Reddoch
Pensacola State College

Michael Redmond
La Salle University

Terri Rentfro
John A. Logan College

Vicki Robertson
Southwest Tennessee Community College

Jennifer Robinson
Trident Technical College

Dianne Ross
University of Louisiana at Lafayette

Ann Rowlette
Liberty University

Amy Rutledge
Oakland University

Candace Ryder
Colorado State University

Joann Segovia
Winona State University

Eileen Shifflett
James Madison University

Sandeep Shiva
Old Dominion University

Robert Sindt
Johnson County Community College

Cindi Smatt
Texas A&M University

Edward Souza
Hawaii Pacific University

Nora Spencer
Fullerton College

Alicia Stonesifer
La Salle University

Jenny Lee Svelund
University of Utah

Cheryl Sypniewski
Macomb Community College

Arta Szathmary
Bucks County Community College

Nasser Tadayon
Southern Utah University

Asela Thomason
California State University Long Beach

Nicole Thompson
Carteret Community College

Terri Tiedeman
Southeast Community College, Nebraska

Lewis Todd
Belhaven University

Barb Tollinger
Sinclair Community College

Allen Truell
Ball State University

Erhan Uskup
Houston Community College

Lucia Vanderpool
Baptist College of Health Sciences

Michelle Vlaich-Lee
Greenville Technical College

Barry Walker
Monroe Community College

Rosalyn Warren
Enterprise State Community College

Sonia Washington
Prince George's Community College

Eric Weinstein
Suffolk County Community College

Jill Weiss
Florida International University

Lorna Wells
Salt Lake Community College

Rosalie Westerberg
Clover Park Technical College

Clemetee Whaley
Southwest Tennessee Community College

Kenneth Whitten
Florida State College of Jacksonville

MaryLou Wilson
Piedmont Technical College

John Windsor
University of North Texas

Kathy Winters
University of Tennessee, Chattanooga

Nancy Woolridge
Fullerton College

Jensen Zhao
Ball State University

Martha Zimmer
University of Evansville

Molly Zimmer
University of Evansville

Mary Anne Zlotow
College of DuPage

Matthew Zullo
Wake Technical Community College

Additionally, we'd like to thank our MyITLab team for their review and collaboration with our text authors:

LeeAnn Bates
MyITLab content author

Jennifer Hurley
MyITLab content author

Becca Lowe
Media Producer

Ralph Moore
MyITLab content author

Jerri Williams
MyITLab content author

Preface

Real World Problem Solving for Business and Beyond

The *Your Office* series provides the foundation for students to learn real world problem solving for use in business and beyond. Students are exposed to hands-on technical content that is woven into realistic business scenarios and focuses on using Microsoft Office as a decision-making tool.

Real world business exposure is a competitive advantage.

The series features a unique running business scenario—the Painted Paradise Resort & Spa—that connects all of the cases together and exposes students to using Microsoft Office to solve problems relating to business areas such as finance and accounting, production and operations, sales and marketing, and more. Look for the icons identifying the business application of each case.

Active learning occurs in context.

Each chapter introduces a realistic business case for students to complete via hands-on steps that are easily identified in blue-shaded boxes. Each blue box teaches a skill and comes complete with video, interactive, and live auto-graded support with automatic feedback.

Coursework that is relevant to students and their future careers.

Real World Advice, Real World Interview Videos, and Real World Success Stories are woven throughout the text and in the student resources. These share how former students use the Microsoft Office concepts they learned in this class and had success in a variety of careers.

Outcomes matter.

Whether it's getting a good grade in this course, learning how to use Excel to be successful in other courses, or learning business skills that will support success in a future job, every student has an outcome in mind. And outcomes matter. That is why we added a Business Unit opener to focus on the outcomes students will achieve by working through the cases and content of each chapter as well as the Capstone at the end of each unit.

No matter what career students may choose to pursue in life, this series will give them the foundation to succeed. And as they learn these valuable problem-solving and decision-making skills while becoming proficient in using Microsoft Office as a tool, they will achieve their intended outcomes, making a positive impact on their lives.

Key Features

The **Outcomes focus** allows students and instructors to focus on higher-level learning goals and how those can be achieved through particular objectives and skills.

- **Outcomes** are written at the course level and the business unit level.
- **Chapter Objectives list** identifies the learning objectives to be achieved as students work through the chapter. Page numbers are included for easy reference. These are revisited in the Concepts Check at the end of the chapter.
- **MOS Certification Guide** for instructors and students directs anyone interested in prepping for the MOS exam to the specific series resources to find all content required for the test.

Business Application Icons

Customer Service

Finance & Accounting

General Business

Human Resources

Information Technology

Production & Operations

Sales & Marketing

Research & Development

Real World Interview Video

Blue Box Videos

Soft Skills

The **real world focus** reminds students that what they are learning is practical and useful the minute they leave the classroom.

- **Real World Success** features in the chapter opener share anecdotes from real former students, describing how knowledge of Office has helped them be successful in their lives.
- **Real World Advice boxes** offer notes on best practices for general use of important Office skills. The goal is to advise students as a manager might in a future job.
- **Business Application icons** appear with every case in the text and clearly identify which business application students are being exposed to (finance, marketing, operations, etc.).
- **Real World Interview Video icons** appear with the Real World Success story in the business unit. Each interview features a real businessperson discussing how he or she actually uses the skills in the chapter on a day-to-day basis.

Features for active learning help students learn by doing and immerse them in the business world using Microsoft Office.

- **Blue boxes** represent the hands-on portion of the chapter and help students quickly identify what steps they need to take to complete the chapter Prepare Case. This material is easily distinguishable from explanatory text by the blue-shaded background.
- **Starting and ending files** appear before every case in the text. Starting files identify exactly which student data files are needed to complete each case. Ending files are provided to show students the naming conventions they should use when saving their files. Each file icon is color coded by application.
- **Side Note** conveys a brief tip or piece of information aligned visually with a step in the chapter, quickly providing key information to students completing that particular step.
- **Consider This** offers critical thinking questions and topics for discussion, set apart as a boxed feature, allowing students to step back from the project and think about the application of what they are learning and how these concepts might be used in the future.
- **Soft Skills icons** appear with other boxed features and identify specific places where students are being exposed to lessons on soft skills.

Study aids help students review and retain the material so they can recall it at a moment's notice.

- **Quick Reference boxes** summarize generic or alternative instructions on how to accomplish a task. This feature enables students to quickly find important skills.
- **Concept Check** review questions, which appear at the end of the chapter, require students to demonstrate their understanding of the objectives.
- **Visual Summary** offers a review of the objectives learned in the chapter using images from the completed solution file, mapped to the chapter objectives with callouts and page references, so students can easily find the section of text to refer to for a refresher.
- **MyITLab™ icons** identify which cases from the book match those in MyITLab™.
- **Blue Box Video icons** appear with each Active Text box and identify the brief video, demonstrating how students should complete that portion of the Prepare Case.

MyITLab® MyITLab®
Grader

Extensive cases allow students to progress from a basic understanding of Office through to proficiency.

- **Chapters all conclude with Practice, Problem Solve, and Perform Cases** to allow full mastery at the chapter level. Alternative versions of these cases are available in Instructor Resources.
- **Business Unit Capstones all include More Practice, Problem Solve, and Perform Cases** that require students to synthesize objectives from the two previous chapters to extend their mastery of the content. Alternative versions of these cases are available in Instructor Resources.
- **More Grader Projects** are offered with this edition, including Prepare cases as well as Problem Solve cases at both the chapter and business unit capstone levels.

Resources

Instructor Resources

The Instructor's Resource Center, available at www.pearsonhighered.com/irc includes the following:

- AACSB mapping that identifies which cases and exercises in the text prepare for AACSB certification
- Business application mapping, which provides an easy-to-filter way of finding the cases and examples to help highlight whichever business application is of most interest
- Annotated Solution Files with Scorecards, which assist with grading the Prepare, Practice, Problem Solve, and Perform cases
- Data and solution files
- Rubrics for Perform cases in Microsoft Word format, which enable instructors to easily grade open-ended assignments with no definite solution
- PowerPoint presentations with notes for each chapter
- Lesson plans that provide a detailed blueprint to achieve chapter learning objectives and outcomes and best use the unique structure of the business units
- Complete test bank, also available in TestGen format
- Syllabus templates for 8-week, 12-week, and 16-week courses
- Additional Practice, Problem Solve, and Perform cases to provide variety and choice in exercises at both the chapter and business unit levels
- Scripted Lectures, which provide instructors with a lecture outline that mirrors the chapter Prepare case

Student Resources

Student Data Files

Access the student data files needed to complete the cases in this textbook at www.pearsonhighered.com/youroffice.

Available in MyITLab

- **Blue Box Videos** walk students through the activity in each blue box, illustrating how to perform a task while explaining the business context of the case.
- **Real World Interview Videos** introduce students to real professionals discussing how they use Microsoft Office in their daily work. These videos provide real world relevance to answer the question "Why is this content important to me?" There are videos in each Business Unit.
- **Audio PowerPoints** provide a lecture review of the chapter content and include narration.
- **Grader Projects** provide live-in-the-application training and assessment with immediate feedback and detailed reports for students to practice, learn, and remediate.
- **eText** is available in some MyITLab courses.

MyITLab for Office 2016 is a solution designed by professors for professors that allows easy delivery of Office courses with defensible assessment and outcomes-based training. The new **Your Office 2016** system will seamlessly integrate online assessment, training, and projects with MyITLab for Microsoft Office 2016!

Dear Students,

If you want an edge over the competition, make it personal. Whether you love sports, travel, the stock market, or ballet, your passion is personal to you. Capitalizing on your passion leads to success. You live in a global marketplace, and your competition is global. The honors students in China exceed the total number of students in North America. Skills can help set you apart, but passion will make you stand above. *Your Office* is the tool to harness your passion's true potential.

In prior generations, personalization in a professional setting was discouraged. You had a "work" life and a "home" life. As the Series Editor, I write to you about the vision for *Your Office* from my laptop, on my couch, in the middle of the night when inspiration struck me. My classroom and living room are my office. Life has changed from generations before us.

So, let's get personal. My degrees are not in technology, but chemistry and law. I helped put myself through school by working full time in various jobs, including a successful technology consulting business that continues today. My generation did not grow up with computers, but I did. My father was a network administrator for the military. So, I was learning to program in Basic before anyone had played Nintendo's Duck Hunt or Tetris. Technology has always been one of my passions from a young age. In fact, I now tell my husband: don't buy me jewelry for my birthday, buy me the latest gadget on the market!

In my first law position, I was known as the Office guru to the extent that no one gave me a law assignment for the first two months. Once I submitted the assignment, my supervisor remarked, "Wow, you don't just know how to leverage technology, but you really know the law too." I can tell you novel-sized stories from countless prior students in countless industries who gained an edge from using Office as a tool. Bringing technology to your passion makes you well rounded and a cut above the rest, no matter the industry or position.

I am most passionate about teaching, in particular teaching technology. I come from many generations of teachers, including my mother who is a kindergarten teacher. For over 12 years, I have found my dream job passing on my passion for teaching, technology, law, science, music, and life in general at the Kelley School of Business at Indiana University. I have tried to pass on the key to engaging passion to my students. I have helped them see what differentiates them from all the other bright students vying for the same jobs.

Microsoft Office is a tool. All of your competition will have learned Microsoft Office to some degree or another. Some will have learned it to an advanced level. Knowing Microsoft Office is important, but it is also fundamental. Without it, you will not be considered for a position.

Today, you step into your first of many future roles bringing Microsoft Office to your dream job working for Painted Paradise Resort & Spa. You will delve into the business side of the resort and learn how to use *Your Office* to maximum benefit.

Don't let the context of a business fool you. If you don't think of yourself as a business person, you have no need to worry. Whether you realize it or not, everything is business. If you want to be a nurse, you are entering the health care industry. If you want to be a football player in the NFL, you are entering the business of sports as entertainment. In fact, if you want to be a stay-at-home parent, you are entering the business of a family household where *Your Office* still gives you an advantage. For example, you will be able to prepare a budget in Excel and analyze what you need to do to afford a trip to Disney World!

At Painted Paradise Resort & Spa, you will learn how to make Office yours through four learning levels designed to maximize your understanding. You will Prepare, Practice, and Problem Solve your tasks. Then, you will astound when you Perform your new talents. You will be challenged through Consider This questions and gain insight through Real World Advice.

There is something more. You want success in what you are passionate about in your life. It is personal for you. In this position at Painted Paradise Resort & Spa, you will gain your personal competitive advantage that will stay with you for the rest of your life—*Your Office*.

Sincerely,

Amy Kinser

Series Editor

Painted Paradise

RESORT & SPA

Welcome to the Team!

Welcome to your new office at Painted Paradise Resort & Spa, where we specialize in painting perfect getaways. As the Chief Technology Officer, I am excited to have staff dedicated to the Microsoft Office integration between all the areas of the resort. Our team is passionate about our paradise, and I hope you find this to be your dream position here!

Painted Paradise is a resort and spa in New Mexico catering to business people, romantics, families, and anyone who just needs to get away. Inside our resort are many distinct areas. Many of these areas operate as businesses in their own right but must integrate with the other areas of the resort. The main areas of the resort are as follows.

- The **Hotel** is overseen by our Chief Executive Officer, William Mattingly, and is at the core of our business. The hotel offers a variety of accommodations, ranging from individual rooms to a grand villa suite. Further, the hotel offers packages including spa, golf, and special events.

  Room rates vary according to size, season, demand, and discount. The hotel has discounts for typical groups, such as AARP. The hotel also has a loyalty program where guests can earn free nights based on frequency of visits. Guests may charge anything from the resort to the room.

- **Red Bluff Golf Course** is a private world-class golf course and pro shop. The golf course has services such as golf lessons from the famous golf pro John Schilling and playing packages. Also, the golf course attracts local residents. This requires variety in pricing schemes to accommodate both local and hotel guests. The pro shop sells many retail items online.

  The golf course can also be reserved for special events and tournaments. These special events can be in conjunction with a wedding, conference, meetings, or other events covered by the event planning and catering area of the resort.

- **Turquoise Oasis Spa** is a full-service spa. Spa services include haircuts, pedicures, massages, facials, body wraps, waxing, and various other spa services— typical to exotic. Further, the spa offers private consultation, weight training (in the fitness center), a water bar, meditation areas, and steam rooms. Spa services are offered both in the spa and in the resort guest's room.

  Turquoise Oasis Spa uses top-of-the-line products and some house-brand products. The retail side offers products ranging from candles to age-defying home treatments. These products can also be purchased online. Many of the hotel guests who fall in love with the house-brand soaps, lotions, candles, and other items appreciate being able to buy more at any time.

  The spa offers a multitude of packages including special hotel room packages that include spa treatments. Local residents also use the spa. So, the spa guests are not limited to hotel guests. Thus, the packages also include pricing attractive to the local community.

- **Painted Treasures Gift Shop** has an array of items available for purchase, from toiletries to clothes to presents for loved ones back home including a healthy section of kids' toys for traveling business people. The gift shop sells a small sampling from the spa, golf course pro shop, and local New Mexico culture. The gift shop also has a small section of snacks and drinks. The gift shop has numerous part-time employees including students from the local college.

- The **Event Planning & Catering** area is central to attracting customers to the resort. From weddings to conferences, the resort is a popular destination. The resort has a substantial number of staff dedicated to planning, coordinating, setting up, catering, and maintaining these events. The resort has several facilities that can accommodate large groups. Packages and prices vary by size, room, and other services such as catering. Further, the Event Planning & Catering team works closely with local vendors for floral decorations, photography, and other event or wedding typical needs. However, all catering must go through the resort (no outside catering permitted). Lastly, the resort stocks several choices of decorations, table arrangements, and centerpieces. These range from professional, simple, themed, and luxurious.

- **Indigo5** and the **Silver Moon Lounge**, a world-class restaurant and lounge that is overseen by the well-known Chef Robin Sanchez. The cuisine is balanced and modern. From steaks to pasta to local southwestern meals, Indigo5 attracts local patrons in addition to resort guests. While the catering function is separate from the restaurant—though menu items may be shared—the restaurant does support all room service for the resort. The resort also has smaller food venues onsite such as the Terra Cotta Brew coffee shop in the lobby.

Currently, these areas are using Office to various degrees. In some areas, paper and pencil are still used for most business functions. Others have been lucky enough to have some technology savvy team members start Microsoft Office Solutions.

Using your skills, I am confident that you can help us integrate and use Microsoft Office on a whole new level! I hope you are excited to call Painted Paradise Resort & Spa *Your Office*.

Looking forward to working with you more closely!

Aidan Matthews
Aidan Matthews
Chief Technology Officer

Common Features of Microsoft Office 2016

Chapter 1 | UNDERSTANDING THE COMMON FEATURES OF MICROSOFT OFFICE

Prepare Case

  Sales & Marketing  General Business

Painted Paradise Resort & Spa Employee Training Preparation

The gift shop at the Painted Paradise Resort & Spa has an array of items available for purchase, from toiletries to clothes to souvenirs for loved ones back home. There are numerous part-time employees, including students from the local college. The gift shop frequently holds training luncheons for new employees. Your first assignment will be to prepare three documents for a meeting with your manager, Susan Brock: a starting file for meeting minutes, the agenda for the meeting, and an Excel budget. To complete this task, you need to understand and work with the common features in the Microsoft Office Suite.

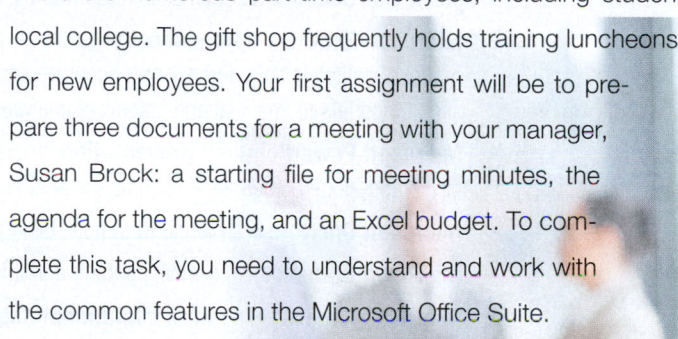

Michaeljung/Shutterstock

Student data files needed for this chapter:

 Blank Word document

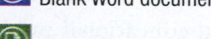 Blank Excel workbook

 cf01ch01Agenda.docx

 cf01ch01Logo.jpg

You will save your files as:

 cf01ch01Minutes_LastFirst.docx

 cf01ch01Agenda_LastFirst.docx

 cf01ch01Budget_LastFirst.xlsx

 cf01ch01Budget_LastFirst.pdf

Working with the Office Interface

When you walk into a grocery store, you usually know what you are going to find and that items are likely to be in approximately the same location, regardless of which store you are visiting. The first items you usually see are the fresh fruits and vegetables, while the frozen foods are typically near the end of the store. This similarity among stores creates a comfortable and welcoming experience for the shopper, even if the shopper has never been in that particular store. The brands may be different, but the food types are the same. Canned corn is canned corn.

Microsoft Office was designed to create that same level of familiarity and comfort with its ribbons, features, and functions. Each application has an appearance or user interface that is similar to the appearance or interface of the other applications. The interface for Microsoft Office 2016 has introduced new color schemes, the default being a colorful appearance. The new look is minimalist; even the ribbon is hidden by default — unless a setting from a prior version of Office carries into your Office 2016 installation. In this section, you will learn to navigate and use the Microsoft Office interface.

Microsoft Office Suite and Different Versions

Microsoft Office 2016 is a suite of productivity applications or programs that are available for purchase separately or as a package. The exact applications available depend on the package installed. Office 2016 is available in greater variety and flexibility than ever before.

QUICK REFERENCE	Programs in Office 2016

- **Microsoft Word** is a word-processing program. This application can be used to create, edit, and format **documents** such as letters, memos, reports, brochures, resumes, and flyers.
- **Microsoft Excel** is a **spreadsheet** program — a two-dimensional grid that can be used to model quantitative data and perform accurate and rapid calculations with results ranging from simple budgets to financial and statistical analyses.
- **Microsoft PowerPoint** is a **presentation** program — an oral performance aid that uses slides or a stand-alone presentation such as those at kiosks.
- **Microsoft OneNote** is a planner and note-taking program.
- **Microsoft Outlook** is an e-mail, contact, and information management program.
- **Microsoft Access** is known as a **relational database** — or three-dimensional database software — because it is able to connect data in separate tables, allowing you to make the most efficient storage of your data.
- **Microsoft Publisher** is a desktop publishing program that offers professional tools and templates to help communicate a message easily in a variety of publication types, saving time and money while creating a polished and finished look.
- **Microsoft Skype for Business** — formerly known as Lync — is a unified communication platform.

With Office 2016 and Windows 10, Microsoft has embraced the concept of flexible versions for multiple platforms such as Windows Phone, iPads, Android devices, and even a web browser. Different versions of Office have different levels of functionality, but Microsoft has tried to keep the universal user interface as similar as possible.

Microsoft Office 2016 is available in several different suite packages from home to enterprise. This book is written with Microsoft Office 365 ProPlus — other packages do not contain the database program Access. Furthermore, most schools have special educational pricing and versions. You should consult your instructor or institution for further information.

For non-educational consumers, Office 2016 is available in two main pricing schemes. You can purchase Office 2016 the traditional way from a retailer for a one-time fee. You can then install the software on exactly one computer. Alternatively, Office 2016 can be purchased by subscription for a yearly or monthly fee. This version is called Office 365. It is the same product as Office 2016, but it comes with more frequent updates, the ability to be installed on more than one computer, more OneDrive storage space, free minutes in Skype, and several other additional perks. At the time of this writing, the Office 365 version is competitively priced to be less expensive for most people despite the monthly or yearly fee. For the latest in pricing and options, you can visit http://office.microsoft.com.

REAL WORLD ADVICE | **Help, I Have a Mac!**

Traditionally, Office has been available in different versions for Windows and Macs with different functionality, such as the absence of the Access program in the Mac versions. Instead of using the Mac version of Office, two other popular options exist for using Office on a Mac: virtualization and dual boot.

Virtualization of Office on a Mac uses software that mimics Windows in order to run Office. In any major search engine, search for "PC virtualization on Mac" and you will find many software options for emulating a PC on a Mac. While many virtualization programs promise to mimic entirely, there can be some — usually minor — differences.

Dual boot is the ability to choose the operating system on startup. **Bootcamp** is the Mac software that allows the user to decide which operating system — Mac operating system or Windows — to run. When the computer is turned on, the user is given the choice of operating system. Thus, the user can run the Windows version of Office under the Windows operating system.

You should consult your instructor about the policy in your course. Policies on the usage of the Mac operating system vary greatly from course to course and from school to school.

Typically, using Office requires you to have a free Microsoft account. If you are working in a computer lab or enterprise version of Windows 10, you may not need to sign into a Microsoft account to run Office or Windows 10. If you are running Office on a personal computer, you will need to have a Microsoft account. You can create the account when you install Windows 10. If you do not have an account, you need to sign up for one at https://signup.live.com and follow the on-screen instructions. Your first name, last name, and profile image for your Microsoft account will appear in various screens of Windows and Microsoft Office.

Start, Save, and Navigate Office Applications

Each Office application has its own specific application Start screen. From the **application Start screen**, you can select a blank document, workbook, presentation, database, or one of many application-specific templates. Files that have already been created can also be opened from this screen. When existing files are double-clicked from a File Explorer window, the Start screen is not needed and does not open.

Opening Microsoft Word and the Start Screen

Once you start working with these applications, you can have more than one application or more than one instance of the same application open at a time. This means that you can open one file in Word in one window and also open another file in Word in a different window. In this exercise, you will start Microsoft Word so you can create a beginning file for meeting minutes.

 **CF01.01**

To Open Microsoft Word and Use the Start Screen

SIDE NOTE
Windows 10
This book is written for Windows 10. If you are using Windows 8, open your charms, click Search, and then type Word. If using Windows 7, search the Start menu for Word.

a. On the taskbar, click into the **Ask me anything** or **Search the web and Windows** box. Type Word. The search results display. Verify the first result is Word 2016, and then press Enter. Pressing Enter automatically selects the first search result. Microsoft Word opens to the Word Start screen.

Troubleshooting

If Word 2016 is not the first option, you will need to use your mouse to select Word 2016 from the search results.

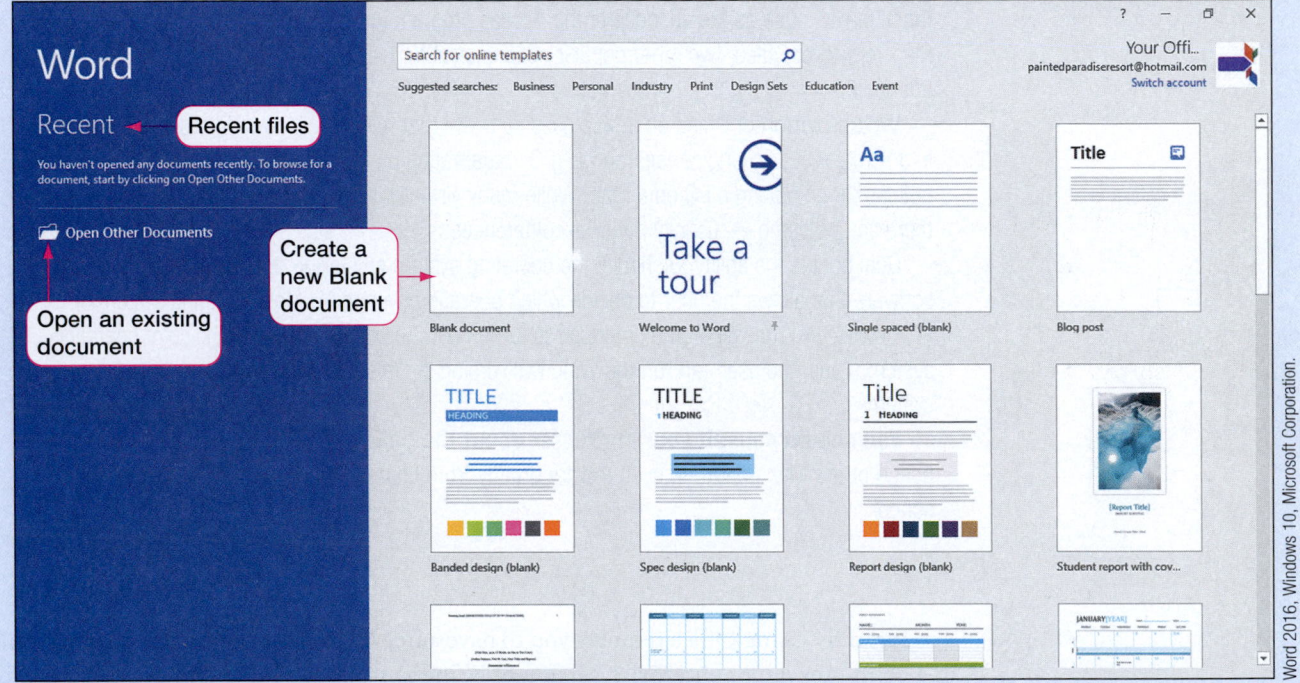

Figure 1 Word Start screen

b. Click **Blank document**. A new Word document opens.

Notice the words Document1 – Word appear on the title bar. This means that the document has not been saved yet. The insertion point is at the beginning of the document.

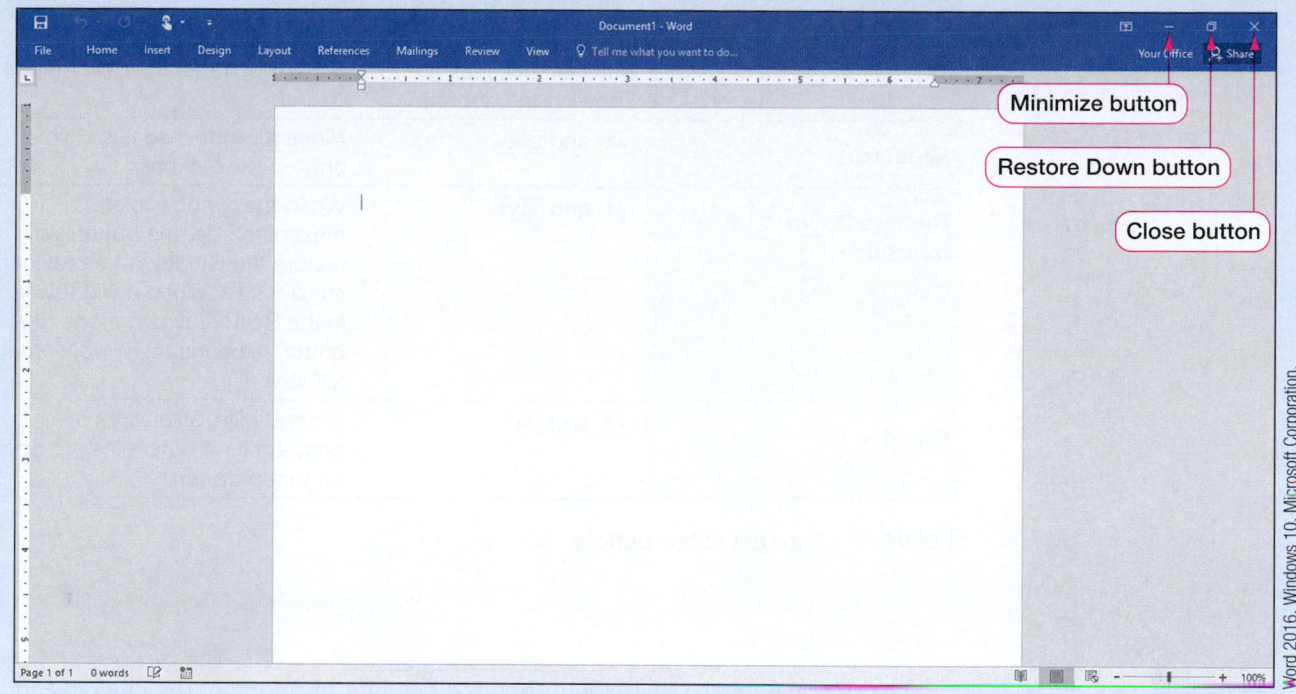

Figure 2 New Word document

Using the Ribbon and Ribbon Display Options

Office has a consistent design and layout that help to make its programs familiar and comfortable to the user. Once you learn to use one Office 2016 program, you can use many of those skills when working with other Office programs. The **ribbon** is the row of tabs across the top of the application. The ribbon display changes according to the screen resolution of your monitor. The figures in this text are set to a screen resolution of 1366×768. When open, the ribbons look like Figure 3.

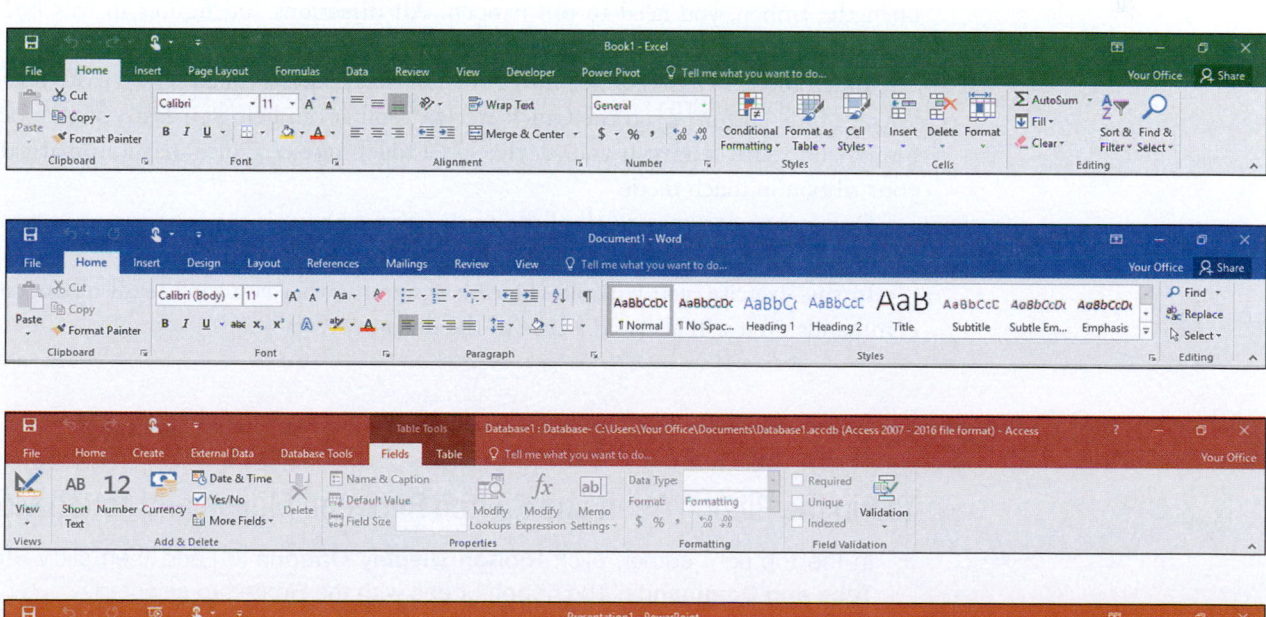

Figure 3 Ribbons of Excel, Word, Access, and PowerPoint

Button	Keyboard Shortcut	Action
Ribbon Display Options ⊞	Ctrl and F1 (toggles between collapsing and showing the ribbon)	Auto-Hide Ribbon, Show Tabs, and Show Tabs and Commands
Minimize −	Alt and Space	Hides a window so it is visible only on the taskbar
Restore Down ⧉ or **Maximize** ◻	Alt and Space	When the window is at its maximum size, the button will restore the window to a previous, smaller size. When a window is in the Restore Down mode, the button expands the window to its full size.
Close ×	Alt and F4	Closes a file; also, exits the program if no other files are open for that program

Table 1 Top right ribbon buttons

The ribbon for each Office application has two tabs in common: the File tab and the Home tab. The File tab is the first tab on the ribbon and is used for file management needs such as saving and printing. The Home tab is the second tab and contains the commands for the most frequently performed activities, such as copying, cutting, and pasting. The commands on these tabs may differ from program to program. Other tabs are program specific, such as the Formulas tab in Excel, the Design tab in Word and PowerPoint, and the Database Tools tab in Access. The ribbon is further subdivided into **groups** — logical groupings of related commands.

By default, the ribbon is hidden. This allows you more room to work with your document rather than having the ribbon take up screen space with buttons and tools. However, hiding the ribbon makes it harder to perform tasks while learning Office. To open the ribbon, you need to pin it open. All directions and figures in this book will assume that the ribbon is pinned open.

Touch mode switches Office into a version that makes a touch screen easy to use. The Touch Mode button 👆 on the Quick Access Toolbar can help you easily switch between mouse and touch modes. If your device has a touch screen, Office may automatically put your ribbon in touch mode.

One feature common to all of the application ribbons is the four buttons that appear in the top right corner of an application title bar as shown in Table 1.

In this exercise, you will pin the ribbon open so that you can see all of the tabs and commands. You will also add a title to the document.

 **CF01.02**

To Pin the Ribbon Open and Switch Between Mouse and Touch Mode

a. In the top right corner, click **Ribbon Display Options** ⊞ and then click **Show Tabs and Commands**. The ribbon opens with the Home tab selected.

Troubleshooting

Does your ribbon looks different? Your ribbon may seem to have condensed or expanded buttons and groups. The most common causes are different screen resolution, auto-detecting touch mode, or a smaller program window. Since the ribbon changes to accommodate the size of the window or screen, buttons can appear as icons without labels, and a group can be condensed into a button that must be clicked to display the group options. So do not worry! All of the same features are on the ribbon and in the same general area.

All of the figures in this book use a screen resolution of **1366 × 768**. Setting your computer to that resolution, if it is available, will minimize this issue. In Windows 10, you can find the screen resolution by right-clicking the desktop, clicking Display settings, and clicking Advanced display settings.

Touch/Mouse Mode in the Quick Access Toolbar

Title bar name for unsaved documents

Ribbon Display Options

Save button

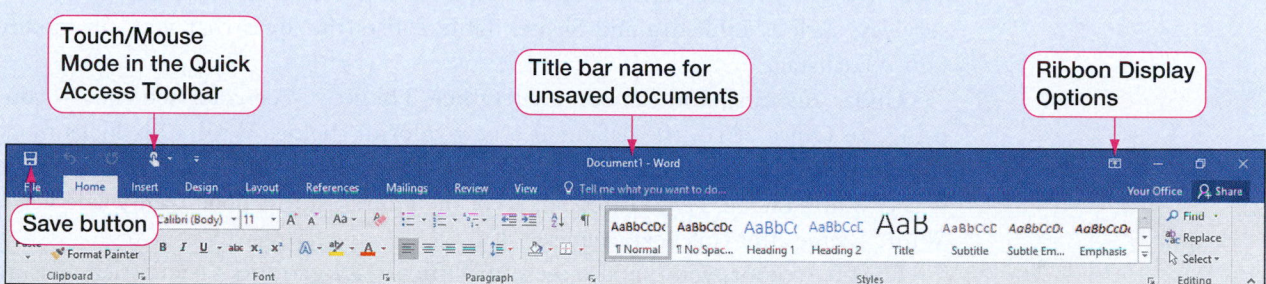

Word 2016, Windows 10, Microsoft Corporation.

Figure 4   Word with ribbon pinned open

b. In the Quick Access Toolbar in the top left corner, click **Touch/Mouse Mode** 👆. Then click **Touch**. If your ribbon does not change, you were already in Touch mode — and you most likely have a device with a touch screen.

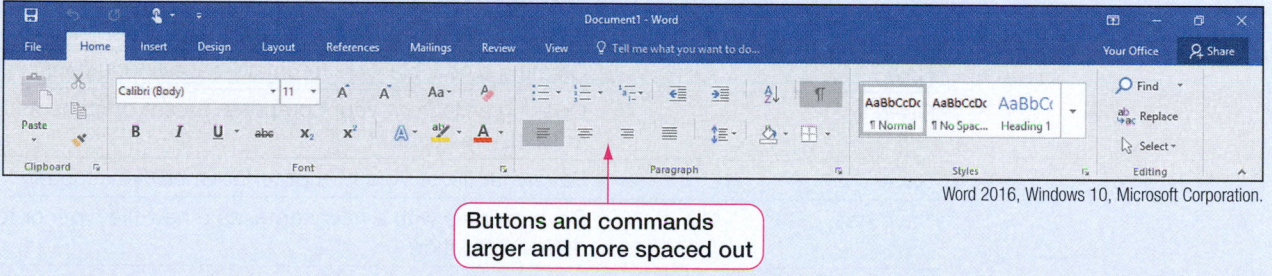

Word 2016, Windows 10, Microsoft Corporation.

Buttons and commands larger and more spaced out

Figure 5   Word ribbon in Touch mode

c. All the figures in this text were made in mouse mode. In the Quick Access Toolbar in the upper left, click **Touch/Mouse Mode** 👆. Then click **Mouse** to ensure that you are in mouse mode.

d. With your insertion point still at the beginning of the document, type Meeting Minutes – Budget Meeting.

Using Office Backstage, Your Account, and Document Properties

Office Backstage provides access to the file-level commands, such as saving a file, creating a new file, opening an existing file, printing a file, and closing a file, as well as program options and account settings. Backstage is accessed via the File tab. Office Backstage includes an area called Account. This enables you to log into your Microsoft account or switch accounts. You can also see a list of connected services and add services, such as LinkedIn and Skype. Table 2 lists the areas that you can modify in Office Backstage.

Under Account, you can see what **Office Theme** — or color scheme — you are using. In Office 2016, the default is a new colorful theme. While this looks modern, the best theme for accessibility for people with vision impairments or color blindness is the White theme. For this reason, all of the figures in this book were made with the White theme after this next exercise.

Under Account, you can also see your **Office Background** — an artistic design in the upper right area of the title bar. Again for accessibility reasons, all the figures in this text were made with No Background. In this exercise, you will look at Backstage for your meeting minutes starting document.

Area	Description
Info	Adding properties, protecting, inspecting, and managing a document.
New	Creating a new blank or template-based document.
Open	Opening a file from your computer, recent documents list, or OneDrive account.
Save	Save your file to your computer or OneDrive account.
Save As	Save your file with a new name, as a new file type, or to a different location.
Print	Preview and print your document.
Share	Share your file by invitation, e-mail, online presentation, or blog post.
Export	Change the file type or create a PDF/XPS document.
Close	Close the file without closing the application.
Account	User and product information, including connected services.
Options	Launches the Application Options dialog box with many options, including advanced options.

Table 2 Office Backstage

 **CF**01.03

To Use Backstage to Set Account Settings and View Document Properties

a. Click the **File** tab and then, in the left pane, click **Info**.

Notice the file properties on the right side of the window. Since you have not saved yet, most of the properties are blank. The properties will appear once the file has been saved.

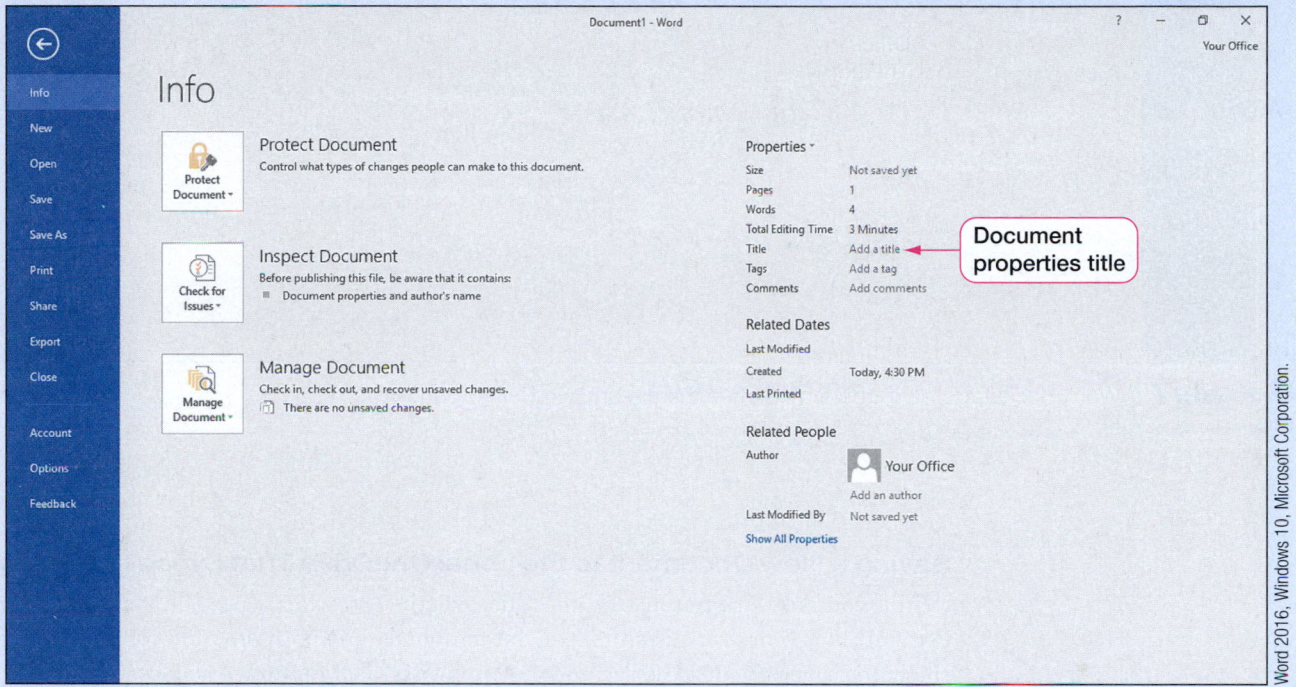

Word 2016, Windows 10, Microsoft Corporation.

Figure 6   Word Backstage, info page

b. In the properties, click **Add a title**, and then type Budget Meeting Minutes LastFirst, using your last and first name.

c. In the left pane, click **Account**.

If your Microsoft account is already connected, you will see your information and links to access and modify your account. If it is not connected, you will see an option to sign in. In a computer lab, you may see something entirely different, depending on your administrator's setup. If desired and needed, you can sign in to your account now.

Notice that you can also check for updates and see your version of Office. As Microsoft updates in between new versions of Office, your version may change the way the interface works slightly from these instructions. This book is written for version 16.0.6001.1033.

d. If you would like your screen to match the figures in this text, ensure that the **Office Background** is set to **No Background** and the **Office Theme** is set to **White**. Leave Backstage open for the next exercise.

The best theme for accessibility for people with vision impairments or color blindness is the White theme and No Background. For this reason, from this point forward all figures in this book were made with the White theme.

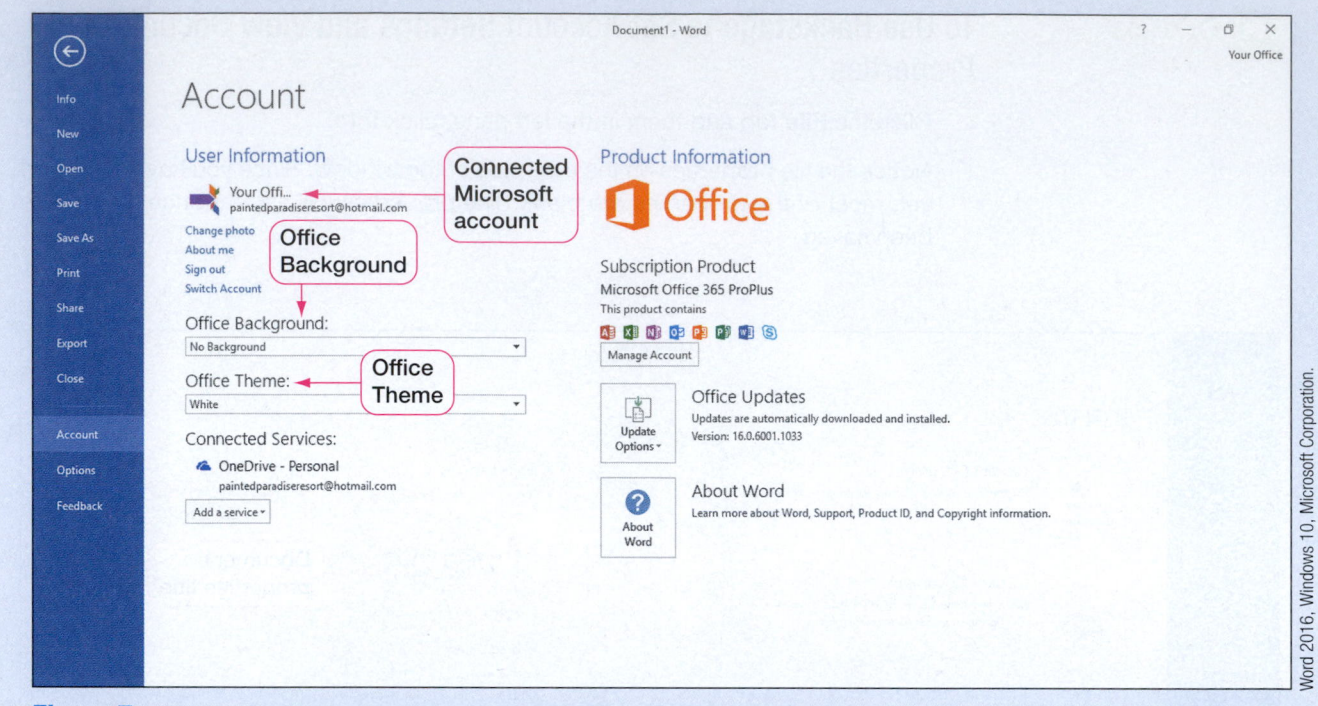

Figure 7 Word Backstage Account name, White theme, and No Background

Saving a New Document to the Local OneDrive That Syncs to the Cloud

While you are working on an Office file, whether creating a new file or modifying an existing file, your work is stored in the temporary memory on your computer, not on the hard drive or your USB flash drive. Any work that you do will be lost if you exit the program, turn off the computer, or experience a power failure or computer crash without you or the program's automatic save function saving your work. To prevent losing your work, you need to save your work and remember to do so frequently — at least every 10 minutes or after adding several changes. That saves you from having to re-create any work you did before the last save.

You can save files to the hard drive, which is located inside the computer; to an external drive, such as a USB flash drive; to a network storage device; or to OneDrive or another cloud storage service. Office has an **AutoRecovery** feature — previously called AutoSave — that will attempt to recover any changes made to a document since your last save if something goes wrong, but this should never be relied upon as a substitute for saving your work manually.

Traditionally, for file storage, files are saved locally on a hard drive or an external storage device such as a USB drive. A **USB drive** is a small, portable storage device — popular for moving files back and forth between a lab, office, and/or home computer. However, USB drives are easily lost, and file versions and backups are usually maintained manually, potentially causing versioning problems.

With Windows 10 and Office 2016, cloud file storage technologies are easier to use than ever. **OneDrive** — Microsoft's cloud storage solution — is fully integrated into File Explorer and Backstage. **Cloud computing** is computing resources, either hardware or software, on remote servers being used by a local computer over the Internet. Apps exist for all of your devices, even Apple and Android devices, that connect to your files on the cloud. Other cloud storage systems also exist, such as Dropbox, Google Drive, and Box.

When you edit a file, your computer or device automatically updates the file in the online storage location. All of the other computers and devices check the online storage for changes and update as needed. Thus, when saving your file, you automatically place a copy online and in all of your synced computers. This creates an online backup if your computer crashes. Additionally, there is no USB drive to lose. File versioning problems are also minimized — in fact, OneDrive by default keeps all versions of your file for you, just in case. Once all applications have been properly set up, you have your files everywhere you want them and shared with exactly who needs them without having multiple copies of files around or e-mailing attachments.

REAL WORLD ADVICE   **Not All Terms of Service Are the Same**

Terms of service for online cloud storage services vary. Some services require you to waive your rights to file content. You really should read the terms of service before signing up for any online service. If you do not, you may not "own" your own files.

Your school's computer lab may or may not be integrated with cloud storage. In this case, you can always log into the cloud storage via a web browser and upload your files. For OneDrive, the URL is http://onedrive.live.com. If you are unsure about your school's computers, ask your instructor.

REAL WORLD ADVICE   **Backing Up to the Cloud**

Best practice still dictates bringing files to important meetings on a physical drive such as a USB drive as backup. Cloud technologies are dependent on an Internet connection. Suppose you show up for a presentation and cannot get to your files because of a poor Internet connection. Your presentation is likely to be a disaster.

The Save As option in Office Backstage gives you direct access to OneDrive, which you can access with your Microsoft account — except Access, which requires you to save locally. With Windows 10, you have a local folder that is directly accessible from the File Explorer and automatically syncs with OneDrive. Thus, you can sync Access files in the local syncing OneDrive folder.

When you save a file, you must provide a name. A file name includes the name you specify and a **file extension** — a few letters that come after the period in the name — assigned by the Office program to indicate the file type. The file extension may or may not be visible, depending on your computer settings. You can check your computer's setting in the File Explorer window under the View tab in the Show/Hide group. The check box for File name extensions should be checked to see file extensions, as shown in Figure 8. Each Office program adds a period and a file extension after the file name to identify the program in which that file was created. Table 3 shows the common default file extensions for Office.

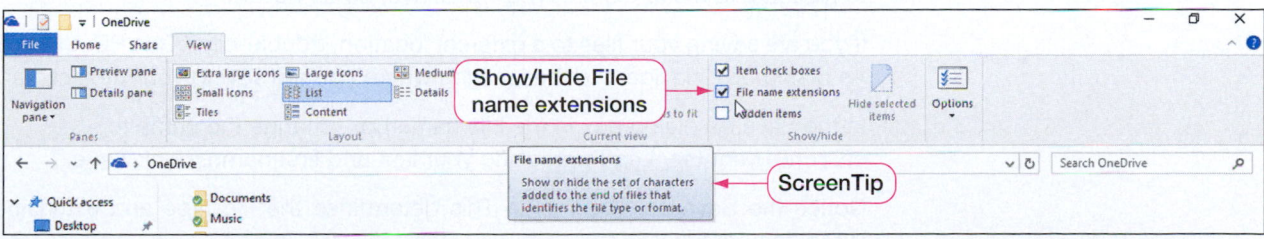

Figure 8   File Explorer extension setting

Word 2016, Windows 10, Microsoft Corporation.

Application	Extension
Microsoft Word 2016	.docx
Microsoft Excel 2016	.xlsx
Microsoft PowerPoint 2016	.pptx
Microsoft Access 2016	.accdb

Table 3 Office 2016 default file extensions

Name your file with a descriptive name that accurately reflects the content of the document, workbook, presentation, or database, such as "January 2017 Budget" or "012017 Minutes". The descriptive name can include uppercase and lowercase letters, numbers, hyphens, spaces, and some special characters — excluding ? " / | < > * : — in any combination.

A file exists on your local machine at a **file path** — the physical location of the file starting with a letter that represents the drive and separating folders with a "\". This could be to your hard drive, usually the C:\ drive. Or it could be a USB drive that could be any letter of the alphabet, such as G:\. Assuming your main hard drive is C:\, the OneDrive location on your local computer is C:\Users\username\OneDrive — where username is the username you logged in with. Thus, if you put a file called Meeting.docx in your local OneDrive — and not in a subfolder — the file path combined with the file name would be C:\Users\username\OneDrive\Meeting.docx.

The file path and name combined can include a maximum of 255 characters including the extension. Even though Windows 10 can handle a long file name, some systems cannot. Thus, shorter names can prevent complications in transferring files between different systems.

In this exercise, you will save the meeting minutes document to OneDrive or the location where you are saving your files.

 **CF**01.04

To Save a Workbook to the Local OneDrive Folder That Syncs to the Cloud

a. If necessary, return to Backstage by clicking the **File** tab. Then, on the left pane, click **Save As**.

Notice there is an option for Save and Save As. Save saves a file to the location in which it already exists with the same name. Since this is a new, never saved file, Save and Save As work the same. You will work with an existing file to understand the difference later in this chapter.

b. Click on **This PC**. You may see a folder icon that links to Documents. You will also see recent locations, potentially your OneDrive. If you see OneDrive here, you can click on it. You can also click on Browse to open the Save As dialog box.

c. If you are logged into your Microsoft account, double-click **OneDrive**. If you want to navigate to a subfolder in your OneDrive, do so now.

If you are saving your files to a different location, double-click This PC. In the Save As dialog box, navigate to the location where you are saving your project files.

d. In the Save As dialog box in the File name box, change the name to cf01ch01Minutes_LastFirst, using your last and first name. Click **Save**.

Notice the Save as type menu. This determines the file type and extension. In Word, the default is .docx.

Troubleshooting

You are not connected to OneDrive! If this is your PC, log into your Microsoft account as directed in the previous exercise. If you cannot do that, such as in a computer lab, double-click **This PC** or **Browse** and navigate to a location where you would like to store your files.

You can store the files on the desktop and then upload them at http://onedrive .live.com when you are finished. If you do this, make sure all files are closed before you upload them.

Alternatively, you can save the files to a USB drive or other location of your choosing.

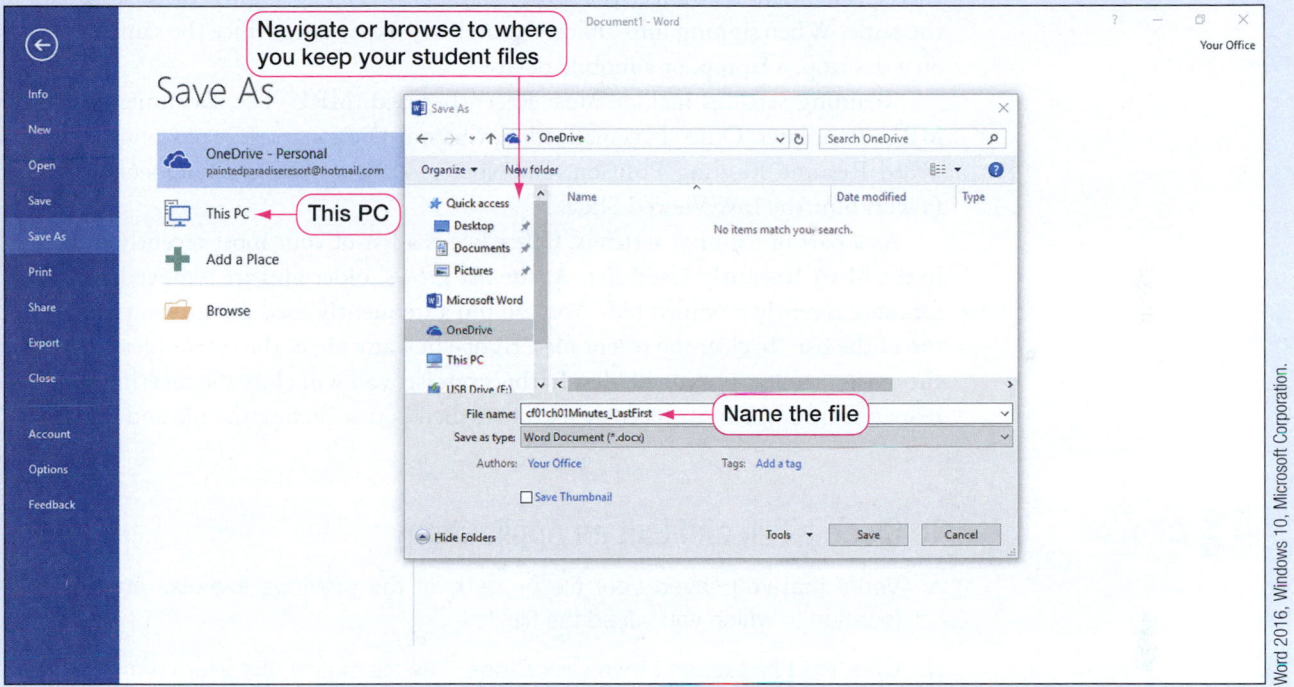

Figure 9   Word Save As

e.   Click **Minimize** ⬚. Then on the taskbar, click **File Explorer** ⬚.

f.   In the left Navigation pane, Click **OneDrive** or otherwise navigate to where you saved your file. In the file list, verify that your file is there.

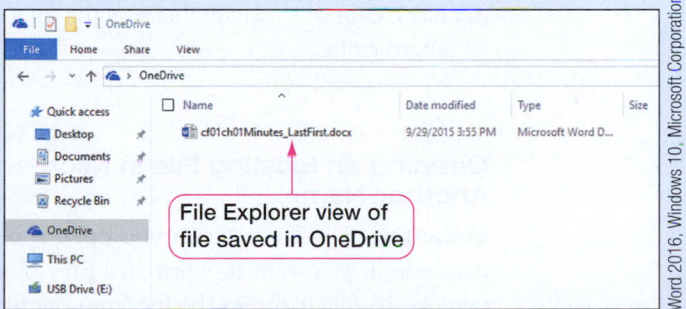

Figure 10   Word file in File Explorer

g.   In the top right corner of File Explorer, click **Close** ⬚.

h.   On the taskbar, point to the **Word icon** until you see the Live Preview of your file. Click the **Live Preview** to maximize your file again.

Closing a File, Reopening from the Recent Documents List, and Exiting an Application

When you are ready to close a file, you can click the Close command in Office Backstage. If the file you close is the only file that's open for that particular program, the program window remains open with no file in the window. You can also close a file by using the Close button ⊠ in the top right corner of the window to exit the window. If you exit the window, it will close both the file and the program. Exiting programs when you are finished with them helps to save system resources and keeps your Windows desktop and taskbar uncluttered. It also prevents data from being accidentally lost. Importantly, files must be closed before being uploaded to the web, copied to a new location, or attached to an e-mail; otherwise you risk corrupting the file.

Office's **roaming settings** are a group of settings that offer easy remotely synced user-specific data that affect the Office experience. Across logins, these settings remain the same. When signing into Office, the user will experience Office the same way, whether on a desktop, a laptop, or a mobile device.

Roaming settings include Most Recently Used (MRU) list, Documents and Places, MRU Templates, Office Personalization, Custom Dictionary, List of Connected Services, Word Resume Reading Position, OneNote — custom name a notebook view, and in PowerPoint the Last Viewed Slide.

As a part of roaming settings, Office keeps a list of your most recently modified files in the **Most Recently Used list**. As the list grows, older files are removed to make room for more recently modified files. You can pin a frequently used file to always remain at the top of the list. To clear the recent files, right-click any file in the recent files list, and select the option to clear unpinned files. In this exercise, you will close the meeting minutes and reopen it from the most recently used list; then you will close the file and Word.

 CF01.05

To Close a File and Exit an Application

a. Verify that you saved your file properly in the previous exercise and know the location to which you saved the file.

b. Click the **File** tab, and then click **Close**. The file closes, but Word remains open.

c. Click the **File** tab, and then click **Open**. On the right, you should see your file in the Most Recently Used list organized by last saved date — labeled Today, Yesterday, Last Week, or Older.

d. Click **cf01ch01Minutes_LastFirst**. Your file opens from the originally saved location.

e. Click **Close** ⊠. Since this was the only open document, the document closes and Word exits.

Opening an Existing File in Microsoft Word and Then Saving as Another Name

You create a new file when you open a blank document, workbook, presentation, or database. If you want to work on a previously created file, you must first open it. When you open a file, it copies the file from the file's storage location to the computer's temporary memory and displays it on the screen. When you save a file, it updates the storage location with the changes. Until then, the file exists only in your computer's memory. If you want to open a second file while one is open, the keyboard shortcut of pressing Ctrl and then pressing O will display the Open tab of Office Backstage. Using the keyboard shortcut of Ctrl + F12 will launch the Open dialog box without taking you to Office Backstage.

Many times, you will open a file that already exists rather than starting a new file. You can open the program and then open the file. You also can double-click a file in File Explorer, and the file will open in the associated program. When you have an existing file open, the Save command saves the file to the current location with the same name. If you want to change the name of a file or save it to a different location, you will need to use the Save As command. This allows you to specify the save options. When you use Save As, it allows you to select any location and give the file a new name.

When you open files that you downloaded from the Internet, accessed from a shared network, or received as an attachment in e-mail, the file usually opens in a read-only format called **Protected View** in Reading Mode. In Protected View, the file contents can be seen and read, but you cannot edit, save, or print the contents until you enable editing. If you see the information bar right under the ribbon and you trust the source of the file, simply click the Enable Editing button on the information bar.

REAL WORLD ADVICE	Sharing Files Between Office Versions

Different Office versions are not always compatible with one another. The general rule is that files created in an older version can always be opened in a newer version but not the other way around — an Office 2016 file is not easily opened in earlier versions of Office. Sharing files with Office 2003 users is a concern because different file extensions were used. For example, .doc was used for Word files instead of docx, .xls instead of .xlsx for Excel, and so on.

It is possible to save the Office 2016 files in a previous file format. To save in one of these formats, use the Save As command, and click the 97-2003 file format. If the file is already in the format of a previous version of Office, it will open in Office 2016 and be saved with the same format in which it was created. However, if a file is saved with the extension of a previous version, it may lose anything created with newer features.

If you have not already done so, you need to download the files for this text at http://www.pearsonhighered.com/youroffice. In this exercise, you will open an existing file and save it with another name. Susan Brock has already started an agenda for your meeting with her but has asked you to finish it.

 CF01.06

To Open an Existing File

a. On the taskbar, click in **Ask me anything** or **Search the web and Windows** and type Word. Click the **Word 2016** search result. The Word Start screen opens.

b. Click **Open Other Documents** in the left pane, and then click **Browse**. Navigate through the folder structure to the location of your student data files, and then double-click **cf01ch01Agenda**.

The agenda previously started by Susan Brock opens in Word.

c. If necessary, click Enable Editing. If you needed to click Enable Editing, your file opened in Protected View.

d. Click the **File** tab, click **Save As**, and then double-click **This PC**. In the Save As dialog box, navigate to the location where you are saving your project files, and then change the file name to **cf01ch01Agenda_LastFirst**, using your last and first name. Click **Save** 💾.

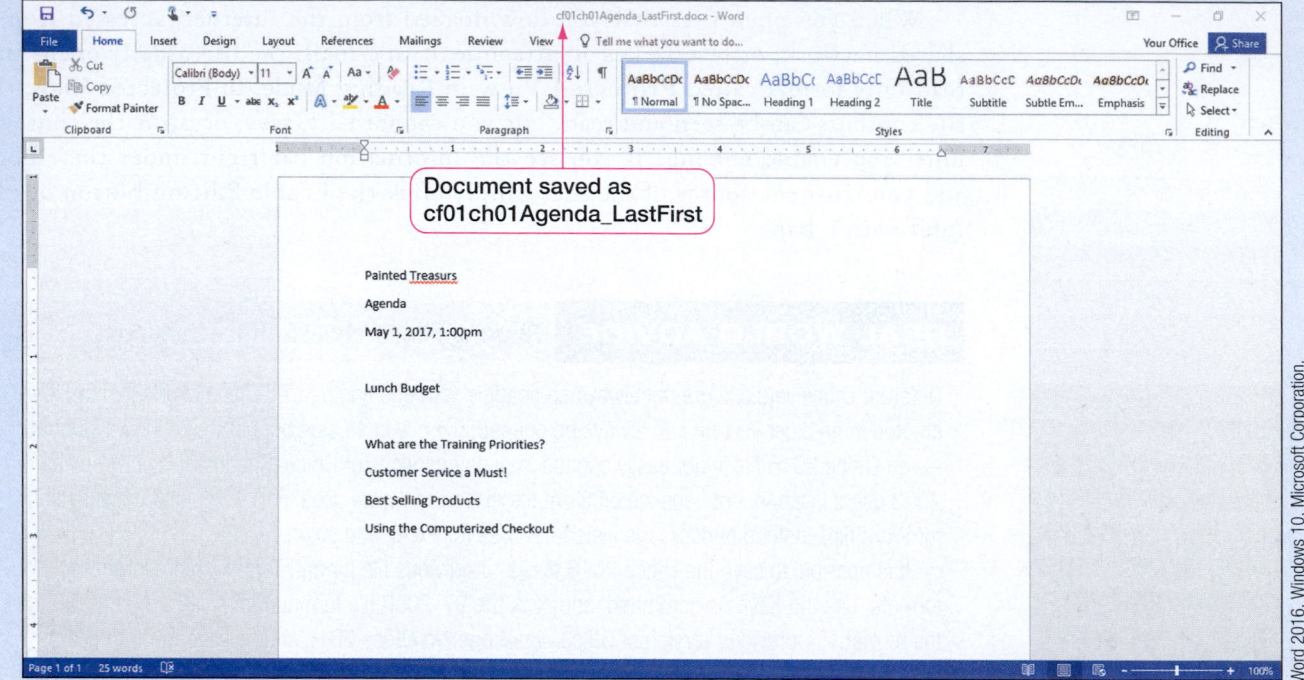

Figure 11 Beginning the Agenda document

Zooming, Scrolling, and Navigating with Keyboard Shortcuts

To get a closer look at the content within the program, you can zoom in. Alternatively, if you would like to see more of the contents, you can zoom out. Keep in mind that the zoom level affects only your view of the document on the screen and does not affect the printed output of the document. It is similar to using a magnifying glass on a page of a book to make the words look bigger — the print on the page is still the same size. Therefore, do not confuse the zoom level with how big the text will print — it affects only your view of the document on the screen.

On the right side of the status bar in the lower right corner is a slide control that permits zooming in Word from 10% to 500%. The minus and plus buttons provide an easy method to change the view size, or you can drag the Zoom Slider ━━━━━━. In Excel and PowerPoint, the zoom range is from 10% to 400%. When zoom is used, text is sometimes shifted off the viewing screen. Depending on the program and the zoom level, you might see the vertical or horizontal scroll bars or both scroll bars, which can be used to adjust what is displayed in the window. The scroll bars have arrows that can be clicked to shift the workspace in small increments in a specific direction and a scroll box that can be dragged to move a work space in larger increments. Touch screens allow you to zoom in and out by using pinch and stretch gestures. In addition to zooming and scrolling, you can navigate the file using keyboard shortcuts.

REAL WORLD ADVICE | Using Keyboard Shortcuts and KeyTips

Keyboard shortcuts — keyboard equivalents of software commands — are extremely useful, and some are universal to all Windows programs. They allow you to keep your hands on the keyboard instead of reaching for the mouse — increasing efficiency and saving time. Some companies have even take the mouse away from their interns to force them to use keyboard shortcuts. Keyboard shortcuts are also very useful for accessibility and people with vision impairments.

Pressing Alt will toggle the display of **KeyTips** — or keyboard shortcuts — for items on the ribbon and Quick Access Toolbar. After displaying the KeyTips, you can press the corresponding letter or number to request the action from the keyboard.

For multiple-key shortcuts, you hold down the first key listed and press the second key once. Some common keyboard shortcuts are listed below.

Ctrl + C	Copy the selected item
Ctrl + X	Cut the selected item
Ctrl + V	Paste a copied or cut item
Ctrl + A	Select all the items in a document or window
Ctrl + B	Bold selected text
Ctrl + Z	Undo an action
Ctrl + Home	Move to the top of the document
Ctrl + End	Move to the end of the document

In this exercise, you will zoom in and out on the agenda document and navigate it with keyboard shortcuts.

 **CF01.07**

SIDE NOTE

Methods for Zooming

Several ways exist to zoom Office applications: Zoom Slider, View tab in the Zoom group, Ctrl and a mouse wheel, and touch gestures.

SIDE NOTE

End of the Document

When this text requests that the insertion point be at the end of the document, use this keyboard shortcut to avoid mistakes.

To Zoom, Scroll, and Navigate with Keyboard Shortcuts

a. The insertion point should be at the beginning of the document right before the word "Painted," and the insertion point should be blinking.

b. On the Word status bar, drag the **Zoom Slider** [– ——— | ——— +] to the right until it reaches **500%**. The document is enlarged to its largest size. This makes the text appear larger.

c. Press Ctrl + End. This takes you to the end of the document.

Troubleshooting

As discussed in the Windows 10 chapter, if the End key is shared with a function key as on many laptops, you may have had a different result. Ensure that your button is behaving as the End key and not as a function key. This is device specific, and you may need to do a web search to figure it out. If necessary, use the scroll bar instead.

d. On the Word status bar, click **500%**.

Notice that this percentage is the Zoom level button that opens the Zoom dialog box. This dialog box provides options for custom and preset settings.

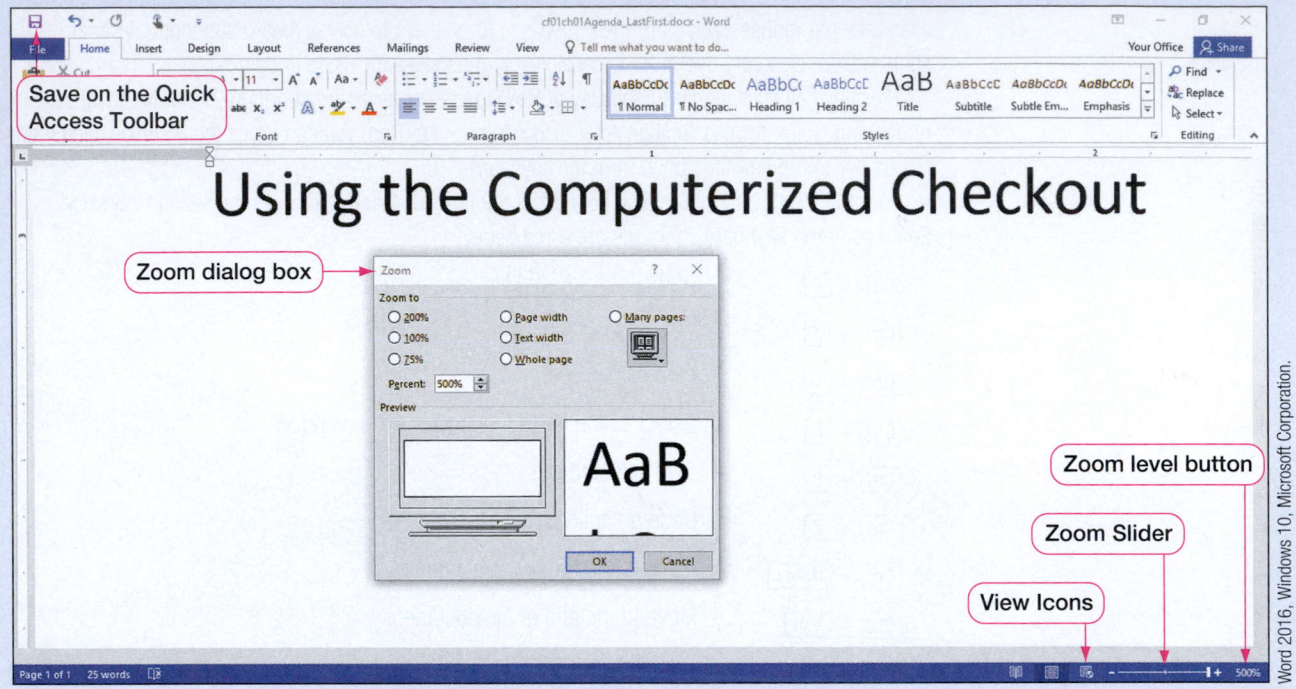

Figure 12 Zoom controls and dialog box

Word 2016, Windows 10, Microsoft Corporation.

e. Click **Page width**, and then click **OK**.

The Word document zooms to its page width. Notice that this zoom level will give you the maximum size without creating a horizontal scroll bar.

f. Right-click the **scroll box** in the scroll bar. Then select **Top** to return to the beginning of the document.

Notice that the document scrolled to the top but did not move the insertion point. The keyboard shortcut of Ctrl + Home takes you to the top and moves the insertion point.

g. Press Ctrl + Home and notice that the insertion point moves to the top as well.

h. Save the document.

Using the Quick Access Toolbar to Save a Currently Open File

In addition to Office Backstage, Office provides several ways to save a file. To quickly save a file, simply click Save on the Quick Access Toolbar or use the keyboard shortcut of pressing Ctrl + S. The **Quick Access Toolbar** is the series of small icons in the top left corner of the title bar that can be customized to display commonly used buttons.

When this method is used, the program simply saves the file to its current location with the same name. Once you save a file the first time, the simple shortcut methods to save any changes to the file work fine to update the existing file — as long as you do not need to change the file name or location with the Save As command. In this exercise, you will save your file to its current location with the same name as previously given.

 **CF**01.08

SIDE NOTE
Save Keyboard Shortcut
You can also save with the keyboard shortcut of Ctrl + S.

To Save an Existing File with the Quick Access Toolbar

a. In the top left corner in the Quick Access Toolbar, click **Save** .

The file is now saved to the same location and with the same name you designated earlier in this chapter. Although you have not made changes since the document was last saved, best practice is to save your files frequently.

Manipulate, Correct, and Format Content in Word

A personal brand is important in business. If a person dresses poorly, colleagues may assume that this person's work is poor as well. In the business world, everything a person does influences the way colleagues and superiors view that person, including the content and formatting of the files he or she produces. Thus, understanding appropriate content and formatting is very important — it is a direct reflection of you as a professional.

 REAL WORLD ADVICE | **It Is Not the Place for Jokes!**

Business documents and files are rarely if ever appropriate for jokes. Consider a job applicant who lists, as the last thing in his or her resume, "Will work for food" — this has actually happened. The job applicant may have wanted to convey that he or she had a good sense of humor. But in reality, the message shows that the job applicant did not understand that humor was inappropriate in this situation or he or she did not take getting the job seriously.

CONSIDER THIS | **Consider Your Personal Brand**

Have you thought about your personal brand? Are you the creative person? Are you the efficient person? Describe your brand. Give an example of how you were influenced positively or negatively by the way another person presented themselves or their work.

Checking Spelling

Checking spelling is a must — and it is easy in Office. There are no excuses for spelling mistakes. Everyone makes typos, but that is no excuse for poor spelling. Further, you need to understand your audience and purpose before using jargon, acronyms, text abbreviations, or other informal language. Using informal language in a business chat in Skype is appropriate. However, in a business meeting agenda, formal language is expected.

In this exercise, you will correct a spelling mistake.

 **CF01.09**

To Correct Spelling

a. Notice the second word on the first line is misspelled as "Treasurs" instead of "Treasures." Since it is misspelled, Word put a wavy red line under the word to indicate the mistake. A green wavy line indicates a grammar mistake. A blue wavy line indicates that there could be a mistake but it is not grammar or spelling — such as using "from" instead of "form".

b. Right-click the misspelled word **Treasurs**. Click the first option for **Treasures**.

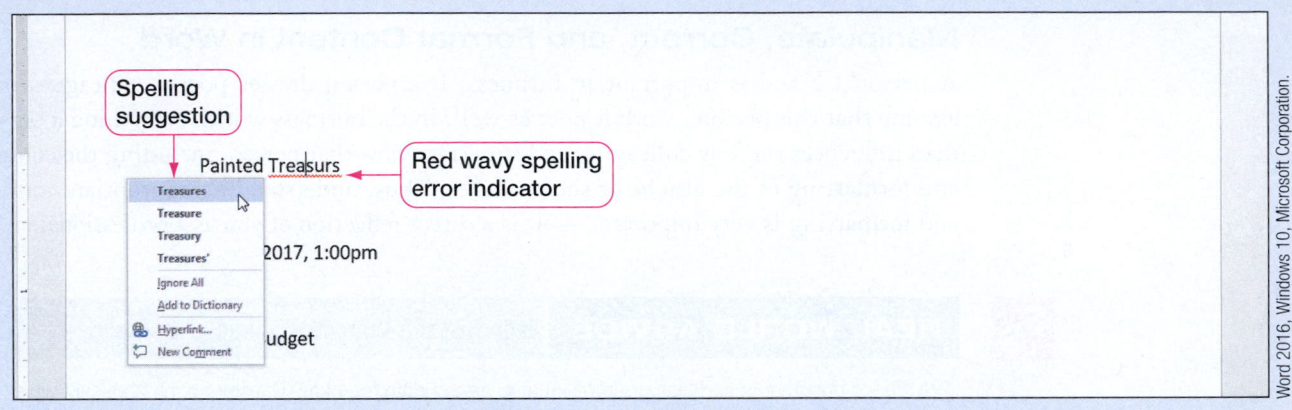

Figure 13   Correcting spelling in a document

c. **Save** 💾 the document.

Showing Formatting Symbols, Entering, Copying, and Pasting Text

Many keys, such as Spacebar, Enter, and Tab, insert nonprinting characters in a document. For example, when you press Tab, text is indented and a tab "character" is inserted. Sometimes called formatting marks, nonprinting characters are by default not displayed on the screen. These formatting marks are not shown when the document is printed, even when they are displayed on the screen. When content is entered, these marks can change the way the text is shown, is located, and is formatted. Thus, displaying formatting symbols can help you see everything in your document.

As you add content, you will inevitably find an occasion when copying and pasting the text will save you time. Of course, someone looking at the end product will have no way of knowing what you typed by hand and what you copied and pasted. In many instances, copy and paste not only will save you time but also will increase accuracy — assuming that you do not copy a mistake! In this exercise, you will enter the top three products at the gift store. Along the way, you will copy and paste to enter text as efficiently as possible.

 **CF01.10**

To Show Formatting Symbols, Enter, Copy, and Paste Text

a. On the Home tab, in the Paragraph group, click **Show/Hide** ¶. The hidden formatting symbols now show. Notice the only hidden symbols in this document are a paragraph mark indicating the end of a paragraph and a dot representing spaces.

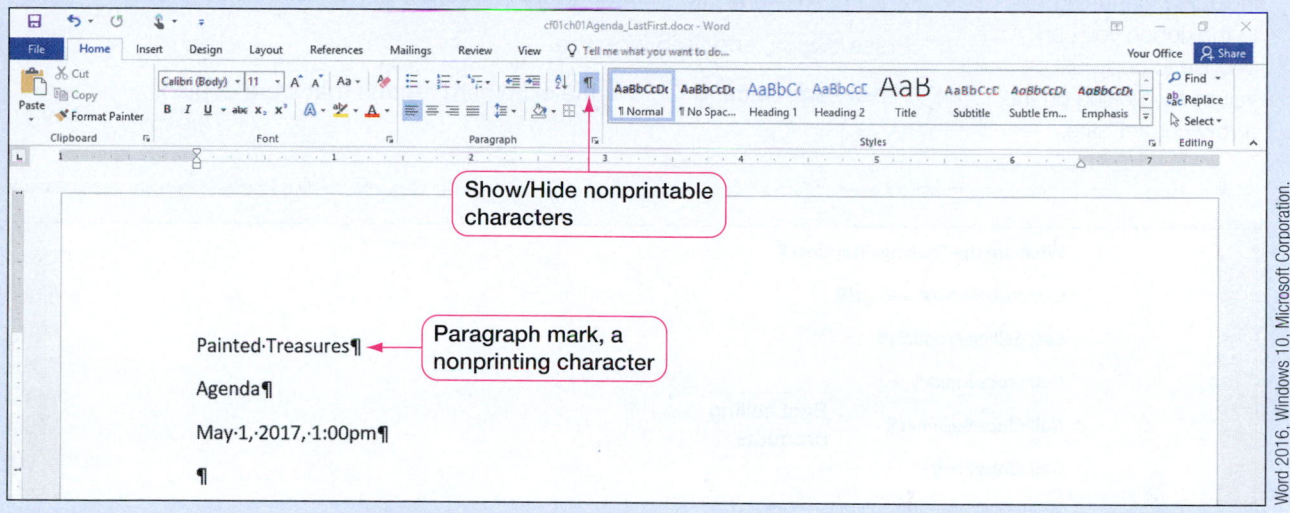

Figure 14 Hidden formatting characters

Word 2016, Windows 10, Microsoft Corporation.

SIDE NOTE
Mouse Versus Keyboard
If you have trouble using the keyboard to select text, use the mouse instead. In the end, it does not change your document. Knowing both methods is about speed.

b. If necessary, scroll until you see the words **Best Selling Products** and then click after the **s** in Products to place your insertion point at the end of that line. Press Enter.

Pressing Enter creates a hard return that creates a new paragraph. Word will automatically wrap text in a paragraph down to the next line.

c. Type **Golf Clubs**. The top three products are three different kinds of golf clubs. To save time, you will use copy and paste.

d. Hold down the Shift key, and press the ← **ten** times to select the words Golf Clubs.

You can use Shift and arrow keys to select, rather than the mouse. Depending on the situation, the mouse could be faster or the keyboard could be faster. Therefore, it is useful to know how to use both. Notice when you pressed the arrow for the tenth time, it automatically selected the paragraph mark.

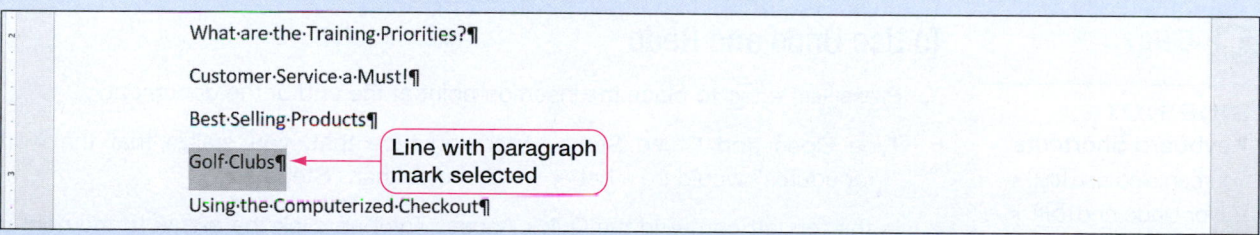

Figure 15 Paragraph mark selected

Word 2016, Windows 10, Microsoft Corporation.

e. Press Ctrl + C. This copies the text to the Office Clipboard to use anytime you want, even multiple times, until the clipboard is replaced with something else.

f. Click after the **s** in Golf Clubs to place the insertion point at the end of the line. Then press Spacebar and type **Junior**.

g. Press `Enter` and then press `Ctrl` + `V`. This pastes the contents of the Clipboard onto that line. Then press `←` to return to the second line that says "Golf Clubs."

h. Press `Spacebar` and then type Beginner.

i. Press `Enter` and then press `Ctrl` + `V`. This pastes the contents of the Clipboard onto that line. Then press `←` to return to the third line that says "Golf Clubs."

j. Press `Spacebar` and then type Pro.

k. Press `Delete` twice to remove the extra hard returns that were copied.

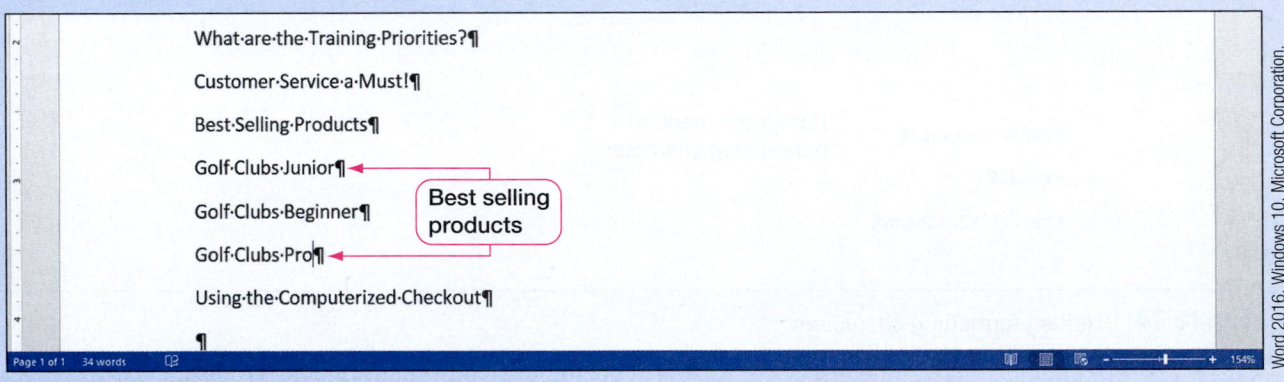

Figure 16 Top products entered

l. **Save**  the document.

Using Undo and Redo

Everyone makes a typo from time to time, and you are going to make mistakes that you need to undo. The easiest way to do that is through the Undo and Redo buttons in the Quick Access Toolbar. In this exercise, you will add some text to your agenda, undo it, and then add better text.

CF01.11

To Use Undo and Redo

a. Press `Ctrl` + `End` to place the insertion point at the end of the document.

b. Type Open and Close Steps. After you type that, you realize that the word "Procedures" would be a better word choice than "Steps."

c. In the top left corner in the Quick Access Toolbar, click the **arrow** to the right of Undo Typing.

SIDE NOTE
Redo
Redo works similar to Undo. If you undo something and then change your mind, you can reverse the Undo by clicking Redo ⟳.

d. Verify that the list is letting you undo by the letter. If not, see the troubleshooting below. Click the item on the list that says **Typing "S"** that was the first letter to the word Steps.

Troubleshooting

If your version of Office does not undo by the letter, you may see an option for only the phrase Typing "Steps." If you do, click that option. You may also see an option for the whole phrase Typing "Open and Close Steps." If you do, click that option and then, in the next step, you will have to redo the entire line by typing Open and Close Procedures.

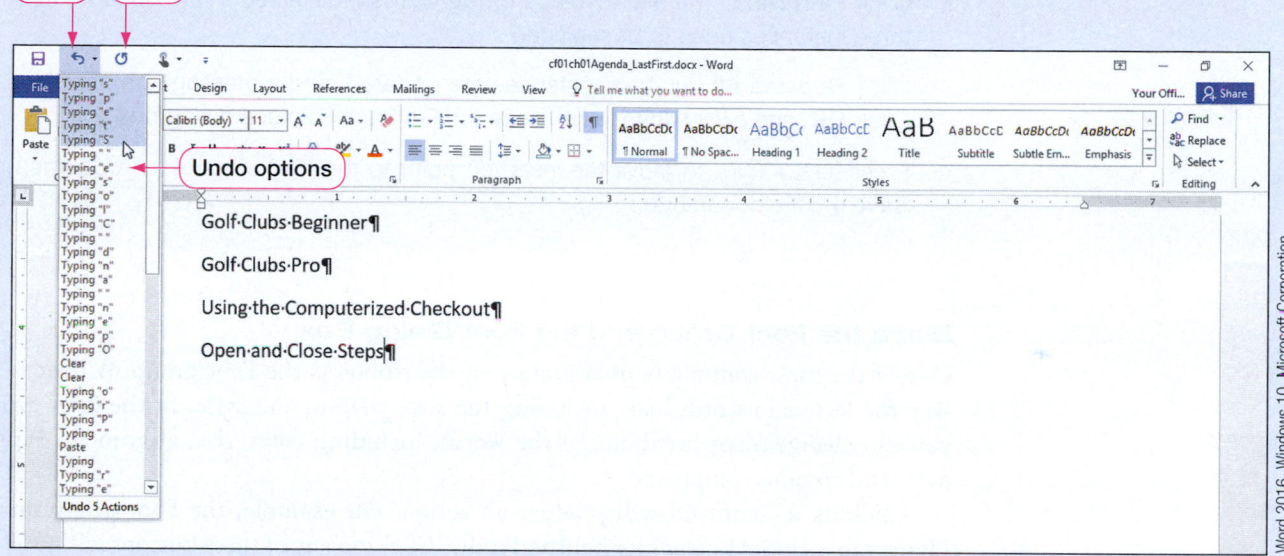

Figure 17 Undo typing steps

e. Type **Procedures**. The word "Steps" is undone, and you have entered a better word choice. Undo and Redo can be used for almost anything you do, not just typing.

f. **Save** 🖫 the document.

Using the Navigation Pane, Finding Text, and Replacing Text

Sometimes, you may not know where certain text is in a document. Or you may need to replace text with something different. You can use Find and Replace on the ribbon rather than manually looking for text and changing it. If you click Find on the Home tab, it opens the Navigation pane on the left side of the window with a search box. A **pane** is a smaller window that often appears to the side of the program window and offers options or helps you to navigate through completing a task or feature. If you click Replace, it opens the Find and Replace **dialog box**, which is a window that provides more options or settings beyond those provided on the Navigation pane. All three of the top-selling products are actually Wilson Golf clubs. In this exercise, you will find the words "Golf Clubs" and replace them with the more precise brand of Wilson Golf Clubs.

REAL WORLD ADVICE **What to "Find" in a Find and Replace?**

Be careful what you look for in a find and replace. If you are not careful, you can end up replacing items that should not have been. If this ever happens, remember the Undo command!

 **CF01.12**

To Use Find and Replace

SIDE NOTE

Be Careful with Replace All

When using Replace All, be very careful. It is easy to unintentionally change text that should not have been changed.

a. On the Home tab, in the Editing group, click **Find**. The Navigation pane appears on the left. You could find all of the instances of Golf Clubs from this pane. However, you cannot do a find and replace operation from here. In the top right corner of the Navigation pane, click **Close** ⊠ to close that pane.

b. On the Home tab, in the Editing group, click **Replace**. The Find and Replace dialog box opens.

c. Click in the **Find what** box, and type Golf Clubs.

d. Click in the **Replace with** box, and type Wilson Golf Clubs.

e. Click **Find Next**. The first instance of the words is selected in the document. All three instances need to be replaced.

f. Click **Replace All**. All three instances are updated, and a message box appears. Click **OK**, and click **Close** ⊠ to close the Find and Replace dialog box.

g. Press Ctrl + Home to move the insertion point to the beginning of the document. **Save** 💾 the document.

Using the Font Group and the Font Dialog Box

One of the most commonly used groups on the ribbon is the Font group. A **font** is the way the letters in words look, including the size, weight, and style. In the Font group, you can change many attributes of the words, including color, size, alignment, type of font, and common emphasis.

Clicking a command will produce an action. For example, the Font group on the Home tab includes buttons for bold and italic. Clicking any of these buttons will produce an intended action. So if you have selected text to which you want to apply bold formatting, simply click the Bold button, and bold formatting is applied to the selected text.

Some buttons are **toggle buttons** — one click turns the feature on and a second click turns the feature off. When a feature is toggled on, the button remains highlighted. Clicking toggles the setting on and off. Bold is an example of a toggle button.

Some buttons have two parts: a button that accesses the most commonly used setting or command and an arrow that opens additional options. A **gallery** is a set of menu options that appears when you click the arrow next to a button. A normal arrow will bring up the options or enable you to scroll through the options. If there is a More arrow ▾, it brings up all of the options.

For example, on the Home tab, in the Font group, the Font Color button **A** ▾ includes a gallery of the different colors that are available for fonts. If you click the button, the default is to apply the last color used, which is displayed on the icon. To access the gallery for other color options, click the arrow next to the Font Color button.

Some commands open other menus. These commands expand to a list of options when the arrow next to the list is selected. Whenever you see an arrow next to a button, this is an indicator that more options are available. Then you can click on the option from the list that you want.

Some ribbon groups include a diagonal arrow in the bottom right corner of the group, called a **Dialog Box Launcher** ▢, which opens a corresponding dialog box. Click the Dialog Box Launcher to open a dialog box. It often provides access to more precise or less frequently used commands along with the commands that are offered on the ribbon; thus, using a dialog box offers the ability to apply many related options at the same time and from one location.

In this exercise, you will change the formatting of the font to be more appropriate.

 **CF**01.13

SIDE NOTE

Text Selection

You can double-click to select a single word or triple-click to select the entire paragraph. You can also use Shift and arrow keys to select text.

To Use the Font Group and Font Dialog Box

a. If necessary, press Ctrl + Home to place your insertion point at the beginning of the document.

b. On the Home tab in the Paragraph group, click **Center** ≡. The title is centered across the top.

c. On the first line, click before the **P** in Painted Treasures, and then drag to right after the **s** to select the words "Painted Treasures."

d. On the Home tab, in the Font group, click **Increase Font Size** A˄ three times. The title is now larger.

e. On the Home tab, in the Font group, click the **arrow** next to the Font gallery. Scroll down the list, and click **Verdana**. The font changes.

f. On the Home tab, in the font group, click the **arrow** next to Font color A˅. Under Standard Colors, select **Dark Red**.

g. On the Home tab, in the font group, click **Bold** B.

h. Click before the **L** in Lunch Budget, and drag to the **t** to select Lunch Budget.

i. On the Home tab, in the Font group, click the **arrow** next to Font Size 11 ˅. Click **14**. The font increases in size to 14 points.

j. On the Home tab, in the Font group, click the **Dialog Box Launcher** ⌜. The Font dialog box opens. Under Font style, click **Italic**.

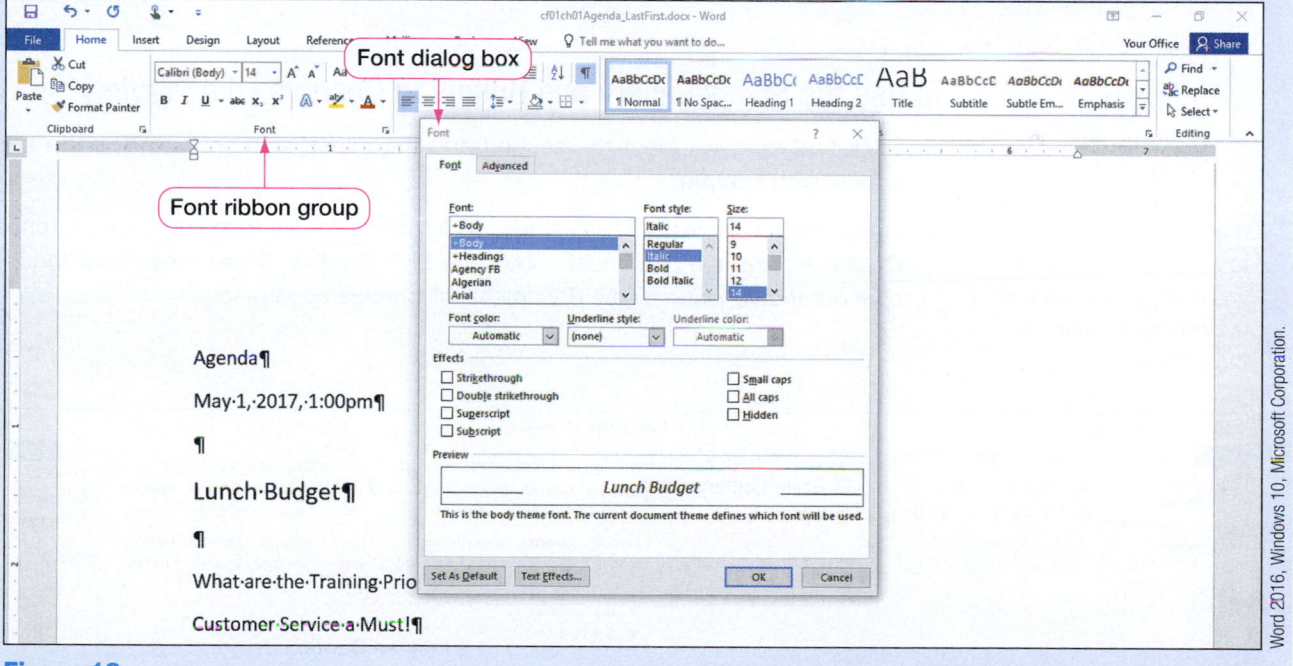

Figure 18 Font dialog box

k. Click **OK**. The dialog box closes.

l. **Save** 🖫 the document.

CHAPTER 1

Word 2016, Windows 10, Microsoft Corporation.

Using the Style Gallery and Bullets with Live Preview

Live Preview lets you see the effects of menu selections on your document file or selected item before making a commitment to a particular menu choice. The menu or grid shows samples of the available options. Not all additional options under arrows have Live Preview. Using Live Preview, you can experiment with settings before making a final choice.

Predefined Styles are a type of preset formatting. You will learn more about styles later. However, styles allow for more advanced features, such as a Table of Contents. They can also be customized. So if you later decide that Heading 2 should be in a larger font size, you change the style, and it changes every instance of Heading 2 in your document. Finally, and for the purpose of this chapter, styles help you apply aesthetically pleasing formatting very quickly — and can also be helpful for users with vision color impairments.

When you click on the More arrow  for styles, you will see the Styles gallery. Point to a text style in the Styles gallery, and the selected text or the paragraph in which the insertion point is located appears with that text style. Moving the pointer from option to option results in quickly seeing what your text will look like before you make a final selection. To finalize a change to the selected option, click the style.

Bullets are symbols that appear before each item to create a list of items. Typically, bullets also have different spacing than a normal paragraph and have the Live Preview option. When you click on the Bullets ⬚ ⌄ arrow, a library menu appears that allows you to pick the symbol you wish to use.

In this exercise, you will add a style to the gift shop agenda using styles and some simple bulleting. In business, agendas usually do not need a lot of formatting. However, a little bit of formatting can actually change what the content conveys to others and provide clarity to your content.

▶ CF01.14

SIDE NOTE
Live Preview

Live Preview shows how formatting looks before you apply it. This feature is available for many of the galleries.

To Use the Styles Gallery and Bullets to Observe Live Preview

a. Click and drag to select the second and third lines starting with **Agenda** and ending with **1:00pm**.

b. On the Home tab, in the Styles group, click **More** ⬚. Point to the option for **Intense Quote**. Notice, the document shows the Live Preview. If you move your mouse over other style options, the document will change accordingly.

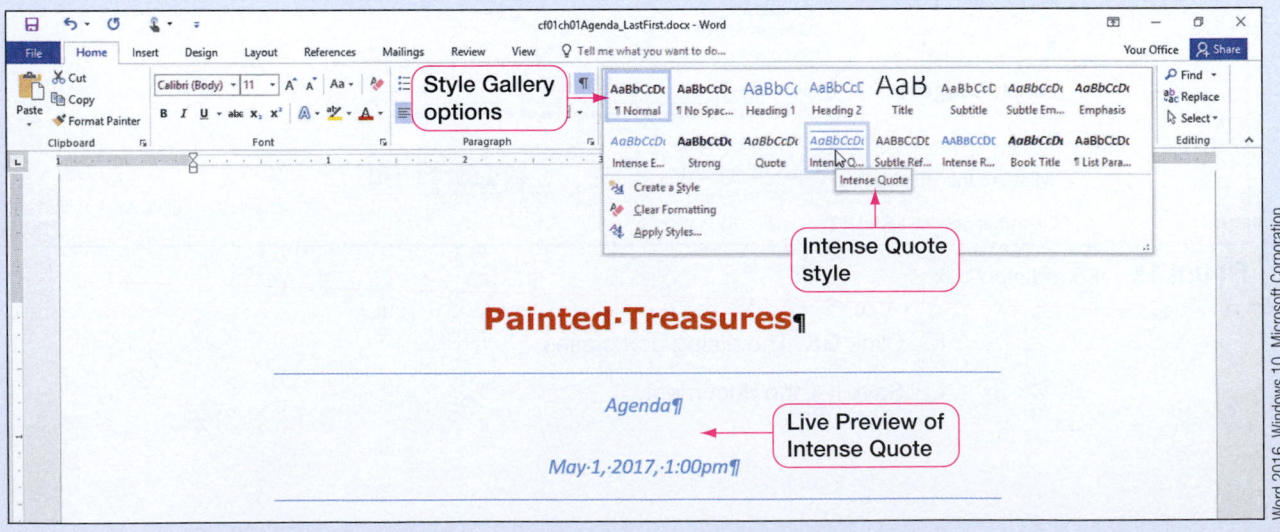

Figure 19   Styles Live Preview

c. Click **Intense Quote**. The Intense Quote style is now applied to those two lines.

d. If necessary, scroll down until you see the golf clubs you entered. Click and drag starting with **Wilson Golf Clubs Junior** down to the last of the three types of golf clubs, **Wilson Golf Clubs Pro**.

e. On the Home tab, in the Paragraph group, click **Bullets** . The lines now display as a bulleted list. Notice that after the bullet symbol, the formatting symbol for a tab appears, indicating space between the symbol and the words.

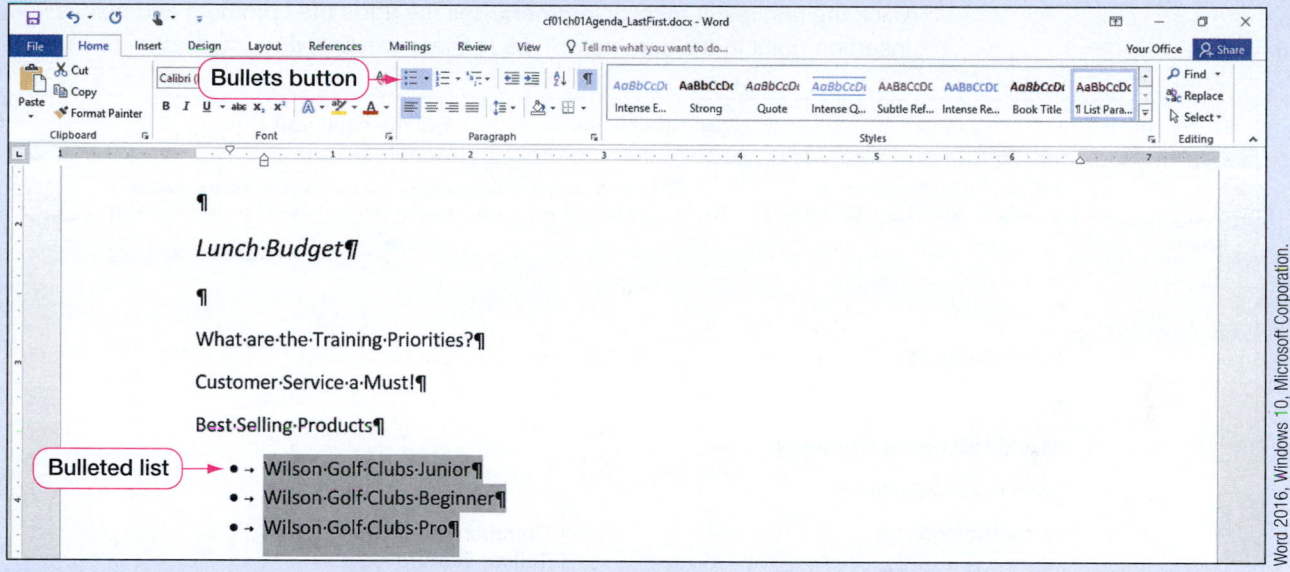

Figure 20 Bulleted list

f. **Save** the document.

Inserting a Comment and Footer Using the Tell me what you want to do Box

New in Office 2016, all of the programs have a **Tell me what you want to do** box in the title bar — "Tell me" for short. This tool is particularly useful when you want to do something but do not know where a command is located in the ribbon. This tool will not just take you to help on that item — though it does provide options for that as well. It actually performs the action for you. Although the Tell me feature is not currently connected to Cortana or speech recognition, it is easy to see that as a potential feature upgrade in the future.

Under the Tell me what you want to do search results, you also have an option for a Smart Lookup, which is new to Office 2016. With Smart Lookup, you can open search results and do research without leaving the application. Instead, it brings up the results in the Inights pane.

A comment allows you to leave a note for another person to read and reply. Comments are great for collaboration and can be easily deleted before the document is final. A footer allows you to put text at the bottom of every page. Footers are great for placing the page number, your name, or even the file name. You will learn more about comments and footers in a later chapter and will add basic ones in this exercise. The Tell me feature is great for using and finding features you do not know a lot about.

In this exercise, you will use this tool to add a comment and a footer to the agenda. Susan, the gift shop manager, has asked you to send back to her the updated agenda. You need to add a comment to ask her a question.

To Use Tell Me to Insert a Comment and Footer

a. Place your insertion point at the end of the line Using the Computerized Checkout so that the insertion point is after the **t** and before the **paragraph** mark.

b. In the title bar, click in the **Tell me what you want to do . . .** box and type Add Comment. Notice that command options are listed first. Next, you have the option to open the Help window on the topic you entered. Finally, you can select Smart Lookup, which opens the Insights pane on the right with Bing web search results.

c. Click the first result **Insert Comment**. Tell me adds the comment and places your insertion point in the comment. Type Is there existing documentation to use?

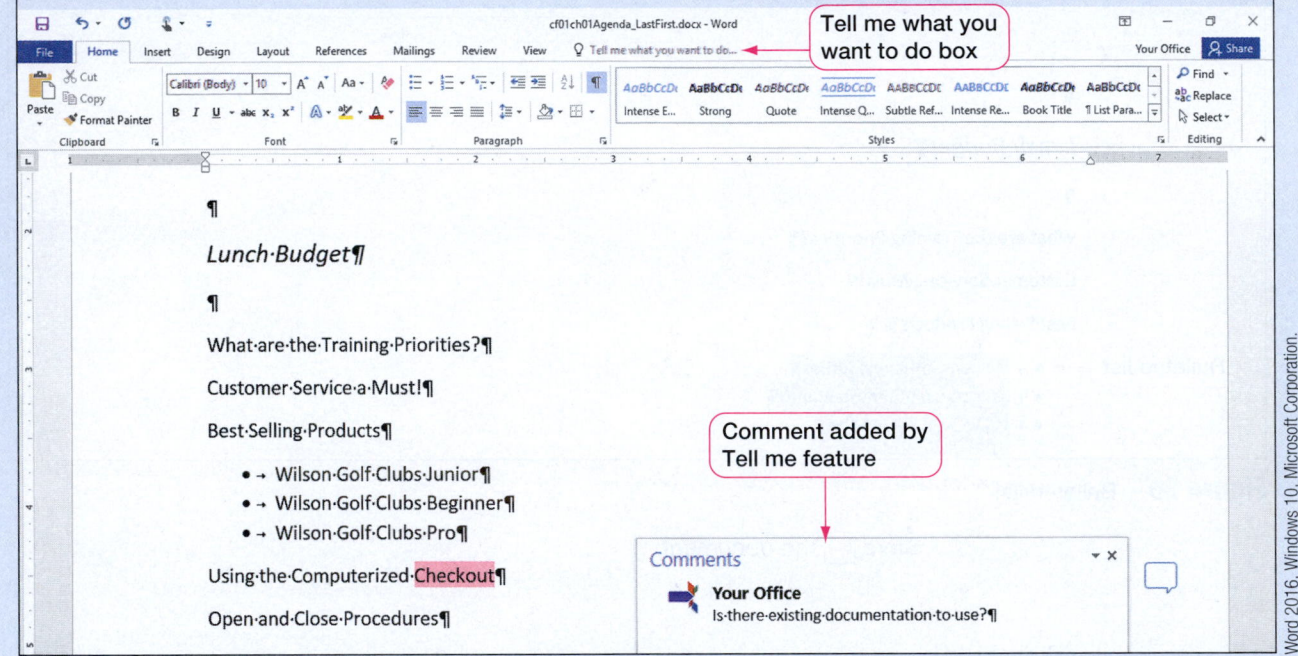

Figure 21 Inserted comment

d. If necessary, scroll to the left and press Ctrl + End to place your insertion point at the end of the document.

e. In the title bar, click in the **Tell me what you want to do . . .** box and type Add a footer, and then click the first result **Add a Footer**. In the submenu, select the second option **Blank (Three Columns)**. Tell me adds the footer and places your insertion point in the footer.

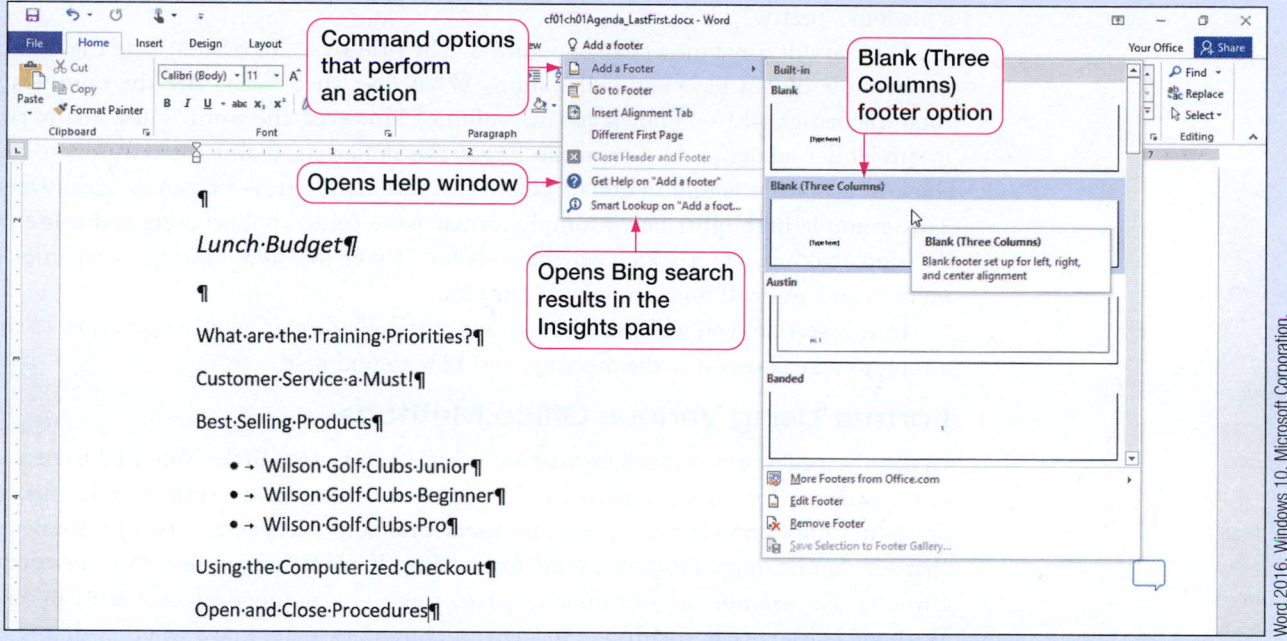

Figure 22 Adding a footer with Tell me

f. On the left side, click **[Type here]** and type First Last, using your first and last name.

g. In the middle, click **[Type here]** and type Course Name, using your class's name.

h. On the right side, click **[Type here]** and type InstructorLast, using your instructor's last name.

i. Press [Esc] to exit the footer, and then press [Ctrl] + [Home] to return to the beginning of the document.

j. **Save** 🖫 the document, and then click **Close** ✕ to close Word. Submit your file as directed by your instructor. If you need to take a break before finishing this chapter, now is a good time.

REAL WORLD ADVICE **Saving Files**

Most programs have an added safeguard or warning dialog box to remind you to save if you attempt to close a file without saving your changes first. Despite that warning, best practice dictates that you save files before closing them or exiting a program. If you select the wrong option on the warning by accident, you will lose work. Remembering to save before you close prevents this kind of accident.

Best practice also dictates saving often. The more often you save, the less work you can lose in the event of an unexpected closing of the application. Pressing [Ctrl] + [S] takes only a few seconds. Train yourself now to use this keyboard shortcut regularly and often. If you do, it will become second nature and save you from losing work in the future!

Formatting, Finding Help, and Printing in Office

The accuracy and quality of your content are the most important aspect of your files. However, even the most high-quality, accurate file is much harder to use if it is formatted poorly causing confusion for anyone who looks at it. After accuracy, clarity of your file to others — and even yourself — is extremely important. It is much more than just making a file look "pretty."

For example, imagine a table of numbers. The title says "2016 Sales," and the numbers in the table do not have any dollar signs. What does that mean? Are the numbers the total quantities sold — known as sales volume? However, the word "sales" many times means dollar amounts. Did someone forget the dollar signs and these numbers really show how much was sold in dollars before costs are removed — known as sales revenue? This example highlights how a simple format issue could confuse users and cause poor decision making. Do a search on the web for "Excel mistakes costing companies big money" and you will find numerous examples.

In this section, you will learn how to appropriately format your budget, how to print a copy to take notes on at the meeting, and how to find help.

Format Using Various Office Methods

Generally speaking, too much formatting is just as bad as too little. You need to be aware of accessibility for vision-impaired individuals — discussed in depth later in this text. Styles in Office provide nice options for users who don't have an artistic eye. Remember that less can be more. However, some formatting, if not done, can lead to incorrect conclusions. For example as mentioned earlier, there is a number labeled Sales in Excel. Without a clearer title or currency formatting, how does a user know whether that is sales in dollars or in quantity sold?

Earlier in the chapter, you added a small amount of formatting that helped the clarity of your agenda. Now you are ready to create your budget in Excel.

Creating a New Excel Workbook

An Excel file is referred to as a **workbook**. Each Excel workbook can contain many different worksheets. Each sheet has rows represented by numbers and columns represented by letters of the alphabet. The intersection of any row and column is a **cell**. For example, cell B2 refers to the cell where column B and row 2 intersect. The **active cell** is the currently selected cell. In a new worksheet, the active cell is the first cell of the first row, cell A1.

On a personal computer, you may prefer to use the Windows Start menu to open the program, but in a computer lab or on an unfamiliar computer, the search method may be preferable. In this exercise, you will search for and open Microsoft Excel to create a new workbook to start a budget for the training budget that you will finish in your meeting with Susan Brock, the gift shop manager.

 CF01.16

To Create a New Excel Workbook

a. On the taskbar, click **Ask Me Anything** or **Search the web and Windows**. Type **Excel**.

b. Click on **Excel 2016** in the search results. The Excel Start screen is displayed.

c. Click **Blank workbook**. A new Excel spreadsheet opens.

Notice, the words Book1 - Excel appear on the title bar. This means that the workbook has not been saved yet. This opens a blank workbook with one worksheet named Sheet1. The active cell is A1.

d. Press Ctrl + F1. The ribbon is pinned open so that you can see all of the commands. on the Home tab.

Troubleshooting

You pressed the keyboard shortcut, but nothing happened or something else happened. Are you working on a laptop? If so, then you may need to hold down the Fn key as well. The function keys on a laptop are generally assigned to other things, such as volume. You can change these key assignments, but they are specific to the device — you may need to search the web to find out how to change them on yours.

On a Microsoft Surface, you can press Fn and CapsLock to make the function keys work without pressing the Fn keys. If you have a laptop, it is worth the time to figure out how to do this on your machine. Keyboard shortcuts greatly increase your speed and efficiency. Finally, you can always use the Ribbon Display Options button ⊡ instead.

e. Click the **File** tab, click **Save As**, and then double-click **This PC**. In the Save As dialog box, navigate to the location where you are saving your project files, and then change the file name to cf01ch01Budget_LastFirst, using your last and first name. Click **Save** 🖫.

Using Excel to Enter Content, Apply Italics, and Apply a Fill Color

As was discussed earlier in the chapter, Office uses a common interface between all of the applications. This does not mean an identical interface. While some things are the same, how they are applied or how they work may be slightly different. For example, in Excel, if you select the cell, the formatting options apply to the entire cell — not just part of the text inside of a cell. By contrast, in Word, you select precisely the words for which to change the font color. To make only a single word a different color in Excel, you must select the specific text you want inside the cell first. Some formatting must be applied to the entire cell, such as number type — Currency, Text, and Date, among others. When exploring features that are common to the Office applications, you need to experience how a feature can be slightly different or very different in an application-specific way.

In this exercise, you will add content to the budget, apply italic to some cells, and apply different background color to others.

 **CF01.17**

To Use the Italic Button and the Fill Color Button

a. Click cell **A6** to make it the active cell. Then type Budget and press Enter. The text is inserted into the cell, and the cell below becomes the active cell.

b. Click cell **A8**. Type Expenses and press Enter.

c. In cell A9, type Food and press Enter.

d. In cell A10, type Drinks and press Enter.

e. Click cell **A8** to make it the active cell. Then, on the Home tab, in the Font group, click **Italic** Ⅰ. The toggle button applies italic to cell A8, and the button is highlighted.

f. Click cell **B6**. Type 500 and press Ctrl + Enter. The value is entered in the cell, and the active cell remains B6.

g. With B6 active, on the Home tab, in the Font group, click the **Fill Color arrow** . The color options appear. Point to the colors to find **Green, Accent 6, Lighter 60%**. At the writing of this text, that is the third color down in the far right column. Click **Green, Accent 6, Lighter 60%**.

> ### Troubleshooting
> What if that color is not there? Microsoft has taken to updating Office more often than just every new version. Thus, things can change over time — and color placement in the galleries is one of those things. The best way to find the color is to point to the name. If the color you need is not there, pick the standard color — which does not change — of light green.

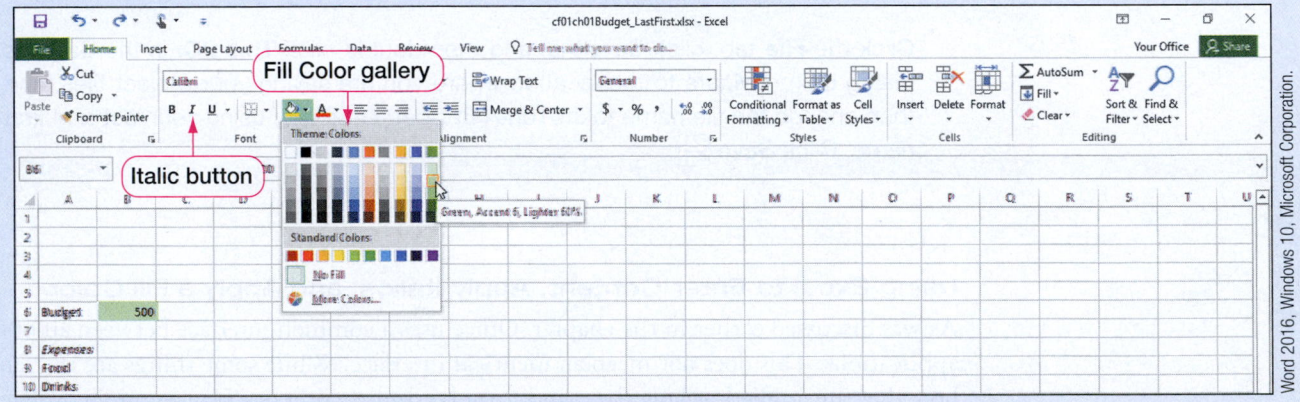

Figure 23   Fill color

h. Save  the spreadsheet.

Opening an Excel Dialog Box

Excel has dialog boxes, just like Word. The Format Cells dialog box is probably the most used dialog box in Excel, as it allows you to specify many things. Most important, it allows you to specify the type of data in the cell, such as Currency or Text. Since spreadsheets use many calculations, specifying the type of data is very important.

In this exercise, you will use a dialog box to format some of the cells in the budget you are beginning for your manager, Susan Brock.

CF01.18   To Use the Dialog Box Launcher to Format a Number

a. If necessary, click cell **B6** to make it the active cell. Then, on Home tab, in the Number group, click on **Number Format Dialog Box Launcher** . The Format Cells dialog box opens to the Number tab.

b. On the left side, under Category, click **Currency**.

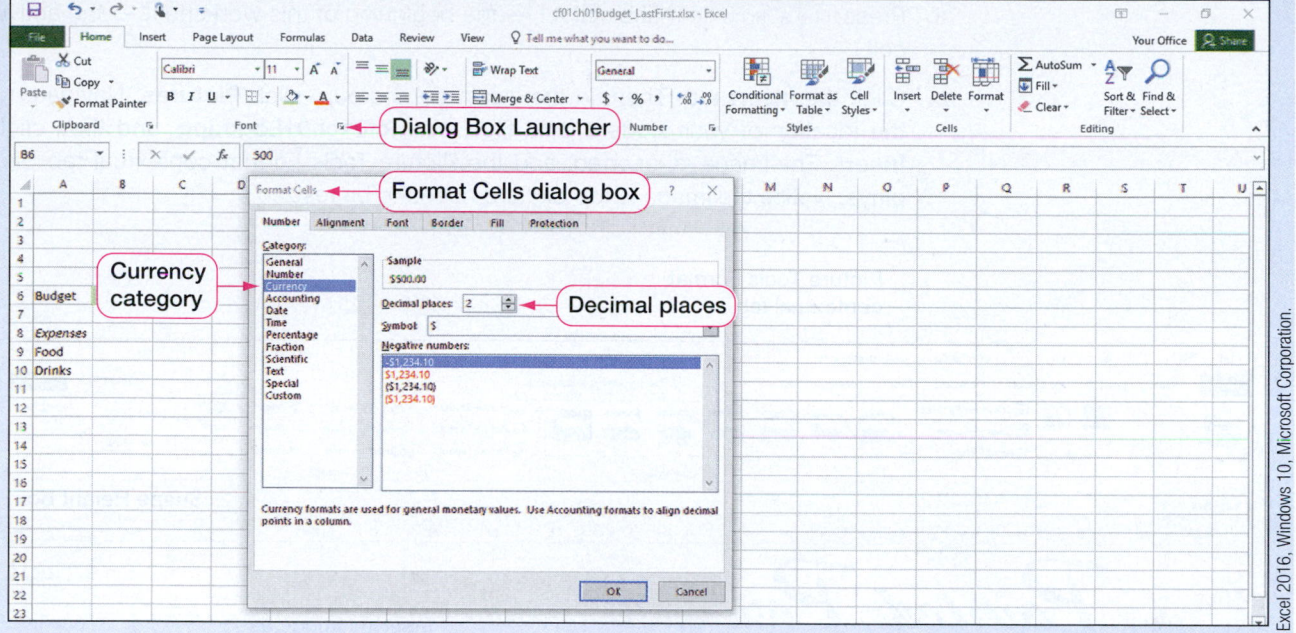

Figure 24 Format Cells dialog box, Number tab

c. Click **OK**. The cell now shows a dollar sign before the number. Notice that the default of two decimals is applied.

d. **Save** 🖫 the spreadsheet.

Inserting Images and Using Contextual Tools to Resize

In Word, Excel, PowerPoint, and Publisher, you can insert pictures from a file, a screen shot, or various online sources. The online options include inserting images within the Office Online Pictures collection, via a Bing search, or from your own OneDrive. Be careful when you insert Online Pictures — you must ensure that you have the right to use the image you selected for the purpose you want.

The term "contextual tools" refers to tools that appear only when needed for specific tasks. Some tabs, toolbars, and menus are displayed as you work and appear only if a particular object is selected. Because these tools become available only as you need them, the workspace remains less cluttered.

A **contextual tab** contains commands related to selected objects so that you can manipulate, edit, and format the objects. Examples of objects that can be selected to display contextual tabs include a table, a picture, a shape, or a chart. A contextual tab appears to the right of the standard ribbon tabs. The contextual tab disappears when you click outside the selected object — in the file — to deselect the object. In some instances, contextual tabs can also appear as you switch views.

In this exercise, you will insert a Painted Treasures Gift Shop logo into the budget you are beginning for your manager, Susan Brock. This budget will become a part of Susan's larger budget that she must present to the CEO of Painted Paradise in an internal memo once a year. Logos are an excellent way to brand both internal and external communications.

 **CF01.19**

To Insert an Image and Use the Contextual Tab to Resize

a. Press ⎡Ctrl⎤ + ⎡Home⎤ to make cell A1 — the beginning of this worksheet — the active cell.

b. Click the **Insert** tab. Then, in the Illustrations group, click **Pictures**. Navigate to the location of your student data files, click **cf01ch01Logo.jpg**, and then click **Insert**. The image is inserted, and the Picture Tools Format contextual tab displays. Notice the image is too big and needs to be resized.

Figure 25 Picture Tools Format contextual tab

c. In Picture Tools, on the Format contextual tab, in the Size group, click in the **Shape Height** box. Then type **1** and press ⎡Enter⎤. The image now fits the spreadsheet more appropriately.

d. Click cell **A6**. The contextual tab disappears because the image is no longer selected.

e. **Save** 🖫 the spreadsheet.

REAL WORLD ADVICE	What Is Creative Commons and Why Should You Care?

Office used to provide clip art pictures that were free to use. Office 2016 instead searches web sources for images. By default, it will find images that have Creative Commons licenses. These are images for which the copyright owner has chosen to allow anyone to use the image without commercial compensation. However, it is up to YOU to make sure that image really is free to use. You must read the specific license for that image to be sure your use is acceptable — otherwise, you could be sued for copyright infringement — which is why you should care. When you insert the image, the source URL will be listed on the bottom. Click the link to open the source URL. From there, it may or may not be easier to find the license that is specific to that URL. When in doubt, do not use the file, or contact the owner before using.

Formatting Using the Mini Toolbar

The **Mini toolbar** appears after text has been selected and contains buttons for the most commonly used formatting commands, such as font, font size, font color, center alignment, bold, and italic. The Mini toolbar button commands vary for each Office program. The toolbar disappears if you move the pointer away from the toolbar, press a key, or click the workspace. All the commands on the Mini toolbar are available on the ribbon; however, the Mini toolbar offers quicker access to common commands, since you do not have to move the mouse pointer far away from the selected text for these commands.

In this exercise, you will edit some of the cells in your budget with the Mini toolbar.

 **CF01.20**

To Use the Mini Toolbar to Make a Cell Bold

a. Double-click cell **A6** to place the insertion point in the cell. Double-clicking a cell enables you to enter edit mode for the cell text.

b. Double-click cell **A6** again to select the text. The Mini toolbar appears, coming into view directly above the selected text. If you move the pointer off the cell, the Mini toolbar becomes transparent or disappears entirely. If you don't move it too far away, you can move the pointer back over the Mini toolbar, and it becomes completely visible again. If it doesn't reappear, double-click on the text again.

Troubleshooting

If you are having a problem with the Mini toolbar disappearing, you may have inadvertently moved the mouse pointer to another part of the document. If you need to redisplay the Mini toolbar, right-click the selected text, and the Mini toolbar will appear along with a shortcut menu. Once you have selected an option on the Mini toolbar, the shortcut menu will disappear and the Mini toolbar will remain while in use — or repeat the prior two steps, then make sure the pointer stays over the toolbar.

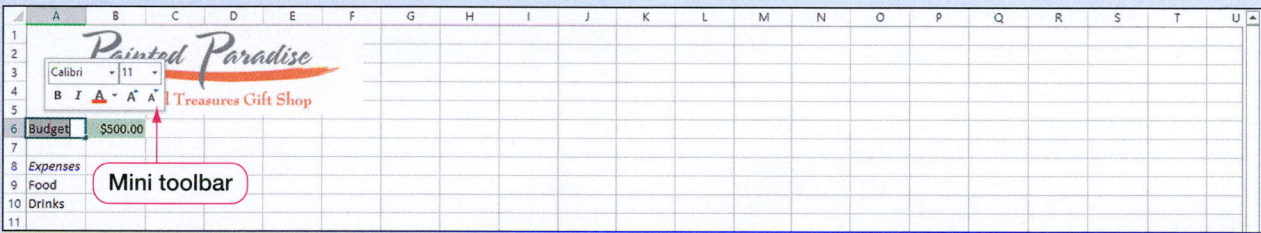

Figure 26   The Mini toolbar

Excel 2016, Windows 10, Microsoft Corporation.

c. In the Mini toolbar, click **Bold** B and press Enter.

d. **Save** 🖫 the spreadsheet.

The Mini toolbar is particularly helpful with the touch interface. When Office recognizes that you are using touch instead of a mouse or digitizer pen, it displays Mini toolbars that are larger and designed to work with fingers more easily. An example of a touch Mini toolbar in Excel Touch mode is shown in Figure 27.

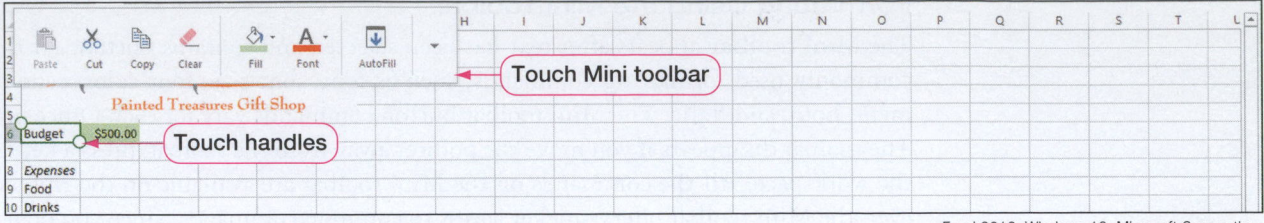

Figure 27   The Mini toolbar in Touch mode

Opening Shortcut Menus and Format Painter

A **shortcut menu** is a list of commands related to a selection that appears when you right-click — click the right mouse button. Shortcut menus are also context sensitive and enable you to quickly access commands that are most likely to be needed in the context of the task being performed. This means that you can access popular commands without using the ribbon. Included are commands that perform actions, commands that open dialog boxes, and galleries of options that provide a Live Preview. The Mini toolbar also opens with the shortcut menu when you click the right mouse button. If you click a button on the Mini toolbar, the shortcut menu closes, and the Mini toolbar remains open, allowing you to continue formatting your selection.

The **Format Painter** allows you to copy a format and apply it to other selections. This allows you to format in one place and quickly apply all of the same formatting elsewhere. If you click the Format Painter button once, Format Painter will turn off after you use it just once. If you double-click the Format Painter, it leaves Format Painter active until you click the Format Painter button again or press Esc; leaving Format Painter active allows you to apply the formatting to multiple locations.

In this exercise, you will add some additional information to the budget you are beginning for your manager. You will also edit some of the cells using a shortcut menu and copy the format using Format Painter.

To Use a Shortcut Menu and Format Painter

a. Click cell B9. Type **450** and press Enter. Cell B10 should now be the active cell.

b. With cell B10 active, type **50** and press Enter.

c. Right-click cell **B9** to display the shortcut menu.

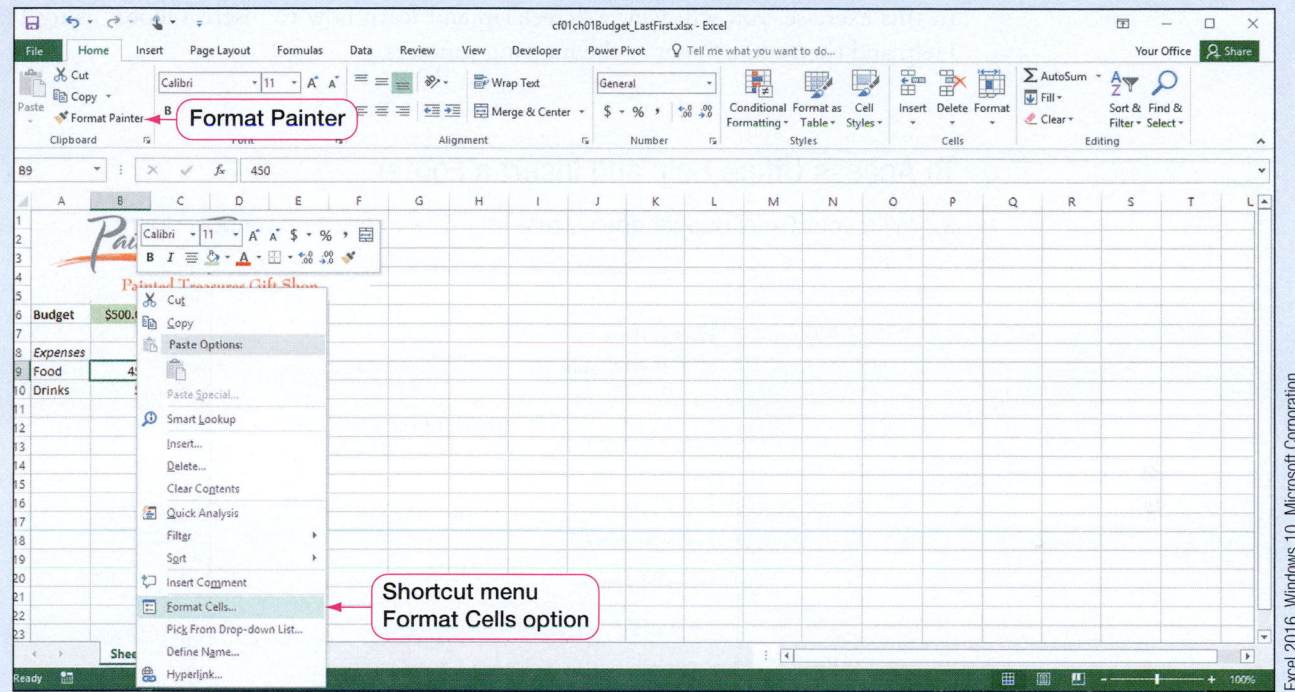

Figure 28 The shortcut menu

Excel 2016, Windows 10, Microsoft Corporation.

SIDE NOTE

Double-click the Format Painter

If you double-click the Format Painter, it will stay on until you click the Format Painter again, allowing you to apply the formatting to more than one cell.

---

d. Click **Format Cells**.

e. In the Format Cells dialog box, under Category, click **Currency** and then click **OK**.

f. With B9 as the active cell, on the Home tab, in the Clipboard group, single-click **Format Painter**. Your insertion point now appears with a paintbrush next to it.

g. Click cell **B10**. Notice that B10 changes to currency format and the Format Painter is turned off.

h. **Save** the spreadsheet.

Find Help, Print, and Share in Office

Office **Help** can give you additional information about a feature or steps for how to perform a new task. Your ability to find and use Help can greatly increase your Office proficiency and save you time from seeking outside assistance. Office has several levels of help, from a searchable search window to more directed help such as ScreenTips.

The Help window provides detailed information on a multitude of topics, as well as access to templates, training videos installed on your computer, and content available on Office.com — the website maintained by Microsoft that provides access to the latest information and additional Help resources. To access the contents at Office.com, you must have access to the Internet from the computer. If there is no Internet access, only the files installed on the computer will be displayed in the Help window. The easiest way to access Help is through pressing F1 — in some of the programs. If available, this will take you directly to an article about what is actively selected.

Pointing to any command on the ribbon will display a **ScreenTip** with screen text to indicate more information. You may have seen these while working earlier in the chapter. They are very useful to learn what the command on the button will do.

Using the Help Window and ScreenTips

In this exercise, you will view a ScreenTip and learn how to insert a footer using Excel Help and then add a footer to the meeting minutes.

 **CF01.22**

To Access Office Help and Insert a Footer

a. With your Excel budget open, press F1. The Excel Help window opens.

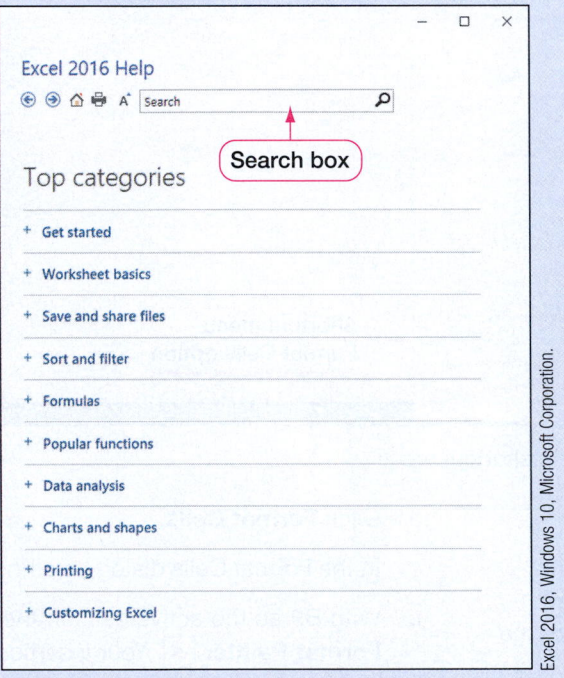

Figure 29   The Excel Help window

b. In the search box, type add a footer and press Enter. Then click the first link, and read about how to add a footer. When you are done, click **Close** ☒ to close the Help window.

c. Click the **Page Layout** tab, and then, in the Page Setup group, point your mouse to **Print Titles**. Notice the ScreenTip with a link for Tell me more. If you clicked on Tell me more, it would take you to the Help window specifically for Print Titles.

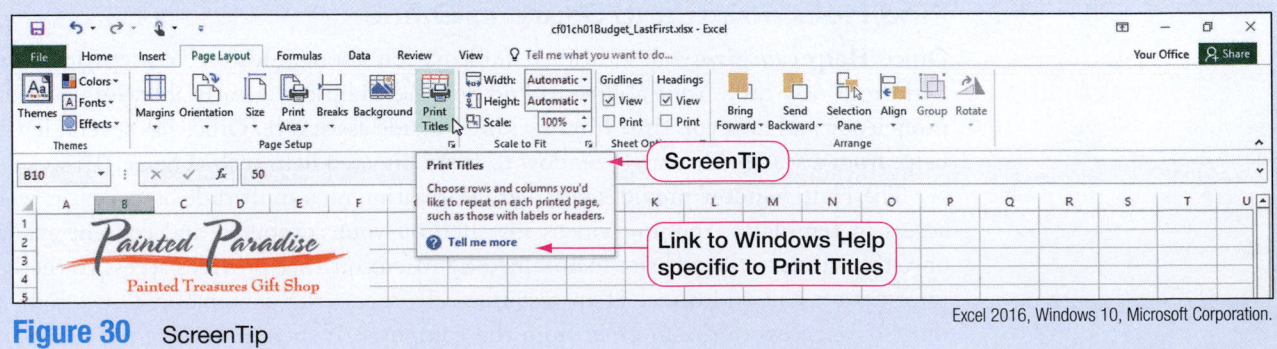

Figure 30   ScreenTip

d. On the **Page Layout** tab, in the Page Setup group, point your mouse to the **Page Setup Dialog Box Launcher** ⌟. Notice the ScreenTip, this time without the Tell me more option. Click the **Page Setup Dialog Box Launcher** ⌟.

e. Click the **Header/Footer** tab, and then click **Custom Footer** to display the Footer dialog box.

f. Click in the **Left section** and type First Last, using your first and last name.

g. Click in the **Center section** and click **Insert File Name** 📄.

h. Click in the **Right section** and type InstructorLast, using your instructor's last name.

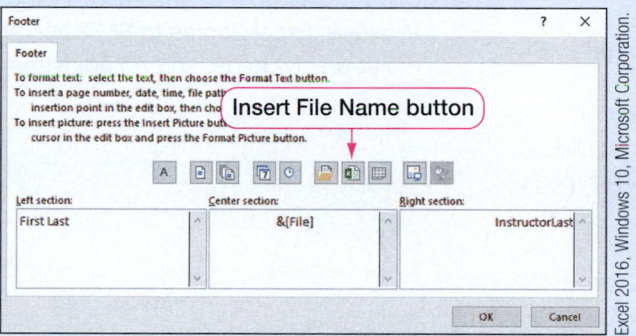

Figure 31 The Footer dialog box

Excel 2016, Windows 10, Microsoft Corporation.

> **SIDE NOTE**
> **ScreenTip and** F1
> If a topic for a ScreenTip does not exist in Help, the window will open to the starting search page.

i. Click **OK**, and then click **OK** again. The footer is inserted. In Normal view, you will not see the footer. You will see the footer in the next exercise.

j. **Save** 💾 the spreadsheet.

Accessing the Share Pane

In Office, many ways exist for sharing files. There are times when you will need a paper copy — also known as a hard copy — of an Office document, spreadsheet, or presentation. When a printed version is not needed, a digital copy will save paper and costs. Office provides many ways to share your document. You can use traditional ways of sharing by printing or exporting a PDF. From the Share link in Office, you can invite other people to share the document, and you can specify whether others are allowed to edit the document if the file is saved to OneDrive. From Office Backstage, the document can be e-mailed to others, transformed into an online, browser-not-required presentation, or posted to a blog.

New in Office 2016, you can share your file without leaving your file. In the top right corner, next to your account image, click Share. This will open the Share task pane. From there, you can add a person, choose whether he or she can edit or just view the file, and even give a personal message. In addition, new with Office 2016, you and those you share with can all be editing the document in real time. You will be able to see the changes being made to the document while you are also making changes. To do this, you must have the file saved in your OneDrive and be logged into your Microsoft account.

Changing Views

In each of the Office applications, there are different ways to view the file. For example, in Word, you can view in Read Mode, as a Web Layout, Outline, or Draft. In Excel, it is particularly important to change your view to Page Break Preview before attempting to print a file. This view shows you where the page breaks will happen and, if needed, allows you to modify them. Also, Page Layout view will allow you to view any headers and footers before printing. In this exercise, you will change to Page Break Preview and the Page Layout view to ensure that everything will fit on one page.

 **CF01.23**

SIDE NOTE
Adjusting Page Breaks
From Page Break Preview you can click and drag to adjust page break lines.

To Change Views to Preview How a File Will Print

a. Click the **View** tab, and then, in the Workbook Views group, click **Page Break Preview**. Excel Zooms to 60% and shows each page with blue lines. The budget will fit on one page, and no adjustments are needed.

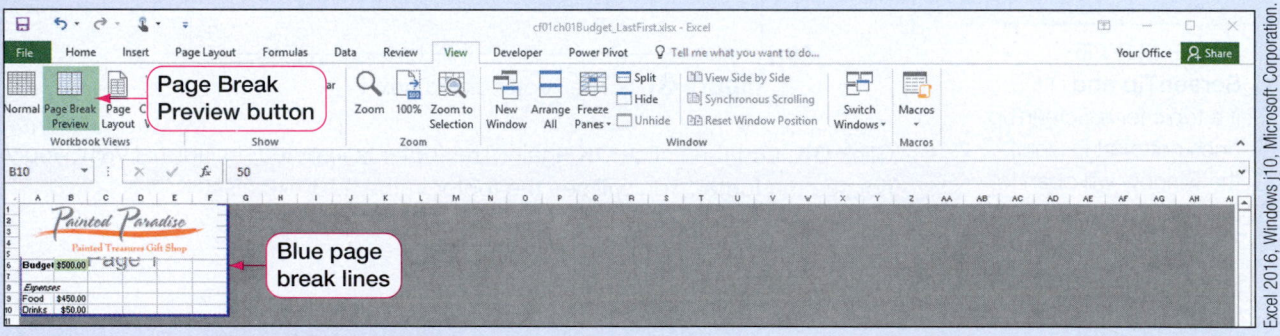

Figure 32 Page Break Preview

b. On the View tab, in the Workbook Views group, click **Page Layout**. Scroll down and verify that the footer you created in a prior exercise looks correct.

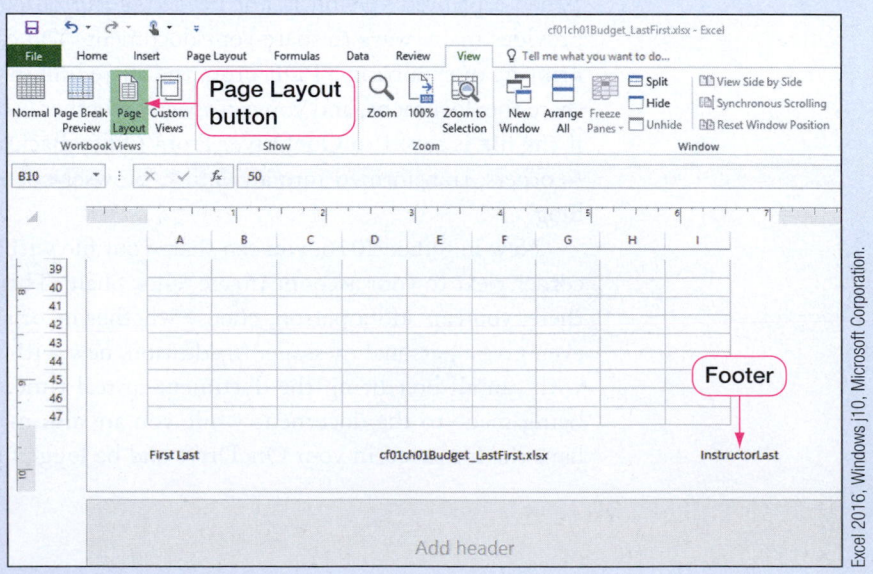

Figure 33 Page Layout view

40 **CHAPTER 1** | Common Features of Microsoft Office 2016

c. On the View tab, in the Workbook Views group, click **Normal** to return to the normal Excel view. Press ⎡Ctrl⎤ + ⎡Home⎤ to make cell A1 the active cell.

d. **Save** 🖫 the spreadsheet.

Printing a File

Before printing, carefully consider whether a paper copy is necessary. Even in the digital world, paper copies of documents make more sense in many situations. Always review and preview the file and adjust the print settings before sending the document to the printer as you did in the prior exercise. Many options are available to fit various printing needs, such as the number of copies to print, the printing device to use, and the portion of the file to print. The print settings vary slightly from program to program. Printers also have varied capabilities; thus, the same file may look different from one computer to the next, depending on the printer that is connected to it. Doing a simple print preview will help to avoid having to reprint your document, workbook, or presentation, which requires additional paper, ink, and energy resources.

In this exercise, you will print the budget on which notes can be handwritten during the meeting so that you can update the spreadsheet with more detail later.

 **CF01.24**

To Print a File

a. In Excel, click the **File** tab to open Office Backstage.

b. Click **Print**. The Print settings and Print Preview appear. Verify that the Copies box displays **1**.

c. Verify that the correct printer — as directed by your instructor — appears in the Printer box. Choices may vary depending on the computer you are using. If the correct printer is not displayed, click the Printer arrow, and then click to choose the correct or preferred printer from the list of available printers.

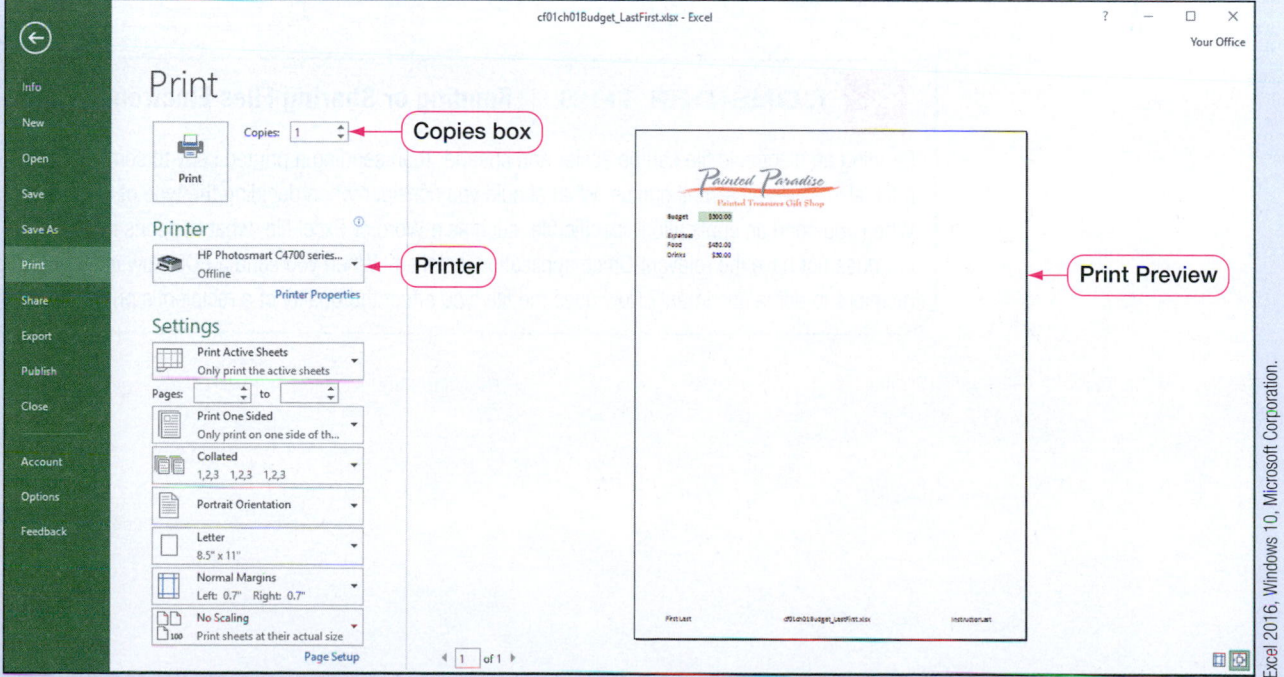

Figure 34   Backstage Print

d. If your instructor asks you to print the document, click **Print**.

Exporting a PDF

When you want to give someone else a document, consider whether an electronic version of the file is better than a printed copy. A **portable document format (PDF)** file is a type of file that ensures that the document will look the same on someone else's computer. For example, different computers may have different fonts installed. A PDF maintains the fonts used in the original document. Even if the computer on which the file is being viewed does not have the same fonts as the computer that was used to create the file, the viewer will see the correct font. PDFs are a common file format used in business to share documents because of the readily available free readers. In Word, you can edit a PDF. Also, in Windows 10, the default PDF reader is now the new Edge browser. You can still install the Adobe reader program and set it as the default if you prefer.

In this exercise, you will export a PDF of the budget file so you can e-mail a copy to your colleagues who are also attending the meeting.

 **CF01.25**

To Create a PDF File

a. If you are not already in Office Backstage, click the **File** tab. Click **Export**, and then click **Create PDF/XPS**.

b. Navigate to the location where your student files are stored. Verify that the file name selected is **cf01ch01Budget_LastFirst.pdf**. Notice settings in the Publish as PDF or XPS dialog box for optimizing for publishing online versus printing. Since your colleague will print this document, the default setting of Standard is appropriate.

c. Click **Publish**. Close the **PDF** file. If the PDF opens in the default reader — in the Windows 10 Edge browser — then close the reader.

d. **Save** the spreadsheet and click **Close** ⊠ to close this file and exit Excel. Submit your files as directed by your instructor.

SS **CONSIDER THIS** | **Sending or Sharing Files Electronically**

Sending an electronic file can be easier and cheaper than sending a printed copy to someone. Sharing a file also saves on e-mail quotas. What should you consider when deciding the type of file to send? When you send an application-specific file, such as a Word or Excel file, what happens if the recipient does not have the relevant Office application installed? When you send a PDF, how easy is it for a recipient to edit a document? How does the file type affect the quality of a recipient's printout?

Insert Office Add-ins

To enhance the features of Office, you can install **Add-ins for Office** from Microsoft's Office Store. These Add-ins run in the side pane to provide extra features such as web search, dictionary, and maps. There are different Add-ins for the different Office programs. You must be signed into Office with your Microsoft account to take advantage of them.

QUICK REFERENCE	Installing Add-ins for Office

1. Open up any Office application in which you want to use apps.

2. Go to the Insert tab, and then select My Add-ins arrow. Select See All from the menu.

3. The Office Add-ins window appears, showing all the apps you have installed to your Microsoft account under My Apps. If you see the app you want, select the app, and then click Insert.

4. If you do not see the app you want, click Store link or Office Store button.

5. Search for the Add-in you want, and then follow the steps online to install the Add-in to your account. You may have to sign into your Microsoft account.

6. Once the Add-in has been installed, return to the Office application and repeat steps 2 and 3.

Concept Check

1. What kind of Microsoft program do you need to create a budget? p. 2

2. What are the advantages of using OneDrive instead of a USB flash drive? p. 10

3. What is the difference between Save and Save As? p. 8

4. How do you pin open the ribbon? Explain what can be done in Office Backstage. p. 6–8

5. Explain a way to copy and paste. What advantages are there to knowing keyboard shortcuts? p. 16

6. What is the Tell me what you want to do feature and how is it different from Help? p. 27

7. Describe three different ways of making text bold. p. 24

8. What is a contextual tab? p. 33

9. Describe ways to obtain help in Office 2016. p. 37

10. How could you share a newsletter with all the members of your business fraternity without printing the document? p. 39, 42

11. What are the Add-ins for Office? p. 43

Key Terms

Visual Summary

Go to Office backstage (p. 9)
Use the Tell me what you to do box (p. 28)
Change how the ribbon displays
cf01ch01Agenda_LastFirst.docx - Word
File
Home
Insert
Design
Layout
References
Mailings
Review
View
Tell me what you want to do...
Share
Undo and redo actions (p. 22)
Touch and Mouse Mode (p. 6)
Find and replace (p. 24)
Find
Replace
Select
Editing
Clipboard
Font
Paragraph
Using the Font group and the Font dialog box launcher (p. 25)
Show formatting symbols (p. 21)
Use the Style gallery and Live Preview (p. 26)
Close a file and exit an application (p. 14)
Create a Style
Apply Styles
Intense Quote
Painted·Treasures¶
Check spelling and use buttons (p. 20)
Agenda¶
May·1,·2017,·1:00pm¶
Paragraph symbol (p. 95)
Lunch·Budget¶
Zoom
Page 1 of 1
5 of 41 words
154%

Word 2016, Windows 10, Microsoft Corporation.

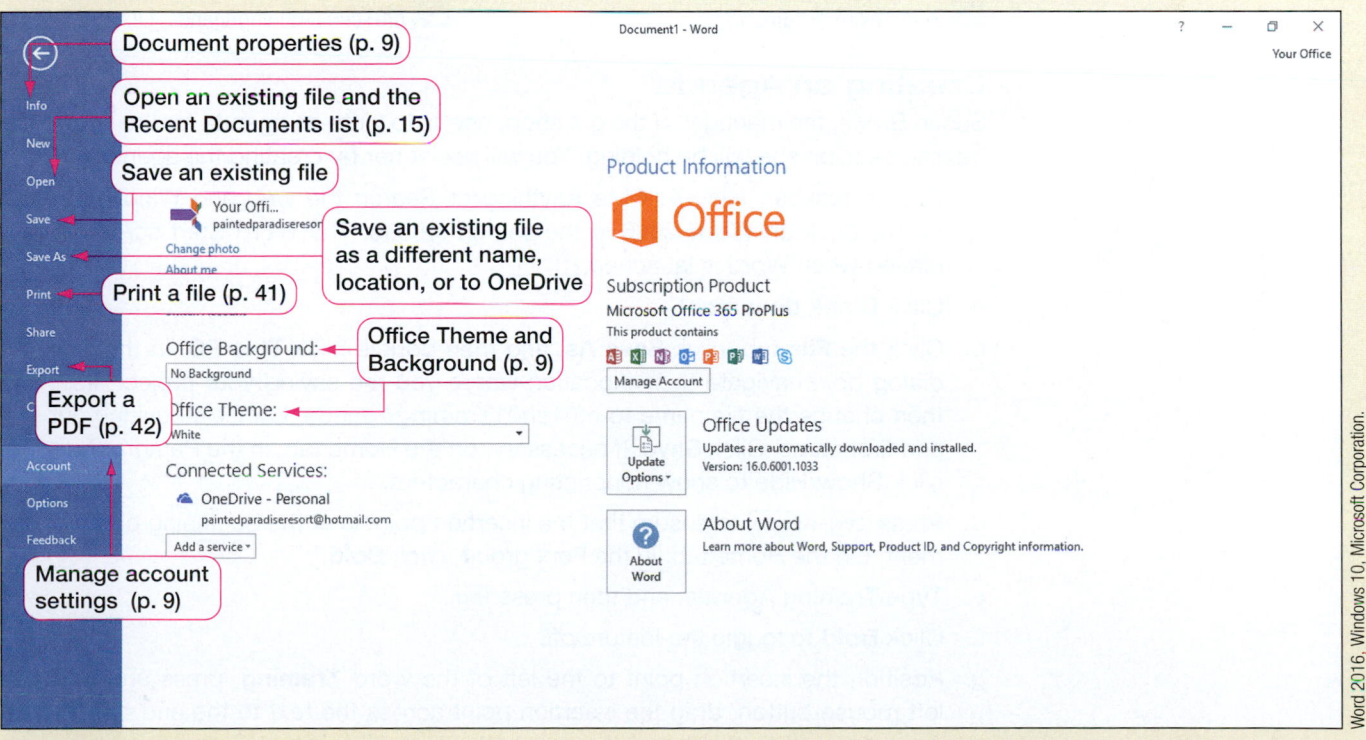

Figure 35

Document1 - Word
Your Office
Document properties (p. 9)
Info
Open an existing file and the Recent Documents list (p. 15)
New
Open
Save an existing file
Save
Save As
Save an existing file as a different name, location, or to OneDrive
Print
Print a file (p. 41)
Share
Export
Export a PDF (p. 42)
Office Theme and Background (p. 9)
Office Background:
No Background
Office Theme:
White
Account
Options
Feedback
Connected Services:
OneDrive - Personal
paintedparadiseresort@hotmail.com
Add a service
Manage account settings (p. 9)
Change photo
About me
Product Information
Office
Subscription Product
Microsoft Office 365 ProPlus
This product contains
Manage Account
Office Updates
Updates are automatically downloaded and installed.
Version: 16.0.6001.1033
Update Options
About Word
Learn more about Word, Support, Product ID, and Copyright information.

Word 2016, Windows 10, Microsoft Corporation.

Figure 36

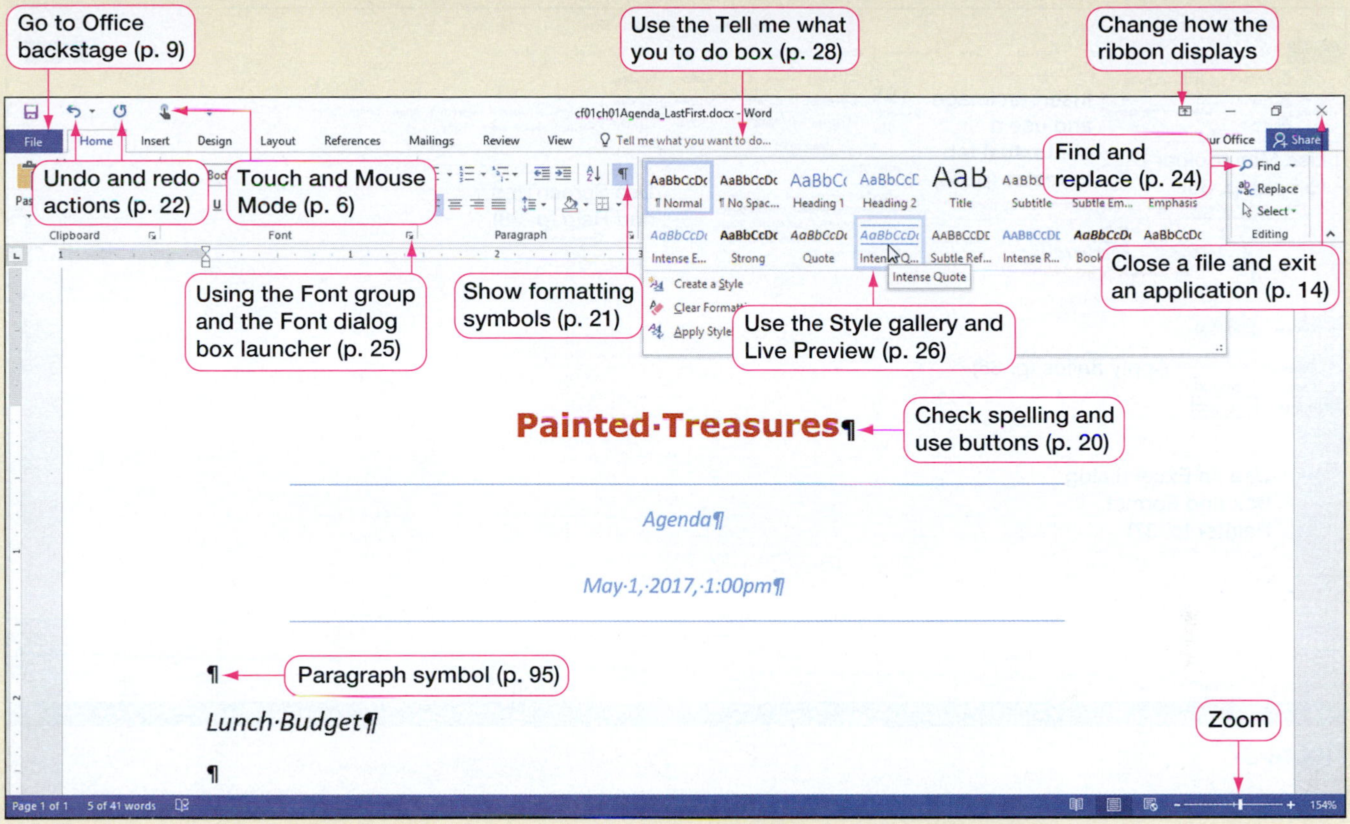

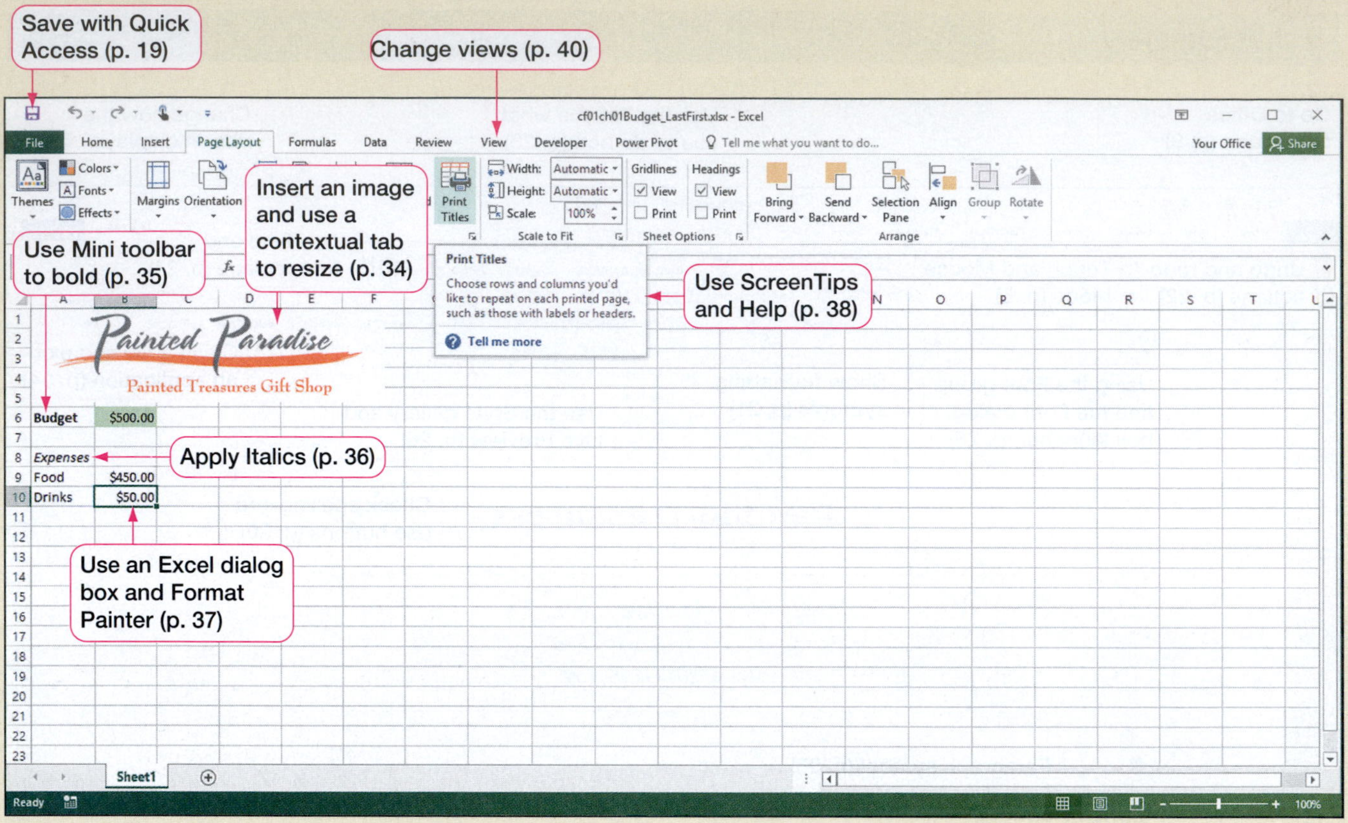

Insert an image and use a contextual tab to resize (p. 34)

Use Mini toolbar to bold (p. 35)

Print Titles
Choose rows and columns you'd like to repeat on each printed page, such as those with labels or headers.

❓ Tell me more

Use ScreenTips and Help (p. 38)

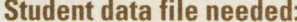

Apply Italics (p. 36)

Use an Excel dialog box and Format Painter (p. 37)

Budget $500.00

Expenses
Food $450.00
Drinks $50.00

Excel 2016, Windows 10, Microsoft Corporation.

Figure 37

Practice 1

Student data file needed:

📄 Blank Word document

You will save your file as:

📄 cf01ch01TrainingAgenda_LastFirst.docx

Human Resources

Creating an Agenda

Susan Brock, the manager of the gift shop, needs to write an agenda for the upcoming training session she will be holding. You will assist her by creating the agenda.

a. On the taskbar, click Ask Me Anything or Search the web and Windows. Type **Word**. Click on **Word 2016** in the search results. The Word Start screen is displayed when Word is launched.

b. Click **Blank document**.

c. Click the **File** tab, click **Save As**, and then double-click **This PC**. In the Save As dialog box, navigate to the location where you are saving your project files, and then change the file name to cf01ch01TrainingAgenda_LastFirst, using your last and first name. Click **Save**. If necessary, on the Home tab, in the Paragraph group, click Show/Hide to show nonprinting characters.

d. Press Ctrl + Home to ensure that the insertion point is at the beginning of the document. On the Home tab, in the Font group, click **Bold**.

e. Type Training Agenda, and then press Enter.

f. Click **Bold** to toggle the feature off.

g. Position the insertion point to the left of the word **Training**, press and hold the left mouse button, drag the insertion point across the text to the end of the word **Agenda**, and then release the mouse button. All the text in the line should be highlighted.

h. On the Home tab, in the Font group, click the **Font Size** arrow. Select **20** to make the font size larger.

i. In the Paragraph group, click **Center** . In the Font group, click the **arrow** next to Font Color and select **Blue**.

j. Click the second line, type **today's date**, and then press Enter twice.

k. In the Paragraph group, click the **Bullets** arrow. Under the Bullet Library, click the **circle** bullet.

l. Type Welcome trainees 2:00 pm, and then press Enter.

m. Type Using the Register, and then press Enter.

n. Type Customer Service Policies, and then press Enter.

o. Type Wrap-Up, and then press Enter twice to turn off bullets.

p. Type Questions?. On the Home tab, in the Styles group, click **Heading 2**.

q. **Save** the document.

r. Click the **Insert** tab, and then, in the Header & Footer group, click the **Footer** arrow, and then select the first option **Blank**.

s. On the Header & Footer Tools Design tab, in the Insert group, click **Document Info**, and then click **File Name**.

t. On the Header & Footer Tools Design tab, in the Close group, click **Close Header and Footer** to exit the footer.

u. **Save** the document, exit Word, and then submit your file as directed by your instructor.

Problem Solve 1

MyITLab® Grader

Homework

Student data files needed:

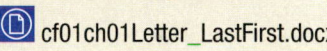

 cf01ch01Letter.docx

 cf01ch01Cookies.jpg

You will save your file as:

 cf01ch01Letter_LastFirst.docx

Midnight Sweetness Loan Letter

Finance & Accounting

Recently, you opened a business with a few partners called Midnight Sweetness. With the slogan "No more starving late-night studies," the business specializes in delivering freshly baked cookies, brownies, and other sweet treats to local college students. Midnight Sweetness has been a huge success. Currently, you rent a small building that includes major kitchen appliances. Now you and your partners are looking for a bank loan to expand your business. As part of your presentation to the bank, you must write a cover letter highlighting some parts of your business. The letter is written, but now you will add formatting to make it easier to read.

a. Open the cf01ch1Letter document. Save your file as cf01ch01Letter_LastFirst, using your last and first name. Click Enable Editing if necessary. If necessary, show nonprinting characters.

b. Place the insertion point before the **M** in Midnight Sweetness. Insert the cf01ch01Cookies image.

c. Resize the image to be **1"** in height.

d. Format the company name, Midnight Sweetness, to **bold**, **Dark Red** font color, font size **36**, and font of **Georgia**.

e. Find the two spelling errors with a red wavy line, and correct the **mistakes** in the text.

f. Midnight Sweetness has three offerings: Freshly baked cookies, Homemade brownies, and Other sweet treats. Change the three paragraphs listing the offerings to a **bulleted** list using regular bullets.

g. Midnight Sweetness is trying to achieve four things: a larger kitchen, more office space, additional baking equipment, and additional baking supplies. Change the four paragraphs of what the company is trying to achieve to a **numbered** list with **Number alignment: Left** style that uses the number without the parenthesis.

h. Select the second and third lines of the document containing the address. Cut the address to the clipboard.

i. Insert a **blank** footer. Paste the **two address lines** to the footer. Verify that the footer does not have any blank paragraphs — only the two address lines. Verify that there is only one blank paragraph between the company name and the line that reads "Dear Mr. Garth."

j. In the footer, change the font color of both lines of the address to **Dark Red**, and **Center** the text.

k. In the blank line between the company name and "Dear Mr. Garth," type the **current date**.

l. After the letter closing, on the paragraph below "Sincerely," type First Last, using your first and last name. Erase any blank paragraphs below your name.

m. Apply the style **Emphasis** to your name, change the font size to **14**, and change the font color to **Dark Red**. Press Ctrl + Home to place the insertion point at the beginning.

n. Save the document, exit Word, and then submit your file as directed by your instructor.

Critical Thinking

These directions told you how to format the letter. Do you have any suggestions for improvements or anything that might be problematic? Do you think the letter looks professional? Is the content of the language in the letter professional and appropriate? You may suggest changes that you have not learned how to make yet. Answer as directed by your instructor.

Perform 1: Perform in Your Career

Student data files needed:

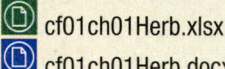 cf01ch01Herb.xlsx

cf01ch01Herb.docx

You will save your files as:

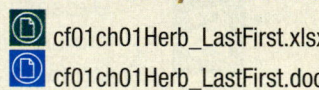 cf01ch01Herb_LastFirst.xlsx

cf01ch01Herb_LastFirst.docx

Harry's Herbs

General Business

You are interning for a local nursery. One of the employees, Harry, specializes in herbs. Every year, he does an herb sale as a fundraiser for the local homeless shelter. Another intern began to create these files — but is unexpectedly unavailable to finish them. Your supervisor has asked you to help get ready for the event by preparing documents associated with the schedule.

a. Open the Excel file **cf01ch01Herb**. Save your file as cf01ch01Herb_LastFirst, using your last and first name.

b. Change the **font, fill color**, and **font color** of the merged cell A1:D1, and make the font size **16 or larger**. Choose professional colors.

c. Format the merged cell from A2:D2 to be **bold**.

d. Format cells A3:A5 as **italic**.

e. Format cell **A6** so that it matches or complements the coloring you applied to the merged cell A1:D1, and make the font size **larger**.

f. Paint the format from cell A6 to **A13**, **A19**, **A24**, and **A28**.

g. Change the text in cell **D7** to **Details**, and make D7 **bold**. Then copy and paste to put the same label in cells **D14**, **D20**, **D25**, and **D29**.

h. Apply bold to all of the cells with one of these three labels **Master Gardener Advice and Classes**, **Daily** and **Hourly**.

i. Add any other formatting that will make this spreadsheet look more professional or have more clarity. Do not change any more of the content or move cells.

j. Add a custom footer that contains **First Last**, using your first and last name, in the Left section and the **File Name** in the Right section. Do not worry if the file will not print on a single page.

k. **Save** the spreadsheet, exit Excel, and then submit your file as directed by your instructor.

l. Open the Word file **cf01ch01Herb.docx**. Save your file as **cf01ch01Herb_LastFirst.docx**, using your last and first name.

m. Correct all spelling mistakes.

n. Before the word Schedule in the title, add the word **Tuesday**.

o. Add **am** and **pm** to the times appropriately — Tuesdays overall hours are 10:00 am to 8:00 pm.

p. Change the **font colors**, **background colors**, **font sizes**, and **styles** to make the schedule easier to read and understand. Match the colors you used in cf01ch1Herb_LastFirst.xlsx.

q. Add a custom footer with **First Last**, using your first and last name.

r. **Save** the document, and close Word. Submit your work to your instructor as directed.

Perform 2: Perform in Your Life

Student data files needed:

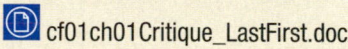 Blank Word document
cf01ch01Vintage.docx
cf01ch01Dinner.xlsx

You will save your file as:

cf01ch01Critique_LastFirst.docx

Improving the Appearance of Files

Human Resources   Finance & Accounting

Your boss at a local vintage clothing store has asked you to review a spreadsheet and a document — made by a prior employee — and make suggestions on what to do to improve the appearance of the document and spreadsheet. Examine the two files cf01ch01Vintage and cf01ch01Dinner. Then do the following.

a. Open a new blank document in Word, and then save the file as **cf01ch01Critique_LastFirst**, using your last and first name.

b. List five items that you would change in the document and why.

c. List five items that you would change in the spreadsheet and why.

d. Add a footer with First Last, using your first and last name, and the file name.

e. Exit Word, and then submit your file as directed by your instructor.

Additional Chapter Cases are available at www.pearsonhighered.com/youroffice

Additional Cases

Excel Business Unit 1

Understanding the Fundamentals

Data is vital to businesses to help them determine their profits or their losses, their place in a competitive market, and/or their ability to branch into new markets. Businesses use Excel to structure and process data to create information to help in decision making purposes. To use Excel effectively, you need to plan, structure, and format workbooks appropriately. This business unit will introduce you to the fundamentals of creating and working with an Excel workbook.

Learning Outcome 1:

Use Excel to enter text, number, date, and time data to create efficient and effective worksheets.

REAL WORLD SUCCESS

"My family has operated the same farm for four generations. When I graduated from college, I decided to become the first woman to run the family farm. I now track all of our production inputs and outputs using Excel. The high-quality information I produce with Excel has made our farm more efficient and more profitable. Farming is a business, and a successful business requires intelligence in handling information as much as, or more than, it requires intelligence in any other critical business activity."

- Leah, recent graduate

Learning Outcome 2:

Use Excel to effectively communicate information through the use of functions and worksheet formatting.

REAL WORLD SUCCESS

"I worked in an insurance agency while I was in college. Part of my job was to administer marketing strategies. Every month, we received data from our parent company that identified prospective clients. I used Excel to calculate a ranking so I could contact prospects with the highest potential value first. Agency performance was significantly improved as a result, and I received a regional award for efficiency improvement."

- Mike, alumnus and insurance agent

Microsoft Excel 2016

Chapter 1 | CREATE, NAVIGATE, WORK WITH, AND PRINT WORKSHEETS

MyITLab® Grader
Homework

$
Finance & Accounting

Prepare Case

Red Bluff Golf Course & Pro Shop Golf Cart Purchase Analysis

The Red Bluff Golf Course & Pro Shop makes golf carts available to its members for a fee. Recently, the resort has been running out of carts. The time has come for the club to add more golf carts to its fleet. Club manager Barry Cheney, wants to use Microsoft Excel to analyze the purchase of golf carts by model, price, and financing parameters.

Laura Gangi Pond / Shutterstock

Student data file needed for this chapter:

 e01ch01GolfCarts.xlsx

You will save your files as:

 e01ch01GolfCarts_LastFirst.xlsx

 e01ch01GolfCarts_LastFirst.pdf

 e01ch01Mowers_LastFirst.xlsx

Getting Started with Excel

Data plays an integral part in supporting business. Without data, businesses cannot determine their effectiveness in the market, let alone their profit or loss performance. In addition, as businesses grow and change, the types of data collected by a particular business are among the few things that remain relatively static over time. Jobs change, products change, and businesses grow, shrink, or evolve into different lines of business — even into different organizations — on the basis of customer and market demands. However, the types of data that businesses gather and analyze are relatively constant. Much of the same information is required about customers, vendors, products, services, materials, transactions, and so on regardless of the type of business or its stage of growth. Data tracking typically expands as new data is made available and deemed necessary for business purposes or as new technologies easily capture data that was prohibitive to track in the past. Many things may change, but the type of information remains the same.

Data requires processing — categorizing, summarizing, counting, averaging, statistical analysis, and formatting for effective communication — to reveal information that the data itself cannot tell you. With an application such as Excel, it is possible to structure data and to process it in a manner that creates information for decision-making purposes.

Understand Spreadsheet Terminology and Components

Excel is a spreadsheet program that can be used to manage, analyze, and share information. With the help of Excel, you can reveal underlying trends, calculate values, make predictions, make recommendations, and display or share information with large or small amounts of data.

To learn the efficient and effective utilization of Excel, you must know the terminology and components of a spreadsheet. If you are unsure where something is located or how Excel is functioning, you can use the Excel Help feature. You can access Excel Help by pressing the F1 key or by typing your question into the *Tell me what you want to do . . .* or *Search the web or Windows . . .* section on the ribbon.

What Is a Spreadsheet?

Excel is a spreadsheet application. A **spreadsheet** is a collection of data that is organized in a row and column format. The intersection of each row and column is called a **cell**. A **row** is a horizontal set of cells that encompasses all the columns in a worksheet. A **column** is a vertical set of cells that encompasses all the rows in a worksheet. Each cell can contain text, numbers, formulas, and/or functions. A **formula** is an equation that produces a result and may contain numbers, operators, text, and/or functions. A **function** is a built-in program that performs a task such as calculating a sum or average. Both formulas and functions must always start with the equal sign (=). In Excel, each instance of a spreadsheet is referred to as a **worksheet**, which is a grid of columns and rows in which data is entered.

From balancing an accounting ledger to creating a financial report, many business documents use Excel spreadsheets. Excel spreadsheets are designed to support analyzing business data, representing data through charts, and modeling real world situations.

Spreadsheets are also commonly used to perform **what-if analysis**. In what-if analysis, you change values in spreadsheet cells to investigate the effects on calculated values of interest. What-if analysis allows you to examine the outcome of the changes to values in a worksheet.

Spreadsheets are used for much more than what-if analysis, however. A spreadsheet can be used as a basic collection of data in which each row is a record and each column is a field in the record. A **record** is all of the categories of data that pertain to one person, place, thing, event, or idea and are formatted as a row in a worksheet. A **field** is an item of information in a worksheet column that is associated with something of interest.

Spreadsheets can be built to act as a simple accounting system. Businesses often use spreadsheets to analyze complex financial statements and information. Excel can calculate statistical values such as mean, variance, and standard deviation. Excel can even be used for advanced statistical models such as forecasting and regression analysis. Spreadsheet applications "excel" at calculations of almost any kind.

What Is a Workbook?

Excel files are known as workbooks. A **workbook** is a file that contains one or more worksheets. In Microsoft Excel 2016, workbooks have a file extension of .xlsx. By default, a new, blank workbook contains one worksheet, identified by a tab at the bottom of the Excel window titled Sheet1. As additional worksheets are added, each is given a default name. For example, two new worksheets would be given the names Sheet2 and Sheet3. The **active worksheet** is the worksheet that is visible in the Excel application window and is denoted by a white tab — unless a tab color has been applied — with bold letters and a thick bottom border. Worksheets that are not active are denoted by gray tabs — unless tab colors have been applied — with normal letters. The number of worksheets that can be contained in a workbook is determined by the amount of available memory.

Once a workbook has been created, any changes to it will need to be saved. Save can accomplish this task; however, Save As is useful for saving a copy of a file with a new name. Save As is also useful for creating a backup of a file or for creating a copy of a workbook when you want to use that workbook as the starting point for another workbook.

In this exercise, to get started on the golf cart analysis, you will open a workbook that club manager Barry Cheney has prepared for you and then will save the workbook with a new name.

E01.00

SIDE NOTE
Windows 10
This book is written for Windows 10. If you are using Windows 8, open your charms, click Search, and then type Excel. If using Windows 7, search the Start menu for Excel.

SIDE NOTE
Pin the Ribbon
If your ribbon is collapsed, pin your ribbon open. Click the Home tab. In the lower right-hand corner of the ribbon, click Pin the Ribbon 📌.

To Start Excel and Open, Save, and Rename a Workbook

a. On the taskbar, click **Ask Me Anything** or **Search the web and Windows**. Type **Excel**.

b. If necessary, click on **Excel 2016** in the search results.

c. As explained in the Common Features chapter, the Excel Start screen is displayed when Excel is launched. Click **Open Other Workbooks** in the left pane, and then double-click **This PC**. Navigate through the folder structure to the location of your student data files, and then double-click **e01ch01GolfCarts**. If a Security Warning message displays, click the **Enable Editing** button.

   A workbook providing data to analyze the purchase of golf carts by model, price, and financing opens.

d. Click the **File** tab, click **Save As**, and then double-click **This PC**. In the Save As dialog box, navigate to the location where you are saving your project files, and then change the file name to **e01ch01GolfCarts_LastFirst**, using your last and first name. Click **Save**.

REAL WORLD ADVICE | **AutoRecover and Quick Save — Outsmart Murphy!**

Computers are not perfect. While life's imperfections often make things interesting, they are also an opportunity for Murphy's Law: Anything that can go wrong, will go wrong. However, never fear — AutoRecover and Quick Save are here!

Excel automatically saves your work every 10 minutes, but you can change that interval. Click the File tab, click Options, and then click Save. In the Excel Options dialog box, change the value in the Save AutoRecover information every box. The saved copies of your work are called AutoRecover files. If your computer shuts down unexpectedly, Office will recognize that the file you were working on was not closed properly and will give you the option of opening the most recent AutoRecover file.

The Ctrl + S shortcut quickly saves your file to the same location as the last save. Whenever you make a significant change to your file, save it immediately using the quick save keyboard shortcut.

QUICK REFERENCE | **Back Up Your Workbook!**

It is a good idea to back up your workbook when you are about to make significant changes to it, when those changes have been made, and/or when you have finished working for the moment.

To make a backup of your workbook, do the following.

1. Click the File tab, click Save As, and then click Browse.
2. In the Save As dialog box, navigate to the location where you are saving your files. In the File name box, type the name of your file, such as YourFile_yyyy-mm-dd, where yyyy-mm-dd is today's date. Click Save.

If possible, best practice is to store backup files on an entirely different drive, such as a USB drive, or to a cloud service such as OneDrive.

Save As not only saves a copy of your file, but also changes the file Excel has open. YourFile_yyyy-mm-dd will be the open file, and the title bar at the top of the Excel application window will display the new file name. Click Close and open your original file before continuing your work.

Navigate Worksheets and Workbooks

Workbooks often contain more than a single worksheet. Sometimes the worksheets are related to each other, such as monthly sales data. Other times, worksheets may be separate from the rest of the data and used only to document the workbook's worksheet(s). To effectively develop and use workbooks and worksheets, you must be able to navigate within worksheets and between worksheets in a workbook.

Navigating Between Worksheets

Workbooks may contain more than one worksheet. The worksheet tabs are located on the bottom left side of the Excel window. Each tab represents a single worksheet in the workbook.

The active worksheet — the worksheet that is visible — is readily identifiable because the background color of its worksheet tab is white and it has a thick bottom border. To make a different worksheet active, click its worksheet tab. When you open a workbook that you have not worked with before, it is a best practice to spend some time familiarizing yourself with its worksheets.

You may have noticed that the golf carts workbook you have opened contains four worksheets. In this exercise, you will navigate among worksheets to familiarize yourself with their contents.

 **E01.01**

To Change the Active Worksheet

a. Click on the **GolfCartPurchases** worksheet tab to make it the active worksheet. This worksheet is the start of a purchase analysis for replacement of the Red Bluff Golf Course fleet of golf carts.

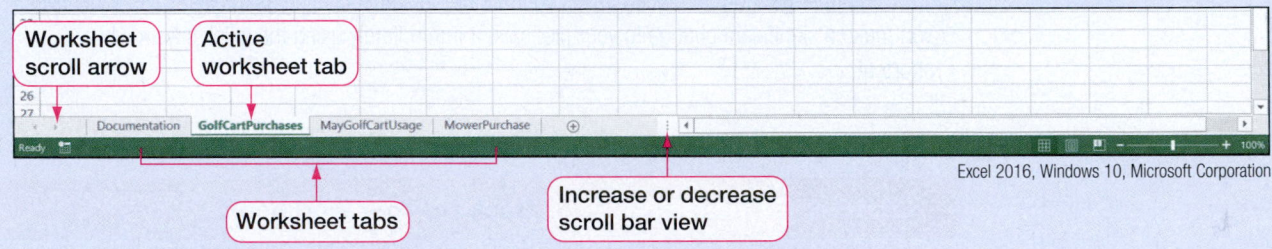

Excel 2016, Windows 10, Microsoft Corporation

Figure 1   Change the active worksheet

SIDE NOTE
Naming Worksheets
It is best practice to not use spaces when naming worksheet tabs. Consider using capitalization if your worksheet tab names contain more than one word.

b. Click the **MayGolfCartUsage** worksheet tab. This worksheet is an analysis of golf cart usage for the month of May that Barry Cheney developed to assess whether the number of carts in the current fleet is optimal.

c. Click the **MowerPurchase** worksheet tab. This worksheet is an analysis of the five different types of mowers available for purchase.

d. Click the **Documentation** worksheet tab. You may need to scroll left using the worksheet scroll arrows to see the Documentation worksheet tab. This worksheet is used to document the contents of the workbook. Documentation is an important component of a well-structured workbook.

e. **Save** 💾 the workbook.

Troubleshooting

All the figures in this text were taken at a monitor resolution of 1366 × 768. Higher or lower resolution will affect the way Excel displays ribbon options.

Once Excel is open, it is important to recognize the components of the worksheet window so that you can effectively use a workbook and navigate within a worksheet. As Figure 2 shows, the worksheet window has many components.

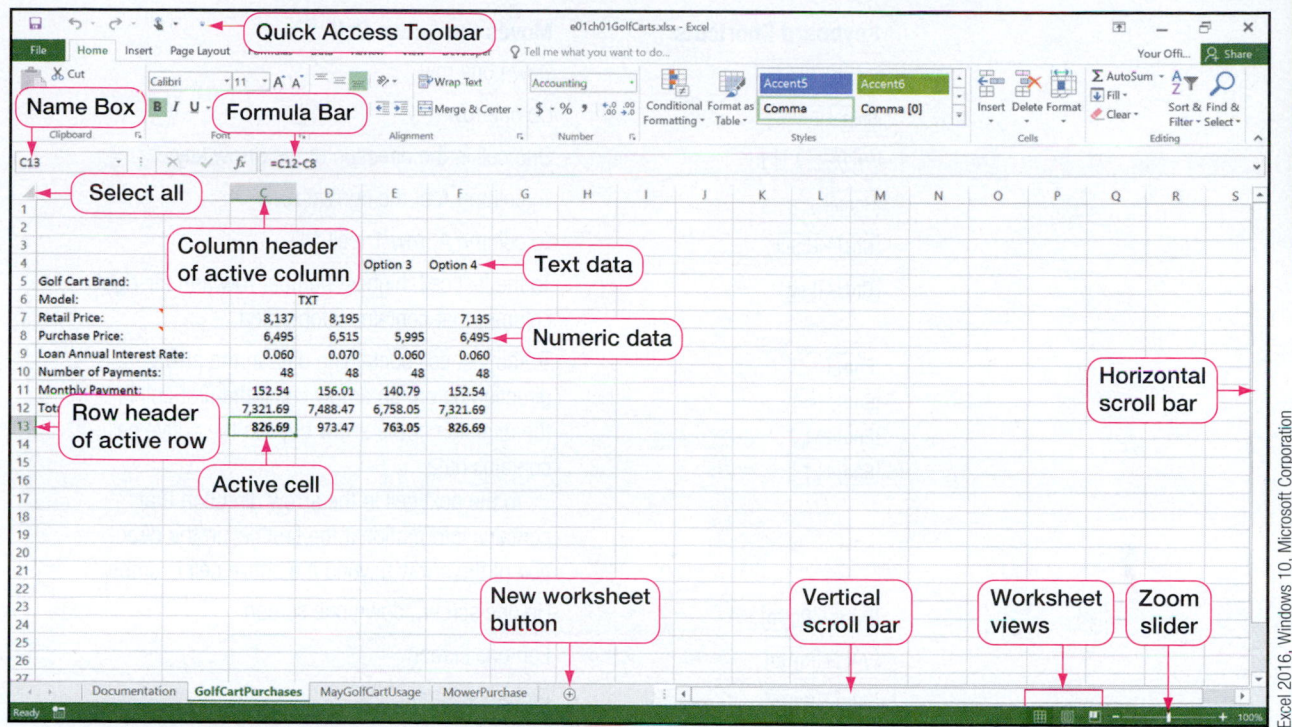

Figure 2 The worksheet window

Navigating Within Worksheets

Whether a worksheet is small or extremely large, navigation from one cell to another is necessary to enter or edit numbers, formulas, functions, or text. Navigation requires an understanding of how Excel handles rows, columns, and cells.

Each row is identified by a number in ascending sequence from top to bottom. Each column is identified by a letter in ascending sequence from left to right. Each cell has a default name called a **cell reference**. A cell reference refers to a particular cell or range of cells within a formula or function instead of a value. The cell reference is a combination of its column letter and row number. For example, the intersection of column A and row 1 has a cell reference of A1, and the intersection of column D and row 20 is cell D20.

Navigating in a small worksheet is simple: Point to the cell, and click to make it the active cell. The **active cell** is the recipient of an action, such as a click, calculation, or paste. When a cell becomes the active cell, the border around it changes to a thick, green line. Any data you enter via the keyboard is placed into the active cell. Worksheet navigation is simply defined as moving the location of the active cell.

When a part of a worksheet is out of view, it may be because the worksheet is too large to be displayed completely in the visible application window. In this case, use the vertical and horizontal scroll bars to shift other parts of the document into view. The vertical scroll bar is on the right side of the application window, and the horizontal scroll bar is at the bottom right of the application window. It is important to note that scrolling does not move the active cell; it only changes your view in the worksheet.

A **keyboard shortcut** is a keyboard equivalent for a software command that allows you to keep your hands on the keyboard instead of reaching for the mouse to make ribbon selections. Keyboard shortcuts allow rapid navigation in a worksheet without having to use the mouse. It is considered best practice to learn and use keyboard shortcuts whenever possible.

There are several keyboard shortcuts that may be used to navigate a worksheet and move the active cell.

Keyboard Shortcuts	Moves the Active Cell
Enter	Down one row
Shift + Enter	Up one row
→ ← ↓ ↑	One cell in the direction of the arrow key
Home	To column A of the current row
Ctrl + Home	To column A, row 1 (cell A1)
Ctrl + End	To the last cell, highest number row and far-right column, that contains information
End + → End + ← End + ↓ End + ↑	To the last cell containing data in the arrow direction before an empty cell if the first cell in the direction of the arrow beyond the active cell contains data To the next cell in the arrow direction that contains information if the first cell in the direction of the arrow beyond the active cell is empty
PgUp PgDn	Up one screen, down one screen
Alt + PgUp	Left one screen
Alt + PgDn	Right one screen
Ctrl + PgUp Ctrl + PgDn	One worksheet left One worksheet right
Tab Shift + Tab	One column right One column left

For large worksheets, Go To allows rapid navigation. Although the worksheet you are currently working with is not large, knowledge of how to use the Go To dialog box to navigate directly to any cell in the worksheet by specifying a cell reference is a skill that you may find useful. In this exercise, you will learn to navigate within a worksheet.

 **E01.02**

SIDE NOTE
Alternate Method
Instead of pressing Ctrl + Enter to finish a cell entry, you can use the Enter button ☑ on the formula bar.

To Navigate Within a Worksheet

a. Click the **GolfCartPurchases** worksheet tab, and then press Ctrl + Home to make **A1** the active cell. Press the ↓ six times, and then press → four times. The active cell should be **E7**. Type 6495, and then press Ctrl + Enter to keep cell E7 active.

b. Press ← once, and then press ↑ two times. The active cell should be **D5**. Type EZ-GO, and then press Enter.
    Notice that the active cell is now **D6**. Pressing Enter moved the active cell down one row.

c. On the Home tab, in the Editing group, click **Find & Select**, and then click **Go To**. The Go To dialog box appears. Click in the **Reference** box, and type D13.

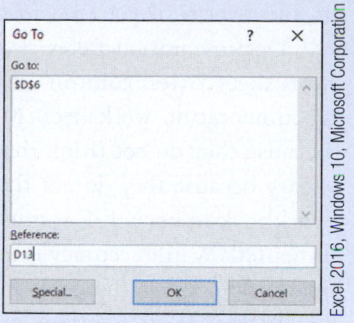

Figure 3 Go To dialog box

Excel 2016, Windows 10, Microsoft Corporation

d. Click **OK**. The active cell is now D13. On the Home tab, in the Font group, click **Bold** B.

e. Press Home. This takes you to column A of the row with the active cell. The active cell should be **A13**. Type Total Interest Cost:, and then press Enter.

f. Press Ctrl+Home to return the active cell to A1.

> **Troubleshooting**
> The active cell is repositioned by using the mouse pointer or keyboard. Even experienced users often scroll through a worksheet and press an arrow key only to find themselves returned to the active cell where they began scrolling.

g. **Save** the workbook.

Touch Devices

If you have a device such as a tablet PC with a touch screen, you can control Excel 2016 using your finger. The commands on the ribbon and in shortcut menus are the same, but Excel recognizes when you have touched the screen and enables **touch mode**. In touch mode, the ribbon and shortcut menus are enlarged to make selecting commands with your fingertip easier. Figure 4 shows the Excel interface in touch mode.

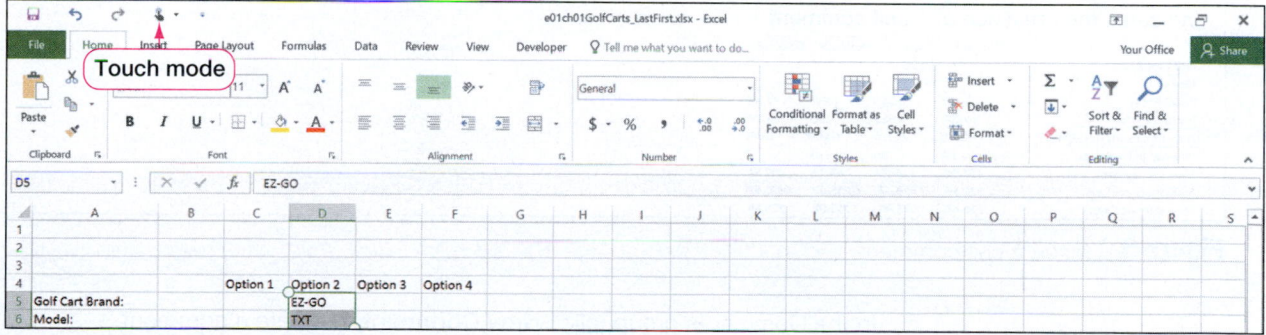

Figure 4 Touch mode in Excel 2016

Excel 2016, Windows 10, Microsoft Corporation

Document Your Work

Workbooks may be used by people who did not develop them. Even if a workbook will never be used by anyone other than its builder, best practice dictates that you document a workbook and its worksheets.

Documentation is vital to ensure that a workbook remains usable. A well-documented workbook is much easier to use and maintain, particularly for a user who did not develop the workbook. You may use a workbook on a regular basis, you may even have developed it, but over time you may forget how the workbook operates.

Documentation takes several forms, such as descriptive file and worksheet names, worksheet titles, column and/or row titles, cell labels, cell comments, or a dedicated documentation worksheet. Many people do not take the time to document adequately because they do not think that it is time spent productively. Some do not think it is necessary because they do not think anyone else will ever use the workbook. However, for a workbook to be useful, it must be accurate, easily understood, flexible, efficient, and documented. While accuracy is most important, an undocumented workbook can later create inaccurate data. Where documentation is concerned, less is not more — more is more.

While documentation worksheets generally include documentation for an entire workbook, comments can be created specifically to add documentation to a worksheet and address individual fields, calculations, and so on and are included as content in an individual cell.

Using Comments to Document a Workbook

A cell **comment** is a text box, similar to a sticky note, that is attached to a cell in a worksheet in which you can enter notes or give instructions. In this exercise, you will insert comments into a worksheet to document a workbook.

 **E01.03**

To Document a Workbook Using Comments

a. On the **GolfCartPurchases** worksheet, notice the red triangles in the upper right corners of cells A7 and A8. The triangle indicates the existence of a comment. Point to cell A7. The comment that appears defines Retail Price.

b. Click cell **A9**. Click the **Review** tab.

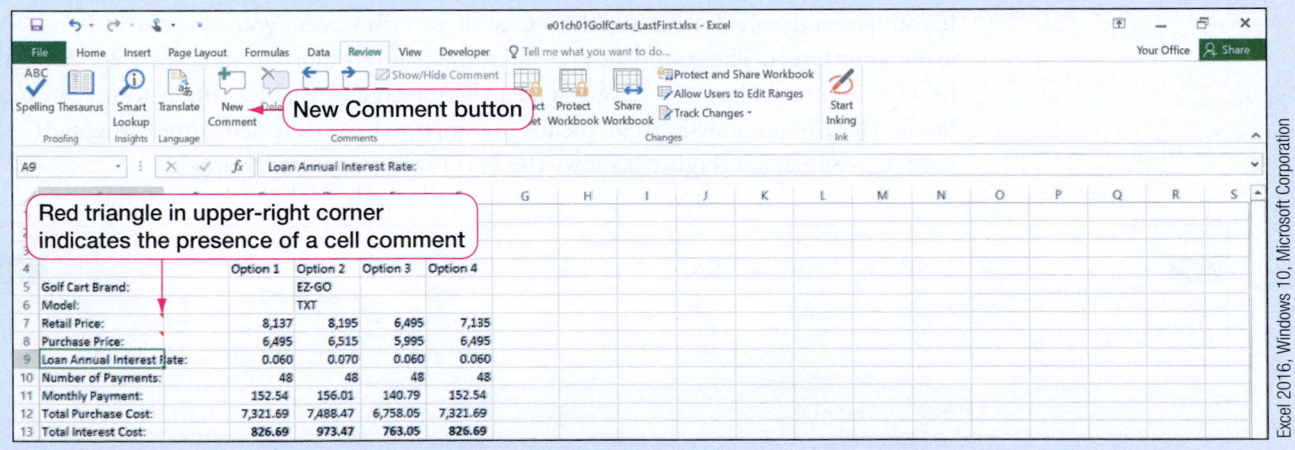

Figure 5   Insert a cell comment

Excel 2016, Windows 10, Microsoft Corporation

SIDE NOTE

Deleting a Comment
To delete a comment, click on the cell that includes the comment, click the Review tab, and in the Comments group, click Delete.

c. In the Comments group, click **New Comment** to create a comment.

d. In the comment box, select the text **user name** — not the colon — that is automatically inserted into the comment. Press Del to delete the text.

e. With the insertion point to the left of the colon, type Annual Interest Rate, and then press the → twice, and then type Annual rate of interest in decimal or percentage format.

4		Option 2	Option 3	Option 4
5	Golf Cart Bra	EZ-GO		
6	Model:	TXT		
7	Retail Price:	8,137	8,195	6,495	7,135
8	Purchase Price:	6,495	6,515	5,995	6,495
9	Loan Annual Interest Ra		0.070	0.060	0.060
10	Number of Payments:		48	48	48
11	Monthly Payment:		156.01	140.79	152.54
12	Total Purchase Cost:		7,488.47	6,758.05	7,321.69
13	Total Interest Cost:	826.69	973.47	763.05	826.69

Comment box

Annual Interest Rate: Annual rate of interest in decimal or percentage format.

Figure 6 Documenting a worksheet using a comment

Excel 2016, Windows 10, Microsoft Corporation

CHAPTER 1

f. Press Esc twice to close the comment. Cell A9 now has a red triangle in the top right corner to indicate the presence of a comment.

g. Save 🖫 the workbook.

> **SIDE NOTE**
> **Cell Comments**
> To close a comment, you can also click any other cell within the worksheet.

Using a Worksheet for Documentation

A well-structured worksheet is self-documenting in that there are descriptive titles, column headings, and cell labels. However, a separate documentation worksheet includes information that is not generally specified in a worksheet, such as authorship, modification dates, modification history, or specific information that should be noted. Documentation worksheets go beyond the file properties that are automatically stored by Excel when a workbook is saved. For example, a documentation sheet could include the indication of cell comments or an explanation of calculations being performed, which could assist the user of the workbook.

In this exercise, you will update the documentation worksheet to include your name as well as the addition of the cell comment you added previously.

▶ E01.04

To Document a Workbook Using a Documentation Worksheet

a. Click the **Documentation** worksheet tab. You may have to scroll left in the worksheet tabs. Click cell **A8**, and then type the **current date** in mm/dd/yyyy format.

b. Press Tab. In cell **B8**, type your name in Firstname Lastname format. Press Tab. In cell **C8**, type Added comment to a key heading on the GolfCartPurchases worksheet, and then press Enter.

c. Save 🖫 the workbook.

REAL WORLD ADVICE | **Failing to Plan Is Planning to Fail**

Winston Churchill said, "He who fails to plan, plans to fail." The first step in building a worksheet should be planning. There are several questions that you should consider before you begin entering information.

- What is the objective of the worksheet? Is it to solve a problem? Is it to analyze data and recommend a course of action? Is it to summarize data and present usable information? Is it to store information for use by another application?
- Do you have all of the data necessary to build this worksheet?

Enter and Edit Data

In building and maintaining worksheets, the ability to enter, edit, and format data is fundamental. As data is entered via the keyboard, the data appears simultaneously in the active cell and in the formula bar. Figure 7 shows the result when a cell is double-clicked to place the insertion point into cell contents. If you click in the formula bar, the insertion point is displayed in the formula bar.

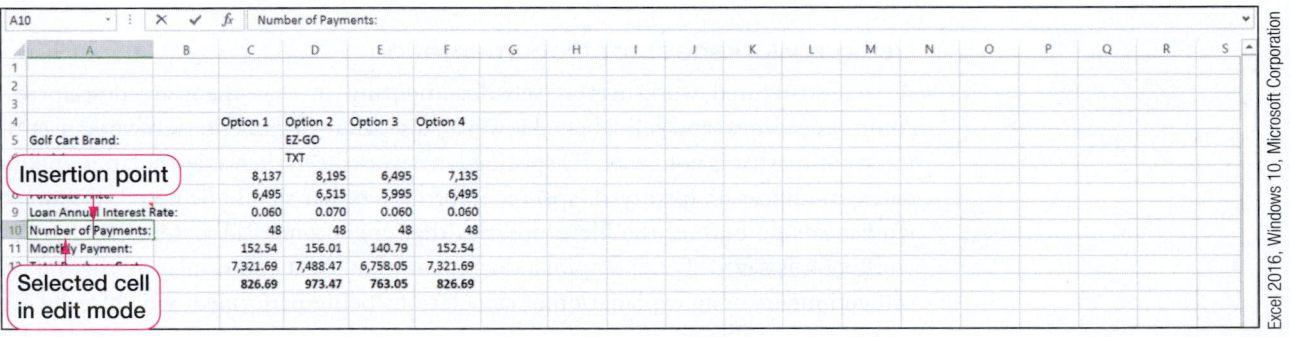

Figure 7 Editing data in a cell

Using Text, Number, Date, and Time Data in Cells

Cell entries can consist of text data or numerical data. **Text data** consists of any combination of printable characters, including letters, numbers, and special characters available on any standard keyboard. By default, text data is left-aligned in a cell

Numeric data consists of numbers (0–9) in any form not combined with letters and special characters such as the period (decimal) and/or hyphen (to indicate negative values). Technically, special characters such as the dollar sign ($) or comma (,) are not considered numeric. They are displayed only for contextual and readability purposes and are not stored as part of a numeric cell value. By default, numeric data is right-aligned in a cell.

In Excel, date data and time data are special forms of numeric data. **Date data** is data recognized by Excel as a date. Data formatted as a date takes the form of a serial number, with the number 1 representing January 1, 1900. **Time data** is data recognized by Excel as representing time. Time data is represented as a decimal value where .1 is 144 minutes, .01 is 14.4 minutes, and so on. Information entered in a recognized date and/or time format will be converted automatically to an Excel date and/or time value. If Excel recognizes a value as a date/time, it will right-align the entry. If you enter a date or time that is not recognized, Excel treats the information as text and left-aligns it in the cell.

Table 1 includes examples of valid dates and times that can be entered into Excel and how they will be displayed by default.

Enter	Excel Displays	Enter	Excel Displays
December 21, 2018	21-Dec-18	1:00 p	1:00 PM
21 Dec 2018	21-Dec-18	1 a	1:00 AM
Dec 21, 2018	21-Dec-18	13:00	13:00

Table 1   Date and time entries and how Excel displays dates

Amy S Kinser, Brant Moriarity, Eric Kinser, Kristyn Jacobson

The GolfCartPurchases worksheet not only contains text, numbers, and date information, it also contains formulas and functions. Although you will not learn about formulas and functions until the next chapter, it is important to note that they appear throughout the Golf Carts workbook. A formula performs a mathematical calculation (or calculations) using data in the worksheet to calculate new values, as in cell D12 of the GolfCartPurchases worksheet. A function is a built-in program that performs operations against data and returns a value, as in cell D11 of the GolfCartPurchases worksheet.

After reviewing the GolfCartPurchases worksheet, you think that the worksheet is missing an appropriate title to help with understanding its contents. In this exercise, you will add worksheet titles and edit existing information.

E01.05

SIDE NOTE
Keyboard Shortcut for Undo
Ctrl + Z is a fast and efficient method of performing an Undo ↩.

SIDE NOTE
Use Undo History
If you need to undo a change but have made other changes since making that change, click the Undo arrow ↩ to see the change history.

To Enter Information into a Worksheet

a. Click the **GolfCartPurchases** worksheet tab, click cell **A2**, type Red Bluff Golf Course & Pro Shop, and then press Enter. Notice the active cell is cell A3.

b. In cell **A3**, type Golf Cart Purchase Analysis, and then press Enter. Notice that Excel displays the text as left-aligned.

c. In cell **A4**, type 6/6/2018, and then press Enter. Notice that Excel displays the date as 6/6/2018 and is right-aligned.

d. In cell **G4**, type Option 5, and then press Enter. Notice that the text in cell G4 is left-aligned.

e. Notice the value in cell D11 of 156.01. Click cell **D9**, type 0.06, and then press Enter.

Notice that the monthly payment in cell D11 changes to 153.00. The values in cells D11, D12, and D13 are automatically recalculated because those cells contain formulas.

f. Click on cell **D11**, and then view the function in the Formula Bar. Also click on cells **D12** and **D13** to view the formulas of those cells in the Formula Bar.

Troubleshooting

If the monthly payment is larger than it should be, you may have entered 0.6. That is actually 60% for calculation purposes. You must enter the percentage 6% or enter 0.06, the decimal equivalent of 6%.

g. **Save** 💾 the workbook.

Wrapping Text and Line Breaks

By default, Excel places all information in a single line in a cell. Text that is too long to fit in a cell is displayed over adjoining cells to the right unless those cells also contain information. If adjoining cells contain information, lengthy text from cells to the left is not fully displayed.

Text truncation can be avoided by changing the alignment of a cell to wrap words or by placing hard returns into text to force wrapping at a particular location. In this exercise, you will wrap text in a cell.

 **E01.06**

To Wrap Text in a Cell

a. Click the **Documentation** worksheet tab, and then click cell **C8**. Notice how the contents of cell C8 appear to be displayed over cell D8.

b. Click the **Home** tab and in the Alignment group, click **Wrap Text**. The vertical size of row 8 is increased to display all content within the boundaries of cell C8.

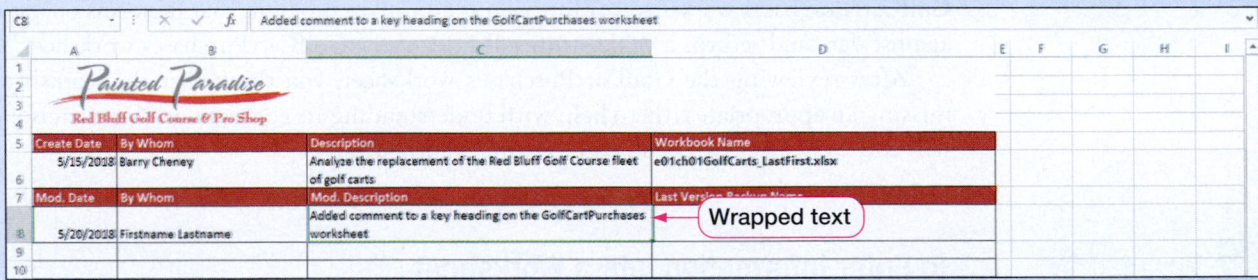

Figure 8 Wrap text in a cell

Excel 2016, Windows 10, Microsoft Corporation

c. Click the **GolfCartPurchases** worksheet tab.

d. Click cell **A3**, and then click in the **Formula Bar** immediately to the right of the word **Cart**. Press Delete to remove the space between Cart and Purchase, and then press Alt + Enter to insert a line break, often referred to as a hard return.

e. Press Ctrl + Enter to complete the entry. Notice how only the words before the hard return are visible on the formula bar.

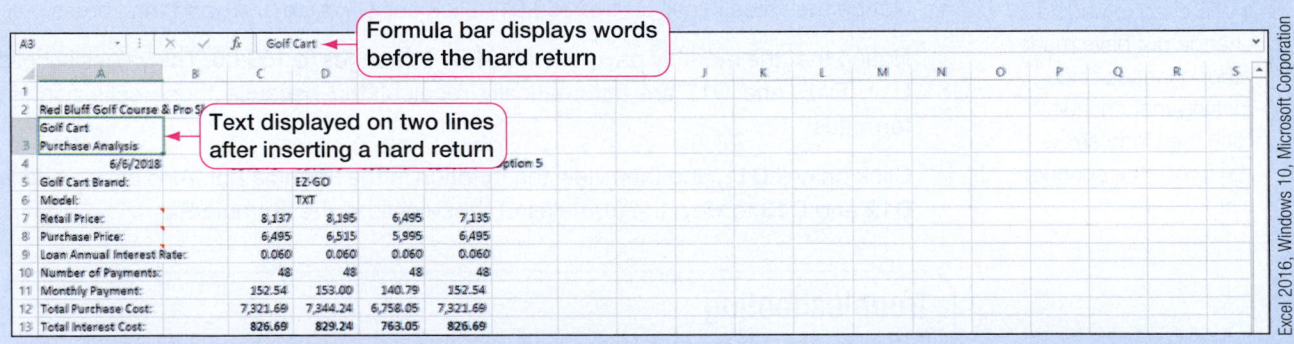

Figure 9 Insert a hard return to control text wrap location

Excel 2016, Windows 10, Microsoft Corporation

f. **Save** the workbook.

Work with Cells and Cell Ranges

Part of what makes a worksheet an efficient tool is the ability to perform actions that affect many cells at once. Knowing how to work with cells and cell ranges is an important part of maximizing your efficiency. **Cell range** refers to the cells in the worksheet that have been selected. A cell range can reference a single cell, several contiguous cells, or noncontiguous cells. A **contiguous cell range** consists of multiple selected cells, all directly adjacent to one another — for example, A1:A10. When you read a range such as A1:A10, the colon stands for "through." A **noncontiguous cell range** consists of multiple selected cells with at least one cell not directly adjacent to other cells.

Cutting, Copying, and Pasting

Copy and paste copies everything in a cell, including formatting. Cut and paste moves everything in a cell, including formatting. However, through Paste Options  and Paste Special, you can control exactly what is placed into the destination cells. When you copy or cut data in Excel, the data is placed in the Clipboard. The **Clipboard** is a temporary storage location where information that was cut or copied is stored until you paste, move, or clear the information. A **destination cell** is the location cell to be modified by a move or paste operation.

In this exercise, you will make changes to the GolfCartPurchases worksheet by using the cut, copy, and paste in Excel.

E01.07

SIDE NOTE
Keyboard Shortcuts
The keyboard shortcut for **Cut** is Ctrl + X; the shortcut for **Copy** is Ctrl + C; and the shortcut for **Paste** is Ctrl + V.

To Cut, Copy, and Paste Cells

a. On the GolfCartPurchases worksheet, click cell **D5**. On the Home tab, in the Clipboard group, notice that the Paste option is unavailable — it is light gray in color.

> ### Troubleshooting
> If the Paste option is not grayed out on your screen, you could have another application open in which you have been copying information and therefore information remains on the Office Clipboard. To clear the Clipboard, click the Clipboard arrow, and select Clear All from the Clipboard pane, and then close the Clipboard pane.

b. In the Clipboard group, click **Cut**. The solid border around cell D5 changes to a moving dashed border.

c. Click cell **C5**.

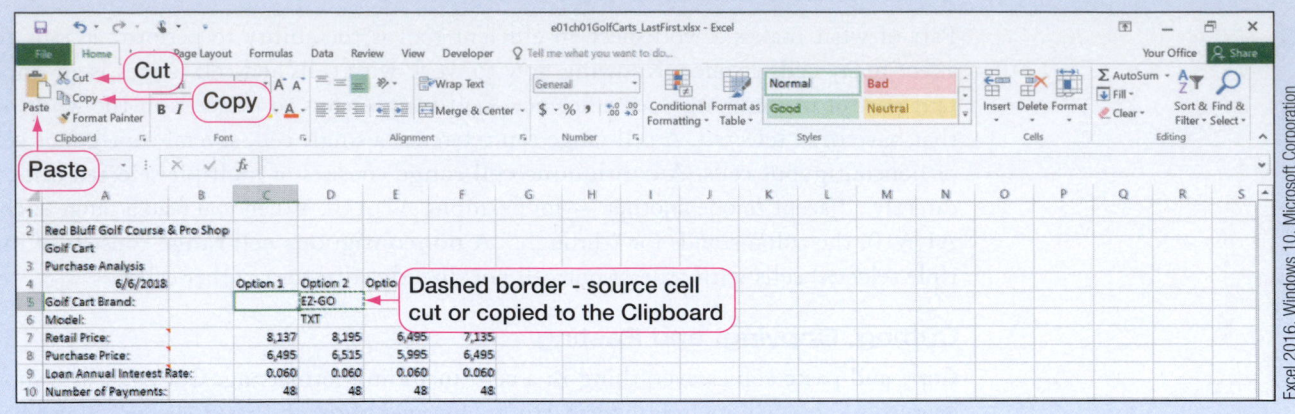

Figure 10   Cut, copy, and paste

d. In the Clipboard group, click **Paste** 📋.

e. Click cell **D6**, and then, in the Clipboard group, click **Copy** 📋. The solid border around cell D6 changes to a moving dashed border. Click cell **C6**, and then, in the Clipboard group, click **Paste** 📋.

f. Press Esc to clear the Clipboard and remove the dashed border from around cell D6. Notice that once the Clipboard has been cleared by pressing Esc, Paste 📋 becomes unavailable again.

g. **Save** 🖫 the workbook.

Selecting Cell Ranges

By using the mouse, multiple cells can be selected simultaneously. Selected cells can be contiguous to each other, or they can be noncontiguous. Once multiple cells have been selected, they can be affected by actions such as clear, delete, copy, paste, formatting, and many others while offering the convenience of performing the desired task only once for the selected cells. In this exercise, you will select, copy, and paste to contiguous and noncontiguous selections.

 E01.08

SIDE NOTE

Shift can be used in combination with other navigation keys and/or the mouse to select a contiguous range of cells.

To Select, Copy, and Paste to Contiguous and Noncontiguous Selections

a. On the GolfCartPurchases worksheet, click cell **C5**. Press Shift+↓. The active cell border expands to include **C5:C6**.

b. Press Ctrl+C to copy the selected cells to the Clipboard. Click cell **E5**, and then press Ctrl+V to paste the Clipboard contents to the selected cell.

Excel 2016, Windows 10, Microsoft Corporation

c. Click cell **D5**, press and hold Ctrl, click cell **F5**, and then release Ctrl.

d. Press Shift+→.

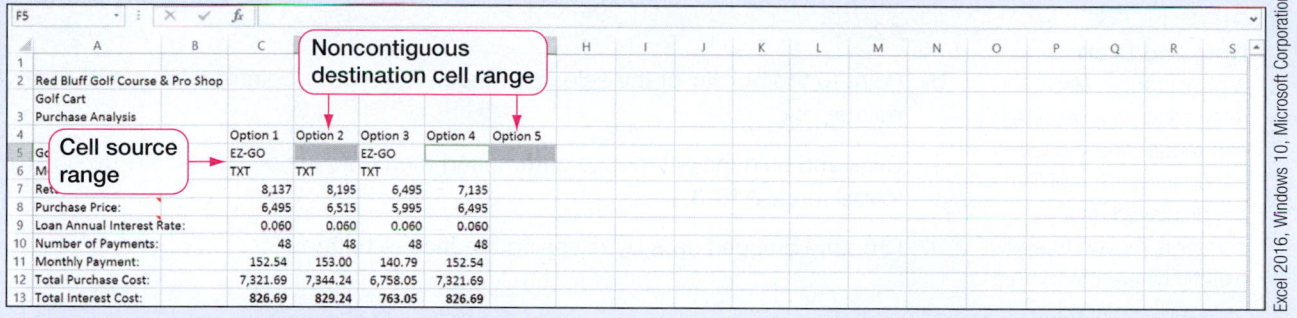

Figure 11 Selecting a noncontiguous cell range

e. Press Ctrl+V, and then press Esc to clear the Clipboard.

> **Troubleshooting**
>
> If nothing pasted when you pressed Ctrl+V, it could be that you lost the copy command by pressing another cell or command. Retry by selecting C5:C6, pressing Ctrl+C, and then repeating step c.

f. **Save** 💾 the workbook.

QUICK REFERENCE	Selecting Cell Ranges

There are several ways to select a contiguous range of cells.

- Expand the active cell by dragging the mouse.
- Select the first cell in the range, press Shift, and click the last cell in the desired range.

A contiguous range of rows or columns can be selected in the following ways.

- Click a row or column header. Drag the mouse pointer across the headers to select contiguous rows or columns.
- Click a row or column header, press Shift, and then click the header of the last row or column you wish to select.

Once a cell or contiguous range of cells has been selected, you can add noncontiguous cells and ranges by pressing Ctrl and using any of the above methods for selecting ranges that do not involve Shift.

Dragging and Dropping

As worksheets are designed, built, and modified, it is often necessary to move information from one cell or range of cells to another. One of the most efficient ways to do this is called "drag and drop." In this exercise, you will drag and drop cells to reorganize a worksheet.

 E01.09

SIDE NOTE
Drag and Drop
A ghost range, also referred to as a destination range, and a destination range ScreenTip are displayed as a pointer is moved to show exactly where the moved cells will be placed.

To Drag and Drop Cells

a. On the GolfCartPurchases worksheet, click and drag to select the cell range **A2:A4**.

b. Point to the **border** of the selected range. The mouse pointer changes to a move pointer.

c. Click and hold the left mouse button, and then drag the selected cells up one row to cell range **A1:A3**.

d. Drop the dragged cells by releasing the mouse button.

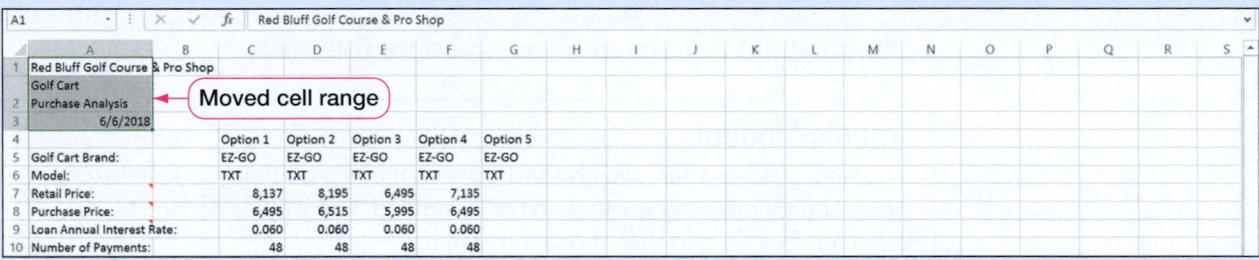

Figure 12   Moved cell range

Excel 2016, Windows 10, Microsoft Corporation

e. Select the range **F7:F13**. Move the mouse pointer until it is over the **border** of the selected range in column F. The mouse pointer changes to a move pointer. Press and hold Ctrl. The move pointer changes to a copy pointer. Drag the selected range until the ghost range is directly to the right of column F, over range **G7:G13**. Release the mouse button, and then release Ctrl.

f. Cell range F7:F13 has been copied to cell range G7:G13.

g. **Save** the workbook.

QUICK REFERENCE	Moving Cells

Moving cells may cause formulas to break. After moving a cell or range of cells, always double-click any formulas to ensure that they still reference the appropriate cells.

Modifying Cell Information

Copying and pasting content from one range of cells to another range or ranges is a highly efficient way to reuse parts of a worksheet. The range you just copied into column G contains information that is calculated by using formulas in the cell range G11:G13.

However, once you have duplicated a cell or cell range, it is usually necessary to change some content.

If only part of the content is to change, a cell can be placed into edit mode. In edit mode, the active cell will contain an insertion point. Double-click the cell to enter edit mode, and use arrow keys or click to position the insertion point at the desired location. Cells can also be edited by using the Formula Bar.

If all the cell content is to be replaced, click the cell once to make it the active cell, and then begin entering the new content. All cell content will be replaced when you begin typing to enter the new content for the selected cell.

In this exercise, you want to correct the GolfCartPurchases worksheet to reflect the correct golf cart brands and prices.

 **E01.10**

SIDE NOTE
Alternate Method
Press the F2 key to place a cell in edit mode.

To Modify Worksheet Contents by Changing Copied Information

a. On the GolfCartPurchases worksheet, click cell **D6**, type **RXV**, and then press →. Notice that the entire contents of the cell are replaced with the new text.

b. Double-click cell **E6**, press Home to go to the left margin of the cell, type **Freedom**, and then press Spacebar once so the formula bar displays **Freedom TXT**. Press Tab.

c. In cell **F6**, type **Freedom RXV**, and then press Tab.

d. In cell **G6**, type **The Drive**, and then press Enter.

e. Click cell **G7**, type **6995**, and then press Enter. In cell **G8**, type **6350**, and then press Ctrl+Enter.

Notice that when you changed the value in cell G8, the Monthly Payment, Total Purchase Cost, and Total Interest Cost were recalculated because these cells contain formulas.

f. Click cell **G5**, type **Yamaha**, and then press Enter.

g. Select the range C6:G6. On the Home tab in the Alignment group, click Wrap Text, and then press Ctrl+Home.

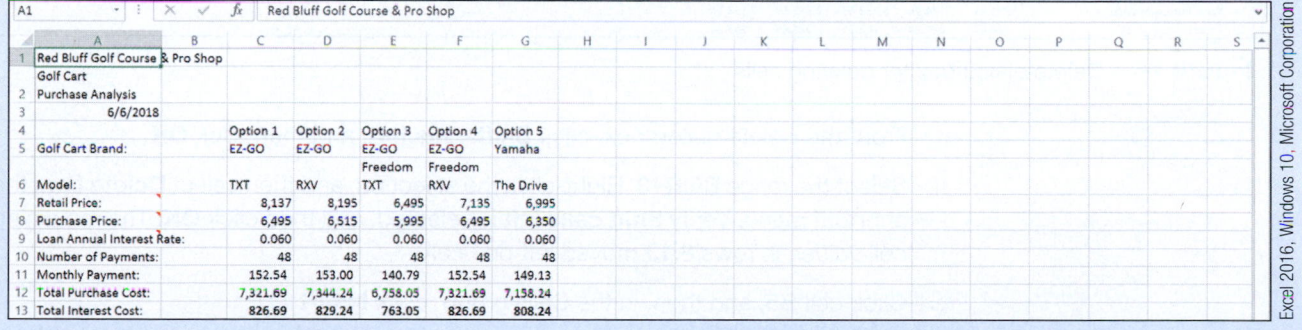

Figure 13 Modified worksheet

h. **Save** the workbook.

Inserting and Deleting Cells, Clearing Cells, and Cell Ranges

It is sometimes necessary to insert or delete cells to make a worksheet easier to read or to improve its appearance. Inserting or deleting cells is not the same as inserting or deleting entire rows or column. If you insert a cell in a worksheet where data already exists, Excel will adjust the current data by shifting cells down or to the right. If you delete a cell in a worksheet where data already exists, Excel will shift cells up or to the left.

Worksheet data can either be cleared or deleted; there is a difference. Clearing contents from a cell does not change the location of other cells in the worksheet. Deleting a cell shifts surrounding cells in a direction determined from a prompt. When you are editing a string of characters in a cell, pressing Delete works exactly as you would expect. When you are not in edit mode, pressing Delete clears content but does not delete the cell or cells.

You want to change the appearance of the golf cart purchase analysis worksheet. In this exercise, you will insert and delete cells.

 **E01.11**

To Insert, Delete, or Clear Cells and Cell Ranges in a Worksheet

a. On the GolfCartPurchases worksheet, click cell **B5**. On the Home tab, in the Cells group, click **Delete**. Notice that the brand headings in row 5 moved to the left one cell.

> ### Troubleshooting
> If nothing happened, you may have pressed the Delete button on the keyboard. Click the Delete button in the Cells group. If you click the Delete arrow, you can then click Delete Cells in the list.

b. Click cell **B4**. Click the **Delete** arrow, and then click **Delete Cells**.

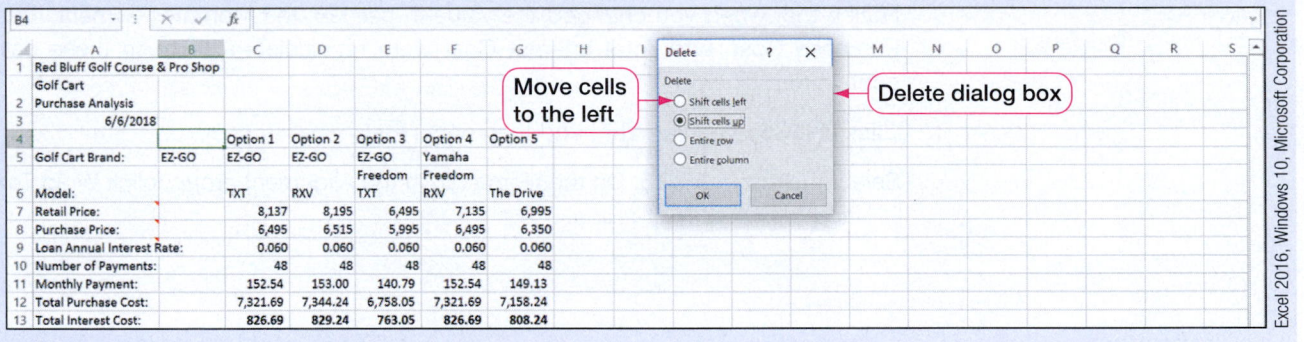

Figure 14 Delete dialog box for deleting cells

c. From the Delete dialog box, click **Shift cells left**, and then click **OK**.

d. Select the range **B6:B13**. Right-click the selection, and then select **Delete** from the shortcut menu. Verify **Shift cells left** is selected, and then click **OK**. The remaining cell values in rows 6:13 moved left one cell.

e. Click cell **B5**, and then, in the Cells group, click **Insert**.

   Notice how the contents of column B shifted down a row and no longer align appropriately with the labels in column A. You will undo this change.

f. Click **Undo** from the Quick Access Toolbar to undo the last action.

g. Click in Cell **B6**, press Delete, and then press Ctrl+Enter. Notice how the content of cell B6 is cleared but the cell is not deleted. Click **Undo**.

h. **Save** the workbook.

Merging and Centering Versus Centering Across

The titles in the golf cart analysis worksheet are in cells A1:A3. Although they contain the correct information to communicate the purpose of the golf cart analysis worksheet, that information might be better presented with some formatting improvements.

Titles that identify the general purpose of a worksheet are often at the top and centered above worksheet content. Clicking the Center button ≣ from the Alignment group of the Home tab will center contents only within the active cell. However, the **Merge & Center** feature ▦▾ combines selected cells into a single cell and then centers the text within that single cell. Merge & Center can be applied to horizontal or vertical cell ranges. Content in the left and/or top cell of the selected range is centered; all other data in the selected range is lost.

If more than one row of cells need to be centered, another option is to use the Center Across Selection command. Center Across Selection removes the borders between cells such that a selected range looks like a single cell, but the original cells remain, the borders between them are hidden, and the content is centered across the cells. Center Across Selection can be applied only horizontally. Additionally, Center Across Selection will never replace the data in the other cells.

In this exercise, you will center the headings in rows 1:3 to improve the appearance of the golf cart purchase analysis worksheet.

 **E01.12**

To Merge & Center Headings

a. On the GolfCartPurchases worksheet, press Ctrl+Home to return to cell **A1**. Left-click and drag until range **A1:F1** is selected. On the Home tab, in the Alignment group, click **Merge & Center** ▦▾.

Notice how the content of cell A1 appears to span across the six columns even though the content still remains in cell A1.

b. Select the range **A2:F3**. In the Alignment group, click **Merge & Center** ▦▾.

Notice the warning message. If you Merge & Center data in more than one cell at a time, only the data in the upper left cell of the selected range will be kept; the rest will be lost.

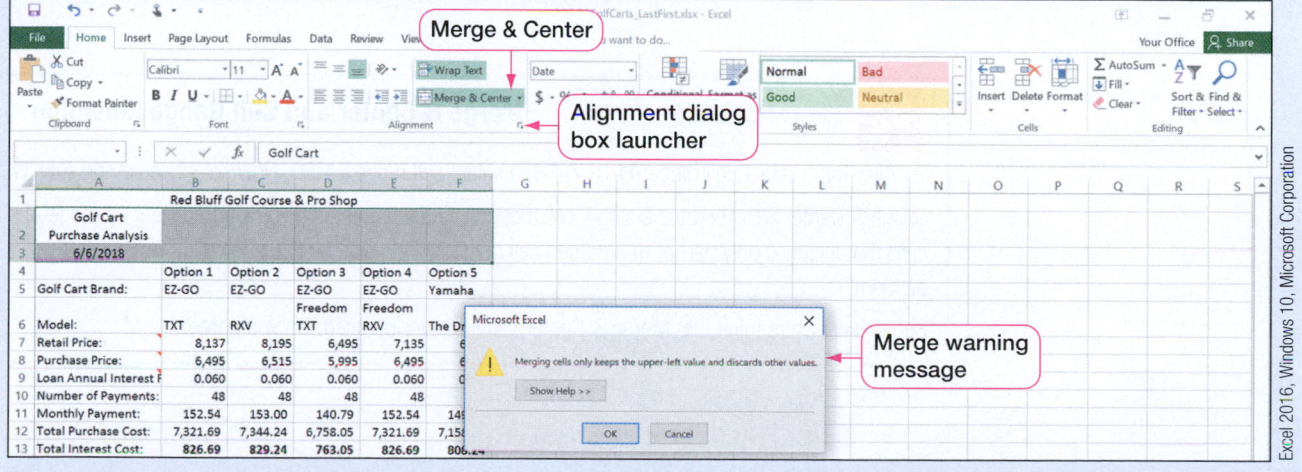

Figure 15 Merge and center a range containing multiple values

c. Click **Cancel**. You do not want to lose the data in cell A3.

> ## Troubleshooting
>
> If you clicked OK instead of Cancel, press Ctrl+Z to undo the last change and go back to step b.

d. With range A2:F3 still selected, on the Home tab, in the Alignment group, click the **Alignment** Dialog Box Launcher. This opens the Format Cells dialog box.

e. With the **Alignment** tab selected, click the **Horizontal** arrow, and then click **Center Across Selection**.

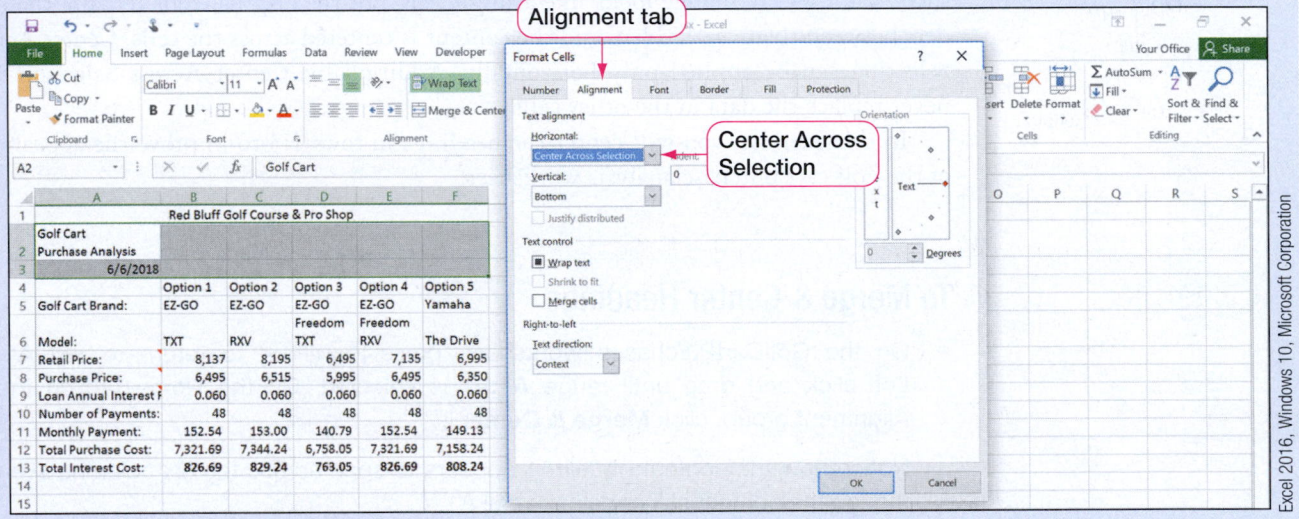

Figure 16 Center Across Selection

f. Click **OK**. Cell A2 content is centered across cell range A2:F2, and cell A3 content is centered across cell range A3:F3.

g. **Save** the workbook.

> ## SS CONSIDER THIS | Merge & Center and Cell Range Selection
>
> Try this: Try to select cell range A1:D17. Try to select cell range A1:B9. Now select cell range A2:F17.
>
> Merge & Center creates a single cell that can cause problems if you want to select a range of cells that includes only part of the merged cell range. Center Across Selection does not cause this problem.
>
> Some Excel users think that Merge & Center should never be used. Do you agree?

Adjust Columns and Rows

Any worksheet created has default column widths and row heights. As you build, refine, and modify a worksheet, it is often necessary to add and/or delete columns and rows or to change column widths and/or row heights for formatting and content purposes. Fortunately, Excel makes these activities easy to accomplish.

Selecting Contiguous and Noncontiguous Columns and Rows

To manipulate columns and rows, you must first indicate which of each you wish to affect by your actions. As with cells and cell ranges, you can select entire columns, entire rows, multiple columns, and multiple rows. You can select noncontiguous columns and rows, and you can even select multiple columns and multiple rows at the same time.

QUICK REFERENCE	Selecting Columns and Rows

- To select a column or row click the header — the letter or number, respectively — in the header.
- To select a range of contiguous columns or rows, point to and click the header at the start of the range you want to select. Hold down the mouse button, and then drag to select additional columns or rows, or click the header of the column or row at one end of the range you want to select, press and hold Shift, and then click the header of the column or row at the other end of the range.
- To select noncontiguous columns or rows, click the header of the first column or row you want to select. Press and hold Ctrl, and then click the headers of any additional columns and/or rows you want to select.
- To select all cells in a worksheet, point to the Select All button, and when the pointer changes to ⊕, click the left mouse button. Click any cell to cancel the selection.

Inserting and Deleting Columns or Rows

It is sometimes necessary to insert or remove rows or columns in a worksheet. The user may need to add or delete data, or perhaps it is necessary to refine the white space in a worksheet to improve its readability. **White space** refers to blank areas of a worksheet that do not contain data or documentation — regardless of the actual color. The blank space gives a document visual structure and creates a sense of order in the mind of the worksheet user.

A selected range is defined as a contiguous set of cells, columns, or rows that are all part of a single contiguous selection. However, how you select cells, columns, and rows determines whether they are a single contiguous range or are considered separate individual selections.

If you click column C, press and hold Shift, and click column E, you have created a contiguous selection of columns C:E. All three columns are highlighted as a group. But if you click column C, press and hold Ctrl, click column D, and then click column E, you have just selected three individual columns — three individual selections. In this situation, Excel treats columns C, D, and E as noncontiguous columns — there is a white border highlighted between the columns. Whether columns or rows are contiguous or noncontiguous has an effect on how actions such as Insert are applied to a worksheet.

You want to make the golf cart analysis worksheet easier to read and to use by refining the white space. There is also a need to add some white space to the golf cart purchases worksheet because the columns and rows of information for the different golf carts are too close together. One way to add white space is to insert blank columns or blank rows to not only separate the data but also add visual interest to the worksheet. In this exercise, you will insert and delete sheet columns and rows to adjust the white space in a worksheet.

 **E01.13**

To Insert or Delete Columns and Rows

a. On the GolfCartPurchases worksheet, click cell **A4**. On the Home tab, in the Cells group, click the **Insert** arrow.

b. Click **Insert Sheet Rows**. Excel inserts a row above the active cell location and moves all cells in row 4 and below down.

c. Right-click the header for **row 8**.

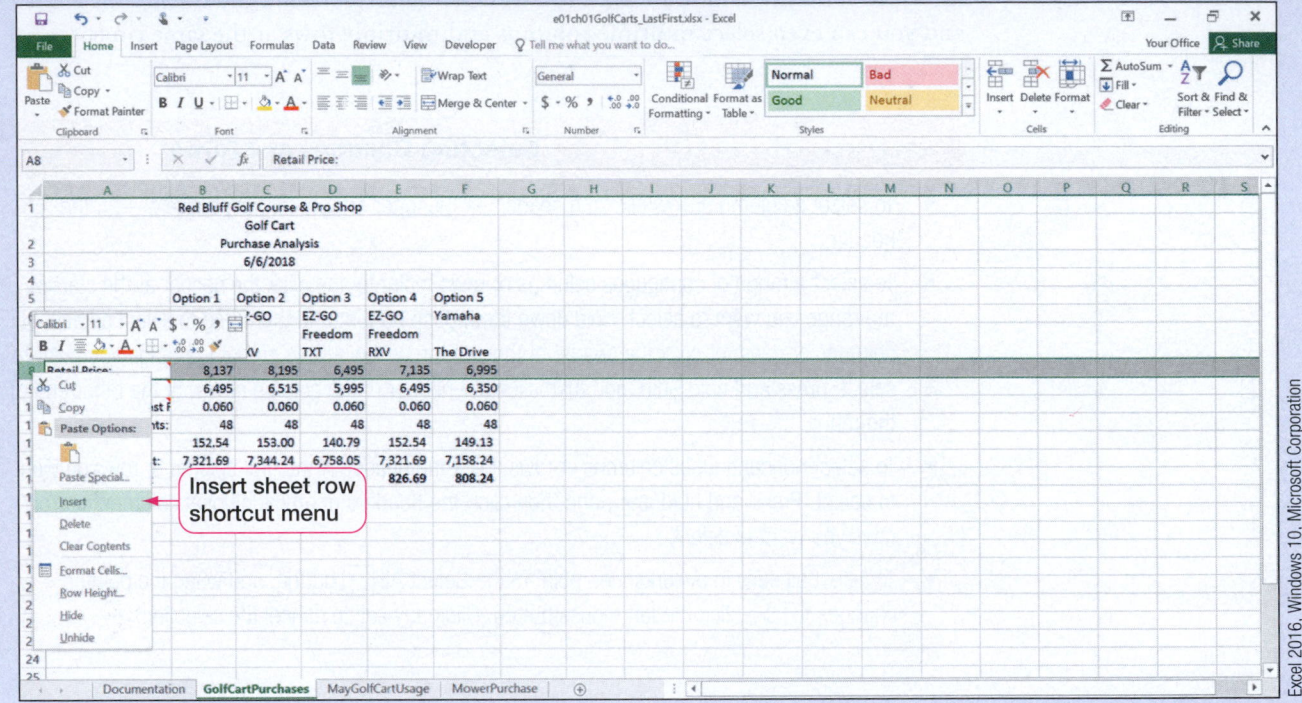

Figure 17 Inserting a sheet row by row header

d. Select **Insert** on the shortcut menu. Excel inserts a row above row 8 and moves all cells in row 8 and below down one row.

e. Select the range **A11:A12**. In the Cells group, click the **Insert** arrow, and then click **Insert Sheet Rows**. Excel inserts a row for each row in the selected range.

> **Troubleshooting**
>
> If you clicked the Insert ⊞ button from the Cells group instead of the Insert arrow, Excel will default to inserting extra cells only, instead of a row. Press Ctrl+Z to undo the last change, and then repeat step e.

SIDE NOTE
Alternate Method
To delete a sheet row, you can also right-click a row header, and select **Delete** from the shortcut menu.

f. Select the **row headers** for rows **15:16**, and in the Cells group, click **Insert** ⊞.

Inserting two rows above and below rows 13 and 14 appears to be too much. Often, you cannot tell until you try, but the worksheet might look better if a couple of the rows of white space were removed.

g. Click the header for **row 11**, press Ctrl, and then click header for **row 15**. In the Cells group, select **Delete** ⊞.

h. Click the header for column C to select column C, and then, in the Cells group, select **Insert** 🔲. A new column is added to the **left** of the selected column.

i. Click the header for **column E**, press and hold ⌃Ctrl, and then select **column F** and **column G** by clicking on each column header individually. Notice the white line between the columns. This is not a selected range of columns; it is three individually selected columns.

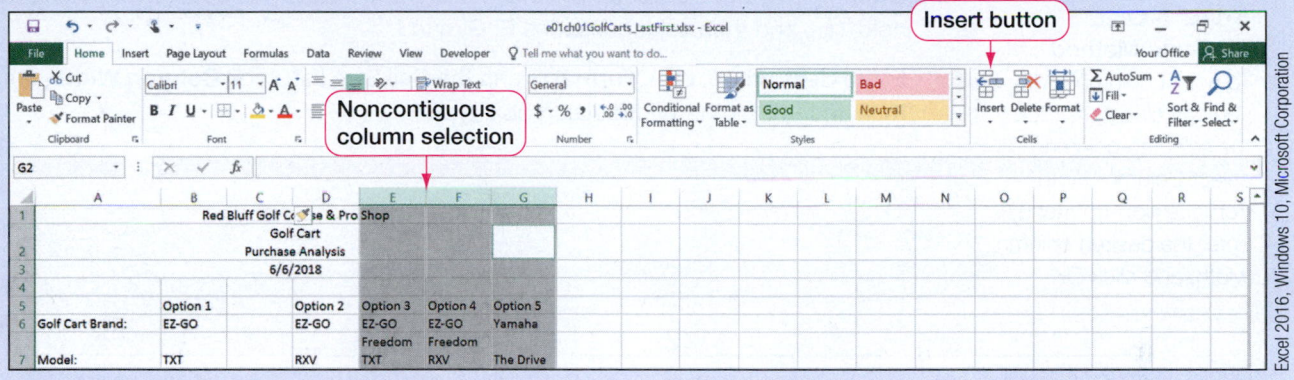

Figure 18 Selecting noncontiguous columns

j. In the Cells group, click **Insert** 🔲.

A column has been inserted to the left of each selected column because columns E, F, and G were selected as noncontiguous individual columns. Had you selected columns E:G as a single contiguous selection, three columns would have been inserted to the left of column E.

> **Troubleshooting**
> If you now have three blank columns to the left of column H, you selected columns E:G as a contiguous selection. Press ⌃Ctrl+Z to Undo, and repeat steps b and c.

Notice also that the merged and centered cells in rows 1:3 expanded to include the inserted columns. This ensures that the content in rows 1:3 remains centered over the columns that were in the original merged range.

k. Save 🔲 the workbook.

Adjusting Column Width and Row Height

You have inserted columns and rows to add additional white space, but there is still a need to refine the amount of white space in the worksheet. At this point, there is too much — the information is spread too far apart.

Column width and row height often need to be adjusted for a couple of reasons. One reason is to reduce the amount of white space a blank column or row represents in a worksheet; the other is to allow the content of cells in a row or column to be displayed properly. Column width is defined in characters. The default width is 8.43 characters. The maximum width of a column is 255 characters. Row height is defined in points. A point is approximately 1/72 of an inch (0.035 cm). The default row height in Excel is 15 points, or approximately 1/6 of an inch (0.4 cm). A row can be up to 409 points in height (about 5.4 inches).

In this exercise, you will manually adjust column width and row height to improve the appearance of a worksheet.

 **E01.14**

To Manually Adjust Column Width and Row Height

a. On the GolfCartPurchases worksheet, select the header for column **C**, press and hold Ctrl, and then select columns **E**, **G**, and **I**.

b. In the Cells group, click **Format** 🔲. In the Cell Size list, click **Column Width**, and then, in the Column Width dialog box, type **2**.

SIDE NOTE
Alternate Method
To adjust column width, you can also right-click the selected columns, select Column Width from the pop-up menu, enter the desired column width, and click OK.

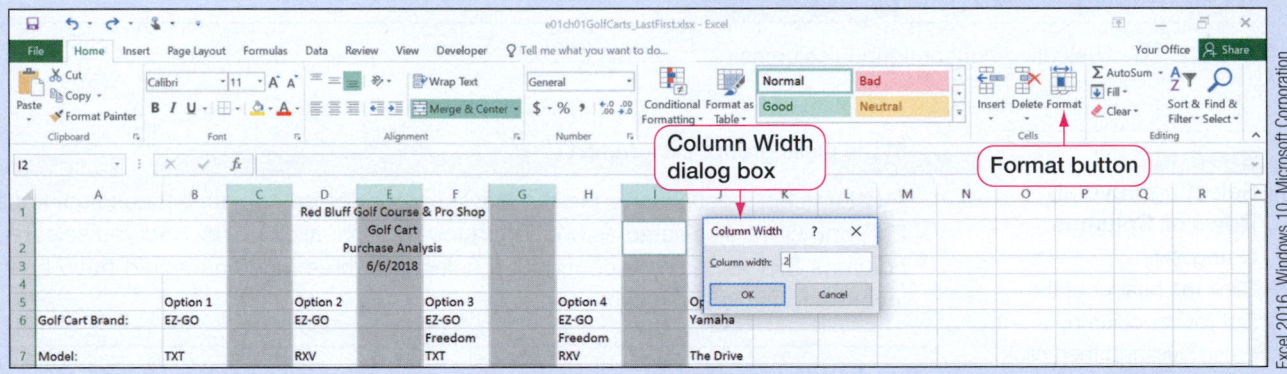

Figure 19 Column Width dialog box

SIDE NOTE
Alternate Method
To adjust row height, you can also right-click the selected rows, select Row Height from the pop-up menu, enter the desired row height, and click OK.

c. Click **OK**. By changing the column width, there is less white space between the columns.

d. Click the **row 4** header, press and hold Ctrl, and then select headers for rows **11** and **14**.

e. In the Cells group, click **Format** 🔲, and then, in the Cell Size list, click **Row Height**. In the Row Height dialog box, type **7**, and then click **OK**.

f. **Save** 💾 the workbook.

Changing Column Widths Using AutoFit

By using the AutoFit feature, column width and row height can be adjusted automatically on the basis of the width and height of selected content. AutoFit adjusts the width of columns and the height of rows to allow selected content to fit. Care is required in adjusting column widths so that data in unselected cells is not truncated or improperly displayed.

In this exercise, you will use AutoFit to adjust column width to adjust the appearance of a worksheet.

 **E01.15**

To Use AutoFit to Adjust Column Width

SIDE NOTE
AutoFit Row Height
AutoFit Row Height works in exactly the same manner as AutoFit Column Width.

a. On the GolfCartPurchases worksheet, click cell **A7**, press and hold Ctrl, and then select cells **B7**, **D7**, **F7**, **H7**, and **J7**.

b. On the Home tab, and then, in the Cells group, click **Format** 📷, and in the Cell Size list, click **AutoFit Column Width**.

Since AutoFit sizes columns to the selected content, which in this case was individual cells, columns B and D are too narrow to display most of their numeric information, so now the information is displayed as a series of number signs (#). Notice also that column A is too narrow to display the content of most of the cells in range A6:A17, so content is truncated on the right.

c. Select column **A** by clicking the column A header, press and hold Ctrl, and then select columns **B**, **D**, **F**, **H**, and **J**.

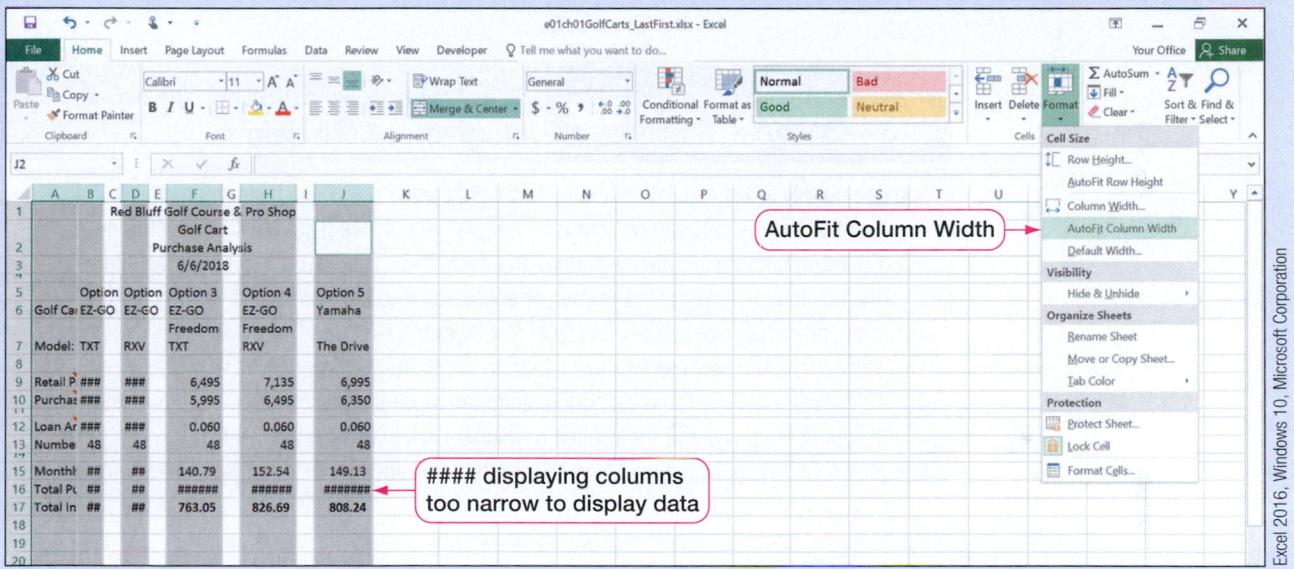

Figure 20 AutoFit Column Width results for selected cells

SIDE NOTE
Alternate Method
If you see number (#) signs in columns, point to the line between two column headers, and when the mouse pointer changes to ✛, double click.

d. In the Cells group, click **Format** 📷. In the Cell Size list, click **AutoFit Column Width**.

Since columns were selected instead of individual cells, the columns are automatically adjusted to the widest content in the column, resulting in no number signs.

Column width can also be set manually. Column A could be a little wider than was set by AutoFit Column Width.

e. Click cell **A1** to deselect the columns. Point to the border between column A and column B. The pointer should change to ✛. Click and hold the left mouse button. Drag the mouse to the right until column A has a width of **26.00** (293 pixels). Notice the column width ScreenTip. NOTE: The number of pixels corresponding to a width of 26.00 may vary based on your monitor's screen resolution.

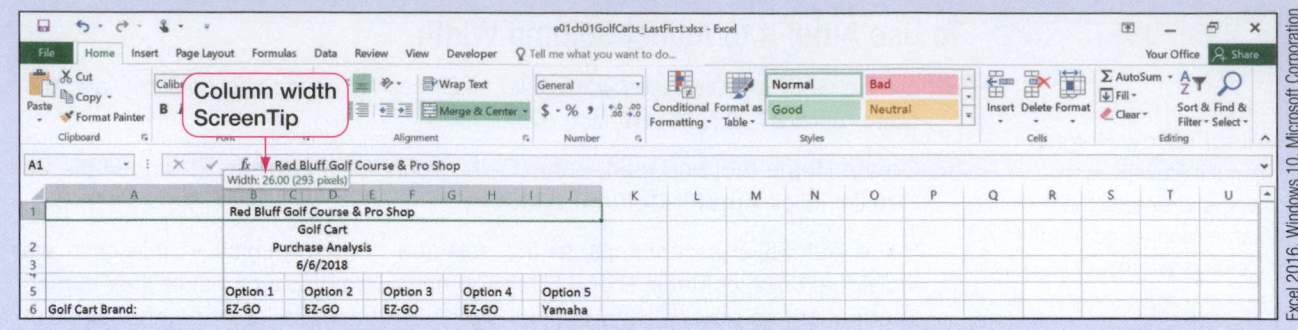

Figure 21 Manually adjust column width

f. Release the left mouse button, and then **Save** 🖫 the workbook.

g. If you need to take a break before finishing this chapter, now is a good time.

Working With and Printing Workbooks and Worksheets

Worksheets must often be printed for discussion at meetings, for distribution in venues where paper is the most effective medium, or to send digitally in a printed file format. Excel has a lot of built-in functionality that makes printed worksheets easy to read and understand. Further, as workbooks grow to include multiple worksheets and evolve to require maintenance, it is necessary to be able to create new worksheets, copy worksheets, delete worksheets, and reorder worksheets.

Manipulate Worksheets and Workbooks

Worksheets can be added to a workbook, deleted from a workbook, moved or copied within a workbook, or moved or copied to other workbooks. Sheet names are displayed on each sheet's tab at the bottom of the application window, just above the status bar (see Figure 22). The white worksheet tab identifies the active worksheet. Gray worksheet tabs identify inactive worksheets.

When a workbook contains a large number of worksheets or when the worksheets have very long names, some worksheet tabs may not be visible in the application window.

To bring tabs that are not visible into view, use the worksheet tab scrolling buttons to the left of the worksheet tabs.

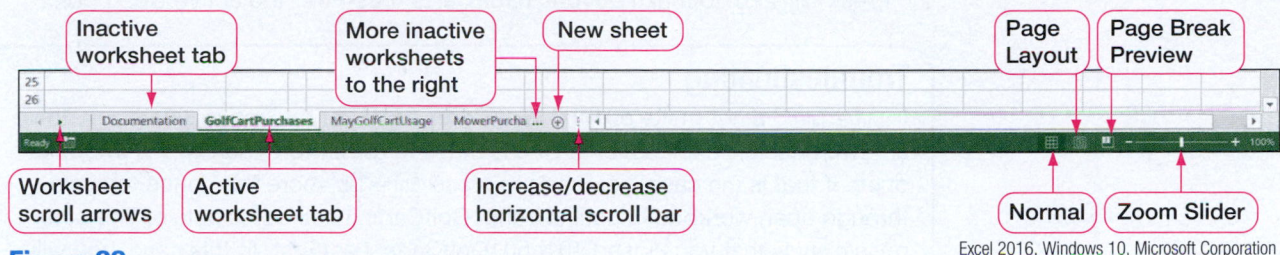

Figure 22   Worksheet tabs and controls

Excel 2016, Windows 10, Microsoft Corporation

Creating a New Workbook

When you first open Excel, you can click Blank workbook to create a new, blank workbook. However, sometimes you may wish to create a blank workbook when Excel is already open. This can be accomplished on the File tab in Backstage view.

Barry Cheney used the golf cart analysis as an example to create an analysis of lawn mowers he is considering for purchase. The MowerPurchase worksheet is located in the Golf Carts workbook. Barry wants to present the mower analysis at an upcoming staff meeting. Therefore, he asked you to create a separate workbook for the mower analysis. In this exercise, you will create a new workbook and move or copy the appropriate worksheets to the new workbook.

 **E01.16**

To Create a Blank Workbook

a. If you took a break, open the **e01ch01GolfCarts** workbook. Click the **File** tab to access Backstage view, and then click **New**.

b. Available templates will appear in the right pane. Click **Blank workbook**. You will leave Backstage view and see the new blank workbook. You now have two files open in Excel.

c. Click the **File** tab, click **Save**, and under Save As, click **Browse**. In the Save As dialog box, navigate to the location where you are saving your files. In the File name box, type e01ch01Mowers_LastFirst using your last and first name.

d. Click **Save**. You have now created a new, blank workbook.

Moving and Copying Worksheets Between Workbooks

Well-developed worksheets are often used as the starting point for new worksheets. Excel makes it easy to copy worksheets from one workbook to another.

Barry has asked you to create a separate workbook for the mower analysis. In this exercise, to save yourself some time, you have decided to copy the MowerPurchase and Documentation worksheets from the GolfCarts workbook to the new Mowers workbook instead of recreating them.

 **E01.17**

To Move or Copy a Worksheet to Another Workbook

a. Press Ctrl + Tab to make **e01ch01GolfCarts_LastFirst** the active workbook.

> **Troubleshooting**
>
> If Ctrl + Tab did not make e01ch01GolfCarts_LastFirst the active workbook, there are two possible explanations. One is that you have more than two workbooks open. If that is the case, you need to press Ctrl + Tab more than once to cycle through open workbooks until e01ch01GolfCarts_LastFirst is active. The other possibility is that you closed e01ch01GolfCarts_LastFirst. In this case, you will need to open the file, at which time it will be the active workbook.

b. Right-click the **MowerPurchase** worksheet tab, and then select **Move or Copy** in the shortcut menu.

c. In the Move or Copy dialog box, click the **To book** arrow, and then click **e01ch01Mowers_LastFirst**. Leave Sheet1 selected in the **Before sheet** section.

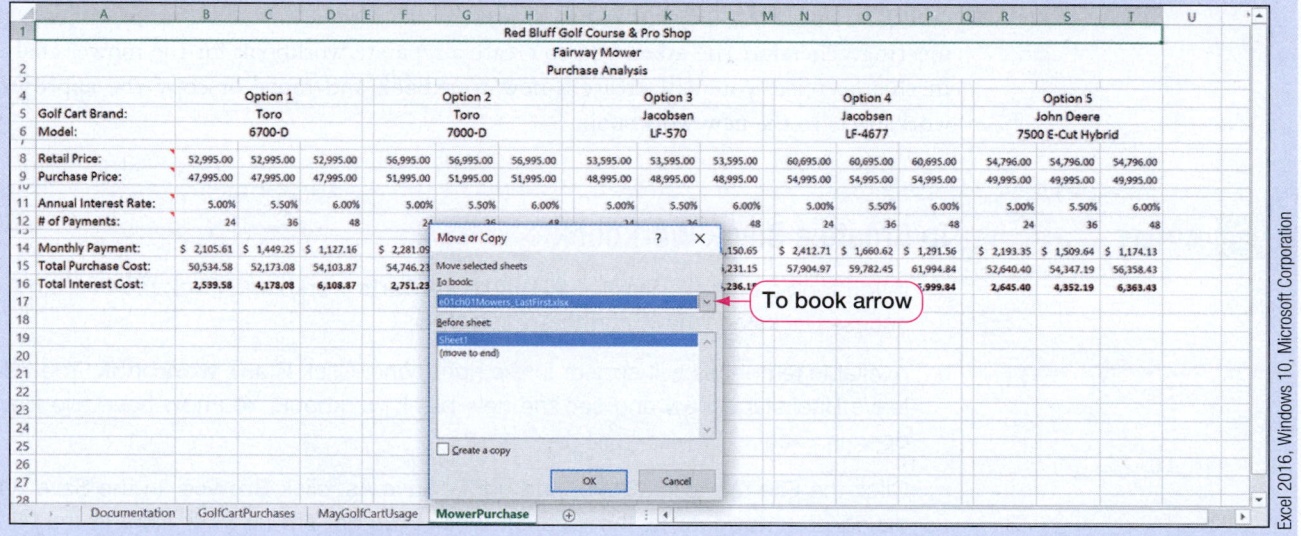

Figure 23 Move or Copy dialog box

d. Click **OK**. The MowerPurchase worksheet is moved to the e01ch01Mowers_LastFirst workbook, which is now the active workbook.

e. Press Ctrl + Tab to make **e01ch01GolfCarts_LastFirst** the active workbook.

f. If necessary, scroll to the left to view the Documentation worksheet. Right-click the **Documentation** worksheet tab, and then select **Move or Copy** in the shortcut menu. In the Move or Copy dialog box, click the **To book** arrow, and then click **e01ch01Mowers_LastFirst**. In the **Before sheet** box, click **Sheet1**, and click the **Create a copy** check box.

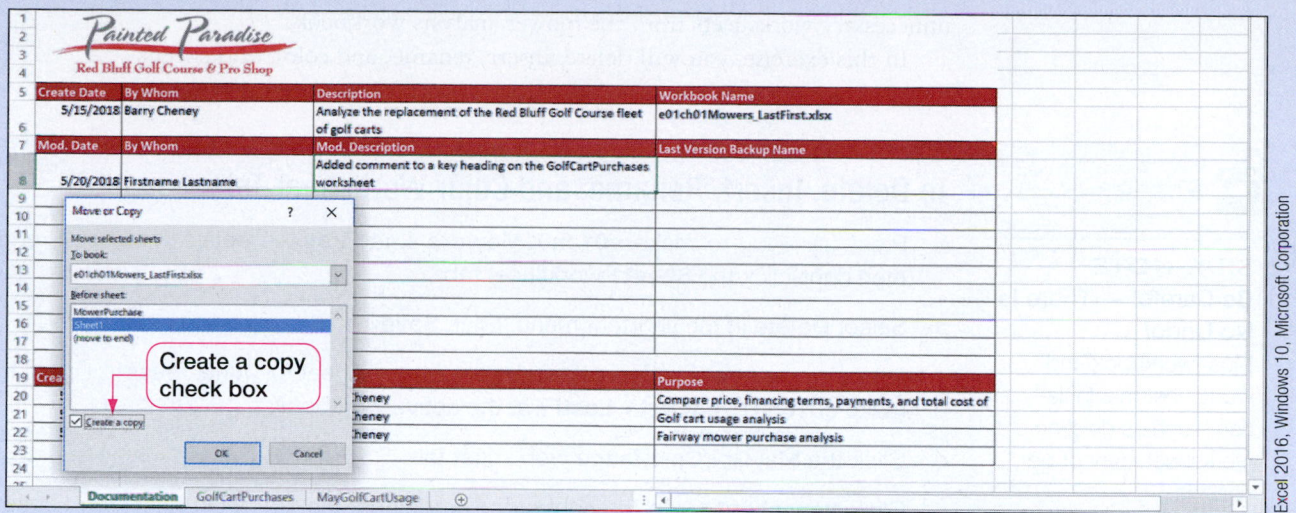

Figure 24 Copy a worksheet to another workbook

g. Click **OK**. The Documentation worksheet is copied to the e01ch01Mowers_LastFirst workbook, which is now the active workbook.

h. In the Documentation worksheet of the **e01ch01Mowers_LastFirst** workbook, select cell range **A20:D21**. Press and hold Ctrl, select cell **C8**, and then press Delete.

i. Right-click the header for row **22**, and select **Cut**. Right-click the header for row **20**, and then click **Paste**. The documentation that had been in line 22 should now be in line 20.

j. Double-click cell **C6**. Position the insertion point after **carts**, delete **fleet of golf carts**, type fairway mowers, and then press Enter. Click **Save** 💾.

k. Press Ctrl+Tab to make **e01ch01GolfCarts_LastFirst** the active workbook. In the **Documentation** worksheet, select cell range **A22:D22**, and press Delete.

l. **Save** 💾 the workbook.

Deleting, Inserting, Renaming, and Coloring Worksheet Tabs

Unused worksheets are a form of clutter in a workbook and add unnecessary size to the stored workbook file, so it is best practice to delete any unused sheets in a workbook. Do so with caution, however, because deleting a worksheet removes it from a workbook. This action cannot be undone. Inserted worksheets are by default given a name such as "Sheet2" in which the number is one larger than the last number used for a worksheet name. An inserted worksheet is automatically the active worksheet. To insert a worksheet, move to the right of the list of worksheet tabs, and click New sheet ⊕. In Excel 2016, new worksheets are always inserted to the right of the active worksheet.

The default worksheet names are not particularly descriptive and do nothing to help document the contents or purpose of a worksheet. Worksheets can be renamed in two ways: by double-clicking the worksheet tab and typing a descriptive name or by right-clicking the worksheet tab and then clicking Rename on the shortcut menu. Worksheet names can be up to 31 characters long. Worksheet tabs can also be colored to add interest or for visual separation of the worksheets.

Now that you have created a separate workbook for the mower purchase analysis, Barry wants you to prepare a worksheet in the golf cart purchase analysis to extend the golf cart usage analysis to the month of June. He has asked you to create a new worksheet and to use the May usage analysis as a starting point. You just need to create the worksheet and get it ready for Barry to enter the data later. First, you should remove any unnecessary worksheets from the mower analysis workbook.

In this exercise, you will delete, insert, rename, and color worksheets.

 **E01.18**

To Delete, Insert, Rename, and Color Worksheet Tabs

SIDE NOTE

Be Careful — There Is No Undo!

Most workbook and worksheet manipulation, such as deleting a worksheet, cannot be undone.

a. Press ⌃Ctrl+⇥Tab to make **e01ch01Mowers_LastFirst** the active workbook, and then right-click the **Sheet1** worksheet tab.

b. Select **Delete** in the shortcut menu. Click **Save** 🖫.

c. Now prepare a new golf cart usage analysis worksheet for June. Press ⌃Ctrl+⇥Tab to make **e01ch01GolfCarts_LastFirst** the active workbook.

d. Click the **MayGolfCartUsage** worksheet tab.

e. Click **New sheet** ⊕ to the right of the worksheet tabs. A new Sheet1 worksheet is inserted to the right of the MayGolfCartUsage worksheet.

f. Double-click the **Sheet1** worksheet tab, type JuneGolfCartUsage, and then press ⏎Enter.

g. Right-click the **JuneGolfCartUsage** worksheet tab, and point to **Tab Color**.

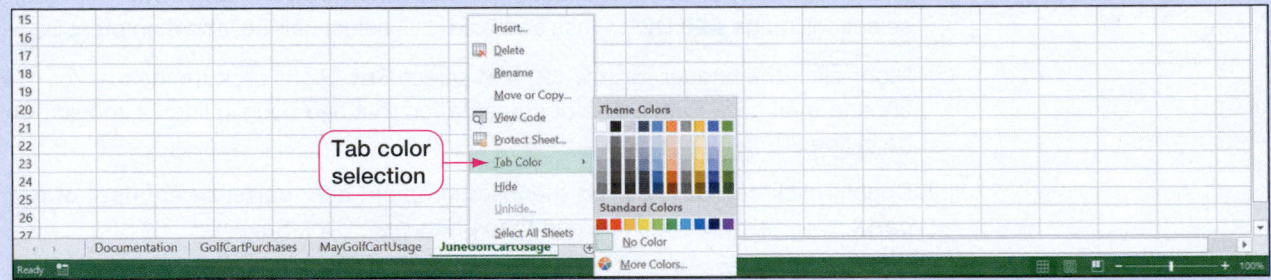

Figure 25 Worksheet tab color

Excel 2016, Windows 10, Microsoft Corporation

h. Select **Blue, Accent 1** in the top row, fifth column.

i. Right-click the **MayGolfCartUsage** worksheet tab, point to **Tab Color**, and then select **Orange, Accent 2** in the top row, sixth column.

j. **Save** 🖫 the workbook.

Using Series (AutoFill)

The AutoFill feature is a powerful way to minimize the effort required to enter certain types of data. **AutoFill** copies information from one cell or a series in contiguous cells into contiguous cells in the direction in which the fill handle is dragged. AutoFill is a smart copy that will try to guess how you want values or formulas changed as you copy. Sometimes, AutoFill will save significant time by changing the contents correctly. Other times, AutoFill changes the contents in a way you did not intend. When that happens, Auto Fill Options 🖽 makes options available that may be helpful.

The fill handle is a small green square in the bottom right corner of the active cell border. To engage the AutoFill feature, drag the fill handle in the direction in which you wish to expand the active cell. When you point to and drag the fill handle, the mouse pointer is a thin black plus sign ➕.

To make the JuneGolfCartUsage worksheet ready for data entry, in this exercise you will copy and then clear some of the May data. You will also generate date information for June.

 **E**01.19

SIDE NOTE
Alternate Method
To select all the data in a worksheet, you can also use the Select All button above the Row 1 header.

To Quickly Generate Data Using AutoFill

a. On the MayGolfCartUsage worksheet, press Ctrl+Home to make cell A1 the active cell, and then press Ctrl+A to select the entire worksheet.

b. Press Ctrl+C to copy the contents of the MayGolfCartUsage worksheet.

c. Click the **JuneGolfCartUsage** worksheet tab, press Ctrl+Home to ensure that cell A1 is the active cell, and then press Ctrl+V to paste the contents from the May worksheet.

d. Click cell **A11**. If necessary, scroll down until you can see cell A41. Press and hold Shift, and then click cell **A41**. Cell range A11:A41 should be selected. Press Delete.

e. June contains one less day than May. Therefore, you need to delete one row of the daily data. Right-click the header for **row 12**, and then select **Delete** in the shortcut menu.

f. Double-click cell **H3**, delete the word **May**, and then type June.

g. Click cell **A11**. Type 06/01/2018, and then press Ctrl+Enter.

h. Click and hold the fill handle, drag the fill handle down until the border around the cell range expands to include cells **A11:A40**, and then release the left mouse button.

Notice that the date is incremented by one day in each cell from top to bottom. Also notice the Auto Fill Options button.

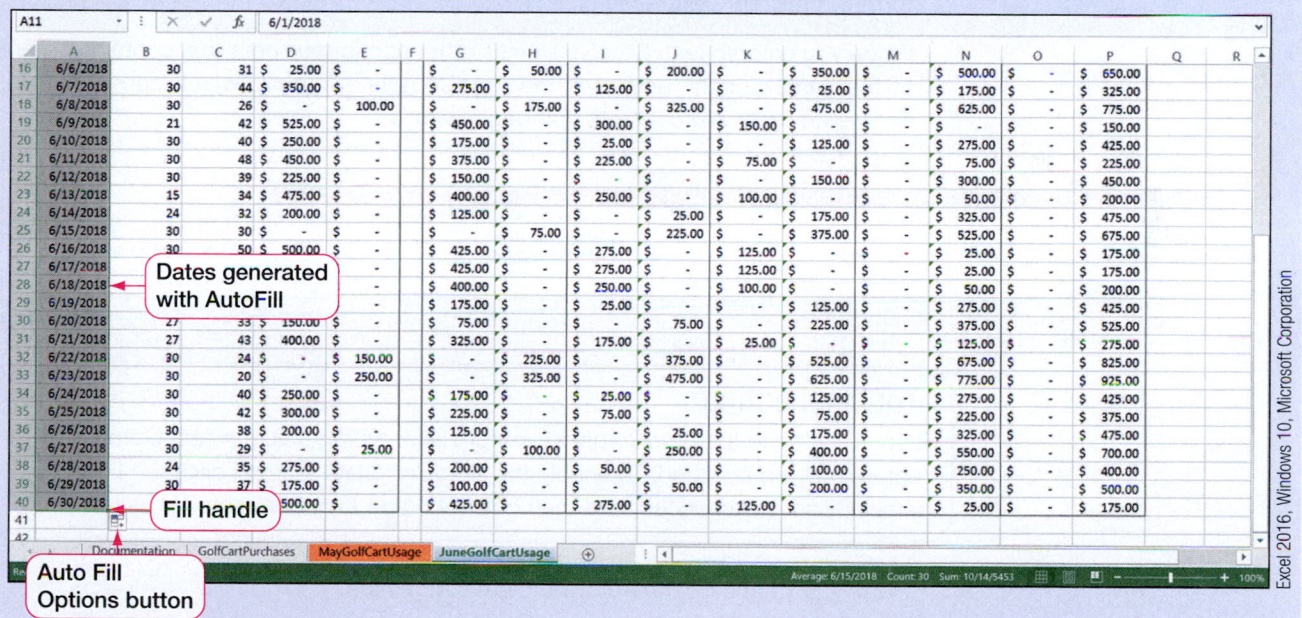

Figure 26 Generate data using AutoFill

i. Click the **Auto Fill Options** button.

Formula bar: A11 = 6/1/2018

A	B	C	D	E	F	G	H	I	J	K	L	M	N	O	P
6/6/2018	30	31	$ 25.00	$ -		$ -	$ 50.00	$ -	$ 200.00	$ -	$ 350.00	$ -	$ 500.00	$ -	$ 650.00
6/7/2018	30	44	$ 350.00	$ -		$ 275.00	$ -	$ 125.00	$ -	$ -	$ 25.00	$ -	$ 175.00	$ -	$ 325.00
6/8/2018	30	26	$ -	$ 100.00		$ -	$ 175.00	$ -	$ 325.00	$ -	$ 475.00	$ -	$ 625.00	$ -	$ 775.00
6/9/2018	21	42	$ 525.00	$ -		$ 450.00	$ -	$ 300.00	$ -	$ 150.00	$ -	$ -	$ -	$ -	$ 150.00
6/10/2018	30	40	$ 250.00	$ -		$ 175.00	$ -	$ 25.00	$ -	$ -	$ 125.00	$ -	$ 275.00	$ -	$ 425.00
6/11/2018	30	48	$ 450.00	$ -		$ 375.00	$ -	$ 225.00	$ -	$ 75.00	$ -	$ -	$ 75.00	$ -	$ 225.00
6/12/2018	30	39	$ 225.00	$ -		$ 150.00	$ -	$ -	$ -	$ -	$ 150.00	$ -	$ 300.00	$ -	$ 450.00
6/13/2018	15	34	$ 475.00	$ -		$ 400.00	$ -	$ 250.00	$ -	$ 100.00	$ -	$ -	$ 50.00	$ -	$ 200.00
6/14/2018	24	32	$ 200.00	$ -		$ 125.00	$ -	$ -	$ 25.00	$ -	$ 175.00	$ -	$ 325.00	$ -	$ 475.00
6/15/2018						$ -	$ 75.00	$ -	$ 225.00	$ -	$ 375.00	$ -	$ 525.00	$ -	$ 675.00
6/16/2018						$ 425.00	$ -	$ 275.00	$ -	$ 125.00	$ -	$ -	$ 25.00	$ -	$ 175.00
6/17/2018						$ 425.00	$ -	$ 275.00	$ -	$ 125.00	$ -	$ -	$ 25.00	$ -	$ 175.00
6/18/2018						$ 400.00	$ -	$ 250.00	$ -	$ 100.00	$ -	$ -	$ 50.00	$ -	$ 200.00
6/19/2018	27	37	$ 250.00	$ -		$ 175.00	$ -	$ 25.00	$ -	$ -	$ 125.00	$ -	$ 275.00	$ -	$ 425.00
	7	33	$ 150.00	$ -		$ 75.00	$ -	$ -	$ 75.00	$ -	$ 225.00	$ -	$ 375.00	$ -	$ 525.00
	7	43	$ 400.00	$ -		$ 325.00	$ -	$ 175.00	$ -	$ 25.00	$ -	$ -	$ 125.00	$ -	$ 275.00
	0	24	$ -	$ 150.00		$ -	$ 225.00	$ -	$ 375.00	$ -	$ 525.00	$ -	$ 675.00	$ -	$ 825.00
	0	20	$ -	$ 250.00		$ -	$ 325.00	$ -	$ 475.00	$ -	$ 625.00	$ -	$ 775.00	$ -	$ 925.00
	0	40	$ 250.00	$ -		$ 175.00	$ -	$ 25.00	$ -	$ -	$ 125.00	$ -	$ 275.00	$ -	$ 425.00
	0	42	$ 300.00	$ -		$ 225.00	$ -	$ 75.00	$ -	$ -	$ 75.00	$ -	$ 225.00	$ -	$ 375.00
	0	38	$ 200.00	$ -		$ 125.00	$ -	$ -	$ 25.00	$ -	$ 175.00	$ -	$ 325.00	$ -	$ 475.00
	0	29	$ -	$ 25.00		$ -	$ 100.00	$ -	$ 250.00	$ -	$ 400.00	$ -	$ 550.00	$ -	$ 700.00
	4	35	$ 275.00	$ -		$ 200.00	$ -	$ 50.00	$ -	$ -	$ 100.00	$ -	$ 250.00	$ -	$ 400.00
	0	37	$ 175.00	$ -		$ 100.00	$ -	$ -	$ 50.00	$ -	$ 200.00	$ -	$ 350.00	$ -	$ 500.00
	0	50	$ 500.00	$ -		$ 425.00	$ -	$ 275.00	$ -	$ 125.00	$ -	$ -	$ 25.00	$ -	$ 175.00

Auto Fill Options selections:
- Copy Cells
- ○ Fill Series
- Fill Formatting Only
- Fill Without Formatting
- Fill Days
- Fill Weekdays
- Fill Months
- Fill Years
- Flash Fill

Figure 27   AutoFill Options menu

j. Click **Fill Without Formatting** so the border of cell A40 does not disappear. Press Home to deselect the AutoFill range.

k. If necessary, scroll to the left, and then click the **Documentation** worksheet tab. Click cell **A22**, and then press Ctrl+; to insert today's date. Press Tab, type **JuneGolfCartUsage**, and then press Tab. Type **your name** in Firstname Lastname format, press Tab, and then type **G**.

Since you entered text, Excel examines other contiguous cells that contain content in the same column and uses the AutoComplete feature, which completes the entry with other cell contents that begin with "G".

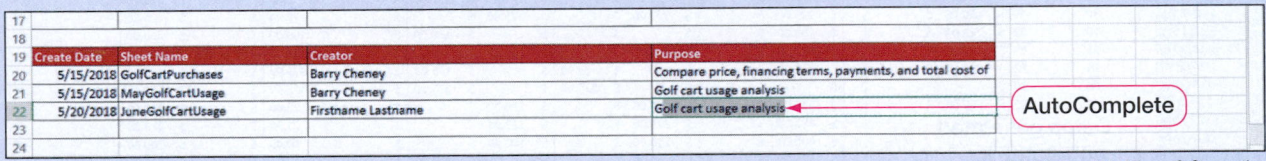

	Create Date	Sheet Name	Creator	Purpose	
19	Create Date	Sheet Name	Creator	Purpose	
20	5/15/2018	GolfCartPurchases	Barry Cheney	Compare price, financing terms, payments, and total cost of	
21	5/15/2018	MayGolfCartUsage	Barry Cheney	Golf cart usage analysis	
22	5/20/2018	JuneGolfCartUsage	Firstname Lastname	Golf cart usage analysis ←	AutoComplete

Figure 28   AutoComplete

Troubleshooting

If you didn't see the AutoComplete feature after typing a G, the AutoComplete feature may be disabled. To enable the AutoComplete feature, click the File tab, select Options, Advanced, and then check Enable AutoComplete for cell values.

l. Press Enter to accept the AutoComplete suggestion.

m. **Save** 💾 the workbook.

Moving or Copying a Worksheet

The order of worksheets in a workbook can be changed by reordering the worksheet tabs. To move a worksheet, make the worksheet you wish to move the active worksheet by clicking on its tab. Click and hold the worksheet tab, drag the worksheet tab to its new location, and drop it by releasing the mouse button. As a worksheet is dragged, a small black triangle will appear between worksheet tabs. This indicates the location where the worksheet will be inserted if the mouse button is released.

If a new worksheet needs to be created that will be similar to another worksheet in the workbook, the worksheet can be copied to save time. To copy a worksheet within a workbook, after clicking on the worksheet tab, press and hold Ctrl, and drag a copy of the worksheet to a new location.

In the golf carts workbook, the Documentation worksheet is the first worksheet tab on the far left. Painted Paradise Resort & Spa standards require the Documentation worksheet to be the far-right worksheet in a workbook. In this exercise, you will move and copy worksheets.

To Move and Copy a Worksheet

a. In the e01ch01GolfCarts_LastFirst workbook, click and hold the **Documentation** worksheet tab. The mouse pointer will change to the move worksheet pointer ![pointer]. Drag the mouse to the right until ![triangle] appears to the right of the JuneGolfCartUsage worksheet tab.

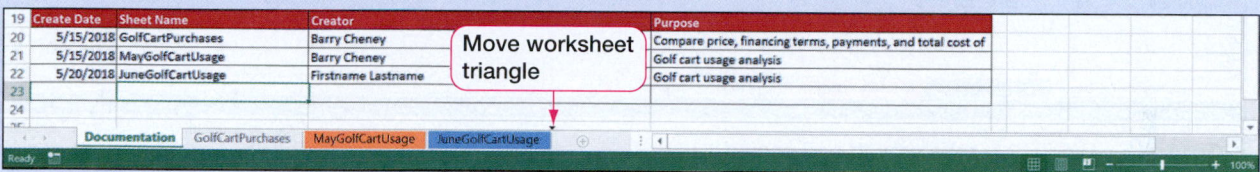

Figure 29 Move a worksheet

Excel 2016, Windows 10, Microsoft Corporation

SIDE NOTE

Copying a Worksheet
Worksheets can also be copied by right-clicking the worksheet tab and selecting **Create a copy** from the Move or Copy dialog box.

b. Release the mouse button. The Documentation sheet is now the last worksheet tab on the right.

Barry has decided that he wants the most recent golf cart usage analysis to be first (leftmost) in the sequence of worksheets. You need to move the JuneGolfCartUsage worksheet tab to the left of the MayGolfCartUsage worksheet tab.

c. Click and hold the **JuneGolfCartUsage** worksheet tab, drag to the left of MayGolfCartUsage, and then release the mouse button. The worksheets are now in the following order from left to right: GolfCartPurchases, JuneGolfCartUsage, MayGolfCartUsage, and Documentation.

Barry also wants you to create a JulyGolfCartUsage worksheet. He has decided that three months of usage data will help him better determine the number of carts to purchase. Rather than creating a new worksheet and then copying a range of cells from another worksheet, this time you will copy the MayGolfCartUsage worksheet in its entirety to a new worksheet.

d. Click and hold the **MayGolfCartUsage** worksheet tab, and then press and hold Ctrl. The mouse pointer will change from ![pointer] to the Copy Worksheet pointer ![pointer]. Move the mouse to the left until ![triangle] appears to the left of the JuneGolfCartUsage worksheet tab. Release the mouse button.

e. A copy of the MayGolfCartUsage worksheet has been created, called "MayGolfCartUsage (2)". Double-click the **MayGolfCartUsage (2)** worksheet tab, type JulyGolfCartUsage, and then press Enter.

f. Right-click the **JulyGolfCartUsage** worksheet tab, point to **Tab Color**, and then select **Gold, Accent 4**, in the top row, eighth column.

g. Double-click cell **H3**, delete the word **May**, and then type July.

h. Click cell **A11**. Type 07/01/2018, and then press Ctrl+Enter.

i. Double-click the **fill handle** to fill the dates in the range A11:A41 Scroll, if necessary, to see row 41. Click the Auto Fill Options 🗗, and then select **Fill Without Formatting**.

j. Press Ctrl+Home to deselect the Auto Fill range.

k. Click the **Documentation** worksheet tab, click cell **A23**, and then press Ctrl+; to insert today's date. Press Tab, type JulyGolfCartUsage, and then press Tab. Type your name in Firstname Lastname format, press Tab, and then type G and press Enter to use Auto Complete to fill in the remainder of the text.

l. Click the **JulyGolfCartUsage** worksheet tab.

SIDE NOTE
Navigating Between Worksheets
Press Ctrl+PgUp to go to the prior worksheet.
Press Ctrl+PgDn to go to the next worksheet.

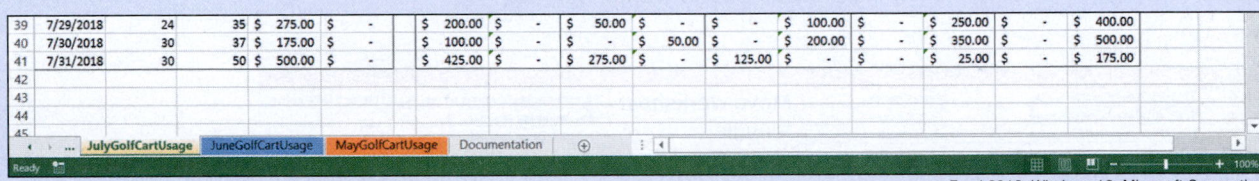

Figure 30 Worksheet tabs moved and copied

Excel 2016, Windows 10, Microsoft Corporation

m. Save 🖫 the workbook.

Preview, Print, and Export Workbooks

Excel has a great deal of flexibility built into its printing functionality. To appropriately present your work in printed form, it is important that you understand how to take advantage of Excel's previewing, printing, and exporting features.

Using Worksheet Views

In the bottom right corner of the application window are three icons that control the worksheet view. **Normal view** 🎛 is what you use most of the time when building and editing a worksheet. Only the cells in the worksheet are visible; print-specific features such as margins, headers, footers, and page breaks are not displayed.

Page Layout view 🗔 shows page margins, print headers and footers, and page breaks. It presents you with a reasonable preview of how a worksheet will print on paper.

Page Break Preview 🗔 does not show page margins, headers, or footers, but it allows you to manually adjust the location of page breaks. This is particularly helpful when you would like to force a page break after a set of summary values and/or between data categories and force part of a worksheet to print on a new page.

Excel places a default page break wherever it is necessary to split content between pages. If the size of content changes, the location of a default break can change. A hard page break remains in its defined location until you move it. Changes in content size have no effect on the location of a hard page break. In this exercise, you will switch among worksheet views and adjust page breaks.

 **E01.21**

To Switch Among Worksheet Views and Adjust Page Breaks

a. Select the **e01ch01Mowers_LastFirst** workbook, and click the **MowerPurchase** worksheet tab.

b. Click the **File** tab, and then click **Print**.

Notice that the worksheet does not print on a single page; nor does information break across pages correctly.

c. Press Esc to leave Backstage view, and then click **Page Break Preview** 🔲 on the status bar.

Only the part of the worksheet that will print is displayed. A dashed blue border indicates where printing will break from one page to another.

d. Use the Zoom Slider ▬▬▬▬▬ to decrease the zoom level to make the pages as large as possible without having any data not be visible in the application window.

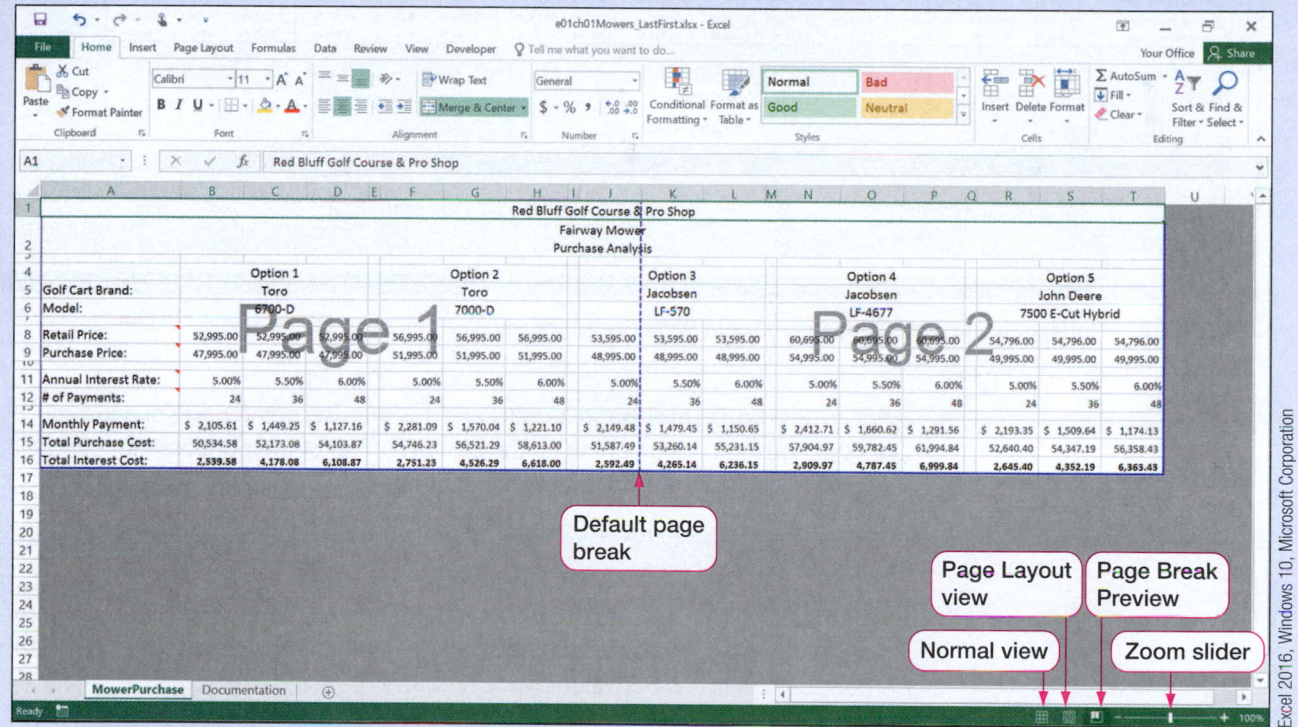

Figure 31   Page Break Preview

Now move the default page break, since it divides Option 3 between two pages.

e. Move the mouse pointer over the **vertical dashed line** between columns **J** and **K** to display the Vertical Page Break pointer ↔. Click and drag the page break between columns **I** and **J**.

Notice that the page break changes to a solid blue line. By moving the page break, you changed it from a default break to a hard page break. Now you need to insert a new page break so that Option 5 will print on a separate page.

f. On the ribbon, click the **Page Layout** tab — not Page Layout on the status bar.

g. Click cell **R2**. In the Page Setup group, click **Breaks**, and then select **Insert Page Break**.

Two page breaks are inserted: a horizontal page break above the active cell and a vertical page break to the left of the active cell. You want only the vertical page break between columns Q and R.

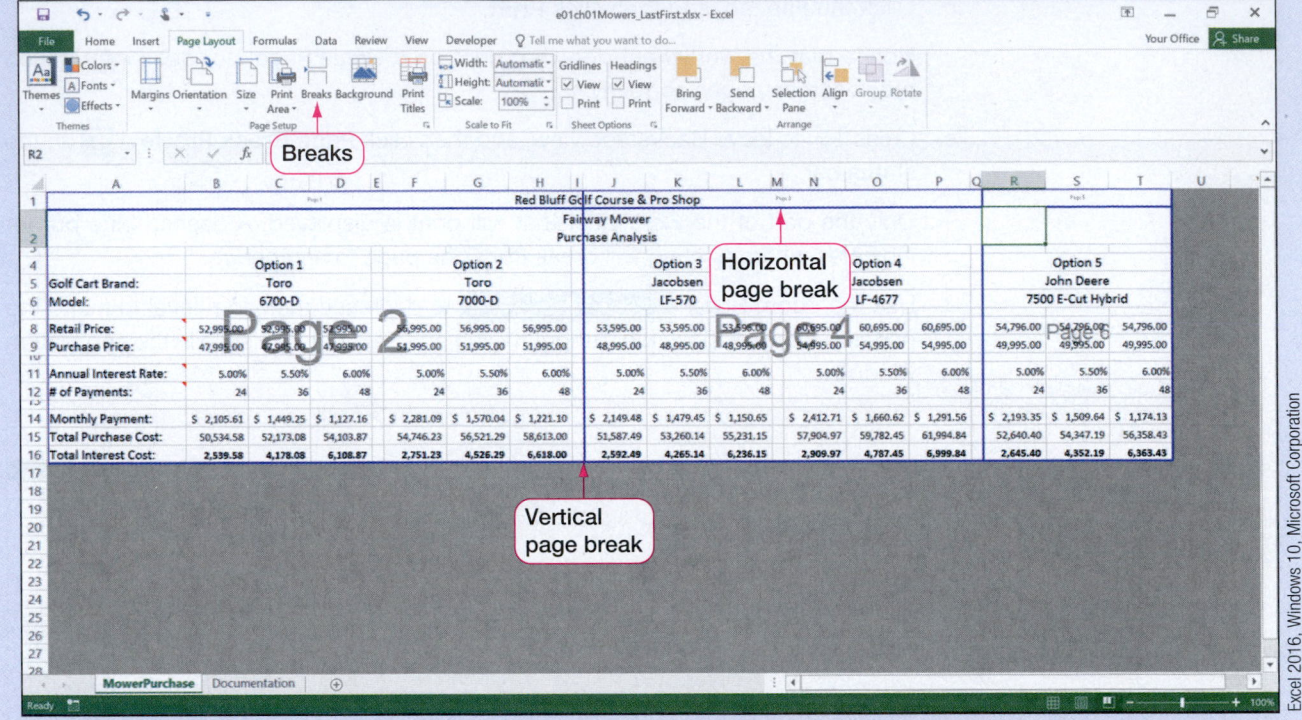

Figure 32 Horizontal and vertical page breaks in Page Break Preview

h. Point to the **horizontal page break**, and the mouse pointer will change to ⬍. Drag the horizontal page break off the bottom or top of the print area to remove it. There should now be a page break after column I and a page break after column Q.

Notice that the titles in rows 1:2 are split between two pages. You need to remove them from the print area.

i. Point to the **top border**, and the mouse pointer will change to the Horizontal Page Break pointer ⬍. Click and hold the left mouse button, and then move the top border down until it is between rows 2 and 3.

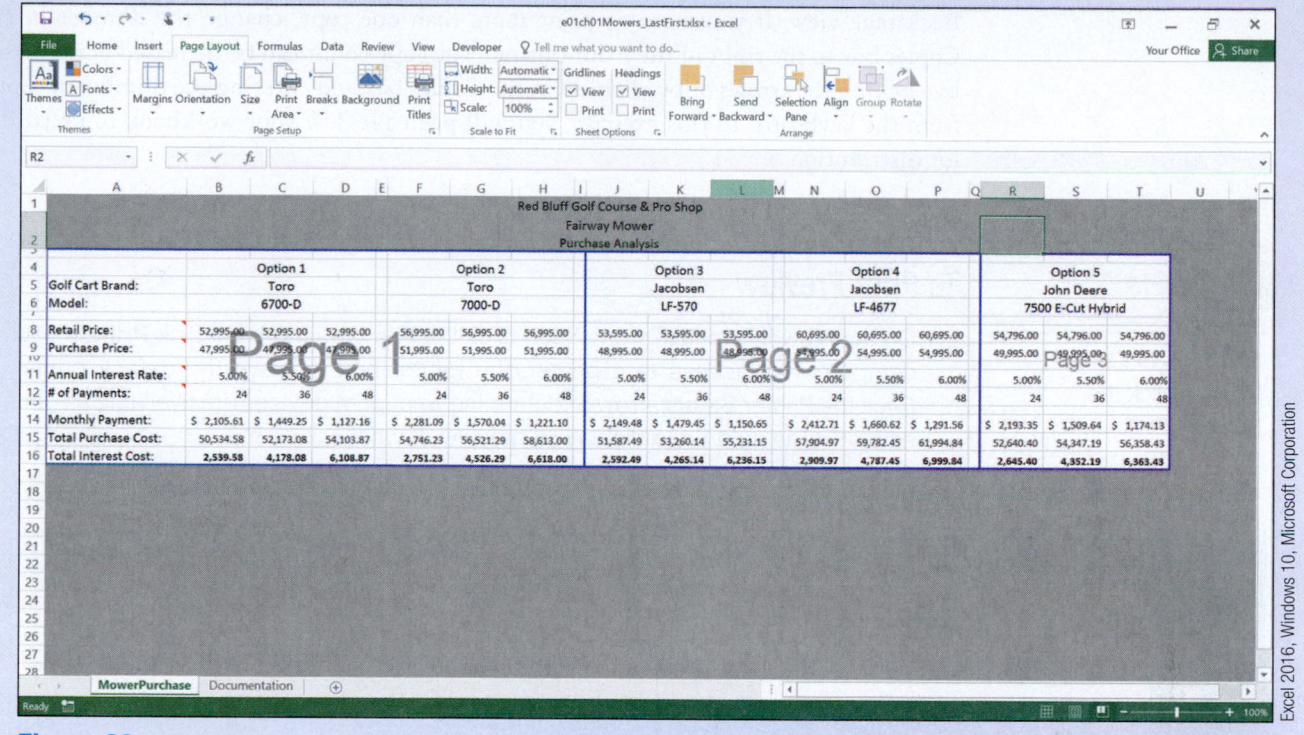

Figure 33 Page Break Preview

j. Click **Page Layout** on the status bar, and then press Ctrl+Home. Page Layout view displays the worksheet with print margins. A thin border shows which part(s) of the worksheet will be printed on a page and also shows the location of the header.

k. Click **Normal** on the status bar. The thin lines between rows 2 and 3, between rows 16 and 17, between columns I and J, and between columns Q and R show the print area and the locations of page breaks.

l. **Save** the workbook.

QUICK REFERENCE	Switching Among Worksheet Views

On the right side of the status bar, do the following.

1. Click for Normal view.

2. Click for Page Layout view.

3. Click for Page Break Preview.

Using Print Preview and Printer Selection

Print Preview is the backstage view of how a document, workbook, presentation, table, or other object will appear when printed. You can use the scroll bar on the right or the page navigation arrows on the bottom to view additional pages if your worksheet requires more than one page to print.

More than one print device can be made available to a computer. Always pay attention to the printer name before printing, and be sure to select the device you want to use. The default printer is selected automatically and is usually acceptable. When a different printer is required, click the Printer Status arrow to see a list of available devices.

Printing a worksheet is as simple as clicking the Print button on the Print tab in Backstage view. If you want to print more than one copy, change the number in the Copies box to the right of the Print button. The copy count can be increased or decreased by clicking the arrows or by clicking in the Copies box and entering the number of copies from the keyboard. In this exercise, you will print preview your workbook to prepare it for distribution.

 **E01.22**

SIDE NOTE
You can click the Previous Page button ◄ to go back a page.

To Print Preview

a. On the MowerPurchase worksheet, click the **File** tab, and then click **Print**. If your computer has access to a printer, the Printer box displays the default printer. Click the Printer Status arrow to determine what print devices are available on your network. The right pane displays a preview of what will print.

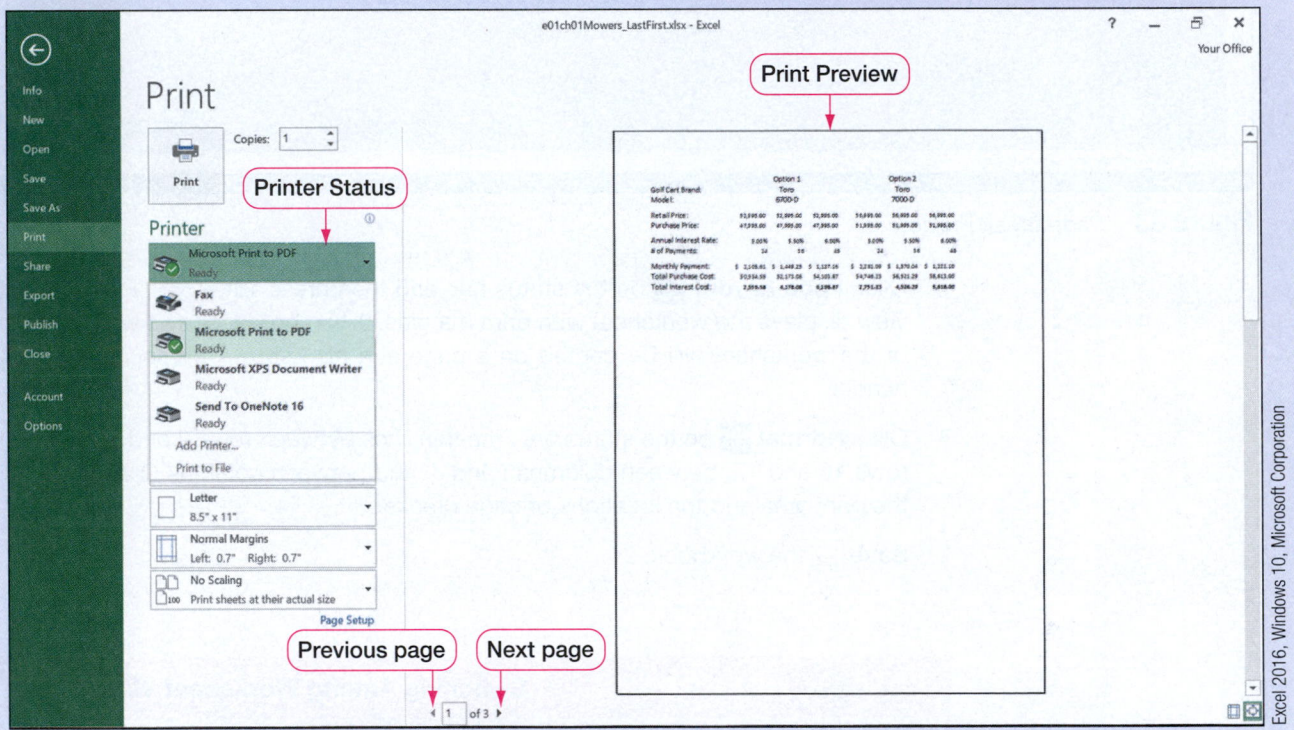

Figure 34   Print Preview and the Printer list

> ### Troubleshooting
> The list of devices displayed in the Printer list is determined by your installation, so the list of available printers will not match those shown in Figure 34.

b. Click the **Next Page** button ▶ to view page 2, and then click the **Next Page** button ▶ to view page 3.

Notice that pages 2 and 3 do not have any row headings. None of the pages have a page title. There is more to be done before this worksheet is ready for printing.

c. Press Esc to leave Backstage view.

d. **Save** 🖫 the workbook.

Using Print Titles

When a worksheet is too large to print on a single page, it is often difficult to keep track of what information is being viewed from one page to another. Headers, such as those in column A of the golf cart analysis, are printed only on the first page.

Print titles can be included on each printed page so every column and/or row is labeled and easily identified from one page to another. Since you set page breaks between cart categories, you should print at least one column on each page that identifies cell contents in each row. In this exercise, you will specify print titles to prepare the worksheet to print.

 E01.23

To Specify Print Titles

a. On the MowerPurchase worksheet, click the **Page Layout** tab, and then, in the Page Setup group, click **Print Titles**. The Page Setup dialog box will appear.

b. On the Sheet tab of the Page Setup dialog box, under Print titles, in the **Columns to repeat at left** box, type **A:A** as shown in Figure 35.

The Print Titles feature requires the specification of a range, even when only a single column will be printed — thus the need to enter column A as A:A.

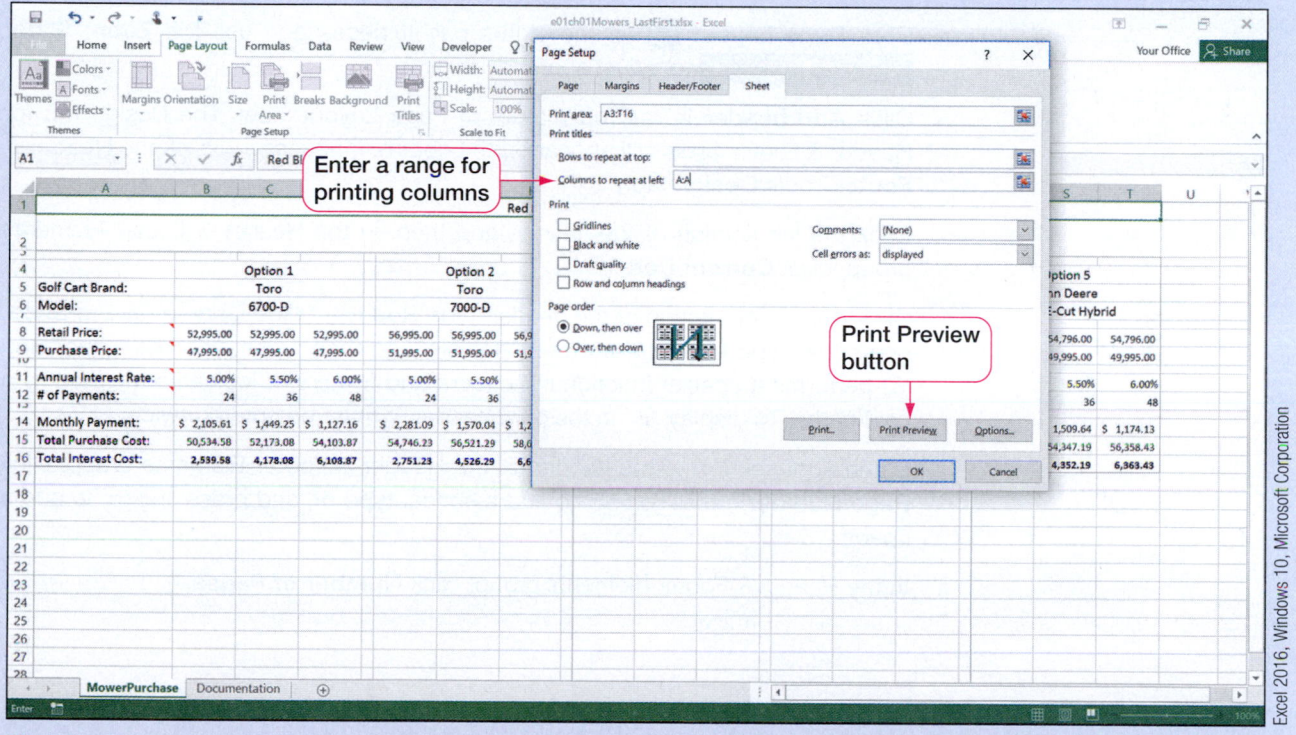

Figure 35 Sheet tab in the Page Setup dialog box for creating print titles

SIDE NOTE
Alternate Method
You can also press the Excel Back button ⊙ to exit Backstage view.

c. Click **Print Preview**. In the Print Preview pane, click ▶ to view page 2, and then click ▶ again to view page 3.

d. Notice that pages 2 and 3 now have row headings. Press [Esc] to exit Backstage view.

e. **Save** 🖫 the workbook.

Adding Headers and Footers

There are often items of information that should be included on a printed document that are not necessary in a worksheet. These items might include the following.

- Print date
- Print time
- Company name
- Page number
- Total number of pages
- File name and location

Headers place information at the top of each printed page. Footers place information at the bottom of each printed page. Headers and footers are divided into three sections: left, center, and right. Information can be placed in any combination of the sections. You may include information in either the header or the footer or both, as deemed necessary. In this exercise, you will add a header and a footer to prepare the worksheet to print.

 **E01.24**

To Add a Header and a Footer

a. On the **MowerPurchase** worksheet tab, press Ctrl+Home to make A1 the active cell.

b. Click **Page Layout** on the status bar. If necessary, use the **Zoom Slider** to adjust zoom to 100%.

c. Click **Add header** in the top margin of Page Layout view. The Design tab for Header & Footer Tools will appear on the ribbon. If necessary, click the **Header & Footer Tools Design** tab.

d. Click the left section of the header, and then, in the Header & Footer Elements group, click **Current Date**.

e. Click the center section of the header, type Red Bluff Golf Course && Pro Shop, press Enter, type Mower Purchase Analysis, and then press Tab. The ampersand (&) performs a special function in headers and footers. It indicates the start of a field name. To display "&" in the print header, it must be entered twice.

f. In the right section of the header, in the Header & Footer Elements group, click **Page Number**, press Spacebar to add a space, type of, and press Spacebar to add a space.

g. In the Header & Footer Elements group, click **Number of Pages**.

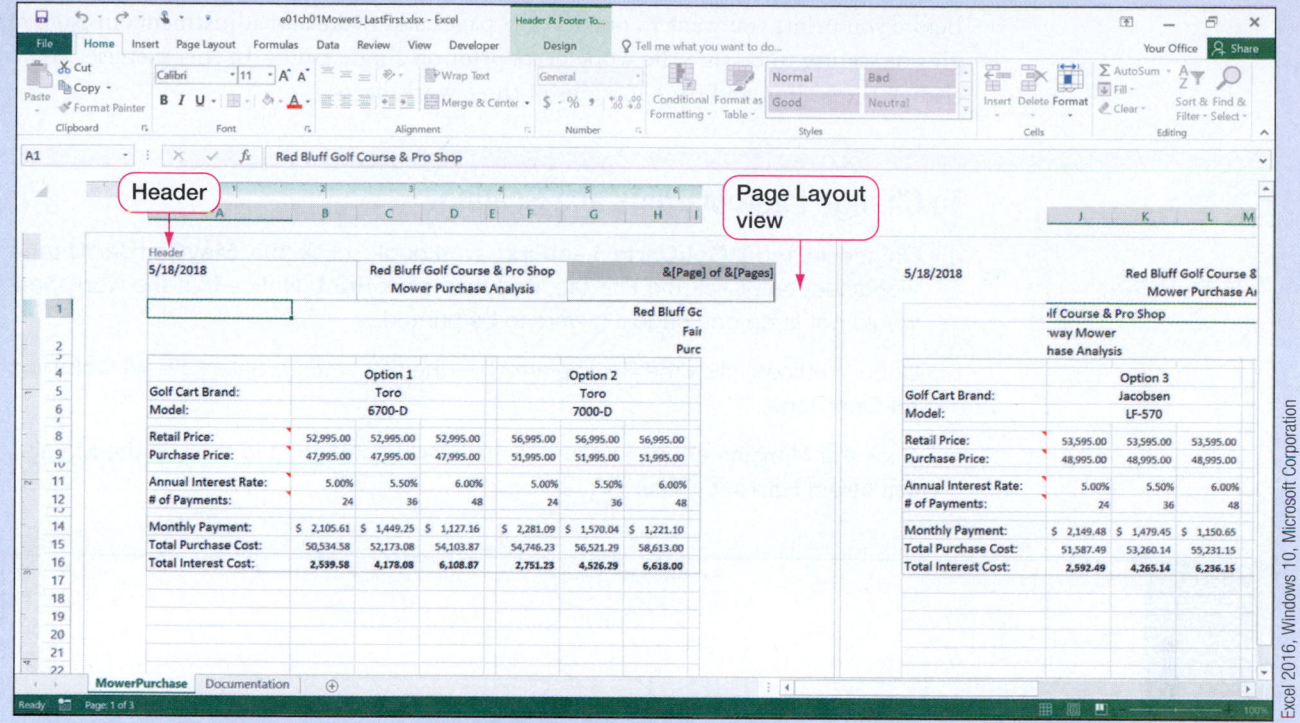

Figure 36 Page Layout view with header information added

h. In the Navigation group, click **Go to Footer**.

i. Click the left section of the footer, and then, in the Header & Footer Elements group, click **File Name**. Select any cell in the worksheet, press Ctrl+Home, and then, on the status bar, click **Normal** ⊞.

j. Click the **File** tab, and then click **Print**. In the Print Preview pane, scroll through the pages to see that the header and footer are added to every page.

k. If your computer is attached to a printer, the Printer Status control displays the default printer. If you want to print to a different printer, click the Printer Status arrow next to the printer name, and then select the desired printer from the list. If requested by your instructor, click **Print**. If you are not instructed to print, press Esc.

l. **Save** 🖫 and **Close** ✕ the e01ch01Mowers_LastFirst workbook, and then submit your file as directed by your instructor.

Changing Page Margins and Scaling

Page margins are the white space at the edges of the printed page. Normal margins for Excel are 0.7 inch on the left and right sides of the page, 0.75 inch on the top and bottom of the page, and 0.3 inch for the header and footer if included.

Margins can be changed to suit conventions or standards for an organization, to better locate information on the page, or to avoid a page break at the last column or line of a worksheet.

It is not uncommon for worksheets to be too large to print on a single page or to be so small that they appear lost in the top left corner of the page. Scaling changes the size of the print font to allow more of a worksheet to be printed on a page or for a worksheet to be printed larger and use more page space. A printed worksheet that has been scaled to fit a sheet of paper generally looks more professional and is easier to read and understand than a worksheet that is printed on two pages that uses only a small part of the second page.

Barry Cheney wants you to prepare the golf cart analysis workbook for printing. Before you print, you want to preview the pages and make and adjustments in page margins or scaling to be sure the worksheets print on single pages. In this exercise, you will change the scaling and page margins of three worksheets.

 **E01.25**

To Change Page Margins and Scaling

a. On the **e01ch01GolfCarts_LastFirst** workbook, click the **MayGolfCartUsage** worksheet tab. Click the **File** tab, and then click **Print**. Notice that the worksheet would not fit on one page if it were to be printed.

b. Under Settings, click the Scaling arrow — the last setting. Select **Fit All Columns on One Page**.

c. Click the **Margins** arrow, just above the Scaling setting, and then, in the Margins list, select **Narrow**. Press Esc.

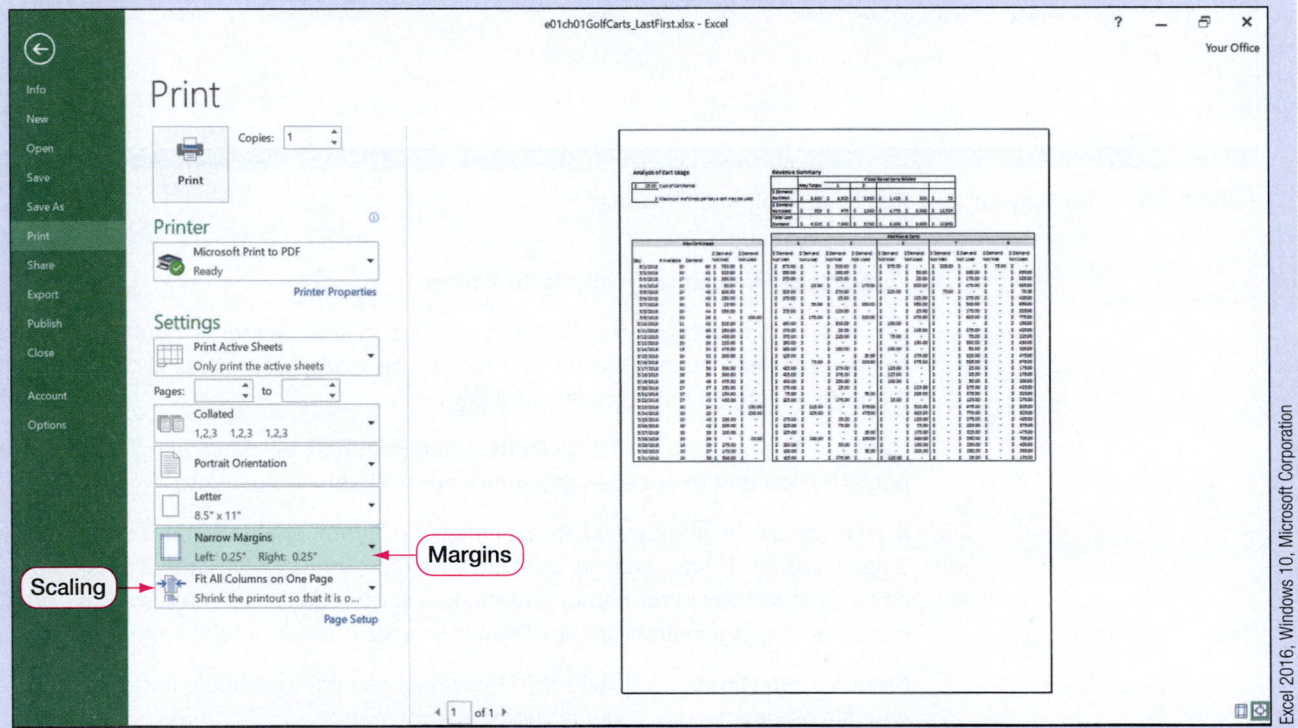

Figure 37 Print Preview with scaling control and narrow margins

d. Repeat steps b through c for the **JuneGolfCartUsage** and **JulyGolfCartUsage** worksheet tabs.

e. **Save** the workbook.

Changing Page Orientation and Print Range

Worksheets can be oriented to print on paper in one of two ways: portrait or landscape. **Landscape orientation** indicates that the page is wider than it is tall. Landscape orientation is generally used when a worksheet has too many columns to print well on a single page in portrait orientation. **Portrait orientation** indicates that the page is taller than it is wide. Scaling the worksheet to fit all columns on a single page can work in portrait orientation, but if scaling makes the data too small to be readable, landscape orientation is an option.

Print range defines what part of a workbook will be printed. The default is Print Active Sheets. This is often adequate, but you can also choose to print only a selected range of cells or to print the entire workbook.

Barry Cheney does not like the last printout you produced of the Documentation worksheet; the print is too small. He suggests changing the page orientation to landscape. In this exercise, you will change the page orientation of a worksheet.

 **E01.26**

To Change Page Orientation and Print Range

a. Click the **Documentation** worksheet tab. Click the **File** tab and then click **Print**.

b. Click the **Orientation** arrow — fourth from the bottom under Settings — and then select **Landscape Orientation**.

c. Click the Print Range arrow — the first setting under Settings — and then select **Print Entire Workbook**. Notice that five pages will print.

d. Scroll through the pages to preview how the workbook would print. Click **Print** if requested by your instructor, or press (Esc).

e. **Save** 🔲 the workbook.

Exporting a Workbook to PDF

Portable Document Format (PDF), which was developed by Adobe Systems in 1993, is a file type that preserves most formatting attributes of a source document regardless of the software in which the document was created. PDF preserves exactly the original "look and feel" of a document but allows the document to be viewed in many different applications. Exporting to PDF is a great way to document your worksheets. One way to distribute a worksheet or workbook in a manner that allows it to be read by anyone with a free PDF reader application is to export the worksheet or entire workbook to PDF.

Now that you have the e01ch01GolfCarts_LastFirst workbook prepared for distribution, Barry wants a PDF version. In this exercise, you will export the workbook to PDF.

 **E01.27**

To Export a Workbook to PDF

a. With the **e01ch01GolfCarts_LastFirst** workbook open, click the **File** tab, and then click **Export**.

b. In the right pane, under Create a PDF/XPS Document, click **Create PDF/XPS**.

c. In the Publish as PDF or XPS dialog box, click **Options**. In the Options dialog box, under Publish what, click **Entire workbook**.

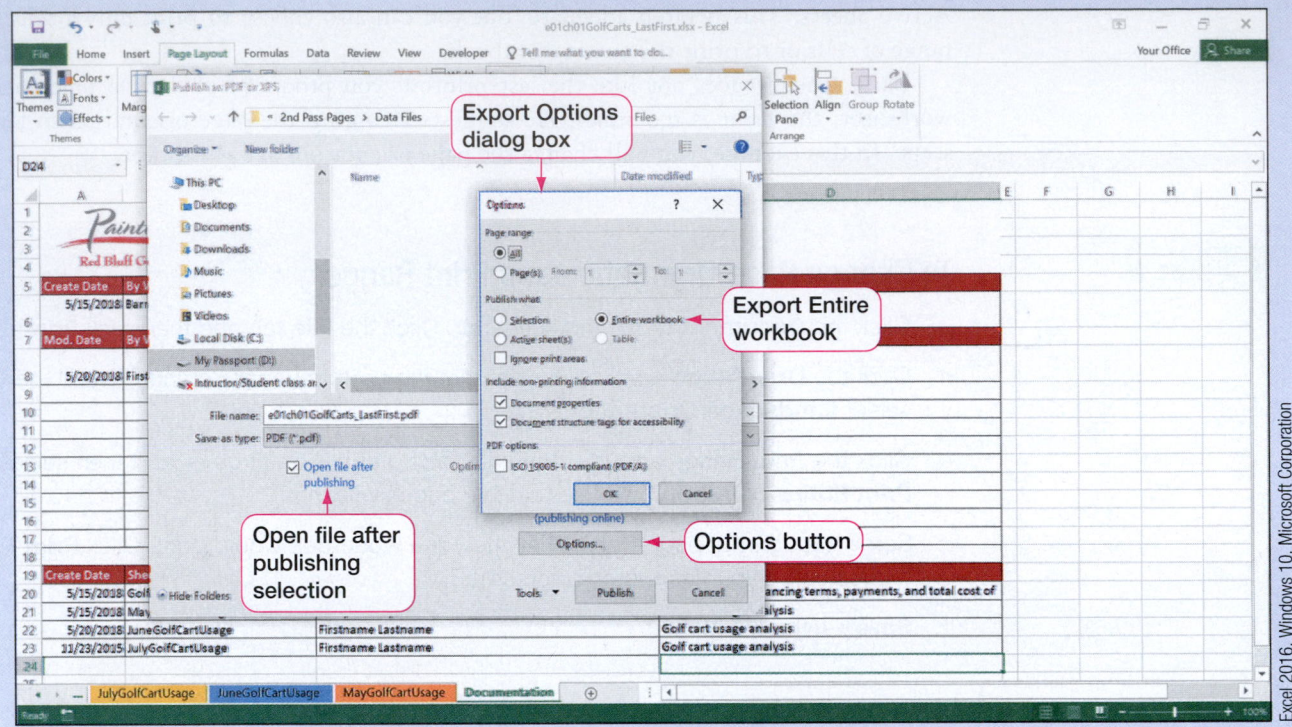

Figure 38 Export Options dialog box

Excel 2016, Windows 10, Microsoft Corporation

> d. Click **OK**. In the Publish as PDF or XPS dialog box, be sure **Open file after publishing** is checked.
>
> e. Navigate to where you are saving your Excel files, verify the file name listed in the File name box to be **e01ch01GolfCarts_LastFirst** using your last and first name, and then click **Publish**.
>
> f. Once the PDF file has been created, it may be opened in Reader, the built-in Windows 10 PDF document viewer.

Troubleshooting

Your PDF file may not open in Reader if a different PDF reader, such as Adobe Reader, is installed as the default PDF file reader. If the PDF file displays in a different reader, close the reader and skip step g.

> g. Right-click anywhere on the screen. A menu bar will appear at the bottom of the screen. Click **More**.
>
> h. Click **Close** to close the PDF file.
>
> i. **Save** 🖫 the workbook, exit Excel, and then submit your files as directed by your instructor.

Concept Check

1. Explain the following terms for a reader who is not familiar with Excel.

   - Worksheet p. 53
   - Workbook p. 54
   - Cell p. 53
   - Row p. 53
   - Column p. 53
   - Spreadsheet p. 53

2. How do you quickly navigate to the last row in a worksheet that contains data? What happens when you press End in Excel? How do you move from one worksheet to another in Excel? What purpose does the Go To dialog box serve? How do you access the Go To dialog box? p. 58

3. Why is documentation important? Why do many people not properly document their workbooks? What are the possible costs associated with inadequate documentation? p. 61

4. What happens if you select a cell that contains important data, type "Your Office", and then press Enter? How does the outcome change if you first double-click a cell that contains important data, type "Your Office", and then press Enter? p. 68–69

5. How do you select noncontiguous cells? Is the ability to select noncontiguous cells important to the effective use of Excel? If yes, why? If no, why make use of noncontiguous cell selection? p. 73

6. Describe two ways in which columns and rows can be inserted and deleted. p. 73

7. How do you reorder worksheets in a workbook? p. 79

8. Explain the purpose of print titles, page headers, and page footers and describe when you would use them. What are page orientation and scaling, and how can they be used in tandem to allow you to efficiently print a professional-looking worksheet? p. 91

Key Terms

Active cell 57
Active worksheet 54
AutoFill 82
Cell 53
Cell range 65
Cell reference 57
Clipboard 65
Column 53
Comment 60
Contiguous cell range 65
Date data 62
Destination cell 65

Field 53
Formula 53
Function 53
Keyboard shortcut 57
Landscape orientation 94
Merge & Center 71
Noncontiguous cell range 65
Normal view 86
Numeric data 62
Page Break Preview 86
Page Layout view 86
Portable Document
    Format (PDF) 95

Portrait orientation 94
Print Preview 89
Record 53
Row 53
Spreadsheet 53
Text data 62
Time data 62
Touch mode 59
What-if analysis 53
White space 73
Workbook 54
Worksheet 53

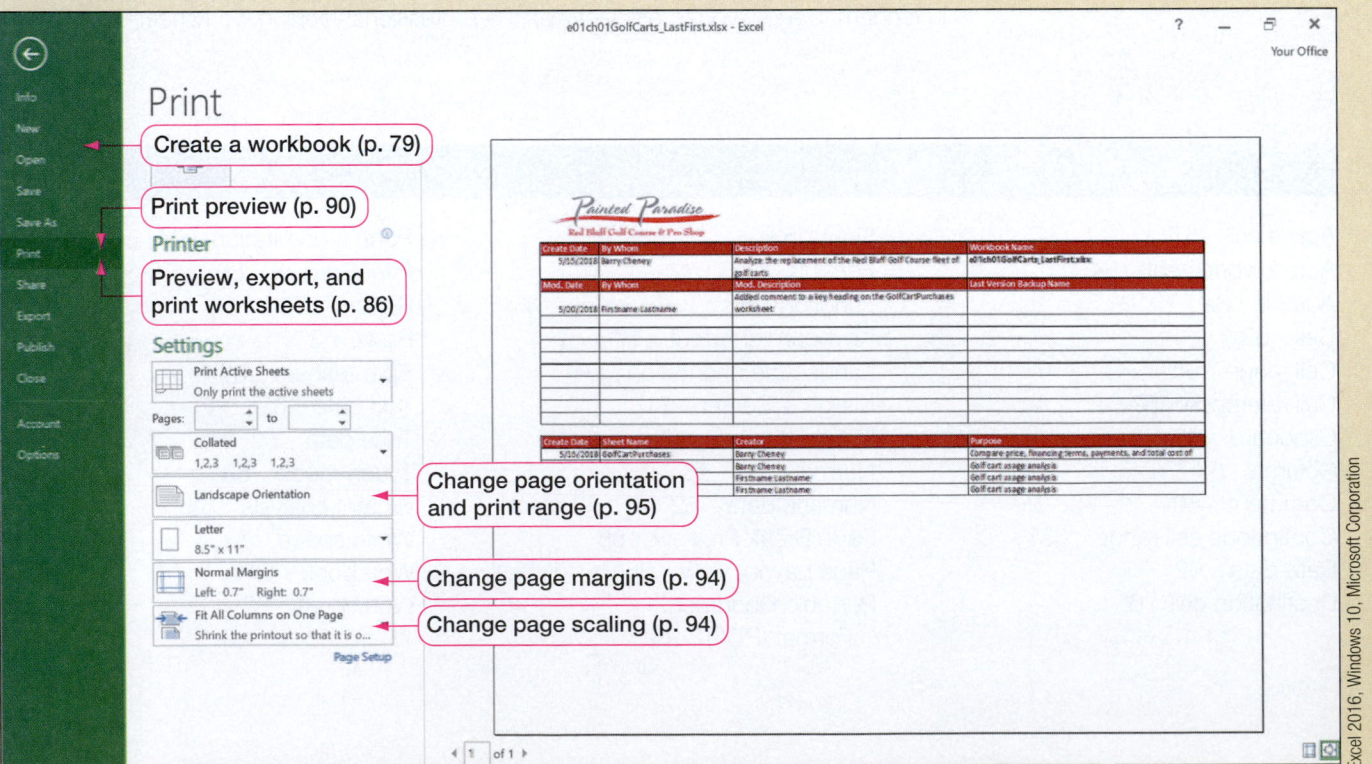

Figure 39

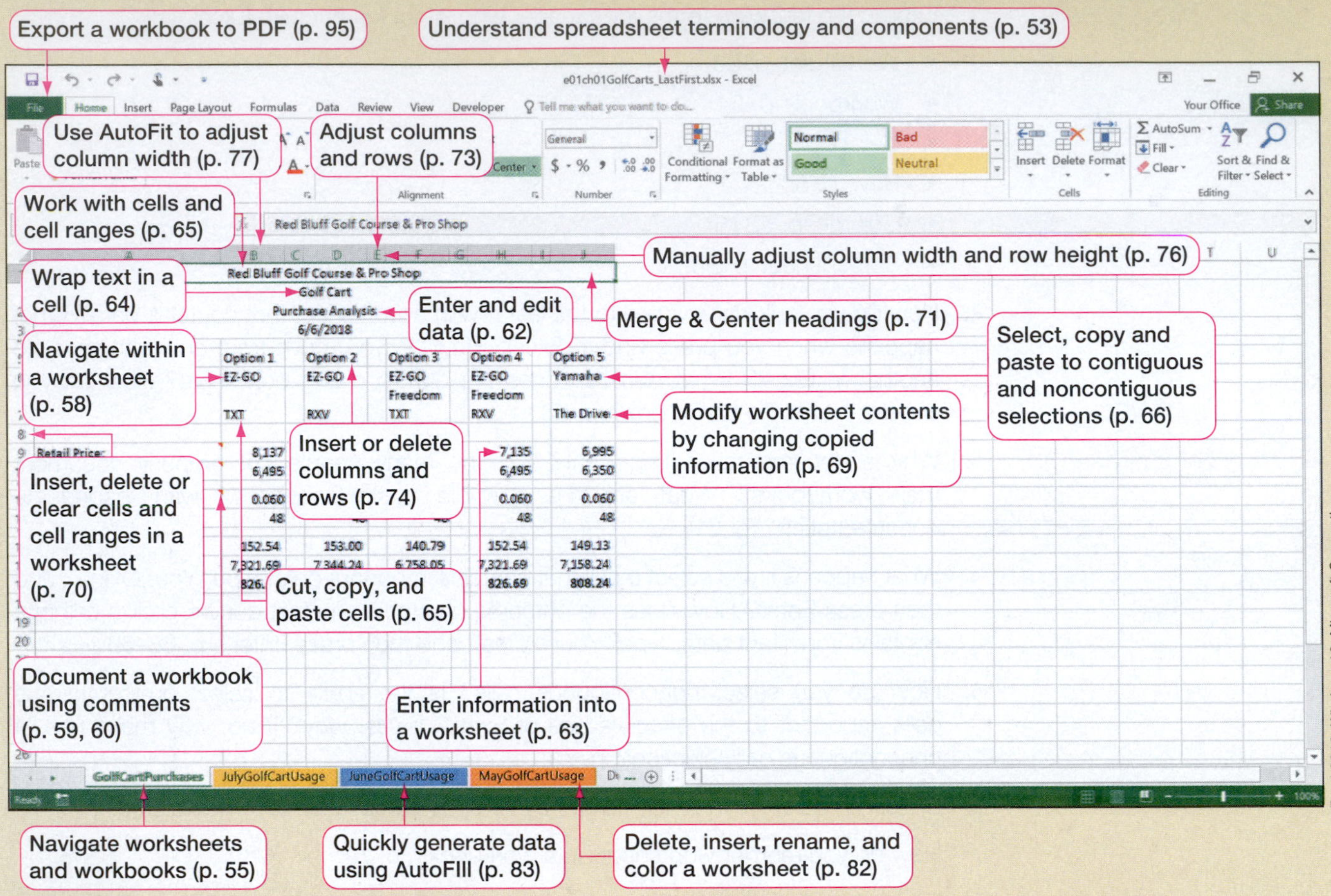

Figure 40

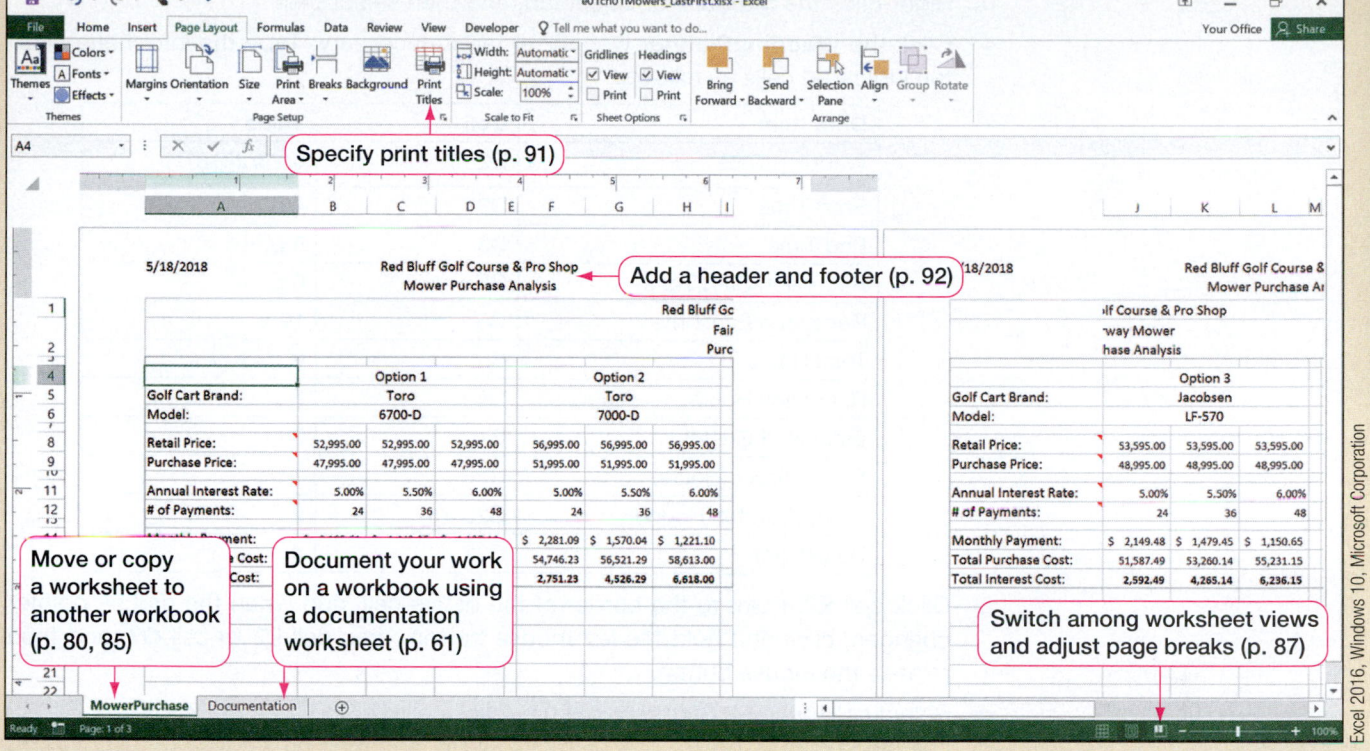

Figure 41

Practice 1

Student data file needed:

 e01ch01WeddingPlan.xlsx

You will save your files as:

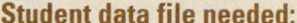 e01ch01WeddingPlan_LastFirst.xlsx

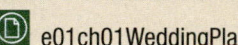 e01ch01WeddingPlan_LastFirst.pdf

Red Bluff Resort Wedding Planning Worksheet

Sales & Marketing

Weddings are becoming an important part of the Painted Paradise Resort & Spa's business, so Patti Rochelle started a worksheet to improve the wedding-planning process for her staff. Last year, the resort hosted three weddings per week, on average, and it has done as many as six in a weekend. The worksheet Patti wants you to finish will allow for changes in pricing to be immediately reflected in the planning process.

You have been given a workbook that includes product/service categories, prices, and an initial worksheet structure to help standardize the process and pricing of weddings. You will build a worksheet that calculates the price of a wedding and doubles as a checklist to use as weddings are set up, to ensure that subcontractors, such as DJs, are reserved in a timely fashion and that all contracted services are delivered.

a. Start Excel, click **Open Other Workbooks** in the left pane, and then double-click **This PC**. Navigate through the folder structure to the location of your student data files, and then double-click **e01ch01WeddingPlan**. If a Security Warning message displays, click the **Enable Editing** button.

b. Click the **File** tab, click **Save As**, and then double-click **This PC**. In the Save As dialog box, navigate to the location where you are saving your project files, and then change the file name to e01ch01WeddingPlan_LastFirst, using your last and first name. Click **Save**.

c. Double-click the active **Sheet3** worksheet tab, type WeddingPlanner, and then press Enter. Double-click the **Sheet1** worksheet tab, and then type Documentation as the new name for the worksheet. Press Enter, click cell **B20**, and then type WeddingPlanner. Press Ctrl+Home.

d. Right-click the **Sheet2** worksheet tab, and then select Delete.

e. Click the **WeddingPlanner** worksheet tab if necessary. Type the information into the indicated cells as follows.

Data Item	Cell	Value
Wedding Date	B2	6/18/2018
Start Time	D2	4 p
End Time	D3	5 p
Reception Start Time	G2	6 p
Reception End Time	G3	12 a
Total Hours	B5	8
Reception Hours	D5	6
Estimated Guests	B7	300
Piano Player (Hours)	C28	1
String Quartet (Hours)	C29	2
DJ (Hours)	C32	4

f. Click cell **E2**. Point to the border of the active cell, and when the mouse pointer changes, click and hold the left mouse button, drag cell E2 to cell **G7**, and then release the mouse button.

g. Select cell range **F2:G3**, press Ctrl+X, click cell **H7**, and then press Ctrl+V. Select cell range **C2:D3**, press Ctrl+X, click cell **H4**, and then press Ctrl+V.

h. Select cell range **A2:B2**, press Ctrl+X, and then click cell **G3** to make it the active cell. Press Ctrl+V, and then select columns **G:I**. On the Home tab, in the Cells group, click the Format arrow, and then click **AutoFit Column Width**.

i. Select columns **B:C**, and in the Cells group, click **Format**, and then click **Column Width**. Type **17** in the Column Width box, and then click **OK**.

j. Click the header for column **E**, and then right-click and select **Delete** from the shortcut menu to delete the column. Right-click column E, select Column Width, type **2** in the Column Width box, and then click **OK**.

k. Press Ctrl+Home. Select **A1:H1** and in the Alignment group, click **Merge & Center**.

l. Right-click the header for Row 1, select Row Height, type **20** in the Row Height box, and then click **OK**.

m. Select cell range **B9:C9**, press Ctrl, and then select cell range **B34:C34**. In the Alignment group, click **Merge & Center**.

n. Click cell **A27**, and then, in the Cells group, click the **Insert** arrow, and then click **Insert Sheet Rows**.

o. Click **Page Layout** view on the status bar, scroll to the bottom of the worksheet, and click in the left section of the Add footer. If necessary, under Header & Footer Tools, click the **Design** tab. In the Header & Footer Elements group, click **File Name**, and then click a cell in the worksheet. Press Ctrl+Home, and then click **Normal** on the status bar.

p. Click the **Documentation** worksheet tab. Repeat step m to insert the file name in the footer.

q. Click cell **A8**, and then type **today's date** in mm/dd/yyyy format. Click cell **B8**, and type your name in Firstname Lastname format. Click cell **C8**, type Completed Ms. Rochelle's initial work; reorganized worksheet to function better as a checklist, and then press Ctrl+Enter. On the Home tab, in the Alignment group, click **Wrap Text** to wrap the text in cell C8.

r. Click and hold the **Documentation** worksheet tab, and then move the Documentation worksheet to the right of the WeddingPlanner worksheet to make it the last sheet.

s. Click the **WeddingPlanner** worksheet tab, click the **File** tab, and then click **Print**. Click the Scaling arrow, and then select **Fit All Columns on One Page**. Exit Backstage view.

t. Click the **Documentation** worksheet tab. Click the **File** tab, and then click **Print**. Click the **Orientation** arrow, and then select **Landscape Orientation**. Click the Scaling arrow, and then select **Fit All Columns on One Page**.

u. Click **Export**, and then click **Create PDF/XPS**. Click **Options**. In the Options dialog box, under Publish what, click **Entire workbook**, and then click **OK**. Navigate to the folder where you are saving your files. In the File name box, type e01ch01WeddingPlan_LastFirst using your last and first name. Verify **Open file after publishing** is checked, and then click **Publish**. View the pages, and then close the PDF.

v. Save the workbook, exit Excel, and then submit your files as directed by your instructor.

Problem Solve 1

MyITLab®
Grader
Homework

Student data file needed:

 e01ch01TCO.xlsx

You will save your file as:

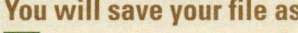 e01ch01TCO_LastFirst.xlsx

Automobile Total Cost of Ownership

Sales & Marketing   Finance & Accounting

Most people own, or will at some time own, an automobile. Few actually take the time to calculate what owning an automobile actually costs — called total cost of ownership. This is an important calculation for both individuals and businesses. You will complete the development of an automobile total cost of ownership worksheet for your supervisor, Jan Bossy, CFO at Kallio Auto Sales.

a. Open the Excel file, **e01ch01TCO**. Save your file as e01ch01TCO_LastFirst, using your last and first name.

b. Rename **Sheet1** Documentation. Rename **Sheet2** AutoTCO.

c. Delete **Sheet3**.

d. On the AutoTCO worksheet, type the Value information into the indicated cells as follows.

Data Item	Cell	Value
Miles Driven / Year	E4	15000
Fuel Cost / Gallon	E5	3.00
MPG	E6	26

e. Merge and center the worksheet heading across cell range **A1:F1**.

f. Select cell range **C16:C22**, and then copy the selected range to the Clipboard. Select cell range **D16:F16**, and paste the Clipboard contents into the selected range.

g. Select cell range **B15:C15**. Use AutoFill to copy the selected range to **B15:F15**.

h. Insert a row above row 15.

i. In cell **B15**, type 5-year Total Cost of Ownership Analysis, and then select cell range **B15:F15**. Apply **Center Across Selection**.

j. Add the file name in the left footer of the AutoTCO and Documentation worksheets.

k. Click cell **A8**, and then enter **today's date** in mm/dd/yyyy format. Click cell **B8**, and then type your name in Firstname Lastname format. Click cell **C8**, and then type Completed Ms. Bossy's automobile total cost of ownership worksheet. Apply **Wrap Text** to cell **C8**. Click cell **B20**, type AutoTCO.

l. On the **AutoTCO** worksheet tab, apply **AutoFit Column Width** to column A. Change the column width of columns **B:F** to **12**.

m. Move the AutoTCO worksheet to the left of the Documentation worksheet.

n. For printing the AutoTCO worksheet, set its orientation to **Landscape Orientation**. For the Documentation worksheet, set its orientation to Landscape Orientation, and then set the scaling to **Fit All Columns to One Page**. Set the Print Range to **Print Entire Workbook**, and then print the workbook as directed by your instructor.

o. Save the workbook, exit Excel, and then submit your file as directed by your instructor.

Perform 1: Perform in Your Career

Student data file needed:

 e01ch01IncProp.xlsx

You will save your file as:

 e01ch01IncProp_LastFirst.xlsx

Property Investment Analysis

Finance & Accounting

You were recently hired by O'Miller Property Investment for an internship. A determining factor in Kelsie O'Miller's decision to give you this opportunity was based on your ability to work with Microsoft Excel. Ms. O'Miller just started a workbook that she wants to use to compare properties under consideration for acquisition.

She has asked you to finish the worksheet by formatting and expanding the worksheet to allow the side-by-side comparison of six properties.

a. Open the Excel file, **e01ch01IncProp**. Save your file as e01ch01IncProp_LastFirst, using your last and first name.

b. Rename the **Sheet3** worksheet PropertyAnalysis, and then rename the **Sheet1** worksheet Documentation. Delete the **Sheet2** worksheet.

c. On the PropertyAnalysis worksheet tab, set the width of column A so that no portion of any row heading is hidden, and then delete column **B**.

d. Insert new rows into the worksheet above Loan APR, Income, Interest Paid Year 1, and Net Carrying Costs.

e. Copy all of the information for a loan, and paste two more loan columns to the right of column F. Use the AutoFit feature to adjust the column width of the new loan columns if necessary.

f. Use AutoFill to number the loans in row 4.

g. Type the following information into the indicated columns.

Data Item	G	H
Purchase Price	450000	499000
Down Payment	50000	60000
Loan APR	0.06	0.055
Income	95000	105000
Property Taxes	6500	7250
Repairs	12000	10000
Insurance	5000	5500
Advertising	600	650

h. Center the worksheet titles — the top two lines — across all columns that contain headings and data. Adjust row height where necessary so that the titles are entirely visible.

i. Insert a column between the columns that contain loan information. For any column to the left of a column that contains loan data, set the column width to **3**.

j. Move the values for Depreciation Years and Income Tax Rate one column to the right to C29:C30.

k. Add a comment to cell **C30** stating Income tax rate may increase.

l. In the **Documentation** worksheet, insert today's date into cell **A8**. Type your name in Firstname Lastname format into cell **B8**, and then type into cell **C8** an appropriate description of your activities in this workbook. Change any other necessary information in the Documentation worksheet.

m. Add the file name to the left page footer on both worksheets.

n. Move a worksheet so that the worksheets are in the following order from left to right: PropertyAnalysis, Documentation.

o. For printing the PropertyAnalysis worksheet, set its orientation to **Landscape**. For printing the Documentation worksheet, set its orientation to **Landscape Orientation**, and then set scaling to **Fit All Columns on One Page**. Set Print Range to **Print Entire Workbook**. Press Esc.

p. Save the workbook, exit Excel, and then submit your file as directed by your instructor.

Additional Chapter Cases are available at www.pearsonhighered.com/youroffice

Additional
Cases

Microsoft Excel 2016

Chapter 2 | FORMATS, FUNCTIONS, AND FORMULAS

Prepare Case

Finance and Accounting

Red Bluff Golf Course & Pro Shop Sales Analysis

The Red Bluff Golf Course & Pro Shop sells products ranging from golf clubs and accessories to clothing displaying the club logo. In addition, the Pro Shop collects fees for rounds of golf and services such as lessons from golf pro John Schilling.

Manager Aleeta Herriott needs to track Pro Shop sales by category on a day-by-day basis. Sales, at least to some extent, are a reflection of traffic in the Pro Shop and can be used to help determine staffing requirements on different days of the week. In addition, summary sales data can be compared to inventory investments to determine whether the product mix is optimal, given the demands of the clientele.

Each item or service at the time of sale is recorded in the Pro Shop point-of-sale (POS) system. At the end of each day, the POS system produces a cash register report with categorized sales for the day. This is the data source of each day's sales for the worksheet. Aleeta has created an initial layout for a sales analysis workbook, but she needs you to finish it.

Bikeriderlondon/Shutterstock

Student data files needed for this chapter:

 e01ch02WeekSales.xlsx

 e01ch02red_bluff.jpg

You will save your files as:

 e01ch02WeekSales_LastFirst.xlsx

 e01ch02WSFormulas_LastFirst.pdf

Worksheet Formatting

To be of value, information must be communicated effectively. Effective communication of information generally requires the information is formatted in a manner that aids in proper interpretation and understanding.

Some of the most revolutionary ideas in history were initially recorded on a handy scrap of paper, a yellow legal pad, a tape recorder — even a paper napkin. Communication of those ideas generally required that they be presented in a different medium and that they be formatted in a manner that aided other people's understanding. The content may not have changed, but the format of the presentation is important. People are more receptive to well-formatted information because it is easier to understand and to absorb. While accuracy of information is of the utmost importance, of what use is accurate data that is misunderstood? In this section, you will manipulate a worksheet by formatting numbers, aligning and rotating text, changing cell fill color and borders, using built-in cell and table styles, and applying workbook themes.

Format Cells, Cell Ranges, and Worksheets

There are several ways to present information. If different technologies, mediums, and audiences are considered, a list of more than 50 ways to present information would be easy to produce. The list could include varied communication methods such as books, speeches, websites, tweets, RSS feeds, and bumper stickers. However, an analysis of such a list would reveal generic communication methodologies.

- Oral
- Written narrative
- Tabular
- Graphical

Excel is an application specifically designed to present information in tabular and graphical formats. **Tabular format** is the presentation of text and numbers in tables — essentially organized in labeled columns and numbered rows. **Graphical format** is the presentation of information in charts, graphs, and pictures. Excel facilitates the graphical presentation of information via charts and graphs based on the tabular information in worksheets.

E02.00

To Get Started

a. Start **Excel**, click **Open Other Workbooks** in the left pane, and then double-click **This PC**. Navigate through the folder structure to the location of your student data files, and then double-click **e01ch02WeekSales**. If a Security Warning message displays, click the **Enable Editing** button.

b. Click the **File** tab, click **Save As**, and then double-click **This PC**. In the Save As dialog box, navigate to the location where you are saving your project files, and then change the file name to e01ch02WeekSales_LastFirst, using your last and first name. Click **Save**.

Number Formatting

Through number formatting, context can be given to numbers, reducing the need for text labeling, such as for date and/or time values. Most of the world's currencies can be represented in Excel through number formatting. Financial numbers, scientific numbers, percentages, dates, times, and so on all have special formatting requirements and can be properly displayed in a worksheet. The ability to manipulate and properly display many different types of numeric information is a feature that makes Excel an incredibly powerful and ubiquitously popular application.

Numbers can be formatted in many ways in Excel. The most common formats are shown in Table 1.

Format Name	Ribbon	Number Format List	Keyboard Shortcut	Example
Accounting	$ ▾	🖼		$ (1,234.00)
Comma*	,		Ctrl + Shift + !	(1,234.00)
Currency		🖼		-1,234.00
			Ctrl + Shift + $	($1,234.00)
General		ABC 123	Ctrl + Shift + ~	-1234
Number		General ▾		-1234.00
Percentage	%	%	Ctrl + Shift + %	-7.00%
Short Date		📅		6/28/2018
			Ctrl + Shift + #	28-Jun-18
Time		🕐		6:00:00 PM
			Ctrl + Shift + @	6:00 PM

*Comma format is Accounting format without a currency symbol.

Table 1 Common number formats   Amy S Kinser, Brant Moriarity, Eric Kinser, Kristyn Jacobson

Your manager, Aleeta Herriott, has asked you to format the WeeklySales worksheet so the data is easier to understand. You think using simple Excel formatting such as the Accounting Number Format, Currency Format, Comma Style, Percent Style, and Decimals will make the worksheet more readable. In this exercise, you will format numbers on the WeeklySales worksheet.

E02.01

SIDE NOTE
Pin the Ribbon
If your ribbon is collapsed, pin your ribbon open. Click the Home tab, in the lower right-hand corner of the ribbon, click Pin the Ribbon ⊞.

SIDE NOTE
Accounting Number Format
The Accounting Number Format also formats a cell with a comma at the thousand and two decimal places.

To Format Numbers

a. On the WeeklySales worksheet tab, select cell range **B6:H6**. Click the **Home** tab, and then, in the Number group, click **Accounting Number Format** $ ▾. The top row of numbers is often formatted with a currency symbol to indicate that subsequent values are currency as well.

> **Troubleshooting**
> If any of the cells you just formatted display a series of number signs (#), select the cell(s), and in the Cells group, click Format ⊞, and then, under Cell Size, click AutoFit Column Width.

b. Select cell range **B7:H8**, and then, in the Number group, click **Comma Style** , .

c. Select cell range **C29:C30**, press and hold Ctrl, click cell **C33**, and then select **C36:C38**. In the Number group, click **Percent Style** %, and then in the Number group, click **Increase Decimal** ⬆.00 once.

d. Click cell **C31**, press Ctrl, and then click **C34**. In the Number group, click the **Number Format** arrow [General ▾], and then select **More Number Formats**. The Format Cells dialog box is displayed. Under Category, select **Currency**.

e. Double-click the Decimal places box, and type **0**.

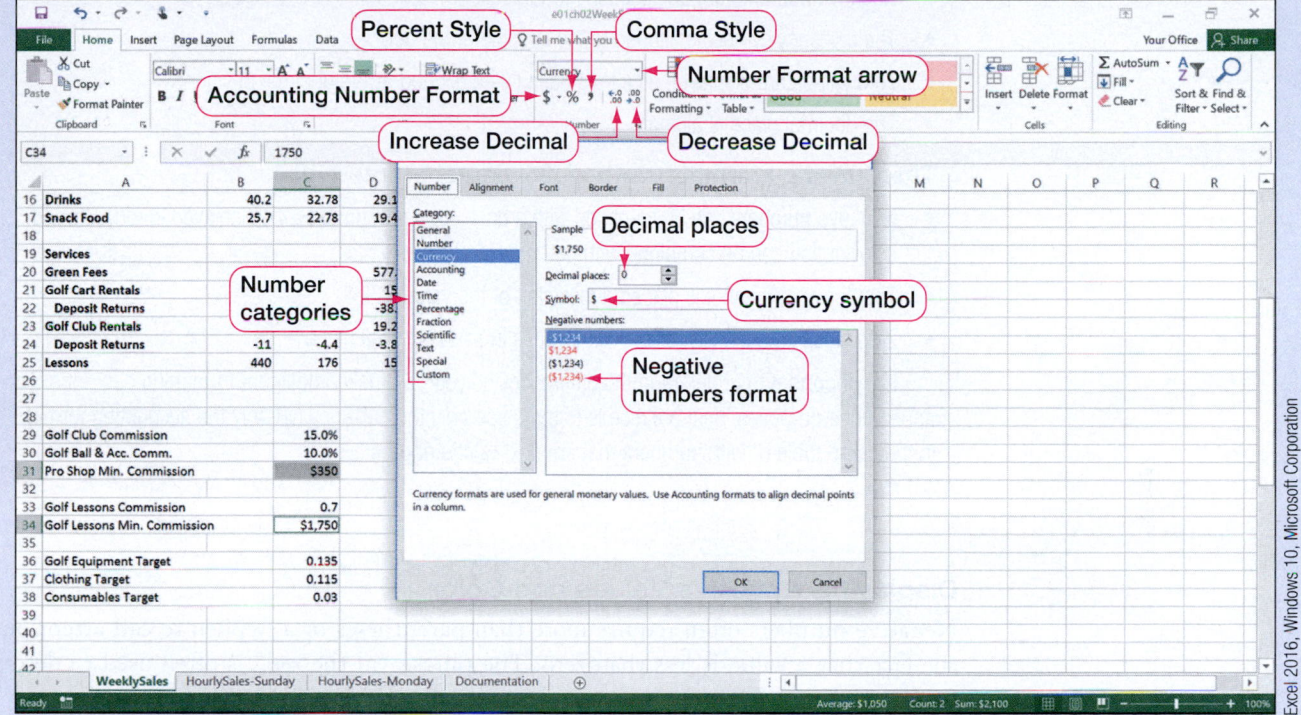

Figure 1 Number Format options

SIDE NOTE

Comma Style
The Comma Style is simply the Accounting Number Format without a monetary symbol.

f. Click **OK**, and then **Save** 🖫 the workbook.

The Accounting and Currency number formats are both intended for monetary values.

The Accounting format has the following characteristics.

- Negative numbers are enclosed in parentheses.
- The currency symbol is aligned to the left side of the cell.
- Zero values are displayed as a long dash (—) aligned at the decimal position.
- The decimal place is aligned.

The Currency format has the following characteristics.

- Negative numbers can be identified with a dash (–), parentheses, or displayed in red. The red color option can be combined with parentheses as well.
- The currency symbol is placed directly left of the value.
- Zero values are displayed as 0 with zeroes in each decimal place.

It is important to understand the differences so you can make intelligent formatting decisions. For appearance purposes, best practice is to try to use only the currency OR only the accounting format in the same table or with numbers that are next to one another.

Displaying Negative Values and Color

Negative numbers often require more than parentheses or a hyphen to call attention to the fact that a value is less than zero. The phrase "in the red" is often used to describe financial values that are less than zero, so, not surprisingly, Excel makes it very easy to display negative numbers in a red font color.

To draw attention to negative numbers, in this exercise you will format the worksheet to display negative numbers in red.

 **E02.02**

To Display Negative Numbers in Red

a. On the WeeklySales worksheet, select cell range **B20:H22**. On the Home tab, in the Number group, click the **Number Format** arrow General , and then select **More Number Formats**.

b. Under Category, select **Number**. If necessary, type a **2** in the Decimal places box. Select **Use 1000 Separator (,)**. Under Negative numbers, select the **red negative number format (1,234.10)**, and then click **OK**. You will change the format of rows 23:25 in a later exercise.

Troubleshooting

If the negative numbers in B22:H22 are not displayed in red, you didn't select the correct negative number format. Press Ctrl +Z, and repeat steps a and b.

c. **Save** 🖫 the workbook.

Formatting Date and Time

Excel stores a date and time as a number in which the digits to the left of the decimal place are the number of complete days since January 1, 1900, inclusive. The right side of the decimal place is the decimal portion of the current day, which represents the current time. This date system allows Excel to use dates in calculations. For example, if you add 7 to today's date, the result is the date one week in the future.

While this is useful for computer systems and applications such as Excel, people have not been taught to interpret time in this manner, so unformatted date and time values — those displayed in General format — mean little or nothing to us. Date and time formatting allows Excel date and time values to be displayed in a fashion that allows human interpretation. A heading that identifies a column as date values gives context to the information, but in the case of date information, without proper formatting, it is for the most part unusable by the reader.

In this exercise, you will format cells with date and time formats.

 E02.03

To Format a Cell or Cell Range as a Date or Time

a. On the WeeklySales worksheet, click cell **B4**; this is an unformatted date in Excel.

b. On the Home tab, and in the Number group, click the **Number Format** arrow `General`, and then select **Short Date**. Click and hold down the left mouse button on the **fill handle,** drag the fill handle right until the border around the active cell expands to include cells **B4:H4**, and then release the left mouse button. The date in cell B4 has been incremented by one day in each of the cells in C4:H4.

c. Notice the series of number (#) signs in F4:H4. Select columns **F:H**. In the Cells group, click **Format**, and then select **AutoFit Column Width**. Next you want to format numbers to appropriately reflect time.

d. Click the **HourlySales-Sunday** worksheet tab. Select cell range **A6:A7**. In the Number group, click the **Number Format** arrow `General`.

Notice the Time format includes hours, minutes, and seconds. You have no need to display seconds, so you need to use the Format Cells dialog box to access additional time formats.

e. Select **More Number Formats**. Under Category, select **Time**. In the Type box, select **1:30 PM**.

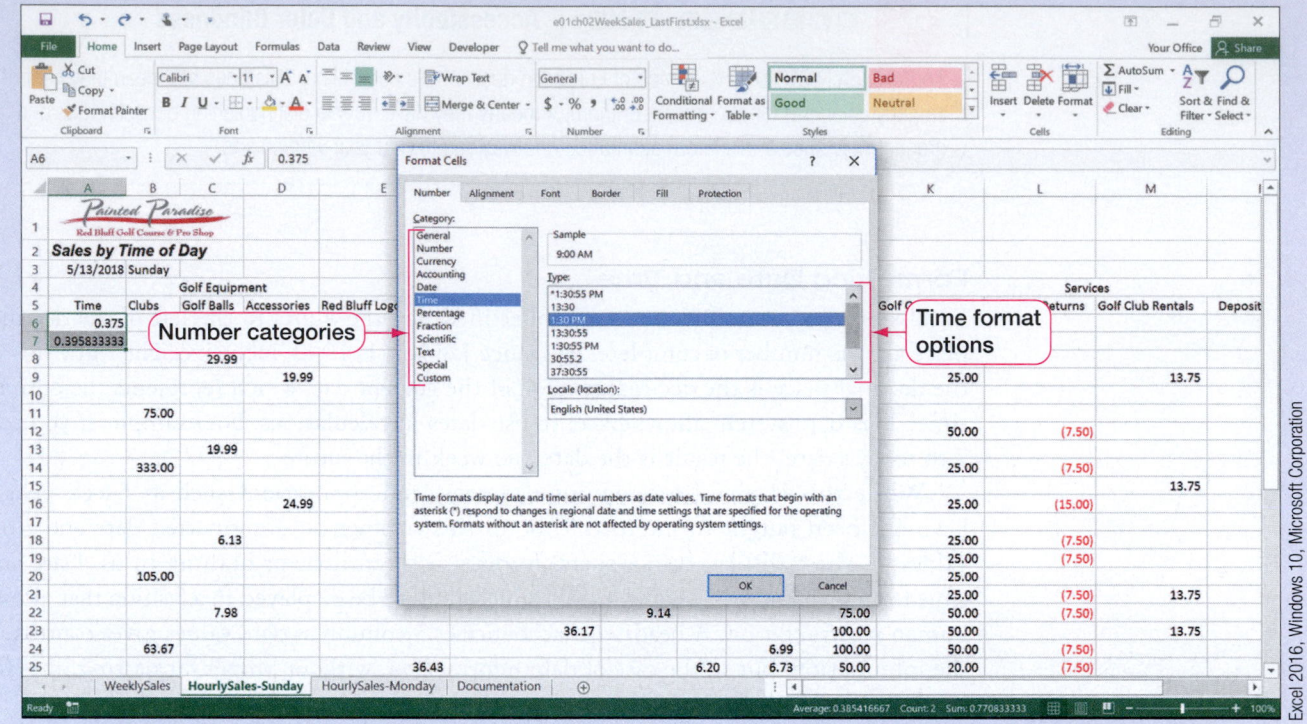

Figure 2 Format Cells dialog box

f. Click **OK**. With A6:A7 still selected, click and hold the **fill handle**, and then drag the **fill handle** down to encompass cells **A6:A28**.

The series in cell range A6:A7 has been expanded through cell A28. Note each cell is incremented by 30 minutes from the cell above. The 30-minute increment was determined by the time difference between cells A6 and A7. That is why you selected two cells before using AutoFill in cell range A6:A28.

g. Save  the workbook.

SS **CONSIDER THIS** | **Excel stores time values as decimal portions of one day as follows.**

- 1 = 1 day = 1,440 minutes

- .1 = 144 minutes = 2:24 AM

- .01 = 14.4 minutes = 12:14:24 AM

For this system to work in conjunction with date values, 0 and 1 are displayed as equivalent time values: 12:00:00 AM. However, in reality, once a time value increases to 1, the date is incremented by 1 day and time reverts to 0. Would you be able to adapt if your digital watch or cell phone showed time the way Excel stores it? Would there be any advantages if time were actually displayed and handled in this format? What about date values?

Aligning Cell Content

Cell alignment allows cell content to be left-aligned, centered, and right-aligned horizontally, as well as top-aligned, middle-aligned, and bottom-aligned vertically. Certain cell formats are aligned left or right by **default** — automatically in place unless you specify otherwise. Number formats are right-aligned, including date and time formats. Text formatting aligns cell contents to the left by default. For the most part, horizontal alignment changes will be made to alphabetic content such as titles, headings, and labels.

To improve the appearance of the data labels, in this exercise you will align text on the WeeklySales worksheet.

 **E02.04**

To Align Text

a. Click the **WeeklySales** worksheet tab, select cell range **A5:A25**.

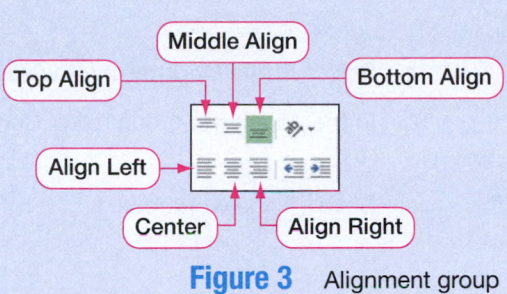

Figure 3   Alignment group

b. In the Alignment group, click **Align Right** .

c. Click cell **A5**, press and hold Ctrl, and then select cells **A10**, **A15**, and **A19**. In the Alignment group, click **Align Left** , and then, in the Alignment group, click **Increase Indent** .

d. Select cell range **I4:J4**, and then click **Align Right** . The content in J4 is truncated (cut off), so the width of column J needs to be increased.

e. Point to the border between the headers for columns J and K. The mouse pointer will change to . Double-click to apply AutoFit to the width of column J.

f. Select cell range **B4:J4**.

g. In the Alignment group, click **Bottom Align** .

In the next exercise, you will rotate the dates in cell range B4:H4. Applying Bottom Align ensures the contents of cell range B4:J4 will align at the bottom of the cell once the dates have been rotated.

h. **Save** the workbook.

Setting Content Orientation

Sometimes it is helpful to display information at an angle or even vertically rather than in the standard horizontal left to right. This is particularly true for tabular information. When you are formatting charts and graphs, rotating textual content can be very helpful in presenting information in a space-efficient yet readable manner.

You think the dates on the WeeklySales worksheet appear too close to one another. In this exercise, you will rotate text on the WeeklySales worksheet.

Excel 2016, Windows 10, Microsoft Corporation

 **E02.05**

To Rotate Text

   a. On the WeeklySales worksheet, select cell range **B4:J4**.

   b. In the Alignment group, click **Orientation** ⬀▾.

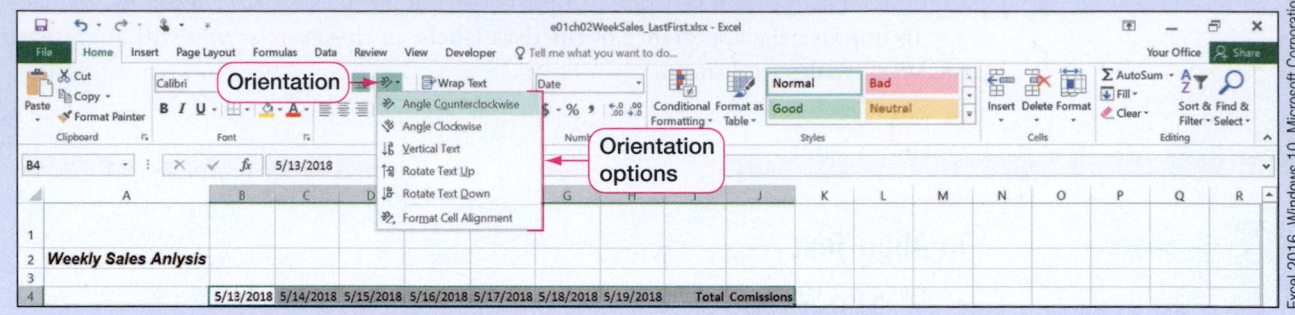

Figure 4   Orientation list

   c. Select **Angle Counterclockwise**.

   d. In the Alignment group, click **Center** ☰, and then, in the Font group, click **Bold** **B**.

   e. **Save** 💾 the workbook.

Changing Fill Color

Fill color refers to the background color of a cell. It can be used to categorize information, to band rows or columns as a means of assisting the reader to follow information across or down a worksheet, or to highlight values.

It is generally best practice to use muted or pastel fill colors. Bright colors are difficult to view for long periods of time and often make reading difficult. Bright background colors should be used sparingly to highlight a value that requires attention, such as a value outside normal operating parameters.

In this exercise, to make some of the worksheet data labels stand out, you will fill cells and cell ranges with background color.

 **E02.06**

To Change Cell Background Color

   a. On the WeeklySales worksheet, select the cell range **B4:J4**. Press Ctrl, and then select cell range **A5:A25**. In the Font group, click the **Fill Color** arrow 🎨▾ to display the color palette. Under Theme Colors, point to any color in the palette, and a ScreenTip will appear identifying the color name.

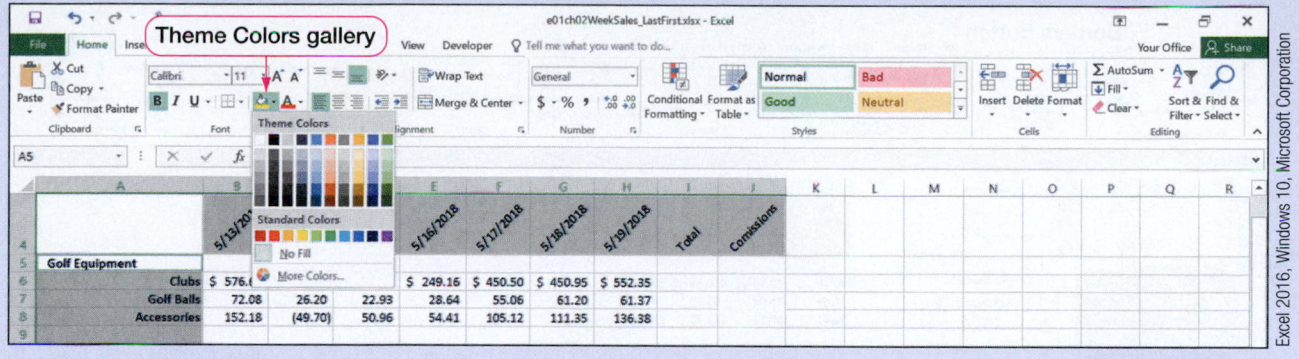

Figure 5 Theme colors

b. Select **Gold, Accent 4, Lighter 40%** (eighth column, fourth row).

c. Click cell **A4**. Click **Fill Color**. Notice that the fill color applied in step b is now applied to A4.

d. Click cell **A9**, press Ctrl, and then select cells **A14** and **A18**. In the Font group, click the **Fill Color** arrow, and then select **No Fill**.

e. **Save** the workbook.

Adding Cell Borders

In the previous exercise, you changed the background color in a range of cells. When the background color is changed for a range of contiguous cells, cell borders are no longer visible. If it would be preferable to have visible cell borders, cell borders can be formatted to make them visible.

In this exercise, on the WeeklySales worksheet, you want to have the worksheet total rows identified, so you have decided to format the cells using borders.

 **E02.07**

To Format Cell Borders

a. On the WeeklySales worksheet, select cell range **B4:J4**, press Ctrl, and then select cell range **A5:A25**.

b. In the Font group, click the **Borders** arrow.

> **Troubleshooting**
> The Borders button may look different in your Excel application window than it does when referenced in this text; this is because the Borders button in the Font group of the Home tab displays the last border setting applied.

Excel 2016, Windows 10, Microsoft Corporation

CHAPTER 2

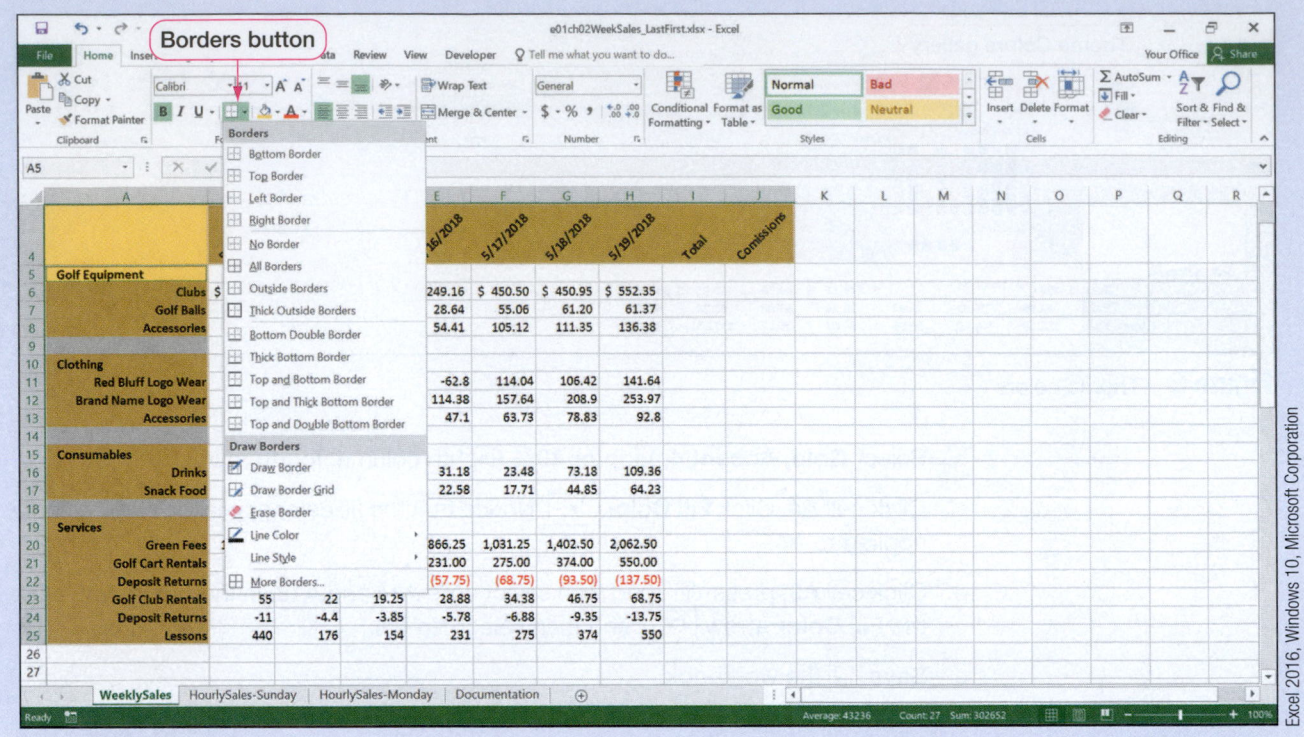

Figure 6 Borders list

SIDE NOTE

Hide the Ribbon
Double-click the Home tab to hide the ribbon and see more of your worksheet. Double-click the Home tab again to unhide the ribbon.

c. In the Borders list, select **All Borders**.

d. Click cell **A5**, press [Ctrl], and then select cells **A10**, **A15**, and **A19**. In the Font group, click the **Borders** arrow [⊞ ▾], and then, in the Borders list, select **Thick Bottom Border**.

e. Click cell **J9**, click the **Borders** arrow [⊞ ▾], and then select **Top and Double Bottom Border**.

f. Select cell range **B9:I9**, press [Ctrl], and then select cell ranges **B14:I14**, **B18:I18**, and **B26:I26**. Click the **Borders** arrow [⊞ ▾], and then select **Top and Bottom Border**.

g. Select cell range **B27:I27**, click the **Borders** arrow [⊞ ▾], and then select **Bottom Double Border**.

h. **Save** [💾] worksheet.

REAL WORLD ADVICE Formatting — Less Is More

Too much formatting results in a worksheet that is difficult to look at, is difficult to read, and conveys a sense that the designer lacked a plan. Here are some formatting guidelines.

- Format for a reason, not just for appearances.
- Use at most three fonts in a worksheet. Use each font for a purpose, such as to differentiate titles.
- Use color only to assist in readability, categorization, or identification purposes. For example, use organization colors for titles, use bright colors to highlight small details, and use background colors for categorization.
- Background colors should be pale, pastel colors. Bright background colors are tiring for the reader and can become painful to look at after a while.
- Special characters such as the dollar sign ($) should be applied only as necessary. A dollar sign in the first value of a column of numbers is often sufficient to identify its values as monetary. Then format subtotals and totals with a dollar sign to differentiate them.

Copying Formats

Formatting a cell can consist of several steps involving fonts, colors, sizes, borders, alignment, and so on. You gain a significant efficiency advantage by reusing your work. Once a cell has been formatted properly, you can apply the formatting properties to other cells. Copying formats from one cell to another saves a great deal of time.

Format Painter is a tool that enables you to copy the format of objects, such as text or pictures, to other objects. To use the Format Painter, simply select the cell that is the source of the format you want to copy, click the Format Painter in the Clipboard group on the Home tab, and then select the cell or range of cells you want to "paint" with the source cell's formatting. To paint a format to more than one nonadjacent cell, you can double-click Format Painter and then select nonadjacent cells. Once you have finished applying the format to nonadjacent cells, press (Esc) or click the Format Painter again to turn off the feature.

In this exercise, to save time formatting the WeeklySales worksheet, you will use the Format Painter to copy formats.

E02.08

SIDE NOTE
How to Use the Format Painter Multiple Times
Double-click the Format Painter, and it will remain active until you click it again or press (Esc).

To Use the Format Painter to Copy Formats

a. On the WeeklySales worksheet, click cell **B22**, and then, in the Clipboard group, click **Format Painter**. The mouse pointer will change to . Select cell range **B23:H25**.

b. Click cell **B6**, double-click **Format Painter**, and then select cell range **B11:H11**. Select cell range **B16:H16**, select cell range **B20:H20**, and then click **Format Painter** to toggle it off.

c. Click **Format**, and then select **AutoFit Column Width**.

d. **Save** the workbook.

Using Paste Options/Paste Special

When a cell is copied to the Clipboard, there is much more than a simple value ready to be pasted to another location. Formats, formulas, and values are all copied and can be selectively pasted to other locations in a workbook.

Different paste options are shown in Table 2. Although there are a large number of paste options, most worksheet activities require only a few of these options. Paste 📋, Paste Formatting 🖌, and Paste Values 📋 will accomplish most of what you will need to do. The various paste options are additive, in that you can first paste a value to a copied cell and then paste the format from the copied cell, after which you could paste the formula from the copied cell.

Button	Function	Pastes
📋	Paste	All content from the Clipboard to a cell
🖌	Formatting	Only the formatting from the Clipboard to a cell
📋	Values	Only the value from the Clipboard to a cell
📋	Formulas	Only the formula from the Clipboard to a cell
📋	Paste Link	A link (e.g., =A25) to the source cell from the Clipboard to a cell
📋	Transpose	A range of cells to a new range of cells with columns and rows switched

Table 2 Paste options   Amy S Kinser, Brant Moriarity, Eric Kinser, Kristyn Jacobson

In this exercise, you will use the Paste Options to copy formats in the WeeklySales worksheet.

 E02.09

To Use Paste Options to Copy Formats

a. On the WeeklySales worksheet, click cell **B7**. In the Clipboard group, click **Copy** 📋 to copy cell B7 to the Clipboard. Select cell range **B12:H13**, press Ctrl, and then select cell range **B17:H17**.

b. Right-click the selected range. The shortcut menu is displayed, which includes options that are determined by the context of the object that is the focus of the right-click.

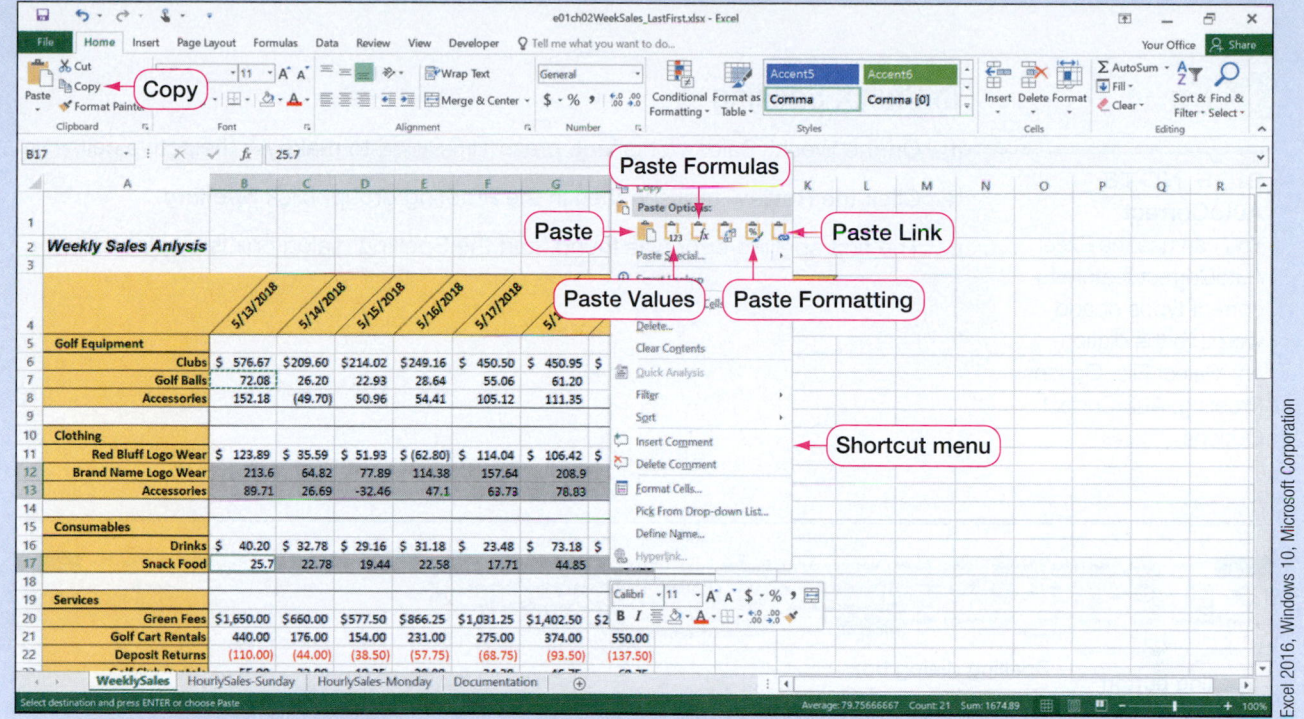

Figure 7 Paste Options menu

c. Point to each button on the Paste Options menu, and notice what happens in the selected cell range.

d. On the Paste Options menu, click **Formatting** 🖼️, and then press ⎋Esc to clear the Clipboard.

e. **Save** 🖫 the workbook.

Checking the Spelling of a Worksheet

Not only should worksheets be professionally formatted, they should also contain correct spelling. Even professionally formatted worksheets can be confusing if they contain misspelled words or phrases. Unlike other Microsoft applications such as Word, Outlook, or PowerPoint, by default Microsoft Excel does not automatically check for misspelled text. Also, Excel does not have a grammar checker, as Word, Outlook, and PowerPoint do.

If a single cell is selected, Excel begins checking the spelling from the active cell. Excel checks spelling only on the active worksheet, not the entire workbook, but it will spell check the entire worksheet, including any comments, page headers, footers, and graphics. If you have a range of cells selected, Excel will check spelling only on the range of cells, not the entire workbook. There are several ways to check the spelling of a worksheet. On the Review tab, in the Proofing group, select the Spelling button. For easy reference, the Spelling 🔤 command can be added to the Quick Access Toolbar.

In this exercise, you will check the spelling on the WeeklySales worksheet.

 **E02.10**

To Check Spelling

a. On the WeeklySales worksheet, press Ctrl + Home to make A1 the active cell.

b. Click the **Review** tab, and then in the Proofing group, click **Spelling**.

c. The first spelling error was found, and the Spelling dialog box is displayed.

SIDE NOTE
AutoCorrect
You can use the Excel AutoCorrect feature to correct typos or add words to the dictionary. Select File, Options, Proofing, AutoCorrect Options.

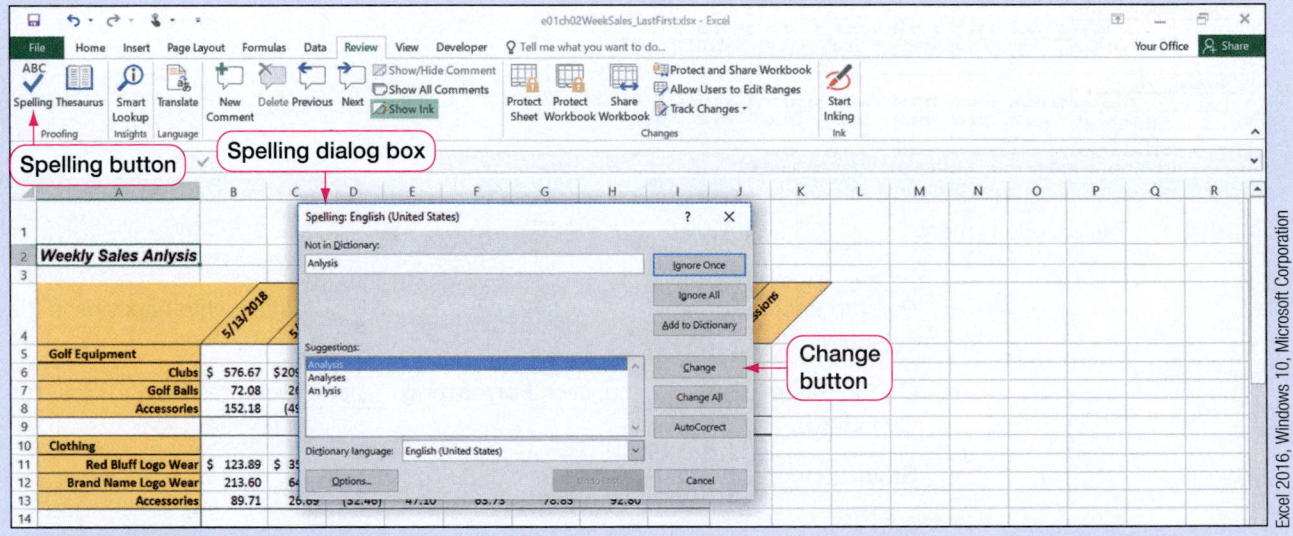

Figure 8   Spelling dialog box

SIDE NOTE
Quick Access Spelling
To add the Spelling button to the Quick Access Toolbar, click the Customize Quick Access Toolbar arrow, and select Spelling.

d. Verify **Analysis** is selected in the Suggestions box, and then click **Change**.

e. A second spelling error was found. Verify **Commissions** is selected in the Suggestions box, and then click **Change**. There were only two spelling errors on this worksheet; therefore, the spell check is finished.

f. Click **OK**, and then **Save** 🖫 the workbook.

SIDE NOTE
Alternate Method
You can also press the F7 key to begin to spell check a worksheet.

Inserting a Picture

Painted Paradise Resort & Spa has logos for each of its core businesses. All documents must include the appropriate logo whenever possible. Excel allows images, such as logos, to be inserted into a worksheet. Images are not contained in a cell, as data is, but can be sized to fit cell borders by using the Snap to Grid feature.

In this exercise, you will insert an image into a worksheet.

 **E02.11**

To Insert an Image into a Worksheet

a. On the WeeklySales worksheet, click cell **A1**.

b. Click the **Insert** tab, and then, in the Illustrations group, click **Pictures**. In the Insert Picture dialog box, navigate to the location where your student data files are stored, click the **e01ch02red_bluff** file, and then click **Insert**.

c. Click the **Picture Tools Format** tab, and then, in the Arrange group, click **Align**. If Snap to Grid is not selected — it does not have a border around it as shown around View Gridlines — then select **Snap to Grid**.

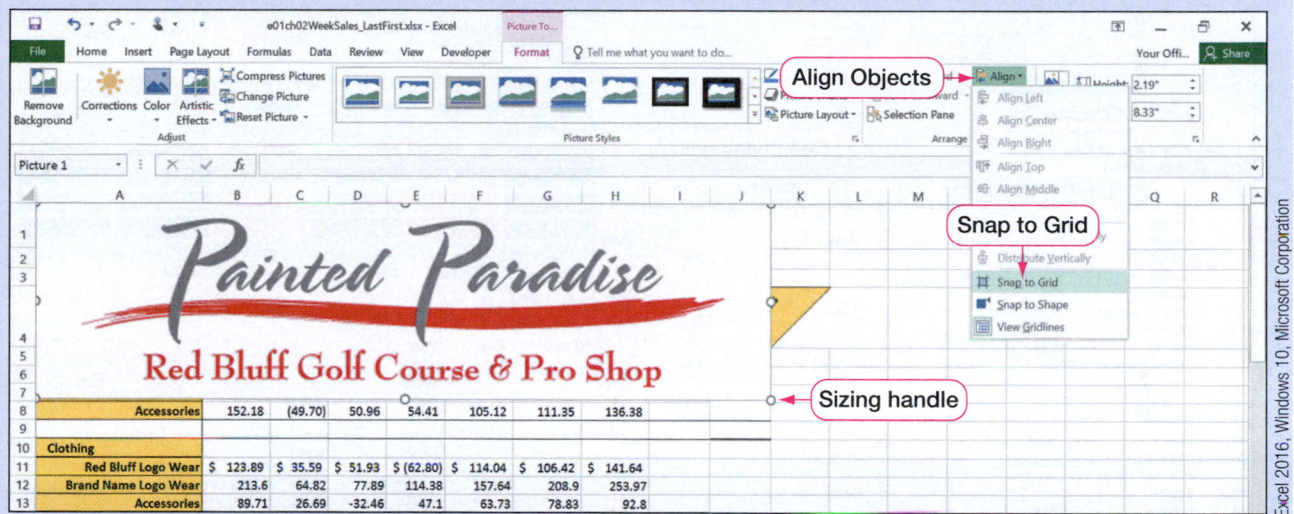

Figure 9 Insert a picture and toggle on Snap to Grid

Painted Paradise Logo, Pearson Education, Inc.; Red Bluff Logo, Pearson Education, Inc

d. Click and hold the right horizontal sizing handle, and then drag the edge of the **logo** to the left until it snaps to the border between columns **B** and **C**. Click and hold the bottom vertical sizing handle, and then drag the bottom edge of the logo up until it snaps to the border between rows **1** and **2**. Click cell **B6** to deselect the picture.

e. **Save** the workbook.

Using Built-In Cell Styles

Built-in cell styles are predefined and named combinations of cell and content formatting properties that can be applied to a cell or range of cells to define several formatting properties at once. A built-in cell style can set the font, font size and color, number format, background color, borders, and alignment with just a few clicks of the mouse. Built-in cell styles allow for rapid and accurate changes to the appearance of a workbook with very little effort.

To change the appearance of the HourlySales-Sunday worksheet, in this exercise you will apply built-in cell styles on the HourlySales-Sunday worksheet.

 **E02.12**

To Apply Built-In Cell Styles

a. Click the **HourlySales-Sunday** worksheet tab, and if necessary click the **Home** tab.

b. Click cell **B4**, press Ctrl, and then select cell **H4**.

c. In the Styles group, click **Cell Styles** 📋. The Cell Styles gallery appears.

> **Troubleshooting**
> If you do not see the Cell Styles button 📋, it may be that your screen has a different resolution and the Cell Styles button has been expanded.

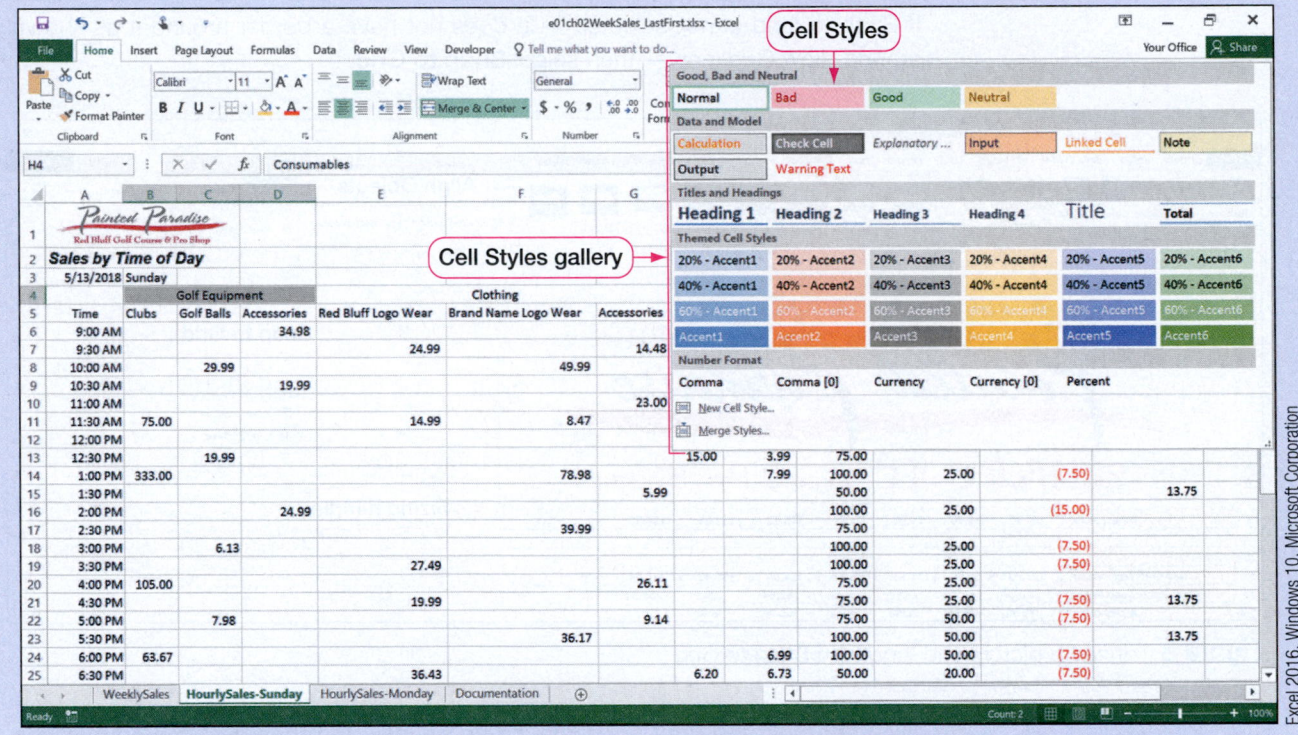

Figure 10 Cell Styles gallery

d. Under Themed Cell Styles, click **20% - Accent1**.

SIDE NOTE

Multiple Styles Can Be Applied to One Cell

How the cell is ultimately formatted is determined by the order in which styles are applied.

e. Click cell **E4**, press Ctrl, and then select cell **J4**. In the Styles group, click **Cell Styles**, and then select **40% - Accent1**.

f. Select cell range **A3:B3**, press Ctrl, select cell range **B4:O5,** and then select **A5:A33**.

g. Click **Cell Styles**, and then, under Titles and Headings, select **Heading 4**. Click cell **B6**.

Notice in cell range B4:O4, the Accent1 cell background colors have not changed.

h. Select cell range **B29:O29**, and in the Styles group, click **Cell Styles**, and then, under Titles and Headings, select **Total**.

i. Press Ctrl+Home, and then **Save** 💾 the workbook.

Applying Table Styles

Data can be formatted as an Excel table. A **table** is a powerful tabular data-formatting tool that facilitates data sorting, filtering, and calculations. Once a collection of data has been defined as a table by the application of a table style, it has special table properties not available to data that is simply entered into rows and columns of cells.

A **table style** is a predefined set of formatting properties that determine the appearance of a table. One of the useful features of a table style is the ability to "band" rows and columns. **Banding** is alternating the background color of rows and/or columns to assist in visually tracking information. Banding can be accomplished manually by changing the background color of a range of cells — a row, for example — and then pasting the formatting into every other row. Manually banding a table is a tedious process at best. By applying a table style to a selected range of rows and columns, banding is accomplished in a couple of clicks. Most important, table banding is dynamic. If a row or column is inserted into — or deleted from — the worksheet, the banding is automatically updated. If banding is done manually, insertions and deletions require the banding to be manually updated as well.

Tables also allow for calculations in a total row such as summations, averages, or counts for each column in the table. These calculations are possible without table formatting; however, a table simplifies them.

In this exercise, you will apply a table style to cell ranges.

 E02.13

To Apply a Table Style to a Cell Range

a. Click the **HourlySales-Monday** worksheet tab.

b. Click the cell range **A5:O28**. Click the **Home** tab, and then, in the Styles group, click **Format as Table**. The Table Styles gallery appears.

c. Under Medium table styles, select **Table Style Medium 2** — second column. The Format As Table dialog box appears.

d. Since row 5 contains column headings, be sure **My table has headers** is checked.

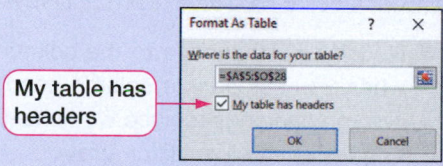

My table has headers

Excel 2016, Windows 10, Microsoft Corporation

Figure 11   Format As Table dialog box

e. Click **OK**. The range is formatted as a table, and the Table Tools Design contextual tab appears.

Notice the rows of table data are in descending order by time. The arrow next to each column heading in the table in row 5 allows you to sort or filter the entire table by the information in each column.

f. In cell **A5**, click the Filter arrow.

CHAPTER 2

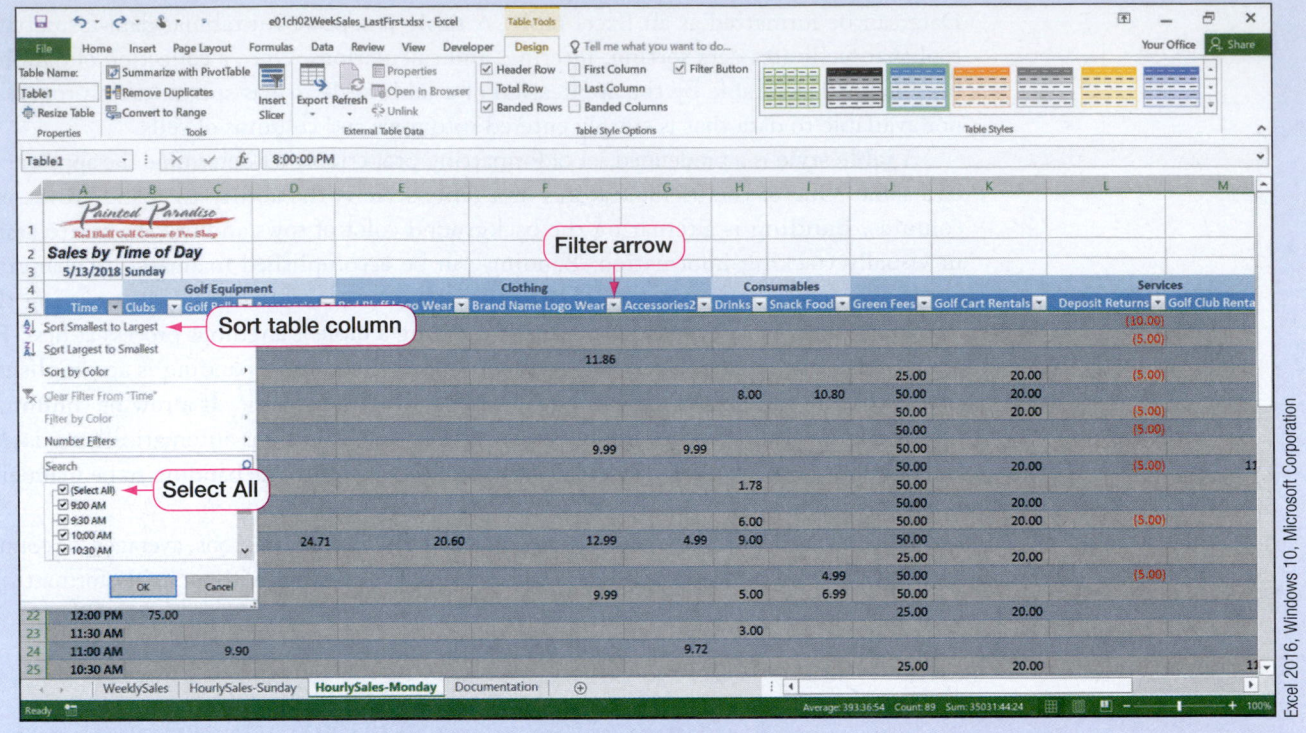

Figure 12 Filter menu

g. On the displayed list, click **Sort Smallest to Largest**. Notice the sort indicator ⌄↑ on the Time column filter arrow.

> **Troubleshooting**
>
> Is the Table Tools Design tab not available when you want to select it? Check to make sure the active cell is somewhere in the table you formatted. A worksheet can contain many tables. Excel makes the Table Tools Design tab available only when the active cell is part of a formatted table.

h. Click cell **B10**. Scroll down until row 5 disappears at the top of the window.

Notice what happens to the column headers. If the active cell is inside a table, when you scroll table column headings off the visible application window, table column headings replace worksheet column headings. Also notice the sort arrow on the Time column filter arrow.

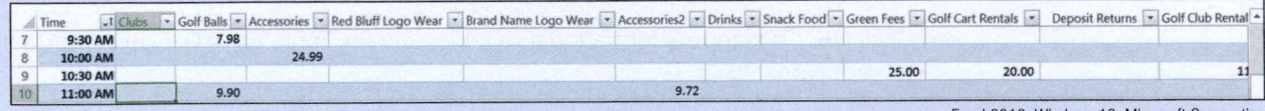

Figure 13 Column headers become table column names

i. Click the **HourlySales-Sunday** worksheet tab. Select cell range **A5:O28**. In the Styles group, click **Format as Table**. Under Medium table styles, select **Table Style Medium 9**. The Format As Table dialog box appears. Be sure **My table has headers** is checked, and then click **OK**.

You do not want the table functionality on the HourlySales-Sunday worksheet, so you will convert the table out of table format.

j. Click the **Design** tab, and then, in the Tools group, click **Convert to Range**. In the alert box that appears, click **Yes**.

Convert to Range removes all table functionality but leaves in place the headers and cell formatting of the selected table design. This is a great way to quickly format a range with a theme and row banding, but if you do not want the data filtering and other table features, you can keep the visual formatting.

k. Click cell **B6**, and then **Save**  the workbook.

Changing Themes

A **theme** is a collection of fonts, styles, colors, and effects associated with a theme name that enables you to create professional, color-coordinated documents quickly. The default theme — the theme that is automatically applied unless you specify otherwise — is the Office theme. Changing the assigned theme is a way to very quickly change the appearance of the worksheets in your workbook. When a different workbook theme is applied, the built-in cell styles in the Styles group on the Home tab change to reflect the new workbook theme. Applying a workbook theme ensures a consistent, well-designed look throughout your workbook.

In this exercise, to ensure all the worksheets in the Week Sales workbook have the same formatting features, you will apply a theme to the workbook.

E02.14

To Change the Theme

a. On the HourlySales-Sunday worksheet, click the **Page Layout** tab, and then, in the Themes group, click **Themes**. The Themes gallery is displayed.

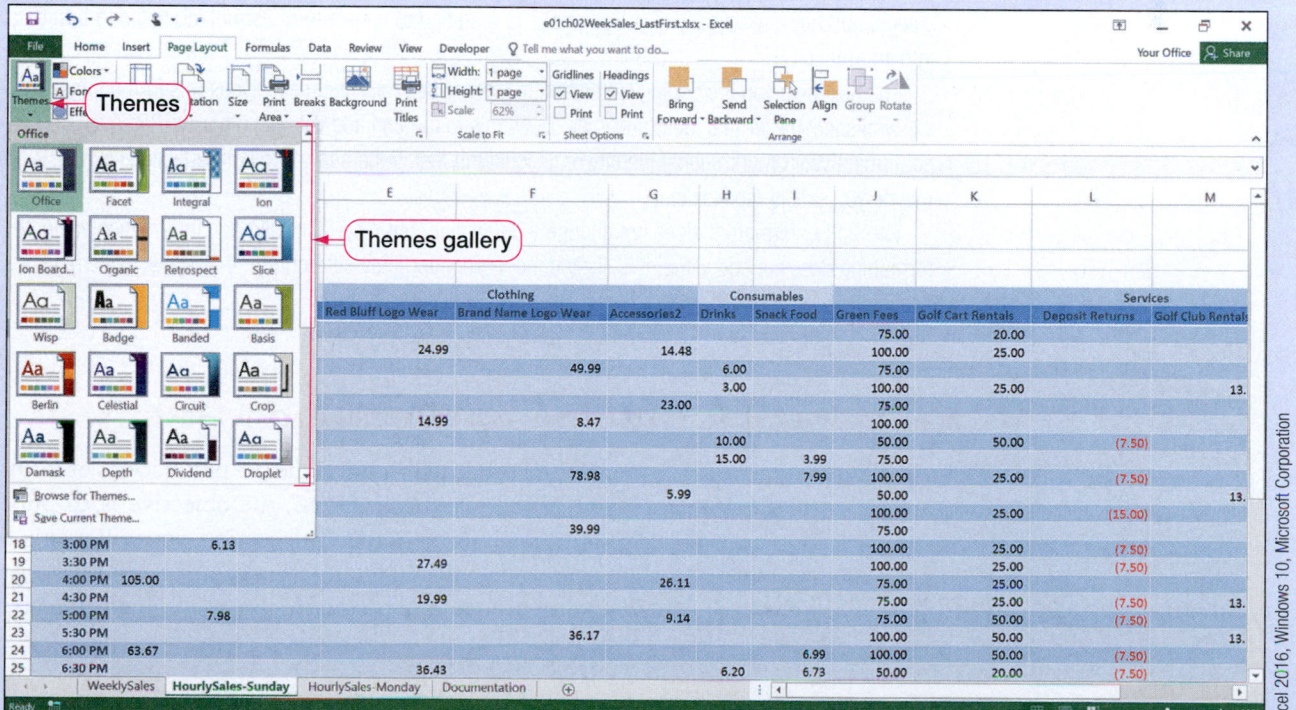

Figure 14 Themes gallery

b. Scroll down, and then select the **Parallax** built-in theme.

Note any cell that was assigned a cell style now reflects the corresponding cell style in the Parallax theme. For example, click the Home tab, and see that the default font has changed to Corbel.

c. Click the **HourlySales-Monday** worksheet tab. Note the Parallax theme has been applied to this worksheet as well as the HourlySales-Sunday worksheet.

d. Click the **Page Layout** tab. In the Themes group, click **Themes**, and then select the **Metropolitan** theme.

The table styles applied to these worksheets reveal the extent to which a change in theme can change the appearance of a worksheet. Note also that themes affect the entire workbook. A theme cannot be selectively applied to individual worksheets in a workbook.

e. Click the **WeeklySales** worksheet tab, and then click the **Home** tab.

Notice the background colors that were set by using cell formatting are also affected by the new workbook theme. Also notice for any cell in which a font was not explicitly set, the font has changed to Calibri Light.

f. **Save** 🖫 the workbook.

g. If you need to take a break before finishing this chapter, now is a good time.

REAL WORLD ADVICE	Formatting Does Not Change the Data Value, but Formatting Can Make Information More Valuable

Formatting affects how information is displayed and understood. It does not change the value stored in a cell. Special formatting characters such as the dollar sign ($) and comma (,) are not stored with values, but they make financial values easier to read and to understand. Formatting helps to turn data into information.

The next time you are adding formatting to a worksheet, ask yourself, "Does this formatting make my worksheet easier to understand?" or "Does this formatting add value in other ways?" such as confirming your organizational identity or its look and feel. If the answer to both questions is "No," maybe you should reconsider.

Remember formatting does not change a data value, but it certainly can add information value. If formatting does not add value, it is likely unnecessary and may detract from the overall value of your worksheet. Consider your formatting decisions carefully.

Creating Information for Decision Making

In Excel, new information is most often produced through the use of functions or formulas to make calculations against data in the workbook. Often, the objective is to improve decision making by providing additional information. In this section, you will manipulate data using functions and formulas, and you will add information using conditional formatting to highlight or categorize information on the basis of problem-specific parameters.

Create Information with Functions

Functions are one of Excel's most powerful features. A **function** is a built-in program that performs operations on data. Function syntax takes the following form:

function name (argument 1, …, argument n)

where "function name" is the name of the function and arguments inside the parentheses are the values the function requires. Different functions require different arguments. **Arguments** are variables or values the function requires in order to calculate a solution. Arguments can be entered as letters, numbers, cell references, cell ranges, or other functions. Some functions do not require any arguments at all. There are more than 400 functions built into Excel that can be categorized as financial, statistical, mathematical, date and time, text, and several others. Collectively, these are referred to — not surprisingly — as **built-in functions**.

Part of what makes functions so useful is the use of cell references as arguments. **Cell references** refer to a particular cell or range of cells within a formula or function instead of a value. Cell references enable you to use information from a particular cell or cell range in a function. Recall that a cell reference is the combination of a cell's column and row addresses. When a function that includes a cell reference as an argument is copied, the cell reference is changed to reflect the copied location relative to the original location. For example, suppose a function in cell B26 calculates the sum of cells B1:B25; if you copy the function from cell B26 to cell C26, the function in cell C26 will automatically be changed to sum C1:C25 — the copied function will be relatively adjusted one column to the right.

Using the SUM, COUNT, AVERAGE, MIN, and MAX Functions

Of the more than 400 functions built into Excel, commonly used functions such as SUM, COUNT, AVERAGE, MIN, and MAX are readily available via the AutoSum Σ AutoSum ▾ button in the Function Library group on the Formulas tab or in the Editing group on the Home tab. There are two ways to use AutoSum functions. You select either the **destination cell(s)**, the cell(s) that received the result of an operation such as Paste or an AutoSum function, or the **source cell(s)**, the cell(s) that contain the data supplied to the function.

When you invoke AutoSum with the destination cell(s) selected, Excel inspects your worksheet and automatically includes a range adjacent to the active cell. Adjacent cells above the active cell are used by default. If there are no adjacent cells above, then adjacent cells to the left are used for the range. Excel does not inspect cell ranges to the right or below the active cell.

If a column of source cells is selected, if the cell at the bottom of the selected range does not contain data, the bottom cell is treated as the destination cell. If a row of source cells is selected, if the far-right cell in the selected range does not contain data, the far-right cell is treated as the destination cell. If the bottom or far-right cell contains data, the next open cell is used as the destination cell. Table 3 contains examples of the different ways in which data can be included in a function.

Type of Data	Function
Numbers	=SUM(1,3,5,7,11,13)
Cell range	=AVERAGE(B3:B25)
List of noncontiguous cells	=COUNT(B3,B9,C5,D14)
Column or columns	=SUM(J:J) or =AVERAGE(J:L)
Row or rows	=MIN(9:9) or =MAX(9:11)
Combination	=MIN(B3,B9:B15,C12/100,D:E)

Table 3   Function variations

Amy S Kinser, Brant Moriarity, Eric Kinser, Kristyn Jacobson

Using the SUM Function by Selecting Destination Cells

The **SUM function** is a commonly used function that adds all numeric information in a specified range, list of numbers, list of cells, or any combination. In this exercise, you will generate new information in the Weekly Sales worksheet by selecting destination cells and inserting the SUM function.

 E02.15

To Use the SUM Function by Selecting Destination Cells

a. If you took a break, open the **e01ch02WeekSales** workbook, and, if necessary, navigate to the **WeeklySales** worksheet tab.

b. Click cell **B9**. On the Home tab, in the Editing group, click **AutoSum** Σ AutoSum ▾ . Excel inspects the cells above B9 and suggests that you want to sum range B6:B8 by surrounding it with a dashed, moving border.

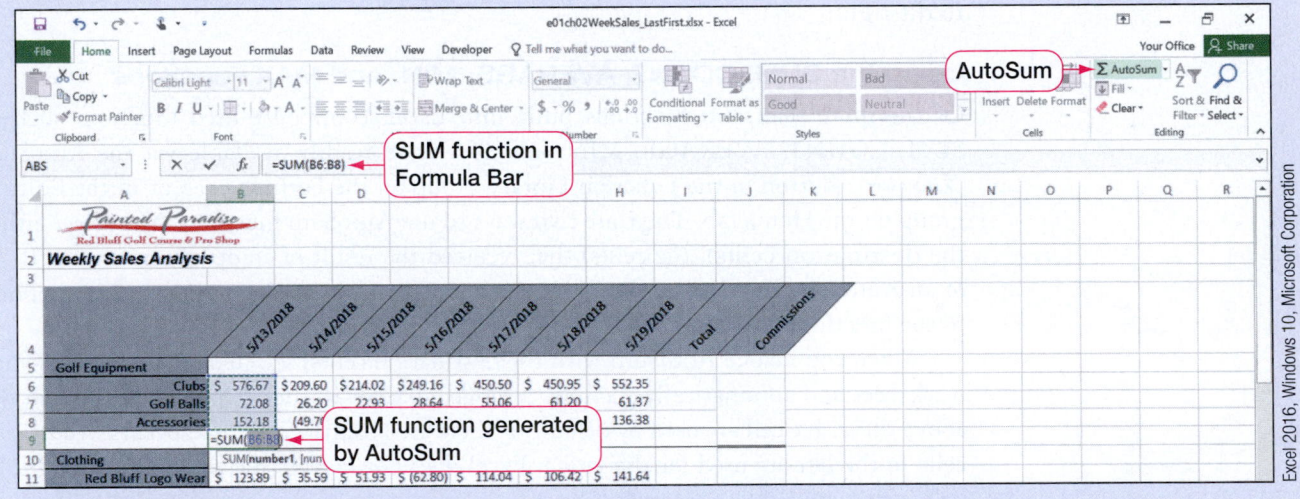

Figure 15 AutoSum range

SIDE NOTE
Double-Click AutoSum

If you are sure Excel will predict the correct range, double-click the AutoSum.

c. Since the suggested range is correct, press Ctrl + Enter. Notice the Accounting Number Format is automatically applied to cell B9. Drag the fill handle to copy the formula to **C9:H9**.

d. Select cell range **B14:H14**, press and hold Ctrl, and then select cell ranges **B18:H18**, **B26: H26**, **I6:I9**, **I11:I14**, **I16:I18**, and **I20:I26**. Click **AutoSum** Σ AutoSum ▾ .

e. In the Cells group, click **Format** , and then select **AutoFit Column Width**.

AutoSum will operate on noncontiguous cell ranges as well, but it must be handled a little differently. To calculate the total sales for each day, you must sum the category totals.

SIDE NOTE
SUM Shortcut

SUM can be quickly invoked by pressing Alt + =.

f. Click cell **B27**, and then click **AutoSum** Σ AutoSum ▾ . AutoSum recognizes that cell B26 contains a SUM function and selects only B26 as the predicted range. Press and hold Ctrl; select cells **B18**, **B14**, and **B9**; and then click **AutoSum** Σ AutoSum ▾ again.

g. Drag the fill handle to copy the formula to **B27:I27**. If any of the cells display a series of number signs (#), in the Cells group, click **Format** , and then select **AutoFit Column Width**.

h. Press Ctrl + Home, and then **Save** the workbook.

Using the SUM Function by Selecting Source Cells

Inserting a function using AutoSum after selecting source cells works particularly well when the source range does not contain contiguous data, as in the HourlySales - Sunday worksheet. In the next exercise, you will generate new information in the HourlySales - Sunday worksheet by selecting source cells and inserting a SUM function using the AutoSum button.

 **E02.16**

To Use the SUM Function by Selecting Source Cells

a. Click the **HourlySales-Sunday** worksheet tab.

b. Select cell range **B29:B6**. If you start your selection with the cell where you wish to insert the SUM function, then when the function is inserted, you will see it in the formula bar.

c. Click the **AutoSum** button Σ AutoSum ▾ to insert a SUM function.

Since the bottom cell in the selected range did not contain data, the SUM function is placed into cell B29.

d. Select cell range **B6:P29**. You have included a row of empty cells below your destination range and a column of empty cells to the right of your destination range. In this case, you are actually selecting both the source and destination cells. Click the **AutoSum** button Σ AutoSum ▾. You may have to scroll to the right to see column P.

Click cell **B6** to deselect the selected range, and then **Save** 💾 the workbook.

> **SIDE NOTE**
> **Error Warning Symbol**
> If you see a green triangle in the upper right corner of a cell, point to the triangle to get a warning symbol ⚠️; Excel believes there may be an error in your formula.

Using COUNT and AVERAGE

The **COUNT function** returns the number of cells in a cell range that contain numbers. It can be used to generate information such as the number of sales in a period by counting invoice numbers, the number of people in a group by counting Social Security numbers, and so on.

The **AVERAGE function** returns the average (mean) from a specified range of cells. The sum of all numeric values in the range is calculated and then divided by the count of numbers in the range. Essentially the AVERAGE function is SUM/COUNT. COUNT and AVERAGE can be inserted in any manner by which the SUM function can be inserted.

In this exercise, you will calculate averages and counts for the HourlySales - Sunday worksheet and take advantage of the AutoSum feature that places results in the first open cell following a selected destination range.

 **E02.17**

To Use the COUNT and AVERAGE Functions

a. On the HourlySales-Sunday worksheet, select cell range **B6:O28**. In the Editing group, click the **AutoSum** arrow ∑ AutoSum ▾ .

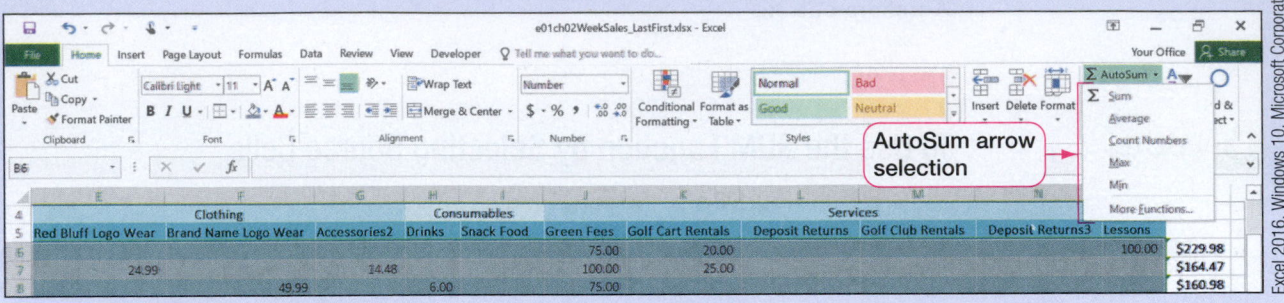

Figure 16 AutoSum arrow selection

b. Select **Average**.

Notice Excel expanded the selected range to include row 29 but inserted the AVERAGE functions into row 30, the first available empty cells below the selected destination range. Click cell O30. Also notice the AVERAGE function in cell O30 does not include row 29; it includes the rows specified in the originally selected range.

c. Select cell range **B6:O28**, click the **AutoSum** arrow ∑ AutoSum ▾ , and then select **Count Numbers**.

Once again, AutoSum expanded the selected range to include row 29, but this time it inserted the COUNT functions into row 31, the first available empty cells below the selected destination range.

d. **Save** 🖫 the workbook.

Using MIN and MAX

An average gives you an incomplete picture. If your instructor states that the average score on the exam is 75%, you do not have any information about the actual score distribution. Everyone in the class may have gotten a C with a low of 71% and a high of 79%. Conversely, no one may have gotten a C; it may be that half the class got an A and half got an F. Both situations could result in a 75% average but with very different distributions. You should never rely on the average without looking at additional statistics that help to complete the picture. While many statistics exist to do this, the minimum value and the maximum value provide at least a little more insight into the distribution of data by defining the extremes. The **MIN function** and **MAX function** examine all numeric values in a specified range and return the minimum value and the maximum value, respectively.

In this exercise, you will use the MIN and MAX functions to find the smallest and largest values in a range of cells.

 **E02.18**

To Use the MIN and MAX Functions

a. On the HourlySales-Sunday worksheet, select cell range **B6:O28**, click the **AutoSum** arrow ∑ AutoSum ▾ , and then select **Max**.

The MAX functions were inserted into row 32, the first available empty row below the selected destination range.

b. Rather than selecting cell range **B6:O28** over again, press Shift + ↑ to remove row 29 from the selected range. Cell range B6:O28 should now be selected. Click the **AutoSum** arrow Σ AutoSum ▾ , and then select **Min**.

The MIN functions were inserted into row 33, the first available empty row below the selected destination range. The functions inserted into the HourlySales - Sunday worksheet can be used to calculate the same values in the HourlySales - Monday worksheet. They simply need to be copied between worksheets.

c. Click the header for **row 29**, press and hold Shift, and then click the header for **row 33**. In the Clipboard group, click **Copy** 📋.

d. Click the **HourlySales-Monday** worksheet tab, click cell **A29**, and then, in the Clipboard group, click **Paste** 📋.

The functions in rows 29:33 in the HourlySales-Sunday worksheet have been copied to the same locations in the HourlySales-Monday worksheet.

e. **Save** 💾 the workbook.

Calculate Totals in a Table

Not only can an Excel table be used to format worksheet data, a table can be applied to a range of cells that is to be managed separately from other data in the same worksheet. When a range is formatted as a table, the range is structured such that every column is assigned a name, either by the user or automatically by Excel. When a range of data is formatted as a table, you will see filter buttons on each column name, the data formatted with a table style, a sizing handle in the lower right corner of the table, and the Table Tools Design tab on the ribbon. Data in a table can be easily sorted and/or filtered by the values in each column. When you filter data, you choose which data is visible and which is not. Visible data is included in table calculations, and hidden data is not.

Using Tables and the Total Row

An Excel table can include a total row that allows you to calculate a number of different statistics for each column in the table. The HourlySales-Monday worksheet has been formatted as a table. In the next exercise, you will add a total row and use the total row to sum each column in the table.

To generate a statistic such as the sum, average, or standard deviation in a total row, you click the filter arrow and select from the menu. A table total row uses the SUBTOTAL function to generate values. The **SUBTOTAL function** is a function that will run calculations only on the data that is in the subset when a filter is applied. Therefore, when the SUBTOTAL function is used in a table, Excel calculates results based on only data that is visible in a table. When you filter table data, the SUBTOTAL values will automatically be recalculated. The SUBTOTAL function can return any of 11 different values, including all of the AutoSum functions, product, standard deviation, and variance.

An extensive discussion of structured references is outside the scope of this text, but since a table is a data structure defined by its column titles, you can perform calculations by referencing the column titles — the structure identifiers — in the table. In this exercise, you will use Sum in a table's total row, and you will filter table results.

 **E02.19**

To Use Sum in a Table Total Row and Filter the Results

a. On the HourlySales-Monday worksheet, click cell **B28** to place the active cell inside the table range. The Table Tools Design tab is displayed. Click the **Design** tab, and then, in the Table Style Options group, click the **Total Row** check box.

This adds a special total row that works with the table format to total each column as you specify. Notice the formulas you copied into this worksheet in the previous exercise have been moved down one row.

b. Click cell **B29**, and then click the **Function List** arrow next to cell B29.

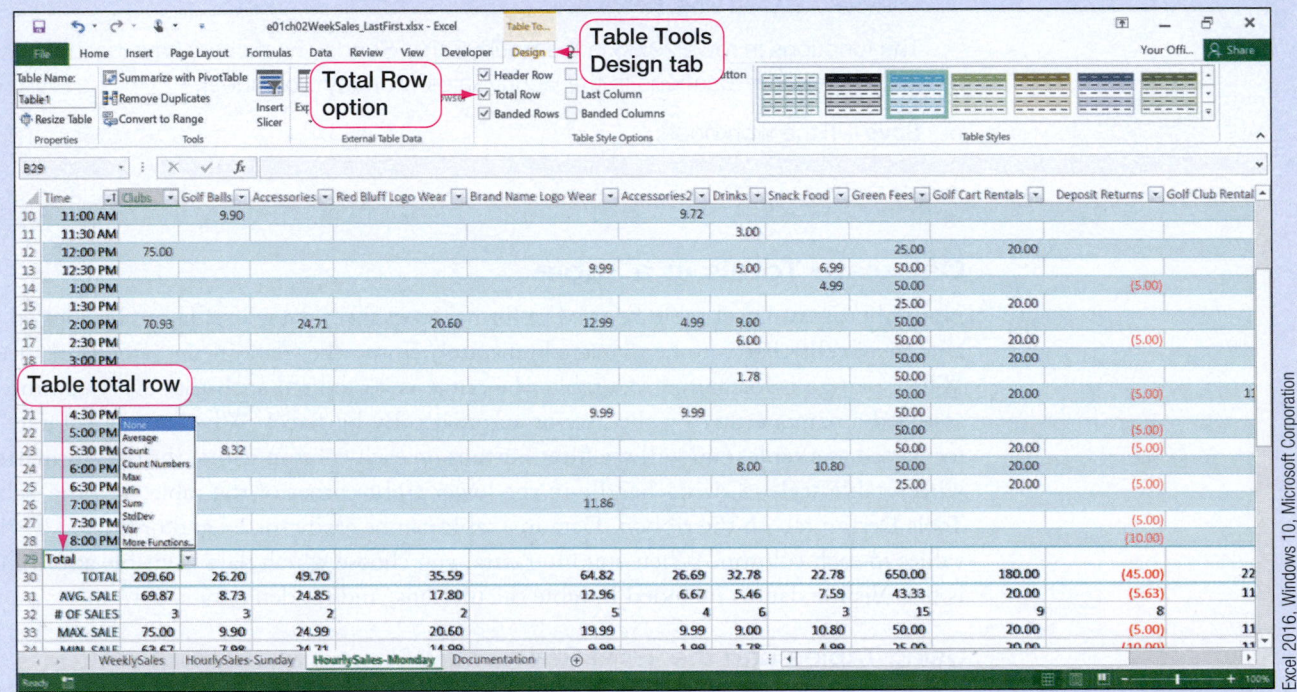

Figure 17 Calculating the sum in a table total row

c. Select **Sum**.

Excel does not need to predict the summed range for a table. It automatically sums all the visible rows in the table column. Notice the formula bar. Even though you selected Sum from the Table Totals menu, Excel uses a SUBTOTAL function in a table total row.

d. Drag the fill handle to copy cell B29 to cell range **C29:O29**. Select AutoFit Column Width if necessary. Notice how rows 28:29 have the same values.

e. In cell **A5**, click the **filter arrow**. Since this is the Time column, you can filter the table data by selecting — or deselecting — values in the time column. Click **(Select All)** to deselect all time values in the table. Then click **9:00**, **9:30**, **10:00**, **10:30**, **11:00** and **11:30**. This will filter the table to display only sales in the morning hours.

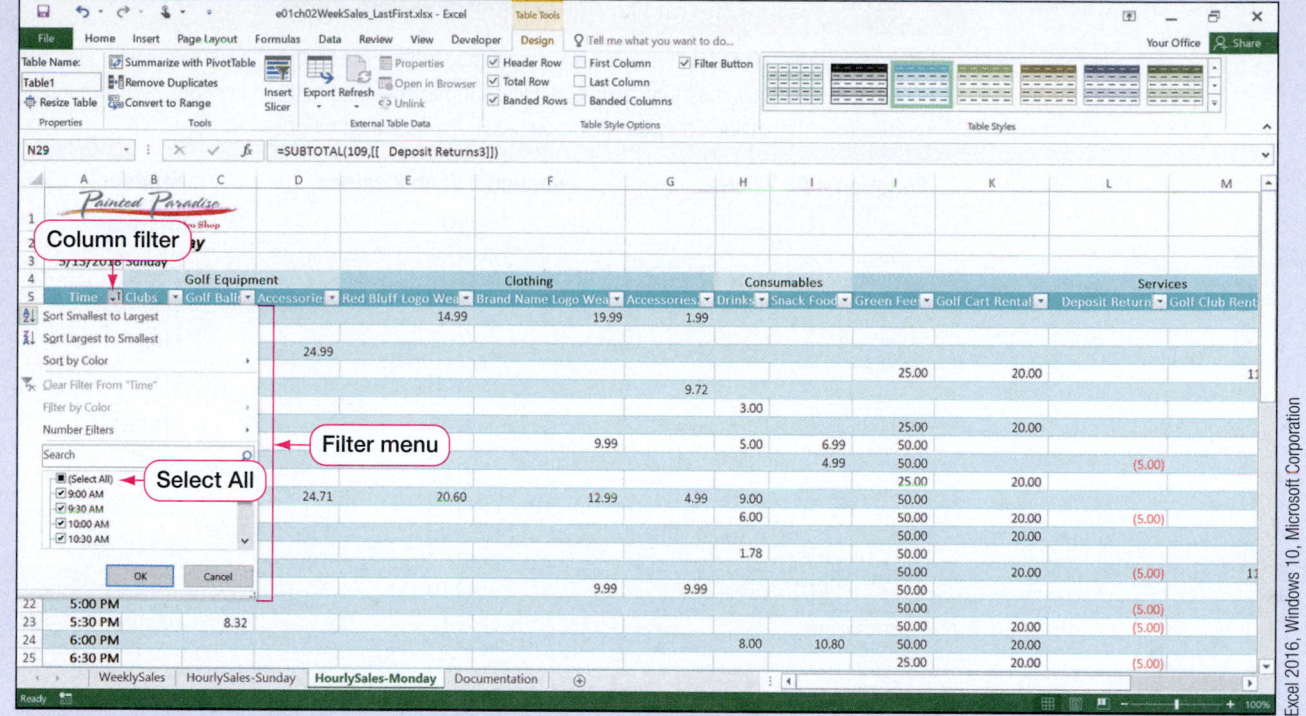

Figure 18 Table filter menu

f. Click **OK**, and then click cell **B29**.

Figure 19 Filtered table total row

Notice in Figure 19 that the Total values in row 29 no longer equal the TOTAL values in row 30. The SUBTOTAL function that calculated the sums in row 29 included only the visible data. You filtered the table to exclude all hours of 12:00 PM or later. Notice rows 12:28 are hidden — rows 12:28 are not included in the SUBTOTAL calculations in row 29.

In Figure 19, notice the formula bar displays the function in cell B29, that is, =SUBTOTAL(109,[Clubs]). This formula uses a structured reference that is unique to tables in Excel. It is the equivalent of =SUBTOTAL(109,B6:B28), but it uses the column name in the table to identify the range against which the function is to act. The number "109" indicates that the SUBTOTAL function is to calculate a sum. The Quick Reference lists the values for different SUBTOTAL statistics.

g. **Save** 🖫 the workbook.

SIDE NOTE
What Is the SUBTOTAL Function?

To learn more about the SUBTOTAL function (or other functions), press [F1], type SUBTOTAL (or the name of another function) into the Search box, and press [Enter].

The first argument listed in the SUBTOTAL function identifies the statistic to be calculated. Functions 1 through 11 return values that include all values in the specified range. Functions 101 through 111 return values that include only the visible values in the specified range.

Function # All values	Function # Visible values	Statistic
1	101	AVERAGE
2	102	COUNT
3	103	COUNTA
4	104	MAX
5	105	MIN
6	106	PRODUCT
7	107	STDEV
8	108	STDEVP
9	109	SUM
10	110	VAR
11	111	VARP

One quirk associated with the SUBTOTAL function is that when it is used to calculate statistics against a table, the function number visibility is irrelevant. For example, if you specify function number 9 and then filter the table data such that only part of the table data is visible, only visible data will be included in the calculation. Value visibility is a factor in SUBTOTAL function calculations only for data not included in a table.

Create Information with Formulas

A **formula** allows you to perform basic mathematical calculations using information in the active worksheet and other worksheets to calculate new values; formulas can contain cell references, constants, functions, and mathematical operators. Formulas in Excel have a very specific syntax. In Excel, formulas always begin with an equal sign (=). Formulas can contain references to specific cells that contain information; a **constant**, which is a number that never changes, such as the value for π (pi); **mathematical operators** such as +, −, *, /, and ^; and functions. Cells that contain formulas can be treated like any other worksheet cell. They can be referenced, edited, formatted, copied, and pasted.

If a formula contains a cell reference, the cell reference in the formula changes when the formula is copied and then pasted into a new location. The new cell reference reflects a new location relative to the old location. This is called a relative cell reference. For example, as shown in Figure 20, when the formula in the left column is copied one column to the right and two rows down, the cell references in the formula change to reflect the destination cell relative to the original cell. Consequently, columns A and J are changed to B and K, respectively — one column right, and rows 3 and 12 are changed to 5 and 14, two rows down. Note that the column and row numbers of the cells that contain the formulas are not shown in Figure 20. The active cell address does not matter in relative addressing. All that matters is the relative shift in columns and rows from source to destination and the cell references in the formula.

SIDE NOTE
Copying a Formula and Not Changing Relative References
Select the formula in the formula bar, click Copy, press [Esc], select the destination cell, and then click Paste.

Excel 2016, Windows 10, Microsoft Corporation

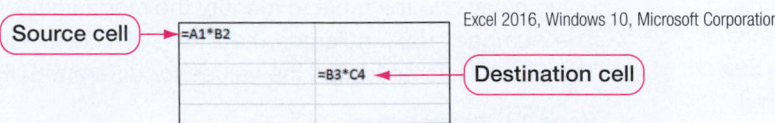

Figure 20 Relative referencing when copying from a source cell to a destination cell
Excel 2016, Windows 10, Microsoft Corporation.

Relative cell references allow you to reuse formulas in a well-designed worksheet. You can enter a formula once and use it many times without having to reenter it in each location and change the cell references. Simply copy the formula and paste it to a new location.

Further, relative references adjust formulas to ensure correctness when the structure of the worksheet changes. If a column is inserted to the left of a cell referenced in a formula or a row is inserted above a cell referenced in a formula, the cells referenced by the formula will be adjusted to ensure the formula still references the same relative locations.

Using Operators

Excel formulas are constructed by using basic mathematical operators very similar to those used in everyday mathematics and exactly the same as those used in most programming languages. Table 4 contains the mathematical operators recognized in Excel.

Operation	Operator	Example	Formula Entered in Current Cell
Addition	+	=B4+B5	Assign the sum of B4 and B5 to the current cell.
Subtraction	-	=B5-B4	Assign the difference of B4 and B5 to the current cell.
Multiplication	*	=B5*3.14	Assign B5 multiplied by 3.14 to the current cell.
Division	/	=B5/B4	Assign the result of dividing B5 by B4 to the current cell.
Exponentiation	^	=B4^2	Assign the square of B4 to the current cell.

Table 4 Mathematical operators in Excel   Amy S Kinser, Brant Moriarity, Eric Kinser, Kristyn Jacobson

Applying Order of Operations

The **order of operations** is the order in which Excel processes calculations in a formula that contains more than one operator. Mathematical operations execute in a specific order, which can be remembered by using the mnemonic PEMDAS.

1. (P) Parentheses
2. (E) Exponentiation
3. (M) Multiplication
4. (D) Division
5. (A) Addition
6. (S) Subtraction

Excel scans a formula from left to right while performing calculations using the above order of operation rules. Thus, you can control which part of a calculation is performed first by enclosing parts of a formula in parentheses. Portions of a formula enclosed in parentheses are evaluated first, following the previously listed order. Table 5 contains some examples of the effect of order of operations on formula results.

Formula	Result	Formula	Result
=4-2*5^2	-46	=(5+5)*4/2-3*6	2
=(4-2)*5^2	50	=(5+5)*4/(2-3)*6	-240
=5+5*4/2-3*6	-3	=(5+5)*4/(2-3*6)	-2.5

Table 5 Order of operations   Amy S Kinser, Brant Moriarity, Eric Kinser, Kristyn Jacobson

Golf pro John Schilling is paid a commission on golf lessons. He earns 70% of all lesson fees received by the Pro Shop. Pro Shop manager Aleeta Herriott is in charge of all golf club sales. She receives a 15% commission on all sales of clubs and a 10% commission on golf balls and accessories. In this exercise, you will calculate commissions using formulas.

 E02.20

To Calculate Commissions Using Formulas

a. Click the **WeeklySales** worksheet tab, and then click cell **J25**. In this cell, you will calculate the commissions John Schilling earned on golf lessons. The total revenue from golf lessons for the week is in cell I25, and the commission paid for golf lessons is in cell C33.

b. Type **=**, click **I25**. Excel puts the cell reference of I25 into the formula.

c. Type *****, click **C33**. Excel puts the cell reference of C33 into the formula.

SIDE NOTE
Alternate Method
To enter the formula in J25, type **=I25*C33**, and then press Enter.

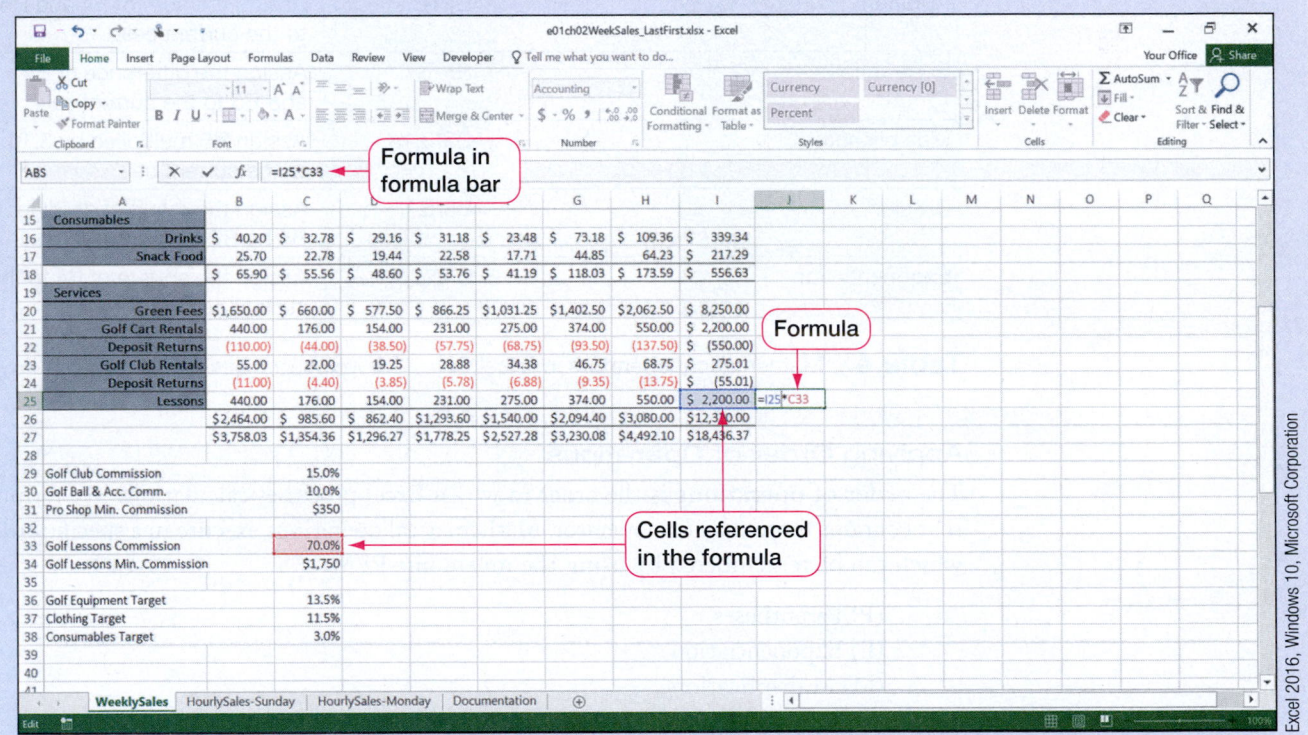

Figure 21   Entering a formula in a cell

d. Press Enter. The active cell is now J26, and the formula in cell J25 multiplies I25 and C33. AutoFit the column width as necessary.

Next, you need to calculate the commissions that Aleeta Herriott earned selling golf clubs in the Pro Shop by multiplying the total golf club sales for the weekly by the commission percentage on golf club sales.

e. Click cell **J6**. Type **=**, click cell **I6**, type *****, click cell **C29,** and then press Enter.

Next, you need to calculate the commission earned on Pro Shop accessories by multiplying the sum of golf ball and accessory sales for the week by the appropriate commission.

SIDE NOTE
Alternate Method
To enter the formula in J7, type **=(I7+I8)*C30**, and then press Enter.

f. Click cell **J7**. This cell has been merged. Type **=(,** click **I7**. Type **+,** click **I8**. Type **)*,** click **C30**, and then press Enter.

You added the parentheses to ensure cells I7 and I8 are added before they are multiplied by cell C30. Next you need to sum Aleeta Herriott's commissions.

> **SIDE NOTE**
> **Alternate Method**
> In cell J9, type =SUM(J6:J7), and then press Enter.

g. Click cell **J9**, and then double-click the **AutoSum** button Σ AutoSum ▾ .

After adding the formula in cell J9, you notice the error message in the upper left corner in cell I9. Excel believes there may be an error in the formula in cell I9 because the formulas in cell I9 and J9 differ. Because both formulas are correct, you want to remove the error message.

h. In cell **I9,** click the **Error** arrow.

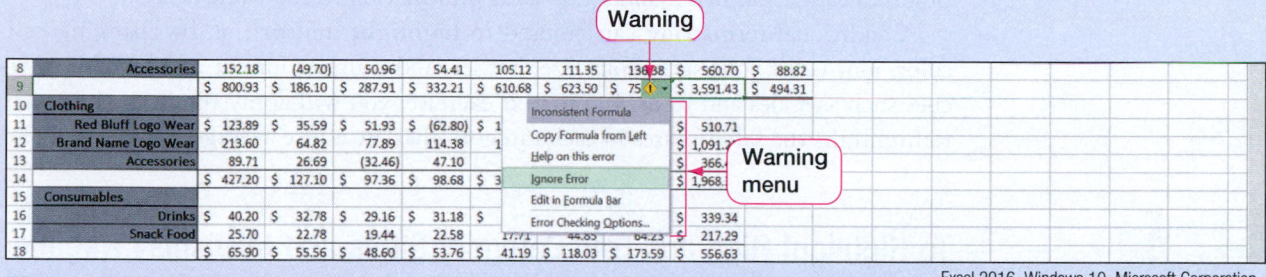

Figure 22 Error Message menu

Excel 2016, Windows 10, Microsoft Corporation

i. Select **Ignore Error**, and then **Save** the workbook.

> ## Troubleshooting
>
> Excel allows you to copy formulas from one location to another and adjusts cell references to ensure calculation accuracy. This is not necessarily true when a formula is moved from one location to another, however. If you move a formula by dragging it from one location to another, cell references do not change. Be sure you double-check a formula after you move it to ensure it is still producing a correct result.

REAL WORLD ADVICE **An Alternative to Typing Cell References**

An alternative — and more accurate — method of typing cell references into a formula is to type only the operators and then select the cells from the worksheet. The steps to enter the daily sales total in the Weekly Sales worksheet would be as follows.

1. Select cell B27.
2. Type =.
3. Click cell B9, and then type +.
4. Click cell B14, and then type +.
5. Click cell B18, and then type +.
6. Click cell B26, and then press Enter.

This method of building formulas is much less error prone than typing cell references.

Use Conditional Formatting to Assist in Decision Making

As was discussed previously, one of the primary purposes of information analysis in Excel worksheets is to assist in decision making. People are often influenced by the format in which information is presented. Worksheets can be very large — thousands of rows and dozens of columns of information. The number of calculated items can be daunting to analyze, digest, and interpret. To the extent to which Excel can be used to assist the decision maker in understanding information, decision-making speed and quality should improve.

Conditional formatting can aid the decision maker by changing the way information is displayed based on rules specific to the problem the worksheet is designed to address.

Highlighting Values in a Range with Conditional Formatting

Conditional formatting allows the specification of rules that apply formatting to a cell as determined by the rule outcome. It is a way to dynamically change the visual presentation of information in a manner that adds information to the worksheet.

Conditional formatting can be used to highlight information by changing cell fill color, font color, font style, font size, border, and number format and by adding visual cues such as scales and icons. In the next exercise, you will apply conditional formatting to highlight the sales figures in each category that are above average for each day's sales.

 E02.21

To Highlight High and Low Category Sales and to Display Negative Accounting Number Formatted Cells in Red

a. On the WeeklySales worksheet, select cell range **B9:H9**. Click the **Home** tab, and in the Styles group, click **Conditional Formatting** 📊. Point to **Top/Bottom Rules**, and then select **Top 10 Items**. In the Top 10 Items dialog box, in the **Format cells that rank in the TOP** box, double-click **10**, and then type **1**.

b. Click the **with** arrow, select **Green Fill with Dark Green Text**.

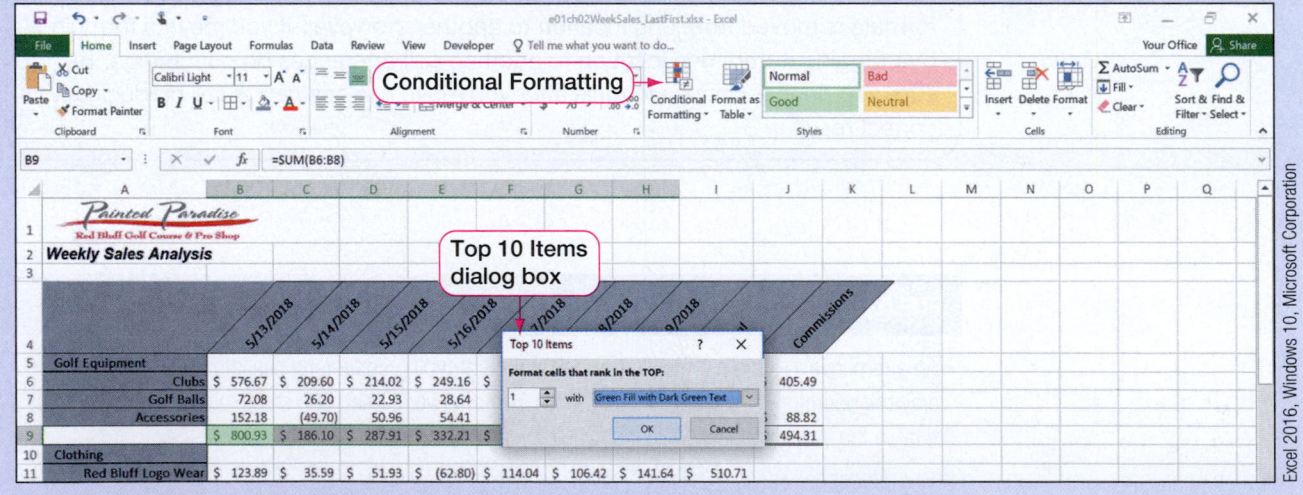

Figure 23 Top 10 Items dialog box

c. Click **OK**. With cell range B9:H9 still selected, in the Styles group, click **Conditional Formatting** 📊, point to Top/Bottom Rules, and then select **Bottom 10 Items**. In the Bottom 10 Items dialog box, in the **Format cells that rank in the BOTTOM** box, double-click **10**, and then type **1**. Click **OK** to accept the Light Red Fill with Dark Red Text.

Now you can copy the formatting you just added to B9:H9 to the other category totals and to the overall totals in the WeeklySales worksheet.

d. With cell range **B9:H9** still selected, in the Clipboard group, double-click **Format Painter** . Select cell ranges **B14:H14**, **B18:H18**, and **B26:H26**. Click **Format Painter** to turn off the Format Painter.

Recall that Accounting Number Format does not include the option to display negative numbers in red — notice cell C8. This can be accomplished with conditional formatting.

SIDE NOTE
Want Negative Numbers in Blue?
In the with box, click Custom Format, click Color, and choose a different color for negative numbers.

e. Select cell range **B6:I27**. In the Styles group, click **Conditional Formatting** , point to **Highlight Cells Rules**, and then click **Less Than**. In the **Format cells that are LESS THAN** box, type **0**. Click the **with** box arrow, and then select **Red Text**. Click **OK**.

f. **Save** the workbook.

Applying Conditional Formatting to Assess Benchmarks Using Icon Sets

Conditional formatting can also be used to highlight whether or not a value satisfies particular criteria such as a benchmark. The staff in the Pro Shop is guaranteed a minimum commission amount — stored in cells C31 and C34. The resort management prefers that a staff member's commissions exceed the minimum. You can use conditional formatting to clearly identify whether or not Aleeta Herriott's commissions in the Pro Shop and John Schilling's commissions for lessons exceed the contractual minimum.

In this exercise, you will use conditional formatting with icon sets to highlight above-minimum commissions.

E02.22

To Use Conditional Formatting with Icon Sets to Highlight Above-Minimum Commissions

a. On the WeeklySales worksheet, click cell **J9**. In the Styles group, click **Conditional Formatting** , point to **Icon Sets**, and then select **More Rules**. In the New Formatting Rule dialog box, under Select a Rule Type, make sure **Format all cells based on their values** is selected.

b. Under Edit the Rule Description, click the **Icon Style** arrow, and then select the first item in the list, **3 Arrows (Colored)** — you will have to scroll up.

c. Under Icon, next to the yellow arrow icon, click the arrow, and then select the red down arrow for the middle Icon box; the Icon Style box will change to Custom. In the bottom Icon box, next to the red arrow icon, click the arrow, select **No Cell Icon**, and then select **Number** in both **Type** boxes.

d. Double-click in the top **Value** box, and then press Delete. Click the **Collapse** button , select cell **C31** — the minimum commission for the Pro Shop manager — and then click the **Expand** button .

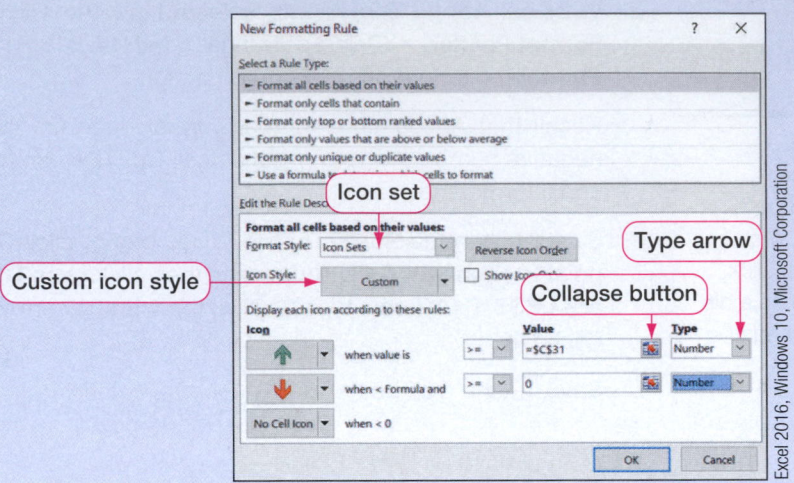

Figure 24   Conditional Formatting icon sets

e. Click **OK**. Now you can use the conditional format you just created for the golf lessons commission in cell J25.

f. With cell **J9** selected, click **Format Painter** 🖌, and then click cell **J25** to paste formatting, including conditional formatting.

g. With **J25** still selected, in the Styles group, click **Conditional Formatting** 📊, and then select **Manage Rules**. The Conditional Formatting Rules Manager dialog box is displayed.

h. In the Conditional Formatting Rules Manager dialog box, click **Edit Rule**. In the Edit Formatting Rule dialog box, under Display each icon according to these rules, double-click the top **Value** box.

i. Click the **Collapse** button 📊 in the top Value box. Click cell **C34** — the minimum commission for the RBGC golf pro — and then click the **Expand** button 📊.

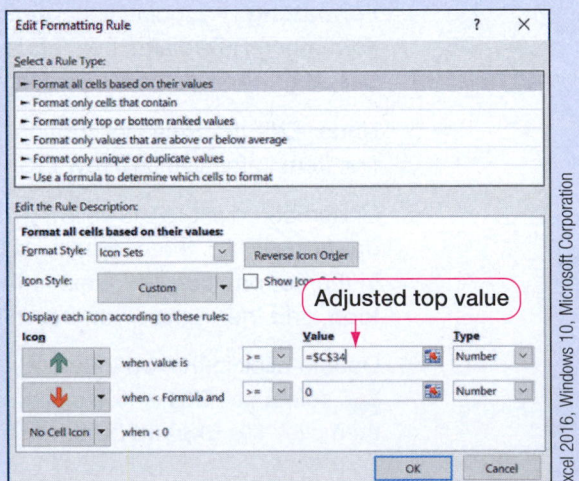

Figure 25   Conditional Formatting modifying an icon set

j. Click **OK**, and then click **OK**. AutoFit the column width of column J.

k. Save  the workbook.

Using Conditional Formatting to Assess Benchmarks Using Font Formatting

In the previous exercise, you used arrow icons to indicate whether or not Aleeta Herriott and John Schilling had met commission minimums. Any of the conditional formatting features can be used to visually highlight benchmark satisfaction. Aleeta has used historical sales data to identify a proportion of weekly sales that is a minimum goal (benchmark) for each product category.

In this exercise, you will format weekly sales totals to be displayed in a bold and green font if they meet or exceed benchmarks.

E02.23

To Highlight Sales That Meet or Exceed Benchmarks

a. On the WeeklySales worksheet, click cell **I9**. In the Styles group, click **Conditional Formatting**. Point to **Highlight Cells Rules**, and then select **More Rules**. In the New Formatting Rule dialog box, under Select a Rule Type, select **Use a formula to determine which cells to format**.

b. In the **Format values where this formula is true box**, type **=I9/I27>=C36** (golf equipment percentage of total sales compared to the golf equipment target percentage of sales).

In using a formula to determine which cells to format, the conditional format always starts with an equal sign, which is followed by a conditional test. If that condition is TRUE then the formatting is applied. If the condition is FALSE, then it will not apply the formatting.

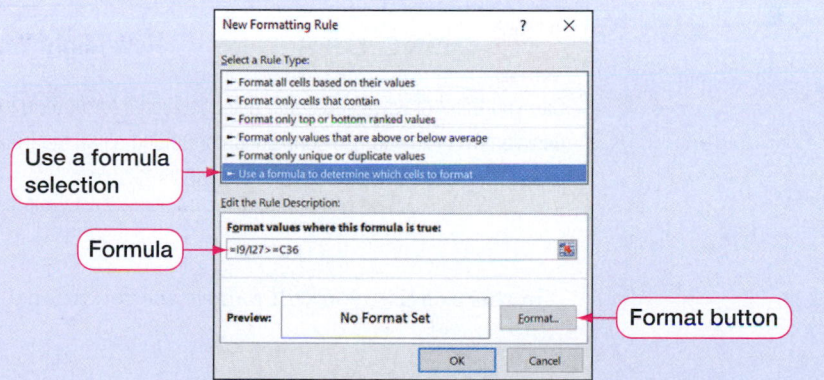

Use a formula selection

Formula

Format button

Excel 2016, Windows 10, Microsoft Corporation

Figure 26   Conditional Formatting using a formula

c. Click **Format**. In the Format Cells dialog box, on the Font tab, in the Font style box, select **Bold**, and then click the **Color** arrow. Under Standard Colors, select **Green**.

d. Click **OK** twice. If necessary, AutoFit Column Width on cell I9.

e. Click cell **I14**. In the Styles group, click **Conditional Formatting** . Point to **Highlight Cells Rules**, and then select **More Rules**. In the New Formatting Rule dialog box, under Select a Rule Type, select **Use a formula to determine which cells to format**. Type **=I14/I27>=C37**. Click **Format**. On the Font tab, in the Font style box, click **Bold**, and then click the **Color** arrow. Under Standard Colors, select **Green**. Click **OK** two times.

f. Click cell **I18**. In the Styles group, click **Conditional Formatting** . Point to **Highlight Cells Rules**, and then select **More Rules**. In the New Formatting Rule dialog box, under Select a Rule Type, select **Use a formula to determine which cells to format**. Type **=I18/I27>=C38**. Click **Format**. On the Font tab, in the Font style box, click **Bold**, and then click the **Color** arrow. Under Standard Colors, select **Green**. Click **OK** two times.

g. **Save** the workbook.

Removing Conditional Formatting

Once conditional formatting has been applied to a cell or range of cells, it may be necessary to remove the conditional formatting without affecting other cell formatting or cell contents. Conditional formatting can be removed from a selected cell or cell range, and it can be removed from the entire sheet, depending on which option is chosen.

When you applied the conditional formatting to cell range B6:I27 to display negative numbers in red regardless of the number format, several cells that did not contain data were also conditionally formatted. Although applying conditional formatting to a large range of cells all at once is efficient, applying it to cells that do not contain data in the current design may cause unforeseen problems as the worksheet is modified in the future. You need to remove the conditional formatting in the empty cells.

S̲s **CONSIDER THIS** | **How Might You Use Conditional Formatting?**

Can you think of ways you could use conditional formatting in worksheets to aid in making personal decisions? Could you use conditional formatting as an aid in tracking your stock portfolio? Monthly budget and expenses? Checking account?

In this exercise, you will remove the conditional formatting in the empty cells.

 E02.24

SIDE NOTE
Alternate Method
To remove conditional formatting, click Conditional Formatting, select Manage Rules, click Delete Rule.

To Remove Conditional Formatting from a Range of Cells

a. On the WeeklySales worksheet, select cell range **B10:I10**, press Ctrl, and then select cell ranges **B15:I15** and **B19:I19**.

b. In the Styles group, click **Conditional Formatting** , and then select **Manage Rules**. Notice the Cell Value < 0 rule that was applied to the selected ranges even though the ranges do not contain any data. Click **Close**.

c. In the Styles group, click Conditional Formatting, and then point to **Clear Rules**. Select **Clear Rules from Selected Cells**.

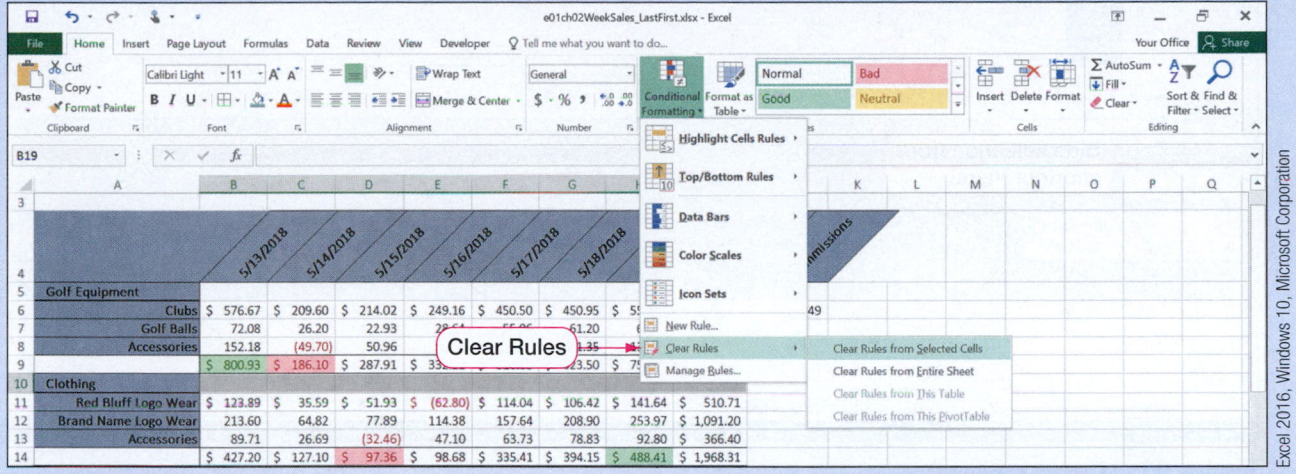

Figure 27 Remove Conditional Formatting

d. Save  the workbook.

Hide Information in a Worksheet

A worksheet can contain information that may not be necessary, or even desirable, to display. For example, detailed information used to calculate totals might be hidden until such time that the person using the worksheet would like to see it.

Hiding information in a worksheet is relatively simple. Entire worksheet rows and columns can be hidden. Simply select the rows and/or columns to be hidden by clicking on the row or column heading. Point to the selected row or column heading(s), right-click, and then select Hide on the displayed shortcut menu.

Gridlines are very helpful in visualizing and navigating a workbook during development, but some users feel gridlines clutter a worksheet. Gridlines can be "hidden" simply by unchecking the Gridlines box in the Show group on the View tab.

Hiding Worksheet Rows

In the WeeklySales worksheet, rows 29:38 contain parameters that are used to calculate commissions, to identify minimum commission levels, and to specify sales percentage benchmarks for golf equipment, clothing, and consumables. Once the WeeklySales worksheet has been fully developed, there is little need to have this data visible. In fact, having this kind of data visible can be problematic in that a user could inadvertently or intentionally change the data and cause the worksheet to display incorrect information.

In this exercise, you will hide rows 29:38 from view in the WeeklySales worksheet.

E02.25

SIDE NOTE
Alternate Method
You can also click and drag to select rows 29:38

To Hide Rows in a Worksheet

a. On the WeeklySales worksheet, click the heading for row **29** in the WeeklySales worksheet, press and hold Shift, and then click the heading for row **38**.

b. Right-click anywhere in the selected rows.

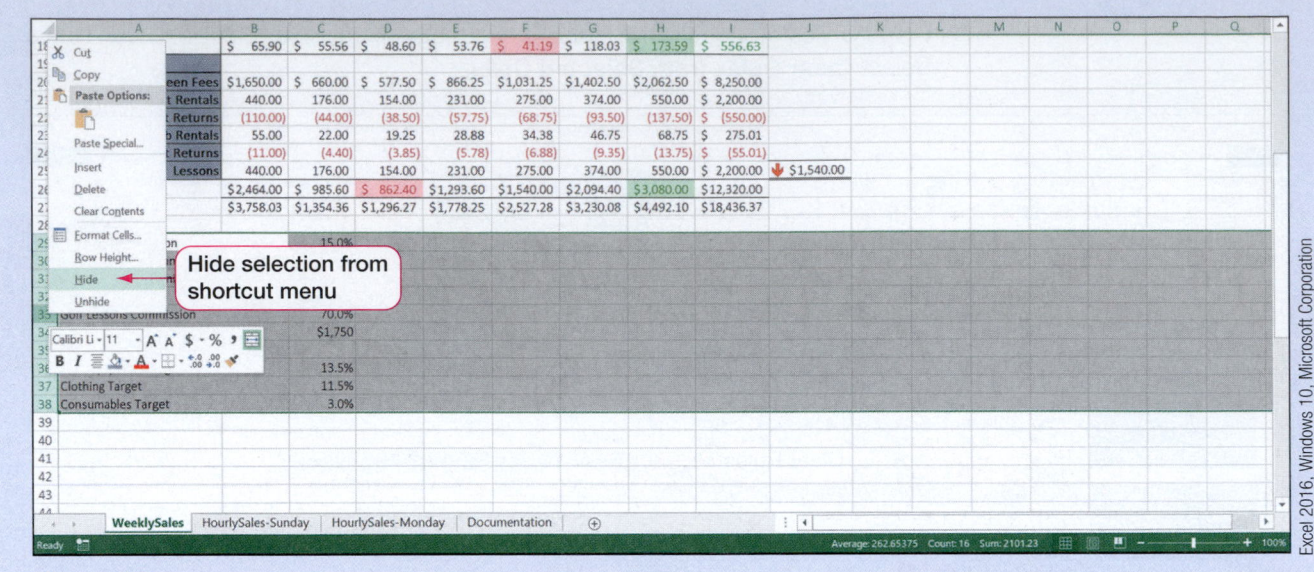

Figure 28 Shortcut menu

c. Select **Hide** on the shortcut menu, and then press Ctrl + Home.

d. **Save** 💾 the workbook.

Hiding Worksheet Gridlines

Gridlines assist in identifying cells in manipulating a worksheet. Once a worksheet is complete, some people think gridlines detract from a worksheet's professional appearance. In this exercise, you will turn off, or hide, gridlines in the WeeklySales worksheet.

▶ E02.26

To Hide Gridlines in a Worksheet

a. On the WeeklySales worksheet, click the **View** tab, and then, in the Show group, click to deselect the **Gridlines** check box and turn the gridlines off.

Notice the worksheet now has a white background. To many users, this is much more visually appealing than a worksheet in which gridlines are visible.

b. **Save** 💾 the workbook.

Document Functions and Formulas

An important part of building a good worksheet is documentation. Aleeta Herriott included the standard documentation worksheet in the Week Sales workbook and updated it to reflect what she had accomplished before assigning completion of the workbook to you.

Showing Functions and Formulas

What is displayed in a cell that contains a function or a formula is the calculated result. The function or formula that generated the displayed value is visible only one cell at a time by selecting a cell and then looking at the formula bar. When the Show Formulas feature is turned on, the calculated results are hidden and functions and formulas are shown in the cells instead, whenever applicable.

Show Formulas is very helpful in understanding how a worksheet is structured. It is an essential aid in correcting errors or updating the function of a worksheet. A worksheet that has Show Formulas turned on can be printed and/or exported for documentation purposes.

In this exercise, you will view worksheet formulas and export a formulas worksheet to a PDF.

 E02.27

To View Worksheet Formulas and Export to PDF

a. On the WeeklySales worksheet, click the **Formulas** tab, and then, in the Formula Auditing group, select **Show Formulas** 📊.

Cells now display formulas rather than values. Notice that Show Formulas also displays cell data without formatting.

b. Use the **Zoom Slider** ⬅——|——➕ on the status bar to move the zoom level so you can view the entire worksheet on the monitor.

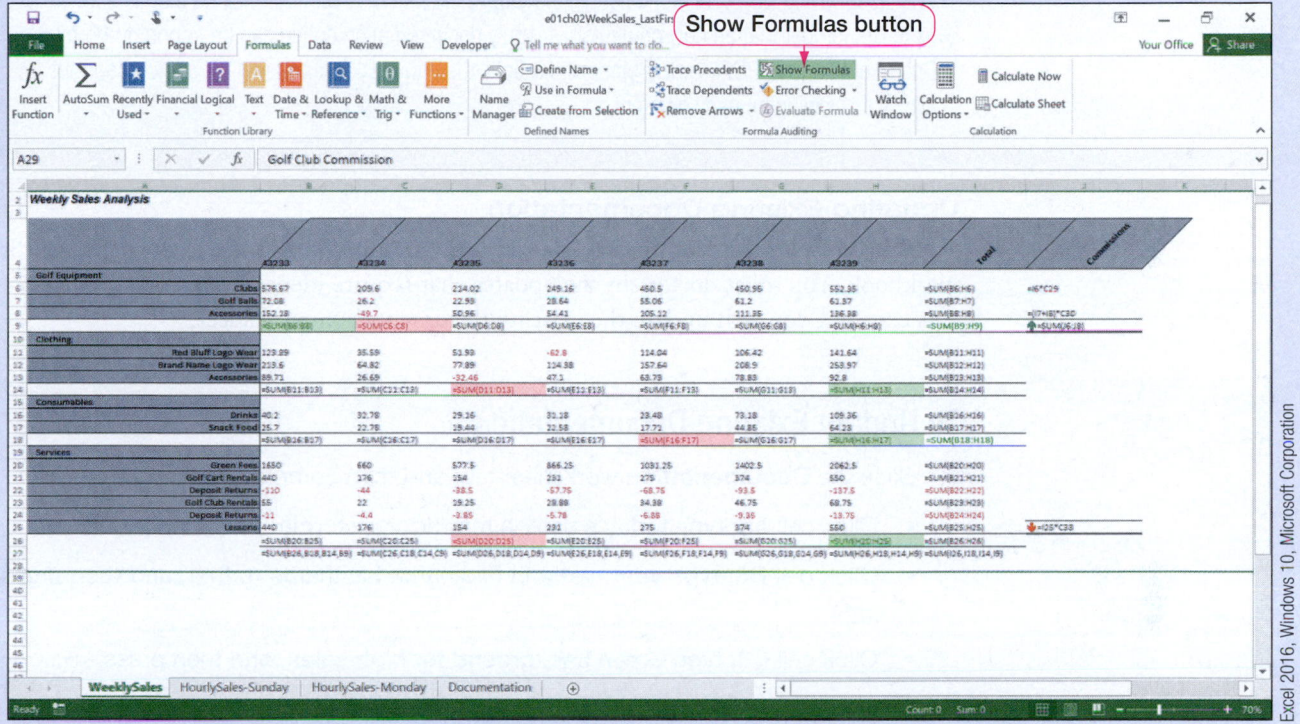

Figure 29 Show formulas

c. Click the **Page Layout** tab, and then, in the Scale to Fit group, click the **Width** arrow, and then select **1 page**. This will scale your worksheet to print in the width of a single page.

d. In the Scale to Fit group, click the **Height** arrow, and then select **1 page**. This will scale your document to print in the height of a single page.

e. In the Page Setup group, click **Orientation**, and then select **Landscape**.

f. Click the **File** tab to enter Backstage view, and then click **Export**. Under Create a PDF/XPS Document, click **Create PDF/XPS**. In the Publish as PDF or XPS dialog box, double-click the File name box, and then type e01ch02WeeklySalesFormulas_LastFirst, using your last and first name. Make sure **Open file after publishing** is checked. Click **Publish**.

g. The WeeklySales worksheet with Show Formulas turned on is displayed as a PDF document in Reader. Close Reader.

h. Click the **Formulas** tab, and then click **Show Formulas**  to toggle off Show Formulas and return to the default Normal view.

i. Use the Zoom Slider on the status bar to set the zoom to 100%.

j. **Save** the workbook.

Updating Existing Documentation

You have made some significant and very important improvements to the Week Sales workbook. You must document the updates that require identification or explanation. In this exercise, you will update the existing documentation worksheet.

E02.28

To Update Existing Documentation

a. Click the **Documentation** worksheet tab, and then complete the following.

- Click cell **A8**, type today's date in mm/dd/yyyy format, and then press Enter.

- Click cell **B8**, type your name in Firstname Lastname format, and then press Enter.

- Click cell **C8**, type Green background for high sales, and then press Enter.

- In cell **C9**, type Red background for low sales, and then press Enter.

b. Add the file name to the left page footer on all worksheets.

c. Click the **WeeklySales** worksheet tab. Click the **File** tab, and then click **Print**. Under Settings, click the **Print Active Sheets** arrow, and then click **Print Entire Workbook.** If requested by your instructor, click **Print**.

d. **Save** the workbook, exit Excel, and then submit your files as directed by your instructor.

Concept Check

1. Why should you format data in Excel? How might you format data for a person who is color-blind? p. 105–109

2. What are the different functions made available via the AutoSum button? What does each function calculate? p. 125

3. What are the advantages of calculating totals in a table total row? p. 129

4. What character precedes all formulas and functions in Excel? What purpose do parentheses serve in Excel formulas? p. 132–133

5. What is conditional formatting? How can conditional formatting assist in decision making? p. 136

6. List two reasons why it may be necessary to hide rows or columns of information in a worksheet. p. 141

7. Why might you choose to print the formulas of a worksheet? Why is the PDF file format good for saving documentation? p. 144

Key Terms

Argument   125
AVERAGE function   127
Banding   121
Built-in cell style   119
Built-in function   125
Cell alignment   111
Cell reference   125
Conditional formatting   136
Constant   132
COUNT function   127

Default   111
Destination cell   125
Fill color   112
Format Painter   115
Formula   132
Function   124
Graphical format   105
Mathematical operator   132
MAX function   128
MIN function   128

Order of operations   133
Source cell(s)   125
SUBTOTAL function   129
SUM function   126
Table   121
Table style   121
Tabular format   105
Theme   123

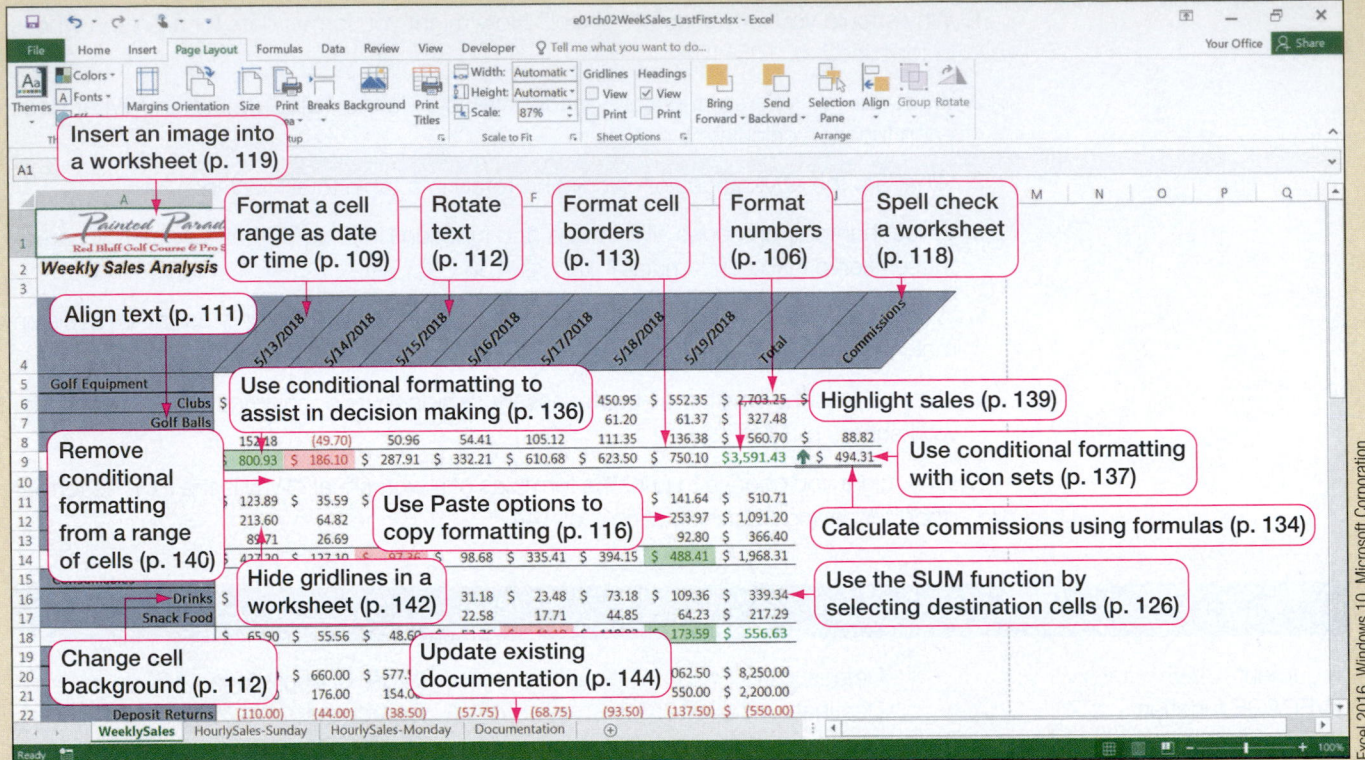

Figure 30

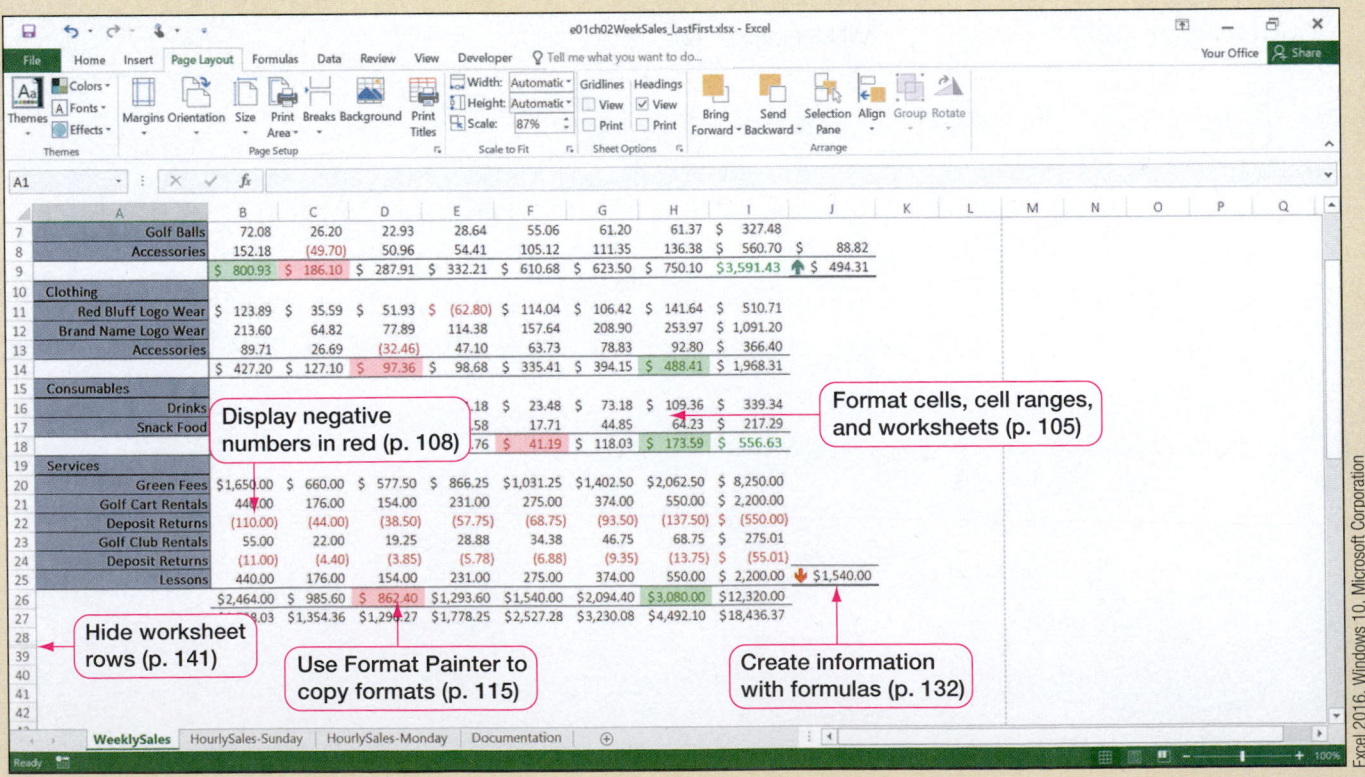

Figure 31

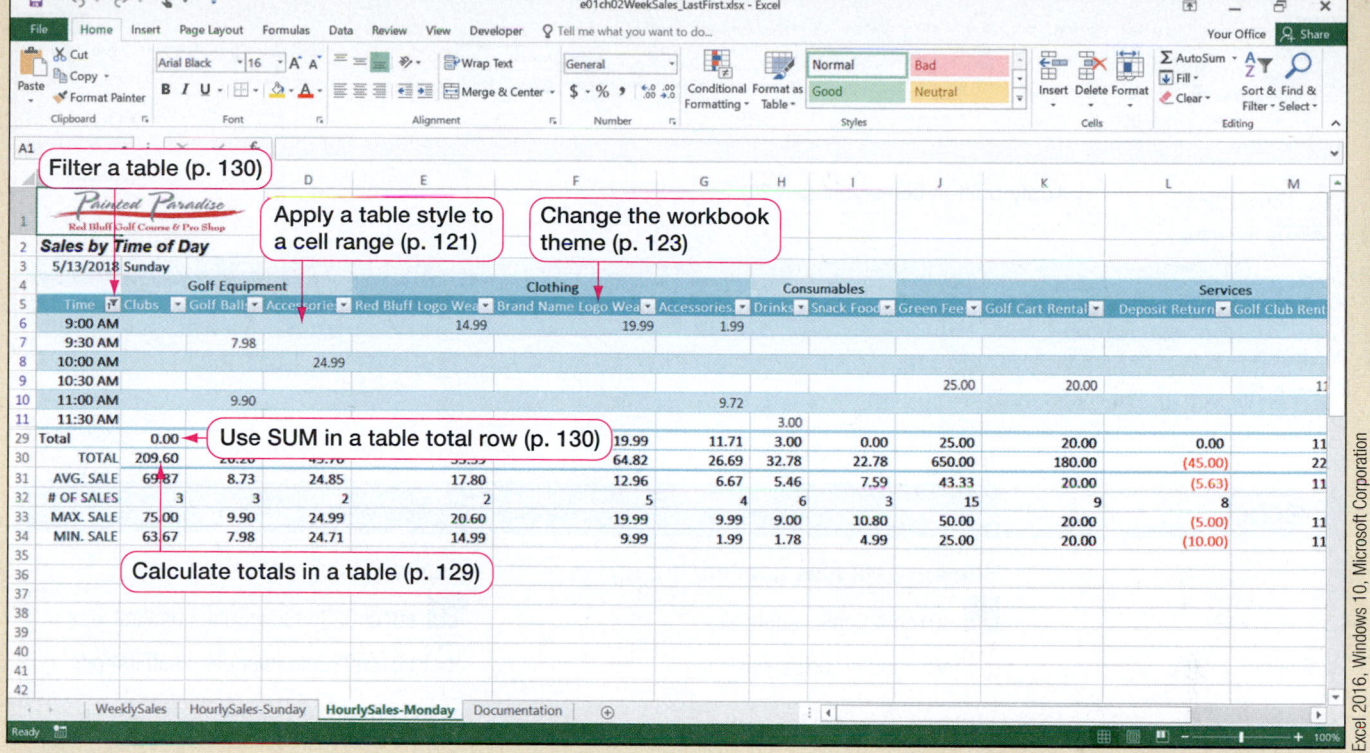

Figure 32

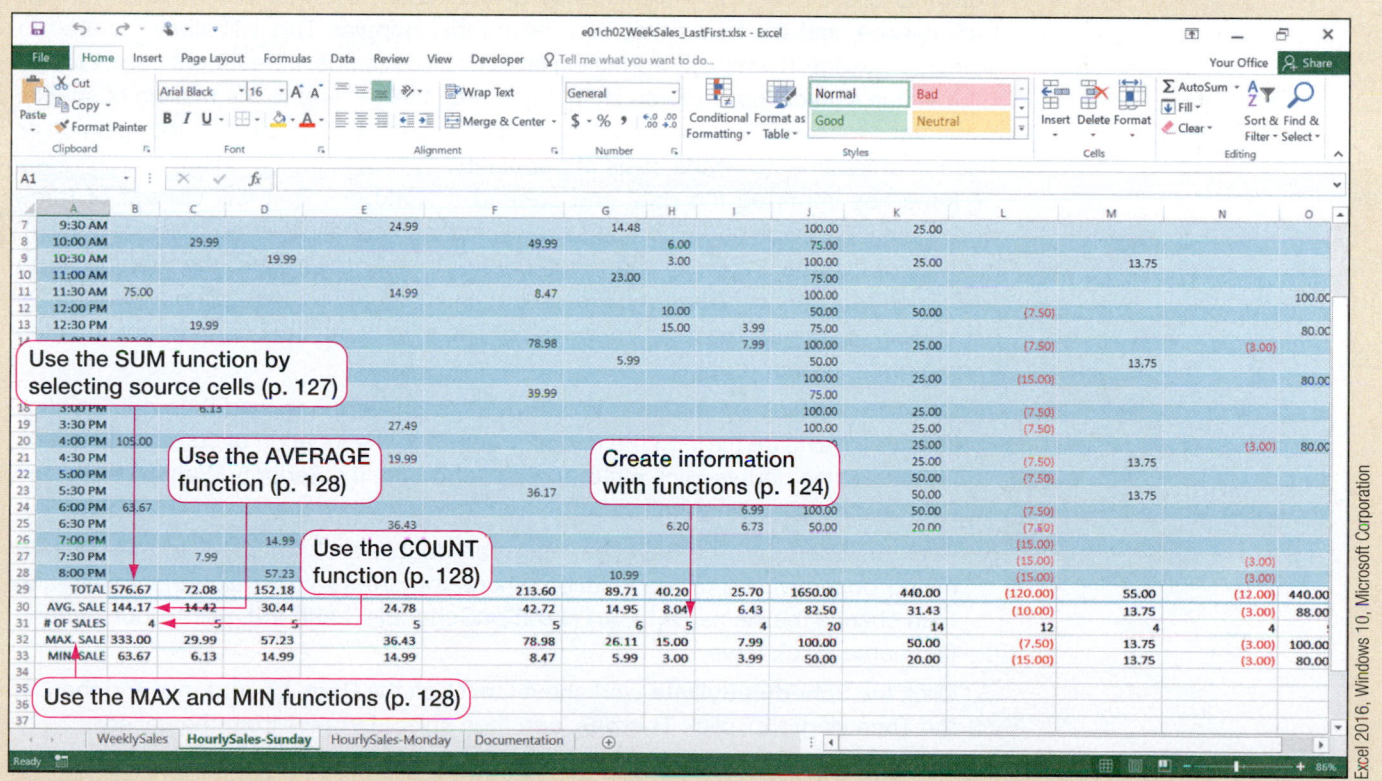

Figure 33

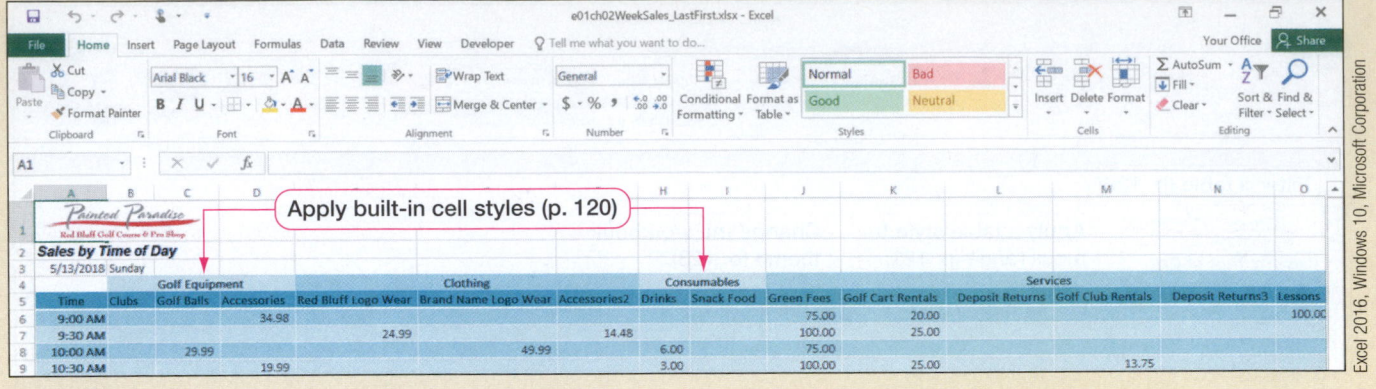

 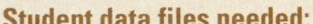 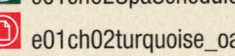 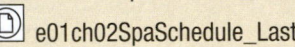

Apply built-in cell styles (p. 120)

Figure 34

Practice 1

Student data files needed:

- e01ch02SpaSchedule.xlsx
- e01ch02turquoise_oasis.jpg

You will save your files as:

- e01ch02SpaSchedule_LastFirst.xlsx
- e01ch02SpaSchedule_LastFirst.pdf

Spa Schedule

Production & Operations

Irene Kai, another manager at the Turquoise Oasis Spa, has exported sales data from a database program into an Excel spreadsheet to facilitate the analysis of services received by a client during a visit to the spa. This spreadsheet is in the initial development stages, but the intention is to keep track of the treatments performed on an individual client during the client's stay at the resort, the therapist who performed each service, and the treatments that seem most popular. This will allow the staff to review spa usage in a visually appealing layout, notice trends in treatment choices, and improve the scheduling of therapist. In the future, it might lead to the mailing of special promotions to regular or repeat customers, a reevaluation of pricing, or the addition or deletion of treatments on the basis of popularity.

Irene has imported the data and created a workbook that will consist of three worksheets. One worksheet contains the clients' names, a list of the dates of service, the type of treatment ad-ministered, the cost of the treatment, and the therapist who performed that service. A second worksheet has a list of spa therapists and the days of the week and times that each is available. The third worksheet contains information to document the workbook.

a. Open Excel, click **Open Other Workbooks** in the left pane, and then double-click **This PC**. Navigate through the folder structure to the location of your student data files, and then double-click **e01ch02SpaSchedule**. If a Security Warning message displays, click the **Enable Editing** button.

b. Click the **File** tab, click **Save As**, and then double-click **This PC**. In the Save As dialog box, navigate to the location where you are saving your project files, and then change the file name to e01ch02SpaSchedule_LastFirst, using your last and first name. Click **Save**.

c. Click the **ScheduleByDate** worksheet tab. Click the **Page Layout** tab, and then, in the Themes group, click **Themes**, and then select **Droplet** from the gallery.

d. Click cell **A1**. Click the **Home** tab, and then, in the Cells group, click **Format**, and then click **Row Height**. Type **60** in the Row height box, and then click **OK**.

e. Click cell **E1**. Click the **Insert** tab, and then, in the Illustrations group, click **Pictures**. Navigate to the location where your student data files are stored, click **e01ch02turquoise_oasis.jpg**, and then click **Insert**. Click the **Picture Tools Format** tab, and then, in the Arrange group, click **Align**. If necessary, select **Snap**

to Grid. Click the right horizontal sizing handle, and snap the right edge of the logo to the border between columns **F** and **G**. Click the bottom vertical sizing handle, and snap the bottom edge of the logo to the border between rows **1** and **2**.

f. Select the cell range **A2:J2**. Click the **Home** tab, and then, in the Alignment group, click **Merge & Center**. In the Styles group, click **Cell Styles**, and then click **Heading 4** in the gallery.

g. Select cell range **A4:J4**, click **Cell Styles**, and then click **Heading 3** in the gallery.

h. Click cell **A2**, and then, in the Clipboard group, click **Copy**. Select cell range **A26:A30**, right-click cell **A26**, and then, in the Paste Options shortcut menu, select **Formatting**. In the Alignment group, click **Align Left**.

i. Click cell **A6**. In the Clipboard group, click **Format Painter**, and then select cell range **A7:A23**.

j. Select cell range **I6:I23**. In the Number group, click the **Number Format** arrow, and then select **Currency**. In the Number group, click **Decrease Decimal** two times.

k. Select cell range **C6:C23**. Click the **Number Format** arrow, and then select **More Number Formats**. In the Type box, select **1:30 PM**, and then click **OK**.

l. Click cell **J10**. Click **AutoSum**, select the cell range **I6:I9**, and then press Enter. Click cell **J13**. Click **AutoSum**, select the cell range **I11:I12**, and then press Enter. Click cell **J18**. Click **AutoSum**, select cell range **I14:I17**, and then press Enter. Click cell **J21**. Click **AutoSum**, select cell range **I19:I20**, and then press Enter. Click cell **J24.** Click **AutoSum**, select cell range **I22:I23**, and then press Enter.

m. Click cell **C28**, type **=MAX(J6:J24)**, and then press Ctrl+Enter. Click cell **J24**, click the **Format Painter**, and then click cell **C28**.

n. Select cell range **A4:J24**. In the Styles group, click **Format as Table**, and then select **Table Style Medium 3** from the gallery. In the Format as Table dialog box, click to select **My table has headers**, and then click **OK**. On the Design tab, in the Table Style Options group, click **Total Row**. On the **Home** tab, click cell **J10**, click **Format Painter**, and then click cell **J25**.

o. In the Editing group, click **Sort & Filter**, and then click **Filter** to turn off column filters.

p. Select cell **J10**, press and hold Ctrl, and then select cells **J13**, **J18**, **J21**, and **J24**. In the Styles group, click **Conditional Formatting**, point to Highlight Cells Rules, and then select **Greater Than**. Type **=C$31** in the Format cells that are GREATER THAN box. Click the **with** arrow, and then select **Custom Format**. In the Format Cells dialog box, on the Font tab, in the Font style box, select **Bold**. Click the Color arrow, and select **Green, Accent2** from the palette. Click **OK**, and then click **OK** again.

q. Click the **TherapistSchedule** worksheet tab. Select cell **C8**, type **Monday**, and then press Ctrl+Enter. Click and hold the fill handle, and then expand the active cell to encompass cell range **C8:C14**. Press Ctrl+C. Click cell **C16**, press and hold Ctrl, and then click cell **C24**. Press Ctrl+V.

r. Select cell range **A6:D6**. In the Styles group, click **Cell Styles**, and then select **40% - Accent5** from the gallery. In the Font group, click **Bold**.

s. Select cell range **A8:A14**. Press Ctrl, and then select cell ranges **B8:B14**, **A16:A22**, **B16:B22**, **A24:A30**, and **B24:B30**. In the Alignment group, click **Merge & Center**. In the Alignment group, click **Orientation**, and then select **Vertical Text**. In the Alignment group, click **Middle Align**. In the Font group, click **Bold**. Select columns A:B. In the Cells group, click **Format**, and select **AutoFit Column Width**.

t. Right-click the header for row **5**, and then click **Delete**.

u. Click the **Documentation** worksheet tab. Click cell **A8**, insert **today's date**, and then press Tab. Type **your name** in cell B8 in the Firstname Lastname format. Click cell **C8**, and then type **Calculated daily totals**. Press Enter. Type **Determined** maximum day's sales. Press [Enter]. Type **Formatted daily sales totals that met target as green and bold**. Press [Enter]. Press [Ctrl]+[Home].

v. Click the **ScheduleByDate** worksheet tab. On the **Page Layout** tab, in the Page Setup group, click **Orientation**, and then select **Landscape**. In the Scale to Fit group, click the **Width** arrow, and then select **1 page**.

w. Spell check the entire workbook. Insert the **file name** on the left page footer on all worksheets.

x. On the **File** tab, click **Export**, and then, under Create a PDF/XPS Document, click **Create PDF/XPS**. Be sure **Open file after publishing** is not checked. Click **Options**. In the Options dialog box, under Publish what, click **Entire workbook**, and then click **OK**. Navigate to the folder where you are saving your files. In the File name box, type **e01ch02SpaSchedule_LastFirst** using your last and first name, and then click **Publish**.

y. Save 💾 the workbook, exit Excel, and then submit your files as directed by your instructor.

Problem Solve 1

Student data file needed:

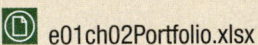
e01ch02Portfolio.xlsx

You will save your file as:

e01ch02Portfolio_LastFirst.xlsx

Stock Portfolio Monthly Dividend Income

Finance & Accounting

One method that people use to provide income during their retirement years is investing in dividend-paying stocks. The dividends allow investors to make withdrawals from their retirement account without having to reduce their invested principal. Michael Malley, president and chief investment officer of your new employer, Excellent Wealth Management, has developed a worksheet to show how a portfolio of stocks can create an additional income stream for his clients. You are asked to determine how much income the current portfolio is generating in order to assist with future investment decisions in the form of adding to current investments or diversifying and adding other dividend-paying investments.

a. Open the Excel file, **e01ch02Portfolio**. Save your file as **e01ch02Portfolio_LastFirst**, using your last and first name.

b. **Center** and **bold** cell range **B2:F3**.

c. Merge & Center cell range **A1:N1**. Apply the **Title** cell style, and then **Bold** the range.

d. Select cell range **N12:N16** and **N20:N24**, and then calculate row totals using the **SUM** function.

e. Calculate the average of Total Dividends Received in cell **G8**.

f. Apply cell style **Heading 3** to cells **G7**, **B10**, and **B18**.

g. Apply the **Currency** format to cell ranges **B4:F4**, **B6:F6**, **B8:G8**, **B12:N16**, and **B20:N25**.

h. In cell **B7**, calculate the yield of Prime Steel — the annual dividends per share divided by the price per share. Copy the formula to cell range **C7:F7**. Format the yield figures as Percent Style with two decimal places.

i. Hide rows **10:17**.

j. Format cell range **A19:N24** as a table with headers. Apply **Table Style Light 11**. Sort by **STOCK** from **A-Z**, and then turn off Filters.

k. Add the Total Row to the table, and calculate the total of columns B:N.

l. Apply a top border to cell range **A25:N25**.

m. Apply cell style **40% - Accent3** to cell ranges **A20:A25**, **B25:N25**, and **N20:N24**.

n. Apply Conditional Formatting to cell range **B20:M24**. Display **the Top 10 Items** as **Green Fill with Dark Green Text**.

o. Turn off **gridlines** in the Dividend Portfolio worksheet.

p. In the **Documentation** worksheet, enter today's date in mm/dd/yyyy format into cells **A8** and **A20**. In cell B8, type your name in the Firstname Lastname format. In cell **C8**, type Completed Mr. Malley's monthly dividend income worksheet. Make cell **A1** the active cell.

q. Spell check the entire workbook. Insert the file name on the left page footer on all worksheets.

r. For the **DividendPortfolio** and **Documentation** worksheets, set the Orientation to **Landscape**, and then set the **Width** to **1 page**. Change Print Settings to **Print Entire Workbook**. Print your workbook as directed by your instructor.

s. Save the workbook, exit Excel, and then submit your file as directed by your instructor.

Critical Thinking

The FIVE stock yields the highest dividends. What decision regarding the FIVE stock can be drawn from this result? The PULSE stock yields the lowest dividends. Should this stock be sold based off of this data? Why or why not?

Perform 1: Perform in Your Life

Student data file needed:
e01ch02PriceChanges.xlsx

You will save your file as:
e01ch02PriceChanges_LastFirst.xlsx

Tracking Stock Price Movements

Finance & Accounting

Excel can be used to track changes in stock prices over time. Not only can you record the actual prices, but by using formulas and some formatting, you can easily calculate the percentage changes in price and pick out the winners and losers in your portfolio.

After you have demonstrated your Excel skills for Mr. Malley, he would like you to work with some real data for a client (your instructor). The client may decide to modify the specifications given below. Because customer service is of the utmost importance to Excellent Wealth Management, be sure to follow any client requests very carefully.

a. Open the Excel file, **e01ch02PriceChanges**. Save your file as e01ch02PriceChanges_LastFirst, using your last and first name.

   Use a website that provides access to historic stock price data for steps b through d. Options include, but are not limited to, finance.yahoo.com and google.com/finance.

b. Select five companies that are publicly traded. Enter the company name in each cell, starting with B3:F3. Format the titles to look professional. In the cells immediately below each company name, enter the ticker symbol — the abbreviation that the company's stock uses.

c. Enter the eight most recent dates that denote the first trading day of a quarter, starting in cell A5:A12. For example, the first trading day of 1Q2016 was 1/2/2016. The first trading day of 2Q was 4/1/2016. Format the dates entered as Long Date. Adjust the widths of columns A:F to fit the data you entered.

d. Look up the historic closing prices for each stock for the dates entered in step c, and then enter these values into the corresponding cells.

e. Under the first company's historic closing price data, calculate the minimum price that was observed. Copy the formula to the cells under each of the other companies' historic price data.

f. Under the minimum price that was calculated, determine the maximum closing price that was observed. Copy the formula to the appropriate cell for each of the other companies.

g. For each company, calculate the Current Gross Margin as the closing price for the most recent quarter minus the closing price of the first quarter.

h. Format the historic price data, the minimum and maximum closing prices, and the current gross margin with an appropriate format.

i. Select the range that contains the historic closing prices for the first company. Apply conditional formatting to the range using the Gradient Fill Green Data Bar.

j. Right-align row headings (A5:A12), and center the company names and tickers for each range. Merge & Center the heading Price Performance across columns B:F. Merge & Center Excellent Wealth Management across all of the columns used in the worksheet, and then apply the Title cell style and bold. Make sure all of the data is visible in each of the cells.

k. Apply an appropriate heading cell style to all row and column headings, and then apply an appropriate cell style to the ticker symbols.

l. Apply an appropriate workbook theme, and then adjust the widths of columns A:F if necessary.

m. Copy the worksheet to a new worksheet named Auditing. Move the Auditing worksheet to the right of the Stocks worksheet. Show the formulas in this worksheet, and then adjust the column widths of columns A:F to fit the displayed content.

n. Update the Documentation worksheet to reflect the changes that have been made to the workbook. Spell check the entire workbook. Insert the file name on the left page footer on all worksheets.

o. Click the Stocks worksheet tab, and then adjust print settings to ensure a usable printed worksheet and to print all worksheets in the workbook. Adjust the Auditing worksheet to print on one page.

p. Save the workbook, exit Excel, and then submit your file as directed by your instructor.

Additional
Cases

Additional Chapter Cases are available at www.pearsonhighered.com/youroffice

Understanding the Fundamentals

This business unit had two outcomes:

Learning Outcome 1:

Use Excel to enter text, number, date, and time data to create efficient and effective worksheets.

Learning Outcome 2:

Use Excel to effectively communicate information through the use of functions and worksheet formatting.

In the Business Unit 1 Capstone, students will demonstrate competency in these outcomes through a series of business problems at various levels from guided practice to problem solving an existing spreadsheet to performing to create new spreadsheets.

More Practice 1

Student data files needed:

e01BeverageSales.xlsx

e01Indigo5.jpg

You will save your files as:

e01BeverageSales_LastFirst.xlsx

e01BeverageSales_LastFirst.pdf

Beverage Sales and Inventory Analysis

Product & Operations

Accounting & Finance

The Painted Paradise Resort & Spa offers a wide assortment of beverages through the Indigo5 restaurant and bar. The resort must track the inventory levels of these beverages as well as the sales and costs associated with each item. Restaurant manager Alberto Dimas has asked you to analyze the inventory and sales data found in the worksheet. There are four categories of beverages: beer, wine, soda, and water. You also have three inventory figures: Starting, Delivered, and Ending. You will work with a beverage sales workbook to generate an analysis of beverage sales in which you identify units sold of each beverage, cost of goods sold, revenue, profit, profit margin, and appropriate totals and averages.

a. Open **Excel**, click **Open Other Workbooks** in the left pane, and then double-click **This PC**. Navigate through the folder structure to the location of your student data files, and then double-click **e01BeverageSales**. If a Security Warning message displays, click the **Enable Editing** button.

b. Click the **File** tab, click **Save As**, and then double-click **This PC**. In the Save As dialog box, navigate to the location where you are saving your project files, and then change the file name to **e01BeverageSales_LastFirst**, using your last and first name. Click **Save**.

c. On the **BeverageSales** worksheet tab, select cell range **C2:K2**, and then click **Merge & Center** for the selected range. Apply the **Title** cell style to the selected range.

d. Select cell range **C3:K3**, and then click **Merge & Center** for the selected range. Apply the **Heading 4** cell style to the selected range.

e. Insert a hard return at the specified locations in the following cells. Be sure to remove any spaces between the words, and then press [Alt] + [Enter] to insert the hard return.

    • Between **Starting** and **Inventory** in C6

    • Between **Inventory** and **Delivered** in D6

    • Between **Ending** and **Inventory** in E6

f. Make the following calculations.

    • Click cell **F7**. Calculate Units Sold by adding Starting Inventory to Inventory Delivered and then subtracting Ending Inventory. Type **=**, click cell **C7**, type **+**, click cell **D7**, type **-**, and then click cell **E7**. Press Ctrl + Enter, and then copy the formula in cell F7 to cell ranges **F8:F12**, **F15:F18**, **F21:F25**, and **F28:F29**. If any cells contain a series of number signs (#), select the column. On the **Home** tab, in the Cells group, click **Format**, and then click **AutoFit Column Width**.

- Click cell **H7**. Calculate Cost of Goods Sold as Units Sold multiplied by Cost Per Unit. Type =, click cell **F7**, type *, and then click cell **G7**. Press Ctrl + Enter, and then copy the formula in cell H7 to cell ranges **H8:H12**, **H15:H18**, **H21:H25**, and **H28:H29**. If any cells contain a series of number signs (#), select the column, and then apply **AutoFit Column Width**.

- Click cell **J7**. Calculate Revenue as Units Sold multiplied by Sale Price Per Unit. Type =, click cell **F7**, type *, and then click cell **I7**. Press Ctrl + Enter, and then copy the formula in cell J7 to cell ranges **J8:J12**, **J15:J18**, **J21:J25**, and **J28:J29**. If any cells contain a series of number signs (#), select the column, and then apply **AutoFit Column Width**.

- Click cell **K7**. Calculate Profit Margin as (Revenue - Cost of Goods Sold)/Revenue. Type =(, click cell **J7**, type -, click cell **H7**, type)/, and then click cell **J7**. Press Ctrl + Enter, and then copy the formula in cell K7 to cell ranges **K8:K12**, **K15:K18**, **K21:K25**, and **K28:K29**.

g. Select cell ranges **C13:F13**, **C19:F19**, **C26:F26**, and **C30:F30** and cells **H13**, **J13**, **H19**, **J19**, **H26**, **J26**, **H30**, and **J30**. Click **AutoSum**. If any cells contain a series of number signs (#), select the cells, and then apply **AutoFit Column Width**.

h. Click cell **C31**. Calculate the total number of items in Starting Inventory for all categories combined by using the SUM() function. Type **=SUM(C13,C19,C26,C30)**, and then copy cell C31 to cell range **D31:F31** as well as cells **H31** and **J31**. If any cells contain a series of number signs (#), select the cells, and then apply **AutoFit Column Width**.

i. Make the following formatting changes.

- Format the row height of row 6 to 30.

- Select cell range **A6:K29**, and then apply **AutoFit Column Width**.

- Select cell range **C6:K6** along with cells **B13**, **B19**, **B26**, **B30**, and **B31**. Apply **Align Right**.

- Select cell ranges **C13:K13**, **C19:K19**, **C26:K26**, and **C30:K30**. Add a **Top and Bottom Border** to the selected cell ranges.

- Select cell range **C31:K31**, and then add a **Bottom Double Border** to the selected range.

j. Select cell range **C7:F31**. Format the selected range as **Number** with a comma separator and **zero** decimal places. Select cell range **G7:J31**, and then format the selected range as **Number** with a comma separator and **two** decimal places.

k. Copy cell **K12**, and then from **Paste Options**, paste **Formulas** into cells **K13**, **K19**, **K26**, **K30**, and **K31**. Select cell range **K7:K31**. Format the selected range as **Percentage** with two decimal places. If any cells contain a series of number signs (#), select the cells, and then apply **AutoFit Column Width**.

l. Select cells **H13**, **J13**, **H19**, **J19**, **H26**, **J26**, **H30**, **J30**, **H31**, and **J31**. Format the selected cells as **Currency**. If any cells contain a series of number signs (#), select the cells, and then apply **AutoFit Column Width**.

m. Select cell range **F7:F12**. Use **conditional formatting** to highlight the beer with the highest number of units sold for the week as **Green Fill with Dark Green Text**. Use **Top 10 Items** in Top/Bottom Rules, and then change the number of ranked items to 1.

n. Copy cell **F12**. Select cell range **J7:J12**. Right-click the selected cell range, and then under **Paste Options**, click **Paste Formatting**. Continue pasting conditional formatting as follows:

- Select cell range **F15:F18**, right-click the selection, and then click **Paste Formatting**.

- Select cell range **J15:J18**, right-click the selection, and then click **Paste Formatting**.

- Select cell range **F21:F25**, right-click the selection, and then click **Paste Formatting**.

- Select cell range **J21:J25**, right-click the selection and then click **Paste Formatting**.

- Select cell range **F28:F29**, right-click the selection and then click **Paste Formatting**.

- Select cell range **J28:J29**, right-click the selection and then click **Paste Formatting**.

o. Select cell range **J7:J12**, press Ctrl, and then select cell ranges **J15:J18**, **J21:J25**, and **J28:J29**. Click **Increase Decimal** two times.

p. Select cell range **A6:K6**, press Ctrl, and then click cells **A14**, **A20**, and **A27**. Click **Cell Styles** and then, in the Themed Cell Styles group, apply **Accent6** to the selected cells. With the cells still selected, press Ctrl, and then select cell ranges **B13:K13**, **B19:K19**, **B26:K26**, and **B30:K31**. Click **Bold**.

q. Delete row **4**.

r. Press Ctrl + Home. Click the **Insert** tab, and then in the Illustrations group, click **Pictures**. Navigate to the location of your student data files, and then click **e01mpIndigo5**. Click **Insert**. Under **Picture Tools**, on the **Format** tab, in the Arrange group, click **Align**, and then click **Snap to Grid**. Drag the square resizing handle on the right side of the logo left until the right border is between columns **B** and **C**. Drag the square resizing handle on the bottom of the logo and up until the bottom border is between rows **4** and **5**.

s. Click the **Page Layout** tab, in the Themes group, click **Themes**, and then click **Organic** to change the workbook theme. Click the **Home** tab, and then in the Cells group, click the **Format** button and select **AutoFit Column Width** to columns A:K. Click the **Page Layout** tab, and in the Page Setup group, click the **Orientation** arrow. Select **Landscape**. In the Scale to Fit group, change the Width to **1 page**, and then press Ctrl + Home.

t. Click the **Documentation** worksheet tab, click cell **A8**. Press Ctrl +; (semicolon), press Ctrl + Enter, and then press Tab. In cell **B8**, type your name in the Firstname Lastname format, and then press Tab. In cell **C8**, type Formatted BeverageSales worksheet, and then press Enter. Press Ctrl + Home.

u. Click the **Insert** tab, in the Text group, click Header & Footer. In the Navigation group, click **Go to Footer**, and then insert the **file name** in the left footer of all worksheets.

v. Check the spelling on both worksheets.

w. Click the **BeverageSales** worksheet tab.

x. Click the **File** tab, click **Export**, and then under Create a PDF/XPS Document, click **Create PDF/XPS**. Be sure Open file after publishing is not checked. Click **Options**. In the Options dialog box, under Publish what, click **Entire workbook**, and then click **OK**. Navigate to the folder where you are saving your files. In the File name box, verify e01mpBeverageSales_LastFirst is the file name, and then click **Publish**.

y. Save the workbook, exit Excel, and then submit your files as directed by your instructor.

Problem Solve 1

Homework

Student data file needed:

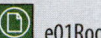 e01RoomService.xlsx

You will save your file as:

 e01RoomService_LastFirst.xlsx

Room Service Analysis

Accounting & Finance

The Painted Paradise Resort & Spa offers an extensive array of food and drinks available for delivery to guests' rooms. For the convenience of in-room delivery, guests pay a premium price for the service. Recently, the resort has asked representatives from both the hotel and the restaurant to start tracking the charges by room type and day of the week. From this information, management hopes to determine which types of guests are ordering room service.

a. Open the Excel file, **e01RoomService**. Save your file as e01RoomService_LastFirst, using your last and first name.

b. Click the **RoomServiceAnalysis** worksheet tab, and then apply the formatting as follows:

- Select cell range **A2:H2**, and then apply Merge & Center.

- Select cell **A2**, and then apply the **Heading 2** cell style.

- Select cell range **B7:H23**, and then apply the **Comma Style** (,) number style.

- Select cell range **B22:H22**, and then set the number of decimals to **0**.

- Format cell ranges **A4:A23** and **B6:H6** as cell style **Heading 4** and **Align Right**. Select cell ranges **A7:A23** and **B6:H6**, and then set the Fill Color to **Green, Accent 6, Lighter 60%**. Click cell **A6**, and then click **Fill Color** to apply the color Green, Accent 6, Lighter 60%.

- Insert a hard return between **Villa** and **Suite** in cell **G6** (remember to remove the space between the two words).

- Set the width of column **A** using **AutoFit Column Width**. Set the width of columns **B:H** to **12**.

c. Increase the height of row 1 to **55**.

d. Select the **picture** in cell A1. Set the picture alignment to **Snap to Grid**. Position the graphic with the right edge between columns **F** and **G** and the left edge between columns **C** and **D**.

e. Calculate the following using **AutoSum** with source cells selected. Use cell range **B7:G13** as the source range for the remainder of this step.

- Add a total in row **14**.

- Average the values in row **15**.

- Calculate the minimum value in row **16**.

- Calculate the maximum value in row **17**.

f. Calculate the total for each row of data in column H in cell ranges **H7:H14** and **H19:H20**, and cell **H22**. Make sure the number of decimal places in cell H22 is set to **0**.

g. Calculate the average individual sales per day for One Double rooms in cell **B23**. Divide the total sales for the week by the number of rooms divided by the number of days in a week (7). Copy the formula to cell range **C23:H23**.

h. Apply the Data Bar conditional formatting to cell range **H7:H13**. Select the **Orange Data Bar** under the Gradient Fill.

i. Apply the Total cell style to cell range **B14:H14**, and then apply Accounting Number Format to cell ranges **B14:H17**, **B19:H20**, and **B23:H23**.

j. Turn off the worksheet **gridlines**. Apply the **Headlines** theme.

k. Insert the file name into the left section of the page footer for both worksheets in the workbook.

l. For both worksheets, set page orientation to **Landscape** orientation, and set scaling to **Fit All Columns on One Page**.

m. Check the spelling of both worksheets.

n. In the **Documentation** worksheet, type today's date in cells **A8**. In cell **B8**, type your name in Firstname Lastname format. In **C8**, type Completed the RoomServiceAnalysis worksheet.

o. Save the workbook, exit Excel, and then submit your file as directed by your instructor.

Critical Thinking After reviewing the completed RoomServiceAnalysis worksheet, which types of guests are ordering room service the most. Identify the top 2 types. Which types of guests are ordering room service the least? Identify the bottom 2 types. What decisions could management make about room service from analysis worksheet?

Problem Solve 2

MyITLab® Grader
Homework

Student data file needed:

 e01AutoBody.xlsx

You will save your files as:

 e01AutoBody_LastFirst.xlsx
e01AutoBody_LastFirst.pdf

Auto Shop Sales Analysis

Accounting & Finance

You are the office manager for Jim's Auto Shop. A new body shop just opened a few blocks away, and your boss, Jim Love, is concerned that sales have declined. He has started a workbook of services offered at the auto shop and included the last six month's sales. He has asked that you complete the workbook by creating formulas to calculate the total sales of each service. Jim also wants you to determine the largest-selling service at the auto shop and to call attention to these services by formatting them appropriately. From this completed workbook, Jim will determine whether he should continue to offer all services or focus on fewer services to stay competitive.

a. Open the Excel file, **e01AutoBody**. Save your file as **e01AutoBody_LastFirst**, using your last and first name.

b. Rename Sheet1 **Sales**. Rename Sheet2 **Documentation**.

c. On the **Sales** worksheet, set the horizontal alignment for A1:H1 and then A2:H2 to **Center Across Selection**.

d. Increase the height of row **1** to **30**. Hide row **3**.

e. Click cell **H4**, and type **Total**. Click in cell **A15**, and type **Total**.

f. Select cell **B4**. Use AutoFill to fill through **G4**. Apply the Angle Counterclockwise orientation to cell range **B4:H4**.

g. In cell range **B15:G15**, use a function to calculate the monthly totals.

h. In cell range **H5:H15**, use a function to calculate the total of each service offered.

i. Select cell range **A4:H4**, and then apply the **Heading 3** style to the cell range. Select cell **A1**, and then apply the **Title** style. Select cell **A2**, and then apply **Heading 4** style.

j. Select cell ranges **B5:H5** and **B15:H15**, and then apply the **Accounting Number Format**.

k. Select cell range **B6:H14**, and then apply the **Comma** style format.

l. Select cell range **B15:H15**, and then apply the **Total** style.

m. Select cell range **B5:H15**, and then decrease the decimals to zero decimal places.

n. In cells **A17**, **A18**, and **A19**, enter the labels **Average**, **Largest**, and **Smallest**, respectively. **Right-align** cell range A17:A19.

o. In **B17**, use a function to determine the average sales for January

p. In **B18**, use a function to determine the largest sale for January.

q. In **B19**, use a function to determine the smallest sale for January.

r. Copy the formulas in cell range B17:B19 to cell range **C17:G19**. If necessary, decrease the decimals to zero decimal places.

s. Select cell range **H5:H14**. Apply the **Gradient Fill Light Blue Data Bar** to the range of cells.

t. Select cell range **B5:G14**, and apply a conditional format to highlight any sales less than $1,000 with **Light Red Fill**.

u. Hide the **Gridlines** of the **Sales** worksheet.

v. Click the **Documentation** worksheet. In cell **A8**, type today's date. In cell **B8**, type your name in the Firstname Lastname format. In cell **C8**, type Calculated totals for the services and products for the past six months. **Wrap the text** of cell **C8**. Type Sales in cell **B20**.

w. Enter the file name in the left footer of both worksheets. Check the spelling of both worksheets.

x. Change the scaling of the **Sales** worksheet to **Fit all Columns on One Page**. Change both worksheets to **Landscape** orientation.

y. Show the formulas of the Sales worksheet, and then export the worksheet to **PDF**. Do not open the file after publishing. Save the PDF as **e01AutoBody_LastFirst** using your last and first name. Remove the formulas view from the Sales worksheet.

z. Save the workbook, exit Excel, and then submit your files as directed by your instructor.

Perform 1: Perform in Your Life

Student data file needed:
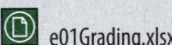 e01Grading.xlsx

You will save your file as:
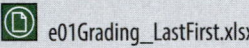 e01Grading_LastFirst.xlsx

Grade Analysis

Information Technology

Most students are concerned about grades and want to have some means of easily tracking grades, analyzing their performance, and calculating their current grade (as much as is possible) in every class. You will create a grade analysis workbook to assist you with tracking, calculating, and analyzing your performance in your classes.

a. Open the Excel file, **e01Grading**. Save your file as e01Grading_LastFirst, using your last and first name. Rename Sheet1 with a name appropriate for this exercise.

b. A grading scale of 90-80-70-60 was entered into the worksheet. If necessary, adjust the grading scale as desired. Classes and class assignments have been entered into the workbook. Adjust to your classes and class assignments as desired.

c. Include the following calculations,

- Using a function, calculate the total possible points for each class.
- Using a function, calculate your total score for each class.
- Using a formula, calculate the percentage earned on each assignment for each class.
- Using a formula, calculate the total percentage earned in each class.

d. In cell E46, using a formula, calculate the average total percent earned in all classes.

e. In cell E47, using a formula, calculate the lowest total percent earn in all classes.

f. You are striving for an A in each course. Apply conditional formatting to the total percentage earned in each course based on the grading scale. For example, when 90% or greater is earned, a format is applied. When less than 90% is earned, a different format is applied.

g. Format the worksheet appropriately. Rename and color the worksheet tab containing your grade data.

h. Include a completed and well-structured Documentation worksheet.

i. Insert the file name in the left footer of all worksheets. Check the spelling of both worksheets.

j. Modify any page settings to ensure that each of your worksheets will print on a single page. Specify portrait or landscape orientation as is appropriate to maximize readability.

k. Save the workbook, exit Excel, and then submit your file as directed by your instructor.

Perform 2: Perform in Your Career

Student data file needed:

 Blank Excel workbook

You will save your file as:

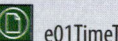 e01TimeTrack_LastFirst.xlsx

Personal Time Tracking

Accounting & Finance

Human Resources

You have started working as a computer programmer with BetaWerks Software Corporation. The company requires you to track the time that you spend doing different things during the day each week. This helps the company to determine how many of your hours are billable to customers. You have several different projects to work on as well as a few training sessions throughout the week. The company pays for one 15-minute coffee break and a one-hour lunch each day. Any additional time is considered personal time.

a. Start Excel, and then open a blank workbook. Save your file as e01TimeTrack_LastFirst, using your last and first name. Rename Sheet1 with a name appropriate to this exercise.

b. Create a worksheet to track your time for the company this week. The following requirements must be met.

- The worksheet should identify the first day of the workweek with a title such as Week of mm/dd/yyyy.

- Your time must be broken down by project/client and weekdays.

- Time not billable to a project should be classified as Unbillable.

- Unbillable time should be broken into at least two categories: Breaks and Work.

c. Set up your worksheet so you can easily calculate the amount of time you spent working on each account, in meetings, in training, and on breaks according to the following information.

- Monday, you spent two hours in a meeting with your development team. You will bill this to the BetaWerks Software company as unbillable hours. After the meeting, you took a 20-minute coffee break. After your break, you spent two hours and 15 minutes working on your project for Garske Advising. After a one-hour lunch, you attended a two-hour training and development meeting. Before heading home for the day, you spent two hours working on the ISBC Distributing project.

- Tuesday morning, you spent four hours on the Klemisch Kompany project. To help break up the morning, you took a 20-minute coffee break at 10:00. You had time for only a 30-minute lunch because you had to get back to the office for a team-building activity. The activity lasted 40 minutes. To finish the day, you spent four hours working on the Garske Advising assignment.

- Wednesday morning, you spent two hours each on the Garske Advising and Klemisch Kompany projects. Lunch was a quick 30 minutes because you had a conference call with Mr. Atkinson from ISBC at 1 p.m. The conference call took one hour, and then you spent an additional three hours working on the ISBC project.

- Thursday, the day started with a 30-minute update with your supervisor. Following the meeting, you were able to spend two hours on the ISBC project. After a 15-minute coffee break, you started on a new project for K&M Worldwide for 90 minutes. You took a 45-minute lunch break and then spent two and a half hours on the Klemisch Kompany project and two hours on your work for L&H United.

- Friday started with a two-hour training and development session about a new software package that BetaWerks is starting to implement, followed by a 15-minute coffee break. After your coffee break, you were able to squeeze in two more hours for L&H United before taking a one-hour lunch. After lunch, you put in four hours on the Klemisch Kompany project before finally going home for the week.

d. BetaWerks bills your time spent on each account according to the following rates.

Klemisch Kompany	$275
Garske Advising	$250
ISBC Distributing	$225
K&M Worldwide	$175
L&H United	$200

e. Your salary is $100,000/year with benefits. Given two weeks of vacation, you cost BetaWerks $2,000 in salary and benefits per week.

f. Include in your worksheet a calculation of your profit/loss to BetaWerks for the week.

g. Be sure to document your worksheet using a separate Documentation worksheet, comments, and instructions.

h. Modify any page settings to ensure that each of your worksheets will print on a single page. Specify portrait or landscape orientation as is appropriate to maximize readability.

i. Insert the file name in the left footer of all worksheets.

j. Save the workbook, exit Excel, and then submit your file as directed by your instructor.

Perform 3: Perform in Your Team

Student data file needed:

 Blank Excel workbook

You will save your file as:

 e01CheckRegister_TeamName.xlsx

Finance & Accounting

Check Register

You volunteer time with a local nonprofit, the Mayville Community Theatre. Because of your business background, the board of directors has asked you to serve as the new treasurer and to track all the monetary transactions for the group.

a. Select one team member to set up the document by completing steps b through e. Then continue with step d.

b. Open your browser, and then navigate to either https://www.onedrive.live.com, https://www.drive.google.com, or any other instructor-assigned location. Be sure all members of the team have an account on the chosen system, such as a Microsoft or Google account.

c. Create a new workbook, and then save it as **e01CheckRegister_TeamName**. Replace Name with the number assigned to your team by your instructor.

d. Rename Sheet1 as **CheckRegister-TeamName**. Replace Name with the number of your team.

e. Share the worksheet with the other members of your team. Make sure that each team member has the appropriate permission to edit the document.

f. Hold a team meeting, and make a plan. Lay out on paper the worksheet you are going to build, discuss the requirements of each of the remaining steps, and then divide the remaining steps (steps g through n) among team members. Note that the steps should be completed in order, so as each team member completes his or her steps, he or she should notify the entire team, not just the team member responsible for the next step.

g. Create the Check Register worksheet to track receipts and expenditures that should be assigned to one of the following categories: **Costumes**, **Marketing**, **Operating and Maintenance**, **Scripts and Royalties**, and **Set Construction**. Also track the following for each receipt or expenditure: the date, amount of payment, check/reference number, recipient, and item description.

h. Enter the following receipts and expenditures under the appropriate category.

Date	Item	Paid To	Check or Ref. #	Amount
11/1/2018	Starting Balance	N/A		$1793.08
11/2/2018	Royalties for "The Cubicle"	Office Publishing Company	9520	−$300.00
11/2/2018	Scripts for "The Cubicle"	Office Publishing Company	9521	−$200.00
11/5/2018	Building Maintenance — Ticket Office	Fix It Palace	9522	−$187.92
11/8/2018	Patron Donation	N/A	53339	$1,000.00
11/12/2018	Costumes for "The Cubicle"	Jane's Fabrics	9523	−$300.00
11/21/2018	Building Materials for set construction of "The Cubicle"	Fix It Palace	9524	−$430.00
11/30/2018	TV and Radio ads for "The Cubicle"	AdSpace	9525	−$229.18
11/30/2018	General Theater Operating Expenses — November	The Electric Co-op, City Water Works	9526	−$149.98
12/15/2018	Ticket Revenue from "The Cubicle"	N/A	59431	$1,115.50
12/31/2018	General Theater Operating Expenses — December	The Electric Co-op, City Water Works	9527	−$195.13

i. Money is deposited periodically into the checking account. Include a column to track deposits.

j. Finally, include a column to track the running balance. This should be updated any time money is deposited into or withdrawn from the account.

k. If the running account balance drops below $1,000, there should be a conditional formatting alert for any balance figure below the threshold.

l. Document the check register using a separate Documentation worksheet and comments where helpful.

m. Modify any page settings to ensure that each of your worksheets will print on a single page. Specify portrait or landscape orientation as is appropriate to maximize readability.

n. Insert the file name in the left footer on all worksheets in the workbook. Include a list of the names of the students in your team in the right section of the footer.

o. Save the workbook, exit Excel, and then submit your file as directed by your instructor.

Perform 4: How Others Perform

Student data file needed:

 e01ProjectBilling.xlsx

You will save your file as:

 e01ProjectBilling_LastFirst.xlsx

Project Management Billing

Finance & Accounting

John Smith works with you at the Excellent Consulting Company. Each week, consultants are required to track how much time they spend on each project. A worksheet is used to track the date, start time, end time, project code, description of work performed, and number of billable hours completed. At the bottom of the worksheet, the hours spent on each project are summarized so clients can be billed. In your role as an internal auditor, you have been asked to double-check a tracking sheet each week. By random selection, you need to check Mr. Smith's tracking worksheet this week. Make sure his numbers are accurate, and ensure that his worksheet is set up to minimize errors. His worksheet is also in need of formatting for appearance and clarity.

a. Open the Excel file, **e01ProjectBilling**. Save your file as e01ProjectBilling_LastFirst, using your last and first name.

b. Check all calculated figures for accuracy. If you subtract Start Time from End Time and multiply the difference by 24, the result is the number of hours between the two times.

c. Calculate the totals for the items in column J.

d. Examine client totals, and then correct any problems with formulas.

e. Apply formatting, such as cell styles, bold, and a theme, to improve the appearance of the worksheet.

f. Apply any data formatting that will make the data easier to interpret.

g. Add workbook documentation as directed by your instructor.

h. Insert the file name in the left footer on all worksheets in the workbook.

i. Modify any page settings to ensure that each of the worksheets will print on a single page. Specify portrait or landscape orientation as is appropriate to maximize readability.

j. Save the workbook, exit Excel, and then submit your file as directed by your instructor.

Excel Business Unit **2**

Conducting **Business Analysis**

Businesses often have to manage large amounts of data on a daily basis. This can be a difficult feat for any business employee. However, Excel can help you organize large amounts of data, making that data easier to manage, update, and analyze. You can also use Excel to report or present information to internal and external customers, company stakeholders, or your supervisor. This business unit will introduce you to the importance of using Excel for business analysis.

Learning Outcome 1

Use Excel to create formulas and functions to perform calculations, analyze data, solve problems, and help in making wise business decisions.

REAL WORLD SUCCESS

"The skills I have learned through Excel have become incredibly valuable in my everyday life. I recently worked at a private golf course and was asked to create an inventory workbook to track beverage cart sales. This would allow the golf course to forecast demand and predict the amount of starting inventory we needed to maintain. In addition, we needed to use functions that would be user-friendly for the beverage cart employees. At the end of the day, the beverage cart employees would count to see how many items from the set amount of inventory were missing, input the numbers into the Excel workbook. Then Excel would compute the amount of sales the beverage cart employee would need to turn in. The remaining amount would equal the tips the employee had earned. The use of Excel functions helped the golf course to track not only its inventory but also its profits."

- Miri, alumnus

Learning Outcome 2

Use Excel to create a variety of detailed charts appropriate to the data that will visually represent and analyze the data.

REAL WORLD SUCCESS

"In my internship, I used a combo chart to analyze inventory trends over time, presenting inventory buildup or shrinkage on one axis and production levels on another. I was able to use this visual representation to better understand supply chain coordination throughout a quarter, providing my superiors with data to improve our operating efficiency. By combining these charts with charts presenting demand variance, our company was able to pinpoint sources of inventory buildup and higher operating costs."

- Steven, alumnus

Microsoft Excel 2016

CELL REFERENCES, NAMED RANGES, AND FUNCTIONS

MyITLab® Grader Homework

Sales & Marketing

Finance and Accounting

OBJECTIVES

1. Understand the types of cell references   p. 165

2. Create named ranges   p. 173

3. Create and structure functions   p. 178

4. Use and understand math and statistical functions   p. 180

5. Use and understand date and time functions   p. 185

6. Use and understand text functions   p. 188

7. Use financial and lookup functions   p. 193

8. Use logical functions and troubleshoot functions   p. 197

Prepare Case

Painted Paradise Resort & Spa Wedding Planning

Clint Keller and Addison Ryan have just booked a wedding at Painted Paradise Resort & Spa. When requested by a happy couple, the Turquoise Oasis Spa coordinates a variety of events including spa visits, golf massages, and gift baskets made up of various spa products. Given the frequency of wedding events at the Turquoise Oasis Spa, Meda Rodate has asked for your assistance in modifying an Excel workbook that can be used and reused to plan these events in the future.

Goran Bogicevic/Shutterstock

Student data file needed for this chapter:

e02ch03Wedding.xlsx

You will save your file as:

e02ch03Wedding_LastFirst.xlsx

Referencing Cells and Named Ranges

The value of Excel expands as you move from using the spreadsheet for displaying data to analyzing data in order to make informed decisions. As the complexity of a spreadsheet increases, techniques that promote effective and efficient development of the spreadsheet become of utmost importance. Integrating cell references within formulas and working with functions are common methods used in developing effective spreadsheets. These skills will become the foundation for more advanced skills.

A **cell reference** refers to a particular cell or range of cells within a formula or function instead of a value. A cell reference contains two parts: a column reference, which is the alphabetic portion that comes first, and a row reference, which is the numeric portion that comes last. For example, cell reference B4 refers to the intersection of column B and row 4. When a formula is created, you can simply use values, such as =5*5. However, writing a formula without cell references is limiting. Formulas with cell references are substantially more powerful. For example, the formula =B4*C4, where cells B4 and C4 contain values to be used in the calculation, allows the formula to reference a cell (or cell range) rather than a value (or values). This means that when data changes in an individual cell, any formulas that reference the cell are automatically recalculated.

A **named range** is a group of cells that have been given a name. The name can then be used within a formula or function. In this section, you will use cell referencing and named ranges to build a worksheet model for planning events at the Turquoise Oasis Spa.

Understand the Types of Cell References

There are three types of cell referencing: relative, absolute, and mixed. A **relative cell reference** is a cell reference that changes automatically when the formula or function is copied to another location. The change in the cell reference will reflect the number of rows and/or columns from which the cell was copied relative to its original location. Relative cell references are the default in Excel. An **absolute cell reference** is the exact address of a cell when both the column and the row need to remain constant regardless of the position of the cell when the formula is copied to other cells. When an absolute cell reference is used, a cell reference does not change if a formula or function is copied to another location. An absolute cell reference is specified by placing a dollar sign ($) in front of both the column letter(s) and the row number(s). For example, to make B4 an absolute reference, you would specify $B$4. A **mixed cell reference** is a combination of relative and absolute cell references. In a mixed cell reference, the column or row portion of the reference is absolute, and the corresponding row or column is relative. For example, $B4 is a mixed reference in which the column is absolute and the row is relative. B$4 is a mixed reference in which the column is relative and the row is absolute. In essence, the dollar sign ($) sign locks down the letter or number it precedes so the letter or number will not change when copied.

QUICK REFERENCE	Types of Cell Referencing

Below are examples of the types of cell referencing for cell A5.

1. Relative cell referencing: =A5+B5
2. Absolute cell referencing: =$A$5+B5
3. Mixed cell referencing: =$A5+B5
4. Mixed cell referencing: =A$5+B5

Cell referencing is a useful feature when formulas need to be copied across ranges in a spreadsheet. When you create a spreadsheet and develop a formula that will not be copied elsewhere, absolute cell referencing and mixed cell referencing are not necessary.

However, data arranged in a table may require a formula to perform calculations on each row, or record. Excel allows this process to be completed quickly and easily by using cell referencing. The formula can be constructed once and then quickly copied across a range of cells.

REAL WORLD ADVICE | **Creating Dynamic Workbooks**

The use of cell references in formulas helps to make spreadsheets in Excel extremely powerful. By using a cell reference to refer to a value in a formula, you can make your spreadsheet flexible. In other words, using cell references makes your spreadsheet easier to use and more efficient. If something about your business changes and requires an update to a value in your spreadsheet, you need only make the update in one place.

Opening the Starting File

Meda Rodate would like for the Turquoise Oasis Spa to become more efficient in planning for wedding events. She has asked for your help in designing an Excel workbook to accomplish this goal. You will begin in this exercise by opening the wedding planning workbook and organizing the number and pricing of spa gift baskets by creating common Excel functions using various types of cell referencing.

E03.00

SIDE NOTE
Pin the Ribbon
If your ribbon is collapsed, pin your ribbon open. Click the Home tab. In the lower right corner of the ribbon, click Pin the Ribbon ⊱.

To Open the Wedding Workbook

a. Start **Excel**, click **Open Other Workbooks** in the left pane, and then double-click **This PC**. Navigate through the folder structure to the location of your student data files, and then double-click **e02ch03Wedding**. If a Security Warning message displays, click the **Enable Editing** button.

b. Click the **File** tab, click **Save As**, and then double-click **This PC**. In the Save As dialog box, navigate to the location where you are saving your project files. Change the file name to **e02ch03Wedding_LastFirst**, using your last and first name. Click **Save**.

c. Click the **Insert** tab, and then, in the Text group, click **Header & Footer**.

Troubleshooting

If you do not see the Text group, look for the Text button and click the Text arrow, which will open the Text group and show the various commands.

---

d. On the Header & Footer Tools Design tab, in the Navigation group, click **Go to Footer**. Click the **left section of the footer**, and then, in the Header & Footer Elements group, click **File Name**.

e. Click any cell on the spreadsheet to move out of the footer, and press Ctrl+Home to return to cell A1.

f. Click the **View** tab, and in the Workbook Views group, click **Normal**, and then click the **Home** tab. Click **Save** 🖫.

Using Relative Cell Referencing

Relative cell referencing (as shown in Figure 1) is the default reference type in constructing formulas in Excel. Remember that relative cell referencing changes the cell references in a formula if it is copied or otherwise moved to another location. This includes the use of copy and paste or the AutoFill feature to copy a formula to another location. If a formula is copied to the right or left, the column references will change in the formula. If a formula is copied up or down, the row references will change in the formula.

Relative cell referencing is useful in situations in which the same calculation is needed in multiple cells but the location of the data needed for the calculation changes relative to the position of the calculation cell. The GiftBaskets worksheet of the Wedding workbook contains a list of individual items that are included in the different types of gift baskets offered at the Turquoise Oasis Spa. The worksheet contains the prices for individual items in the baskets, the number of each item in the basket, and the prices of each basket.

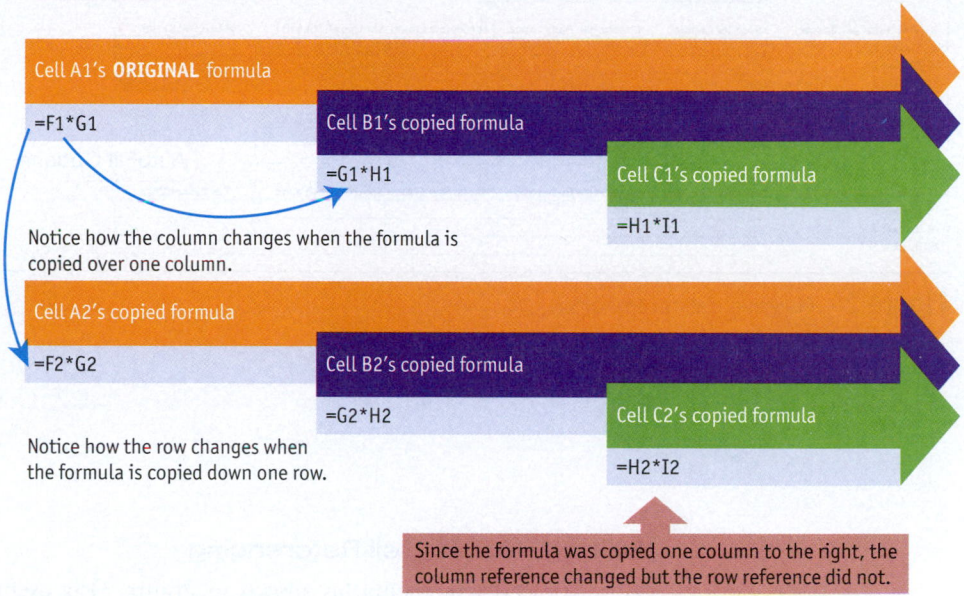

Figure 1 Understanding cell referencing

Excel 2016, Windows 10, Microsoft Corporation.

The Turquoise Oasis Spa allows wedding parties to specify up to three different kinds of custom gift baskets. Each gift basket can contain up to four different items in each basket. The workbook has been set up such that cells with a blue fill need to be changed from one event to another. In this exercise, you will use relative cell referencing to display the total number of items in each type of gift basket.

 **E03.01**

SIDE NOTE
You can also use AutoFill with a formula in a vertical range by selecting the range, pressing Ctrl, and typing D.

SIDE NOTE
Viewing Formulas
You can view your formulas by pressing Ctrl+~.

To Use Relative Cell Referencing

a. Click the **GiftBaskets** worksheet if necessary, and then click cell **F9**.

b. On the Home tab, in the Editing group, click **AutoSum** Σ AutoSum ▾ , and then press Ctrl+Enter.

c. Click the **AutoFill handle** on the bottom right corner of cell **F9**, and then drag down to copy the formula to cell **F11**.

Notice that the formula in cell F11 refers to cells B11:E11. Since the formula was copied down, the row reference changed from 9 to 10 and finally to 11.

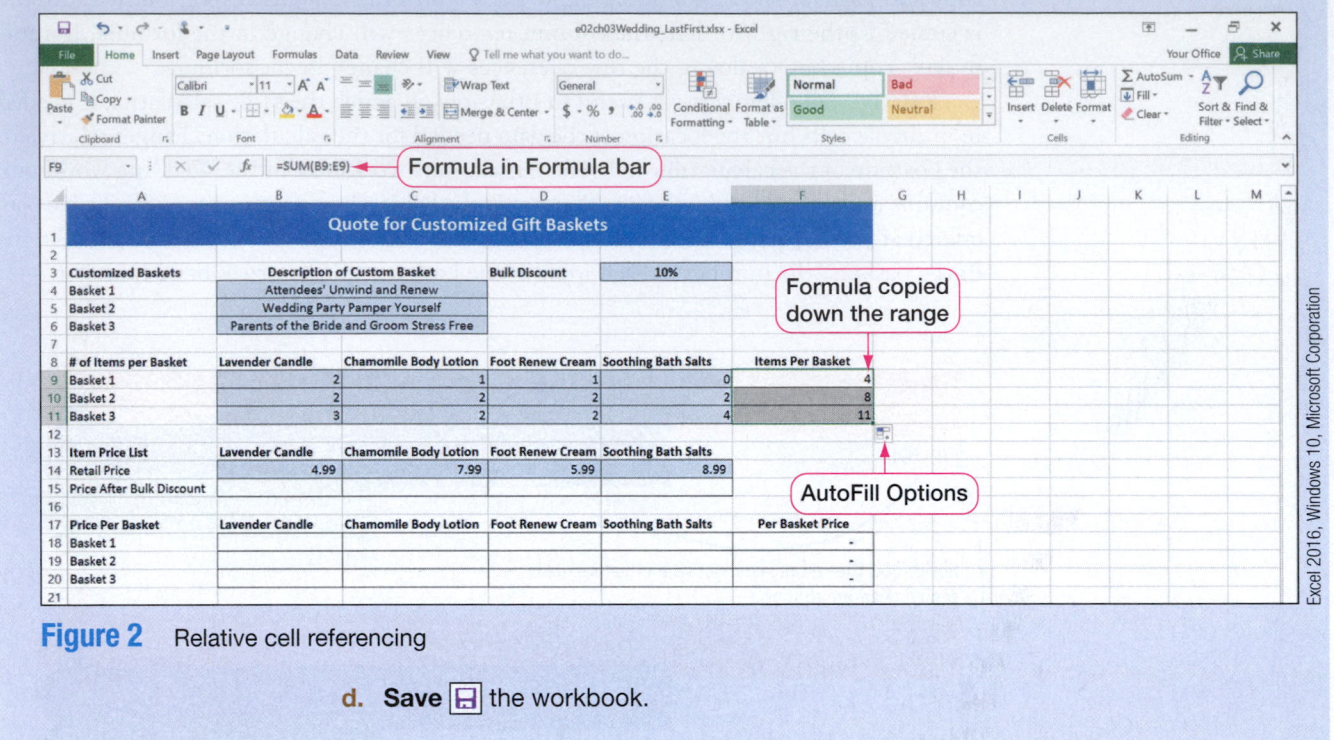

Figure 2 Relative cell referencing

d. **Save** 🖫 the workbook.

Using Absolute Cell Referencing

Absolute cell referencing (as shown in Figure 3) is useful when a formula needs to be copied and the reference to one or more cells within the formula must not change as the formula is copied. Thus, the column and row address of a referenced cell remains constant regardless of the position of the cell when the formula is copied to other cells.

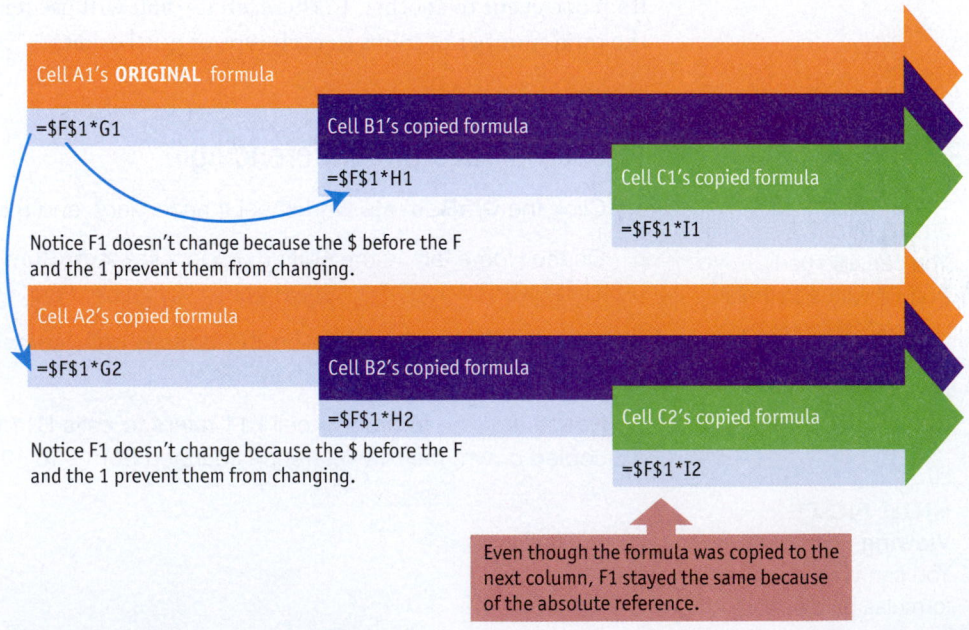

Figure 3 Understanding absolute cell referencing

Excel 2016, Windows 10, Microsoft Corporation

Meda has decided to offer a bulk percentage discount on all gift baskets purchased for this event because of the large number being ordered. In this exercise, you will modify the formulas in cells B15:E15 of the GiftBaskets worksheet using absolute cell referencing to include this discount.

E03.02

SIDE NOTE
Using F4
An alternative to typing the dollar sign is to press F4 after typing or selecting the cell reference.

SIDE NOTE
Alternate Method
You can also use AutoFill with a formula in a horizontal range by selecting the range, pressing Ctrl, and typing R.

To Use Absolute Cell Referencing

a. On the **GiftBaskets** worksheet, click cell **B15**.

b. Type **=B14-(B14*$E$3)**, and then click **Enter** ✓ to the left of the Insert Function button fx.

c. Click the **AutoFill handle** on cell **B15**, and then drag to the right to copy the formula to cell **E15**.

Notice that the formula in cell E15 refers to cell E3. The dollar signs in front of the column letter and row number force Excel to keep the same cell reference as the formula is copied.

Also, notice that the dollar sign before row 3 is not required, since the formula was not copied to a different row. However, no matter where this formula is copied to on the worksheet, the calculation should always use cell E3. Thus, common practice is to put a dollar signs before the column and row, making the cell reference absolute.

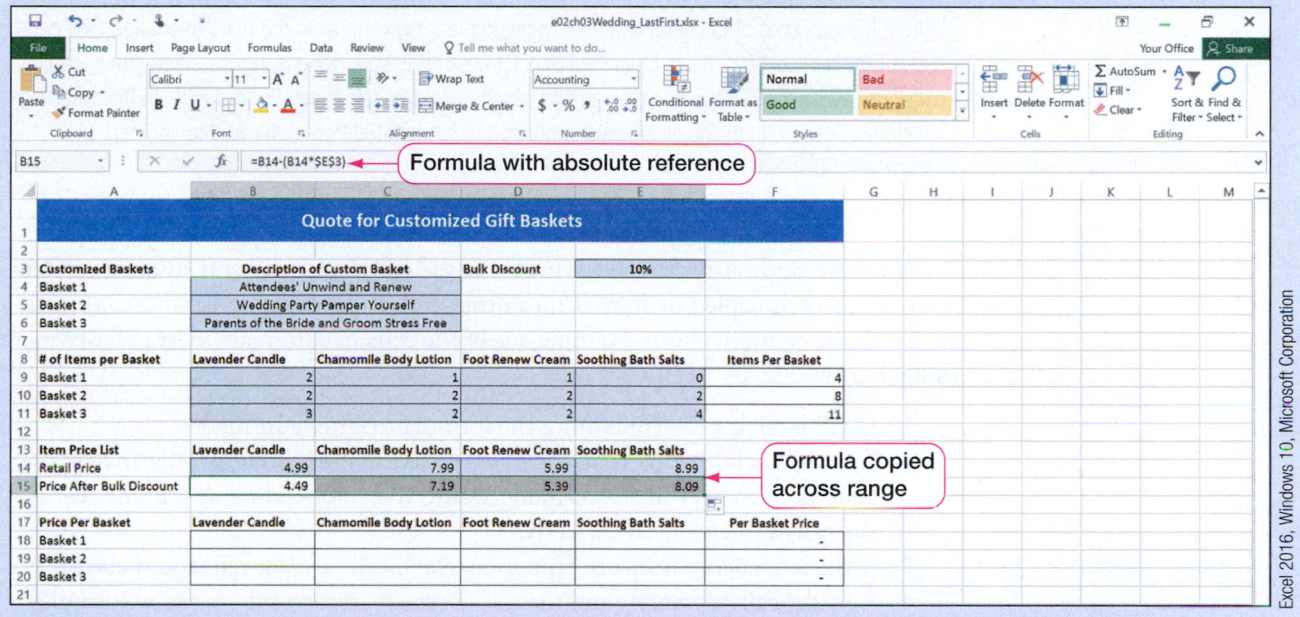

Figure 4 Absolute cell referencing

d. **Save** 🖫 the workbook.

Using Mixed Cell Referencing

Mixed cell references can be very useful in the development of spreadsheets. Mixed cell references refer to referencing a cell within the formula where part of the cell address is preceded by a dollar sign to lock — either the column letter or the row value — as absolute reference. This will leave the other part of the cell as relatively referenced when the formula is copied to new cells. Figure 5 shows a representation of how mixed cell referencing works.

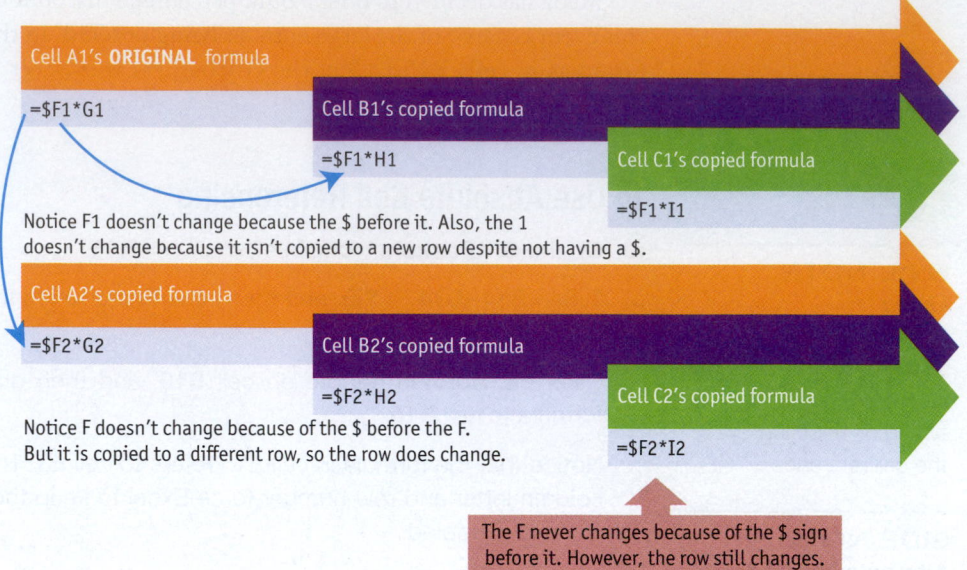

Cell A1's **ORIGINAL** formula

=$F1*G1

Cell B1's copied formula

=$F1*H1

Cell C1's copied formula

=$F1*I1

Notice F1 doesn't change because the $ before it. Also, the 1 doesn't change because it isn't copied to a new row despite not having a $.

Cell A2's copied formula

=$F2*G2

Cell B2's copied formula

=$F2*H2

Cell C2's copied formula

=$F2*I2

Notice F doesn't change because of the $ before the F. But it is copied to a different row, so the row does change.

The F never changes because of the $ sign before it. However, the row still changes.

Figure 5   Understanding mixed cell referencing   Excel 2016, Windows 10, Microsoft Corporation

---

REAL WORLD ADVICE   **Layout of a Spreadsheet Model**

Think of a spreadsheet model as an interactive report. Some of the data is static and may not change often, if ever. Some of the data, as in the wedding planning workbook, will need to change with each use of the spreadsheet. It can be helpful to color code cells so anyone using the spreadsheet can easily see which cells require a change and which should be left alone. For example, in the Wedding workbook, cells with a blue fill are cells that need to be updated from one event to another.

If you need to verify that the formula has the correct relative and absolute referencing after it has been copied or moved into other cells within the spreadsheet, a quick and easy verification method is to examine one of the cells in edit mode. Best practice dictates following these steps.

1. Double-click a cell containing the formula to enter edit mode.
2. In edit mode, notice that the color-coded borders around cells match the cell address references in the formula. Using the color-coding as a guide, verify that the cells are referenced correctly.
3. If the referencing is incorrect, notice which cells are not referenced correctly.
4. Edit the cell references, and then, if necessary, recopy the corrected formula.
5. Always recheck the formula again to see whether your correction worked when it was copied into other cells or cell ranges.

To exit out of edit mode, press Esc to return to the original formula. Another way of entering edit mode is to press the A key.

Repeat this process as needed. Instead of typing the dollar signs within your cell references, F4 can be used to change the type of cell referencing. If the insertion point is placed within a cell reference in your formula, press F4 one time, and Excel will insert dollar signs in front of both the row reference and the column reference. If you press F4 again, Excel places a dollar sign in front of the row number only. If you press F4 a third time, Excel places a dollar sign in front of the column reference and removes the dollar sign from the row reference. Pressing F4 a fourth time returns the cell to a relative reference.

F4 can be used to change the type of cell referencing.

1. Press F4 one time to place a dollar sign in front of both the column and row values (absolute reference).

2. Press F4 a second time to place a dollar sign in front of the row value only (mixed reference).

3. Press F4 a third time to place a dollar sign in front of the column value only (mixed reference).

4. Press F4 a fourth time to remove all dollar sign characters (relative reference).

Meda has asked you to update the range B18:E20 to include formulas that calculate the price of individual items included in each basket type. In this exercise, you will do so, using mixed cell referencing.

E03.03

SIDE NOTE

Alternate Method

You can click the Enter button ✔ to the left of the Insert Function button f_x on the Formula Bar for the same result as Ctrl+Enter.

To Use Mixed Cell Referencing

a. On the **GiftBaskets** worksheet, click cell **B18**.

b. Type =B9*B$15, and then press Ctrl+Enter.

c. Click the **AutoFill handle** on cell **B18**, and then drag down to copy the formula to cell **B20**.

   Notice that the formula in cell B20 still refers to cell B15. The dollar sign in front of the row heading forces Excel to use row 15 as the referenced row no matter where the formula is copied to. However, the column will change as the formula is copied to the left or right in the worksheet.

d. With range **B18:B20** still selected, click the **AutoFill handle** on cell B20, and then drag to the right to copy the formulas to the range **E18:E20**. Notice that as the formulas are copied, column B changes, while the row reference to row 15 remains unchanged as the formula is copied to the range.

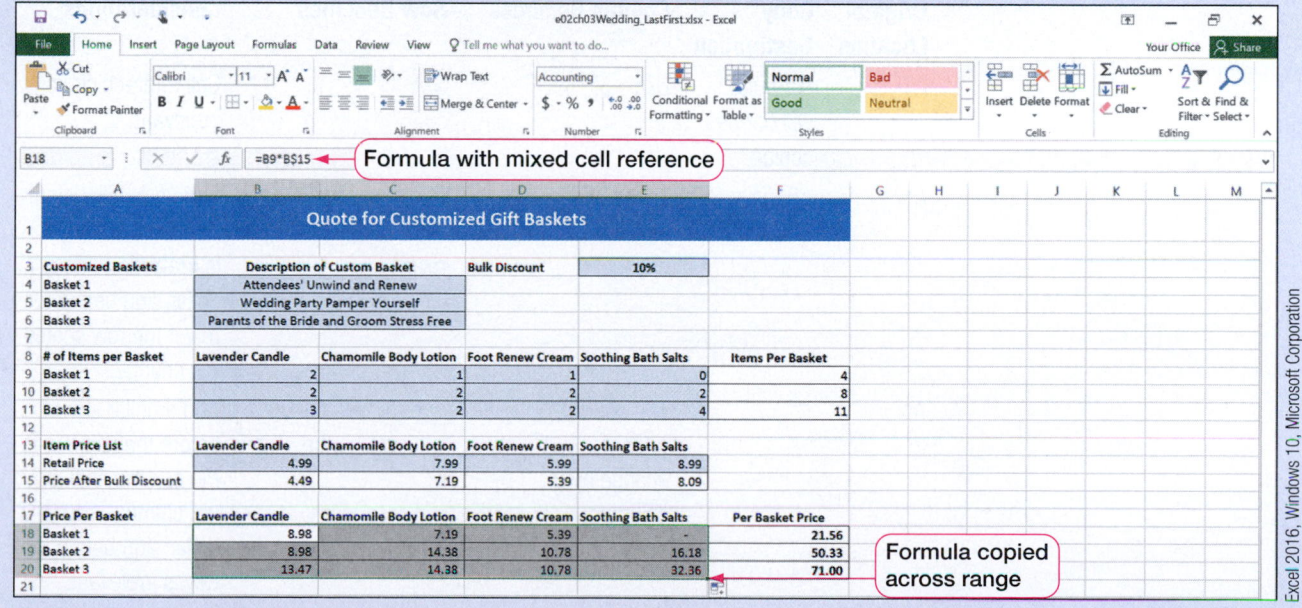

Figure 6 Mixed cell referencing

e. Click cell **E14**, type **11.99**, and then press ⏎.

Notice that the values in cells E19:E20 have been updated. For reference, E20 previously displayed 32.36; now it displays 43.16.

f. **Save** 🖫 the workbook.

SS CONSIDER THIS | **Cell Referencing**

In cell B18 of the GiftBaskets worksheet, the formula uses mixed cell referencing by referring to cell B$15. Would there have been a different result if absolute referencing ($B$15) had been used? Would there have been a different result if relative referencing (B15) had been used? Why would these options be incorrect?

REAL WORLD ADVICE | **Building for Scalability**

When you develop a spreadsheet, you should consider the potential for the model to expand. A good spreadsheet model allows the user to add more data as needed. Instead of assuming that current conditions will never change, your spreadsheet should be built to accommodate growth. While developing the model, you may consider using hypothetical data so you can see how the model will look when it has real data.

QUICK REFERENCE | **Understanding Referencing Based on Copy Destination**

Cell references in a formula can change when copied. To understand where to put a dollar sign, you must understand how the cell references will change when copied. Excel determines what to change by the original location and the copy destination. Remember that the dollar sign locks down the letter (column) or number (row) it precedes so it will not change.

Original Location	Copy Destination	Column Becomes	Row Becomes	Considerations
A1	Formula will not be copied.	N/A	N/A	Cell referencing is irrelevant.
A1	A5	The column reference will not change.	The row reference will change by 4 rows.	Adding a dollar sign before the column is irrelevant. Add a dollar sign before the row if the row should not change.
A1	C1	The column reference will change by 2 columns.	The row reference will not change.	Add a dollar sign before the column if the column should not change. Adding a dollar sign before the row is irrelevant.

(Continued)

QUICK REFERENCE	Understanding Referencing Based on Copy Destination (Continued)			
Original Location	Copy Destination	Column Becomes	Row Becomes	Considerations
A1	C5	The column reference will change by 2 columns.	The row reference will change by 4 rows.	Since both the column and row references will change, add a dollar sign before any references that should not change.

Create Named Ranges

Once you are comfortable working with formulas and cells, there is a natural progression to using named ranges and functions. As has been mentioned, a named range is a group of cells that have been given a name that can then be used within a formula or function. Named ranges are an extension of cell references and provide a quick alternative for commonly used cell references or ranges.

Spreadsheet formulas that use cell references, such as =C5*C6, may be easy to interpret when they are simple. However, as the size and complexity of the workbook increase, so do the difficulty and time needed to incorporate cell references in formulas. This is especially the case with workbooks that use multiple worksheets. The use of named ranges enables a developer to quickly develop formulas that make sense. It also increases the readability of formulas to other individuals who are using the same workbook. For example, the formula =SUM(BasketSubtotals) is much easier to interpret than =SUM(C23:C25). Also, named ranges create absolute referencing when used in a formula. You can quickly understand the formula if it is written with assigned names you designate.

Creating Named Ranges Using the Name Box

Named ranges are easy to create as you develop a spreadsheet. A named range can be either a single cell or a group of cells. Most named ranges are groups of cells used within multiple formulas. A simple way to name a range is to select the range and use the Name Box to create the name. This allows for a custom name to be given to the range. In naming ranges, a descriptive name should be used for the range being named. Named ranges do have some restrictions on the types of characters that can be used. Named ranges cannot start with a number and cannot contain spaces, and the name cannot resemble a cell reference.

QUICK REFERENCE	Conventions for Naming Ranges

Below is a list of conditions that must be meet when creating named ranges.

1. Names for ranges must start with a letter, an underscore (_), or a backslash (\ ).
2. Create names that provide specific meaning to the range being named.
3. Spaces cannot be used in creating a named range. Instead, use an underscore or a hyphen character, or capitalize the first letter of each word (e.g., HairStyles).
4. Do not use combinations of letters and numbers that resemble cell references.

In this exercise, you will create a named range using the Name box. This named range can then be used in future calculations as an absolute cell reference.

 **E03.04**

To Create a Named Range Using the Name Box

a. On the **GiftBaskets** worksheet, select the range **C23:C25**.

b. Click in the **Name Box** to select the existing text. Type BasketSubtotals, and then press Enter to create a new named range. Notice that when the range C23:C25 is selected, the text BasketSubtotals is displayed in the Name box.

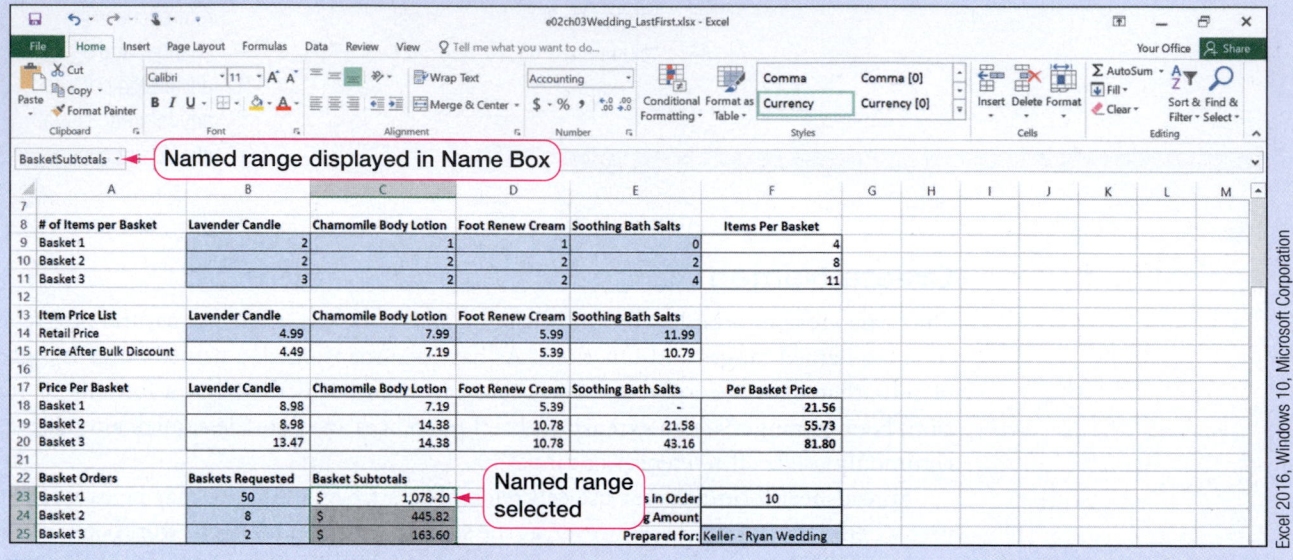

Figure 7 Name range applied to C23:C25

SIDE NOTE

Selecting a Range

Click the Name Box arrow to display a list of all named ranges in a workbook. Click any named range in the Name Box to select that range in a worksheet.

Troubleshooting

If you click outside of the Name Box before pressing Enter, the named range will not be created.

c. **Save** 💾 the workbook.

Modifying Named Ranges

If a named range has been created incorrectly, it can be redefined by selecting the correct data and naming the range again. Alternatively, the Name Manager can be used to modify an existing range or to view a list of already defined ranges. The **Name Manager** can be used to create, edit, delete, or troubleshoot named ranges in a workbook.

Currently, the range BasketsRequested includes only gift basket options 2 and 3. In this exercise, you will modify the named range that was previously created in the workbook to include all basket options.

174   CHAPTER 3 | Microsoft Excel 2016

 **E03.05**

To Modify a Named Range

a. On the **GiftBaskets** worksheet, click the Name box arrow, and then click **BasketsRequested**.

Notice that the range selected is B24:B26. This is the incorrect range. The correct range is B23:B25.

b. Click the **Formulas** tab, and then, in the Defined Names group, click **Name Manager**.

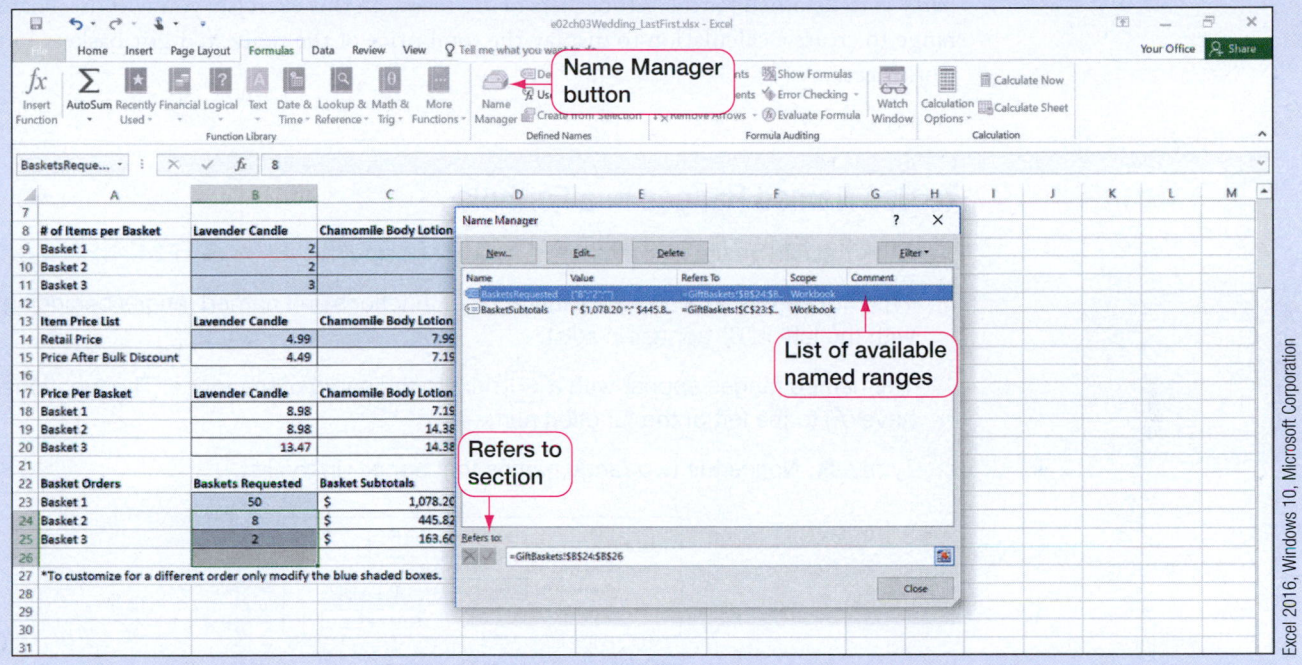

Figure 8 Name Manager dialog box

c. From the displayed list of names, click **BasketsRequested**, and then, in the Refers to section in the box, select the text **GiftBaskets!$B$24:$B$26**.

d. Type **$B$23:$B$25**, click **Close**, and then click **Yes** to accept the changes to the named range.

e. Click the Name box arrow, and then click **BasketsRequested**. Notice that the correct range, B23:B25, is now selected.

f. **Save** the workbook.

Using Named Ranges

Using named ranges in place of cell references is a simple process. Instead of typing in the cells that you want to use in a formula, you can type the range name you have created. Excel will begin to recognize the name you are typing and offer to automatically complete the name for you. Another method of using named ranges is to use the Paste Name feature in Excel. While typing a formula, you can press F3 to view a list of named ranges in the workbook and then insert it into the formula you are constructing. A third way of using named ranges is the Use in Formula button in the Defined Names group of the Formulas tab. When typing a formula, click the Use in Formula arrow and select an available range name.

Meda has requested that the worksheet display the total amount that the wedding party is to be billed for the gift baskets being made. In this exercise, you will use a named range to create a calculation to display the total price of the requested gift baskets in the worksheet.

 E03.06

To Use Named Ranges in a Formula

a. Click the **GiftBaskets** worksheet if necessary, and then click cell **F24**.

b. Type **=SUM(B**, and then notice that a list of functions and named ranges beginning with the letter "B" appear in a list.

The named ranges appear with a ⊞ next to the name of the range. The functions have ƒx to the left of the function name.

c. Type **ask**. Notice the two range names that appear in the list.

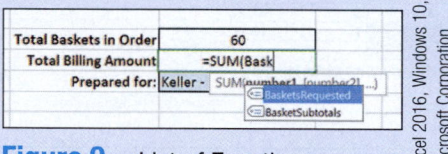

Figure 9   List of Functions

Excel 2016, Windows 10, Microsoft Corporation

d. Press ↓, and then press Tab to select the BasketSubtotals named range. Press Ctrl + Enter to complete the formula.

e. **Save** 🖫 the workbook.

Creating Named Ranges from Selections

At times, your worksheet's data will be organized in such a way that the names for your ranges exist in a cell in the form of a heading for each row or each column in the data set. Rather than selecting each row or column separately, which is a time-consuming process, you can use the Create from Selection method.

The Create from Selection method produces multiple named ranges from the headings in rows, columns, or both from the data set. The key element is to realize that the names for the ranges need to exist in a cell adjacent to the data range. Most commonly, these names are row or column headers that make for very convenient names for each row or column of data.

Meda has asked you to create named ranges for the item subtotals for each type of gift basket. In this exercise, you will create the named ranges. You will then apply them to the formulas in cells F18:F20.

 **E03.07**

To Create Named Ranges and Apply the Names to Formulas

a. On the **GiftBaskets** worksheet, select the range **A18:E20**.

b. On the **Formulas** tab, in the Defined Names group, click **Create from Selection**. The Create Names from Selection dialog box opens.

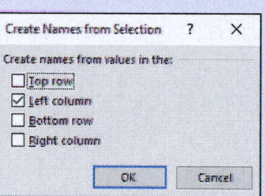

Figure 10 Create Names from Selection dialog box

Excel 2016, Windows 10, Microsoft Corporation

c. Confirm that the **Left column** check box is selected, and then click **OK**.

d. Select the range **B18:E18**.

Notice that the Name box displays the name Basket_1. In creating the named range, Excel replaced all space characters in the name with underscore characters. Ranges B19:E19 and B20:E20 will appear similarly.

e. Select the range **F18:F20**, and then, in the Defined Names group, click the **Define Name** arrow, and then click **Apply Names**. Notice that Excel has detected three potential named ranges that can be substituted into the formulas in the selected range.

Apply Names dialog box

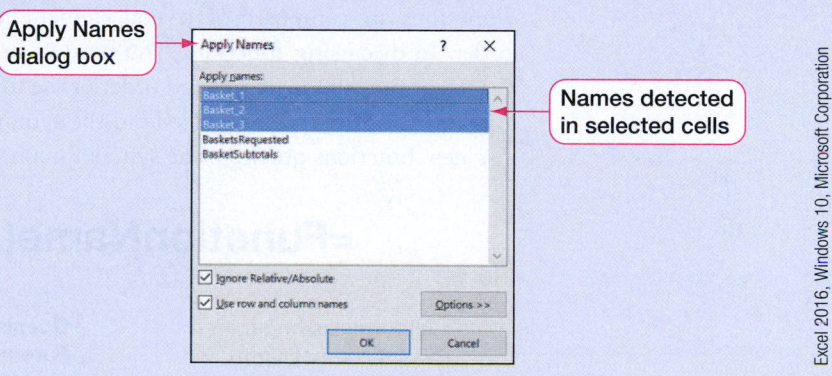

Names detected in selected cells

Figure 11 Apply Names dialog box

Excel 2016, Windows 10, Microsoft Corporation

f. Click **OK**. Notice in the Formula Bar that the formula in cell F18 now reads =SUM(Basket_1).

g. **Save** the workbook. If you need to take a break before finishing this chapter, now is a good time.

Understanding Functions

A **function** is a built-in formula that performs operations against data based on a set of inputs. Excel uses functions to calculate output on the basis of the input provided. Functions can be fairly simple, such as using the SUM function that totals the contents of the cells in a range. Functions can also be more complex. For example, calculating a monthly loan payment is accomplished by providing various arguments: the loan amount, number of payments, and interest rate. An **argument** is a variable or value the function requires to calculate a solution. As long as you have the correct inputs, Excel will perform the calculation for the function. Some functions do not require arguments. In this section, you will use common business functions to continue building the worksheet to be used for planning events at the Turquoise Oasis Spa.

Create and Structure Functions

Functions are composed of several elements and need to be structured in a particular order. In discussing functions, you need to be aware of the syntax of an Excel function. The **syntax** is the structure and order of the function and the arguments needed for Excel to run a function. If you understand the syntax of a function, you can easily learn how to use new functions quickly. The syntax for a function is represented in Figure 12.

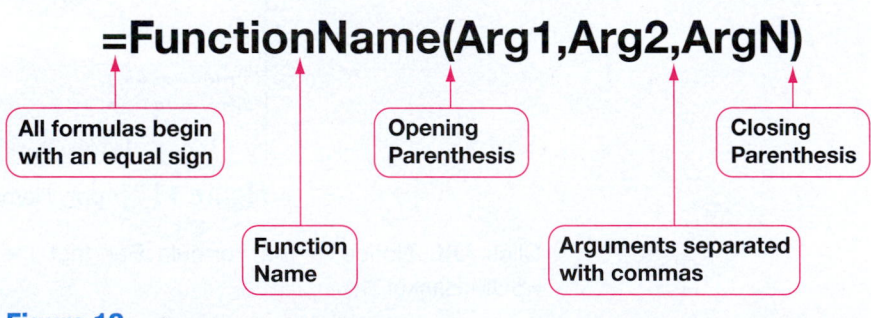

Figure 12   Syntax of a function   Excel 2016, Windows 10, Microsoft Corporation

The FunctionName is any function that is in the Excel library. Examples are SUM, COUNT, and TODAY. With all functions, a pair of parentheses () are required after the FunctionName that may contain arguments associated with the function. Functions such as SUM() have one or more arguments that are required. If the required argument or arguments are not supplied, an error will occur. Some functions, such as TODAY(), do not have any arguments. These functions do not need any inputs to be able to generate output. The TODAY() function uses the clock on the computer to return the current date. Even though no arguments are needed, the () parentheses are always included, which helps Excel understand that a function is being used.

Arguments can be either required or optional. The required arguments always come before any optional arguments. Arguments are separated by commas. Optional arguments are identified by square brackets [] around the argument name. You never type the square brackets into the actual construction of the function; they are used only to inform you that the argument is optional.

For example, the syntax for the SUM function is

=SUM(number1, [number2], . . .)

The first argument is required; the SUM function must have a number, cell, or range to begin the calculation. The second argument — a second cell or range — is optional. Notice that the second argument uses square brackets to identify that it is optional. The periods after the second argument indicate that one or more arguments can be added as needed. The SUM function can hold up to 255 arguments.

Arguments, like variables in a math equation, need to be appropriate values that are suitable for the function. With Excel, the acceptable values can take six common forms, including other functions, as shown in Table 1.

Form of Input	Example	Explanation
Numeric value	5	Type the value
Cell reference	C5	Type the cell or range of cells
Named range	SALES	Type the name of the range
Text string	"Bonus"	Type the text with quotation marks so Excel will recognize it as a text string rather than a named range
Function	SUM(C5:C19)	Type a function using the correct syntax of the function name, pair of parentheses, and any arguments
Formula	(C5+D5)/100	Type the formula using correct mathematical formula structure

Table 1   Function argument formats

Functions are typically categorized for easy access. The primary categories are shown in Table 2. Functions can be found on the Formulas tab under these categorical names. They can also be searched to find the usage and syntax of functions that are unfamiliar.

Category	Description
Compatibility	A set of functions that are compatible with older versions of Excel
Cube	Working with data and filtering, similar to pivot tables
Date & Time	Working with serial date and time values
Engineering	Working with engineering formulas and calculations
Financial	Working with common financial formulas
Information	Providing data about cell content within a worksheet
Logical	Evaluating expressions or conditions as being either true or false
Lookup & Reference	Working with indexing and retrieving information from data sets
Math & Trig	Working with mathematics
Text	Working with text strings
Statistical	Working with common statistical calculations
Web	Working with URL, XML, and web services connections

Table 2   Function categories

Use and Understand Math and Statistical Functions

At the most fundamental level, spreadsheets are used to perform calculations. These calculations may result in loan payments, GPA calculations, profit margins, or even age calculations. Excel has a large array of functions available for simple and complex mathematical functions. There are functions available to sum, count, perform algebra or trigonometry, and create a wide range of statistical calculations.

Using Math and Trig Functions

The math and trigonometry functions are useful for various numerical manipulations. For example, there are several functions that round data in a cell or calculation. The **ABS function** returns the absolute value of the number analyzed by the function. A cell or calculation resulting in the number −4 would be returned as 4 by the ABS function. The **INT function** rounds down any decimal values associated with a number to the nearest whole integer. The **ROUND function** is important when you want to round a number to a specific number of digits. The ROUND function can round values to the left or right of the decimal in a number. For example, using the ROUND function, you could change the number 115.89 to 116 by rounding to the ones place. You could also display 120 by rounding to the integer value to the tens place. While ROUND will round to the nearest digit, ROUNDDOWN and ROUNDUP can be used to force the rounding in a particular direction.

When a function is used to round data, the result of that function is used in future calculations. This is different from formatting a cell to a specific number of decimal places, as formatting does not change the underlying data.

Commonly used math functions are shown in Table 3.

Function	Usage
ABS(number)	Returns the absolute value of a number
INT(number)	Rounds a number down to the nearest integer
RAND( )	Returns a random number from 0 to less than 1
RANDBETWEEN(bottom,top)	Returns a random integer between the numbers you specify
ROUND(number,num_digits)	Rounds a number to a specified number of digits
ROUNDDOWN(number,num_digits)	Rounds a number down to a specified number of digits
ROUNDUP(number,num_digits)	Rounds a number up to a specified number of digits

Table 3   Commonly used math functions

There are two common methods for creating functions: by using the Function Arguments dialog box and by typing the function in the cell. The **Function Arguments** dialog box provides additional information and previews results of the function being constructed. When you are first developing the skills for using functions in Excel, the Function Arguments dialog box can be very valuable. As you gain more experience with functions, you will depend less on the Function Arguments dialog box, particularly when nesting multiple functions together.

Meda has received some historical data on wedding events that she would like to have summarized. In planning new events, referring to this historical data will be helpful. The data contains four items of interest.

1. The number of days spent by wedding parties at the Painted Paradise Resort & Spa. Previously, the value was calculated by using decimal values based on check-in and checkout times. Meda would like this data to be in integers, or whole numbers of days. Since wedding parties receive a late checkout time, these values would need to be rounded down to the nearest whole number.

2. The price of merchandise that was returned after the wedding took place — the price in the column represents the money refunded to customers for the merchandise. The system used at the spa erroneously allowed employees to enter some of this data as either negative or positive values. In the new system, this data must be displayed as positive values.

3. Data displaying the amount spent in total by each wedding party at the Turquoise Oasis Spa. The average of this column has been calculated in the WeddingSummary worksheet cell C2. Currently, the average is formatted to display too many decimal places. However, the actual value of the cell has many more than two decimals. Meda plans to use this average in subsequent calculations. Formatting the cell to two decimals will not change the value of the cell. Thus, the value needs to be rounded to two decimals.

4. Data indicating whether the bridal party from the wedding is a member of the spa. The system used by the spa indicates a 1 for spa members and a null value for nonmembers. When this data was imported into Excel, the result for nonmembers was the text "Null".

In this exercise, you will summarize these data items, using the INT and ABS functions.

 **E03.08**

To Use the INT and ABS Functions

a. If you took a break, open the **e02ch04Wedding** workbook, click the **WeddingSummary** worksheet, and then click cell **C9.**

b. To the left of the formula bar, click **Insert Function** _fx_. Click the **Or select a category** arrow, and then select **Math & Trig**.

c. In the Select a function box, scroll down, click **INT**, and then click **OK**.

d. Type **B9**, and notice that to the right of the dialog box, you see the value currently in cell B9. Under the current value, you will see a preview of the result of the INT function.

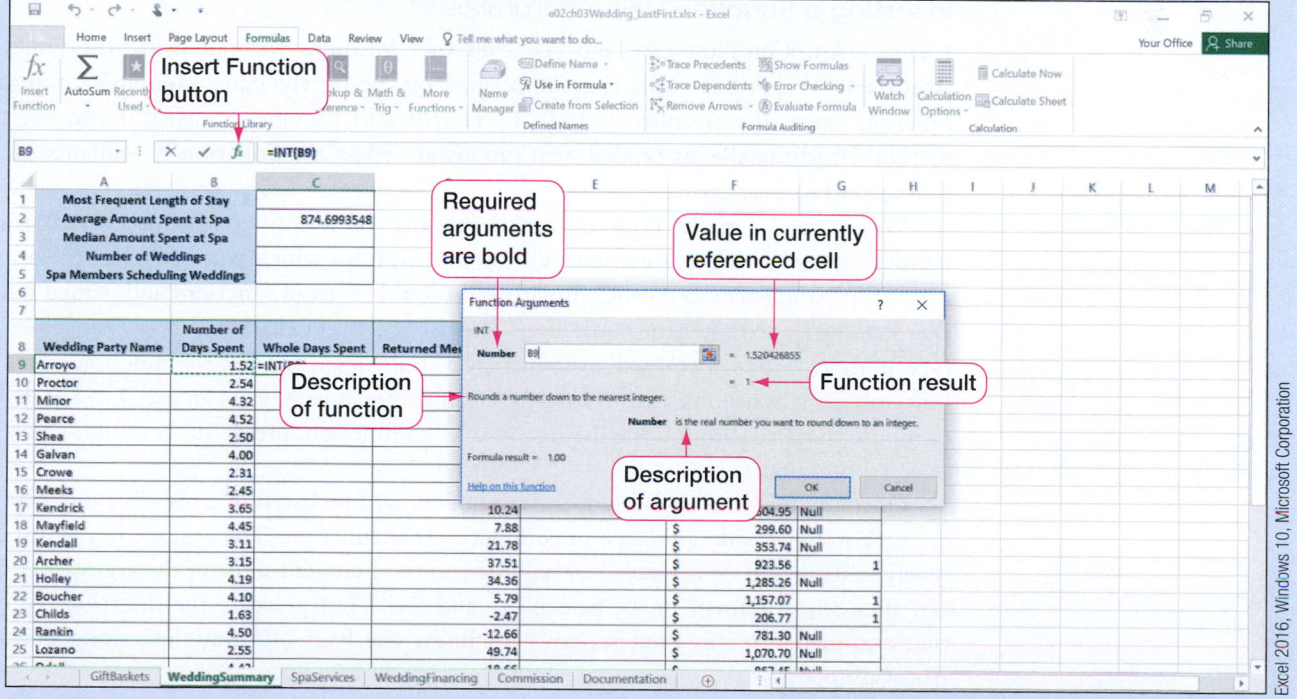

Figure 13 Function Arguments dialog box

e. Click **OK**, and then double-click the **AutoFill handle** to copy cell **C9** down to **C39**.

Notice that the values in column B have now been rounded down to the nearest whole number. Illustratively, the value of cell C24 is 4.00 even though the value in cell B24 is 4.50. Since all of the values are now whole days without a decimal value, the format for C9:C39 should have decimals decreased to zero decimals.

f. With the range **C9:C39** selected, click the **Home** tab, and then, in the Number group, click **Decrease Decimal** twice.

g. Click cell **E9**, and then click **Insert Function** . If necessary, click the **Or select a category** arrow, and then verify that **Math & Trig** is selected.

h. In the Select a function box, click **ABS**, and then click **OK**.

i. In the Function Arguments dialog box, in the Number box, type **D9**, and then click **OK**. Double-click the **AutoFill handle** to copy cell **E9** down to **E39**. All values in column E now appear as positive numbers.

j. **Save** the workbook.

SIDE NOTE
Function Help
Click the Help on this function link in the lower left of the Function Arguments dialog box to open Excel Help for the function being used.

SS | **CONSIDER THIS** | **Exploring Functions**

Use the Insert Function button in the formula bar to find a function with which you are not familiar. Read the description for the function in the Insert Function dialog box. Use Microsoft Help or the Internet to learn more about the function, and share your findings with another person. Did you have any trouble understanding the function? Is the Insert Function button a useful tool for exploring new functions?

Inserting a Function Using Forumlas

Formula AutoComplete can help you construct formulas without using the Function Arguments dialog box. This is accomplished by typing the equal sign and typing the function name directly into the cell. Excel will still provide guidance if you use this method. Additionally, as needed, you can always enter the Function Arguments dialog box to get more assistance.

When you initially type in the beginning of a function name, the Formula AutoComplete listing of functions will be shown, from which you can select the appropriate function. Formula AutoComplete will provide a list of functions and named ranges that match the text after the equal sign. The list will automatically reflect changes as you type in more letters. Excel will even display a short description of the function when the function name is highlighted. As the function names appear, you can use ↑, ↓, →, ←, or mouse to move through the listing. To select a function, press Tab or double-click the selected function.

Once the function is selected, the arguments will be listed in a movable tag, called a ScreenTip, to provide guidance in completing the function. The argument you are currently editing will be displayed in bold. If you have entered some of the arguments, you can click the argument in the ScreenTip, and Excel will relocate the insertion point to that argument. In this exercise, you will insert the ROUND function, using Formula AutoComplete.

E03.09

SIDE NOTE
Alternate Method
You can also edit a cell by pressing the F2 key.

To Insert a Function Using Formula AutoComplete

a. On the **WeddingSummary** worksheet, double-click cell **C2** to begin editing the function.

b. Click after the **equal sign** to place the insertion point before the AVERAGE function. Type **ROUND(** to begin the new function.

Notice how the Formula AutoComplete suggested possible functions while you typed "round". Also, notice that the number argument is shown in bold to indicate that this is the argument being edited.

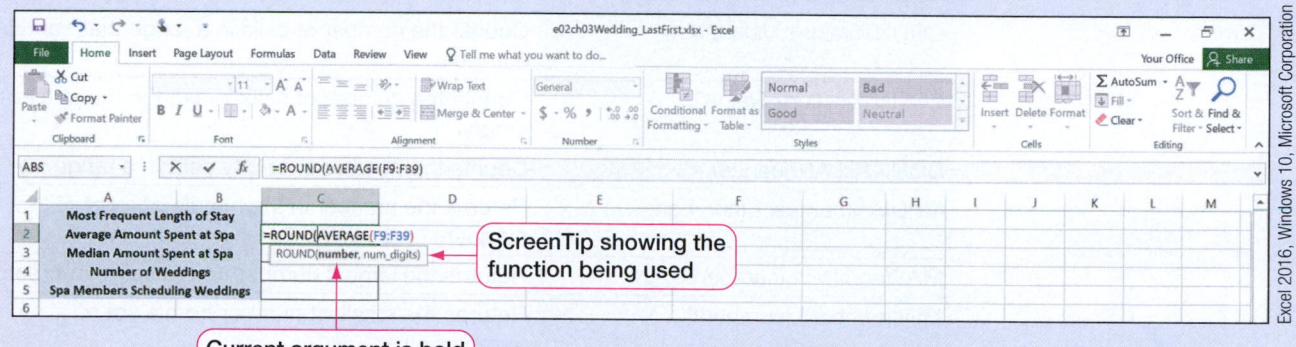

Figure 14   Screen Tip showing ROUND function

SIDE NOTE
Formula AutoComplete
To reduce typing and possible errors, you can use the arrow keys or the mouse to select functions from the Formula AutoComplete list.

c. Click after the **ending parenthesis** for the AVERAGE function, type **,** — a comma — and then notice in the ScreenTip that the num_digits argument of the ROUND function is in bold.

d. Type **2)** to complete the num_digits argument. This will round the result of the AVERAGE function to two decimal places. Press Ctrl+Enter.

Notice that the value in cell C2 is now $874.70, rounded to two decimal places. It is important to know that if you had formatted cell C2 to display only two decimal places, the cell would also show $874.70 on the screen. However, formatting does not change the value. So even though the cell would show $874.70, the cell value used in subsequent mathematical calculations would still be $874.6993548. If you increase the number of decimals for cell C2 after using the ROUND function, you will see that the cell value is changed to $874.700000.

e. **Save** 🖫 the workbook.

REAL WORLD ADVICE   **Rounding Versus Formatting**

Formatting text as currency will only give the appearance of true rounding. Any calculations using a cell formatted as currency but containing extra decimal places will include all decimal places in the calculation. Using the ROUND function will eliminate extra decimal places. Thus, future calculations will use the value displayed as a result of the ROUND function.

Using Statistical Functions

Similar to mathematical functions, statistical functions, as shown in Table 4, handle common statistical calculations such as averages, minimums, and maximums. Statistical functions are extremely useful for business analysis, as they aggregate and compare data. Common descriptive statistics are used to describe the data. The average, median, and mode are common descriptive statistics that help describe the nature of a data set. They help understand and predict future data.

Statistical Functions	Usage
AVERAGE(number1,[number2],…)	Returns the average from a set of numbers
COUNT(value1,[value2],…)	Counts the number of cells in a range that contain numbers
COUNTA(value1,[value2],…)	Counts the number of cells in a range that are not empty
COUNTBLANK(range)	Counts the number of empty cells in a range
MEDIAN(number1,[number2],…)	Returns the number in the middle of a set of numbers
MAX(number1,[number2],…)	Returns the largest number from a set of numbers
MIN(number1,[number2],…)	Returns the smallest number from a set of numbers
MODE.SNGL(number1,[number2],…)	Returns the value that occurs most often within a set

Table 4   Commonly used statistical functions

The **MEDIAN function** is used to measure the central tendency or the location of the middle of a set of data. For example, in the number set 1 to 3, 2 would be the middle of the data or the median.

Another measure commonly used to locate data in a range is mode. There are two methods for calculating the mode — the value that occurs most often — of a range of data in Excel 2016. The **MODE.SNGL** function returns the most frequently occurring value in a range of data. If more than one number occurs multiple times in a range of data, the **MODE.MULT** function can be used to return a vertical array, or list, of the most frequently occurring values in a range of data.

The **MODE function**, like MODE.SNGL, returns the most frequently occurring value in a range of data. It is important to note that in Excel 2010, this function was replaced by MODE.SNGL and MODE.MULT. The MODE function is still available in Excel 2010, 2013, and 2016 to provide backwards compatibility with earlier versions of Excel. Because of this, the function will appear in the Formula AutoComplete menu with a warning icon 🔒 next to it.

The **COUNTA function** is a useful function for counting the number of cells within a range that contain any type of data. Using COUNTA is a great method to count the number of records in a data set that may include numbers and letters. This is different from the COUNT function.

The **COUNT function** returns the number of cells in a range of cells that contain numeric data.

On the WeddingSummary worksheet, column G contains a list indicating whether or not the bridal party were members of the spa. When the data was imported into Excel, the system used by the spa marked members with the number one. Nonmembers were marked with the text "Null". Meda has asked you to find the most frequently occurring number of days stayed by a wedding party, the median amount spent by wedding parties at the spa, the number of weddings held at the spa, as well the number of members who have scheduled weddings. In this exercise, you will find this data using statistical functions.

 **E03.10**

To Use Statistical Functions

a. On the **WeddingSummary** worksheet, click cell **C1**.

b. Type **=MODE.SNGL(C9:C39)**, and then click Enter ✓.

Cell C1 now displays 4, the most frequently occurring number of days stayed by a wedding party.

c. Click cell **C3**, type **=MEDIAN(F9:F39)**, and then press Enter.

Cell C3 now displays the median amount spent by wedding parties at the spa, $899.77, representing the middle value as compared to the data for the average amount spent at the spa.

d. Click cell **C4**, type **=COUNTA(A9:A39)**, and then press Enter.

The COUNTA function counts all of the cells that contain values in the range A9:A39 to display the 31 wedding parties represented in the data.

e. Click cell **C5**, type **=COUNT(G9:G39)**, and then press Ctrl+Enter.

The COUNT function counts the numbers occurring in the range G9:G39 to display 16 spa members scheduled weddings.

f. **Save** 💾 the workbook.

1	Most Frequent Length of Stay	=MODE.SNGL(C9:C39)
2	Average Amount Spent at Spa	=ROUND(AVERAGE(F9:F39),2)
3	Median Amount Spent at Spa	=MEDIAN(F9:F39)
4	Number of Weddings	=COUNTA(A9:A39)
5	Spa Members Scheduling Weddings	=COUNT(G9:G39)

Figure 15 Statistical functions in formula view
Excel 2016, Windows 10, Microsoft Corporation

Use and Understand Date and Time Functions

Date and time functions are useful for entering the current day and time into a worksheet as well as for calculating the intervals between dates. This category of functions is based on a serial date system in which each day is represented sequentially from a starting point. In Microsoft applications, that standard is 1/1/1900, which has a serial number of 1. Thus, dates before January 1, 1900, will not be recognized by the system. Interestingly, when Apple initially made its starting point, it began in 1904. Excel settings can be changed to use the Apple starting point, but it is generally accepted practice to keep the default setting of 1/1/1900 as the starting point. Using two different starting points for dates in Excel spreadsheets can cause significant problems. Common date and time functions are shown in Table 5.

Function	Usage
DATE(year,month,day)	Returns the number that represents the date in Microsoft Excel date-time code
DATEDIF(date1,date2,interval)	Returns the time unit specified between two dates, including the two dates (inclusive)
DAY(serial_number)	Returns the day of the month, a number from 1 to 31
MONTH(serial_number)	Returns the month, a number from 1 to 12
NETWORKDAYS(start_date,end_date,[holidays])	Returns the number of whole workdays between two dates, inclusive; does not count weekends and can skip holidays that are listed
TODAY( )	Returns the computer system date
WEEKDAY(serial_number, [return_type])	Returns a number from 1 to 7 representing the day of the week. Can be set to return 0–6 or 1–7
WEEKNUM(serial_number, [return_type])	Returns the week number in the year, which week of the year the date occurs
YEAR(serial_number)	Returns the year of a date, an integer in the range 1900–9999

Table 5 Common date functions

 CONSIDER THIS | **Dates in Microsoft Applications**

Do you suppose the same Microsoft employees developed Access, Excel, Word, and PowerPoint? Is it possible that even within a company, there may have been differences in the starting date? Does Access use the same 1/1/1900 for its date starting point? See if you can find out.

Using Date and Time Functions

Since Excel tracks time by the number of days that have occurred since 1/1/1900, time is represented by the decimal portion of this number. The decimal is based on the number of minutes in a day (24*60=1440). Thus, a 0.1 decimal is equal to 144 minutes. A full date and time value — such as 5/14/2018 8:35 AM — would appear as 43234.35763. There are 43234 days between 1/1/1900 and 5/14/2018. The time of 8:35 AM is represented by the .35763 portion of the number.

The TODAY and NOW functions are two common functions for inserting the current date into a spreadsheet. There is a difference between these functions. The key difference is that the **TODAY function** simply inserts the current date into a cell, while the **NOW function** inserts the current date and time into a cell. If you think about it, the TODAY function works only with integer representation of days, while the NOW function uses decimals to include the time in addition to the day. Both functions can be formatted to show just the date, and you can work with time calculations that mix the two functions. Common time functions are listed in Table 6.

Function	Usage
HOUR(serial_number)	Returns the hour in a time value, from 0 to 23
MINUTE(serial_number)	Returns the minute in a time value, from 0 to 59
SECOND(serial_number)	Returns the number of seconds in a time value, from 0 to 59
NOW( )	Returns the computer system date and time

Table 6 Common time functions

REAL WORLD ADVICE — NOW Versus TODAY

Be careful when using NOW versus TODAY, especially when doing date calculations. Both functions use a serial number, counting from 1/1/1900. But the NOW function also includes decimals for the time of day, while TODAY works with integer serial numbers. At noon on 5/1/2018, the NOW function has the value of 43221.5, while the TODAY function has a value of 43221.0. If you are using these date functions inside another function, this could change the result if you are comparing a date the user provided. The TODAY function should be used if a user will be inserting the date into Excel by hand so the hand-typed value will be compared or used in a calculation with the function, eliminating the decimal issue.

DATEDIF function is a useful date function because it enables you to calculate the time between two dates. The function can return the time unit as days, months, or years. However, while all the other functions are listed and can be found in Excel, neither Help nor the Function Library offers any information about the DATEDIF function. You will not find any information on the DATEDIF function unless you search the Microsoft site. Since no information exists on it within Excel, this is one function that you must hand type and do the research to understand the syntax. Nonetheless, DATEDIF is one of the more useful date functions.

The syntax of the function is

=DATEDIF(date1, date2,interval)

The first argument is the starting date in time — the older date — and the second argument is the ending date in time — the newer, more recent date. It may be helpful to remember that time lines are usually depicted as moving from left to right, just as they would be listed in the DATEDIF function. The third argument is the interval that should be used, such as the number of months or days between the two dates. The interval is expressed as a text value and therefore must be surrounded by quotes for correct syntax. The viable interval options are shown in Table 7.

Interval	Description
"D"	Returns the number of complete days between the dates
"M"	Returns the number of complete months between the dates
"Y"	Returns the number of complete years between the dates
"MD"	Returns the difference between days in two dates, ignoring months and years
"YM"	Returns the difference between months in two dates, ignoring days and years
"YD"	Returns the difference between days in two dates, ignoring years

Table 7 Unit value options for DATEDIF

The options "D", "M", and "Y" are commonly used to calculate differences between dates. For example, using "Y" for the Interval argument is common practice for calculating an age. The options "YM", "YD", and "MD" are not as commonly used because they ignore certain aspects of the date structure. For example, using "YM" for the Interval argument with the dates 7/1/2017 and 9/12/2018 will result in a value of 2. This is because the "YM" unit value ignores the years in the two dates and calculates only the number of whole months between July (7) and September (9). Using "M" in the Interval argument will result in the value 14, the more commonly expected result.

Meda has asked for your help in completing an analysis of customers in the Keller-Ryan wedding party who have requested spa services. She would like the current date to appear in cell B1 of the spreadsheet and the current age of customers to appear in column C. In this exercise, you will use common date functions to complete the analysis.

 E03.11

To Use Date and Time Functions

a. Click the **SpaServices** worksheet tab, and then click cell **B1**.

b. Type **=TODAY()**, and then press ⎇Ctrl⎇+⎇Enter⎇.

Notice that cell B1 now displays the current date. Each time the worksheet is opened or when a cell is edited, the current date will be updated and displayed in cell B1. Since the time of day is not relevant here, the TODAY function is preferred over the NOW function.

SIDE NOTE
Alternate Method
You could also use the TODAY function in the formula in place of the absolute reference to B1. For example, the formula could be =DATEDIF(B5,TODAY(),"Y").

c. Click cell **C5**, type **=DATEDIF(B5,$B$1,"Y")**, and then press ⎇Ctrl⎇+⎇Enter⎇.

In this formula, B5 is the start date, $B$1 is the end date, and the "Y" stands for years. Using an absolute reference to cell **B1** will allow you to copy the formula down a range. Since the interval is set to year, the result is that the age of the guest is always current in this calculation.

Troubleshooting

No ScreenTip will appear when you type the DATEDIF function. If the DATEDIF function returns a #NUM! error, the most likely problem is mixing up the order of the two dates within the function. The first date should be the earliest date, and the second date should be the most recent one. The other common error is actually typing in a date as the argument. Typing 12/3/2018 will be interpreted as division instead of a date. The value must be either in serial date format or typed inside of quotation marks.

d. Double-click the **AutoFill handle** to copy cell **C5** down to **C22**. The current ages of all guests are now displayed in column C.

e. **Save** 🖫 the workbook.

 CONSIDER THIS | Calculating Days

Do you really need to use the DATEDIF function to calculate the difference between days — the "D" unit? In what other way could you calculate the difference? What would that formula look like?

Use and Understand Text Functions

Excel is frequently used to bring data together from multiple different locations and/or systems, including text data. Many times, the data is inconsistent from one source to another. For example, one workbook could list names as First Name Last Name — Olivia Stone — and the next may list names as Last Name, First Name — Stone, Olivia. In situations like this, knowing how to alter text data is extremely valuable and can save a lot of time.

There are many reasons why text data in a cell may need to be altered. Names in a cell may need to be separated or combined. Several pieces of data may be stored in a single cell but need to be separated into many columns of data for easier analysis. Excel contains a wide array of functions and features that allow for the manipulation of text data. Some newer features when Excel are optimized for touch screen devices. This makes it easier to manipulate data when using Excel on a mobile device such as a tablet computer.

Text functions are functions that manage, manipulate, and format text data. They can be used to change the appearance of data, such as displaying text in all lowercase letters. Text functions can also be used to cleanse text. **Cleansing text** involves removing unwanted characters, rearranging data in a cell, or correcting erroneous data.

Using Text Functions

Data stored as text is commonly referred to as a string. Text functions can change the way data is viewed, cut a string of text into multiple pieces, or combine multiple pieces of text together into one string of text. While most text functions can be used individually, they become increasingly powerful when nested together to transform text. Common text functions are defined in Table 8.

Function	Usage
CONCATENATE(text1,text2,...)	Joins textl, text2,...,textn together into a single string value.
FIND(find_text,within_text,[start_num])	Finds find_text in within_text. The search begins at start_ num (start_num defaults to 1) and is case sensitive. The starting position of find_text is returned. If the find_text is not present, an error will be returned.
LEFT(text,[num_chars])	Returns a string num_chars long from the left side of text. Num_chars defaults to 1.
LEN(text)	Returns a number that represents the number of characters.
MID(text,start_num,num_chars)	Returns a string extracted from text beginning in position start_num that is num_chars long.
RIGHT(text,[num_chars])	Returns a string num_chars long from the right side of text. Num_chars defaults to 1.
TRIM(text)	Returns text with any leading, trailing, or extra spaces between words removed.
UPPER(text)	Returns text with all characters in uppercase.
PROPER(text)	Returns text with only the first letter in uppercase. All other letters will return in lowercase.
SEARCH(find_text,within_text,[start_num])	Finds find_text in within_text. The search begins at start_ num (start_num defaults to 1) and is case insensitive. The starting position of find_text is returned. If the find_text is not present, an error will be returned.
TEXT(value,format_text)	Returns a number value as a string with the format specified in format_text.

Table 8   Common text functions

The **LEFT function** returns the characters in a text string based on the number of characters you specify, starting with the far-left character in the string. The number of characters the LEFT function will return is defined in the num_chars argument. This number can be simply typed in, or it can be more dynamically calculated by using other functions. The **FIND function** searches for a specified string of text in a larger string of text and returns the position number where the specified text begins. By using the FIND function in the num_chars argument of the LEFT function, a dynamic formula can be constructed to separate a portion of text from one cell into another.

Meda has asked that you rearrange some of the data on the SpaServices worksheet. Column A contains a list of guests' first and last names. To provide better customer service, Meda would like the first names of the guests in a separate column that can be used later. The names in column A are arranged in a consistent format. The text in the cell begins with the guest's first name followed by a single space character. After the space character is the guest's last name. Given this format, the space character can be used by text functions to separate the first name from the last name. In this exercise, you will use the FIND and LEFT functions to display only the first name of the guests in column D.

 **E03.12**

To Nest the FIND and LEFT Functions

a. On the **SpaServices** worksheet, click cell **D5**.

b. Type **=LEFT(A5,** to begin the text function. The LEFT function will begin at the left side of cell A5 and return all characters from position 1 until the number specified by the num_chars argument.

c. Type **FIND(" ",A5))**, and then press Ctrl+Enter to complete the function. Be sure to enter a space between the quotation marks.

   Notice that the name Olivia appears in cell D5. To separate the first name, you take advantage of the text pattern of the space. To separate text, you must identify the text pattern. To use text functions, the pattern must be consistent in some way. Here, the FIND function looks for the space character that separates the first and last names. For cell A5, the FIND function returns a 7 because the name Olivia contains six characters and the space after the name is the seventh character. Since you will not want to include the space character, the TRIM function can be used to remove it.

d. Double-click cell **D5** to begin editing the function. Click after the **equal sign** to place the insertion point before the LEFT function. Type **TRIM(** to begin the TRIM function.

e. Click after the last **closing** parenthesis. Type **)**, and then press Ctrl+Enter to complete the TRIM function. The number of characters displayed in cell D5 is now 6, as the trailing space character has been removed.

f. Double-click the **AutoFill handle** to copy cell **D5** down to **D22**. The first names of all guests are now displayed in column D.

The TRIM function with LEFT and FIND functions nested

D5 | =TRIM(LEFT(A5,FIND(" ",A5)))

	A	B	C	D	E	F	G	H
1	Today's Date	10/15/2018						
2			Spa Service Requests					
3								
4	Guest Name	Date Of Birth	Age	First Name	Service Requested	City & State	City	State
5	Olivia Stone	2/20/1978	40	Olivia	Hair Treatment	Bernalilo, NM		
6	Mia Ramos	11/11/1972	45	Mia	Hair Color Treatment	Farmington, NM		
7	Isabella Hudson	10/19/1975	42	Isabella	Makeup Service	Benson, AZ		
8	Rhonda Griffith	1/2/1969	49	Rhonda	Women's Facial	Benson, AZ		
9	Steven Lucas	2/26/1970	48	Steven	Golf Massage	Bisbee, AZ		
10	Elizabeth Anderson	4/14/1977	41	Elizabeth	Hair Color Treatment	Bernalilo, NM		
11	Jessica Montgomery	10/6/1969	49	Jessica	Women's Facial	Santa Fe, NM		
12	Ella West	5/26/1978	40	Ella	Makeup Service	Farmington, NM		
13	Joseph Wallace	6/19/1986	32	Joseph	Golf Massage	Farmington, NM		
14	Joshua Pierce	5/12/1969	49	Joshua	Pedicure	Bernalilo, NM		
15	Ryan Jennings	6/5/1971	47	Ryan	Full Massage	Bisbee, AZ		
16	Judy Brown	11/8/1967	50	Judy	Manicure	Benson, AZ		
17	Hannah Rowe	5/8/1974	44	Hannah	Hair Color Treatment	Bisbee, AZ		
18	Jill Mcdonald	6/9/1976	42	Jill	Full Massage	Bernalilo, NM		
19	Glenn Barker	8/22/1974	44	Glenn	Pedicure	Santa Fe, NM		
20	Mia Rivera	3/9/1985	33	Mia	Pedicure	Santa Fe, NM		
21	Jane Montgomery	5/12/1986	32	Jane	Makeup Service	Farmington, NM		

Excel 2016, Windows 10, Microsoft Corporation

Figure 16 Result of nesting the LEFT and FIND functions

g. **Save** 💾 the workbook.

Using Flash Fill

The Flash Fill feature in Excel 2016 makes data cleansing easier and faster than using traditional text functions. **Flash Fill** recognizes patterns in data as you type and automatically fills in values for text and numeric data. Flash Fill involves less typing than text functions, and this makes it easier to use on mobile or touch screen devices.

To work correctly, Flash Fill must be completed in a column adjacent to the data being manipulated. There are two ways to use Flash Fill. Providing two suggested values will initiate the automatic Flash Fill to a suggestion for cleansing your data. This suggestion will be previewed along the column adjacent to the data. Pressing [Enter] will accept the suggestion and populate the column of cells. Flash Fill can also be initiated on the Data tab. This is useful for cleansing data in cells that are not directly adjacent to the data or for numeric data. Flash Fill will not automatically suggest values for numeric data.

The SpaServices worksheet includes a list of the city and state of origin for each guest who will be attending the wedding. Separating these values into individual columns will be helpful for future tasks such as counting the number of guests from each state. In this exercise, you will use the Flash Fill feature to separate the guests' city and state of origin into individual columns.

E03.13

To Use Flash Fill

a. On the **SpaServices** worksheet, click cell **G5**.

b. Type Bernalilo, and then press [Enter] to move to cell **G6**.

c. Type F, and notice that the Flash Fill suggestion appears down the column of data. Press [Enter] to accept the suggestion.

Notice that column G now contains only the city names from the list of cities and states in column F.

d. Click cell **H5**, type **NM**, and then press (Ctrl)+(Enter).

Since the State column is not next to the column with the city and state text, typing a suggested value for Flash Fill will not work. Using the Flash Fill button from the Data tab will accomplish the task of isolating the state from column F.

e. Click the **Data** tab, and then, in the Data Tools group, click **Flash Fill**.

Notice that column H now contains only the state abbreviations from the list of cities and states in column F.

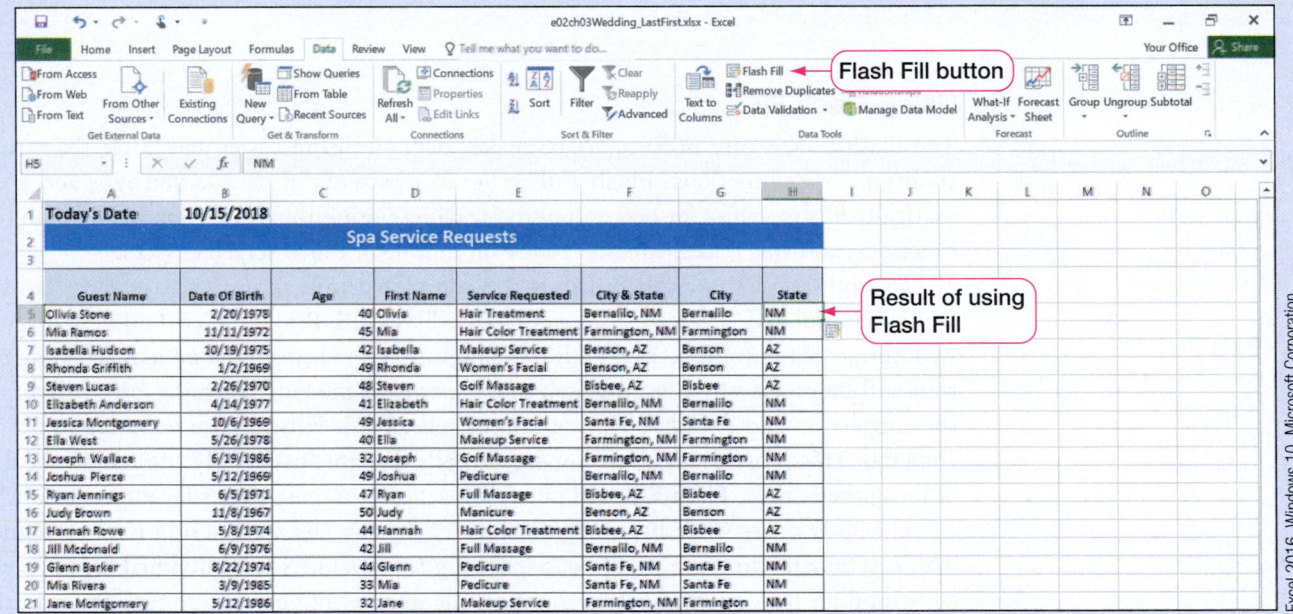

Figure 17 City names and state abbreviations separated with Flash Fill

f. **Save** 🖫 the workbook.

Use Financial and Lookup Functions

Excel has many functions available to help businesses make decisions. These decisions may include calculating payments on a loan or returning data from a table based upon a specific value in a worksheet. The ability to combine these processes in more complex tasks is even more powerful. For example, a lookup function can retrieve an interest rate from a table of data to be used in a subsequent loan calculation. As with other functions, lookup and reference functions can be very effective when combined with financial functions.

Using Lookup and Reference Functions

Lookup and reference functions look up matching values in a table of data. Lookup and reference functions can be used for simple matches or complex retrieval tasks. This can be as simple as retrieving a value from a vertical or horizontal list or as complex as finding the value of a cell within a table of data at a given row and column intersection. Common lookup and reference functions can be found in Table 9.

Function	Usage
HLOOKUP(lookup_value,table_array, row_index_num,[range_lookup])	Finds lookup_value in the top row of table_array and returns a value from row_index_num
INDEX(array,row_num,[column_num])	Returns a value from array by indexes specified as row_num and column_num
MATCH(lookup_value,lookup_array, [match_type])	Finds lookup_value in lookup_array
VLOOKUP(lookup_value,table_array, col_index_num,[range_lookup])	Finds lookup_value in the first column of table_array and returns a value from col_index_num

Table 9 Common lookup and reference functions

The **VLOOKUP function** matches a provided value in a table of data and returns a value from a subsequent column — similar to looking up a phone number in a phone book. The "V" signifies that the function matches the provided value vertically in the first column of the table of data. The syntax of a VLOOKUP is

=VLOOKUP(lookup_value, table_array, col_index_num, [range_lookup])

The lookup_value argument can be any text, any number, or a reference to a cell that contains data. The table_array argument is a range in a spreadsheet. The range can be a single column of cells or multiple columns of cells. The VLOOKUP function will match the lookup_value in the first column of the supplied table_array. The col_index_num is the column number of the corresponding value that will be returned. The optional range_lookup argument allows the VLOOKUP to perform an approximate or exact match.

The range_lookup argument is TRUE for an approximate match. An approximate match allows the VLOOKUP to return the first value less than the range_lookup in the first column of the table_array. For example, looking up the value 50 on a range containing 45 and 55 would return 45. To get an exact match, the range_lookup argument should be set to FALSE. An exact match will force the VLOOKUP to find the same value supplied in the lookup_value in the first column of the table_array. If the value cannot be found, the function will return an error.

The Turquoise Oasis Spa has recently partnered with a local bank to offer financing to customers who are booking large, costly events. Booking spa services is usually one of the last things guests will do. Thus, some guests will book fewer services than they desire because of budget concerns. The spa is hoping that offering a financing package and discounts for large events will increase revenue.

As part of the workbook you are building for the spa, Meda has asked that you finish the WeddingFinancing worksheet that she started. This worksheet contains cells to enter information about guest weddings being planned. The worksheet already has cells prepared for entering the cost of the event, the down payment supplied by the guest, the annual interest rate, and the term of the loan in years.

You have been asked to complete this worksheet so that when a wedding is scheduled, the guest will have an understanding of the basic elements of the financing plan. In this exercise, you will use a lookup function to return the discount that the spa will provide based on the total cost of the wedding event being planned.

 E03.14

To Use the VLOOKUP function

a. Click the **WeddingFinancing** worksheet tab, and then click cell **B7**.

b. Click **Insert Function** f_x. In the Search for a function box: type **VLOOKUP**, click **Go**, and then click **OK**. The Function Arguments dialog box is now open.

c. In the Lookup_value, type **B3** as the lookup value to match on the list of discounts, and then press Tab.

d. In the Table_array, type **E4:F8**, and then press Tab.

e. In the Col_index_num, type **2**, and then press Tab.

f. In the Range_lookup, type **TRUE**.

The VLOOKUP matches the value in B3 on the range E4:E8. When a match is found, the corresponding row value from column F will be returned. By placing TRUE as the range_lookup argument, the VLOOKUP will perform an approximate match; true is the default setting for this function. This means that an event costing $37,000 will return a 5.0% discount.

SIDE NOTE
Lookup Table Array
Notice the values in the table array (E4:F8) are listed in ascending order; otherwise, the correct value may not be returned.

SIDE NOTE
Table Array Text
Uppercase text and lowercase text are equivalent in lookup table arrays.

Troubleshooting

If the VLOOKUP function returns a #N/A error, check to make sure the range_lookup argument is TRUE. Using FALSE for the argument will force the VLOOKUP into an exact match. Since $37,000 is not listed in E4:E8, an error will be returned.

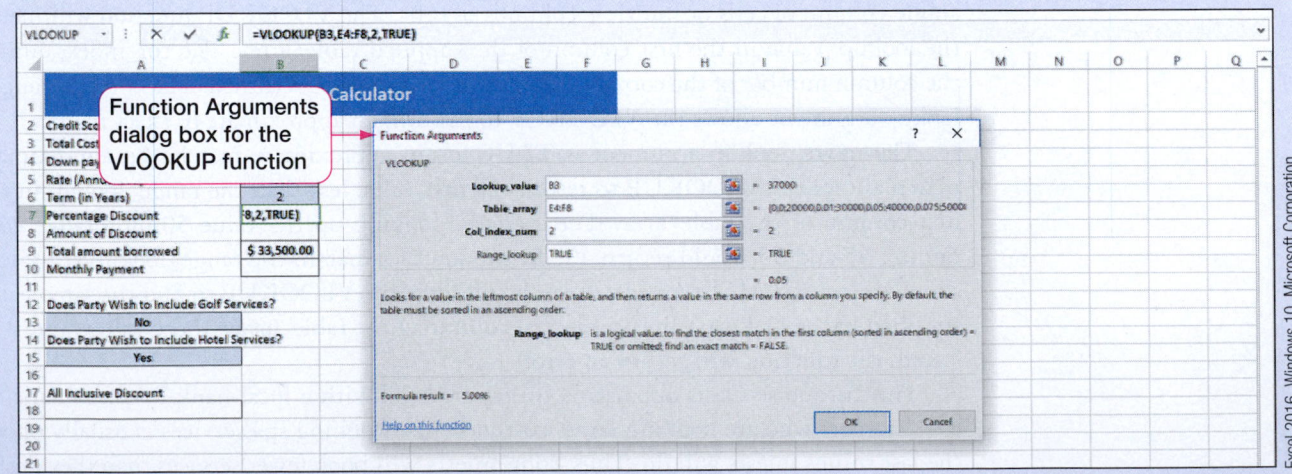

Figure 18 Function Arguments dialog box for the VLOOKUP function

g. Click **OK** to complete the VLOOKUP function and get a result of 5.00%.

h. Click cell **B8**, type =B3*B7, and then press Enter. This will apply the 5.00% discount to the $37,000 event cost, resulting in a discount of $1,850.00.

i. **Save** 💾 the workbook.

REAL WORLD ADVICE	Approximate and Exact Matches

If the range_lookup argument is left blank, it will default to TRUE for an approximate match. If the range_lookup should be FALSE but is mistakenly left blank, an incorrect result will be returned.

Using Financial Functions

Having a foundational knowledge of financial terms is an important element of succeeding in both your personal life and your professional life. Some common financial terms that you will see and hear or possibly use in an Excel spreadsheet are shown in Table 10.

Financial Term	Definition
APR	The annual percentage rate; an interest rate expressed in an annual equivalent
Compound interest	The interest charged on both the principal and the interest that accumulates on a loan
Interest payment	The amount of a payment that goes toward paying the interest accrued
NPV	The net present value of future investments
Period	The time period of payments, such as making payments monthly
Principal payment	The amount of a payment that goes toward reducing the principal amount
Principal value	The original amount borrowed or loaned
PV	Present value — the original value of the loan
Rate (and APR)	The interest rate per period of a loan or an investment
Simple interest	The interest charged on the principal amount of a loan only
Term	The total time of a loan, typically expressed in years or months

Table 10   Financial terminology

Financial functions are a set of predefined functions that can be used for common financial calculations, such as interest rates, payments, and analyzing loans. Some common financial functions are listed in Table 11.

PMT(rate,nper,pv,[fv],[type])	Calculates periodic payment for a loan based on a constant interest rate and constant payment amounts
IPMT(rate,per, nper,pv,[fv],[type])	Calculates periodic interest payment for a loan based on a constant interest rate and constant payment amounts
PPMT(rate,per,nper,pv,[fv],[type])	Calculates periodic principal payment for a loan based on a constant interest rate and constant payment amounts
NPV(rate,value1,[value2]…)	Calculates the net present value based on a discount interest rate, a series of future payments, and future income

Table 11 Common financial functions

A common and useful financial function is the PMT function. The **PMT function** determines the periodic payment for a loan based upon constant payments and interest rate. The PMT function by default returns a negative value. The function is really calculating an outflow of cash, a payment to be made. Within the financial and accounting industry, an outflow of cash is considered a negative value. In other words, this function assumes that you are actually making a payment — taking money out of your pocket to give to someone else, or a negative value to you. Since some people may be confused by seeing the value as negative, the value can be made positive by simply inserting a negative sign before the function or placing the absolute value function — ABS() — around the PMT function.

The syntax of the PMT function is

=PMT(rate,nper,pv,[fv],[type])

The first argument is the rate, which is the periodic interest rate. It is important to remember that the interest rate must be for each period. Most loans are discussed in terms of annual percentage rate (APR), while the period would be a shorter time period such as quarterly or monthly. The APR would need to be divided by 12 to get an equivalent monthly interest rate.

The second argument is nper, which is the number of periods or total number of payments that will be made for the loan. Again, many loans are discussed in years, while the payments would be monthly. Therefore, you will often need to determine the total number of periodic payments with a calculation.

The third required argument is PV, which is the present value of an investment or loan — the amount borrowed that needs to be paid back. The last two arguments are optional. The FV argument is the future value attained after the last payment is made. If this argument is left blank, the PMT function assumes FV to be zero. The type argument indicates when a payment is due. If it is left blank, the PMT function assumes that payments are due at the end of a period; if the type argument is supplied, payments are assumed to be due at the beginning of a period.

In this exercise, you will calculate the monthly payment for the customer for the event being planned, using the PMT function.

 E03.15

To Use the PMT Function

a. On the **WeddingFinancing** worksheet, click cell **B10**.

b. Type **=-PMT(** to begin the PMT function.

As was mentioned previously, the PMT function is calculated by default as a negative value. The negative sign before the PMT function will display the final result as a positive number.

Unit Conversions
Be careful when converting the arguments of the PMT function. Monthly payments are converted by using 12; quarterly payments are converted by using 4.

c. Type **B5/12,** to complete the rate argument. Because the interest rate in cell B5 is annual, you need to divide by 12 to get the interest rate per payment — in this case, monthly.

d. Type **B6*12,** to complete the number of periods argument. Because the term of the loan is in years, you will need to multiply the term by 12 to get the total number of payments — in this case, months — in the loan.

e. Type **B9),** and then press Ctrl+Enter to supply the present value of the loan and complete the PMT function.

f. The original loan amount was $37,000. Cell B9 takes the original amount in B3, subtracts the down payment supplied in cell B4, and subtracts the amount of the discount in cell B8.

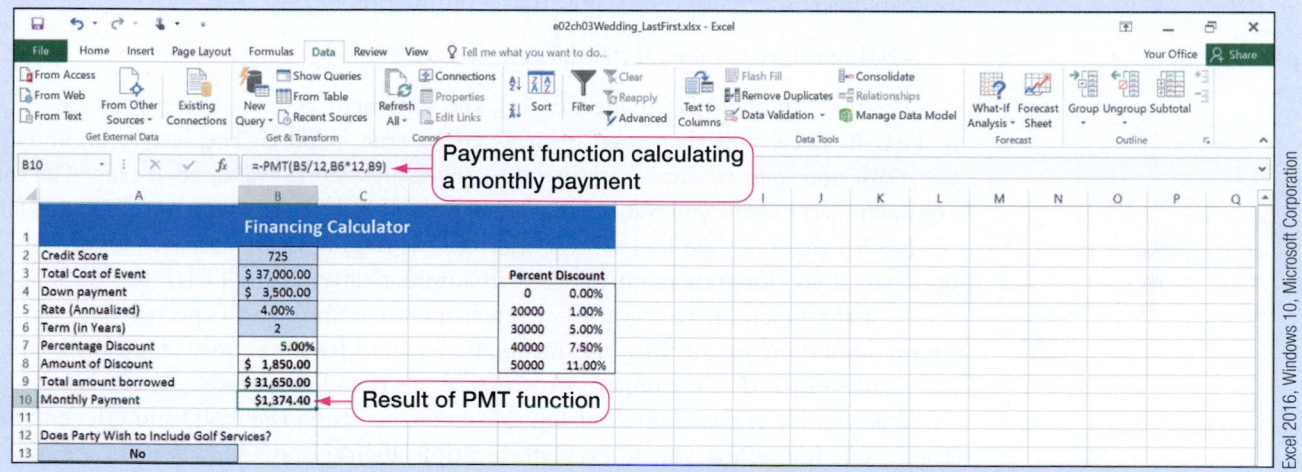

Figure 19 PMT function used to calculate a monthly payment

g. **Save** 💾 the workbook.

Use Logical Functions and Troubleshoot Functions

In constructing a spreadsheet, the need will often arise to evaluate criteria in a range of cells and make a decision based on those criteria. Excel contains functions that can evaluate a wide range of criteria and return customized results. For example, a comparison of two cells to see whether their values are the same may result in a cell displaying TRUE, a customized text response, or even performing another calculation. As the formulas become more complicated, errors may occur in the spreadsheet. Understanding some basic spreadsheet troubleshooting techniques can help you to easily correct these errors.

Using Logical Functions

Logical functions return a result based upon evaluating whether a logical test is true or false. For example, the statement "The sky is blue" is a declaration that can be evaluated as true. If the statement was "Is the sky blue?" the response would be a yes/no instead of true/false. So all logical functions are structured around the concept of declaring a position or statement that Excel will evaluate and return as True or False.

The best way to think of a declaration is to think of using comparison symbols such as the =, >, <, or >= symbols as shown in Table 12. When you set up a statement of X > Y, Excel can evaluate that comparison as true or false.

Comparison Operator Symbol	Example	Declarative Clause
<	A < B	A is less than B
>	A > B	A is greater than B
=	A = B	A is equal to B
<=	A <= B	A is less than or equal to B
>=	A >= B	A is greater than or equal to B
<>	A <> B	A does not equal B

Table 12   Comparison operators

The IF function is the most commonly used logical function. The **IF function** will return one of two values depending upon whether the supplied logical test being evaluated is true or false. The syntax of the IF function is

=IF(logical_test,[value_if_true],[value_if_false])

The first argument is the logical_test, the statement you want to evaluate as TRUE or FALSE. Excel will then evaluate it as either true or false. The second argument is the result you want to display in the cell if the expression is evaluated as true. The third argument is the result you want to display in the cell if the expression is evaluated as false.

Notice that only the logical_test argument is required. The last two arguments are optional. If you leave them out, Excel will automatically return TRUE or FALSE as the result of the function. However, it is much more common and expected that you will supply something for all three arguments. If you consider the context, logical statement, and results of the IF function, the structure begins to fall into place.

It is possible to create intricate logical statements using the AND and OR functions. These functions allow you to evaluate multiple logical statements within a single IF function. The **AND function** is a logical function that returns TRUE if all logical tests supplied are true; otherwise, it returns FALSE. The **OR function** is a logical function that returns TRUE if any one logical test supplied is true; otherwise, it returns FALSE. The components can incorporate values, cells, named ranges, and even other functions. Common logical functions and their usage are listed in Table 13.

Logical Functions	Usage
IF(logical_test,[value_if_true],[value_if_false])	Returns one of two values depending upon whether the logical statement is evaluated as being true or false
IFERROR(value,value_if_error)	Returns a specified value if a function or formula returns an error; otherwise, it returns the value of the function or formula
AND(logical1,logical2,…)	Returns true if logical1, logical2,…logical255 all return true
OR(logical1,logical2,…)	Returns true if any one of logical1, logical2,…logical255 return true

Table 13   Common logical functions

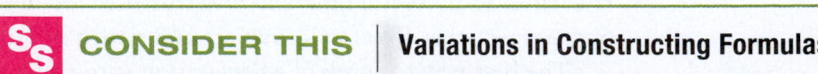 **CONSIDER THIS** | **Variations in Constructing Formulas**

In Excel, a formula can be written in many ways. Some are more efficient than others. At a minimum, every IF statement can be written in two ways. Why? Provide an example for each way.

To encourage couples getting married to use the resort for all of their wedding services, the Painted Paradise Resort & Spa is offering an all-inclusive discount of $500.00. The availability of the discount to the guests must be evaluated in two steps. First, the discount can be offered only if the guest's credit score is at least 650. Second, the wedding party must use both the golf course and the hotel as part of the event.

In this exercise, you will use common logical functions to evaluate whether a wedding party is eligible for the all-inclusive discount. If the wedding party is eligible, they will receive a $500 discount. If they are not eligible, the cell should display a zero.

 E03.16

To Use the IF and the AND functions

a. On the **WeddingFinancing** worksheet, click cell **C10**.

b. Click the **Formulas** tab, and in the Function Library group, click **Logical**, and then click **IF** to begin the IF function and enter the Logical_test argument.

The credit score of the guest is located in cell B2. The IF function will need to test for a value in this cell of greater than or equal to 650.

c. With the insertion point in the Logical_test, type **B2>=650** for the logical_test argument. Press ⎡Tab⎤ to enter the value_if_true argument.

The IF function should return the text "Sufficient Credit Score" if the value in B2 is 650 or greater. If the value is less than 650, the text "Insufficient Credit Score" should be returned.

d. Type **Sufficient Credit Score**, and then press ⎡Tab⎤ to enter the Value_if_false argument.

e. Type **Insufficient Credit Score**.

SIDE NOTE
Using Text in Formulas

Note in the Functions Arguments dialog box how Excel supplied quotation marks around the Value_if_true text. If you type this formula in a cell, you must add the quotation marks.

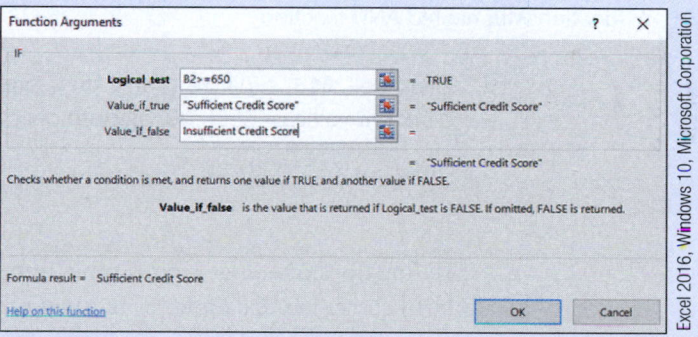

Figure 20 Function Arguments dialog box

f. Click **OK** to complete the IF function. Use the AutoFit feature on column C. Notice that since the value in B2 is 725, the text "Sufficient Credit Score" is returned by the IF function.

g. Click cell **A18**, and then type **=IF(** to begin the IF function.

Since the discount requires both golf services and hotel services to be used by the wedding party, the AND function will be used in the logical test of the IF function to evaluate this criterion.

h. Type **AND(A13="Yes",A15="Yes"),** to insert the AND function into the IF function and complete the logical_test argument.

The AND function will now return TRUE if cells A13 and A15 both contain the text "Yes". Otherwise, it will return FALSE to the IF function.

i. Type **500,** to complete the Value_if_true argument.

If the AND function returns TRUE, the number 500 will be displayed in cell A18. This will give a $500 discount to the wedding party.

j. Type **0)** to complete the Value_if_false argument and complete the IF function. Press Ctrl and Enter.

If the AND function returns FALSE, the number 0 will be displayed in cell A18, and no discount will be given. Notice that no discount is currently given, as cell A13 displays No.

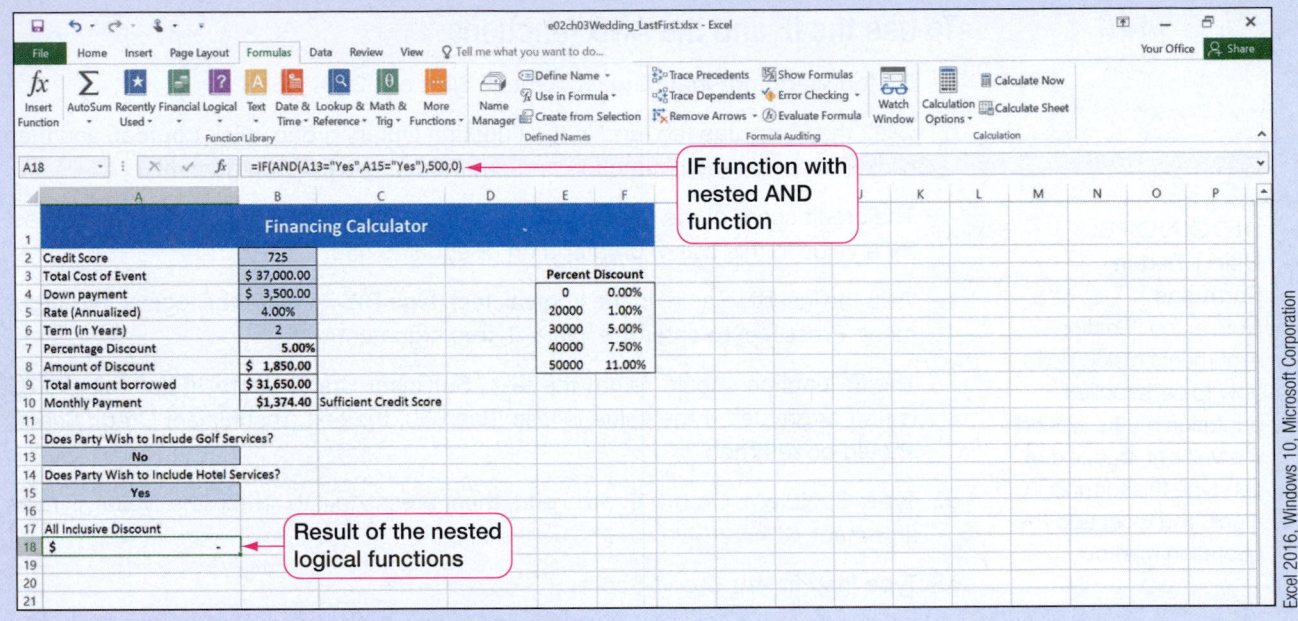

Figure 21 IF function with nested AND function

k. Click cell **A13**, type **Yes**, and then press Ctrl+Enter. Cell A18 now displays the discount value of $500.00, as both cells A13 and A15 display Yes.

l. **Save** the workbook.

IF functions can range from simple tests of a statement to complex, nested formulas. Table 14 shows four examples of IF functions with varying levels of complexity.

Context: Display the word "Good" if the exam score in J10 is greater than or equal to the target goal of 80 which is in cell B2. If it is worse than 80, display the word "Bad".

Example: =IF(J10>=$B$2,"Good","Bad")

Interpretation: If the value in cell J10 is greater than or equal to the value in B2, the text "Good" is displayed. Otherwise, the text "Bad" is displayed.

Context: Display the status of an employee meeting his or her goal of getting a number of transactions where transactions are listed in the range of A2:A30 and the target number of transactions are in cell C3.

Example: =IF(COUNT(A2:A30)>=C3,"Met Goal"," ")

Interpretation: If the count of transactions that are listed in range A2:A30 is greater than or equal to the value in C3 (the target goal for the employee), the employee met his or her goal and the text "Met Goal" should be displayed. Otherwise, the goal was not met, and no value should be displayed. This can be accomplished by supplying two quotation marks with no characters typed between them.

Context: For tracking any projects that have not been completed, check the text in H20, and if it does not say "Complete", assume that the project is not complete and calculate how many months are left when A3 has today's date and A4 has the targeted completion date.

Example: =IF(H20<>"Complete", DATEDIF(A3,A4,"M"),0)

Interpretation: If H20 does not say "Complete" to represent a completed project, calculate the number of months left based on dates in cells A3 and A4. Otherwise, show a zero.

Context: Determine salary by checking whether the employee generated less revenue than his or her goal listed in B2. If so, the employee simply gets the base pay. If the employee does meet his or her goal or generates more revenue than the goal, the employee gets a bonus, which is a percent of sales added to the base pay. Since this may result in a value that has more than two decimals, the result needs to be rounded to two decimals.

Example: =ROUND(IF(SUM(Sales)<B2,Base,Base+BonusPercent*(SUM(Sales))),2)

Interpretation: The ROUND() function will round the result to two decimals. Inside the ROUND function, the SUM(Sales) functions will sum the range named Sales to give the total sales. The IF statement then indicates that IF the total Sales is less than the value in B2 (the sales goal), provide the value that is in the range called Base (Base pay). Otherwise, the total Sales must be greater than or equal to B2, and the pay would be calculated as the Base (Base pay) plus the value in the named range BonusPercent times the total Sales.

Table 14   Examples of IF functions

 CONSIDER THIS | **What IF There Are Three Options?**

An IF statement can handle just two results: true and false. Are most real world situations that simple? How could you use an IF statement if there are more than two results? It is possible!

Troubleshooting Functions

Logical functions dramatically increase the value of a spreadsheet. However, on the path to learning how to use functions, and even as an experienced spreadsheet user, you will still make typing errors during the development of functions. Excel does an excellent job of incorporating clues to help you determine where you have gone astray with a function.

When you make a mistake with a function that prevents Excel from returning a viable result, Excel will provide an error message. While these may seem cryptic initially, they can be interpreted. Typically, an error message will be prefaced with a number symbol (#).

Examples are #VALUE!, #N/A, #NAME?, or #REF!. Over time, you will learn to recognize common issues that would cause these error messages.

QUICK REFERENCE	Common Error Messages

1. **#NAME?** — This error indicates that text in a formula is not recognized. Excel treats unrecognized text as a named range that does not exist. This is often the result of missing quotes around a text string or mistyping the function or range name.

2. **#REF!** — This error indicates a reference that Excel cannot find. This is often the result of changes such as a deleted worksheet, column, row, or cell.

3. **#N/A** — This error indicates that a value is not available in one or more cells specified. Common causes occur in functions that try to find a value in a list but the value does not exist. Rather than returning an empty set — no value — Excel returns this error instead.

4. **#VALUE!** — This error occurs when the wrong type of argument or operand is being used, such as entering a text value when the formula requires a number. Common causes include the wrong cell reference that contains a text value rather than a numeric value.

5. **#DIV/0!** — This is a division by zero error and occurs when a number is divided by zero or by a cell that contains no value. While it can occur as a result of an actual error in the design of a formula, it may also occur simply as a result of the current conditions within the spreadsheet data. In other words, this is common when a spreadsheet model is still in the creation process and data has not yet been entered into the necessary cells. Once proper numeric data does exist, the error disappears.

There are numerous ways to troubleshoot erroneous functions in Excel. When you encounter an error, you can quickly check the cell references and arguments of the function by double-clicking the cell to edit the function. This is beneficial because while a function is being edited, Excel will outline any cells or ranges included in the function and display the ScreenTip for the function. You can also press the F2 key to place a cell in edit mode. Auditing options are available in the Formula Auditing group of the Formulas tab as well.

QUICK REFERENCE	Troubleshooting Cells with Error Messages or Incorrect Results

1. Double-click a cell to enter edit mode of the cell.
2. Press the F2 key to enter edit mode of a cell.
3. In the Formula Auditing group of the Formulas tab, select Error Checking-Trace Error.

On the Commission worksheet, Meda has set up a quick analysis that rewards the employee who schedules the event with a commission on the total cost of the event. The commission earned is then added to the base event pay for the employee. The base event pay is contingent upon the employee level. After setting up the worksheet, Meda noticed an error in one of the cells. Additionally, the table located in the Commission worksheet states that managers have a base event pay of $1,250. However, the value shown for the manager in the worksheet is only $750. In this exercise, you will troubleshoot the problem.

 **E03.17**

To Troubleshoot a Function

a. Click the **Commission** worksheet tab, and then click cell **B4**.

Notice the #N/A error being returned by the VLOOKUP function in the cell. Recall that this error commonly occurs because a value cannot be found on a list.

b. Click the **Error Message** button next to cell **B4**. Notice the error message states that a value is not available.

c. Click cell **B4** again, and then press F2 to edit the formula.

Notice the outlines around the cells that are part of the VLOOKUP function. From this view, you can verify that cell B3 is correctly referenced as the lookup value. Cells E4:F8 are correctly referenced as the table array. The column index number will return a value from column F if a value is found in column E.

Notice that the range_lookup argument is set to FALSE. This means that the lookup is performing an exact match. Since $17,000 does not occur in the range E4:E8, the VLOOKUP will return a #N/A error.

d. Place the insertion point at the end of the **range_lookup** argument, and then delete the text **FALSE**. Type TRUE, and then press Ctrl+Enter to fix the formula. Notice that the value 5.00% now appears in cell B4.

e. Double-click cell **B8** to edit the formula.

Notice that the range_lookup argument is set to TRUE. This means that the lookup is performing an approximate match and is returning the incorrect base event pay rate.

f. Place the insertion point at the end of the **range_lookup** argument, and then **delete** the text **TRUE**. Type FALSE, and then press Ctrl+Enter to fix the formula. Notice that the value $1,250 now appears in cell B8.

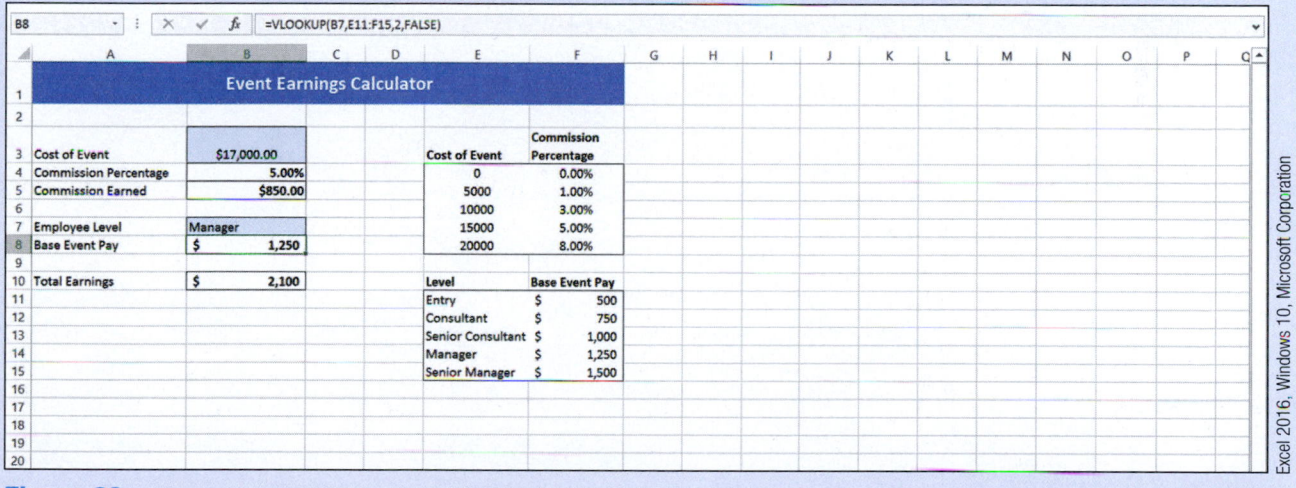

Figure 22 Worksheet with IF functions corrected

g. Complete the Documentation worksheet according to your instructor's directions.

h. Insert the file name in the left footer of all worksheets.

i. **Save** the workbook, exit Excel, and then submit your file as directed by your instructor.

As you develop a spreadsheet, follow these guidelines for creating formulas and functions.

1. Use parentheses for grouping operations in calculations in order to get the correct order. However, do not overuse parentheses, as this quickly adds to the complexity of the formula. For example, use =SUM(Sales) instead of =(SUM(Sales)).

2. When inserting numbers into a function, use formatting such as 10000. Do not enter 10,000, with a comma. In Excel, the comma is a formatting element and is used to separate arguments. Best practice for functions and formulas dictates entering the 10000 value in a cell and then using the cell address in the formula.

3. Insert currency as 4.34 instead of $4.34 to avoid confusion with relative and absolute cell referencing. Then format the cell that will contain the result as Accounting or Currency. Best practice for functions and formulas dictates entering the 4.34 value in a cell and then using the cell address in the formula.

4. Enter percentages as decimals, such as .04. Then format the number as a percentage.

5. Logical conditions have three parts: two components to compare and the comparison sign. Do not type >5 when there is no value to evaluate as being greater than 5.

6. Use the negative sign, as in -333, to indicate negative numbers in formulas, rather than (333).

7. Always put quotation marks around text unless it is a named range. Numeric values do not require quotation marks unless the number will be used in a textual context and not for a mathematical calculation. An example of numbers in a textual context would be a zip code or telephone number.

8. Avoid unneeded spaces in formulas. Excel will allow a function such as =SUM(A2:A10). Best practice dictates typing the function as =SUM(A2:A10) with no extra spaces.

Concept Check

1. Explain the three different types of cell referencing. p. 165

2. Why are named ranges useful? What limitations are there in creating the names for ranges? p. 173

3. Why is the syntax of an Excel function important? How can you distinguish between required and optional portions of a function? p. 178–179

4. In the mathematical and statistical functions, what are the differences between the ROUND function and the INT function? Give a business example of when you would use each. p. 180

5. What is the difference between the TODAY() function and the NOW() function? Why is this difference important? p. 186–187

6. What are common uses for text functions? Why is the Flash Fill feature useful on mobile devices? p. 189–191

7. Explain the difference between the TRUE and FALSE arguments for the range_lookup argument of a VLOOKUP function. Give a business example of how you would use a VLOOKUP with a PMT function. p. 193–196

8. Give a business example in which an IF function would be useful. How would using the AND or OR functions in the logical_test argument change the way the IF function works? p. 197–201

Key Terms

ABS function   180
Absolute cell reference   165
AND function   198
Argument   178
Cell reference   165
Cleansing text   189
COUNT function   184
COUNTA function   184
Date and time functions   185
DATEDIF function   187
Financial functions   195
FIND function   190

Flash Fill   191
Function   178
Function arguments   180
IF function   198
INT function   180
LEFT function   189
Logical functions   197
Lookup and reference functions   193
MEDIAN function   184
Mixed cell reference   165
MODE function   184
MODE.MULT function   184

MODE.SNGL function   184
Name Manager   174
Named range   165
NOW function   186
OR function   198
PMT function   196
Relative cell reference   165
ROUND function   180
Syntax   178
Text function   189
TODAY function   186
VLOOKUP function   193

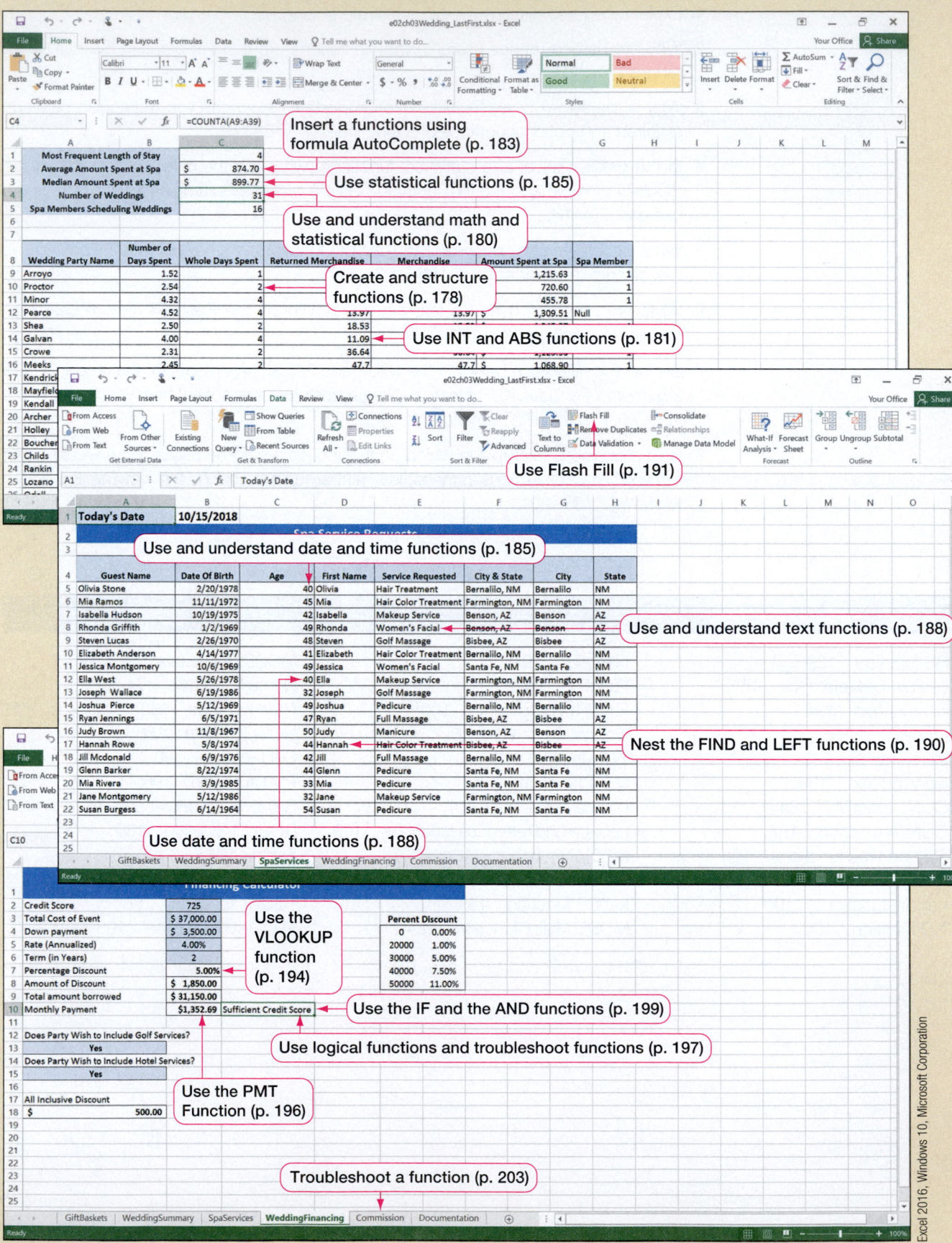

Figure 23

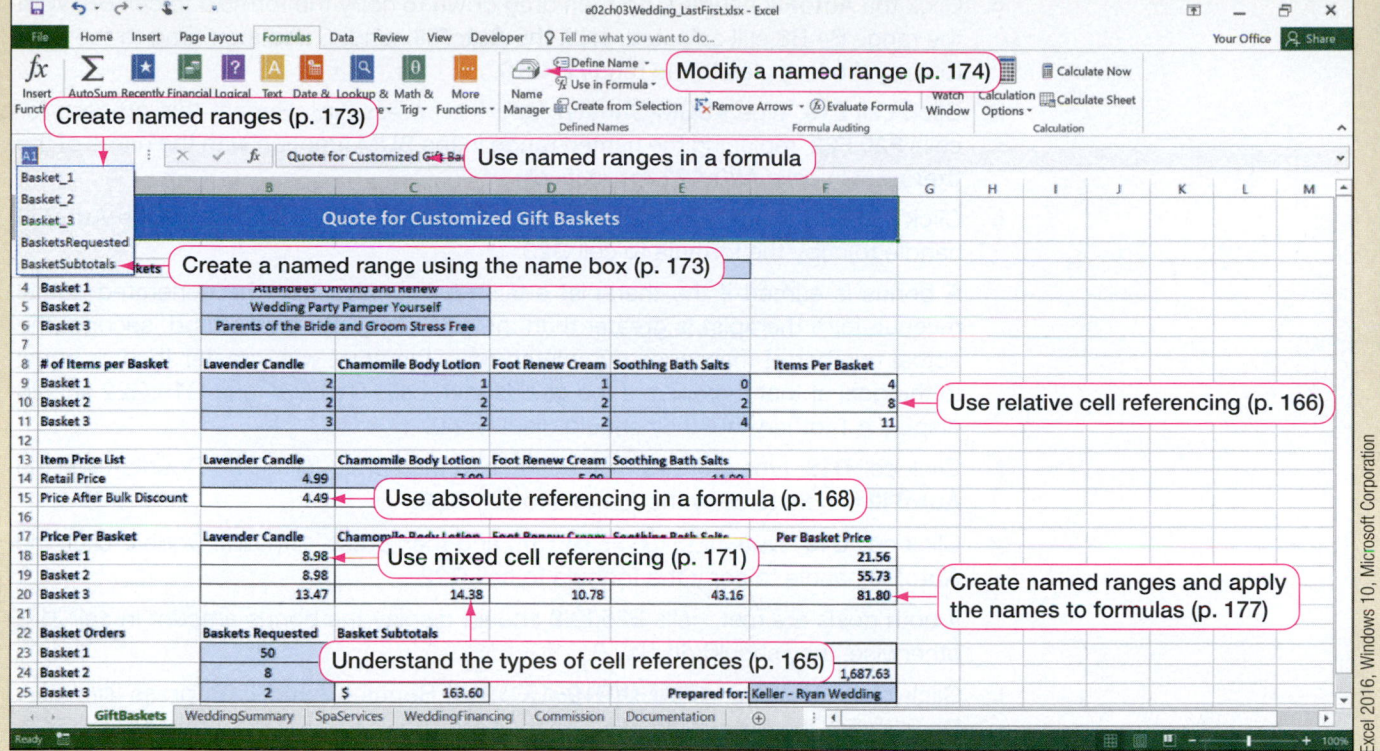

Figure 24

Practice 1

Student data file needed:

 e02ch03Bonus.xlsx

You will save your file as:

e02ch03Bonus_LastFirst.xlsx

Massage Therapist Bonus Workbook

Human Resources

Finance and Accounting

Meda Rodate has been constructing a workbook that will enable her to analyze the goals for massage therapists and calculate their pay. The massage therapists have a base pay and earn commission on massages along with a bonus. Meda has asked that you make some modifications to the workbook that she began to facilitate her analysis.

a. Start **Excel**, click **Open Other Workbooks** in the left pane, and then double-click **This PC**. Navigate through the folder structure to the location of your student data files, and then double-click **e02ch03Bonus**. If a Security Warning message displays, click the **Enable Editing** button.

b. Click the **File** tab, click **Save As**, and then double-click **This PC**. In the Save As dialog box, navigate to the location where you are saving your project files, and then change the file name to e02ch03Bonus_LastFirst, using your last and first name. Click **Save**.

c. Click the **Bonus** worksheet tab, and then click cell **J17**. Click in the Name box, type Bonus, and then press Enter.

d. Click the **Formulas** tab, and then, in the Defined Names group, click **Name Manager**. Click **Christy** in the list of named ranges in the workbook.

e. In the **Refers to** box, delete the existing range, and then type =Bonus!$B$12:$K$12. Click **OK**, and then click **Close**.

f. Click cell **B4**, type =B3, and then press F4 twice to create the mixed cell reference B$3. Type *A4, and then press F4 three times to create the mixed cell reference $A4. Press Ctrl+Enter.

Practice 1   207

g. Click the **AutoFill** handle, and then drag down to copy the formula to cell **B8**. With the range B4:B8 still selected, click the **AutoFill** handle, and then drag to the right to copy the formulas to the range **B4:K8**.

h. Click cell **F19**, type =SUM(Christy), and then press Enter. Repeat this process for cells **F20:F22**, replacing the named range in the SUM function with the name of the **therapist** in cells **A20:A22** respectively.

i. Click cell **D25**, type =C19*C25, and then press Ctrl+Enter. Double-click the **AutoFill** handle to copy the formula to cell **D28**.

A bonus is earned if the therapist attains two goals: first, the generated actual revenue for a therapist is greater than the goal for that therapist and, second, the actual number of massages completed for a therapist was greater than or equal to the goal of that therapist. If the goal is met, cells D19:D22 and G19:G22 should display a 1; otherwise, they should display a 0.

j. Click cell **D19**, type =IF(C19>=B19,1,0), and then press Ctrl+Enter. Double-click the **AutoFill** handle to copy the formula to cell **D22**.

k. Click cell **G19**, type =IF(F19>=E19,1,0), and then press Ctrl+Enter. Double-click the **AutoFill** handle to copy the formula to cell **G22**.

If both goals are met, cells E25:E28 should display the bonus amount in cell J17; otherwise, they should display 0.

l. Click cell **E25**, type =IF(AND(D19=1,G19=1),Bonus,0), and then press Ctrl+Enter. Double-click the **AutoFill** handle, and then drag down to copy the formula to cell **E28**.

m. Click cell **F25**, type =B25+D25+E25, and then press Ctrl+Enter. Click the **AutoFill** handle, and then drag down to copy the formula to cell **F28**.

n. On the **Insert** tab, in the Text group, click **Header & Footer**. On the Header & Footer Tools Design tab, in the Navigation group, click **Go to Footer**. Click in the left footer section, and then, in the Header & Footer Elements group, click **File Name**.

o. Click any **cell** on the spreadsheet to move out of the footer, and then press Ctrl+Home. On the **View** tab, in the Workbook Views group, click **Normal**.

p. Click the **Documentation** worksheet. Click cell **A8**, and then type in today's date. Click cell **B8**, and then type your name in the Firstname Lastname format. Complete the remainder of the Documentation worksheet according to your instructor's directions.

q. Save the workbook, exit Excel, and then submit your file as directed by your instructor.

Problem Solve 1

Student data file needed:

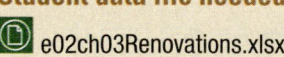 e02ch03Renovations.xlsx

You will save your file as:

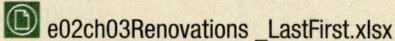 e02ch03Renovations _LastFirst.xlsx

Painted Paradise Resort & Spa Scenario

Productions and Operations

Finance and Accounting

Lesa Martin, a member of the support/coordination staff for the conference center at Painted Paradise Resort & Spa, has created a worksheet to keep track of the renovations being made to the three rooms that are used for conferences and the two technology centers that are used for computer-based presentations and interactive sessions. The technology centers are equipped with workstations, are networked, and have Internet accessibility. This spreadsheet is simple and designed only for Lesa and her associates to keep a handle on the renovation progress and estimate the increase in capacity and revenue that might occur as a result of the renovations.

a. Open the Excel file, **e02ch03Renovations**. Save your file as e02ch03Renovations_LastFirst, using your last and first name.

b. On the **Renovations** worksheet in cell **G6**, enter a formula using an absolute reference to determine the new capacity that the Musica Room will hold based on the capacity in cell F6 and the percentage in cell B13.

c. Copy this formula to the range **G7:G10**.

d. Assign the name range IncreaseInRevenue to cell **B14**.

e. In cell **I6**, enter a formula to determine the increase in revenue for the Musica Room based on the revenue figure in cell H6 and the percentage in cell B14. Use the named range in cell B14 when entering this formula.

f. Copy this formula to the range **I7:I10**.

g. In cell **D6**, enter the appropriate date function to determine the length in days of the expected renovation for the Musica Room.

h. Copy this function to the range **D7:D10**.

i. In cell **B15**, enter the function to calculate the median length of renovations in days. Give the cell the name range MedianDays.

j. In cell **J6**, enter a logical function to display the word **Under** in the cell if the renovations are going to take fewer than or equal to the median number of days calculated in cell B15; otherwise, have the word **Over** display. Use the named range for B15 when entering this formula.

k. Copy this function to the range **J7:J10**.

l. In cell **B21**, enter a function that will calculate the monthly payment for the loan amount in cell B18, based on the Annualized Rate in B19, and the number of years in the Term in cell B20. Display the monthly payment as a positive value.

m. Assign the named range **RoomClassification** to A24:B27.

n. In cell **K6**, using a lookup function, create a formula to determine the projected room classification based on the projected quarterly revenue after renovations in cell I6. Use the name range RoomClassification when entering this formula.

o. Copy this formula to the range **K7:K10**.

p. Add the file name in the left footer of the Renovations sheet. Return to Normal view if necessary.

q. On the **Documentation** worksheet in cell **A8**, type today's date. In cell **B8**, type your name in the Firstname Lastname format. Complete the remainder of the Documentation worksheet according to your instructor's directions.

r. Save the workbook, exit Excel, and then submit your file as directed by your instructor.

Critical Thinking

The Renovations workbook contains named ranges. What are the benefits of using named ranges in formulas?

Not all workbooks benefit from naming cells or ranges of cells. Can you explain a scenario in which it would not be wise to use names or named ranges?

Perform 1: Perform in Your Life

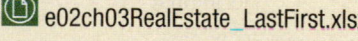

Student data file needed:

 e02ch03RealEstate.xlsx

You will save your file as:

e02ch03RealEstate_LastFirst.xlsx

Finance and Accounting

Real Estate Workbook

You are interning at Schalow Real Estate firm. Your supervisor has asked you to cleanse the data in a spreadsheet so that she can analyze it and look for trends. She asks that you create new columns as directed. Format all currency spreadsheet values using the Currency Number Format, and display two decimal places. Fill all formula and functions through the appropriate rows.

a. Open the Excel file, **e02ch03RealEstate**. Save your file as e02ch03RealEstate_LastFirst, using your last and first name.

b. On the Sold worksheet, create a column named Price/SqFt in column N, and then create a formula to calculate the price per square foot based on of the square footage and the price sold.

c. Create a column named Down PMT, and then create a formula that will calculate a down payment of 20% of the sold price.

d. Create a column named Days on MKT, and then create a formula to calculate the number of days each property was on the market.

e. Create a column named Monthly Payment. Create a formula to calculate the monthly mortgage payment for each property. With a mixed reference, use the interest rate found in cell V2. With a mixed reference, use the term in cell W2. Deduct the down payment from the sold price to calculate the amount financed. Edit the function to display positive numbers.

f. Create a column named Monthly Taxes. Each development has a different tax rate. Use a lookup function to look up the **Development ID** from the Sold worksheet, and determine that development's **Tax Rate** from the Development worksheet. Then, to determine the actual tax, multiply the tax rate by the sold price, and divide the tax by 12. This will determine the amount to save each month to pay the taxes at the end of the year (Month Tax).
    To reference a lookup table on a different worksheet, click on the worksheet tab that contains the lookup table, select the range, type a comma (,), and then click the original worksheet tab.

g. Create a column named Monthly Insurance. The cost to insure homes is different in different neighborhoods. Use a lookup function to look up the **Development ID** and determine that development's Insurance Rates from the Development worksheet. Then multiply the insurance rate by the sold price, and divide by 12 to determine the monthly payment.

h. Create a column named Total Payment. Add the monthly tax and insurance to the monthly payment to determine how much the homeowner needs to live in the newly purchased home.

i. Ensure that your columns are sufficiently wide to display their content fully. Wrap the text in the header rows on each worksheet as necessary. Format the workbook professionally.

j. On the **Documentation** worksheet in cell **A8**, type today's date. In cell **B8**, type your name in the Firstname Lastname format. Complete the remainder of the Documentation worksheet according to your instructor's directions.

k. Add the file name to the left footer on all sheets.

l. Save the workbook, exit Excel, and then submit your file as directed by your instructor.

Additional
Cases

Additional Chapter Cases are available at www.pearsonhighered.com/youroffice

Microsoft Excel 2016

Chapter 4 | EFFECTIVE CHARTS

Prepare Case

Sales & Marketing

Turquoise Oasis Spa Sales Reports

The Turquoise Oasis Spa managers, Irene Kai and Meda Rodate, are pleased with your work and would like to see you continue to improve the spa spreadsheets. They want to use charts to learn more about the spa. Meda has given you a spreadsheet with some data and would like you to develop some charts. Visualizing the data with charts will provide knowledge about the spa for decision-making purposes.

Sea Wave/Fotolia

Student data files needed for this chapter:

 e02ch04SpaSales.xlsx

 e02ch04TurquoiseOasis.jpg

You will save your file as:

 e02ch04SpaSales_LastFirst.xlsx

Designing a Chart

With Excel, you can organize data so it has context and meaning. **Data visualization** is the graphical presentation of data with a focus on qualitative understanding. It is central to finding trends and supporting business decisions. Modern data visualization can involve beautiful and elegant charts that include movement and convey information in real time. Charts are at the heart of data visualization. Charts enlighten you as you compare and contrast data and examine how it changes over time. Learning how to work with charts means not only knowing how to create them but also realizing that each type of chart can discover or emphasize different knowledge.

While it may seem simple to create a pie chart or a bar chart, there are many considerations in creating charts. Like a picture, a chart can be worth a thousand words. However, different people may interpret a chart differently if it is not well developed. A well-developed chart should provide context for the information without overshadowing key points. Finally, it is easy to confuse people with the choice and layout of a chart. A chart should use accurate and complete data. The objective should be to provide a focused, clear message. In today's data-rich world, many interpretations or messages can be extracted from the data. Businesses have three primary objectives in charting: data analysis, hypothesis testing, and persuasion.

In data analysis, the Excel chart is used to manipulate the data to try to evaluate and prioritize all the interpretations or messages. There may be a need to create multiple charts, using a variety of data sources, layouts, and designs as data is interpreted.

Ideas or hypotheses may be made about the data. Charts can visually support or refute hypotheses. For example, maybe you have the impression that a certain salesperson performs better than the other salespeople. You could support or refute your hypothesis by charting their sales data.

If you have a position you want the data to support visually, you could consider using an Excel chart to help persuade your audience of your position. You will need to select a specific and appropriate chart layout, use the necessary data, and design a chart that conveys your message clearly and unambiguously. Further, you have an ethical obligation to represent the data accurately. Misrepresenting data can result in lawsuits or termination of employment.

Regardless of the objective, even a small set of data allows you to create a variety of charts, each offering a different understanding of the data. In this chapter, you will start with understanding the concepts for creating a chart in Excel and understanding which type of chart will depict the information in the best and most efficient manner.

Explore Chart Types, Layouts, and Styles

When you decide to represent data visually, you need to make some initial decisions about the basic design of the chart. These initial decisions include the location of the chart, the type of chart, the general layout and style, and what data you will be using. These elements can be set initially and modified later. Best practice dictates that you first consider and develop the basic design of the chart.

Regardless of the location or type of chart, the process of creating a chart starts with the organization of the data on the spreadsheet. The typical structure is to have labels across the top of the data, along the left side of the data, or both. While the labels do not have to be directly next to the data, this position helps in selecting data and making your chart. The data may have been brought in from an external data source, such as Access. The data may need to be filtered, calculated, or reorganized before a chart is created. Keep in mind that not all data is organized in a way that allows for the creation of charts.

When you are ready to create a chart, select the cells that contain both the label headings and the data. People rarely create a perfect chart the first time. You might start a chart, work with it for a while, and then realize that a different chart type would better convey the information. Fortunately, Excel provides ample flexibility in designing charts. Thus, if you change your mind, you can modify the chart or simply start over.

Opening the Starting File

In this exercise, you will review a pie chart that displays the use of portable massage tables by different therapists at the Turquoise Oasis Spa.

E04.00

SIDE NOTE

Pin the Ribbon

If your ribbon is collapsed, pin your ribbon open. Click the Home tab. In the lower right corner of the ribbon, click Pin the Ribbon ⊞.

SIDE NOTE

Screen Size

Not all screen sizes are the same. If you cannot see all of a tab's groups, you may need to click a arrow to make a button visible.

To Open the SpaSales Workbook

a. Start **Excel**, click **Open Other Workbooks** in the left pane, and then click **This PC**. Navigate through the folder structure to the location of your student data files, and then click **e02ch04SpaSales**. The workbook containing sales data for the Turquoise Oasis Spa opens.

b. If necessary, click Enable Editing. Click the **File** tab, and then click **Save As,** and then click **This PC**. In the Save As dialog box, navigate to the location where you are saving your project files, and then change the file name to **e02ch04SpaSales_LastFirst** using your last and first name. Click **Save**.

c. On the **TableUse** worksheet, click the **Insert** tab, and in the Text group, click **Header & Footer**.

d. On the **Header & Footer Tools Design** tab, in the Navigation group, click **Go to Footer**. If necessary, click the left section of the footer, and then, in the Header & Footer Elements group, click **File Name**.

e. Click any **cell** on the worksheet to move out of the footer, press Ctrl+Home, and then, on the status bar, click **Normal** ⊞.

f. Click **Save** 🖫.

Modifying an Existing Chart

A chart is an object in Excel. Clicking on the chart will allow you to modify aspects of the chart or even change the type of chart. When you click an existing chart, you are activating the chart area. The border of the chart will be highlighted, while the middle of the sides and the corners of the chart will have selection handles, which can be used to resize the chart. The chart border can also be used to move the entire chart to a new location within the spreadsheet. When a chart is selected, the Chart Tools contextual tab will appear on the ribbon. To the right of the chart, the Chart Formatting Control will appear as three buttons that provide quick access to common functions such as chart elements, chart layout, and filtering of chart data.

When a chart is selected by clicking on the chart, the data used in creating the chart will be highlighted in the worksheet, offering a visual clue of the associated data. In the TableUse worksheet, you will see a pie chart describing the use of massage tables by individual therapists at the spa. When the chart is selected, a purple border surrounds the data that represents the legend labels. The range with a blue border is the data that represents the data series for the pie slices. A **data series** is a group of related data values to be charted. A **data point** is an individual data value in a data series. A chart may contain multiple data series or a single data series.

REAL WORLD ADVICE	**First Impressions**

First impressions are important with charts. You want the audience to receive the correct message during the initial moments. An audience that is distracted by the look and feel of the chart may stop looking for the message in the chart or extend the chaotic personality of the chart to the presenter. Thus, the chart can become a reflection on you and your company.

To quickly identify the value of the data series, Meda Rodate has asked you to modify the existing pie chart on the TableUse worksheet by adding data labels, which you will do in this exercise. Since you will be modifying a pie chart, Meda prefers the addition of percentage labels over the value labels for each data series. She has also asked you to change the chart style to improve its appearance. In this exercise, you will modify an existing chart.

 **E04.01**

SIDE NOTE
Alternate Method
Any action completed in the Chart Formatting control can also be completed through the Chart Tools contextual tab on the ribbon.

To Modify an Existing Chart

a. On the **TableUse** worksheet, notice the pie chart located to the right of the data on this worksheet.

b. Click the **chart border** of the chart to select the chart and display the Chart Tools contextual tabs.

c. To the right of the chart, click **Chart Elements** ➕, and then click to select **Data Labels**. This will display the number of times each therapist used a portable massage table in the corresponding slice of the pie chart.

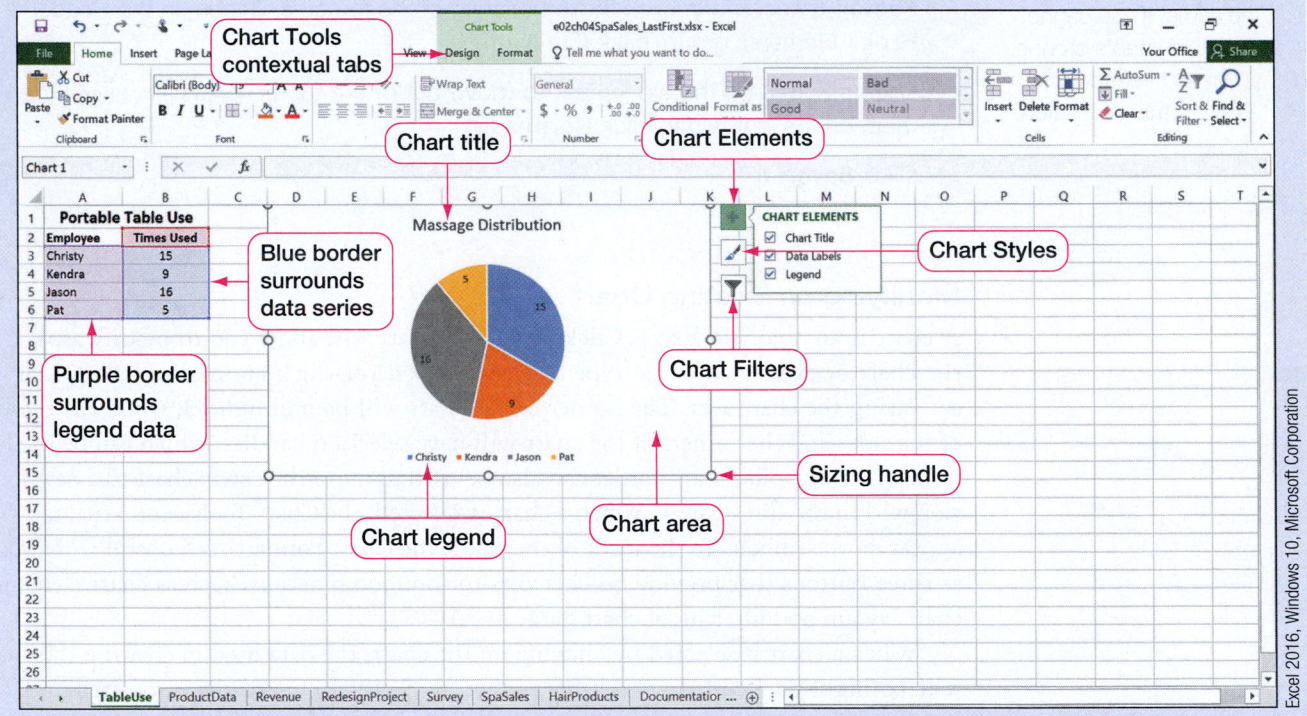

Figure 1 Selected pie chart

SIDE NOTE
Point to See Icon Information
When you are presented with a set of icons, point to an icon. A ScreenTip will appear offering descriptive information.

d. Click the **Data Labels** arrow, and then select **More Options**. This will open the Format Data Labels task pane.

e. Under Label Options, click to select **Percentage**, and then click to deselect **Value**. On the Format Data Labels task pane on the right side of the screen, click close ✕.

f. Click the **chart border** of the pie chart, click **Chart Styles** 🖌, and then scroll down and point to **Style 3**. Notice that the chart changes to display a live preview of the style.

g. Click **Style 3**, and then click **Chart Styles** 🖌 to close the control. The chart now displays the percentage of portable table use for each massage therapist at the spa.

h. **Save** 🖫 the workbook.

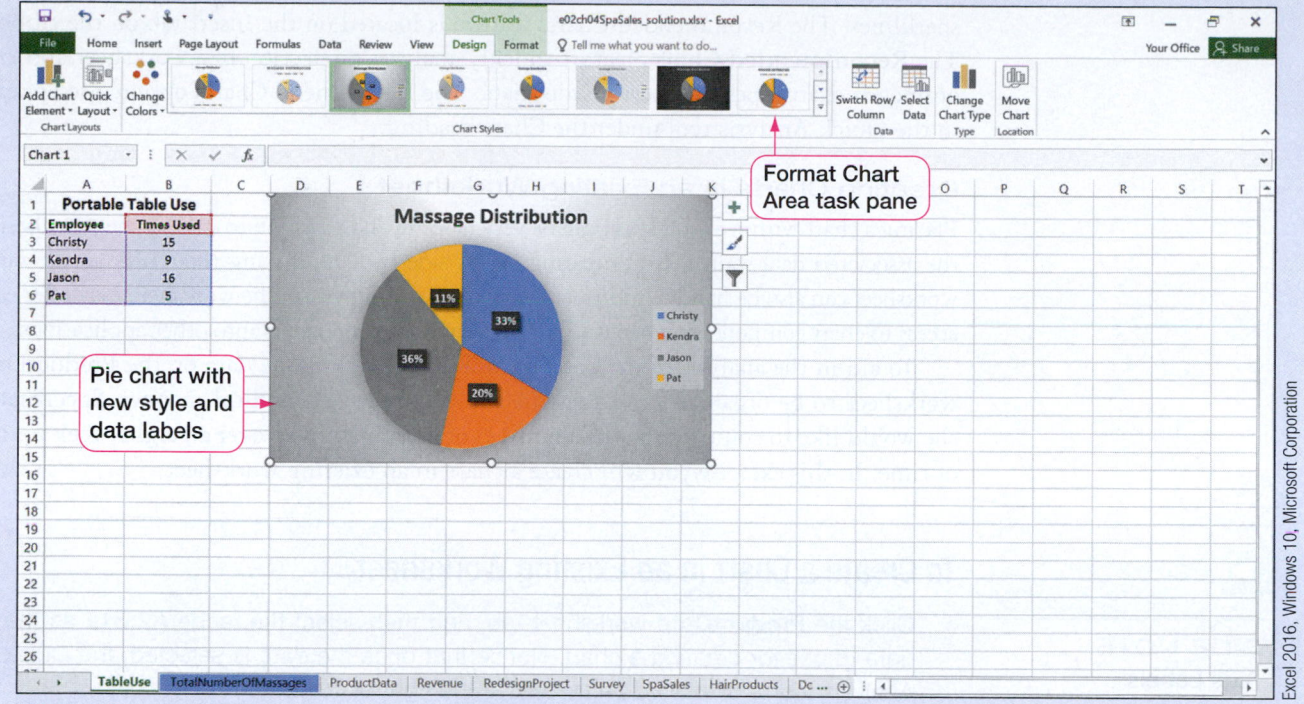

Figure 2 Modified chart

SS **CONSIDER THIS** | **Misleading Charts**

Charts are supposed to frame information. However, charts in newspapers, online articles, and magazines sometimes lead the viewer to an incorrect assumption or conclusion. Look for a chart that is misleading. Discuss the context and possible incorrect conclusions that could be drawn from the chart, and consider the ethical aspect for the creator of the chart.

QUICK REFERENCE | **Working with Chart Objects**

It is possible to navigate through a chart using some of these guidelines.

- Click the chart border to activate the Chart Tools contextual tabs.
- Click chart objects to select individual chart components.
- Click outside a chart object or press Esc to deselect an object.
- On the Chart Tools contextual tabs, on the Format tab, in the Current Selection group, use the Chart Elements box to select specific chart objects.
- Use border corner handles to resize selected objects.
- Click a chart object and drag to move the chart object.

Explore the Position of Charts

When designing a chart, consider the chart location, as this might affect the flexibility of moving and resizing your chart components. There are two general locations for a chart: either within an existing worksheet as an embedded chart or on a separate worksheet, referred to as a chart sheet. An **embedded chart** exists as an object on the same worksheet with the data. **A chart sheet** is a special worksheet that is dedicated to displaying chart objects. Excel 2016 has several features that allow you to quickly analyze data. Two of these are the Quick Analysis tool and the Recommended Charts feature. The **Quick Analysis** tool is a contextual tool that appears when you select data in a worksheet and offers single-click access to formatting, charts, formulas, PivotTables, and sparklines. The Recommended Charts feature is located on the Insert tab on the ribbon. The **Recommended Charts** feature quickly analyzes a selection in a worksheet and recommends chart types that best fit your data. The Recommend Charts option also appears in the Quick Analysis tool under the Chart heading.

Creating Charts in an Existing Worksheet

Placing a chart within a worksheet can be very helpful, allowing you to display the chart beside the associated data source. In comparing charts side by side, placing the charts on the same worksheet can also be handy. Additionally, placing a chart within the worksheet may offer easy access to chart components when copying and pasting components into other applications.

To aid in the analysis of the data, Irene Kai would like the data on the ProductData worksheet to be organized and presented in an effective graphical manner. Specifically, she would like to compare the total number of massages given over an eight-week period of time. In this exercise you will create a chart in an existing worksheet.

 E04.02

SIDE NOTE
Axis Labels
When creating a chart, be sure to select the appropriate data labels as well as the data. Failure to do so may produce an incomplete and confusing chart.

To Create a Chart in an Existing Worksheet

a. Click the **ProductData** worksheet tab, and then select the range **A2:B12** as the data to use for creating a chart. Notice that once the data is selected, the Quick Analysis tool is displayed below and to the right of cell B12.

b. Click **Quick Analysis**, and then click **Charts**.

c. Point to the **Clustered Column** chart suggestion. Notice that a Live Preview of the chart is displayed.

Troubleshooting

If Live Preview is not displaying, it may be that your taskbar is in triple height. Try changing your taskbar to double or single height.

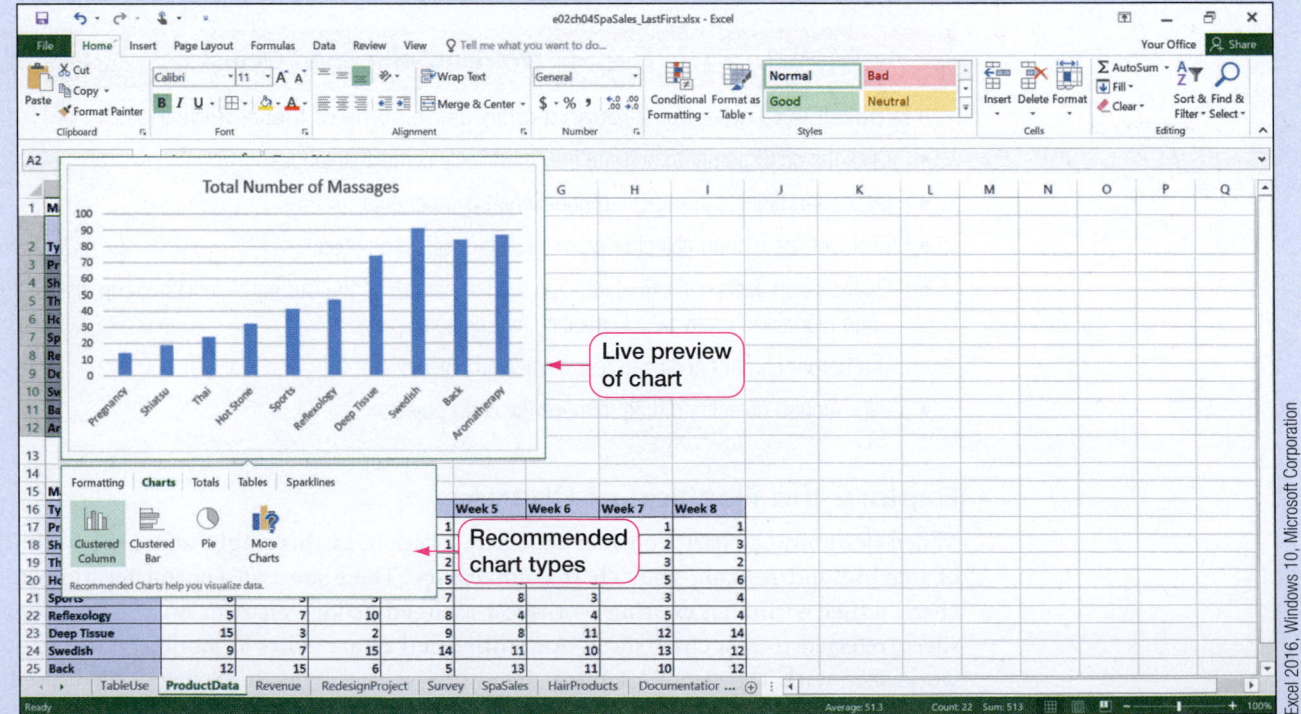

Figure 3   Quick Analysis tool with a suggested chart

SIDE NOTE
Resizing a chart
You can resize a chart by clicking and dragging a sizing handle. Be careful not to click the corners or middle areas of the chart border if you want only to move a chart.

d. Click **Clustered Column** to insert the chart into the worksheet.
Notice that the chart appears on the currently active worksheet and shows colored borders surrounding the associated data linked to the chart. This chart displays the total number provided of each type of massage offered by the spa.

e. Click the **chart border.** When the pointer appears as a four-way arrow , drag the border to move the chart to the right of the data so the top left chart corner is in cell **D2**.

f. **Save** 🖫 the workbook.

Modifying a Chart's Position Properties

When a chart is created in Excel, it is placed by default on a worksheet as an embedded chart. The default property settings resize the chart shape if any of the underlying rows or columns are changed or adjusted. Therefore, if the width of a column that lies behind the chart is increased, the chart width will increase accordingly. It is possible to change this setting, locking the size and position of the chart so it does not resize or move when columns or rows are resized, inserted, or deleted.

Meda is concerned that if additional data is added to the ProductData worksheet, the data may require the underlying columns to be widened or new columns to be inserted. If the default settings on the chart are not adjusted, the chart could become distorted when changes are made to the worksheet. In this exercise, you will modify the chart's position properties.

E04.03

To Modify the Chart Position on a Worksheet

a. On the **ProductData** worksheet, right-click the **chart border** of the clustered column chart, and then select **Format Chart Area**. This will open the Format Chart Area task pane.

b. In the Format Chart Area task pane, click **Size & Properties** 🖾, and then click the **Properties** arrow to expand the **Properties** group.

c. Click **Move but don't size with cells**.

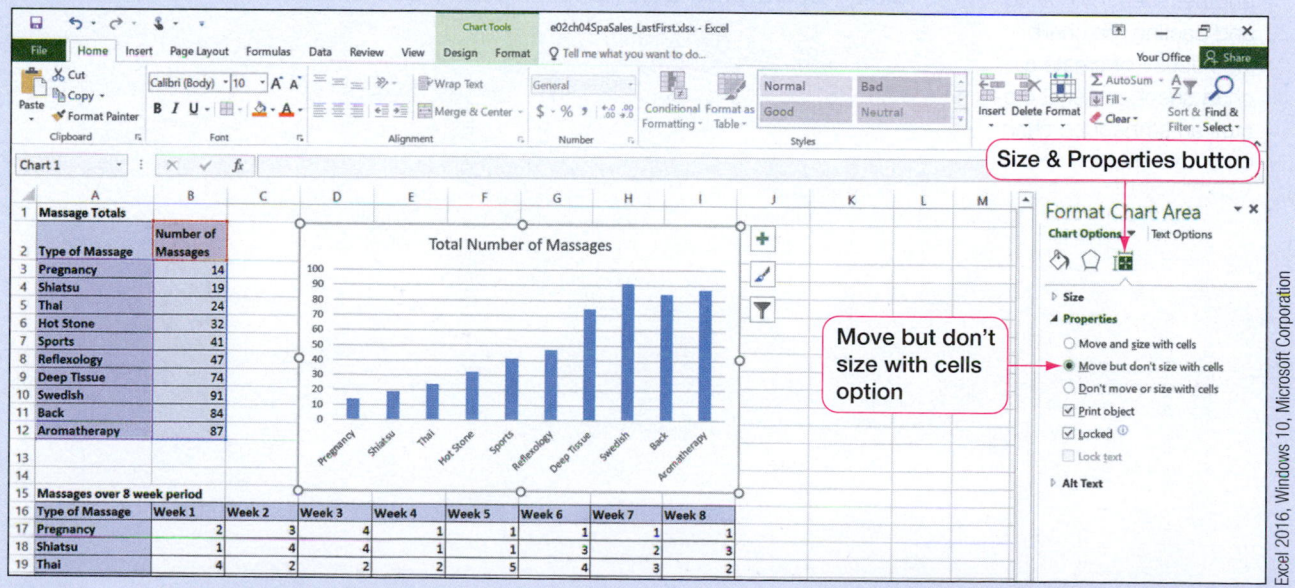

Figure 4 Format Chart Area task pane

d. On the Format Chart Area task pane, click **Close** ☒. **Save** 🖫 the workbook.

The chart size will not be resized if the width or height of the columns or rows underneath are changed or adjusted, but the chart will move along with the cells beneath the chart. From here, you can easily move the chart by dragging the border, or you can resize the chart by clicking and dragging the sizing handles.

Placing Charts on a Chart Sheet

A chart sheet is a worksheet that contains only a chart object. The familiar cell grid is replaced with the actual chart. Having the chart on a separate chart sheet can make it easier to isolate and print on a page. Chart sheets are also useful when you want to create a set of charts and easily navigate between them by worksheet names rather than by looking for them on various worksheets. Because of the nature of chart sheets, the data associated with the chart will be on a different worksheet.

Irene has mentioned that she would like to use this chart in future presentations and would like to be able to easily isolate and print the chart. To facilitate this, in this exercise, you will move the chart to a chart sheet.

 E04.04

SIDE NOTE
Alternate Method
To move a chart to a chart sheet, you can also right-click the chart and select Move Chart from the shortcut menu.

SIDE NOTE
Cutting and Pasting a Chart
You can move a chart to another sheet by cutting and pasting the chart. This does not create a chart sheet; rather, it creates an embedded chart on a new sheet.

To Move a Chart to a Chart Sheet

a. On the **ProductData** worksheet, select the **clustered column chart**.

b. On the **Chart Tools Design** tab, in the **Location** group, click **Move Chart**. The Move Chart dialog box is displayed.

c. In the Move Chart dialog box, click the **New sheet** option. In the New sheet box, clear the **existing name**, and then type TotalNumberOfMassages. Click **OK**.

Notice that you now have a new chart sheet tab in your workbook. By default, the new sheet is placed to the left of the current sheet. This chart sheet is exclusively for the chart and will not have the normal worksheet appearance.

d. Applying a color to the worksheet tab will allow the chart sheet to be easily distinguished from the rest of the worksheets in the workbook. Right-click the **TotalNumberOfMassages** worksheet tab. Point to **Tab Color**, and then click **Blue, Accent 1** in the first row, fifth column as the tab color.

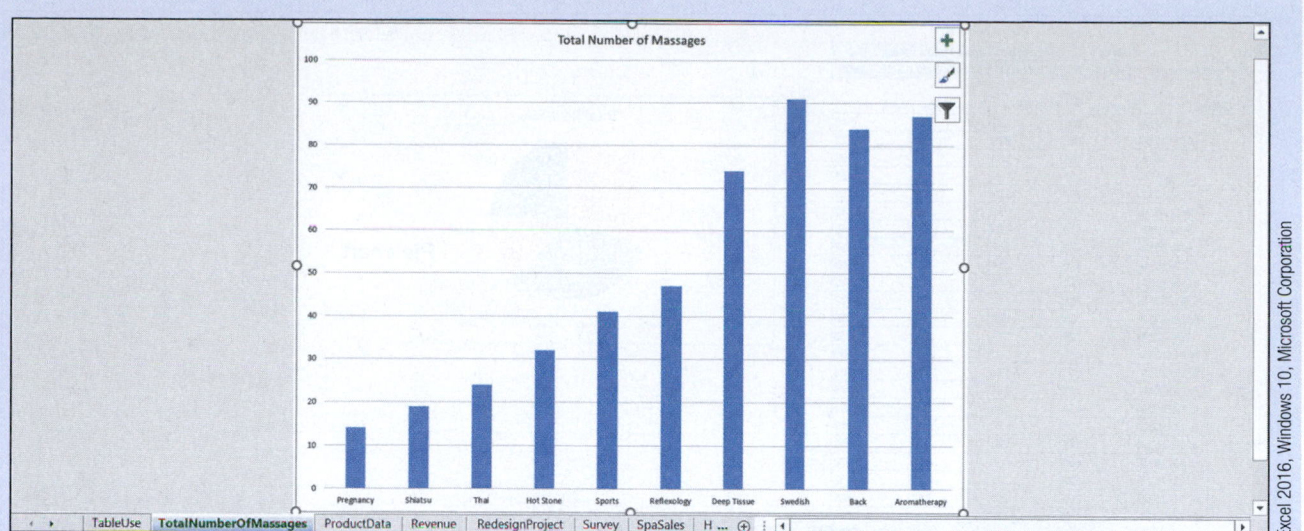

Figure 5 Total number of massages bar chart sheet

e. **Save** the workbook.

Understand Different Chart Types

In creating a chart, it is important to choose the correct type of chart to use. Each chart type conveys information in a particular way. The chart type sets the tone for the basic format of the data and what kind of data is included. Thus, it helps if you become familiar with the types of charts that are commonly used for business decision making and for presentations. Always consider which type is appropriate for the message you are trying to convey.

Creating Pie Charts

Pie charts are commonly used for depicting the relationships of the parts to the whole, such as comparing staff performance within a department or comparing the number of transactions of each product category within a time period.

For a pie chart, you need two data series: the labels and a set of corresponding values. This is similar to the data selection made in the TableUse sheet to indicate the percentage of times each person used the portable massage table. Note that the data can be described as a percentage of the whole, as in the chart.

The questions you have will influence what textual data you will include in any chart. If you are exploring a usage fee for each time a table is used, then having the percentage would indicate which therapist is contributing the most fees, and the actual numbers may not be a crucial element. When you create a chart, examine it to see whether it answers your questions.

In this exercise, you will create a simple pie chart that shows the proportion of total revenue each of four different massage types earned for the spa in the month of June.

▶ E04.05

SIDE NOTE

Resizing a chart
When resizing a chart, consider pressing [Alt] and then dragging the sizing handle to snap the chart to a cell.

To Create a Pie Chart

a. Click the **Revenue** worksheet tab, and then select the range **A1:E2**.

b. Click **Quick Analysis** [icon], click **Charts**, and then click **Pie**.

c. Click the **chart border**, and then drag to move the chart to the top left corner of cell **G4**. This will place the chart to the right of the data set.

d. Point to the **bottom right corner** of the chart until the pointer changes to [icon], and then drag to the chart so the bottom right corner is over cell **M17**. The chart displays the proportion of revenue generated by each massage type.

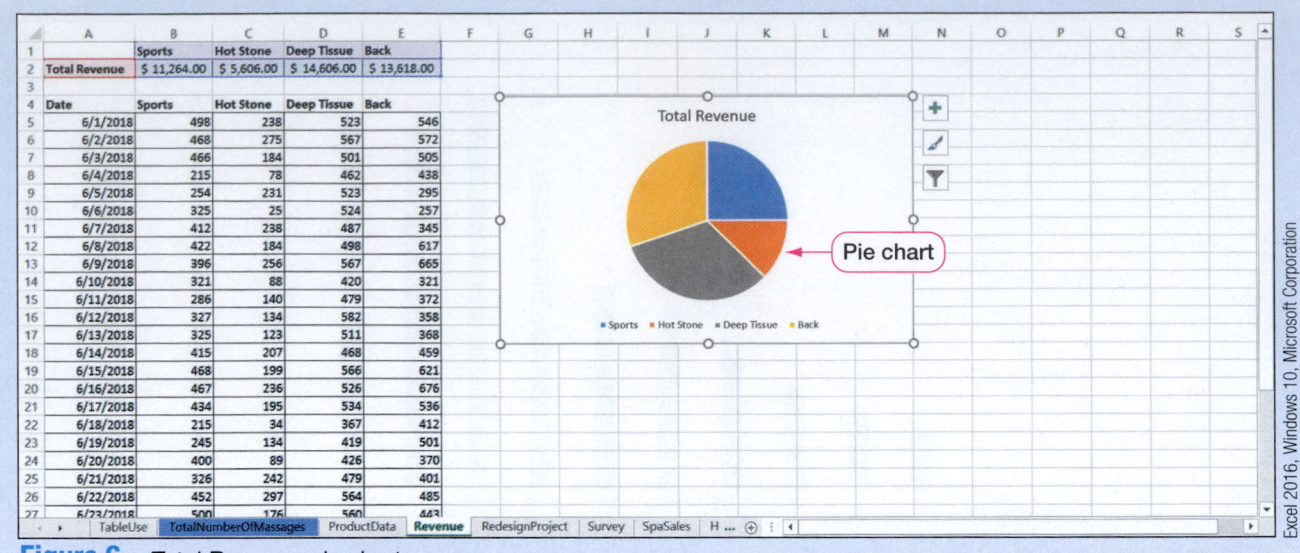

	A	B	C	D	E
1		Sports	Hot Stone	Deep Tissue	Back
2	Total Revenue	$ 11,264.00	$ 5,606.00	$ 14,606.00	$ 13,618.00
3					
4	Date	Sports	Hot Stone	Deep Tissue	Back
5	6/1/2018	498	238	523	546
6	6/2/2018	468	275	567	572
7	6/3/2018	466	184	501	505
8	6/4/2018	215	78	462	438
9	6/5/2018	254	231	523	295
10	6/6/2018	325	25	524	257
11	6/7/2018	412	238	487	345
12	6/8/2018	422	184	498	617
13	6/9/2018	396	256	567	665
14	6/10/2018	321	88	420	321
15	6/11/2018	286	140	479	372
16	6/12/2018	327	134	582	358
17	6/13/2018	325	123	511	368
18	6/14/2018	415	207	468	459
19	6/15/2018	468	199	566	621
20	6/16/2018	467	236	526	676
21	6/17/2018	434	195	534	536
22	6/18/2018	215	34	367	412
23	6/19/2018	245	134	419	501
24	6/20/2018	400	89	426	370
25	6/21/2018	326	242	479	401
26	6/22/2018	452	297	564	485
27	6/23/2018	500	176	560	443

Total Revenue — Pie chart — Sports, Hot Stone, Deep Tissue, Back

TableUse | TotalNumberOfMassages | ProductData | Revenue | RedesignProject | Survey | SpaSales

Excel 2016, Windows 10, Microsoft Corporation

Figure 6 Total Revenue pie chart

e. **Save**  the workbook.

Even though all the data is used to show every massage type, you do not have to use all the data. If the goal is to examine the data and extract a portion of the information, such as the fact that several massage types have low or high average ratings, it may be better to show only a few massage types rather than including too much information. Showing a subset of massage types may help to emphasize particular ratings.

In determining how to proceed once the data has been initially examined, start developing hypotheses and questions. For example, it may be that hot stone massages are too new and need to be marketed more, as they currently represent a small portion of revenues. Develop questions, and then use the data to determine the validity of the questions and make strategic decisions.

Creating Line Charts

Line charts help to convey change in data over a period of time. They are great for exploring how data in a business, such as sales or production, changes over time. Line charts help people to interpret why the data is changing and to make decisions about how to proceed. For example, in examining a heart rate on an electrocardiogram, a doctor is looking at data over time to see what has been happening. The doctor wants to determine if there are issues, and then make decisions about whether the patient should go home, be given medications, or have surgery.

To create a line chart, you need to have at least one set of labels and at least one set of corresponding data. It is possible to have multiple data series, each series representing a line on the chart. You have been provided with data that lists revenue generated by four different types of massages. The data is organized by day throughout the month of June.

In this exercise, you will create a line chart displaying daily revenue by massage type in June. Irene would like each day to appear as a point on the line that is created and each massage type to be a separate line on the chart.

E04.06

To Create a Line Chart

a. On the **Revenue** worksheet tab, click cell **A4**, press Ctrl, and then press A to select the entire data set, including the labels.

b. Click **Quick Analysis**, click **Charts**, and then click **Line**. The chart displays the revenue generated by each type of massage through the month of June.

c. Click the **Chart Tools Format** tab. In the Current Selection group, click the **Chart Elements** arrow, and then click **Chart Title** to select the chart title. Type **Revenue by Massage Type for June**, and then press Enter.

d. Click the **chart border**, and then drag to move the chart to place the top left corner in cell **G20**. This will place the chart to the right of the data set.

e. Point to the **bottom right corner** of the chart until the pointer changes to ⬚, and then drag to resize the chart so the bottom right corner is over cell **M34**.

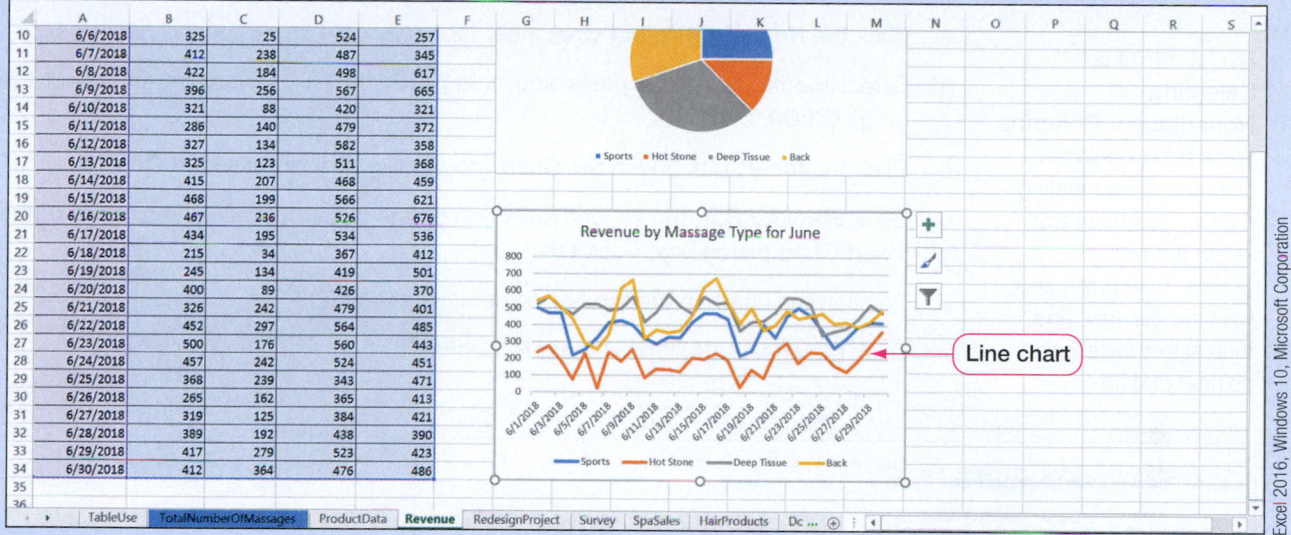

Figure 7 Revenue by Massage Type for June line chart

> ## Troubleshooting
>
> If you end up with a chart that looks dramatically different from what you would expect, check the colored borders around the linked data set. It is very common to select all the data in a table when the intention was to select just part of the data. If too much data was selected, you can delete the selected chart by pressing Delete and then try recreating the chart with the appropriate data. Alternatively, you could select the corner of a colored link data border and drag the border to adjust the set of data. The blue border data is displayed in the chart. When that border is adjusted, the associated label data is automatically adjusted accordingly. The chart is also automatically adjusted so changes can be immediately seen.

f. **Save** 🖫 the workbook.

Creating Column Charts

Column charts are useful for comparing data sets that are categorized, such as departments, product categories, or survey results. Column charts are also useful for showing categories over time where each column represents a unit of time. Column charts are good for comparisons either individually, in groups, or stacked. Column chart data can easily allow for grouping of data so comparisons of the groups can occur.

On the TotalNumberOfMassages chart sheet, it is easy to interpret that pregnancy massages represent a small portion of the total massages provided. By contrast, Swedish, aromatherapy, back, and deep tissue massages represent a large portion of the data.

Creating Bar Charts

Bar charts are useful for working with categorical data. Bar charts are similar to column charts except the bars are horizontal representations of the data rather than vertical. Like column charts, bar charts can depict a single piece of data, can be grouped data series, and can be stacked.

Stacked bar charts can be useful when you want to see how the individual parts add up to create the entire length of each bar. A stacked bar chart can display changes over time for products or services. Stacked charts should be considered when the sum of the data values is as important as the individual items.

In this exercise, you will create a stacked bar chart that will assist Meda and Irene to visualize the status of a project to redesign the massage therapy rooms.

 E04.07

SIDE NOTE
Selecting Nonadjacent Columns
To select nonadjacent columns when creating a chart, you must first select the first column of data, then press and hold the Ctrl key, and then select the second column of data.

To Create a Stacked Bar Chart

a. Click the **RedesignProject** worksheet tab.

b. Select the range **A3:A8**, press and hold down the Ctrl key, and then select the range **C3:D8**.

c. Click the **Insert** tab, and in the Chart group, click **Recommended Charts**.

d. Click **Stacked Bar**, the second selection on the Recommended Charts tab of the Insert Chart dialog box. Click **OK**.

e. Position the chart so the top left corner is over cell **A10**.

f. Click the **chart title**, type Project Redesign Status, and then press Enter.

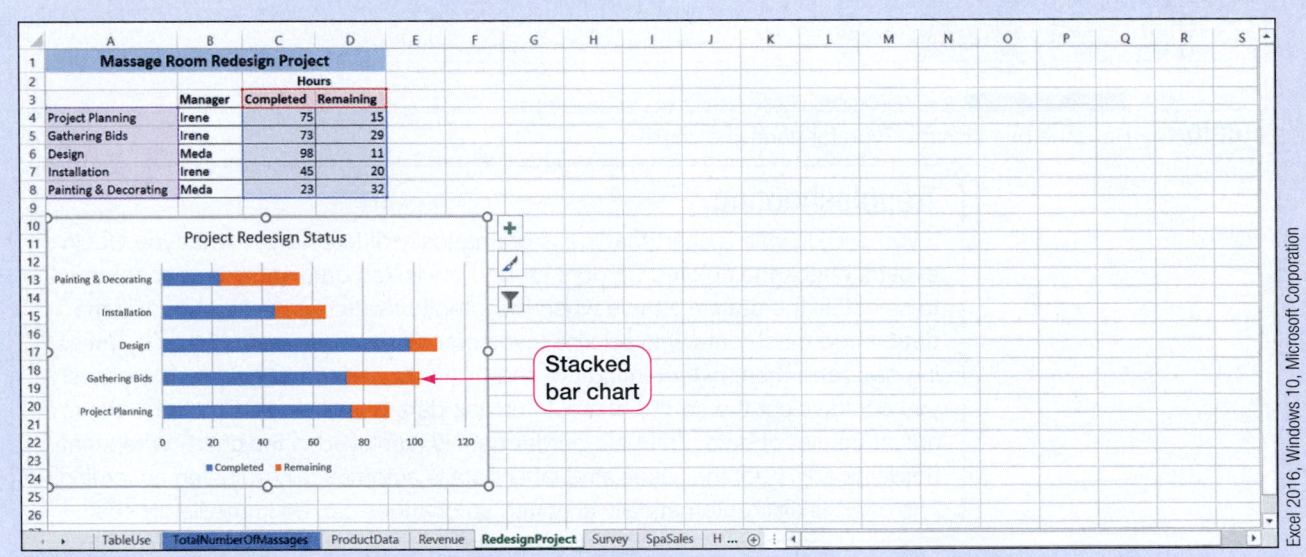

Figure 8 Project Redesign stacked bar chart

g. **Save** the workbook.

The stacked bar chart helps Irene and Meda to determine the status of the redesign phases The chart shows which phases are nearly complete and which phases still need more time to complete. They can use the information to determine whether they need to assign more resources to a phase, such as painting and decorating, to be sure it gets completed in the desired time.

Creating Scatter Charts

A **Scatter chart**, also called XY (Scatter), is a particular type of chart that conveys the relationship between two numeric variables. This type of chart is very common as a statistical tool depicting the correlation between the two variables. The standard format is to have the x-axis (horizontal) data in the left column and the y-axis (vertical) data in the right column(s).

Irene and Meda have data from a survey showing the requested temperature of the room used for massages and the age of the customer. This data may reveal important information about what temperature is typically requested by customers in different age groups. In this exercise, you will create a scatter chart of the requested temperatures of rooms and ages of customers.

 **E04.08**

To Create a Scatter Chart

a. Click the **Survey** worksheet tab, and then select the range **A2:B53**. This will include the data and labels for Age and Temp.

b. Click **Quick Analysis** 📊, click **Charts**, and then click **Scatter**.

c. Click the **chart border**, and then drag to move it to the right of the data so the top left corner is over cell **E2**.

The default scale of the chart does not bring out any trends in the data. Adjusting the scaling of the y-axis will help to display any trends. You will adjust the scale of the y-axis later in this chapter.

d. Click the **Chart Title**, type Relationship Between Age and Temperature, and then press Enter. This chart shows the relationship between increasing age and temperatures requested for massages.

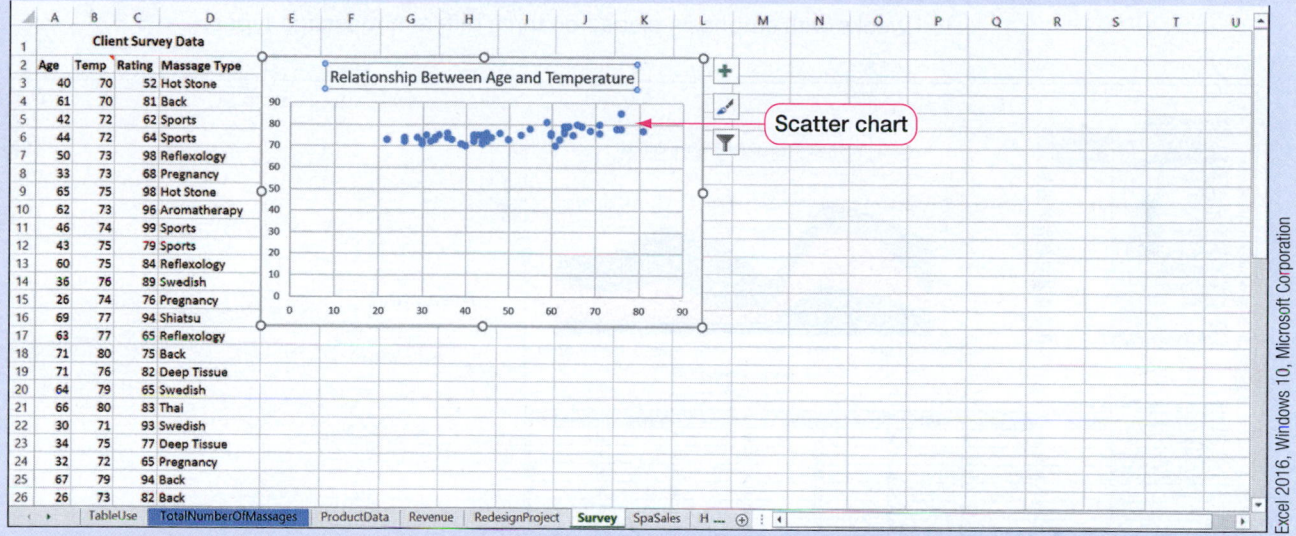

Figure 9 Scatter chart of temperature

e. **Save** 💾 the workbook.

Creating Area Charts

An **area chart** is a variation of a stacked line chart that emphasizes the magnitude of change over time and visually depicts a trend. The area chart stacks a set of data series and colors each area that is created. This type of chart provides a nice visual presentation because each colored layer changes, by growing or shrinking as it moves across time periods. With an area chart, the horizontal x-axis is typically a time sequence. The area chart could also use categories instead of time on the horizontal x-axis, where each layer again is showing the individual contribution to the area; thus, it is a quantitative chart that shows growth or change in totals.

Irene has asked you to create a chart to further understand the differences in the types of massages given over the past eight weeks at the spa. She is particularly interested in Pregnancy, Shiatsu, and Thai massages. In this exercise, you will create an area chart for this purpose.

To Create an Area Chart

a. Click the **ProductData** worksheet tab, and then select the range **A16:I19**.

b. Click **Quick Analysis**, click **Charts**, and then click **Stacked Area.** Notice that there are two chart choices for stacked charts. You will select the second for Stacked Area.

c. Click the **Chart Title**, type Massage Types Over 8 Week Period, and then press Enter.

d. Click the **chart border**, and then drag to move the chart so the top left corner is over cell **D2**.

e. With the chart border still selected, point to the lower right sizing handle, and then drag to resize the chart so the lower right corner of the chart is over **I14**.

This chart shows the total number of massages offered for each of the past eight weeks with emphasis placed on three different massage types.

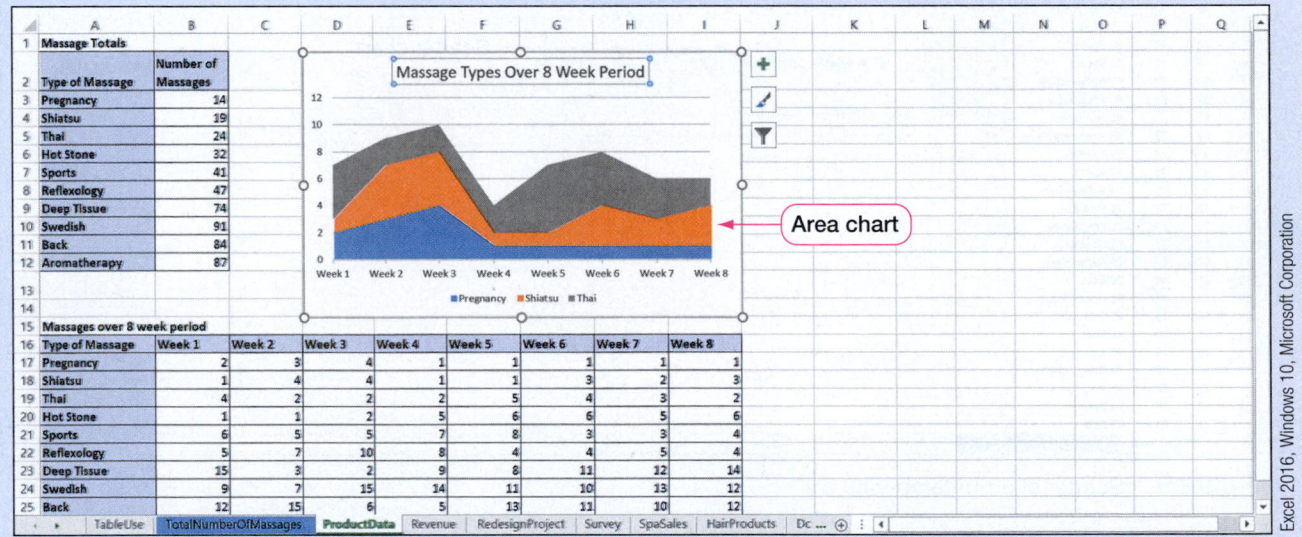

Figure 10   Area chart of three types of massages over past eight weeks

f. **Save** the workbook.

Creating Combination Charts

A **combination chart** displays two different types of data by using multiple chart types in a single chart object. Combination charts can enhance the understanding of data when the scale of data being charted varies greatly. For example, consider monitoring the number of items sold in the spa to customers over a 12-month span of time. To fully comprehend the data, it would be helpful to explore both the number of items sold and the profit from items sold. However, a single item may cost hundreds of dollars. This makes creating a chart to compare these two pieces of data difficult. In prior versions of Excel, creating a combination chart was a difficult and time-consuming process. In Excel 2016, combination charts are a standard chart type.

Meda has asked you to analyze the quantities of spa products sold from the prior year's sales and compare the result to the profits over the same time span. Currently, only data from January to November is available. In this exercise, you will create a chart to which the December data can be added when it becomes available.

 **E**04.10

To Create a Combination Chart

a. Click the **SpaSales** worksheet tab, and then select the range **A2:C13**.

b. Click **Quick Analysis** 📊, click **Charts**, and then click **More Charts**.

c. In the Insert Chart dialog box, click the **All Charts** tab. From the list of charts, click **Combo**.

Before you insert the chart, you will have an opportunity to customize how the data will look. The default chart shows the month on the x-axis while using a line chart for profit (in red) and a clustered column chart for quantity sold (in blue).

d. At the bottom of the dialog box, to the right of **Profit**, click to select the **Secondary Axis** check box. This scales the line chart for profit on a separate axis from quantity, allowing the trend over time between the two to be compared. Click **OK**.

e. Click the **Chart Title**, type Quantity Sold and Profit, and then press Enter.

f. Click the **chart border**, and then drag to move the chart so the top left corner is over cell **E1**.

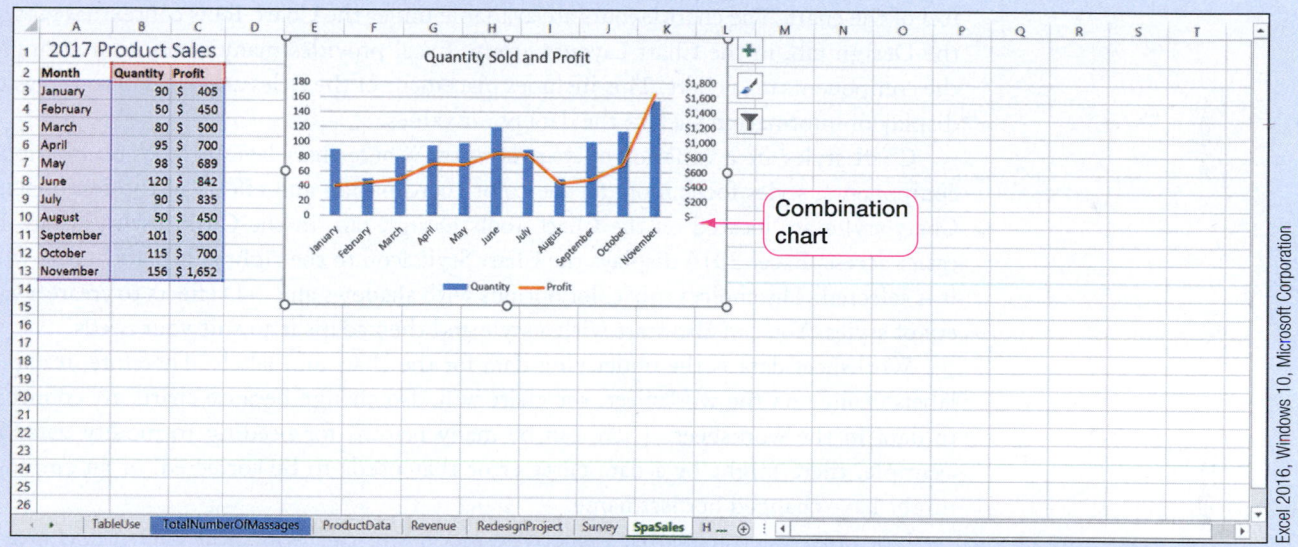

Figure 11 Combination chart of quantity sold and profit

Excel 2016, Windows 10, Microsoft Corporation

g. **Save** 💾 the workbook.

This chart compares the number of spa products sold and the profit from products sold in the same chart. Notice that in January, the profit for items sold is lower than might be expected from the quantity sold.

h. If you need to take a break before finishing this chapter, now is a good time.

QUICK REFERENCE	Chart Selection Guidelines

- **Pie**   Used for comparing the relationship of parts to a whole
- **Line**   Shows changes within a data series; often used with time on the x-axis
- **Column**   Compares data vertically; can incorporate a time element and groups
- **Bar**   Compares data horizontally; stacked bar can show progress or growth
- **Scatter**   Used for correlations, exploring the relationship between two variables
- **Area**   Used to highlight areas showing growth over time or for categories; a variation of a line chart
- **Combination Chart**   Used to display two different types of data in a single chart

Exploring Chart Layouts

As you have seen, a chart can help to answer questions and may even generate more questions. This can help in moving toward the understanding of information, which can also lead to better decision making. Creating these initial charts to explore data is quick and efficient and informs the user.

When a chart is presented to other people, the context of the chart is of utmost importance. Without context, your audience must try to guess the context. You need to provide meaning. Providing context means providing textual guidance to the audience. The audience will see the chart, but you need to inform them more about the data. Thus, labels are another crucial element needed to provide context in charts. The labels include the chart title and axes titles, legend, and data labels. All these elements should work cohesively to complete a picture of what the chart is trying to convey to the audience. In this section, you will change the appearance of charts by altering their layout and color patterns. You will also modify chart titles and the titles of the chart axes.

Change Chart Data and Styles for Presentations

While the default chart settings are pleasant visually, you can still improve the look and feel of the chart. The chart layouts are available under the Chart Tools contextual tabs, on the Design tab, in the Chart Layouts group. Excel provides many options for arranging the components on a chart. This includes placement of the titles and legend as well as the display of information such as the data point values.

Chart styles are a variation of chart layouts. Where chart layouts focus on location of components, styles focus more on the color coordination and effects of the components. Chart styles are located on the Chart Tools Design tab, in the Chart Styles group. For easier access, Excel 2016 displays the Chart Style icon to the right side of any chart when it is selected. The choices mix color options with shadows and 3-D effects to create a variety of styles. You can also start with a style and then adapt it to suit your needs.

Worksheet data is the underlying data for the chart and labels. Therefore, if data or labels change on the worksheet, the chart will also change because charts are connected to data in the worksheet. There can be many reasons for needing to modify data. For example, there might be a data entry error that needs to be corrected, or an employee might have changed her last name.

Not only can you modify a chart by modifying the worksheet data it was created from, you can also modify how the chart is displaying the data. For example, if the data needs to be swapped between the data points and the axis data, you can use the Data group to switch rows and columns or select new data for a chart.

Changing the Data and Appearance of a Chart

Because charts in Excel are connected to data on the worksheet, changes to the data are automatically reflected in the chart. This is extremely useful if you have a model that is using some calculations that are then used in a chart. You can do what-if analysis by changing data in a worksheet; the corresponding changes will appear on the chart.

Charts may need to be modified when the amount of data being charted needs to be changed. For example, a chart might have too much information included, making it difficult to get a clear picture. Conversely, a chart may need to be modified as new data becomes available. If the new data is adjacent to the existing data, it is a simple process to expand the existing data series. This is achieved by resizing the borders around the data series after activating the chart.

Irene has just provided you with the December data for quantity and profit for the spa. She has also mentioned that there is an error in the quantity in January sales. In this exercise, you will add the December data to the SpaSales worksheet, adjust the combination chart accordingly, and correct the January data. You will also modify the appearance of the chart.

 **E04.11**

To Modify the Layout and Data in an Existing Chart

a. If you took a break, open the **e02ch04SpaSales** workbook and, if needed, navigate to the **SpaSales** worksheet. Click cell **A14**.

b. Type December, and then press Tab↹. Type 165, and then press Tab↹. Type 1701, and then press Ctrl+Enter.

c. Click the **chart area** portion of the chart. Click the **sizing handle** on the lower edge between cells **A13** and **B13**, and then drag the sizing handle down one row so the range **A2:C14** is now being charted. The chart will now include the quantity sold and profits for the month of December.

d. On the **Chart Tools Design** tab, in the Type group, click **Change Chart Type**.

e. Near the bottom of the Change Chart Type dialog box, next to the **Profit** series, click the **Chart Type** arrow. Select **Area**, and then click **OK**.

f. To the right of the chart, click **Chart Styles** ✏, scroll down, and then click **Style 6**. Click **Chart Styles** ✏ to close the style gallery.

g. On the **Chart Tools Design** tab, in the Chart Layouts group, click **Quick Layout**. In the displayed gallery, click **Layout 9**.

Notice that the new layout added labels for the x-axis and y-axis on the chart. These axis titles will be revised at a later point.

h. On the worksheet, click cell **B3**, enter 125, and then press Tab↹. In cell **C3**, type 650, and then press Enter. Notice that the combination chart reflects the new values.

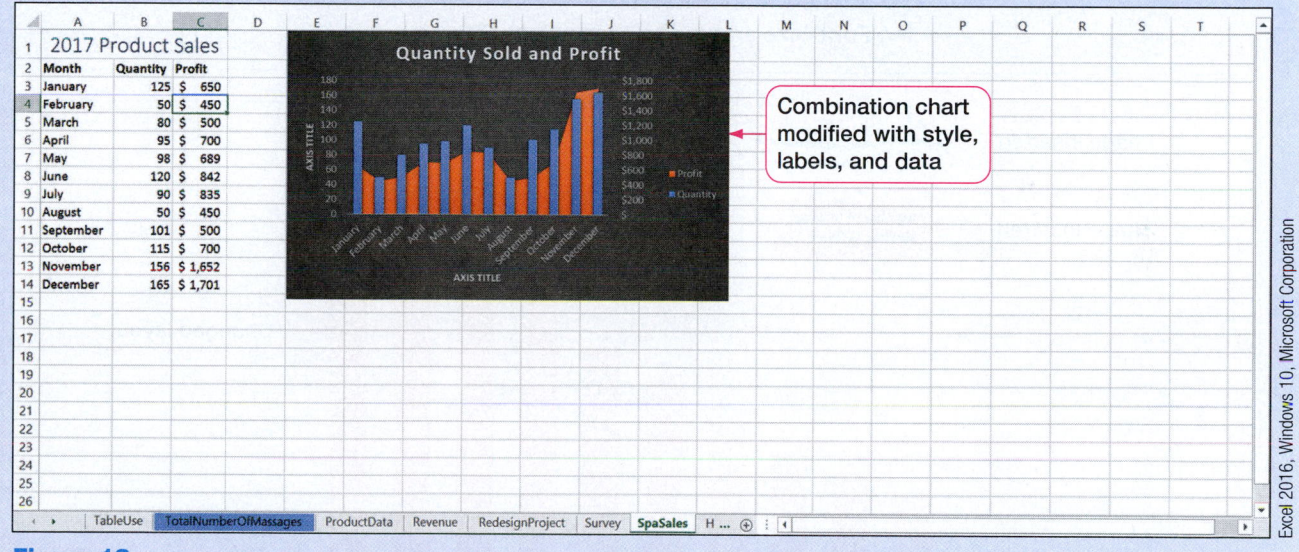

Figure 12 Modified combination chart

i. **Save** 💾 the workbook.

Inserting Objects

If you work for a company, it can be useful to insert the company logo into any chart that is used outside the company. After all, marketing occurs everywhere. It may also be useful to use images to help convey the tone of the presentation. This can be accomplished by inserting an image into the chart.

Irene mentioned that she would be using the chart sheet in the workbook in a variety of presentations and would like it to contain the Turquoise Oasis Spa logo. In this exercise, you will modify the appearance of the chart by inserting the logo and a shape object containing the title of the chart.

 **E04.12**

To Insert Objects into a Chart

a. Click the **TotalNumberOfMassages** worksheet tab.

b. Click the **Insert** tab, and then, in the Illustrations group, click **Pictures**. In the left pane of the Insert Picture dialog box, navigate to the location where you store your student data files, and then click **e02ch04TurquoiseOasis**. Click **Insert**.

c. On the **Picture Tools Format** tab, in the Size group, click the **Shape Height** box. Clear any existing text, type **0.9**, and then press Enter.

d. Click in the **Chart Area**. Click the **Chart Tools Design** tab, and in the Chart Layouts group, click **Quick Layout**. In the gallery that appears, click **Layout 4**. Notice that the new layout added labels for the x-axis on the chart.

e. Click any of the columns in the chart. On the **Chart Tools Format** tab, in the Shape Styles group, click the **More** arrow, and then click **Subtle Effect - Orange, Accent 2** in the fourth row, third column.

f. Click the **Insert** tab, and then, in the Illustrations group, click **Shapes**. In the displayed gallery, in the Rectangles group, click **Rounded Rectangle** — the second option. Click below the Turquoise Oasis Spa logo to place the rectangle.

g. Type Number of Massage Services by Type. On the **Drawing Tools Format** tab, in the Size group, click the Shape Height box, type **0.8**, and then press Enter. In the Shape Width box, type **2.2**, and then press Enter.

h. In the Shape Styles group, click the **More** arrow, and then select **Subtle Effect - Orange, Accent 2** in the fourth row, third column.

i. Select the text in the rectangle. Click the **Home** tab, and in the Font group, click the **Font Size** arrow, and then select **16**.

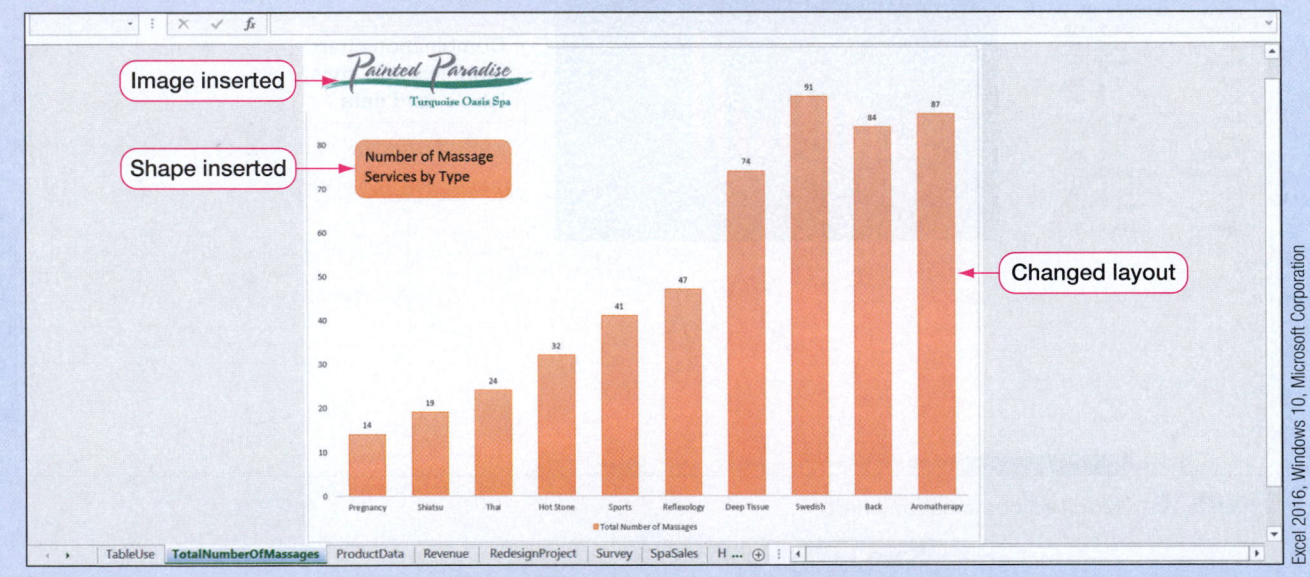

Figure 13 Picture and shape inserted into a chart

j. **Save** the workbook.

Exploring Titles for the Chart and Axes

Chart and axes titles are added easily under the Chart Tools Format tab or with the Chart Elements button that appears on the right side of charts in Excel 2016. Chart titles can be added within the chart, or they can reference cells on the spreadsheet for easy updating.

In this exercise, you will alter the title of the stacked bar chart on the RedesignProject worksheet to match the text in cell A1. You will also clarify the horizontal and vertical axis labels on the combination chart in the SpaSales worksheet.

To Modify Chart Titles and Axis Labels

a. Click the **RedesignProject** worksheet tab, and then click the **chart border** of the stacked bar chart.

b. Click the **chart title** at the top of the chart, and then click the Formula Bar. Type **=**, and then click cell **A1**.

c. Press Enter.

Notice that the title of the chart now matches the contents of cell A1. If the text in cell A1 is changed, the chart title will be updated automatically.

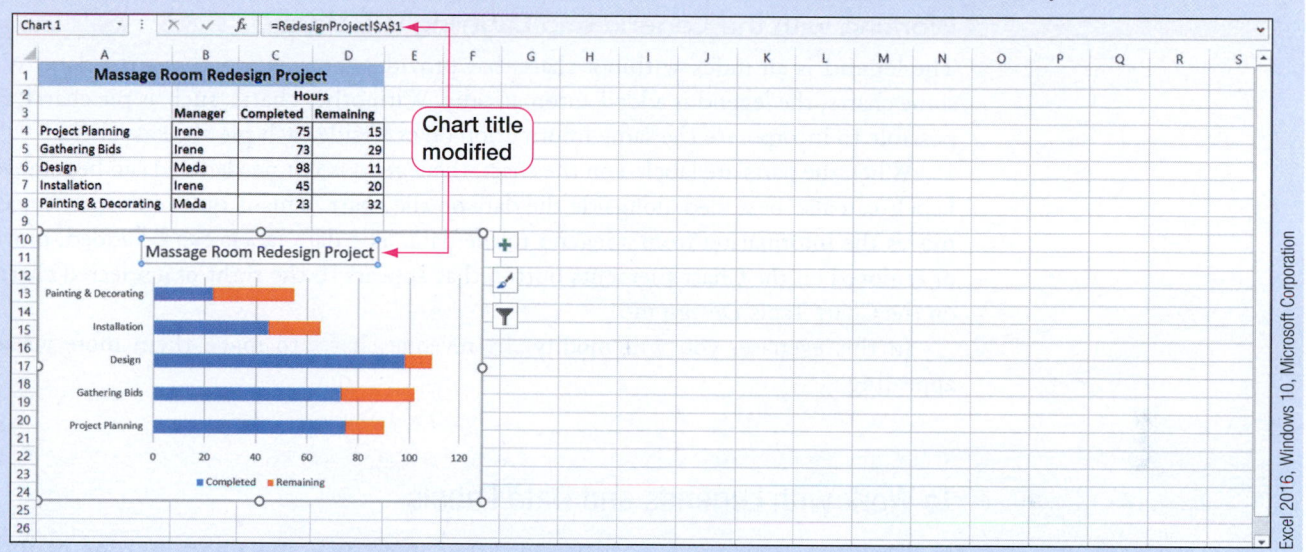

Figure 14 Chart with modified title

d. Click the **SpaSales** worksheet tab, and then click the **chart border** of the combination chart. Click the **Horizontal (Category) Axis Title** box, and then press Del.

e. Click the **Vertical (Value) Axis Title**, type Quantity, and then press Enter.

f. On the **Chart Tools Design** tab, in the Chart Layouts group, click **Add Chart Element**.

g. Point to **Axis Titles**, and then select **Secondary Vertical**. Type Profit, and then press Enter.

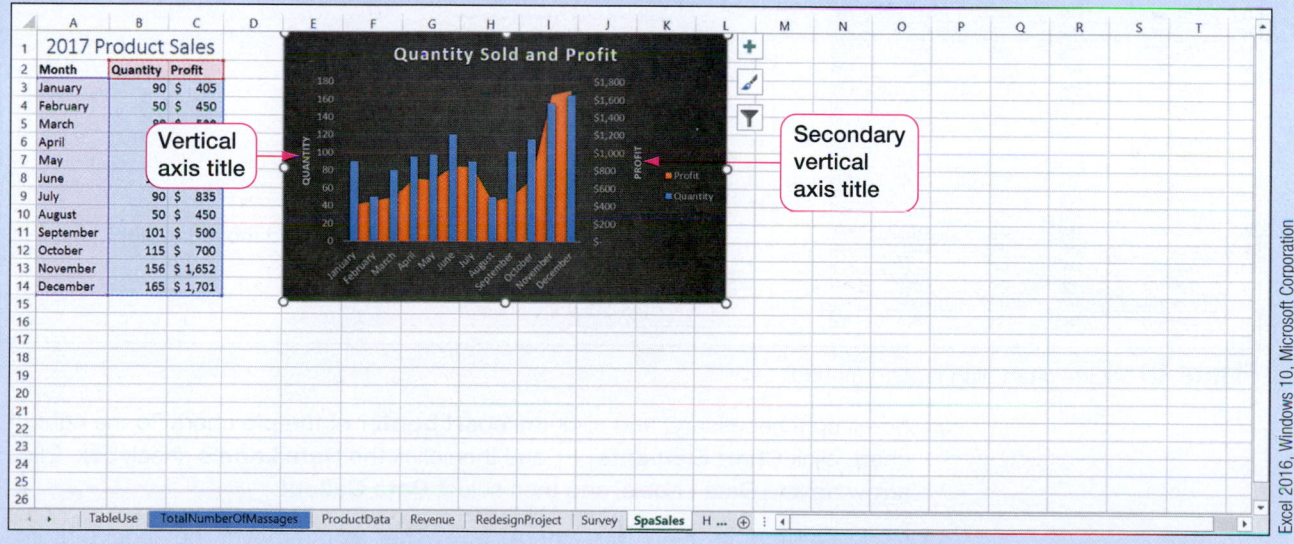

Figure 15 Chart with modified axis labels

h. **Save** the workbook.

CONSIDER THIS | **The Unit of Analysis**

You are presented with a chart titled "2018 Sales Report," and the x-axis is showing 20, 30, 40, and so on for the scale. What is the report depicting? Is it the number of sales transactions, the number of items sold, or the revenue for 2018? Are the 20, 30, and 40 the actual numbers of items sold, or are they quantities in hundreds or thousands? What context should be provided to make certain the audience knows the meaning of the chart?

Working with the Legend and Labeling the Data

The **legend** is an index within a chart that provides information about the data. With some charts, the legend is added automatically. With other charts, such as pie charts, it is possible to incorporate the same information on or beside each pie slice as labels.

When the parts are labeled on the chart, the legend is not needed and can be removed. Labels can also be added alongside the data on the chart. This is quite informative, as it moves the information from a legend to the data. The data labels can be added, moved, or removed on the Chart Elements button that appears to the right of a selected chart or on the Chart Tools Design tab.

In this exercise, you will modify the revenue charts to make them more visually appealing.

E04.14

To Work with Legends and Data Labels

a. Click the **Revenue** worksheet tab, and then click the **chart border** of the **line** chart.

b. To the right of the chart, click **Chart Elements** ⊞, point to Legend, click the **Legend** arrow, and then click **Right**. This moves the legend to the right side of the chart. Click **Chart Elements** ⊞ again to close it.

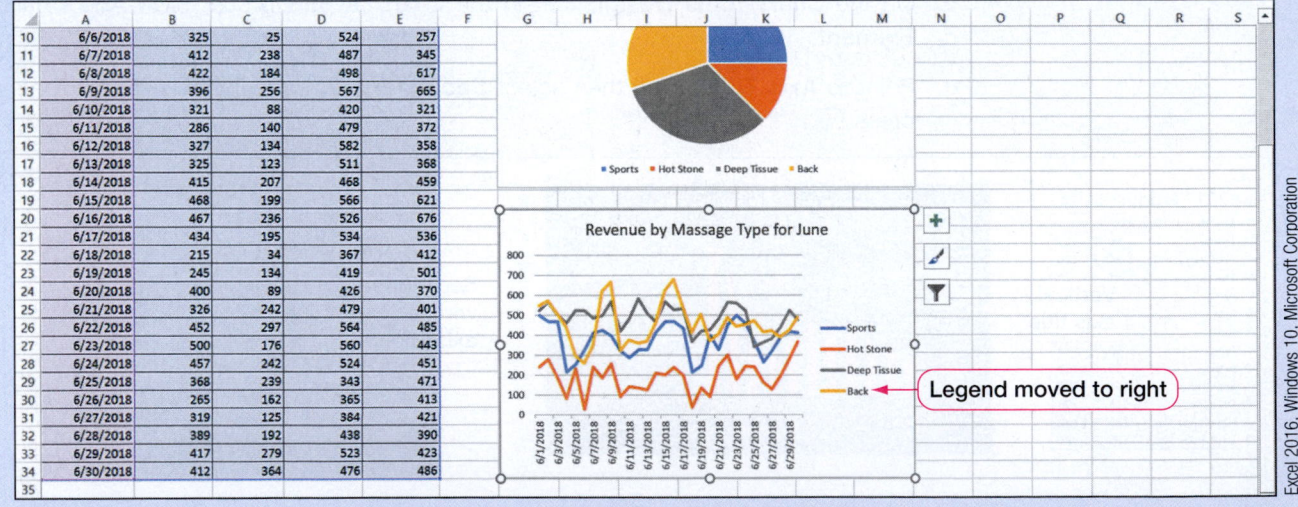

Figure 16   Line chart with legend moved

c. Scroll up if necessary, and click the **chart border** of the **pie** chart. To the right of the chart, click **Chart Elements** ⊞, and then click the **Data Labels** check box. Click the arrow next to Data Labels, and then select **Data Callout**.

d. Click **Legend** to clear the check box. This will remove the legend from the pie chart.

e. Click **Chart Elements** ⊞ again to close the gallery.

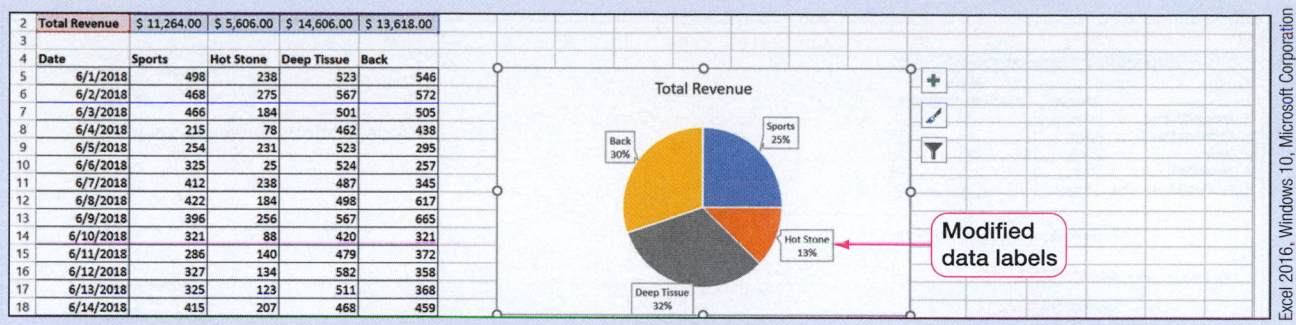

2	Total Revenue	$ 11,264.00	$ 5,606.00	$ 14,606.00	$ 13,618.00
3					
4	Date	Sports	Hot Stone	Deep Tissue	Back
5	6/1/2018	498	238	523	546
6	6/2/2018	468	275	567	572
7	6/3/2018	466	184	501	505
8	6/4/2018	215	78	462	438
9	6/5/2018	254	231	523	295
10	6/6/2018	325	25	524	257
11	6/7/2018	412	238	487	345
12	6/8/2018	422	184	498	617
13	6/9/2018	396	256	567	665
14	6/10/2018	321	88	420	321
15	6/11/2018	286	140	479	372
16	6/12/2018	327	134	582	358
17	6/13/2018	325	123	511	368
18	6/14/2018	415	207	468	459

Figure 17   Pie chart with modified legend and data labels

    f.   Save 💾 the workbook.

> ## Troubleshooting
>
> Adding and removing chart elements may alter the position of other elements of your chart. You may need to reposition existing or new elements in the chart to clarify the meaning of the chart.

Modifying Axes

The horizontal x-axis and vertical y-axis scales are automatically created through a mathematical algorithm within Excel. However, sometimes the scale needs to be modified, as you have already seen. For example, when the scale of numbers is large, a significant gap can exist from 0 to the first data point. In this case, you can modify the scale to start at a more appropriate number instead of 0, which is the default minimum value for Excel. When you need to compare two or more charts, the scales must be consistent. Any time you put charts side by side, you also need to make sure your x-axis and y-axis scales are the same. Otherwise, your audience may not notice the difference and may make incorrect assumptions or decisions. The axis data may also be too crowded, making it difficult to read. In this situation, you would be able to modify the layout of the scale by adjusting the alignment of the data. The data on the axis can be vertical, horizontal, or even placed at an angle.

    The Format Axis task pane is used to manually set the axis options for consistency between a set of charts. Under the Axis Options, the default Excel scale minimum and maximum values are set automatically on the basis of the data. This setting can be changed to allow for customized minimum and maximum values to be applied to the chart. If the source data for the chart is changed, the scale will remain fixed and will not automatically be updated; therefore, any fixed values may also need to be reevaluated as source data changes. In this exercise, you will change the minimum value of a chart.

▶ **E04.15**

To Modify a Chart Axis

a. Click the **RedesignProject** worksheet tab, and then click the **chart border** of the stacked bar chart.

b. Double-click **Horizontal (Value) Axis** for corresponding hours completed and hours remaining. This will open the Format Axis task pane to the Axis Options group. In the Format Axis task pane, if necessary click the Axis Options arrow to expand the **Axis Options** group, and then click in the box for **Minimum**.

c. In the Minimum box, delete the **existing value**, type **20**, and then press Enter .

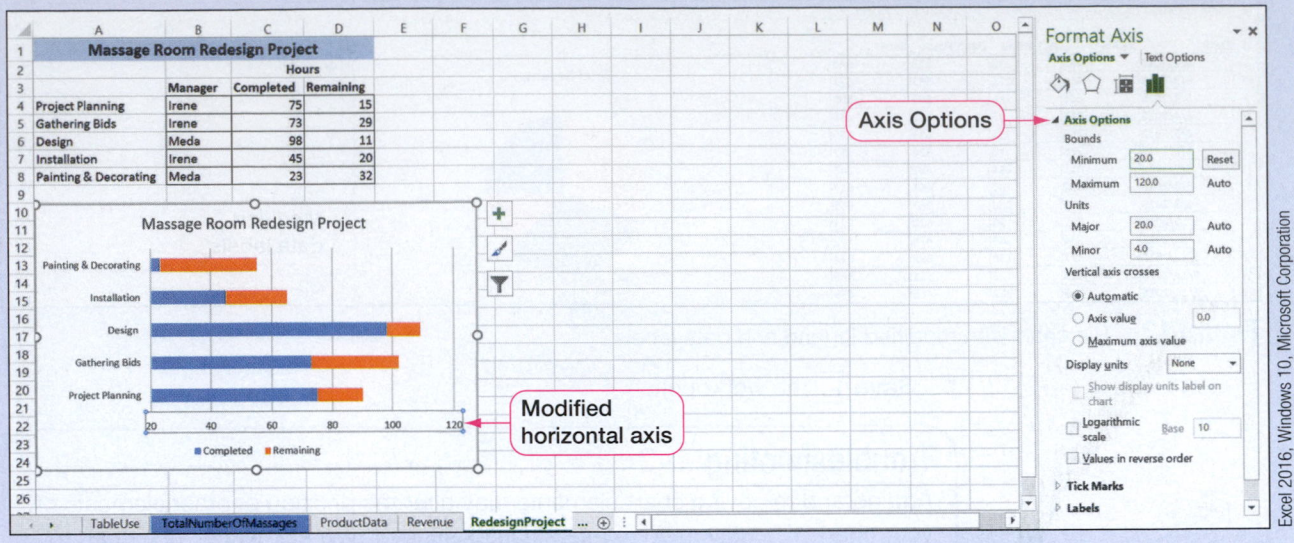

Figure 18 Stacked bar chart with modified chart axis

d. Click the **Survey** worksheet tab, and then select the scatter chart. Double-click the **Vertical (Value) Axis** corresponding to the temperature requested. In the **Axis Options** group, under Bounds, click in the box for **Minimum**.

e. Select the existing number, type **65**, and then press Enter. Notice that the resulting scatter plot has a slight upward trend as the age of the customer increases. This knowledge may lead to decisions that help provide better customer service. You will learn more about modifying axes later in this chapter.

f. On the Format Axis task pane, click Close ☒.

> **Troubleshooting**
> If the value you type in any of the Axis Options boxes does not work for your chart, click the Reset button to the right of the box to change the value back to the chart default.

g. **Save** ☐ the workbook.

Analyzing with Trendlines

A common analysis tool to use within a chart is the trendline. A **trendline** is a line that uses current data to show a trend or general direction of the data. However, data can have a variety of patterns. For scatter plots that explore how two variables interact, a linear trend may be seen. If data fluctuates or varies a great deal, it may be more desirable to use a moving average trendline. Instead of creating a straight line based on all the current data, the moving average trendline uses the average of small subsets of data to set short trend segments over time. The moving average trendline will curve and adjust as the data moves up or down.

The trend or pattern of the data may suggest or predict what will happen in the future. For linear trends, the predicted data can be charted by using a linear trendline added to a scatter chart and the current trend of the data.

Adding a trendline for the scatter chart on the Survey worksheet data may help to confirm the hypothesis that older customers desire a warmer room than younger customers. This may lead the staff to adjust the room temperature before a customer arrives. The staff could predict the desired temperature based on the age of the customer. This could help to improve customer satisfaction. The spa may also want to consider other demographics or characteristics of the customers that allow for providing a customized and personalized service that will build customer loyalty and repeat business. It is easier to retain existing customers than find new ones.

The scatter chart on the Survey worksheet shows that as the age of the customer increases, so does the temperature of the room they request. In this exercise, you will add a trendline to this chart to further illustrate this relationship.

 E04.16

SIDE NOTE
Types of Trendline
The type of trendline you apply to your chart will depend on your chart's data. You can fine-tune trendline settings in the Trendline Format task pane.

To Insert a Trendline

a. On the **Survey** worksheet, click the **chart border** of the scatter chart.

b. To the right of the chart, click **Chart Elements** [+], and then click to select **Trendline**.

c. Click the **Trendline** arrow, and then click **More Options**. In the Format Trendline task pane, click **Fill & Line** ⬧.

d. Click the **Dash type** arrow, and then click **Solid** (the first option).

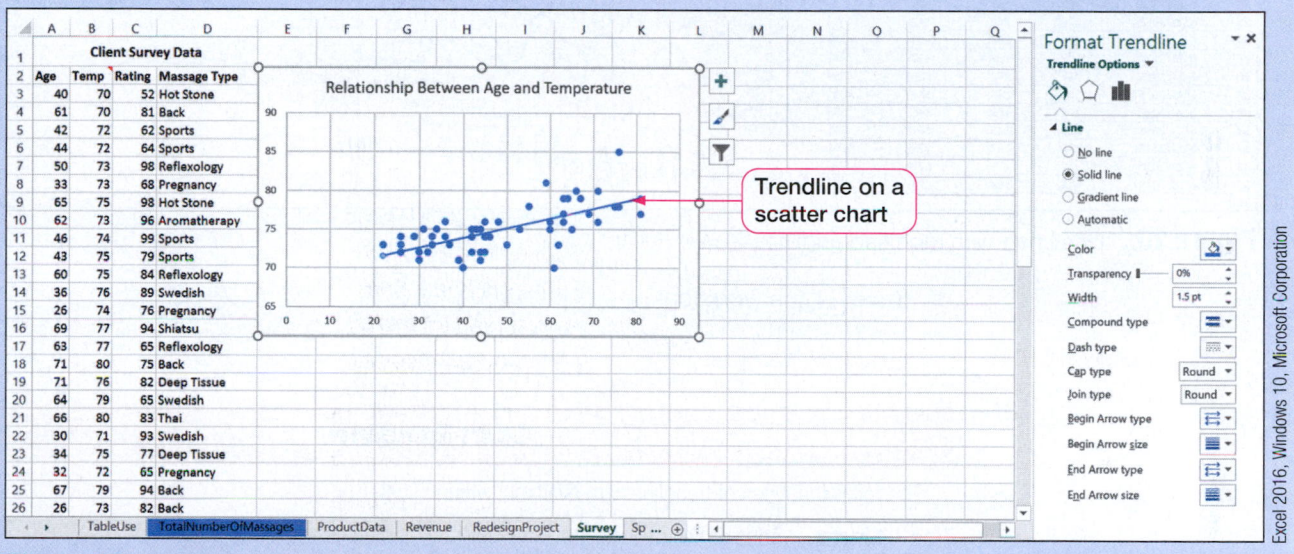

Figure 19 Scatter chart with trendline added

e. In the Format Trendline task pane, click Close [X].

f. **Save** [💾] the workbook.

Changing Gridlines

Gridlines are the lines that go across charts to help gauge the size of the bars, columns, or data lines. In Excel, the default is to display the major gridlines (the gridlines at the designated label values) and not to display the minor gridlines (the gridlines between the label values). If the chart is a line or column chart, Excel puts in the horizontal major gridlines; if it is a bar chart, Excel puts in vertical major gridlines. The default is a good starting point, but personal preferences can dictate which lines to display. The Format Major Gridlines task pane allows for the customization of gridlines in a chart.

In this exercise, you will customize the gridlines in your revenue chart.

 **E04.17**

To Modify Gridlines on a Chart

a. Click the **Revenue** worksheet tab, and then click the **chart border** of the line chart.

b. To the right of the chart, click **Chart Elements** ⊞ , point to over Gridlines, click the **Gridlines** arrow, and then select **Primary Major Vertical**.

c. Click **Chart Elements** ⊞ again to close the gallery.

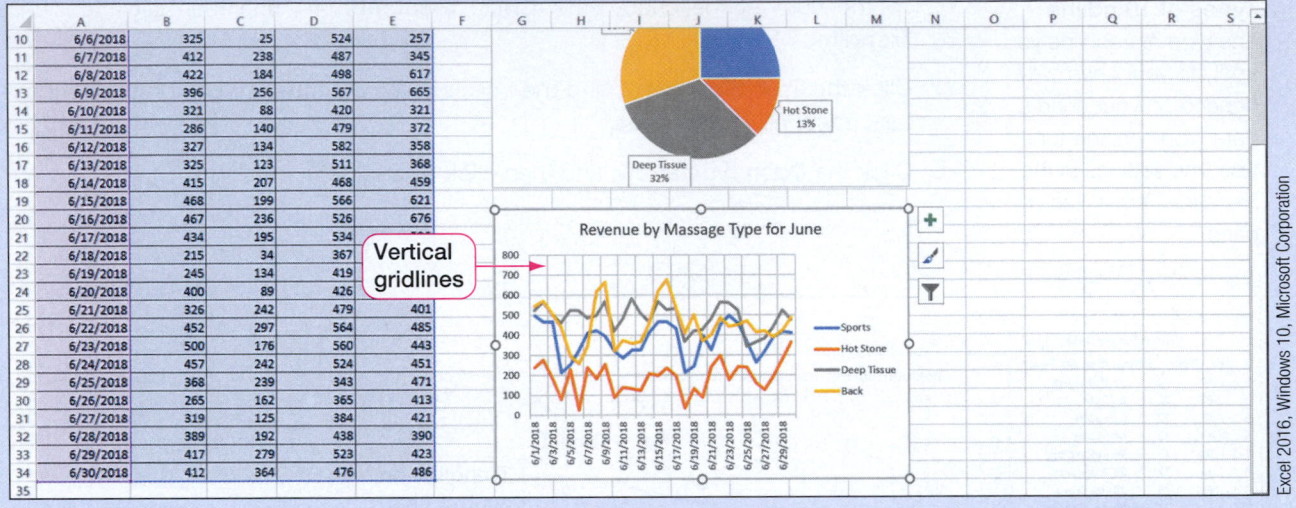

Figure 20 Line chart with modified gridlines

d. **Save** 🖫 the workbook.

Edit and Format Charts to Add Emphasis

In formatting a chart, it is important to have a plan in mind as to the overall layout and look and feel. With a well-thought-out plan, it will be easy to apply the desired adjustments to the components with regard to position, color, and emphasis. Typically, you can either create a unique layout or modify one of Excel's many layouts. Either way, being able to make formatting changes is easy and a very useful and powerful way to convey information. In this section, you will explore various ways to format a chart.

Adding Color to Chart Objects

Working some color into charts can be helpful from a marketing perspective. Excel offers options that allow changing the fill color as well as the border color. Chart colors can be added to match a company's color scheme or to highlight certain important aspects of the data. Remember, however, that while it is possible to add value to charts with color, it is also possible to overdo it.

Irene has mentioned to you that she will be using the pie chart on the Revenue worksheet in a presentation. In this exercise, you will enhance the visual appeal of the chart before her presentation.

 **E04.18**

To Change the Coloring of a Chart

a. On the **Revenue** worksheet, click the **chart border** of the pie chart.

b. On the **Chart Tools Design** tab, in the Chart Styles group, click **Change Colors**, and then, in the gallery that appears, click **Color 4** (the fourth option).

c. On the **Chart Tools Format** tab, in the Shape Styles group, click **Shape Fill**, and then click **Gold, Accent 4, Lighter 60%**.

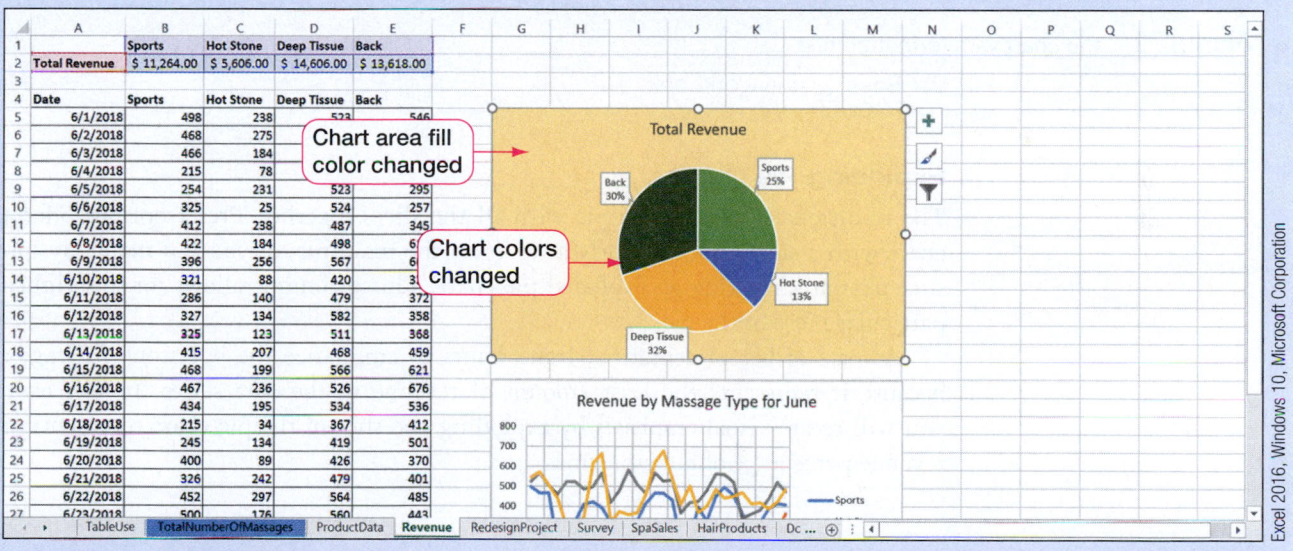

Figure 21 Pie chart with color added

d. **Save** the workbook.

Working with Text

Whether the text is in a shape, title, legend, or axis scale, you can change the formatting of text and the backgrounds of the text objects in charts. The text can be formatted as WordArt, and shapes can be modified to common Shape Styles.

Irene has decided that the pie chart you modified with a new color scheme now has a title that is too difficult to read. In this exercise, you will increase the font size and apply bold to the font in the chart title box to address this problem.

 **E04.19**

To Format Text Within a Chart

a. On the **Revenue** worksheet, if necessary click the **chart border** of the pie chart.

b. Click the **Chart Title**, click the **Home** tab, and then, in the Font group, click **Bold** **B**. In the Font group, click the **Font Size** [11] arrow, and then select **16**.

c. With the title still selected, click the **Chart Tools Format** tab, and in the WordArt Styles group, click the Quick Styles More arrow [▾] to expand the WordArt gallery. Select **Pattern Fill – White, Text 2, Dark Upward Diagonal, Shadow** in the first column, fourth row.

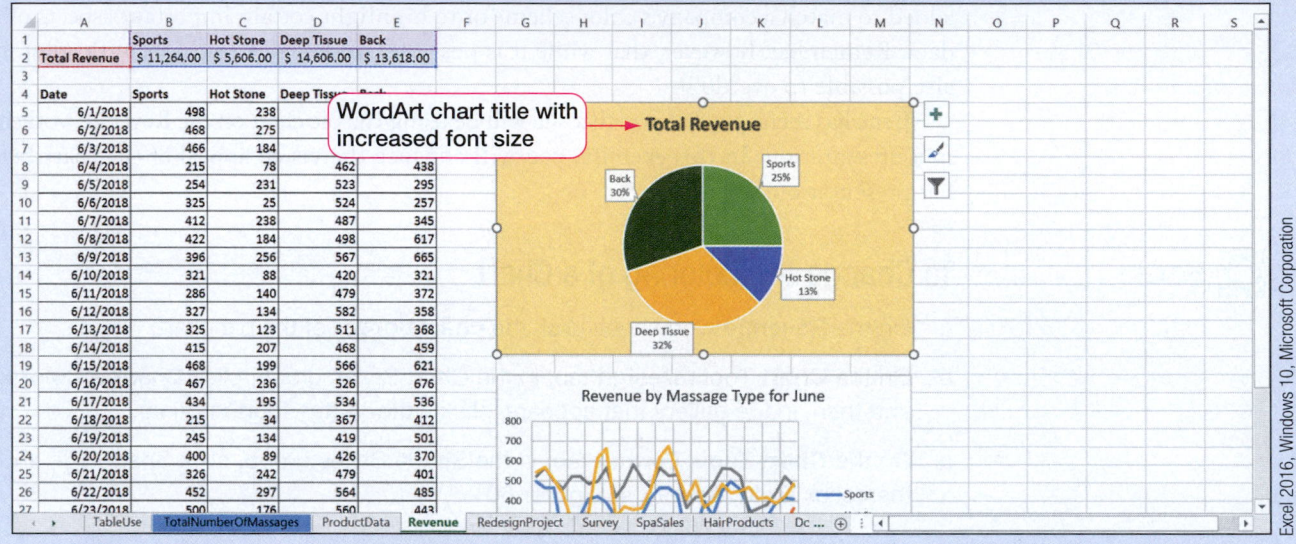

Figure 22 Pie chart with formatted title

d. **Save** 💾 the workbook.

Exploding Pie Charts

The traditional pie chart is a pie with all the slices together. Preset options offer a pie chart with a slice pulled slightly away from the main pie, or you can manually move a slice outward, creating an exploded pie chart. This technique allows for highlighting a particular piece of the pie.

As part of her presentation, Irene wants to emphasize the hot stone massage type because it represents the least amount of revenue in the data series. In this exercise, you will create visual emphasis by exploding the slice of the pie chart representing the revenue percentage of hot stone massages.

 **E04.20**

To Create an Exploding Pie Chart

a. On the **Revenue** worksheet, if necessary click the **chart border** of the pie chart.

b. Click the **pie**. Notice that the entire pie is selected.

c. Click the **Hot Stone** slice of the pie. Notice that only the Hot Stone slice is now selected.

d. Drag the Hot Stone data **slice** slightly to the **right**. The Hot Stone slice is now exploded to show emphasis.

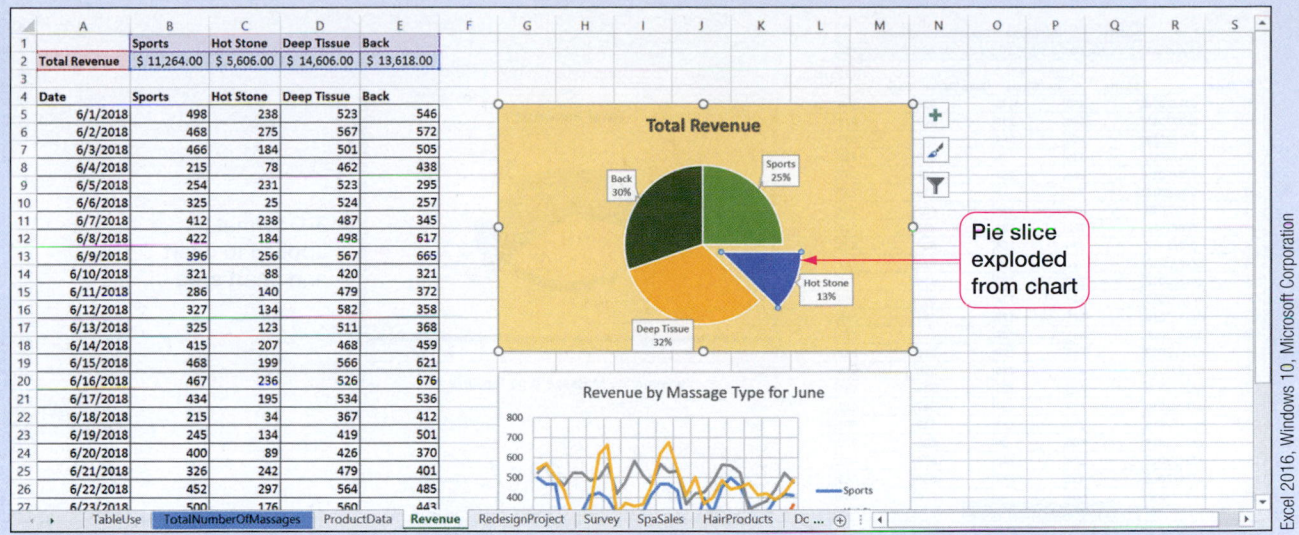

Figure 23 Exploded pie chart

e. **Save**  the workbook.

Changing 3-D Charts and Rotation of Charts

The 3-D effect and rotation of a chart are effects that should be used conservatively. They can be done well, or they can be overused, resulting in a chart that goes overboard and distracts from the intended message. You can choose the 3-D effect when starting to develop a chart, or you can apply the effect after creating the chart. Additionally, options are available to rotate the 3-D effect, giving the chart a crisp, distinctive look. The 3-D format can be applied to a variety of objects. The 3-D Rotation setting is intended for the chart area only.

In this exercise, you will use the 3-D effect and rotation to enhance the pie chart showing the total revenue by massage type.

E04.21   To Change the Chart Type to 3-D

a. On the **Revenue** worksheet, if necessary, click the **chart border** of the pie chart.

b. Click the **Chart Tools Design** tab, and then, in the Type group, click **Change Chart Type**.

c. In the Change Chart Type dialog box, if necessary, click the **All Charts** tab. In the left pane, click **Pie**, click **3-D Pie**, and then click **OK**.

d. Double-click the **chart area** to open the Format Chart Area task pane. Click **Effects** ◻, and then click the **3-D Rotation** arrow to expand the 3-D Rotation group.

e. Click in the box for **Y Rotation**, delete the existing value, and then type 50. Click in the box for **Perspective**, delete the existing value, and then type 30.

f. Click the **3-D Format** arrow to expand the 3-D Format group. Click the **Top bevel** arrow, and then click **Cool Slant** in the first row, fourth column. In the Format Chart Area task pane, click Close ☒.

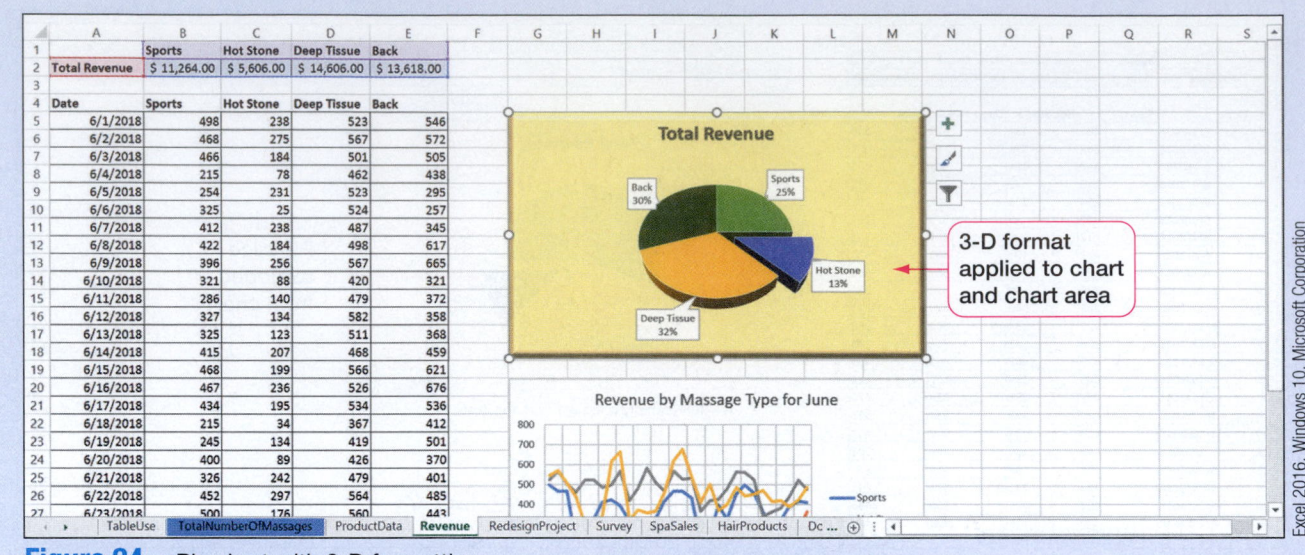

Figure 24 Pie chart with 3-D formatting

g. **Save** 🖬 the workbook.

h. If you need to take a break before finishing this chapter, now is a good time.

| **QUICK REFERENCE** | **Formatting Options for Chart Objects** |

Below are format options for charts and their descriptions.

- **Number**   Format data as currency, date, time, and so on.
- **Fill**   Fill the background of a component with a color, picture, or pattern.
- **Border Color**   Set the color of the border for a component.
- **Border Styles**   Set the thickness and type of border for a component.
- **Shadow**   Add shadowing effect to a component.
- **Glow and Soft Edges**   Add glow and edge effects to a component.
- **3-D Format**   Add 3-D effects to a component.
- **Alignment**   Align text direction for a component, such as left, top, vertical, or horizontal.

Using Charts Effectively

The effectiveness of a chart depends on the chart type, the layout, and the formatting of the data. Charts should provide clarity and expand the viewer's understanding of the data. Charts used in a presentation should support the ideas you want to convey. The charts should highlight key components about an issue or topic being addressed in the presentation. In this section, you will use sparklines and data bars to emphasize data. You will also recognize and correct confusing charts.

Use Sparklines and Data Bars to Emphasize Data

The same data can be viewed through various perspectives, emphasizing different parts of information. Charts typically do three things.

- Support or refute assertions
- Clarify information
- Help the audience understand trends

Sparklines and data bars are tools in Excel that can accomplish these three goals.

Emphasizing Data

As with any set of data, you can reasonably expect to find multiple ideas that could be emphasized in a chart. Typically, in a business setting, one to three key issues might be chosen for discussion. The idea is to eliminate any extraneous data from the chart that does not pertain to the issues being emphasized. Common methods can be employed to emphasize the idea in the chart. When using a single chart, highlight a particular data set within the chart to help focus attention to a key point. Depending on the chart type, the emphasis may be depicted differently, as shown in Table 1.

Single Chart Types	Common Emphasis Methods
Pie chart	Explode a pie slice
Bar/column	Use an emphasizing color on the bar/column
Line	Use line color, weight, and marker size
Scatter	Add a trendline

Table 1 Emphasis methods for single chart types

Exploring Sparklines

Sparklines are small charts that are embedded into the cells in a worksheet, usually beside the data, to facilitate quick analysis of trends. A sparkline can be used within a worksheet to give an immediate visual trend analysis, and it adjusts as the source data changes. The sparkline can graphically depict the data over time through either a line chart or a bar chart that accumulates the data. Sparklines can also depict data points in the series as a win/loss chart. The default setting is for values above 0 to be a win while values below 0 are a loss. This value can be modified under the Format tab by using the Sparkline Axis button.

Irene and Meda would like to better examine sales of hair products at the spa. They have collected some data for you to analyze from the last eight weeks. In this exercise you will add sparklines adjacent to the data to emphasize the trend in products over time.

 E04.22

SIDE NOTE
Alternate Method
Sparklines can also be inserted to the right of data by using the Quick Analysis tool.

To Insert Sparklines

a. If you took a break, open the **e02ch04SpaSales** workbook, and then click the **HairProducts** worksheet tab. Select the range **A3:A7**.

b. Click the **Insert** tab, and in the Sparklines group, click **Line**. In the Create Sparklines dialog box, in the **Data Range** box, type **C3:N7** and then click **OK**.

c. On the **Sparkline Tools Design** tab, in the Style group, click the **More** arrow, and then select **Sparkline Style Accent 2, Darker 50%** (first row, second column).

The sparklines show the changes in hair products sold over the 12 months represented by the data. Notice that sales of the For Men products were steady until Month 7, when they spiked, then came back down in month 9, and then spiked again in Month 11. This is very easy to visualize with sparklines next to the data.

d. Click cell **A1** to deselect the sparklines.

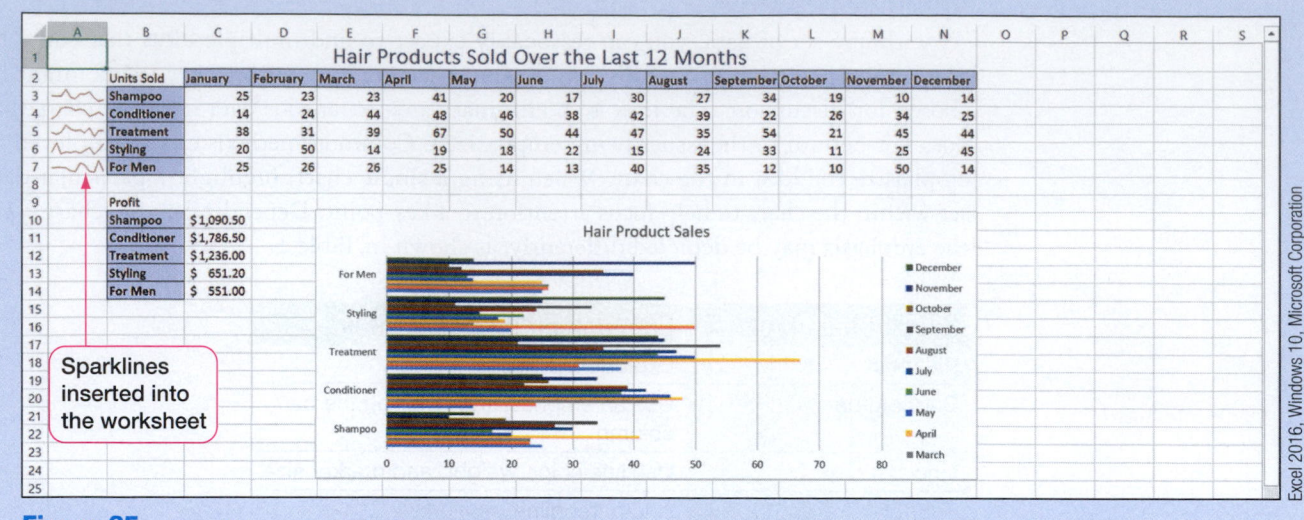

Figure 25 Sparklines applied to hair products data

e. **Save** 🖫 the workbook.

QUICK REFERENCE	Working with Sparklines

Using the following process will help in the development of sparklines.

- Select any cell within the added sparklines to display the Sparkline Tools contextual tabs.

- Ungroup sparklines using the Ungroup button on the Sparkline Tools Design tab.

- Group sparklines again using the Group button on the Design tab.

- Change colors and styles using the options available in the Style group.

- Choose to show high or low points using the options in the Show group.

Inserting Data Bars

Data bars are graphic components that are overlaid onto data in worksheet cells. The graphic component is added to a cell and interprets a set of data in a range in which the bar and, if necessary, the bar color are adjusted to help a spreadsheet user gain a quick understanding of the data. Data bars can be applied as a one-color solid fill or as a gradient fill from left to right as the numerical value gets bigger. Data bars are components of the Conditional Formatting feature. This technique can be employed with scores, ratings, or other data for which the user would want to do a visual inspection to see a relative scale on the data.

Irene and Meda have requested one more enhancement to the hair products analysis you have already begun. They would like a small visual cue added to a list of profits by hair product type. In this exercise, you will add data bars to the profits of all hair products sold at the spa over the past 12 months to emphasize which products were profitable and which were not profitable.

 E04.23

SIDE NOTE
Alternate Method
Data bars can also be inserted from the Quick Analysis tool. The default color is blue if you are using this method.

To Insert Data Bars

a. On the **HairProducts** worksheet, select the range **C10:C14**.

b. Click the **Home** tab, and in the Styles group, click **Conditional Formatting**, and then point to **Data Bars**. Under Gradient Fill, click **Green Data Bar** (row one, second option). The inserted data bars clearly show that Conditioner is the highest-grossing product, while For Men is the lowest-grossing product.

c. Click cell **A1** to deselect the data bars.

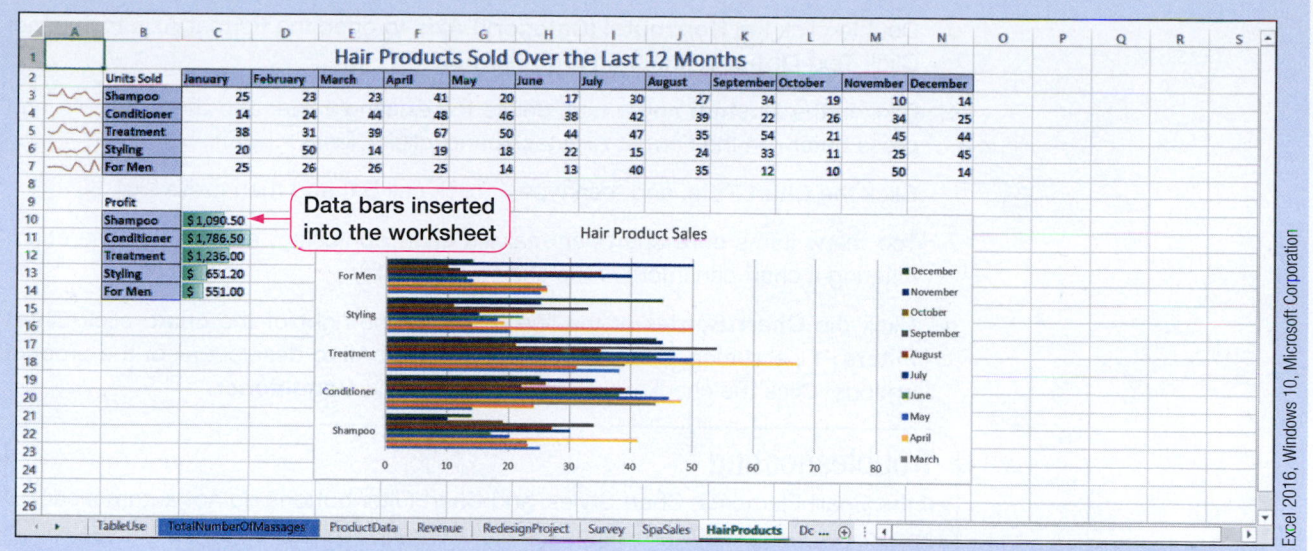

Figure 26 Data bars added to profit data

    d. **Save** 🖫 the workbook.

Recognize and Correct Confusing Charts

The process of working with and creating visually appealing charts with clear messages involves recognizing when you have a confusing chart. It is possible to have too much information or ambiguous information. This could include missing labels or legends, or there might be textual information on a chart that is not clear. Additionally, a common error is to use the incorrect chart type in analyzing data.

Correcting a Confusing Chart

Irene has pointed out that on the HairProducts sheet, a clustered bar chart was created that is difficult to interpret. The chart is based on the same data from which you created sparklines. Irene would like to be able to use the chart to compare different lines of product. The chart that was created shows the number of units sold as the bars, each product having a different bar for each month in the data. In this exercise, you will correct the chart so that it provides a meaningful representation of the data.

 E04.24

SIDE NOTE
Suggested Charts
Depending on your data, Excel may suggest a chart with the x-axis and y-axis already switched, saving you a step.

To Correct a Confusing Chart

a. On the **HairProducts** worksheet, click the **chart border** of the clustered bar chart.

    Notice that this chart is showing time as a bar chart. Earlier in this chapter, you learned that a line chart is better for trends over time.

b. Click the **Chart Tools Design** tab, and in the Type group, click **Change Chart Type**. In the Change Chart Type dialog box, on the **All Charts** tab, click **Line**, and then click **OK**.

c. In the Data group, click **Switch Row/Column**. Since the data being charted is time sensitive, the time element should be shown on the x-axis.

d. Double-click the **Horizontal (Category) Axis** to open the Format Axis task pane. Click **Text Options**, and then click **Textbox** 🔠.

e. Click in the **Custom angle** box, delete the existing value, and then type **-45** and press Enter. On the Format Axis task pane, click Close ✕.

f. Click the **Chart Title**, and then type **=**, click cell **B1**, and then press ⏎.

Too many items on a chart can make a chart confusing, as with this line chart. Filtering a chart can improve the chart's readability.

g. Click the **Chart Border** of the line chart. To the right of the chart, click **Chart Filters** 🔽, and then, under Series, click **Select All** to deselect all of the product options. Click the check boxes for **Shampoo** and **Conditioner**.

> ### Troubleshooting
>
> If the Chart Elements, Chart Styles, and Chart Filter buttons do not automatically appear to the right of the selected chart, use the horizontal scroll bar to create more space to the right of the selected chart. The buttons will appear only if there is enough space beside the chart.

h. Click **Apply** at the bottom of the Chart Filters gallery, and then click **Chart Filters** 🔽 again to close the gallery. Notice that the lines for these two products do not show similar trends, as might be expected.

> ### Troubleshooting
>
> If you cannot see the Apply button on your screen, you may need to close the dialog, move the worksheet up, and try the steps again.

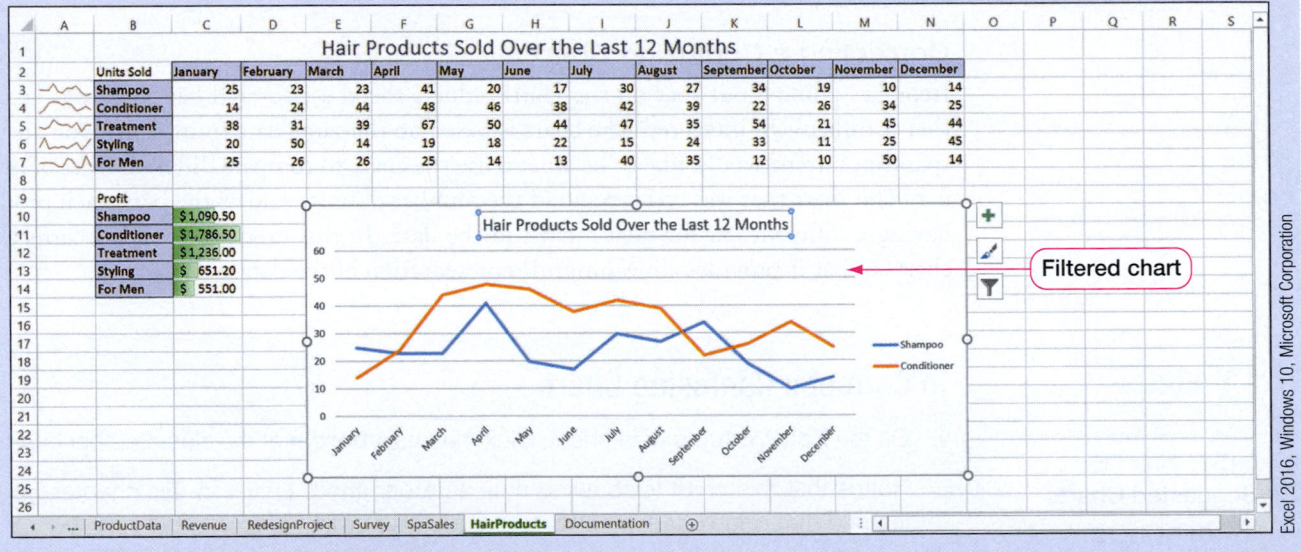

Figure 27 Corrected line chart

> ### Troubleshooting
>
> If you click the chart to see the source data associated with the chart and see only some of the data selected with a blue border, you might have clicked a chart component by mistake instead of the full chart area. To get the data set associated with the entire chart, under Chart Tools, click the Format tab. In the Current Selection group, change the Chart Element to Chart Area. Data associated with the selected component will be highlighted with a colored border.

i. **Save** 💾 the workbook.

Preparing to Print a Chart

Printing charts uses essentially the same process as printing a worksheet. When printing a chart sheet, select the chart sheet, go through the normal printing process, and adjust print options as you would for a worksheet. The chart will be a full-page display. If the chart is on a regular worksheet, it will be printed if you choose to print everything on the worksheet. In this case, the chart will be the size you developed on the worksheet. This is convenient when you want to print some tables or other data along with the chart. Finally, if you want to print just the chart on the worksheet, select the chart first, then choose the Print Selected Chart print option to print only the current chart.

Another useful technique in exploring data through charts is the ability to create static copies of the chart that can be used to compare with later versions. You can, in essence, take a picture of a chart that will not retain the underlying data. In this manner, subsequent versions of the chart can be made into images for comparisons. The process of creating a picture of the chart is to select the chart, copy it, then use the Paste Special option and paste it as a picture. When you paste as a picture, there are multiple picture format options, such as a PNG, JPEG, or GIF files.

In this exercise, you will print the HairProducts chart.

QUICK REFERENCE	Common Charting Issues

These are common issues you should try to avoid in the development of charts.

1. Not enough context; users do not understand the chart.

   - Add titles to the horizontal and vertical axes.
   - Add a chart title that conveys context of time and scope.
   - Add data labels to show percentages or values of chart elements.

2. Too much information is on the chart.

   - Use a subset of the data rather than all the data.
   - Summarize the data so it is consolidated.

3. Incorrect chart type is used.

   - Choose a more appropriate type of chart, such as a line chart for trends.

4. Chart has issues with readability.

   - Check the color scheme to ensure that the text is readable.
   - Check font characteristics such as font type or font size.
   - Move data labels, and remove excess information.
   - Resize the overall chart to provide more area to work.
   - Check the color scheme and formatting so it is professional and does not hide chart information or text.
   - Information or labeling is misleading.
   - Check the scaling to ensure that it is appropriate and labeled with the correct units.
   - Consider the following wording: Does "Sales" mean the number of transactions or the total revenue?

 **E**04.25

To Print a Chart

a. On the **HairProducts** worksheet, click the **chart border** of the line chart.

b. Click the **File** tab, and then click **Print**. Notice that under Settings, the option for Print Selected Chart is selected by default. Also notice that only the chart is displayed in the preview pane. This is because you had the chart selected, not a cell within the worksheet.

c. Click the **Portrait Orientation** arrow, and select **Landscape Orientation**.

d. Verify that the correct printer — as directed by your instructor — appears in the Printer box. Choices may vary depending on the computer you are using. If the correct printer is not displayed, click the Printer arrow, and then click to choose the correct or preferred printer from the list of available printers. If your instructor asks you to print the document, click the **Print** button.

e. Complete the **Documentation** worksheet as directed by your instructor.

f. Insert the file name in the left footer on all worksheets in the workbook.

g. **Save** 🖫 the workbook, exit Excel, and then submit your file as directed by your instructor.

Concept Check

1. What are some important items to consider in choosing the design and layout of a chart? p. 212

2. What are the two possible locations for a chart in Excel? Why would you choose one over the other? p. 215

3. Compare the purpose of a column chart and a pie chart. Give an example of a scenario in which you would use the two different types of charts. When would you create a combination chart to display worksheet data? p. 219–224

4. Why is it important to add elements and styles to charts such as titles, legends, and labels? p. 226

5. List two possible ways to add emphasis to an existing chart. p. 239

6. How are sparklines and data bars different from other chart objects in Excel? What are they commonly used for? p. 239–240

7. What are common mistakes that can be made in designing charts? Why is it important to correct these mistakes in existing charts? p. 241–242

Key Terms

Area chart   223
Bar chart   221
Chart sheet   215
Column chart   221
Combination chart   224
Data bar   240
Data point   213

Data series   213
Data visualization   212
Embedded chart   215
Gridlines   233
Legend   230
Line chart   220
Pie chart   219

Quick Analysis   215
Recommended Charts   216
Scatter chart   222
Sparkline   239
Trendline   232

Visual Summary

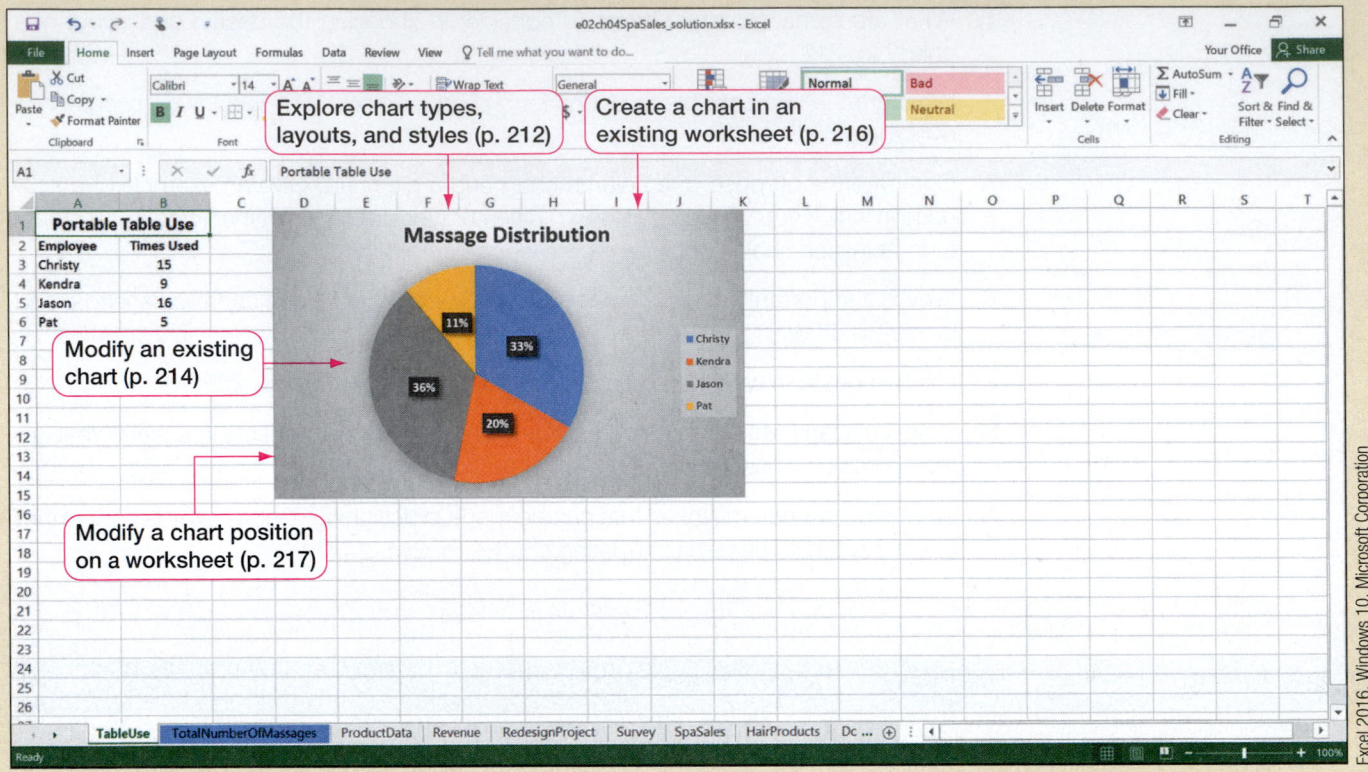

Figure 28

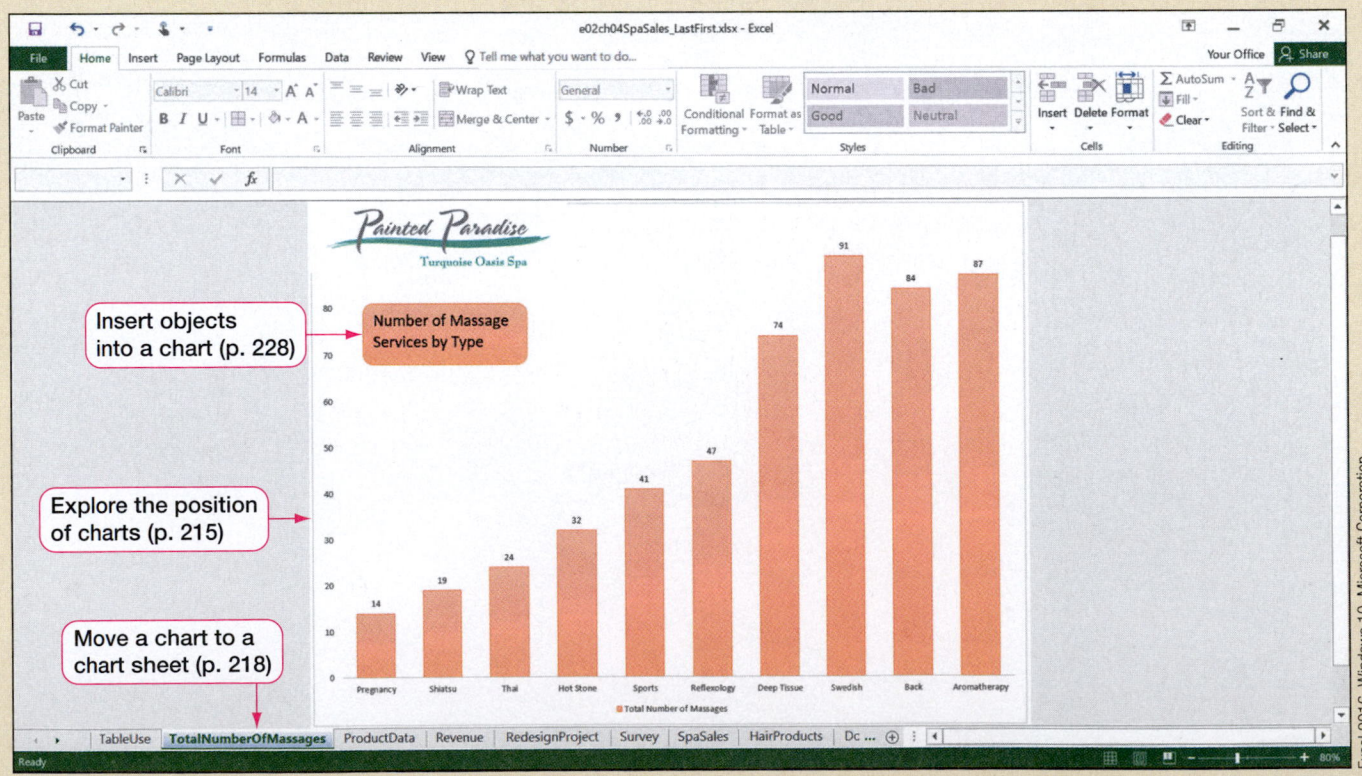

Figure 29

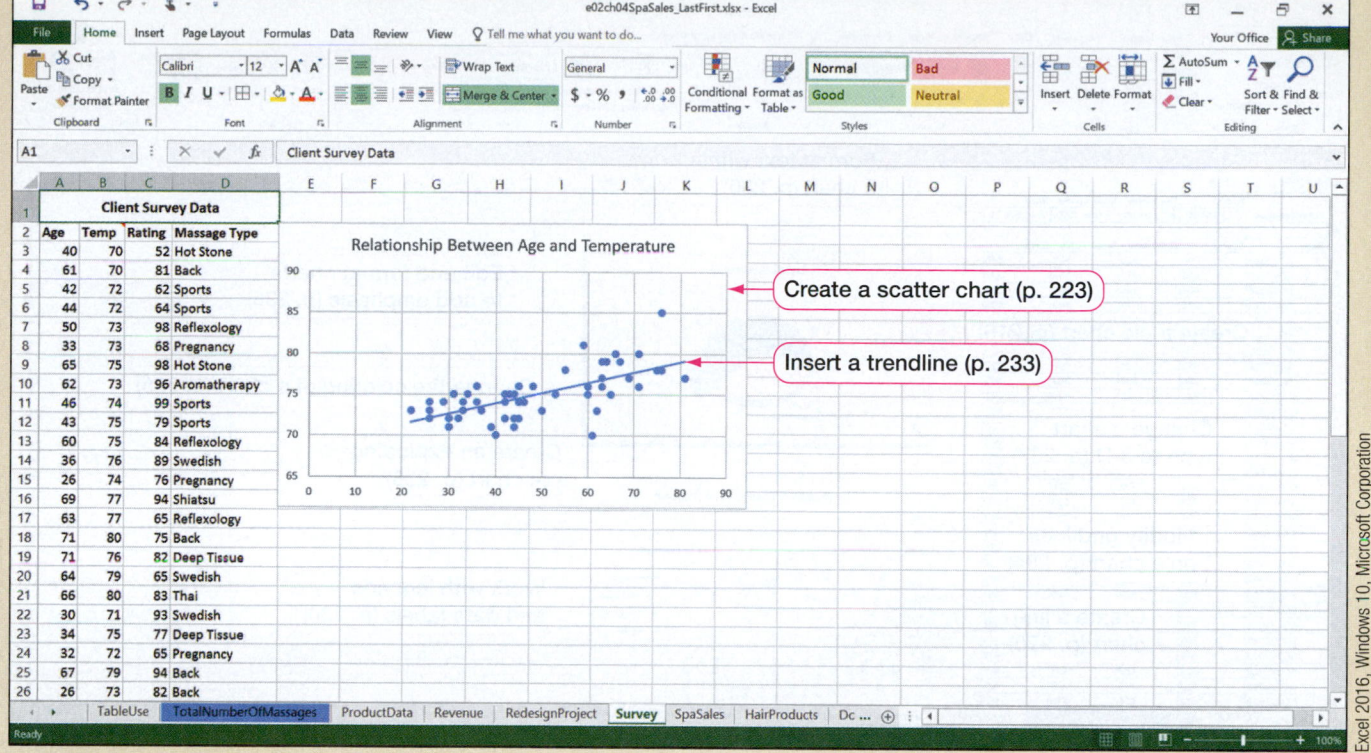

Figure 30

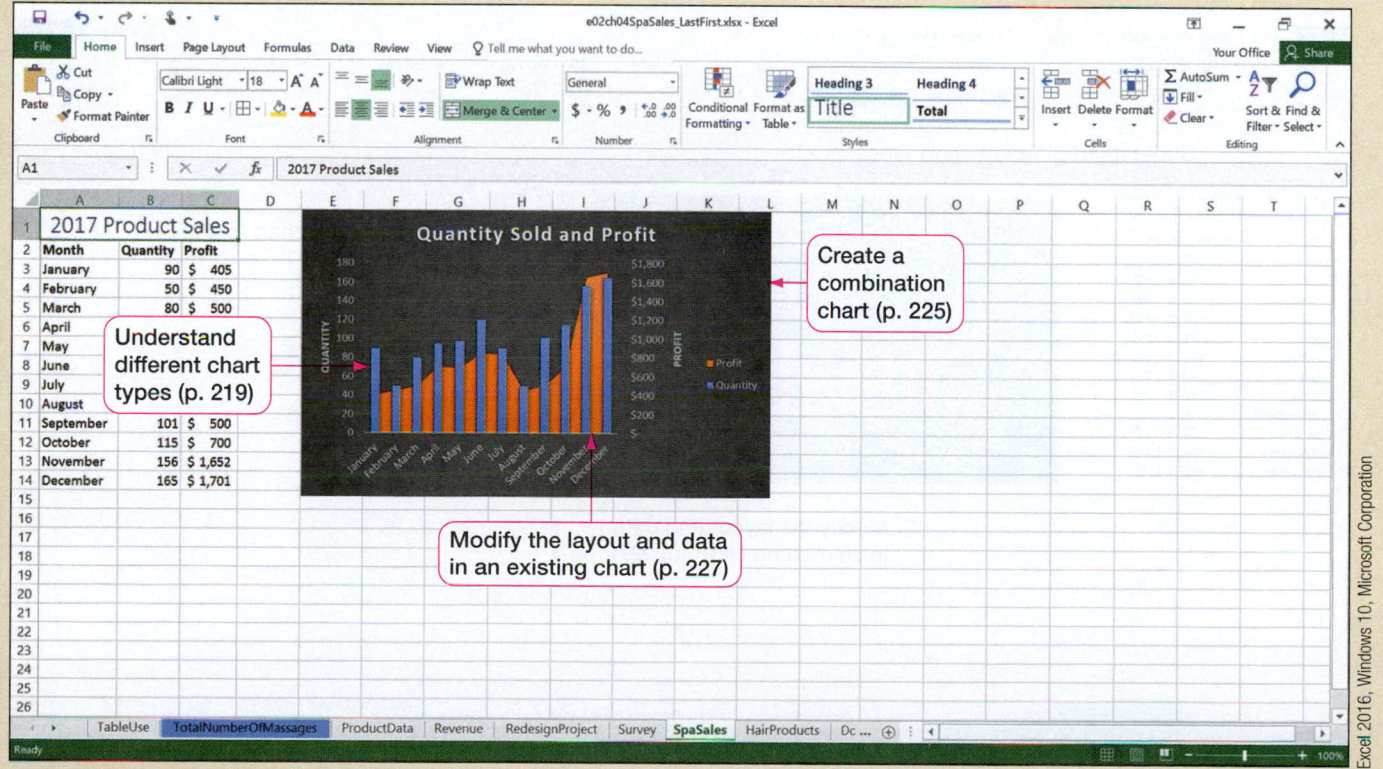

Figure 31

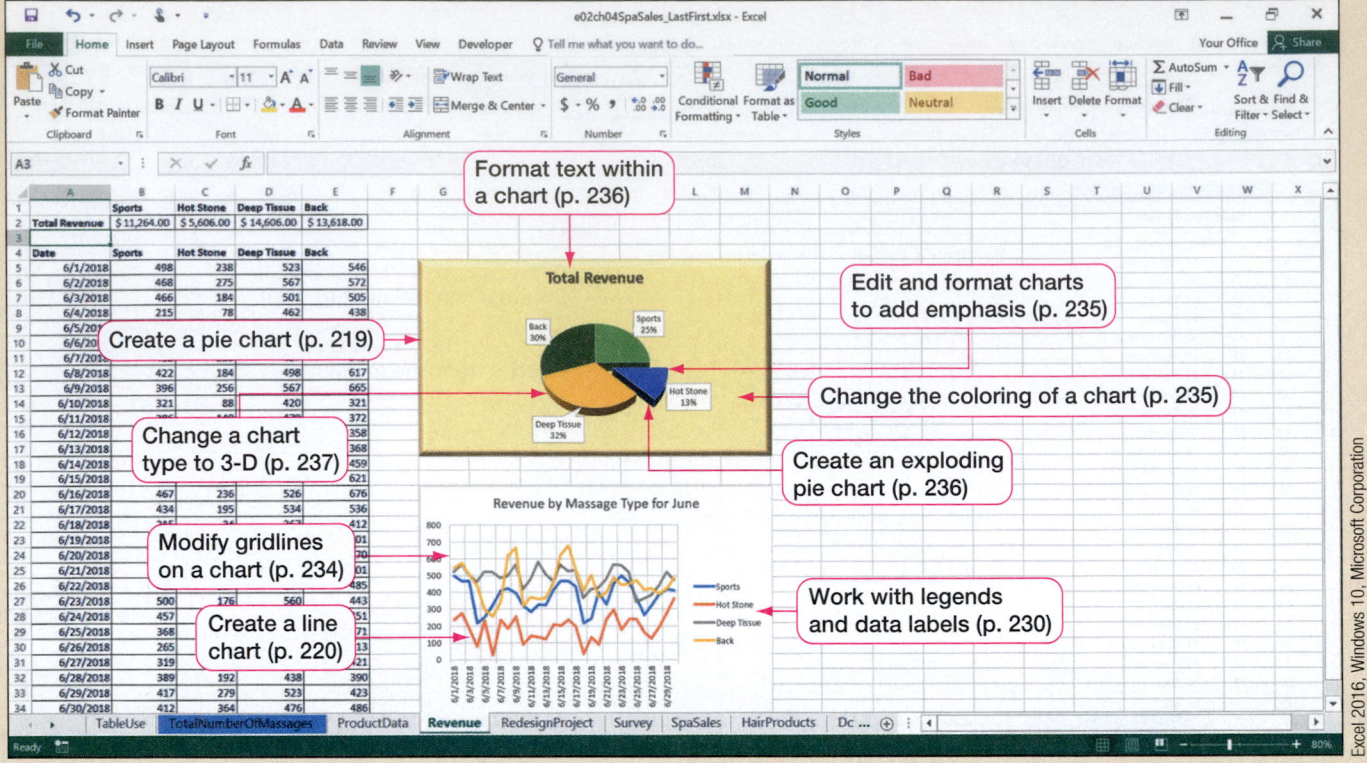

Figure 32

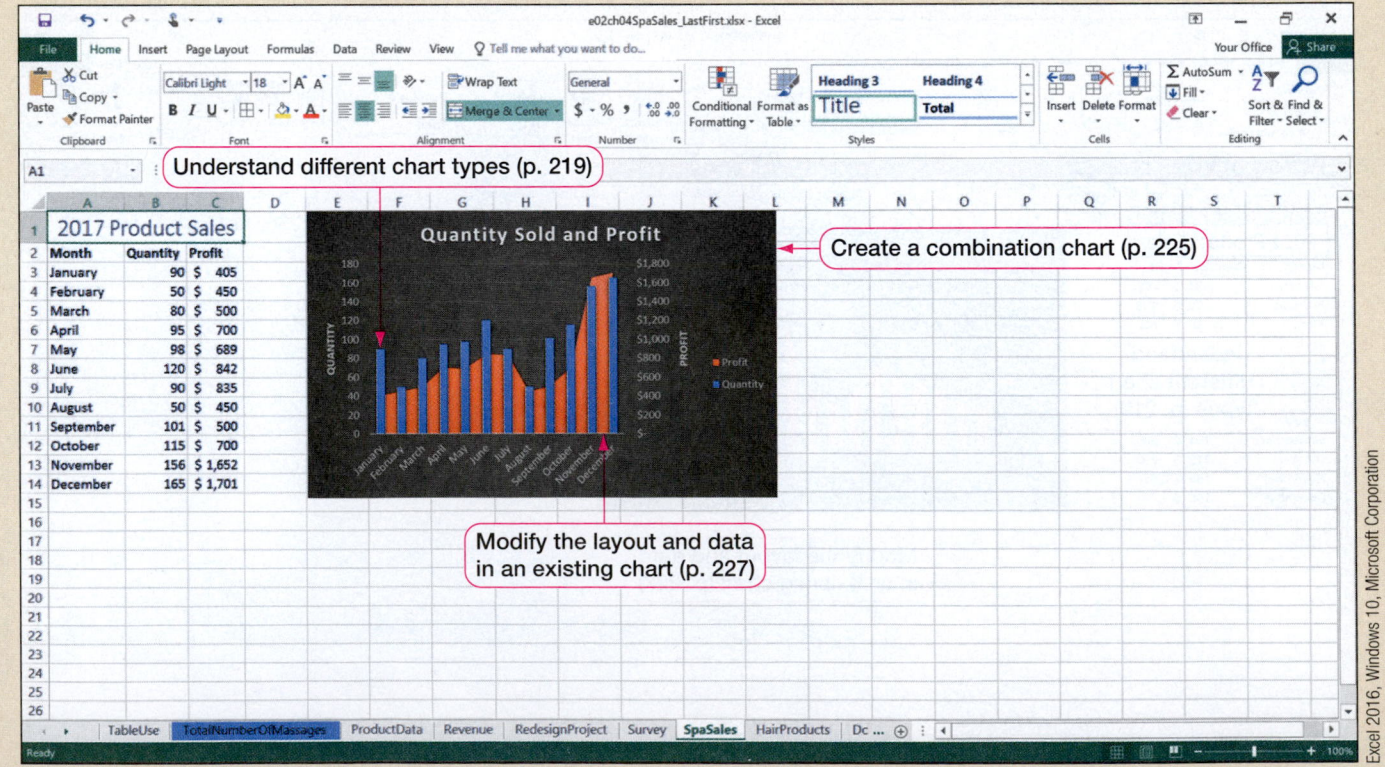

Figure 33

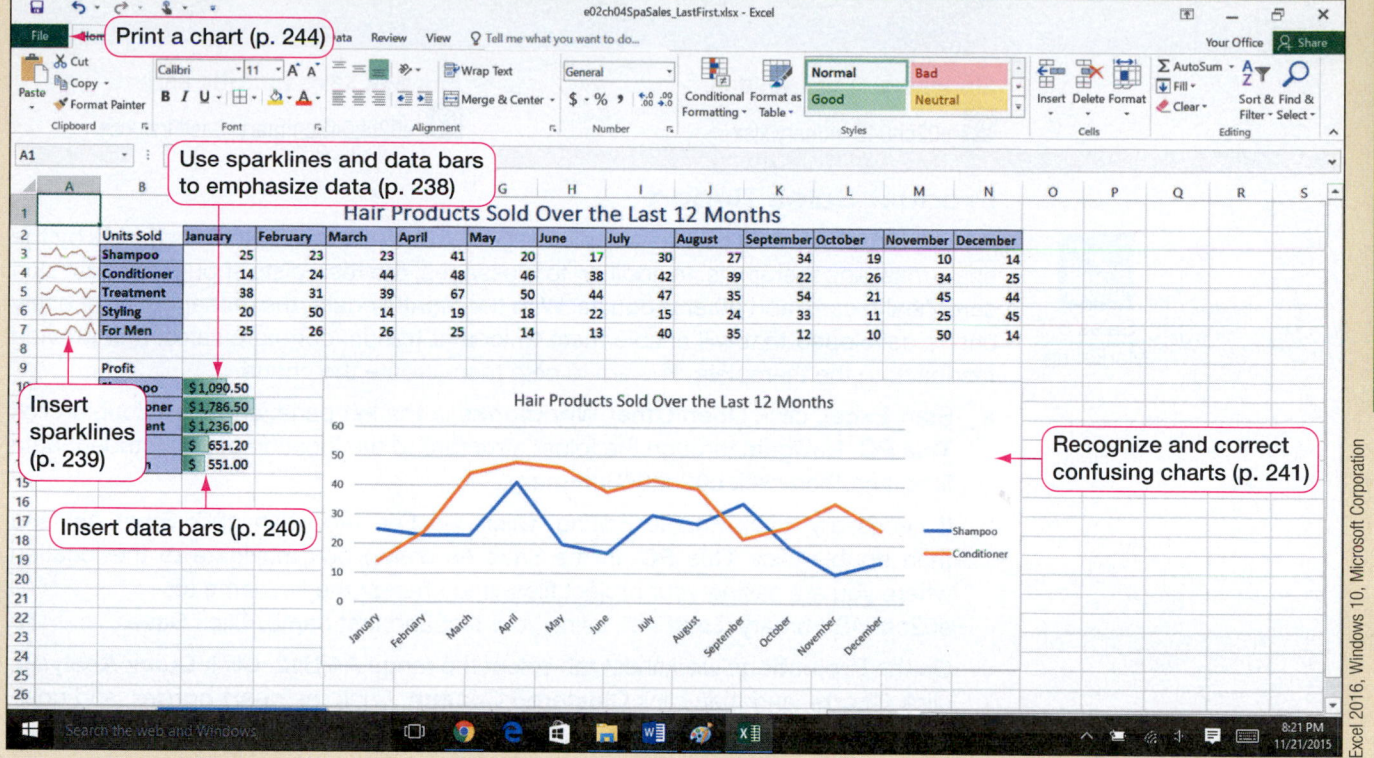

Figure 34

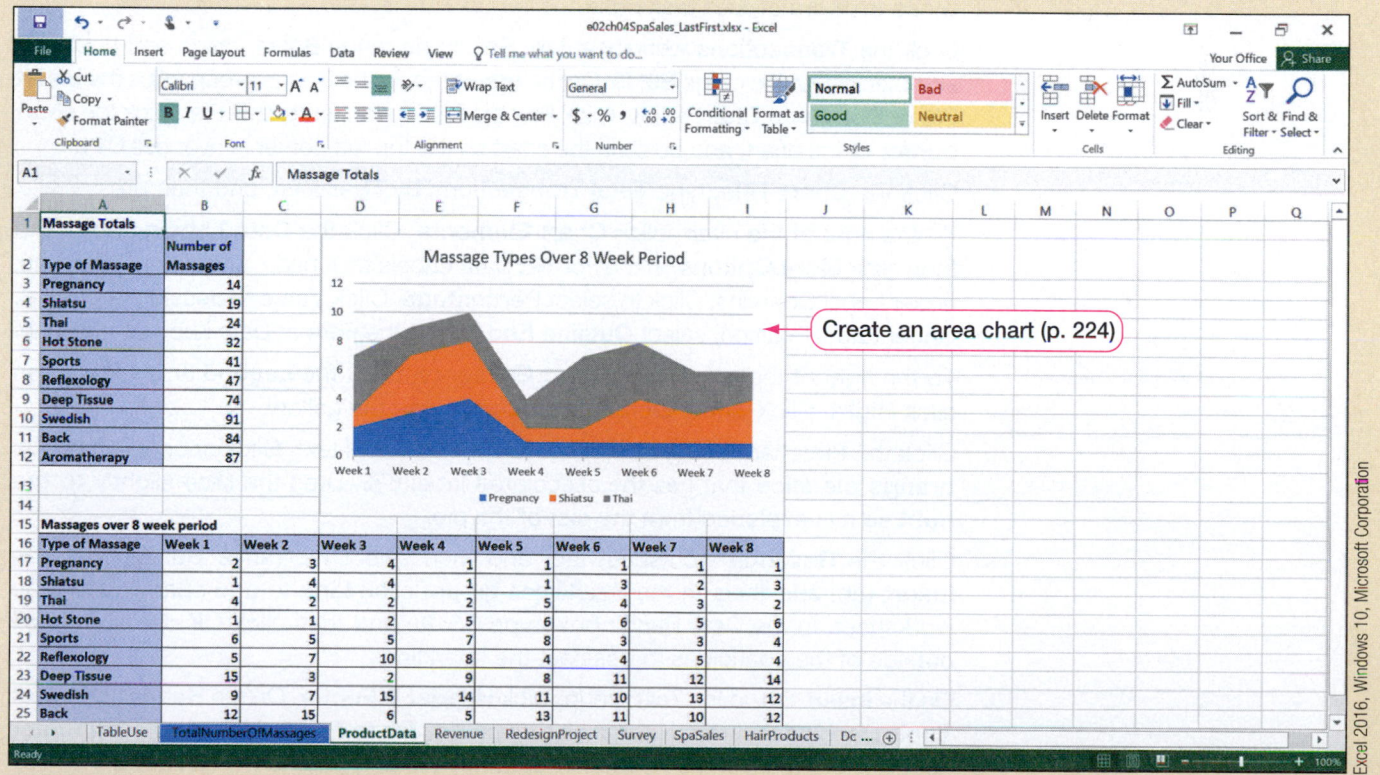

Figure 35

Student data file needed:

 e02ch04Summary.xlsx

You will save your file as:

 e02ch04Summary_LastFirst.xlsx

Product Sales Report

Sales & Marketing

Irene Kai and Meda Rodate have pulled together data pertaining to sales made by the spa's massage therapists. In addition to massages, the therapists should promote skin care, health care, and other products. With the monthly data, the managers want a few charts developed that will enable them to look at trends, compare sales, and provide feedback to the therapists. You are to help them create the charts.

a. Start **Excel**, click **Open Other Workbooks** in the left pane, and then double-click **This PC**. Navigate through the folder structure to the location of your student data files, and then click **e02ch04Summary**.

b. If necessary, click Enable Editing. Click the **File** tab, then click **Save As**, and then double-click **This PC**. In the Save As dialog box, navigate to the location where you are saving your project files, and change the file name to e02ch04Summary_LastFirst, using your last and first name. Click **Save**.

c. On the **Projections** worksheet tab select the range **A4:B12**. Click **Quick Analysis**, click **Charts**, and then click **Clustered Column**. Click the **chart border**, and position the chart so the top left corner is over cell **D4**. Adjust the size of the chart so the bottom right corner is over cell **J17**.

d. Click the **Chart Title**, and then click in the **formula bar**. Type **=**, click cell **A1**, and then press Enter.

To the right of the chart, click **Chart Styles**, and then click **Style 6** from the list. Click **Chart Styles** again to close the gallery.

e. Double-click the **Vertical (Value) Axis** to open the Format Axis task pane. In the Axis Options, click in the **Minimum** box, clear the existing text, and then type 100. Close the Format Axis task pane.

f. Click the **Transactions** worksheet tab. Select the range **B4:J4**, press and hold Ctrl, and then select the range **B9:J9**. On the **Insert** tab, in the Charts group, click the **Insert Pie or Doughnut Chart** arrow. Click **Pie**, the first option under 2-D Pie. Click the **chart border** of the chart, and position the chart so the top left corner is over cell **C11**.

g. Click the **Chart Title**, type Total Transactions by Therapist, and then press Enter.

h. To the right of the chart, click **Chart Elements**. Click the **Data Labels** arrow, and then click **More Options**. In the Format Data Labels task pane, under Label Options, under Label Contains, Click to select **Percentage**. Click **Value** to deselect that label. Under Label Position, select **Outside End**. Close the Format Data Labels task pane.

i. To the right of the chart, click **Chart Elements**. Click the **Legend** arrow, and then click **Right**. Click **Chart Elements** again to close the gallery.

j. Click the **Pie** chart, being careful not to click the label text. Click once again on the **orange pie slice** that has the associated label 6%. Drag the slice slightly **to the right** so it is exploded from the rest of the pie.

k. Click the **Revenue** worksheet tab, and then select the range **B9:J9**. Click the **Insert** tab, and then, in the Sparklines group, click **Line** to add sparklines to the worksheet. In the Data Range box, type B5:J8, and then click **OK**. Click any **cell** outside of the sparklines to deselect the sparklines.

l. On the **Insert** tab, in the Text group, click **Header & Footer**. On the **Header & Footer Tools Design** tab, in the Navigation group, click **Go to Footer**. Click in the **left footer section**, and then, in the Header & Footer Elements group, click **File Name**.

m. Click any **cell** on the worksheet to move out of the footer, and then press Ctrl+Home. On the status bar, click **Normal**.

n. Click the **Documentation** worksheet tab. Click cell **A8**, and then type in today's date. Click cell **B6**, and then type your name in the Firstname Lastname format. Complete the remainder of the **Documentation** worksheet according to your instructor's directions.

o. **Save** the workbook, close Excel, and then submit your file as directed by your instructor.

Problem Solve 1

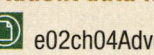

Student data file needed:	You will save your file as:
 e02ch04Advertising.xlsx	e02ch04Advertising_LastFirst.xlsx

Advertising

Sales & Marketing

Finance & Accounting

The marketing manager of the Painted Paradise Golf Resort & Spa, Timothy Smith, has created a spreadsheet of the first six months (first two quarters) of advertising expenses for the various amenities of the resort. He is planning to display the data at the next Board of Directors meeting and wants to create a few charts to make the figures easier to view and the presentation more visually appealing.

a. Open the Excel file, **e02ch04Advertising**. Save your file as e02ch04Advertising_LastFirst, using your last and first name.

b. On the **AdvertisingCosts** worksheet, create a **Line** chart of the data for the total spent on advertising each month from January through June. The primary Horizontal (Category) Axis should be the months of the year, and the Vertical (value) Axis should be the total spent on advertising each month.

c. Change the line chart title to Total Advertising Expenses per Month. Change the Vertical Axis minimum to **$26,000**, and change the chart style to **Style 10**.

d. Move the line chart to a **chart sheet**, and rename the sheet AdvertisingPerMonth. If necessary, move the chart sheet to the **right** of the AdvertisingCosts sheet.

e. Click the **AdvertisingCosts** worksheet tab. Create a **3-D Pie chart** of the amenities and their six-month totals in the range **A16:B22**. Reposition the chart so the left corner of the chart is in cell **C14**.

f. On the 3-D pie chart, insert the title Semi-Annual Advertising Costs. Apply **Style 8** to the chart.

g. Add **Data Callout** as data labels to the 3-D pie chart. Include the **category name** and **percentage** in the data labels.

h. On the 3-D pie chart, slightly explode the segment of the chart that was allocated the **smallest amount** of advertising funds.

i. Double-click the chart area. Select **Effects** in the Format Chart Area task pane, click to expand **3-D Rotation**, and adjust the 3-D rotation to the following:

    a. X rotation of **20**

    b. Y Rotation of **40**

    c. Perspective of **10**

j. On the 3-D pie chart, expand **3-D Format** in the Format Chart Area task pane. Change the Top bevel to **Relaxed Inset** in the second column, first row. Close the Format Chart Area task pane. Resize the chart so the lower-right corner is in H28.

k. In cells **H5:H11**, add **Column sparklines** that chart the advertising expense by amenity type over the months January to June. Apply the style **Sparkline Style Accent 5, Darker 50%**.

l. Update the Documentation worksheet according to your instructor's directions.

m. Insert the file name in the left footer on all worksheets in the workbook.

n. **Save** the workbook, close Excel, and then submit your file as directed by your instructor.

Student data file needed:

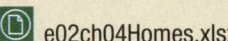 e02ch04Homes.xlsx

You will save your file as:

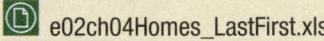 e02ch04Homes_LastFirst.xlsx

Real Estate

Research/
Development

You are interning at Schalow Real Estate Company. Your supervisor needs to know why some houses sell quickly and others take more time. She asks you to create charts from data to help her analyze and look for trends.

a. Open the Excel file **e02ch04Homes**. Save your file as e02ch04Homes_LastFirst, using your last and first name.

b. On the **SoldProperties** worksheet, create a line chart showing the number of days on the market over time. Plot the days on the market on the y-axis and the sold date on the x-axis.

c. Add a **linear trendline** to your chart. Change the trend line Dash type to **Solid**.

d. Format the chart using an appropriate style, and position it below the data in the approximate range **A40:F54**.

e. Create a line chart that shows how the price per square foot of the sold properties has changed over time.

f. Add a **linear trendline** to your chart. Change the trend line Dash type to **Solid**.

g. Format the chart using a style of your choice, and position it below the data in the approximate range **H40:N54**.

h. On the **Summary** worksheet, the first group of data in A2:D11 describes homes sold in all developments. Use that data to create three charts using a style of your choice, and show the following on the three different charts.

- The Average Number of Days on Market by Development

- The Average Percent of List Price by Development

- The Average of Sold Price by Development

i. Create a **new worksheet** in your workbook. Name the new worksheet Charts.

j. Move the three charts showing averages by development to the **Charts** worksheet. Position them in the approximate ranges **A1:I15**, **A17:I31**, and **A33:I47**.

k. On the **Summary** worksheet, type your last name in cell **A38**.

l. Create a chart that shows the average number of days it took a home to sell by salesperson.

m. Format this chart using **Style 8**. Position the chart on the **Charts** worksheet in the range **K1:R15**.

n. Complete the **Documentation** worksheet according to your instructor's directions. Insert the file name in the left footer on all worksheets in the workbook.

o. **Save** the workbook, close Excel, and submit your file as directed by your instructor.

Additional
Cases

Additional Chapter Cases are available at www.pearsonhighered.com/youroffice

Conducting Business Analysis

This business unit had two outcomes:

Learning Outcome 1

Use Excel to create formulas and functions to perform calculations, analyze data, solve problems, and help in making wise business decisions.

Learning Outcome 2

Use Excel to create a variety of detailed charts appropriate to the data that will visually represent and analyze the data.

In Business Unit 2 Capstone, students will demonstrate competence in these outcomes through a series of business problems at various levels from guided practice to problem solving an existing spreadsheet and creating new spreadsheets.

More Practice 1

Student data file needed:

e02Sales.xlsx

You will save your file as:

e02Sales_LastFirst.xlsx

Sales & Marketing

Finance & Accounting

Restaurant Marketing Analysis

The accounting system at the Indigo5 Restaurant tracks data on a daily basis that can be used for analysis to gauge its performance and determine any needed changes. The restaurant is considering entering into a long-term agreement with a poultry company and getting a new refrigeration unit to store the chicken. If Indigo5 enters the agreement, the poultry company agrees to give Indigo5 a substantial discount for a specified period of time. Management would like to stimulate sales for the lowest-revenue-producing chicken item and any chicken items that do not meet a sale performance threshold. To accomplish this, some of the savings will be passed on to the guests by having these chicken items put on special at a lower price.

a. Open **Excel**, click **Open Other Workbooks** in the left pane, and then double-click **This PC**. Navigate through the folder structure to the location of your student data files, and then double-click **e02Sales**. If a Security Warning message displays, click the **Enable Editing** button.

b. Click the **File** tab, click **Save As**, and then double-click **This PC**. In the Save As dialog box, navigate to the location where you are saving your project files, and then change the file name to **e02Sales_LastFirst**, using your last and first name. Click **Save**.

c. Click the **Indigo5ChickenSales** worksheet, and then click cell **D2**. Enter the formula =**TODAY()**, and then press Enter.

Notice the data on the worksheet. The range A13:E18 contains four months of actual sales quantities for each menu item. The range A22:E27 contains the sales projections that Indigo5 made for the same four months before the start of each month.

d. Click cell **B4**, enter the formula =**SUM(B22:E22)**, and then press Ctrl+Enter. In cell B4, double-click the AutoFill handle to automatically fill cell range B4:B9. The range now returns the total quantity projection over the four months for each item.

e. Format range **B4:B9** with comma style, zero decimal places.

f. Click cell **C4**, enter the formula =**SUM(B13:E13)**, and then press Ctrl+Enter. In cell C4, double-click the AutoFill handle to automatically fill cell range C4:C9. The range now returns the total quantity of actual sales over the four months for each item.

g. Format range **C4:C9** with comma style, zero decimal places.

h. Click cell **D4**, enter the formula =AVERAGE(B13:E13), and then press Ctrl+Enter. In cell D4, double-click the AutoFill handle to automatically fill cell range D4:D9. The range now returns the average monthly quantity for actual sales over the four months for each item.

i. Format range **D4:D9** with comma style, two decimal places.

j. Now you need to determine the price for each item to use in revenue calculations. Notice that a list of menu prices is in cells A30:B44. Select the range **A30:B44**. Click the **Name Box**, type Prices, and then press Enter. The price listing is now named Prices to use in later calculations.

k. Now you want to assign the price of each item by looking up the item and exactly matching the item name in the Prices list. Click cell **E4**, enter the formula =VLOOKUP(A4,Prices,2,FALSE), and then press Ctrl+Enter. Be sure to use the range name Prices in the formula. In cell E4, double-click the **AutoFill** handle to automatically fill the cell range **E4:E9**.

l. To determine the total revenue for each item, click cell **F4**, enter the formula =E4*C4, and then press Ctrl+Enter. In cell **F4**, double-click the AutoFill handle to automatically fill cell range **F4:F9**.

m. Now you need to determine whether the item fell short of the sales projection or exceeded it. Click cell **G4**, enter the formula =ROUND(C4/B4,2), and then press Ctrl+Enter. In cell **G4**, double-click the **AutoFill** handle to automatically fill cell range **G4:G9**. The range now returns a projection percentage. An item that fell short of the sales projection will be under 100%. An item that exceeded the sales projection will be over 100%.

n. Now you need to determine what item has the highest revenue. Click cell **H4**, enter the formula =IF(F4=MAX($F$4:$F$9),"Best Item",""), and then press Ctrl+Enter. In cell **H4**, double-click the **AutoFill** handle to automatically fill cell range **H4:H9**. The range now returns a blank for all items except the one with the highest sales revenue, which returns Best Item.

o. Next you need to determine which items to put on sale to stimulate sales. An item should be put on sale if its % of Projection is less than the Sale Threshold in cell L4 or if its sales revenue is the lowest. Click cell **I4**, enter the formula =IF(OR(G4<$L$4,F4=MIN($F$4:$F$9)),"Put on Sale",""), and then press Ctrl+Enter. In cell **I4**, double-click the **AutoFill** handle to automatically fill cell range **I4:I9**.

The range now returns Put on Sale for two items: the item with the lowest sales revenue and the item with a % of Projection less than 95%. All other items return a blank.

p. You also need to know how many days the sale will last based on dates given by the poultry company. Click cell **L7**, enter the formula =DATEDIF(L5,L6,"D"), and then press Ctrl+Enter.

q. Select the range **B13:E18**. Click the **Insert** tab, and then, in the Sparklines group, click **Line**. Select the location range **F13:F18**, and then click **OK**. Click the **Sparkline Tools Design** tab, and then, in the Show group, click the **Markers** check box.

r. To represent the data, you want to create a chart comparing the percentage of all sales each item represents. Select the range **A3:A9**. Press and hold Ctrl, and then select the range **F3:F9**.

- Click the **Insert** tab, and then, in the Charts group, click the Insert Pie or Doughnut Chart button. Select the first option for a Pie Chart.

- Click the chart border, and then drag to move the chart so the top left corner is over the top left corner of cell G10. Click on the right resizing handle, and then drag the right chart border to the border between columns L and M. Click the bottom resizing handle, and then move the bottom of the chart to the border between rows **22** and **23**.

- On the **Chart Tools Design** tab, in the Chart Styles group, select **Style 3**.

- Click the chart title, **Total Revenue**. Click a second time on **Total Revenue** to place your insertion point in the title. Erase "Total Revenue", and then type Chicken Sales

Revenue by Menu Item. Decrease the font size of the title text to **14**. Click cell **D1** to deselect the chart.

s. You need to look at loan options for the new refrigeration unit by looking at a quarterly payment as it varies for different numbers of payments — or terms in years — and the annual interest rate. Click the **PoultryLoan** worksheet tab. Indigo5 would like to make quarterly payments (four payments per year). Click cell **C12**, enter the formula **=-PMT($B12/4,C$11*4,$C$6)**, and then press Ctrl+Enter. In cell **C12**, double-click the **AutoFill** handle to automatically fill cell range **C12:C14**. With C12:C14 selected, drag the **AutoFill** handle to column **E** to fill the range **C12:E14**.

Notice that the mixed cell addressing of the dollar sign before the B will make the B stay the same and not change when copied, and the same holds true for the dollar sign before the 11. Notice that when copied, the formula will always contain $C$6, since it has an absolute reference of a dollar sign before both the column and the row.

t. Indigo5 would like to use the option that keeps the payment under $2,000, has the shortest term, and has the lowest interest rate. Click cell **D12**, and then click the **Bold** button to indicate that option as the best.

u. Click the **Indigo5ChickenSales** worksheet tab. Click the **Page Layout** tab, and then, in the Page Setup group, click the **Page Setup Dialog Box Launcher**. Click the **Header/Footer** tab. Click **Custom Footer**, then click the **Insert File Name** button to place the file name in the left section of the footer. Click **OK** twice. Repeat this step for the **PoultryLoan** worksheet.

v. Click the **Documentation** worksheet. Click cell **A8**, and then type in today's date. Click cell **B8**, and then type your name in Firstname Lastname format. Complete the remainder of the **Documentation** worksheet according to your instructor's directions.

w. **Save** the workbook, close Excel, and then submit your file as directed by your instructor.

Problem Solve 1

Student data file needed:

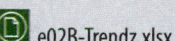 e02B-Trendz.xlsx

You will save your file as:

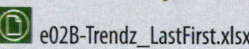 e02B-Trendz_LastFirst.xlsx

Sales Data Analysis

Finance & Accounting

You are the executive assistant to the director of sales at B-Trendz, Inc., a trendy retail store that has locations in only ten states. The company is considering branching into the online retail market. Your supervisor, Kayla Zimmerman, wants to review last year's sales data and make predictions about this year's sales data before making any decisions on whether or not to begin selling online and, if so, which products may sell well online. You have been asked to determine the best-selling women's and men's clothing line by ranking them on a scale from A to E. Only products that have a ranking of A or B will be considered for online sales. To branch into the online market in the future, next year's total sales must be at least $3,000,000. Finally, if B-Trendz, Inc. begins selling products online, you will need help setting up and maintaining the online store. Several companies have given you their information, and you need to determine which company would best fit the needs for the B-Trendz online website.

a. Open the Excel file, **e02B-Trendz**. Save your file as e02B-Trendz_LastFirst, using your last and first name.

b. The Retail sheet contains 2017 quarterly sales data. You need to complete several calculations on this sheet.
- Calculate the quarterly sales totals for the women's and men's clothing lines.
- Calculate the yearly sales totals for the women's and men's clothing lines.
- In **B36:F36**, calculate the grand totals of women's and men's clothing sales.
- In **B37:E37**, calculate the percentage of sales from women's clothing. Display zero decimal places.

- In **B38:E38**, calculate the percentage of sales from men's clothing. Display zero decimal places.

c. You have been asked to determine whether the grand total yearly sales goals were met. The 2017 yearly sales goals were met if the yearly sales were $25,000,000 or more.
- In cell **G36**, using a logical function, determine whether the yearly sales goals were met. Set the formula to return a value of **Yes** if the goal was met or a value of **No** if the goal was not met.

d. You want to create quick visuals of the quarterly sales of each product line, so you decide to use Sparklines to view the sales at a glance. In **G5:G16**, insert **Line** sparklines based on the data in B5:E16. Add High Point markers. Also add **Line** sparklines for the Men's clothing data in **G21:G32**. Add High Point markers.

e. To determine which clothing lines may sell well online, you decide to rank them on a scale from A to E. First, you want to give the ranking table a range name.
- Select **M4:N8**, and give the range the name Rank.
- In cell **H5**, using a Vlookup function, determine the product line ranking of each product based on the Yearly Sales. Use the range name assigned to the lookup table.
- Copy the formula through **H16**.
- In cell **H21**, using a Vlookup function, determine the product line ranking of each product based on the Yearly Sales. Use the range name assigned to the lookup table.
- Copy the formula through **H32**.

f. You have been told that each product line will be considered for online sales only if the product line has a ranking of A or B. You need to determine which product lines will be considered for online sales.
- In cell **I5**, using a logical function, determine whether the product will be an online product. The product will be an online product if it has a ranking of A or B. Set the formula to return a value of **Yes** if the rank was met and a value of **No** if the rank was not met.
- Copy the formula through **I16**.
- Repeat the same formula for the men's clothing lines starting in cell **I21**, and copy the formula through **I32**.

g. You want to visually compare the women's sales and the men's sales of the product lines. Create two charts.
- Create a 3-D clustered column chart that represents the women's clothing sales based on each product line and the product line's yearly sales. Enter a chart title of Women's Clothing Sales.
- Move the chart so the top left corner of the chart is in cell **K10** and the bottom right corner of the chart is in cell **Q22**.
- Apply **Style 3** to the chart.
- Create a second 3-D clustered column chart that represents the men's clothing sales based on each product line and the product line's yearly sales. Enter a chart title of Men's Clothing Sales.
- Move the chart so the top left corner of the chart is in cell **K23** and the bottom right corner of the chart is in cell **Q38**.
- Apply **Style 3** to the chart.
- Adjust the vertical axis Bounds and Units of the men's clothing chart to match the vertical axis of the women's clothing chart.

h. You want to compare sales percentages of women's and men's clothing and have this chart as a separate chart sheet for ease of printing.
- Create a clustered column chart to compare the sales percentages of women's and men's clothing sales for all four quarters.

- Move the chart to a new chart sheet, and name the new worksheet SalesComparison. Position the SalesComparison worksheet to the right the Retail worksheet.
- Apply **Style 4** to the chart.
- Enter the chart title Sales Comparison. Change the chart title format using WordArt, **Pattern Fill - Blue, Accent 1, Light Downward Diagonal, Outline - Accent 1**. Increase the font of the chart title to **40**.
- Insert a rounded rectangle shape in the top left corner of the chart. Enter the text Women's products consistently outsold men's products.
- Change the size of the rounded rectangle shape to **.6"** high and **2.25"** wide.

i. B-Trendz management believes that with the growing popularity of its clothing products, the company can reach the overall yearly goal of $30,000,000 in sales (the sales goal of 2017 was $25,000,000). You have been asked to determine the approximate increase in sales of each product that would be needed to reach this goal. Assume the same percentage increase for all the products.

- Select the **Predictions** worksheet tab. In cell **B5**, multiply the percent increase in sales in B1 by the 2017 sales for women's Quarter 1 Activeware (B5 of the Retail worksheet). (Hint: To use data from another worksheet in this formula, click the worksheet tab, click the cell you want to multiply by the percentage in cell B1 and then press Enter.) Don't forget that you want at least the amount from the Retail worksheet plus the predicted increase.
- Copy this formula to the range **B5:E16**.
- Total the women's clothing sales as well as the women's quarterly sales.
- Repeat all the above steps for the men's clothing sales.
- In **B36:F36**, total the quarterly and yearly sales for both women's and men's clothing.
- In cell **G36**, using a logical function, you will determine whether the sales goal is met. The sales goal is met if the yearly sales total is greater than or equal to $30,000,000. Set the formula to return a value of **Yes** if goal was met and a value of **No** if goal was not met.
- Using trial and error in cell **B1**, determine the approximate percentage increase that is needed for all products to meet the total sales goal of $30,000,000 in cell G36. Use only whole number percentages.

j. To launch online sales, B-Trendz will need to hire a website development company to set up and maintain the website. To do so, B-Trendz will need to take out a loan to cover the cost of the development and maintenance of the website. You have solicited and received bids from three different companies. For each bid, you need to determine the monthly payment, total loan payment, and total interest.

- Select the **Online** worksheet. In cell **B11**, calculate the monthly payment for the loan given the loan amount, term, and interest for the Online Solutions company. The result should be a positive value.
- In cell **B12**, calculate the total payments over the life of the loan.
- In **B13**, calculate how much total interest will be paid over the life of the loan.
- Copy the range B11:B13 to **D11:D13**.
- You need to recommend which company B-Trendz should use to create and maintain the online website. The best option is based on the company maintaining the website for at least two years and a monthly payment of $2,100 or less. Use a logical function in cell **B15:D15** to return the company name from row 2 if the website will be maintained for at least two years and the monthly payment is $2,100 or less. If the value is false, the cell should remain blank.

k. Complete the **Documentation** worksheet according to your instructor's directions. Insert the **file name** in the left footer section on all worksheets in the workbook.

l. **Save** the workbook, exit Excel, and then submit your file as directed by your instructor.

Critical Thinking

When calculating the payment for the three potential loans, you were asked to have the function return a positive value. Why is it important to return a positive value of a loan payment? Identify at least two ways to make a payment function return a positive value.

Sales & Marketing

Student data file needed:

e02Advertise.xlsx

You will save your file as: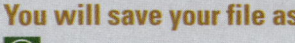

e02Advertise_LastFirst.xlsx

Advertising Review

The Painted Paradise Resort & Spa has been investing in advertising using different media. When guests check in, the employee asks them how they heard about Painted Paradise Resort & Spa. Based on the customer's response, the employee then notes in the system either magazine, radio, television, Internet, word of mouth, or other. Since almost every guest is asked, the number surveyed represents a significant portion of the actual guests. The past year's data is located on the GuestData worksheet. Every time a guest answers the question by mentioning an advertising source, it is considered a guest result. Ideally, the resort wants to purchase advertising at a low cost but then see as many guest results from that advertising as possible.

Every year, upper management sets the advertising budget before the beginning of the fiscal year, July 1. For the coming year, upper management has given you a larger television budget because of a new video marketing campaign. Also, the advertising contracts get negotiated every year, because the media vendors require a one-year commitment. The contracts are negotiated after the budget has been set. You will develop charts for an upcoming presentation that will discuss a marketing strategy, potential changes to the budget given the new media prices, anticipated monthly guest results, and the prospect of hiring a marketing consulting company with a high retainer that would require a loan.

a. Open the Excel file, **e02Advertise**. Save your file as e02Advertise_LastFirst, using your last and first name.

b. On the **GuestData** worksheet, in cells **A6:J17**, the data indicates the number of guests responding that they heard of the resort from the listed method — Guest Results. Add the following.

- In cell **H2**, add a COUNTA function to determine the number of months listed in cells A6:A17.

- In cell **J2**, add a DATEDIF function to calculate the survey duration in years using the 2017 Fiscal Start date and 2018 Fiscal Start date.

- In cells **B6:B17**, use Flash Fill to return the three-character code for the month — JUL for July.

- Select cells **L6:M17**, and then name the range **Season**.

- In cells **C6:C17**, add a VLOOKUP that will exactly match the month in column **B** to return the correct season — Low, Mid, or High — based on the named range **Season**.

- In cells **D19:J19**, calculate the averages for each column with a rounded value — not just formatted — to zero decimal places.

- For later use, create the following named ranges.

Cell	Name
D19	AvgMagazine
E19	AvgRadio
F19	AvgTelevision
G19	AvgInternet

c. On the **AdvertisingPlan** worksheet, an analysis of past Guest Results and the new budget have been started. First, you need to finish out the past year analysis. Add the following:

- In cell **F2**, enter a function that will return the current date.

- Set the following cells to these formulas.

Cell	Name
D6	=AvgMagazine
D7	=AvgRadio
D8	=AvgTelevision
D9	=AvgInternet

* Note that these are monthly averages. Thus, all calculations on this worksheet are estimates based on the monthly average.

- In cells **E6:E9**, calculate the Amount Spent — a monthly figure — by multiplying the Cost Per Ad and the Ads Placed.

- In cells **F6:F10**, calculate the Cost per Guest Result by dividing the Amount Spent by the Past Guest Results.

- In cells **C10:E10**, calculate the appropriate totals for each column.

d. On the **AdvertisingPlan** worksheet, you need to finish out the new budget year analysis. Add the following.

- In cells **I6:I9**, calculate the Number of Ads that can be purchased based on the New Budget and the New Cost Per Ad in columns **G** and **H**. (Hint: A partial ad cannot be purchased. Further, $300 would not be enough to purchase one radio ad, since the new cost per ad is $325, so you need to create a formula that will round the number down to the nearest integer.)

- In cells **J6:J9**, calculate the Amount to Spend — this is a monthly figure — by multiplying the New Cost Per Ad and the Ads to Place.

- In cells **G10** and **I10:J10**, calculate the appropriate totals for each column. If necessary, change the format for cell I10 to general.

- In cell **H11**, calculate the amount of the budget remaining by subtracting the Amount to Spend total from the New Budget total. Note that the totals are in row 10. A negative number indicates that the new plan is over budget. A positive number indicates that the new plan is under budget and has excess spendable funds.

- In cells **K6:K9**, add a formula that will return **Increase?** if the Ads to Place is equal to zero or if the New Cost Per Ad is less than or equal to the Budget +/- in cell **H11**. Any others should return **Decrease?**. This column now indicates the media types for which the resort may want to consider an increase or decrease in the Ads to Place, along with any necessary budget adjustment.

- In cells **L6:L9**, calculate the Anticipated Guest Results by dividing the Amount to Spend by the Cost per Guest Result — column F. The resulting value — not the just the format — should be rounded to zero decimals.

- In cell **L10**, calculate the appropriate total for Anticipated Guest Results.

- In cell **L11**, calculate the number of anticipated guest results compared to the past by subtracting the Past Guest Results total from the Anticipated Guest Results total. Note that the totals are in row 10. A negative number indicates an anticipated decrease in Guest Results. A positive number indicates an anticipated increase in Guest Results.

e. Starting on the **AdvertisingPlan** worksheet, you need to make two charts for your presentation. Create the following two charts.

- Based on the data in cells **A5:A9**, **D5:D9**, and **L5:L9**, add a **3-D Clustered Column** chart to compare the past guest results to the anticipated guest results based on the new monthly advertising.

- Under chart styles, set the chart to **Style 6**. Then change the title to read PAST VS. ANTICIPATED MONTHLY GUEST RESULTS.

- Move and resize the chart so the top left corner is in cell **A11** and the bottom right corner is in cell **F22**. Set the chart title to **12** pt font size.

- Based on the data in cells **A5:A9**, **D5:D9**, and **E5:E9**, add a **Clustered Column - Line on Secondary Axis Combo Chart**. Move this chart to its own worksheet — chart sheet — named **GuestResultsBySpending**.
- Under chart styles, set the chart to **Style 6**. Then change the title to read **Past Advertising Amount Spent Compared to # of Guest Results Experienced**.
- Set the chart title to **18** pt font size, set all axis data labels to **12** pt font size, and set all legend text to **12** pt font size.

f. On the **MarketingConsultants** worksheet, a monthly loan payment analysis has been started. The resort is considering hiring marketing consultants. However, they require a large up-front retainer fee. The resort would need to take out a loan to cover the cost. The resort needs an analysis of the loan payment by varying interest rate and down payment amount. Add the following.

- In cells **D10:H13**, add a **PMT** function to calculate the monthly payment. Enter one formula that can be entered in cell **D10** and filled to the remaining cells. (Hint: Think carefully about where dollar signs are needed for mixed and absolute cell addressing. Also, the down payment can be subtracted from the Retainer — or Principal — Amount in the third argument of the PMT function. Adjust the formula so the result is positive.)

g. Complete the **Documentation** worksheet according to your instructor's directions. Insert the **file name** in the left footer section on all worksheets in the workbook.

h. **Save** the workbook, exit Excel, and then submit your file as directed by your instructor.

Perform 1: Perform in Your Life

Student data file needed:

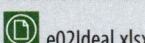 e02Ideal.xlsx

You will save your file as:

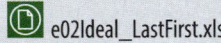 e02Ideal_LastFirst.xlsx

Your Ideal Career Start

Human Resources

Even if this is your first semester, you have probably already begun to think about the type of job or career you want. Further, when you are spending long hours studying, it can be fun to imagine the new car you might buy at your ideal career start after graduation. For this project, pretend — if you need to — that you are graduating this semester. In this project, you need to find currently available jobs and establish criteria to help you pick your most desired position. Then you will find the ideal new car to purchase, but your new position's salary must allow you to afford the monthly payment.

a. Open the Excel file, **e02Ideal**. Save your file as **e02Ideal_LastFirst**, using your last and first name. Keep the workbook professional, but feel free to optionally add elements such as a picture of your ideal career start or new car.

b. Go to the Internet, and find five or more jobs that interest you. You can select data from multiple websites or just one website (from the same website will be easiest). Search for jobs that you may apply for after graduation. Copy and paste that data into the **JobData worksheet**. Feel free to add columns, move columns, or rename columns to fit your data and style needs.

c. On the **JobData** worksheet, accomplish the following.
- In cell **A1**, add an appropriate title for your career goals.
- In cell **B3**, indicate the website you used to find the job posting (e.g., Monster.com or CareerBuilder.com).
- In cell **B4**, indicate the date you gathered the information.

- In the center header of your worksheet, insert your full name.
- Starting in row 7, complete the columns of data listed on Table 1 below by copying from the Internet and separating — or cleansing — the data using Excel's Flash Fill feature and/or text functions as necessary. You can gather more data than is listed below if it is relevant to picking the ideal job for you. At a minimum, you must have the following.

Data (no extra characters in or around the data)	Description
Company Name	Full name as you would address a letter to the company.
Job Title	Full job title, which needs to be descriptive of the position. For example, "Entry Level" is not a sufficient title. "Application Support Analyst — Entry Level" is a sufficient title.
State	State in which the position is located. State should be in a column by itself, not in combination with the city or address.
Salary	Try not to mix pay types. For example, if you are looking for a salaried position, choose all salaried positions.

Table 1   Required minimum job position data

- Add headers, comments, and/or notes to make clear to your instructor what Excel steps you took to get to the final job data. Leave all formulas you create in the worksheet — show your work, don't delete it. If Flash Fill was used, indicate the range. Keep your work organized.
- Format the JobData worksheet as needed.

d. On the **JobAnalysis** worksheet, copy data from the JobData sheet that you intend to use to help you determine which position(s) to apply for. Add the following elements to this worksheet.

- In cell A1, enter an appropriate worksheet title, and then copy data from the JobData sheet beginning in row 3.
- In Column D, use an IF statement in combination with any other Excel formulas or functions to indicate whether a job is in a state you find desirable. You should indicate a minimum of two states as desirable.
- In cell A16:A18, fill in salary data to establish pay range categories for Below Expected, Expected, and Above Expected based on your personal job expectations.
- Give the salary table data an appropriate range name.
- In column F, use this table in a VLOOKUP to determine the category for each of the positions you are evaluating using the salary table range name.
- In column G, determine whether you will apply for the job. You will apply for the job if the salary has a category of Expected or Above Expected.
- Add any other additional formulas and functions to help you determine the most desirable position.
- The worksheet must ultimately indicate one final Most Desired job position.
- Format the JobAnalysis worksheet as needed.

e. On the **MyNewCar** worksheet, add the following elements.

- In B2:B7, enter data for the ideal car you wish to purchase. In B13:B15, enter three current interest rates for the type of car you wish to purchase. In C12:E12, enter possible terms of the loan in years for the type of car you wish to purchase.
- In cells C13:E15, calculate the monthly payment for your ideal car using the three different interest rates and three different terms of loans.

- In cell **B17**, input the monthly gross salary by referencing the salary from your most desired job on the JobAnalysis worksheet.
- You need to be able to afford the car you pick. The amount you will be able to afford will vary greatly depending on individual circumstances, such as marital status, credit card debt, and homeowner status. For the purposes of this project, the car you pick cannot have a monthly payment greater than **10%** of your gross salary for your Most Desired job. In C22:E24, determine the percentage of your monthly salary the loan payment would represent.
- Use a conditional format to indicate feasible loan options. If none of the loan options are under 10%, you will have to do one or a combination of the following: pick a new car, increase your down payment, extend your term, or find a lower interest rate.
- Format the MyNewCar worksheet as needed.

   f. Build at least one meaningful chart on either the JobAnalysis or MyNewCar worksheet. Include at least a one-sentence explanation near the chart explaining the chart's significance.

   g. Complete the **Documentation** worksheet according to your instructor's directions. Insert the **file name** in the left footer on all worksheets in the workbook.

   h. **Save** the workbook, exit Excel, and then submit your file as directed by your instructor.

Perform 2: Perform in Your Career

Student data file needed:

 e02Investment.xlsx

You will save your file as:

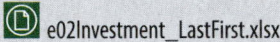 e02Investment_LastFirst.xlsx

Investment Portfolios

Finance & Accounting

You have started working as an investment intern for a financial company that helps clients invest in the stock market. Your manager, Roger Hedding, gives you a spreadsheet detailing some periodic investments in Nobel Energy, Inc. (NBL) made by one of the clients. The client would like a report and charts on the NBL investment and the stock's performance. Your manager has asked you to finish this report.

   a. Open the Excel file, **e02Investment**. Save your file as **e02Investment_LastFirst**, using your last and first name.

   b. On the **NBLInvestment** worksheet, add the following calculation.
- In column **F**, starting in row 21, your manager has already entered a formula to calculate total value. Update the formula to return a value of only **two decimals**. (Hint: The cell value needs to change, which is different from merely formatting to two decimals.)
- In column **G**, starting in the second row — cell **G22** — enter a formula to sum up the quarterly investments as of the date in column A to provide a cumulative total. For example, cell G22 should return the sum of the Quarterly investments on 1/2/2016 and 4/1/2016. Next, cell G23 should return the sum of the Quarterly investments on 1/2/2016, 4/1/2016, and 7/1/2016. Thus, column G returns a running total of investments so the last cell — G33 — reflects the total of all investments from 1/2/2016 thru 1/3/2019.
- In column **H**, calculate the Total Growth. The total growth is the Total Value minus the Total Investment. (A result of a negative value means that the investment shrank instead of growing.)
- In column **I**, calculate the Total Growth %. The Total Growth% is the Total Growth divided by the Total Investment.
- In cell **J21**, type 0. In cell **J22**, calculate the Quarterly Growth. The Quarterly Growth is the Total Growth minus the Total Growth from the previous quarter.

- In column **K**, calculate the Quarterly Growth %: The Quarterly Growth % is the Quarterly Growth divided by the Total Investment.
- In column **L**, using a lookup function, calculate the Quarterly Rank based on the lookup table in M1:N7. Assign the range name **Rank** to the lookup table, and use the range name in the formula.
- In column **M**, using a logical function, determine the Portfolio Status Recommendation. The Portfolio Status is "Good" if the Quarterly Rank is A or B. Otherwise, the Portfolio Status will return a value of "Diversify".

c. Create a **combo chart** for Total Portfolio Performance that displays the Total Value, Total Investment, and Total Growth over time. (Hint: You will need to show a secondary axis for Total Growth.) Apply a chart style. Position the chart above the data in row 20.

d. Create a **combo chart** for Quarterly Performance that displays the Quarterly Growth and the Quarterly Growth % over time. (Hint: You will need to show a secondary axis for Quarterly Total Growth %.) Apply a chart style. Position the chart above the data. You may need to change the Label Position to Low.

e. Complete the **Documentation** worksheet according to your instructor's directions. Insert the **file name** in the left footer on all worksheets in the workbook.

f. **Save** the workbook, exit Excel, and then submit your file as directed by your instructor.

Perform 3: Perform in Your Team

Student data file needed:

 e02Paintball.xlsx

You will save your file as:

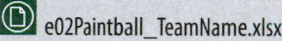 e02Paintball_TeamName.xlsx

Paintball Facility Expansion

Productions & Operations

You work for Splat Attack Paintball Range, a popular outdoor paintball facility near a metropolitan area. The range is open Wednesdays through Sundays from the first of April until the end of October every year. With the popularity of the sport of paintball rising and the facility's inability to accommodate the number of paintball party bookings being requested, Splat Attack is considering an expansion of its paintball range. You have been assigned to a team to help with the analysis for an expansion of the range area and overall capacity. Your manager, Amy Trilling, needs help looking at past sales, sales trends, and loan options. Located in the upper Midwest of the United States, Splat Attack has typical Midwest weather. Therefore, part of the facility's marketing strategy is to offer discounted season passes in the colder months if the temperature is 60 degrees or below. Following is a description of the data Amy has provided to you.

Date	Description
Month	The first day of the month for the data in that row.
Passes Sold	The number of paid players and season pass holders who entered the paintball range that month. Attendance does not reflect the time spent on the range. If a player leaves the range and returns, the player is counted only once.
Ticket Sales	All ticket sales that month, including single-day and season passes. If a player buys a season pass in April, the sale is accounted for only in April, yet the player can play throughout the remaining months of that season.
Other Sales	All other revenue besides ticket sales. This is primarily equipment rental and paintballs.
Avg High Temp (Degrees)	The average high temperature for the park that particular month.

a. Select one team member to set up the document by completing steps b through d.

b. Open your browser, and navigate to **https://www.onedrive.live.com, https://www.drive.google.com**, or any other instructor-assigned location. Be sure all members of the team have an account on the chosen system, such as a Microsoft or Google account.

c. Open the Excel file, **e02Paintball**. Save your file as e02Paintball_TeamName, replacing TeamName with the name assigned to your team by your instructor.

d. Share the spreadsheet with the other members of your team. Make sure each team member has the appropriate permission to edit the document.

e. Hold a team meeting to discuss the requirements of the remaining steps. As a team, make an action plan to assign individual and team work and set deadlines for each step.

f. The **Sales** worksheet includes data about past revenue — earned income before any costs. The data on the Sales worksheet could be analyzed in several ways. Add the following to the worksheet.
   - As a team, determine possible range names that can be used in creating formulas for the Sales worksheet.
   - In cell **E4**, add a field labeled Total Sales. In column E, calculate the total sales for each month using range names if appropriate.
   - In cell **F4**, add a field labeled Average Sales per Pass Sold. In column F, calculate the average sales per pass sold for each month.
   - In cell **G4**, add a field labeled % of Total Sales. In column G, using a mixed or absolute reference, calculate each month's percent of the total sales.
   - In cell **J4**, add a field labeled Discount Passes?. In column J, determine whether Splat Attack will offer discount passes based on the facility's marketing strategy.
   - In cell **A12**, add a field labeled Totals. In the cell range **B12:E12**, use a function to calculate the totals.
   - In cell **A13**, add a field labeled Averages. In the cell range **B13:E13**, use a function or formula to calculate the averages.
   - Add any other calculations your team feels are relevant for analyzing Splat Attack's past revenue.
   - As a team, format the worksheet in a professional manner. Adjust column width and row height as appropriate. Apply cell format as necessary for data interpretation.
   - Each team member should independently create and format one or two charts about the data on this worksheet.
   - With a focus on displaying sales peaks and trends, the team should meet to decide which three to five charts to include in the final file.

g. On the **Loan** worksheet, you will find the basic information about two loan options to finance Splat Attack's range expansion. Make the following updates to the loan worksheet.
   - In cells **B8** and **C8**, calculate the Monthly Payment amount for the two loan options for the range expansion. Splat Attack is considering only terms of three or five years.
   - In cells **B12** and **C12**, calculate the Total Loan Payments for the two loan options.
   - In cell **B13**, identify which loan is preferred for Splat Attack's expansion project. The loan is preferred if the total loan payment is the lower of the two.
   - Add any other calculations your team feels are relevant to determining the best loan for Splat Attack.
   - As a team, format the worksheet in a professional manner, applying appropriate theme and cell styles. Adjust column width and row height as appropriate. Apply cell formatting as necessary for data interpretation.

h. Fill out the **TeamComments** worksheet as directed by your instructor.

i. Complete the Documentation worksheet according to your instructor's directions. At the minimum, include enough detail to identify which parts of the worksheets or workbook each team member completed.

j. Insert the **file name** in the left footer on all worksheets in the workbook. In a custom header section, include the names of the students in your team, spreading the names evenly across each of the three header sections: left section, center section, and right section.

k. **Save** the workbook, exit Excel, and then submit your file as directed by your instructor.

Perform 4: How Others Perform

Student data file needed:

 e02Sport.xlsx

You will save your file as:

 e02Sport_LastFirst.xlsx

Sports Facility Operations

Productions & Operations

You have recently been hired as an account representative in the business office of Sports Plus, a fitness facility. Your supervisor, Tim Kerr, has requested that you finish an already-started Excel workbook file that identifies the expenses of the sports facility and projects by quarter for the current year. Beyond performing calculations for total expenses by expense category and per quarter, you are expected to create and format a series of professional-looking charts that will assist in the interpretation of the workbook data. The spreadsheet data and visual charts will not only be included in an annual report but also be presented to the board of directors of the company.

You have also been asked to look at the sales of the specific exercise classes for the year and determine which courses should continue to be offered at the facility the following year and which courses should no longer be offered. Finally, you have been asked to predict what percentage increase in the cost of classes would be needed to reach the total sales goal of $40,000.

a. Open the Excel file, **e02Sport**. Save your file as e02Sport_LastFirst, using your last and first name.

b. Rename Sheet1 Expenses. Complete the worksheet by making the following changes.

- In cell D6, adjust the existing formula by taking **Last Year's Avg Qtr** and multiplying it by the **Target Factor for Increases** for **Qtr 1**. Use mixed referencing when correcting this formula. Copy the formula though **G14**.

- Check to be sure the SUM function and cell range are correct in cell H6, in which you are calculating the **Total** for **Rent** for the current year only (**Qtr 1 - Qtr 4**). Fill the formula down through Column **H14**.

- Correct the SUM function in cell **D16**, and then fill the corrected function across through column G.

- For cell range **D19:D22**, use functions to perform calculations for Qtr1 through Qtr4. Fill the formulas in **D19:D21** across through column G.

- Apply formatting to improve the appearance of the worksheet as necessary. Apply any data formatting that will make the data easier to interpret.

- Create a chart to display each expense category and expense amounts for each quarter. Reposition the chart below the worksheet data beginning in A24. Resize the chart so the bottom left corner is in cell D38. Format the chart, and add a descriptive title that represents the information displayed in the chart.

- Create a chart to display the expense categories and total expenses for the current year. Add percentages as data labels. Reposition the chart below the worksheet data beginning in row 24. Resize the chart so the bottom left corner of the chart is in cell H38. Format the chart, and add a descriptive chart title.

- In I6:I14, insert column Sparklines of the data for Qtr1:Qtr4.
- Modify the page settings to ensure your worksheet will print on a single page. Specify page orientation as is appropriate to maximize readability.

c. Select **Sheet2**, and rename the sheet SalesData. The SalesData worksheet contains sales information for exercise classes offered at the facility. You will finish this worksheet by completing the following.
   - In column D, create a formula to calculate the sales total for adult classes and youth classes.
   - Calculate the totals of yearly sessions sold and sales total for both adult and youth classes.
   - Calculate the total sales of the exercise classes for the fitness facility.
   - To determine exercise class ranking for both the adult and youth classes, you will use the lookup table in I2:J7. Give the lookup table the range name Rank, and use the range name when creating the formula.
   - Only classes with a ranking of Silver, Gold, or Platinum will be continued the following year. Create a formula to help your supervisor determine whether the courses should continue to be offered for both the adult and youth classes.

d. Select **Sheet3**, and rename the sheet SalesGoal. On the SalesGoal worksheet, you have been asked to predict how much to raise the cost of classes to reach the total sales goal of **$40,000**. You will increase all classes by the same percentage. Finish the SalesGoal sheet by completing the following.
   - Referencing the 2016 data from the SalesData sheet, determine the percentage of increase needed in the 2017 cost per class session. The increase is determined by multiplying the 2016 Cost per Class by the Sales Increase Percentage Recommendation. (Hint: Be sure to add 1 to the percentage found in cell D22 to get an accurate increase for the 2017 classes.)
   - Since the results on the SalesData worksheet indicated that the low-selling courses should be discontinued, change the yearly sessions sold for Racquetball in cell B15 to 0. You may need to re-determine the percentage increase of cost per class session after deleting the row.
   - Through trial and error, determine the recommended percentage of increase in the cost per class session in cell D22 to reach the 2017 sales goal of at least $40,000.

e. Complete the **Documentation** worksheet according to your instructor's directions. Insert the **file name** in the left footer section on all worksheets in the workbook.

f. **Save** the workbook, exit Excel, and then submit your file as directed by your instructor.

Excel Business Unit 3

Integrating Complex Functions into Business Analysis

Analyzing data can be vital to your decision-making process, either on the job or for personal use. However, it may seem overwhelming when you have a large volume of data to analyze. Excel has retrieval functions that help you to analyze large amounts of data. You can also format data as an Excel table to make it more manageable. This business unit will introduce you to the importance of using Excel's complex retrieval functions for business analysis.

Learning Outcome 1:

Use Excel conditional and retrieval functions for a powerful method of extracting data from a table.

REAL WORLD SUCCESS

"During the summer after my sophomore year, I obtained an internship with a top technology consulting firm. Several students from other local colleges worked with me. One day, three of the interns, including me, were assigned to work on a project. Our manager asked us if anyone knew how to create a VLOOKUP in Excel. I was the only one who did!"

- Sahiba, current student

Learning Outcome 2:

Use Excel Tables, PivotTables, and PivotCharts to quickly summarize and analyze large amounts of data.

REAL WORLD SUCCESS

"My instructor taught my class how to work with large amounts of data and explained that we will need to use these skills when we enter the work force. I never imagined that as a marketing analyst I would be working with so much data and that I would have to use the skills my instructor taught. PivotTables have become a way of life for me. I could never have been able to make sense of all the data I collect had it not been for PivotTables and PivotCharts. Thank goodness I learned how to work with these data analysis tools!"

- Stephanie, recent graduate

Microsoft Excel 2016

Chapter 5 | COMPLEX CONDITIONAL AND RETRIEVAL FUNCTIONS

Prepare Case

Accounting & Finance

Productions & Operations

Red Bluff Golf Course & Pro Shop Sales Analysis

The Red Bluff Golf Course & Pro Shop generates revenue through its golfers, golfer services, and pro shop sales. Aleeta Herriott, the pro shop manager, receives revenue data on a monthly basis. She would like to have some reports developed that will help to track sales and to analyze her profit margins. She has a workbook started with some sample data and wants you to continue developing some reports. These reports will help Aleeta make educated decisions about the business, such as which items to place on sale or discontinue.

Four Oaks/Shutterstock

Student data file needed for this chapter:

 e03ch05GolfSales.xlsx

You will save your file as:

 e03ch05GolfSales_LastFirst.xlsx

Integrating Logical Functions

Making decisions, whether they are personal or business driven, involves evaluation and choices. Golfers use logic as they play, evaluating the scene — distance to the green; wind speed and direction; obstacles such as water features, sand traps, or trees; and terrain, including grass height and elevation — as it changes with every shot. For instance, a golfer who is 300 yards away from the green and has an unobstructed shot might choose a driver or a 1-iron. If the golfer is in a sand trap and 20 feet from the hole — pin — a sand wedge would be chosen. Similarly, business success depends on the ability to choose whether to buy or lease, build or buy from a supplier, or advertise in a magazine or on television. Being able to evaluate conditions and apply logic in choosing the best option is the foundation of logical functions. A **logical function** is a function that returns a result, or output, based on evaluating whether a logical test is true or false. Logical functions enable evaluation and choices to be integrated into a worksheet. The most common logical functions include IF, AND, OR, and NOT. Another logical function, IFERROR, is a special function that is discussed at the end of this chapter.

The foundation of a logical function is a logical expression or logical test. A **logical test** is an equation with comparison operators that can be evaluated as either true or false. It is also known as a logical expression. For example, the logical expression "the distance to the green is more than 300 yards" compares the actual distance to 300 yards. The test — determining whether the ball is lying more than or less than 300 yards away from the green — will help to determine which club will be chosen.

Logical operators, as listed in Table 1, are used to create logical tests.

Operator	Description	TRUE	FALSE
<	Less than	5 < 7	10 < 3
>	Greater than	10 > 3	3 > 10
<=	Less than or equal to	5 <= 5	5 <= 4
>=	Greater than or equal to	5 >= 4	3 >= 10
<>	Not equal to	2 <> 4	2 <> 2

Table 1   Logical operators

Preview the Data

Aleeta Herriott, the Red Bluff Golf Course & Pro Shop manager, has asked you to develop a worksheet to assist her with decision making. Another staff member had developed the worksheet and populated it with some sample data. When Aleeta realized that the person was simply entering values for the calculated fields rather than using formulas, she decided to turn the project over to you. She entered additional data to demonstrate how she would like it to look; however, the manually entered calculations need to be replaced with formulas.

Opening the Starting File

To create complex conditional and retrieval functions, you first need to open the GolfSales workbook. In this exercise, you will open a workbook and then will save the workbook with a new name.

To Save the Golf Sales Workbook

a. Start **Excel**, click **Open Other Workbooks** in the left pane, and then double-click **This PC**. Navigate through the folder structure to the location of your student data files, and then double-click **e03ch05GolfSales**. If a Security Warning message displays, click the **Enable Editing** button.

b. Click the **File** tab, click **Save As**, and then double-click **This PC**. In the Save As dialog box, navigate to the location where you are saving your project files, and then change the file name to e03ch05GolfSales_LastFirst, using your last and first name. Click **Save**.

The DataInputs worksheet has been created to store the data that will be used in formulas. Keeping the supporting data on a separate sheet makes it easier to streamline the printed report. Additionally, the worksheet needs to be formatted to analyze different amounts of data. For example, there could be 113 transactions in one time period and 154 in another. Aleeta Herriott believes that having enough room for 200 transactions will be sufficient for managing the business.

Within the workbook, named ranges have been created for most, but not all, of the data. Using named ranges makes creating formulas easier because you do not need to worry about adding absolute and mixed cell references.

The data on the Transactions worksheet is created with two sections. The first section contains data that Aleeta will receive on a monthly basis from the IT staff. It contains the transaction data listed in Table 2.

Data Field	Description
Trans_ID	Transaction number
Trans_Time	Time of the transaction
SKU	Product ID number
Pay_Type	Method of payment
Trans_Qty	Purchase quantity
Coupon_Num	Coupon number, if used
Emp_ID	Employee that completed the transaction
Cust_Cat	Customer category

Table 2   Sales data descriptions

The second section of data contains fields that need to be calculated. Currently, the data has been manually calculated — **static data** — and then typed into the worksheet, a very inefficient practice. You will replace the static data in this section with calculations. The fields' descriptions are briefly detailed in Table 3.

Data Field	Description for Calculated Fields
SKU_Cat	Product category
Emp_Position	Employee position
Shift	Time period when the transaction occurred
Coupon_Target	Type of customer targeted for the coupon
Coupon_Hit	Whether the coupon was submitted by the correct customer type
Coupon_Amt	Percentage off for the coupon
Retail	Retail price of the product
Line_Item_Total	Total revenue (price qty – coupon)
Card_Charge	Whether the transaction used a credit card
Trans_Group	Category of transaction based on the amount of the transaction
Big_Ticket_Item	Category of non-accessory items
Sales_Point1	Incentive points calculation for sales team
Sales_Point2	Additional incentive points calculation for sales team

Table 3 Calculated fields' descriptions

Aleeta would like you to analyze the monthly Red Bluff Golf Course & Pro Shop sales data to transform the data into information that she can use to make sound business decisions. Being able to address the following questions may provide insight into how she can increase sales, decrease expenses, or provide better customer service.

- What types of products sell well? What types do not sell well?
- What percentage of the transactions come from credit card sales?
- What is the average transaction amount?
- Who purchases more in terms of quantity or dollar amount: hotel guests or local customers?
- Which sales team members sell the most? Which sell the least?

S₅ CONSIDER THIS | **How Would These Questions Help Any Business?**

Aleeta's questions are not unique to Red Bluff. Any business that wants to generate revenue would ask questions like these. On the basis of the analysis, Aleeta might create a marketing strategy to increase the average sales to local customers or ask the human resource department to provide sales training to all employees. How would these help management make decisions? What might management surmise from the answers to the questions Aleeta needs to consider?

Exploring the data, finding the answers to questions, and developing knowledge from the Red Bluff Golf Course & Pro Shop information will help management to gain and maintain a competitive advantage. A **competitive advantage** is the strategic advantage that a business has over its competition. Attaining a competitive advantage strengthens a business and positions it better within the business environment. Aleeta hopes that developing the worksheets properly will help with decision making.

CONSIDER THIS | **Can You Identify a Business That Has a Competitive Advantage?**

Think about businesses you visit or ads you see on TV. When you go to McDonald's, do you think about Burger King or Wendy's? What makes you choose one over another? In 2011, Wendy's became the second most popular fast-food hamburger restaurant, surpassing Burger King, which had held the position for 40 years. How did Wendy's do this? How does McDonald's keep its first-place position? How much money do these companies spend to maintain or gain a competitive advantage?

Use IF Functions

The **IF function**, the most common logical function in Excel, returns one of two values depending on whether the supplied logical test being evaluated is true or false. The logical test evaluates a logical condition, or statement, and can involve either values or other functions. The IF function has three arguments

=IF(logical_test, [value_if_true], [value_if_false])

Suppose you want a list of all golf club members who have a handicap — a method used to level the playing field for golfers of different skill levels — at or below 0. A golfer who has a handicap of 0 or below is known as a scratch golfer. An IF function could be created that would check the handicap and return the words "Scratch Golfer" if the handicap is less than or equal to 0 or "Handicapped Golfer" if the handicap is greater than 0. For example, an IF function could be

=IF(C5<=0,"Scratch Golfer","Handicapped Golfer")

In this formula, C5<=0 is the logical test; the value_if_true is "Scratch Golfer", and the value_if_false is "Handicapped Golfer". In other words, the user would see "Scratch Golfer" if the value in C5 is less than or equal to 0; otherwise, "Handicapped Golfer" would be displayed. When using words — referred to a text string — in formulas such as the IF function, you must enter the words in quotation marks.

Although the IF function has three arguments, two arguments are optional. For example, you could have the IF function

=IF(C5<=0)

Since the [value_if_true] argument is not defined, if cell C5 contains a value that is less than or equal to 0, Excel will return the word TRUE in the cell that has the function. Since the [value_if_false] argument is not defined, if cell C5 contains a value that is greater than 0, Excel will return the word FALSE. However, simply returning TRUE or FALSE is not valuable for a manager and is not usually best practice or the desired result. The IF function is exclusive because it only has two outcomes: one when the logical test is true and one when the logical test is false.

CONSIDER THIS | **Why Is It Better to Display Specific Values?**

The IF function can be written to include only one argument, and the results will either be TRUE or FALSE if the optional arguments are not defined. Why is it better to provide specific values for Excel to display? How can this help the user analyze the results?

One of the easiest ways to begin working with IF functions is to use a decision tree. A **decision tree** is a diagramming tool that allows you to break down potential decisions in a logical, structured format. By using the decision tree, you can take a problem or decision and break down the potential possibilities. Consider the previous example. If the formula =IF(C5<=0,"Scratch Golfer","Handicapped Golfer") were inserted into a decision tree, it would be diagrammed with three labeled branches in black, the values for each argument in blue, and finished with the IF function syntax in red, as shown in Figure 1.

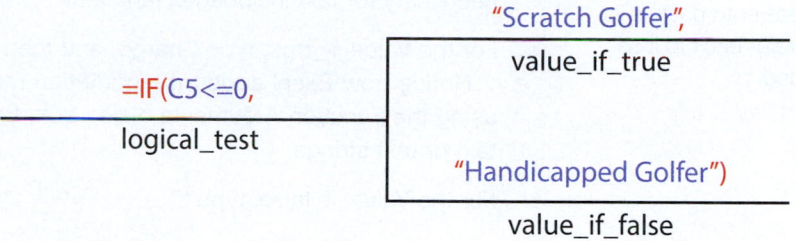

Figure 1   Decision tree

QUICK REFERENCE	Diagramming a Decision Tree

A decision tree helps to keep your thoughts organized as you work through writing your formula. Complete the following steps to create your decision tree.

1.   Draw and label the three branches.
2.   Determine and write the logical test argument.
3.   Determine and write the [value_if_true] argument.
4.   Determine and write the [value_if_false] argument.
5.   Fill in the IF function syntax.
6.   Type your formula into Excel.

Constructing an IF Statement

Credit card companies charge vendors a fee to process each transaction. Aleeta would like to track credit card usage versus other types of transactions — cash and check. In the worksheet, she needs a column to indicate whether a customer used a credit card to pay for their items. If so, Aleeta wants Excel to display the word "Charge". Otherwise, she does not want anything to appear in the cell. You will also determine if the coupon the customer used was a match based on the Customer Category and the Coupon_Target.

In this exercise, you will create logical IF functions.

E05.01

To Create an IF Function

a.   Click the **DataInputs** worksheet. Click cell **I48**, and then press [F3].

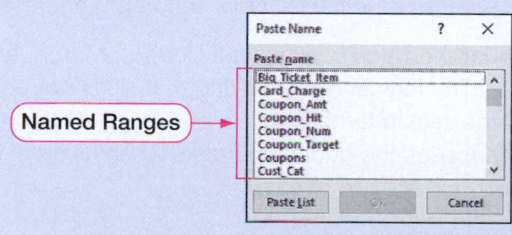

Figure 2   Paste Name dialog box

Excel 2016, Windows 10, Microsoft Corporation.

b. Click **Paste List** so the current ranges with the names are listed. Next you will determine whether or not a customer used a credit card for payment.

c. Click the **Transactions** worksheet, and then click cell **Q9**. Click the **Formulas** tab, and in the Function Library group, click **Logical** arrow, and then select **IF** to open the Function Arguments dialog box.

d. For the Logical_test, type **D9="Ccard"**, and then press Tab. Quotation marks are necessary for text included in functions.

e. For the Value_if_true, type **Charge**, and then press Tab.

   Notice how Excel added the quotation marks around the word Charge. When using the Function Arguments dialog box, Excel will add quotation marks around text or text strings.

f. For the Value_if_false, type **""**.

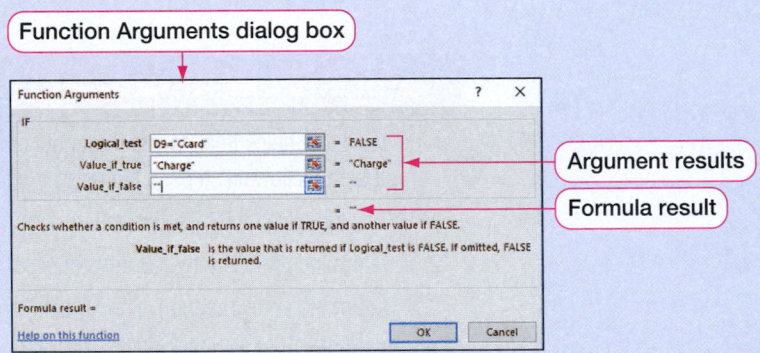

Figure 3 Function Arguments dialog box

g. Click **OK**.

   This checks whether the Pay_Type value in D9 is equal to "Ccard". If so, the word "Charge" will be returned. Otherwise, an empty set, indicated by double quotes with nothing between, will be returned.

h. With cell **Q9** selected, use AutoFill to copy the formula down to cell **Q208** to overwrite the static values. Rows where there are no records will be evaluated as FALSE and return an empty set.

   Next, you will determine if there is a coupon match or no match. The coupon is a match when the Cust_Cat (Customer Category) is the same as the Coupon_Target. When they are different, it is not a match.

i. Click cell **M9**. On the Formulas tab, in the Function Library group, select **Logical** arrow, and then click **IF** to open the Function Arguments dialog box.

j. For the logical test, type **H9<>L9**, and then press Tab.

k. For the value if true, type **No Match**, and then press Tab.

l. For the value if false, type **Coupon Match**, and then click **OK**.

   The logical test is stating that H9 is not equal to L9. Thus, when they are equal, the test returns a value of FALSE which is Coupon Match. Notice how Excel supplies the quotation marks when using the Function Arguments dialog box.

m. With cell **M9** selected, use AutoFill to copy the formula down to cell **M208** to overwrite the static values.

Although the formula is not giving an error message, the result is not correct in the rows where there are no records. This issue will be addressed later in this chapter.

n. **Save** 🖫 the workbook.

Using Different Elements in an IF Statement

As was previously mentioned, the [value_if_true] and [value_if_false] arguments are both optional and could be omitted from the function. In this case, the values TRUE and FALSE are returned when the function is evaluated. While this may be intuitive, it is not user friendly. You can use a variety of elements, including numerical values, text strings, cell references, named ranges, and other functions for the arguments in an IF function. Figure 4 provides an example.

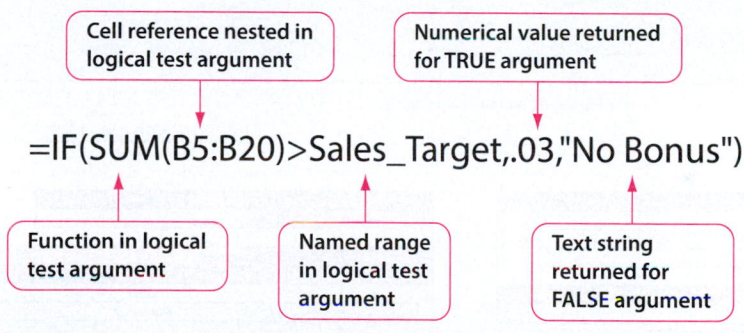

Figure 4   Function Argument example

In this example, .03 is a numerical value. "No Bonus" is a text string and should have quotes around the string. Straight quotation marks that are used in functions and formulas — shown as **double prime symbols**, not the curly double quotation marks you use when writing papers — let Excel know that the element is a text string and not a numeric value, cell reference, or named range. Sales_Target is a named range. This may look like a text string, but because it does not have straight double quotes, Excel will look for a range with that named range. If a Sales_Target named range does not exist, Excel will return the #NAME? error message, which occurs when Excel does not recognize text in a formula.

Finally, SUM(B5:B20) is a function that is part of the logical test. Excel will automatically recognize function names.

In this exercise, you will use different elements of an IF statement.

E05.02

To Use Different Elements in an IF Statement

a. Click the **RevenueReport** worksheet, and then click cell **E21**.

Aleeta Herriott wants to evaluate the number of items being sold. If the total number of items sold is more than 50, then the current goal is met. If that is true, she wants to have "Goal Met" displayed; otherwise, she wants "Under Goal" displayed.

b. Type **=IF(SUM(**, and then press F3 to open the Paste Name dialog box. Scroll down as needed, click to select **Trans_Qty**, and then click **OK**. Type **)>50, "Goal Met","Under Goal")**.

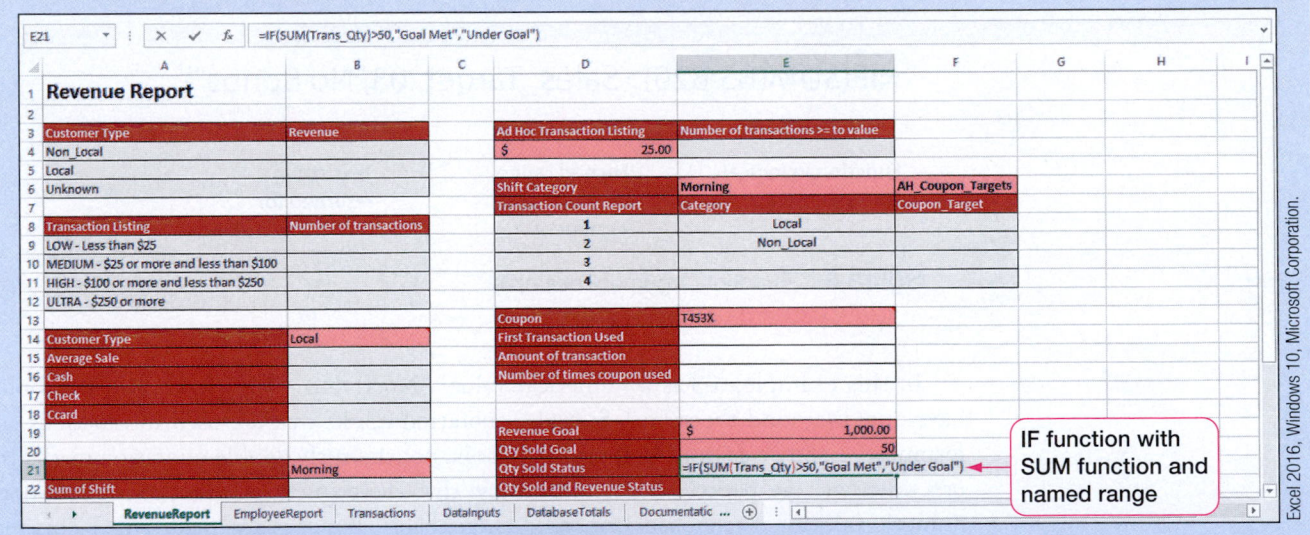

Figure 5 IF function

c. Press Ctrl + Enter.

This will evaluate whether the sum of the quantity sold is greater than 50. However, Excel uses a static value — 50 — in the logical test. If the goal changes, the function will no longer be valid.

d. With cell **E21** selected, press F2 to enter edit mode. Select **50** within the formula, and then type **E20** to replace 50 with the cell reference.

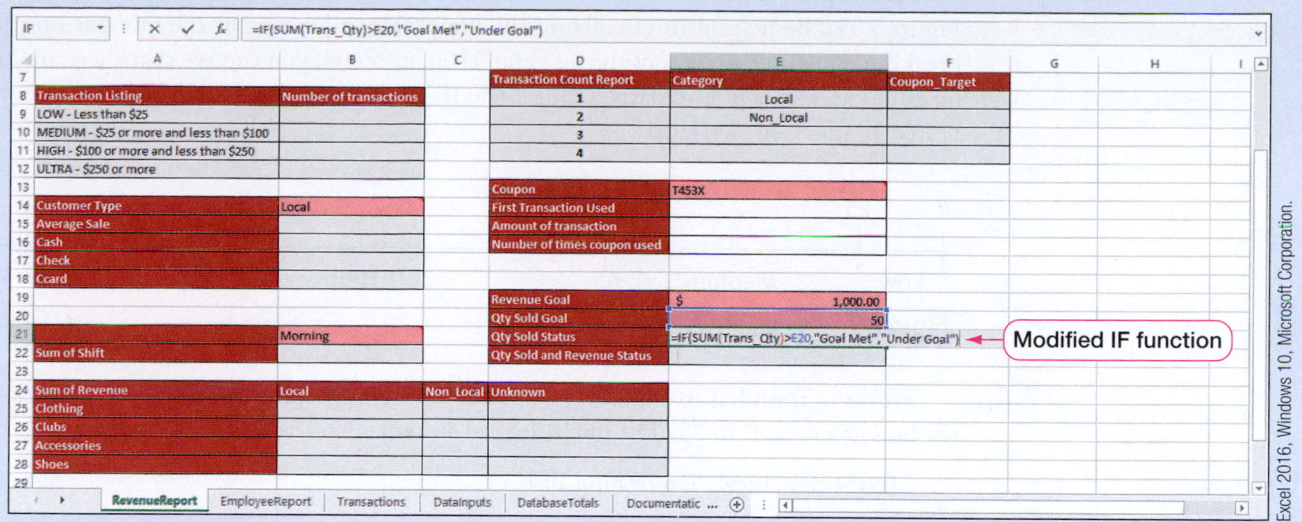

Figure 6 IF function

e. Press [Ctrl] + [Enter], and then **Save** 💾 the workbook.

Notice that as E20 was typed in the formula, Excel recognized it as a valid cell reference and changed the font within the formula to blue and then placed a blue border around E20. By using a cell reference rather than a numeric value, when the goal value in cell E20 changes, the Qty Sold Status formula will still calculate the correct result.

Build Nested IF Functions

The function =IF(SUM(Trans_Qty)>E20,"Goal Met","Under Goal") is a **complex function**, a function that combines multiple functions into one formula, because the logical test involves evaluating a function. A special type of complex function is a nested IF function. A single IF statement provides two outcomes for a single logical test. But what happens if you have more than two options or possible outcomes? A **nested IF function** uses IF functions as arguments within another IF function and increases the number of logical outcomes that can be expressed.

Building Nested IF Functions

The purchase price is included in the sales data, and Aleeta would like to categorize the transactions as Low, Medium, High, or Ultra depending on the purchase price amount. The business requirements for each category are provided in Table 4.

	Greater than or equal to	Less than
Low	$0	$25
Medium	$25	$100
High	$100	$250
Ultra	$250	

Table 4 Transaction ratings

Creating a number line of the business requirements similar to the one shown in Figure 7 can be helpful in visualizing the logic. When looking at the number line and breaking it up on the basis of the $25 and $100 amounts, you can see that there are four possible categories or alternatives. Since one IF function cannot handle four outcomes, a nested IF function is needed.

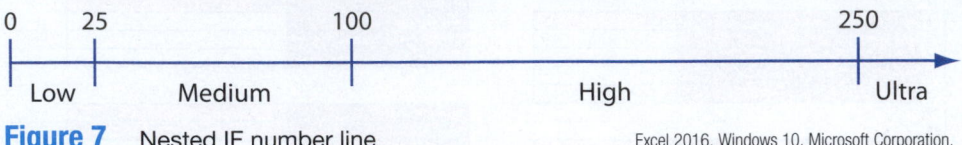

Figure 7   Nested IF number line   Excel 2016, Windows 10, Microsoft Corporation.

Working from left to right across a number line, an initial logical test will check for the far left range: 0 to 25. The initial logical statement starts with

=IF(P9<25,"Low","Everything Else")

Excel checks whether the value in cell P9 is less than $25 and will categorize the type of transaction. If the logical test is true, the value of "Low" will be returned as the outcome. If it is false, Excel will return "Everything Else", which for now replaces the Medium, High, and Ultra categories. This is similar to assuming that there are only two options — Low if the test is true; Everything Else if the test is false, as shown in Figure 8, Part 1. Parts 2 and 3 of Figure 8 will be discussed in a later section in this chapter.

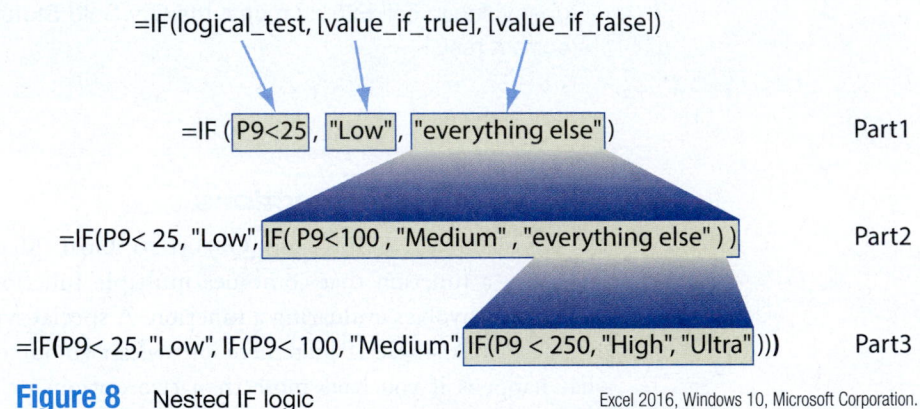

Figure 8   Nested IF logic   Excel 2016, Windows 10, Microsoft Corporation.

In this exercise, you will write a nested IF function to determine transaction groups based on total revenue.

 E05.03

To Begin Writing a Nested IF Formula

a. Click the **Transactions** worksheet. Click cell **R9**, type **=IF(P9<**, click on the **DataInputs** worksheet, and then click cell **K20**. Press the [F4] key, and then type a **,** (comma).

b. Click cell **I20**, press the [F4] key, and then type a **,** (comma). Type **"Everything Else")**, and then press [Ctrl] + [Enter].

    Notice that you are checking to see whether Line_Item_Total on the Transactions worksheet is less than $25, and then you are referencing cells on the DataInputs worksheet that are in the different transactions groups, outlined in Table 4.

c. With cell **R9** selected, click the **AutoFill**, drag down to copy the formula down to cell **R208** to overwrite the static values.

Notice that "Low" shows up for Purchase Prices less than $25 and "Everything Else" is displayed for all other values. Also, note that when there is no price in the column P cell references — no value — the IF statement is returning a result of Low. This will be explored in a later exercise in this chapter.

d. **Save** 🖫 the workbook.

REAL WORLD ADVICE	Working with IF Function Ranges

In the real world, it helps to work with real numbers, such as 25, 100, and 250, in developing the logic of the formula. However, it is hazardous to use the numbers in the formula when they may change. It is much better to build the worksheet for flexibility. It is easier to change a worksheet cell value than it is to search formulas to find the number you need to update. Whenever possible, use a cell reference in a formula instead of a number.

Adding Another Outcome

The initial function works well when there are two outcomes, such as "Low" and "Everything Else". However, when the value is greater than $25, you have established that it is not a low transaction, but you still do not know whether it is Medium, High, or Ultra. Therefore, you need a second logical statement for the [value_if_false] argument, replacing the "Everything Else" as depicted in Figure 8, Part 2. The values below $25 have been eliminated by the first IF function and do not need to be checked again. The second IF function should check for values below $100. If the outcome is true, you want Excel to display "Medium". If the outcome is false, you will not need to write a third IF function. Since there are three possible outcomes and the first two are false, the outcome cannot be anything other than High or Ultra — replaced by "Everything Else". Development of the function would continue as

=IF(P9<25,"Low",IF(P9<100,"Medium","Everything Else"))

QUICK REFERENCE	Easy Tricks for a Nested IF Function

There are two important items to note in writing nested IF functions.

- First, consider the number of outcomes. The number of IF functions needed is always one less than the number of outcomes. For example, if you had five possible outcomes of Very Cold, Cold, Warm, Hot, and Very Hot, you immediately know that you will need to nest four IF functions, three of which are nested inside the main IF function.

- Second, the number of parentheses needed to close your functions at the end of your formula is always the same number as the number of IF functions you used. In the previous example, in which you use four IF functions, you know immediately that you will need four closing parentheses at the end of your formula. Keep in mind that this would not include any parentheses that may be needed in the final [value_if_false] argument.

In this exercise, you will create a nested IF function.

 E05.04

To Nest an IF Function

SIDE NOTE
Alternate Method
Instead of typing
DataInputs! in a formula,
you can click on the
DataInputs tab and
then select the cell.

a. On the Transactions worksheet, click cell **R9**, and then press F2 to enter edit
   mode. Select **"Everything Else"**, including the quotes, and replace it by typing
   IF(P9<DataInputs!$K$21,DataInputs!$I$21,DataInputs!$I$22).

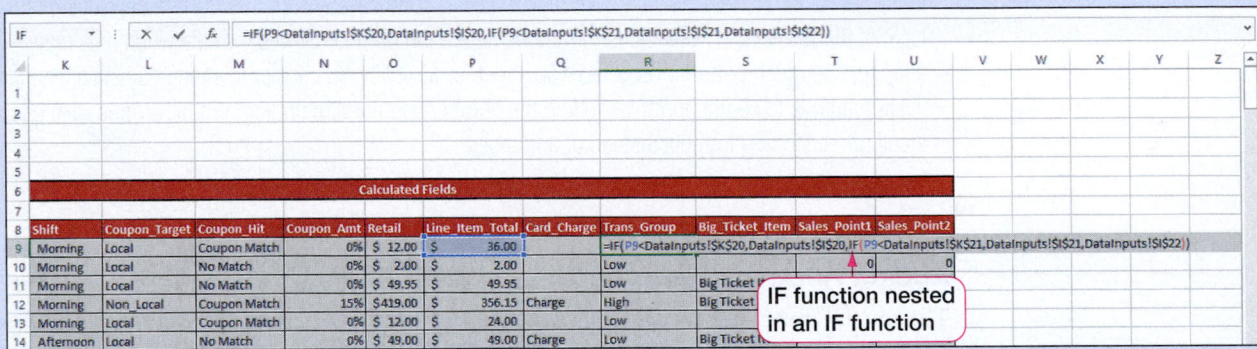

Figure 9   Nested IF function

Excel 2016, Windows 10, Microsoft Corporation.

b. Press Ctrl + Enter so R9 remains the active cell.

> ## Troubleshooting
>
> If you receive an error after typing your formula, ensure that you enclosed
> DataInputs inside apostrophes followed by an exclamation point. These are
> needed in referencing another worksheet.

c. Copy the formula down to cell **R208**, and then **Save** 🖫 the workbook.
   Notice that "Low" is displayed when the Line_Item_Total price is less than $25
   and "Medium" is displayed when the Line_Item_Total price is less than $100 but
   greater than or equal to $25. "High" is displayed for all other values unless the
   price column cell is empty.

If the Line_Item_Total price is not Low — not less than $25 — the second nested IF
function will check whether it is less than $100. If it is, then the text "Medium" will be
displayed. The possibility of the price being less than $25 was eliminated with the first
logical test. This is why best practice dictates working from left to right — from low to
high — on the number line. It allows you to take advantage of the process of elimination
without having to nest additional functions — such as AND — within the nested IF
function. The function checks for the far-left range first — $0 to $25 — and if the first
logical test evaluates to TRUE, then Excel knows it is in that range, knows the outcome,
and ends; the other nested IF functions will not be evaluated. However, if the first logical
test is FALSE, indicating that the price is $25 or greater, you need a second IF function

to determine whether the outcome is Medium (if the second test returns TRUE) or High (if the second test returns FALSE).

CONSIDER THIS | **Left or Right When Working with Nested IFs**

Consider the process of working with the ranges on a number line in a left-to-right fashion. Would it be possible to start on the right side and work to the left? Do you suppose it would be possible to start with any range and construct the logic of the options in any order?

Completing the Nested IF Function

What if you decided to add another category? Perhaps you would like to categorize any Line_Item_Total price that is greater than or equal to $250 as Ultra. This would require adding one more IF function in the [value_if_false] at the end of the second IF function, as shown in Figure 8, Part 3. The nested function would be expanded to be

=IF(P9<25,"Low",IF(P9<100,"Medium",IF(P9<250,"High","Ultra")))

In this exercise, you will nest a third IF function.

 E05.05

To Nest a Third IF Function

SIDE NOTE
Pairing Parentheses
Each function needs a pair of parentheses. Excel color codes each parenthesis to indicate which parentheses are paired.

a. On the Transactions worksheet, click cell **R9**, and then press F2 to enter edit mode. Select **DataInputs!$I$22**, replace it by typing **IF(P9<DataInputs!$K$22, DataInputs!$I$22,DataInputs!$I$23)**, and then press Ctrl + Enter so that R9 remains the active cell.

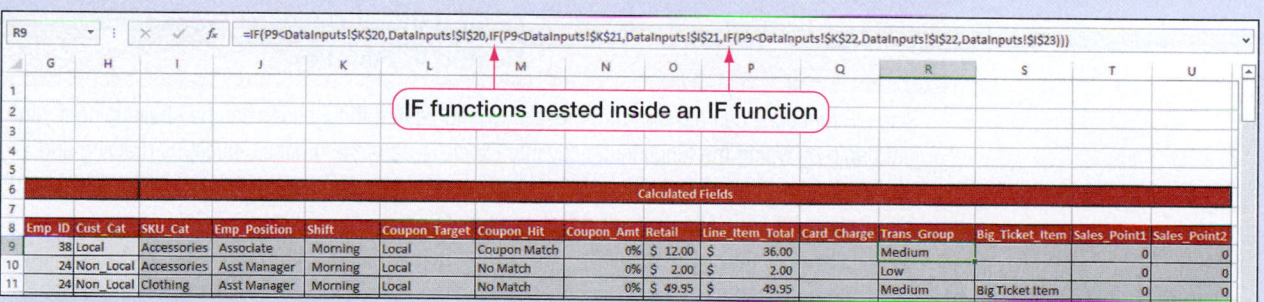

Figure 10   Nested IF function

Excel 2016, Windows 10, Microsoft Corporation.

b. With cell **R9** selected, copy the formula down to cell **R208**, and then **Save** 💾 the workbook.

Recall that "Low" is still displayed for empty price cells; this will be addressed in a later section of this chapter. Notice the cells that contain data have one of four outcomes returned appropriately for each Line_Item_Total price. There are three parentheses at the far right of the formula, one for each IF function. The options are exhaustive because any number that is provided for the Line_Item_Total price will fall into one of the four groups.

Nested IF functions can be challenging to write. One way to simplify the development process is to use a decision tree as shown in Figure 11. Begin by drawing and labeling the first three branches. You can then begin to construct the first IF function — also called the first level of the formula — using the first two possible outcomes by completing the logical test and [value_if_true] arguments. Because Excel stops evaluating an IF function once the [value_if_true] argument has been reached, the additional branches will always "grow" off of the [value_if_false] branch. If the result is not "Low", then it has to be either "Medium", "High", or "Ultra". Thus, the [value_if_false] branch becomes another logical test and another level in the formula — the second level. As you add possible outcomes, such as Ultra, you can continue adding branches to the [value_if_false] branches. Not only does this assist in keeping your thoughts organized, it also helps you understand the logic of what you are doing.

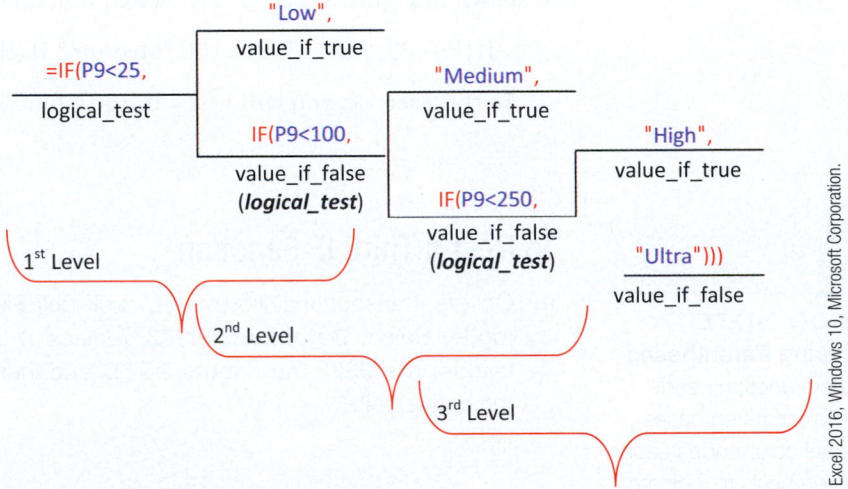

Figure 11   Nested IF decision tree

QUICK REFERENCE	Diagramming Decision Trees for a Nested IF Function

Since IF functions can have up to 64 levels, writing nested IF functions can be challenging if you just begin by typing the function directly into Excel. To ease the process, begin by drawing and labeling the first three branches, and then complete the following steps to create your decision tree.

1. Determine and write the logical test argument.
2. Determine and write the [value_if_true] argument.
3. Determine and write the [value_if_false] argument, which will serve as the next IF function.
4. Continue steps 1–3 until all levels have been written.
5. Fill in the IF function syntax.
6. Type the formula into Excel.

In addition to the decision tree, realizing that nested IF statements are a process of elimination can also help you write them. In this example, the function can return one of four outcomes — Low, Medium, High, or Ultra. Also, notice that you had to use only three IF statements. The very last outcome — Ultra — is returned only if the other three possibilities are eliminated by the three logical tests for Low, Medium, and High. Thus, you need one fewer IF statement than outcomes. Knowing this rule of thumb can help you figure out the syntax given that the number of IF statements needed will vary from problem to problem. Figure 12 shows the syntax for a nested IF statement and the location of the outcome determined by the process of elimination.

Last value_if_false determined by a process of elimination.

=IF(logical_test,value_if_true,IF(logical_test,value_if_true,IF(logical_test,value_if_true,value_if_false)))

=IF(P9<25,"Low",   )

        IF(P9<100,"Medium",   )

              IF(P9<250,"High","Ultra"   )

OR

=IF(P9<25,"Low",IF(P9<100,"Medium",IF(P9<250,"High","Ultra")))

Figure 12   Nested IF syntax   Excel 2016, Windows 10, Microsoft Corporation.

REAL WORLD ADVICE | **Working with IF Function Ranges**

You will want to consider whether your ranges go to the left or right of infinity or whether you have actual lower and upper bounds. If a value should never be negative, then it may be necessary to incorporate a starting point for the far left range. The same would apply for the right side. For some values, such as the credit limit, you may want to check that the value is not above $50,000. While data validation can be used to limit the values, if you actually have a lower or upper limit, you will need to consider whether to test for this in the IF statements.

Integrate Conjunction Functions into IF Functions

While nesting IF functions allows handling more than two outcomes, conjunction functions allow evaluation of multiple logical tests and enable linking or joining of functions or formulas. The conjunction functions within Excel are AND, OR, and NOT.

- The **AND function** returns TRUE if all logical tests supplied are true; otherwise, it returns FALSE.
- The **OR function** returns TRUE if any one logical test supplied true; otherwise, it returns FALSE.
- The **NOT function** is used when there are many options that fit the desired criteria and only one option that does not fit the criteria.

It is important to realize that the syntax for these functions is similar to that for any other function: The arguments are parenthetical following the function name. A user might think the syntax would be something like

    X AND Y

However, the correct syntax is

    AND(logical1,[logical2],…)
    OR(logical1,[logical2],…)
    NOT(logical1)

Using the AND Function

At least one logical test must be included, and additional logical test arguments are optional for the AND function. For example, students who want to be eligible for a university scholarship must have an ACT score of 30 or more AND a high school GPA of 3.5 or better. Using named ranges to evaluate whether or not a student achieved these goals, the AND function would be written as

AND(ACT>=30,GPA>=3.5)

Both conditions must be met to display TRUE.

Like the outcomes of the IF function, the outcomes of either TRUE or FALSE are not valuable to a manager. Generally, conjunction functions are nested within other functions, such as an IF function. An AND function could be used in an IF statement

IF(AND(ACT>=30,GPA>=3.5),"Eligible","Not Eligible")

In this case, the ACT>=30 is the first logical argument, and the GPA>=3.5 is the second logical argument.

The logic for evaluating an AND function with two logical tests — AND(Logical Test 'A',Logical Test 'B') — is shown in Table 5 in a logical truth table. When the AND function is nested in the logical test argument of an IF function, both logical tests need to be evaluated as TRUE for the [value_if_true] argument to be returned. If either test evaluates to FALSE, then the AND function will return a FALSE for the logical test. Of the four outcomes, only one would return a value of TRUE.

Logical Test 'A'	Logical Test 'B'	AND Function Result
TRUE	TRUE	TRUE
TRUE	FALSE	FALSE
FALSE	TRUE	FALSE
FALSE	FALSE	FALSE

Table 5   AND logical truth table

Aleeta wants to evaluate the status of employees. If an employee is an assistant manager and the Percent of Goal is greater than 25%, then Aleeta wants to have the status be "On Target". Otherwise, it should return a result of "Increase Sales". Because there are two conditions that lead to the results and both must be true, an AND function can be used within the logical test for the IF function.

In this exercise, you will use the AND function within an IF Function.

 **E05.06**

To Use the AND Function Within an IF Function

a. Click the **EmployeeReport** worksheet, and then click cell **B17**.

b. Enter the formula =IF(AND(B4="Asst Manager",B9>0.25),"On Target","Increase Sales"), press Enter, and then **Save** 🖫 the workbook to see a result of "Increase Sales" in cell B17.

Both logical tests in the AND function must be evaluated to TRUE for the AND to return a TRUE. When this happens, the [value_if_true] argument — On Target — is executed, or the [value_if_false] argument — Increase Sales — is executed.

Using the OR Function

The OR function works in the same way as an AND function except that the logical evaluation of the arguments is different. Where the AND function requires all arguments to be TRUE, the OR function requires only one of the arguments to be evaluated as TRUE. Thus, the OR function with two logical tests — OR(Logical Test 'A', Logical Test 'B') — as depicted in the logical truth table in Table 6 shows that three of the four combinations would return a result of TRUE.

Logical Test 'A'	Logical Test 'B'	OR Function Result
TRUE	TRUE	TRUE
TRUE	FALSE	TRUE
FALSE	TRUE	TRUE
FALSE	FALSE	FALSE

Table 6 OR logical truth table

Aleeta wants to determine if the local customers are using local coupons. Because there are two Non_Local coupons listed in the Coupons table on the DataInputs worksheet tab, the Coupon_Num value on the Transactions worksheet can be either coupon. Thus, an OR function can be used in conjunction with an IF statement to evaluate the data. Once the target for the coupon is known, it is possible to determine whether a nonlocal customer used a nonlocal coupon, which is the desired use. In this exercise, you will use the OR function within the IF function.

 E05.07

To Use the OR Function Within an IF Function

a. Click the **Transactions** worksheet, and then click cell **L9**.

b. Type **=IF(OR(F9=**, click the **DataInputs** worksheet, click cell **I5**, and then press `F4`. Type **,F9=**, click cell **I7**, and then press `F4`. Type **),"Non_Local","Local")**, and then press `Ctrl` + `Enter`.

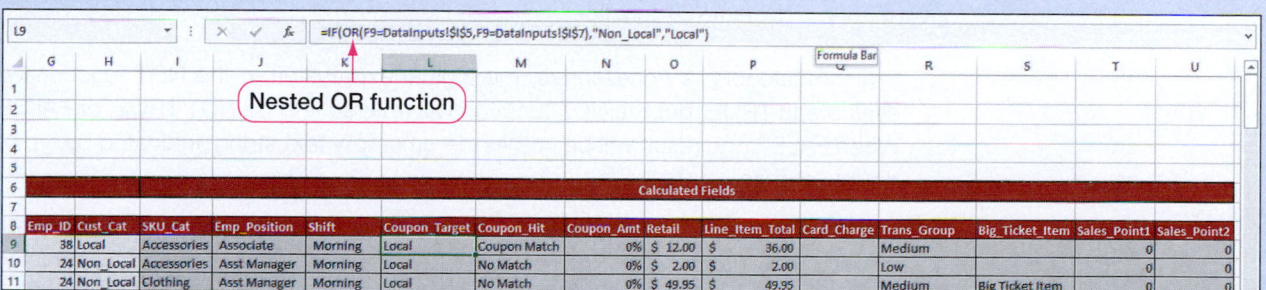

Figure 13 OR function nested in an IF function

Excel 2016, Windows 10, Microsoft Corporation.

If either one of the logical tests in the OR evaluates to TRUE, then the logical test for the IF function will be TRUE and "Non_Local" is displayed.

c. Copy the formula down to cell **L208** to overwrite the static values. **Save** 💾 the workbook.

Notice that this provides a "Local" result for rows where there is no data. This will be explored and changed in a later section of this chapter.

Using the NOT Function

The NOT function allows creation of logical statements in which it creates the opposite or reverse result of its argument. It evaluates to TRUE or FALSE. If the logical test is TRUE, then FALSE is returned. If the logical test is FALSE, then TRUE is returned. This is particularly useful when there are many values that would result in a TRUE and only one that would return a FALSE. For example, if you wanted to charge state tax to all states except Texas, you could use NOT(State="Texas"). In this example, if the value were Texas, that is TRUE, and the result of the NOT function would be FALSE. If the state was Ohio, then Ohio=Texas is FALSE, and NOT FALSE is TRUE. So all other states would return the same result.

Aleeta recognizes that the accessories items do not cost a lot or take up much space. All of the other categories of products found in the SKU_Cat column are big-ticket items, which have a larger profit margin. Because the shop makes a larger profit from selling the big-ticket items, Aleeta may want some analyses on just those items. She would like a column that distinguishes the big-ticket items, regardless of the category. You can accomplish this task in one logical test, using the NOT function. In this exercise, you will use the NOT function within an IF function.

 **E05.08**

To Use the NOT Function Within an IF Function

a. On the Transactions worksheet, click cell **S9**, enter the formula =IF(NOT(I9="Accessories"),"Big Ticket Item",""), and then press Ctrl + Enter.

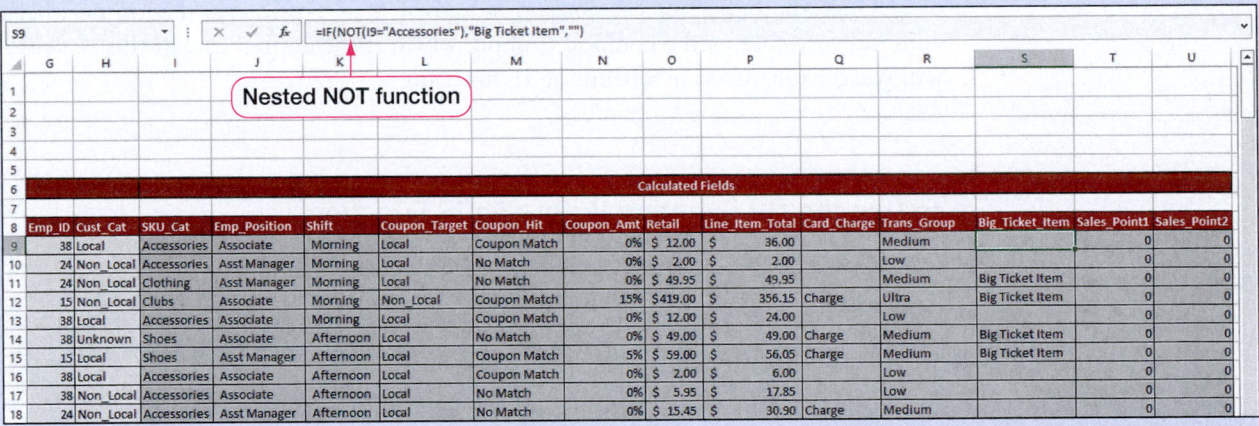

Figure 14   Nested NOT function

Excel 2016, Windows 10, Microsoft Corporation.

> If the category is Accessories, the logical expression in the NOT function will evaluate to TRUE, but the NOT function will reverse it to be NOT TRUE, or FALSE. When FALSE, the result will be nothing — an empty text string, indicated by typing double quotes.

b. With cell **S9** selected, copy the formula down to cell **S208** to overwrite the static values.

c. **Save** 🖫 the workbook.
> Notice that this provides a "Big Ticket Item" result for rows where there is no data. The formula should check whether there is a transaction. This will be evaluated and changed later in this chapter.

Combining an OR Function in an AND Function

There are more complex situations in which it is necessary to combine the OR with the AND function. This can be challenging because you need to determine whether to put the AND inside the OR or vice versa. A lot depends on the situation, and just as in math, you need to be careful with grouping.

Aleeta wants to give motivational points to the sales team for certain transactions. Sales_Point1 will look for Trans_Group results of High or Ultra transactions that occur in the morning or afternoon shift and will award one point. Otherwise, it will return zero points. The logic for this is illustrated in Figure 15. The formula requires both an OR function and an AND function within the IF statement. The initial step is to think through the situation and organize the conditions, using pseudocode. **Pseudocode** is the rough draft of a formula or code. It is intended to help you understand the logic and determine the structure of a problem before you develop the actual formula. Pseudocodes are used to structure a function but with wording that is written for understanding the function's structure logically. Here, there are four conditions to evaluate. The first two are Shift is Morning or Shift is Afternoon. They cannot be joined with an AND, since they are exclusive, that is, only one can be true. So you need to use an OR function. The same applies to the Trans_Group because a transaction cannot be both High and Ultra. The requirement mentions that High transactions have to occur in one of the two shifts, so an AND function needs to be used to combine the High transaction with either of the shifts. Thus, the AND is the outer function with two OR functions inside.

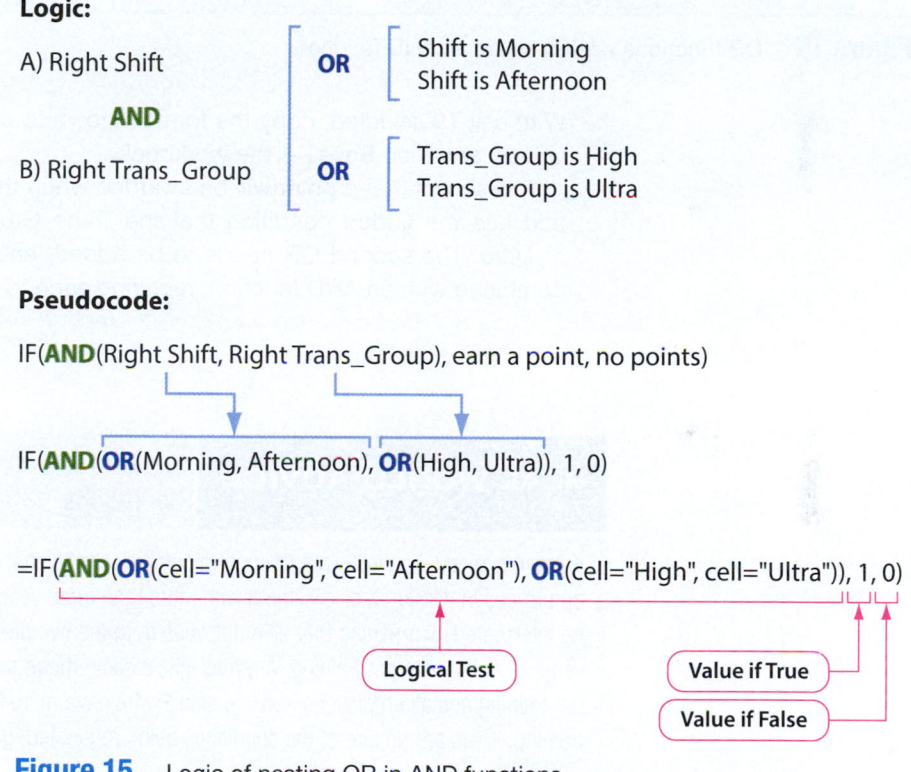

Figure 15 Logic of nesting OR in AND functions
Excel 2016, Windows 10, Microsoft Corporation.

In this exercise, you will use the OR function nested within an AND function.

 E05.09   **To Use the OR Function Nested Within an AND Function**

a. On the Transactions worksheet, click cell **T9**, enter the formula
=IF(AND(OR(K9="Morning",K9="Afternoon"),OR(R9="High",R9="Ultra")),1,0),
and then press Ctrl + Enter.

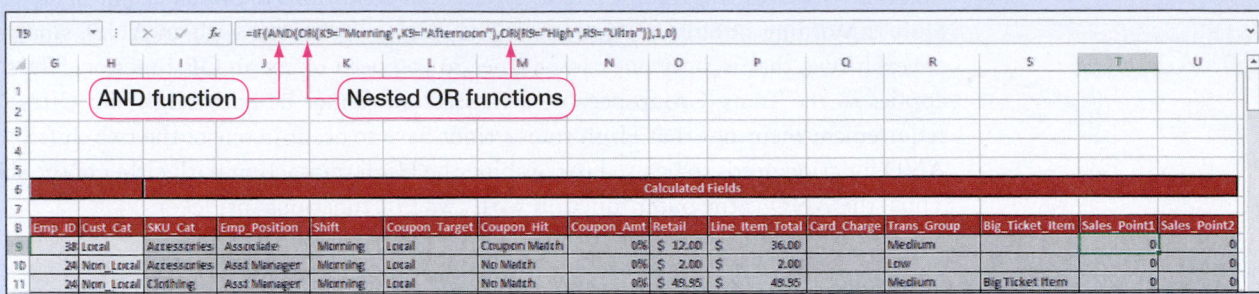

Figure 16   OR functions nested inside an AND function

Excel 2016, Windows 10, Microsoft Corporation.

b. With cell **T9** selected, copy the formula down to cell **T208** to overwrite the static values, and then **Save** 🖫 the workbook.

This shows that a point will be awarded when the shift is Morning or Afternoon and has the added condition that the Trans_Group results display either High or Ultra. The second OR needs to be added, and the two OR functions will be combined with an AND function, requiring each to return a TRUE result.

REAL WORLD ADVICE   **Working with Complex AND and OR Conditions**

In the real world, you will want to confirm complex conditions. For example, the statement "All employees in division X or division Y with more than three years of experience receive training" can be interpreted as meaning that all employees from the two divisions who have more than three years of experience get training. Alternatively, it could mean that all employees from division X get training and all employees from division Y who have more than three years of experience get training. If you are unsure of the conditions being requested, get clarification before proceeding.

Combining an AND Function in an OR Function

For the second set of motivational points, Aleeta wants to give points to encourage the sales team to increase the purchasing of both the local and nonlocal (out-of-town) customers. She believes that nonlocal customers tend to purchase more than local customers do, so the transaction amount for nonlocal customers is set higher than that for the local customers. Ultimately, she would like to see the average transactions increase for all customers. She may change the transaction amounts that determine the points, so these have been included in the workbook. For a point to be earned, the transaction needs to be either a local customer who spent more than $50 or a nonlocal customer who spent more than $100. The structure of this logical statement is shown in Figure 17 with pseudocode. It shows there are two ways to earn the points, and either will work; therefore,

The OR function is the outer function. The two ways of earning points both require an AND function. The AND functions combine the Line_Item_Total condition with the Cust_Cat condition, requiring both to be evaluated as TRUE.

an OR function is the outer function. The two ways of earning points both require an AND function. The AND functions combine the Line_Item_Total condition with the Cust_Cat condition, requiring both to be evaluated as TRUE.

Logic:

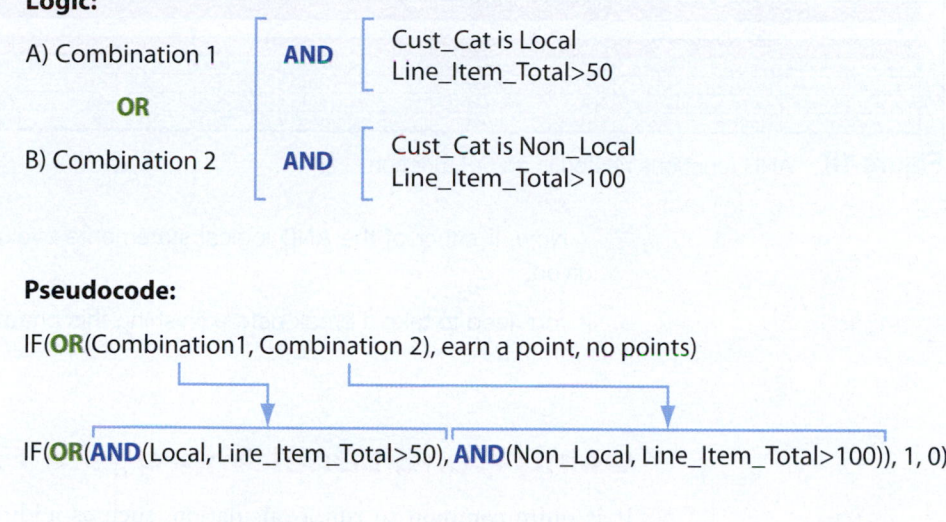

Pseudocode:

IF(**OR**(Combination1, Combination 2), earn a point, no points)

IF(**OR**(**AND**(Local, Line_Item_Total>50), **AND**(Non_Local, Line_Item_Total>100)), 1, 0)

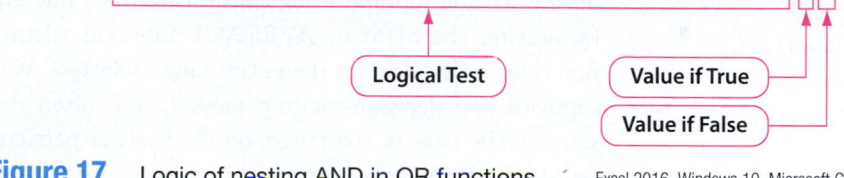

=IF(**OR**(**AND**(cell="Local",cell>50), **AND**(cell="Non_Local", cell>100)),1,0)

Logical Test   Value if True   Value if False

Figure 17   Logic of nesting AND in OR functions   <small>Excel 2016, Windows 10, Microsoft Corporation.</small>

In this exercise, you will use the AND function nested within an OR function.

 **E05.10**

To Use the AND Function Nested Within an OR Function

SIDE NOTE
Referencing Cells
Values on the DataInputs worksheet allow managers to change or adapt their criteria without having to change values in formulas.

a. On the Transactions worksheet, click cell **U9**. Type **=IF(AND(H9=**, click the **DataInputs** worksheet tab, click **I14**, and then press F4. Type **,P9>**, click **J14**, press F4, type **),1,0)**, and then press Ctrl + Enter.

b. Copy the formula down to cell **U208** to overwrite the static values.

This will show that transactions from local customers spending more than $50 will get 1 point, but no other customers will get a point. The second inside logical AND condition to test for nonlocal customers spending more than $100 needs to be added with the OR as the outside joining function.

c. Click cell **U9**, press F2, and then position the cursor to the right of the IF(. Type **OR(AND(H9=DataInputs!$I$13,P9>DataInputs!$J$13),**. Place the cursor to the right of $J$14), and then type **)**, so there is a closing parenthesis for the OR function that was just added. Press Ctrl + Enter.

d. Copy the formula down to cell **U208**.

e. **Save** the workbook.

Integrating Logical Functions 289

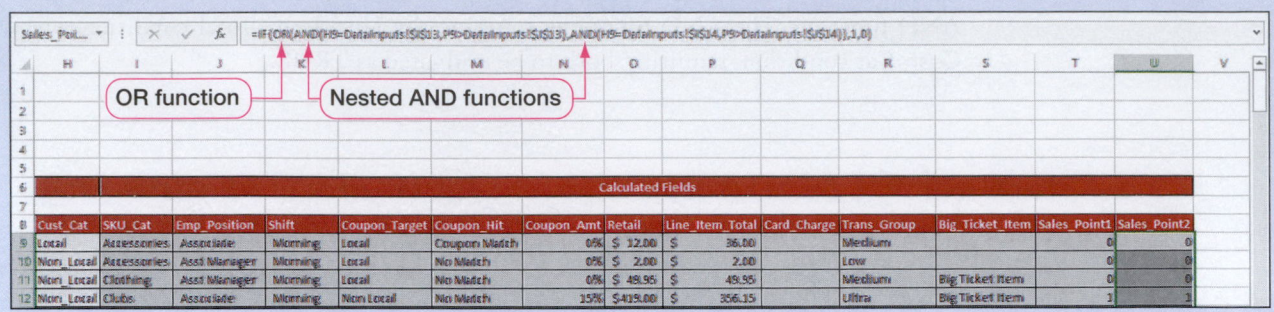

Figure 18 AND functions nested in an OR function

Excel 2016, Windows 10, Microsoft Corporation.

Now, if either of the AND logical statements evaluate to TRUE, a point will be given.

e. If you need to take a break before finishing this chapter, now is a good time.

Using Conditional Aggregate Functions

It is quite common to run a calculation, such as adding or averaging sales, and then evaluate whether the average or total met a specific goal or benchmark. This incorporates both a calculation and a logical decision into one equation. This is possible to handle by nesting the SUM or AVERAGE function within the IF function. However, these functions will calculate the entire range selected. With a workbook that includes more sophisticated decision-making models, it is often desirable to perform calculations on some of the data in the range, on the basis of particular criteria. For example, in a data set of sales transactions, it may be useful to sum all of the credit card sales, ignoring the cash or check sales.

The addition of conditional aggregate functions in Excel makes this task manageable. **Conditional aggregate functions** are functions that consolidate or summarize a subset of data that has been filtered based upon one or more criteria. This is different from the traditional functions that calculate by using all cells that are in a specified range. If SUM(A1:C10) is used, it adds all the values in all the cells in that range. With an aggregate function, a range would still be provided, but the aggregation would use only cells that meet one or more criteria. The criteria can be on the data that is being aggregated or on associated data.

The criteria for determining which subset of data is chosen can be constructed in a variety of ways, as defined in Table 7. Quotes are needed with the logical operators. The ampersand is used for combining the logical operator with another component. Elements such as named ranges and cell references cannot go inside quotes because Excel would interpret them as text strings rather than named ranges or cell references. For example, "> B4" would check for values greater than the string >B4 instead of a value that is in cell B4. This applies to all the functions discussed here.

In this section, conditional functions and database functions will be developed by using this foundation. The functions will provide analysis of a data set for the purpose of gaining knowledge from the information.

Criterion	Action
B4	Selects if the value equals the value in B4
">10"	Selects if the value is **greater than** 10
">="&Goal	Selects if the value is **greater than or equal to** the value in the named range 'Goal'
"><"&B5	Selects if the value is **not equal to** the value in B5

Table 7 Criteria options

Use Conditional Statistical Functions

Excel recognizes the need for having statistical functions that can calculate a subset of data that meets the specified criteria. There is a set of common functions that have been merged with the logical functions, including the COUNT and AVERAGE functions. They have been set to handle both a single criterion and multiple criteria for filtering.

Using the COUNTIF Function

The **COUNTIF function** counts the number of cells that meet a specified criteria. This differs from the SUMIF and SUMIFS functions, which sum the data in the cells that meet the given criteria. For example, a COUNTIF function that uses a range with 12 cells would return a value between 1 and 12 because the cells are counted. If the same range was used with a SUMIF function, the result is the sum of the values within the cells, not the number of cells. The COUNTIF function has two arguments: range and criteria. The syntax for the COUNTIF function is

=COUNTIF(range, criteria)

The range is the cells that will be counted, and the criteria is the logical statement that will determine which cells to count within the formula cell range. For example, if there was a range of data in which the cells contained the data "Handicapped Golfer" or "Scratch Golfer" and the criterion was "Scratch Golfer", the function would count every occurrence in the cell range where the cell data content (criterion) equals "Scratch Golfer".

Aleeta wants to count the transactions based on the transaction amount. You can accomplish this using the Trans_Group data range that has been classified as Low, Medium, High, and Ultra. Counting each of those will give the number by each classification. Additionally, Aleeta would like to count the number of times a specific coupon is used and the number of transactions greater than or equal to a specific value.

In this exercise, you will create a COUNTIF function.

 E05.11

SIDE NOTE
Without Formatting
It is recommended that you copy the formula down without formatting so that you do not need to fix your border styles.

To Create a COUNTIF Function

a. If you took a break, open the **e03ch05GolfSales_LastFirst** workbook, and click the **RevenueReport** worksheet.

b. Click cell **B9**. Click the **Formulas** tab, and in the Function Library group, click the **More Functions** arrow, and then select **Statistical**. Scroll if necessary, and select **COUNTIF**.

c. For the Range, type Trans_Group, and then press Tab.

d. For the Criteria, press the **Collapse** button, select the **DataInputs** worksheet, and then click cell **I20**. Press the **Expand** button, and then click **OK**.

e. With cell B9 selected, copy the formula down, without formatting, to cell **B12**.

Notice the 190 value seems unusually high in comparison to the remaining values. This is because the formula returns a value of "Low" in any remaining cells on the Transactions worksheet where reference cells in the formula are blank. This is an example of why a formula needs to account for all possibilities when validating the information. This will be addressed later in the chapter.

f. Click cell **E16**, enter the formula **=COUNTIF(Coupon_Num,E13)**, and then press Enter.

    This will count the number of times the coupon listed in E13 was used in the Coupon_Num range found on the Transactions worksheet. The coupon T453X was used 2 times.

g. Click cell **E4**, enter the formula **=COUNTIF(Line_Item_Total,">="&D4)**, and then press Enter.

h. Save 💾 the workbook.

    This is different because the criteria uses the value in D4 instead of looking for the string "D4". The number of line item transactions greater than or equal to $25 is ten.

REAL WORLD ADVICE | **Testing Your Functions**

In the real world, you will check for errors as you develop a workbook, looking for numbers that do not make sense or seem out of line. Try testing data to ensure that formulas work the way you expect them to. It may be that an issue is caused by cells being referenced in a formula rather than by the formula itself. Develop techniques, such as using formula auditing and testing a range of data, to ensure that calculations are correct.

Using the COUNTIFS Function

The **COUNTIFS function** allows for multiple criteria in multiple ranges to be evaluated and counted. The syntax for the COUNTIFS function is

    =COUNTIFS(criteria_range1, criteria1, [criteria_range2, criteria2],...)

There is no distinction between a criteria_range argument found in COUNTIFS and a range argument used in COUNTIF. When counting, it simply counts the cells that meet the criteria; thus, the range of cells to count and the criteria_range are the same range. However, in using multiple criteria, all criteria ranges must have exactly the same shape — the same number of rows and same number of columns. Then the cells within the multiple ranges are compared and all criteria have to evaluate to TRUE to be counted.

In Figure 19, the first set of cells will be TRUE if the value is 392. Cells A1 and B3 would be TRUE. In the second range, the cells will be evaluated as TRUE if they have a value of 28. Cells F1, F2, and G3 meet that second criteria. However, cells in the same relative position within the two ranges must both be TRUE to be counted. Thus, the pairs A1 and F1 and B3 and G3 are both TRUE, so the COUNTIF would return a value of 2 for this COUNTIFS example. The criterion is met for the cell in F2 — the first column, second row, for the second range — but is not met for cell A2 in row 2, column 1, for the first criteria range, so that set is not counted. Thus, the number of cells in one range determines the maximum count that can be obtained.

COUNTIFS(A1:B3,"=392", F1:G3,"=28")

	A	B
1	**392**	439
2	439	375
3	827	**392**

	F	G
1	**28**	83
2	28	37
3	48	**28**

Figure 19 COUNTIFS calculation
Excel 2016, Windows 10, Microsoft Corporation.

Aleeta wants to count the number of transactions, grouped by coupon target and shift. The table on the Transactions worksheet has been set up to show the coupon targets and the current shift desired. The shift may change, so it needs to be referenced. Two criteria must match for a count to occur. The two ranges that will be checked will be the Shift and the Coupon_Target, and since both are the same shape, the first cell in both ranges will be evaluated. If both are true for their criteria, that pair will be counted, continuing for the remaining cells in the two ranges.

In this exercise, you will create a COUNTIFS function.

 **E05.12**

To Create a COUNTIFS Function

a. On the RevenueReport worksheet, click cell **F8**. Click the **Formulas** tab, and in the Function Library group, click the **More Functions** arrow, and then select **Statistical**. Scroll if necessary, and select **COUNTIFS** to open the Function Arguments dialog box.

b. For Criteria_range1, type **Shift**, and then press ⎆Tab.

c. For Critera1, type **$E$6**, and then press ⎆Tab.

d. For Criteria_range2, type **Coupon_Target**, and then press ⎆Tab.

e. For Criteria2, type **E8**. This formula checks for the Shift category of "Morning" and for "Local" coupon targets. When both occur, the set is counted. There are four coupon targets that meet the criteria of morning and local.

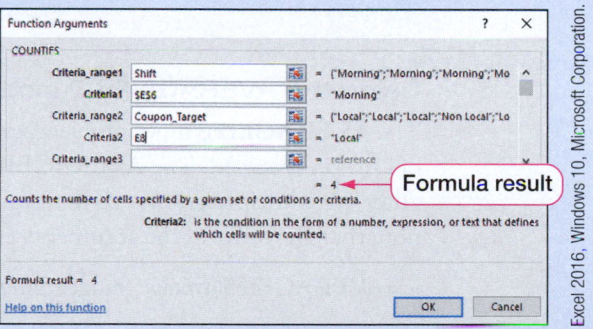

Figure 20 COUNTIFS Function Arguments dialog box

f. Click **OK**. With cell **F8** selected, copy the formula to cell **F11**, and then **Save** 🖫 the workbook.

Troubleshooting

If your borders change once you copy the formula down, you click the Auto Fill Options button and then select Fill Without Formatting.

Using the AVERAGEIF Function

The **AVERAGEIF function** averages the cells that meet the specified criteria. This differs from the AVERAGE function, which averages the data in the selected cells. The AVERAGEIF function has three arguments, two required and one optional. The syntax for the AVERAGEIF function is

=AVERAGEIF(range, criteria, [average_range])

If the [average_range] argument is omitted, Excel assumes that the same range specified in the range argument will be used for filtering the data and for averaging. For example, if Aleeta wanted to find the average for only the scratch golfers, she would average the handicaps for people who have a handicap less than or equal to 0. This would filter the data on the basis of the handicap and would average the same range.

With the AVERAGEIF function, the third argument is required only if one range of data is being averaged on the basis of criteria of a second range.

For the Revenue Report, the average sales will be calculated for local customers. Additionally, an average will be calculated for the type of transaction used for the local customers. Thus, the Excel function will retrieve the local customers who used cash, and then average the line item total for those records. The same thing will be done for the checks and credit card transactions for the local customers.

In this exercise, you will create an AVERAGEIF function.

 **E05.13**

To Create an AVERAGEIF Function

a. On the RevenueReport worksheet, click cell **B15**. Click the **Formulas** tab, and in the Function Library group, click the **More Functions** arrow, and then select **Statistical**. Select **AVERAGEIF**.

b. For the Range, type Cust_Cat, and then press Tab.

c. For the Criteria type B14, and then press Tab.

d. For the Average_range, type Line_Item_Total, and then click **OK**. The average sales for local customers is 27.95.

e. **Save** 🖫 the workbook.

Using the AVERAGEIFS Function

The **AVERAGEIFS** function averages a range of data, selecting data to average on the basis of criteria specified. The AVERAGEIFS function expands on the AVERAGEIF function, allowing multiple criteria to determine the subset of data. However, it is important to note that the order of the arguments changes. The syntax for the AVERAGIFS function is

=AVERAGEIFS(average_range, criteria_range1, criteria1, [criteria_range2, criteria2], …)

The average range is moved to become the first argument on the assumption that different ranges would be used for determining the filtered subset of data. After the average range, there are pairs of criteria ranges and criteria. In this fashion, multiple criteria can be used to filter the data to be averaged. Similar to the COUNTIFS function, the two ranges must be the same shape, having the same number of rows and columns. With the AVERAGEIFS function, all ranges must be the same size, although they do not have to be adjacent or even on the same worksheet, as shown in Figure 21.

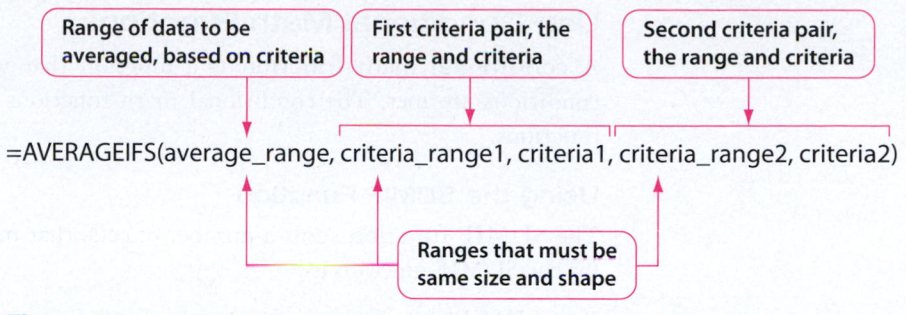

Figure 21 AVERAGEIFS calculation   Excel 2016, Windows 10, Microsoft Corporation.

Aleeta wants to find the average Line_Item_Total based on the Cust_Cat and the Pay_Type. She would like flexibility, so cells will need to be referenced in the formula. In this exercise, you will create an AVERAGEIFS function.

 **E05.14**

To Create an AVERAGEIFS Function

a. On the RevenueReport worksheet, click cell **B16**. Click the **Formulas** tab, and in the Function Library group, click the **More Functions** arrow, and then select **Statistical**. Select **AVERAGEIFS**.

b. For the Average_range, type Line_Item_Total, and then press Tab.

c. For Criteria_range1, type Cust_Cat, and then press Tab.

d. For Critera1, type $B$14, and then press Tab.

e. For Criteria_range2, type Pay_Type, and then press Tab.

f. For Criteria2, type A16.

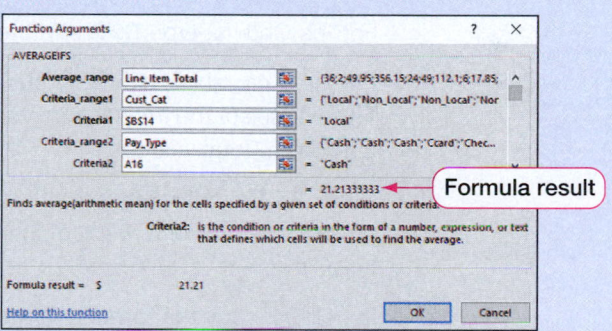

Figure 22 AVERAGEIFS Function Arguments dialog box

Excel 2016, Windows 10, Microsoft Corporation.

g. Click **OK**.

This formula checks for the pay type of Cash and for Local coupon targets. When both occur, the set is counted. Now the Customer Type can be changed in B14, and the Average will automatically be adjusted.

h. Click cell **B16**, and then copy the formula to cell **B18**.

i. Click cell **B14**, and then type Non_Local to test your formulas. Notice that your numbers will be updated because you changed the criteria that the AVERAGEIFS function is referencing.

j. Press Ctrl + Z to change the value in B14 back to "Local".

k. **Save** 🖫 the workbook.

Use Conditional Math Functions

A **conditional math function** is a function that will calculate only when specified conditions are met. The conditional math functions include the SUMIF and SUMIFS functions.

Using the SUMIF Function

The **SUMIF function** sums a number of cells that meet a specified criteria. The syntax for the SUMIF function is

=SUMIF(range, criteria, [sum_range])

For the SUMIF function, because only one criteria is allowed, the first argument is the range associated with the criteria. The second argument is the criteria itself, which will determine which values are summed. The third argument, [sum_range], is optional because you can set the criteria on the actual sum range. If the [sum_range] argument is omitted, the default is to assume that the range and the sum_range are the same. However, a great feature with this function is that the criteria can be set on one range, such as the payment type, while the function sums a second range, such as the payment amount.

In this exercise, you will create a SUMIF function.

To Create a SUMIF Function

a. On the RevenueReport worksheet, click cell **B22**. If necessary, click the **Formulas** tab, and in the Function Library group, click the **Math & Trig** arrow, and then scroll to select **SUMIF**.

b. For the Range, type Shift, and then press Tab.

c. For the Criteria, type B21, and then press Tab.

d. For the Sum_range, type Line_Item_Total, and then click **OK** for a result of $468.10. This will select the transactions that occurred during the morning shift and sum the Line_Item_Total values.

e. Click cell **B4**, enter the formula =SUMIF(Cust_Cat,A4,Line_Item_Total), and then press Ctrl + Enter for a result of $744.11. This will total the revenue for the customer type.

f. In cell B4, copy the formula through cell B6, and then **Save** the workbook.
   Now each subset of the line item totals has been summed and then grouped by the customer type.

Using the SUMIFS Function

The **SUMIFS function** sums a range of data, selecting data to total based on the criteria specified. With the SUMIFS function, it is assumed that multiple criteria would be set, thus having a sum_range different from at least one criteria_range. Thus, the order is changed to have the sum_range first, then add a criteria_range and criteria for each constraint or filter. For example, you could indicate the sales range to sum and have a criterion of summing only transactions that were made online and were set up as gifts. The syntax for the SUMIFS function is

=SUMIFS(sum_range, criteria_range1, criteria1, [criteria_range2, criteria2],...)

The structure for the arguments is the same as that in the AVERAGEIFS function. The criteria ranges have to match the sum_range in shape. If there are multiple criteria, the cells are evaluated for each criterion with a result of TRUE to be used in the subset of data, as shown in Figure 23.

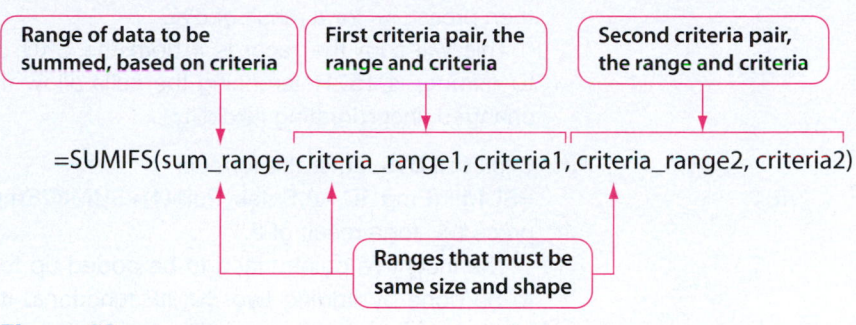

Figure 23   SUMIFS calculation   Excel 2016, Windows 10, Microsoft Corporation.

The report has been set up to sum the Line_Item_Total range filtered by the SKU_Cat and the Cust_Cat. Thus, the report will show a grid indicating revenue from Local or Non_Local, grouped by the Product Categories of Clothing, Clubs, Accessories, and Shoes.

In this exercise, you will create a SUMIFS function.

 **E05.16**

To Create a SUMIFS Function

a. On the RevenueReport worksheet, and click cell **B25**. If necessary, click the **Formulas** tab, and in the Function Library group, click the **Math & Trig** arrow, and then scroll to select **SUMIFS**.

b. For the Sum_range, type Line_Item_Total, and then press Tab .

c. For the Criteria_range1, type SKU_Cat, and then press Tab .

d. For the Criteria1, type $A25, and then press Tab .

e. For the Criteria_range2, type Cust_Cat, and then press Tab .

f. For the Criteria2, type B$24, and then press **OK** for a result of $0. The mixed cell referencing is used so the formula can be copied to the other cells within the grid.

g. In cell B25, copy the formula to cell **B28**.

h. With the range B25:B28 selected, copy the formula to cell range **B25:D28**. Press Ctrl + Home .

i. Click the **EmployeeReport** worksheet, and then click cell **B6**.
   The Employee Sales Report also needs some conditional sums. The Total Sales Revenue for the sales staff needs to be calculated. The current Sales Staff is an Assistant Manager named Hample who has a Staff ID Number of 15, which will be used as the conditional filter.

j. Enter the formula =SUMIF(Emp_ID,A6,Line_Item_Total), and then press Enter for a result of $483.91.

k. Click cell **B13**.

The staff has a goal for each product category. Currently, Clothing is listed in B11, and the associated goal for Hample is also provided. The percentage of that goal is Hample's sales for clothing divided by the goal.

l. Enter the formula **=SUMIFS(Line_Item_Total,SKU_Cat,B11,Emp_ID,A6)/B12**, and then press Enter for a result of 6%.

This will sum the records if both the SKU category is clothing and the staff ID number is 15. Referencing the cells allow the category and sales staff to be changed, incorporating flexibility.

m. Click cell **B15**, enter the formula **=SUMIF(Emp_ID,A6,Sales_Point1)+SUMIF(Emp_ID,A6,Sales_Point2)**, and then press Enter for a result of 2.

The incentive points need to be added up for the staff person listed. This has to be done by adding two SUMIF functions. It cannot be done in one SUMIFS function, as that sums on multiple criteria, and the only criterion in this case is the Emp_ID. The sales point columns cannot be combined into one sum range because the Sales_Point1 and Sales_Point2 data would not match up in the same cells for the same range shape; therefore, they need to be tallied separately and then combined.

n. **Save** the workbook.

SS **CONSIDER THIS** | **Using the SUMIF Function Versus the SUMIFS Function**

The SUMIF and SUMIFS functions are very similar in what they accomplish. Could you simply use the SUMIFS function all the time and become comfortable with its format? Could any situation that would use SUMIF be written by using SUMIFS?

Construct Database Functions

Excel's worksheet structure of rows and columns allows the use of certain kinds of simple databases, and database functions are specifically designed to work with this type of data. An **Excel database** is a way of storing data that is made up of records (rows) and fields (columns). Different types of data can be organized in this manner, including common information such as a contact list or a catalog of your smartphone applications. In a database, each record is one unit of data, such as an application in your collection, and each field is a specific piece of information, such as the application's name. An important aspect of databases is that each record contains the same fields. Thus, each application record will contain a title field, a rating field, a price field, a developer field, and so on. Furthermore, Excel databases must include field names that are always listed in the first row.

Database functions execute common calculations such as sum, average, and count and are designed specifically for use with an Excel database. The power of database functions lies in the fact that they permit you to identify which records to include in the calculation. Consider the smartphone application database example. The database functions let you calculate things such as the following.

- The total number of applications in your collection that were created by Rovio
- The highest-rated application in your collection
- The most expensive application in your collection

All database functions are named by using the format DXXX(), where XXX is the name of the corresponding non-database Excel function. For example, in the DSUM function, the D indicates that the function is a database function, and SUM is the name of the corresponding non-database Excel function. Additionally, all database functions include the same three arguments. Using the DMAX() function as an example, the syntax is

=DMAX(database, field, criteria)

For the DMAX function, because the function is using data included in an Excel database, the database argument specifies the range containing the database, including the field names in the first row. The second argument — field — is the name of the database field that the calculation will use. The third argument — criteria — is the range containing the criteria that tells the function which records to use in the calculation and is a two-cell range that is one column wide and two rows high. The upper cell contains the field name to which the criterion applies; the lower cell contains the value that you want to match. For example, you could use the DMAX function to find the Line_Item_Total that contains the highest price within the filter criteria listed in range L1:U2, as shown in Figure 24.

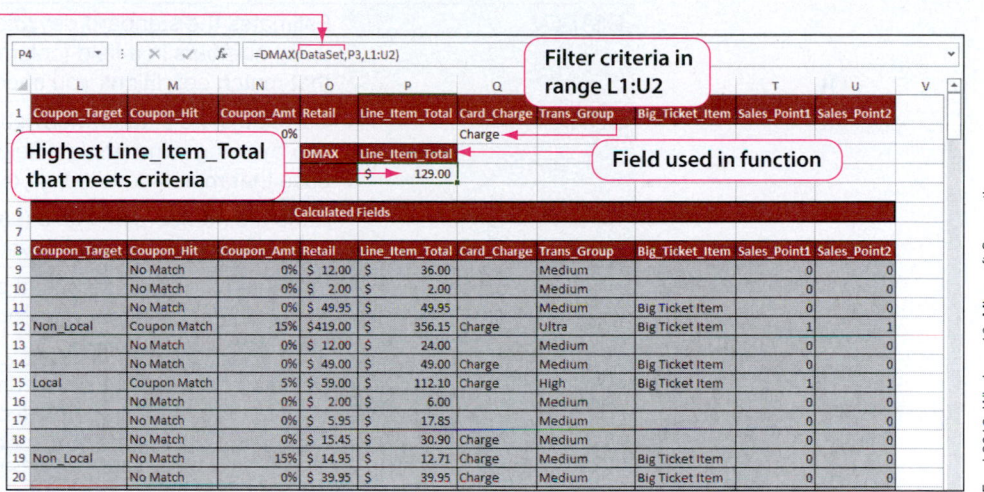

Figure 24   DMAX function

Using the DSUM Function

The **DSUM function**, which is similar to the SUMIFS function, is a database function that is ideal for setting up a criteria range and then calculating the sum based on the filters within that criteria range. An advantage of using the DSUM function is that you can see the criteria on the worksheet and understand the calculation much more easily. Second, the criteria can be modified on the worksheet, and the result is updated automatically. Thus, instead of editing a SUMIFS function, the DSUM criteria are changed in cells on the worksheet, and there is no need to actually alter the function. The syntax of the DSUM function is

=DSUM(database, field, criteria)

The database argument is a range of cells that make up the data set, such as transaction data, which includes records and fields. The field is the field label of the column to be summed, such as Line_Item_Total. The criteria is a range of cells that contains the conditions you specify. The criteria range includes a column field label or list of field labels on the top row and one or more cell rows below the field label(s) for the criteria condition. Criteria can be put onto multiple fields at the same time. When this is done, all the criteria must be evaluated to TRUE for the record to be included in the summation of the fields. Common database functions are described in Table 8.

Database Function	Description
DAVERAGE	Averages the values in the field (column) of records in a list or database that match conditions you specify
DCOUNT	Counts the cells that contain numbers in a field (column) of records in the database that match the conditions you specify
DCOUNTA	Counts nonblank cells in the field (column) of records in the database that match the conditions you specify
DGET	Extracts a single value from a field (column) of a database that matches the conditions you specify
DMAX	Returns the largest number in the field (column) of records in the database that match the conditions you specify
DMIN	Returns the smallest number in the field (column) of records in the database that match the conditions you specify
DPRODUCT	Multiplies the values in the field (column) of records in the database that match the conditions you specify
DSTDEV	Estimates the standard deviation based on a sample by using numbers in a field (column) of records in a database that match conditions you specify
DSTDEVP	Calculates the standard deviation based on the entire population by using numbers in a field (column) of records in a database that match conditions you specify
DSUM	Adds the numbers in a field (column) of records in the database that match conditions you specify
DVAR	Estimates the variance based on a sample by using the numbers in a field (column) of records in a database that match conditions you specify
DVARP	Calculates the variance based on the entire population by using the numbers in a field (column) of records in a database that match conditions you specify

Table 8 Database functions

In this exercise, you will create a DSUM function.

To Create a DSUM Function

a. Click the **DatabaseTotals** worksheet. Click cell **G2**, type Non_Local, and then press Enter.
   This value is the constraint for filtering the records. Only records that are nonlocal customers will be used in the DSUM function.

b. Click cell **B5**. Click the **Formulas** tab if necessary, and in the Function Library, click **Insert Function** to open the Insert Function dialog box.

c. Click the **Or select a category** arrow, select **Database**. In the Select a function box, scroll to select **DSUM**.

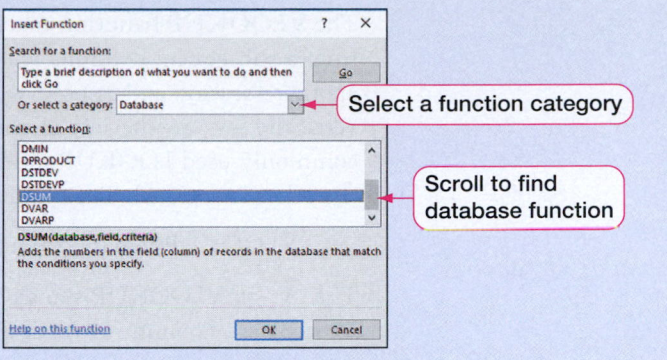

 annotations: "Select a function category" and "Scroll to find database function"

Excel 2016, Windows 10, Microsoft Corporation.

Figure 25   Insert Function dialog box

d. Click **OK**. For the Database, type DataSet, and then press Tab.

e. For the Field, type B4.

f. For the Criteria, type A1:K2, and then click **OK** for a result of $466.90.

The DataSet is the transaction database data found on the Transactions worksheet. B4 is the field that will be summed. A1:K2 is the two rows of information that are the criteria.

g. Click cell **A2**, type Check, and then press Enter.

This changes the value reflected in B5 immediately to $32.95, and once again, flexibility has been integrated into the formula. B4 is the field to be summed. If Aleeta wants to sum the line item total or the transaction quantity, she simply puts the field name into B4. The formula will automatically be updated. The field chosen for B4 should be a numerical field such as the Line_Item_Total or the Trans_Qty.

h. Press Ctrl + Home, and then **Save** 💾 the workbook.

i. If you need to take a break before finishing this chapter, now is a good time.

Retrieving Data Using Lookup and Reference Functions

With sets of data, it is useful to be able to look for and retrieve specific data. For example, you may have exam scores and you need to convert the numerical score into a letter grade. Within a business, you may need to convert a coupon number into a percentage number so the amount of the discount can be calculated. In both cases, you want to search for or look up a value and then retrieve some corresponding information. You need to refer to or retrieve specific information. A variety of functions exist for this type of data analysis. In this section, you will create functions that will look up information based on the initial data set. Then you will work to evaluate and eliminate errors within the worksheet model.

Explore LOOKUP Functions

There are two LOOKUP functions — VLOOKUP and HLOOKUP — you can use to look up a value and then, using that value as a reference, return data that is associated with that value. LOOKUP functions are extremely valuable when working with tables in which the data is in rows or columns. LOOKUP functions are also valuable when you need to retrieve values that are located in another location within your workbook.

Using the VLOOKUP Function with an Approximate Match

The **VLOOKUP function** matches a provided value in a table of data and returns a value from a subsequent column. The VLOOKUP function helps to retrieve values located in another location and is used when your comparison values are located in a column — vertically — to the left of the data you want to find. The VLOOKUP is the more commonly used LOOKUP function. It has four arguments, three of which are required; the other is optional. The syntax for the VLOOKUP function is

=VLOOKUP(lookup_value, table_array, col_index_number, [range_lookup])

The "V" in VLOOKUP stands for vertical and is used when your comparison values are located in a column — vertically — to the left of the data that you want to find. For example, a teacher could use a VLOOKUP to look up an exam score and retrieve the corresponding letter grade.

The setup for the VLOOKUP function shown in Figure 26 uses a TRUE value for the optional [range_lookup] argument. It should be noted that if this optional argument is omitted, Excel defaults to the TRUE argument, which will find the next lower value for a specified value. Because a TRUE argument will not search for an exact match and will return the next lower match that it finds, it should also be noted that the far left lookup_value column must be sorted in ascending order to ensure that the appropriate value is returned. In Figure 26 the lookup_value is 72, and when Excel encounters the value of 80, Excel will assume that the closest value in this example will be approximate to the lower 70 score value. A score of 79 will also drop down to the closest match less than that value, so 79 would also return the 70 value result.

VLOOKUP(B1, table, 2, TRUE)

Cell A1	Cell B1		1	2
C	72		SCORE	GRADE
			0	F
			60	D
			70	C
			80	B
			90	A

Figure 26   Approximate match VLOOKUP function
Excel 2016, Windows 10, Microsoft Corporation.

For the Employee Report, Aleeta wants to give incentives to staff members who do well in selling products. She is awarding points for certain transactions, and a set of rewards has been set up for redeeming points earned during the time period. The more points earned, the better the rewards. She will adjust the awards and point levels needed to attain the various choices. On the Employee Report worksheet, the incentive points have been added. The point value needs to be converted to show the reward level. There are four reward levels, and "no reward" is an additional possibility. As Figure 26 illustrates, a VLOOKUP can be used to find the approximate match and return the appropriate result for the points attained.

In this exercise, you will find an approximate match with a VLOOKUP function.

 **E05.18**

To Find an Approximate Match in VLOOKUP

a. If you took a break, open the **e03ch05GolfSales_LastFirst** workbook, and then click the **EmployeeReport** worksheet.

b. Click cell **B16**. A table has been set up as IncentivePts and resides on the DataInputs worksheet.

c. Click the **Formulas** tab, click the **Lookup & Reference** arrow, scroll down, and then select **VLOOKUP** to open the Function Arguments dialog box.

d. For the Lookup_value, type **B15**, and then press Tab.

e. For Table_array, type IncentivePts, and then press Tab.

f. For Col_index_num, type 2, and then press Tab.

g. For Range_lookup, type TRUE.

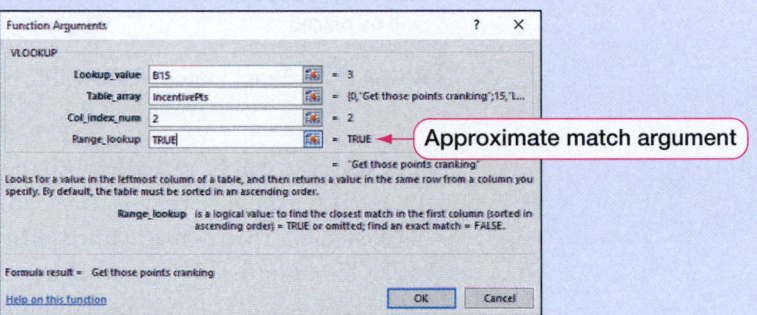

Figure 27 Function Arguments dialog box

h. Click **OK** for a result of "Get those points cranking". With only a few incentive points, Hample needs to improve sales to the target customers. **Save** 🖫 the workbook.

Using the VLOOKUP Function with an Exact Match

The other optional argument for a VLOOKUP searches for an exact match. You search for an exact match daily in a contact list when looking for a phone number associated with a name. You search for a name and from the name obtain the phone number or other data that has been stored in the little table such as the one shown in Figure 28 that demonstrates the process and components of a phone contact list within the structure of a VLOOKUP. Each row contains the information for a person. The value you look up is the name. The information returned is in the adjacent columns to the right of the name. The lookup_value is the value Excel will look for in the far left column of the table array. For a phone number, an exact match is needed. This is achieved with the optional [range-lookup] argument set to FALSE or a 0. If the VLOOKUP does not find an exact match in the left column of the table_array, it will return a #N/A error — not available. If the fourth argument is assigned a FALSE, or 0 value, the VLOOKUP will return an exact match, and it will not be necessary to sort the lookup_value column in ascending order.

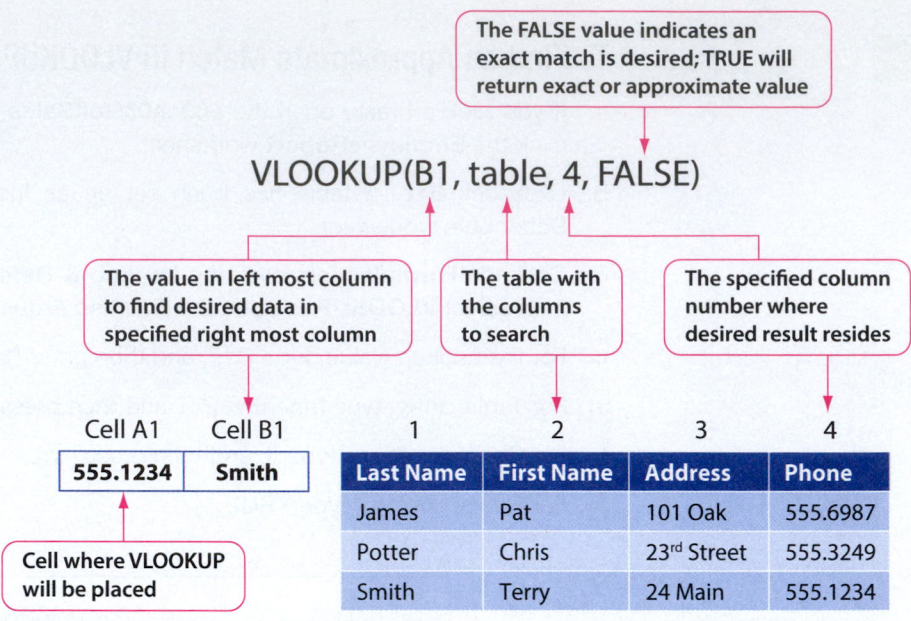

The FALSE value indicates an exact match is desired; TRUE will return exact or approximate value

VLOOKUP(B1, table, 4, FALSE)

The value in left most column to find desired data in specified right most column

The table with the columns to search

The specified column number where desired result resides

Cell A1   Cell B1   1   2   3   4

555.1234	Smith	Last Name	First Name	Address	Phone
		James	Pat	101 Oak	555.6987
		Potter	Chris	23rd Street	555.3249
		Smith	Terry	24 Main	555.1234

Cell where VLOOKUP will be placed

Figure 28 Exact match VLOOKUP   Excel 2016, Windows 10, Microsoft Corporation.

The SKU_Cat will be included with the data brought into the Transactions worksheet, but the retail purchase price will not be included. This data can be found by referencing a SKU_List table that is maintained on the DataInputs worksheet. The Item ID will need to be found in the SKU_List table, and the corresponding Retail_Price can then be included. This means that the first column of the range where the search will occur must contain the Item ID. Because an exact match must be found, the table does not have to be sorted.

In this exercise, you will create a VLOOKUP function to find an exact match.

 E05.19

SIDE NOTE
Alternative Method
Consider using the Function Arguments dialog box to enter a VLOOKUP function by pressing f_x.

To Find an Exact Match in VLOOKUP

a. Click the **Transactions** worksheet. Click cell **O9**, enter the formula **=VLOOKUP(C9,SKU_List,6,FALSE)**, and then press Ctrl + Enter.

The SKU_List on the DataInputs worksheet has the list and is a named range. The Item ID in cell reference C9 is also located in the first column of the table. The corresponding Retail Price is pulled from the sixth column, counting from left to right within the SKU_List table. The Item ID must be an exact match to the data on the SKU_List for a result of $12.00.

b. With cell O9 selected, copy the formula down to cell **O208** to overwrite the static values. The formula will display a #N/A error for any cells that reference a blank cell in column C, but this will be corrected in a later exercise when the worksheet is checked and updated for errors.

c. Click cell **N9**.

The coupon percentage needs to be determined from the coupon number provided in column F. The Coupons table is set up on the DataInputs worksheet and is a range named Coupons.

d. Enter the formula **=VLOOKUP(F9,Coupons,2,FALSE)**, and then press Ctrl + Enter.

Note the #N/A error that appears. Because no coupon was used in the column F cell reference, Excel cannot find an exact match and returns an error message that means "not applicable" or "not available."

e. With cell N9 selected, copy the formula down to cell **N208** to overwrite the static values.

   Note error messages occur for all the transactions that do not have a Coupon_Num entry listed in the column F cell. This will be corrected when the worksheet is checked and updated for errors.

f. Click cell **I9**, enter the formula =VLOOKUP(C9,SKU_List,3,FALSE), and then press Ctrl + Enter for a result of "Accessories".

   The SKU_Cat needs to be determined by looking at the SKU in column C. The SKU_List on the DataInputs worksheet has the Item ID on the left side so it can be searched. In the SKU_List table, the Category is listed in the third column. The search needs to find an exact match, not an approximate one. From that, the VLOOKUP can be created.

g. In cell I9, copy the formula down to cell **I208** to overwrite the static values.

   The formula will display a #N/A error for any cells referencing a blank cell in column C. This will be corrected in a later exercise when the worksheet is checked and updated for errors.

h. **Save** 💾 the workbook.

REAL WORLD ADVICE **The VLOOKUP Function in Business**

Businesses use LOOKUP functions on a regular basis because they have a tremendous amount of data stored in multiple workbooks. Employers will expect you to be comfortable with LOOKUP functions when you seek employment. An interviewer may even ask you whether you know how to work with them.

Using the HLOOKUP Function

The **HLOOKUP function** works in the same manner as the VLOOKUP function — helping to retrieve values located in another location — but is used when your comparison values are located in a row horizontally. As Figure 29 shows, the HLOOKUP wants a row_index_number indicating which row below the lookup row the target value can be found. By comparison, the VLOOKUP used a col_index_num. All the remaining arguments are the same and operate in a similar manner. The HLOOKUP function also uses the optional [range_lookup] argument with the same approximate or exact match options.

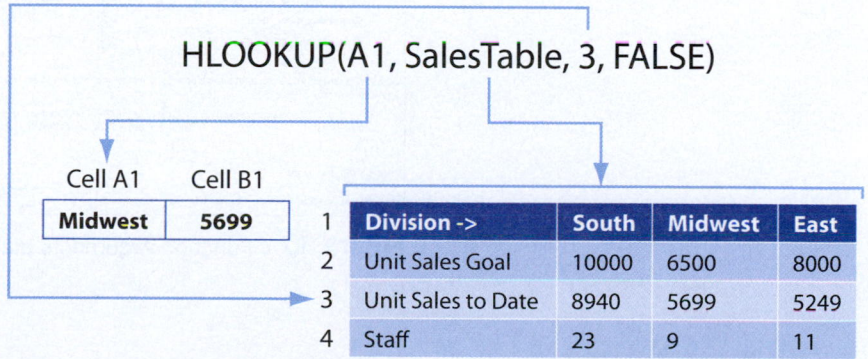

Figure 29   HLOOKUP function   Excel 2016, Windows 10, Microsoft Corporation.

For the report, a section is set up to analyze individual staff members. With an individual listed, formulas will be created to retrieve information pertaining to that person, such as each employee's revenue goal.

Aleeta would also like to be able to retrieve data about the Transaction Groups, the Shifts, or the Coupons that have been established on the DataInputs worksheet. Because the worksheet needs to be flexible, she wants to be able to choose one of those options and have the categories appear for that option and then calculate the sum when it can be applied to appropriate categories on the Transactions worksheet. But first, an adjustment to the Revenue Report worksheet will be developed.

In this exercise, you will create an HLOOKUP function.

 **E05.20**

To Create an HLOOKUP Function

a. Click the **DataInputs** worksheet, and then select cell range **B12:G17**.
   This range is the data and headings for the HLOOKUP function. It will be used to search in the first row for the different reporting groups as needed.

b. Click the **Formulas** tab, and then, in the Defined Names group, click **Define Name**.

c. In the New Name dialog box, replace AH_Shifts by typing AH_ReportTable in the Name box, and then click **OK**. Now the table can be referenced easily in formulas.

d. On the Formulas tab, in the Defined Names group, with the range B12:G17 still selected, click **Create from Selection**. Uncheck the Left column check box, leaving only Top row checked, and then click **OK**. Now each report group has also been named, so they can easily be referenced.

e. Click the **RevenueReport** worksheet, and then click cell **E8**. On the Formulas tab, in the Function Library group, click the **Lookup & Reference** arrow, and then select **HLOOKUP**.

f. For Lookup_Value, type F6, press the [F4] key, and then press [Tab].

g. For Table_array, type AH_ReportTable, and then press [Tab].

h. For Row_index_num, type D8+1, and then press [Tab].

i. For Range_lookup, type FALSE.
   This will look for the Ad Hoc Report Name listed in F6 within the AH_ReportTable range on the DataInputs worksheet. Once that data has been found, Excel will retrieve the category item. Because the function has FALSE as the last argument, Excel will look for an exact match to the value in F6.

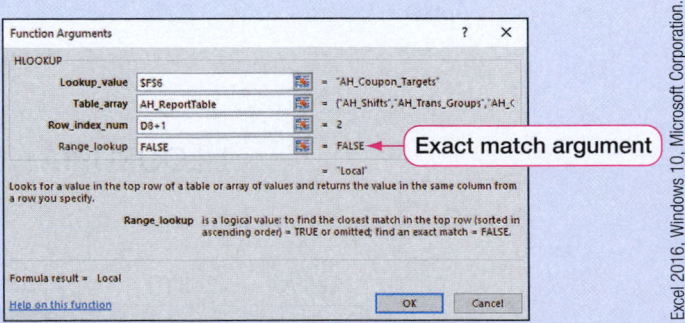

Figure 30 Function Arguments dialog box

j. Click **OK**. Copy the formula down through **E11**.

Using the numbers in column D allows the formula to be copied without having to edit the row_index_num within each formula. If it had been hard-coded into the formula, it could not have been copied to the other cells without editing them.

k. Click the **Transactions** worksheet, and then click cell **K9**.

The Shift needs to be determined from the time of the transaction. The Shifts named range has been created on the DataInputs worksheet for range B20:D21. The times fall within time ranges. Thus, searching for an exact match would rarely succeed. Instead, an approximate match is needed.

l. Enter the formula **=HLOOKUP(B9,Shifts,2,TRUE)**, and then press [Ctrl] + [Enter]. This will find an approximate match, and then pull the corresponding result from the second row in the table.

m. In cell **K9**, copy the formula down to cell **K208** to overwrite the static values. Ignore the #N/A errors, which will be corrected later.

n. Click the **EmployeeReport** worksheet, and then click cell **B8**.

The overall goal for the staff, currently Hample, needs to be retrieved. The staff's goals are listed on the DataInputs worksheet. The data can be pulled from the table and can be flexible so it will be updated when the staff member listed in A4 changes.

o. Enter the formula **=HLOOKUP(A4,DataInputs!B4:F9,6,FALSE)**, and then press [Enter] for a result of $1,250.00.

p. Click cell **B9**, enter the formula **=B6/B8**, and then press [Enter] so the percentage of goal is now determined to be 38.7%. **Save** [disk icon] the workbook.

SS | **CONSIDER THIS** | **Using VLOOKUP or Nested IF**

Take the situation of converting an exam score to a letter grade. Could you create an IF function statement that would accomplish the same task? What logical issues would lead you to use a VLOOKUP versus a nested IF? Which one would be more efficient?

Retrieve Data Using MATCH, INDEX, and INDIRECT

VLOOKUP and HLOOKUP search the first column or row of data and "look" to the right or down to retrieve a value. What if you wanted to find the name of the person with the phone number (412) 555-8767 in the phone book? Would that be easy to do? Unfortunately, the task is difficult because a traditional phone book is organized by name, not by phone number.

To overcome this limitation in the VLOOKUP and HLOOKUP functions, the MATCH and INDEX functions work to accomplish the same type of process. The primary difference is that these two functions together overcome the limitation of data arrangement. With the MATCH and INDEX functions, you have the added flexibility of multiple data ranges that can be located throughout the worksheet. The ability to use

MATCH and INDEX together is a powerful capability within Excel. Several benefits of using the MATCH INDEX function in Excel are as follows.

- MATCH INDEX allows for left-to-right lookup.
- Columns can be added or deleted in a table array without breaking the formula with MATCH INDEX.
- VLOOKUP values are limited in size (255 characters), but with the MATCH INDEX, there is no limit to the lookup value size.

Using the MATCH Function

If you need the position of an item in a range instead of the item itself, use the MATCH function. The **MATCH function** looks for a value within a range and returns the position of that value within the range. The position is a relative location starting from the top row of the table array. The syntax for the MATCH function is

=MATCH(lookup_value, lookup_array, [match_type])

The optional [match_type] argument uses a value of –1, 0, or 1. The default value of 1 is assumed if it is omitted. A [match_type] value of 0 is used for an exact match, a 1 returns a match for the largest value that is less than or equal to the lookup_value, and a –1 finds the smallest value that is greater than or equal to the lookup_value.

The exact match will return the row where the first occurrence of the match resides. This means that if there are multiple occurrences of a value, Excel will return the first one it finds, from the top, and will not find subsequent values.

The match_type of 1 will find the location of the value that is closest to the value but not greater than the value. The –1 value will return the position of the value that is closest to the lookup_value but not less than the lookup_value.

Thus, by being able to return either the next lowest or next highest value, the match has a little more flexibility than the VLOOKUP function. In either the 1 or –1 option, the data has to be sorted in ascending order or descending order, respectively, or the match process will not work correctly.

The MATCH function returns a number that indicates the position, or row, in which the match was found. This value will be relative to the top row of the range. While the function indicates the lookup_array is one range, the range must be one continuous range that is only in one column. If you try to use a range that includes more than one column, the MATCH function will not work.

For the Revenue Report, Aleeta wants to be able to check the transactions and see when the first transaction that used a coupon occurred. In this exercise, you will create a MATCH function.

 **E05.21**

To Create a MATCH Function

a. Click the **RevenueReport** worksheet. Click cell **E14**, type **=MATCH(E13,Coupon_Num,0)**, and press Ctrl + Enter.
The coupon listed in E13 will be searched in the Coupon_Num field as the lookup_array within the Transactions worksheet. The third argument in the function is 0, indicating that the search should be for an exact match.

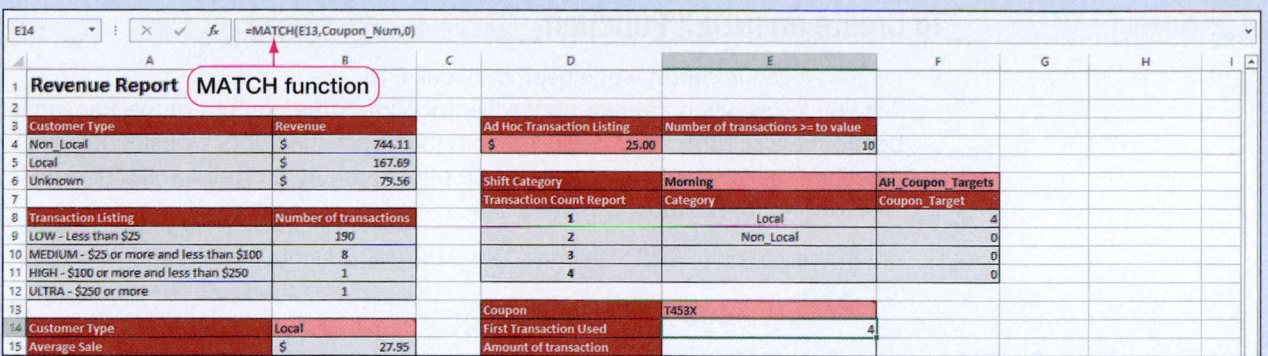

Figure 31 MATCH function

Excel 2016, Windows 10, Microsoft Corporation.

b. **Save** 💾 the workbook.

If the coupon listed in E13 is not used in any of the transactions, it will return the #N/A error, which indicates it could not find the coupon listed. If the coupon listed was typed incorrectly, this would also return a #N/A error. It would not be easy to determine whether a #N/A error indicates that the discount coupon typed in was simply not used or that it was not a valid coupon.

REAL WORLD ADVICE | **Handling Typing Errors**

With a short list of options, such as coupon numbers, using a comment to list the coupon codes is a reasonable solution. But, it is still possible to make typing errors. To minimize typing errors, you will typically create a drop-down list of the options. This eliminates typing errors and is a more efficient method. Learning to incorporate drop-down lists in a cell is handled in chapter 7. It is a valuable tool to use in validating data.

Using the Index Function

The **INDEX function** works in conjunction with the MATCH function. The INDEX function returns the value of an element in a table or array selected by the row and column number indices and has two argument lists to select. The first list of arguments uses an array and returns a value from a specified cell or range. The second list of arguments uses a reference and returns a reference to specified cells. The more common set of arguments, which will be discussed here, is with the array that returns a value. The value gets returned from a range on the basis of the row and column indicated. The indexing starts from the top left corner of the table. Thus, the left column, first row, of the table would be row 1 and column 1. The index is relative based on the top left corner of the array. The syntax for the INDEX function is

=INDEX(array, row_number, [column_number])

The array is the range of data; the row_number is the row in which the value will be found; and if the [column_number] is provided, it will be the column number, starting from the left of the range, from which the result will be retrieved.

The INDEX function works with the MATCH function extremely well because the MATCH function indicates the row where a match was found, and then the INDEX can go to that row and another column to retrieve associated data. In this exercise, you will create an INDEX function.

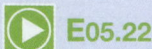 **E05.22**

To Create an INDEX Function

a. On the RevenueReport worksheet, click cell **E15**.

If you know when the first transaction occurred, the amount of the transaction before the discount could be pulled from the transaction data by using the INDEX function. The transaction total would be price*quantity for that transaction, which is in row 4 of the data.

b. Enter the formula **=INDEX(Trans_Qty,E14)*INDEX(Retail,E14)**, and then press Ctrl + Enter.

E15		▼ : ✕ ✓ fx	=INDEX(Trans_Qty,E14)*INDEX(Retail,E14)						
	A	B	C	D	E	F	G	H	I
1	**Revenue Report**		INDEX functions						
2									
3	Customer Type	Revenue		Ad Hoc Transaction Listing	Number of transactions >= to value				
4	Non_Local	$ 744.11		$ 25.00	10				
5	Local	$ 167.69							
6	Unknown	$ 79.56		Shift Category	Morning	AH_Coupon_Targets			
7				Transaction Count Report	Category	Coupon_Target			
8	Transaction Listing	Number of transactions		1	Local	4			
9	LOW - Less than $25	190		2	Non_Local	1			
10	MEDIUM - $25 or more and less than $100	8		3		0			
11	HIGH - $100 or more and less than $250	1		4		0			
12	ULTRA - $250 or more	1							
13				Coupon	T453X				
14	Customer Type	Local		First Transaction Used	4				
15	Average Sale	$ 27.95		Amount of transaction	$ 419.00				

Figure 32 INDEX function

Excel 2016, Windows 10, Microsoft Corporation.

This goes to the fourth record in the Trans_Qty field found on the Transactions worksheet, retrieves the value, then retrieves the value from the fourth record in the Retail field range and multiplies the two values to compute the total amount of the transaction.

c. Press Ctrl + Home. Click the **EmployeeReport** worksheet tab, and then click cell **B20**.

Aleeta wants to be able to list the rewards for the different levels so this information is available as she talks with her staff. Currently, the worksheet shows Level_1 in B19. Aleeta wants the three Level_1 rewards to be listed below. You can use the INDEX function and the numbers in column A to retrieve the information.

d. Enter the formula **=INDEX(Level_1,A20)**, and then press Ctrl + Enter.

e. In cell B20, copy the formula down to **B22**.

The items available for Level_1 are now listed. However, the formulas would need to be changed if a different level were desired. In a later section of this chapter, this will be modified to be updated automatically when cell B19 is modified.

f. Click cell **B4**.

The position for the staff member, currently listed as Hample, needs to be retrieved. However, in the table, Hample is not the first column. It could still be searched, but using a VLOOKUP would not work because the position field is to the left of the Last Name field in the table on the DataInputs worksheet. The MATCH function can locate the row where Hample exists and then go to the same row for the positions and retrieve his position.

g. Type **=MATCH(A4,DataInputs!L27:L31)**, and then press Ctrl + Enter. This will show the row where Hample is located — row 1.

Next, you will add the INDEX function to retrieve the position description by using the position found with the MATCH function.

h. Press F2 to edit cell B4. Click in the **Formula Bar** to position the insertion point to the right of the = sign, and then type INDEX(DataInputs!I27:I31,. Position the cursor at the end of the formula, type), and then press Enter. The formula is now set to retrieve Hample's position value of Asst Manager, using the nested MATCH function to determine the row_num argument.

i. Click the **Transactions** worksheet, and then click cell **J9**. The employee position for all the transactions needs to be retrieved and accomplished in a manner similar to that used in retrieving Hample's position.

j. Type =INDEX(DataInputs!$I$27:$I$31,MATCH(G9,DataInputs!$J$27:$J$31,0)), and then press Ctrl + Enter. The dollar signs, which make the references absolute, are necessary because the ranges need to stay in place as the formula is copied down the column.

k. In cell J90, copy the formula down to cell **J208** to overwrite the static values. The errors will be fixed later, when the sheet is error checked.

l. Click the **EmployeeReport** worksheet, and then click cell **B12**.

Currently, the value is $200 for the clothing goal for Hample. But for flexibility, Aleeta wants this number to be updated if the staff member changes and if the product category changes. Fortunately, the Sales Goals table found on the DataInputs worksheet has all the goal values listed for each category for each staff member, and the named range has been saved as Goals.

SIDE NOTE
Viewing Named Ranges

To navigate to the Goals named range, you can also press F5 to open the Go To dialog box, select Goals, and then click OK.

m. Click the **Name box**, and then choose **Goals** from the list of named ranges.

You will see the named range Goals selects the data associated with the staff and the goals for each category. If the row and column within the table is known, the INDEX function can be used to pull the value for the appropriate goal value. By using the MATCH functions within the INDEX function, the goal can be retrieved. Building test MATCH functions a piece at a time will help with the development of the INDEX MATCH function by testing the subcomponents.

n. Click the **EmployeeReport** worksheet. Click cell **D12**, type =MATCH(B11, DataInputs!A5:A9,0), and then press Ctrl + Enter. This will be deleted once you have created the entire formula piece by piece.

This is the first piece and shows the row where the lookup_value from B11 — Clothing — is found in the Goals named range. The last argument, with 0, indicates that an exact match should be found.

o. Click cell **D13**, type =MATCH(A4,DataInputs!B4:F4,0), and then press Ctrl + Enter.

This will be deleted once you have created the entire formula piece by piece. The formula returns the column where the staff member is located in the Goals named range on the DataInputs worksheet.

p. Click cell **B12**. Since the MATCH functions work, the complex function can be constructed. Type =INDEX(Goals,MATCH(B11,DataInputs!A5:A9,0),MATCH(A4, DataInputs!B4:F4,0)), and then press Enter.

The Goals range on the DataInputs worksheet array is used. The first MATCH function is the row within the table, and the second MATCH function is the column within the range. Using those coordinates, the INDEX function returns the correct goal value.

q. Select cells **D12:D13**, press Delete to remove the test functions, and then **Save** 🖫 the workbook.

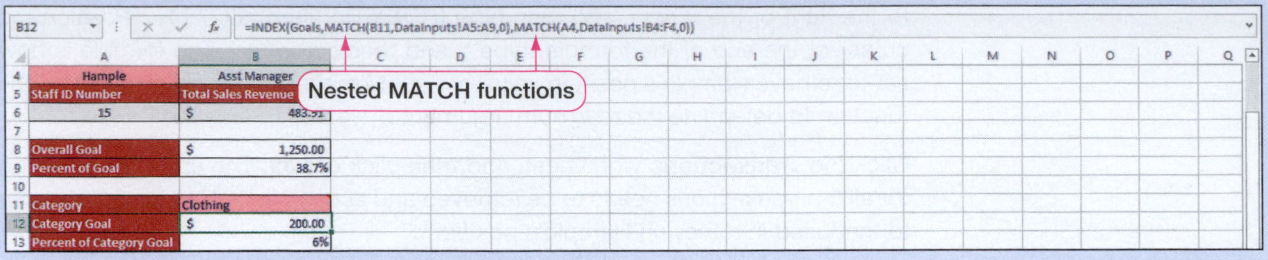

| B12 | ▼ : × ✓ fx | =INDEX(Goals,MATCH(B11,DataInputs!A5:A9,0),MATCH(A4,DataInputs!B4:F4,0)) |

	A	B	C	D	E	F	G	H	I	J	K	L	M	N	O	P	Q
4	Hample	Asst Manager															
5	Staff ID Number	Total Sales Revenue															
6	15	$ 483.51															
7																	
8	Overall Goal	$ 1,250.00															
9	Percent of Goal	38.7%															
10																	
11	Category	Clothing															
12	Category Goal	$ 200.00															
13	Percent of Category Goal	6%															

Nested MATCH functions

Figure 33 INDEX function with nested MATCH functions

Excel 2016, Windows 10, Microsoft Corporation.

Using the INDIRECT Function

The **INDIRECT function** is another reference function that can be used to add flexibility to a worksheet. The INDIRECT function is valuable because it can change a text string within a cell to a cell reference. The syntax for the INDIRECT function is

=INDIRECT(ref_text, [A1])

The argument typically is a cell reference or a text string, and within that cell, you can enter in another cell, range, or named range. The function tells Excel to interpret the cell's value as a reference rather than a text string. In other words, the cell referenced in the INDIRECT function reroutes to a new reference.

In Figure 34, the formula in cell A1 does not use a specific named range. The AVERAGE function does not go directly to the named range. It goes indirectly, to B1, which redirects the function to use the range listed in B1. The INDIRECT function pulls the value in B1, the range named "Pat" as a range to be averaged. Instead of changing the named range in the formula, the name can be changed in cell B1 from "Pat" to "Chris" and it would give the average for Chris. This adds flexibility to choose which named range to average.

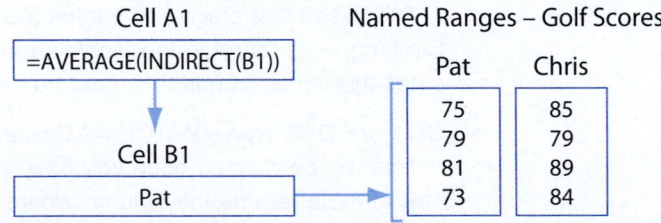

Figure 34 INDIRECT function logic   Excel 2016, Windows 10, Microsoft Corporation.

The optional INDIRECT argument will not be a concern for the average user. The function defaults to the **A1 reference method** if the A1 argument is omitted, which merely refers to the A1 reference method for cell references. If letters appear for the column headings, the reference style for Excel is currently A1. In this mode, cells are referenced by using a letter for the column and a number for the row.

The alternative method is referred to as the **R1C1 reference style**. With R1C1 style, if numbers appear for the column headings, the reference style for Excel is currently R1C1. For example, if a value is in the third row and fourth column, the cell reference would be R3C4. Excel allows you to set the R1C1 reference style check box as a default option under Formulas within the Excel Options dialog box. Whichever reference style mode Excel is in, all cell references typed in formulas must be in that reference style form — A1 or R1C1. If not, an error will be produced. The A1 reference style is the easiest to use in Excel and is the default method.

On the Employee Report worksheet, if Aleeta wants to look at the different rewards in the different levels, the formulas would need to be changed again. Preferably, the value in B19 could show the level that is to be displayed. And since it is the name of the range that holds the list of rewards, it could be used in the three formulas. Using the INDIRECT function would allow the value in cell B19 to change, and the reward list would automatically be updated.

In this exercise, create an INDIRECT function.

 **E05.23**

To Create an INDIRECT Function

a. On the **EmployeeReport** worksheet, and click cell **B20**.

b. Click in the **Formula Bar**. In the formula, select the **Level_1** text, type **INDIRECT($B$19)**, and then press Ctrl + Enter.

c. Copy the formula to cell **B22**, and then press Ctrl + Home.

d. **Save** 💾 the workbook.

The complete formula in B20 should now appear as =INDEX(INDIRECT($B$19),A20). Now, instead of hard-coding the named range, the formula goes to A20 and pulls the value in A20 to use as the range, indirectly, by going first to B19, and B19 is directing the formula to use the Level_1 value contained in the cell as the named cell range.

Handle Errors with the IFERROR Function

Because logical functions are used in decision-making scenarios in which flexibility and scalability are desirable, there are times in the development of the formulas when the functions may return error messages. Because there could be multiple users of varying skills, it is important to minimize the occurrence of error messages within the workbook. Error messages tend to make users uncomfortable because they believe the error message means that they did something wrong. Additionally, if the error message is legitimate and other calculations reference those cells, the errors will carry forward into the next formulas, compounding the problem.

The solution is to be aware of when errors may occur — such as dividing by 0 or because you are referencing an empty cell — and create functions in a way that eliminates the error message from being viewed. During development, it is possible to anticipate and handle errors within the formula if you consider the values to be used and the possible answers.

Using the IFERROR Function

The **IFERROR function** is used for detecting an error and displaying something more user-friendly than the error message. With the IFERROR function, it is possible to evaluate whether an error will occur and replace one of Excel's default error messages with another value that you specify; otherwise, the formula result will be returned. The syntax for the IFERROR function is

=IFERROR(value, value_if_error)

The first argument — value — is the formula that is going to be checked for existing errors. If the value works and a valid output exists, that formula result will be returned. However, if the value returns any error message, such as #N/A or #DIV/0!, then the value_if_error value will be returned.

When examining the Transactions worksheet, you will see error messages showing up within the range in two different contexts. First, when there are not any transaction records, error messages exist throughout. Second, in a few columns, error messages occur even when there are transactions. The #N/A is not only distracting, it is confusing to users because they may believe that there are calculation errors when in actuality the errors are valid errors.

In the process of checking the values and eliminating errors, it is best to start with formulas that are simple and do not reference other cells that have formulas. For example, if an error exists in a formula in cell A1, that error will create an error in any other formula that references A1. For the Transactions data, it also makes sense to first correct fields in which the error message occurs only where data does not exist. In checking the formulas, it appears that fields such as SKU_Cat, Emp_Position, and Shift have errors only when cells are empty. A simple way to eliminate this type of error is to leave the cell blank if an error message occurs.

In this exercise, you will eliminate errors with the IFERROR function.

 E05.24

To Eliminate Errors using the IFERROR Function

a. Click the **Transactions** worksheet, and then click cell **I9**. Click in the Formula Bar, place the insertion point to the right of the equal sign, and then type **IFERROR(**.

b. Reposition the cursor at the end of the formula, type **,"")**, and then press Ctrl + Enter.

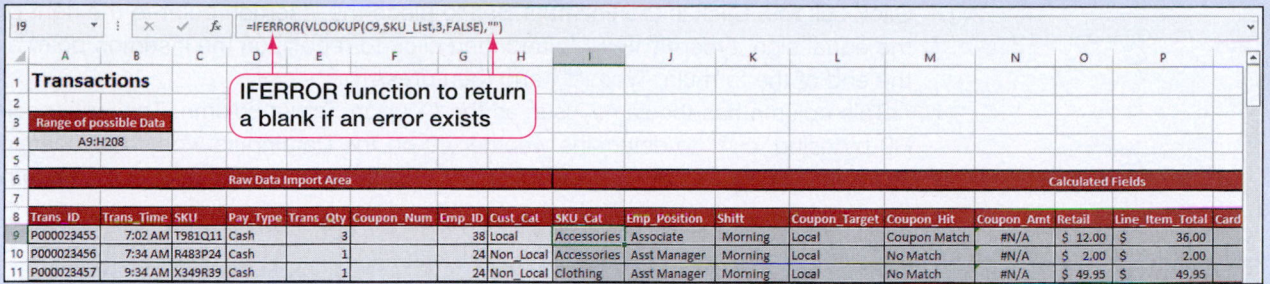

Figure 35 IFERROR function

Excel 2016, Windows 10, Microsoft Corporation.

c. In cell I9, copy the formula to cell I208. This will update any error cells with a blank cell whenever there is no record for the formula cell references in those fields.

d. Click cell **J9**, click in the **Formula Bar** to place the insertion point to the right of the equal sign, and then type IFERROR(. Click to place the insertion point at the end of the formula, type ,""), and then press Ctrl + Enter.

e. Click cell **K9**, click in the **Formula Bar** to place the insertion point to the right of the equal sign, and then type IFERROR(. Click to place the insertion point at the end of the formula, type ,""), and then press Ctrl + Enter.

f. Select range **J9:K9**, and then copy the formulas down to **J208:K208** to overwrite the existing formulas.

g. Click cell **L9**.

   With this column, there are no error messages. However, "Local" is displayed whenever there is not a value in the Coupon_Num field. Evaluating any calculations on the formula results, such as a COUNT formula, would be erroneous because of the incorrect "Local" values. The formula needs to show nothing when there is no coupon. An IF function that checks whether the Coupon_Num field is empty will eliminate the issue.

h. Click in the **Formula Bar** to place the insertion point to the right of the equal sign, type IF(F9<>"",, and then click to reposition the insertion point at the end of the formula. Type ,""), and then press Ctrl + Enter.

i. In cell L9, copy the formula down to **L208** to cell overwrite the existing formulas.

   This will check to see if F9 has a value. If F9 is not blank, this will check whether I5 and I7 on the DataInputs worksheet contains values. If either does, the Excel function will check for the type of coupon and return the corresponding value. If either does not contain a value, the cell will remain blank.

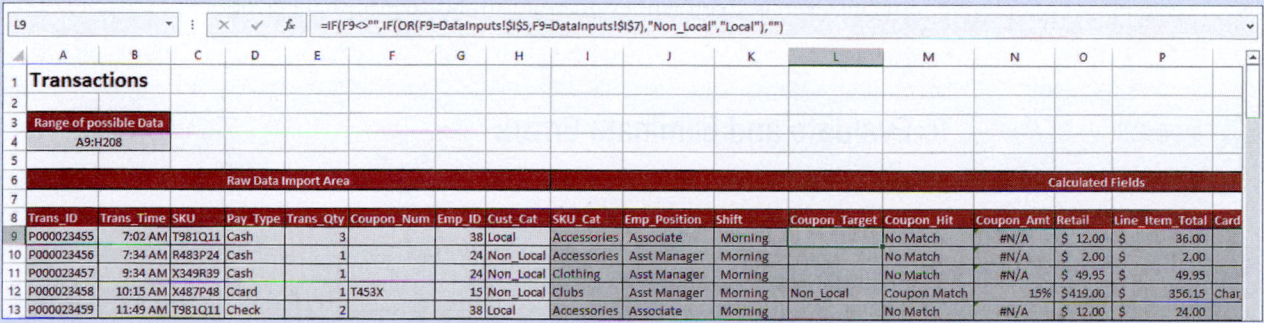

Figure 36 Return a blank result in a cell

Excel 2016, Windows 10, Microsoft Corporation.

j. Click cell **M9**. Click in the **Formula Bar** to place the insertion point to the right of the equal sign, type IF(H9<>"",, and then click to reposition the insertion point at the end of the formula. Type ,""), and then press ⌃Ctrl + ⏎Enter.

This column has the same issue as the Coupon_Target column. This will check H9 by using <> "" to determine whether L9 on the DataInputs worksheet contain values. If either does, the Excel function will check for the type of coupon and return the corresponding value. If it does not contain a value, the cell will remain blank.

k. In cell M9, copy the formula down to cell **M208**.

l. Click cell **N9**.

This cell has the #N/A error because the formula cannot locate an exact VLOOKUP value to match a blank cell found in the Coupon_Num field. The IFERROR function will correct this issue.

m. Click in the **Formula Bar** to place the insertion point to the right of the equal sign, and then type IFERROR(. Click to reposition the insertion point at the end of the formula, type ,0), and then press ⌃Ctrl + ⏎Enter. Copy the formula down to **N208**.

n. Click cell **O9**, click in the **Formula Bar** to place the insertion point to the right of the equal sign, and then type IFERROR(. Click to reposition the insertion point at the end of the formula, type ,0), and then press ⌃Ctrl + ⏎Enter. Copy the formula down to **O208**.

o. Click cell **P9**, and then type =ROUND(O9*E9-(O9*E9*N9),2). This function will round the calculation to take Retail price times Trans_Qty and then subtract the discount calculations.

p. Press ⌃Ctrl + ⏎Enter. Copy the formula down to **P208**.

q. **Save** 💾 the workbook.

Because column P still contained hard-coded values, this formula will display the correct calculation for the Line_Item_Total.

Eliminating Errors

Earlier, you used the IFERROR function to correct the values in column N (Coupon_ Amt) by placing a zero for any error references. What if you had used a blank cell correction instead? When a 0 or "" is placed in a formula, the worksheet should be checked to ensure that the 0 or blank does not interfere with formulas that reference those cells. For example, a 0 would affect the AVERAGE function. If there is a 0 where there is no record, this would cause miscalculation of the average.

In this exercise, you will evaluate formulas to eliminate errors.

 **E05.25**

To Evaluate and Eliminate Errors

a. On the Transactions worksheet, click cell **N9**. Click in the **Formula Bar**, select the **0** at the end located before the last closing parenthesis, and then type "" to replace the zero with an empty text string. Press ⌃Ctrl + ⏎Enter. Notice the #VALUE! error is displayed in cells P9, R9, T9, and U9.

b. In cell N9, copy the formula down to **N208**. Notice the #VALUE! errors that appear in numerous cells for the affected columns.

c. Press ⌈Ctrl⌉ + ⌈Z⌉ to undo the AutoFill. Press ⌈Ctrl⌉ + ⌈Z⌉ again to undo the formula change to cell N9. The worksheet should return to normal without the errors.

d. Click cell **R9**. The formula in column R returns a value of Low for records that have no transactions.

e. Click the **RevenueReport** worksheet, and then click cell **B9**.

Recall that B9 counts the number of Low values on the Transaction worksheet for the Trans_Group column; thus, the 190 is correct for the current amount of Low values, but the count is not valid or accurate. This supports the need to carefully evaluate the formulas throughout the entire worksheet.

f. Click the **Transactions** worksheet, and then, if necessary, click cell **R9**. Click in the Formula Bar to place the insertion point to the right of the equal sign, type **IF(A9<>"",**, and then click to reposition the cursor at the end of the formula. Type **,"")**, and then press ⌈Ctrl⌉ + ⌈Enter⌉.

This checks whether there is a transaction ID in Trans_ID. If there is a transaction ID, the formula does the calculation; otherwise, it leaves the cell blank. Using the "" is appropriate, as the field is a text-oriented field.

g. Click the **RevenueReport** worksheet. View the result of this change in cell B9, and then click the **Transactions** worksheet.

h. In cell R9, copy the formula down to **R208**.

i. Click cell **S9**. Click in the **Formula Bar** to place the insertion point to the right of the equal sign, type **IF(A9<>""**, and then click to reposition the cursor at the end of the formula. Type **,"")**, and then press ⌈Ctrl⌉ + ⌈Enter⌉.

This column has the same issue of values for the nonexistent transactions. Setting it up like column R will correct this issue. If there is a transaction, the formula calculation continues; otherwise, the cell remains blank. Using the "" is appropriate, as the field is a text-oriented field.

j. In cell S9, copy the formula down to **S208**.

k. Complete the **Documentation** worksheet as directed by your instructor.

l. **Save** 🖫 the workbook, exit Excel, and then submit your file as directed by your instructor.

SIDE NOTE
Expand the Formula Bar

If you cannot see the end of your formula, expand the Formula Bar. Place your cursor between the Formula Bar and the column headings until it changes into a double arrow. Drag your cursor down until you see the entire formula.

Concept Check

1. When is it not best practice to use static data? p. 270

2. Describe three types of data inputs that can be used for arguments within an IF function. p. 270

3. Explain how a decision tree can help you write a nested IF function. p. 272

4. Construct pseudocode for the following situation: The result "Loan" is displayed for an applicant who has either salary greater than $100,000 and a credit score of at least 700 or a salary greater than $50,000 and a credit score of at least 750. Otherwise, the result displayed is "No Loan". p. 287

5. Describe three conditional statistical functions. p. 291–294

6. Describe two conditional math functions. p. 296

7. What is an Excel database? Explain how database functions may differ from non-database functions. p. 298–299

8. Provide examples of when you would use the TRUE/FALSE options for the fourth argument in a VLOOKUP. p. 302

9. What is the primary advantage of using the MATCH and INDEX combination rather than a VLOOKUP function? p. 307–309

10. What benefit is there to using the IFERROR function when it increases the complexity of the formulas? p. 314

Key Terms

A1 reference method   p. 312
AND function   p. 283
AVERAGEIF function   p. 294
AVERAGEIFS function   p. 294
Competitive advantage   p. 271
Complex function   p. 277
Conditional aggregate
    functions   p. 290
Conditional math function   p. 296
COUNTIF function   p. 291
COUNTIFS function   p. 292

Decision tree   p. 273
Double prime symbol   p. 275
DSUM function   p. 299
Excel database   p. 298
HLOOKUP function   p. 305
IF function   p. 272
IFERROR function   p. 314
INDEX function   p. 309
INDIRECT function   p. 312
Logical function   p. 369
Logical operator   p. 269

Logical test   p. 269
MATCH function   p. 308
Nested IF function   p. 277
NOT function   p. 283
OR function   p. 283
Pseudocode   p. 287
R1C1 reference style   p. 312
Static data   p. 270
SUMIF function   p. 296
SUMIFS function   p. 296
VLOOKUP function   p. 302

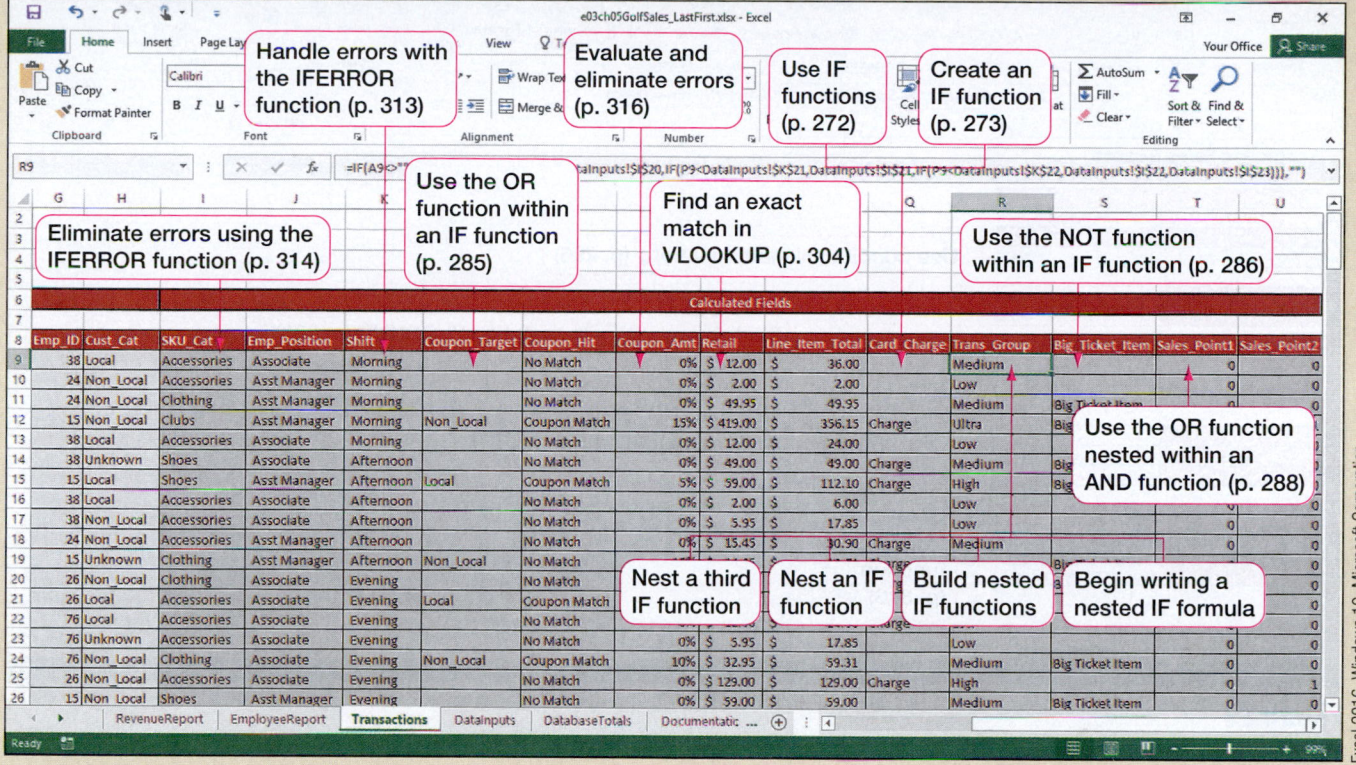

Figure 37

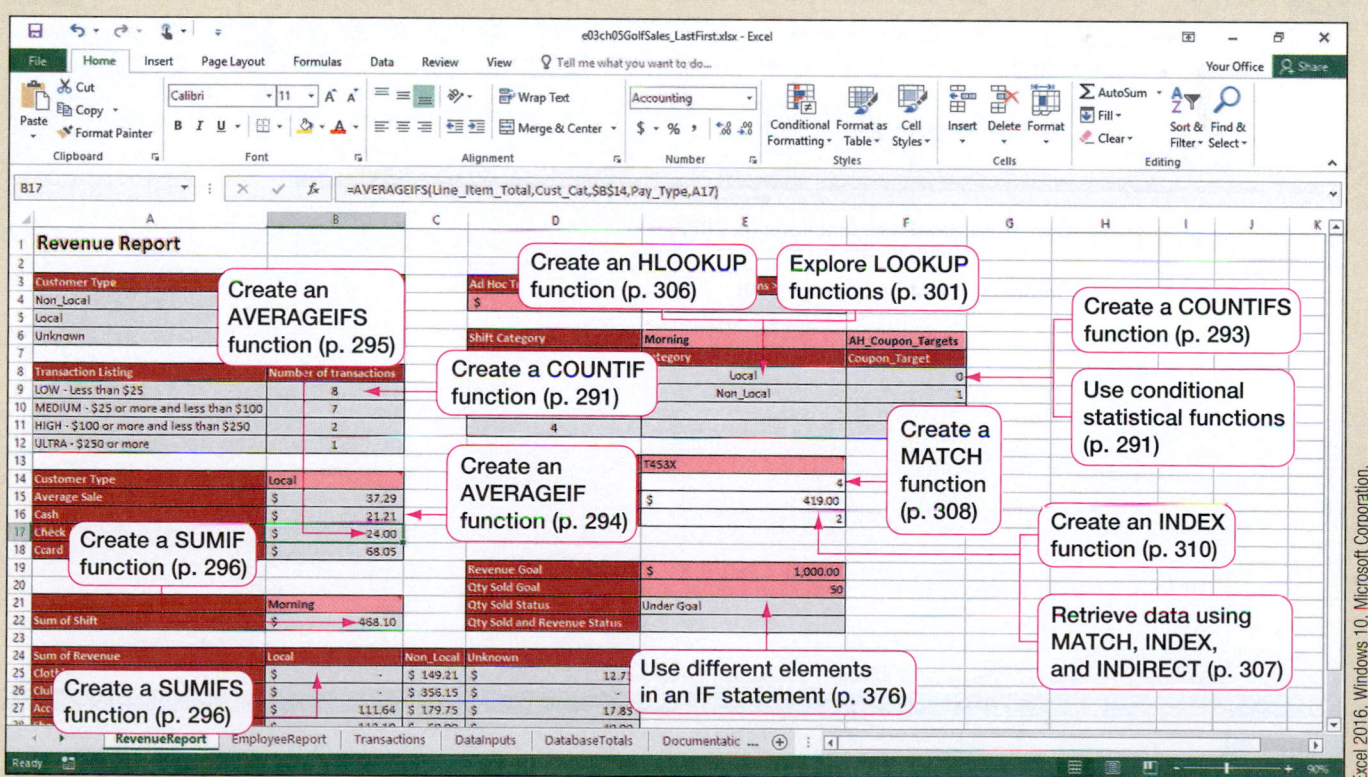

Figure 38

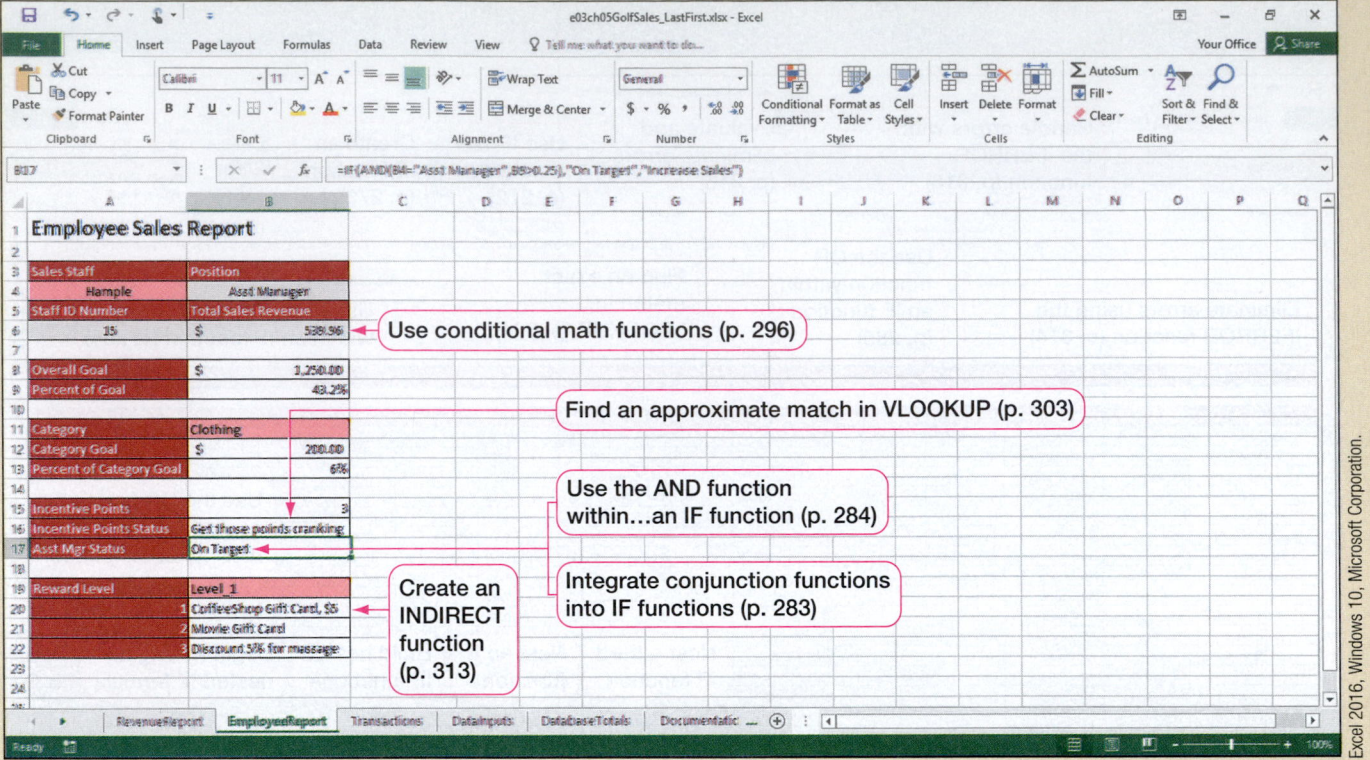

Figure 39

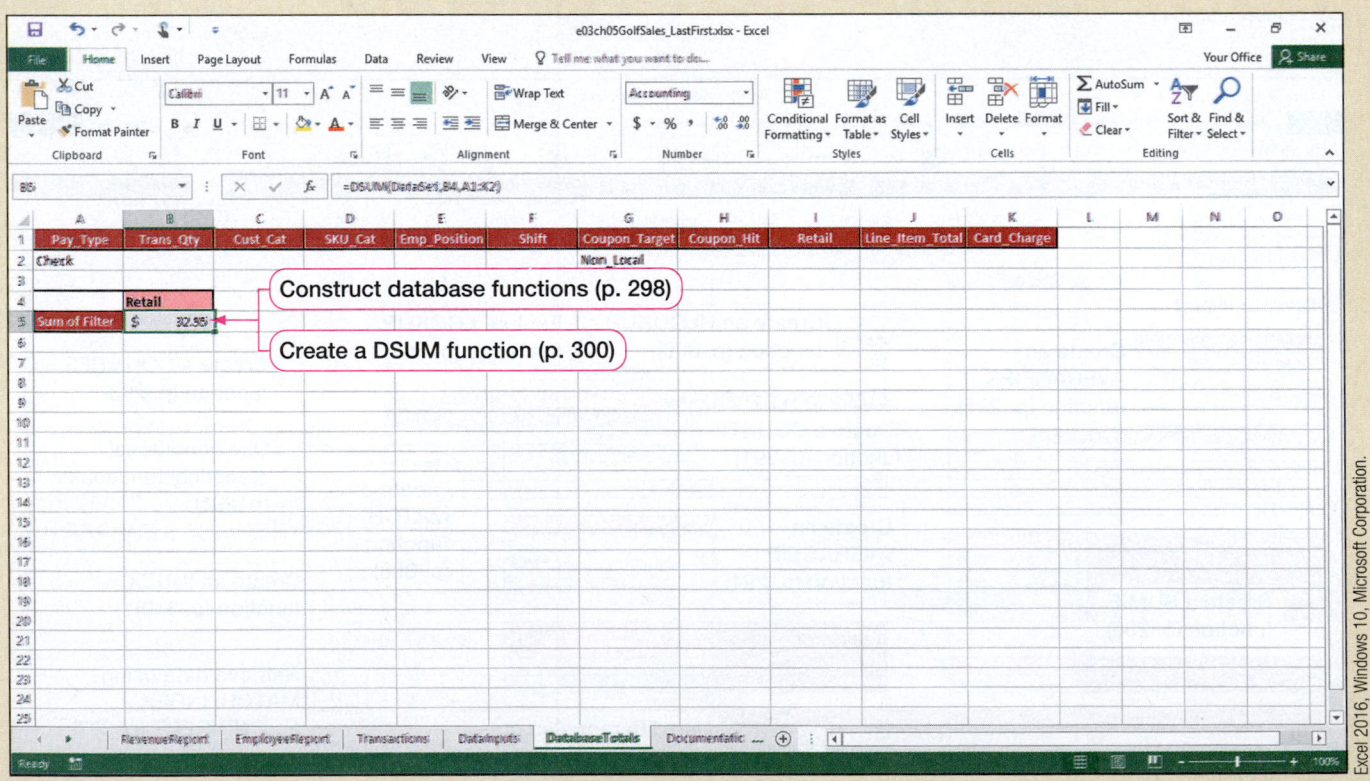

Figure 40

Student data file needed:

 e03ch05Scramble.xlsx

You will save your file as:

 e03ch05Scramble_LastFirst.xlsx

Production & Operations

Managing Golf Scramble Registrations

The Red Bluff Golf Course & Pro Shop is getting ready for another charity golf scramble tournament. Because it holds charity events on a regular basis, Aleeta Herriott, the manager, would like a workbook developed that will track information about the registrations such as foursomes, registrations, T-shirts, and fees. You have been asked to continue the development of reports to support decision making for the tournament.

a. Start **Excel**, click **Open Other Workbooks** in the left pane, and then double-click **This PC**. Navigate through the folder structure to the location of your student data files, and then double-click **e03ch05Scramble**. If a Security Warning message displays, click the **Enable Editing** button.

b. Click the **File** tab, click **Save As**, and then double-click **This PC**. In the Save As dialog box, navigate to the location where you are saving your project files, and then change the file name to e03ch05Scramble_LastFirst, using your last and first name. Click **Save**.

c. Create named ranges that will help in the development of the formulas.

- Click the **Registrations** worksheet, click cell **B8**, and then press Ctrl + A to select the range of data.

- Click the **Formulas** tab, and then, in the Defined Names group, click **Define Name**. Type ScrambleData in the Name box, and then click **OK**.

- On the Formulas tab, in the Defined Names group, click **Create from Selection**. In the Create Names from Selection dialog box, verify the **Top row** check box is checked, and then click **OK**.

- Click the **DataInputs** worksheet, and then select range **B24:E27**. On the Formulas tab, in the Defined Names group, click **Create from Selection**. In the Create Names from Selection dialog box, verify the **Top row** check box is checked, and then click **OK**.

- Select cell range **B13:D15**, click in the Name box to the left of the formula bar, type Sponsor_Fees, and then press Enter.

- Select cell **B2**, click in the Name box, type Mulligan_Fee, and then press Enter.

d. Click the **Registrations** worksheet, and then click cell **M8**. To create a level playing field, there is a maximum score per hole based on a player's handicap. Enter the formula =IF(E8<>"",VLOOKUP(H8,DataInputs!$A$6:$C$10,3),""), and then press Ctrl + Enter. Copy the formula down to **M79**. The Max Hole score will be calculated only if there is a player name.

e. Click **E2**, type Hole in One, and then press Enter. In cell **F5**, enter the formula =DSUM(ScrambleData,F4,E1:M2), and then press Enter. This will create a DSUM function that will use the filtering in range E1:M2 for the criteria and the field listed in F4 for the summation field.

f. Determine each player within a particular foursome.

- Click the **Report** worksheet, click cell **C12**, and then enter the formula =MATCH(E2,Foursome_Name,0) to determine the position of the first player in the foursome, located on the Registrations worksheet. Press Enter.

- In cell **C13**, type =C12+1, and then press Enter. Click cell **C13**, and then copy the formula down to **C15**. This will find the row position for the other players in the foursome within the Registration data set.

- Click cell **B12**, enter the formula =INDEX(Sponsor_Level,C12), and then press Enter. This will determine the sponsor level if applicable.
- Click cell **A12**, enter the formula =INDEX(Early_Bird,C12), and then press Enter. This will retrieve the early bird information for each of the players in the foursome.
- Select cell range **A12:B12**, and then copy the formula down to cell range **A15:B15**.

g. To complete the information for each player, his or her data can be retrieved from the Registration data based on the row where the player's data exists. The row was determined in column C. Each person was listed for his or her team, but each person still needs to register and submit a shirt size and other information. If the player has not registered, he or she will need to be reminded to register.

- Click cell **E12**, enter the formula =IF(INDEX(Shirt_Size,C12)="","No","Yes"), and then press Tab. This will look to see whether a shirt size has been input, indicating the player has registered.
- Click cell **F12**, enter the formula =INDEX(Registrations!$D$8:$D$79,C12), and then press Tab. This will display the person's first name.
- Click cell **G12**, enter the formula =INDEX(Registrations!$E$8:$E$79,C12), and then press Tab. This will display the last name of the person.
- Click cell **H12**, enter the formula =IF(INDEX(Registrations!$I$8:$I$79,C12)= "","Missing",INDEX(Registrations!$I$8:$I$79,C12)), and then press Tab. This will return "Missing" if the person did not sign up for any Mulligans. If the person did sign up, it will return how many were purchased.
- Click cell **I12**, enter the formula =IF(INDEX(Captain,C12)="Y","Yes",""), and press Tab. This will check the record to determine whether the person was designated in column C on the Registration worksheet as the captain. If so, it will return "Yes". Otherwise, it will remain blank.
- Select cell range **E12:I12**, and then copy the formulas without formatting to cell range **E12:I15**.

h. Compile data about the foursome listed in cell E2.
- Click cell **E3**, enter the formula =AVERAGEIF(Foursome_Name,E2,Handicap), and then press Enter.
- Click cell **E4**, enter the formula =IF(I12="Yes",B12,IF(I13="Yes", B13,IF(I14="Yes",B14,B15))), and then press Enter.
- Click cell **E5**, enter the formula =IF(I12="Yes",A12,IF(I13="Yes",A13,IF(I14= "Yes",A14,A15))), and then press Enter.
- In cell **E6**, enter the formula =IF(E3<DataInputs!A19,DataInputs!B19,IF(E3< DataInputs!A20,DataInputs!B20,DataInputs!B21)), and then press Enter.
- Click cell **E7**, enter the formula =SUM(H12:H15), and then press Enter.
- Click cell **E8**, enter the formula =IF(OR(SUM(H12:H15)>=8,AND(E5="Yes", SUM(H12:H15)>=6)),2,0)+VLOOKUP(E4,DataInputs!E6:F9,2,FALSE), and then press Enter.

Click cell **E18**. The listing of team names needs to be retrieved from the registration table. Enter the formula =IFERROR(INDEX(Foursome_Name, MATCH(D18,Registration_Number,0)),""), and then press Enter. Click cell **E18**, and then copy the formula down to cell **E35**.

i. Click cell **F18**, enter the formula =SUMIF(Foursome_Name,E18,Mulligans), and then press Ctrl + Enter. Copy the formula down to cell **F35**.

j. Click cell **H3**, enter the formula =HLOOKUP(E4,Sponsor_Fees,IF(Report!E5= "Yes",2,3),FALSE), and then press Enter.

k. In cell **H4**, enter the formula =SUMIF(Foursome_Name,E2,Mulligans)*Mulligan_Fee, and then press Enter.

l. In cell **H5**, enter the formula =SUM(H3:H4), and then press Enter.

m. Click cell **K4**, enter the formula =COUNTIF(Shirt_Size,J3) and then press Enter.

n. In cell **K5**, enter the formula =INDEX(DataInputs!B25:E27,MATCH(K4, DataInputs!A25:A27,1),MATCH(J3,DataInputs!B24:E24,0)), and then press Enter.

o. Select columns **A:C**, right-click, and then click **Hide** to hide the columns from the user.

p. Click the **Documentation** worksheet. Click cell **A8**, and then type in today's date. Click cell **B8**, and then type in your name in the Firstname Lastname format. Complete the remainder of the Documentation worksheet according to your instructor's directions.

q. Save the workbook, exit Excel, and then submit your file as directed by your instructor.

Problem Solve 1

MyITLab® Grader

Homework

Student data file needed:

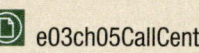 e03ch05CallCenter.xlsx

You will save your file as:

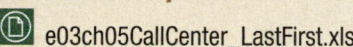 e03ch05CallCenter_LastFirst.xlsx

University Call Center

IT

Information & Technology

Human Resources

The University's call center needs a workbook developed that will use data to analyze the performance of the call center. The call center contacted your professor and she recommended you for the task. The workbook will set up a variety of tools that will help assess the efficiency of the center and its staff. You will develop a workbook for the call center manager that will help with the center's data analysis.

a. Open the Excel file, **e03ch05CallCenter**. Save your file as e03ch05CallCenter_LastFirst, using your last and first name.

b. On the **Lists** worksheet, create named ranges to use within formulas.
   - Name the range **A2:A6**, Department.
   - Name the range **A14:B18**, GradeScale.
   - Name the range **B9:H9**, DayofWeek.
   - Select cell range **E1:I5**, and create named ranges using the top row as the range values.

c. On the **CallData** worksheet, create a table and calculated fields.
   - In cell **A9**, format the data as an Excel table with Table Style Light 1 using the current data set.
   - In cell **H9**, add Issue as the field label.
   - In cell **I9**, add Grade as the field label.
   - In cell **J9**, add Weekday as the field label.
   - Select range **A9:J128**, and then name the entire data set, including the labels, CallDataAll.
   - Create named ranges for **A9:J128** using the top row as the range values.

d. In cell **H10**, enter an INDEX function that will use a nested INDIRECT reference to the Dept named range listed in column C (C10), and use the Reason field in column B (B10) as the row number to return for the department name in the referenced named range. Nest the function inside an IF function so that issues currently displaying as a 0 will display as a blank cell. Resize the column width as needed.

e. In cell **I10**, enter a VLOOKUP function that will convert the Satisfaction Rating to a grade found in the second column of the GradeScale named range.

f. In cell **J10**, enter an INDEX function that will convert the Call Day to the actual weekday found in row 1 of the DayofWeek named range. Resize the column width as needed.

g. On the **CallData** worksheet:

- In cell **C2**, type Public_Affairs.

- In cell **G2**, and then type Y.

- Run an advanced filter on the table data using the criteria range **A1:J2**.

h. On the **CallCenterReport** worksheet, add formulas that will summarize the issues for the department entered in cell B3.

- In cell **B6**, add an INDEX function that will use an INDIRECT function to retrieve the department issue list for the department listed in cell B3. Use an absolute reference to B3, and then use a relative cell reference to A6 as the row_num argument. Copy the formula down to cell B9.

- In cell **C6**, add a COUNTIFS function that will count the number of departments on the CallData worksheet. Use the Dept named range as criteria_range1, and then use an absolute reference to B3 as criteria1. Use the Reason named range as criteria_range2, and then use cell A6 as criteria2. Copy the formula down to cell C9.

- In cell **D6**, add a COUNTIFS function that will count the number of calls coming from the department listed in B3. Use the Dept named range as criteria_range1, and then use an absolute reference to B3 as criteria1. Use the Reason named range as criteria_range2, and then use cell A6 as criteria2. Use the On_Hold named range as criteria_range3, and then use "Y" as criteria3. Copy the formula down to cell D9.

- In cell **E6**, add an IF statement with a nested AND that will enter a status notice. If the number of calls on issue in cell C6 is greater than 3 and the number of calls on hold in cell D6 is greater than 2, then "Check Hold Issue" should display. Otherwise, nothing should display. Copy the formula down to cell E9.

i. Add the following formulas for this report.

- In cell **B12**, add an AVERAGEIF function that will find the average call length for the Dept named range and the criteria specified in cell A12.

- In cell **C12**, add a COUNTIF function that will count the number of calls for the Dept named range and the criteria specified in cell A12.

- In cell **D12**, add a formula that sums two COUNTIFS formulas. The first COUNTIFS will count the number of calls associated with the Dept named range and criteria specified in cell A12 that received a Grade "F", and the second COUNTIFS will do the same for Grade "D".

- In cell **E12**, add an IF statement using a nested OR function that will return a note associated with the issue. If there are more than 10 issues reported with a grade below a C in cell D12, or when the number of scores below a C divided by the total calls in cell C12 is greater than 50%, then "Explore Issues" should display. Otherwise, nothing should display.

- Copy the formulas in B12:E12 down through row 16.

j. Because calls should be handled quickly, the longest call will be noted and checked.

- In cell **H11**, add a MAX function that will show the maximum call length minutes using the Call_Length named range.

- In cell **H12**, add an INDEX function that will use the Dept named range as the array associated with a MATCH function to determine the longest call referenced in H11 in the lookup array Call_Length with an exact match.

- In cell **H13**, add an INDEX function that will use the Satisfaction_Rating named range as the array associated with a MATCH function to determine the longest call referenced in H11 in the lookup array Call_Length with an exact match.

k. A final section is needed that will use database functions for some reports. The criteria can be easily changed to determine the satisfaction and call length for any subset of data.

- In cell **G19**, type Y, and then in cell **J19**, type Friday.
- Name the range **A18:J19**, Call_Criteria.
- In cell **B22**, add a DCOUNT function for the CallDataAll database to find the count of the satisfaction rating currently listed in cell B21 using the Call_Criteria range.
- Add corresponding database functions in **B23:B26** that find the DAVERAGE, DSUM, DMAX, and DMIN for the Satisfaction_Rating named range.
- Select range **B22:B26**, and then copy the formulas to column C.

l. Complete the Documentation worksheet according to your instructor's directions.

m. Save the workbook, exit Excel, and then submit your file as directed by your instructor.

Perform 1: Perform in Your Career

Student data file needed:

 e03ch05College.xlsx

You will save your file as:

 e03ch05College_LastFirst.xlsx

Choosing a College

General Business

You live in Lebanon, Kansas, which is the geographic center of the United States. You are looking for a college that will be near your home or near your relatives in Illinois. By doing a little research online at various websites, you have been able to obtain some information about the colleges in your area which you plan on using to rate the colleges and choose the best one for you.

a. Open the Excel file, **e03ch05College**. Save your file as e03ch05College_LastFirst, using your last and first name.

b. On the **SchoolData** worksheet, create named ranges for the range A13:Q54 using the names in row 13.

c. In M14, enter an IF function that tests if the state is equal to KS. Nest a VLOOKUP function that will return the Value from the COA (Cost of Attending) range from the Lists worksheet based on the resident cost of attendance if the college is in Kansas (KS). If the college is outside of Kansas, nest a VLOOKUP function that will return the value of the non-resident cost of attendance. If there is no cost of attendance in the schedule, the formula should return the word "Missing".

d. In cell N14, enter an HLOOKUP function that uses the MilesGrade range from the Lists worksheet to return the Score based on the distance of the school from your home.

e. In cell O14, enter a formula that will return 5 points if the Fresh Satis (Freshman Satisfaction) and Grad Rate (Graduation Rate) are greater than 50%. If both conditions are not met, the college will only receive 1 point.

f. In cell P14, enter a formula that will return 5 points if the Size of the school is less than 1,000 or the school meets the financial needs of its students more than 50% of the time. If neither condition is met, the school will only earn 1 point.

g. In cell Q14, enter a formula to total the number of points the school has earned (Columns M through P).

h. Fill the formulas from the range M14:Q14 to row 54. The current formatting should not be replaced.

i. In cell C1, enter a formula that will count the number of schools if the state is Kansas.

j. In cell C2, enter a formula that will count the number of schools in the state of Kansas that have a low cost of attendance. You decided that a low cost of attendance is any school that earned a 4 or 5 cost point value in Column M. (Hint: You will need to add the count for colleges in the state that earned 4 points to the count of colleges in the state that earned 5 points.)

k. In cell G1, calculate the average resident cost of attendance for colleges located in the state of Kansas.

l. In cell G2, Calculate the average cost of attendance for colleges in the state of Kansas that have a low cost of attendance. To ensure that you only calculate the average for the lowest-cost schools, you decide to only average schools that earned a 5 cost point value.

m. In cell L1, total the number of students enrolled in the state of Kansas.

n. Enter a formula in cell L2 that will determine the number of students at low-cost schools in the state of Kansas. You should consider any school that earned 4 or 5 cost points to be a low-cost school. (Hint: You will need to add the sum for colleges in the state that earned 4 points to the sum of colleges in the state that earned 5 points.)

o. In cell B8, using the criteria in row 5, enter a database function to determine the school with the maximum number of points.

p. In cell B9, use a database function to total the number of points based on the criteria.

q. In cell B10, use a database function to count the number of schools that meet the criteria in row 5.

r. In cell K9, enter a formula based on the total points you calculated that will determine the maximum number of points that were earned for all schools.

s. In cell K10, enter an INDEX and MATCH function to determine the name of the college that matches the number of points you found in cell K9. To allow you to quickly change from the name of the college to any other attribute, you should use an INDIRECT function to the name in cell J10. To test your formula, replace the word Name in cell J10 with Distance. The name of the college in K10 should be updated to how far the college is from home.

t. Update the Documentation worksheet according to your instructor's directions.

u. Save the workbook, exit Excel, and then submit your file as directed by your instructor.

Additional
Cases

Additional Workshop Cases are available on the companion website and in the instructor resources.

Microsoft Excel 2016

Chapter 6 | INTEGRATING COMPLEX FUNCTIONS INTO BUSINESS ANALYSIS

Sales & Marketing

Prepare Case

Golf Course Marketing Strategies

Barry Cheney, the manager of the Red Bluff Golf Course & Pro Shop, would like to develop marketing strategies for increasing golf course patronage. He has requested data about the golf course's activity over the past years. He needs to be able to work with the data to understand the current patronage, such as where the patrons were from, how many patrons were on each transaction, the tee time, and so forth. Exploring the data is key in determining the marketing strategy because it helps him learn about customer preferences. After analyzing the data, Barry will present his ideas to the board of directors.

Milosz Aniol/Shutterstock

Student data file needed for this chapter:

 e03ch06GolfMarketing.xlsx

You will save your file as:

 e03ch06GolfMarketing_LastFirst.xlsx

Organizing Data with Tables

While Excel can analyze large amounts of data, users can sometimes be overwhelmed by the volume of data that needs to be evaluated. Information overload can quickly set in as it becomes difficult to track the data across many rows and columns. However, using tools contained in Excel can help you understand the data more easily. For example, viewing data in tables allows you to examine the data in an organized manner. By organizing data, you can easily make decisions based on your analysis. In this section, you will work with data and information in data tables.

Work with Data and Information

Barry Cheney, the Red Bluff Golf Course & Pro Shop's manager, wants to analyze data collected over the years. Daily transactions from the past ten years exist within the Red Bluff Golf Course & Pro Shop's database, but there is too much data to import into Excel — there are over one million rows of data! Therefore, he has requested a random sample of data for his initial analysis. The database administrator was able to run a query on the database and provide a set of data to explore.

Opening the Starting File

To work with data tables, you first need to open a workbook. In this exercise, you will open the Golf Marketing workbook.

E06.00

To Save the Golf Marketing Workbook

a. Start **Excel**, click **Open Other Workbooks** in the left pane, and then double-click **This PC**. Navigate through the folder structure to the location of your student data files, and then click **e03ch06GolfMarketing**. If a Security Warning message displays, click the **Enable Editing** button.

b. Click the **File** tab, click **Save As**, and then double-click **This PC**. In the Save As dialog box, navigate to the location where you are saving your project files, and then change the file name to e03ch06GolfMarketing_LastFirst, using your last and first name, and then click **Save**.

 CONSIDER THIS | **Is Data Really That Important?**

Data is one of the most valuable assets within an organization. Without data, managers would have an extremely difficult time making decisions. Think about the daily decisions you make. For example, think about the last time you went out to lunch. You probably considered location, menu, and price — all of which is data. What else might you consider before choosing where to eat lunch? What data do you use to make other decisions throughout the day?

Work with Data and Information in Data Tables

Regardless of the career you choose, the need to work with data is common. **Raw data** is considered to be elements or raw facts — numeric or text — that may or may not have meaning or relevance. For example, data such as "blue" or "brown" is raw data without context and therefore of minimal value to anyone. **Information**, however, is data that has context, meaning, and relevance and therefore is valuable to a user. The value is determined by the user and may vary from one user to another. Thus, information is created by users when they organize, interpret, and present data in a meaningful context.

Data sets are named collections of related sets of information that are composed of separate elements — the data. If a set of data is not organized, it is difficult to determine the context and transform the data into information. The user is informed by understanding the method by which the data has been gathered and organized and the purpose of doing so. For example, the raw pieces of data "blue" and "brown" by themselves may not have any significance. Knowing that these pieces of data were collected from a set of subjects in the context of studying the eye color of men and women allows information to be created. By having information, a user can determine whether one eye color is more prevalent in males.

Excel is an excellent tool for manipulating data. It can be used to transform data into information, which can lead to good decision making. Organizing the data by using an Excel table is a good first step toward creating and evaluating information effectively.

Organizing Data Sets

In working with data, care should be taken to protect its integrity. This includes keeping a backup of the original data so if errors occur, it is possible to return to the original data and start over. Whenever possible, check your data for completeness and accuracy. Also, strive to organize data within the workbook in a meaningful and efficient manner that allows for new data to be added as needed. Finally, it is best to keep sets of data separated. Avoid using cells immediately surrounding the sets of data. This will minimize the possibility of mistakenly assuming that the content in the adjacent cells is part of the main data set. When possible, keep related data on one worksheet while reporting and analyzing the data on another worksheet.

In this exercise, you will prepare a backup copy of the data on the GoldData worksheet.

 E06.01

To Prepare a Backup Copy of Data

a. Right-click the **GolfData** worksheet, and then select **Move or Copy**. The Move or Copy dialog box opens.

b. In the Before sheet box, click **(move to end)**, click the **Create a copy** check box, and then click **OK**. A new worksheet is displayed with the name GolfData (2).

c. Right-click the **GolfData (2)** worksheet, and then select **Rename**. Type GolfDataBackup, and then press Enter to rename the worksheet.

d. Click the **GolfData** worksheet to return to the worksheet that will be modified.

e. Select rows **1** through **10**. Click the **Home** tab, and then, in the Cells group, click **Insert**. This will insert ten rows and move the data set down to row 11 starting with the field headings.

f. **Save** ⊟ the workbook.

 CONSIDER THIS | **Placement of Calculations and Analysis**

You could place the data and subsequent analysis anywhere within a spreadsheet. Why place the analysis at the top of the data set? Why not place it at the bottom of the data set? What are the advantages and disadvantages of each? How about placing the analysis on another worksheet?

Creating a Data Table in Excel

While the data may already be arranged in a spreadsheet, an Excel table establishes the data as more than a simple collection or range of raw facts presented in rows and columns. An Excel table can help to provide context to the user by organizing the data in a meaningful way. Data can be converted to an Excel table that offers additional capability, allowing the user to manipulate the data and to generate information and value for a variety of needs.

In this exercise, you will create a data table in Excel.

 E06.02

SIDE NOTE
Cell Selection
Any cell within the table range may be used when you create a table.

SIDE NOTE
Range Selection
There is no need to select the entire table range, but do not select a small subset of data. Excel may use that range for the table instead of the entire data set.

SIDE NOTE
Creating Tables
A table can also be created on the Home tab. Select the range. In the Styles group, click the Format as Table button, and then select a table style.

To Create a Data Table in Excel

a. On the GolfData worksheet, click cell **A12**.

b. Click the **Insert** tab, and then, in the Tables group, click **Table**. The Create Table dialog box opens.

c. In the **Where is the data** for your table box, verify that the range **$A$11:$H$211** is selected, and then verify that the **My table has headers** check box is checked.

> **Troubleshooting**
> If Excel fails to guess the correct range selection, you can either adjust the range by typing in the correct range or drag to select the correct range.

d. Click **OK**, and then click cell **A12**. An Excel table will be created with banded coloring. Additionally, the Table Tools Design contextual tab will appear, containing all the options available for working with a table.

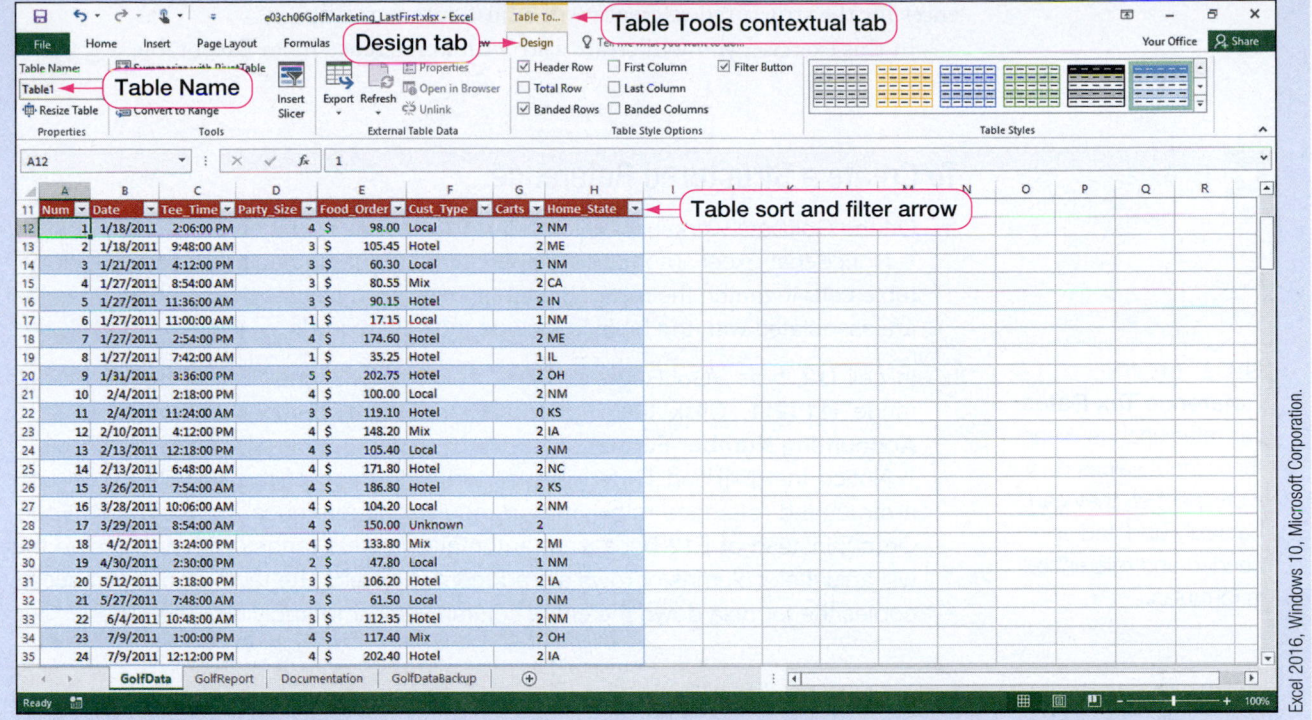

Figure 1 Excel data table

Excel 2016, Windows 10, Microsoft Corporation.

SIDE NOTE

Table Names

Because of the way that Excel is configured, table names cannot include spaces.

SIDE NOTE

Alternate Method

To select the table, you can also click any cell in the table and then press Ctrl + A.

SIDE NOTE

Changing Table Styles

Access the Style gallery to change the look of the table to one of the variety of styles that offer different color schemes.

---

e. Click the **Table Tools Design** tab if necessary. In the Properties group, click in the **Table Name** box. Replace **Table1** with GolfData, and then press Enter. This will name the table GolfData and create a named range for the entire data set, excluding the field headings.

f. Select cells **A11:H211** if necessary. Click the **Formulas** tab, and then, in the Defined Names group, click **Create from Selection**. Verify that the **Top row** check box is selected, click the check box next to **Right column** to deselect it if necessary, and then click **OK**. The named ranges will be used in your formulas.

g. On the **Formulas** tab, in the Defined Names group, click **Name Manager**. In the Name Manager dialog box, click the **GolfData** named range in the list if necessary, and then notice at the bottom of the dialog box that the Refers to range is displayed as =GolfData!$A$12:$H$211.

   The tag beside the GolfData range is a small table, indicating that it is associated with the table. The option to delete this range is not available, since it is associated with the Excel table. You also can see all the other named ranges that you created.

h. Click **Close**.

i. **Save** the workbook.

Creating a Structured Reference in a Table

The Excel table has both flexibility and scalability. New columns and rows can be added, and the table will extend to include them automatically. Formatting and formula references automatically adjust as well. You can use a structured reference in an Excel table to make the formula easier to understand. A **structured reference** is a formula that refers to table columns by names that were generated when the table was created. Structured references can be useful because table data ranges may change. If they do, the cell references for the structured reference will adjust automatically.

In this exercise, you will create a structured reference in an Excel table.

 E06.03

To Create a Structured Reference

a. On the GolfData worksheet, click cell **I11**, type **Tax**, and then press Enter.

Notice that Excel automatically applied the formatting color to the newly added table cells to match the rest of the table. Excel also adjusts the named ranges that are associated with the table to include the new records.

SIDE NOTE
Reference Tax Rates
Tax rates change. Keep these input values on a worksheet so they can be easily updated as needed and referenced in formulas.

b. In cell **I12**, type **=GolfReport!$B$3***, click cell **E12**, and then press Enter. Select range **I11:I211**. Click the **Home** tab, and then, in the Number group, click **Accounting Number Format**.

Notice that [@[Food_Order]] is inserted at the end of the formula. Excel uses a structured reference rather than a regular cell reference. It inserted [@[Food_Order]] instead of E12 because it automatically sets ranges within the table that will adjust as columns or rows are added or deleted. The table also automatically copies the formula down the entire column, similar to applying Auto Fill.

Troubleshooting

If your table did not automatically update, Excel may be configured to not update data tables automatically. Click the Formulas tab, and in the Calculation group, click the Calculation Options arrow, and then select Automatic.

c. Scroll down until cell A212 is visible. Notice that the field headings in row 11 replace the column lettering when you scroll.

d. Click cell **A212** to add a new record to the data.

The field headings disappear and are replaced with column letters when you click in cell A212 because this cell is outside the table range. However, the field headings reappear after you type the data for the first cell in the new row.

e. Using the following data, add a new record in row 212, pressing Tab after each entry. Notice that the banded color formatting appears as soon as data is initially entered and that the Tax field is copied down automatically because it is a calculation.

Field	Data
Num	201
Date	12/31/2017
Tee_Time	8:30 AM
Party_Size	4
Food_Order	104.80
Cust_Type	Hotel
Carts	2
Home_State	WI

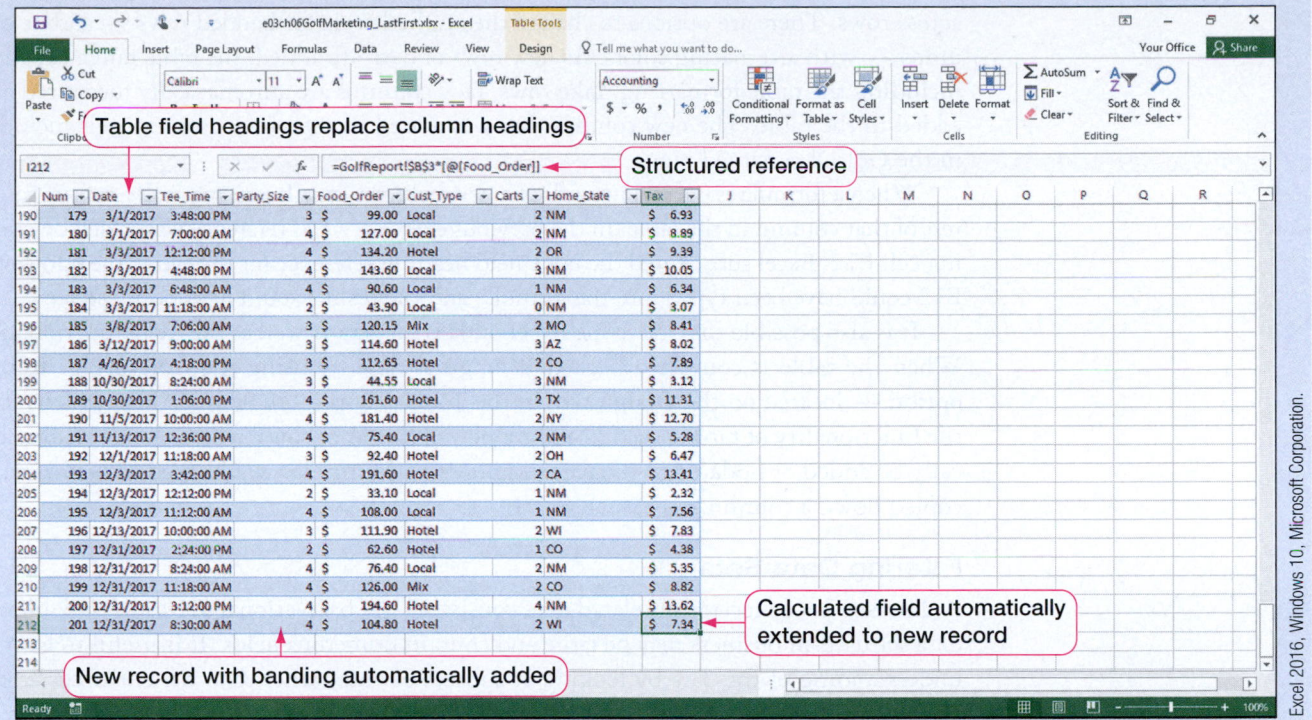

Figure 2 Adding a new record to an Excel table

f. Click the **Formulas** tab, and then, in the Defined Names group, click **Name Manager**. The Name Manager dialog box opens. In the list, click the **GolfData** named range, and then notice that the range is now $A$12:$I$212. The range has changed to include the newly created column and row.

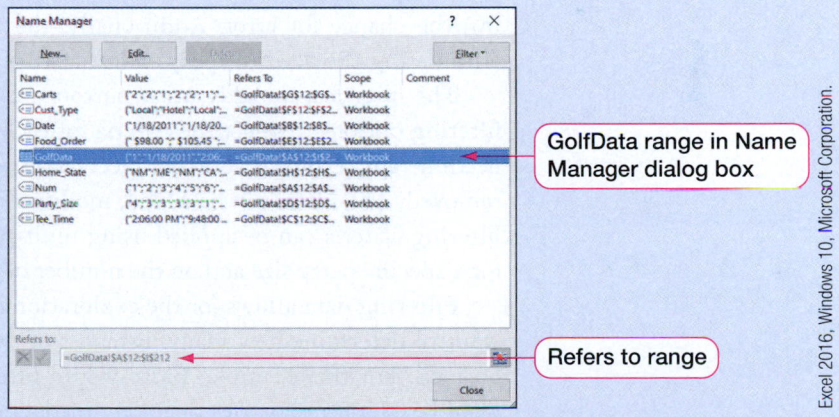

Figure 3 Name Manager dialog box with GolfData named range selected

g. Click **Close**. Press Ctrl + Home to return to cell A1.

h. **Save** 🖫 the workbook.

CHAPTER 6

A table defaults to a table style that has banded rows, making it easier to read data across rows. There are options to change the applied style for banded rows — and/or columns — with alternating colors. As new rows of data are added, the table range expands, including the table formatting. Like rows, new columns are automatically formatted and added to the table. The new column that was added in the previous exercise is included in the GolfData named range.

When a formula is created in a cell of a new column, it will automatically copy it to the rest of that column in the table. In the previous exercise, a cell reference was added by clicking cell E12. Excel substituted the table field heading reference for the cell name. However, E12 could have been typed into the formula, and the result would have been the same.

It is also possible to remove the Excel table structure as well as the extra functionality. When the table is converted back to a range of data by using the **Convert to Range** option — located on the Design tab, in the Tools group — the formatting remains, but the functionality of tables, such as adding new columns or rows, will no longer automatically be added or updated to the named ranges, and formulas would need to be manually copied down a column.

Filtering Data Sets

A **data set** is a collection of related data consisting of observational units and variables. A data set used in business may be large and contain numerous fields. It is useful to gain an understanding of the data by looking at subsets of data rather than the entire set at one time. Filtering data sets is useful and makes it possible to view specific data. Filtering is also useful for selecting and copying a subset of data to move to a new worksheet. **Filtering** is a process of hiding records that do not meet specified criteria in a data set. Filtering enables a user to examine and analyze, if desired, a subset of records.

Filters can be established either on a range of data or on an Excel table. For a range of data, a filter can be set by clicking the Filter button in the Sort & Filter group on the Data tab. When applying a filter to a data range, be sure the active cell is within the range to help ensure that the correct data range is selected. However, if an Excel table has been created, the range will be established on the basis of the initial creation process, decreasing the chance for error. Additionally, the filter is a standard part of the Excel table, eliminating the need to apply a filter feature to the data set.

The filter feature adds arrow buttons for each field heading, which offer menus with filtering options to select the criteria for each field. By selecting criteria for a certain field heading, any records that do not meet the criteria will be hidden until the filter criterion is removed. The filters can be added, modified, and cleared as needed. Additionally, various filtering criteria can be applied using multiple fields. Thus, it would be possible to filter for a specific party size and on the number of golf carts used within the GolfData table.

Filtering data allows for the exploration of the data. For example, Barry Cheney may want to determine how many instances of two-person golf parties spend more than $75 on food. For this example, Barry would filter for parties containing two people, which would exclude any parties that contained a number other than two. Then the data would be explored further by filtering the records on the basis of the total each two-person party spent on food. The two-person golf parties that spent more than $75 would then be displayed and available for easy analysis.

In this exercise, you will filter data in a table.

 ### To Filter Data in a Data Table

a. On the GolfData worksheet, click the **Party_Size** filter arrow ⏷ , and then click **(Select All)** to deselect it. Click the **2** check box.

b. Click **OK**. All the other options will be hidden or filtered, showing only the records that meet the checked criteria.

c. Click the **Food_Order** filter arrow ▾, point to **Number Filters**, and then select **Greater Than**.

d. In the Custom AutoFilter dialog box, click in the box on the top right side of the dialog box. Type **75**, and then click **OK**.

   Notice the Filter icon is displayed on the filter button as a visual cue that the field heading has a filter applied. Examine the row numbers and notice the visible row numbers start at 81 and jump to 88, 108, 110, and 159. The other rows of data are still there but are hidden. The data still exists, and it can be redisplayed.

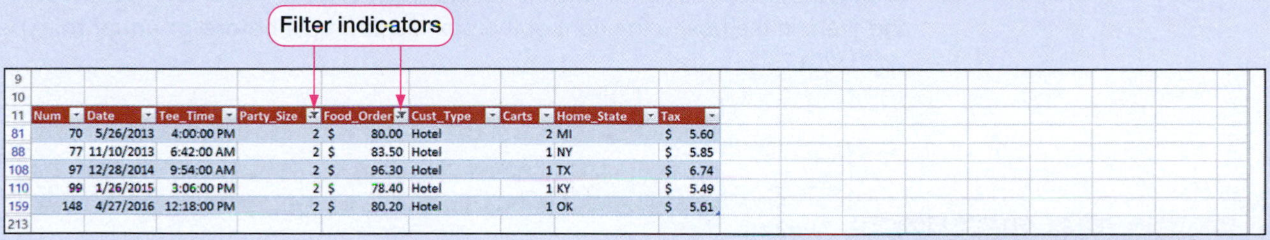

Filter indicators

	Num	Date	Tee_Time	Party_Size	Food_Order	Cust_Type	Carts	Home_State	Tax
9									
10									
11									
81	70	5/26/2013	4:00:00 PM	2	$ 80.00	Hotel	2	MI	$ 5.60
88	77	11/10/2013	6:42:00 AM	2	$ 83.50	Hotel	1	NY	$ 5.85
108	97	12/28/2014	9:54:00 AM	2	$ 96.30	Hotel	1	TX	$ 6.74
110	99	1/26/2015	3:06:00 PM	2	$ 78.40	Hotel	1	KY	$ 5.49
159	148	4/27/2016	12:18:00 PM	2	$ 80.20	Hotel	1	OK	$ 5.61
213									

Figure 4 Filtered data

Excel 2016, Windows 10, Microsoft Corporation.

e. **Save** 💾 the workbook.

Filtering hides the rows of data that do not fit the selected criteria. In this case, both criteria must be true for the rows to be displayed. It is easy to remove, or clear, filters and apply other filters. The **standard filter** displays the values in the field that can be toggled on and off through the use of check boxes. If the check boxes are not able to provide a filter for the desired criteria, there are options above the check boxes that are specific for the type of data contained in the field. For example, the options available for fields with numeric values will differ from the options available if the field data contains date or text values.

REAL WORLD ADVICE   Developing Questions for Data Analysis

It is vital to have an understanding of the company data so relevant questions can be explored. The managers could find the average size of the golf parties, but this does not provide much value. However, it may be useful to know whether larger groups tend to order more food per person than smaller groups do. Based on the answer, a marketing strategy could be developed and implemented. Always consider the value of the question.

Clearing and Changing Filters

There are times when you have several filters to apply or the current filter is not providing the output needed to answer your question. Then clearing and changing the filters becomes an important task.

In this exercise, you will clear and change filters on a worksheet.

E06.05

To Clear and Change Filters

a. On the GolfData worksheet, in cell D11, click the **Party_Size** filter arrow, and then select **Clear Filter From "Party_Size"**.

b. Click the **Date** filter arrow in cell B11. Notice that it has a listing of years with plus signs. Click the **plus sign** beside 2017. It will expand to months, and if needed, individual days could be shown and selected.

c. Point to Date Filters and notice the list of options are specific for dates. Select **Between** to display the Custom AutoFilter dialog box.

d. Click in the box to the right of the box displaying **is after or equal to**, type **1/1/2017**, and then, in the box to the right of the box displaying **is before or equal to**, type **12/31/2017**.

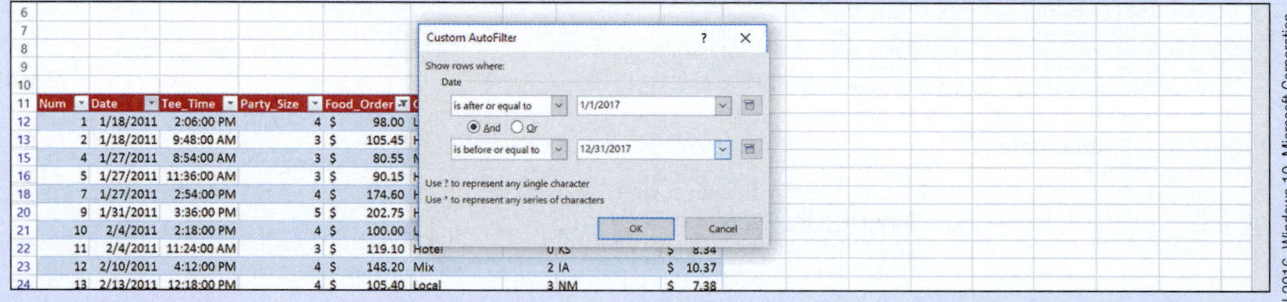

Figure 5 Custom AutoFilter dialog box

e. Click **OK**. The results will display food orders over $75 that occurred in 2017.

f. In cell B11, point to the Date filter arrow to display a ScreenTip indicating the details of the filter. The filter arrow button will also have a smaller triangle next to a filter icon, which indicates that the field has a filter applied.

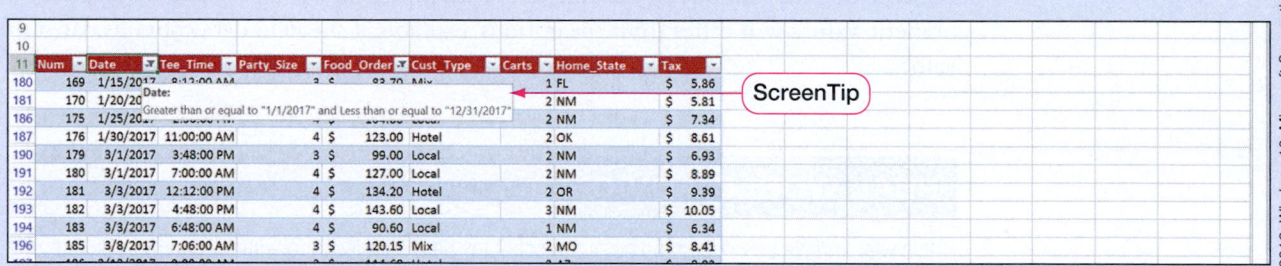

Figure 6 Display filter information

g. Select the filtered range **A11:I212**, and then press Ctrl + C.

h. Click **New Sheet**. This will create a new worksheet with cell A1 as the active cell. Press Ctrl + V. The subset of data will be pasted into the new worksheet. Press Esc.

Having data filtered can be useful, especially when there is a complete data set and someone else needs to examine some, but not all, of the data. The filtered data can be copied and pasted to a new worksheet so it can be analyzed separately.

i. Right-click the **Sheet2** worksheet, and then select **Rename**. Type **2017Data**, and then press Enter. Verify columns A:I are selected. Click the **Home** tab if necessary, and then, in the Cells group, click **Format**. Select **AutoFit Column Width** so the columns are wide enough to view all the data. Press Ctrl + Home.

j. **Save** the workbook.

Using the Advanced Filter Feature

While the filtering feature is great for ad hoc and spur-of-the-moment exploration of data, the filtering mechanism makes it difficult to easily see what filters exist. A user would need to hover over or click the displayed filter arrows to evaluate which filters are applied. With the **Advanced Filter** feature, the filtering criteria are set up on the spreadsheet. The filtering criteria must be set up in a specific format. A top row with field headings that are identical to the data set must be established. Then criteria can be set up in one or more cells below the field names. Advanced filtering will hide records in the same manner as the filters on the data set, but only records matching the criteria will be displayed.

Once the criteria area has been set up, the Advanced Filter can be applied. Criteria entered on one row creates an And filter criteria. Records that meet all the specified criteria in a criterion row will be displayed. Criteria entered on separate rows creates an Or filter criterion. Records that meet the criteria on either row in a criteria range will be displayed.

In this exercise, you will create an advanced filter.

 E06.06

To Create an Advanced Filter

a. Click the **GolfData** worksheet. Select range **A11:I11**, press Ctrl + C to copy the range, select cell **A1**, and then press Ctrl + V to paste the range. Press Esc.

b. Click cell **A11**. Click the **Data** tab, and then, in the Sort & Filter group, click **Clear** to clear all current filters that have been applied to the data set.

c. Click cell **F2**, type Hotel, and then press Ctrl + Enter.

   The range B1:I2 will be the data criteria area. The first row contains the field names that could potentially be used for setting constraints or criteria. The second row and below could be used for the criteria for particular fields. In this case, there is only one criterion set: the customer type of Hotel. With this arrangement, the advanced filter is ready to be created and will find the records that meet the criterion entered in the data criteria area.

d. Click cell **A11**. On the Data tab, in the Sort & Filter group, click **Advanced** to display the Advanced Filter dialog box.

e. Verify the range $A$11:$I$212 appears in the List range box.

f. Click in the **Criteria** range box, click the **Collapse Dialog** button 🔲, and then select **A1:I2**. Click the **Expand Dialog** button 🔲. Verify **Filter the list, in-place** is selected.

SIDE NOTE

Alternate Method

To select the List range, you can also select the range A11:I212. The List range will change to display GolfData[#All], recognizing the data range of the table.

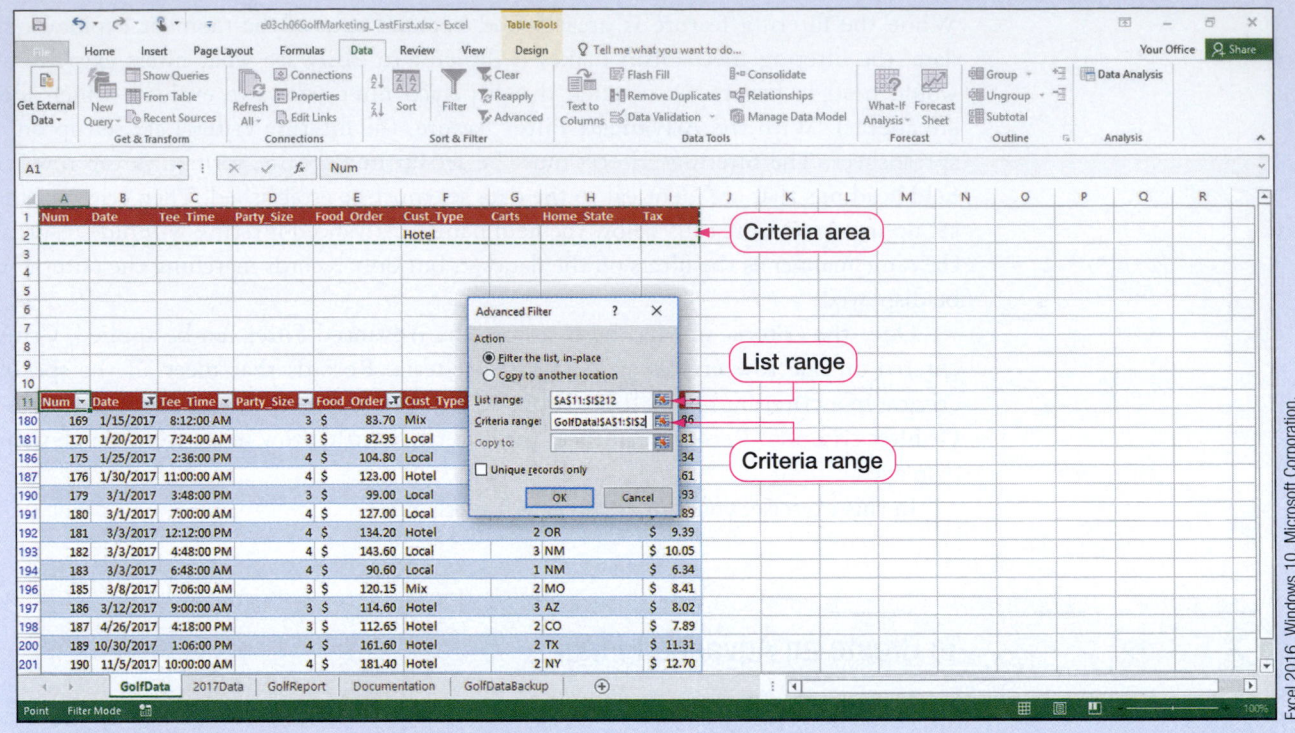

Figure 7 Advanced filter with Hotel Customer Type

g. Click **OK**. The data in the table is filtered to show only the Hotel Cust_Type transactions.

It is possible to add additional criteria. All criteria have to be met for the record to be shown. If only Hotel customers from Texas with food orders over $100 are to be shown, all three of those constraints must be true for the record to be displayed. The three constraints are therefore joined with an AND clause. If Cust_Type equals Hotel AND Home_State equals TX AND Food_Order is greater than $100, the record will be displayed. Because all three constraints are listed on one row, Excel will know to have all three arguments set to true for the record to be included in the results.

h. Click cell **E2**, type **>100**, and then press ⟨Tab⟩ three times. In cell **H2**, type **TX**, and then press ⟨Tab⟩.

i. On the Data tab, in the Sort & Filter group, click **Advanced**. Verify that the range in the List range box is $A$11:$I$212 and the range in the Criteria range box is $A$1:$I$2. Click **OK**.

The settings in the Advanced Filter will remain from the previous time, so the List range and Criteria range are the same as the first time the advanced filter was run. The data set should adjust to show Hotel customers from Texas with food orders greater than $100.

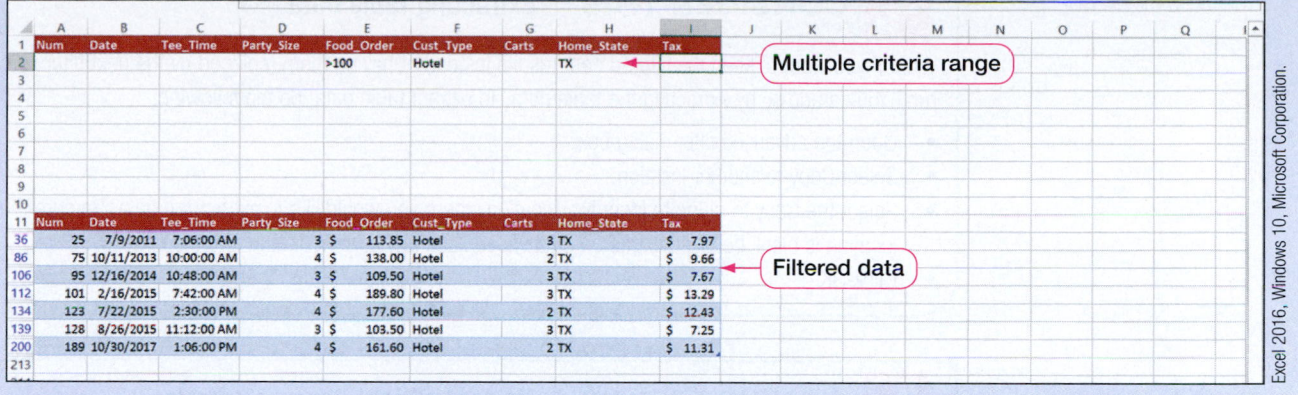

Figure 8 Filtered data using multiple criteria

To add additional criteria, add each criterion to the criteria range. For example, to also include all records that have a Party_Size of 1 with customer type of Local, a second row would be used. Criteria on an individual row must all be true, as has been mentioned. Each row of criteria acts as an OR, joining the two sets of filtering criteria. Records that meet either the first row of criteria or the second row of criteria will be displayed.

SIDE NOTE

Empty Rows of Criteria

If the criteria range for the Advanced Filter includes a row with no criteria, the entire record set will be returned because nothing is constraining the records.

j. Click cell **D3**, type **1**, and then press Tab twice. In **F3**, type **Local**, and then press Tab.

k. On the Data tab, in the Sort & Filter group, click **Advanced**. Click to place your insertion point at the end of the text in the Criteria range box, press Bksp to delete the 2, and then type **3**, so the Criteria range displays $A$1:$I$3. Click **OK**.

When adding a second row of criteria as shown in Figure 9, the criteria in the Advanced Filter must also be adjusted. The same would apply if the additional row of criteria were removed from the Advanced Filter. The results will show records for food orders greater than $100 from Texas Hotel customers and all parties of one for Local customers. The constraints on one row will not affect the constraints on another row. Thus, there are parties of one that did not spend more than $100.

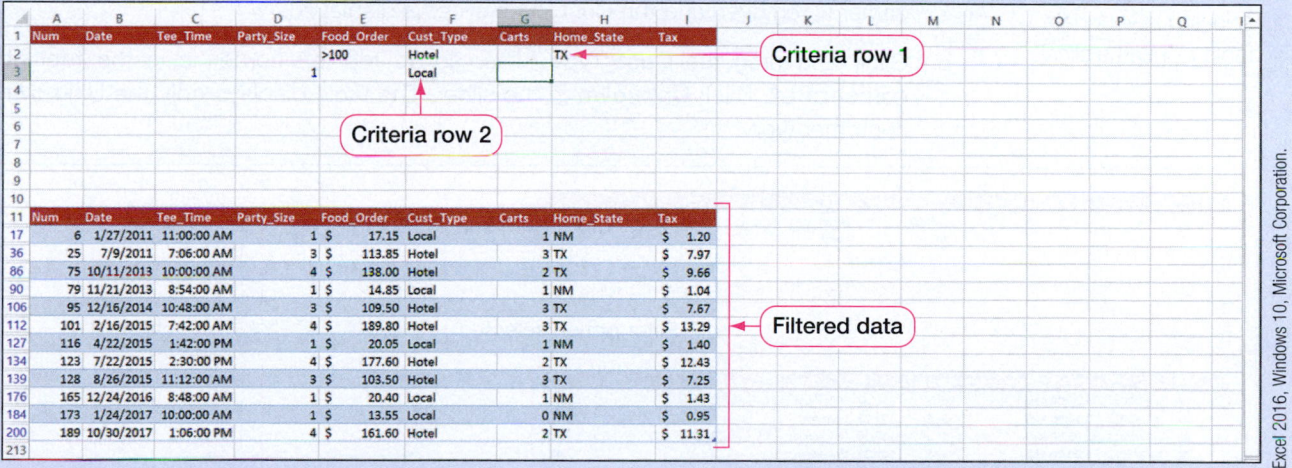

Figure 9 Filtered data using multiple criteria

l. **Save** 💾 the workbook.

What if you want to keep the filtered data results instead of having them replaced by the next filter you run? You can do so by extracting the table data. To extract table data, do the following.

- Open the advanced filter dialog box.
- Select Copy to another location.
- Select the Copy to range to identify a location where you would like to extract the data. Be sure the location is blank because extracted data will replace any current data in a range of cells.
- Click OK.

What will happen if you forget to adjust the criteria range? What will happen if you do not extend the range to include a new row of criteria? What will happen if you delete a row of criteria but leave that row in your criteria range? Do you think you will get the same filter results? How would it affect your decision making?

Using Slicers to Filter Data

A **slicer** is a window that is used for quickly filtering data in an Excel table, PivotTable, or data table. Also, it is a visual control that allows you to quickly and easily filter your data in an interactive way to replace filter icons in PivotCharts or data tables. One of the benefits to using slicers is that they are easy to generate and use. Additionally, slicers indicate the current filter, so you will know exactly what data you are viewing.

In this exercise, you will create a filter for data using a Slicer.

 **E06.07**

To Create a Filter Using a Slicer

SIDE NOTE
Inserting Slicers
You must have a cell selected in your data table to insert a slicer.

a. On the GolfData worksheet, click cell **A17**. Click the **Insert** tab, and then, in the Filters group, click **Slicer**. The Insert Slicers dialog box opens.

b. Click the **Cust_Type** check box, and then click **OK**. Notice the filter you applied earlier is removed and the Cust_Type slicer is displayed.

c. Click and drag the **Cust_Type** slicer so its top left corner is in the top left corner of **L2**. Click **Unknown** in the slicer. The table displays only the Unknown customer type.

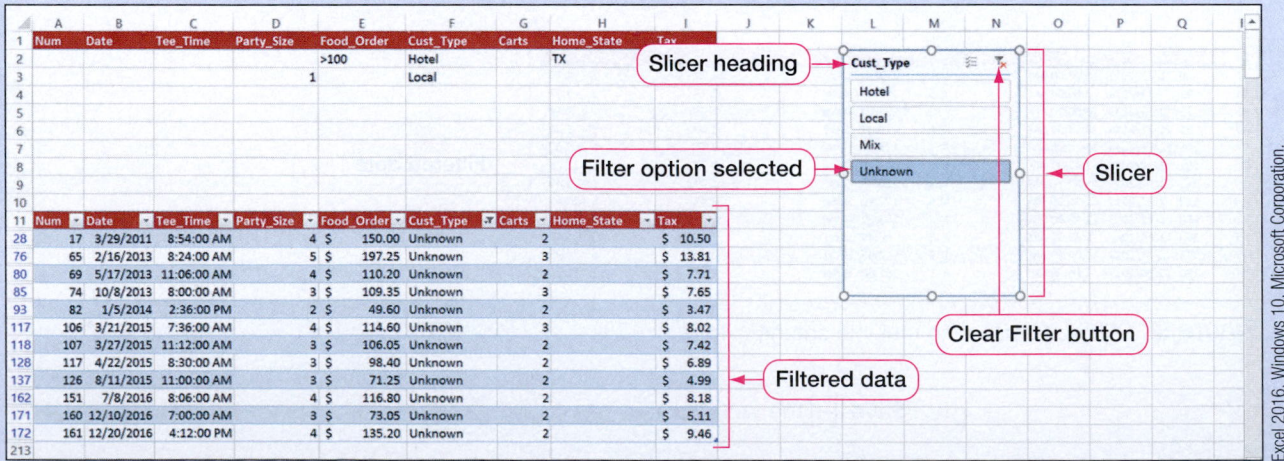

Figure 10 Filter data using a slicer

d. Press Ctrl, and then click **Local** in the slicer. Notice once you release Ctrl, the table displays both the Unknown and Local customer types.

e. Click **Clear Filter** in the top right corner of the slicer to remove the filter.

f. Drag the **bottom edge** of the Cust_Type slicer to adjust the height so that the extra white space is no longer visible. Do not drag it so far that you see a scroll bar on the right side.

g. Click cell **H12**. Click the **Insert** tab, and then, in the Filters group, click **Slicer**. Click the **Home_State** check box, and then click **OK**. The Home_State slicer is displayed.

h. Drag the **Home_State** slicer so its top left corner is in the top left corner of **L11**. Click **Unknown** in the Cust_Type slicer. The table displays only the Unknown customer type.

i. Right-click the **Home_State** slicer, and then select **Slicer Settings**. The Slicer Settings dialog box opens.

j. Under the Header section, in the Caption box, replace **Home_State** with **Home State**, and then click **OK**.

k. Right-click the **Home State** slicer, and then select **Size and Properties**. The Format Slicer pane opens.

l. Click the **Position and Layout** arrow, and then, under Layout, change the number of columns to **3**, and then press Enter.

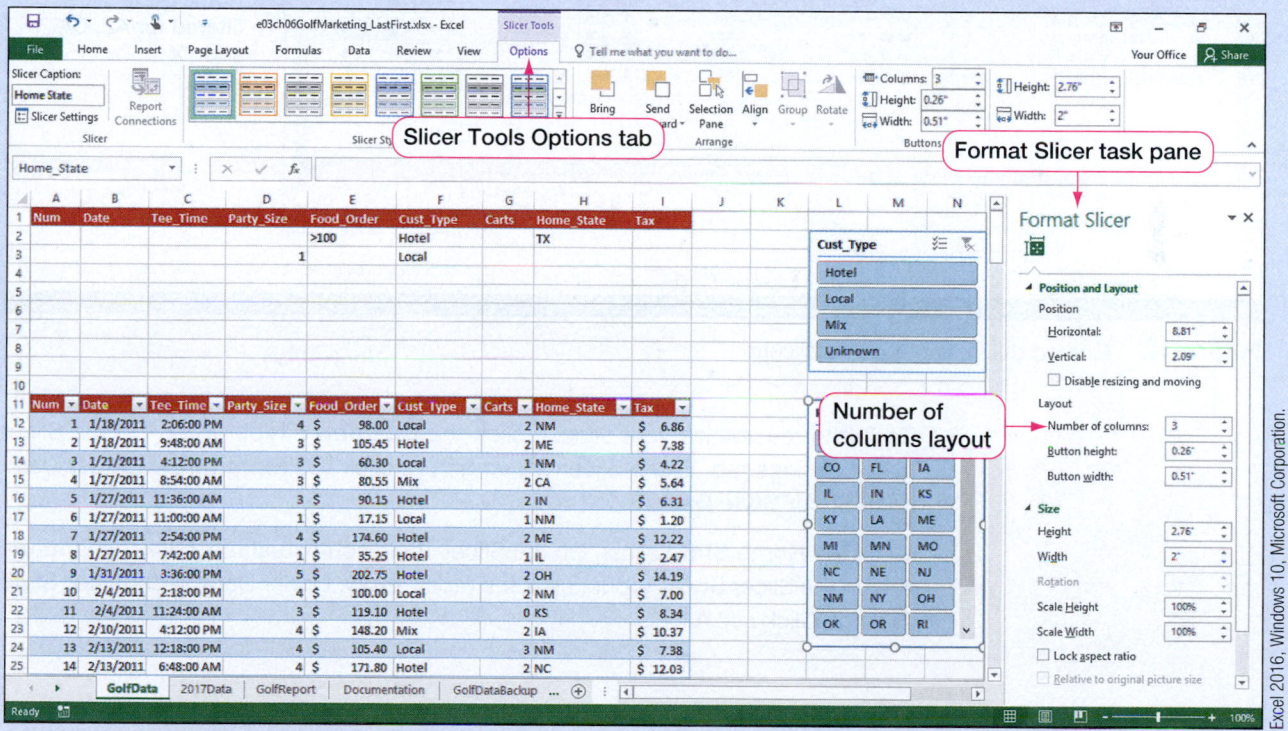

Figure 11 Filter data using a slicer

m. **Close** ☒ the Format Slicer pane. Notice that the states are much easier to see.

n. Right-click the **Cust_Type** slicer, and then select **Slicer Settings**. The Slicer Settings dialog box opens.

o. Under the Header section, in the Caption box, replace **Cust_Type** with Customer Type, and then click **OK**.

p. In the Customer Type slicer, click **Mix**. Notice that the Home State slicer automatically filters the states where the Mix customer type live.

q. In the Home State slicer, click **AZ**. Press Ctrl, click **CA**, and then click **TX**. You may need to scroll up to find the states.

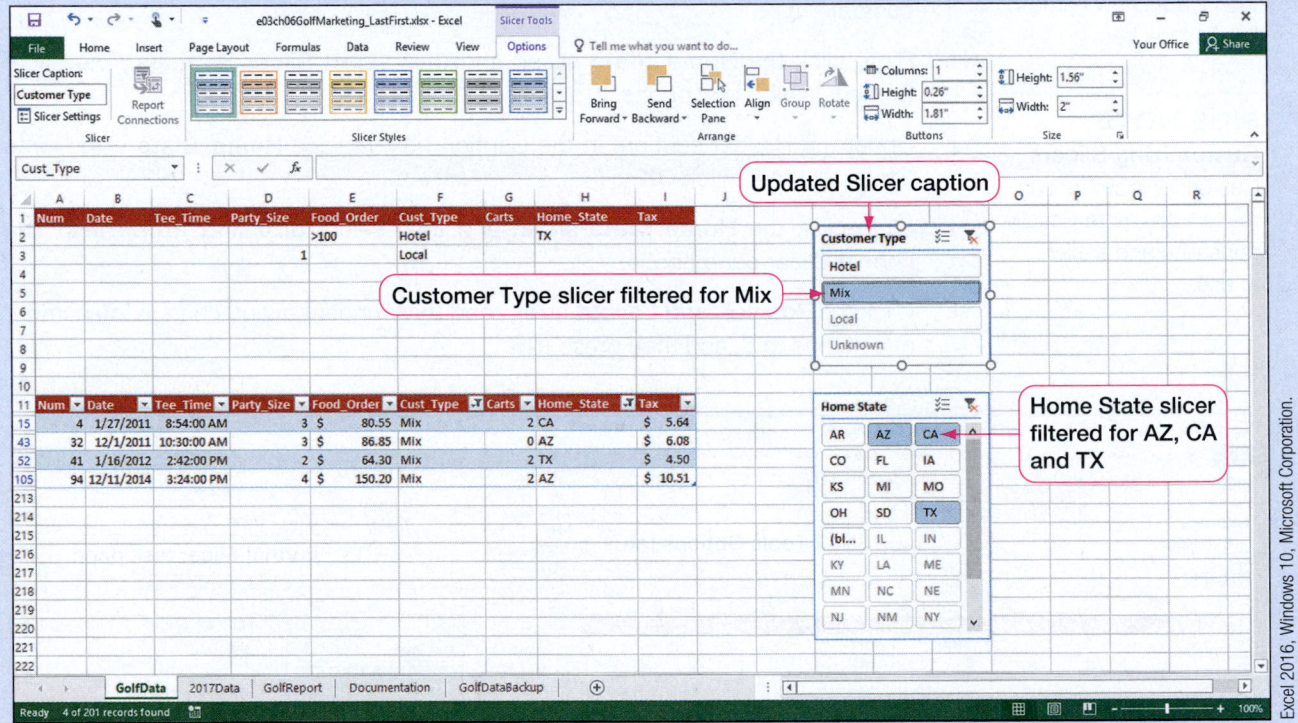

Figure 12 Filtered data using multiple slicers

r. To further customize your slicers, click the **Customer Type** slicer. On the Slicer Tools Options tab, in the Slicer Styles group, click the **More** arrow. Under Dark, click **Slicer Style Dark 2**.

s. Click the **Home State** slicer. On the Slicer Tools contextual tab, click the **Options** tab. In the Slicer Styles group, click the **More** arrow. Under Dark, click **Slicer Style Dark 2**. Click cell **A1**.

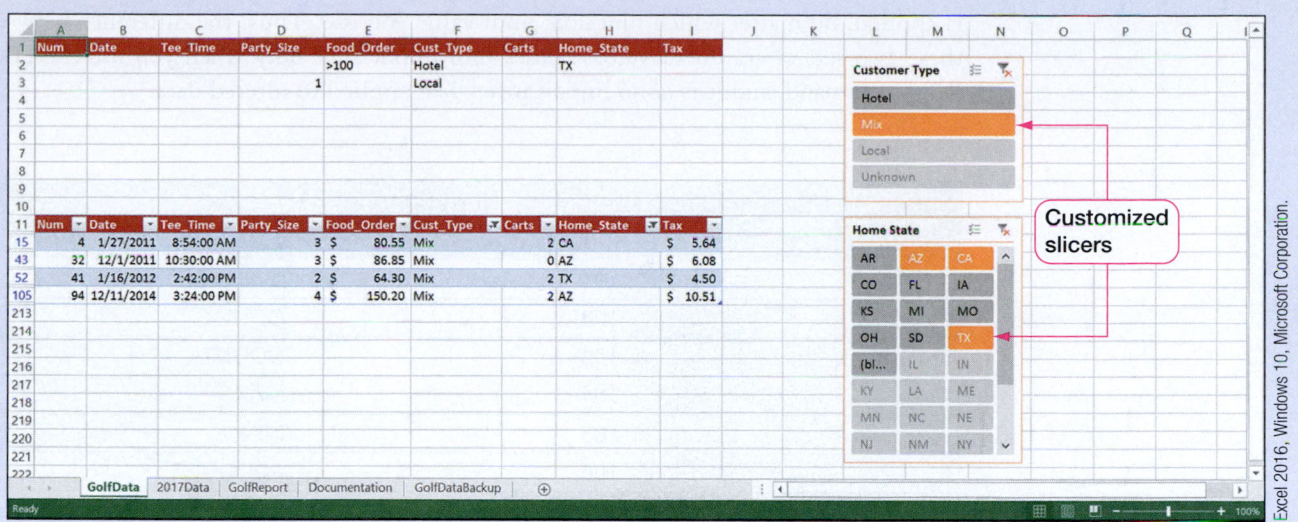

Figure 13 Customized slicers

> **t.** **Save** 🖫 the workbook.

Use the SUBTOTAL Function and Filters in Data Tables

To **aggregate** data means to consolidate or summarize the data, similar to the way an executive summary consolidates and summarizes a project or a report. Functions such as SUM or AVERAGE aggregate an entire set of data. However, when a set of data is filtered to show a subset of the entire data set, it would be useful to be able to aggregate the subset of data instead of the entire set of data. This is impossible to conduct with standard functions, as they will run calculations on the data regardless of whether the records — or rows — are hidden or displayed. Thus, the applied data filters have no impact on standard functions.

While the subset of data could be copied to another worksheet and then aggregated, it would be an inefficient method of analyzing data. By copying the subset of data, it duplicates the data and complicates the analysis. It would be more efficient to have the flexibility of adjusting the filter and having the aggregation of the subset of data also adjust. It is possible to accomplish this by using the SUBTOTAL function.

The **SUBTOTAL function** is specific to the filtering mechanism and will run calculations only on the data that is in the subset when a filter is applied; it can return 11 different values. Any records that are in hidden rows will not be used in the calculation of the SUBTOTAL function. The SUBTOTAL function has two arguments. The first argument requires a function number to indicate which aggregate function to apply, such as SUM, AVERAGE, or COUNT. The second argument is one or more ranges to be aggregated. The syntax of the SUBTOTAL function is as follows

=SUBTOTAL(function_num, ref1, [ref2],…)

The function_num argument informs Excel which function to use on the subset of records. When you are typing this function, a list will appear to help if you are not familiar with which argument number to use. There are two sets of function numbers, 1–11 and 101–111, as shown in Table 1. The first set, 1–11, will return result values for rows that are visible and rows that have been hidden by using the Hide Rows command. The second set, 101–111, will ignore rows that have been formatted to be hidden, again by using the Hide Rows command; thus, it returns a value of visible rows only.

Keep in mind that the SUBTOTAL function ignores any rows not included when a filter is applied, no matter which function_num value you use. Thus, the difference between these two sets of argument values comes into importance only when you use the Hide Rows command, and it is of no importance when applied to filtered data.

Function_Num (includes hidden values)	Function_Num (ignores hidden values)	Function
1	101	AVERAGE
2	102	COUNT
3	103	COUNTA
4	104	MAX
5	105	MIN
6	106	PRODUCT
7	107	STDEV.S
8	108	STDEV.P
9	109	SUM
10	110	VAR.S
11	111	VAR.P

Table 1 Subtotal function list

 CONSIDER THIS | **Selecting a Function Number from the List**

The purpose of analyzing data is to aid in decision making. Perhaps you wanted to use all the data, including the hidden rows. What would happen if you chose a function number — function_num — that does not include hidden values? How would it affect your decision making?

REAL WORLD ADVICE | **Hiding Rows and Filtering**

It is unusual to use the Hide Rows feature when filtering, and this is not a recommended practice. Any time filters are removed, any hidden rows will become unhidden. It becomes complicated to try to work with both filtering data and hiding rows. All records should be visible when you are filtering. Any records that should not be used in the SUBTOTAL calculations should be excluded by using the filtering process.

Summarizing a Data Set

Filters can provide answers to many questions, but they may not give you all the results you need to make sound decisions. Functions such as SUBTOTAL, AVERAGE, and AVERAGEIF functions can help to summarize the data in the data set.

In this exercise, you will summarize a data set using the SUBTOTAL, AVERAGE, and AVERAGEIF functions.

To Summarize a Data Set

a. On the GolfData worksheet, click cell **A5**, type Average, and then press Enter. In cell **B6**, type Overall, and then press Enter. In cell **B7**, type Filtered, and then press Enter.

b. In cell **B8**, type By State, and then press Enter. In cell **B9**, type Customer Type, and then press Enter.

c. Click cell **D8**, type NM, and then press Enter. In cell **D9**, type Local. Click cell **E8**, type Number of Records, and then press Enter. In cell **E9**, type Sum of Food Order, and then press Enter.

d. Select columns **B:E**, and then double-click the border margin between column B and column C to automatically fit the text in columns B through E.

e. Select range **A5:B9**, press and hold Ctrl, and then select range **E8:E9**. Press Ctrl, and then press B to bold the text.

f. Click cell **C6** type =AVERAGE(Food_Order), and then press Enter.
   The overall average uses the named range and will calculate the average using every record. The AVERAGE function uses all data even if it is hidden.

g. In cell **C7** type =SUBTOTAL(. Notice that a listing for the function number will appear with the available choices for the function that will be used on the filtered records.

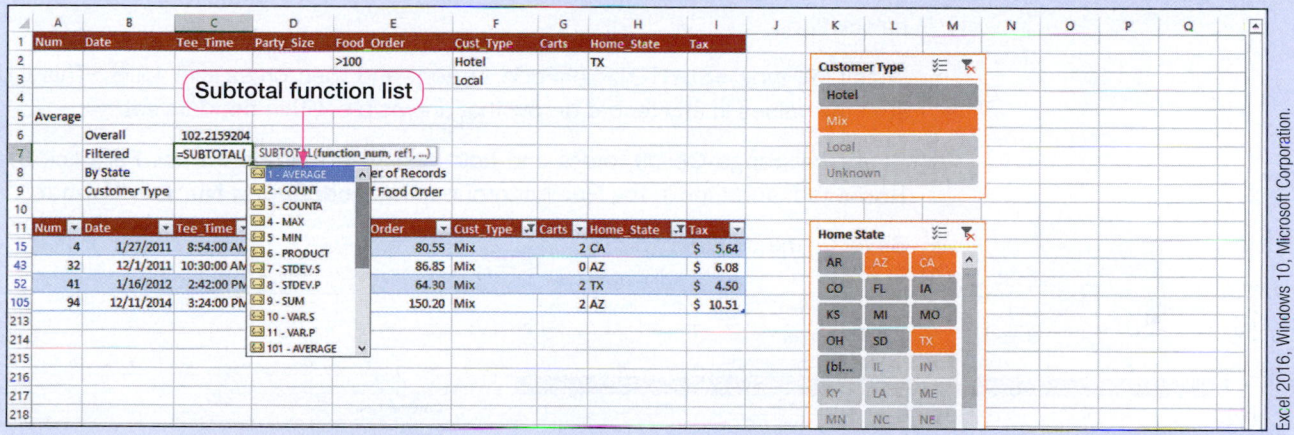

Figure 14 Subtotal function

> **Troubleshooting**
> If the SUBTOTAL function ScreenTip covers the 1 - Average selection, click the border of the ScreenTip and drag it to the left or to the right away from the listing.

h. Double-click **1 - AVERAGE** from the list.

i. Type ,Food_Order), and then press Enter. The SUBTOTAL function ignores any data that is hidden because of the filter you previously applied.

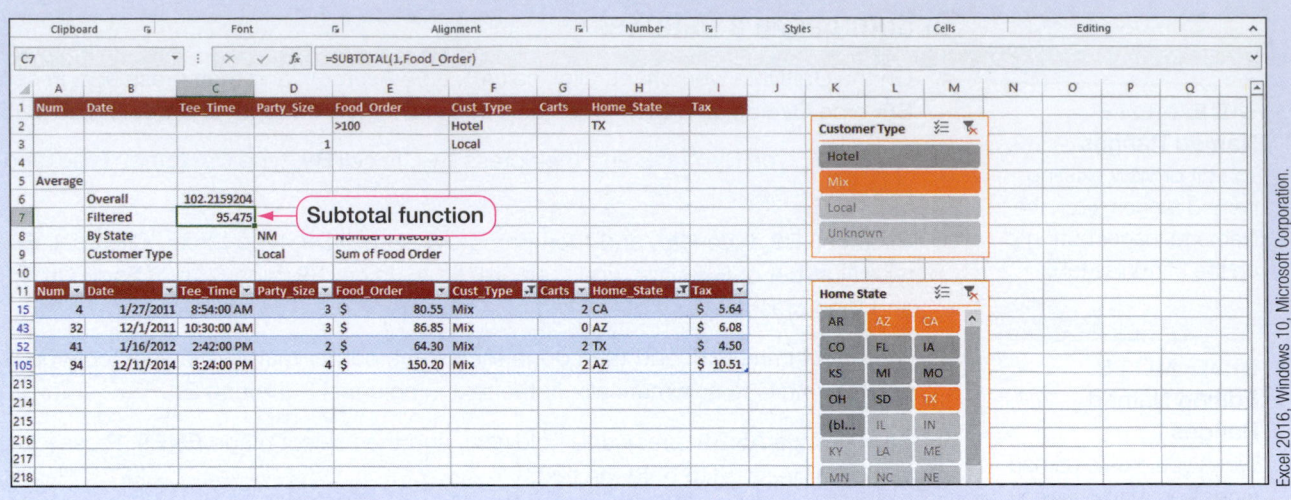

Figure 15 Subtotal function result

j. In cell **C8**, type **=AVERAGEIF(Home_State,D8,Food_Order)**, and then press Enter. The AVERAGEIF function will include hidden records, just like the AVERAGE function.

k. In cell **C9**, type **=AVERAGEIF(Cust_Type,D9,Food_Order)**, and then press Enter.

l. Click cell **F8**, type **=SUBTOTAL(2,Num)**, and then press Enter. This will count the number of records that are visible and would be included in any subtotal calculation.

m. In cell **F9**, type **=SUBTOTAL(9,Food_Order)**, and then press Ctrl + Enter. This will sum the values in any record or row that are visible within the data set.

n. Select cell range **C6:C9**, press and hold Ctrl, and then select cell **F9**. Click the **Home** tab, and then in the Number group, click **Accounting Number Format**.

o. **Save** 💾 the workbook.

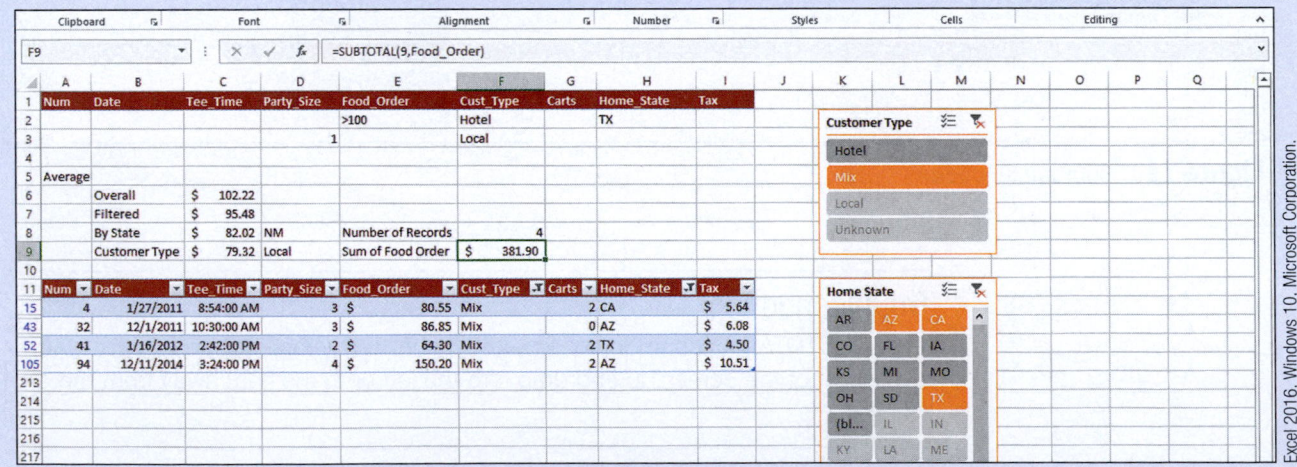

Figure 16 Subtotal function

p. If you need to take a break before finishing this chapter, now is a good time.

Because you have entered several different formulas, it is now possible to see the variance within the different averages that have been calculated. Notice that only the SUBTOTAL function ignores hidden records and uses only visible filtered records to calculate the average. The other functions provide results based on all the records, without regard to visible and hidden records.

Organizing and Analyzing with PivotTables and PivotCharts

It is possible to accomplish a great deal through the use of tables and filters — the SUBTOTAL function and other aggregate functions such as SUMIF or AVERAGEIF. However, what if there is a need to really dig deep and explore a data set so you have the ability to answer all kinds of questions? What if those initial questions drive subsequent questions?

PivotTables provide a more expanded solution for exploring data. They are especially useful when you are looking at a huge table of data that can become overwhelming. A **PivotTable** is an interactive table that extracts, organizes, and summarizes source data. PivotTables are used for data analysis and looking for trends and patterns for decision-making purposes. Among other functions, a PivotTable can automatically sort, count, total, or give an average of the data stored in one table or spreadsheet. Excel then displays the results in a separate table, called a PivotTable. Here are some examples of questions PivotTables can help to answer for the Red Bluff Golf Course & Pro Shop.

- How often are clubs rented for a round of golf?
- How many customers came from each state last year?
- Has the mix between hotel customers and local customers changed over time?
- How much revenue has each employee generated over the last 12 months?

These questions can easily be answered with a PivotTable report because PivotTables can easily group the time period to years, quarters, months, or all three. The flexibility comes from using an interface that allows the table to be built without having to create formulas and functions to do the grouping, summarizing, or calculating. And because PivotTables are interactive, they can be adjusted with a few clicks, rearranged by dragging fields, or cleared to start the process over if the layout becomes too muddled. In this section, you will develop skills for working with PivotTables and PivotCharts.

Develop and Customize PivotTables

An understanding of the general process is helpful in working with PivotTables. First, it is important to make sure the data set is well organized. A PivotTable can be created on an existing worksheet or a new worksheet. When it is created, a link or connection is established to a source range of data. After the data source and where to insert the blank PivotTable have been determined, the interactive part begins. The PivotTable is blank or clear to begin with, but it can be developed by considering what data to group and what data to summarize. The final step is to explore and work with the options within the PivotTable to fine-tune the layout to fit your specific needs. If needed, it is possible to create PivotCharts, covered later in this chapter, with chart data based on PivotTable adjustments, thus offering charted data based on extracted subsets of data analysis.

Creating PivotTables

The creation of a PivotTable is a two-step process: selecting the data set and location where the PivotTable will be created and working with the data fields to group and summarize the selected data. When creating a PivotTable, ensure the source data is arranged in an area with column headings representing each field and the rows representing each record, preferably with no other information or content in cells that are adjacent to the data set just like with a data table. In addition, there should be clear, concise field headings in the top cell for each column of data. Excel will use these as the labels within the PivotTable. Finally, if there are automatic subtotals or other summary functions at the bottom of the data, be sure to remove these. They will cause confusion if they are incorporated into a PivotTable.

There are only two options with regard to the location of a PivotTable: A PivotTable can be created on a new worksheet or on the worksheet where your data is. PivotTables automatically expand and contract on a worksheet as variables are added, removed, and rearranged. Creating a PivotTable on a new worksheet will set it apart and reduce the chance that the PivotTable will interfere with or disturb other data. If a PivotTable is placed on an existing worksheet with other data, it is best to choose a location where it is below or to the right of any existing data. This allows the PivotTable room to expand to the right or down as needed, without interfering with the existing data. While it is possible to create multiple PivotTables from the same data set, only one PivotTable is permitted per worksheet.

 CONSIDER THIS | **PivotTables and Hidden Data**

A filter applied to the data set will not affect the PivotTable creation process. The PivotTable will ignore the filter and use all the data — including the hidden data. Why is this important when using the data for decision making?

Similar to creating an Excel table, when a PivotTable is being created from a data set, one cell within the data set should be the active cell. Excel will automatically detect the range in the process of setting up the initial PivotTable area. It is possible to adjust the data range used if Excel mistakenly includes other information that is not needed in the PivotTable data range. If the data has been established as a table, the creation of a PivotTable is based on the current range for the table.

In this exercise, you will create a PivotTable from an Excel table.

 E06.09

To Create a PivotTable from an Excel Table

a. If you took a break, open the **e03ch06GolfMarketing** workbook, navigate to the **GolfData** worksheet, and then click cell **A15**.

Troubleshooting

If you have a few cells selected in a data set when you begin creating a Pivot-Table, you may end up creating a PivotTable that has only the subset selection as the range. It is best to have only one cell selected in your data set when you create the PivotTable.

b. Click the **Design** tab, and then, in the Tools group, click **Summarize with PivotTable**. The Create PivotTable dialog box opens.

Troubleshooting

If the data you are using is not in a table, click the Insert tab, and then, in the Tables group, click PivotTable.

c. Verify that the **GolfData** table/range is selected. Verify that **New Worksheet** is selected, and then click **OK**. The PivotTable is inserted on a new sheet named Sheet3.

d. Double-click the **Sheet3** worksheet, replace Sheet3 with PivotAnalysis, and then press Enter. Notice the PivotTable Tools contextual tabs that appeared.

e. Click cell **A1**. Notice that the PivotTable Tools contextual tabs disappear and only a blank PivotTable area is showing below cell A1.

f. Click cell **A3**.

The PivotTable Fields pane will reappear on the right side of the screen. The PivotTable Tools contextual tabs are now available.

g. **Save** 🖫 the workbook.

SIDE NOTE
Selecting Cells
You can select any cell within the PivotTable to redisplay the PivotTable Tools contextual tabs.

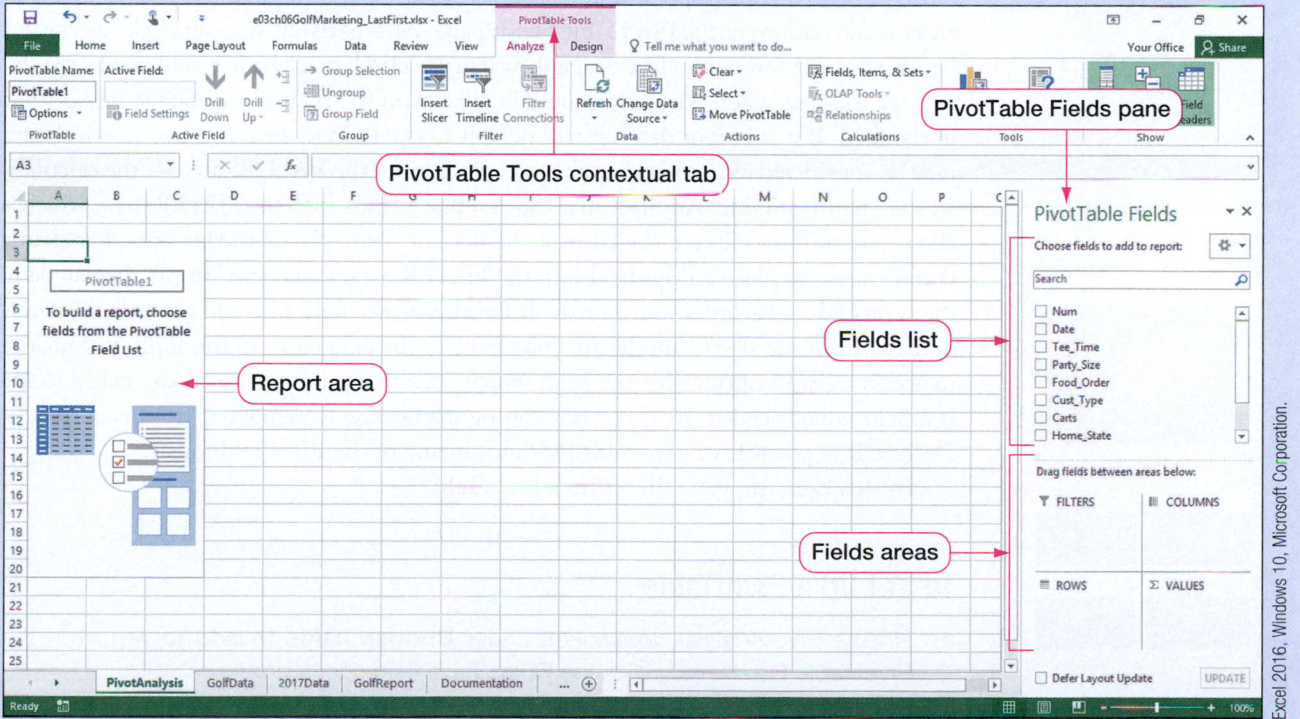

Figure 17 PivotTable layout

Building a PivotTable

Once the worksheet is set up for constructing the PivotTable, the interactive part of the process begins. The focus is to construct a table that will group and summarize subsets of the data in a useful and meaningful manner. There are a few guidelines for choosing how to arrange the fields.

It helps to distinguish fields as either grouping variables or summary variables, because these two types get placed in different areas within the PivotTable. A **grouping variable** can be thought of as any field within the data set that could be used to categorize or group for the purpose of comparison. For example, gender is a common variable used to group and analyze data. It may be necessary to compare the salaries of females with those of males. Dates are also useful for grouping data into months, quarters, and years to explore trends over time. Conversely, a **summary variable** is data that is not categorical in nature and can be aggregated by summing, counting, or averaging, such as gross revenue, quantity, or price.

Grouping variables are placed along the top or the left side of the PivotTable. The aggregation of data occurs when records in the data are grouped by selected variables. The results would be placed in the bottom-right areas of the aggregate summary. This layout is shown in Figure 17.

The grouping variables are positioned in the COLUMNS or ROWS areas at the bottom of the PivotTable Fields pane. The summary variables are positioned in the VALUES area below the PivotTable Fields list. Fields can be chosen from the PivotTable Fields list. Fields can be dragged and dropped from the PivotTable Fields list to any of the four quadrant areas at the bottom of the PivotTable Fields pane. Alternatively, you can click the check box beside the field names to select the field. When the check box beside a field is selected, Excel will try to guess where that field should be placed on the basis of the data values contained in the field. If it is text or dates, it will default to the ROWS area. If it is numerical data, it may be considered a summary variable and placed into the VALUES area — the calculations area of the PivotTable. Additionally, you can place fields into the FILTER area, which will allow you to filter data on the basis of the field or fields placed in that area. For example, if you choose to place a Days field into the FILTER area, you could simply display data for the weekend — Saturday and Sunday. If Excel puts the field into the wrong area, it can be dragged from one area to another, or you can click the field name in the applicable area's box to access a list of options for the field, which include options to move the field's location. If a field is not needed, its check box can be unchecked to remove it from the PivotTable Design. It is possible to have multiple fields in any of the PivotTable areas.

In this exercise, you will set up a PivotTable.

 **E06.10**

To Set Up a PivotTable

a. On the PivotAnalysis worksheet, under **Choose fields to add to report** in the PivotTable Fields area, click the **Cust_Type** field check box.

Cust_Type appears in the PivotTable in column A and displays all the customer types under the Row Labels heading. Additionally, Cust_Type is also displayed under the ROWS area on the PivotTable Fields pane.

b. Scroll if necessary, and click the **Home_State** field check box.

Excel will add both fields to the Row Labels area. The Home_State is displayed for each Cust_Type, which you can view if you scroll down the worksheet. If you prefer that each Home_State be listed with the Cust_Type grouped for each state, the order of the grouping can be switched.

c. In the **ROWS** area, click the **Home_State** field arrow.

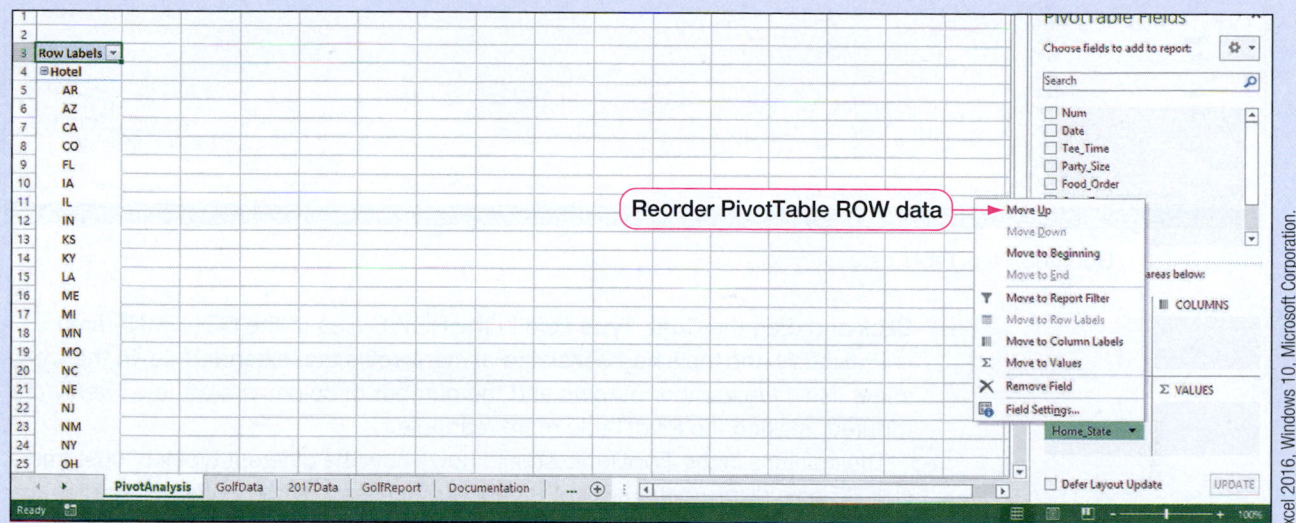

Figure 18 Reorder grouping of PivotTable data

d. Select **Move Up**. This will change the order of the groups for the two fields by switching the ROWS area.

e. In the PivotTable Fields list, click the **Food_Order** check box, and then click cell **B5**.

When Excel detects numerical data, it puts this into the VALUES area and defaults to summing the values. Notice the label in B3 indicates the field being aggregated and what calculation is being applied — in this case, Sum. Cell B4 displays the sum of the golf parties that stayed at the hotel with a home state of Arkansas. The value is calculated, but there is no formula within the cell.

f. Click the **GolfData** worksheet. Click cell **H15**, type **AR**, and then press Enter. Click cell **E15**, and then press Delete. Select **D43:F43**, and then press Delete.

g. Click the **Data** tab, and then, in the Sort & Filter group, click **Clear**. On the Customer Type slicer, click **Hotel**. On the Home State slicer, click **AR**. Notice the Sum of Food Order in cell F9 is now $545.20.

h. Click the **PivotAnalysis** worksheet tab.

Notice the Sum of Food Order in cell B5 is the same as the value in cell F9 on the GolfData worksheet. While it is possible to use formulas and filtering to obtain an answer, the PivotTable generates the answers for all the groups with less effort involved. Thus, PivotTables facilitate comparing summary data more efficiently.

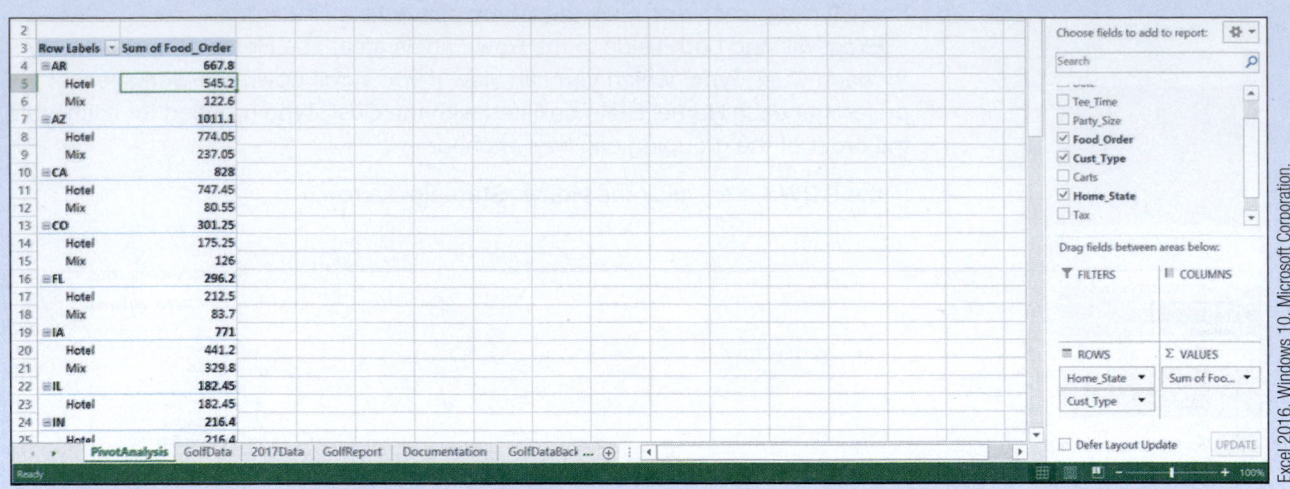

Figure 19 Updated PivotTable data

i. Click and drag the **Cust_Type** field in the ROWS area to the COLUMNS area.

Previously, the table had consisted of many rows that extended down the worksheet. Now the number of rows and the number of columns are more evenly distributed, making the PivotTable more readable.

The columns in the PivotTable should now show the different types of customers. Cell B5 now displays the sum of the food purchased by the hotel golf parties that are from Arkansas. In cell A33, the value indicates blanks — the records where no home state is indicated. Finally, notice how the PivotTable expands in both rows and columns as the fields are added and removed. This is the interactive attribute of a PivotTable and also why it is best to have a PivotTable on a worksheet by itself.

j. In the PivotTable Fields list, click the **Home_State** check box to remove the field from the PivotTable, and then click the **Date** check box. Date will now be in the ROWS area. Most of the time, data will group within each unique date, so it would be helpful if the dates could be aggregated.

k. Right-click **A9**, and then select **Group**. The Grouping dialog box opens with Months, Quarters, and Years highlighted in the By list.

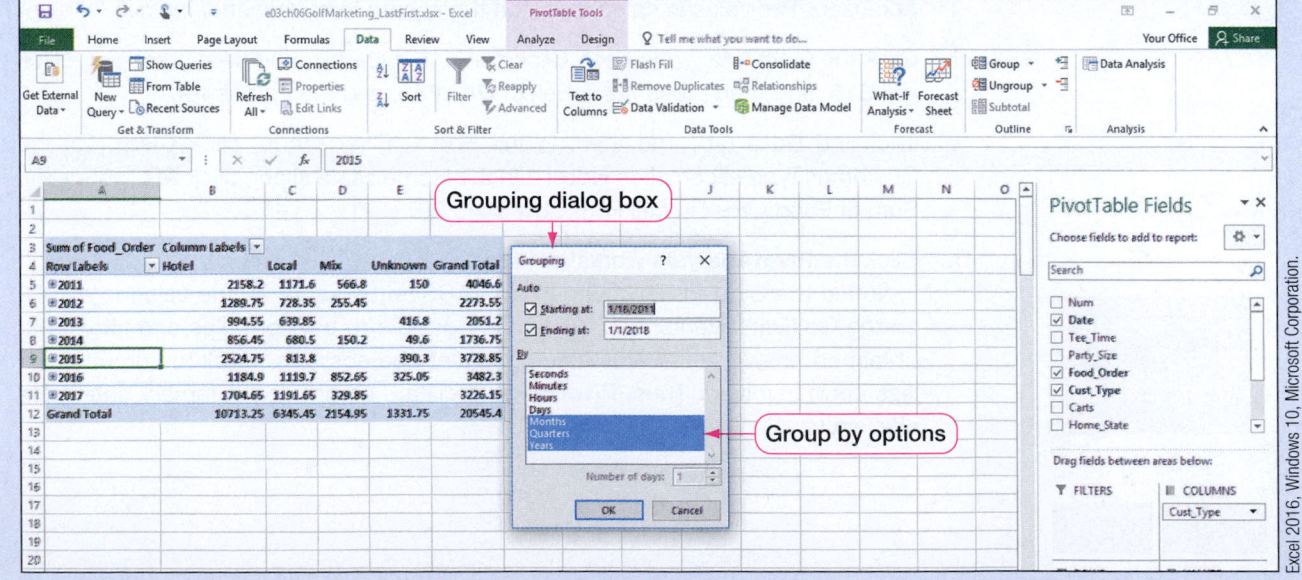

Figure 20 Grouping by dates

l. Click **Months** to remove the blue highlighting. **Quarters** and **Years** should still be selected as grouping levels. Click **OK**.

The dates will now be grouped by year, and within each year, all four quarters within the year will be listed. On the PivotTable Fields list, a Years field is now displayed. In the ROWS area, notice the first grouping is Years. Within each Year, the subgroup is Date, which is the Quarters. If the grouping needs to be changed, you can right-click one of the cells in column A and select Group again to change the grouping options, or you can select Ungroup and the individual dates will reappear.

m. **Save** the workbook.

 CONSIDER THIS | **Group on Rows or Columns**

The fields for grouping could be all in the ROWS area, all in the COLUMNS area, or a mixture. What issues may arise if you have all the grouping fields as row labels or all as column labels? What would you use as a rule of thumb for the number of groups within each area?

REAL WORLD ADVICE | **Which Fields Are Better for Row Labels?**

While it is possible to choose any grouping field on either the ROWS or COLUMNS, there are some guidelines. Typically, you want your PivotTable to go down more than across. People are more accustomed to scrolling up or down in a document than to scrolling left or right. So if you have a lot of groups within a field, it is better to put those fields along the row side of the PivotTable instead of across the top in columns. It is better to have the user scroll up or down instead of across.

Configuring PivotTable Options

With PivotTables, two contextual tabs are available to aid in the control of PivotTable elements: Analyze and Design. The Analyze tab has all the options for fine-tuning the PivotTable. Many of these options can also be accessed by right-clicking any cell within the PivotTable. Some are very useful in creating the structure of the PivotTable.

The Design tab focuses on formatting and on the appearance of designing the PivotTable. Options include choosing from a variety of styles and whether or not to display band row and/or column colors, report layouts, and so forth. Additionally, formatting can always be done through the traditional Format Cells dialog box found by right-clicking any cell in the PivotTable. This is not recommended, though, as it will format only the selected cell. Formatting of data through the Value Field Settings dialog box applies to all other cells within the same field. This eliminates the need to select a range of data and to be concerned with how the formatting will change as the PivotTable changes shape or is restructured.

Additionally, new fields can be added. Remember that when data is in an Excel table, it is possible to add a new field that is automatically included. If, while working with the PivotTable, you need a new calculation, it is possible to add a calculated field directly to the PivotTable without changing the original data set. You also can return to the underlying data, add the new fields, and then use the Refresh button on the Analyze tab to update the PivotTable data for any changes made to the source data.

Finally, it is possible to change the layout, adding totals, grand totals, and labels within the PivotTable to enhance the look and feel of the PivotTable. This is useful in creating a structure that will be used in a presentation.

In this exercise, you will work with the PivotTable options.

 **E06.11**

To Work with PivotTable Options

SIDE NOTE

PivotTable Formatting

It is not recommended to use the standard formatting techniques found on the Home tab with PivotTables. The PivotTable is dynamic, and the regular formatting techniques will not make use of the dynamic attributes.

a. On the PivotAnalysis worksheet, click cell **B6**, which displays the data for the Sum of Food_Order in the first quarter of 2011 for all parties staying at the hotel.

b. On the PivotTable Tools contextual tab, click the **Analyze** tab. In the Active Field group, click **Field Settings**. The Value Field Settings dialog box opens.

c. Click **Number Format**. The Format Cells dialog box opens. Click **Currency** in the Category list. Click **OK**, and then click **OK** in the Value Field Settings dialog box. Notice that all values within the Values section have now changed to Currency format.

d. Mouse over cell B6. A ScreenTip appears, informing you about the data within that cell.

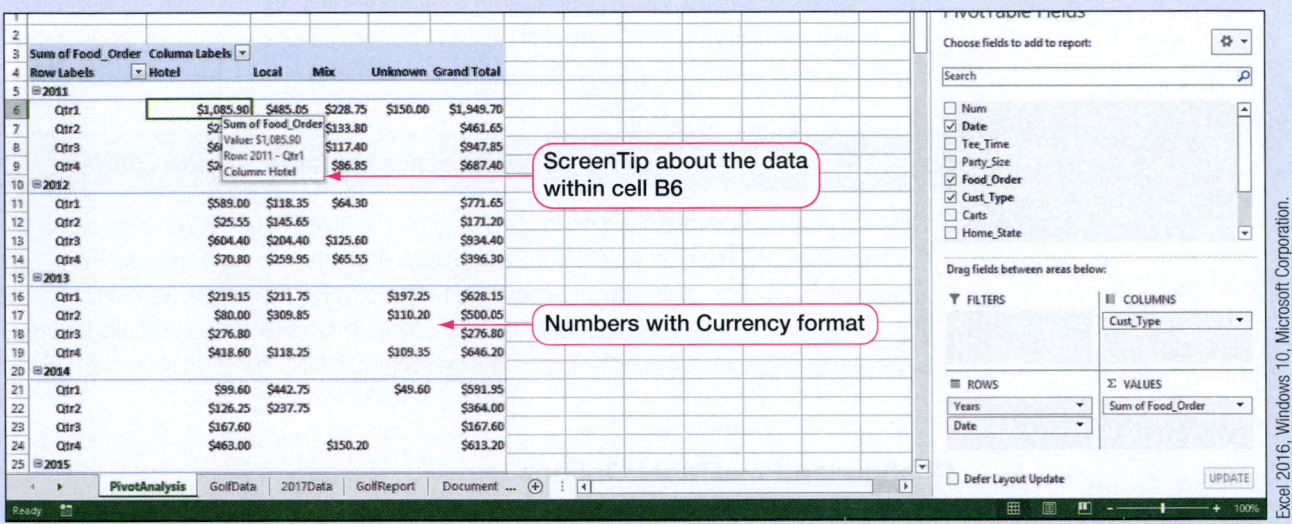

Figure 21   Currency format in PivotTable

e. Right-click cell **B6**, point to **Summarize Values By**, and point to **Average**.

It may be useful to compare the values. For example, it may be important to know how the hotel average sales compares with the overall average of the Painted Paradise Resort & Spa within each time period.

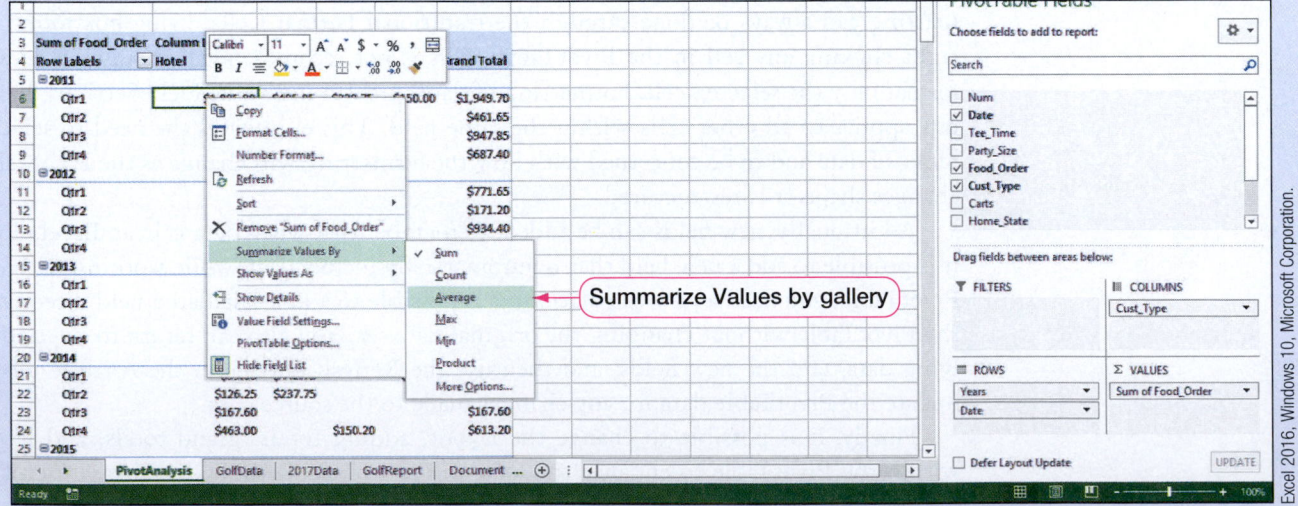

Figure 22   Summarizing data by average

f. Click **Average**. After viewing the results, right-click cell **B6**, point **to Summarize Values By**, and then select **Sum**. Right-click cell **B6**, point to **Show Values As**, and then select **% of Row Total**.

Because the values are sums, the Grand Total row average is 100%. So in Qtr 1 of 2011, the three percentages — Hotel, Local, and Mix — add up to the 100%.

Keep in mind that this average is based on the average Food_Order purchases for each Cust_Type golfing party. However, golfing parties have anywhere from one to five people, so if the average purchases per person was desired, the PivotTable would need to be adjusted to calculate an average by dividing the Food_Order by Party_Size.

g. In the PivotTable Fields list, uncheck the **Food_Order** field.

h. On the Analyze tab, in the Calculations group, click **Fields**, **Items**, & **Sets**. Select **Calculated Field**. The Insert Calculated Field dialog box opens.

i. In the Name box, type Food Per Person, and then press Tab. In the Formula box replace =0 with =Food_Order/Party_Size. Click **Add**, and then click **OK**.

The average food cost per person is now displayed. For example, B6 is the total food order for all hotel parties during Qtr 1 of 2011 divided by the sum of all the party sizes during that same time period. Notice there are some #DIV/0! errors in the table. This is because those are cells where there was no activity, so Excel is trying to divide by 0. Because this error message is a valid error that could reasonably be expected, it can also be hidden.

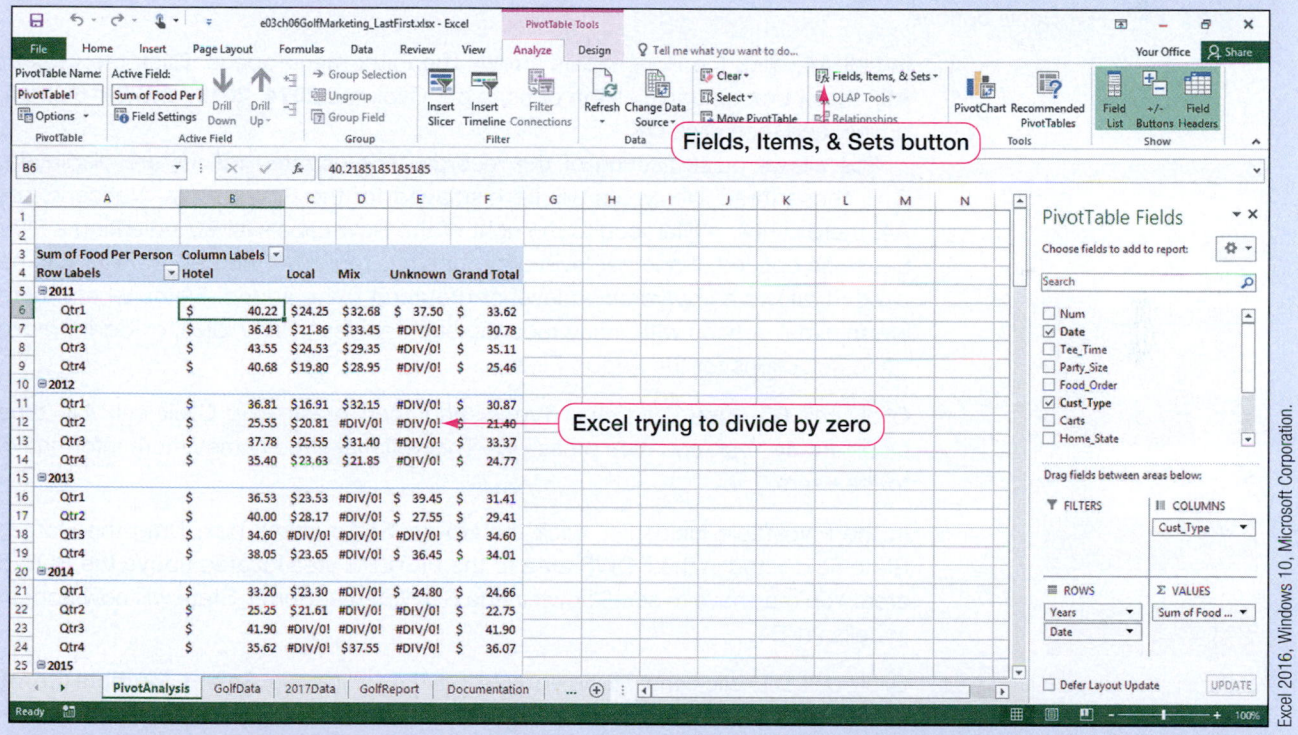

Figure 23 Calculated field

Excel 2016, Windows 10, Microsoft Corporation.

j. Click cell **B6** if necessary. On the **Analyze** tab, in the PivotTable group, click **Options**. The PivotTable Options dialog box opens.

k. Click the **Layout & Format** tab if necessary, and then, under the Format section, click the **For error values show** check box. Because you want nothing to be displayed when there is an error, leave the box blank, and then click **OK**.

Notice the error messages are now replaced with a blank cell. Now the data from 2011 through 2017 should be showing, by quarter. However, if the analysis were to focus on just a couple of years, the data could be filtered even more.

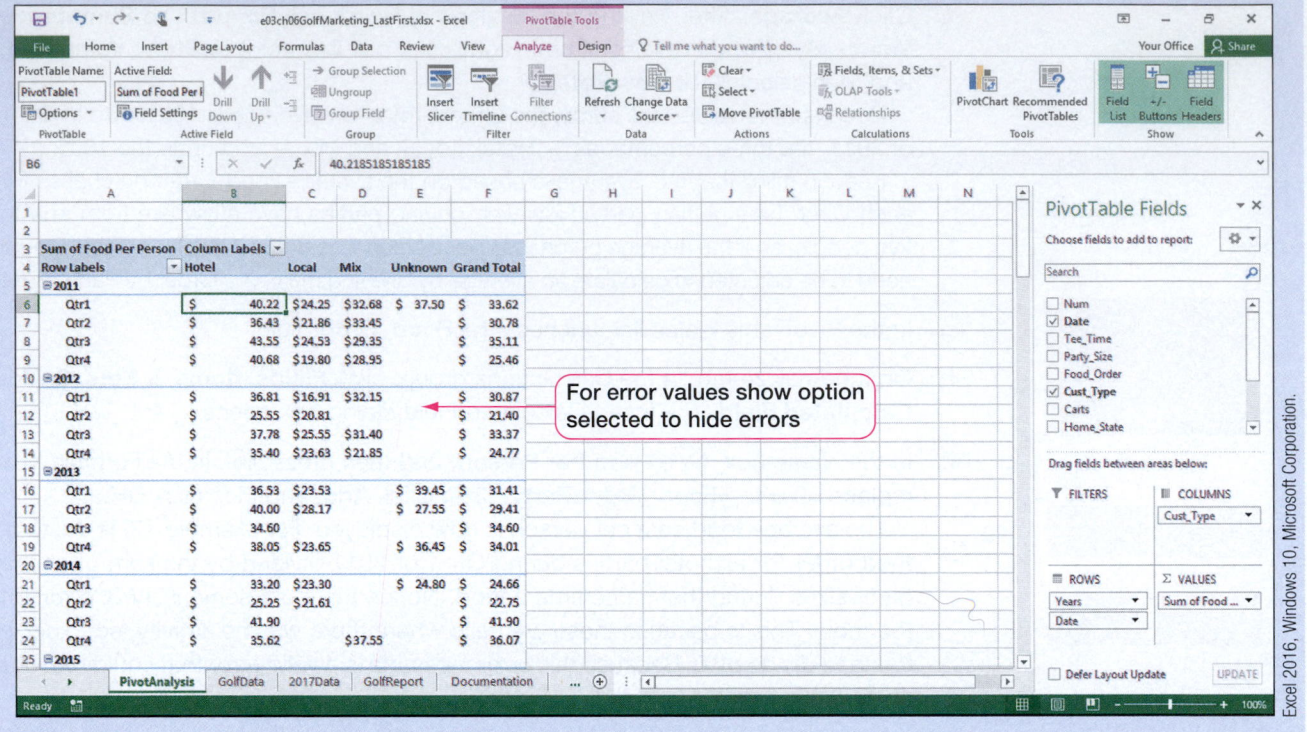

Figure 24 PivotTable options

l. In cell **A4**, click the Row Labels arrow. The Filter menu opens. Click the **(Select All)** check box to toggle all the options off. Click the **2014**, **2015**, and **2016** check boxes, and then click **OK**.

This allows quick filtering of the records. The updated results are displayed. Only those three filter years will be displayed for the Row Labels. Notice in cell A4, there is now a filter icon to the right of the Row Labels label, indicating a filter has been applied. If another level of grouping is required, the Report Filter can be used. It allows an overarching level of grouping to be added. Fields where there are minimal options with many records, such as Year, Party_Size, or Carts, make good selections for the Report Filter.

m. Click cell **B3**, type Customer Types, and then press Enter. Click cell **A4**, type Quarters by Year, and then press Enter. This will make the names more informative to the users.

n. In the PivotTable Fields list, click the **Home_State** check box. Drag the Home_State field listed in the ROWS area to the FILTERS area located above the ROWS area. You may have to scroll down in the ROWS area. Home_State will now appear in cells A1:B1.

o. Click cell **B1**, click the **Filter** arrow, and then click the **Select Multiple Items** check box. Click the **(All)** check box to clear all the check boxes, and then click the **AR** and **AZ** check boxes to display the Arizona and Arkansas data.

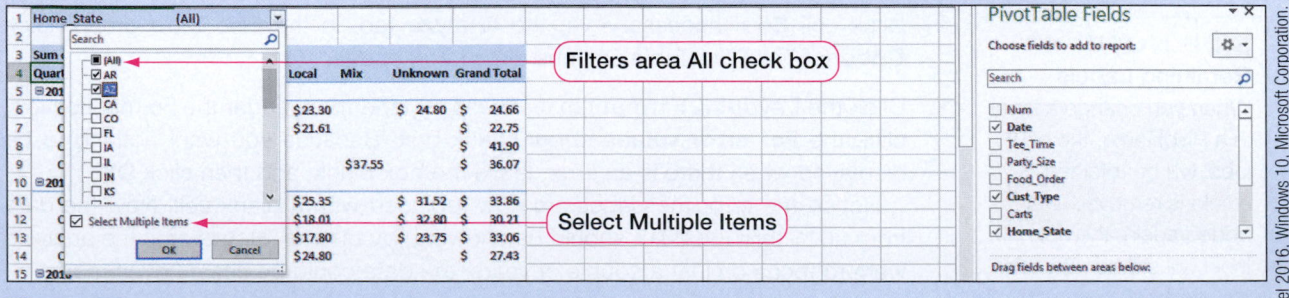

Figure 25 Filtered table

p. Click **OK**. On the PivotTable Tools contextual tab, click the **Design** tab. In the PivotTable Styles group, click the **More** arrow. Under Light, click **Pivot Style Light 3**.

q. Save the workbook.

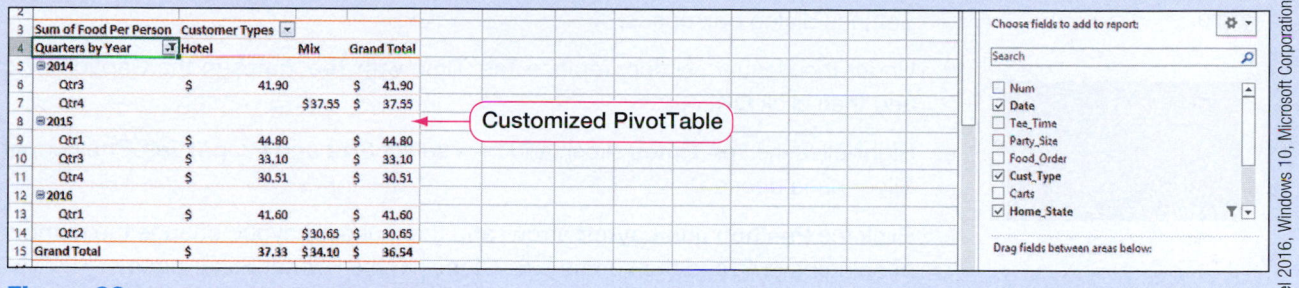

Excel 2016, Windows 10, Microsoft Corporation.

Figure 26   Report filter with customization

REAL WORLD ADVICE   **Choosing Report Filter Fields**

In general, the Report Filter field should be an overarching field that gives a big picture perspective of the data. If a Date field is used, the year should be the grouping criterion, rather than months. Fields that can be further manipulated by other fields make for good report filters. A Product field would not be as suitable a report filter as a Product Category field because a product category is a bigger picture field that can be filtered further as needed.

Adding a Slicer to the PivotTable

Finally, more options can be added by using a slicer to create yet another layer of slicing to the data. A slicer is a visual mechanism for quickly filtering data in a PivotTable. A slicer is an object that sits or floats on top of the spreadsheet that lists the data options of a field. The user can quickly select one or more of the list items to filter on the fly.

In this exercise, you will insert and customize a slicer.

E06.12

SIDE NOTE

Moving the Slicer

The slicer will not move as the PivotTable changes shape. Point to the border of the slicer, and then, when the Move pointer appears, drag the border edge to a new location.

To Insert and Customize a Slicer

a. On the PivotAnalysis worksheet, click the **Analyze** tab. In the Actions group, click the **Clear** arrow, and then select **Clear Filters**. In cell **A4**, click the **Quarters by Year** arrow. The Filter menu opens. Click the **(Select All)** check box to toggle all the options off. Click the **2015**, **2016**, and **2017** check boxes, and then click **OK**.

b. On the PivotTable Tools Analyze tab, in the Filter group, click **Insert Slicer**. The Insert Slicers dialog box opens. Click the **Tee_Time** check box, and then click **OK**. Click the **8:30:00 AM** time slot in the Tee_Time slicer. Press and hold Shift, scroll down, and then click the **11:30:00 AM** time slot. The data for those time slots will be incorporated into the PivotTable.

The slicer floats on the spreadsheet with all available Tee_Times. The PivotTable will reflect the filters applied to the slicer. Shift can be used to select a range of options, or you can use Ctrl to pick and choose options to include in the PivotTable. There are no records in the subset of data that have other tee times.

c. Right-click the **Tee_Time** slicer, and then select **Slicer Settings**. The Slicer Settings dialog box opens.

d. Under the Header section, replace Tee_Time with Tee Times in the Caption box, and then click **OK**.

e. Right-click the **Tee Times** slicer, and then select **Size and Properties**. The Format Slicer pane opens.

f. Click the **Position and Layout** arrow, and then, under Layout, change the number of columns to 3, and then press Enter. **Close** ☒ the Format Slicer pane.

g. Drag the **Tee Times** slicer so its top left corner is in the top left corner of **H3**.

h. Drag the bottom right corner of the **Tee Times** slicer to cell **L17**.

i. To further customize your slicers, click the Tee Times slicer if necessary. On the Slicer Tools contextual tab, click the **Options** tab. In the Slicer Styles group, click the **More** arrow. Under Dark, click **Slicer Style Dark 2**.

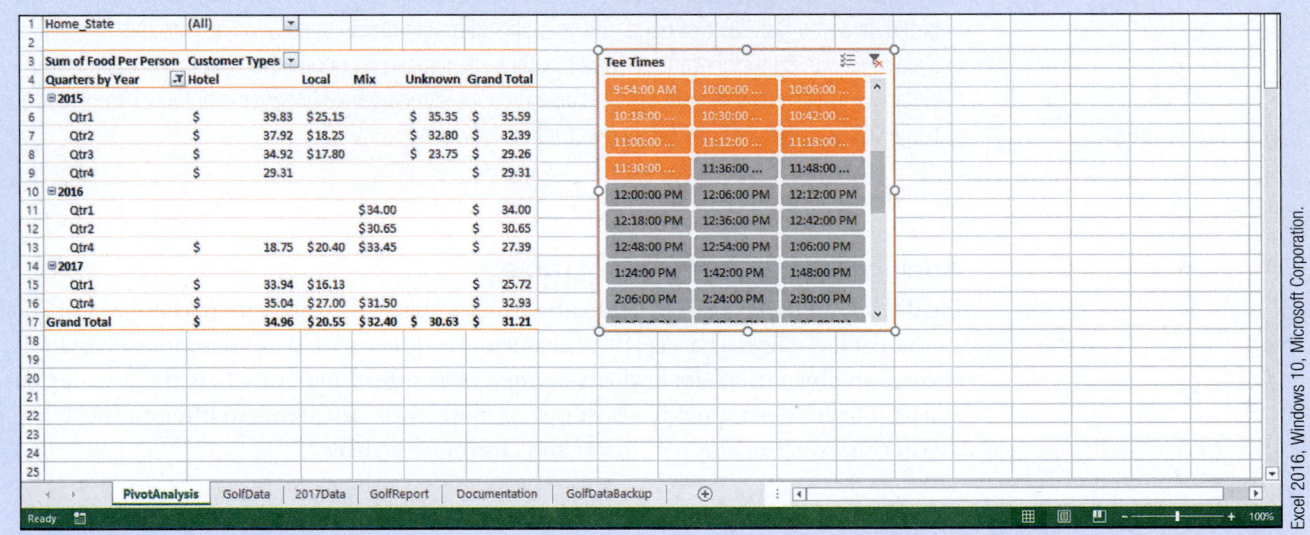

Figure 27 PivotTable and slicer with customization

j. **Save** 🖫 the workbook.

REAL WORLD ADVICE | The Power of Data Modeling

Businesses can collect thousands upon thousands of rows of data every day. Some businesses can collect even more than that per hour! Think of how many transactions a large banking organization has every minute. This vast amount of data collected on a regular basis may be stored in multiple locations, making it difficult to combine in one location to perform data analysis. Basic data model functionality that is built into Excel — called PowerPivot — allows experienced Excel users to conduct more advanced data analysis and build sophisticated data models. PowerPivot allows a user to import up to one million rows of data from multiple sources, such as large corporate databases, public data feeds, spreadsheets, and text files on your computer.

Modifying a PivotTable Design and Working with PivotTable Totals

Design options on the PivotTable Tools Design tab focus on the look and feel of the PivotTables. The options available include layout and styles. To get a perspective of the design options, it will be useful to clear the filters from the current PivotTable and begin with a basic structure. An important piece of data within a PivotTable can be totaled or summed numbers.

In this exercise, you will modify the design and work with totals in a PivotTable.

 E06.13

To Modify the Design and Work with Totals

a. Click the **GolfData** worksheet, and then click cell **A11**. Click the **Insert** tab, and then under Tables group, click **PivotTable** 🔃. The Create PivotTable dialog box opens.

b. Verify that the **GolfData** table/range is selected. Verify that **New Worksheet** is selected, and then click **OK**. The PivotTable is inserted on a new sheet named Sheet4. Rename Sheet4 PivotSubtotals.

c. In the PivotTable Fields list, click the check boxes to select **Date**, **Cust_Type**, **Food_Order**, and if necessary **Years**.

> **Troubleshooting**
>
> You may need to scroll down in the ROWS area to find fields.

d. In the ROWS area, drag the **Cust_Type** field to the **COLUMNS** area.

e. Right-click cell **A5**, and then select **Group**. Verify that **Quarters** and **Years** are selected, and then click **OK**.

f. On the PivotTable Tools contextual tab, click the **Design** tab. In the Layout group, click the **Subtotals** arrow. Select **Show all Subtotals at Bottom of Group**.

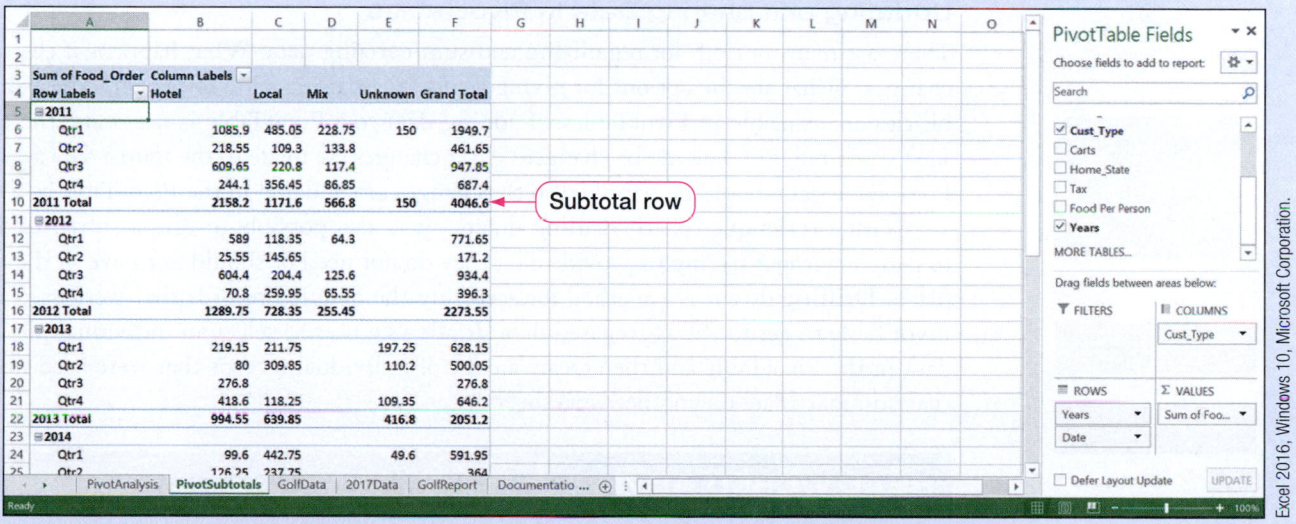

Figure 28   PivotTable subtotals

g. On the Design tab, in the PivotTable Style Options group, click the **Banded Rows** check box.

   This will put alternating colors on the rows. A PivotTable style, which consists of templates, can also be selected if desired.

h. Right-click cell **B6**, and then select **Number Format**. Under Category, click **Currency**, and then click **OK**.

i. On the Design tab, in the Layout group, click **Report Layout**. Select **Show in Tabular Form**.

j. Click cell **A3**, and then type Food Order Totals. Press Tab two times. In cell C3, type Customer Type, and then press Enter. Click cell **B4**, and then type Quarters. Press Enter.

k. Select columns **B:C**. Click the **Home** tab, and then, in the Cells group, click **Format**. Select **AutoFit Column Width** so the columns are wide enough to view all the data. Press Ctrl + Home.

l. **Save** 🖫 the workbook.

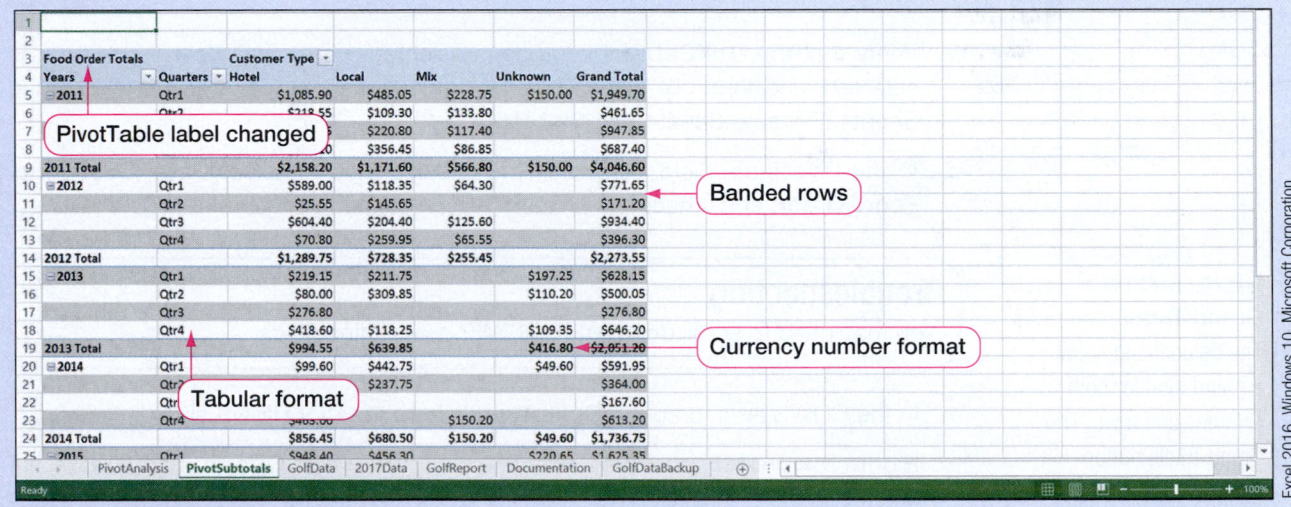

Figure 29   Stylized PivotTable

Updating and Sharing Data in PivotTables

There are many options for organizing and summarizing data. What happens if the data changes? What are the options for giving a subset of data to another person? These capabilities are available in PivotTables. If adding data to a PivotTable is necessary, the data source and range of data can be changed. After changes are made to the source data set, the PivotTable data should be refreshed so the changes are updated in the PivotTable as well.

With a technique called "drilling down," it is also possible to give a subset of data to people without having to provide data they do not need or should not have in the first place. **Drilling down** is a method for accessing the detailed records that were used in a PivotTable to get to the aggregated data. It allows a user to select an individual piece of data in the PivotTable and then create a copy of individual records that were used to get that summary data on another worksheet.

REAL WORLD ADVICE   **Managers Use Drilled-Down Data**

The level of management position that a manager holds determines the type of data that is needed. Lower-level managers need very detailed data — data that is drilled down — to make daily decisions. Senior-level managers mainly use summarized data. Think about that from a PivotTable perspective. Lower-level managers will click the plus signs to expand the fields, while senior-level managers will not. Because of these different information needs, it is important to know your audience before constructing your PivotTable.

In this exercise, you will update, refresh, and drill down data.

 **E06.14**

To Update, Refresh, and Drill Down

SIDE NOTE
Cell Versus Table References

When adding the new field "Region", you typed the cell references. If you click cell H12, Excel will insert [@[Home_State]] into the formula instead of H12. The two methods will yield the same result.

a. Click the **GolfData** worksheet. Click the **Data** tab, and then, in the Sort & Filter group, click **Clear** to clear all the filters in the table.

b. Click cell **J11**, type Region, and then press Enter. In cell **J12**, type =IF(OR(H12="NM",H12="TX",H12="AZ"),"Tri_State",""), and then press Enter. Notice the formula will automatically fill in the new column.

c. Click the **PivotSubtotals** worksheet. Click cell **A6**, and then click the **Analyze** tab. In the Data group, click **Refresh**. Scroll through the field list to notice the new field for Region now appears in the PivotTable Fields list and could be integrated into the PivotTable as needed.

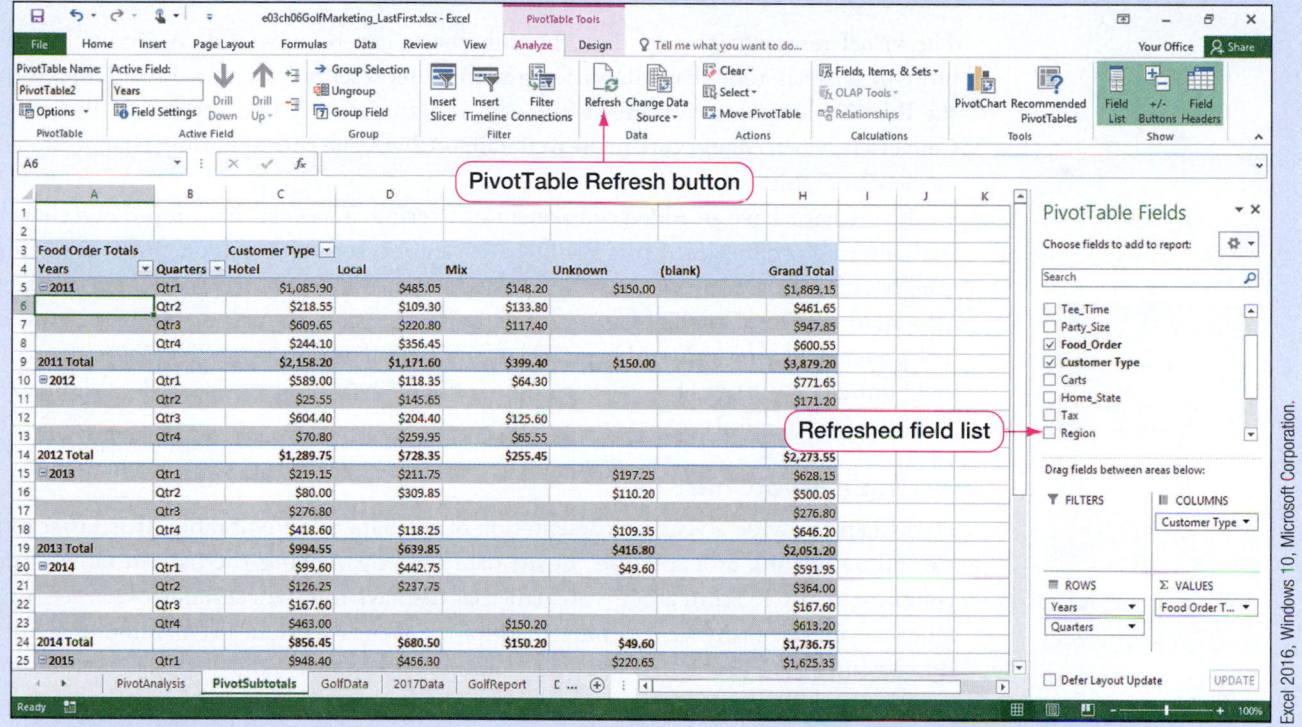

Figure 30   Refreshed PivotTable Field list

d. Click cell **C35**.

This is the food order revenue from customers during the first quarter of 2017. The underlying records that were used in generating the $491.10 total need to be retrieved.

e. Double-click cell **C35**. The action of double-clicking any cell within the PivotTable initiates the drill-down process, in which Excel will copy and paste the records that are associated with that value to another worksheet.

f. Double-click the **Sheet5** worksheet, replace Sheet5 with 2017Local, and then press Enter.

g. Select columns **B:C**. Click the **Home** tab, and then, in the Cells group, click **Format**. Select **AutoFit Column Width**.

h. On the 2017Local worksheet, click cell **E7**. Type **=SUM(E2:E6)**, and then press [Ctrl] + [Enter]. Notice the sum is 491.10, which corresponds to the data in the PivotTable.

i. **Save** [💾] the workbook.

REAL WORLD ADVICE | **Dates on the Row Labels**

In general, if dates are going to be a grouping variable, it is customary to put them in the Row Labels area. Typically, grouping by quarter or month with the date in the Row Labels area follows a financial or accounting format. If you are grouping only by year, it may be suitable to put the date field in the Column Labels area.

Develop and Customize PivotCharts

The visual representation of data through charts can be powerful. A **PivotChart** is a built-in analysis tool that allows for graphical representations of a PivotTable. When the PivotTable data is rearranged, the data is automatically updated in the PivotChart. Conversely, when changes are made to the PivotChart, the corresponding changes are seen in the PivotTable.

PivotCharts have an added component of filtering. The chart has drop-down elements with filtering options. Multiple PivotCharts can be associated with one PivotTable; however, because they are all tied together, best practice dictates having only one PivotChart associated with one PivotTable. Additionally, be careful when making use of a PivotChart in a presentation so that no changes occur accidentally within the PivotTable that could yield unwanted changes to the chart. Once a PivotChart has been created, all formatting elements from a regular chart are available.

Adding a PivotChart

PivotCharts provide a visual representation of the data in a PivotTable. It is easier to see a trend by looking at a "picture" of the data than by viewing the data in table format. For example, by looking at a PivotChart that displays the spa's revenue over the past 12 months, you can easily see the movement of the trends without even thinking about it. By viewing data in a PivotTable, you would need to think about whether the numbers are higher or lower than the one you previously viewed. Once you view the data in a PivotChart, it is easy to read details such as month and total revenue for each month.

In this exercise, you will add a PivotChart to a worksheet.

 **E06.15**

SIDE NOTE
Choosing a Chart
Some chart types are not available for use with a PivotTable.

To Add a PivotChart

a. Click the **PivotSubtotals** worksheet, and then click cell **A6**. Under the PivotTables Tools contextual tab, click the **Analyze** tab.

b. In the Tools group, click **PivotChart**. The Insert Chart dialog box opens. Click the **Clustered Column** chart in the first position if necessary, and then click **OK**.

c. With the chart selected, under the PivotChart Tools contextual tab, click the **Design** tab. In the Location group, click **Move Chart**. The Move Chart dialog box opens. Select **New sheet** if necessary, and then in the New sheet box, replace

Chart1 with PivotChart. Click **OK**. There will be filtering options on the chart that allow you to change the filters within the chart.

d. On the **PivotChart** worksheet, click the **Customer Type** filter button to display the filter menu. Click to uncheck the **Mix**, **Unknown**, and **Blank** check boxes, and then click **OK**.

e. Click the **Years** filter button to display the filter menus. Click **(Select All)** to uncheck all years, and then click **2015**, **2016**, and **2017**.

f. Under the PivotChart Tools contextual tab, click the **Design** tab. In the Chart Layouts group, click **Add Chart Element**, point to **Chart Title**, and then select **Above Chart**.

g. Enter the chart title Food Purchases by Customer Type, 2015–2017.

h. On the Design tab, in the Chart Styles group, select **Style 6**.

i. In the Chart Layouts group, click **Add Chart Element**, point to **Axis Titles**, and then select **Primary Vertical**.

j. Replace Axis Title with Revenue.

k. On the Design tab, in the Chart Styles group, click **Change Colors**. Under Monochromatic, select **Color 6**. Close the PivotChart Fields pane.

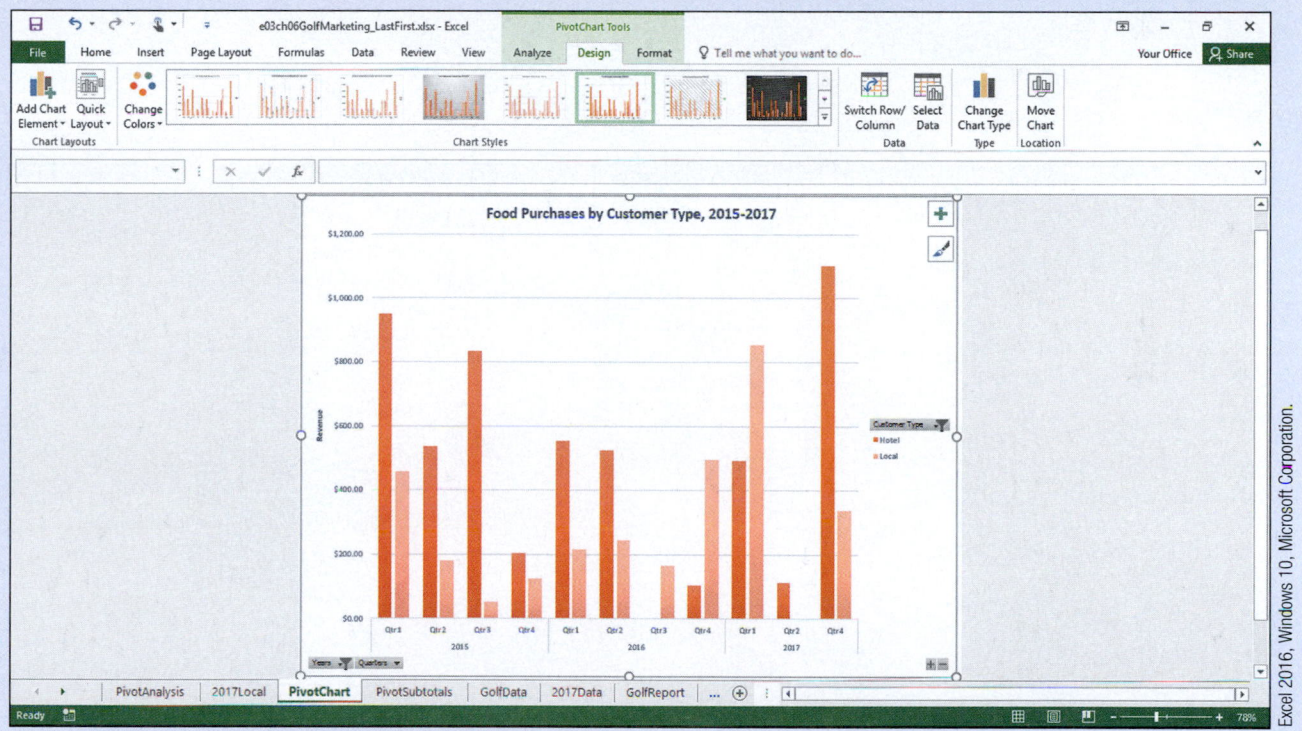

Figure 31 Customized PivotChart

l. Complete the **Documentation** worksheet as directed by your instructor.

m. **Save** the workbook, exit Excel, and then submit your file as directed by your instructor.

When creating a PivotTable or PivotChart, remember the following.

- Once you have selected your data, ensure that the source data is arranged in an area with column headings representing each field and the rows representing each record.

- Distinguish fields as either grouping variables or summary variables.

- Format the PivotTable or PivotChart so it is easy to read and your audience understands what it is you are trying to communicate.

- Know who your audience is before you develop your PivotTable or PivotChart. It could make a difference in how much detail you display.

Concept Check

1. You have delete data in a spreadsheet that you are going to analyze. What are some tips for working with the data set to help prevent and correct errors? p. 329

2. You are talking with a colleague who mentions that the SUBTOTAL function performs sum, average, count, or other functions and questions why a person would use that function when the SUM, AVERAGE, and COUNT functions already exist. What is the difference between using the SUBTOTAL to sum data and using the SUM function? p. 343

3. What type of data would work well for the row and column labels within a PivotTable? What are some examples? p. 347

4. Describe two benefits of using an Excel PivotChart rather than an Excel PivotTable. p. 362

Key Terms

Advanced Filter   337
Aggregate   343
Convert to Range   334
Data set   334
Drilling down   360
Filtering   334

Grouping variable   350
Information   328
PivotChart   362
PivotTable   347
Raw data   328
Slicer   340

Standard filter   355
Structured reference   331
SUBTOTAL function   343
Summary variable   350

Visual Summary

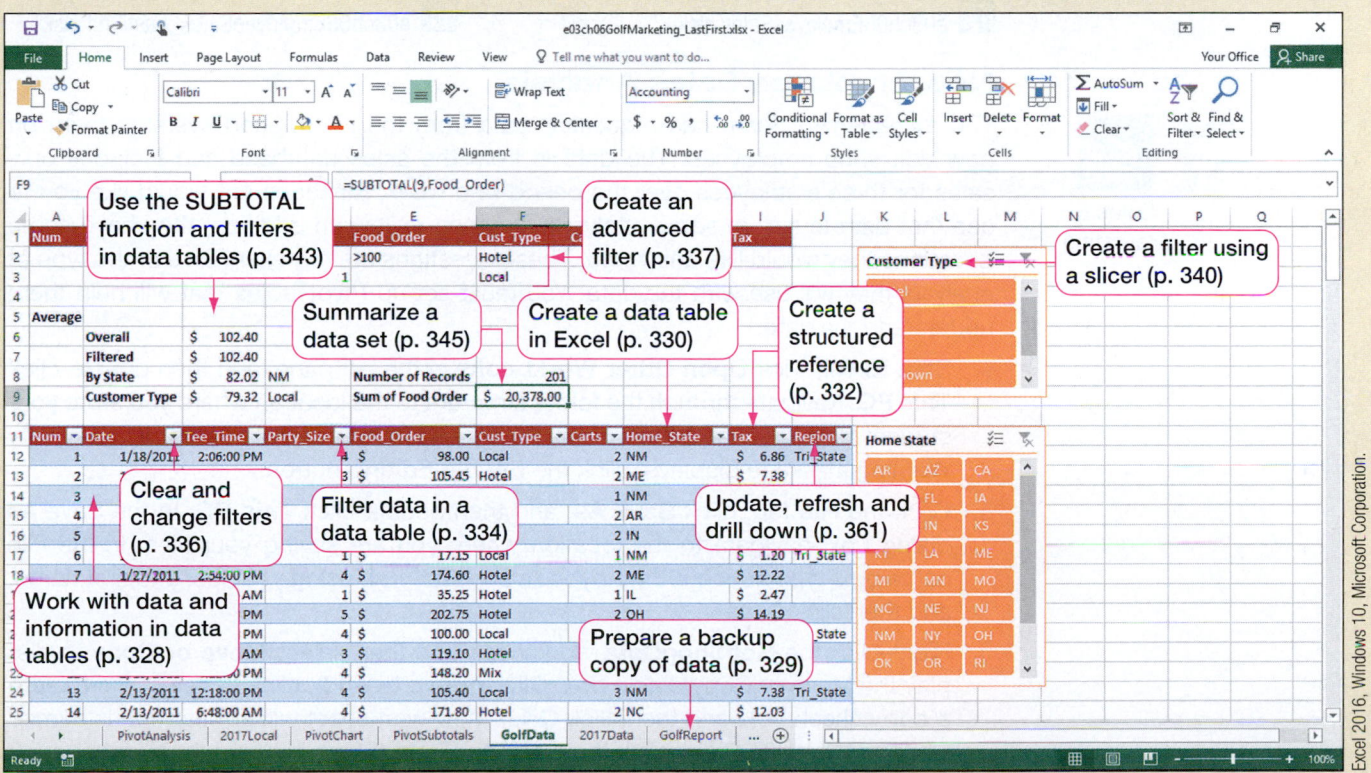

Figure 32

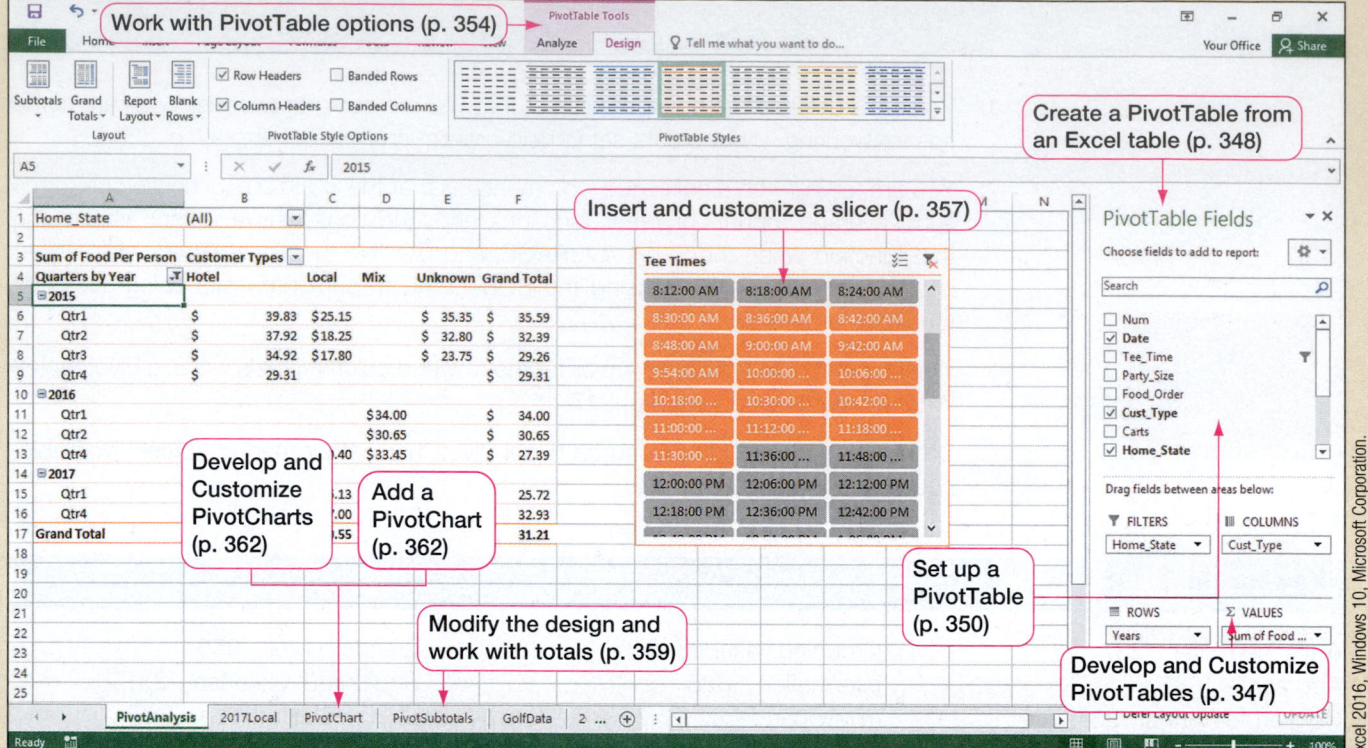

Figure 33

Practice 1

Student data file needed:

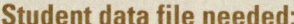 e03ch06EmployeeSales.xlsx

You will save your file as:

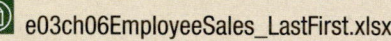 e03ch06EmployeeSales_LastFirst.xlsx

Sales & Marketing

New Employee Sales Analysis

The management team has requested data from the information systems team on new golf shop employees. The data is from the sales database and includes only sales for three employees over the period of a week. Management would like you to use that data to set up some analyses they can review. In addition, they have some questions they would like answered. These questions are representative of the type of analysis they will use with the data. You must set up PivotTables that will help them understand the data.

a. Start **Excel**, click **Open Other Workbooks** in the left pane, and then double-click **This PC**. Navigate through the folder structure to the location where you store your student data files, and then double-click **e03ch06EmployeeSales**. If a Security Warning message displays, click the **Enable Editing** button.

b. Click the **File** tab, click **Save As**, and then double-click **This PC**. In the Save As dialog box, navigate to the location where you are saving your files. In the File name box, type e03ch06EmployeeSales_LastFirst, using your last and first name, and then click **Save**.

c. Right-click the **GolfShopData** worksheet, and then select **Move or Copy** to display the Move or Copy dialog box. Click **(move to end)**, click to select the **Create a copy** check box, and then click **OK**. A new worksheet will appear that is named GolfShopData (2). Right-click the **GolfShopData (2)** worksheet tab, and then click **Rename**. Type GolfShopDataBackup, and then press Enter.

d. Click the **GolfShopData** worksheet. Click cell **C20**, click the **Insert** tab, and then, in the Tables group, click **Table**. Verify that the table range box displays $A$20:$K$90 and the **My table has headers** check box is checked, and then click **OK**. With the data still selected, click the **Formulas** tab, and then, in the Defined Names group, click **Create from Selection**. Verify that only the **Top row** check box is checked, uncheck the Left column if necessary, and then click **OK**.

e. Select cell range **A20:K20**, and then press ⌃Ctrl and Ⓒ to copy the range. Click cell **A1**, and then press ⌃Ctrl and Ⓥ to paste the field labels in row 1. Click cell **C2**, and then type Accessories. Click cell **K2**, type Friday, and then press Enter.

f. Click cell **C20**, click the **Data** tab, and then, in the Sort & Filter group, click **Advanced**. If a message asking to include the column labels in the selection to allow the Filter command to work properly appears, click **Yes**. In the Advanced Filter dialog box, click in the **Criteria range** box, and then select **A1:K2**. Verify that Filter the list, in-place is selected. Ensure that Excel automatically made the criteria range an absolute reference, and then click **OK**.

g. Select cell range **A20:K72**, and then press ⌃Ctrl and Ⓒ to copy the filtered data. Click **New sheet** to insert a new worksheet. Select cell **A1** if necessary, and press ⌃Ctrl and Ⓥ to paste the subset of data. Press Esc, select columns **A:K**, and then click the **Home** tab. In the Cells group, click **Format**, and then select **AutoFit Column Width**. Right-click the **Sheet2** worksheet, and then select **Rename**. Type FridayFilter, and then press Enter. Press ⌃Ctrl + Home.

h. Click the **GolfShopData** worksheet, press Esc to clear the copy range, and then click cell **C20**. Click the **Insert** tab, and then, in the Filters group, click **Slicer**. Click the **Category** check box, and then click **OK**. Drag the Category slicer so its top left corner is in the top left corner of L2. In the slicer, click **Accessories**, press ⌃Ctrl, and then click **Clothing**. Drag the bottom edge of the Category slicer to adjust the height so that the extra white space is no longer visible. To further customize your slicers, click the Category slicer if necessary. Under the Slicer Tools contextual tab, click the **Options** tab. In the Slicer Styles group, click the **More** arrow. Under Light, click **Slicer Style Other 1** in the first row, seventh column.

i. On the GolfShopData worksheet, click the **Table Tools Design** tab, and then, in the Tools group, click **Summarize with PivotTable**. Select **Existing Worksheet**, and then click in the **Location** box. If necessary, clear any existing text. Click the **GolfReport** worksheet tab, click cell **A10**, and then click **OK**.

j. In the PivotTable Fields pane, in the PivotTable Fields list, click the **Category**, **QTY**, and **Emp_ID** check boxes.

k. In the VALUES area, click the **Sum of Emp_ID** arrow, and then click **Move to Column Labels**.

l. The Employee IDs are not informative, so they should be changed to the employee's first names.

- Click cell **B11**, and then type Chuck.
- Click cell **C11**, and then type Jennifer.
- Click cell **D11**, and then type Allie.
- Select columns **B:D**, and then click the **Home** tab. In the Cells group, click **Format**, and then select **AutoFit Column Width** so the employee names can be seen.
- Apply **Pivot Style Light 17** to the PivotTable.
- Select cell **B12**. Right-click the range, and then select **Value Field Settings**. Click **Number Format**, and then select **Number**. Click **OK**, and then click **OK**.

m. View the data in the PivotTable. In cell **A2**, type your answer to question 1. In cell **A4**, type your answer to question 2. You will answer question 3 later in this project.

- View the data in the PivotTable to answer question 1. By looking at the Grand Total column, you find that the total units of clothing sold is 26. Click cell **A2**, and then type 26.

- View the data in the PivotTable to answer question 2. By looking at the Clothing row, you find that Allie sold the most clothing with 10 units. Click **A4**, and then type Allie. Click **B4**, and then type 10.

n. Click any cell in the PivotTable, and then uncheck the **Category**, **QTY**, and **Emp_ID** fields.

o. Click cell **A10**. Click the **Analyze** tab, and then, in the Calculations group, click **Fields, Items, & Sets**. Select **Calculated Field**.
- In the Name box, type Subtotal, and then press ⟨Tab⟩.
- Click Retail in the Fields list, and then click **Insert Field**.
- Type *.
- Click **QTY** in the Fields list, and then click **Insert Field**.
- Click **OK**.

p. Click the **GolfShopData** worksheet, and then select cell **K20**. Click the **Data** tab, and then, in the Sort & Filter group, click **Clear**. Click cell **L20**, type Subtotal, and then press ⟨Enter⟩. Type =. Click cell **F21**, type *, and then click cell **G21**. Press ⟨Enter⟩ to calculate the subtotal for each line item.

q. Click the **GolfReport** worksheet, and then click cell **A10**.
- Click the **Analyze** tab, and then, in the Calculations group, click **Fields, Items, & Sets**, and then select **Calculated Field**.
- In the Name box, type Tax, and then press ⟨Tab⟩.
- Click **Subtotal** in the Fields list, and then click **Insert Field**.
- Type *.07, and then click **OK**.

r. In the PivotTable Fields list, click **Product ID**, **Category**, and **Day**. Verify that the Subtotal and Tax fields are checked.
- Drag the **Day** field from the ROWS area to the FILTERS area.
- Drag the **Product ID** in the ROWS area below the Category field.
- Click cell **B12**. Click the **Analyze** tab, and then, in the Active Field group, click **Field Settings**. If necessary click the **Show Values As** tab, and then click **Number Format**. Click **Currency**, click **OK**, and then click **OK**.
- Click cell **C12**. On the **Analyze** tab, in the Active Field group, click **Field Settings**, and then click **Number Format**. Click **Currency**, click **OK**, and then click **OK**.

s. On the **Analyze** tab, in the Filter group, click **Insert Slicer**. Click the **Emp_ID** check box, and then click **OK**. Click **Allie** in the Emp_ID slicer. Drag the Emp_ID slicer so its top left corner is in the top left corner of E10. Drag the bottom edge of the **Emp_ID** slicer to adjust the height so the extra white space is no longer visible. Right-click the **Emp_ID** slicer, and then select **Slicer Settings**. In the Caption box, replace Emp_ID with Employee, and then click **OK**. To further customize your slicer, click the Employee slicer if necessary. On the Slicer Tools contextual tab, click the **Options** tab. In the Slicer Styles group, click the **More** arrow. Under Light, click **Slicer Style Other 1** in the first row, seventh column.

t. In cell **B8**, click the Filter arrow. Click the **Select Multiple Items** check box. Deselect the **(All)** check box, click the **Friday** and **Saturday** check boxes, and then click **OK**.

u. Click cell **B10**. Click the **Design** tab, and then, in the Layout group, click the **Subtotals** arrow. Select **Show all Subtotals at Bottom of Group**.

v. View the data in the PivotTable to answer question 3. By looking at the Sum of Subtotal column and the Clubs Total row, you find that the total clubs revenue Allie generated is $419. Click cell **A6**, type $419, and then press ⟨Enter⟩.

w. Complete the following to create a PivotChart.

- On the GolfReport worksheet, click **Clear Filter** on the slicer, and then close the PivotTable Fields pane. Click cell **A10**, type Categories, and then press Tab. In cell **B10**, type Pre-tax Total, and then press Tab. In cell **C10**, type Tax Total, and then press Tab.

- Click cell **A12**. Under the PivotTables Tools contextual tab, click the **Analyze** tab. In the Tools group, click **PivotChart**. Click the **Line** tab, and then click **Line with Markers** in the fourth position. Click **OK**.

- With the chart selected, under the PivotChart Tools contextual tab, click the **Design** tab. In the Location group, click **Move Chart**. Select New sheet if necessary, and then, in the New sheet box, replace Chart1 with PivotChart Analysis. Click **OK**.

- Under the PivotTables Tools contextual tab, click the **Design** tab. In the Chart Layouts group, click **Add Chart Element**, point to Chart Title, and then select **Above Chart**. Triple-click the **Chart Title** box, and then replace Chart Title with Total Sales and Tax by Category. Press Enter.

- In the Chart Layouts group, click **Add Chart Element**, point to Axis Titles, and then select **Primary Horizontal**. Select the Axis Title box, replace Axis Title with Category, and then press Esc.

- On the Design tab, in the Chart Styles group, click the **More** arrow. Select **Style 8**, in the first row, eighth column.

x. Click the **Documentation** worksheet. Click cell **A8**, and then type today's date. Click cell **B8**, and then type in your name in the Firstname Lastname format. Complete the remainder of the Documentation worksheet according to your instructor's directions.

y. Click **Save**, exit Excel, and then submit your file as directed by your instructor.

Problem Solve 1

 Student data file needed:

 e03ch06ShopSales.xlsx

You will save your file as:

e03ch06ShopSales_LastFirst.xlsx

Painted Treasures Gift Shop Sales Review

Human Resources

Sales & Marketing

The sales team at the Painted Treasures Gift Shop would like to review its staff's sales after some of the new staff members have finished a sales training program. You have been given the data for May 2018, and more data will be added in the future. The sales team wants you to review the data, perform some data analyses, and answer some specific questions. This will help the sales team determine how well the staff is performing and who needs further training.

a. Open the Excel file, **e03ch06ShopSales**. Save your file as e03ch06ShopSales_LastFirst, using your last and first name.

b. Create a copy of the Sales worksheet, and then place it at the end of the workbook. Rename the Sales (2) worksheet as SalesBackup.

c. On the **Sales** worksheet, insert a table with headers that uses the range $A$15:$I$212. With the data table selected, create named ranges using the top row as the names.

d. Copy range **A15:I15**, and then paste the range in cell **A1**. In cell **G2**, type Receptionist. In cell **I2**, type Card.

e. Create an advanced filter, using the data in range **A1:I2**. Filter the list in-place to display the filtered data on the Sales worksheet. Insert a new sheet, and then rename it Filter. Copy the filtered data, and then paste it in cell **A1** on the Filter worksheet. Resize the columns so all the data is visible.

f. On the Sales worksheet, in cell **J15**, type Subtotal. In cell **J16**, enter a formula that multiplies Units and Retail_Price. Format the Subtotal column as **Accounting Number Format**. Create a named range for the Subtotal column that uses the column heading as the name.

g. Use the SUBTOTAL function to complete the following.

- In cell **H7**, insert a formula that counts the number of cells in the Category field that are not empty.
- In cell **H8**, insert a formula that sums the cells in the Units field.
- In cell **H9**, insert a formula that sums the cells in the Subtotal field.
- In cell **H10**, insert a formula that averages the cells in the Retail_Price field.

h. Using the cell range **A15:J212**, insert a PivotTable in cell A12 on the **SalesAnalysis** worksheet.

i. Configure the PivotTable, using the following.

- Add **Units**, **Staff**, and **Staff Category** to the PivotTable.
- Move **Staff Category** to the COLUMNS area.
- Using the Column Labels arrow, uncheck **Manager**.
- Right-click cell **E14**, point to **Sort**, and then sort the data in ascending order.

Critical Thinking 1
View the PivotTable data to determine the employee with the highest number of units sold. Click cell **A2**, click the drop-down arrow, and then select the name of the employee with the highest number of units sold. In cell **A3**, click the drop-down arrow, and then select the name of the employee with the second highest number of units sold.

Critical Thinking 2
View the PivotTable data to determine the employee with the lowest number of units sold. Click cell **A5**, click the drop-down arrow, and then select the name of the employee with the lowest number of units sold. In cell **A6**, click the drop-down arrow, and then select the name of the employee who sold 30 units.

j. Modify the PivotTable as follows.

- Add the **Category** field to the PivotTable.
- Move **Category** to the FILTERS area.
- Add the **Hotel_Guest** field to the PivotTable.
- In cell **A15**, replace **No** with Non-hotel Guest. Resize column A so Non-hotel Guest is visible.
- In cell **A16**, replace **Yes** with Hotel Guest.
- Click cell **B18**, and then modify the display to show the percent of the grand total.
- On the Design tab, modify the grand totals so they display for just the columns. Modify the subtotals so they display at the bottom of the group.

Critical Thinking 3
View the PivotTable data to determine the percentage of revenue for the massage therapists. Click cell **A8**, click the drop-down arrow, and then select the percentage of revenue for massage therapists.

k. On the **SalesAnalysis** worksheet, insert a slicer for the Trans_Type field. Click **cash** and **check** in the Trans_Type slicer. Drag the Trans_Type slicer so the **top left corner** is in the top left corner of G12. Drag the bottom edge of the Trans_Type slicer to adjust the height so the extra white space is no longer visible. Replace the Trans_Type heading with Payment Type.

l. Using the PivotTable, create a Clustered Column PivotChart. Format the PivotChart as follows.

- Move the PivotChart to a new sheet named SalesChart.

- Add an Above Chart title. Replace **Chart Title** with Percent Revenue Contribution.

m. Complete the Documentation worksheet according to your instructor's directions.

n. Save the workbook, exit Excel, and then submit your file as directed by your instructor.

Perform 1: How Others Perform

Student data file needed:

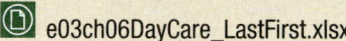 e03ch06DayCare.xlsx

You will save your file as:

e03ch06DayCare_LastFirst.xlsx

Small Business Ownership

Finance & Accounting

You run a small day care out of your home. Many of the parents who love your interactions with their children, have begun talking to you about expanding your operations. Never having thought about opening a day care business, you have begun to research the costs involved in opening your own center. After gathering some data, you believe you can open a business. But you realize you need to analyze the data and make the data look more presentable to your investors.

a. Open the Excel file, **e03ch06DayCare**. Save your file as e03ch06DayCare_LastFirst, using your last and first name.

b. Make a backup copy of the **Revenue** and the **Expenses** worksheets. The new worksheets should be labeled RevenueBackup and ExpensesBackup.

c. On the Revenue worksheet, select the cell range **A5:E131** and format the range as a Table.

d. In cell F5 of the Revenue worksheet, enter the column heading Budget. To calculate the budget, in cell F6 enter a formula that will multiply the number of children by the Income Per (Column E). If the number of children is zero (the income isn't based on a per-child cost), then the formula should return the figure in the Income Per column.

e. Create named ranges for all columns of the table.

f. Create and apply an advanced filter that will show all field trips prior to 1/1/2017 and where the budget is less than 1000.

g. On the Expenses worksheet, select the cell range A10:E338 and format the range as a Table. Add the heading Budget to F10. To calculate the budget, in cell F11 enter a formula that will multiply the number of people by the cost per person. If the number of people is zero, then the formula should return the figure in the cost per person.

h. Using filters, answer the questions on rows 1 and 2 on the Expenses worksheet. Use the table Total Row feature to get the correct answer for question 2.

i. Insert two slicers formatted to match your table. Select multiple criteria for each slicer. Ensure that the slicers do not cover any data.

j. Insert SUBTOTAL functions into cells C4, C5 and C6 that will answer the questions in column A based on the filtered data.

k. Using the data on the Expenses worksheet, create a PivotTable on a new worksheet.

l. Rename the worksheet appropriately.

m. Your PivotTable should show the Budget by Category by Date.

n. Create a calculated field on the PivotTable named BudgetPerPerson that divides the Budget by the # People.

o. Group the Date by Quarters and Years and only show 2017 data.

p. Subtotals should be shown at the bottom of your data.

q. Add a slicer and format the slicer appropriately.

r. Format the table appropriately and hide any error values if necessary.

s. Add a PivotChart based on your PivotTable results. Insert an appropriate title and format appropriately. Move the PivotChart so that it does not cover any of your data.

t. Drill down on one of the items in your PivotTable to display all the detail behind the number. Change the tab name on the newly created worksheet appropriately. Adjust column widths as necessary.

u. Update the Documentation worksheet according to your instructor's directions.

v. Save the workbook, exit Excel, and then submit your file as directed by your instructor.

Additional Cases

Additional Workshop Cases are available on the companion website and in the instructor resources.

Integrating Complex Functions into Business Analysis

This business unit had two outcomes:

Learning Outcome 1:

Use Excel conditional and retrieval functions for a powerful method of extracting data from a table.

Learning Outcome 2:

Use Excel Tables, PivotTables, and PivotCharts to quickly summarize and analyze large amounts of data.

In Business Unit 3 Capstone, students will demonstrate competence in these outcomes through a series of business problems at various levels from guided practice to problem solving an existing spreadsheet.

More Practice 1

Student data file needed:

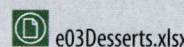 e03Desserts.xlsx

You will save your file as:

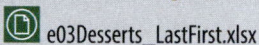 e03Desserts_LastFirst.xlsx

Indigo5 Dessert Analysis

Sales & Marketing

Robin Sanchez, the chef at Indigo5, has been discussing dessert sales with the restaurant manager, Alberto Dimas. They want to examine the production levels and the sales of their signature desserts. To do so, they have collected data from last week's sales and included it in a workbook so you can analyze the data. Once you have completed the analysis, you will present it to Chef Sanchez and Mr. Dimas so they can make marketing decisions about the restaurant's dessert menu.

a. Open **Excel**, click **Open Other Workbooks** in the left pane, and then double-click **This PC**. Navigate through the folder structure to the location of your student data files, and then double-click **e03Desserts**. If a Security Warning message displays, click the **Enable Editing** button.

b. Click the **File** tab click **Save As**, and then double-click **This PC**. In the Save As dialog box, navigate to the location where you are saving your project files. Change the file name to e03Desserts_LastFirst, using your last and first name. Click **Save**.

c. Right-click the **DessertSales** worksheet, and then select **Move or Copy** to display the Move or Copy dialog box. Click to select **(move to end)**, click to check the **Create a copy** check box, and then click **OK**. A new worksheet named DessertSales (2) will appear. Rename the DessertSales (2) worksheet DessertSalesBackup.

d. Click the **InputData** worksheet. You will create named ranges to use in formulas.

- Select **A3:D9**. Click in the **Name** box, type DessertList, and then press Enter.
- Select **A12:B19**. Click in the **Name** box, type EmployeeList, and then press Enter.
- Select **G3:M4**. Click in the **Name** box, type DailyGoal, and then press Enter.
- Select **F12:G15**. Click in the **Name** box, type GoalGrade, and then press Enter. Press Ctrl + Home.

e. Click the **DessertSales** worksheet, and then click cell **B10**. Click the **Insert** tab, and then in the Tables group, click **Table**. Verify the range is =$A$10:$D$210 and that the **My table has headers** check box is checked. Click **OK**.

f. To begin your analysis, create the following fields and formulas.

- Click cell **E10**. Type Dessert, and then press Tab. In cell **F10**, type Day, and then press Tab. In cell **G10**, type Category, and then press Tab. In cell **H10**, type Emp Name, and then press Tab. In cell **I10**, type Revenue, and then press Enter.

- Click cell **E11**, enter the formula =VLOOKUP(B11,DessertList,2,FALSE), and then press Tab. The VLOOKUP will look up the Dessert ID from the DessertList named range and return the name of the dessert. FALSE indicates an exact match will be needed.

- In cell **F11**, enter the formula =INDEX(DailyGoal,1,WEEKDAY(C11,1)), and then press Tab. This will pull the value from the DailyGoal named range, looking in Row 1. The WEEKDAY function will pull the day of the week, returning a number from 1 to 7, which will translate to the column field name within the DailyGoal table.

- In cell **G11**, Creme Brulee and Dutch Apple Pie are the two desserts that are prepared just before serving and are served warm. Thus, if the dessert is either of those, the category should be "Warm"; otherwise, it should be "Cool." In cell **G11**, enter the formula =IF(OR(E11="Creme Brulee",E11="Dutch Apple Pie"),"Warm","Cool"), and then press Tab.

- In cell **H11**, enter the formula =VLOOKUP(A11,EmployeeList,2,FALSE), and then press Tab. The VLOOKUP will look up Emp ID in the EmployeeList named range and retrieve the employee's name from the second column of the named range. FALSE indicates an exact match will be needed.

- In cell **I11**, enter the formula =VLOOKUP(B11,DessertList,4,FALSE)*D11, and then press Enter. This will look up the Dessert ID in the DessertList named range and retrieve the selling price. Then the selling price is multiplied by the quantity sold to calculate the total dessert revenue generated.

g. Select cell range **I11:I210**. Click the **Home** tab, and then, in the Number group, click **Accounting Number Format**. Select columns **G:I**. On the Home tab, in the Cells group, click **Format**, and then select **AutoFit Column Width**.

h. On the **DessertSales** worksheet, create the following named ranges.
   - Click cell **E10**, press Ctrl + A to select the entire table. Click in the **Name** box, type **DessertAll**, and then press Enter.
   - Click the **Formulas** tab, and then, in the Defined Names group, click **Create from Selection**. Verify that only the **Top row** check box is selected, and then click **OK**.

i. Select cell range **A10:I10**, and then press Ctrl + C to copy the header information. Click cell **A1**, and then press Ctrl + V to paste the headers. Press Esc to deselect range A10:I10.

j. Click cell **F2**, and then type **Tuesday**. Press Tab, and then in cell G2 type **Cool**. Press Enter.

k. Click cell **C10**. Click the **Data** tab, and then, in the Sort & Filter group, click **Advanced**. Confirm **$A$10:$G$210** is displayed in the List range input box, and if necessary, edit the range as specified to select the entire table. Click in the **Criteria range** input box, select cell range **A1:I2**, and then click **OK** to filter the data.

l. Calculate the following subtotals.
   - Click cell **C5**, and then enter the formula =SUBTOTAL(1,Revenue) to calculate the average dessert check. Press Enter. The "1" indicates that the formula will average the filtered records on the Revenue field for records currently displayed in the table.
   - Click cell **C6**, and then enter the formula =SUBTOTAL(3,Dessert_ID) to count the number of different desserts by different servers. Press Enter. The "3" indicates that the formula will count the nonblank cells in the Dessert ID field for records currently displayed in the table.
   - Click cell **C7**, and then enter the formula =SUBTOTAL(9,Qty) to sum the number of desserts sold. Press Enter. The "9" indicates that the formula will sum the numbers in the Qty field for records currently displayed in the table.

m. Click cell **G10**. Click the **Insert** tab, and then, in the Filters group, click **Slicer**. In the Insert Slicers dialog box, click the **Dessert** and **Emp Name** check boxes. Click **OK**. Format the slicers as follows.

- Drag the **Emp Name** slicer so its top left corner is in the top left corner of cell **K1**. Right-click the **Emp Name** slicer, and then select **Slicer Settings**. In the Caption box, replace **Emp Name** with Employee. Click **OK**.

- To further customize your slicer, click the Employee slicer if necessary. On the **Slicer Tools Options** tab, in the Slicer Styles group, click the **More** arrow. Under Dark, select **Slicer Style Dark 4** in the second row, fourth column.

- Right-click the **Employee** slicer, and then select **Size and Properties**. In the Format Slicer pane, click the **Position and Layout** arrow, and then change the **1** in Number of columns to **2**. **Close** the Format Slicer pane. Drag the **bottom edge** of the slicer to adjust the height so that the extra white space is no longer visible.

- Drag the **Dessert** slicer so its top left corner is in the top left corner of cell **K10**. Drag the **bottom right corner** of the slicer to adjust the height and width so that the extra white space is no longer visible and all dessert names are visible.

- To further customize your slicer, click the Dessert slicer if necessary. On the Slicer Tools Options tab, in the Slicer Styles group, click the **More** arrow. Under Dark, select **Slicer Style Dark 4** in the second row, fourth column.

- In the Employee slicer, click **Joe**, press Ctrl, and then click **Wayne**. In the Desserts slicer, click **Carrot Cake**, press Ctrl, click **Double Chocolate Delight**, and then click **New York Cheesecake**.

n. Click the **Report** worksheet, create the following formulas.

- Click cell **B3**, enter the formula =SUMIF(Dessert,A3,Qty), and then press Ctrl + Enter. Double-click the **AutoFill** handle to copy this formula down through **B8**.

- Click cell **B11**, enter the formula =SUMIFS(Qty,Dessert,$A11,Day,B$10), and then press Ctrl + Enter. Double-click the **AutoFill** handle to copy this formula down though **B16**, and then drag the **AutoFill** handle to copy across to **H16** so the formula is copied to the cell range **B11:H16**. This sums the Qty field where both the dessert and day criteria are true.

- Click cell **B18**, enter the formula =SUM(B11:B16)/HLOOKUP(B10,DailyGoal,2,FALSE), and then press Enter. This sums the day's quantity sold and divides this value by the day's goal. The goal is found by using the HLOOKUP in the DailyGoal named range.

- Click cell **B19**, enter the formula =VLOOKUP(B18,GoalGrade,2), and then press Enter.

- Select cell range **B18:B19**, and then drag the **AutoFill** handle to copy the formulas through the cell range **C18:H19**.

- Click cell **B23**, enter the formula =IF(B21="Employee","Emp_Name","Dessert"), and then press Enter. This determines which data named range is associated with the category that is in cell B21. It will then be used in other formulas to select that named range.

- Click cell **B24**, enter the formula =SUMIF(INDIRECT(B23),B22,Qty), and then press Enter. This uses the named range in B23 as the criteria range and sums the Qty field.

- Click cell **B25**, enter the formula =AVERAGEIF(INDIRECT(B23),B22,Qty), and then press Enter. This averages the Qty field, using the named range listed in B23 as the criteria field.

- Click cell **F3**. The End Level is either Low or Okay. If the Bake Time is Day Bake and has an ending quantity lower than the Day Bake level listed in G6 on the Input Data worksheet, the formula will return Low. The formula also returns Low if the Bake Time is Fresh Bake and the ending quantity for the Fresh Bake item is less than the Fresh Bake value listed in cell G7 on the Input Data worksheet.

- In cell F3, enter the formula =IF(OR(AND(E3="DayBake",C3<InputData!$G$6), AND(E3="Fresh Bake",C3<InputData!$G$7)),"Low","Okay"), and then press Ctrl + Enter.

- Double-click the **AutoFill** handle to copy the formula down to cell **F8**.

- The Adjust column checks if either of two situations is true. If either is true, the chef will need to produce more; otherwise, the cell can remain blank. If requests are more than 5, indicating that the item sold out, more will need to be produced. Or if the end level is low and the Bake Time is Day Bake, then more will need to be produced. Click cell **G3**, enter the formula =IF(OR(D3>5,AND(F3="Low",E3="Day Bake")),"Produce More","")), and then press Ctrl + Enter. Double-click the **AutoFill** handle to copy the formula down to cell **G8**. Press Ctrl + Home.

o. Click the **DessertSales** worksheet, and then click cell **B10**. Click the **Insert** tab, and then, in the Tables group, click **PivotTable**. Select the **New Worksheet** option, and then click **OK**. Double-click the **Sheet2** worksheet, replace **Sheet2** with PivotTableAnalysis, and then press Enter to rename the worksheet.

p. Complete the following to create your PivotTable.

- In the PivotTable Fields List, check the **Qty**, **Dessert**, **Day**, and **Category** check boxes.
- Drag the **Dessert** field to the **COLUMNS** area.
- In cell **B3**, select the **Column Labels** filter button, and then click **(Select All)** to deselect all the items. Click the **Creme Brulee**, **Dutch Apple Pie**, and **New York Cheesecake** check boxes, and then click **OK**.
- Click the **PivotTable Tools Design** tab, and in the PivotTable Styles group, click the **More** arrow. Under Medium, select **Pivot Style Medium 5**. In the PivotTable Style Options group, click the **Banded Rows** check box.
- Click cell **A3**, type Total Quantity, and then press Tab. In cell **B3**, type Desserts, and then press Enter. In cell **A4**, type Day and Dessert Type, and then press Enter. Select columns **A:D**. Click the **Home** tab. In the Cells group, click **Format**, and then select **AutoFit Column Width**.
- Click cell **A3**, and then click the **PivotTable Tools Design** tab. In the Layout group, click **Subtotals**, and then select **Show all Subtotals at Bottom of Group**.
- Click cell **A5**. Click the **PivotTable Tools Analyze** tab, and in the Tools group, click **PivotChart**. Click **Line**, click **Stacked Line**, the second option, and then click **OK**. Close the PivotChart Fields pane.
- Click the **Design** tab, and then, in the Location group, click **Move Chart**.
- In the Move Chart dialog box, select **New sheet**. Click in the **New Sheet** box, replace **Chart1** with PivotChartAnalysis, and then click **OK**.
- Click the PivotChart Tools Design tab, and in the Chart Layouts group, click **Add Chart Element**, point to **Chart Title**, and then select **Above Chart**. Select the chart title, type Total Quantity Sold by Day and Dessert Type, and then press Enter.
- In the Chart Styles group, click **Change Colors**, and then select **Color 4**. In the Chart Styles group, click the **More** arrow, and then select **Style 13**.

q. Click the **Documentation** worksheet. Click cell **A8**, and then type in today's date. Click cell **B8**, and then type in your name in the Firstname Lastname format. Complete the remainder of the Documentation worksheet according to your instructor's directions.

r. Save the workbook, exit Excel, and then submit your file as directed by your instructor.

Problem Solve 1

MyITLab® Grader
Homework

Student data file needed:

 e03Inventory.xlsx

You will save your file as:

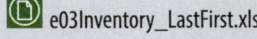 e03Inventory_LastFirst.xlsx

Production & Operations

Managing Gift Shop Inventory

The gift shop staff wants to track inventory so it can reduce out-of-stock inventory items and reorder inventory more efficiently. The staff needs a template designed that will hold all the product information and then analyze daily transactions at the end of every month. You have been asked to help the gift shop employees develop a workbook that will help them manage the store's inventory. Because the staff currently does not collect this data, the gift shop manager has given you a template with a small amount of fictitious data so you can create the needed formulas and worksheets. The worksheet also contains named ranges that you will use to create formulas in the template.

a. Open the Excel file, **e03Inventory**. Save your file as **e03Inventory_LastFirst**, using your last and first name.

b. On the **Inventory** worksheet, click cell **L19**, and enter a nested IF and AND function to determine the reorder status. If the current inventory in cell H19 is blank and the reorder point in I19 is blank, then a blank value should be returned. If not, then if Discontinue in K19 is equal to N and current inventory is less than or equal to the rush reorder point in J19, Rush should be returned. If not, then if Discontinue is equal to N and current inventory is less than the reorder point, return the value of Reorder, or else OK. Copy the formula down the column.

c. On the **DailyTransactions** worksheet, in cell **D2**, type Food, and in cell **E2**, type Fri.

d. In cell **F11**, the data in the Trans_Sold column is the number of items sold. Negative Trans_Qty numbers are the quantity that was sold. Positive Trans_Qty numbers are the total number received from the supplier. Enter an IF function to determine if the Trans_Qty is less than zero. If the Trans_Qty is less than zero, then return the absolute value of the Trans_Qty, or else the cell is left blank. Copy the formula down the column.

e. In cell **C6**, enter a DSUM function to determine the sum of the field in C5 in the table range data in A10:G40 and the criteria range established in rows 1:2.

f. In cell **C7**, enter a DAVERAGE function to determine the average of the field in cell C5 from the table range data in A10:G40 and the criteria range established in rows 1:2. Format the cell with no decimal places.

g. In cell **G11**, enter an IF function to determine if there were transactions delivered. If the value in the Trans_Qty is greater than zero, then the result is the value, or else the cell is left blank. Copy the formula down the column.

h. On the **InventoryAudit** worksheet, the cells in range A2:D17 need to be filled in based on the category that is listed in cell B1 — Massage. The table will then contain the information about each product within the listed category. Using named ranges already created in the Inventory worksheet, complete the following:

- In cell **B3**, create a formula to retrieve the item within each category in cell B1. Enter an INDIRECT function nested in an INDEX function to return the item numbers by category. The function will reference cell B1 and index the value of the intersection of row 3 and column 1. Nest the function in an IFERROR function to return a blank cell if no items exist within the category.

- In cell **C3**, create a formula to retrieve the projected sales for each item within the category in cell B1. Enter an INDIRECT function nested in an INDEX function to return the item numbers by category. The function will reference cell B1 and index the value of the intersection of row 3 and column 2. Nest the function in an IFERROR function to return a blank cell if no items exist within the category.

- In cell **D3**, create a formula to determine the total quantity sold within the category in cell B1. Enter a SUMIF function nested in an IF function to determine if B3 has a value. If B3 has a value, then you will sum Trans_Sold if the Trans_Item meets the criteria in B3. If B3 does not have a value, then the cell is left blank.

- Select cell range **B3:D3**, and then copy the formulas through cell range B4:D17.

i. In cell **C21**, using a SUMIFS function, calculate the total quantity sold per category per day in cell range B20:I26 based on two sets of criteria — C20 and B21. Use an appropriate mixed reference on the criteria cell references to be able to copy to the formula through cell I26.

- Trans_Sold is the sum range.
- WeekDay is the criteria range for cell C20.
- Trans_Category is the criteria range for cell B21.
- Copy the formula through cell range D21:I26.

j. Calculate the total quantity sold per category in cell range **D32:D51** based on the item in column B. Once this has been calculated, the total quantity delivered and ending inventory can be calculated.

- In cell **D32**, create a formula to sum the range Trans_Sold if the criteria in B32 is found in the range Trans_Item.
- In cell **E32**, create a formula to sum the range Trans_Delivered if the criteria in B32 is found in the range Trans_Item.
- In cell **F32**, create a formula that subtracts the Total out from the Beginning inventory and then adds in the Total in.

k. In cell **G32**, create a VLOOKUP formula for the value in cell B32 from the cell range A19:M38 on the Inventory sheet in the seventh column with an exact match.

l. Select cell range **D32:G32**, and then copy the formulas through cell range **D33:G51**.

m. There is an error in a table array in the formulas in K33:K51. In cell **K32**, review the formula, and then make any necessary corrections to correct the formula. Copy the corrected formula through cell range K33:K51.

n. Make a copy of the DailyTransactions worksheet, and place it to the right of the DailyTransactions worksheet. Name the new sheet DailyTransactionsFilter. In cell **D2**, enter Clothing. Format **A10:G40** as a Table. Create an advanced filter using the criteria in A1:G2.

o. Click cell **A11** of the **DailyTransactions** worksheet. Create a PivotTable, and place it on a new worksheet named PivotTableAnalysis. Add the Transaction, Trans_Category, and Trans_Item fields.

- Sort the transaction categories in Descending order.
- Count the number of transaction items.
- Change the text in A3 to Items Sold, and the text in cell B3 to # of Transactions.
- Apply Pivot Style Dark 2 to the PivotTable.
- Filter the PivotTable for Golf, Food, and Clothing.

p. Update the **Documentation** worksheet according to your instructor's directions.

q. Save the workbook, exit Excel, and then submit your file as directed by your instructor.

Problem Solve 2

Student data file needed:

 e03ShareClub.xlsx

You will save your file as:

 e03ShareClub_LastFirst.xlsx

Repair and Share Club

Information Technology

You have been asked to advise a new club on campus called the Repair and Share Club. The purpose of the club is to collect used desktop and laptop computers donated from area companies and refurbish them for members of the college community. The students in this club are responsible for collecting and rebuilding these computers. The dean requires a report of the club's activities over the academic year in spreadsheet format that tracks student involvement as well as donation information.

a. Open the Excel file, **e03ShareClub**. Save the file as e03ShareClub_LastFirst, using your last and first name.

b. On the **ClubInformation** worksheet, format **A5:J16** as a Table. Assign named ranges using the **Top row**.

c. A grade table appears in the spreadsheet assigning letter grades to grade point averages. In cell **J6**, enter a VLOOKUP function to determine a letter grade for the grade point average in cell I6. Use absolute references in your formula as necessary.

d. Insert a new column to the left of column H. In cell **H5**, type Courses Completed. Resize the column as needed.

e. In cell **H6**, enter an IF function with a nested AND function to analyze the content of F6 and G6. Return **Complete** if both cells contain a Y or **Incomplete** if one or both cells contain a N.

f. The dean has requested a report of the student's information. She wants a breakdown of the student's year in high school, volunteer hours, and their grades. Complete the following to create the dean's report.

- In cells **B22:B24**, using named ranges, create functions that count the number of students if their year in school matches the years listed in A22:A24.

- In cells **C22:C24**, using named ranges, create functions that total the number of volunteer hours if their year in school matches the years listed in A22:A24.

- In cells **C25:C26**, using named ranges, create functions that total the number of volunteer hours if the criteria in A26:A27 is met.

g. The dean has also requested an analysis regarding the companies involved in donating computers to the club. The club's goal is to have each company donate a minimum of 30 computers. Complete the following.

- In cell **A38**, type Totals. Create a formula in cells **B38:E38** to find the total sum for the Value, Donated, Desktops, and Laptops columns respectively.

- In cell **F33**, enter an IF function that evaluates the total number of computers donated from Safety Inc. If a minimum of 30 computers have been donated, the function will return **Goal Met**. If fewer than 30 computers are donated, the function will return **Under Goal**. Copy the formula through cell range F34:F37.

h. Using the data table, in cells A5:K16 insert a PivotTable in cell **A10** on the **PivotAnalysis** worksheet. Use the following criteria to create the PivotTable.

- Add the **Major** and **GPA** fields to the **FILTERS** area.
- Add the **Grade**, **Year**, and **FirstName** fields to the **ROWS** area.
- Add the **Volunteer Hours** and **LastName** fields to the **VALUES** area.
- Display subtotals at the bottom of each group.
- In cell **A10**, type Grades. In cell **B10**, type Total Hours. In cell **C10**, type Total Students. Resize the columns as needed.
- Insert a **slicer** for the **Grade** field. Format the slicer with **3** columns. Resize the slicer to remove the extra white space at the bottom. Move the slicer so the upper left corner is in cell **F10**.
- In the slicer, select **A**, **A-**, **B+**, and **B-**.

Critical Thinking 1

View the PivotTable data to determine how many students have a grade of an A or a B. Click cell **A2**, click the drop-down arrow, and then select the number of students.

- Clear the slicer filter, and then in the slicer, select the grade of an **A**. In cell **B8**, filter the data so the student with the highest GPA displays.

Critical Thinking 2

View the PivotTable data to determine which student has the highest GPA. Click cell **A4**, click the drop-down arrow, and then select the name of the student with the highest GPA.

- Clear the filters. Remove the **Grade** and **Year** fields from the ROWS area. Sort the Total Hours field in largest to smallest order.

Critical Thinking 3

View the PivotTable data to determine the student with the most volunteer hours and the least volunteer hours. Click cell **A6**, click the drop-down arrow, and then select the name of the student with the most volunteer hours. In cell **B6**, click the drop-down arrow, and then select the name of the student with the least amount of volunteer hours.

- Apply **Pivot Style Medium 9** to the PivotTable. Apply **Slicer Style Dark 1** to the slicer. Sort the PivotTable by Grades A to Z.

i. Insert a **Clustered Column PivotChart** on a new worksheet named PivotChartAnalysis. Remove the Total Students field from the VALUES area. Delete the legend. In the chart title, replace Total with Volunteer Hours by Student. Apply **Style 4** to the PivotChart.

j. Complete the Documentation worksheet according to your instructor's directions.

k. Save the workbook, exit Excel, and then submit your file as directed by your instructor.

Perform 1: Perform in Your Career

Student data file needed:

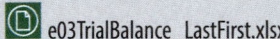 e03TrialBalance.xlsx

You will save your file as:

e03TrialBalance_LastFirst.xlsx

Analyze the Trial Balance

General Business

Finance & Accounting

You work for an optics manufacturing company that was recently purchased by another company. As part of the acquisition, the acquiring company changed your ledger account numbers to match their ledger account numbers. It is your responsibility to remap the trial balance for the prior years so it can be used for trending analysis.

a. Open the Excel file, **e03TrialBalance**. Save your file as e03TrialBalance_LastFirst, using your last and first name.

b. Make a backup copy of the TrialBalance worksheet. The new worksheet should be labeled TrialBalanceBackup, and placed as the last worksheet in the workbook.

c. On the TrialBalance worksheet, add a new field label in G1 named New Account, and a new field label in H1 named New Dept. Format both labels appropriately.

d. In cell G2, create a formula that will look up the account number in the Account worksheet and return the Target. Fill the formula down the column.

e. In cell H2, create a formula that will look up the account number in the Department worksheet and return the Target Department.
   - Hint: Because the Target Department column is to the left of the Source Account, you cannot use a lookup function.
   - If the function returns an error, it should display [None] rather than the error.
   - Fill the formula down the column. Adjust the column width as necessary.

f. Convert cell range A1:H8404 to a table, and then name it TB. Apply a style of your choice to the table.

g. Create named ranges for the range A1:H8404 using the top row as range names.

h. Add 15 blank rows above the table. Create and apply an advanced filter using the table headings and two rows of criteria. If entering criteria for Month, be sure to enter your criteria in date format.

i. In cell A5, type 1/31/2018. In cell B5, type Total, and then right align the cell contents. In cell C5, create a formula to calculate the total of the Balance range if the Month is equal to cell A5.

j. In cell E5, type E. In cell D5, create a formula to calculate the total of the Balance range if the Month is equal to cell A5 and the Type is equal to E.

k. In cell A6, type GeneralAdmin. In cell B6, type Average, and then right align the cell contents. In cell C6, create a formula to calculate the average of the Balance range for the new Dept in cell A6.

l. In cell B7, type Filtered Average, and right align the data. In cell C7, create a formula to average the Balance of the filtered data.

m. In cell B8, type Filtered Sum, and right align the data. In cell C8, create a formula to total the Balance of the filtered data.

n. Format all columns and values appropriately.

o. Insert a slicer from the table data, and apply a style similar to your table. Apply a new filter to the data by selecting multiple criteria for the slicer. Ensure that the slicer does not cover any data.

p. In row 10, copy the headers of your table. In row 11, add criteria to select the account 3010-01-82 and a balance less than –6,000,000.

q. In cell C13, type the word Balance.

r. In cell C14, add a database function using the TB database that will total the Balance based on the criteria you entered in row 11.

s. Insert a PivotTable on a new worksheet using the data in the TB table.
  - In the PivotTable, show the total Balance by quarter for every Description. (Quarters should go across the columns, Descriptions and Years should go down the rows.)
  - Ensure that the data can be filtered by New Dept. Select one department to display in your PivotTable.
  - Rename the worksheet and format the data appropriately.

t. Update the **Documentation** worksheet according to your instructor's directions.

u. Save the workbook, exit Excel, and then submit your file as directed by your instructor.

Perform 2: Perform in Your Life

Student data file needed:

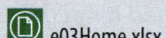 e03Home.xlsx

You will save your file as:

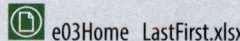 e03Home_LastFirst.xlsx

Change the Floors

Production & Operations

You have decided to replace the flooring in your home. However, you have a limited budget and need to review several possibilities and options. Since you are familiar with Excel, you will use an Excel workbook to help you with your decision.

a. Open the Excel file, **e03Home**. Save your file as e03Home_LastFirst, using your last and first name.

b. On the Searches worksheet, create named ranges for the range A12:C53 using the names in the top row.

c. Convert cell range A12:C53 to a table. Name the table range Flooring_Data.

d. Enter a slicer for Type. Select multiple criteria in the slicer. Format the slicer.

e. In cell A2, type Vinyl Tile. In cell A3, enter an AVERAGEIF function that will return the average cost per square foot for the type of flooring entered in A2.

f. In cell B3, enter a COUNTIFS function to count the number of flooring choices entered in B2 that have an average cost less than the average calculated in cell A3. Hint: Use the criteria of "<"&A3 for the average cost.

g. In cell C3, enter a database function that calculates the Max Cost per Sq Foot for the Criteria in row 6 & 7. (The Cost per Sq Foot in cell C7 has been rounded to 2 decimal places.)

h. In cell A10, create an INDEX with a nested MATCH function that will return the description of the flooring that matches the cost per sq foot in cell C3.

i. Copy the name in cell A10 to the MyChoices worksheet to the appropriate row in Column E.

j. Choose another flooring type from column D and copy the flooring type to cell A2 on the Searches tab. Again copy the result of your search from cell A10 to the MyChoices worksheet to the appropriate row in Column E. Repeat until all Descriptions have been chosen.

k. On the MyChoices worksheet, in Column F, create a lookup function that will return the cost per square foot based on the Description of the flooring.

l. In Column G, create a formula that multiplies the length by the width of the room to determine the total square footage.

m. In Column H, create a formula that multiplies the cost per sq. foot by the number of square feet to determine the total cost.

n. In cell H7, sum the total cost of your flooring.

o. Create a PivotTable on a new worksheet, based on the flooring data information on the Searches worksheet, that shows the average cost per square foot by type of flooring. Create a PivotChart from the PivotTable. Add an appropriate title and format both the PivotTable and PivotChart appropriately.

p. Complete the Documentation worksheet according to your instructor's directions.

q. Save the workbook, exit Excel, and then submit your file as directed by your instructor.

Perform 3: Perform in Your Team

Student data file needed:

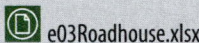 e03Roadhouse.xlsx

You will save your file as:

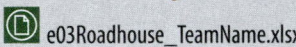 e03Roadhouse_TeamName.xlsx

Managing Inventory at the Roadhouse Bar and Grill

Production & Operations

You and your team manage the Roadhouse Bar and Grill, a local restaurant that specializes in home-cooked meals for breakfast, lunch, and dinner. The owner has given you a scaled-down version of the data with one day's worth of transactions. Your team needs to manage the inventory of beverage items to ensure you have enough beverages for each day you are open for business. You decided to create a shared folder in the "cloud" so you can share the workbook with your management team. All members of the management team will be responsible for updating portions of the database and sharing the updated database via the shared cloud folder.

a. Select one team member to set up the document by completing steps b – d.

b. Open your browser, and navigate to https://www.onedrive.live.com, https://www.drive .google.com, or any other instructor-assigned location. Be sure all members of the team have an account on the chosen system, such as a Microsoft or Google account.

c. Open the Excel file, **e03Roadhouse**. Save your file as **e03Roadhouse_TeamName**, replacing TeamName with the name assigned to your team by your instructor.

d. Share the spreadsheet with the other members of your team. Make sure each team member has the appropriate permission to edit the document.

e. Hold a team meeting, and discuss the requirements of the remaining steps. Make an action and communication plan. Consider which steps can be done independently and which steps require completion of prior steps before being started.

f. In Excel, your team members will need to complete the following. Apply formatting such as resizing fields, and use absolute cell references and relative cell references as deemed necessary.

- On the GeneralReport worksheet, create named ranges for the Servings List and Employee List. On the BeverageData worksheet, create named ranges for the beverage data list. Name the beverage data list range Beverage_Data.

- On the Transactions worksheet, use lookup functions to complete columns F, G, and I. Create a formula in column J to calculate the total spent on beverages based on the quantity sold and price.

- Using the data in cell range A10:J210, insert a table and then create appropriately named ranges. Enter rows of filter criteria in rows 2 and 3 that will be used to create an advanced filter, and then apply the filter. In cell range B6:B8, create appropriate database functions based on the specifications listed in cell range A6:A8. In cell range G6:G8, create appropriate subtotal functions based on the specifications listed in cell range F6:F8.

- Create a PivotTable for the data in your table, and insert it on the PivotTableAnalysis worksheet in row 10. Format the PivotTable with appropriate headings, titles, colors, and other formatting as you deem necessary. Use the PivotTable to answer the three questions at the top of the worksheet.

- Create a PivotChart on a new worksheet. Format the PivotChart with appropriate headings, titles, colors, and other formatting as you deem necessary. Name the new worksheet appropriately.

- On the BeverageData worksheet, insert a function in column G that retrieves the serving type from the Servings List on the GeneralReport worksheet.

- On the GeneralReport worksheet, create a formula to calculate the number of transactions in cell range C3:C5 based on the criteria in cell range A3:A5 and in the table. Create a formula to calculate the shift analysis in cell range F3:F5 based on the criteria in cell range E3:E5.

g. Complete the Documentation worksheet according to your instructor's directions. Minimally, include enough detail to identify which parts of the worksheets and/or workbook each team member completed.

h. In a custom header section of the Documentation worksheet, include the names of the students in your team. Spread the names evenly across each of the three header sections: left section, center section, and right section.

i. Save the workbook, exit Excel, and then submit your file as directed by your instructor.

Perform 4: How Others Perform

Student data file needed:

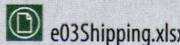 e03Shipping.xlsx

You will save your file as:

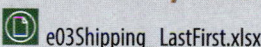 e03Shipping_LastFirst.xlsx

Shipping at ABC Distributor

Production & Operations

ABC Distributor ships to retail companies across the United States. Products are typically shipped in quantities of 20 to 500 units. The company examines shipping data to evaluate and adjust the shipments of items and reduce shipping expenses. In the spreadsheet provided, data with some analysis has been started. The company knows there are issues and would like help getting things straightened out, along with setting up and customizing additional information.

a. Open the Excel file, **e03Shipping**. Save your file as e03Shipping_LastFirst, using your last and first name.

b. On the ShippingData worksheet, a table has been set up and a calculated field was added, but formulas need to be developed and possibly corrected.

- In cell H16, the function that will retrieve the weight from the ProductWeights named range was set up, but it seems to be giving an error message in some cells. Check the formula, and make sure it will retrieve the weight correctly. Format the column appropriately.

- In cell I16, create a formula that will retrieve the Category in the second row of the Size_Category_List array, using the Weight field as the lookup value.
- In cell J16, create a formula that will find the shipping Unit_Cost by dividing ShipCost by Qty shipped.

c. On the ShippingData worksheet, create an advanced filter.

d. Set up calculations on the filtered data based on one of three data fields specified in cell B5.
  - In cell B6, create a formula that will find the average of the filtered data based on the field name listed in B5.
  - In cell B7, create a formula that will find the sum of the filtered data based on the field name listed in B5.
  - Clear the criteria in row 2, and then, in cell E2, type CA as criterion for the State.
  - In cell E6, create a formula that will average the field listed in E5 for the ShipData_All database using the criteria range A1:J2.
  - In cell E7, create a formula that will find the minimum of the field listed in E5 for the ShipData_All database using the criteria range A1:J2.
  - In cell E8, create a formula that will find the maximum of the field listed in E5 for the ShipData_All database using the criteria range A1:J2.
  - In cell E9, create a formula that will find the sum of the field listed in E5 for the ShipData_All database using the criteria range A1:J2.
  - In cell J5, create a formula to find the largest ShipCost from the ShipData.
  - In cell J6, knowing the largest shipping cost value in G6, create a formula to find the City location in conjunction with the row number for the largest shipping cost value in G6.
  - In cell J8, create a formula to find the largest Qty shipped from the ShipData.
  - In cell J9, similar to the function developed in cell G7, create a formula to find the City location for the row number that had the largest shipment quantity value in G9.

e. On the ShippingReport worksheet, database statistics need to be created or corrected. Summary data was partially created and needs to be completed for the cities where shipments have been fulfilled.
  - In cell B2, create a formula to find the average ShipCost of shipments to the City range listed in A2. Copy the formula down the column.
  - In cell E2, create a formula to find the total number of shipments to the City listed in A2. Copy the formula down the column.

f. Using the ShippingData worksheet as a basis, create a PivotTable on a new worksheet named PivotTableAnalysis. Analyze the data. Insert a slicer. Format with appropriate heading, colors, and other formatting as you deem necessary.

g. Create a 3-D Clustered Column PivotChart on a new worksheet. Format with appropriate headings, titles, colors, and other formatting as you deem necessary. Name the new worksheet appropriately.

h. Complete the Documentation worksheet according to your instructor's directions.

i. Save the workbook, exit Excel, and then submit your file as directed by your instructor.

Excel Business Unit 4

Build an Application with Multiple Worksheets and Workbooks

It is quite common for businesses or individuals to need to create worksheets and workbooks that are designed specially to meet their needs. Excel workbooks can also be structured to make it easier for other people to use the workbook. This business unit will explore using multiple worksheets, workbooks, and templates to tailor workbooks to meet specific needs. The business unit will also explore refining workbooks by auditing formulas, creating validation, making the workbooks user-friendly, and protecting worksheets and workbooks.

Learning Outcome 1:

Use multiple worksheets, workbooks, and templates to create an Excel application.

REAL WORLD SUCCESS

"During my internship I worked in the sales department, and one of my jobs was to summarize weekly reports sent in from the various salespeople. Everyone sent their information to me in different formats, and it took a long time to pull it all together — sometimes a day or more! I finally remembered that Excel can consolidate data, so I sent a template to the salespeople and asked them to fill it in each week. Now I could open their files, consolidate the data, and in a few hours have what used to take me days to complete. The salespeople really liked how easy the template was to use, and my boss was totally impressed with my ingenuity and said she will use the method with the next intern."

- Rebecca, recent graduate

Amy S Kinser, Brant Moriarity, Eric Kinser, Kristyn Jacobson

Learning Outcome 2:

Perform formula auditing, use data validation, create macros, and explore worksheet and workbook protection to refine an Excel application.

REAL WORLD SUCCESS

"As an intern, one of my jobs is to do a lot of data entry each week. When I started, I was given a workbook from the last intern to use, and I had to delete the data from the previous week, then save the workbook with a different name, and then enter the new weekly data. It often took me more time to set up the workbook each week than it did to enter the data. So I created a macro to clear the data for me, and now, with the click of a button, I have the worksheet cleared and am ready to enter the new data. After that, I set up macros for all the repetitive tasks I have to do in Excel. Not only has this made my job easier, but it gives me more time to be creative, which definitely gets the attention of my boss!"

- Jarrett, intern

Amy S Kinser, Brant Moriarity, Eric Kinser, Kristyn Jacobson

Microsoft Excel 2016

Chapter 7 | MULTIPLE WORKSHEETS, WORKBOOKS, AND TEMPLATES

Prepare Case

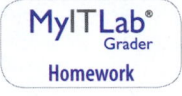

MyITLab® Grader
Homework

Human Resources

Turquoise Oasis Spa Therapist Sales and Service Analysis

The Turquoise Oasis Spa serves resort guests with a full range of services from traditional and alternative massage to aromatherapy and detoxification therapy. The spa is open seven days a week. Meda Rodate, the spa manager, would like a workbook that allows her to summarize and compare the sales of each therapist and services used for each day the spa is open.

Andrey Popov/Shutterstock

Student data files needed for this chapter:

 e04ch07Spa.xlsx

 e04ch07SpaLink.xlsx

 e04ch07SpaLogo.jpg

 e04ch07SpaPrices.xlsx

 e04ch07SpaSales.xlsx

You will save your files as:

 e04ch07Spa_LastFirst.xlsx

 e04ch07SpaKia_LastFirst.xlsx

 e04ch07SpaPrices_LastFirst.xlsx

 e04ch07SpaToDo_LastFirst.xlsx

 e04ch07SpaLink_LastFirst.xlsx

 e04ch07SpaRodate_LastFirst.xlsx

 e04ch07SpaTemplate_LastFirst.xltx

 e04ch07SpaCal_LastFirst.xlsx

Working with Multiple Worksheets

An Excel workbook can contain many worksheets — potentially hundreds of them. A single worksheet is a two-dimensional object; the rows are one dimension, and the columns represent a second dimension. When a workbook contains more than one worksheet, the multiple worksheets can represent a third dimension as long as the worksheets share an identical layout. Data from multiple worksheets can be referenced to generate new data via formulas, functions, and consolidation. Data can be copied and pasted from one worksheet to another and can be filled from one worksheet to many worksheets. Multiple worksheets can be selected at the same time, called **grouping**, and actions such as data entry and formatting can affect all the worksheets in the group at once, greatly increasing efficiency.

Data can be accessed between worksheets by using three-dimensional (3-D) references, and even named ranges can include cells from multiple worksheets. These are called, not surprisingly, 3-D named ranges.

In this section, you will work with the Spa workbook, which contains multiple worksheets. There are three sheets — one for each therapist — that need additional information to be added as well as two additional worksheets with schedule and price information about the therapists' services. You will complete the therapists' worksheets and then add additional worksheets to come up with summary information for the three therapists.

Group Worksheets

Grouping worksheets allows you to perform certain tasks once and have those tasks affect the same cells for all worksheets in the group. There are multiple ways to group worksheets. You can click the tab of a worksheet, hold down Ctrl, and then click the worksheet tab of additional worksheets you want to include in the group. The tabs of each worksheet included in the group will be highlighted with a white — or light — background color as a visual indicator. The file name in the title bar of the window will also show [Group] to remind you that you have worksheets grouped. Alternatively, if all of the worksheets you would like to group are contiguous, you can click the worksheet tab of a worksheet on one end, hold down Shift, and then click the worksheet tab on the other end of the contiguous worksheets.

Ungrouping worksheets is accomplished either by right-clicking a grouped worksheet tab and selecting Ungroup Sheets from the shortcut menu or by clicking the tab of a worksheet that is not grouped.

Opening the Starting File

Meda Rodate, the spa manager, has already started a workbook. She included data for product pricing in the PriceList worksheet and sales for December 16, 2018, in the SpaSales worksheet. She also created three additional worksheets, one for each of the spa therapists: Christy Istas, Kendra Mault, and Jason Niese. You will work with the existing worksheets to add formatting and formulas to make the workbook more useful.

In this exercise, you will open the Spa workbook.

E07.00

To Open the Spa Analysis Worksheet

a. Start **Excel**, click **Open Other Workbooks** in the left pane, and then double-click **This PC**. Navigate through the folder structure to the location of your student data files, and then double-click **e04ch07Spa**. If a Security Warning message displays, click the **Enable Editing** button.

b. Click the **File** tab, click **Save As**, and then double-click **This PC**. In the Save As dialog box, navigate to the location where you are saving your project files, and then change the file name to e04ch07Spa_LastFirst, using your last and first name.

c. Click **Save**.

Grouping Worksheets

When worksheets are grouped, what you do to one worksheet happens to the other worksheets in the group. For example, you can enter data, add formatting, insert and delete rows or columns, and delete or clear cells on all the worksheets in the group. While grouping worksheets is often the most efficient way to modify a workbook, there are some Excel features that are not available for grouped worksheets. For example, conditional formatting cannot be directly applied to grouped worksheets; in that case, conditional formatting would have to be applied to each worksheet individually.

In the Spa workbook, you will group the worksheets for each of the therapists and change the tab color for all the worksheets so they are easy to identify. You will do the same for the PriceList and SpaSales worksheets. The PriceList and SpaSales worksheets contain source data; the IstasChristy, MaultKendra, and NieseJason worksheets contain the analysis. By coloring their respective worksheet tabs differently, you will create a visual differentiation between the two types of worksheets in the workbook.

In this exercise, you will group worksheets and change tab colors.

 **E07.01**

SIDE NOTE

Pin the Ribbon

If your ribbon is collapsed, pin your ribbon open. Click the Home tab. In the lower right-hand corner of the ribbon, click Pin the Ribbon ⊞.

To Group Worksheets and Change the Tab Color

a. Click the **IstasChristy** worksheet. Press and hold Shift, and then click the **NieseJason** worksheet.

The IstasChristy, MaultKendra, and NieseJason worksheets are now grouped. Notice the [Group] tag next to the filename in the title bar, which indicates that you are in grouped worksheet mode.

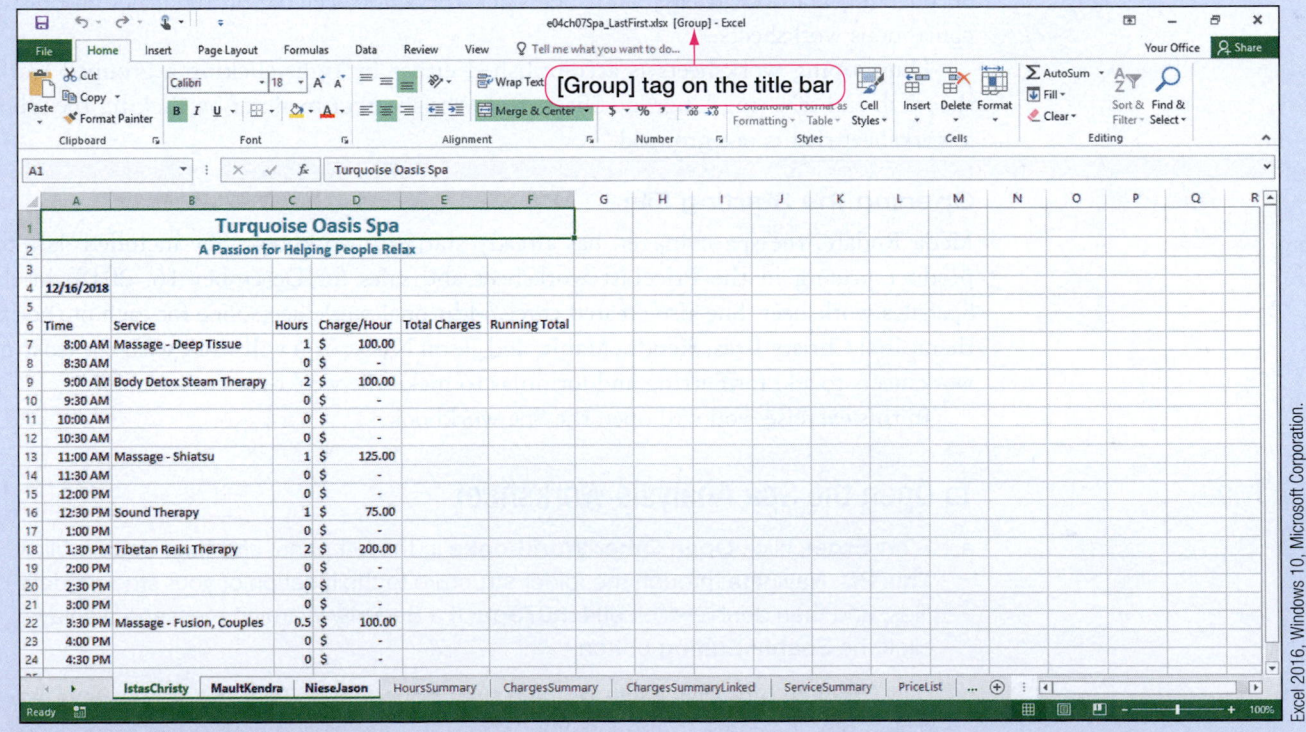

Figure 1　Worksheets grouped

b. Right-click the **IstasChristy** worksheet, point to **Tab Color**, and then select **Dark Blue, Text 2, Lighter 60%**, fourth column, third row.

c. Right-click the **IstasChristy** worksheet, and then click **Ungroup Sheets**.

d. **Save** 🖫 the workbook.

REAL WORLD ADVICE	Do Not Forget to Ungroup

Anyone who works with grouped worksheets occasionally forgets to ungroup them and then makes changes to several worksheets when the objective was to make changes to the visible worksheet only. If you forget to ungroup worksheets, you can quickly create more work than you saved by grouping worksheets in the first place. If you realize immediately that you still have your worksheets grouped, you can use the Undo command and then start again after you ungroup the worksheets.

Entering Data

Grouping worksheets can save a lot of data entry time. Grouped worksheets make the entry of worksheet structural elements such as titles, column headings, and row labels fast and efficient. Be careful, though. Errors made, such as misspellings or misplacement of a heading, are compounded across all grouped worksheets.

In the Spa workbook, you will group the therapist's worksheets again and enter information that will pertain to all the therapists. By grouping, the therapist's worksheets will all have the same structure, be visually consistent, and make data entry in the future much more efficient.

In this exercise, you will enter data into grouped worksheets.

 E07.02

SIDE NOTE
Flash Fill Not Available
Since the worksheets are grouped, many options, including Flash Fill, are not available to use with the group.

To Enter Data into Grouped Worksheets

a. On the **IstasChristy** worksheet, press and hold Shift, and then click the **NieseJason** worksheet.

b. Click cell **A25**, type Total, and then press Ctrl + Enter.

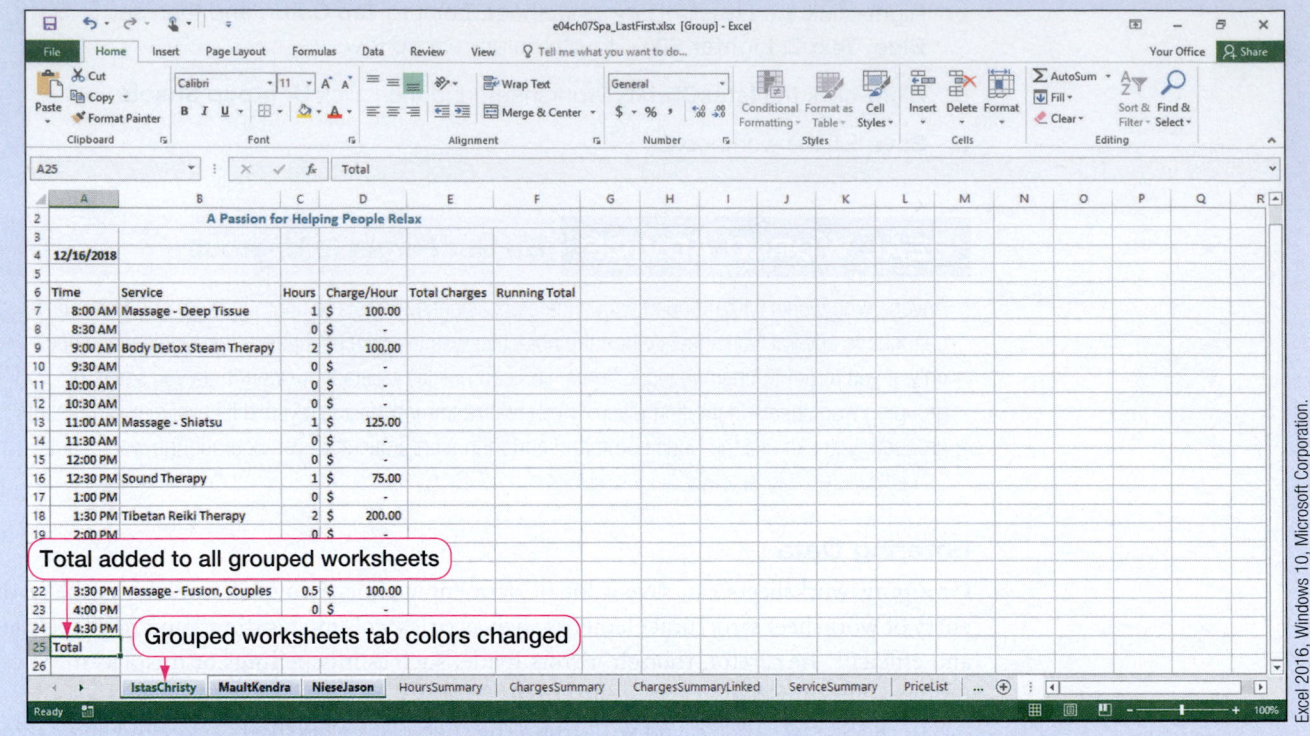

Figure 2 Data entered on IstasChristy worksheet

c. Click the **MaultKendra** worksheet. Notice that the text entered into the IstasChristy worksheet is also in the MaultKendra worksheet. Click the **NieseJason** worksheet, and you will see the same result.

d. Right-click the **IstasChristy** worksheet, and then select **Ungroup Sheets**.

e. **Save** 🖫 the workbook.

Entering Formulas

Entering formulas into grouped worksheets is a very efficient way to simultaneously create new data in multiple worksheets and is the same as entering data in grouped worksheets. Occasionally, while a formula may appear to work on multiple grouped worksheets, the data may appear too similar on the worksheets or even incorrect. It is very important to carefully check the results of your formulas to ensure that they show the intended results.

In the Spa workbook, part of the therapists' worksheets has been added, but two columns have no data. You will add formulas to these columns to calculate both the Total Charges for each therapist and the Running Total for each therapist.

In this exercise, you will enter formulas and functions into multiple worksheets.

 **E07.03**

To Enter Formulas and Functions into Multiple Worksheets

a. Click the **IstasChristy** worksheet, press and hold Shift, and then click the **NieseJason** worksheet.

b. Click cell **E7**, type **=C7*D7**, and then press Ctrl + Enter. Copy the formula to cell range **E8:E24**.

This formula multiplies the Charge/Hour by the number of hours to get the total charge for each service listed. Dashes appear in place of zeroes because the Accounting Number Format is applied to this range of cells on the IstasChristy worksheet.

c. Click cell **F7**, type **=E7**, and then press **Enter**. In cell **F8**, type **=F7+E8**, and then press **Ctrl** + **Enter**. Copy the formula in cell F8 to cell range **F9:F24**.

The Running Total should be the cumulative total for services performed. The first service will simply be the amount of that service, but all services after the first one will be the cumulative amount for the day, so each service in column E will be added to the previous service total charges in column F.

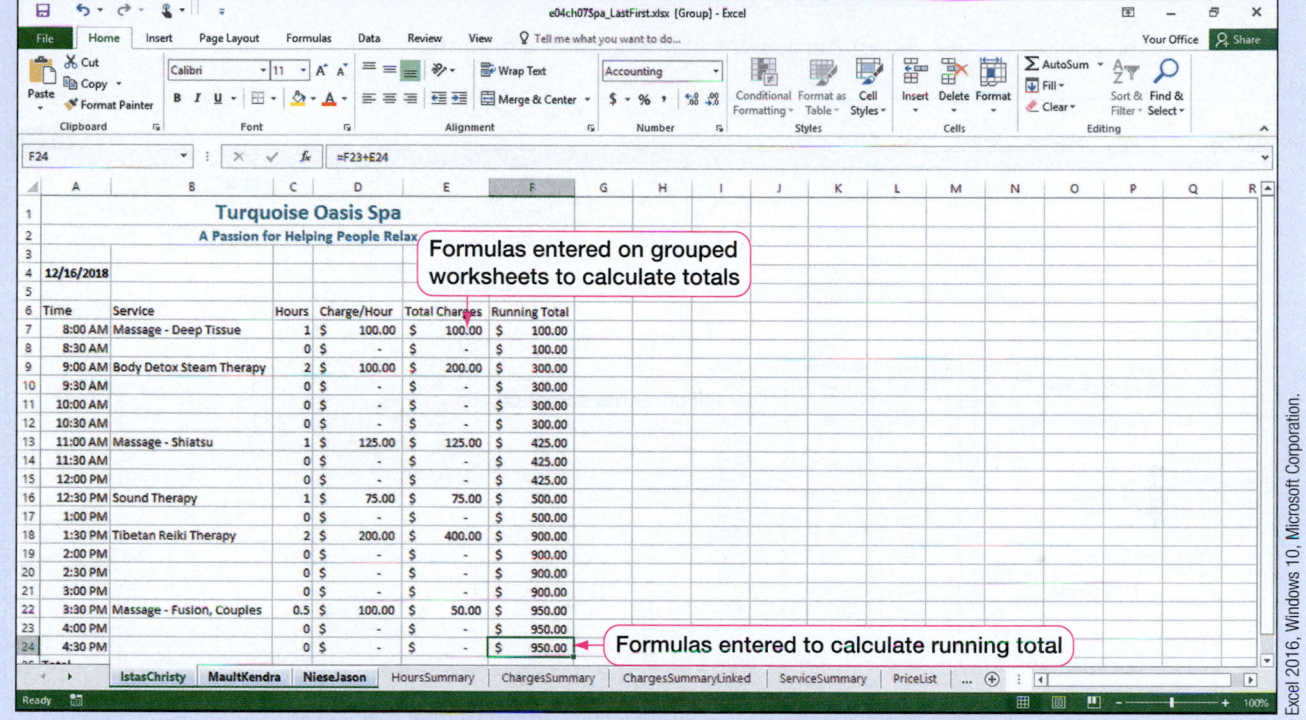

Figure 3 Formulas entered to calculate Total Charges and Running Total

d. Click the **HoursSummary** worksheet to ungroup the worksheets.

e. Save the workbook.

Filling Contents Across Worksheets

Fill Across Worksheets is a command that can be used to copy cell contents, formats, or both contents and formats to worksheets in a group. The source and destination worksheets must all be included in the group. Unlike copy and paste, in which cells can be copied from one location in a worksheet to a different location in the same worksheet or a different worksheet, Fill Across Worksheets will only fill to the same location in different worksheets; for example, cell A5 in Sheet1 can only be filled to cell A5 in other worksheets.

When using Fill Across Worksheets, the decision of whether to fill All, Contents, or Formats depends on what exactly you need to copy. Choose Contents when the target worksheets are already formatted or will be formatted differently than the source worksheet.

In this exercise, you will complete the IstasChristy worksheet and then apply the content and format to the other therapists' worksheets.

 **E07.04**

To Fill Contents Across Worksheets

a. Click the **IstasChristy** worksheet. Select cell range **C25:E25**, and on the Home tab, in the Editing group, click **AutoSum** [Σ AutoSum ▾].

b. With the cell range C25:E25 still selected on the **IstasChristy** worksheet, press and hold [Shift], and then click the **NieseJason** worksheet. On the Home tab, in the Editing group, click **Fill** [↓].

c. Select **Across Worksheets**. Click **Contents**.

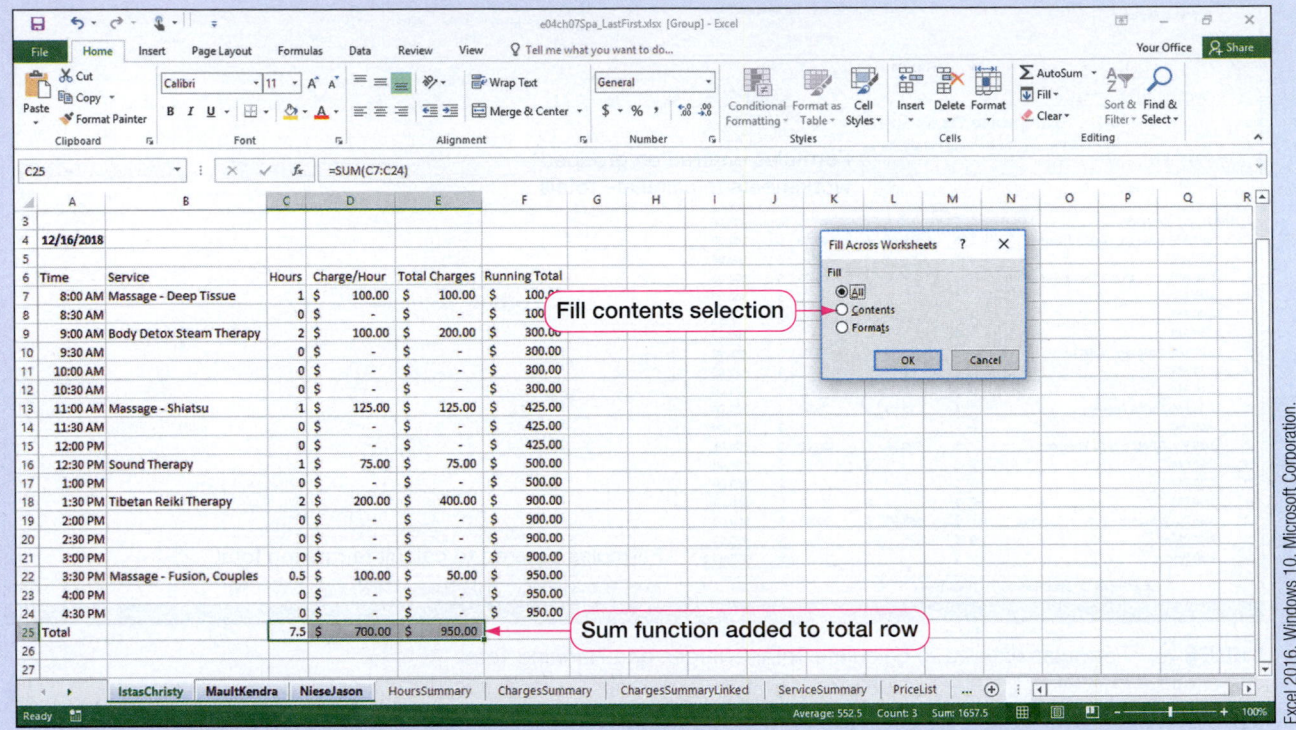

Figure 4 Fill Across Worksheets dialog box

d. Click **OK**.

   The SUM functions in cell range C25:E25 on the IstasChristy worksheet should be copied to both the MaultKendra and NieseJason worksheets.

e. Click the **HoursSummary** worksheet to ungroup the sheets.

f. **Save** [💾] the workbook.

Formatting Cells

By grouping worksheets, you can apply cell formatting to multiple worksheets at once. For example, any of the formatting tools in the Font, Alignment, and Number groups on the Home tab can be applied to grouped worksheets. Any ribbon tools that are not available when worksheets are grouped will be grayed out. Note that table formatting cannot be applied to grouped worksheets, nor can any modifications to cell formats — or cell contents — inside a table be applied when worksheets are grouped.

In this exercise, you will format cells on grouped worksheets.

 **E07.05**

To Format Cells on Grouped Worksheets

a. Click the **IstasChristy** worksheet, press and hold ⇧Shift, and then click the **NieseJason** worksheet. Select cell range **A6:F6**, and on the Home tab, in the Styles group, click **Cell Styles**, and then select **Accent5**.

b. Select cell range **C25:E25**, click **Cell Styles**, and then select **Total**. Click cell **F25** to see the formatting changes.

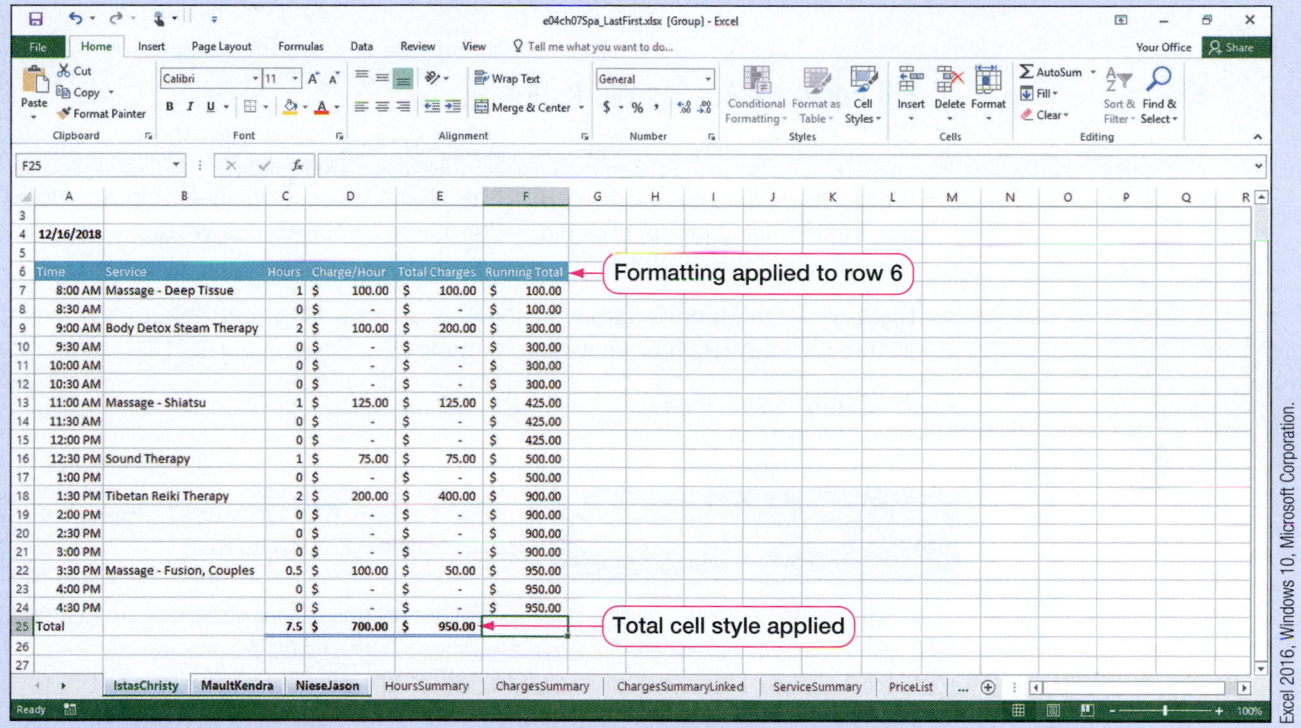

Figure 5   Cells formatted

c. Right-click the **IstasChristy** worksheet, and select **Ungroup Sheets**.

d. Save 🖫 the workbook.

REAL WORLD ADVICE	Copying and Pasting Data in Grouped Worksheets

Data can be copied from a single worksheet into grouped worksheets. Data can be copied from one set of grouped worksheets and then pasted into the same or a different set of grouped sheets. The criteria that determines whether or not Clipboard data can be pasted into a new location are as follows:

- The new location must have room available such that the pasted range has exactly the same shape as the copied range.

- When multiple worksheets are grouped, the pasted range cannot overlap the copied range in any dimension; for example, copied cells from group Sheet1:Sheet2 cannot then be copied to a paste range in group Sheet2:Sheet3, but they could be pasted to Sheet1:Sheet2 as long as the rows and columns of the copied range and the paste range do not overlap.

Filling Formats Across Worksheets

Filling formats across worksheets is similar to filling content across worksheets, but in this case, only the formatting is applied. By using the Fill Across Worksheets command, you can copy formatting without affecting formulas and other data. You will fill the formatting from columns E and F in the IstasChristy worksheet to the MaultKendra and NieseJason worksheets. Since the content of each therapist's worksheet is unique, using Fill Across Worksheets for the formats will create identical formatting without affecting therapist-specific content.

In this exercise, you will fill formats across worksheets.

 **E07.06**

To Fill Formats Across Worksheets

a. On the **IstasChristy** worksheet, select cells **E7:F24**.

b. Press and hold Shift, and then click the **NieseJason** worksheet. On the Home tab, in the Editing group, click **Fill** ⬇, and then select **Across Worksheets**. Click **Formats**, and then click **OK**.

c. Right-click the **MaultKendra** worksheet, and select **Ungroup Sheets**. Verify that all three worksheets have matching formatting.

d. **Save** 🖫 the workbook.

REAL WORLD ADVICE | Some Things Are Different When Worksheets Are Grouped

- You can use worksheet grouping to reorder your worksheets, but remember that the group will move as one in the reordering process. If you want to reorder the placement of worksheets within a group, the worksheets need to be ungrouped, and the reorder placement must be done manually.

- Be careful when printing. If you print when worksheets are grouped, every worksheet in the group is available to print, not just the active worksheet. The Print Preview navigation information will display the available pages for printing from the group. If you want only one worksheet to print, either specify which page or pages to print in the print options or ungroup and select the target worksheet.

- Many of Excel's commands and features are not available when worksheets are grouped — for example, the entire Data tab, table features and formatting, conditional formatting, shapes, charts, and sparklines.

Create Summary Worksheets

If your workbook contains multiple worksheets, you may want to summarize — or consolidate — the data on the multiple worksheets onto one summary worksheet. This can be useful when the worksheets represent different months' worth of data and you want to come up with a year-end summary or, in the case of the spa, you have multiple therapists and want to combine all their individual data on one summary worksheet.

One of Excel's more powerful features is the ability to reference data between worksheets. If you think of a worksheet as a two-dimensional array, then multiple worksheets in a workbook can be thought of as a three-dimensional array. Multiple worksheets represent a third dimension; therefore, references that address data across multiple worksheets are called 3-D references and 3-D named ranges. By using a 3-D formula with 3-D references, you can easily create a summary worksheet from multiple worksheets that are updated automatically as the source data is updated.

If your multiple worksheets contain either an identical structure or data with identical row and/or column labels, another option is to create a summary worksheet using the Consolidate feature. Consolidated data can be generated with or without links to the original source data. Summary data created using the Consolidate feature that is not linked is not automatically updated when the source data is changed. But if you create a summary and link the consolidated data back to the source data, then changes to source data are automatically reflected in the linked consolidation.

There are two ways in which data can be consolidated: by position and by category. **Consolidate by position** aggregates data in the same position in multiple worksheets. **Consolidate by category** aggregates data in cells with matching row and/or column labels; the data does not need to be in the same relative position to create a summary sheet. There can be a different number of labels among the worksheets, and there can be a different mix of labels among the worksheets.

QUICK REFERENCE	When and How to Consolidate

If you want to summarize data from multiple places (worksheets or workbooks), you have several options. The option you choose will depend on where the data is located and how it is organized.

- Consolidate by position — Use this method if you want to arrange the data in all the worksheets in identical order and location.

- Consolidate by category — Use this method if you want to organize the data differently than how it is presented in the separate worksheets, but use the same row and column labels so the consolidated worksheet matches the data.

- Consolidate by formula — Use this method if you want to use formulas with cell references or 3-D references to the other worksheets that you are combining because you do not have a consistent position or category of data to use.

- PivotTable report — Use this method if you want to use a PivotTable instead of a consolidation.

Creating a 3-D Reference

SIDE NOTE

A Space in a Worksheet Name

In a 3-D reference, if a worksheet name includes a space, the space is replaced with an underscore.

Three-dimensional references, or **3-D references**, allow formulas and functions to use data from cells and cell ranges across worksheets. A 3-D reference has the following structure: =worksheet name!cell reference. For example, the 3-D reference to cell C25 in worksheet Sheet3 is Sheet3!C25. Individual cells in multiple worksheets can be referenced by using a range of worksheets as well. For example, to reference cell C25 in Sheet1, Sheet2, and Sheet3 — assuming that the three sheets are in that order and contiguous — the reference is specified as Sheet1:Sheet3!C25. Finally, a range of cells can be referenced across several worksheets. For example, the cell range C3:C25 in worksheets Sheet1 through Sheet3 is specified as Sheet1:Sheet3!C3:C25.

On the Spa workbook, you will delete the date entered in cell A4 of the three therapists' worksheets. Then you will change the date so it is entered on the IstasChristy worksheet and the other two worksheets have a 3-D reference to it.

In this exercise, you will create a 3-D reference.

 **E07.07**

To Create a 3-D Reference

a. On the **MaultKendra** worksheet, press and hold [Shift], and then click the **NieseJason** worksheet. Click cell **A4**, and then press [Delete].

b. In cell A4, type **=**, and then click the **IstasChristy** worksheet. Click cell **A4**, and then press [Ctrl] + [Enter]. This should insert a reference to cell A4 from the IstasChristy worksheet in cell A4 on both the MaultKendra and NieseJason worksheet.

c. Click the **IstasChristy** worksheet to ungroup the sheets.

d. **Save** 🖫 the workbook.

Naming a 3-D Reference

A **3-D named range** references the same cell or range of cells across multiple worksheets in a workbook. A 3-D named range cannot be defined in the Name box; you must use the Define Name command in the Defined Names group on the Formulas tab.

    In this exercise, you will name ranges of cells so you can refer to them at a later time by the name and not the cell reference.

 **E07.08**

To Create a 3-D Name

a. On the **IstasChristy** worksheet, click cell **E25**.

b. Click the **Formulas** tab, and in the Defined Names group, click **Name Manager**.
    There is already one named range in the workbook: ProductTable. This name refers to cell range A2:D26 on the PriceList worksheet and is used in the VLOOKUP function in cell range D7:D24. The VLOOKUP in cell D7 is used to look up the Charge/Hour for the service entered in cell B7. The Charge/Hour is found in the table called ProductTable.

c. Click **New** in the Name Manager dialog box, and then in the Name box, type TotalCharges3D. To the right of the Refers to box, click the **Collapse Dialog** button 📑. Press and hold [Shift], click the **NieseJason** worksheet, and then click the **Expand Dialog** button 📑. The Refers to box should now show ='IstasChristy: NieseJason'!$E$25.
    This reference is to cell E25 on the IstasChristy worksheet, the MaultKendra worksheet, and the NieseJason worksheet, in that order.

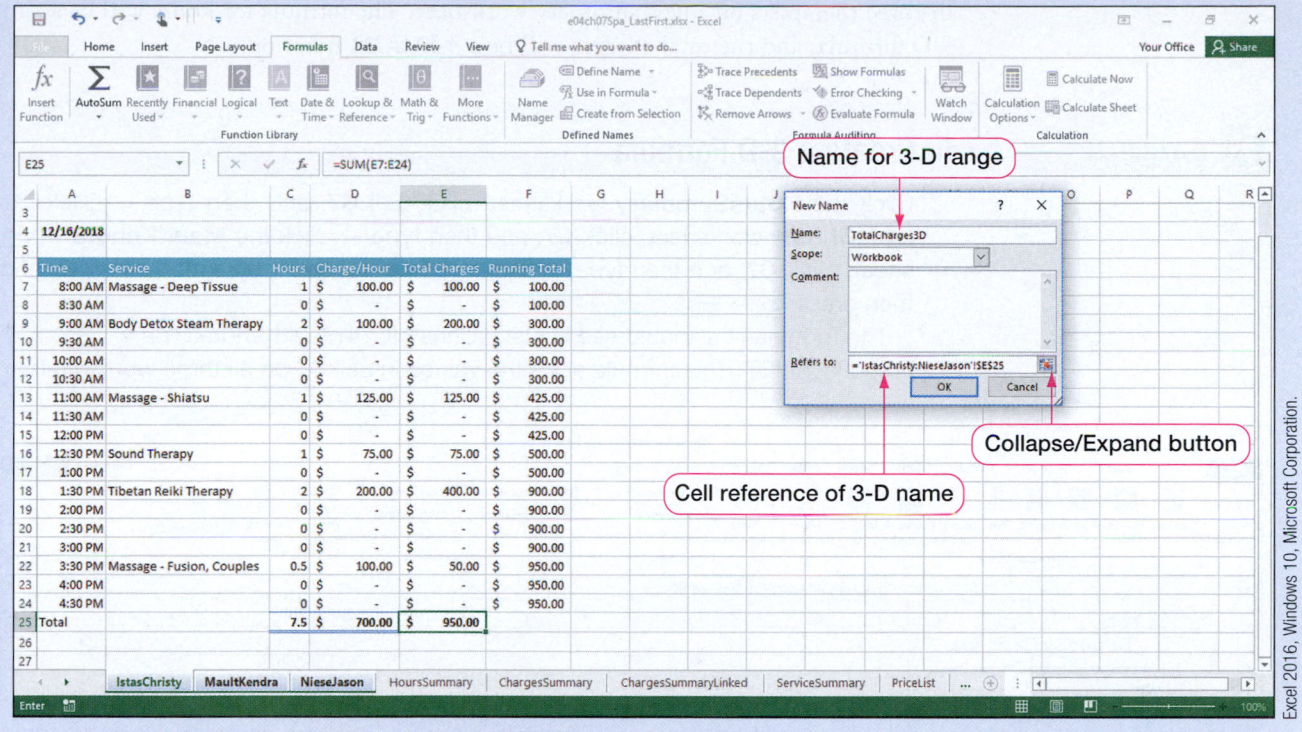

Figure 6 3-D named range added to a worksheet

    d. Click **OK**, notice that TotalCharges3D is now listed in the Name Manager, and then click **Close**.

    e. Save 💾 the workbook.

REAL WORLD ADVICE **Order Matters When Working with Grouped Worksheets**

When you assign a name to a range of cells, the first cell reference and the last cell reference are recognized, and all the cells in between are included in the range. For example, a cell range A1:C25 named "Profits" will always use the values in cell range A1:C25, no matter how you move the cells around.

    Naming ranges that span multiple worksheets works the same way. The difference is that if you start with a range of worksheets, as in the case example that looks like IstasChristy:NieseJason, when you rearrange the worksheets, the range will no longer be accurate. For example, if you decide to move the MaultKendra tab to the right of the NieseJason worksheet, it would no longer be included in the named range IstasChristy:NieseJason. You therefore must be extremely careful when you have named ranges and want to rearrange the worksheets. One option is to name a blank worksheet "Begin" to use for the first worksheet in the named range and another blank worksheet named "End" to use as the last worksheet in the range. This way, you are always reminded to keep the actual worksheets with data between the Begin and End worksheets.

Creating a 3-D Formula

When you have data on multiple worksheets and want to consolidate that data into a summary worksheet, you can use a 3-D formula. A **3-D formula** references the same cell or range of cells across multiple worksheets in a workbook. Creating a 3-D formula is very similar to creating any other formula, but instead of typing the formula, it is generally easier to point to and click the cells. That way, you can avoid spelling errors that may make the formula incorrect.

In the Spa workbook, you will summarize the number of hours and total charges for all three therapists on a new summary worksheet. The formula for hours will be a simple 3-D formula, and the total charges will be a 3-D SUM function.

 **E07.09**

To Create a 3-D Formula

a. Click the **HoursSummary** worksheet, click cell **B7**, and then type **=**. Click the **IstasChristy** worksheet, click **C7**, and then type **+**. Click the **MaultKendra** worksheet, click **C7**, and then type **+**. Click the **NieseJason** worksheet, click **C7**, and then press Ctrl + Enter.

The formula you should see is =IstasChristy!C7+MaultKendra!C7+ NieseJason!C7. This formula adds the values in cell C7 on all three worksheets.

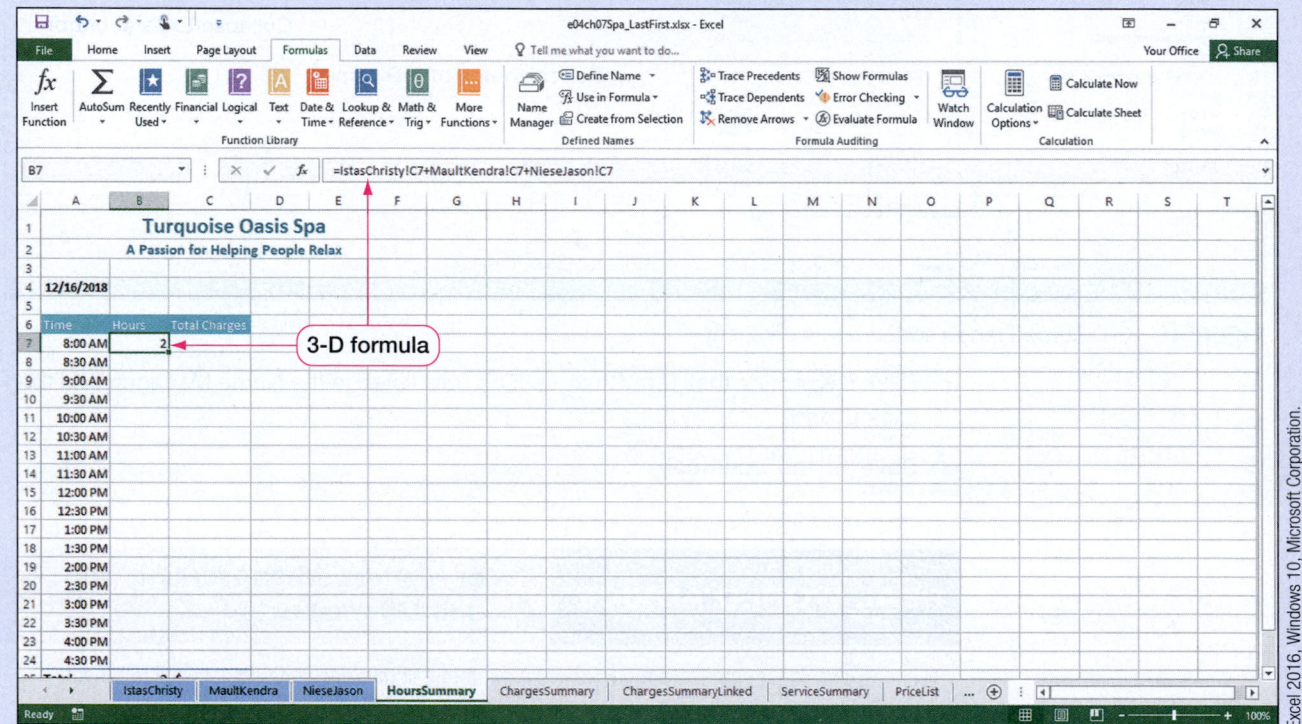

Figure 7   3-D formula added to worksheet

b. Copy the formula to cell range **B8:B24**.

c. Click cell **C7**, and then type **=SUM(**. Click the **IstasChristy** worksheet, click **E7**, press and hold Shift, click the **NieseJason** worksheet, type **)**, and then press Ctrl + Enter.

The formula you should see is =SUM(IstasChristy:NieseJason!E7). This formula sums the values in cell E7 on sheets IstasChristy through NieseJason.

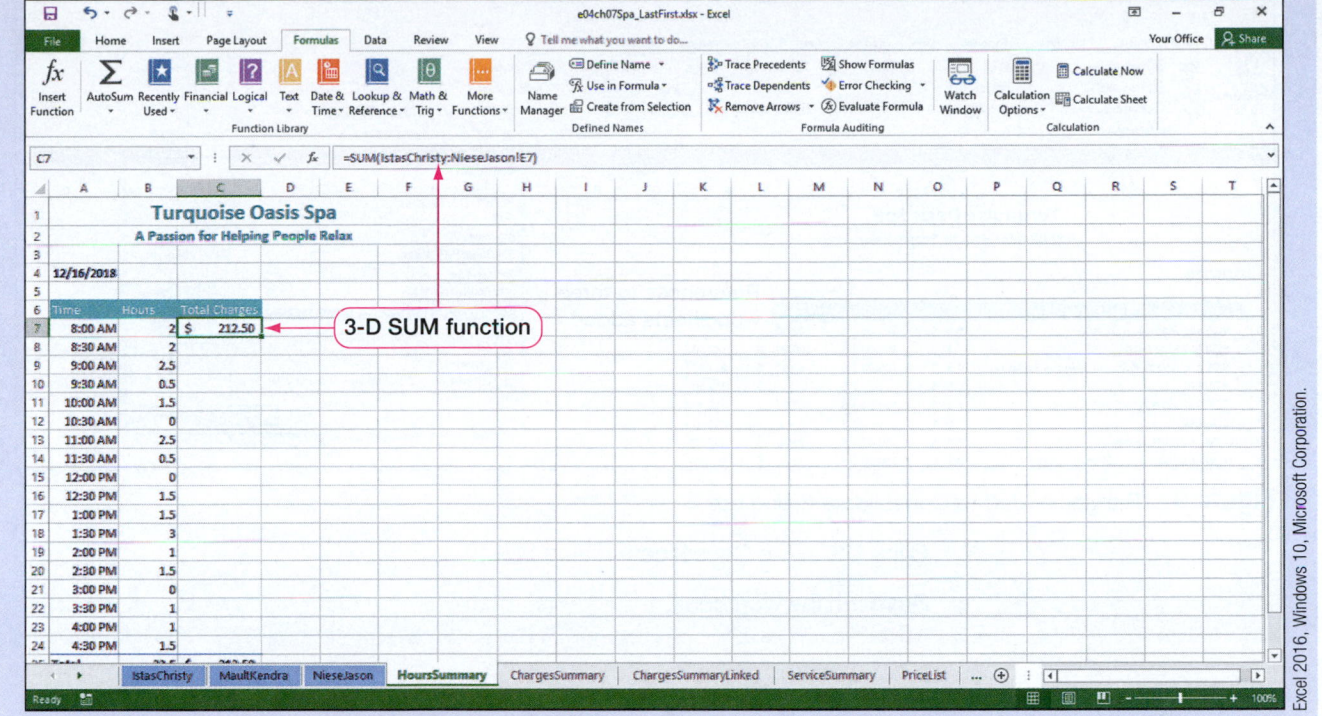

Figure 8 3-D SUM function added to worksheet

d. Copy the formula to cell range **C8:C24**.

e. **Save** the workbook.

Consolidating Data by Position

Consolidate by position can be used to create a summary worksheet when the source worksheets all have an identical structure, such that the same location in each worksheet contains the same relative data. For example, if cell A5 contains sales discounts for bulk sales in the January worksheet, cells A5 in worksheets February through December also contain sales discounts for bulk sales. The range selected in each worksheet must include the exact same number of rows and columns in each worksheet that is part of the consolidation.

In this exercise, you will consolidate data by position.

 **E07.10**

SIDE NOTE
Only One per Worksheet

A worksheet can store only one consolidation. If you want to create more than one consolidation, they should be placed on different worksheets.

To Consolidate Data by Position

a. Click the **ChargesSummary** worksheet, and then click cell **B7**. Click the **Data** tab, and then, in the Data Tools group, click **Consolidate**. In the Consolidate dialog box, make sure **Sum** is selected in the Function box.

b. Click the **Reference** box, click the **IstasChristy** worksheet, and then select cell range **E7:F24**. If necessary, scroll to the left of the worksheet tabs and move the Consolidate dialog box to make the selection.

c. Click **Add** in the Consolidate dialog box.

d. Click the **MaultKendra** worksheet, and notice that cell range E7:F24 is still selected. Click **Add** in the Consolidate dialog box.

e. Click the **NieseJason** worksheet, and notice that cell range E7:F24 is still selected. Click **Add** in the Consolidate dialog box.

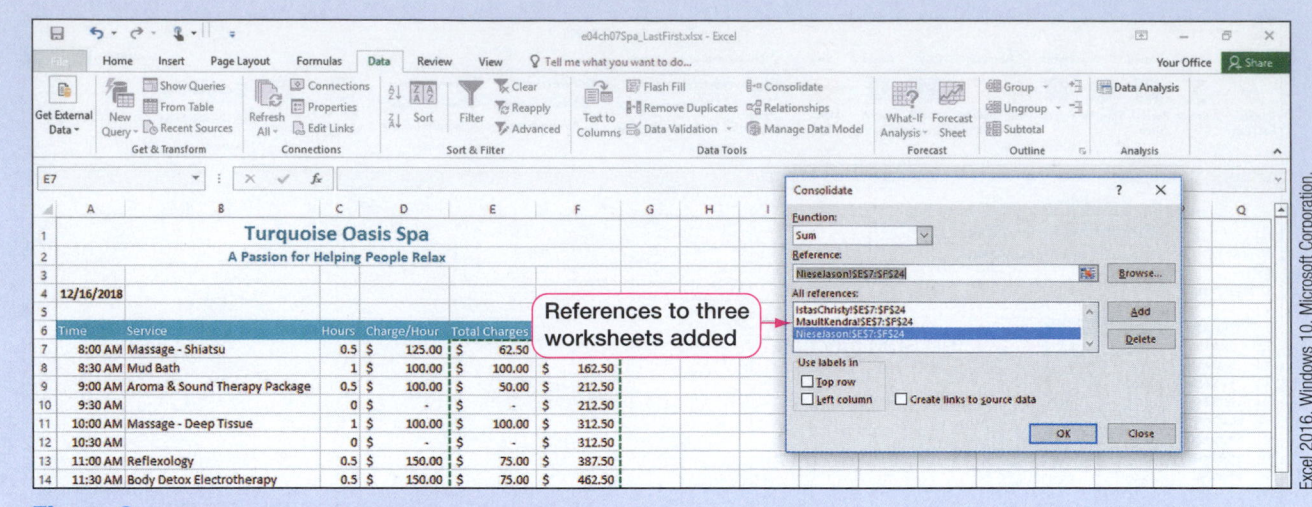

Figure 9 Ranges added to Consolidate dialog box

    f. Click **OK** in the Consolidate dialog box.

    g. Save  the workbook.

Consolidating Data by Category

Consolidating by category is more flexible than consolidating by position. When consolidating by category, Excel examines row and/or column headings to determine which cells should contribute to a given calculation. Data does not need to be in the same relative position between and among worksheets; it simply needs to share the same row and/or column labels. Labels can even be repeated multiple times in a single worksheet.

In the Spa workbook, you will consolidate therapists' sales by service rather than by time. Because there is no way of knowing ahead of time where specific services will be located in the source worksheets, consolidation by category is the only realistic option.

In this exercise, you will consolidate data by category.

E07.11 To Consolidate Data by Category

    a. Click the **ServiceSummary** worksheet, and then click cell **A6**. On the **Data** tab, in the Data Tools group, click **Consolidate**. In the Consolidate dialog box, make sure **Sum** is selected in the Function box, and then click the **Reference** box.

    b. Click the **IstasChristy** worksheet, and then select cell range **B6:E24**. Note that you do not include the Running Total because a sum of Running Total by category would be a meaningless number. Click **Add**.

    c. Click the **MaultKendra** worksheet, verify that cell range B6:E24 is selected, and then click **Add**. Click the **NieseJason** worksheet, verify that cell range B6:E24 is selected, and then click **Add**.

    d. Under the Use labels in section, select the **Top row** and the **Left column** check boxes.

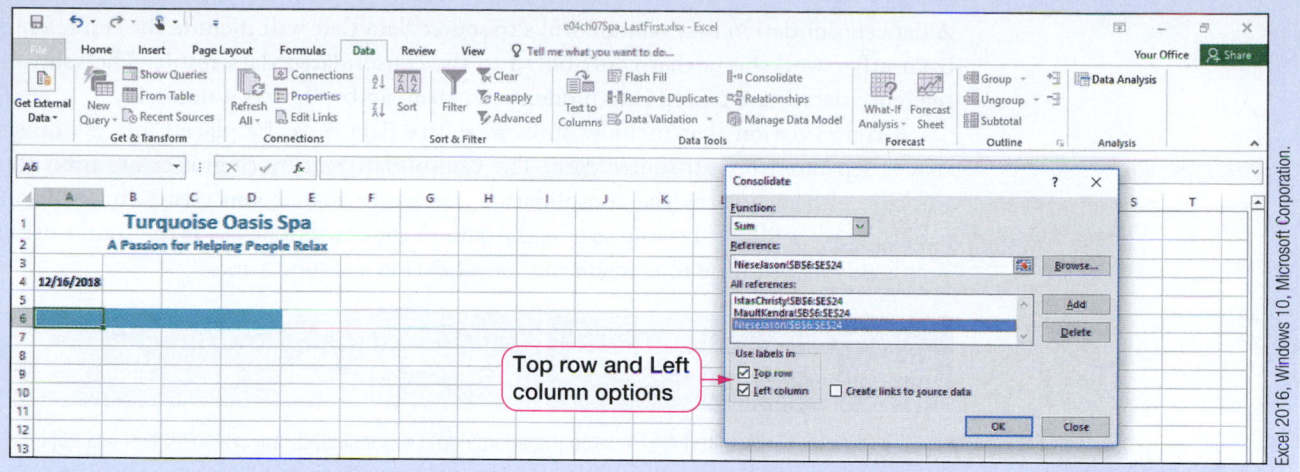

Figure 10 Consolidate dialog box options

e. Click **OK** in the Consolidate dialog box. Click cell **A6**, and then type Service. The Consolidate function does not copy the title of the far-left column. Press Ctrl + Enter. Row 10 will be blank because there are rows in each worksheet for times that are blank, and this is the consolidation of those rows.

f. Select columns **A:D**. Click the **Home** tab, and in the Cells group, click **Format**, and then select **AutoFit Column Width**.

g. Click cell **D20**, type =SUM(TotalCharges3D), and then press Ctrl + Enter. This SUM function uses the 3-D named range created in an earlier exercise.

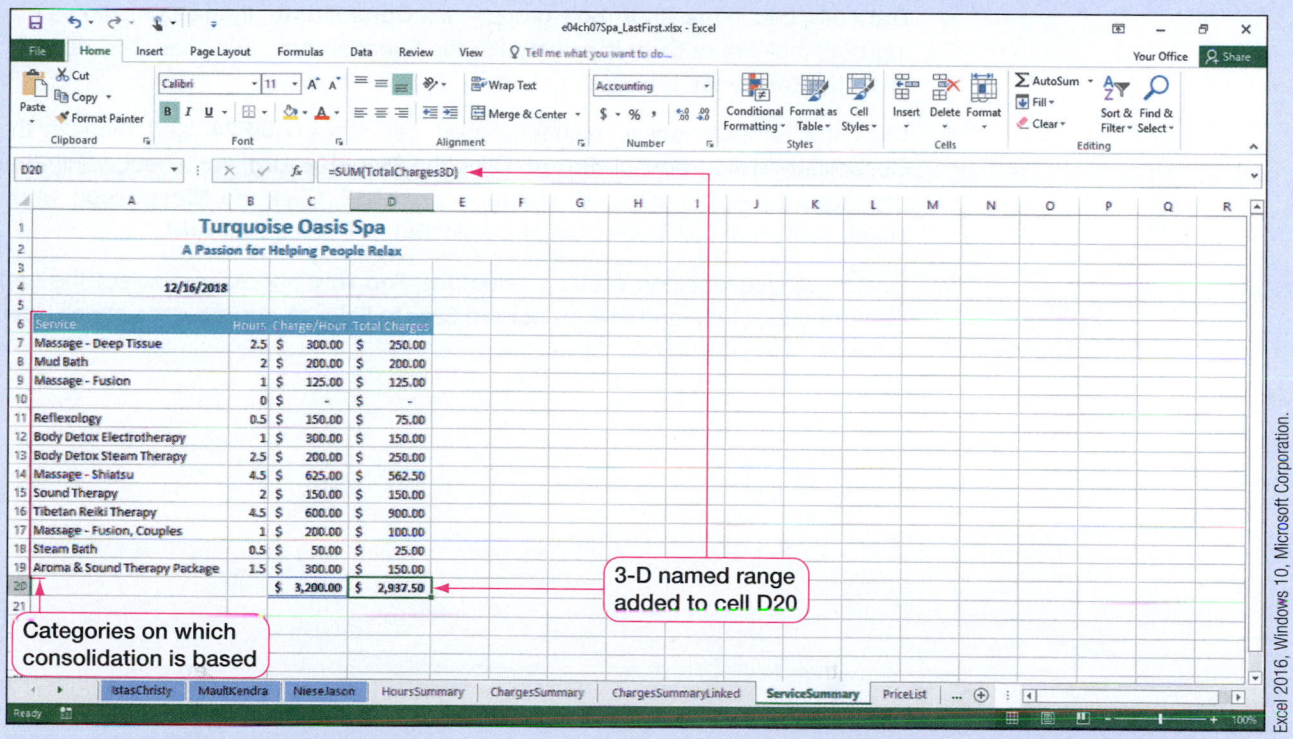

Figure 11 Consolidate by category

h. **Save** the workbook.

Creating Links to Source Data in a Consolidation

A data consolidation may contain links to source data that will include the cell references from other worksheets that contributed to the consolidated data result. The source cell reference details are placed into hidden rows that can be viewed if necessary.

A consolidation that includes links to source data must be placed into a worksheet that is separate from all source data. The Consolidate feature cannot create links to the worksheet that contains the consolidation. Be aware that if you create links to source data then you will not be able to edit the data in the consolidation. If the source data has changed, you will have to recreate the consolidation a second time.

REAL WORLD ADVICE	Considerations for Including Links to Source Data

When data is consolidated and links to the source data are included, the consolidation will not be automatically updated when changes are made to the source data.

In such a case, the entire data consolidation must be deleted and then regenerated. Some experienced Excel users would recommend that you avoid linking to source data in situations in which a consolidation by category will need to be occasionally updated unless consolidation by position could be used as well.

In this exercise, you will create a linked consolidation of sales by appointment time.

 **E07.12**

To Consolidate with Links to Source Data

a. Click the **ChargesSummaryLinked** worksheet, and then click cell **A6**. Click the **Data** tab, and in the Data Tools group, click **Consolidate**. In the Consolidate dialog box, make sure **Sum** is selected in the Function box, and then, if necessary, click the **Reference** box.

b. Click the **IstasChristy** worksheet, select cell range **A6:F24**, and then, in the Consolidate dialog box, click **Add**. Click the **MaultKendra** worksheet, verify that cell range A6:F24 is selected, and then click **Add**. Click the **NieseJason** worksheet, verify that cell range A6:F24 is selected, and then click **Add**.

c. Under the Use labels in section, select the **Top row** check box, select the **Left column** check box, and then select the **Create links to source data** check box.

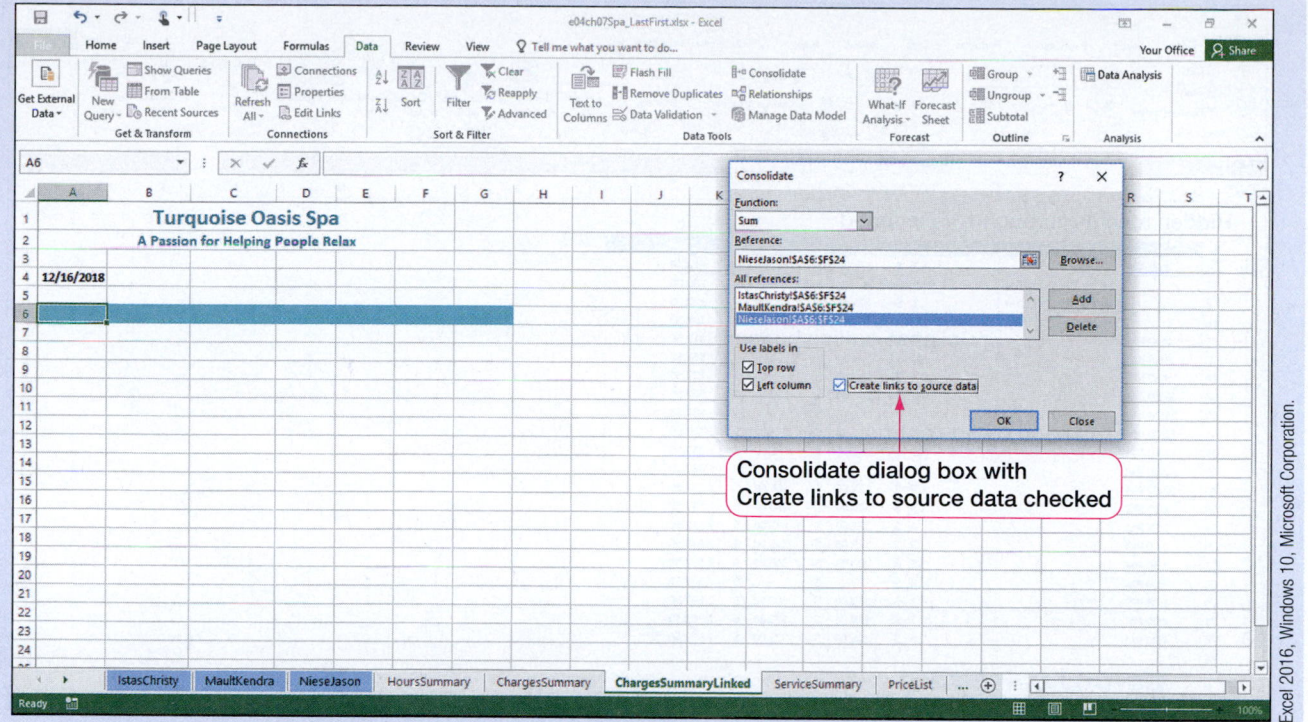

Figure 12   Consolidate dialog box with link box checked

---

d. Click **OK**. Select columns **A:G**. Click the **Home** tab, and in the Cells group, click **Format**, and then select **AutoFit Column Width**.

e. Select cell range **A10:A78**. The hidden rows include the links to the consolidated data. On the Home tab, in the Number group, click the **Number Format** arrow, and then select **More Number Formats**. In the Category box, click **Time**, and then in the Type box, click **1:30 PM**. Click **OK**.

f. Click the **Expand Outline** button ⊞ next to row 14.

Rows 11:13, which were previously hidden, are revealed. Notice that the filename for your workbook is shown in column B. Consolidation can be used among multiple workbooks, and column B identifies the source workbook for each item of data. Because you are consolidating sheets in a single workbook, column B is irrelevant.

Notice that column C is empty. Service names are text and cannot be summated, so column C does not contain any information. Further, Charge/Hour in column E is not particularly informative. A sum of Charge/Hour is not a meaningful number — its inclusion, while necessary for consolidation, is not meaningful.

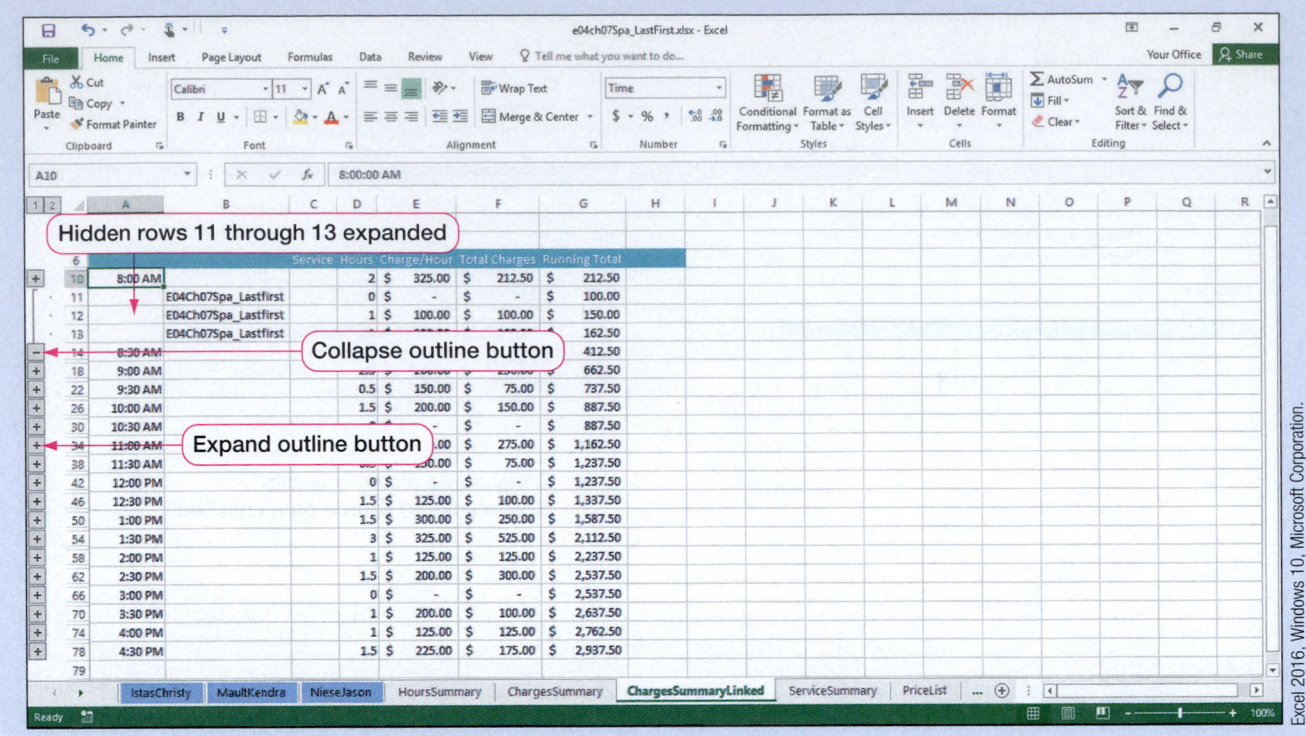

Figure 13 Hidden rows in consolidated summary

g. Click the Level 2 outline button ☐2☐ just to the left of the Select All button ◢. The source data that contributes to each of the subtotals for a category — time in this case — is expanded.

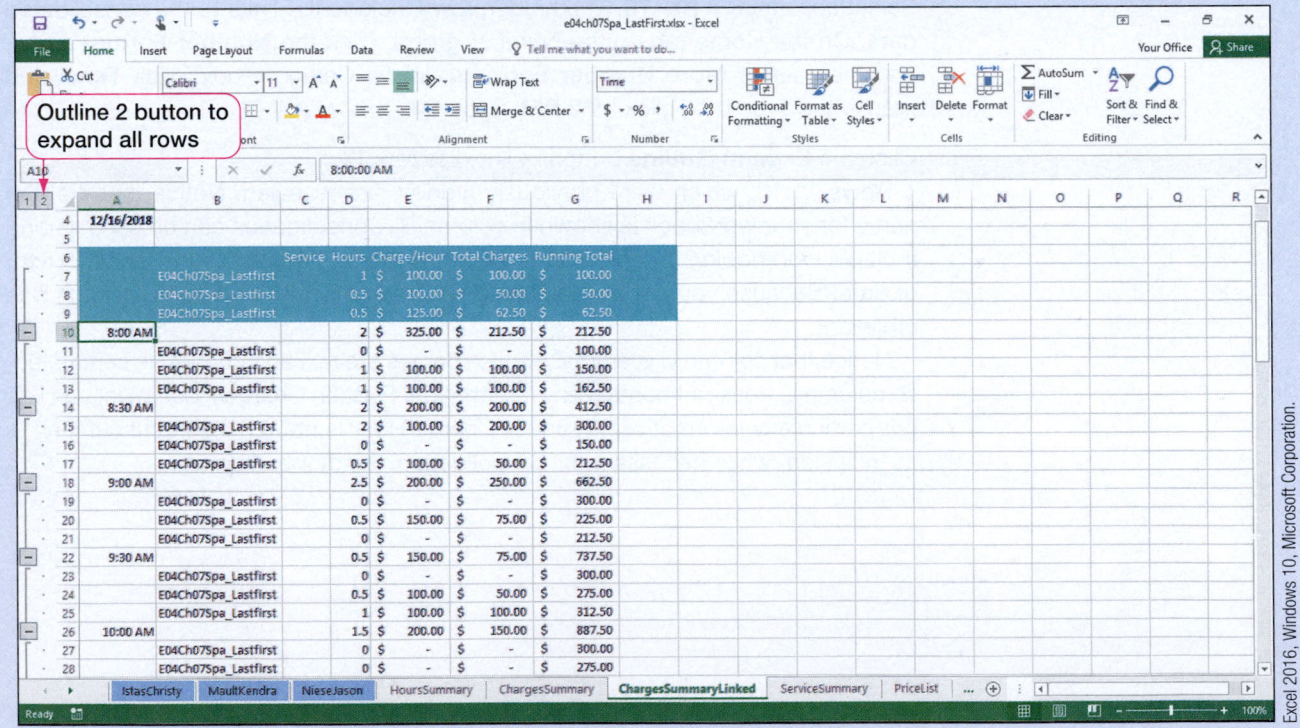

Figure 14 Level 2 outline in consolidated summary

h. Click cell **G8**.

Notice the contents in the formula bar. The 50.00 in cell G8 came from source data in the MaultKendra worksheet, in cell F7. Because a linked consolidation keeps track of the locations of source data, any changes to source data are automatically reflected in the consolidation.

i. Click the **IstasChristy** worksheet, and then press Ctrl + Home.

j. **Save** 🖫 the workbook. If you need to take a break before finishing this chapter, now is a good time.

REAL WORLD ADVICE	Consolidating Between Different Workbooks

You can consolidate not only worksheets, but also workbooks. The easiest way to do this is to have all the source workbooks open, start defining the consolidation, and then navigate to each workbook, select the source range with the mouse, and add the reference to the consolidation. This type of consolidation is useful if you have staff members using similarly structured workbooks and need to combine the data for a summary. If you know you are going to need this kind of summary information, it may be useful to provide your staff or group members with templates to work from or some other standard worksheet so that, when it comes time to collaborate, it will be quick and easy for one person to do.

Using Multiple Workbooks

Excel can access data in other workbooks using external references in formulas and functions. A primary advantage of the ability to reference data in multiple workbooks is that you can access data at its source — in its original location. You do not need to copy the data to your workbook and then be concerned about keeping the copied data up to date when the original data changes.

In this section, you will work with multiple workbooks at the same time. You will create a copy of the Spa workbook and link it to the SpaPrices workbook. Then you will create copies of the SpaPrices workbook in order to collaborate by using two source workbooks and one master workbook. You will change data in the two source workbooks, and then merge the changes into the master workbook.

Work with Multiple Workbooks

Working with multiple workbooks is very similar to working with multiple worksheets. Excel 2016 opens each workbook in an individual window, so you can use multiple monitors to view different workbooks, or you can arrange the windows on one monitor to see multiple workbooks at one time.

Data can be referenced between workbooks using 3-D ranges and formulas, so when the source workbook is updated, the changes flow through to the summary workbook. You can also choose whether or not to link workbooks to make the updating automatic or not.

Viewing Multiple Workbooks at One Time

When you want to view multiple workbooks on one screen, you can choose how they are arranged. Once you have all the workbooks open on your desktop, you can choose to arrange them in four different ways: Tiled, Horizontal, Vertical, or Cascade. How you choose to view them will be determined by how you want to work with them and your personal preference.

In this exercise, you will open another workbook along with the Spa workbook that is already open, and then you will view the two workbooks in different views.

 **E07.13**

To View Multiple Workbooks at One Time

a. If you took a break, open the **e04ch07Spa** workbook.

b. Click the **File** tab, and then click **Open**. Navigate to where your student data files are located, click **e04ch07SpaPrices**, and then click **Open**. Click **Enable Editing** if necessary. The two workbook windows will cascade, one in front of the other.

> **Troubleshooting**
>
> Do you have more than two workbooks open? All open workbooks will be included in this arrangement, so if you do not want to see a particular workbook, be sure to close it and arrange the workbooks again.

c. Click the **View** tab, and in the Window group, click **Arrange All**, click the **Tiled** option, and then click **OK**. Notice that the workbooks are resized to fit on one screen. To edit a workbook, click that workbook to make it active, and then make your changes.

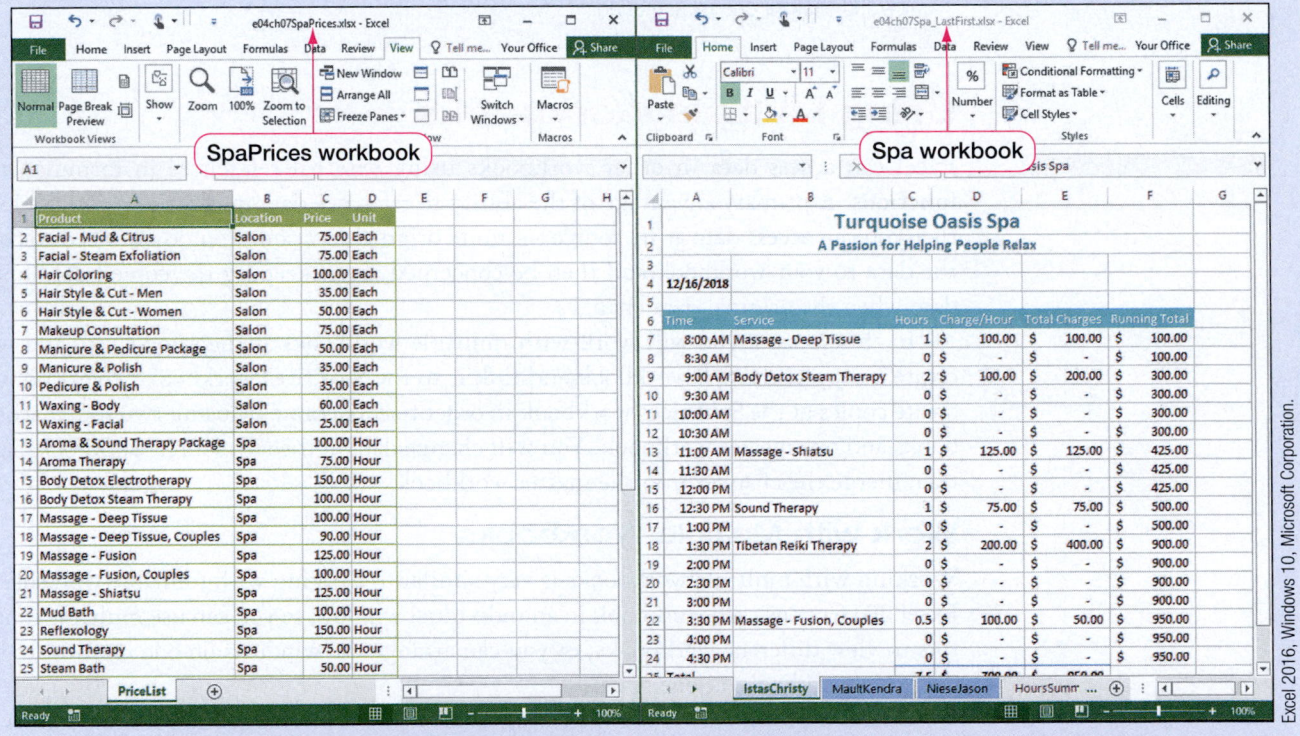

Figure 15   Workbooks arranged with the Tiled option

d. On either of the workbooks, click **Arrange All** again, click the **Horizontal** option, and then click **OK**. Notice that the workbooks are resized to fit the width of the screen, one above the other.

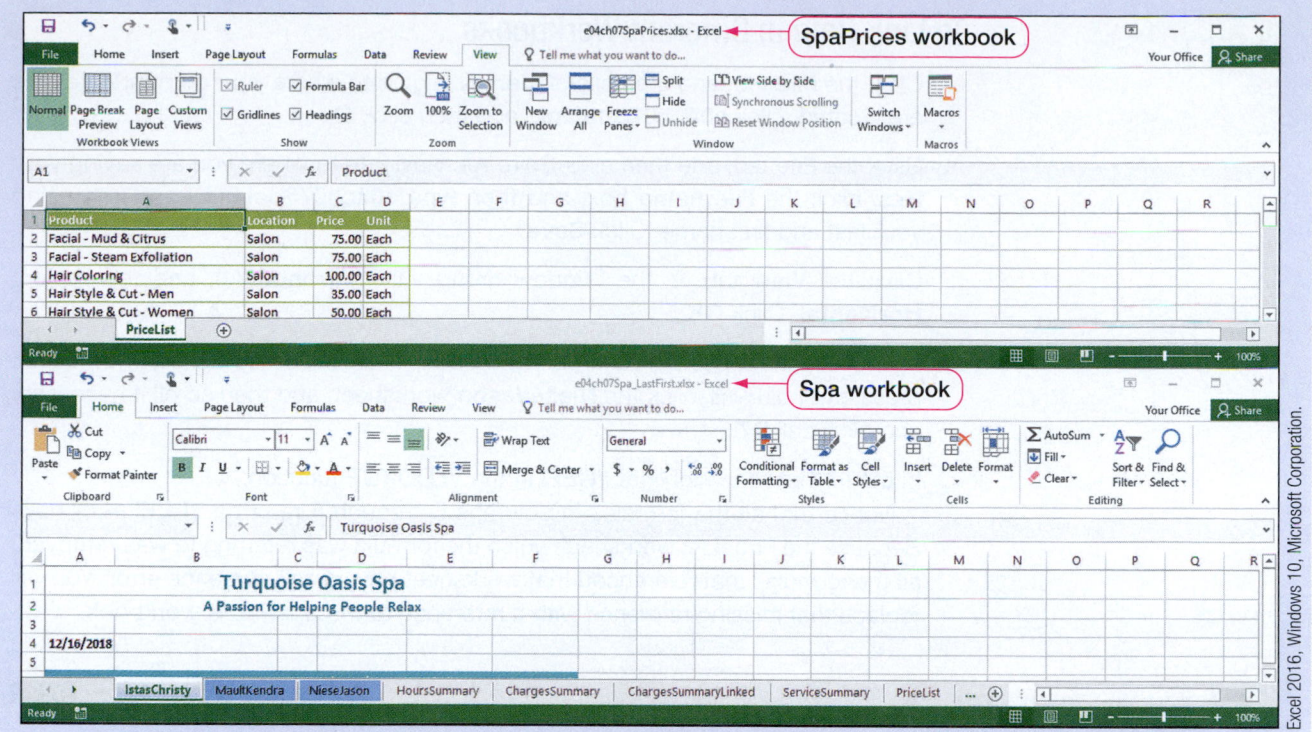

Figure 16 Workbooks arranged with the Horizontal option

e. Close **e04ch07Spa_LastFirst**, but keep **e04ch07SpaPrices** open for use in the next exercise. **Save** the workbook.

f. **Maximize** the e04ch07SpaPrices window.

Linking Workbooks

When you need data from a different workbook, the advantage to referencing that data at its source rather than copying it into your workbook is that when the source data is changed, your workbook can also be changed to reflect the most current data.

Excel recognizes when a workbook is linked to another workbook or workbooks through external references, and it will prompt you when the workbook is opened and ask whether or not you want to update links. Which option you choose will depend on whether or not you want the workbook to be updated.

Linking to other workbooks does create some potential problems, however. Links to workbooks are easily broken, especially if files are moved or deleted. Excel tries to prevent this from happening by using relative addresses. In a relative link, the address of a linked workbook is defined by its location in relation to the location of the destination workbook. If either workbook is moved when the destination workbook is closed, the links will be broken. It is considered good practice to store all workbooks that are in a linked relationship together in the same folder if possible.

When you use a relative link, the reference will include the file name in brackets, the sheet name, an exclamation point, and then the following cell reference.

=[filename.xlsx]worksheet name!cell reference

In this exercise, you will use a copy of the Spa workbook that excludes the PriceList worksheet and then link to the SpaPrices workbook to use the pricing data from there. By linking to the SpaPrices workbook, you will correct the errors that appear when you first open the SpaLink workbook.

 **E07.14**

To Link Data in Different Workbooks

a. Click the **File** tab, and then click **Open**. Navigate to where your student data files are located, click **e04ch07SpaLink**, and then click **Open**.

b. Click the **File** tab, and then click **Save As**. Navigate to where you are saving your files, click the **File name** box, and then type e04ch07SpaLink_LastFirst, using your last and first name. Click **Save**.

c. Click the **View** tab, in the Window group, click **Arrange All**, and then select **Horizontal**. Click **OK**.

d. In the e04ch07SpaLink_LastFirst workbook, click the **IstasChristy** worksheet, press and hold Shift, click the **NieseJason** worksheet, and then scroll if necessary and click cell **D7**.

e. In the formula bar, highlight **#REF!** in the VLOOKUP function.

Notice that all the formulas in columns D through F return a #REF! error now. Because the PriceList worksheet which the formula was referring to was removed, all the formulas that referenced that worksheet have a cell reference error. You will replace that missing reference with a reference to the SpaPrices workbook.

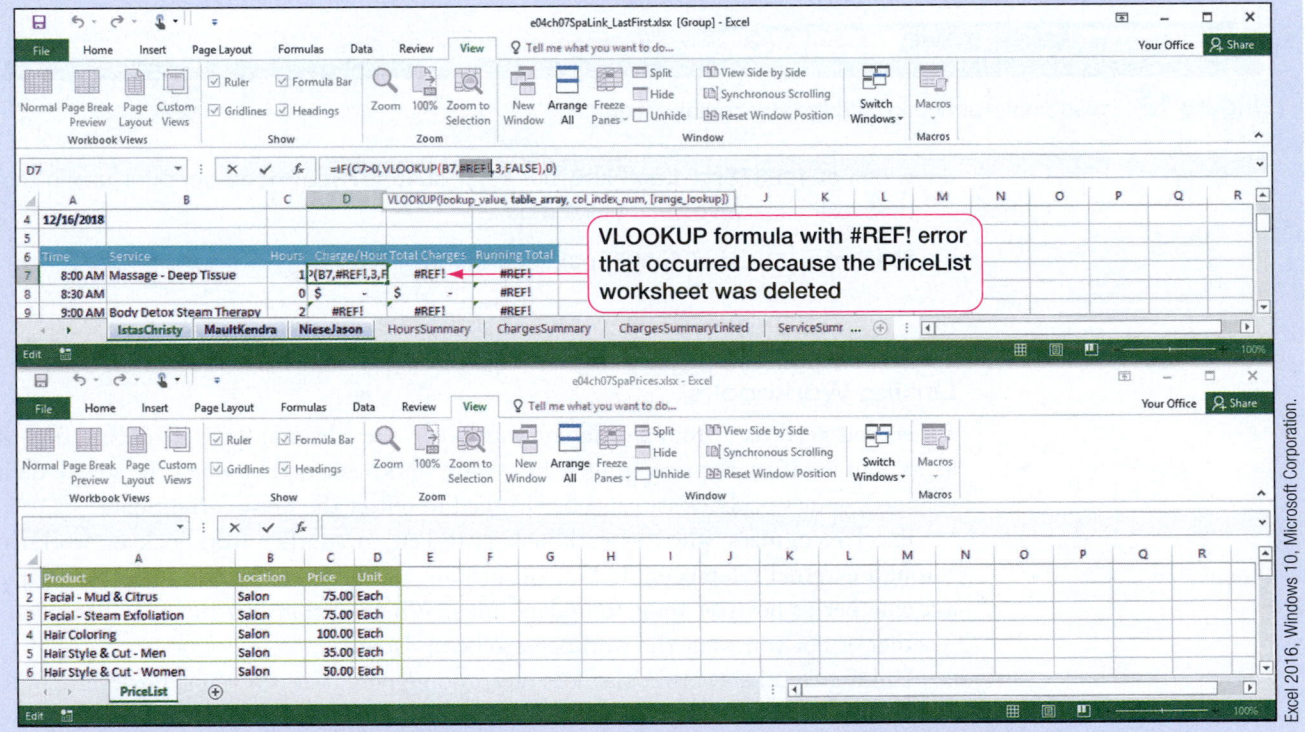

Figure 17 #REF error in the formula

f. Click the **e04ch07SpaPrices** workbook, and then select cell range **A2:D26**. This becomes the new lookup range for the VLOOKUP function. The formula bar should show =IF(C7>0,VLOOKUP(B7,[e04ch07SpaPrices.xlsx]PriceList!$A$2: $D$26,3,FALSE),0).

> ### Troubleshooting
> Remember that the #REF! error in Excel ends with an exclamation point! Be sure to highlight all of #REF! in the above step, or the correction to the formula will not work.

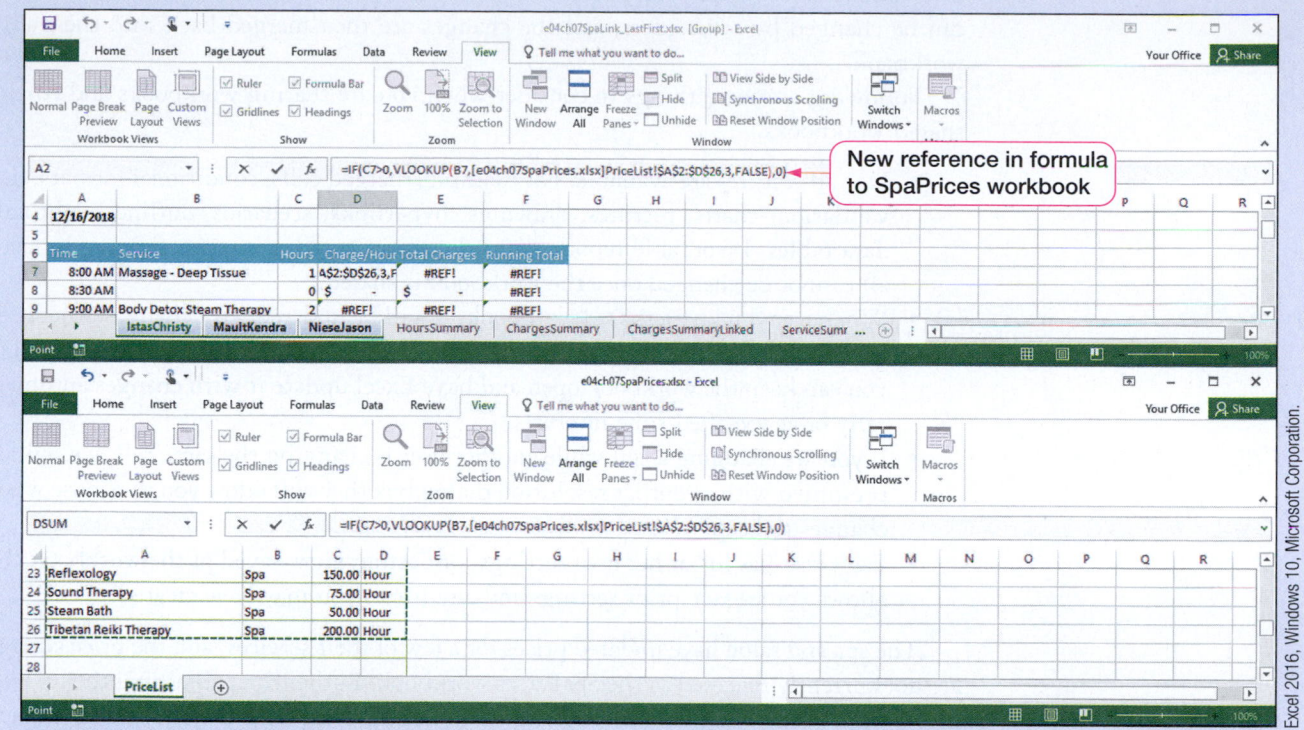

Figure 18 New reference to a workbook

g. Press Ctrl + Enter. Copy the formula in cell **D7** to cell range **D8:D24**, and then press Ctrl + Home. This will eliminate all the #REF! errors on the worksheet.

h. Click the **ChargesSummary** worksheet to ungroup the worksheets, and then **Save** 🖫 the workbook.

Keep the two workbooks open for the next exercise.

REAL WORLD ADVICE | **Planning Linked Workbooks**

- Make your links easy to track — Consider changing the formatting of a linked cell to something identifiable so you can easily identify cells with a linked formula.

- Avoid circular links — Workbooks should not have links to each other. The links should be one-way from one workbook to another. A circular link will slow down opening and updating the workbooks.

- Turn on Automatic Calculation — Source workbooks to which you link should have automatic calculation turned on to make updating quicker and error free. This is the automatic default setting, but it can be verified under Options on the File tab by opening the Options dialog box and scrolling to the Formulas section.

- Consider where you will store your files — If one file is stored on a network drive, and the other linked file is stored on your computer's hard drive, someone opening the file on the network drive will not have access to the linked file on your hard drive. This means that links will not be updated.

Collaborate Using Multiple Workbooks

Collaboration allows workbooks to be shared among different users and then merged together for a final product. Excel allows users to collaborate in the creation of a workbook; however, it is more common for users to collaborate in keeping data in a workbook up to date once the workbook has been developed. When a workbook is shared, you can save additional copies of your workbook for distribution to other users. The shared copies can be changed by other users, and the changes are then merged back into the master workbook.

Following are some things to consider when you are sharing workbooks and editing shared workbooks.

- Not all features are available. For example, merged cells, conditional formats, data validation, charts, pictures, drawings, hyperlinks, scenarios, outlines, subtotals, data tables, PivotTable reports, worksheet and workbook protection, and macros all cannot be changed once the workbook is shared.
- Whenever you save a shared workbook, it will be updated with changes other users have made since the last time you saved it. If you want to monitor these changes, you can keep the workbook open and have Excel update it with changes automatically or at specified time intervals.
- If you are changing a cell while another user is changing the same cell, you will be prompted with a conflict resolution dialog box that will allow you to choose whose changes to keep.
- Each user has his or her own settings, or custom view, saved of the workbook that allows you to save print settings and any filters you may have created.

The spa and salon have updated prices for a few of their services, and the price changes are not currently reflected in the SpaPrices workbook. Rather than obtaining the updated prices from Meda Rodate and Irene Kia and entering them into the worksheet yourself, it is better to have Meda and Irene update copies of the workbook directly to avoid any errors.

In this exercise, you will play three roles.

1. Yourself, as you create copies of a workbook for collaboration and later merge updated data from the copies back into the master workbook

2. Meda Rodate, as you update prices for spa services in a collaboration copy of the SpaPrices workbook created for Meda

3. Irene Kia, as you update prices for salon services in a collaboration copy of the SpaPrices workbook created for Irene

Sharing a Workbook

You will need to share the SpaPrices workbook with Meda Rodate and Irene Kia and then merge their updated data into your master copy. Merging workbooks is not a functionality that is available by default on the ribbon or the Quick Access Toolbar, so you need to customize the Quick Access Toolbar to include the Compare and Merge Workbooks icon.

 E07.15

To Share a Workbook for Collaborative Work

a. Make **e04ch07SpaPrices** the active workbook, and then click **Maximize** ☐. Press Ctrl + Home to return to cell **A1**. Click the **File** tab, click **Save As**, and then in the Save As dialog box, navigate to the folder where you are saving your files. In the File name box, type e04ch07SpaPrices_LastFirst, using your last and first name. Click **Save**.

Because e04ch07SpaLink is open and is linked to e04ch07SpaPrices, saving e04ch07SpaPrices with a new name will automatically update the links in e04ch07SpaLink_LastFirst.

Sharing a Linked Workbook

If workbook A is linked to workbook B, then workbook A must be closed when shared copies of workbook B are created; if not, the references in workbook A will be automatically changed to reference the new files.

b. Make **e04ch07SpaLink_LastFirst** the active workbook. Click the **IstasChristy** worksheet. Click cell **D7**, to view the updated link reference. Click **Save** 🔲, and then click **Close** ☒. The e04ch07SpaPrices_LastFirst workbook should be the only workbook that is open.

c. Above the Home tab, click the **Customize Quick Access Toolbar** button ⬇, and then select **More Commands** from the menu. You must do this before sharing the workbook because customizing the Quick Access Toolbar is not allowed in shared workbooks.

d. Click the **Choose commands from** arrow, and then select **All Commands**. Scroll through the list of Commands, click **Compare and Merge Workbooks**, and then click **Add**.

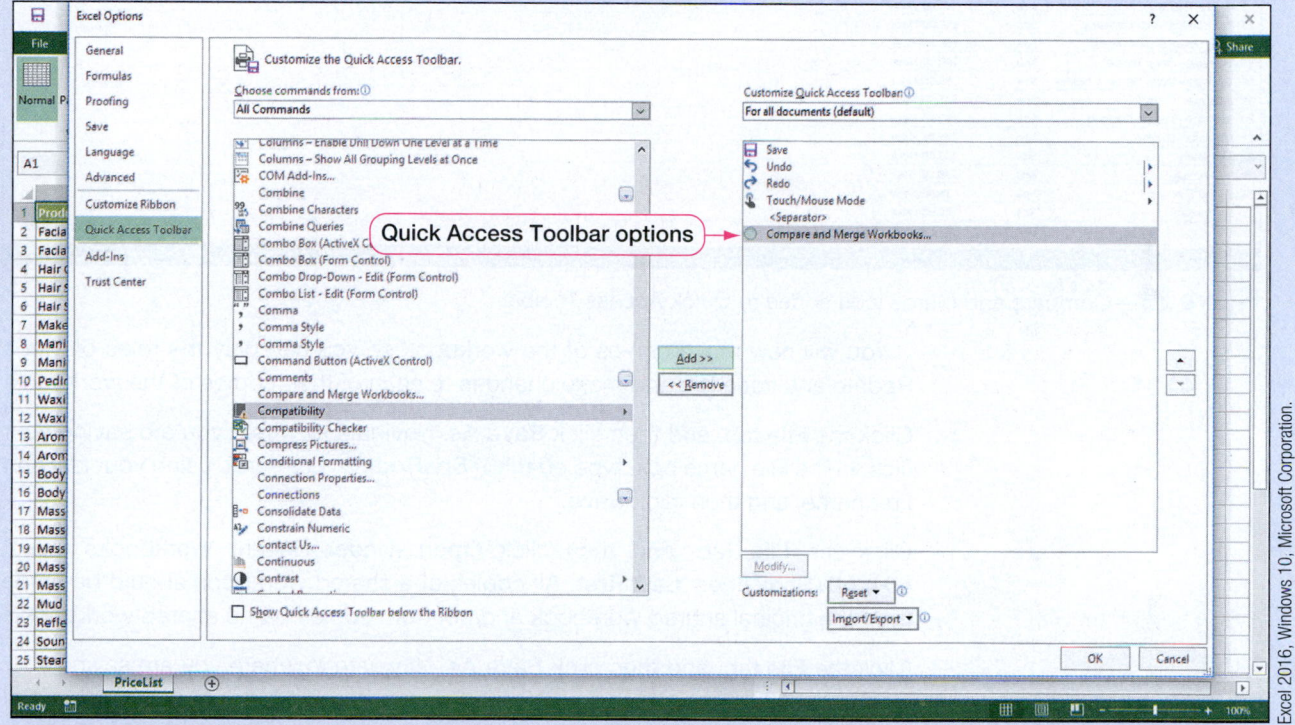

Figure 19 Excel Options dialog box for customizing the Quick Access Toolbar

e. Click **OK**. Compare and Merge Workbooks icon ◉ now appears on the Quick Access Toolbar.

f. Click the **Review** tab, and in the Changes group, click **Share Workbook**. If necessary, in the Share Workbook dialog box, click the **Editing** tab, select the **Allow changes by more than one user at the same time** check box, and then click **OK**.

g. Click **OK** in the alert box that says This action will now save the workbook. Do you want to continue? Notice that once a workbook is shared, the Compare and Merge Workbooks icon changes to a green color.

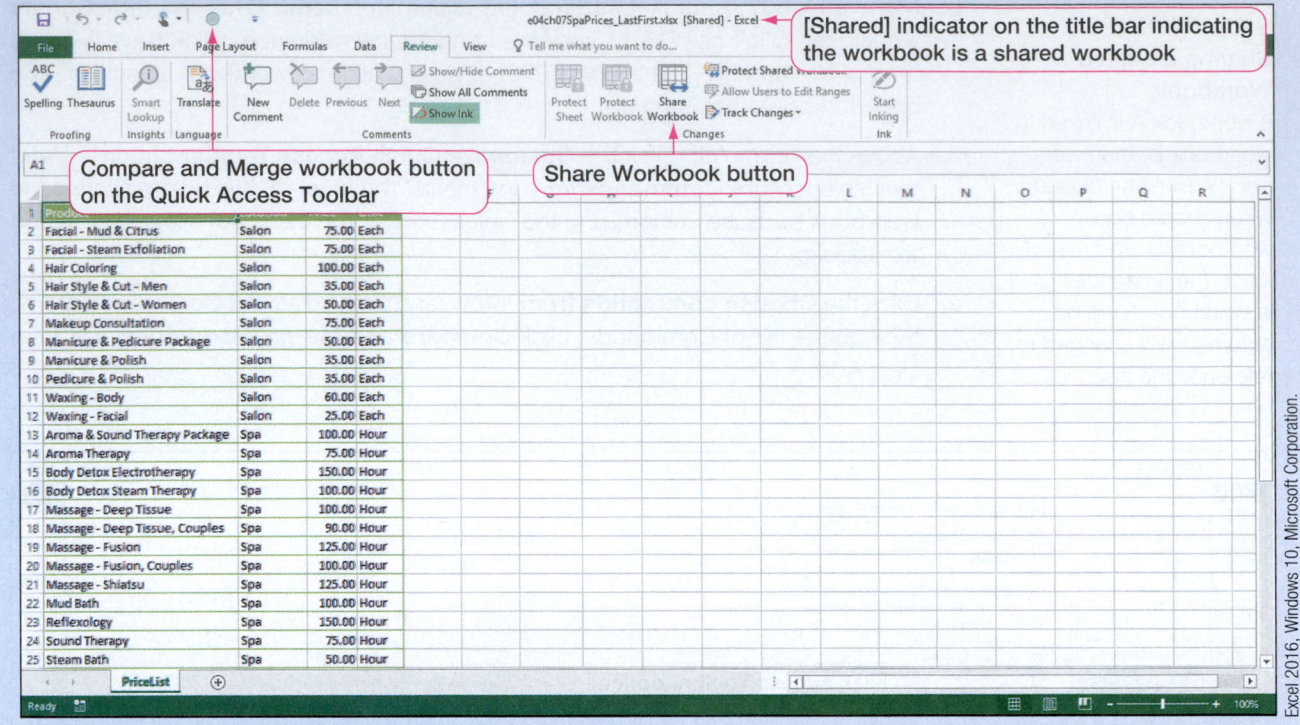

Figure 20 Compare and Merge icon added to Quick Access Toolbar

You will now make copies of the workbook so you can play the roles of Meda Rodate and Irene Kia and make changes to each of their copies of the workbook.

h. Click the **File** tab, and then click **Save As**. Navigate to where you are saving your files. In the File name box, type **e04ch07SpaRodate_LastFirst**, using your last and first name, and then click **Save**.

i. Click the **File** tab, and then click **Open**. Under Recent Workbooks select **e04ch07SpaPrices_LastFirst**. All copies of a shared workbook should be made from the original shared workbook and not from copies of the shared workbook.

j. Click the **File** tab, and then click **Save As**. Navigate to where you are saving your files. In the File name box, type **e04ch07SpaKia_LastFirst**, using your last and first name, and then click **Save**.

k. In the **e04ch07SpaKia_LastFirst** workbook, make the following changes in the Price column for the listed products.

Product	Cell	New Price
Facial - Mud & Citrus	C2	100
Makeup Consultation	C7	100
Manicure & Pedicure Package	C8	70
Manicure & Polish	C9	45
Pedicure & Polish	C10	45
Waxing - Body	C11	75

l. Click **Save**, click the **File** tab, and then select **Close** to close the SpaKia workbook.

Troubleshooting

If you close Excel along with the file by mistake, just restart Excel and continue with the next step.

m. In the **e04ch07SpaRodate_LastFirst** workbook, make the following changes in the Price column for the listed products.

Product	Cell	New Price
Massage - Deep Tissue	C17	125
Massage - Deep Tissue, Couples	C18	112.50
Massage - Fusion	C19	150
Massage - Fusion, Couples	C20	137.50
Massage - Shiatsu	C21	150
Steam Bath	C25	75
Tibetan Reiki Therapy	C26	225

n. Click **Save** 🔲, click the **File** tab, and then select **Close** to close the workbook. Keep Excel open for the next exercise.

Merging Shared Workbooks

The **Compare and Merge Workbooks** command will compare the changes made in each shared workbook and then provide the option to update the workbook with those changes. Following are some things to consider when you are comparing and merging shared workbooks.

- You can merge a shared workbook only with copies of that workbook that were made from the same shared workbook.
- You cannot merge workbooks that are not shared.
- The shared workbooks must have unique file names that are different from the name of the original workbook.
- All copies of the shared workbooks should be saved in the same folder as the shared workbook.

Now that the changes have been made to the individual workbooks, you will compare and merge the changes back into the original SpaPrices workbook.

 E07.16

To Compare and Merge Workbooks

a. Click the **File** tab, and then, in the Recent Workbooks list, click **e04ch07SpaPrices_LastFirst**. Notice that the title bar of the window displays [Shared] after the file name. This is to remind you that the workbook is shared.

b. On the Quick Access Toolbar, click **Compare and Merge Workbooks** 🔘. If necessary, navigate to the location where you saved your files, select **e04ch07SpaKia_LastFirst**, and then click **OK**.

Any cell values that are changed as a result of the merge are highlighted.

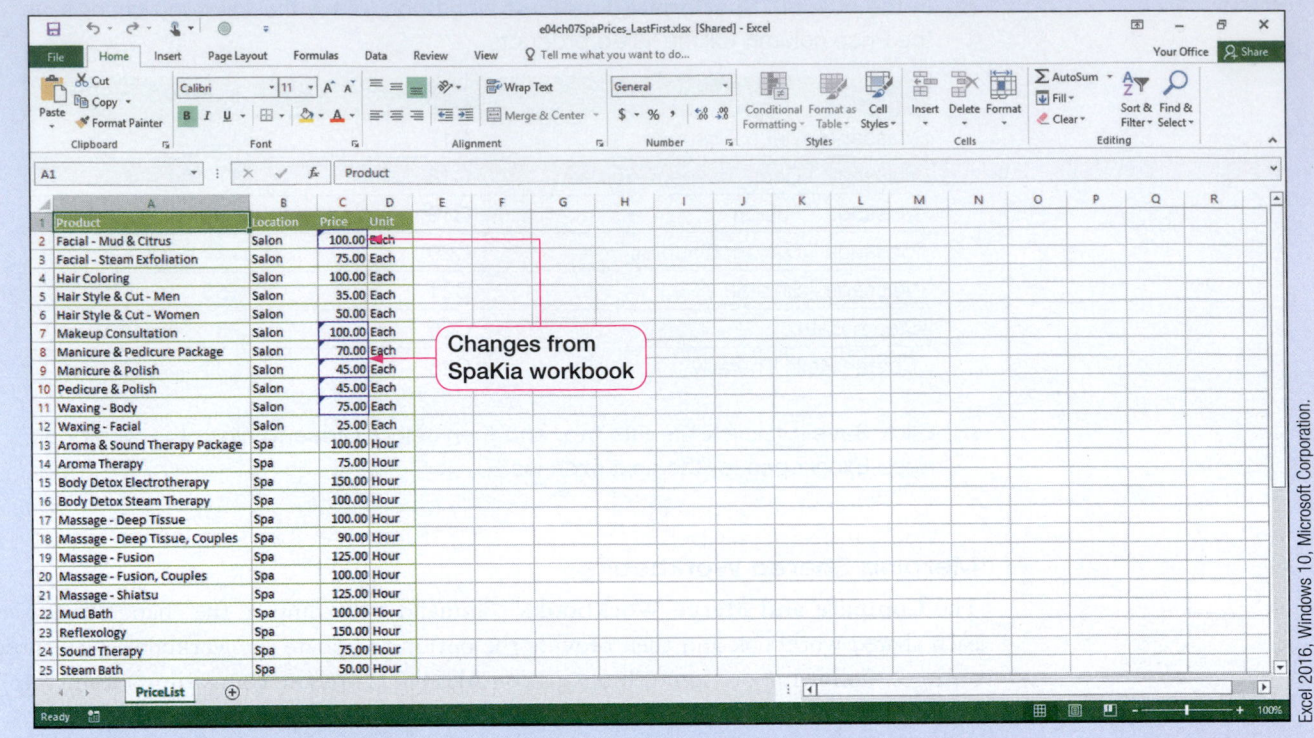

Figure 21 Changes showing in merged workbook

c. On the Quick Access Toolbar, click **Compare and Merge Workbooks** 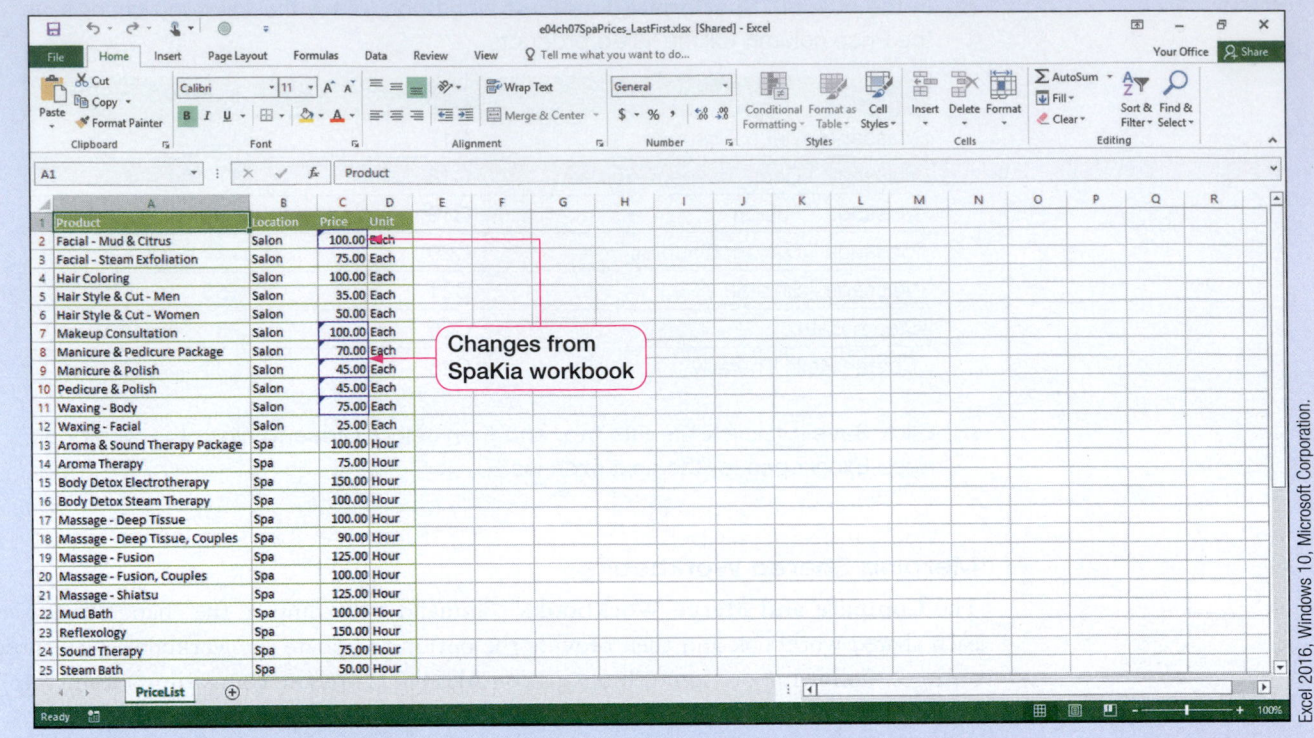, and then, if prompted, click **OK** to save the workbook. Select **e04ch07SpaRodate_LastFirst**, and then click **OK**.

d. **Save** the workbook.

Keeping Track of Changes

As long as workbooks are shared, you can view the changes made and continue making changes to the shared workbooks. The **change history** is information that is maintained about all changes made to the shared workbooks in past editing sessions. The information includes who made the change, when the change was made, and what data was changed. When you save the workbook, the History worksheet will be hidden, and you will have to use the Track Changes options to add the History worksheet again. However, once you stop sharing the workbook, the change history will be deleted and no longer be available.

For this exercise, you will not stop sharing the workbook so the change history will be saved to review in the future.

REAL WORLD ADVICE | **Keeping Track of Changes**

When you share a workbook, Excel creates a change history log so you can keep track of changes made to the workbook from the other shared workbooks. Once you stop sharing the workbook though, Excel assumes that you have accepted all the changes and therefore have no need to keep the history. If you want to view the history after you turn off sharing, you should copy and paste the history data to another worksheet or workbook. Your other option would be to not stop sharing the workbook so the History worksheet is not deleted.

E07.17   **To Save the Change History**

a. On the SpaPrices workbook, click the **Review** tab. In the Changes group, click **Track Changes**, and then click **Highlight Changes**.

b. Click the **When** arrow, and then select **All**. Select the **List changes on a new sheet** check box.

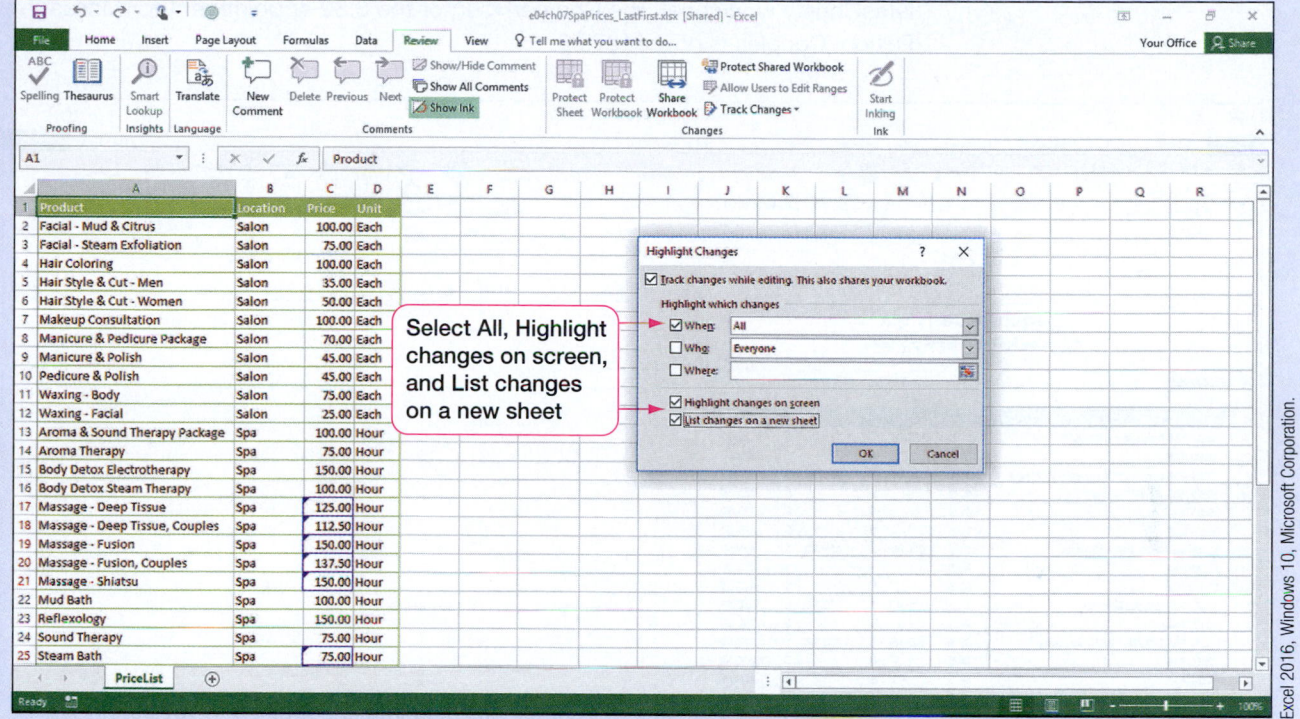

Figure 22   Highlight Changes dialog box

c. Click **OK**. A new worksheet named History will be added to the workbook that shows all the details about the changes made.

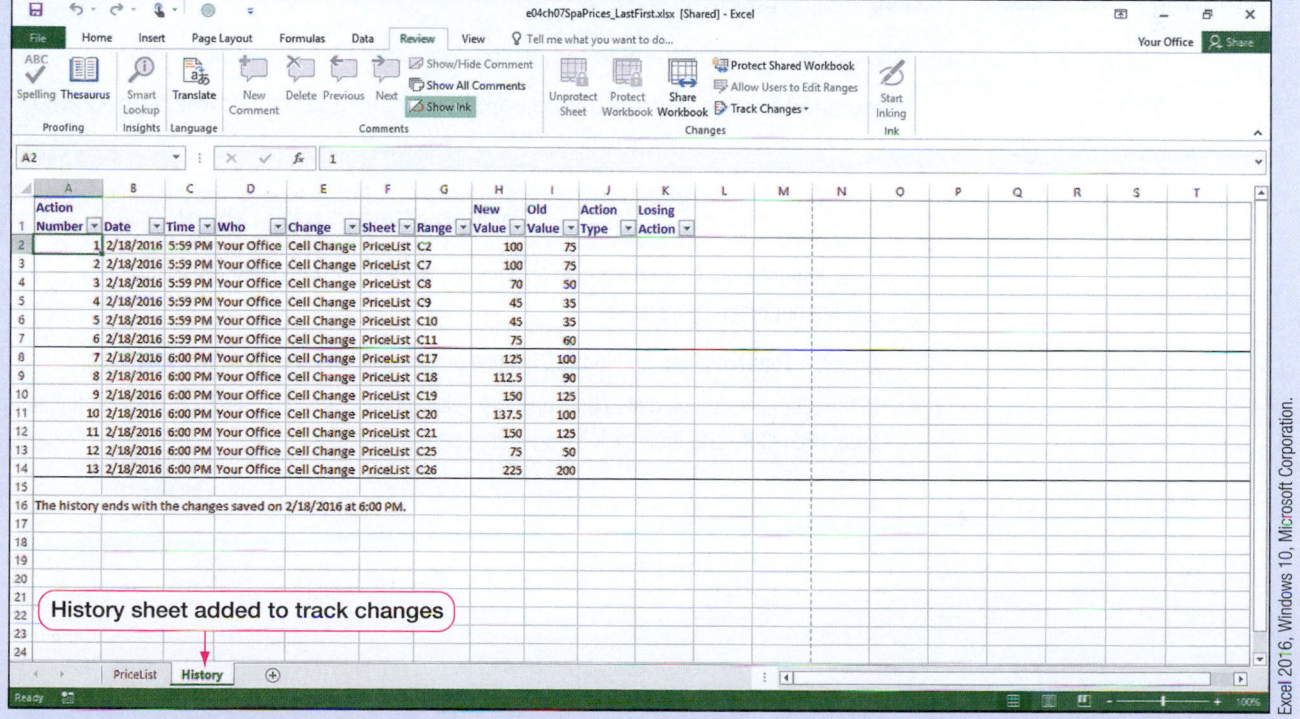

Figure 23   New History worksheet

d. Click **Save** 🖫, click the **File** tab, and then select **Close** to close the workbook.

e. Click the **File** tab, and then, in the Recent Workbooks list, click **e04ch07SpaLink_LastFirst**. Click **Enable Content** to update all the links with the new data.

f. If necessary, click the **IstasChristy** worksheet. Notice that, for example, on the IstasChristy worksheet, the Charge/Hour for the 3:30 appointment for Massage - Fusion, Couples is now $137.50.

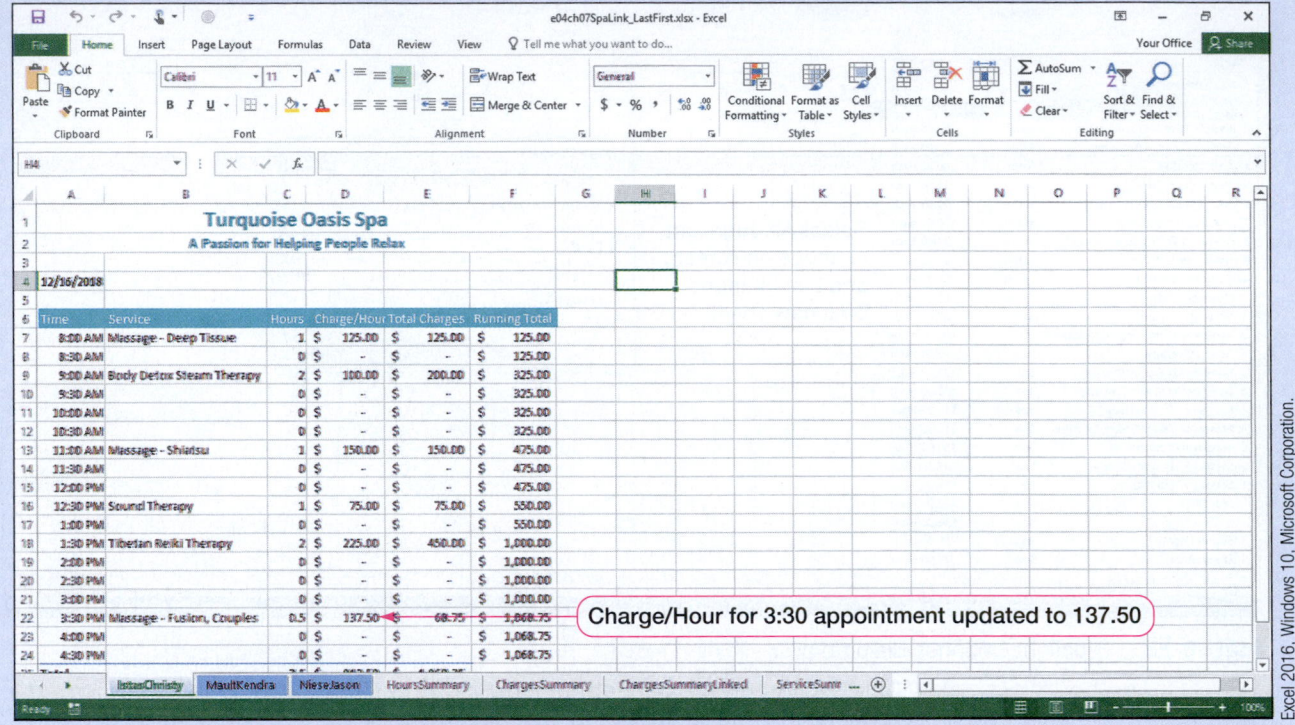

Figure 24 New data from shared and merged workbooks

g. Click **Save** 🖫, click the **File** tab, and select **Close** to close the workbook.

h. If you need to take a break before completing this chapter, now is a good time.

QUICK REFERENCE	To Stop Sharing a Workbook

When you are done tracking changes in a shared workbook, it is good practice to stop sharing it so changes are not made by mistake.

1. Click the **Review** tab, and in the Changes group, click **Share Workbook**.

2. In the Share Workbook dialog box, uncheck Allow changes by more than one user at the same time, click **OK**, and then click **Yes** in the alert that appears.

It may seem easier to keep sharing workbooks, especially if the same workbook will be shared over a period of time or on a regular basis, but this could lead to unforeseen problems. As long as your workbook is shared, the users can make changes. A user who is not aware that you are no longer merging the workbooks on a regular basis may assume that you are seeing those changes when you are not even looking for them. A much better business practice is to share workbooks only when all users understand the time frame for sharing, and then, when the deadline for sharing is reached, the shared files become unavailable. Thus, you can better control who is making changes and when they are being made.

Using and Creating Templates

In its simplest form, an Excel **template** is a workbook that provides a starting point for building other, similar workbooks. In its intended form, a template is a worksheet framework — a worksheet that contains cell formats, structural data such as column headings and data labels, and formulas necessary to achieve the template's purpose, such as totaling invoice line items, calculating sales tax, or tracking and totaling the time spent on a project.

In reality, a template is just a workbook saved with a different file extension — the .xltx extension. If stored in the default location, templates do have one special differentiator that may make their creation advantageous: They are readily available via the File tab when a new workbook is being created. In addition, when a template is opened from the default template location, the file will be saved by default as a normal Excel workbook with the .xlsx extension, thereby leaving the original template file in its original form, ready to use again for future development needs.

Templates, by default, are saved to the system drive in the Users\User name\AppData\ Roaming\Microsoft\Templates folder. Any templates added to that folder are available from the File tab.

Any workbook can be used as a template for another workbook. Simply open a workbook and save it with the template extension and a new file name.

In this section, for the spa, you will use a local template for a to-do list. Then you will search online for a template to use for a group calendar. Finally, you will use the SpaSales workbook to create a template that the managers can use for each of the staff members.

Use Existing Templates

Microsoft Excel has a number of local templates. On your hard drive, local templates are most likely stored in the Program Files\Microsoft Office\Templates\1033 folder. The number 1033 is the language ID number for English (US). This folder will change depending on which language version of Office you have installed. Templates for all the Office applications are stored in this folder.

Local templates are accessed from the File tab. You can add your own templates to the built-in templates folder by saving or moving your templates to that folder.

Using Local Templates

Local templates are the templates that are stored in the default Templates folder on your hard drive, and these are the templates you see when you click the File tab. They are commonly used, have formatting and other features already applied, and are ready for you to enter your personal data. Any data that appears in the template is there as an example, so be sure to delete that sample data before you save your workbook.

In this exercise, you will choose the Project tracker from the local templates to create a project list for the spa employees.

 **E07.18**

To Find, Open, and Use a Local Template

a. If you took a break, open Excel. Click the **File** tab, click **New**, scroll through the list of templates, and then click **Project tracker**.

> ### Troubleshooting
>
> Microsoft frequently changes its templates, so you may not be able to find the Project tracker template as a local template. Either choose a different template that is local for this activity or search for the Project tracker template as an online template.

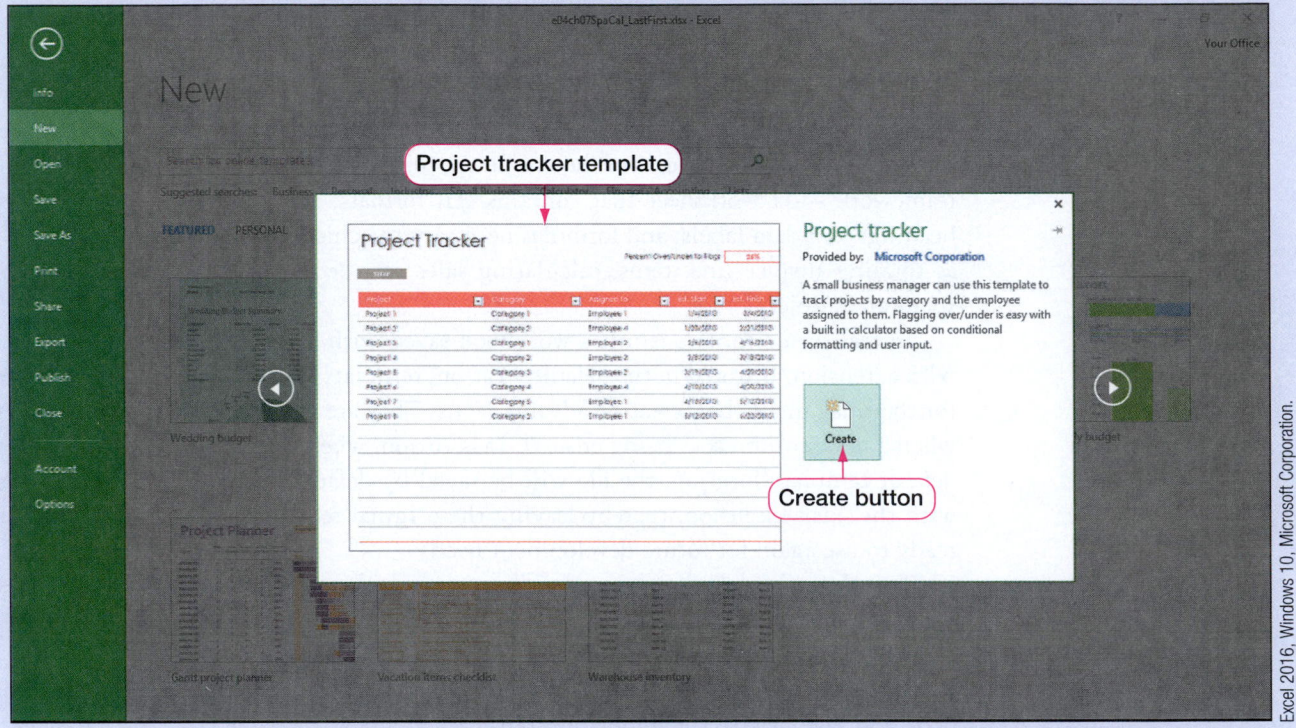

Figure 25 Creating a new template

b. Click **Create** to start using the template. Click the **File** tab, and then click **Save As**. Navigate to the folder where you are storing your files, and type **e04ch07SpaToDo_LastFirst**, using your last and first name. Click **Save**.

c. Click the **Setup** worksheet, and then enter the following categories and employees starting in row B5.

Category	Employee
Supplies	Istas
Inventory	Niese
Subscriptions	Mault

d. Delete the contents of cell range B8:B10 and cell D8.

e. Click the **Project Tracker** worksheet. Enter the following data for the Spa in rows 6 and 7, replacing the sample data already there. Notice the lists available when you click certain cells. You have the option to make a selection from the list or to type in your value.

Project	Category	Assigned To	Est. Start	Est. Finish	Est. Work
Order supplies	Supplies	Mault	5/7/18	5/9/18	2
Purge inventory	Inventory	Istas	4/3/18	4/10/18	7

f. Select cell ranges **B8:G13** and **J6:L13**, and then press ⌈Delete⌉ to delete the contents of the cells. This will delete only the content and none of the formatting in these cells.

g. **Save** 🖫 the workbook, click the **File** tab, and then click **Close**. Keep Excel open for the next exercise.

 CONSIDER THIS | **How Could Excel Facilitate Work as a Team?**

So far in this chapter, you have learned how to group worksheets, consolidate worksheets, merge data from individual worksheets into a master worksheet, and build and use templates. Think about a couple of group or team projects you have been involved with in your educational career, and consider how the Excel capabilities listed above might have aided your efforts with the following.

- Tracking team member contributions to a project

- Tracking project progress toward completion

- Bringing the work of team members together into one coherent final product

- Supporting a team member who is struggling with a part of the project by facilitating the involvement of other team members' assistance

How else might Excel facilitate team work in your education? How about in your career?

Using Online Templates

Online templates are templates stored online that can be downloaded to your hard drive. There are literally hundreds of Excel templates available online. Microsoft, through its template site at Office.com, fosters a community of Office users who download templates posted by other users. Users can rate templates on a scale of 1 to 5 stars. User ratings are averaged, and the average is posted next to each template.

Some people are very good at generating data through formulas and functions; others are experts at presenting information graphically or at formatting tabular content attractively. Office users can post their templates to Office.com so others can benefit from their expertise.

In this exercise, you will search for an online template and then use it to create an event calendar for the spa to provide to their customers.

 E07.19

To Find, Open, and Use an Online Template

a. Click the **File** tab, and then click **New**.

b. In the Search for online templates box at the top of the window, type small business calendar.

c. Click the **Search** button 🔍. Scroll if necessary, and then click the full-page yearly calendar named **Small business calendar (any year Mon-Sun)**. The whole title is visible when you point to the icon for the template.

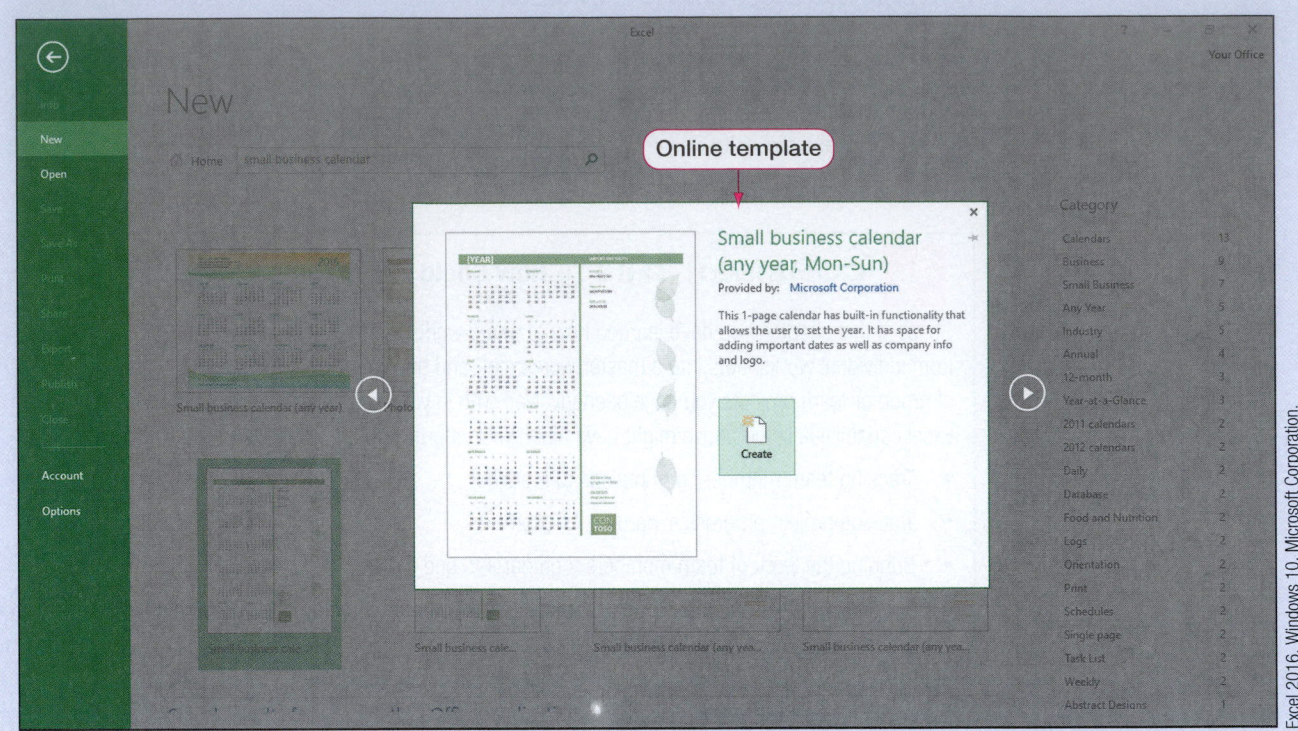

Figure 26   Small business calendar online template

d. Click **Create**. If necessary, in the Protected View bar at the top of the window, click **Enable Editing**.

e. Click the **File** tab, click **Save As**, and then navigate to where you are saving your files. In the File name box, type **e04ch07SpaCal_LastFirst**, using your last and first name, and then click **Save**.

f. In the top left corner of the workbook, click the spinner ⧫ next to the year, and then change the year to **2018**.

g. Click cell **U44**, and change the contents to **3356 Hemmingway Circle**. Change cell **U45** to **Santa Fe, NM 87594**. Change cell **U47** to **505.555.1564**. Change cell **U48** to **kmasters@paintedparadise.com**. Change cell **U49** to **www.paintedparadiseresort.com**.

h. Right-click the image below the resort's website address, and select **Change Picture**. In the Insert Pictures dialog box, next to From a file, click **Browse**. Navigate to your student files, select **e04ch07SpaLogo**, and then click **Insert**.

i. Click any cell to deselect the graphic, and then press Ctrl + Home. Click **Save** ⊟.

j. Click the **File** tab, and then click **Close** to close the workbook. Keep Excel open for the next exercise.

Create Templates from an Existing Workbook

Creating templates is really not different from creating workbooks. You simply remove any specific data and save the workbook as a template. You can create templates from your own workbooks, or you can create them by modifying a template to better fit your needs.

Creating a Template from a Workbook

The SpaSales workbook has the time slots and schedules for one particular day: December 16, 2018. This is a good format to use for other dates, especially since the Spa workbook uses this format to summarize the data. You will delete the date, service, and duration details but leave the appointment times and therapist names so each day can be updated easily. You will also change the tab name to something less specific.

 **E07.20**

To Create a Template from a Workbook

a. Click the **File** tab, click **Open**, navigate to your student files, and then click **e04ch07SpaSales**. Click **Open**. If necessary, click **Enable Editing**.

b. Select cell range **A2:A55**, and then press Delete to delete the dates.

c. Select cell range **D2:E55**, and then press Delete to delete the service descriptions and hours.

d. Right-click the **MondaySales** worksheet, select **Rename**, type DailySales, and press Enter. Press Ctrl + Home.

e. Click the **File** tab, click **Save As**, and then navigate to the location where you are saving your files. In the File name box, type e04ch07SpaTemplate_LastFirst, using your last and first name. In the Save as type list, click **Excel Workbook**, and then select **Excel Template**. Navigate to the location where you are saving your files, and then click **Save**.

Notice the file extension of .xltx. This indicates that the file has been saved as a template.

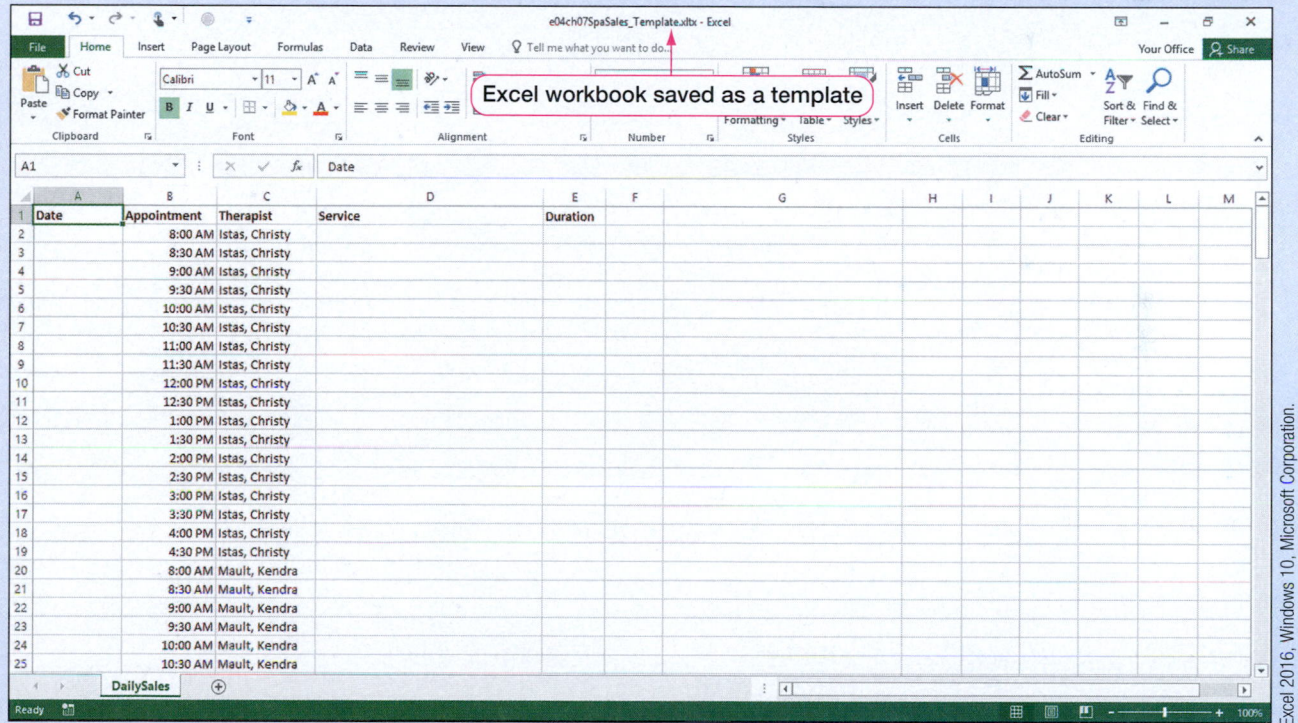

Figure 27 Excel workbook saved as a template

f. Exit Excel, and then submit your files as directed by your instructor.

Concept Check

1. The ability to group worksheets creates an opportunity for you to greatly increase the efficiency of your work. List three ways in which grouping worksheets can increase your efficiency. p. 387

2. What are the three ways in which you can consolidate data across worksheets? When would you use each of the three ways? p. 395

3. What are the different ways in which you can see multiple workbooks on one screen at the same time? When might you want to do this? p. 405

4. What is the advantage of sharing a workbook? How can you keep track of all the changes made to the workbook? pp. 410–416

5. What are local templates? With so many templates available, how do you know which ones might be better than others? pp. 398–400

6. How do you create a custom template? Once you do, how do you make sure it shows on the File tab? p. 402

Key Terms

3-D formula   397
3-D reference   395
3-D named range   396
Change history   414
Collaboration   409

Compare and Merge
  Workbooks   413
Consolidate by category   395
Consolidate by position   395
Fill Across Worksheets   391

Grouping   387
Local templates   417
Online templates   419
Template   417

Visual Summary

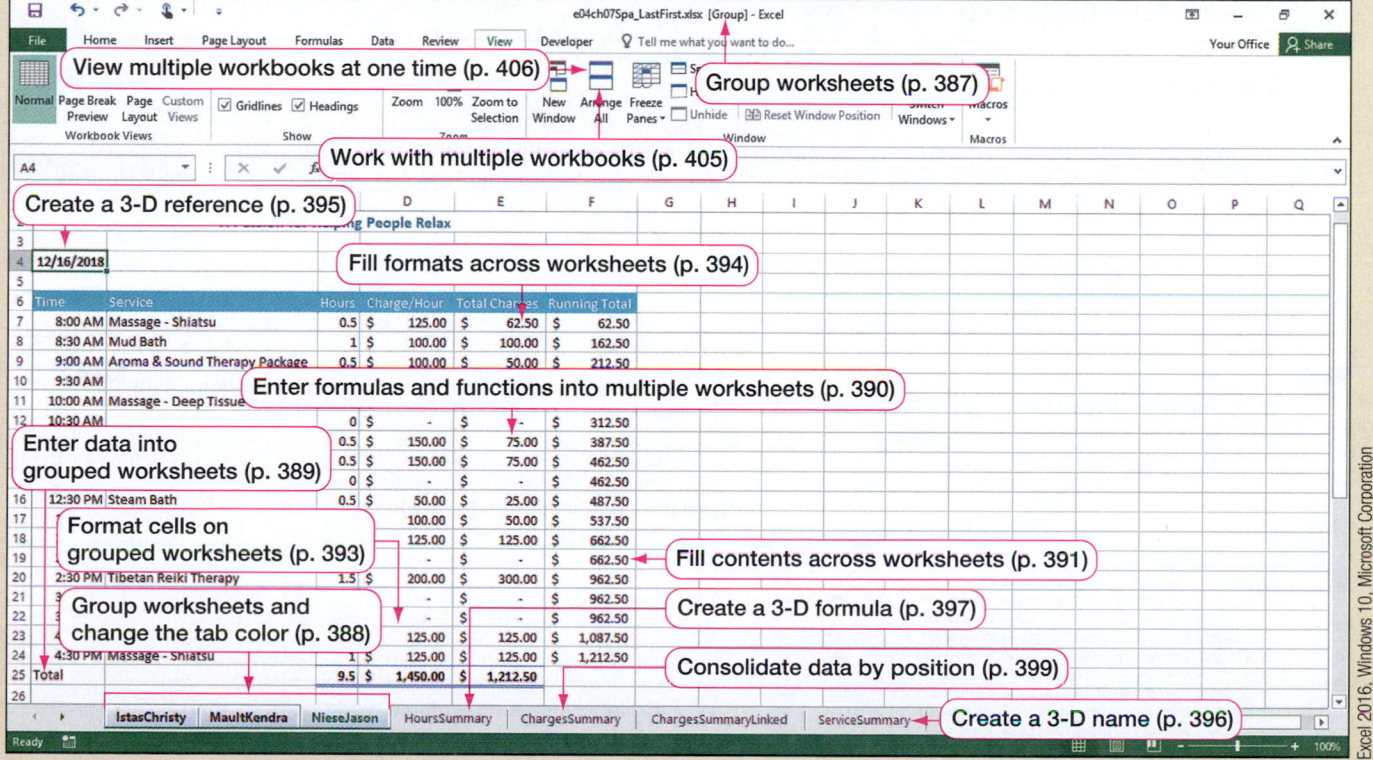

Figure 28

Excel 2016, Windows 10, Microsoft Corporation

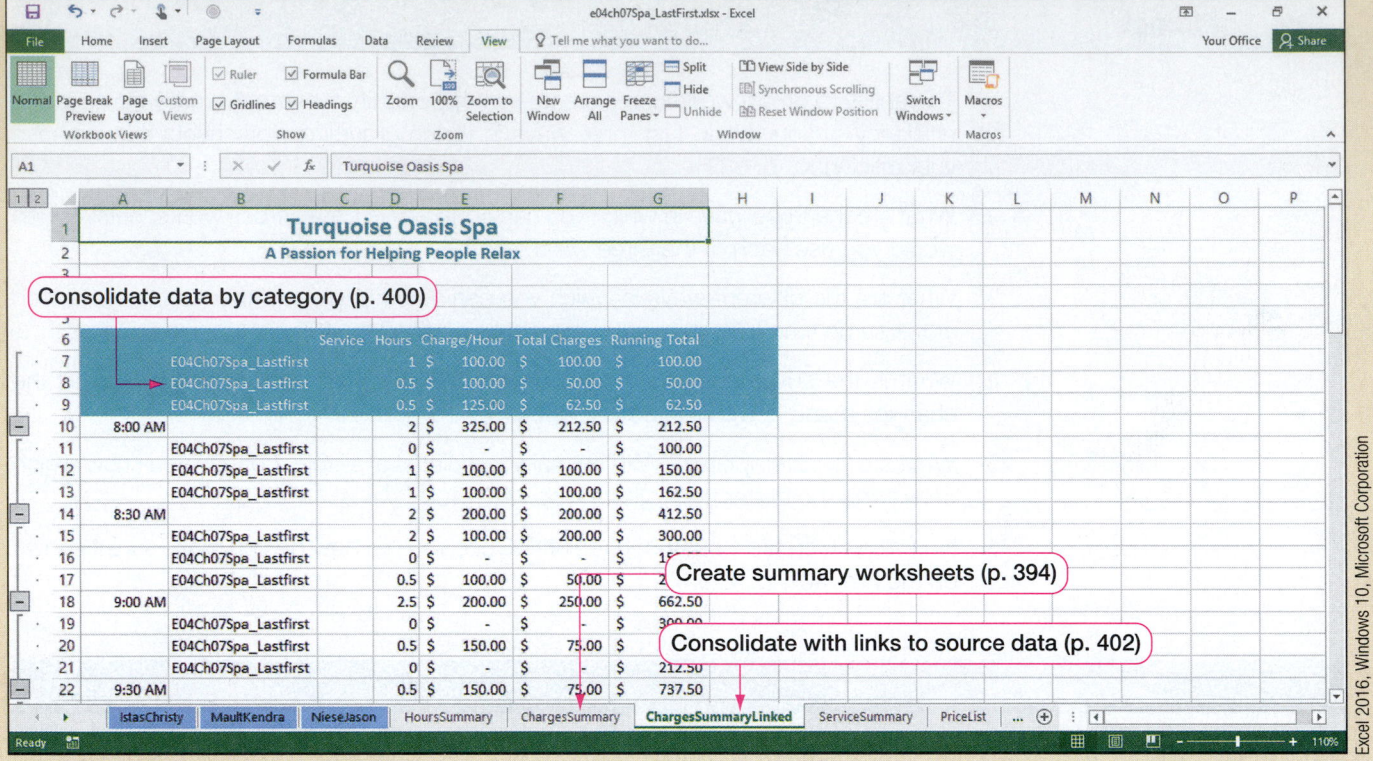

Figure 29

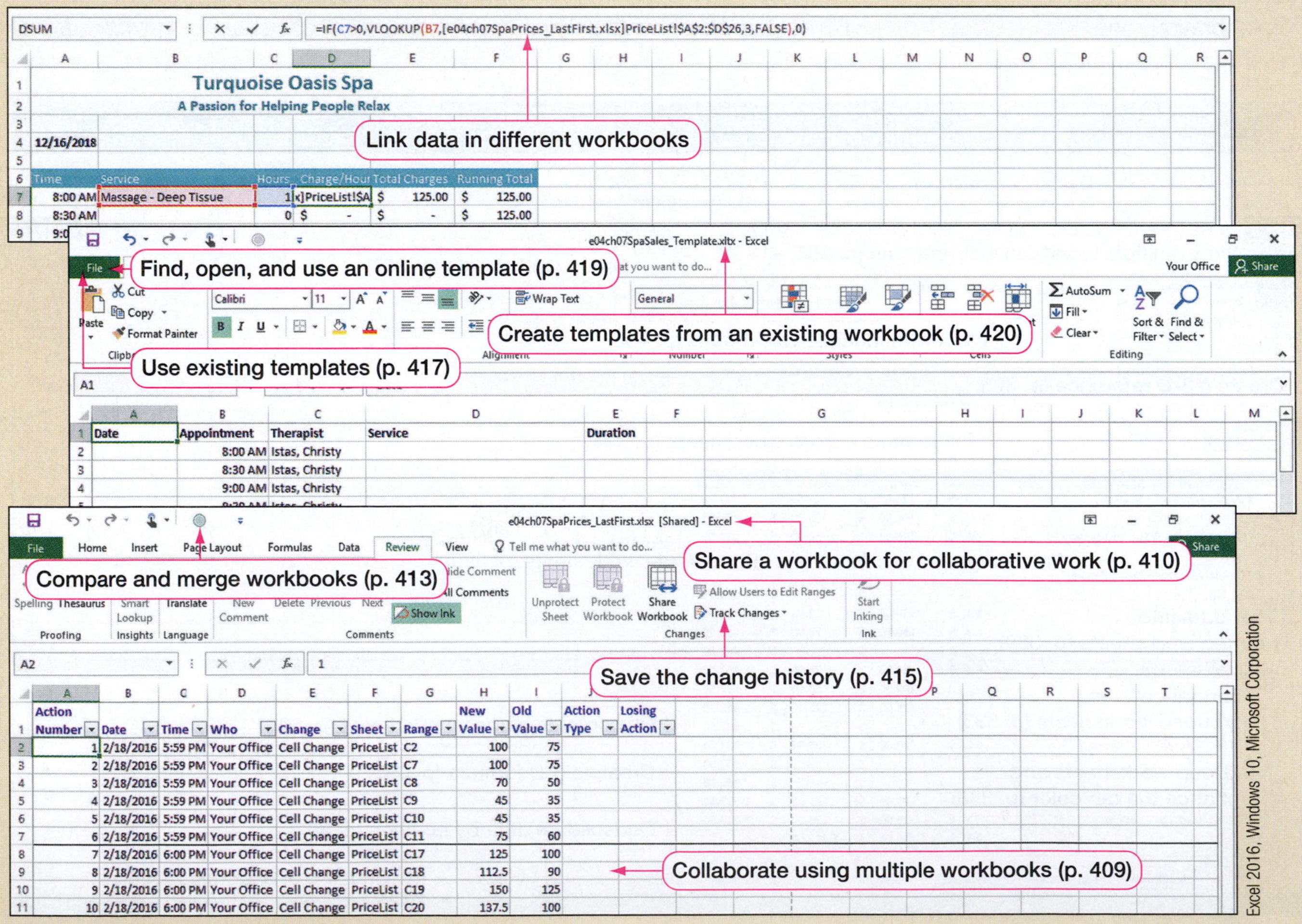

Figure 30

Practice 1

Corporate Event Planning at the Resort

Production & Operations

The Painted Paradise Resort & Spa has three rooms that can be used to host events. Corporate events generally include small meetings, seminars, and conventions that require tables, seating, and often a meal. Room setup and a standard number of tables and chairs are included in the daily room rate, as are refreshments for the guests during the event.

Patti Rochelle, the corporate event planner, has started a workbook to track each month's daily events in each of the three rooms. The first month's data has been entered, but she needs help finishing the workbook and consolidating all the data into a monthly report. She would like to show the total number of guests and the total charges incurred for each day of the month and each type of event. She would also like to create a template to use every month, and she would like the daily rate to link to the external workbook that contains this information so that if the rates change, her workbook will be updated. She would also like to share her workbook with her staff so they can make changes where necessary.

a. Open **Excel**, click **Open Other Workbooks** in the left pane, and then double-click **This PC**. Navigate through the folder structure to the location of your student data files, and then double-click **e04ch07Event**. If a Security Warning message displays, click the **Enable Editing** button.

b. Click the **File** tab click **Save As**, and then double-click **This PC**. In the Save As dialog box, navigate to the location where you are saving your project files, and then change the file name to e04ch07Event_LastFirst, using your last and first name. Click **Save**.

c. Click the **JanMusica** worksheet, press and hold Shift, and then click the **JanPueblo** worksheet.

- Right-click the **JanMusica** worksheet, point to **Tab Color**, and then select **Olive Green, Accent 3**.

- Click cell **E8**, and then enter a formula to calculate the total charges. The formula should multiply the # Days and the Room Rate, using an absolute reference for the Room Rate. Enter the formula =D8*$C$5. Copy the formula to cell range **E9:E38**.

- Select cell range **A7:E39**. On the Home tab, in the Editing group, click **Fill**, click **Fill Across Worksheets**, select **Formats**, and then click **OK**.

- Click cell **E39**, click the **Formulas** tab, and in the Defined Names group, click **Name Manager**. Click **New**, and then type TotalCharges3D in the Name box. In the Refers to box, click at the end of the **cell reference**, press and hold Shift, and then click the **JanPueblo** worksheet. Click **OK**, and then click **Close**.

- Right-click the **JanMusica** worksheet, and then select **Ungroup Sheets**. Review the changes made to the JanEldorado and JanPueblo worksheets.

d. Click the **JanEldorado** worksheet, press and hold Shift, and then click the **JanPueblo** worksheet. Click cell **A3**, type =, and then click the **JanMusica** worksheet. Click cell **A3**, and then press Enter.

e. Click the **GuestSummary** worksheet to ungroup the worksheets.

- Click cell **B8**, type **=**, click the **JanMusica** worksheet, click cell **C8**, and then type **+**. Click the **JanEldorado** worksheet, click cell **C8**, type **+**, click the **JanPueblo** worksheet, click cell **C8**, and then press Ctrl + Enter. Copy the formula to cell range **B9:B38** on the GuestSummary worksheet.

- Click cell **C8**, and then type **=SUM(**. Click the **JanMusica** worksheet, click cell **E8**, and then press and hold Shift. Click the **JanPueblo** worksheet, type **)**, and then press Ctrl + Enter. Copy the formula to cell range **C9:C38**.

f. Click the **RoomSummary** worksheet.

- Click cell **B8**, click the **Data** tab, and then, in the Data Tools group, click **Consolidate**.

- In the Consolidate dialog box, make sure **Sum** is selected in the Function box. Click the **Reference** box, click the **JanMusica** worksheet, and then select cell range **C8:E38**. Click **Add**.

- Click the **JanEldorado** worksheet, verify that cell range **C8:E38** is selected, and then click **Add**.

- Click the **JanPueblo** worksheet, verify that cell range **C8:E38** is selected, and then click **Add**. Click **OK**.

- Click cell **D39**, type **=SUM(TotalCharges3D)**, and then press Enter.

g. Click the **EventSummary** worksheet.

- Click cell **A7**, and then on the Data tab, in the Data Tools group, click **Consolidate**. In the Consolidate dialog box, make sure **Sum** is selected in the Function box, and then click the **Reference** box.

- Click the **JanMusica** worksheet, and then select cell range **B7:E38**. Click **Add**.

- Click the **JanEldorado** worksheet, verify that cell range **B7:E38** is selected, and then click **Add**.

- Click the **JanPueblo** worksheet, verify that cell range **B7:E38** is selected, and then click **Add**.

- Select the **Top row** and **Left column** check boxes.

- Click **OK**. Click cell **A7**, and then type **Event**.

h. Click the **EventSummaryLinked** worksheet.

- Click cell **A7**, and then, on the Data tab, in the Data Tools group, click **Consolidate**. In the Consolidate dialog box, make sure **Sum** is selected in the Function box, and then click the **Reference** box.

- Click the **JanMusica** worksheet, select cell range **A7:E38**, and then click **Add**. Click the **JanEldorado** worksheet, and then click **Add**. Click the **JanPueblo** worksheet, and then click **Add**.

- Select the **Top row** and **Left column** check boxes, and then select the **Create links to source data** check box. Click **OK**.

- Select cell range **A11:A131**, and then, on the Home tab, in the Number group, click the **Number Format** arrow, and select **Short Date**.

- Select columns **A:F** and then, on the Home tab, in the Cells group, click **Format**, and then select **AutoFit Column Width**.

- Save and close the workbook, but keep Excel open.

i. Click the **File** tab, and then open **e04ch07EventLink**. If necessary, click **Enable Content**. Save the file as an **Excel Workbook** with the name e04ch07EventLink_LastFirst, using your last and first name.

j. Click the **File** tab, and then open **e04ch07EventRooms**. If necessary, click **Enable Content**. Save the file as an Excel workbook named e04ch07EventRooms_LastFirst, using your last and first name.

k. Click the **View** tab, and in the Window group, click **Arrange All**. Click the **Tiled** option, and then click **OK**.

l. In the **e04ch07EventLink_LastFirst** workbook, the RoomRates worksheet has been deleted, so the reference to that worksheet shows an error.

- Click the **JanMusica** worksheet, click cell **C5**, and then replace the reference with a new reference to cell **B8** in the e04ch07EventRooms workbook by typing **=**, and then clicking on cell **B8** in e04ch07EventRooms.
- Click the **JanEldorado** worksheet, click cell **C5**, and then replace the reference with a new reference to cell **B7** in the e04ch07EventRooms workbook.
- Click the **JanPueblo** worksheet, click cell **C5**, and then replace the reference with a new reference to cell **B6** in the e04ch07EventRooms workbook.
- Save, and then close the **e04ch07EventLink_LastFirst** workbook.

m. Make **e04ch07EventRooms_LastFirst** the active workbook, and then **maximize** the screen.

- If necessary, click the **Customize Quick Access Toolbar** button, and then select **More Commands** from the menu. Click the **Choose commands from** arrow, select **All Commands**, select **Compare and Merge Workbooks**, and then click **Add**. Click **OK**.
- Click the **Review** tab, and in the Changes group, click **Share Workbook**. Check the **Allow changes by more than one user at the same time** box, and then click **OK**. Click **OK** again.

n. Click the **File** tab, and then click **Save As**. Navigate to where you are saving your files. In the **File name** box, type e04ch07EventRooms2_LastFirst, using your last and first name, and then click **Save**.

- Change the Daily Rate for **Pueblo** in cell B6 to 825, and then change the Daily Rate for **Eldorado** in B7 to 1750.
- Save and close the workbook, but keep Excel open.

o. Open **e04ch07EventRooms_LastFirst**. On the Quick Access Toolbar, click **Compare and Merge Workbooks.** Navigate to the location where you are saving your files, select **e04ch07EventRooms2_LastFirst**, and then click **OK**.

- On the **Review** tab, click **Track Changes**, and then click **Highlight Changes**. In the **When** list, select **All**. Check the **List changes on a new sheet** box, and then click **OK**.
- Save and close the workbook, but keep Excel open.

p. Open **e04ch07Event_LastFirst**. Click the **Documentation** worksheet. Click cell **A8**, and then type in today's date. Click cell **B8**, and then type in your name in the Firstname Lastname format. Complete the remainder of the Documentation worksheet according to your instructor's directions. **Save** the workbook.

q. Click the **JanMusica** worksheet, press and hold Shift, and then click the **JanPueblo** worksheet.

- Select cell range **B8:D38**, and then clear the **Contents** from the cells. Ungroup the worksheets.
- Change the name of the **JanMusica** worksheet to Musica. Change the name of the **JanEldorado** worksheet to Eldorado, and then change the name of the **JanPueblo** worksheet to Pueblo.
- Save the workbook in your student folder as a **template** named e04ch07EventTemplate_LastFirst, using your last and first name.

r. Click **Save**, close Excel, and then submit your files as directed by your instructor.

Student data files needed:

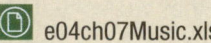 e04ch07Music.xlsx

e04ch07MusicRates.xlsx

You will save your files as:

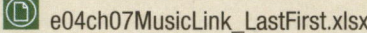 e04ch07Music_LastFirst.xlsx

e04ch07MusicLink_LastFirst.xlsx

e04ch07Music2_LastFirst.xlsx

e04ch07MusicTemplate_LastFirst.xltx

General
Business

Finance &
Accounting

Ingrid's Instrument Rental

You have been hired as an intern to help Ingrid Theobald, the owner of Ingrid's Instrument Rentals, to evaluate how her business is doing by using an Excel workbook. She has created a simple workbook with four worksheets, one for each school to which she rents instruments. She wants to know how much she is making from each school as well as summary data for all four schools. Each worksheet lists the type of instruments Ingrid is renting to the school, the number of students, and the rate per student. She would like to see the total charges for each instrument, a total number of students, and total charges for the school on each worksheet. The rate per student comes from the RentalRates worksheet, but she would like it to come from a separate workbook. She would also like to be able to share the workbook with the music directors at each school so they can update their number of students each semester.

a. Open the Excel file, **e04ch07Music**. Save your file as e04ch07Music_LastFirst, using your last and first name.

b. Group the **Valley** through **Mills** worksheets. Create a formula in cell range **D5:D15** to calculate the total charges for each instrument. Format cell range **C5:D16** with the **Accounting Number Format**. In cells **B16** and **D16**, calculate the total number of students and total charges for the school. Ungroup the worksheets, and save the workbook.

c. On the **Summary** worksheet, enter a 3-D SUM function in cell range **B5:B15** to calculate the total students for all four schools.

d. Use **Fill Across Worksheets** to copy the contents and formatting of cell range **C5:D16** from the **Mills** worksheet to the **Summary** worksheet. Save the workbook.

e. On the **LinkedSummary** worksheet, in cell **A4**, create a linked consolidation using cell range **A4:D15** from each of the school worksheets. In the Consolidate dialog box, be sure to select **Top Row**, **Left Column**, and **Create links to source data**. Change the column width of column **A** to **13**, hide column **B**, and **AutoFit Column Width** of columns **C:E**. Save the workbook.

f. Save **e04ch07Music_LastFirst** as e04ch07MusicLink_LastFirst, using your last and first name. Delete the **RentalRates** worksheet.

g. Open **e04ch07MusicRates**, click **Enable Content**, and save your file as e04ch07MusicRates_LastFirst, using your last and first name. Arrange the workbooks side by side.

h. In **e04ch07MusicLink_LastFirst**, group the **Valley** through **Summary** worksheets. Click cell **C5**, and in the formula bar, replace **RentalRates** in the VLOOKUP (which is no longer a valid range name) with a link to the range **InstrumentRates** (cell range A4:B14) in the **e04ch07MusicRates** workbook. Copy the formula to cell range **C6:C15**. Ungroup the sheets.

i. Save the workbooks. Close **e04ch07MusicRates_LastFirst**.

j. In **e04ch07MusicLink_LastFirst**, if necessary, add the **Compare and Merge Workbooks** button to the Quick Access Toolbar.

k. Share **e04ch07MusicLink_LastFirst**, and allow changes to be made. Save **e04ch07MusicLink_LastFirst** as e04ch07Music2_LastFirst, using your last and first name.

l. Change the Valley Day Schools #Students for violin to **22** and that for tuba to **2**. Save the changes, and then close the workbook.

m. Open **e04ch07MusicLink_LastFirst**, click **Enable Content**, and compare and merge the workbook with **e04ch07Music2_LastFirst**. Save the changes to a new sheet, but do not stop sharing.

n. Update the **Documentation** worksheet according to your instructor's directions. Save and close the workbook.

o. Create a template from **e04ch07Music_LastFirst** to use for the next school year. Group the **Valley** through **Mills** worksheets, and clear the contents from cell range **B5:B15**. Clear the contents from cell **A3**. Press ⌃ Ctrl + Home . Ungroup the sheets. Save the template as **e04ch07MusicTemplate_LastFirst**, using your last and first name.

p. Close the workbook, exit Excel, and then submit your files as directed by your instructor.

Perform 1: Perform in Your Life

Student data file needed:

 e04ch07Prices.xlsx

You will save your files as:

 e04ch07Prices_LastFirst.xlsx

 e04ch07Food_LastFirst.xlsx

 e04ch07FoodLink_LastFirst.xlsx

 e04ch07FoodTemplate_LastFirst.xltx

 e04ch07FoodShared_LastFirst.xlsx

 e04ch07FoodTime_LastFirst.xlsx

Softball Fundraiser

General Business

Finance & Accounting

You have volunteered to help your child's softball team raise money for uniforms. As part of the fundraiser, food booths will be set up at four locations around town. You need to develop a spreadsheet that will track sales and income by product at each location. The file will need to be shared with the four booth locations so the booth volunteers can update their sales on a regular basis. In addition, because the team will be recognizing the person with the most volunteer hours, you need to develop a time card to track the hours.

a. Open the Excel file, **e04ch07Prices**. Save your file as e04ch07Prices_LastFirst, using your last and first name.

- Click the **Sheet1** worksheet, rename it as Prices, and add a heading in row 1 to identify what the workbook contains.

- Format each column appropriately.

- Save the workbook.

b. Open a new workbook, and save it as e04ch07Food_LastFirst, using your last and first name.

c. Rename the first worksheet as Summary, and add four additional worksheets. Rename the four worksheets for each food booth location. Color the tabs for the four locations to visually show that they contain similar data.

d. Format all five worksheets as follows.

- All columns must print on one page.

- There should be at least two rows at the top of the worksheet to hold the location of the booth and the names of the volunteers working the booth. Include a blank row between the heading above and the detail data below.

- Include columns for the item description, units sold, sales price, total sale, cost per unit and total cost.
- Allow at least four rows for the list of products to be sold. Input a formula that will calculate the total sale and the total cost based on the number of units sold and the sales price or cost per unit price as appropriate.
- Add a total row to the units sold, total sale, and total cost columns. Label the row, and format as appropriate.
- Format the column headings using a cell style to highlight them from the rest of the data.
- Center the Location over the columns of data, and size the font appropriately.
- Format any columns that will contain values appropriately.

e. On the Summary worksheet, in row 1, type Summary. Create a 3-D formula that will add the units sold from each location worksheet. Leave the formulas in the total sale and total cost columns as previously entered. Save your changes.

f. Save the file as e04ch07FoodLink_LastFirst, using your last and first name.
- Using the Prices workbook you created earlier, link the item descriptions, sales price, and cost per unit to all five worksheets as appropriate.
- Insert another worksheet to consolidate the location worksheets, and show links from the consolidation. Format appropriately, and change the sheet name to Linked.
- Enter test values in all four location sheets to validate that your formulas are correct and everything is working properly.
- Save your changes.

g. Clear any contents that are not necessary to a template. Save the file as a template with the name e04ch07FoodTemplate_LastFirst, using your last and first name. Close the file.

h. Open **e04ch07FoodLink_LastFirst**. Share the file. Add the Compare and Merge Workbooks button to the Quick Access Toolbar if necessary. Save the file as e04ch07FoodShared_LastFirst, using your last and first name.
- Change the sales on the Location1 sheet, and save the file.
- Reopen the **e04ch07FoodLink_LastFirst** workbook. Compare and merge the workbook with the **e04ch07FoodShared_LastFirst** workbook.
- Create a new sheet with the change history. Do not stop sharing the workbooks.
- Save and close both workbooks.

i. You have decided to use the Built-In template Time Card rather than creating a file from scratch.
- Open the Time Card template.
- Change Employee to Volunteer.
- Delete columns E:H.
- Delete rows 29:39.
- Change the Week ending date to 5/27/2018.
- Save the file as e04ch07FoodTime_LastFirst, using your last and first name.

j. Save the workbook, exit Excel, and then submit your files as directed by your instructor.

Additional Cases

Additional Workshop Cases are available on the companion website and in the instructor resources.

Microsoft Excel 2016

Chapter 8

BUILDING AN APPLICATION WITH MULTIPLE WORKSHEETS AND WORKBOOKS

Prepare Case

Finance & Accounting

Turquoise Oasis Spa Application

Meda Rodate, manager of the Turquoise Oasis Spa, wants to improve the layout of the existing spa invoice and automate the invoice process as much as possible to ensure data accuracy and consistency. The invoice currently has formulas in the Charge/Hour and Amount columns, but they often get deleted by mistake. The Therapist name is often misspelled, the room number is often wrong, and Meda thinks the subtotal amount may not be calculating correctly. Another problem arises when the description of the service is not entered correctly, and then the charge/hour cannot be found in the lookup table.

In this chapter, you will modify an invoice application for the Turquoise Oasis Spa. Meda Rodate has started the application, but she is unable to finish it, so you will assist her. The invoice application has several requirements she cannot satisfy:

- Data validation to minimize data entry errors
- Automatically generated invoice number
- Automated data cleanup using macros
- Protection of the application to stop users from mistakenly changing application content and structure

Andresr/Shutterstock

Student data file needed for this chapter:

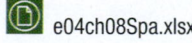 e04ch08Spa.xlsx

You will save your files as:

 e04ch08Spa_LastFirst.slsx

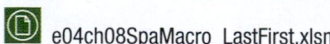 e04ch08SpaMacro_LastFirst.xlsm

Auditing Formulas

Formula auditing tools show you which cells are used in a formula and how the cells are used. Whether you are working with a worksheet you developed or one developed by someone else, being able to see all the cells that are part of a formula makes evaluating the accuracy and relevance of the formula easier. Excel's formula auditing tools include Trace Precedents, Trace Dependents, and Evaluate Formula.

Both tracing a formula and evaluating a formula are useful in understanding how a worksheet is structured. They are particularly useful if a complex formula is not producing a correct result. In this section, you will use formula auditing tools to gain a clearer understanding of how the invoice worksheet is structured and to correct an error in an invoice formula.

View Formula Precedents and Dependents

Tracing formulas draws lines from a formula to cells that supply source data (precedents) and to formulas that use the result of a formula (dependents). A **precedent cell** is a cell that supplies a value to the formula in the active cell, and a **dependent cell** is a cell whose value depends on the value in the active cell for its result. When you select to **trace precedents**, Excel automatically draws arrows from the precedent cells to the active cell. When you select to **trace dependents**, Excel automatically draws arrows from the active cell to its dependent cells. This is helpful for seeing which cells will be affected by a change to the active cell.

Opening the Starting File

Since you did not create the Spa workbook, you will audit the worksheet before you start making changes to it. This will allow you to better understand how the invoice is set up and to check for any possible errors in the formulas.

In this exercise, you will open the Spa workbook.

E08.00

To Open the Spa Workbook

a. Start **Excel**, click **Open Other Workbooks** in the left pane, and then double-click **This PC**. Navigate through the folder structure to the location of your student data files, and then double-click **e04ch08Spa**. If a Security Warning message displays, click the **Enable Editing** button.

b. Click the **File** tab, click **Save As**, and then double-click **This PC**. In the Save As dialog box, navigate to the location where you are saving your project files, and then change the file name to e04ch08Spa_LastFirst, using your last and first name. Click **Save**.

Auditing Formulas with Trace Dependents and Trace Precedents

Every formula has precedents, and some formulas may also have dependents. While you can always click a cell to see the cell references included in a formula, sometimes a visual cue is helpful to see how the formula works. When you choose to trace dependents and trace precedents, Excel puts arrows on the workbook to show you how the formula in the cell is constructed. These arrows make it easier to find errors than just by looking at the cell references in the formula.

In this exercise, you will use trace precedents and trace dependents to look at the formulas to make sure they are constructed properly and work the way they are supposed to work.

 **E08.01**

SIDE NOTE
Pin the Ribbon
If your ribbon is collapsed, pin your ribbon open. Click the Home tab. In the lower right-hand corner of the ribbon, click Pin the Ribbon [→|].

To Trace Precedents and Trace Dependents

a. Click the **Invoice** worksheet, select cell **F31**, and then, on the **Formulas** tab, in the Formula Auditing group, click **Trace Precedents**.

   A blue arrow is displayed that begins with a blue dot in cell F16 and ends with an arrow in cell F31. The cell range F16:F30 is outlined in blue. This outlined range is a precedent to the calculation in cell F31. Notice that the precedent range F16:F30 is determining the subtotal, and is missing cell F15, the first row of the invoice.

b. In the Formula Auditing group, click **Trace Dependents**.

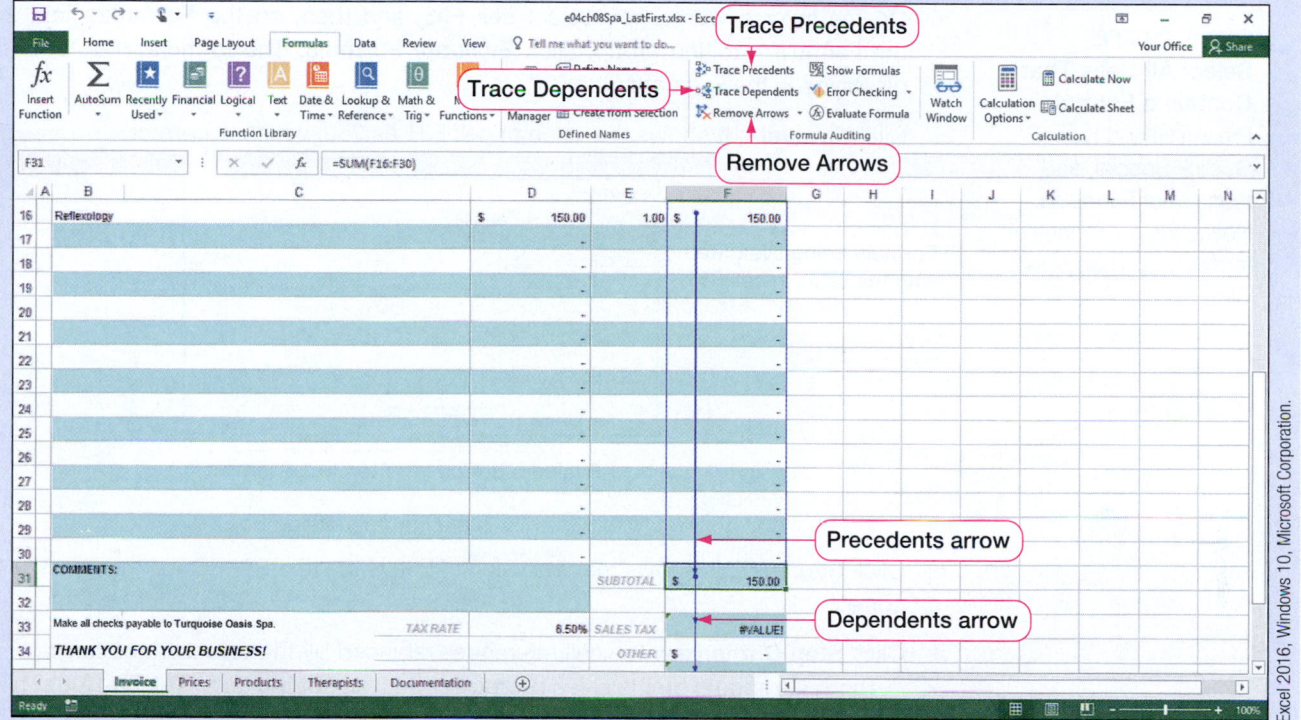

Figure 1 Trace Precedents and Trace Dependents arrows

An arrow is displayed from cell F31 to cell F33, and another arrow is displayed from cell F33 to cell F35. The formula in cell F33 is a dependent cell to the formula in cell F31, and the formula in cell F35 is a dependent cell to the formula in cell F33. This means that the value in cell F33 will depend on the value in cell F31, and the value in cell F35 will depend on the value in cell F33.

c. In the Formula Auditing group, click **Remove Arrows**.

d. If necessary, select cell **F31**, and in the formula bar, change **F16** to **F15** to correct the SUM function so it includes all the rows of the invoice. Press Ctrl + Enter.

e. **Save** [💾] the workbook.

Evaluate Formulas

Evaluating a formula walks you through the steps taken in calculating the result of a formula. **Evaluate Formula** is a tool that breaks down a formula into its individual pieces and evaluates each part separately so you can see how the formula works. It is similar to using trace precedents and trace dependents but without the arrows filling up the screen.

Using the Evaluate Formula Tool

In the Spa workbook, there is a problem with the calculation of the Sales Tax and the Total invoice amount because it is showing a #VALUE! error instead of a result.

In this exercise, you will use Evaluate Formula to determine what is wrong with the formula in cell F33.

 **E08.02**

SIDE NOTE

Select All Cells That Contain a Formula

Press Ctrl and type G, click Special, and then select Formulas. Notice the categories of formulas you can select. Click OK.

To Evaluate Formulas

a. On the Invoice worksheet, select cell **F33**, and then, on the **Formulas** tab, in the Formula Auditing group, click **Evaluate Formula**. The formula =F31*E33 is displayed in the Evaluation box.

b. Click **Evaluate**. It shows the value of cell F31 as 250, which is correct.

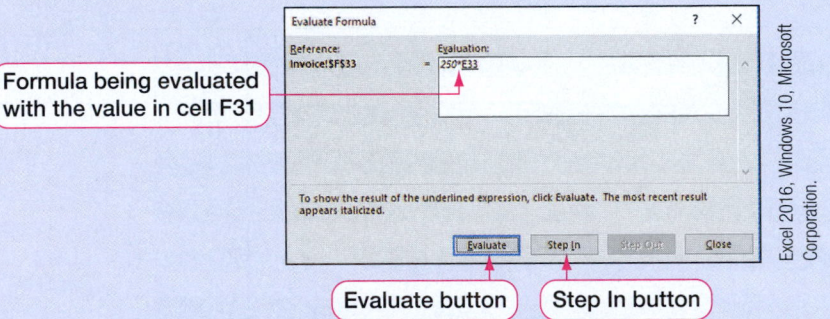

Formula being evaluated with the value in cell F31

Evaluate button   Step In button

Figure 2   Evaluate Formula dialog box

c. Click **Step In**. This shows that the value of E33 is the text SALES TAX, which is not correct.

d. Click **Step Out** to view the cell references replaced by the values in the formula. The value should be the sales tax rate, or 6.50%, not the text "SALES TAX." This is what is causing the #VALUE! error in the cell.

e. Click **Close**. You cannot edit a formula in evaluation mode. Click in the formula bar, and then change E33 to **D33**. Press Ctrl + Enter.

f. Click **OK** in the circular reference warning dialog box. You will correct this problem in the next exercise.

g. **Save** 💾 the workbook.

Correct Circular References

A **circular reference** is an error in a worksheet indicating a single formula that references itself or multiple formulas that reference each other. Technically, the formulas are precedents and dependents of one another. A circular reference is a problem for Excel because it means that action A requires action B to complete before it can be executed but action B requires action A to complete before it can be executed.

Finding and Correcting Circular References

In the Spa workbook, when you corrected the formula referencing the Sales Tax value in the preceding exercise, you saw a circular reference warning dialog box. This means there is a circular reference somewhere in the worksheet. The message in the status bar indicates that the circular reference is in cell F35.

In this exercise, you will identify and correct a circular reference.

 **E08.03**

To Identify and Correct Circular References

a. On the Invoice worksheet, select cell **F35**, and then, on the Formulas tab, in the Formula Auditing group, click **Trace Precedents**.

The arrow is red, indicating an error. Notice that the SUM function in cell F35 includes a cell reference to cell F35, which is causing the circular reference.

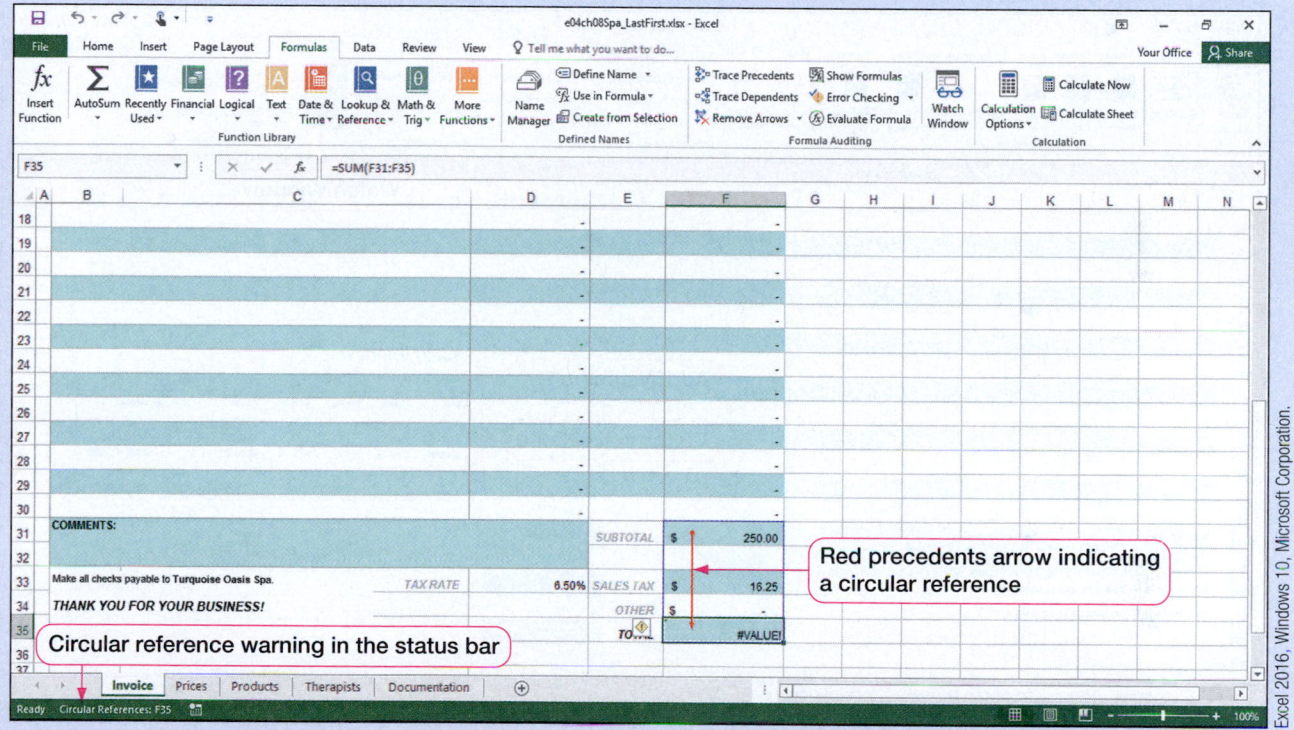

Figure 3 Circular reference as shown by Trace Precedents

b. Click in the **Formula Bar**, and change F35 to **F34**. Press Ctrl + Enter. This removes the trace arrow and corrects the formula.

c. **Save** 🖫 the workbook.

Use the Watch Window

The **Watch Window** is an Excel feature that makes it possible to monitor cells the user considers important in a separate window. The Watch Window is particularly useful when you are making changes in one worksheet or workbook and you want to monitor the effect of your changes to values in several other worksheets or workbooks.

To include a cell in the Watch Window, the workbook that contains the cell must be open and must remain open. As soon as the workbook is closed, any cells in that workbook that are being watched are removed from the Watch Window.

Opening and Using the Watch Window

In the Spa workbook, you will set up a Watch Window to watch the subtotal, sales tax, and total cells. This way, as rows are being added to the invoice, there will be no need to scroll to the bottom to see the total.

In this exercise, you will track changes using the Watch Window.

 E08.04

To Track Changes Using the Watch Window

a. On the Invoice worksheet, click the **Formulas** tab. In the Formula Auditing group, click **Watch Window**. This will open the Watch Window, which will be empty.

b. If necessary, move the Watch Window out of the way. Click cell **F31**. Press and hold Ctrl, and then select cells **F33** and **F35**. In the Watch Window, click **Add Watch**. In the Add Watch dialog box, click **Add** to confirm the cells you selected.

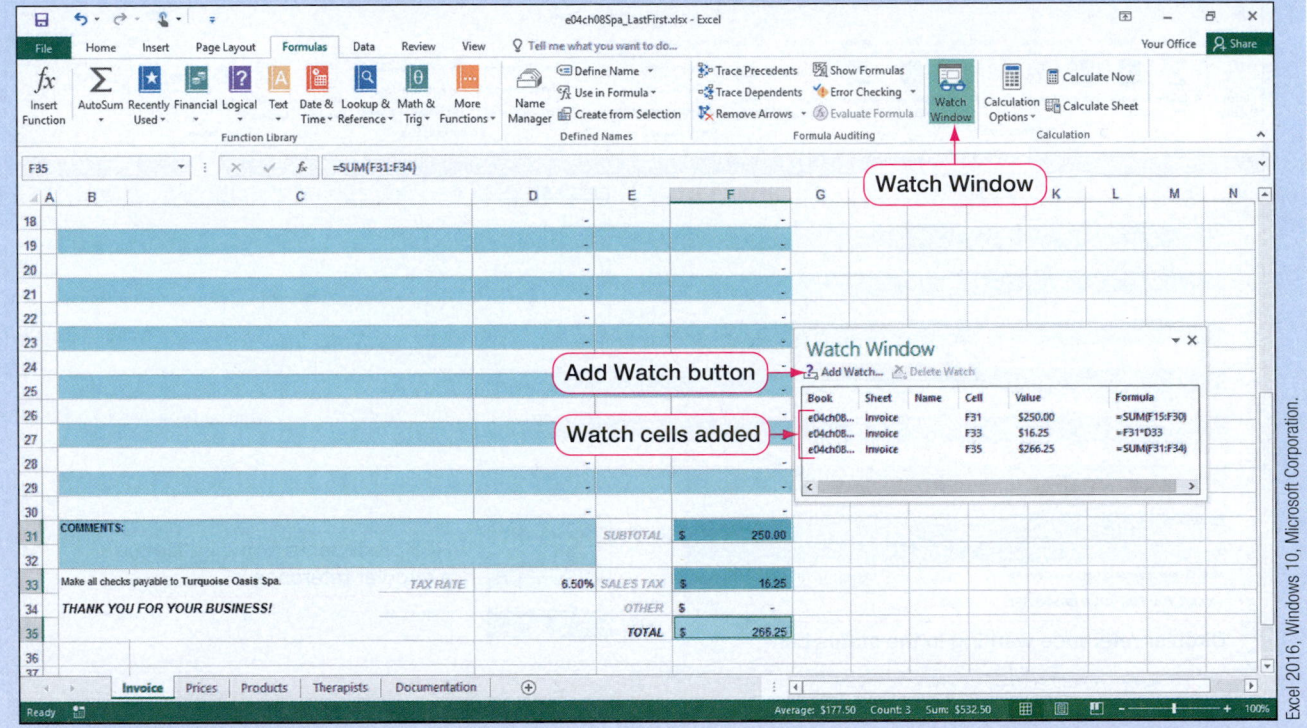

Figure 4 Watch Window

c. Drag the title bar of the Watch Window to the top of the worksheet window.

The Watch Window will dock below the ribbon and stay there. You can also dock the Watch Window on the bottom, left, or right of the worksheet window. To undock the Watch Window, simply drag the title bar toward the middle of the application window.

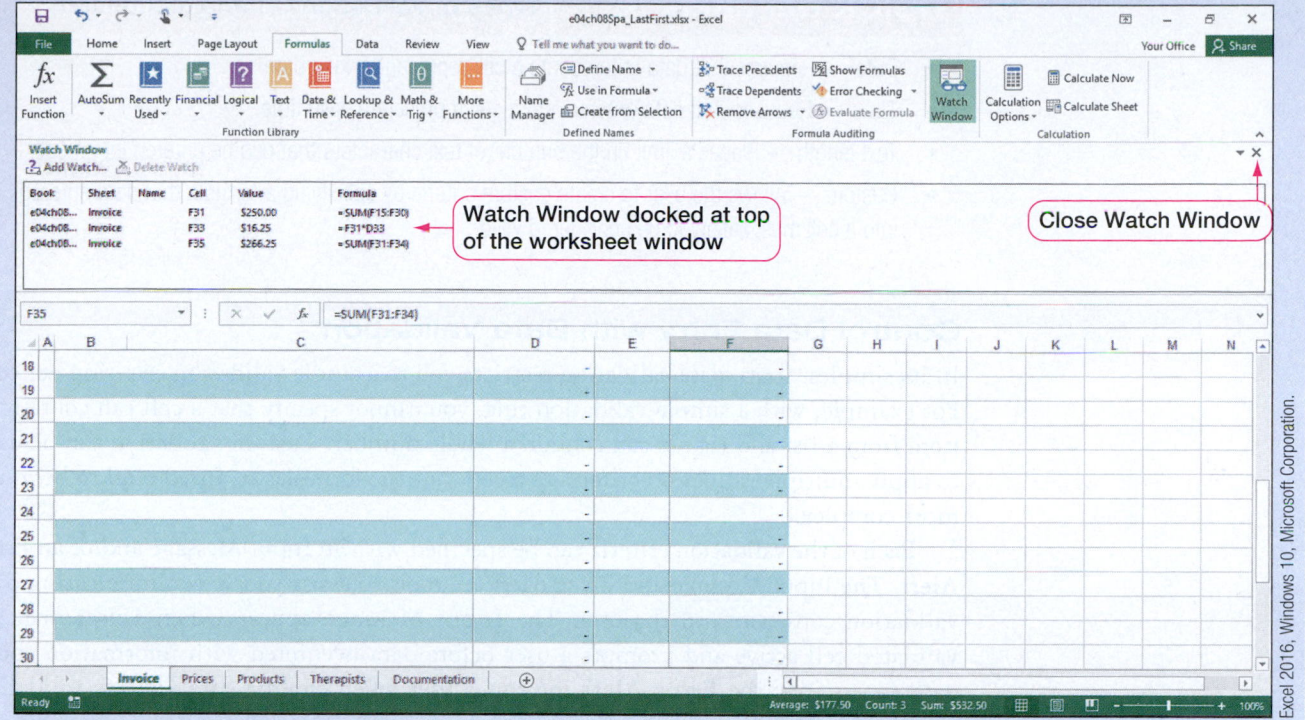

Figure 5 Watch Window docked

d. Select cell **E15**, type **2**, and then press ⌃ Ctrl + Enter. Notice that all the cells in the Watch Window changed.

e. In the Formula Auditing group, click **Watch Window** to close the Watch Window. The Watch Window also closes when you close the workbook, so each time you open the workbook, you will have to open the Watch Window to use it; however, you will not have to add the cells again, since they will be saved.

f. **Save** 🖫 the workbook.

SIDE NOTE

Alternate Method

You can also close the Watch Window by clicking the X in the top right-hand corner of the window.

Creating Data Validation Rules

Probably the greatest single source of errors in a workbook is human error. While it is impossible to completely eliminate human error while editing a workbook, Excel provides data validation tools that can help to ensure that data entry errors are kept to a minimum. **Data validation** includes rules that determine what can and cannot be entered in specific cells. **Validation criteria** are constraints that limit what users are allowed to enter into a particular cell. In this section, you will create various data validation rules for different cells throughout the workbook.

QUICK REFERENCE	Types of Validation Criteria

- Any value — Does not validate data but does allow the use of an input message to give data entry instructions.

- Whole number — Limits the data value in a cell to a specified range of integers.

- Decimal — Limits the number of decimal places that can be used in a cell.

- List — Requires the user to select a value from a list of predefined values.

(continued)

- Date — Requires that data entered into a cell represent a valid date.

- Time — Requires that data entered into a cell represent a valid time.

- Text length — Places a limit on the number of text characters that can be entered into a cell.

- Custom — Allows the user to create custom criteria by specifying a formula that data entered into a cell must satisfy to be considered valid.

Control Data Entry with Data Validation

In its simplest form, data validation restricts you to a single validation criterion per cell. For example, with a simple validation rule, you cannot specify that a cell can contain an item from a list and that it can contain a whole number. Custom validation can be used to apply multiple validation criteria to a cell, but the formulas required tend to be much more complex.

Each of the validation criteria can be specified with an Input Message and/or an Error Alert. The Input Message and Error Alert are tools to assist you in communicating data validation constraints to the user. The **Input Message** appears when a user makes a validated cell active and prompts a user before data is entered with information about data constraints; the **Error Alert** informs a user when entered data violates validation constraints.

There are three types of error alerts that can be assigned to a cell or range of cells with data validation: stop, warning, and information. A stop alert is the most restrictive of the data validation alerts. With a stop alert, if invalid data is entered, the user can only cancel or retry entering valid data. A warning alert will warn the user of an invalid data entry but allows the user to proceed or to cancel the entry. The information alert displays an error message with an information icon but allows the user to enter the invalid data.

Setting Up a List Validation

List validation is a type of data validation that presents a list of data values that the user can choose from. Data for the list must be included as part of the workbook; it cannot be in an external workbook.

The Spa workbook has one validation rule created for the Description lines of the invoice. You will add more data validation rules to limit what can be entered in other cells and cell ranges.

In this exercise, you will create a list validation on the Therapist field to choose from a list of therapists that can be found on the Therapists worksheet.

 E08.05

To Create and Use a List Validation

a. On the Invoice worksheet, select cell **E10**. Click the **Data** tab, and then, in the Data Tools group, click **Data Validation**. Click the **Settings** tab, click the **Allow box** arrow, and then select **List**. Verify that the **Ignore blank** and **In-cell dropdown** options are checked.

b. Click the **Source** box, click the **Therapists** worksheet, and then select the cell range **A2:A4**. The Source box should show =Therapists!$A$2:$A$4. Click the **Source** box again to return to the Data Validation dialog box.

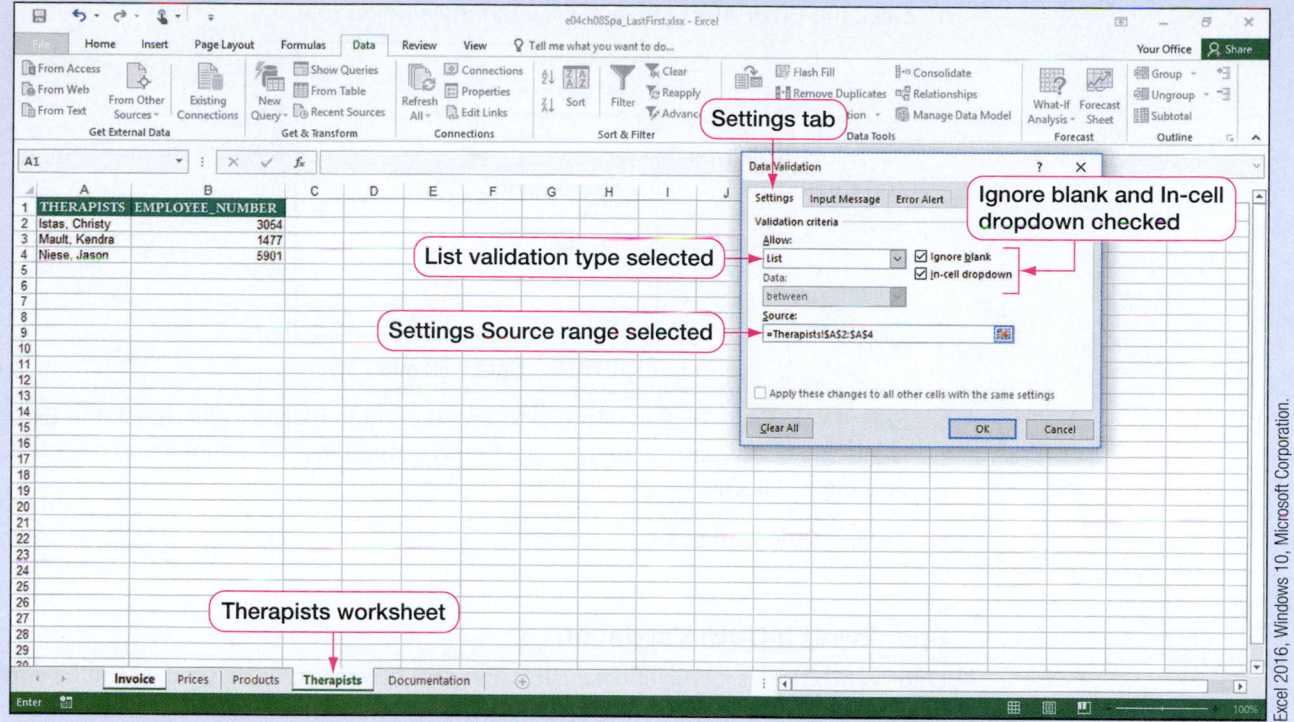

Figure 6 List validation rule

Excel 2016, Windows 10, Microsoft Corporation.

SIDE NOTE
Named Ranges
Consider using named ranges to identify source data for list validation. They can make your worksheet easier to interpret and understand.

c. In the Data Validation dialog box, click the **Input Message** tab. Click the **Title** box, and then type Select a therapist. Click the **Input message** box, and then type Select the therapist who delivered the services listed.

d. In the Data Validation dialog box, click the **Error Alert** tab. Click the **Title** box next to the Stop alert, and then type Not a valid name. Click the **Error message** box, type The name you entered is not a valid name. Please select a name from the list., and then click **OK**.

e. Click the list arrow  next to cell **E10**, and then select **Istas, Christy**.

f. **Save** 💾 the workbook.

Specifying a Decimal Validation

Decimal validation restricts users to only entering data that contains digits and allows decimal places. Validation of this type may require a minimum or maximum value depending on the criteria chosen, such as equal to, between, not equal to, not between, greater than, or less than.

In this exercise, you will specify a decimal validation rule.

🅴 E08.06

To Specify a Decimal Validation Rule

a. On the Invoice worksheet, select the cell range **E15:E30**. Click the **Data** tab, and in the Data Tools group, click **Data Validation**.

b. In the Data Validation dialog box, click the **Settings** tab, click the **Allow box** arrow, and then select **Decimal**. Verify that **Ignore blank** is checked. Click the **Data** box, select **less than or equal to**, and then, in the Maximum box, type 2.

c. Click the **Input Message** tab, click the **Title** box, type Hours, click the **Input message** box, and then type Enter the number of service hours.

d. Click the **Error Alert** tab, and click the Style box arrow.

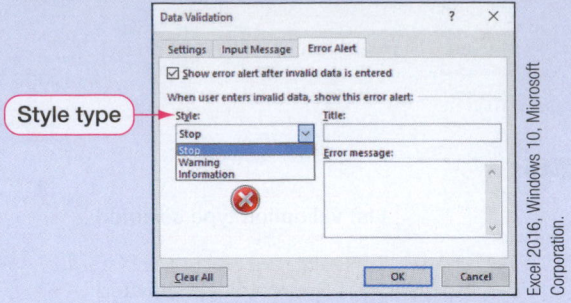

Style type

Figure 7 Data validation style

e. Select **Warning**. Click the **Title** box, and then type Invalid value. Click the **Error message** box, type The hours you entered exceed the maximum recommended., and then click **OK**.

f. Save  the workbook.

Specifying a Date Validation

Date validation is a type of data validation that specifies that only a date can be entered into a cell. Date criteria values can be explicitly entered, referenced by a cell address, or derived from a formula.

In the Spa workbook, the date entered in cell E6 should be restricted to the current date or earlier. Thus, invoices may not be dated with a future date. The TODAY function will be used for the date criteria, so the date entered will always be compared to the current date based on the function.

In this exercise, you will limit data entry to a date.

E08.07

To Limit Data Entry to a Date

a. On the Invoice worksheet, select cell **E6**. Click the **Data** tab, and in the Data Tools group, click **Data Validation**. In the Data Validation dialog box, click the **Settings** tab, click the **Allow box** arrow, and then select **Date**. Verify that **Ignore blank** is checked.

b. Click the **Data box** arrow, and then select **less than or equal to**.

c. Click in the **End date** box, and then type =TODAY(). This function represents the current date, which means that the invoice cannot have a date later than the current date.

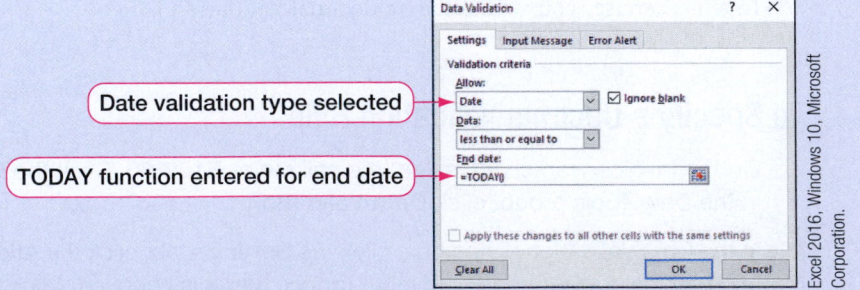

Date validation type selected

TODAY function entered for end date

Figure 8 Data validation with formula

d. Click the **Input Message** tab, click the **Title** box, and then type Invoice date. Click in the **Input message** box, and then type Enter the date in the following format: MM/DD/YYYY.

e. Click the **Error Alert** tab. If necessary, click the Style box arrow, and then select **Stop**. Click in the **Title** box, and then type Error. Click the **Error message** box, type Future dates are not allowed., and then click **OK**.

f. Select cell **E6**, type =TODAY() to enter the current date, and then press [Ctrl] + [Enter]. If you wanted to enter a date manually, that is, not using the TODAY function, as long as the date is in the correct format (MM/DD/YYYY) and is on or before the current date, it would be allowed.

g. **Save** 🔲 the workbook.

Specifying a Time Validation

Time validation is a type of data validation that specifies that only time values can be entered into a cell. Time validation is similar to date validation; the only difference is that in time validation, the data entered must be a time value.

In the Spa workbook, you will add validation criteria to cell E8 to ensure that only a time value between 8:00 AM and 4:30 PM — the spa hours — can be entered.

In this exercise, you will limit data entry to a time value.

 E08.08

To Limit Data Entry to a Time Value

a. On the Invoice worksheet, select cell **E8**. Click the **Data** tab, and in the Data Tools group, click **Data Validation**. In the Data Validation dialog box, click the **Settings** tab, click the **Allow box** arrow, and then select **Time**. Verify that **Ignore blank** is checked and that the Data selection is **between**.

b. Click the **Start time** box, and then type 8:00 AM. Click the **End time** box, and then type 4:30 PM.

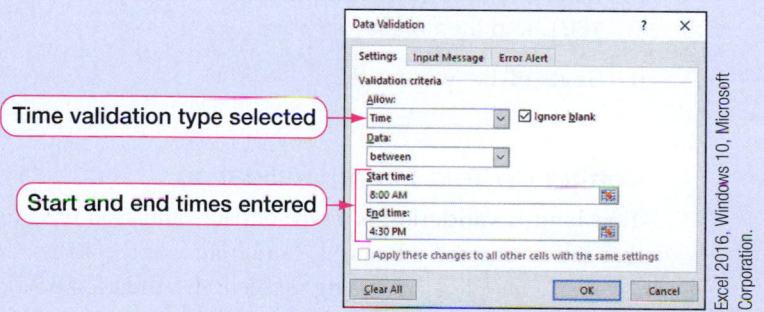

Time validation type selected

Start and end times entered

Figure 9 Start and end time validation

c. Click the **Input Message** tab, click the **Title** box, and then type Appointment time. Click in the **Input message** box, and then type Enter the appointment time as HH:MM AM/PM.

d. Click the **Error Alert** tab, click the **Title** box, and then type Error. Click the **Error message** box, type The time must be between 8:00 AM and 4:30 PM., and then click **OK**.

e. Select cell **E8**, type 2:30 PM, and press [Ctrl] + [Enter].

f. **Save** 🔲 the workbook.

Using Whole Number Validation

Whole number validation is a type of data validation that requires that only integer (whole number) values can be entered in a cell. A valid range or a minimum and a maximum value may also be specified.

In the Spa workbook, you will set the range of numbers allowed in cell E12 to be between 1001 and 5140. These refer to the highest and lowest guest room numbers in the resort. You also decide to not set an input message or an error alert.

In this exercise, you will limit data entry to a whole number with a minimum and a maximum value.

 **E08.09**

To Limit Data Entry to a Whole Number with a Minimum and a Maximum Value

a. On the Invoice worksheet, select cell **E12**. Click the **Data** tab, and in the Data Tools group, click **Data Validation**. In the Data Validation dialog box, click the **Settings** tab, click the **Allow** box arrow, and then select **Whole number**. Verify that **Ignore blank** is checked and that Data is **between**.

b. Click the **Minimum** box, and then type **1001**. Click the **Maximum** box, and then type **5140**.

Whole number validation type →

Minimum and maximum values entered →

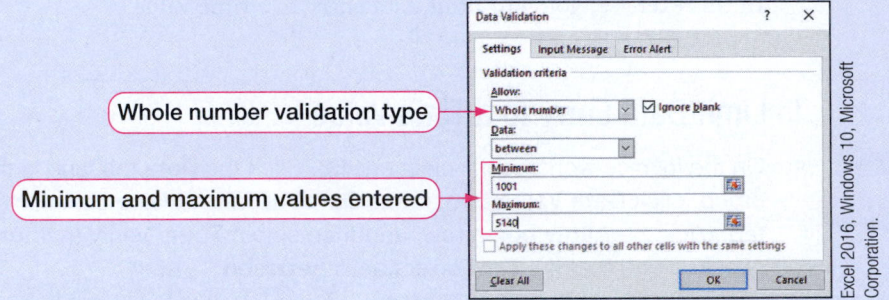

Figure 10 Whole number data validation

c. Click **OK** to skip entering an input message or error alert. Select cell **E12**, type **1001**, and then press Ctrl + Enter.

d. **Save** 💾 the workbook.

Setting Up Text Length Validation

Text length validation is a type of data validation used to limit the number of characters that can be entered into a cell. Data from workbooks is often imported into databases that have fixed field lengths. Using text length validation on a cell that will be imported into a database can help to prevent the data from being truncated (cut off) when it is imported. Text length validation can also prevent cells from becoming too long, which may prevent a range from printing on one page, which is often a requirement for an invoice or other worksheet.

In this exercise, you will limit data entry by the length of text entered in a cell.

 **E08.10**

To Limit the Length of Text Entered in a Cell

a. On the Invoice worksheet, select cell **C31**. Click the **Data** tab, and in the Data Tools group, click **Data Validation**. In the Data Validation dialog box, if necessary, click the **Settings** tab, click the **Allow** box arrow, and then select **Text Length**. Verify that **Ignore blank** is checked.

b. Click the **Data** box arrow, and select **less than or equal to**. Click the **Maximum** box, and then type **180**.

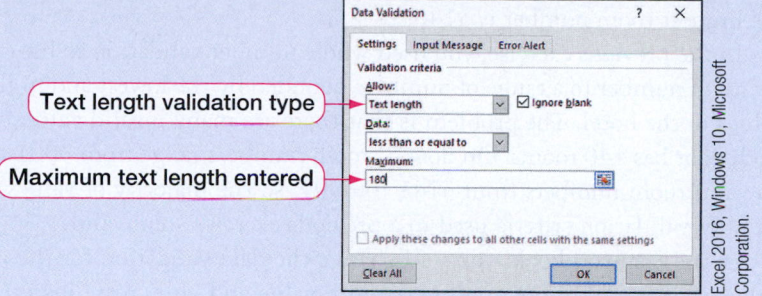

Excel 2016, Windows 10, Microsoft Corporation.

Text length validation type

Maximum text length entered

Figure 11   Maximum length of text data validation

c. Click the **Input Message** tab, click the **Title** box, and then type Comments. Click the **Input message** box, type Comments may not be more than 180 characters. Click the **Error Alert** tab, click the **Title** box, and then type Error. Click the **Error message** box, and then type Must be 180 characters or less. Click **OK**.

d. **Save**  the workbook.

Using Any Value Validation

Any value validation is a type of validation that utilizes the input message as a way to communicate rules to enter data in a cell. The moment an Any Value validated cell is made active, the Input Message is displayed as a prompt to the user. There are no criteria, data restrictions, or error messages set up with an Any Value validation.

In the Spa workbook, you will create a prompt so that when the user clicks on the Tax Rate in cell D33, a prompt appears with more information about the tax rate. There will be no value associated with the data validation and no error message, just the input message to provide information.

In this exercise, you will use data validation to display data entry prompts.

E08.11

To Use Data Validation to Display Data Entry Prompts

a. On the Invoice worksheet, select cell **D33**. Click the **Data** tab, and in the Data Tools group, click **Data Validation**.

b. In the Data Validation dialog box, if necessary, click the **Input Message** tab. Click the **Title** box, and then type Tax rate. Click in the **Input message** box, type All items and services require sales tax., and then click **OK**. Since you are not restricting data in this cell, changes to the Settings tab and Error Alert tab should not be made.

c. **Save**  the workbook.

Creating a Custom Data Validation

Custom validation is a more complex type of data validation that allows the user to apply multiple criteria simultaneously by using formulas. Using custom validation, you can apply multiple criteria simultaneously; for example, you can specify a valid range of whole numbers if a number is entered and limit the length of a text value if a text value is entered.

The Painted Paradise Resort & Spa has 700 hotel rooms: 140 rooms on each of five floors. Rooms are numbered according to a codified data value. A **codified data value** is a value created by following a system of rules in which the position of information is tied to its context. Turquoise Oasis room numbers are codified values; the first digit is the floor the room is located on, and the next three digits are the room number on that floor. For example, the 79th room on floor 3 is room 3079. The lowest room number is 1001, and the highest room number is 5140.

In the previous exercise, you used whole number validation to limit the value entered for room number to a range of numbers bounded by the lowest and highest room number values in the hotel. The problem is that there are many invalid values within that range. Each floor has 140 rooms. On floor 3, room numbers range from 3001 to 3140. There are no valid room numbers from 3141 to 3999; so the majority of values allowed by whole number validation criteria used in a previous exercise are invalid.

In the Spa workbook, you will change the data validation for the room number that only specifies a minimum and maximum value and will create instead a custom validation rule that will allow only the following numbers to be entered in cell E12 for the room number: 1001-1140, 2001-2140, 3001-3140, 4001-4140, and 5001-5140.

In this exercise, you will create a custom validation rule.

 **E08.12**

To Create a Custom Validation Rule for Room Numbers

a. On the Invoice worksheet, select cell **E12**. Click the **Data** tab, and in the Data Tools group, click **Data Validation**.

b. In the Data Validation dialog box, click the **Settings** tab, and in the **Allow** box, select **Custom**. In the Formula box, select the existing text, and then replace it with =AND (LEFT(E12,1)<="5",LEFT(E12,1)>="1",RIGHT(E12,3)>="001",RIGHT(E12,3)<="140", LEN(E12)=4).

> ### Troubleshooting
> If you have trouble entering the data validation formula without making an error, type the formula into a blank cell on the Invoice worksheet. If there is no error, then copy and paste from the formula bar into the Data Validation dialog box.

Custom validation type →

Multiple criteria entered in the form of a function →

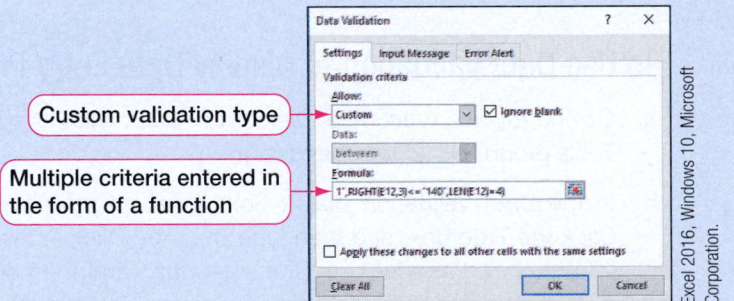

Excel 2016, Windows 10, Microsoft Corporation.

Figure 12 Custom data validation rule

By starting with an AND function, the rule requires all the criteria in the function to be true for there not to be an error. So Excel will check the number entered in cell E12, and as long as it meets *all* of the following criteria, the room number will be accepted. Otherwise, the Alert Message will appear.

- The LEFT(E12,1)<="5" tests to make sure that the first digit (the digit on the left) of the room number in cell E12 is less than or equal to 5, since the resort has only five floors.

- The LEFT(E12,1)>="1" tests to make sure that the first digit of the room number is greater than or equal to 1. So together with the criterion above, this criterion ensures that the first digit is between 1 and 5.

- The RIGHT(E12,3)>="001" tests to make sure that the three digits to the right are greater than or equal to "001", since the room numbers on each floor start with 1.
- The RIGHT(E12,3)<="140" tests to make sure that the three digits to the right are less than or equal to 140, since the highest room number on each floor is 140.
- The LEN(E12)=4 limits the total characters entered into the cell to four.

c. Click the **Input Message** tab. Click the **Title** box, and then type Room number. Click in the **Input message** box, type Enter the 4-digit room number., and click the **Error Alert** tab. Click the Title box, and type Error. Click the Error message box, type You must enter a 4-digit room number., and then click **OK**.

d. In cell E12, type 3120, and then press Ctrl + Enter.

e. **Save** the workbook.

SS CONSIDER THIS | **When Data Validation Might Not Be the Best Option**

Data validation is an excellent tool to use in workbooks where you want to restrict data entry to certain values or ranges of values. There may be times when a list of data is required, and data validation can require the use of that list for choosing a value.

However, there may be times when data validation rules can hinder data entry rather than enhancing it. Can you think of a time when data validation might hinder a user who is trying to enter data in a workbook? In what types of situations might that occur? Can you think of any other options available other than data validation?

Using Formulas to Generate a Value

Codification schemes consist of rules that combine data values in specific formats and locations to generate a new data value. A codification scheme is entered not through data validation but rather as a formula in the cell. The spa would like to use a codification scheme to automatically generate invoice numbers.

The invoice number will be the combination of the appointment date in "yyyymmdd" format, appointment time in "hhmm" format, and employee number, all separated by single spaces. For example, an appointment with Christy Istas, whose employee ID number is 3054, on 5/14/2018 at 2:30 PM would have an invoice number of "20180514 1430 3054."

In the Spa workbook, you will create this codification scheme in a formula that will automatically generate the invoice number based on the data entered in the invoice. You will build the formula one piece at a time until all the pieces of the codification scheme are included.

In this exercise, you will create a codification scheme.

 **E08.13**

To Create a Codification Scheme for the Invoice Number

a. Select cell **E4**, type =IF(E6>0,TEXT(E6,"YYYYMMDD"),""), and then press Ctrl + Enter. This formats the invoice number so that the date is the first part of the invoice number in the format YYYYMMDD, but it displays nothing if cell E6 — the date — is empty.

SIDE NOTE
Use of Ampersand in Formulas
Use the ampersand (&) in a formula to concatenate two strings, or join two strings together, to return one string.

b. Click in the **formula bar**. Place the insertion point at the end of the formula, type &" "&IF(E8>0,TEXT(E8,"HHMM"),""), and then press Ctrl + Enter.

There should be a space between the quotation marks that are between the ampersands so there will be a space between the time of the appointment in HHMM format and the invoice number. There should be no space between the quotation marks at the end of the IF function so that the result displays nothing for the time portion if cell E8 (the time) is empty.

c. Click in the **formula bar**. Place the insertion point at the end of the formula, type &" "&IF(E10>0,VLOOKUP(E10,Therapists,2),""), and then press Ctrl + Enter.

There should be a space between the quotes that are between the ampersands so there will be a space between the employee number of the therapist selected and the end of the invoice number, but there should be no space between the quotation marks at the end of the IF function so it displays nothing for the therapist's employee number if cell E10 is empty. The therapist's employee number comes from the named range Therapists on the Therapists worksheet and is found by using the VLOOKUP function. The final invoice number in cell E4 should be YYYYMMDD 1430 3054, where YYYY is the four-digit year, MM is the two-digit month, and DD is the two-digit day of the current date entered in the invoice.

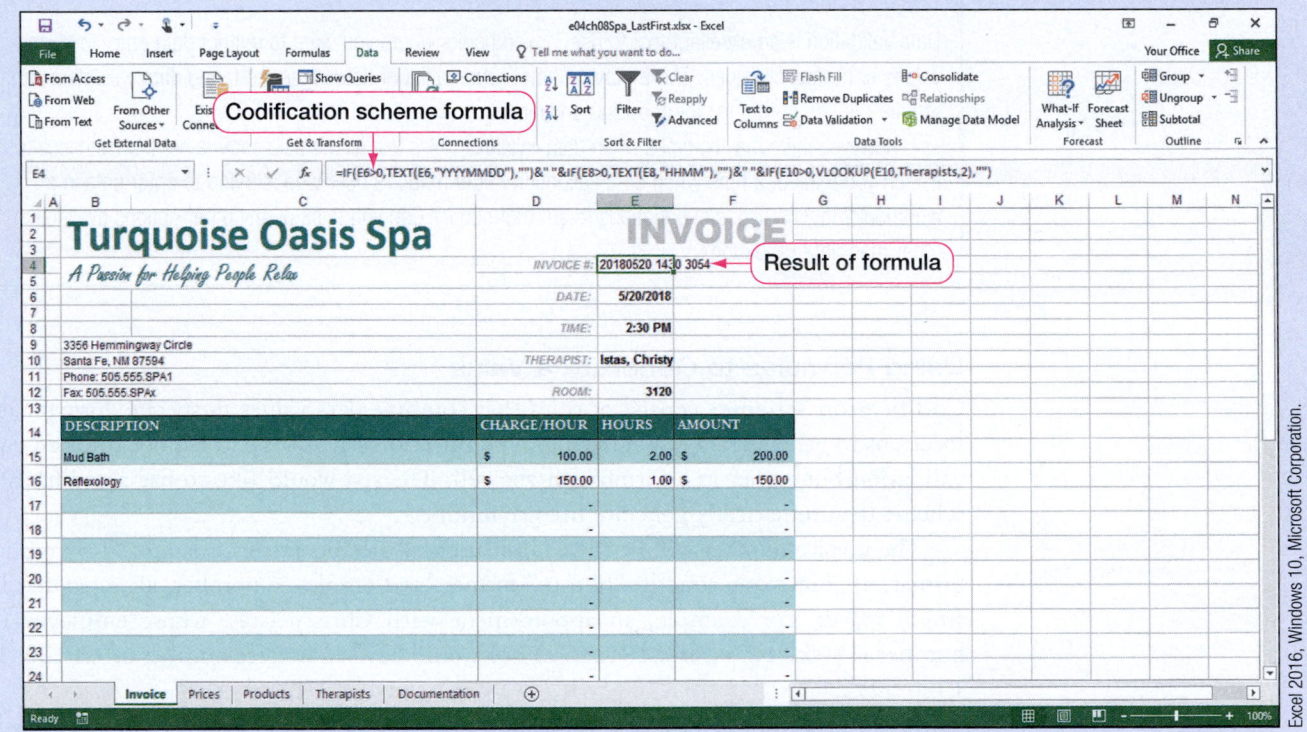

Figure 13 Codification scheme for invoice number

d. **Save** 💾 the workbook.

Validating with Text-to-Speech Manually

Excel includes a **text-to-speech** feature that reads the values of text back to you. This feature requires speakers or headphones. To use the text-to-speech feature, you have to add at least one text-to-speech button to the ribbon. There are five buttons available to choose from, described in the Quick Reference.

<table>
<tr><td>QUICK REFERENCE</td><td>Text-to-Speech Options</td></tr>
</table>

There are a number of text-to-speech buttons you can add to the ribbon. The button or buttons you choose will determine how you can use the text-to-speech feature.

- Speak Cells — Click to hear the contents of the selected cell and adjacent cells.
- Speak Cells - Stop Speaking Cells — Click to stop hearing the cell contents read.
- Speak Cells by Columns — Click to hear the cell contents read in the column selected.
- Speak Cells by Rows — Click to hear the cell contents read in the row selected.
- Speak Cells on Enter — Click to hear the cell contents read when you press [Enter].

This type of editing allows you to hear what you entered as well as see what you entered and can help you find mistakes you might otherwise overlook. This feature has replaced the speech recognition feature in earlier versions of Excel; however, speech recognition is still available in the different versions of Windows.

In the Spa workbook, you will add two of the Speak Cells buttons to a new group on the Review tab and use it to have the contents of a cell read to you.

In this exercise, you will use text-to-speech for data proofing.

 E08.14

To Use Text-to-Speech for Data Proofing

a. Click the **File** tab, click **Options**, and then, in the Excel Options dialog box, click **Customize Ribbon**.

b. Click the **Choose commands from** arrow, and then select **Commands Not in the Ribbon**.

c. In the Main Tabs list, right-click **Review**, and then select **Add New Group** from the shortcut menu. Right-click **New Group (Custom)**, and then select **Rename** from the shortcut menu. Type Text-to-Speech in the Display name box.

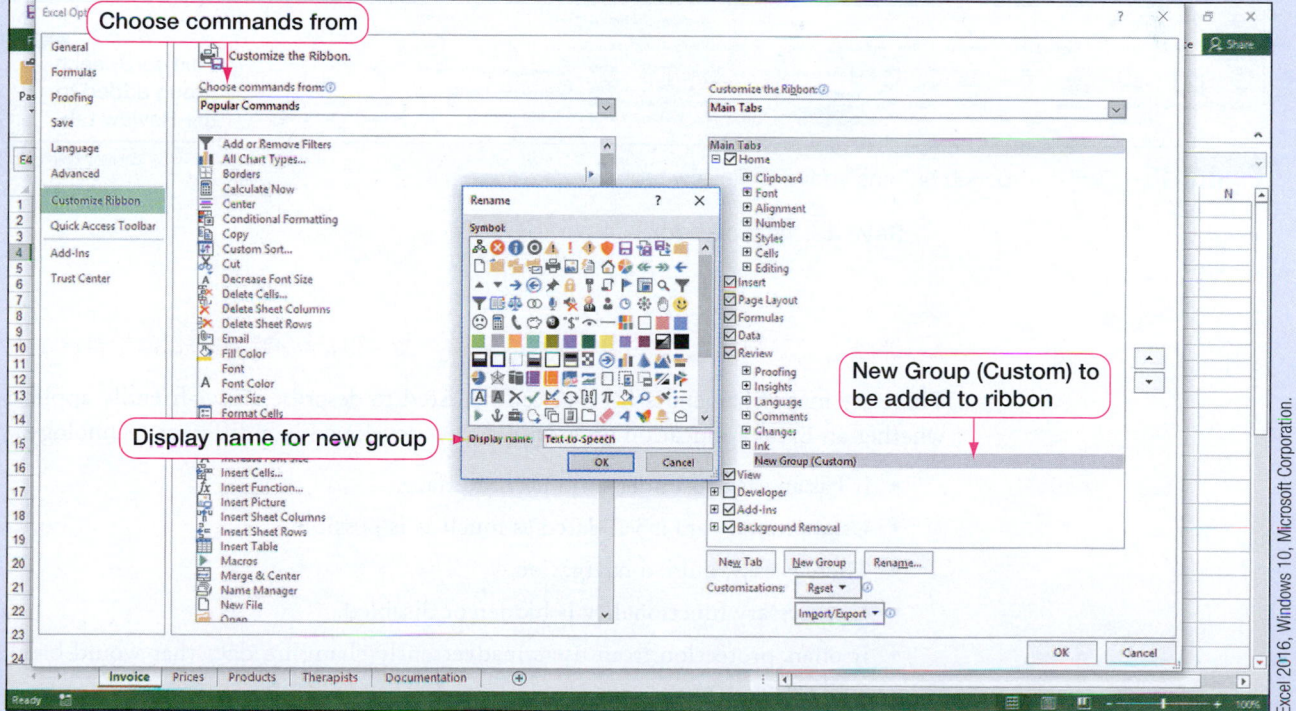

Figure 14   New group for the ribbon

Excel 2016, Windows 10, Microsoft Corporation.

d. Click **OK**, and then, in the Main Tabs list box, click **Text-to-Speech (Custom)**.

e. In the Commands list, scroll down, select **Speak Cells**, and then click **Add**. Select **Speak Cells - Stop Speaking**, and then click **Add**.

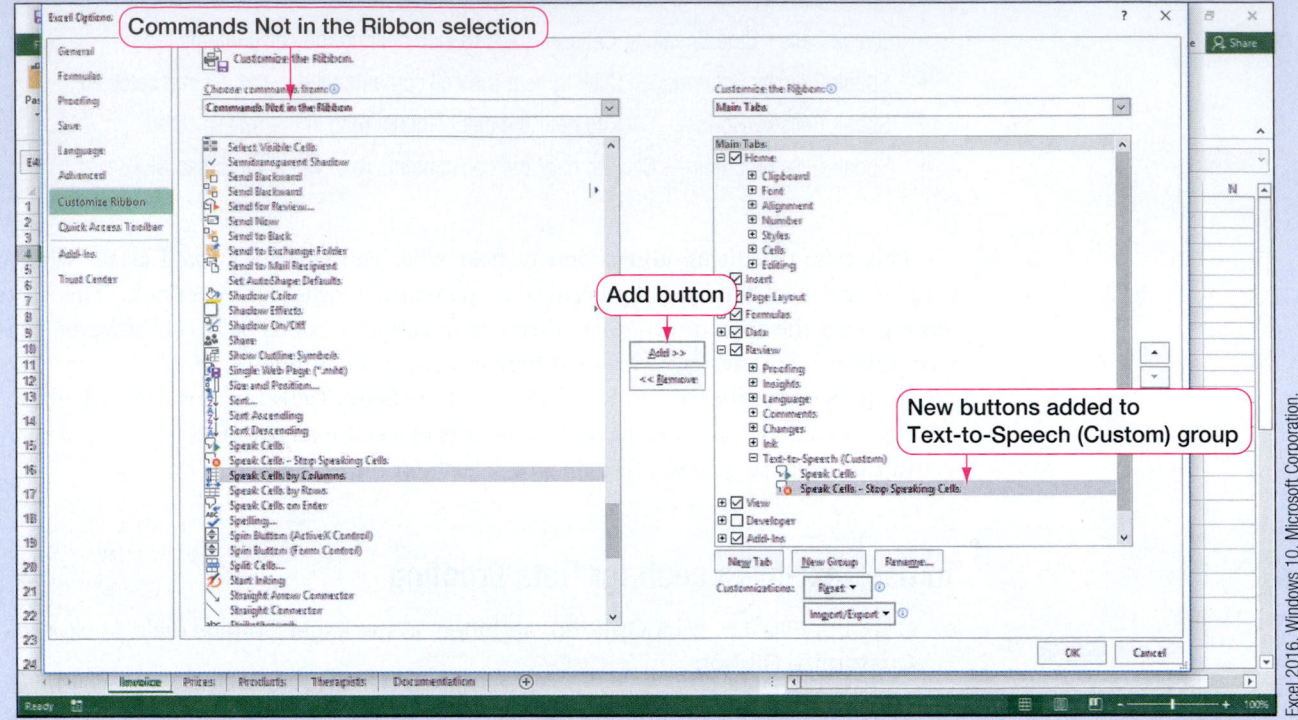

Figure 15 Text-to-speech buttons to add to the ribbon

f. Click **OK**. Select cell **B15**, and then click the **Review** tab. In the Text-to-Speech group, click **Speak Cells**. When several lines have been read, click **Stop Speaking**.

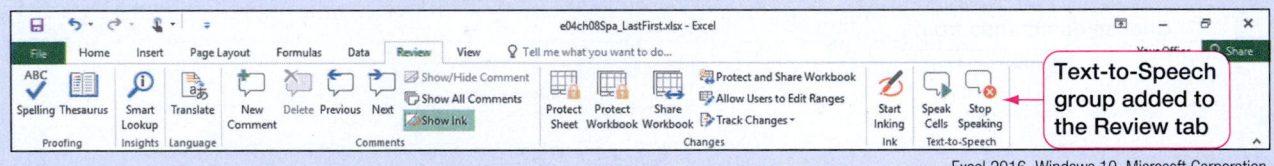

Figure 16 Text-to-speech buttons added to Review tab

Excel 2016, Windows 10, Microsoft Corporation.

g. **Save** 💾 the workbook.

Developing User-Friendly Excel Applications

There are many characteristics that can be listed to describe a user-friendly application, whether an Excel application or an application developed in a different technology.

- It has an easy-to-understand user interface.
- User-entered data is validated as much as is possible.
- There is easy, guided navigation.
- Unnecessary functionality is hidden or disabled.
- It offers protection from users inadvertently changing data that would break the application.
- Only essential content is visible.
- Good documentation exists.

So far, in developing the invoice application, the workbook is easy to understand — it is modeled after a standard invoice design and layout, and data validation has been applied to ensure correct data entry as much as possible.

In this section, you will modify the invoice workbook to make it an even better application by implementing macros, hiding unnecessary workbook parts such as scroll bars and gridlines, and protecting the cells that should not be changed by a user.

Create and Use Macros

Visual Basic for Applications (VBA) is a computer programming language that is part of most Microsoft Office products that users can use to implement a wide variety of enhancements to Microsoft Office applications. VBA is used to record macros in Excel. A **macro** is a group of programmed instructions in Excel that automate tasks and play them back when the macro is run. A macro is often used to automate repetitive tasks. For example, a macro may perform menu selections, data entry, data formatting, or even calculation. If a task is performed repeatedly in a worksheet, it is probably a candidate to be recorded as a macro, particularly if incorrectly performing the task could damage the worksheet. The three locations where a macro can be store are described in Table 1.

This Workbook	This option stores the macro in the active workbook. The macro is available to the active workbook as well as any other open workbooks. Once the active workbook is closed, however, the macro is no longer available to other open workbooks.
New Workbook	This option saves the macro in a new workbook. The macro is available to the active workbook and any open workbooks. Once the new workbook is closed, the macro is no longer available to the active workbook or any other open workbooks.
Personal Macro Workbook	This option stores the macro in a hidden workbook that automatically opens every time you open Excel. The macro is then available to any open workbooks as well as any new workbooks that may be created.

Table 1 Locations where macros can be stored

In the Spa workbook, you will create two different macros. One macro will clear the data from the invoice, and the other will automatically apply formatting to a range of cells. Since a macro records every keystroke and mouse click, it is best practice to plan a macro before recording it to avoid recording unnecessary mouse clicks or keystrokes. If you did record any unnecessary mouse clicks or keystrokes, they can be removed from the macro; in a later exercise, you will learn how to modify a macro. Best practice is also to test your macro to make sure it works as you had planned.

First, you will set up a Trusted Location for your macro-enabled workbook so when you open it, the macros will not be blocked.

Creating a Trusted Location

When you save a workbook that contains a macro, Excel recognizes it as a potential threat, primarily because macros can contain viruses as well as legitimate commands. A **Trusted Location** is a folder that has been identified in the Microsoft Office Trust Center as a safe location for opening files that contain active code that includes macros. If a workbook in a Trusted Location is opened, macros contained in the document will be automatically enabled. If the location where the file is stored is not a Trusted Location, the Trust Center will block any macros and other items that could contain malicious code, and you will have to manually enable the content when you open it.

By default, Excel already has some Trusted Locations set up for templates and other start files. In this exercise, you will add the folder where you are saving your student files as a trusted folder.

 **E08.15**

To Create a Trusted Location

a. Click the **File** tab, click **Options**, click **Trust Center**, and then click **Trust Center Settings**.

b. Click **Trusted Locations**, and in the trusted locations section, click **Add new location**. In the Microsoft Office Trusted Locations dialog box, click **Browse**, navigate to the folder where you save your student files, and then select that folder.

c. Click **OK**, click **OK** again, and then verify that your folder has been added to the list of User Locations. Click **OK**, and then click **OK** again.

d. **Save** 🖫 the workbook.

Adding the Developer Tab to the Ribbon

Recording macros is generally considered an activity for worksheet developers. The **Developer tab** is not visible by default in Excel, so in order to record a macro, the Developer tab needs to be added to the ribbon. The Developer tab contains the buttons needed to create, edit, and run macros.

In this exercise, you will add the Developer tab to the ribbon so you can access the buttons necessary to create macros for the Spa workbook.

 **E08.16**

To Add the Developer Tab to the Ribbon

a. Click the **File** tab, click **Options**, and then click **Customize Ribbon**.

b. In the **Main Tabs** list on the right-hand side of the Excel Options dialog box, click the **Developer** check box, and then click **OK**.

c. **Save** 🖫 the workbook.

Creating an Absolute Macro Reference

As with cell references in formulas, cell references in macros can be absolute or relative. **Absolute macro references** affect the same cell address every time the macro is run. Absolute macro references are set when the macro is recorded. The location of the active cell when the macro is run is irrelevant. Macros are recorded with absolute references by default.

In this exercise, you will record an absolute macro to clear the current data but leave all the formulas necessary for the invoice to calculate correctly.

 **E08.17**

SIDE NOTE
Naming a Macro
A macro name cannot have a space. Consider using capitalization or underscores when assigning macro names.

To Record an Absolute Macro

a. If necessary, click the **Invoice** worksheet. Click the **Developer** tab, and in the Code group, click **Record Macro**.

b. In the Record Macro dialog box, in the Macro name box, type **ClearCells**. Click in the Shortcut key box, press and hold the Shift key, and then type **C**. Ensure that the Store macro in box is **This Workbook**. In the Description box, type **To clear contents from cells**.

Troubleshooting

Make sure you use an uppercase "C" when recording the macro so the shortcut keys will be $\boxed{\text{Ctrl}}$ + $\boxed{\text{Shift}}$ + $\boxed{\text{C}}$. Shift is added because $\boxed{\text{Ctrl}}$ + $\boxed{\text{C}}$ is the keyboard Copy shortcut.

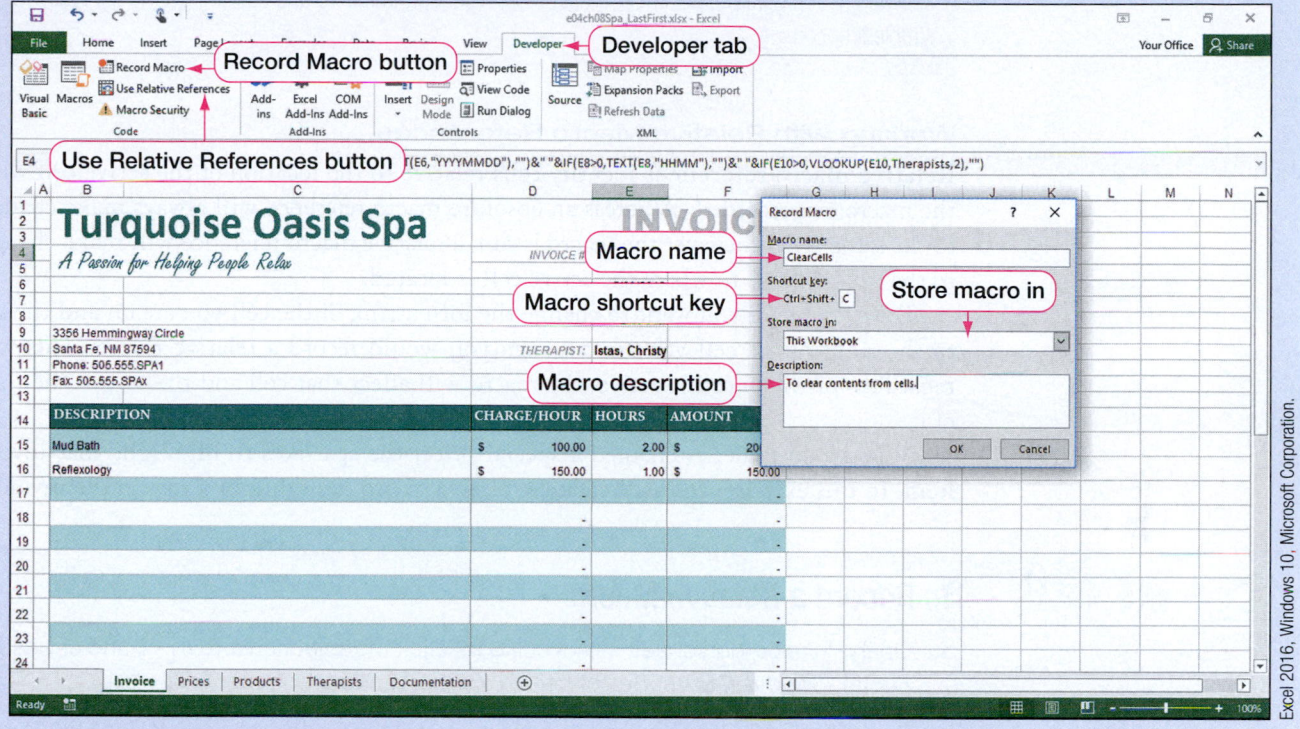

Figure 17   Macro dialog box

c. Click **OK**. Select cell **E6**, press and hold $\boxed{\text{Ctrl}}$, and then select cells **E8**, **E10**, **E12**, and **C31** and the cell ranges **B15:B30** and **E15:E30**.

d. Click the **Home** tab, and in the Editing group, click **Clear**, and then select **Clear Contents**. Click cell **E6**.

e. Click the **Developer** tab, and in the Code group, click **Stop Recording**.

f. Click the **File** tab, and click **Save**. Click **No**.

   To save the macro, you will have to save the workbook as a macro-enabled workbook.

SIDE NOTE
Deleting a Macro

To delete a macro, click the Developer tab, and in the Code group, click Macros, select the macro you want to delete, and then click Delete.

g. In the Save As dialog box, in the **File name** box, type **e04ch08SpaMacro_LastFirst**, using your last and first name. Click the **Save as type** box, and then select **Excel Macro-Enabled Workbook**. Click **Save**. Notice that the file extension of the Macro-Enabled workbook changes to **.xlsm**. You can add data to the invoice, then run the macro to see whether it works correctly.

h. Click in cell **E6**, enter **today's date**. Click in cell **E8**, and enter 2:30 PM. Click in cell **E10**, and select **Istas, Christy**.

i. Press $\boxed{\text{Ctrl}}$ + $\boxed{\text{Shift}}$ + $\boxed{\text{C}}$ to test the macro.

j. **Save** 💾 the workbook.

Working with Relative Macro References

Relative macro references identify cells relative to the location of the active cell when the macro was recorded. Whereas an absolute macro reference will always make changes to the same cells whenever the macro is run, a relative macro reference will make changes to the cells relative to where the active cell is located.

For example, if you want to change the formatting of the cell you are on and the cell to the right of the cell you are on, then you would record a relative macro. This way, regardless of which cell is active, the macro will affect that cell and the cell to the right of it.

When a customer is charged a special price, the spa likes to highlight that invoice item. In this exercise, you will create a relative macro to highlight a row in the invoice.

 E08.18

To Record a Relative Macro

a. On the Invoice worksheet, select cell **B15**, click the selection arrow ▾, and choose **Facial - Mud & Citrus**. Select cell **E15**, type **1**, and then press Ctrl + Enter.

b. Select cell **B15**. Click the **Developer** tab, and in the Code group, click **Use Relative References**. This will toggle the Use Relative References button on, which is evident by the color to which the button changes.

c. Click **Record Macro**, and type **HighlightItem** for the macro name. Click in the shortcut key box, and then type **h**. Ensure the Store macro in box is **This Workbook**. Click in the Description box, type **To highlight an invoice special.**, and then click **OK**.

d. Select cells **B15:F15**, click the **Home** tab, and in the Font group, click **Bold** B. Click the **Font Size** arrow `11 ▾`, and then select **14**.

e. Click the **Developer** tab, and in the Code group, click **Stop Recording**.

f. Click cell **B16**, and then select **Hair Coloring**. Press Ctrl + H to test the macro.

g. **Save** 🖫 the workbook.

Adding a Macro to a Button

Macros can be run by using the keyboard shortcuts you apply when creating the macro, from the Developer tab, or even from a button that you can add to a worksheet. A button makes it easy for a user to run a macro with little or no knowledge of how a macro works.

In this exercise, you will create a macro button to run the ClearCells macro.

 **E08.19**

SIDE NOTE

Running a Macro from the Ribbon

To run a macro from the ribbon, click the Developer tab, and in the Code group, click Macros, select the macro name, and then click Run.

To Create a Macro Button

a. On the Invoice worksheet, click the **Developer** tab, and in the Controls group, click **Insert**. Select the **Button (Form Control)** in the top left corner. Click in the top left corner of cell **G2**, and then drag to the bottom right corner of cell **H3** to draw the button.

b. In the Assign Macro dialog box, under Macro name, click **ClearCells**.

> ### Troubleshooting
>
> Be very careful once you have created a button to run a macro. Even when you are editing the button and its properties, if you left-click the button, the macro will run.

c. Click **OK**. Right-click the button, select **Edit Text**, delete the text, and then type Clear Invoice. Right-click the button, and then select **Exit Edit Text**.

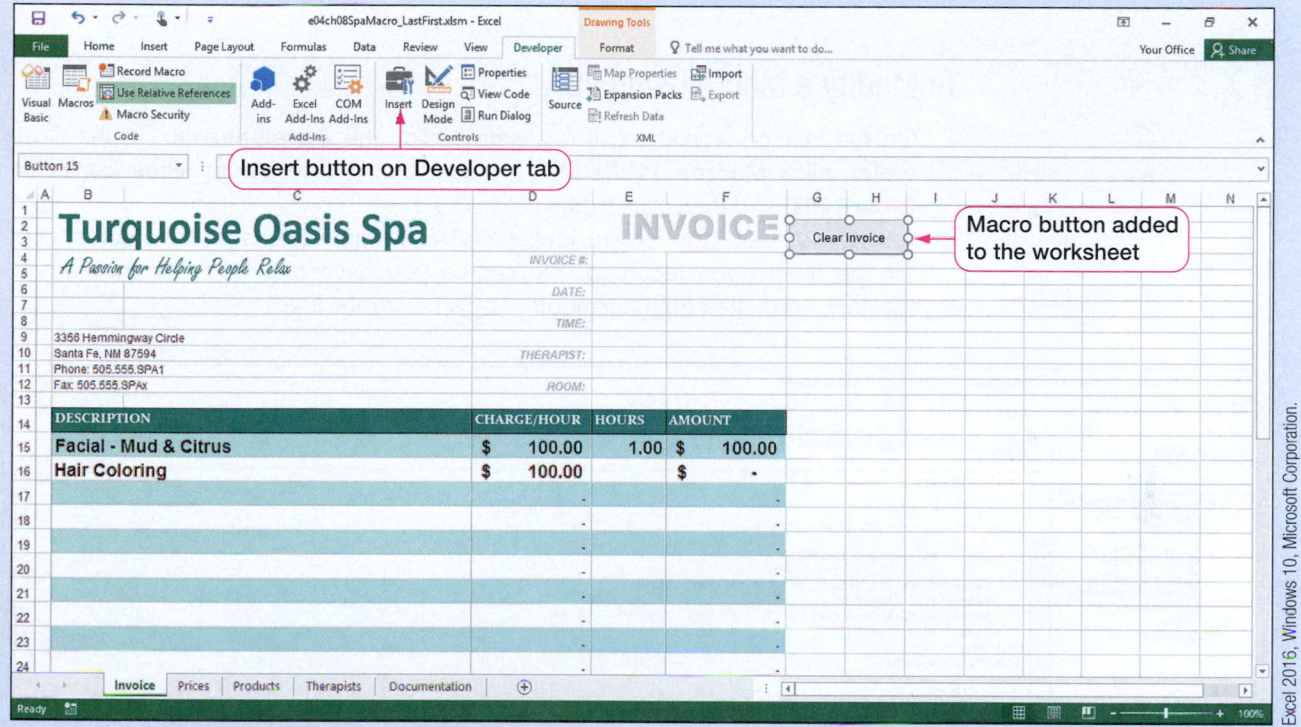

Figure 18 Macro button on the worksheet

d. Select cell **G5** to deselect the button. Click the **Clear Invoice** button to run the macro, and verify that the data in the invoice is cleared.

The clear cells macro in this example clears the contents of the cells but does not clear the formatting, so the special formatting you applied with the HighlightItem macro is still applied to the cell range B15:F15. You will create an absolute macro to clear the formatting.

e. Click the **Developer** tab. In the Code group, click **Use Relative References** to toggle it off. Click **Record Macro**. In the Macro name box, type ClearFormatting. In the shortcut key box, type k. Ensure that the Store macro in box is **This Workbook**. Click in the Description box, type To clear special highlighting from the invoice., and then click **OK**.

f. Select the cell range **B15:F30**. Click the **Home** tab, and in the Font group, click **Bold** B. In the Font group, click the **Font Size** arrow `11 ▾`, and then select **9**. Click cell **B15**.

g. Click the **Developer** tab, and in the Code group, click **Stop Recording**.

h. **Save** 🖫 the workbook.

Modifying a Macro

If you make a mistake when recording a macro, you can delete the macro and record a new one. Or if you know VBA, you can edit a macro and change the VBA code that Excel produced.

In the previous exercise, you recorded a ClearFormatting macro to clear any formatting applied from the HighlightItem macro. To eliminate having to run an extra macro, you will edit the ClearCells macro to include the step recorded in the ClearFormatting macro.

In this exercise, you will modify a macro using VBA.

 E08.20

To Modify a Macro Using VBA

a. On the Invoice worksheet, if necessary, click the **Developer** tab. In the **Code** group, click **Macros**. In the Macro dialog box, in the Macro name list, select **ClearCells**, and then click **Edit**.

A new Visual Basic for Applications (VBA) window opens with the actual code for the macro you recorded. All macros you have recorded will show in the window, separated from one another by a horizontal line.

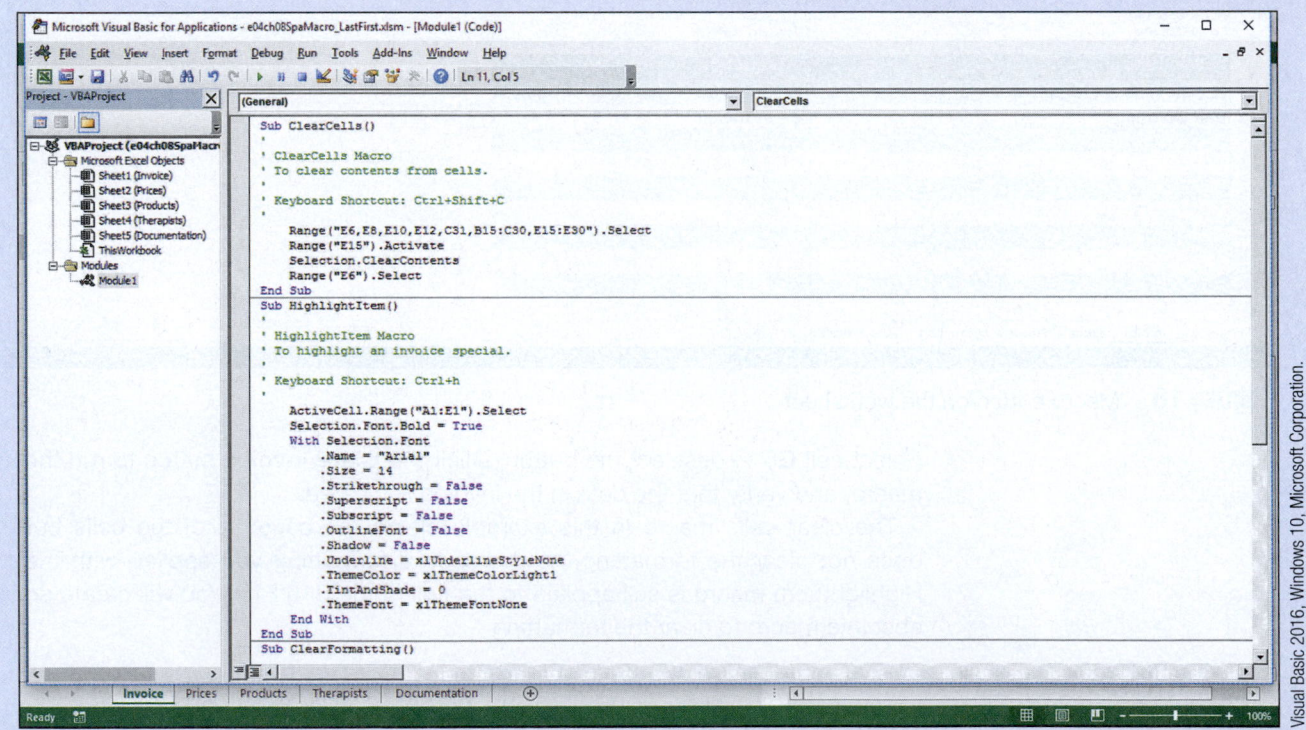

Figure 19   VBA window

Troubleshooting

The code you see in the VBA code window may not exactly match the code shown in Figure 19. Excel converts every keystroke and mouse click to VBA code when recording a macro, so any deviation from the steps in the exercise in which you created the macros — including keystrokes to correct deviations — are recorded.

b. Scroll if necessary to see the VBA code for the **ClearFormatting** macro.

c. Select the text that starts with **Range ("B15:F30")** and ends with **Range ("B15:C15").Select**. Press Ctrl + C.

d. Scroll to the top of the VBA window to see the ClearCells macro. Place your insertion point after the line **Range ("E6").Select**. Press Enter, and then press Ctrl + V.

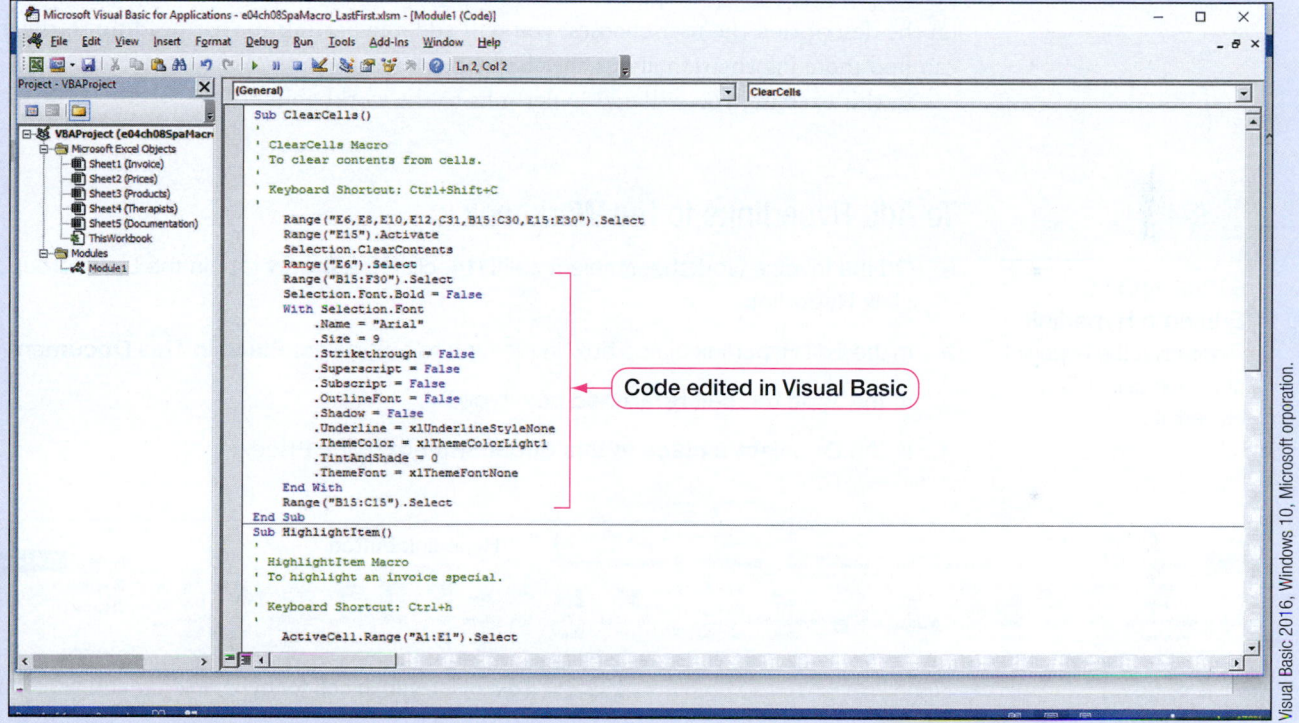

Figure 20   Edited VBA code

e. On the menu, click **File**, and then select **Close and Return to Microsoft Excel**. Your changes will be saved automatically, and the VBA window will close.

f. Click cell **B15**, and select **Facial - Mud & Citrus**. Press Ctrl + H to apply formatting from the HighlightItem macro.

g. Click the **Clear Invoice** button. If necessary, click the Home tab, and verify that the formatting in row 15 was changed back to size 9, not bold.

h. **Save** 💾 the workbook.

Change How to Navigate a Workbook

Workbook navigation is defined as moving from one cell to another in a worksheet and moving between worksheets. Assisting workbook users by adding navigational aids to a workbook and by hiding worksheets and features that the user does not need makes that workbook much more usable and easier to understand, and it makes the workbook's appearance much cleaner and less intimidating.

In the Spa workbook, you will add a hyperlink to navigate to a different worksheet, then hide unnecessary worksheets, worksheet tabs, scroll bars, row and column headings, and gridlines. This will give the invoice a cleaner look and make it look less like an Excel workbook.

Navigating with Hyperlinks

A **hyperlink** is a link that opens another page or file when you click on it. In Excel, a hyperlink can open a worksheet, another workbook, a file, a picture, an e-mail address, a photo, a web page, or another program. The hyperlink can be text or a picture and makes it easy for a user to get additional information that is in another location. Screen tips can be assigned to hyperlinks to give the user more description on the purpose of the hyperlink.

In the Spa workbook, there are multiple worksheets with information about the prices, products, and therapists. Since the charge per hour is automatically filled in based on the description the user chooses, you will add a hyperlink to that heading so the user can find more information about the charge per hour.

In this exercise, you will add hyperlinks to the workbook.

 **E08.21**

SIDE NOTE
Editing a Hyperlink
Right-click the hyperlink, and then select Edit Hyperlink.

To Add Hyperlinks to the Workbook

a. On the Invoice worksheet, select cell **D14**, click the **Insert** tab, in the Links group, click **Hyperlink**.

b. In the Edit Hyperlink dialog box, in the **Link to** box, select **Place in This Document**.

c. In the **Type the cell reference** box, type **F2**.

d. In the **Or select a place in this document** box, click **Prices**.

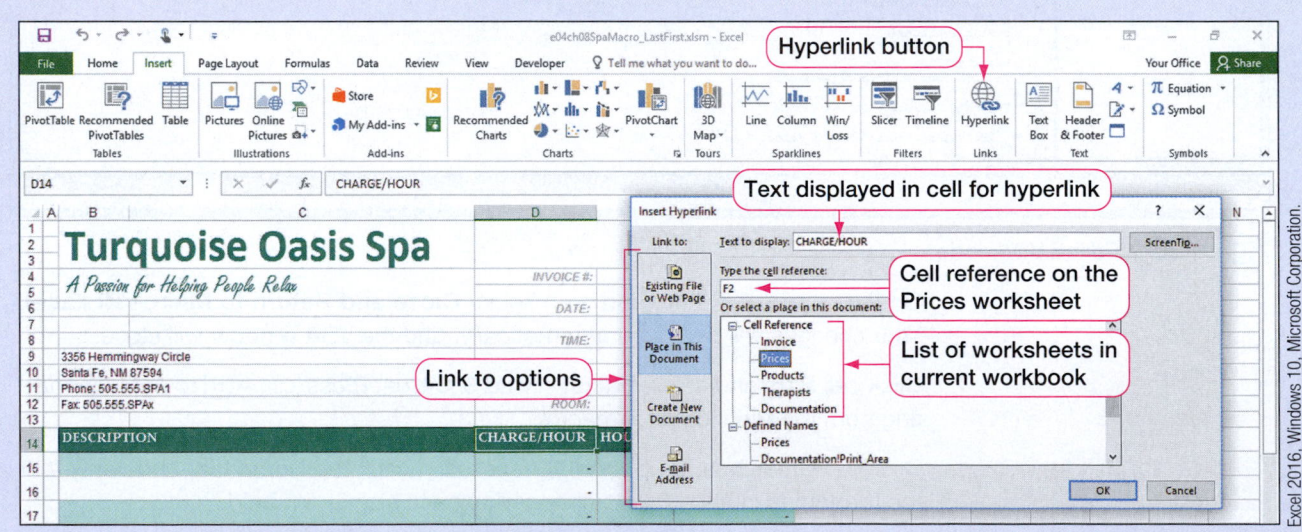

Figure 21   Inserting a hyperlink

e. Click **ScreenTip**. In the **Set Hyperlink ScreenTip** dialog box, type Go to Prices worksheet.

Set Hyperlink ScreenTip dialog box

Hyperlink ScreenTip button

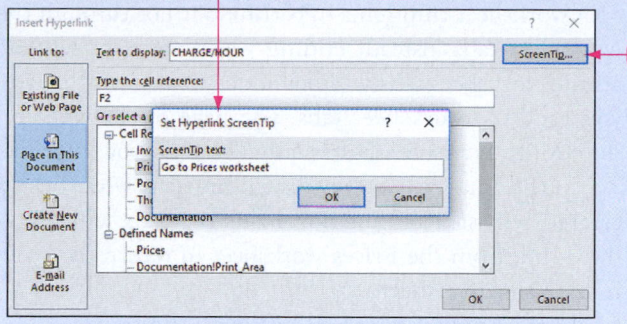

Figure 22 ScreenTip dialog box

f. Click **OK**, and then click **OK**. The font color of the text in cell D14 will change to the default font color for a hyperlink; the text will also be underlined.

g. Click the hyperlink in cell **D14**. The Prices worksheet should be the active worksheet, and cell F2 should be the active cell.

h. In cell **F2,** click the **Insert** tab, and in the Links group, click **Hyperlink**. In the **Type the cell reference** box, type D14. In the **Or select a place in this document** box, select **Invoice**. Click **ScreenTip**. In the **Set Hyperlink ScreenTip** dialog box, type Return to Invoice worksheet, click **OK**, and then click **OK**.

i. Click cell **F2** to return to the **Invoice** worksheet.

> **Troubleshooting**
>
> Click and hold on a cell that contains a hyperlink until the mouse pointer changes to ⊕. The cell will be selected without accessing the hyperlink.

j. **Save** the workbook.

Hiding Worksheets

A workbook with data stored in multiple worksheets can seem cluttered and difficult to navigate. There may be times when you would prefer that users not see data or have access to background calculations and code that has been placed in another worksheet. Since this data is often required for formulas, functions, and other calculations in a workbook, the worksheets can be hidden so a user cannot easily access them.

The employee number listed on the Therapists worksheet could be considered confidential information, so you want to hide this worksheet.

In this exercise, you will hide the Therapists worksheet.

 E08.22

SIDE NOTE
Unhide a Worksheet
Right-click any worksheet tab, select Unhide, select the name of the hidden worksheet, and click OK.

To Hide a Worksheet

a. Right-click the **Therapists** worksheet, and then select **Hide** from the shortcut menu. This will hide the worksheet so it can no longer be accessed by a worksheet.

b. **Save** the workbook.

Hiding Worksheet Tabs

When you hide a worksheet, any hyperlinks to that worksheet will no longer work. Excel assumes that if you want the data on the worksheet hidden, then you would not want to provide access to the data through a hyperlink. However, if you do want to access the data on a worksheet through a hyperlink but not through the worksheet tab, you can hide the worksheet tabs instead. Hiding worksheet tabs will affect the whole workbook: Either all the worksheet tabs will be hidden or none of the worksheet tabs will be hidden. Once you hide the worksheet tabs, you have to show them again to continue navigating to individual worksheets, especially if you do not have hyperlinks set up to each worksheet.

In the Spa workbook, you will hide the worksheet tabs so the Charge/Hour link you created will still be functional but the tabs will not be visible. Because you created a hyperlink from the Prices worksheet to return to the Invoice worksheet, it will be okay to hide the worksheet tabs.

In this exercise, you will hide worksheets.

 **E08.23**

SIDE NOTE

Show Worksheet Tabs
On the File tab, click Options, click Advanced, scroll down, and check Show sheet tabs. Click OK.

To Hide Worksheet Tabs

a. Click the **Invoice** worksheet. Click the **File** tab, click **Options**, and then click **Advanced**. Scroll down until the **Display options for this workbook** group is visible.

Troubleshooting

If the Invoice worksheet is not the active worksheet when you hide it, you will have no way to get back to that worksheet if you do not have any hyperlinks set up. If this happens, repeat the steps to hide the worksheets, check Show sheet tabs, and click OK.

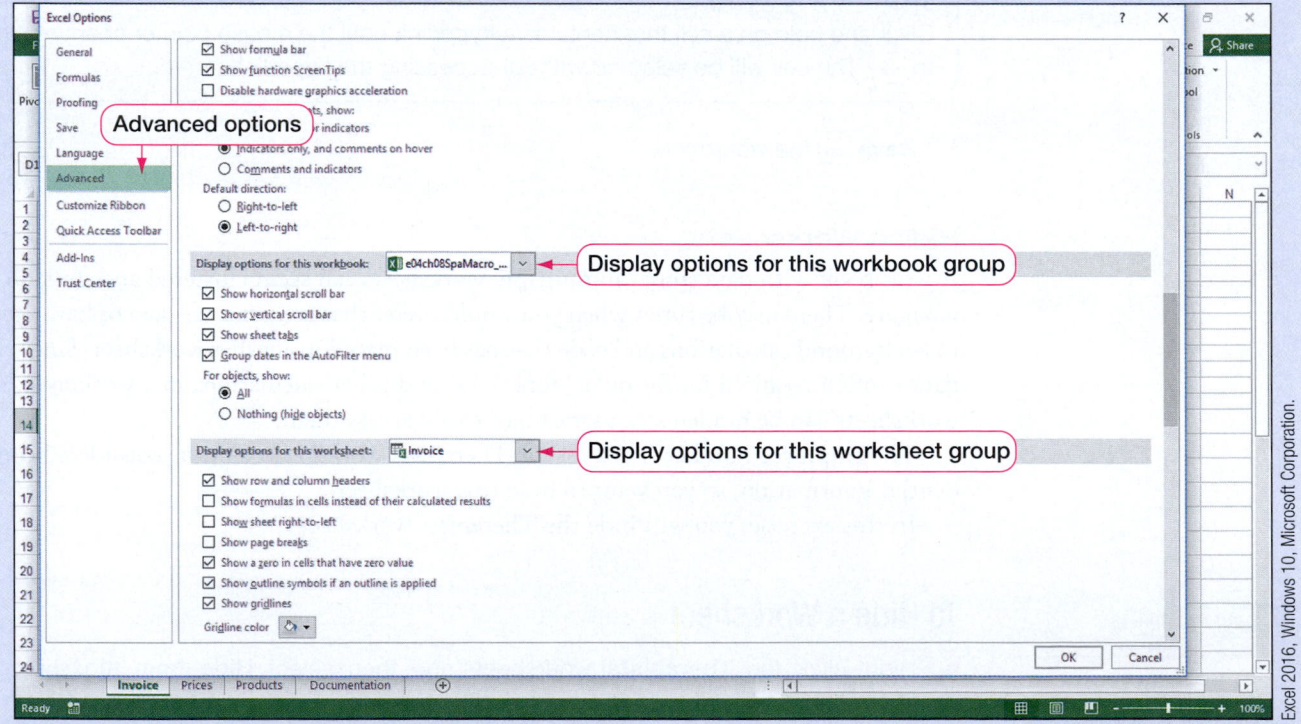

Figure 23   Display options for this workbook

b. Click **Show sheet tabs** to uncheck the option, and then click **OK**. Notice that the sheet tabs at the bottom of the window are no longer visible.

c. **Save** 🖫 the workbook.

Hiding Scroll Bars

Depending on the size of the worksheet and the resolution of your monitor, vertical and/or horizontal scroll bars may or may not be necessary. You can choose to hide the scroll bars, but you should do so only if all cells will be visible on one screen, regardless of the screen size. This option will affect the whole workbook, not just one worksheet.

The Spa workbook does require some scrolling, but you will hide and then unhide the scroll bars as practice. You will be able to use your mouse to scroll or the keyboard arrows to scroll if necessary, but those will be your only ways to scroll with the scroll bars hidden.

In this exercise, you will hide scroll bars.

 E08.24

To Hide Scroll Bars

a. On the Invoice worksheet, click the **File** tab, click **Options**, and then click **Advanced**. Scroll down until the **Display options for this workbook** group is visible. Click **Show horizontal scroll bar**, and click **Show vertical scroll bar** to uncheck the options, and then click **OK**.

   Notice that both scroll bars are gone from the application window, but you can still scroll with your mouse or the arrow keys on the keyboard. Assuming that the invoice width fits and just the length is too long for the window, you will unhide the vertical scroll bar.

b. Click the **File** tab, click **Options**, and then click **Advanced**. Scroll down until the **Display options for this workbook** group is visible. Click **Show vertical scroll bar**, and then click **OK**.

c. Save the workbook.

REAL WORLD ADVICE | **Options for Worksheets and Workbooks**

Some navigation options are for the whole workbook, while some are for individual worksheets. When you are thinking about changing these options, you should carefully consider what each worksheet looks like and how the option will affect each worksheet. Hiding the scroll bars for one worksheet might be fine, but if another worksheet needs them to navigate, then you should probably not hide them. On the other hand, when you hide row and column headings, this is an option for each worksheet, so one worksheet can have them hidden while another worksheet can have them showing.

Hiding Row and Column Headings

Row and column headings are helpful when you are building a formula or even a workbook, but once the workbook is complete and ready to use for data entry, the row and column headings often become unnecessary. This option is available for individual worksheets, so hiding them on one worksheet will not hide them on all the worksheets.

Data entry into the Spa workbook will not rely on cell references, since the cells are well labeled. You will hide the row and column headings that will make the workbook look more like an invoice than an Excel workbook.

In this exercise, you will hide row and column headings.

 **E08.25**

To Hide Row and Column Headings

SIDE NOTE
Display Row and Column Headings
Repeat step a, and then, in the Display options for this worksheet group, click Show row and column headers.

a. On the Invoice worksheet, click the **File** tab, click **Options**, and then click **Advanced**. Scroll down until the **Display options for this worksheet** group is visible, and then click **Show row and column headers** to uncheck the option.

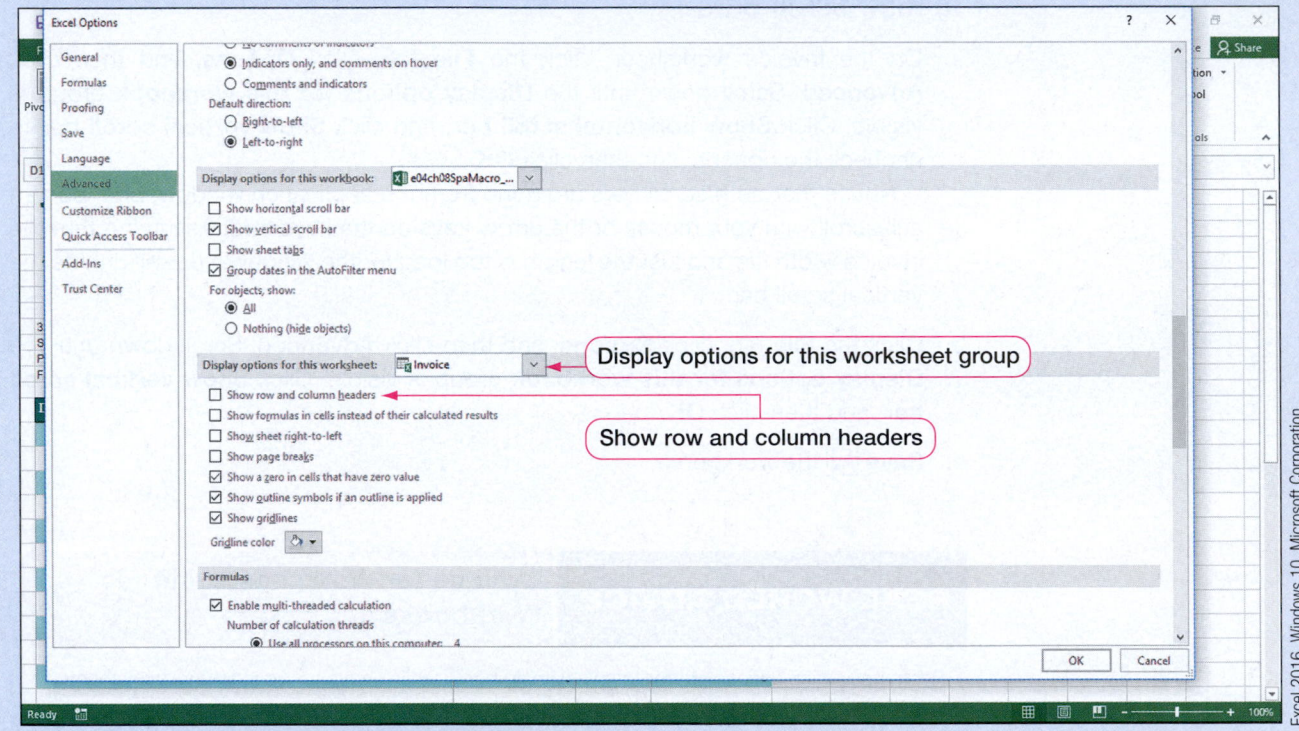

Figure 24 Display options for this worksheet

b. Click **OK**. Notice that the column headers (A, B, C) and row numbers (1, 2, 3) are no longer showing.

c. **Save** the workbook.

Hiding Gridlines

Gridlines, the vertical and horizontal lines on a worksheet that help define a cell's boundaries, are helpful, but they are not always necessary to use in a workbook. The gridlines you see when creating a workbook are not printed unless you select the print option to actually print the gridlines. This print option is available even if the gridlines are hidden on the workbook.

The Spa workbook has little need for gridlines, since most of the areas for data entry are clearly marked. Therefore, you will hide the gridlines.

In this exercise, you will hide worksheet gridlines.

 E08.26

SIDE NOTE
Display Gridlines
On the View tab, in the Show group, click Gridlines.

To Hide Gridlines

a. On the Invoice worksheet, click the **View** tab, and in the Show group, click **Gridlines** to deselect this option.

b. **Save** 🖫 the workbook.

Protect Workbooks and Worksheets

Once a workbook or worksheet has been developed and tested but before you give it to other users, you may want to protect parts of the workbook that you do not want users to be able to change. If a user clicks on a cell that contains a formula and inadvertently presses Delete, a critical part of the application could be erased. Unless the user thinks quickly enough to undo the mistake, the Excel application could be broken.

Excel allows for protection of applications in two layers: the workbook level to control who has access to the workbook and the worksheet level to protect worksheets from alteration. Ideally, only users who are authorized to use a workbook can access it, and only those who are authorized can change the contents of cells or change worksheet structures where appropriate.

At the worksheet level, there are many options available to customize the type of editing that will be allowed on the worksheet. These options are described in the following Quick Reference.

QUICK REFERENCE	Ways to Protect a Worksheet

When an option in the Protect Sheet dialog box is checked, that option will be allowed when the worksheet is protected. By default, only the first two options listed here are allowed when the worksheet is protected. The Protect Sheet dialog box lists the following options.

- Select locked cells — This is selected by default and allows the user to select cells with the Locked check box selected in the Format Cells dialog box.

- Select unlocked cells — This is also selected by default and allows the user to select cells with the Locked check box cleared in the Format Cells dialog box.

- Format cells — Enables all items in the Format cells dialog box, as well as conditional formatting. However, the Protection tab and Merge Cells command remain unavailable.

- Format columns — Enables every item in the Column submenu of the Format menu.

- Format rows — Enables every item in the Row submenu of the Format menu.

- Insert columns — Allows a user to insert columns.

- Insert rows — Allows a user to insert rows.

- Insert hyperlinks — Allows a user to insert hyperlinks.

- Delete columns — Allows a user to delete any column that does not contain a locked cell.

- Delete rows — Allows a user to delete any row that does not contain a locked cell.

- Sort — Enables the Sort option on the Data tab for data in a range that does not contain a locked cell.

- Use AutoFilter — Allows a user to change filter criteria for an existing filter but not to add or delete a filter.

- Use PivotTable & PivotChart — Allows a user to make changes to an existing PivotTable or PivotChart.

- Edit objects — Removes any protection from an object except any related to the object's properties.

- Edit scenarios — Removes protection from scenarios.

Protection at the workbook level is not nearly as flexible as is protection at the worksheet level. Worksheet protection allows many options for protection at the individual cell level, whereas workbook protection allows you only to require a password to open a worksheet, to lock down the structure of the workbook — prohibiting the adding, deleting, or moving of worksheets — and to mark a workbook as Final, which tells users that the worksheet they are using is the final version intended for their use.

REAL WORLD ADVICE | **Use Passwords with Caution**

Any user can turn the worksheet or workbook protection on or off. Therefore, you may want to use a password when you turn on protection. Passwords are case sensitive; can be up to 256 characters long; and can contain letters, numbers, and symbols such as #,$,! — basically any character than can be entered via the keyboard.

However, there is no way to retrieve this password if you forget what it is. This means that if you forget the password, you will not be able to turn the protection off and edit your worksheet or workbook again.

Unlocking Cells

By default, all cells in a worksheet are locked. This does not affect your worksheet until you turn on worksheet protection. Once Protect Sheet is turned on, locked cells cannot be edited. To allow editing, the cells must be unlocked before the protection is turned on.

The Spa workbook has some cells that should be locked and protected, and it has some cells into which the user will need to enter data.

In this exercise, you will unlock the cells that require data entry and then protect the worksheet but without a password. First you will show the row and column headers to make your navigation of the worksheet easier.

 **E08.27**

To Unlock Cells and Protect a Worksheet

a. On the Invoice worksheet, click the **File** tab, click **Options**, and then click **Advanced**. Scroll down to **Display options for this worksheet**, click **Show row and column headers** to select it, and then click **OK**.

b. Select cell **E6**, press and hold Ctrl, and then select cells **E8**, **E10**, **E12**, **D14**, **C31**, and **F34** and cell ranges **B15:B30** and **E15:E30**. Click the **Home** tab, and in the Cells group, click **Format**.

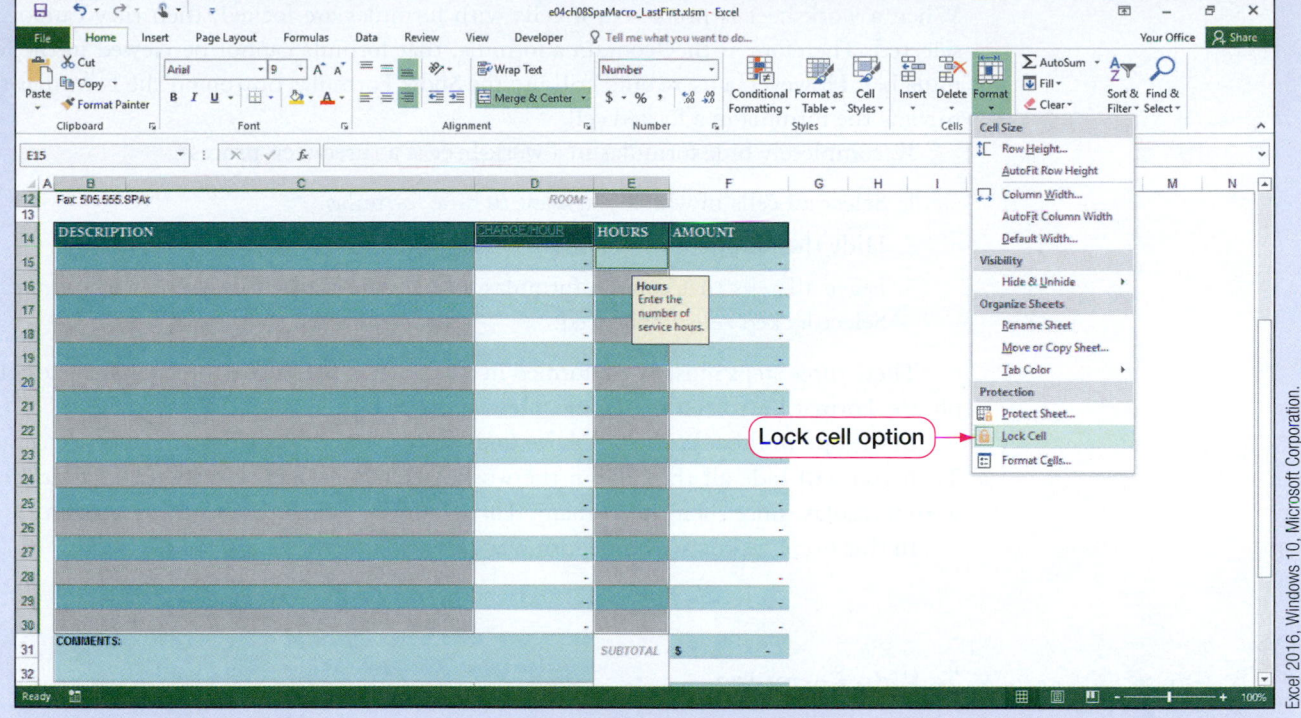

Figure 25 Lock cell option

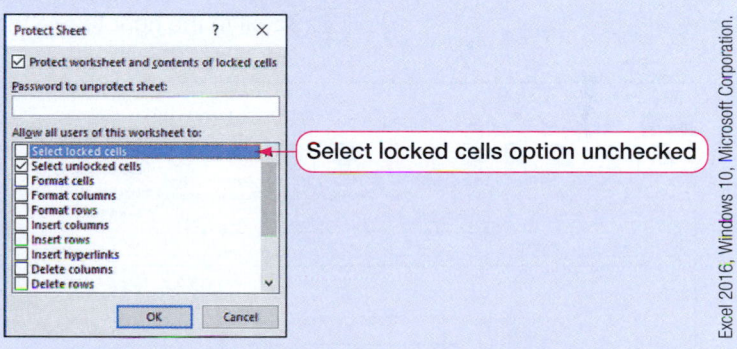

Figure 26 Protect Sheet dialog box

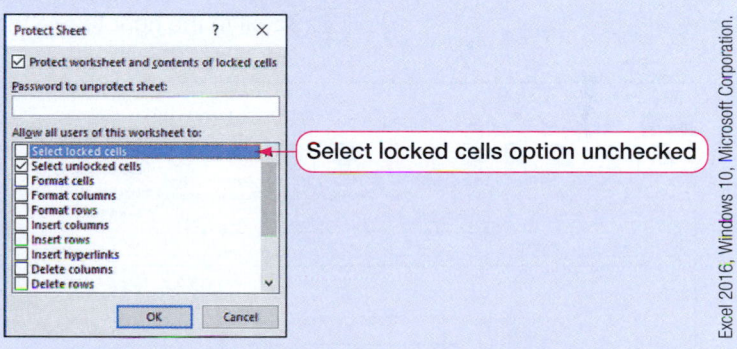

Lock cell option

Select locked cells option unchecked

Excel 2016, Windows 10, Microsoft Corporation.

Excel 2016, Windows 10, Microsoft Corporation.

CHAPTER 8

---

c. Select **Lock Cell** to unlock the selected cells. Click cell **E6**. For the hyperlink in cell D14 to work, the cell must be unlocked.

d. On the Home tab, in the Cells group, click **Format**, and then select **Protect Sheet**. Click Select locked cells to deselect the option.

e. Click **OK**, click cell **B20**, and then press Home.

Notice that the function of Home changes when the sheet is protected. Rather than moving the active cell to column A of the current row, it moves the active cell to the topmost and leftmost unlocked cell in the worksheet — in this case, cell E6.

f. **Save** the workbook.

SIDE NOTE

Alternate Method

To unlock cells, you can also right-click the selection, select Format Cell, click the Protection tab, and click Locked.

Hiding Formulas

When a worksheet is protected, if cells with formulas are locked, then they cannot be selected. Therefore, if they contain a formula, that formula cannot be viewed in the formula bar. However, a user could still use the Show Formulas button on the Formulas tab to view the formula in a locked cell.

To completely hide formulas in a worksheet is a three-step process.

1. Select all cells in which you want to hide formulas.

2. Hide the formulas.

3. Leave all cells that contain formulas locked, and then protect the worksheet with Select locked cells unchecked.

These three steps must be performed in this order, since once Protect Sheet is toggled on, the Format button on the Home tab will not be available.

In the Spa workbook, you will have to unprotect the worksheet to make any changes. Then you will hide all the cells in the workbook rather than selecting individual cells with formulas, since there are so many. Then you will protect the worksheet again.

In this exercise, you will hide formulas in a worksheet.

 E08.28

To Hide Formulas

a. On the Invoice worksheet, click the **Review** tab, and in the Cells group, click **Unprotect Sheet**.

b. Click the **File** tab, click **Options**, and then click **Advanced**. Scroll down, and then, under **Display options for this workbook**, click **Show horizontal scroll bar** to select it. Click **OK**.

c. Click the **Formulas** tab, and in the Formula Auditing group, click **Show Formulas** . Scroll to the right to see the cells with formulas.

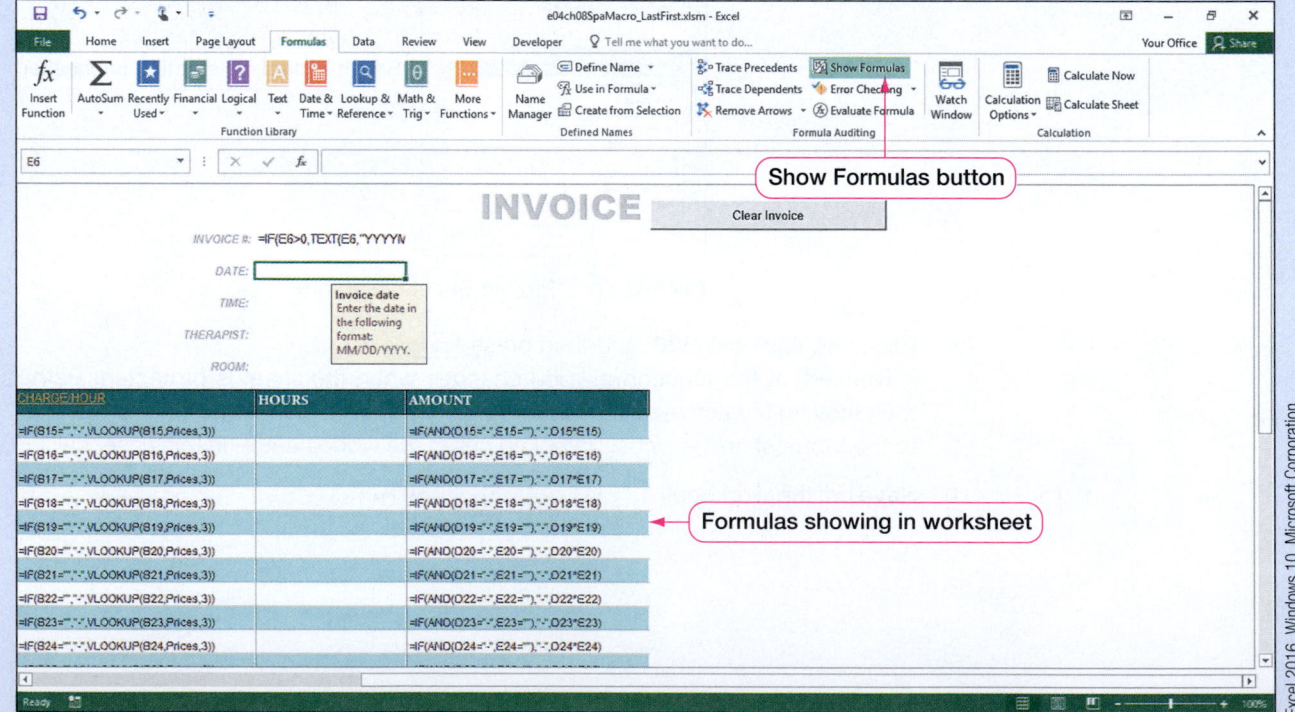

Figure 27 Worksheet in Formula View

d. Select cell **E4**, press and hold Ctrl, and select the cell ranges **D15:D30** and **F15:F30** and cells **F31**, **F33**, and **F35**. Click the **Home** tab, and in the Cells group, click **Format**, and then select **Format Cells**.

e. In the Format Cells dialog box, click the **Protection** tab, and then click **Hidden** to select it. Click **OK**.

f. In the Cells group, click **Format**, click **Protect Sheet**, and then, in the Protect Sheet dialog box click **OK**.

   Notice that formulas are no longer displayed. All cells that contain formulas are locked, so viewing formulas in the formula bar is not possible. The Show Formulas button will toggle on, but the formulas still will not be visible.

g. Click the **Formulas** tab, and in the Formula Auditing group, click **Show Formulas** to toggle it off. This will resize the columns to their normal width when the formulas are not showing.

h. Scroll to the left as needed to make column **A** visible.

i. Click the **File** tab, click **Options**, and then click **Advanced**. Scroll down to the **Display options for this workbook**, and then click the **Show horizontal scroll bar** check box to deselect it. Scroll down to **Display options for this worksheet**, click the **Show row and column headers** check box to deselect it, and then click **OK**.

j. **Save** 🖫 the workbook.

SS **CONSIDER THIS** | **Changing Navigation Tools and Other Features**

By hiding areas of the workbook, including gridlines, row and column headings, and scroll bars as well as hiding, protecting, and locking cells, you certainly make your workbook more secure. Users who are not familiar with Excel may appreciate these enhancements because it makes navigating and using the workbook simpler and often less intimidating. When you are deciding which features to hide and lock, take into consideration your end user. If your users are more advanced in Excel, can you see any frustrations they could encounter in working with a protected and locked workbook? What features might be more helpful to them, and which would be less helpful?

Protecting Workbook Structure

If a user accidentally deletes a formula from a cell, and if the user recognizes the error, Undo can be used to fix the problem. But Undo cannot undelete a worksheet that has been deleted. Protecting the workbook structure stops users from inserting, deleting, hiding, unhiding, and moving worksheets in a workbook.

Further, if a user decides to rename a worksheet, any unopened workbook that accesses data in the renamed worksheet will have its 3D references broken, and Undo will not fix it. If a worksheet in your workbook is accessed by other workbooks and you want to ensure that a user cannot delete or rename a critical worksheet, using Protect Workbook Structure will secure the worksheets and their names.

Protecting the workbook structure includes an optional password. Like the worksheet protection password, if the password is lost, then the protection cannot be turned off. Use passwords with caution.

In this exercise, you will protect the workbook structure.

 **E08.29**

To Protect Workbook Structure

SIDE NOTE

Turn Off Workbook Protection

To turn off workbook protection, click the Review tab, and in the Changes group, click Protect Workbook.

a. On the Invoice worksheet, click the **Review** tab, and in the Changes group, click **Protect Workbook**.

b. In the Protect Structure and Windows dialog box, verify that **Structure** is checked, and then click **OK**.

   You will not add a password in this exercise. On the Review tab, notice that the Protect Workbook button is now toggled on — it is a different color.

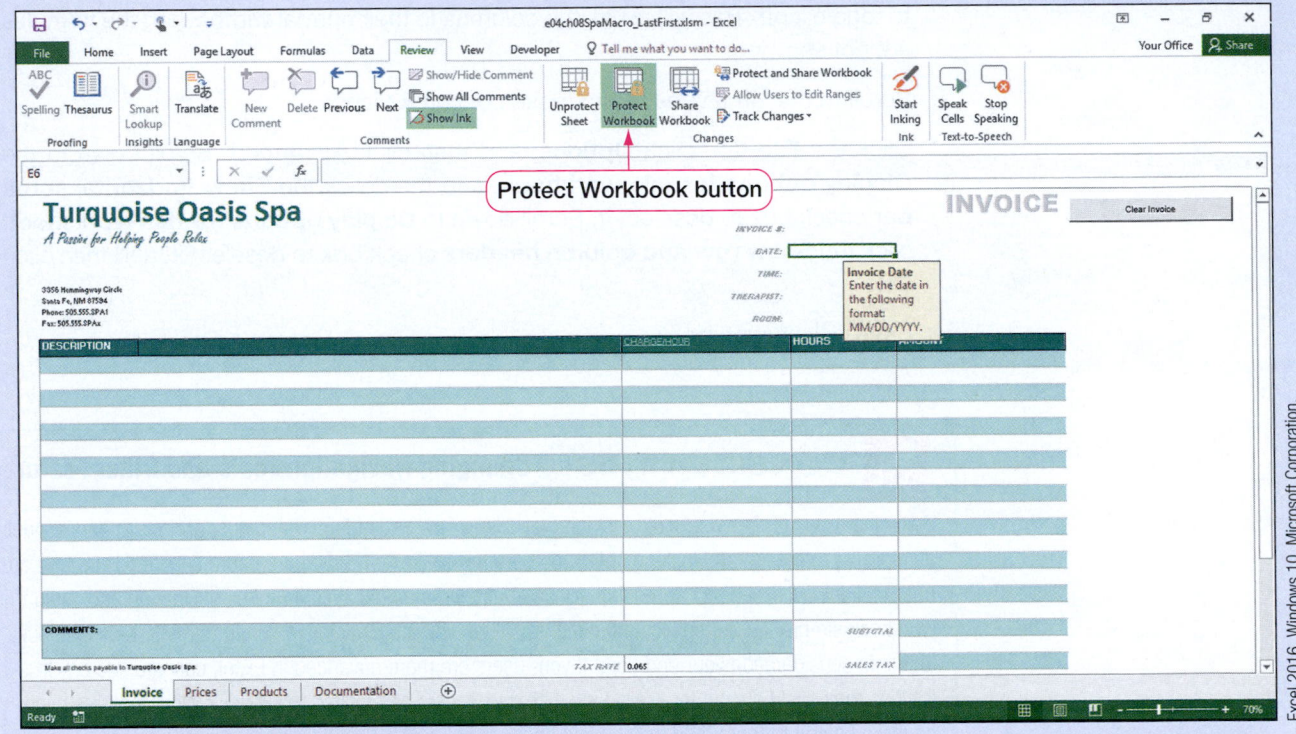

Figure 28 Protect Workbook button

c. Save 💾 the workbook.

REAL WORLD ADVICE   **Do Not Rely Solely on Workbook Protection**

Workbook protection by itself does not lend much protection to your application. Even though a user cannot delete a worksheet, the user can still delete all the content in a worksheet unless worksheet protection is enabled. Protect your workbooks with both workbook-level and worksheet-level protection.

Encrypting a Workbook

The highest level of protection is to encrypt the workbook with a password; this prevents the workbook from being opened without the password. When a password is entered into the Encrypt Document dialog box, the workbook is encrypted when it is saved. **Encryption** is a method of protecting a workbook by assigning a password that unscrambles the code once it has been opened. For the user, the net result is that after a workbook has been saved with an encryption password, the password is required to open the workbook again.

Again, use caution when assigning passwords. If the password is lost, the workbook cannot be opened. If a workbook needs to be protected because it contains sensitive content such as social security numbers, worksheet or workbook passwords are not recommended, as they can be broken with VBA coding. Instead, workbook encryption should be used.

REAL WORLD ADVICE   Back Up Before You Encrypt Your Workbook

If you are going to encrypt your workbook with a password, it is a good idea to make a backup copy of the workbook without the password first. Thus, if you forget your password, you still have a copy of the workbook that you can open.

If you are concerned about security, you can always save the backup with a different name so that someone else might not be able to determine that it is the same workbook as the one with the password.

In this exercise, you will encrypt the workbook with a password.

 E08.30

To Encrypt a Workbook

a. Click the **File** tab, click **Protect Workbook**, and then select **Encrypt with Password**.

b. In the **Encrypt Document** dialog box, in the Password box, type invoice. In Excel, passwords are case sensitive, so type very carefully.

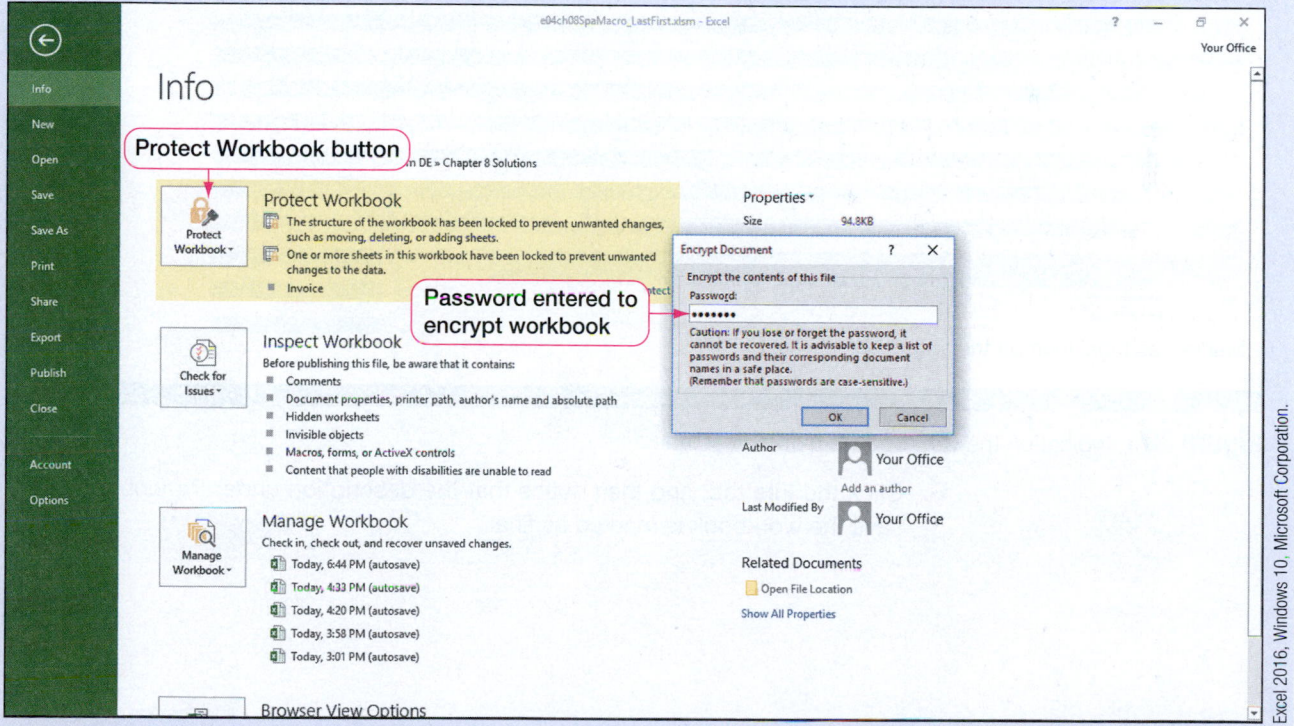

Figure 29   Encrypt Document dialog box

c. Click **OK**, and then type invoice again. Click **OK**. When you close and open the workbook, you will be prompted for the password.

d. Click the **Back** button ⊙. **Save** 🖫 the workbook.

Marking a Workbook as a Final Draft

When you are creating a workbook for someone else to use and have the final version complete, it is helpful to use the Mark as Final option. Mark as Final represents a means of communicating the development status of a workbook to indicate that the workbook is complete and ready for use. Mark as Final is a form of workbook protection by making a workbook read-only. However, Mark as Final is a very weak form of protection. A workbook that has been marked as final will display the Marked as Final icon on the status bar; but even though a workbook has been marked as final, users are given the option to "Edit Anyway".

In this exercise, to indicate to Meda Rodate that the Spa workbook updates she requested are now complete, you will mark this version of the workbook as final.

E08.31

To Mark a Workbook as Final

a. Click the **File** tab, click **Protect Workbook**, and then select **Mark as Final**. Click **OK** in the alert box, and then click **OK** in the next alert box.

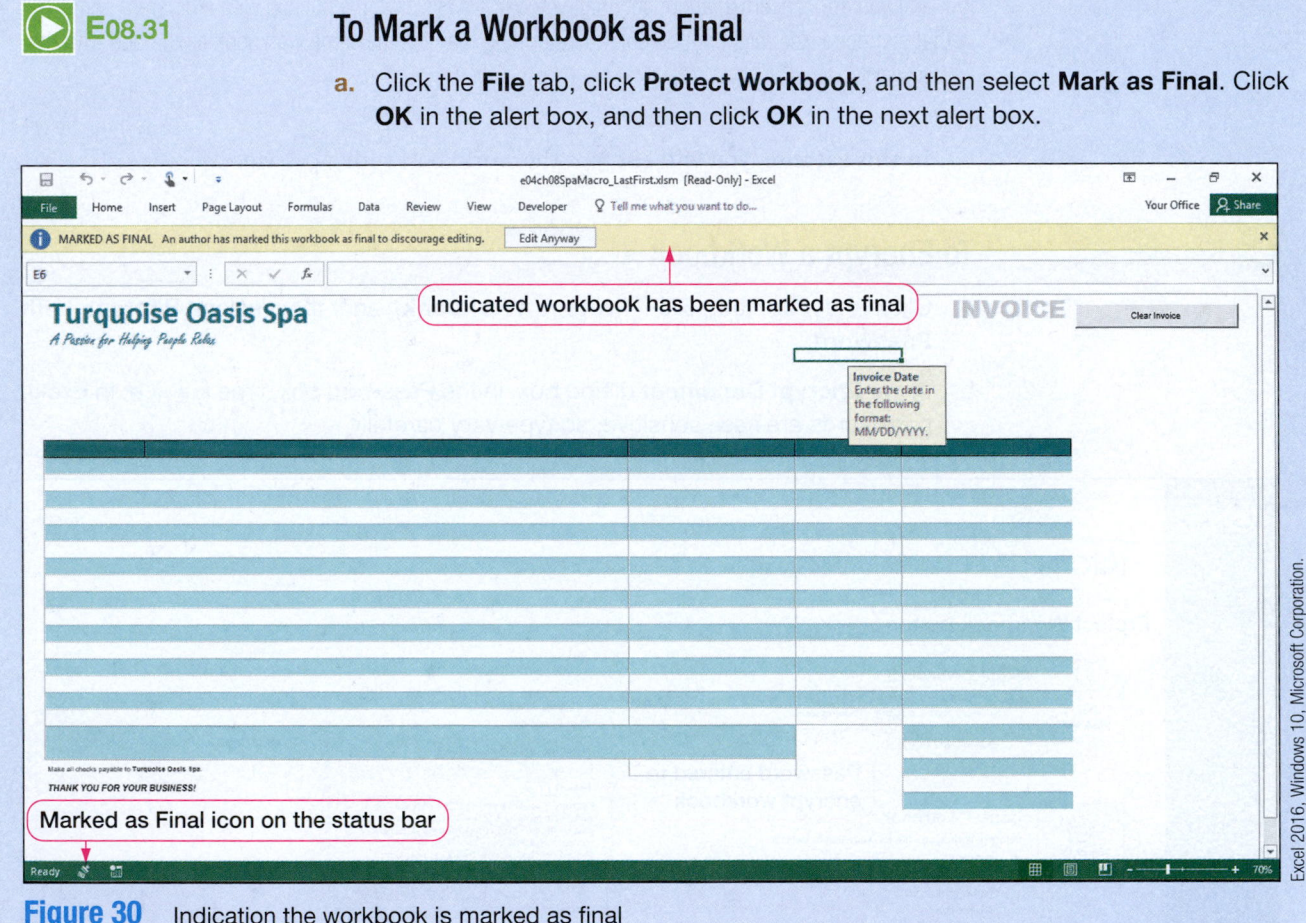

Figure 30   Indication the workbook is marked as final

b. Click the **File** tab, and then notice that the description under Protect Workbook says the workbook is marked as final.

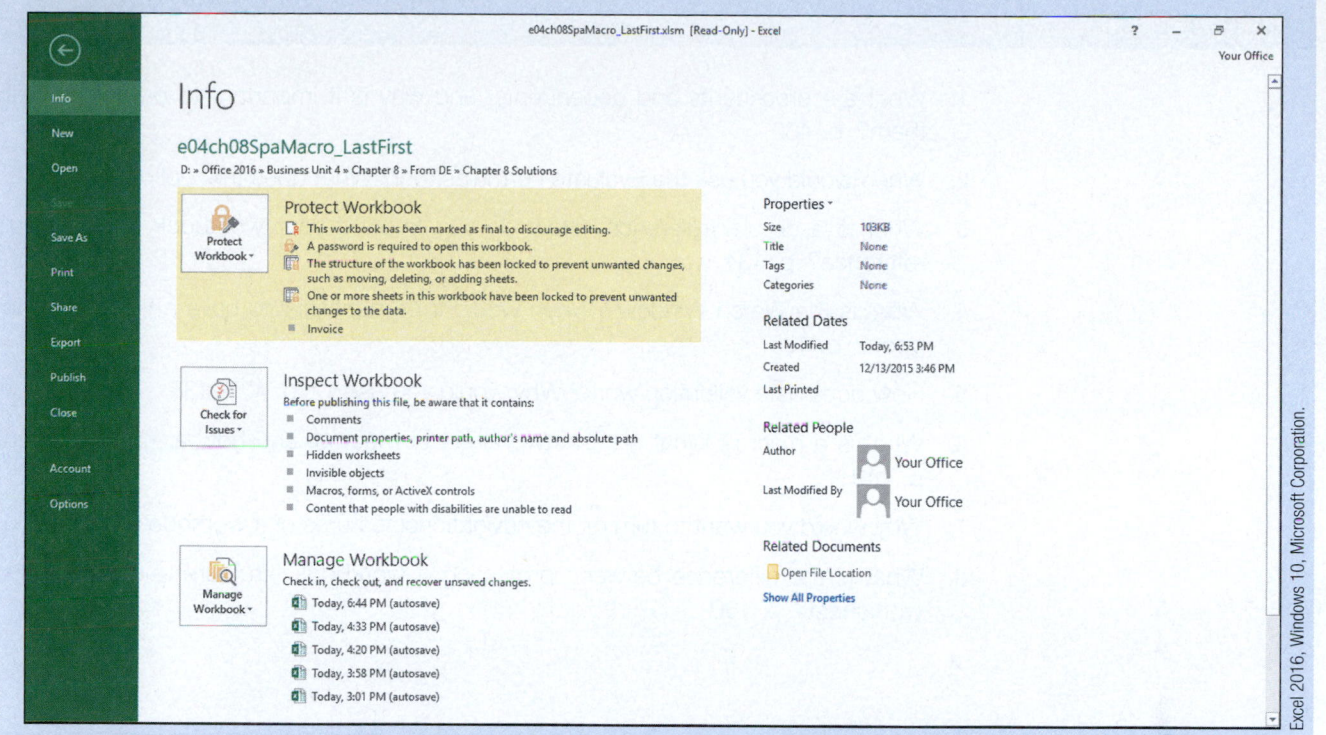

Figure 31   Workbook protection in Backstage view

        c. **Close** the workbook, exit Excel, and then submit your file as directed by your instructor.

Concept Check

1. What are precedents and dependents, and why is it important to be able to trace them? p. 432

2. When would you use the Evaluate Formulas tool? What does the tool do? p. 433

3. What is a circular reference? How do you know if your workbook has a circular reference? p. 434

4. What is the Watch Window? When would it be beneficial to have a Watch Window open? p. 435

5. How does data validation work? Why would you use it? p. 437–438

6. What is a macro? What are the two kinds of macros, and how are they different? p. 449

7. Why would you want to turn off the navigational features of a workbook? p. 455

8. What is the difference between protecting a workbook structure and protecting a worksheet? p. 460

Key Terms

Absolute macro reference   450
Any value validation   443
Circular reference   434
Codification scheme   445
Codified data value   443
Custom validation   443
Data validation   437
Date validation   440
Decimal validation   439
Dependent cell   432
Developer tab   449

Encryption   466
Error Alert   438
Evaluate Formula   434
Gridlines   460
Hyperlink   456
Input Message   438
List validation   438
Macro   449
Precedent cell   432
Relative macro reference   452
Text length validation   442

Text-to-speech   446
Time validation   441
Trace dependents   432
Trace precedents   432
Trusted Location   449
Validation criteria   437
Visual Basic for Applications
   (VBA)   449
Watch Window   435
Whole number validation   442

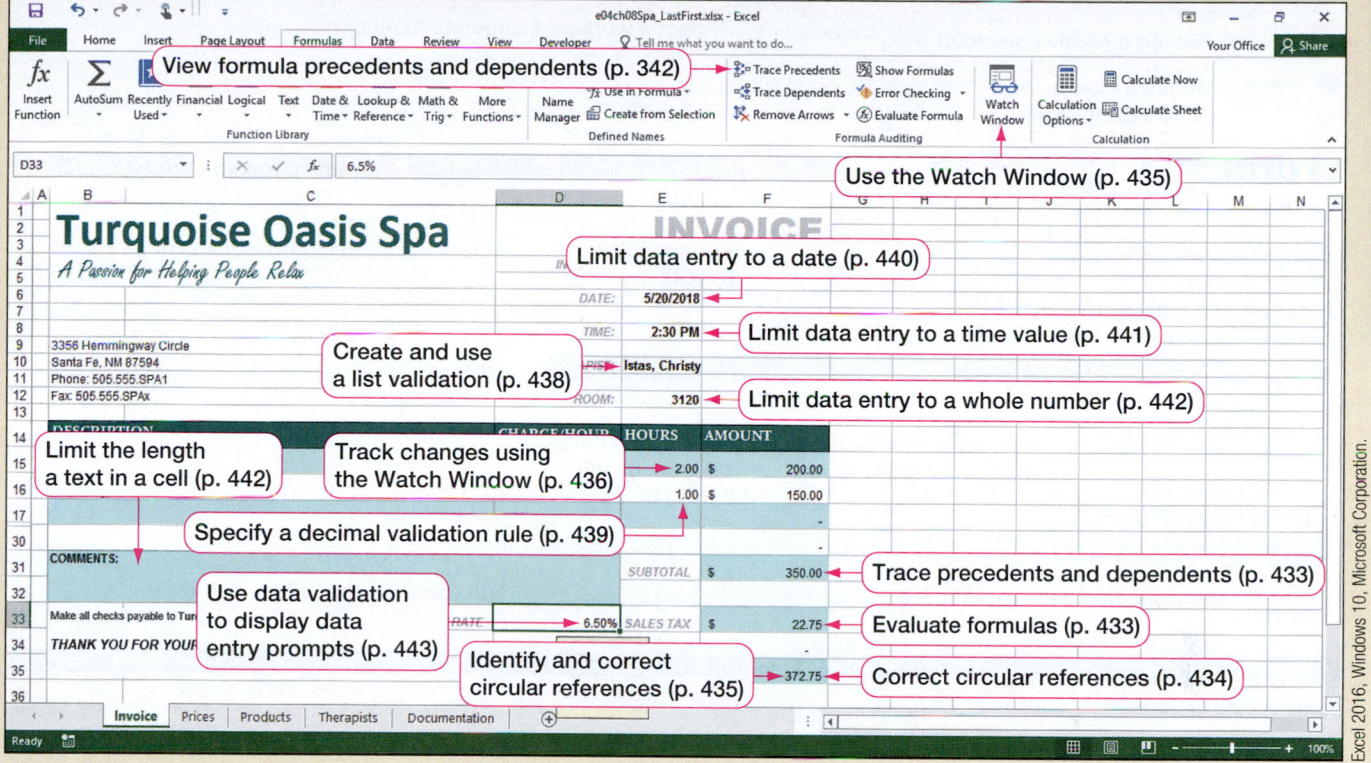

Figure 32

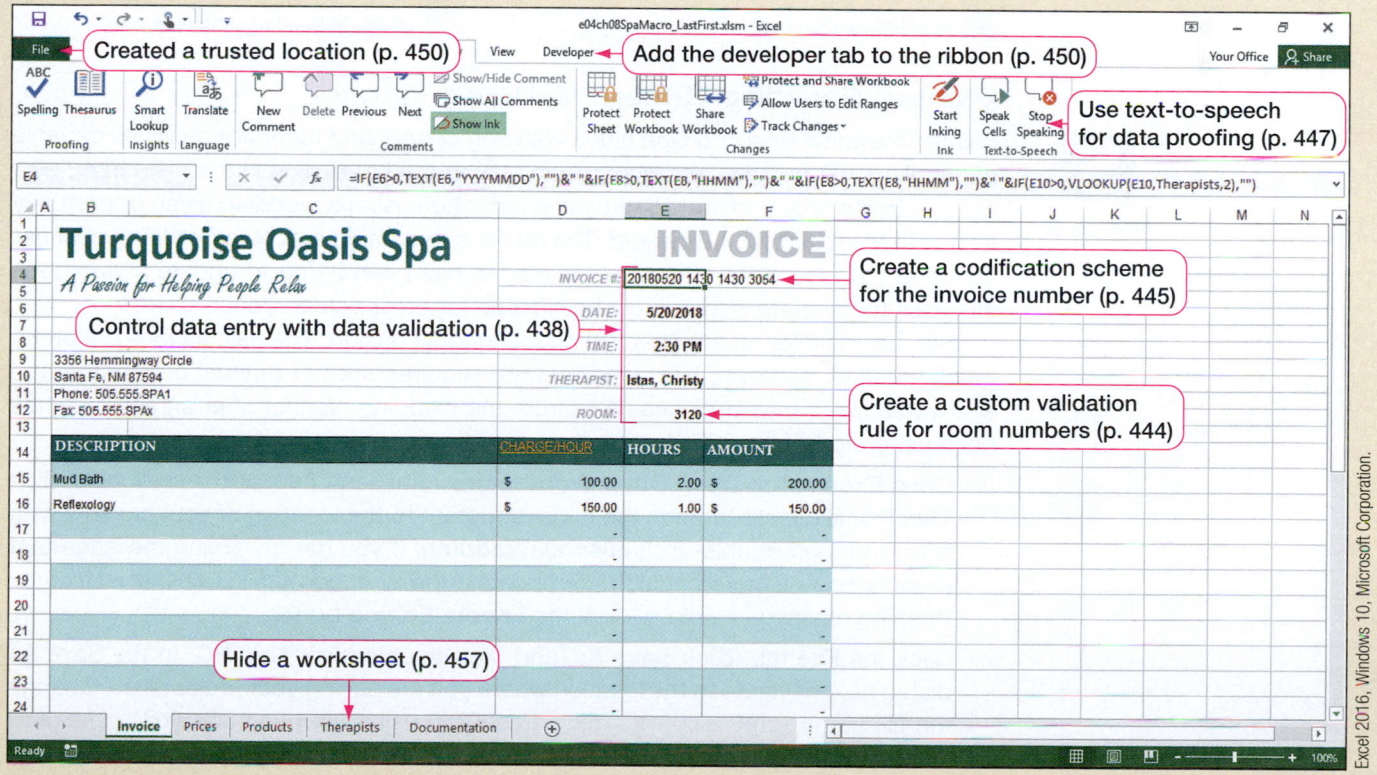

Figure 33

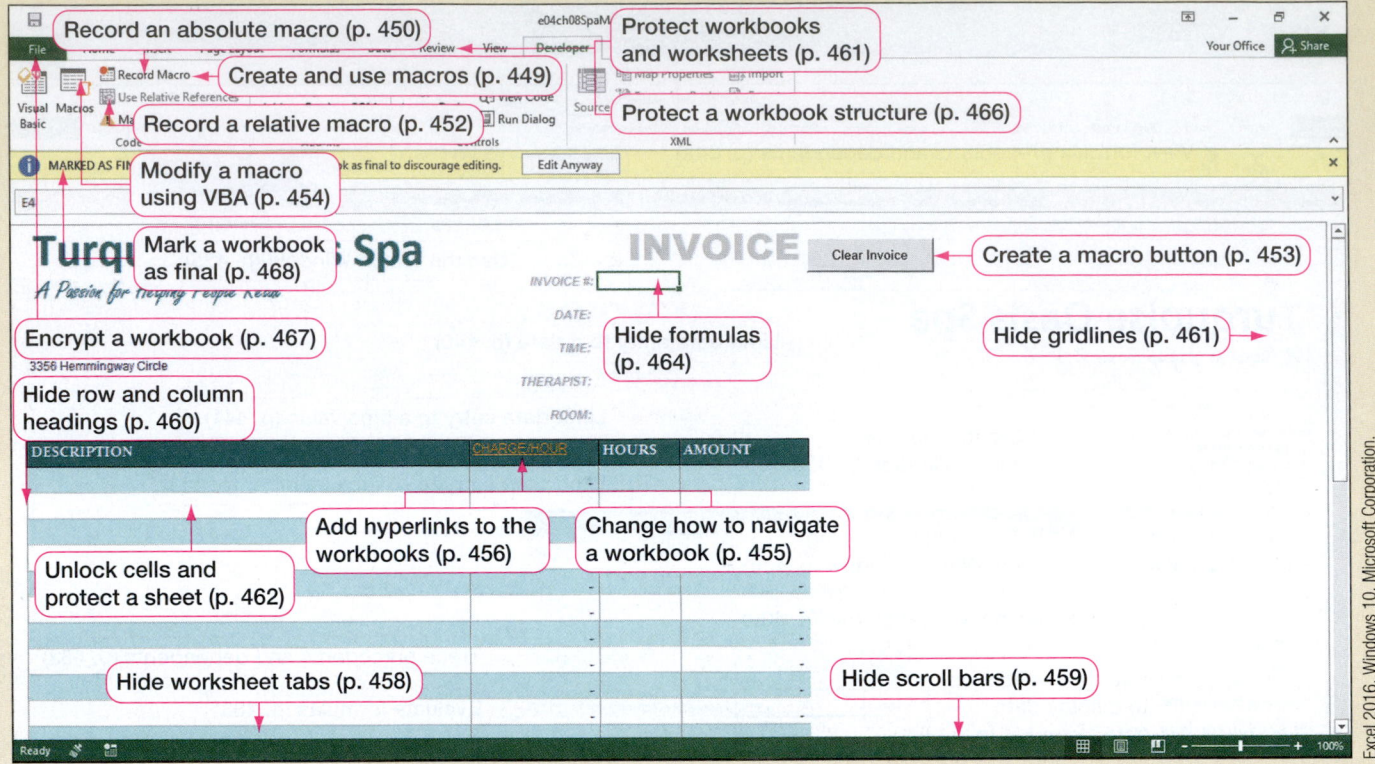

Figure 34

Practice 1

Student data file needed:

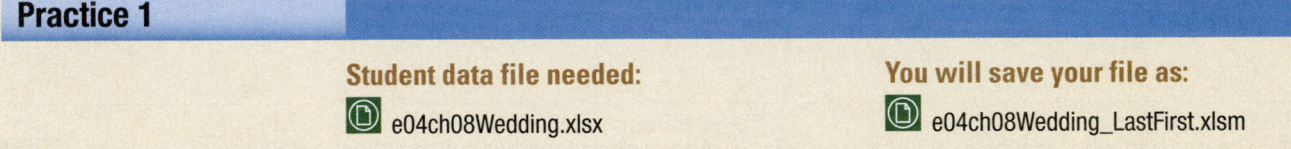 e04ch08Wedding.xlsx

You will save your file as:

e04ch08Wedding_LastFirst.xlsm

Painted Paradise Resort Wedding Planner

Finance &
Accounting

Painted Paradise Resort & Spa has a wedding chapel and reception facilities capable of handling 300 people. Wedding guests stay at the hotel, dine in the restaurant, play golf, go to the spa, and shop in the gift shop, often using a wedding as an opportunity to stay at the resort for a weekend. The resort is becoming a popular wedding destination, and Patti Rochelle, the events manager, has been trying to update a workbook she uses to generate wedding cost estimates for prospective clients.

She has developed an attractive and functional design. The calculations are pretty much handled; however, her worksheet still requires a lot of manual data entry, and she would like a macro to clear data from the wedding planner after an estimate has been generated and printed.

a. Open **Excel**, click **Open Other Workbooks** in the left pane, and then double-click **This PC**. Navigate through the folder structure to the location of your student data files, and then double-click **e04ch08Wedding**. If you get a warning message that there is one or more circular references in the workbook, click **OK**. If a Security Warning message displays, click the **Enable Editing** button.

b. Click the **File** tab, click **Save As**, and then double-click **This PC**. In the Save As dialog box, navigate to the location where you are saving your project files. Change the file name to e04ch08Wedding_LastFirst, using your last and first name, and then select **Excel Macro-Enabled Workbook** in the Save as type box. Click **Save**.

c. On the WeddingPlanner worksheet, select the estimated cost total in cell **E34**. On the **Formulas** tab, in the Formula Auditing group, click **Trace Precedents**.

- Notice the Circular Reference warning in the status bar for cell E34. The SUM function in cell E34 includes a reference to E34 that is causing the circular reference.

- Click in the **Formula Bar**, and then change **E34** to E32.

d. On the Formulas tab, in the Formula Auditing group, click **Watch Window**. Select cells **E16**, **E21**, **E25**, **E28**, **E32**, and **E34**, and then click **Add Watch**. In the Add Watch dialog box, click **Add**. Verify that the cells were added to the Watch Window. Dock the Watch Window to the top of the worksheet. Close the Watch Window.

e. Select cell **C8**. On the Data tab, in the Data Tools group, click **Data Validation**. You will create a rule so the number entered is between 25 and 300.

- On the **Settings** tab, in the **Allow** box, select **Whole number**. In the **Data** box, verify that **between** is selected. In the **Minimum** box, type 25, and then, in the **Maximum** box, type 300.

- Click the **Input Message** tab, and then, in the **Title** box, type Guests. In the **Input message** box, type Enter the estimated number of guests.

- Click the **Error Alert** tab, and then, in the **Title** box type Error. In the **Error message** box, type The number of guests must be between 25 and 300., and then click **OK**.

- In cell **C8**, type 150.

f. Select cell **C10**. In the Data Tools group, click **Data Validation**. You will create a rule so the date entered must be the current date or later.

- Click the **Settings** tab. In the **Allow** box, select **Date**. In the Data box, select **greater than or equal to**. In the **Start date** box, type =TODAY().

- Click the **Input Message** tab, and then, in the **Title** box type Date. In the **Input message** box, type Enter the wedding date.

- Click the **Error Alert** tab, and then, in the **Title** box, type Error. In the **Error message** box, type The wedding date must be today or later., and then click **OK**.

- In cell **C10**, type =TODAY().

g. Select cell **C11**. In the Data Tools group, click **Data Validation**. You will create a rule so the time entered must be between 10:00 AM and 8:00 PM.

- Click the **Settings** tab, and then, in the **Allow** box select **Time**. In the **Data** box, select **between**. In the **Start time** box, type 10:00 AM and then, in the **End time** box, type 8:00 PM.

- Click the **Input Message** tab, and then, in the **Title** box, type Time. In the **Input message** box, type Enter the wedding start time.

- Click the **Error Alert** tab, and then, in the **Title** box, type Error. In the **Error message** box, type The start time must be between 10:00 AM and 8:00 PM., and then click **OK**.

- In cell **C11**, type 2:00 PM.

h. Select the cell range **C20:C21**. In the Data Tools group, click **Data Validation**. You will create a rule so the data entered must come from a list of cells on the Parameters worksheet.

- Click the **Settings** tab, and then, in the **Allow** box, select **List**. Click the **Source** box, click the **Parameters** worksheet, and then select the cell range **A9:A10**.

- Click the **Input Message** tab, and then, in the **Title** box, type Amenities. In the **Input message** box, type Select an option from the list., and then click **OK**.

- In cell **C20**, click the arrow, and then select **Standard**.
- In cell **C21**, click the arrow, and then select **Deluxe**.

i. Select the cell range **C24:C25** and cell **C28**. In the Data Tool group, click **Data Validation**. You will create a rule so the data entered can be selected from a list.

- Click the **Settings** tab, and then, in the **Allow** box, select **List**. Click the **Source** box, type Yes, No. Click **OK**.
- In cell **C24**, click the arrow, and then select **Yes**.
- In cell **C25**, click the arrow, and then select **Yes**.
- In cell **C28**, click the arrow, and then select **No**.

j. Select cell **F10**. In the Data Tools group, click **Data Validation**. You will create a custom rule so the room number entered starts with the number 1 or 2 and ends with a number less than 7; the available room numbers are 10–16 and 20–26.

- Click the **Settings** tab. In the **Allow** box, select **Custom**. Click the **Formula** box, then type =AND(LEFT(F10,1)<="2",LEFT(F10,1)>="1",RIGHT(F10,1)<"7",LEN(F10)=2).
- You will not add an Input message for this cell. Click the **Error Alert** tab. In the Title box, type Room #. In the Error message box, type Invalid room number. Click **OK**.
- In cell **F10**, type 15.

k. If necessary, add the **Developer** tab to the ribbon.

- Click the **File** tab, click **Options**, click **Customize Ribbon**, and then, under Customize the Ribbon, check **Developer**. Click **OK**.

l. Assign the folder where you save your student files as a trusted location.

- Click the **File** tab, click **Options**, click **Trust Center**, click **Trust Center Settings**, and then click **Trusted Locations**.
- Click **Add new location**, browse to the folder where you save your student files, and then click **OK**. Click **OK**, click **OK**, and then click **OK** again.

m. Click the **Developer** tab, and in the Code group, click **Record Macro**.

- In the Macro name box, type ClearContents. In the Shortcut key box, press Shift, and then type C. Verify that the Store Macro in box is **This Workbook**. In the Description, type Delete all user-entered data from the worksheet., and then click **OK**.
- Select the cell range **C5:C6**, press and hold Ctrl, and then select the cell ranges **C8**, **C10:C11**, **C20:C21**, and **C24:C25** and cells **C28** and **F10**. Press Delete.
- Select cell **C5**. On the Developer tab, in the Code group, click **Stop Recording**.

n. Click **Undo** to undo the changes you made recording the macro.

o. On the Developer tab, in the Controls group, click **Insert**, and then select **Button (Form Control)**.

- Click in the top left corner of cell **E5** next to the Bride's name, and then drag to the bottom right corner of cell **F6** to size and add the button.
- Select **ClearContents**, and then click **OK**.
- Right-click the button, and then select **Edit Text**. Delete the current text, and then type Clear Information. Right-click the button, and then select **Exit Edit Text**.
- Test the button.

p. Select cell **B19**. Click the **Insert** tab, and in the Links group, click **Hyperlink**.

- Select **Place in This Document**, and then select **Parameters**. Click **ScreenTip**, and then type Click to view amenities. Select **Type the cell reference**, and then type D15. Click **OK**, and then click **OK**.
- Click the hyperlink to go to the Parameters worksheet.

- On the Parameters worksheet, select cell **D15** if necessary, and then insert a **Hyperlink** to the **WeddingPlanner** worksheet. Click **ScreenTip**, and then type Return to Wedding Planner worksheet. Select **Type the cell reference**, and then type B19. Click **OK**, and then click **OK**.
- Click the hyperlink to return to the WeddingPlanner worksheet.

q. Click the **Documentation** worksheet. Click cell **A8**, and then type in today's date. Click cell **B8**, and then type in your name in the Firstname Lastname format. Complete the remainder of the Documentation worksheet according to your instructor's directions. Right-click the **Documentation** worksheet, and then select **Hide**.

r. Click the **WeddingPlanner** worksheet, select cell **B19**, cell range **C5:C6**, cell **C8**, cell range **C10:C11**, cell **F10**, cell ranges **C20:C21** and **C24:C25**, and cell **C28** — the cells are all formatted with gray where the data is entered. Click the **Home** tab, and in the Cells group, click **Format**, and then **Format cells**. Click the **Protection** tab, and click **Locked** to uncheck the option. Click **OK**.

s. Click the **File** tab, click **Options**, click **Advanced**, and do the following.
- Scroll down to **Display options for this workbook**, and then click **Show horizontal scroll bar** to deselect it.
- Scroll down to **Display options for this worksheet**, and then click **Show row and column headers** to deselect it. Click **OK**.

t. Click the **View** tab, in the Show group, click to deselect the **Gridlines** check box.

u. Click the **Formulas** tab, in the Formula Auditing group, click **Show Formulas**.
- Select all the cells that show a formula.
- Click the **Home** tab. In the Cells group, click **Format**, select **Format Cells**, click the **Protection** tab, and then click **Hidden**. Click **OK**.
- Click the **Formulas** tab, and in the Formula Auditing group, click **Show Formulas** again to remove the formula view.

v. On the Home tab, in the Cells group, click **Format**, and then select **Protect Sheet**. Ensure that **Selected unlocked cells** is checked, and then click **OK**.

w. On the Review tab, in the Changes group, click **Protect Workbook**, verify that **Structure** is selected, and then click **OK**.

x. Click the **File** tab, click **Protect Workbook**, and then select **Mark as Final**. Click **OK** to save the workbook, click **OK** again, and then close **Excel**. Submit your file as directed by your instructor.

Problem Solve 1

MyITLab® Grader
Homework

Student data file needed:
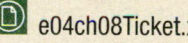 e04ch08Ticket.xlsx

You will save your file as:
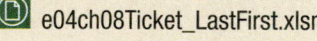 e04ch08Ticket_LastFirst.xlsm

Ticket Order Form

Accounting & Finance General Business

You have just started working in the ticket office of a local theater. The theater has five employees who take ticket orders over the phone. Until now, they have been taking the orders on paper and then retyping the information for each order on an invoice.

Jill, one of the employees, started an Excel workbook in which to enter the ticket orders, but the other employees kept making mistakes and deleting the formulas, so they ended up retyping the invoices anyway. You will help Jill modify her workbook so that data validation makes data entry easier, macros help to clear all the data except the formulas, and various types of workbook protection prevent formulas from being deleted by mistake.

a. Open the Excel file, **e04ch08Ticket**. Save your file as a macro-enabled workbook named e04ch08Ticket_LastFirst, using your last and first name.

b. Use **Trace Precedents** to illustrate the formula error in cell **B21**. Correct the formula in cell **B21** by entering the correct cells (the formula should multiply the Number of tickets by the Cost of Ticket). Note the #VALUE! error will not go away until values are entered in the cells, which you will do in the following steps.

c. In cell **B21**, add an IFERROR formula to display a blank cell if there no result.

d. Add data validation to cell **B4** that allows only the current date. The =TODAY() function should be used. Enter the Input Message Title Date. Enter the Message Enter today's date. Enter the Error Alert Title Error, and the Error Message Date must be today's date. In cell **B4**, type today's date.

e. Add **data validation** to cell **B5** so that only a time between 9:00 AM and 4:00 PM can be entered. Enter the Input Message Title Time, and the Input Message Enter the time in the HH:MM AM/PM format. Enter the Error Alert Title Error, and the Error Message Time must be between 9:00 AM and 4:00 PM. In cell **B5**, type 2:00 PM.

f. Add **data validation** to cell **B6** to look up a list of names from the Employees worksheet. Do not enter an Input Message title. The Input Message should say, Choose an employee name from the list. In cell **B6**, select **Ned**.

g. Add a formula to cell **B7** that creates an Invoice Number from the date in cell B4, the time in cell B5, and the ID number on the Employees worksheet for the employee listed in cell B6. The formula will include an IF function, the TEXT function, and a VLOOKUP function. (Hint: Use the formula in the Prepare Case on page 446 as an example.)

h. Add **data validation** to cell **B18** so only a whole number between 1 and 25 can be entered in the cell. Enter the Input Message Enter a number between 1 and 25. In cell **B18**, type 4.

i. Add **data validation** to cell **B19** to look up a list of ticket locations from the TicketData worksheet. Enter the Input Message Select a location from the list. In cell **B19**, select **Balcony Front**.

j. Insert a hyperlink in cell **A17** on the TicketOrder worksheet that links to cell A8 on the TicketData worksheet. Add the ScreenTip Go to Ticket Data. Insert a hyperlink in cell **A8** on the TicketData worksheet that links to cell A17 on the TicketOrder worksheet. Add the ScreenTip Go to Ticket Order.

k. If necessary, add a Text-to-Speech group to the Review tab, and include the Speak Cells and Stop Speaking buttons.

l. If necessary, add the Developer tab to the ribbon. Create an absolute macro that will clear the contents of all cells containing data that is entered by the user. This includes the cell ranges **B4:B6**, **B10:B15**, and **B18:B19**. Make cell **B4** the active cell after the macro is run. Name the macro ClearData, and assign the letter d as the shortcut key. After creating the macro, click the **Undo** button to undo the changes you made.

m. Add a form control button in the cell range **D3:E4** that will run the macro ClearData. Change the text on the button to read Clear Data. Test the button.

n. Unlock cell **A17** and the cell ranges **B4:B6**, **B10:B15**, and **B18:B19**.

o. Hide all cells that have formulas.

p. Update the Documentation worksheet according to your instructor's directions.

q. Return to the TicketOrder worksheet. Hide the horizontal and vertical scroll bars, the sheet tabs, and the row and column headers.

r. Hide the gridlines. Protect the worksheet. Do not allow for locked cells to be selected.

s. Protect the workbook structure. Do not set a password.

t. Mark the workbook as final. Exit Excel, and then submit your file as directed by your instructor.

Critical Thinking

In this chapter, you learned how to protect a worksheet as well as a workbook. Describe a scenario in which it would be wise to protect a worksheet. Describe a scenario in which it would be wise to protect a workbook.

Student data file needed:

 e04ch08Budget.xlsx

You will save your file as:

 e04ch08Budget_LastFirst.xlsm

Accounting & Finance

Watching Your Money

You and your spouse have decided to create a 2018 budget plan to track your income and expenses. Your spouse is not very familiar with Excel, so you have decided to create a workbook that can be shared between the two of you and can easily be updated. As part of monitoring your expenses, you and your spouse have decided that any expense greater than $500 should pop up with a warning to remind you to double-check the expense.

a. Open the Excel file, **e04ch08Budget**. Save your file as a macro-enabled workbook named e04ch08Budget_LastFirst, using your last and first name. Click **OK** at the circular error message; you will correct this in the next step.

b. Find and correct the circular references in the worksheet.

c. On the Budget worksheet, add a blank column between columns B and C, and enter Type in cell C5.

d. Add data validation to the cell ranges A7:A34, C7:C34, and D7:D34. Use the data on the Lists tab as appropriate. Include input and error messages to ensure that the correct data is entered. You may need to reread the situation to determine the appropriate validation rules. Note that expenses will be entered with a negative value, and income will be entered with a positive value.

e. Enter at least three rows of data to test your validation rules. Income items should be entered as a positive number, and Expense items should be entered as a negative number. Increase column width as appropriate to accommodate your data validations.

f. Format any input cell as unlocked. All other cells should be locked, and formulas should be hidden.

g. Enter a hyperlink for the Type heading on the Budget worksheet to the Lists worksheet, and include a ScreenTip. Enter a hyperlink on the Lists worksheet to switch to the Budget worksheet, and include a ScreenTip. Note that on the Budget worksheet, you may need to unlock the cell which contains the hyperlink.

h. If necessary, add the Developer tab to the ribbon.

i. Add an absolute macro for use at the end of each month to clear the contents of the data entry areas of the worksheet. The macro should make a copy of the Budget worksheet to keep for future use and then clear all the data that was entered for the month. Ensure that you select the appropriate worksheet and protect and unprotect as necessary.

j. Insert a macro button on the Budget worksheet, and assign the macro to the button and name the button appropriately.

k. Protect the Budget worksheet so that users are allowed to select locked and unlocked cells.

l. Update the Documentation worksheet according to your instructor's directions. Hide the gridlines on the Budget worksheet. Hide the sheet tabs, scroll bars as appropriate, and row and column headings on all worksheets.

m. Mark the workbook as final. Close Excel, and then submit the file as directed by your instructor.

Additional Cases

Additional Workshop Cases are available on the companion website and in the instructor resources.

Build an Application with Multiple Worksheets and Workbooks

This business unit had two outcomes:

Learning Outcome 1:

Use multiple worksheets, workbooks, and templates to create an Excel application.

Learning Outcome 2:

Perform formula auditing, use data validation, create macros, and explore worksheet and workbook protection to refine an Excel application.

In Business Unit 4 Capstone, students will demonstrate competence in these outcomes through a series of business problems at various levels from guided practice to problem solving an existing spreadsheet and creating new spreadsheets.

More Practice 1

Student data file needed:

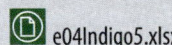 e04Indigo5.xlsx

You will save your file as:

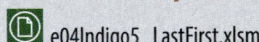 e04Indigo5_LastFirst.xlsm

Indigo5 Meal and Menu Tracking

General Business

To help plan the menu at the Indigo5 restaurant, Alberto Dimas, the restaurant manager, would like to be able to see how many meals in each category are being sold each season. He has created a spreadsheet that has the meals broken down by season with the average price, average cost, and dishes sold for each category, but he is having trouble consolidating and summarizing the data. He would also like to include a form to fill out for estimates for special events. When guests plan a special event, they can pick up to four food categories. Based on the average prices of each category, Alberto would like an estimated cost for the event.

a. Open **Excel**, click **Open Other Workbooks** in the left pane, and then double-click **This PC**. Navigate through the folder structure to the location of your student data files, and then double-click **e04Indigo5**. Click **OK** for the Circular Reference warning dialog box. If a Security Warning message displays, click the **Enable Editing** button.

b. Click the **File** tab, click **Save As**, and then double-click **This PC**. In the Save As dialog box, navigate to the location where you are saving your project files. Change the file name to **e04Indigo5_LastFirst**, using your last and first name, and then select **Excel Macro-Enabled Workbook** in the Save as type box. Click **Save**.

c. Click the **Winter** worksheet, press and hold [Shift], and then click the **Fall** worksheet.
   - Right-click the **Winter** worksheet, point to **Tab Color**, and then select the standard color **Purple**.
   - On the Winter worksheet, click cell **A20**, and then type Total.
   - Select cell **D20**, and then type =SUM(D5:D19).
   - Select the cell range **A20:D20**, and on the Home tab, in the Styles group, click **Cell Styles**, and then select **Total**.
   - Right-click the **Winter** worksheet, and then select **Ungroup Sheets**.

d. Click the **YearSummary** worksheet. Click cell **D5**, and then type =SUM(. Click the **Winter** worksheet, and then click **D5**. Press and hold [Shift], click the **Fall** worksheet, type), and then press [Ctrl] + [Enter]. Use the fill handle to copy this formula to cell range D6:D19.

e. Click the **Fall** worksheet, press and hold ⇧Shift, and then click the **YearSummary** worksheet. On the Fall worksheet, select cell range **D5:D19**. On the Home tab, in the Editing group, click **Fill**, and then select **Across Worksheets**. In the **Fill Across Worksheets** dialog box, click **Formats**, and then click **OK**.

f. On the Fall worksheet, select cell range **A20:D20**, and on the Home tab, in the Editing group, click **Fill**, select **Across Worksheets**, verify that **All** is selected, and then click **OK**.

g. Click the **YearSummaryLinked** worksheet.

- Click cell **A5**, and then, on the **Data** tab, in the Data Tools group, click **Consolidate**. In the **Consolidate** dialog box, make sure **Sum** is selected in the Function box, and then click in the **Reference** box.

- Click the **Winter** worksheet, select cell range **A4:D19**, and then click **Add**. Click the **Spring** worksheet, and then click **Add**. Click the **Summer** worksheet, and then click **Add**. Click the **Fall** worksheet, and then click **Add**.

- Click to select the **Top row** box, click to select the **Left column** box, and then click to select the **Create links to source data** box. Click **OK**.

- Use the AutoFit feature on columns A through E to adjust the column widths, select cell **A5**, and then type Category.

- Select **column B**, and on the Home tab, in the Cells group, click **Format**, point to **Hide & Unhide**, and then select **Hide Columns**.

h. Click the **SpecialEvents** worksheet. Select cell **D15**, the estimated total. On the Formulas tab, in the Formula Auditing group, click **Trace Precedents**.

- Notice the Circular Reference warning in the status bar for cell D15. The SUM function in cell D15 includes a reference to D15, which is causing the circular reference. Click in the **Formula Bar**, and then change D15 to D14.

i. On the **Formulas** tab, in the Formula Auditing group, click **Watch Window**. Select cells **B6**, **B8**, and **D15**, and then click **Add Watch**. Click **Add**, and then **close** the Watch Window.

j. Select cell **B8**. On the **Data** tab, in the Data Tools group, click **Data Validation**. You will set a rule so the number entered is a whole number between 10 and 100.

- Click the **Settings** tab, and in the **Allow** box, select **Whole number**. In the **Data** box, verify that **between** is selected. In the **Minimum** box, type 10, and then, in the **Maximum** box, type 100.

- Click the **Input Message** tab. In the Title box, type Guests, and then, in the **Input message** box, type Enter the estimated number of guests.

- Click the **Error Alert** tab. In the **Title** box, type Error, and then in the **Input message** box type The number of guests is not valid. Click **OK**.

- In cell **B8**, type 90.

k. Select cell **B6**. On the **Data** tab, in the Data Tools group, click **Data Validation**. You will set a rule so the date entered must be after the current date.

- Click the **Settings** tab. In the **Allow** box, select **Date**. In the **Data** box, select **greater than**. In the **Start date** box, type =TODAY().

- Click the **Input Message** tab. In the **Title** box, type Date. In the **Input message** box, type Enter event date.

- Click the **Error Alert** tab. In the Title box, type Error. In the **Error message** box, type The date must be later than today. Click **OK**.

- In cell **B6**, type =TODAY() +1. This will enter tomorrow's date.

l. Select cell range **B11:B14**. On the **Data** tab, in the Data Tools group, click **Data Validation**. You will set a rule so the data entered must come from a list of cells on the YearSummary worksheet.

- Click the **Settings** tab. In the Allow box, select **List**. Click the **Source** box, click the **Year-Summary** worksheet, and then select cell range **A5:A19**.

- Click the **Input Message** tab. In the **Title** box, type Category. In the **Input message** box, type Select an option from the list. Click **OK** (you will not enter an error alert).
- Select cell **B11**, click the **arrow**, and then select **Appetizer**.
- Select cell **B12**, click the **arrow**, and then select **Fish**.
- Select cell **B13**, click the **arrow**, and then select **Poultry**.
- Select cell **B14**, click the **arrow**, and then select **Desserts**.

m. You will enter a formula to create the Estimate No. based on the event date and season.

- Select cell **E6**, and then type =IF(B6>0,TEXT(B6,"YYYYMMDD"),"")"&"&B7. This will convert the date into text based on the format YYYYMMDD and add the text value entered in B7 to the end of it.
- Select cell **B7**, click the **arrow**, and then select **Winter**.

n. **Save** your workbook.

o. If necessary, add the Developer tab to the ribbon. Click the **File** tab, click **Options**, click **Customize Ribbon**, and then, under Customize the Ribbon, click **Developer**. Click **OK**.

p. If necessary, add the location where you save your student files as a trusted location.

- Click the **File** tab, click **Options**. Click **Trust Center**, click **Trust Center Settings**, and then click **Trusted Locations**.
- Click **Add new location**, browse to the folder where you save your student files, and then click **OK**. Click **OK** again, click **OK** again, and then click **OK** again.

q. Click the **Developer** tab, and in the Code group, click **Record Macro**.

- In the **Macro name** box, type ClearContents. In the **Shortcut** key box, press and hold Shift, and then type C. Store the macro in **This Workbook**. In the **Description** box, type Delete all user-entered data from the worksheet. Click **OK**.
- Select cell range **B3:B4**, press and hold Ctrl, and then select cell ranges **B6:B8** and **B11:B14**. Press Delete.
- Select cell **B3**. On the **Developer** tab, in the Code group, click **Stop Recording**.

r. Click **Undo** to undo the changes you made in recording the macro.

s. On the Developer tab, in the Controls group, click **Insert**, and then select **Button (Form Control)**.

- Click in the top left corner of cell **G1**, and then drag to the bottom right corner of cell **H2** to size and add the button.
- Select **ClearContents**, and then click **OK**.
- Right-click the button, and then select **Edit Text**. Delete the current text, and then type Clear Form. Click cell **G4** to deselect the button.

t. Select cell **A10**. Click the **Insert** tab, and in the Links group, click **Hyperlink**.

- Select **Place in This Document**, and then select **YearSummary**. Click **ScreenTip**, and enter the ScreenTip Go to YearSummary. Click **OK**, and then click **OK**.
- Click the **YearSummary** worksheet. Select cell **H2**, type Special Events, and then insert a hyperlink to the SpecialEvents worksheet. Enter a ScreenTip Back to SpecialEvents.

u. Click the **Documentation** worksheet. Click cell **A8**, and then type today's date. Click cell **B8**, and then type your name in the Firstname Lastname format. Complete the remainder of the Documentation worksheet according to your instructor's direction.

v. Right-click the **Documentation** worksheet, and then select **Hide**.

w. Click the **SpecialEvents** worksheet if necessary. Select cell ranges **B3:B4**, **B6:B8**, and **B11:B14**. On the Home tab, in the Cells group, click **Format**, and then select **Lock Cell**.

x. Click the **File** tab, click **Options**, click **Advanced**, and then scroll down to the **Display options for this workbook** section.

- Click **Show horizontal scroll bar** and **Show vertical scroll bar**. This will turn off all the scroll bars for the workbook.

- In the Display options for this worksheet section, click **Show row and column headers**. This will turn off the row and column headers for the SpecialEvents worksheet. Click **OK**.

y. Click the **View** tab, and in the Show group, click **Gridlines**. This will turn off the gridlines for the SpecialEvents worksheet.

z. Click the **Formulas** tab, and in the Formula Auditing group, click **Show Formulas**.

- Select all the cells that show a formula EXCEPT for the Event date, which is entered by the user. Also select cell **A10**, which contains the hyperlink.

- Click the **Home** tab, and in the Cells group, click **Format**, select **Format Cells**, click the **Protection** tab, and then click **Hidden**. Click **OK**.

- Click the **Formulas** tab, and in the Formula auditing group, click **Show Formulas**.

aa. Click the **Home** tab, and in the Cells group, click **Format**, and then select **Protect Sheet**. Click **Select locked** cells to uncheck the option, and then click **OK**.

bb. On the **Review** tab, in the Changes group, click **Protect Workbook**, verify that **Structure** is selected, and then click **OK**.

cc. Click the **File** tab, click **Protect Workbook**, and then select **Mark as Final**. Click **OK** to save the workbook, click **OK** again, and then close Excel. Submit your file as directed by your instructor.

Problem Solve 1

Homework

Student data file needed:

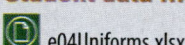 e04Uniforms.xlsx

You will save your files as:

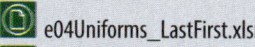 e04Uniforms_LastFirst.xlsm

e04UniformsTemplate_LastFirst.xltm

Hotel Uniform Order Tracking

Production & Operations

The staff at Painted Paradise Resort & Spa are required to wear uniforms every day. While the hotel provides uniforms each year to staff members, occasionally employees want to order items in addition to what is provided to them. One of the recent interns at the hotel created a spreadsheet order form but never finished it. You will finish working on it so it can be distributed to the staff. You will add data validation rules, record a macro, and make the spreadsheet look less like an Excel spreadsheet and more like an online order form so it is easy to use. You will also save it as a template to make it easy for the staff members to open each time.

a. Open the Excel file, **e04Uniforms**. Click **OK** in the circular reference warning box, and save your file as an **Excel Macro-Enabled Workbook** named e04Uniforms_LastFirst, using your last and first name.

b. Locate and correct the circular reference. The affected cell is identified on the status bar at the bottom of the window.

c. Select cell **C8**. Enter a calculated value for the Order Number that uses the employee name followed by the order date in the MMDDYY format. The order number should be created only if C6 and C7 are not blank, and there should be a space between the employee name and order number.

d. Select cell **C10**, and enter a data validation rule to look up the department name from the cell range named Departments on the Options worksheet. The input message should read Select a department from the list. The error message should read Invalid department. Select cell **C10**, and select **Front Desk**.

e. On the OrderForm worksheet, select cell range **C13:C18**, and enter a data validation rule to look up the top options from the cell range named **TopOptions** on the Options worksheet. The input message and error message can be left blank.

f. Select cell **C13**, and select **Vest**.

g. On the OrderForm worksheet, select cell range **C19:C24**, and enter a data validation rule to look up the bottom options from the cell range named **BottomOptions**. The input message and error message can be left blank.

h. On the OrderForm worksheet, select cell range **C25:C30**, and enter a data validation rule to look up the other options from the cell range named **OtherOptions**. The input message and error message can be left blank.

i. On the OrderForm worksheet, select cell range **D13:D30**, and enter a data validation rule to look up the size options from the cell range named **Sizes**. The input message and error message can be left blank. Select cell **D13**, and select **Large**. Select cell **E13**, and type **2**.

j. Select cell **A13**, and insert a hyperlink to the defined name **Tops**. Add a screen tip Go to Top Options. Select cell **A19**, and insert a hyperlink to the defined name **Bottoms**. Add a screen tip Go to Bottom Options. Select cell **A25**, and insert a hyperlink to the defined name **Other**. Add a screen tip Go to Other Options.

k. If necessary, add the Developer tab to the ribbon. Record a macro named ClearForm with the shortcut key F in This Workbook. Add the description To clear the form for another order. Clear cell range **C6:C7**, cell **C10**, cell range **C13:E30**, and cell **C33**. Then select cell **C6** as the last step in your macro, and stop the recording. Undo the changes you made while recording the macro.

l. Insert a macro button to run the ClearForm macro in cell range **F6:G7**. Change the button text to say Clear Form.

m. If necessary, add a new group to the Review tab on the ribbon called Text-to-Speech, and add the **Speak Cells** and **Stop Speaking Cells** buttons.

n. Modify the workbook for easier navigation.
- Update the Documentation worksheet according to your instructor's directions, and then hide the worksheet.
- On the OrderForm worksheet, unlock the cells required for data entry (the same cells the macro clears) as well as the cells containing the hyperlinks.
- Hide all formulas except the Order Date in cell C7.
- Hide the gridlines on the OrderForm worksheet.
- Hide the horizontal scroll bar on both worksheets.
- Hide row and column headings on the OrderForm worksheet.
- Protect the OrderForm worksheet to not allow the user to click in locked cells (do not use a password).

o. **Save** the workbook.

p. Save the workbook as an **Excel Macro-Enabled Template** named e04UniformsTemplate_LastFirst, using your last and first name.

q. Save the workbook, exit Excel, and then submit your files as directed by your instructor.

Student data file needed:

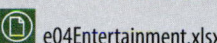 e04Entertainment.xlsx

You will save your files as:

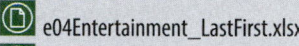 e04Entertainment_LastFirst.xlsx

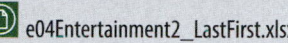 e04Entertainment2_LastFirst.xlsx

Production & Operations

Entertainment Expenses

The Painted Paradise Resort & Spa is a favorite spot for many locals to visit on a Friday night because of the live entertainment in the Silver Moon Lounge. The lounge has quarterly contracts with 13 popular local bands; each band will play in the lounge once a quarter. Lounge manager Will Diaz would like to keep track of quarterly and yearly expenses for the entertainment. He has started a workbook but has asked you to complete it. You will begin by summarizing the quarterly worksheets and consolidating the data. You will also share a copy with the assistant manager to update any necessary items.

a. Open the Excel file, **e04Entertainment**. Save your file as e04Entertainment_LastFirst, using your last and first name.

b. Group the **Q1** through **Q4** worksheets. Change the color of the **Q1**, **Q2**, **Q3**, and **Q4** worksheet tabs to **White, Background 1, Darker 50%**.

c. With the sheets still grouped, on the **Q1** worksheet, select cell range **E4:E16**. Fill All across the worksheets (Q1:Q4).

d. With the worksheets still grouped, on the **Q1** worksheet, select cell range **A3:E3**. Fill the format across the worksheets (Q1:Q4).

e. With the sheets still grouped, enter a formula in cell **E17** to calculate the total of column E prices.

f. A data validation to select from the Type list on the Type worksheet has been created on the Q1 worksheet but is not on the Q2 through Q4 worksheets. With the sheets still grouped, on the Q1 worksheet, select cell range **C4:C16**. Fill All across the sheets, and then press Ctrl + Home.

g. Ungroup the sheets.

h. On the **Year** worksheet, in cell range **B4:B16**, enter a 3-D formula to calculate the total amount spent on each entertainment group during Q1:Q4. In cell **B17**, enter a formula to total the Price column.

i. Update the **Documentation** worksheet according to your instructor's directions.

j. Hide the **Type** and **Documentation** worksheets. **Save** the workbook.

k. If necessary, add the Compare and Merge Workbooks button to the Quick Access Toolbar. Share the workbook, and then save a copy of the workbook as e04Entertainment2_LastFirst, using your last and first name.

l. You received notification from the entertainment group Singing in the Rain that the price of their services has increased to 450. Make this price adjustment on the Q1:Q4 worksheets in cell **E10**.

m. Save and close the workbook, but leave Excel open.

n. Open **e04Entertainment_LastFirst**. Compare and merge the workbook with **e04Entertainment2_LastFirst**. Save all the changes on a new worksheet. Do not stop sharing the workbook.

o. Save the workbook, exit Excel, and then submit your files as directed by your instructor.

Student data file needed:

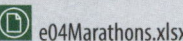 e04Marathons.xlsx

You will save your file as:

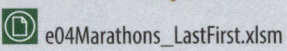 e04Marathons_LastFirst.xlsm

Marathons Around the World

Finance & Accounting

You started running five years ago and have set a personal goal to participate in as many marathons as possible next year. However, you are not sure of all the costs that will be involved so you can budget appropriately. Fortunately, you have two upcoming marathons you can use to assist you in determining your expenses and creating your plan.

You will create a workbook that contains four worksheets. Two of the worksheets will consolidate your expenses for each marathon. You will consolidate the data from the two marathons on the third worksheet. The fourth worksheet will be used to track your expenses. At a minimum, you will need to track the following categories.

- Entrance fees
- Running club dues
- Gym memberships
- Medical
- Clothing
- Footwear
- Miscellaneous supplies
- Travel
- Lodging

a. Open the Excel file, **e04Marathons**. Save your file as an **Excel Macro-Enabled Workbook** named **e04Marathons_LastFirst**, using your last and first name.

b. Rename Sheet1 as **Summary**. Rename Sheet2 and Sheet3 as **Marathon1** and **Marathon2**, respectively. Color the tabs to visually show related tabs.

c. The Summary and the two Marathon tabs should all be set up the same, as follows.
- Ensure that there is a Heading Row for **Category** and the **Amount**.
- List your specific categories under the heading Category.
- Format the cells under the Amount heading appropriately. Enter appropriate amounts for the categories. Not all categories need an amount entered.
- Ensure that there is a total row, and format it appropriately.
- On the Summary tab, use a 3-D reference to consolidate the data from the two marathon tabs under the Amount heading.

d. Sheet4 will contain a table that will track your expenses. Rename the sheet tab appropriately.

e. In cell **A1**, type **Marathon1**, and then, in cell **B1**, type **Philadelphia Marathon**. In cell **A2**, type **Marathon2**, and then in cell **B2**, type **Death Valley Trail Marathon**.

f. Leave at least one row below your headings, and create the following.
- A column for the date of the expense. Only dates in the current year and future years should be allowed.
- A column to indicate whether the expenses belong to Marathon1 or Marathon2 listed in cell range B1:B2. You should be able to choose only from these two marathons.
- A column for the category of expenses. These expenses should be limited to the categories on the Summary worksheet.
- The fourth column is for a detailed description of your expense. It should be limited to no more than 30 characters.
- The next column should contain the actual amount of your expense.

- The last column should be a running total of your expenses.
- Format the values in the amount and the running total as currency.
- Fill formats from the top row of your data, down at least eight rows.
- Create a named range for the data input area you just created, excluding the Running Total column.

g. Enter at least **six rows** of data to test your formulas, perform data validation, and ensure that you enter at least one line of test data for each marathon. Auto Fit all column widths as necessary.

h. Enter a formula on the Marathon1 and Marathon2 worksheets that will total the data entered on the expenses worksheet. There are two criteria that need to be met for a value to appear: The expense must be for the correct marathon, and it must match the correct category. (Hint: Use a SUMIFS formula.)

i. Create a macro that will clear the data from the expenses worksheet. (This will allow you to use the same file for your next two marathons.) Ensure that the first step of your macro is to select the Expenses worksheet.

j. Undo the actions of your macro so your data remains.

k. Add a button to the Summary worksheet that will run the macro.

l. Hide gridlines, headers, and scroll bars on all worksheets in the workbook. Protect the Summary, Marathon1, and Marathon2 worksheets.

m. Update the Documentation worksheet according to your instructor's directions. Hide the Documentation worksheet.

n. Protect the structure of the workbook; do not set a password.

o. Save the workbook, exit Excel, and then submit your file as directed by your instructor.

Perform 2: Perform in Your Career

Student data files needed:

- e04Miles.xlsx
- e04Account.xlsx
- e04Expense.xlsx

You will save your files as:

- e04Miles_LastFirst.xlsx
- e04Expense_LastFirst.xlsx
- e04Expense_LastFirst.xltx

Expense Report Application

Finance & Accounting

You have just started working at a new job. Your boss, Elda Rust, has asked you to recreate the current expense report, which is old and outdated. She would like users to be able to enter data only in appropriate cells and wants to ensure that invalid data is not entered. To be properly designed, your workbook should be easy to use, even for people who are unfamiliar with Excel. You have been instructed to have one worksheet for each day of the week with a consolidation worksheet.

a. Open the Excel file, **e04Miles**. Save your file as e04Miles_LastFirst, using your last and first name.

b. Create a named range for cell range A2:B7.

c. Open the Excel file, **e04Expense**. Save your file as e04Expense_LastFirst, using your last and first name.

d. Open the Excel file, **e04Account**. Save your file as e04Account_LastFirst, using your last and first name. Copy the data on the **Lists** worksheet into the **e04Expense** workbook on a new worksheet. Close the e04Account_LastFirst workbook.

e. On the Expense report worksheet, type **# of Miles** in cell **J10**.

f. Select cell range **B10:B26**, and then delete the Table Column.

g. Clear All in cell range **K4:M5**.

h. In cell **K4**, type Date. Format cell K4 the same as the SSN label.

i. Insert a bottom border in cell **L4**.

j. Adjust the formula in cell **L11**. Using a VLOOKUP function, multiply the number of miles by the appropriate rate from e04Miles_LastFirst and sum the remainder of the items in the row.

k. Format cell range **I11:I26** appropriately.

l. Change the order of cells **C10** and **B10**. (Description will come before Account.)

m. Ensure that only a date of today or before today can be entered in cell **L4**.

n. Cell range **B11:B25** should allow for a list of descriptions from the Lists worksheet.

o. Insert a formula in cell range **C11:C25** that will look up the account number based on the description selected in the adjacent column. Adjust the formula so that errors will return a blank.

p. Hide the Lists worksheet.

q. Update the Documentation worksheet according to your instructor's directions. Hide the Documentation worksheet.

r. Format the column widths appropriately across the entire table.

s. Unlock cells that would be needed for data entry. Hide all formulas. Protect the worksheet, and do not allow the selecting of locked cells.

t. Hide gridlines and row and column headers of the ExpenseReport worksheet. Protect the structure of the workbook. Save the workbook.

u. Save the workbook as a template named **e04Expense_LastFirst**, using your last and first name for future use.

v. Close Excel, and then submit your files as directed by your instructor.

Perform 3: Perform in Your Team

Student data file needed:

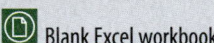 Blank Excel workbook

You will save your file as:

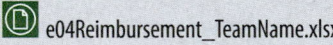 e04Reimbursement_TeamName.xlsx

Team Expense Reimbursement with Summary

Finance & Accounting

The organization you work for has used paper forms for years, but now that so many employees have smartphones, tablets, laptops, or other such devices, the organization would like to create electronic forms. In the past, team members have submitted their expenses individually, and it was up to the payroll manager to consolidate the information to be able to create a team summary of expenses for a project.

Your supervisor has asked you to create a workbook that can be used by teams of employees to track expenses for a project. The workbook should contain one worksheet for each team member as well as a worksheet to summarize team expenses.

a. Select one team member to set up the document by completing steps b through e.

b. Open your browser and navigate to https://www.onedrive.live.com, https://www.drive.google.com, or any other instructor-assigned location. Be sure all members of the team have an account on the chosen system, such as a Microsoft or Google account.

c. Create a new workbook, and then name it e04Reimbursement_TeamName, using the team name assigned to your team by your instructor.

d. Share the spreadsheet with the other members of your team. Make sure each team member has the appropriate permission to edit the document.

e. Hold a team meeting, and discuss the requirements of the remaining steps. Make an action and communication plan. Consider which steps can be done independently and which steps require completion of prior steps before starting.

f. Team member 1 should complete the following.
   - Create a worksheet to track expenses. Include the following columns: Date, Description, Hotel, Transportation, Meals, Phone, Mileage, Other, and Total. Format at least 19 rows as a table.
   - Create data validation rules in the Date column to accept only dates less than or equal to today.
   - Create data validation in the expense columns to restrict the values to decimals between $2.00 and $999.
   - Create three more copies of the worksheet just created, one for each team member. Name each of the worksheets with the first name of one of the team members.
   - Enter at least five lines of expenses on the worksheet for team member 1.

g. Team member 2 should complete the following after team member 1 has uploaded the workbook.
   - On the worksheet for team member 2, enter at least five lines of expenses.
   - For all four worksheets (one for each member), insert a formula in the Total column to add the columns Hotel through Other and add a total line to total expenses by each column.

h. Team member 3 should complete the following after team member 2 has uploaded the workbook.
   - On the worksheet for team member 3, enter at least five lines of expenses.
   - Insert a new worksheet, call it TeamSummary, and then move it to follow the team member 4 worksheet.
   - Add a title to the new worksheet.
   - On the four member worksheets, unlock all cells that need to be opened for data entry. Hide any formulas.

i. Team member 4 should complete the following after team member 3 has uploaded the workbook.
   - On the worksheet for team member 4, enter at least five lines of expenses.
   - On the TeamSummary worksheet, consolidate all four team members' expense reports by Description. Format the results as appropriate. (Hint: Do not include the date column in the consolidation.)
   - On the TeamSummary worksheet, create hyperlinks from the TeamSummary worksheet to all four member worksheets.
   - Protect the four team members' worksheets without a password, and prevent clicking on locked cells.

j. In a custom header section of the TeamSummary worksheet, include the names of the students in your team. Spread the names evenly across each of the three header sections: left section, center section, and right section.

k. On the TeamDescriptions worksheet, each team member must list his or her first and last name as well as a summary of his or her contributions.

l. Team member 1 should save the workbook and mark the workbook as final.

m. Exit Excel, and then submit the team file as directed by your instructor.

Student data file needed:

 e04College.xlsm

You will save your file as:

 e04College_LastFirst.xlsm

Education Costs Worksheet

Finance & Accounting

A fellow student has created a workbook to track his expenses for the next two semesters of school. You like the idea of being able to do this and have asked him for the workbook so you can use it as well. You will adjust the workbook to make it work for you. You are a little confused about how the workbook works, and since he did not leave any instructions, you have to figure out on your own what he has done.

a. Open the Excel file, **e04College**. Save it as an Excel Macro-Enabled workbook named **e04College_LastFirst**, using your last and first name. Click **OK** in the circular warning dialog box.

b. Locate and correct the circular reference.

c. On the Fall2017 and Spring2018 worksheets, create formulas in the Amount column to sum the expenses identified in column A.

d. On the TotalCosts worksheet, create a 3-D reference that sums the data from the Fall2017 and Spring2018 worksheets.

e. On the TotalCosts worksheet, if appropriate, unlock any cells for data entry, and protect the rest of the worksheet. Add hyperlinks to both the Fall2017 and Spring2018 worksheets.

f. On both the Fall2017 and Spring2018 worksheets, create a hyperlink to return to the TotalCosts worksheet.

g. Click the Fall2017 worksheet. Look at the cells with the comments (they have red triangles in the top right corner). On the Documentation worksheet, comment on what the macro does. Also comment on what kind of macro it is.

h. Save the workbook, and mark it as final. Submit your workbook as directed by your instructor.

Excel Business Unit 5

Manipulating Data Sets for Decision Making

Data is a big part of business, and its value and importance are increasing as collecting it from a variety of sources becomes ever easier. Learning how to collect and organize all relevant data for use in analyses is extremely important in every business. Excel is one of the most commonly used applications for data analysis in the world, and it has a variety of tools built-in to facilitate sound, data-driven decision making.

Learning Outcome 1:

Understand the benefits of analyzing data sets and learn techniques to import, organize, and clean data sets from a variety of sources.

REAL WORLD SUCCESS

"I was recently asked to develop a series of reports on enrollments at the university I work for. The data on students enrolling at the university was made available to us in an Access database. By importing the data into Excel from Access, I was able to create a broad range of statistics, graphs, and reports spanning several years of data. The result was a comprehensive view of our data that provided unique insights for our university."

- Dave, alumnus

Amy S Kinser, Brandt Moriarity, Eric Kinser, Kristyn Jacobson

Learning Outcome 2:

Utilize various forecasting and optimization tools, such as data tables, Scenario Manager, and Solver to support decision making.

REAL WORLD SUCCESS

"I recently created a workbook detailing changes to several products our company manufactures. In the workbook, I used a data table to analyze the changes in profits resulting from different cost and demand combinations. The use of form controls and conditional formatting made the worksheet intuitive and easy to use."

- Joseph P., manager

Amy S Kinser, Brandt Moriarity, Eric Kinser, Kristyn Jacobson

Microsoft Excel 2016

| Chapter 9 | ORGANIZE, IMPORT, EXPORT, AND CLEANSE DATA SETS |

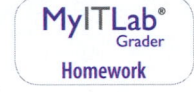 

Sales & Marketing

OBJECTIVES

1. Understand the importance of external data sets   p. 491

2. Understand and import XML data   p. 497

3. Connect to an Access database   p. 505

4. Use Flash Fill and Text functions to cleanse imported data   p. 510

5. Manipulate data using text functions   p. 515

6. Separate data using wizards   p. 524

7. Cleanse date-related data   p. 527

Prepare Case

Red Bluff Golf Course & Pro Shop Data Integration

The Red Bluff Golf Course & Pro Shop manager, Aleeta Herriott, has asked you to create a report that analyzes costs and revenues from tournaments hosted over the past year. In the past, her staff had to reenter data manually from different sources to create this report because no one at the resort knew how to import the data. As a result, they rarely completed the report. Aleeta worries about the accuracy of the reports that were compiled because of the manual data entry. However, she did keep all the original files. Recently, a new Golf database was created to track sales and allow for easy export to Excel for analysis. Aleeta wants you to design a spreadsheet that will help her automate the process of gathering and standardizing the data from the past for analysis.

MNStudio/Shutterstock

Student data files needed for this chapter:

 e05ch09TournamentData.xlsx

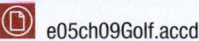 e05ch09Customers.csv

e05ch09TournamentReport.xlsx

e05ch09Golf.accdb

e05ch09MenuOptions.xml

You will save your files as:

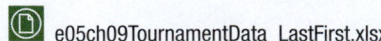 e05ch09TournamentData_LastFirst.xlsx

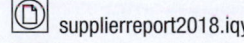 supplierreport2018.iqy

e05ch09TournamentReport_LastFirst.xlsx

Working with Data Sets

One reason for the popularity of spreadsheets is their ability to combine data and information from a wide variety of sources. Once you have advanced beyond the novice level to become a more advanced user, you will very likely need to integrate data from multiple sources. Most organizations have their data spread throughout the organization in a variety of formats on a variety of devices. Your organization may collect data on websites or network servers or in word-processing programs, databases, or even paper reports. In this section, you will learn about external data sets and how to connect to them. You will also work with web queries and import data.

Understand the Importance of External Data Sets

Anything that is not stored in an Excel format (.xls or .xlsx) or not stored locally is considered to be **external data**. Spreadsheet applications such as Excel offer a wide variety of tools to help the user extract external data and integrate it into reports so that it can be actively used to make better decisions. By using the import tools, one can avoid a lot of extra typing. Microsoft has continued to expand the file types that can be easily imported, and this feature has improved considerably in recent versions of Excel. Common file formats that you can import include HTML, XML, text, and .accdb files from Microsoft Access.

One of the reasons that spreadsheets are such powerful tools is that they have evolved into the de facto means of consolidating diverse types of data. For example, an organization may want you to work on an analysis or report but cannot grant you access to their databases. One solution would be for them to export their data to a text format, which you can then easily import into Excel.

QUICK REFERENCE	Common Data Sources for Excel
Source	**Description**
Microsoft Access (.mdb, .accdb)	Import data from relational database tables created in Access (.mdb, .accdb) formats.
HTML (.html)	Link to data stored in tabular form on websites.
Comma separated (.csv)	Convert data stored in a comma-delimited (.csv) format. Even though this is a separate file type, you cannot choose it when importing data into Excel. Excel will automatically open a .csv file.
XML (.xml)	Import data stored in .xml format.
Text (.txt)	Exchange data between mainframes and other systems that use the .txt format.
SQL Server	A popular relational database server for corporate web servers.
Analysis Services	Designed to import data formatted as a data cube in SQL Server Analysis Services.
Windows Azure Marketplace	An online service in which one can subscribe to data sets, build queries, and import the queries to Excel.
Microsoft Query	A query wizard to help in importing data from less common or unlisted sources using ODBC (standard data conversion drivers).
Data Connection Wizard	Another query wizard for creating and maintaining connections with unlisted data sources; uses OLEDB drivers.

Opening the Starting File

Data can be easily shared online between companies, within companies, and between companies and their customers. While this data can be placed into a workbook by copying from the website and pasting into a workbook, linking to a web page is a more efficient process. When the web page is linked to a workbook, the data can be updated without having to visit the web page and perform a copy-and-paste process every time the data is updated. Aleeta Herriott has asked you to import data from a web page that lists online transactions related to golf tournaments through the Painted Paradise website. In this exercise, you will begin by opening the starting file.

E09.00

To Open the Starting File

a. Start **Excel**, click **Open Other Workbooks** in the left pane, and then double-click **This PC**. Navigate through the folder structure to the location of your student data files, and then double-click **e05ch09TournamentData**. An Excel workbook will open with a variety of blank worksheets that you will use throughout this chapter.

b. Click the **File** tab, click **Save As**, and then double-click **This PC**. In the Save As dialog box, navigate to the location where you are saving your project files, and then change the file name to **e05ch09TournamentData_LastFirst** using your last and first name. Click **Save**.

Importing Web Data into Excel

One popular way to integrate information from web pages is to use a web query. A **query** is a question that you would ask a database such as Access. Access allows users to formulate queries in a variety of tools or languages to search for information in the database. You might think of a web query as something you could type into a search engine such as Google or Bing to search the web. However, in Excel, a **web query** is a way of importing data into a spreadsheet directly from a web page. This could be stock prices from a financial website such as http://money.msn.com, or it could be sales data from a company web server or even a table of data in a Wikipedia article.

More and more, companies are using websites to make their data available to users. Financial, governmental, and even college-related data is uploaded and refreshed daily. By linking this data to a spreadsheet via a web query, users can automatically update the data for use in their spreadsheet applications. Web queries are tied to specific URLs; if the URL changes, the web query will no longer be able to access the data. This makes it important to have the exact URL address when you are importing data. In this exercise, you will import data from the Red Bluff Golf Course & Pro Shop Customer Supplier Report using a web query.

 **E09.01**

To Import Web Data into Excel

a. Be sure the Suppliers worksheet is active.

b. Click the **Data** tab, and in the Get External Data group, click **From Web**.

c. In the New Web Query dialog box, click in the **Address** box, and then delete any text. Type the following URL: http://www.paintedparadiseresort.com/redbluffreports2018 .html. If you get a security warning message, select **No**, and continue.

d. Click **Go**.
The New Web Query window now displays the target website.

e. Click the **Supplier Report** link.
The yellow selection arrows indicate data that Excel can easily import into a spreadsheet.

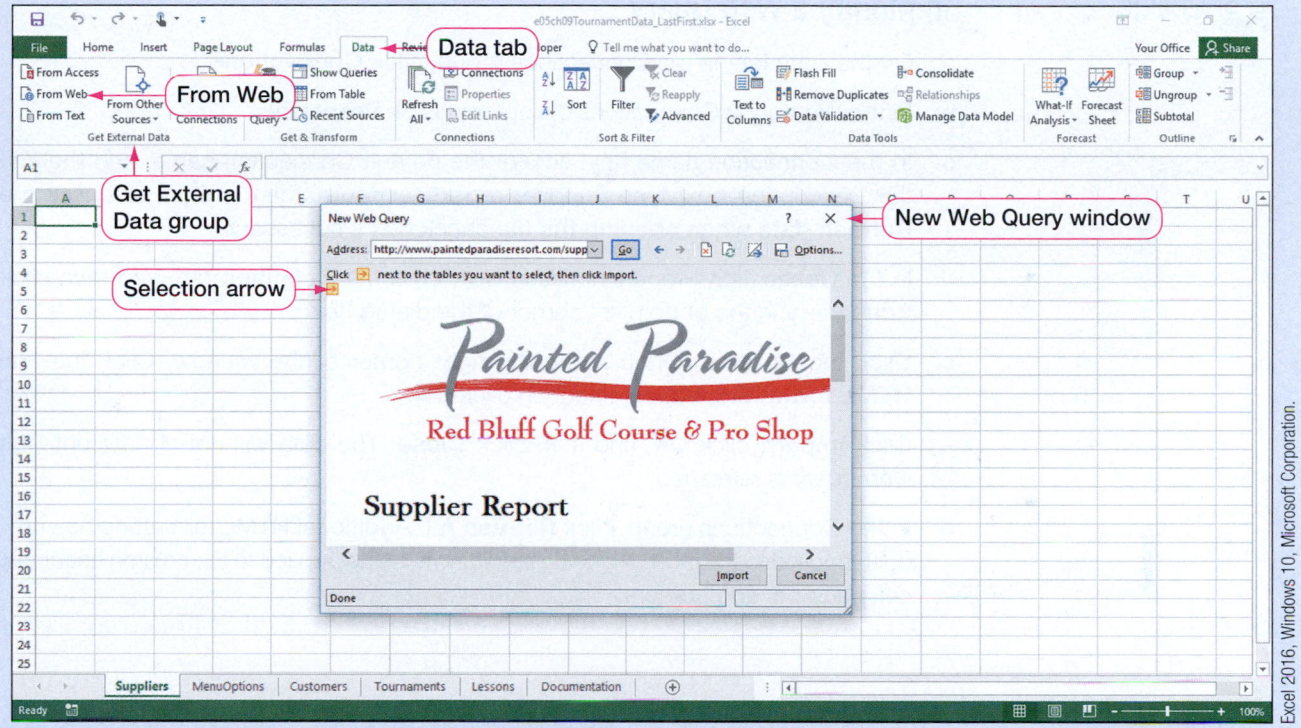

Figure 1 Creating a web query

f. If necessary, scroll down, click the yellow **Selection** arrow next to the table of data to select the table.

g. Click **Import**, accept the default location of cell A1, and then click **OK**. The data from the website is now located in the Suppliers worksheet.

h. **Save** ⊟ the workbook.

Modifying a Web Query

You may have noticed that the data you pulled into your spreadsheet from the web page with your original web query retained some, but not all, of the web page formatting. For example, the data in the Date column is formatted as Date, and the data in the Amount column is formatted as Currency. However, the padding around the data, the bold font of the column headings, and the table borders were not retained. Web queries can be modified so that they are set to retain all the formatting from the target HTML tables. Excel gives you several options for formatting your web query. The default None option retrieves the text with some basic formatting. The Rich Text Formatting only option retains most of the text formatting. The Full HTML formatting option allows you to import more advanced features, such as tables and hyperlinks. If this data is used in meetings or reports, the formatting from the website would make the data more presentable. In this exercise, you will modify the web query to include full HTML formatting.

 E09.02

To Modify a Web Query

a. On the Data tab, in the Connections group, click **Connections**.

b. In the Workbook Connections dialog box, click **Properties**.

c. In the Connection name box, accept the default Connection name, and then, in the Description box, type Supplier report for tournaments. Click to check the **Refresh data when opening the file** check box if necessary.

d. In the Connection Properties dialog box, click the **Definition** tab, and then click **Edit Query** in the bottom left corner of the dialog box.

e. Click the **Options** button in the top right corner of the window. Click the **Full HTML formatting** option, and then click **OK**.

f. Click **Import**, click **OK**, and then click **Close**. The data will not update until the web query is refreshed.

g. In the Connections group, click **Refresh All**. Additional HTML formatting has now been applied to the table, including a bold style being applied to the column headings, cell padding, and borders.

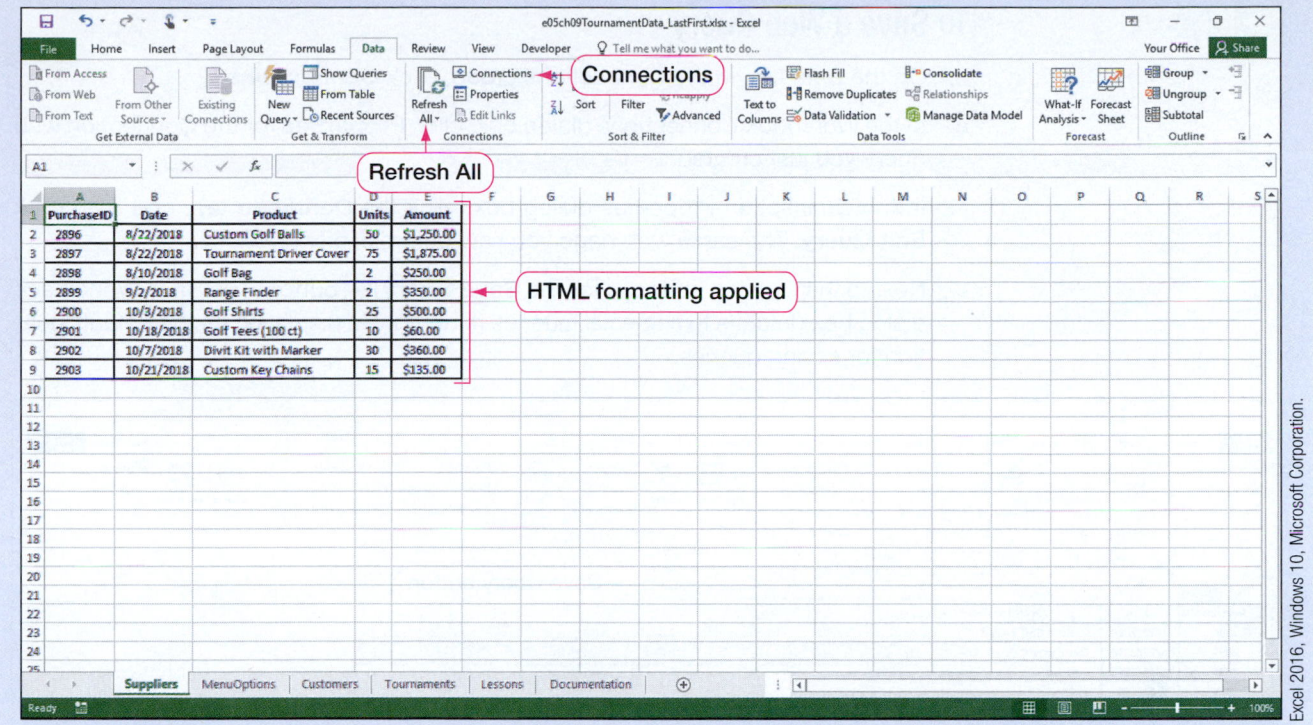

Figure 2 Modified web query

h. **Save** the workbook.

Saving a Web Query

At times, you will want to share your completed web query with other users. By saving a copy of your web query, you create a permanent file that contains a connection to the data. This file can then be used in any Microsoft Office application, including Microsoft Word. In this exercise, you will save the web query that you created in the previous exercise.

 **E09.03**

To Save a Web Query

a. On the Data tab, in the Connections group, click **Connections**.

b. In the Workbook Connections dialog box, click **Properties** for the Connection web query you just created.

c. In the Connection Properties dialog box, click the **Definition** tab, and then click **Edit Query**. The same web page you saw before is displayed.

d. Next to the Options button, click the **Save Query** 🖫 button. The Save Workspace dialog box defaults to a special Queries folder that is displayed as the default location for saving queries.

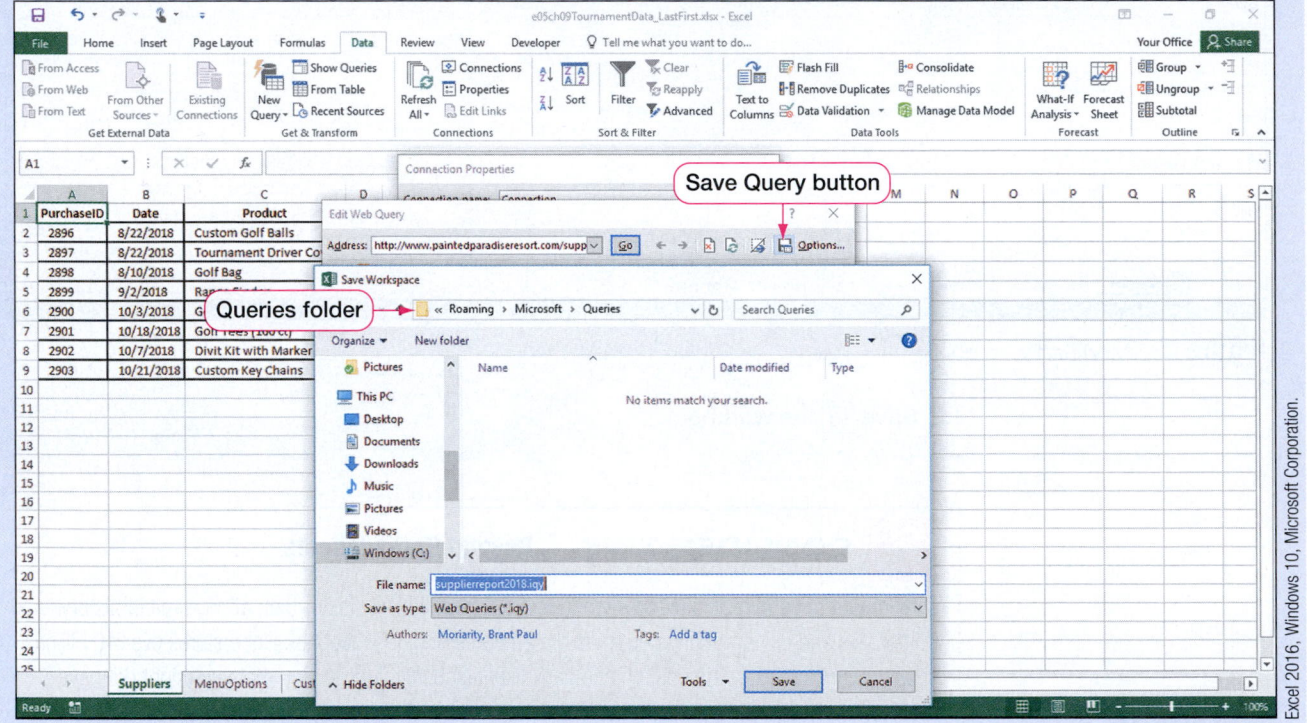

Figure 3 Saving a web query

e. Navigate to the location where you are saving your project files, accept the default file name, click **Save**, and then click **Cancel** twice. Click **Close** to exit the remaining dialog box.

f. Click **Save** 🖫. If you need to take a break before finishing this chapter, now is a good time.

REAL WORLD ADVICE **How Is Connecting to Web Data Different from Copying and Pasting?**

It may seem simpler just to copy the web data and paste it into your worksheet than to use a web query. In fact, you can copy and paste for the occasional import of web data. With a newer browser, you can right-click a web table and copy it to Excel with the Export to Microsoft Excel option. However, when you use the copy-and-paste method, you will have to spend time reformatting the data to use it in your formulas in Excel. More important, web queries provide a great advantage when you are creating an application that needs to be updated frequently. The web query will create a connection to the web page and automatically update the data in your Excel file.

Working with XML Data and Text Files

Two of the most common data formats for importing data into Excel are XML data and text files. In this section, you will learn how to import data in these two formats into Excel.

Understand and Import XML Data

XML, or Extensible Markup Language, is an increasingly popular tool working behind the scenes in Excel. A little understanding of how it is used will take you well beyond the usual beginner's knowledge of spreadsheets. In an earlier exercise, you imported data that was stored in a table on a web page. This made it easier to import the data into Excel without reformatting it. However, in some cases, data on web pages is not stored in an organized manner. That is to say, the data may not be in a table that is easily accessible with Excel. **XML** was created to help give structure to web page data so it can be searched and processed more efficiently. XML allows users to define their own tags in order to define the content of the document.

Most web pages are programmed in **HTML**, or Hypertext Markup Language. Both XML and HTML are examples of markup languages. **Markup languages** use special sequences of characters or "markups" inserted in the document to indicate how the document should look when it is displayed or printed. The markup indicators are often called "tags" and are enclosed in angle brackets (< >). These tags tell the device that will process the document what to do with it. HTML is used to format and display the web data, whereas XML was developed to help convert web data into a tabular structure so it could be easily stored and transported. Unlike HTML tags, the tags in XML actually describe the content of the data between the tags. For instance, HTML uses tags such as <H1></H1> to help describe the formatting of the document, but XML uses tags to describe the actual content between the tags <revenue></revenue>. Because of this, XML capabilities were soon extended to databases, spreadsheets, and word processors and became the de facto standard for transmitting data between systems and different applications.

One of the most powerful aspects of XML is that you can define custom tags for content that is specific to a particular industry. In HTML, all the tags are predetermined so the browser knows how to interpret them. XML is different in that as long as you follow the rules for creating XML tags and documents, you can define the tags any way you like.

The goal of XML is to allow users to automate the storage, transmission, and processing of content. To accomplish this, XML separates the content from the format and structure of the document. To understand how to process an XML document, it is crucial to understand its structure. The structure of an XML document is described in the XML schema or data map. The **XML schema** describes the structure of an XML document in terms of what XML elements it will contain and their sequence. In Excel, the term **XML map** is synonymous with XML schema. An **XML element** includes the start and stop tags and everything in between, such as <revenue>$345,678</revenue>. The document structure is separate from the actual content of the document itself and uses a completely separate file with an .xsd extension. It is similar in concept to the idea of a mail merge. The content is contained in the .xml file, the formatting is described in an .xsl file, and the structure of all the data elements is laid out in the schema or .xsd file. All of these files are merged in the resulting XML document, just as a list of names and addresses is merged with a form letter in Word, as illustrated in Figure 4.

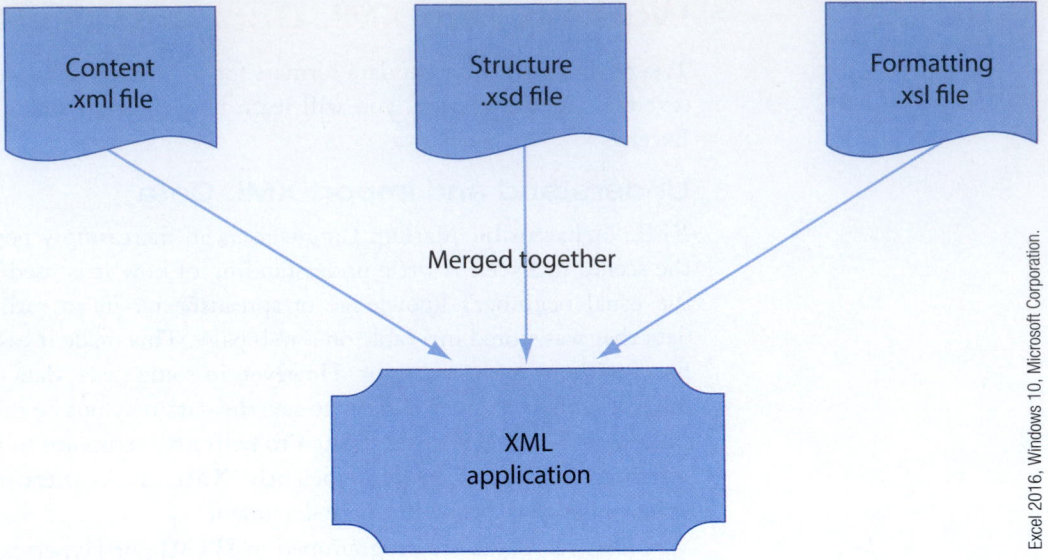

Content
.xml file

Structure
.xsd file

Formatting
.xsl file

Merged together

XML
application

Excel 2016, Windows 10, Microsoft Corporation.

Figure 4   XML document files

Determining the structure of any document may not be obvious. If you were to look at a book index or a table of contents, you would know just by glancing at them what these two different documents were. This is because over the years, publishers have defined what the structure of an index or table of contents should look like. It is the same way with schemas. You can define the structure of a sales order document to contain the customer number, name, date, product ID, cost, and total cost. All of these would be represented as elements within the XML schema. So when processing an XML file, Excel looks for an existing XML schema to check whether it has received a valid XML document. Thus, it can automate the processing of XML files, since it knows what to expect because the parts of the document are defined by the schema.

Adding the Developer Tab to the Ribbon

To import XML data into an Excel document, you first need to activate the Developer tab. The Developer tab provides access to many useful Excel features, such as macros, Visual Basic, and form control tools. In this exercise, you will add the Developer tab to the ribbon.

 E09.04

To Add the Developer Tab to the Ribbon

a. If you took a break, open the **e05ch09TournamentData** workbook.

b. Click the **File** tab, and then click **Options** in the left pane.

c. From the list on the left of the Excel Options dialog box, click **Customize Ribbon**. In the list of tabs on the right, select **Developer**.

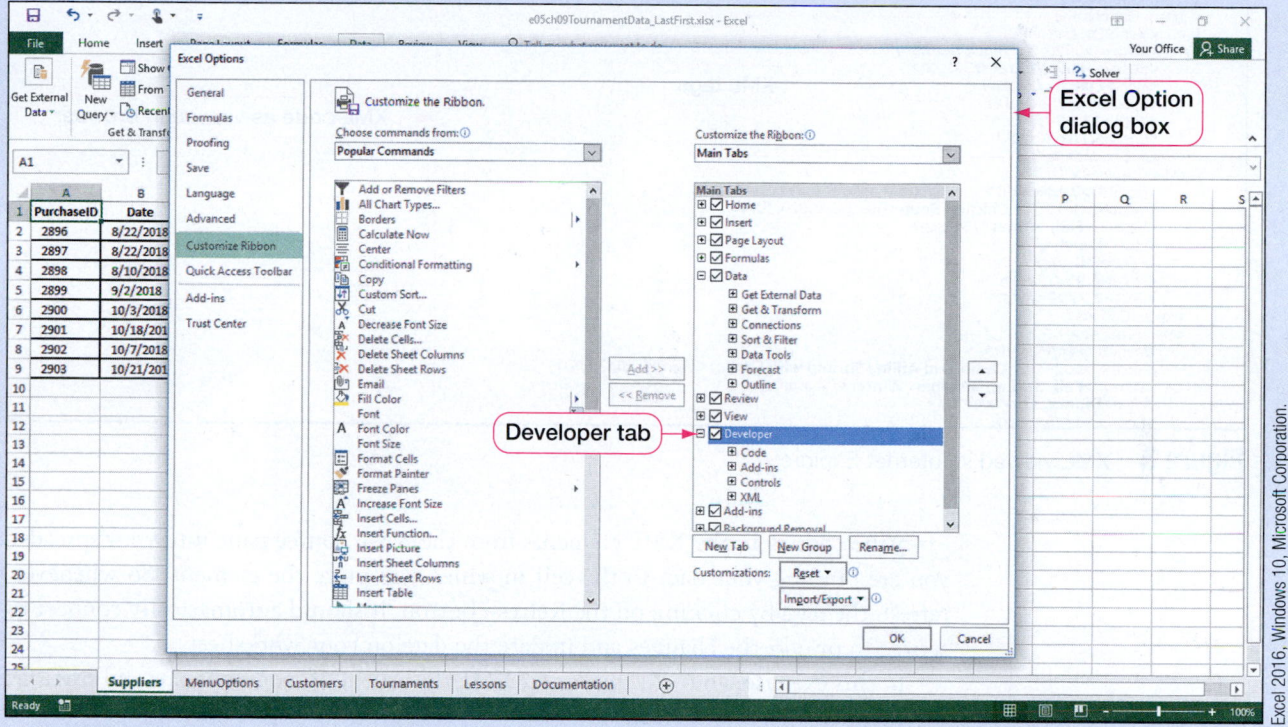

Figure 5   Adding the Developer tab

d. Click **OK**. Click the **Developer** tab to view it on the ribbon.

Importing XML Data

The Red Bluff Golf Course & Pro Shop uses the Indigo5 restaurant to cater food and drinks for many of its hosted tournaments. A list of current menu options and pricing has been sent to you as an XML file. By being saved in this XML document, the data can be electronically transmitted, queried, and stored. When Excel imports the menu options data into a worksheet, it automatically creates an XML schema — or XML map, as it is called in Excel. When viewing an XML file in Internet Explorer (IE) 6.0 and above, you can also export an XML file into Excel by right-clicking anywhere in the browser window, selecting Export to Microsoft Excel, and following the directions. The two methods give the same results. XML files can also be viewed using Microsoft's Edge browser but at the time of this publication the Edge browser does not support exporting to Excel. Figure 6 shows the XML file used in this exercise as viewed in the Edge browser.

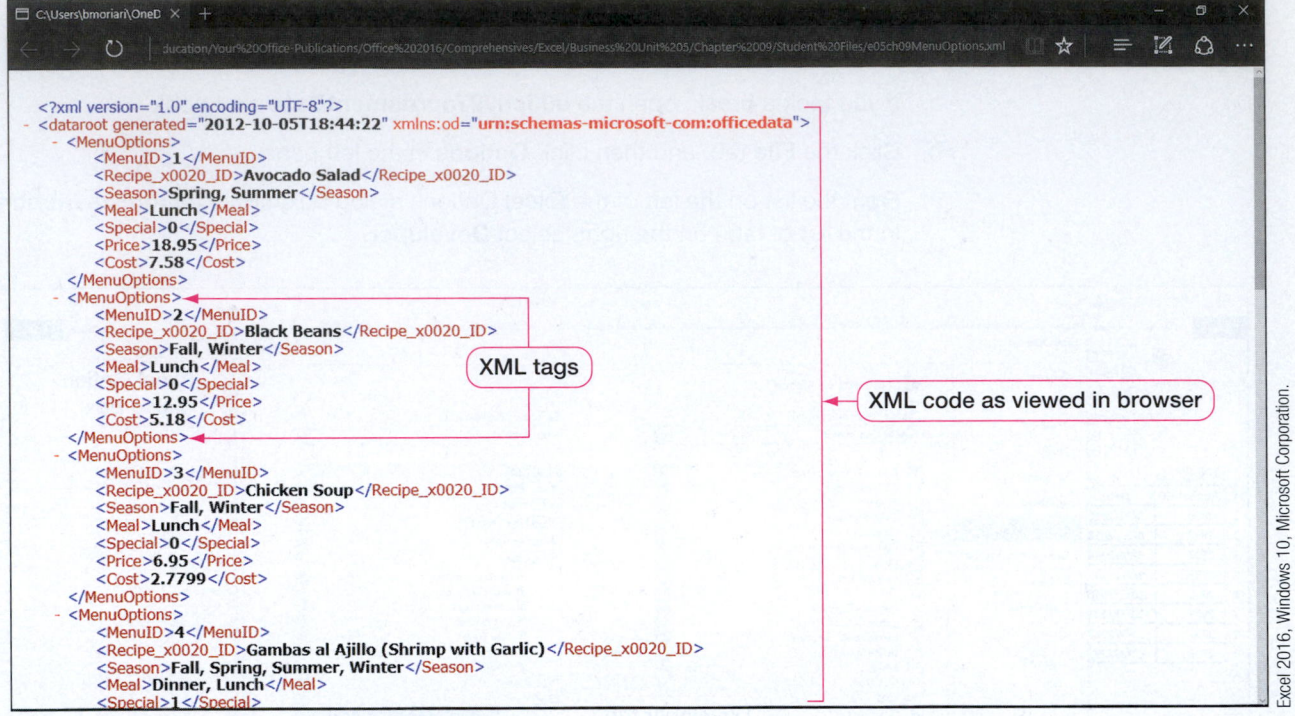

```
<?xml version="1.0" encoding="UTF-8"?>
- <dataroot generated="2012-10-05T18:44:22" xmlns:od="urn:schemas-microsoft-com:officedata">
  - <MenuOptions>
      <MenuID>1</MenuID>
      <Recipe_x0020_ID>Avocado Salad</Recipe_x0020_ID>
      <Season>Spring, Summer</Season>
      <Meal>Lunch</Meal>
      <Special>0</Special>
      <Price>18.95</Price>
      <Cost>7.58</Cost>
    </MenuOptions>
  - <MenuOptions>
      <MenuID>2</MenuID>
      <Recipe_x0020_ID>Black Beans</Recipe_x0020_ID>
      <Season>Fall, Winter</Season>
      <Meal>Lunch</Meal>
      <Special>0</Special>
      <Price>12.95</Price>
      <Cost>5.18</Cost>
    </MenuOptions>
  - <MenuOptions>
      <MenuID>3</MenuID>
      <Recipe_x0020_ID>Chicken Soup</Recipe_x0020_ID>
      <Season>Fall, Winter</Season>
      <Meal>Lunch</Meal>
      <Special>0</Special>
      <Price>6.95</Price>
      <Cost>2.7799</Cost>
    </MenuOptions>
  - <MenuOptions>
      <MenuID>4</MenuID>
      <Recipe_x0020_ID>Gambas al Ajillo (Shrimp with Garlic)</Recipe_x0020_ID>
      <Season>Fall, Spring, Summer, Winter</Season>
      <Meal>Dinner, Lunch</Meal>
      <Special>1</Special>
```

XML tags

XML code as viewed in browser

Excel 2016, Windows 10, Microsoft Corporation.

Figure 6 XML viewed in Internet Explorer

When you drag the XML elements from the XML Source pane into your spreadsheet, you are binding your data to the cell in which you place the element. So whenever you refresh the data by clicking on the Refresh button, it should automatically connect to the source to import the changes and update the data on your worksheet.

In this exercise, you will import an XML document of menu options and pricing into the MenuOptions worksheet.

 **E09.05**

To Import XML Data

a. Click the **MenuOptions** worksheet.

b. On the Developer tab, in the XML group, click **Source**. The XML Source pane is displayed on the right side of your worksheet.

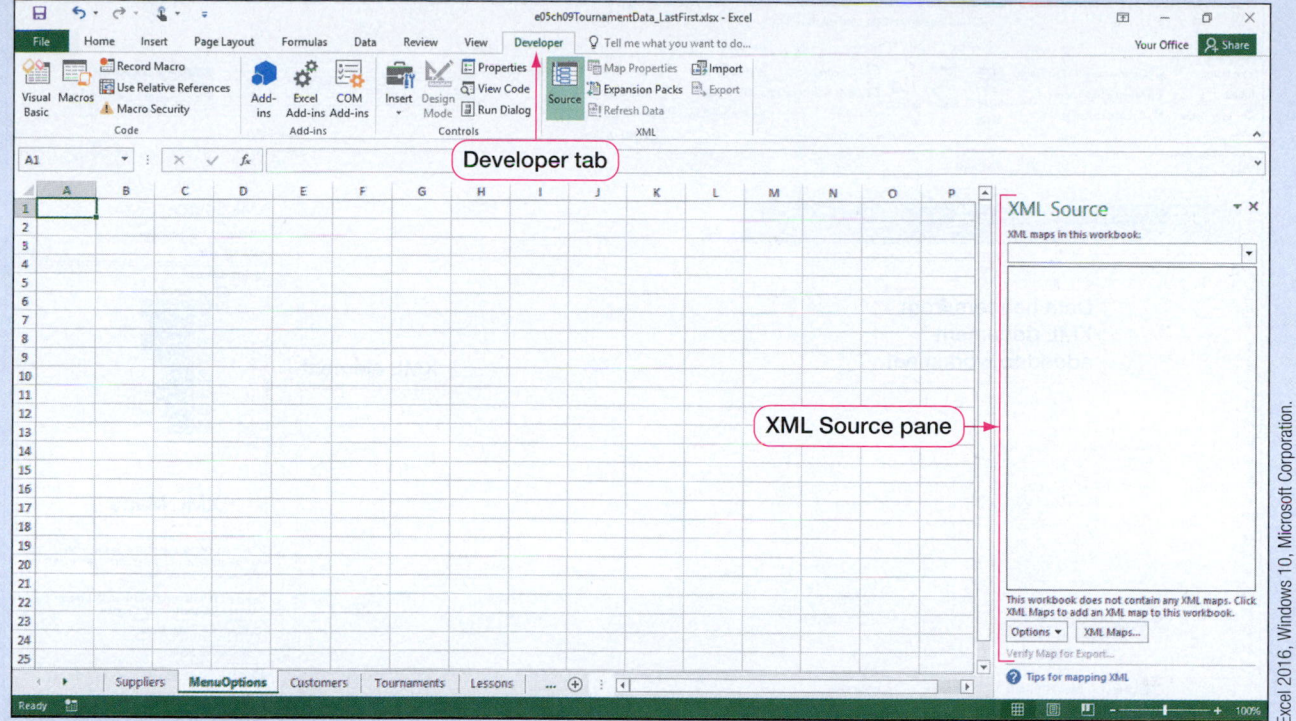

Figure 7 The Developer tab and XML Source pane

c. In the bottom right corner of the XML Source pane click **XML Maps**. A list of XML maps attached to the current workbook is displayed. In this instance, no maps have been attached yet, so you will not see any displayed in the dialog box.

d. In the XML Maps dialog box, click **Add**. In the Select XML Source dialog box, navigate through the folder structure to the location of your student data files, and then double-click **e05ch09MenuOptions**. A dialog box opens stating that no schema exists for this file. Click **OK** two times to close the dialog boxes.

e. Drag the **MenuOptions** element with all of its child elements from the XML Source pane to cell **A1**. Only the data headers from the XML file will appear initially. The XML data will be imported as an Excel table.

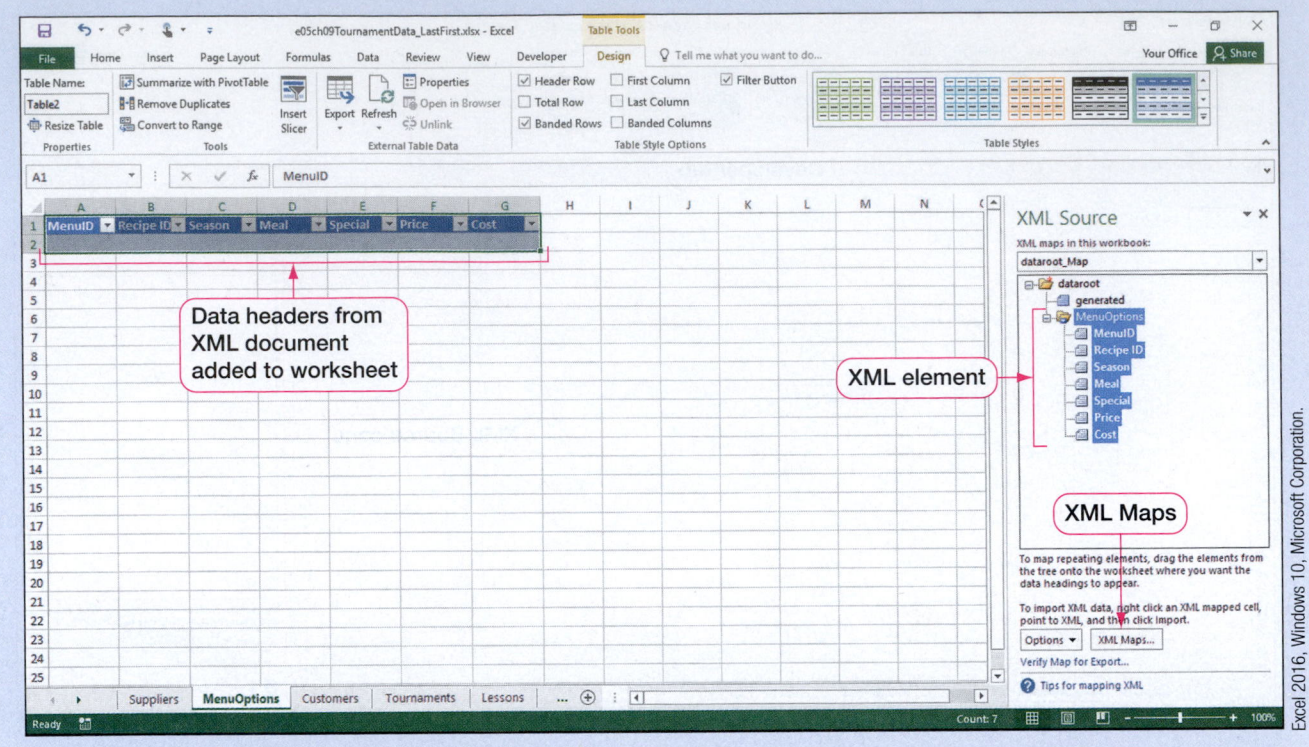

Figure 8 XML document imported into Excel

f. In the External Table Data group, click **Refresh**. The data has now been imported into the spreadsheet.

g. **Close** ☒ the XML Source pane.

h. **Save** 🖫 the workbook.

Importing Text Files

Text data files used to be called flat files because they were structured as simple lines of data separated by delimiters. **Text data** consists of any grouping of characters, numbers, or dates. A **text file** is just a simple container of text data that is structured by the use of delimiters. A **delimiter** is a way of indicating the beginning and end of a text data segment. As a container of data, a text file can transmit virtually any kind of data. Text files are simple to understand and transmit but are not as efficient as binary files because they take up more space in memory. Many different computer systems share data by transmitting text files back and forth. For that reason, text files are one of the most commonly used computer file formats. Text files — also called ASCII files — have no metadata associated with them, so they are not used for transmitting graphics, formulas, or any special formatting. In this context, **metadata** is simply data about data. For digital graphics, metadata could include when the image was created, source information, keywords, format instructions, and captions.

Like XML and HTML files, text files can be imported in two different ways: either one file at a time by opening the file in Excel or by creating a connection that is maintained between the file source and the target workbook. If you are going to use the application often and the external data will change frequently, you will want to maintain a live connection. Otherwise, you can just import the text files as needed. The two methods are similar and easy to accomplish in Excel.

Text files are known as plain text because they contain just text, without any formatting. No special fonts, images, or hyperlinks are allowed. What makes the text understandable is the use of delimiters to separate the data. The use of a delimiter tells the receiving computer when the next data value begins. The most common file types that use delimiters are .csv, .txt, and .prn, as shown in Table 1.

File Type	Sample		
.csv — comma separated	ProductNum,ProductName,DateShipped,Quantity Shipped		
	59313,XL Golf Shirts,3/15/18,35		
	72316,Men's Shoe,2/5/18,10		
	47423,Head covers,3/6/18,20		
.txt — tab delimited	PNum	PName	Shipped	Quantity
	59313	XL Golf Shirts	3/15/18	35
	72316	Men's Shoe	2/5/18	10
	47423	Head covers	3/6/18	20
.prn — space delimited	PNum PName Shipped Quantity		
	59313 XL_Golf_Shirts 3_15_18 35		
	72316 Mens_Shoe 2_5_18 10		
	47423 Head_covers 3_6_/18 20		

Table 1 Common delimited text file formats

You can import a text file by simply clicking the File tab to open Backstage view, clicking Open, navigating to the file, and then clicking Open. This is a quick way to view the data, and it often works well enough for your immediate needs. However, if you want to take advantage of all the text import features, you can use the Text Import Wizard, which can be initiated by clicking the From Text button on the Data tab in Excel.

REAL WORLD ADVICE **More Advanced Features of the Text Import Wizard**

If you do not want to include all the headings or if there is a comment at the beginning of the file, you can tell Excel to start in any row below a target row so it will omit extraneous text. Sometimes Excel will incorrectly identify the language used in the text file, and this may throw off the Text Import Wizard. You can manually change this by clicking the File tab, clicking Options, and then clicking Language. Also, you will occasionally get a text file that is too big to import into Excel. By previewing the data in the Text Import Wizard, you can see exactly how much will be imported and can then split the file into two or more files, using one of the free file-splitting utilities, such as GSplit.

Red Bluff's web developer has exported some customer data from the new Red Bluff website and saved it as a text file. The customers in this list have indicated that they are interested in attending future golf tournaments. In this exercise, you will import the data from the text file into the Customers worksheet.

 **E09.06**

To Import Text Files

a. Click the **Customers** worksheet. On the Data tab, in the Get External Data group, click **From Text**.

b. In the Import Text File dialog box, navigate through the folder structure to the location of your student data files, and then double-click **e05ch09Customers**.

c. The Text Import Wizard recognizes that the file is delimited and has this option selected. Since the first line in the text file contains headings for the data, select **My data has headers**, and then click **Next**.

d. Notice that the sample data from the file is separated by commas. Under Delimiters, select the **Comma** check box, and then click as needed to deselect any other check boxes that may already be selected. Excel shows you a preview of how the data will be separated into cells when imported.

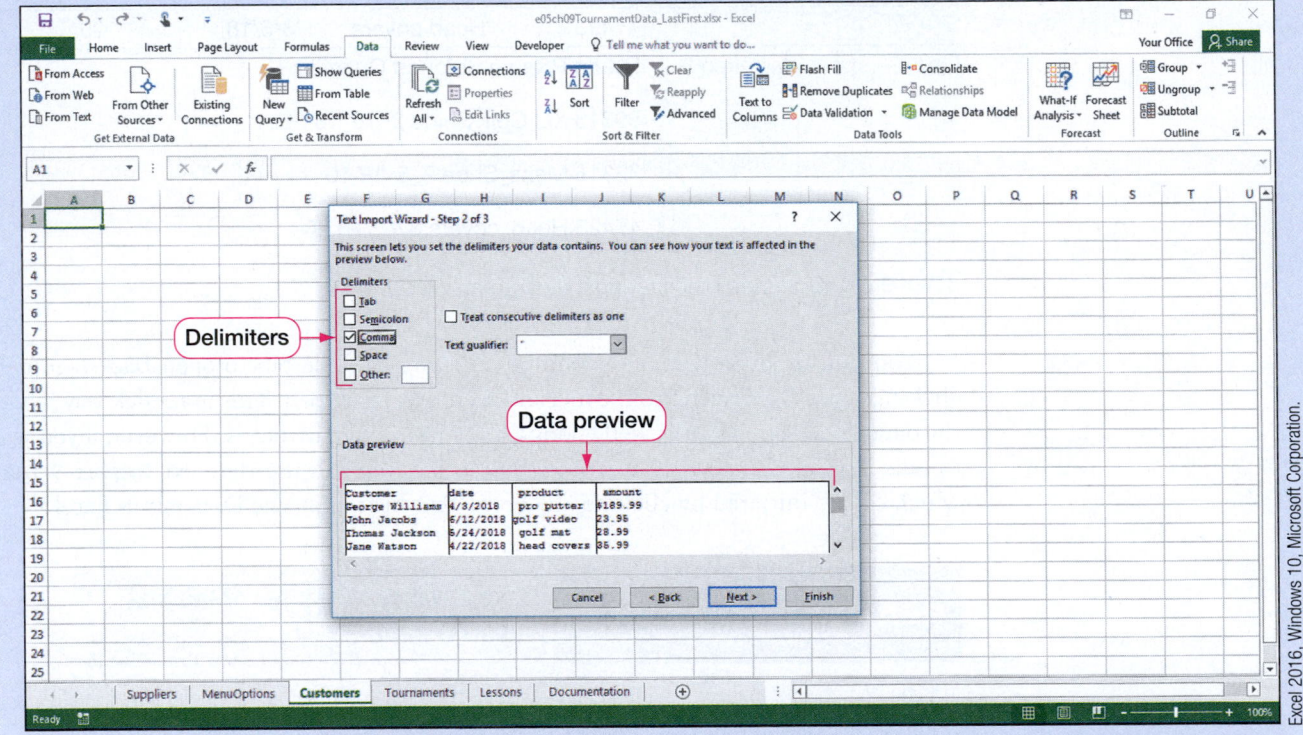

Figure 9 Importing a comma-delimited file

e. Click **Next**. Click **Finish**, and then in the Import Data dialog box, click **OK** to accept cell **A1** as the location to import the data.

f. **Save** 💾 the workbook.

Connect to an Access Database

Data may be collected and stored in a database such as Access and then imported into Excel. This process leverages Excel's powerful charting and analysis features. It also protects the data in the Access database, as Excel will import only a copy of the data, leaving the original data safely in the Access database. Over the years, Excel has evolved, making it easier to move data back and forth between Access and Excel. In this section, you will learn how to connect your Excel spreadsheet to the data in an Access database.

Connecting to an Access Database

At the most basic level, you can copy and paste data from an Access table into a blank Excel worksheet. Within Access, users also have the option of exporting tabular data into an Excel format. For longer-term projects, you can create a permanent connection between an Access database and the Excel application by using the Access Import feature. This live data can be imported as a simple table or even as a PivotTable report or PivotChart.

To understand how to import data from an Access database into Excel, it is important to review how the data is stored in Access. As a tool for using relational databases, Access stores data as a set of one or more tables. By definition, a **relational database** is a collection of tables linked together by shared fields. Each table consists of rows and columns, each row being uniquely identified by a primary key field. The **primary key** functions as a unique identifier for each row or record. Fields such as Customer_Number or Part_Number are commonly used as primary keys. Multiple tables are designed to be linked by joining a common field. In such cases, the primary key field of one table is connected to a common field of another table in which the field for the other table is not a primary key. This field is then known as a **foreign key** field when linked to a primary key field in another table.

With a little background, you can quickly understand the basics of relational databases such as Access. Figure 10 shows the tblPayments table from the Red Bluff Golf Course & Pro Shop database that tracks payments for upcoming tournaments. Across the top, you can see all the field labels, and each row represents a single payment record. The PaymentID field is the unique identifier for each payment. This field functions as the primary key field. The primary key is automatically generated by Access. Important data for the golf course and the pro shop is kept in other tables for employees, members, and member lessons. Information in each of these different tables is linked through the primary key in one table being shared as the foreign key in another table.

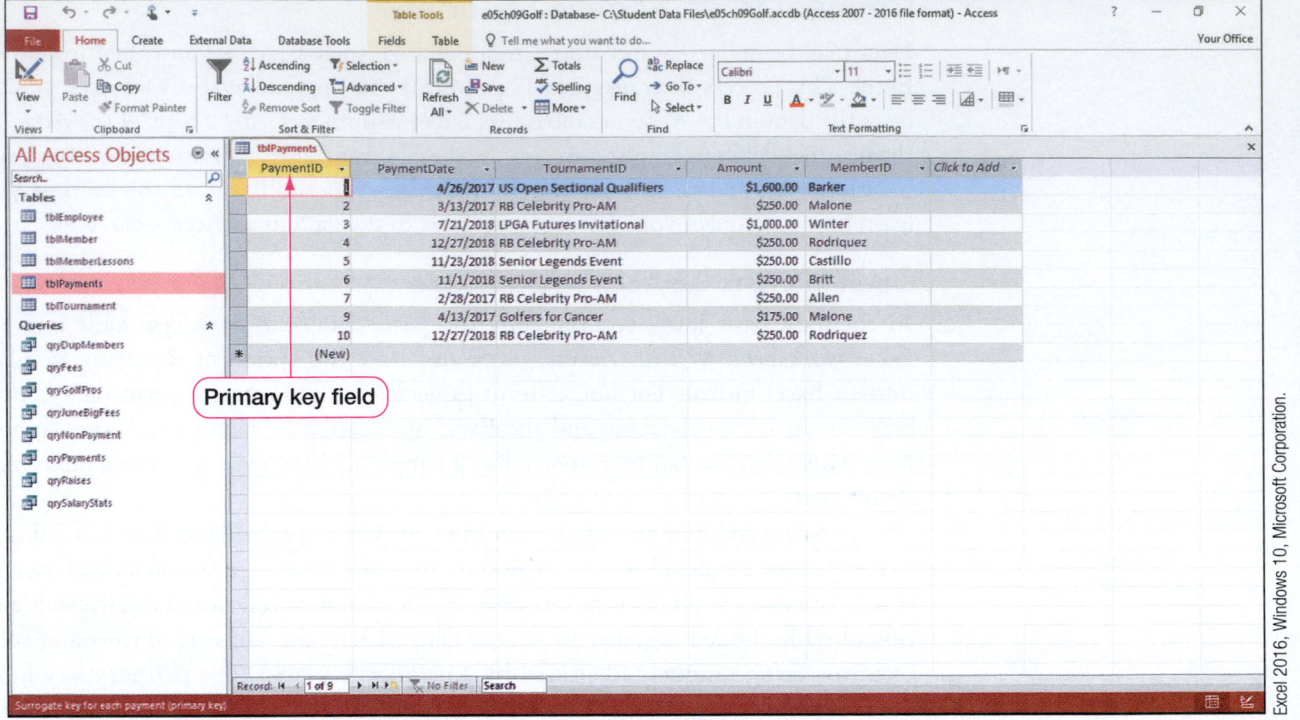

Figure 10 Payment table in Access for the Red Bluff Golf Course & Pro Shop

In this exercise, you will import the qryPayments query results from the Golf database into the Tournaments worksheet. This query organizes various data from the database concerning the tournaments that Red Bluff members have paid entry fees to attend. After the data has been imported into Excel, it can be analyzed further.

 **E09.07**

To Connect to an Access Database

SIDE NOTE

Drag Access Data into Excel

You can import tables and queries from Access by dragging the object from the Navigation Pane and dropping it into the desired starting cell.

a. Click the **Tournaments** worksheet.

b. On the Data tab, in the Get External Data group, click **From Access**. This will display the Select Data Source dialog box. Navigate through the folder structure to the location of your student data files, and then double-click **e05ch09Golf.accdb**.

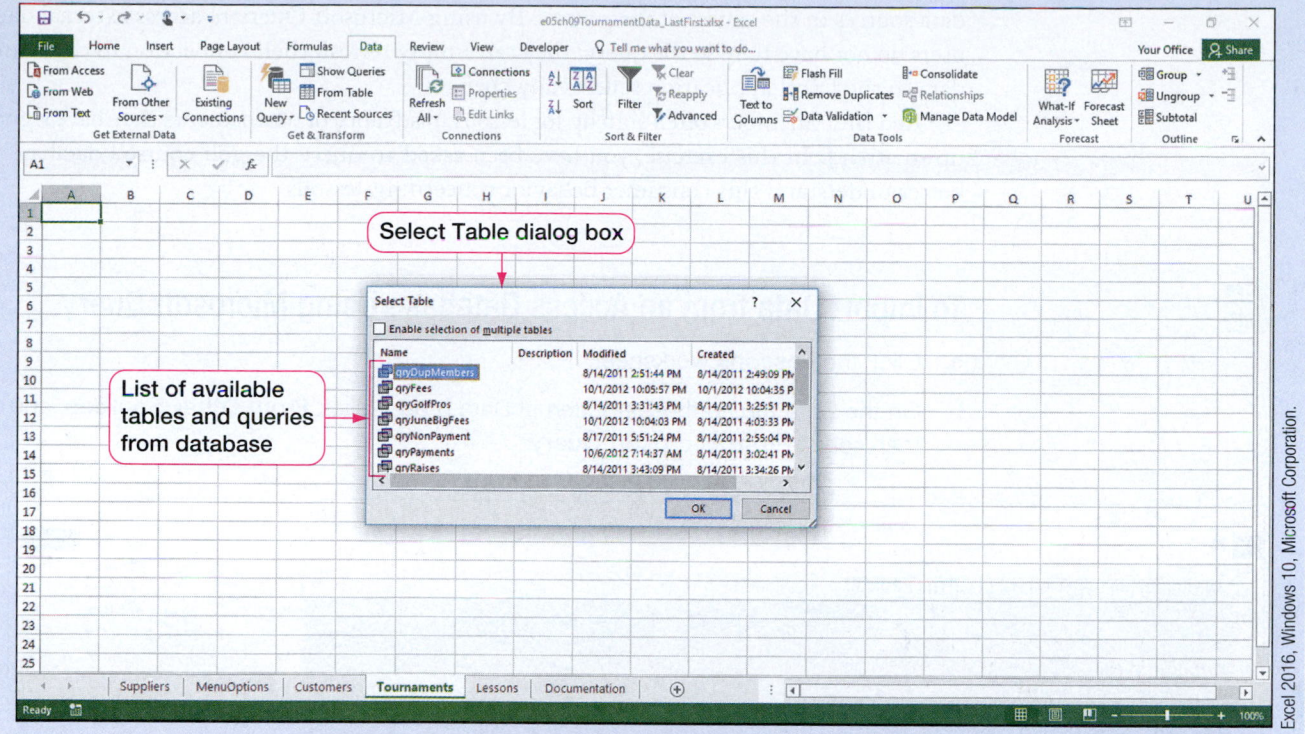

Figure 11 Connecting to an Access database

c. In the Select Table dialog box, select **qryPayments**, and then click **OK**.

d. The Import Data dialog box provides the option to import this data as a table, PivotTable Report, or PivotChart. Make sure the default option **Table** is selected, and then verify that the **Existing worksheet** option is selected and the input box displays =$A$1 to indicate that the data will be imported into cell A1.

e. Click **OK**.

f. **Save** 🖫 the workbook.

Importing Data from an Access Database Using Microsoft Query

Sometimes, instead of importing a complete table into an Excel worksheet from Access, users prefer to pick and choose specific fields. Perhaps you want to create a PivotTable report showing sales by region and country. **Microsoft Query** is a special tool to help users import individual data fields into their Excel applications. Excel has a query wizard built into its Microsoft Query function that can be a very powerful aid for linking a worksheet to an Access database.

QUICK REFERENCE	Microsoft Query

Microsoft Query has built-in drivers that make it easy to retrieve data from these common databases:

- Access
- SQL Server
- Paradox
- Oracle
- dBASE
- Text files
- FoxPro

It is very common for business users to use Excel to routinely access a wide variety of data sources in the course of their work. By using Microsoft Query to access external data, users do not have to redo the query; they can simply refresh their connection to the source data so the Excel application reflects any changes.

Red Bluff members often sign up for lessons in advance of tournaments they have signed up to attend. In this exercise, you have been asked to query the golf course's database to better understand this consumer behavior concerning lessons.

 **E09.08**

To Import Data from an Access Database Using Microsoft Query

a. Click the **Lessons** worksheet.

b. On the Data tab, in the Get External Data group, click **From Other Sources**, and then select **From Microsoft Query**.

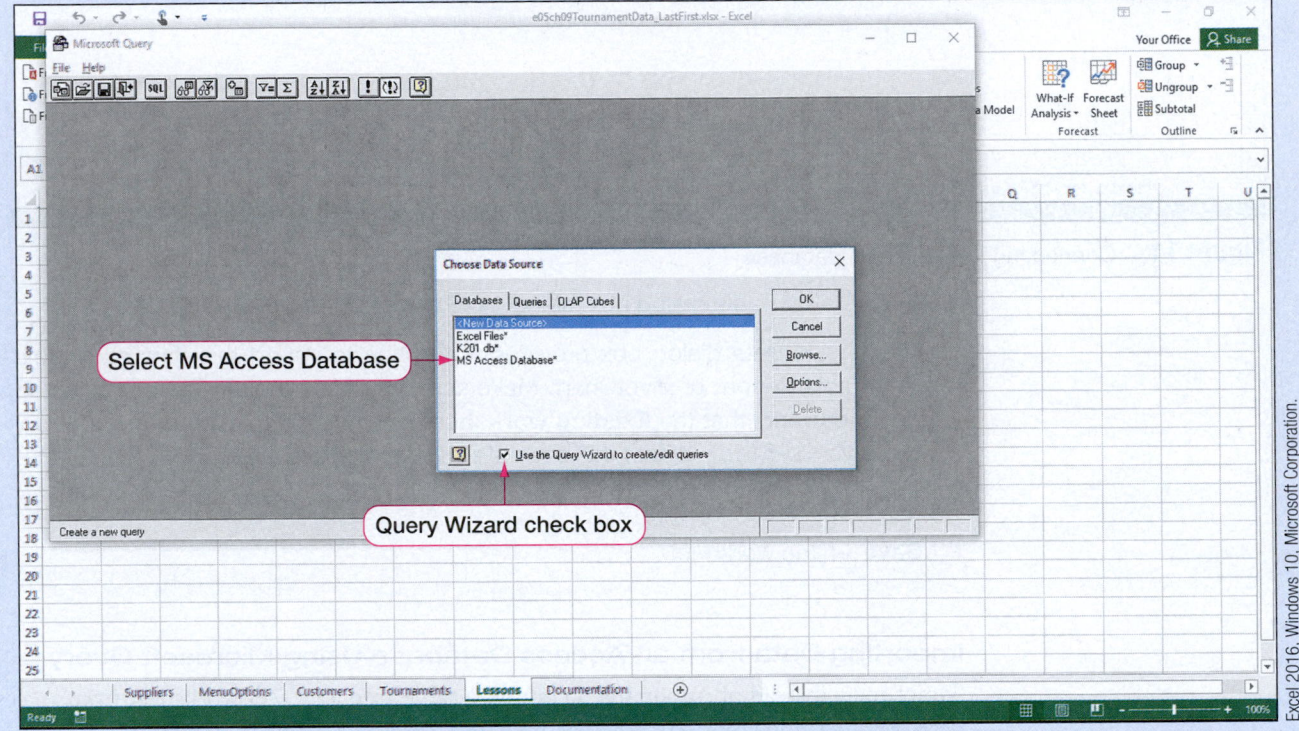

Figure 12   Connecting to an Access database with Microsoft Query

c. In the Choose Data Source dialog box, select **MS Access Database**, ensure that **Use the Query Wizard to create/edit queries** is checked, and then click **OK**.

d. In the Select Database dialog box, under Directories, double-click the **folder** where your student data files are stored, and then, under Database Name, select **e05ch09Golf**. Click **OK**.

e. In the Query Wizard - Choose Columns dialog box, scroll through the list of tables and columns until you see the qryFees query, and then click the **Expand Outline** button [+], to the left of qryFees, to see the available fields.

f. Double-click to select and move **LastName** to the Columns in your query box. Using the same technique, double-click the **FirstName**, **ScheduledDate**, and **Fee** fields to move them into the Columns in your query list.

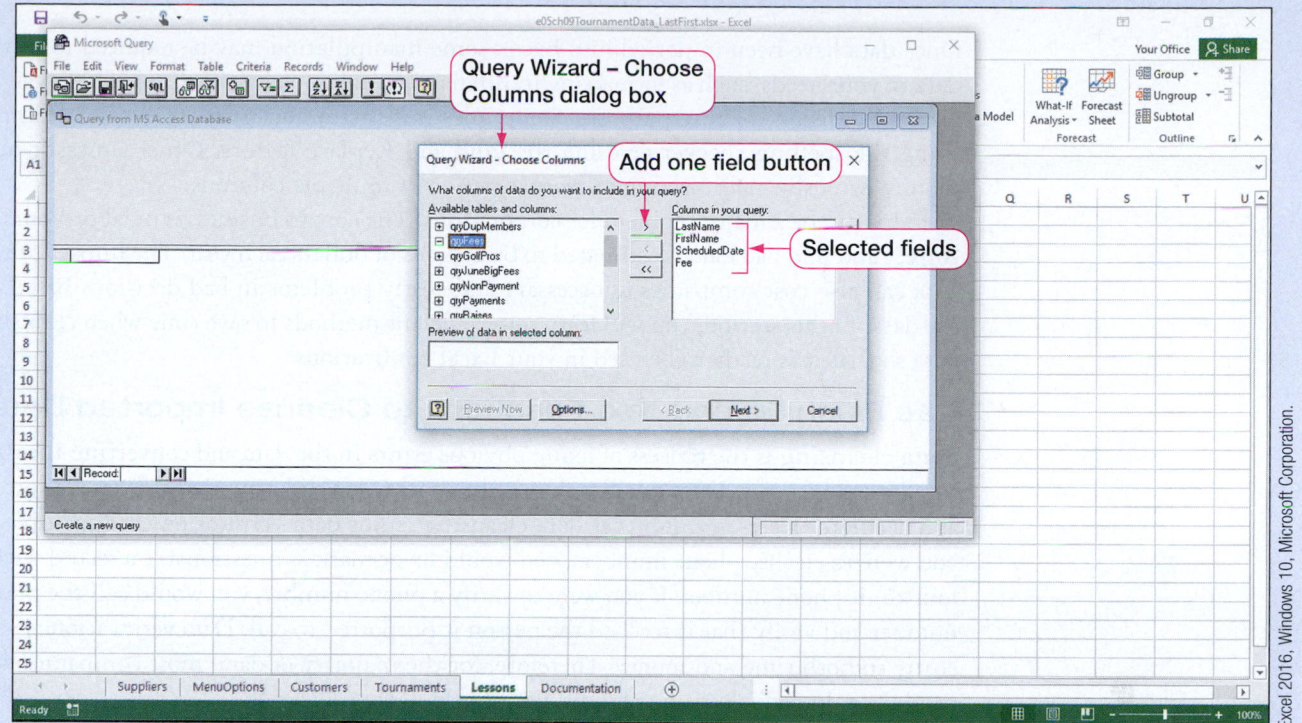

Figure 13   Selecting fields for Microsoft Query

g. Click **Next**, click to select the **ScheduledDate** field, click the first **Filter** arrow, and then click **is greater than or equal to**. In the input box to the right, type 6/1/2018.

h. Ensure that the **And** operator is selected, click the next **Filter** arrow, and then click **is less than or equal to**. In the input box to the right, type 6/30/2018.

i. Click **Fee**, click the first **Filter** arrow, and then click **is greater than or equal to**. In the input box to the right, type 150.

j. Click **Next**. Click the **Sort by** arrow, select **LastName**, and then accept the default Ascending order. Under Then by, click the **Sort by** arrow, select **FirstName**, and then keep the Ascending option.

k. Click **Next**, verify that Return Data to Microsoft Excel is selected, and then click **Finish**.

l. Verify that **Existing worksheet** is selected and that the input box displays =$A$1, and then click **OK**. The Access data is imported and displayed, starting in cell A1.

m. Complete the **Documentation** worksheet as directed by your instructor.

n. **Save** the workbook. Click the **File** tab, click **Close** to close the workbook, and then submit your files as directed by your instructor. If you need to take a break before finishing this chapter, now is a good time.

Making Data Useful

Once data have been imported into Excel, some manipulation may be required to fit the data to your needs, such as formatting it differently and cleansing the data before it can be used for decision-making purposes. Sometimes this is straightforward and entails simply using the spelling checker or using the Find and Replace feature. Other times, it may require extensive reformatting or reorganization of multiple columns.

This can be a major problem for corporations. The cost to businesses in labor-hours to correct and find bad data is estimated to be billions of dollars each year. The impact of bad data can also cost companies unnecessary and costly problems in bad decisions based on the data. In this section, you will learn some efficient methods to save time when cleansing data so that it is ready to be used in your Excel applications.

Use Flash Fill and Text Functions to Cleanse Imported Data

Data cleansing is the process of fixing obvious errors in the data and converting the data into a useful format. **Data verification** is the process of validating that the data is correct and accurate. Keep in mind that data cleansing is not data verification. For example, if you were to cleanse phone numbers, you would fix or mark as questionable a record with a four-digit phone number. If you were to verify a phone number, you would call the phone number and verify that it reached the person it purported to call. Data verification is very costly in both time and money. Therefore, for the majority of data, most companies will conduct only data cleansing and not necessarily data verification.

Using Flash Fill to Cleanse Text Data

Excel 2016 has a feature call Flash Fill that can make data cleansing easier and faster than using traditional text functions. **Flash Fill** recognizes simple patterns in data as you type and automatically fills in values for text and numeric data. Because Flash Fill involves less typing than traditional text functions, it can be easier to use on touch-enabled devices. Before you use the Flash Fill feature, there are a couple of key points to keep in mind. For Flash Fill to work, you must type in a column or row that adjoins your existing data. There cannot be a blank column or row between the data and where you are typing. Also, Flash Fill works only on relatively simplistic data sets and does not update automatically if data is changed or added.

Flash Fill works by examining the pattern of data in the cell next to where you are typing. If a pattern can be detected, a suggested fill will be displayed in the column in which you are typing. On the RegistrationData worksheet, the first names and middle initials of the customers from the tournament golf club giveaway are still in a single column. In this exercise, you will use Flash Fill to separate the First Name into a separate column so that letters can be prepared to send to the entrants.

 E09.09

To Use Flash Fill to Cleanse Text Data

a. Open the Excel file, **e05ch09TournamentReport**. Save your file as e05ch09TournamentReport_LastFirst, using your last and first name.

b. On the RegistrationData worksheet, click cell **B2**.

c. Type Rachel, and then press Enter to move to cell B3.

d. Type Charl.
    Notice that as you type, Flash Fill recognizes the pattern of the data you are trying to enter. A list of all of the first names from column A will appear as suggestions in column B.

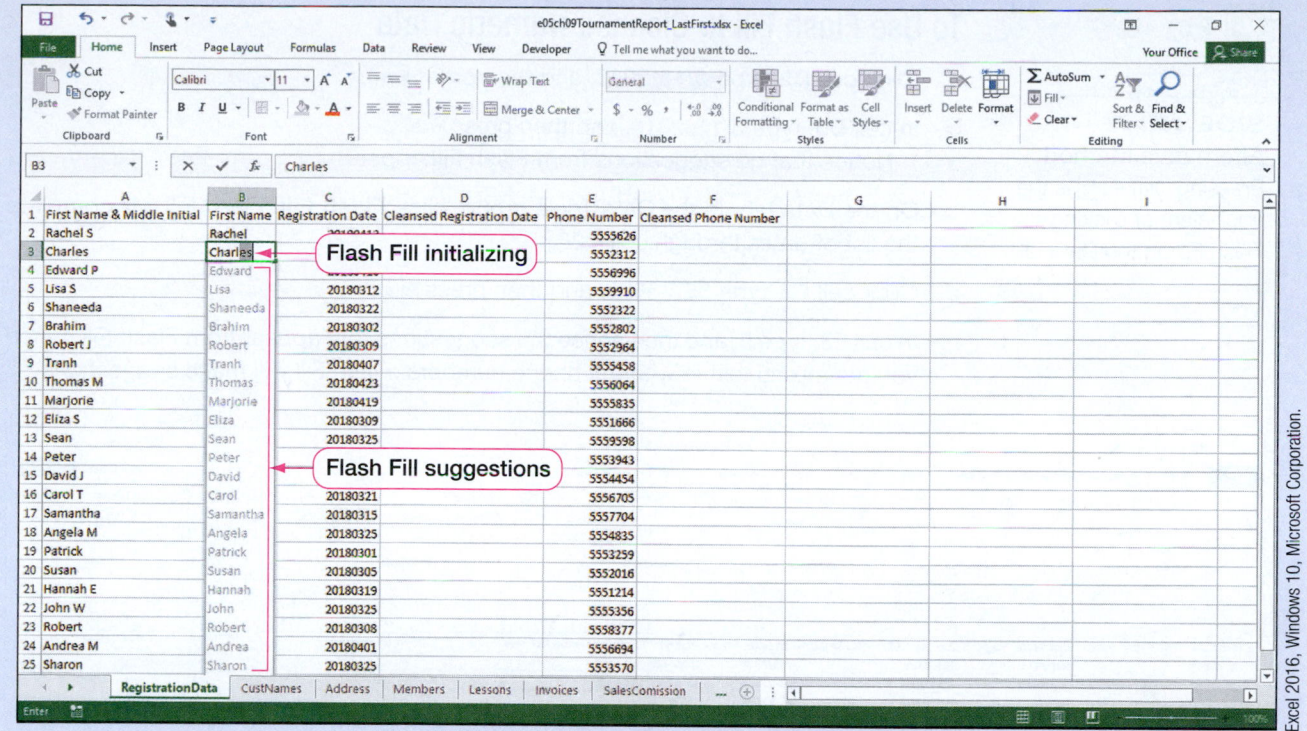

Figure 14 Using Flash Fill to cleanse text data

e. Press [Enter] to accept the changes suggested by Flash Fill.

> **Troubleshooting**
>
> Flash Fill relies on consecutive actions in order to offer a suggestion. If you click on another cell or press a button on the keyboard between typing "Rachel," pressing [Enter], and typing "Charles," Flash Fill will not offer a suggestion.

f. **Save** 🖫 the workbook.

Using Flash Fill to Cleanse Numeric Data

Flash Fill is disabled by default on numeric data. When using the Flash Fill feature on numeric data, you may need to provide an additional example of how the data should be arranged. The Flash Fill feature can then be used through the Data tab in the ribbon.

The registration dates that were provided are in numeric format but not in a format that Excel recognizes as a date. The dates provided are in YYYYMMDD format; for cell C2, the date appears as 20180413. Flash Fill can be used in this situation to reorganize the date into the MM/DD/YYYY format, or 4/13/2018 for cell C2. Additionally, the phone number in cell E2 was provided as 5555626 and needs to be displayed as 555-5626.

In this exercise, the registration date and entrant phone numbers will be properly formatted by using Flash Fill.

 **E09.10**

SIDE NOTE
Alternative Method
Pressing [Ctrl] + [E] is the equivalent of clicking Flash Fill on the Data tab.

To Use Flash Fill to Cleanse Numeric Data

a. Click cell **D2**, type 4/13/2018, and then press [Enter].

b. In cell D3, type 3/18/2018, and then press [Enter]. Notice that no suggestions from Flash Fill appear.

c. On the Data tab, in the Data Tools group, click **Flash Fill**. Flash Fill will complete the list of dates through cell D26.

d. Click cell **F2**, type 555-5626, and then press [Enter].

e. In cell F3, type 5, and then notice the suggestions that appear from Flash Fill. Since you are mixing text in with the phone numbers, Flash Fill will make suggestions.

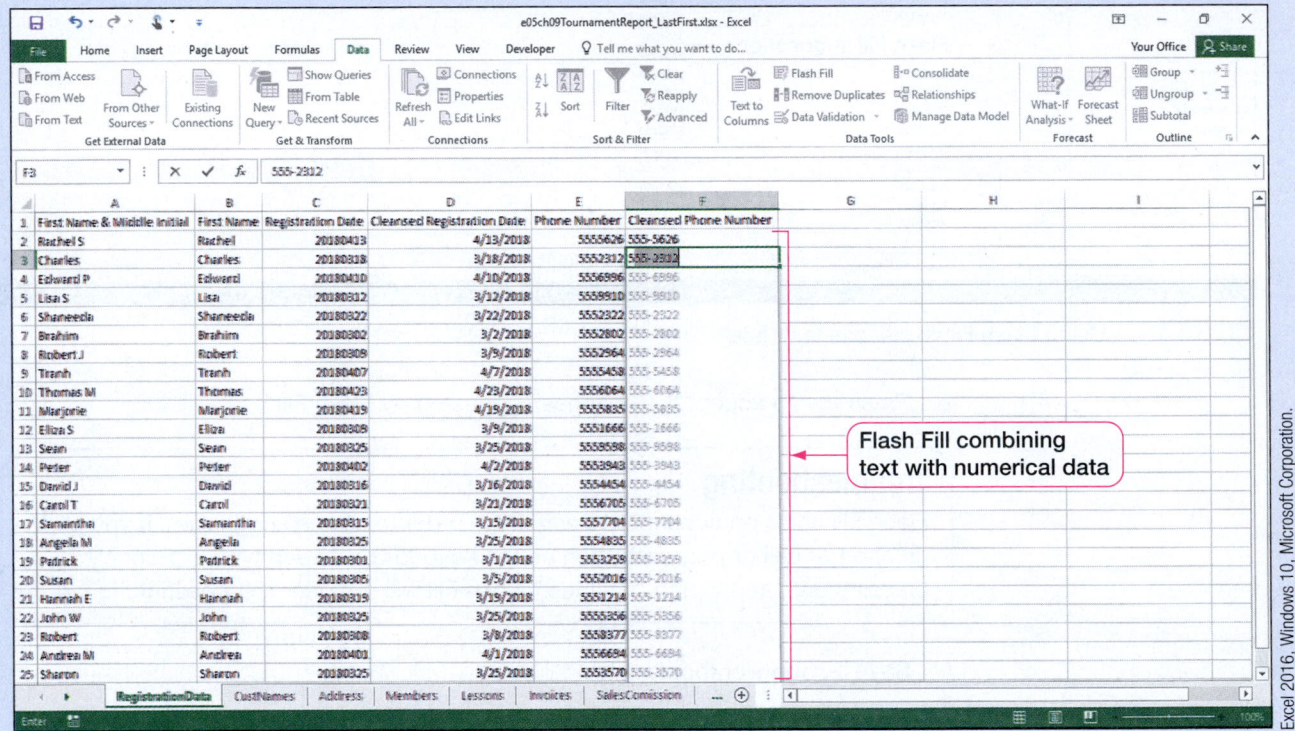

Figure 15 Using Flash Fill to cleanse numeric data

f. Press [Enter] to accept the suggestions.

g. **Save** 💾 the workbook.

Using Text Functions to Cleanse Data

Previously, you imported text data into Excel with some of the built-in tools. Recall that text data involves strings of characters. Do not be confused by this term, since it can include special characters, spaces, and numbers as well as letters. Text is a very generic data type. Often, data from external sources can easily be cleaned up with proper formatting, for example, formatting number values into currency values. Excel offers a range of **text functions** that help to manage text data. Excel text functions help to manipulate and standardize data and can offer additional tools to automate the process.

Common Text Functions

Function Name	Description	Example
CLEAN(text)	Removes any nonprinting characters from a text string. The CLEAN function removes the first 32 nonprinting character codes, but it does not remove nonprinting character codes for higher values.	If cell A2 contains =CHAR(6)&"text", =CLEAN(A2) will leave only "text".
LOWER(text)	Converts a text string to all lowercase characters.	=LOWER(Apt. 4B) will result in "apt. 4b".
PROPER(text)	Capitalizes only the first letter in each word of a text string; the remaining characters are in lowercase.	Given that cell A2 contains the string "this is a TITLE", =PROPER(A2) returns "This Is A Title".
TRIM(text)	Removes all spaces from text except for single spaces between words; this includes extra spaces at the beginning or the end of the string.	Given that cell A2 contains the string " profit margin", =TRIM(A2) would remove the extra spaces to yield "profit margin".
UPPER(text)	Converts all the characters in a text string to uppercase.	=UPPER("total") will result in the word "TOTAL".

**S
S** **CONSIDER THIS** | **Why Should You Care About Bad Data?**

Have you ever received mail in which your name or address was misspelled? This is one example of how bad data is propagated. At some point, your name was entered into a database incorrectly, and then that list of names was sold to others. Studies indicate that the total cost to businesses from bad data is well into the billions of dollars. How else does bad data get into the system? What are some basic steps you could take to prevent or minimize the problem?

Text functions help users to extract and standardize their data in ways that make life easier; a little knowledge of these functions can reap big rewards. One of the golf club manufacturers is sponsoring a hole-in-one prize for an upcoming tournament. If one of the tournament participants gets a hole in one on hole 9, he or she will receive a free set of golf clubs. To be eligible for the prize, customers filled out entry cards, and the information was entered into a database.

The formulas you use in other spreadsheet applications will malfunction when they encounter the irregular spacing found in the Name column of the spreadsheet you have been given (see Figure 16). Consider the contents of cell A2. The text is typed in all capital letters, and there are additional spaces and nonprinting characters. Only the first letter of each string of text should be capitalized. There is also an extra space between the "RACHEL" and the "S" that needs to be removed.

Three helpful functions can change the case of characters in a string of text. The **LOWER** function can be used to change uppercase characters to lowercase, and the **UPPER** function can be used to change all characters in a cell to uppercase. The **PROPER** function will capitalize only the first letter of each word in the text string while changing the other characters to lowercase. The **TRIM** function will remove extra spaces from a string of text.

The **CLEAN** function removes nonprintable characters, such as line breaks, but will leave other characters.

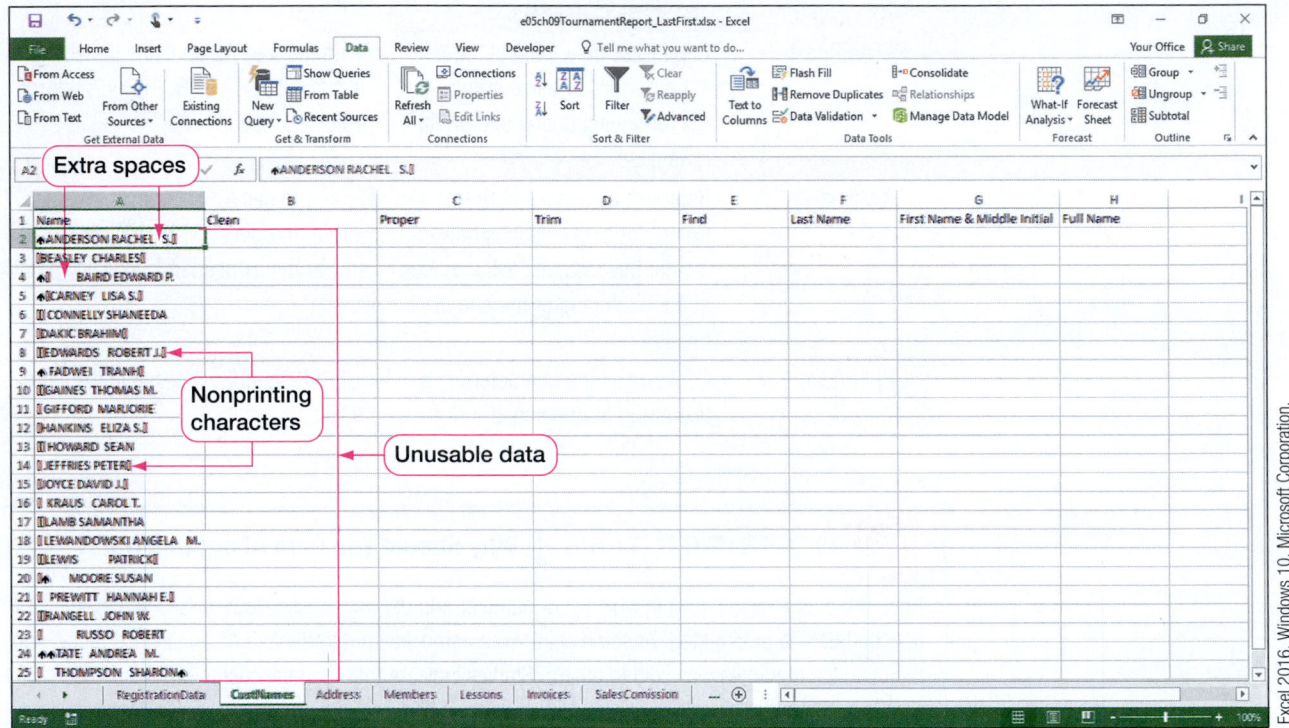

Figure 16 Unusable data needing to be cleansed

In this exercise, you will use text functions to cleanse the data in the spreadsheet.

 E09.11

To Use Text Functions to Cleanse Data

a. Click the **CustNames** worksheet, click cell **B2**, type **=CLEAN**, and then press Tab to insert the function. Click cell **A2**, and then press Enter to complete the function. Notice that the function has removed the nonprinting characters that were found on either side of the name.

b. Click cell **B2**, and then double-click the **AutoFill** handle to copy the function down to B26. Resize the columns as needed to fit the contents.

c. Click cell **C2**, type **=PROPER**, and then press Tab to insert the function. Click cell **B2**, and then press Enter to complete the function. Notice that the function capitalized only the first letter of each name; the rest of the characters were left in lowercase.

d. Click cell **C2**, and then double-click the **AutoFill** handle to copy the function down to C26. Resize the columns as needed to fit the contents.

Alternate Method

Text functions can be nested together to achieve more efficiency. =CLEAN(PROPER (TRIM(B2))) will provide the same result.

e. Click cell **D2**, type **=TRIM(**, and then press ⎯Tab⎯. Click cell **C2**, and then press ⎯Enter⎯. The TRIM function will remove any extra spaces before or after the names as well as extra spaces between names.

f. Click cell **D2**, and then double-click the **AutoFill** handle to copy the function down to D26. Resize the columns as needed to fit the contents.

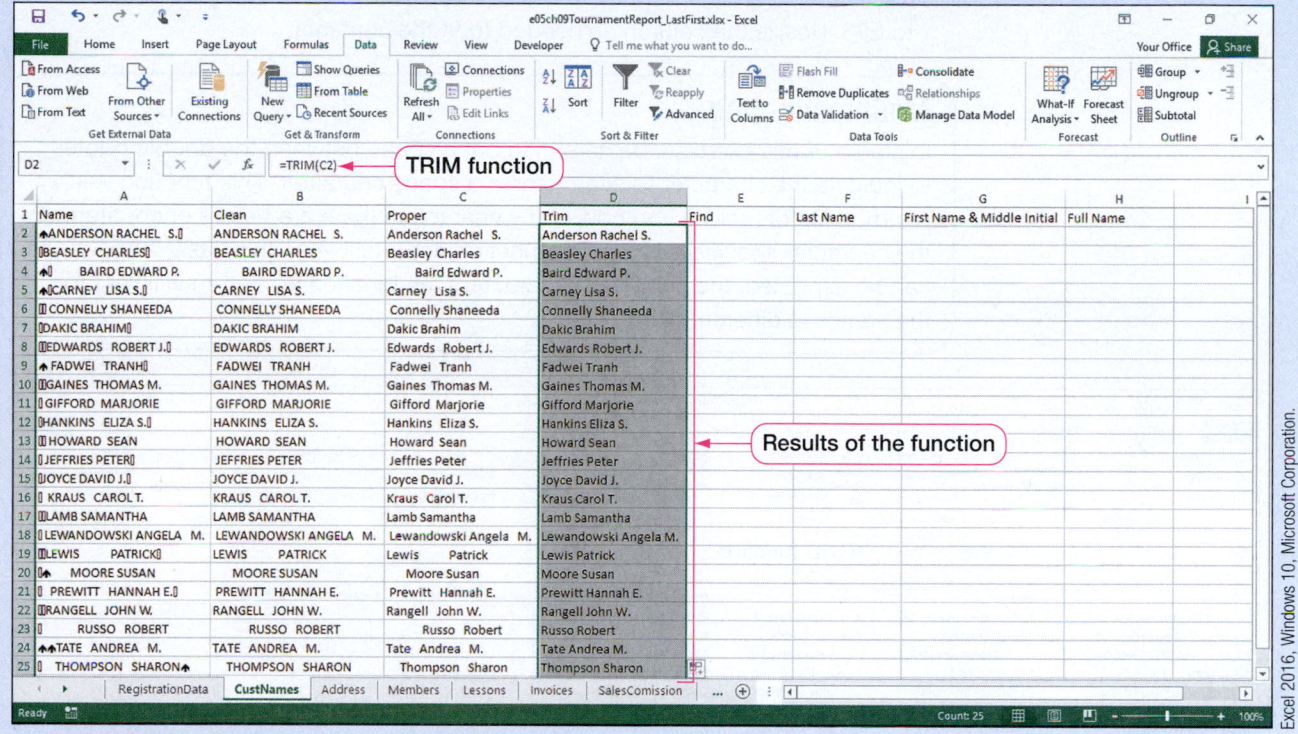

Figure 17 CLEAN, PROPER, and TRIM functions applied

g. **Save** 🖫 the workbook.

Manipulate Data Using Text Functions

Imported data can often contain strings of text that need to be manipulated in addition to being cleansed to be useful in a spreadsheet analysis. The text functions in Excel can be used to separate or reorganize strings of text so they can be better used.

Using the LEFT and FIND Functions to Separate Data

Consider the contents of cell D2 on the CustNames worksheet. For tasks such as mail merges, breaking the name into first, middle, and last columns would be useful. This can be accomplished in many ways. One method would be to find the space character between the last name and first name in the string of text. Once it has been located, everything in front of that space could be removed, leaving only the first name and the middle initial.

The **FIND** function is useful for finding where a specific string of text is located within a larger string. The FIND function returns a number that represents the position, from the left, where a specific string of text begins. The **LEFT** function can be used to extract a specific number of characters from a string of text beginning at the left side of the string.

In this exercise, you will use the LEFT and FIND function to separate the Last Name from the full name in column D.

 **E09.12**

To Use Text Functions to Separate Data

a. On the CustNames worksheet, click cell **E2**, type **=FIND**, and then press ⎆Tab⎆ to insert the function. Type **" "**, to use the space character as the find text, click cell **D2**, and then press ⎆Enter⎆.

    The FIND function returns the position number of first space character in cell D2. The position of this space character is important because throughout the entire column of names, the space character is always located just after the last name.

b. Click cell **E2**, and then double-click the **AutoFill** handle to copy the formula down to E26. Resize the column as needed to fit the contents.

> ### Troubleshooting
> In step a of this exercise, be careful to put a space between the double quotes to indicate the character to search for is a space character. This function will return a number telling you how many characters there are before encountering the character specified as the first function argument — in this case, a space. As can be expected, the number of characters the function will return will vary for the names in different cells.

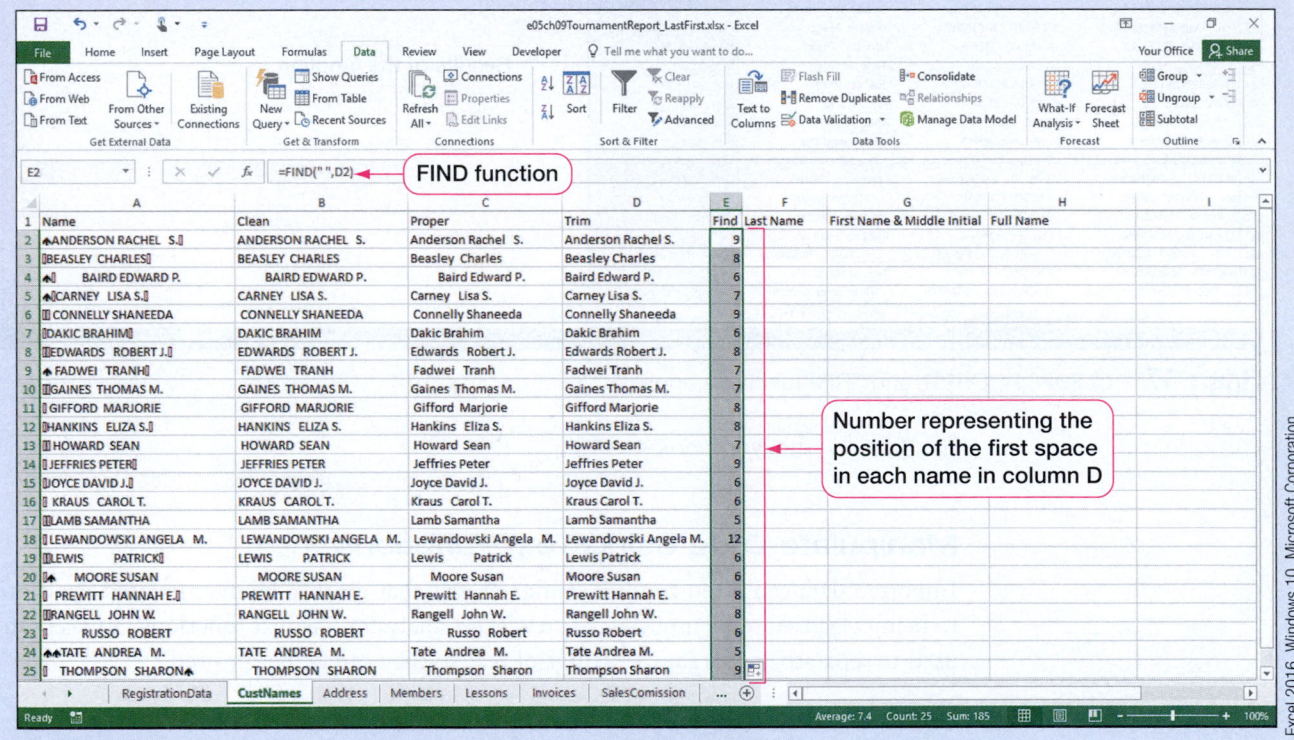

Figure 18 Using the FIND function

c. Click cell **F2**, type **=LEFT**, and then press ⎆Tab⎆ to insert the function. Click cell **D2**, type **,** and click cell **E2**, type **-1**, and then press ⎆Enter⎆.

d. Click cell **F2**, and then double-click the **AutoFill** handle to copy the formula down to F26. Resize the column as needed to fit the contents.

    The LEFT function examines the text in cell D2. The second argument tells the LEFT function how many characters to return from the left. Consider the last name in cell D2: "Anderson". This name is eight characters long. Since the space found in D2 occurs at the ninth position, you can subtract one from E2 to return the first eight characters.

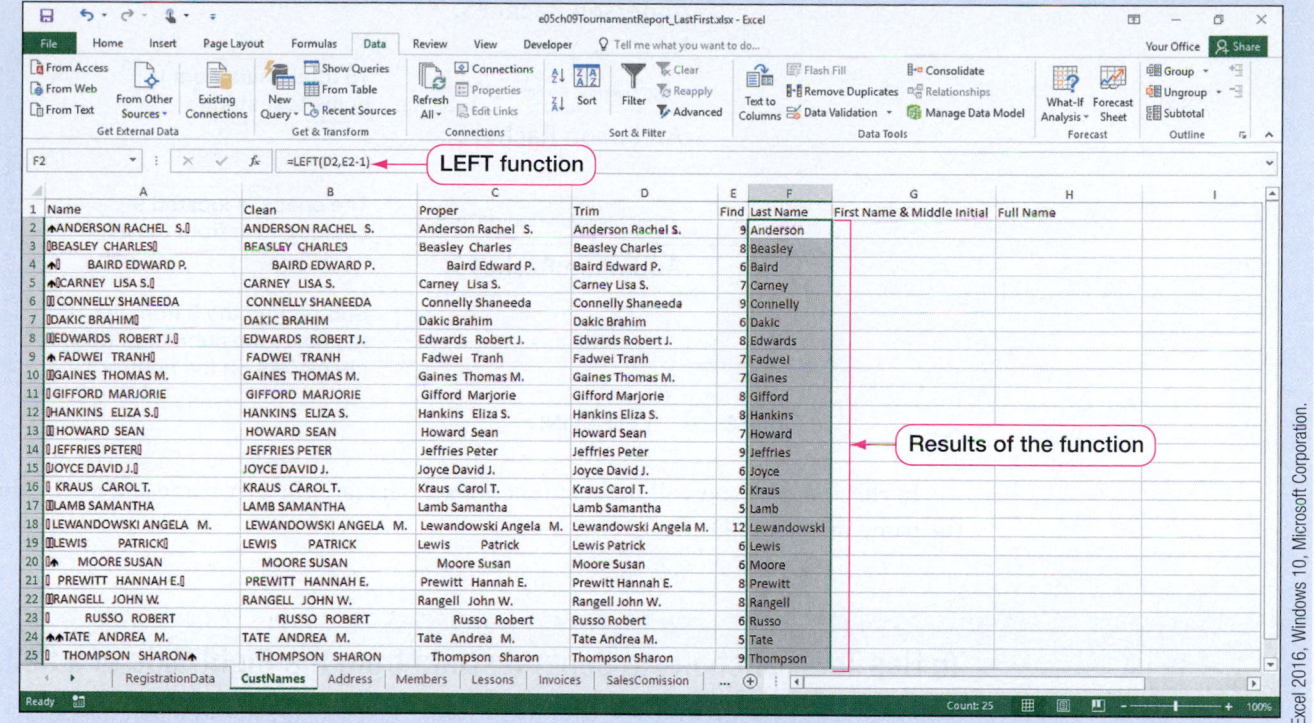

Figure 19 Using the LEFT function

e. **Save** 💾 the workbook.

Using Text Functions to Separate Data from the Right Side of a Cell

Again, consider the contents of cell D2 on the CustNames worksheet. The customer's first name and middle initial are located on the right side of the cell. To separate the data from the right side of a cell, it is best to use the RIGHT function. The **RIGHT** function can be used to extract a specific number of characters from a string of text beginning at the right side of the string.

There are challenges that are unique to using the RIGHT function, as it is the only text function that starts from the right side of a text string. If the desired number of characters is not a static number for all records in the data set, then the number of characters must be calculated by subtracting the result of the FIND function from the result of the LEN function.

The **LEN** function is a useful way to calculate the length of a specified string. The basic syntax contains only one argument: the string of text of which you want to know the length. So if you typed =LEN("Anderson Rachel S."), the function would return the result of 18, which includes the space characters and the period at the end. The FIND function, as you may recall, returns a number that represents the position, from the left, where a specific string of text begins.

Examine all of the names in column D, and you will see that the space character (" ") is what consistently appears directly to the left of the text to be extracted. So if you typed =FIND(" ", "Anderson Rachel S."), the function would return the result of 9, the location of the first space in the string. Subtracting the first 9 characters from the 18 total characters, results in 9, which is the number of desired characters from the right to extract "Rachel S.". See Figure 20 for an illustration of how these functions work together.

Making Data Useful   517

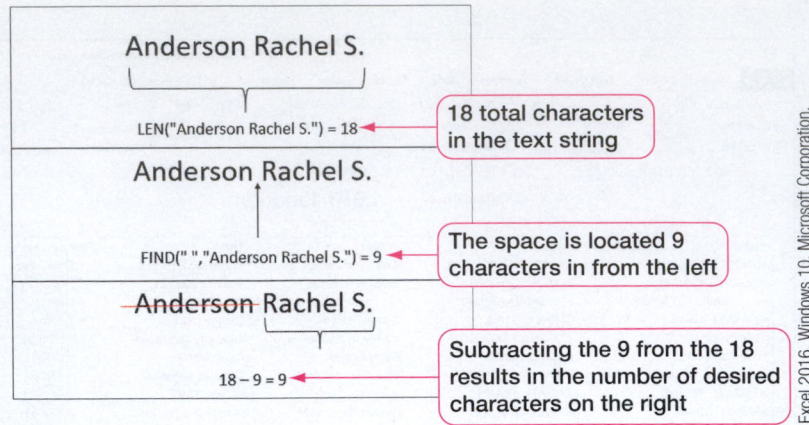

Figure 20 LEN – FIND

In this exercise, you will use text functions to separate the first name and initial from the name in column D.

 **E09.13**

To Use Text Functions to Separate Data from the Right Side of a Cell

a. Click cell **G2**, type **=RIGHT**, and then press Tab to insert the function. Click cell **D2**, type **,LEN**, and then press Tab to insert the function. Click cell **D2**, type **)-**, and then click cell **E2**. Type **)**, and then press Enter.

b. Click cell **G2**, and then double-click the **AutoFill** handle to copy the formula down to G26. Resize the columns as needed to fit the contents.

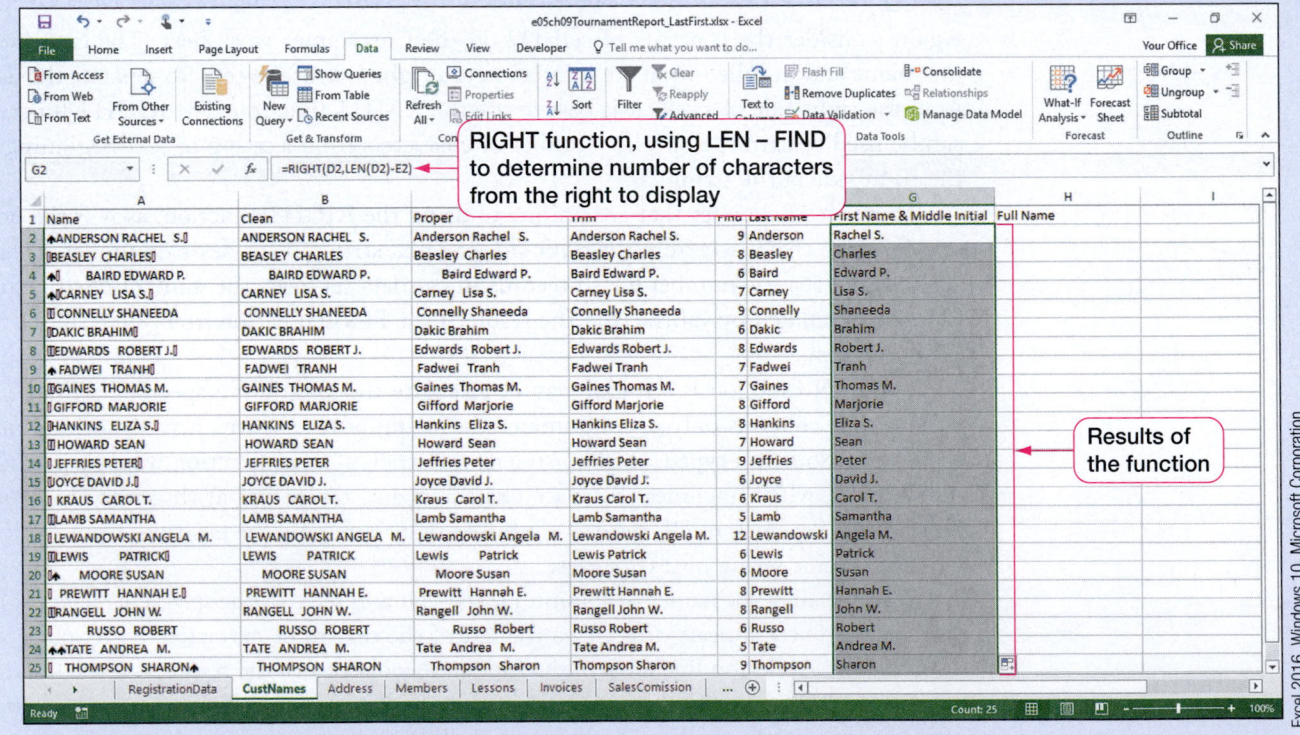

Figure 21 Text string separated from the right

c. **Save** the workbook.

Here are some additional text functions to consider along with a description of what each one does.

Function Name	Description	Example
CONCATENATE(Text1, [Text2], …[Textn])	This function is used to join up to 255 text strings into one text string.	=CONCATENATE(A1," ",B1) will return the value of A1, a space, and the value of B1 in one text string.
FIND(find_text, within_text, [start_num])	Locates a particular string of data within a second text string and returns the number of the starting position of the first text string from the starting position of the second text string. The "start_num" is an optional parameter giving a position within the string where the search will start. If the "start_num" is omitted, the position is assumed to be 1.	=FIND(" ","ABC corp.") will return the value of 4, since the space is the fourth character.
LEFT(text,[num_chars])	This function returns the characters in a text string based on the number of characters you specify, starting with the far-left character in the string. The text argument is a string of text or a cell reference to text data, and the num_chars argument specifies the characters to extract.	If cell A2 contains the text string "sale price", then =LEFT(A2,4) will return the word "sale".
LEN(text)	This function returns the number of characters, including spaces, in a text string.	If cell A2 contains the string "Excel 2016", then =LEN(A2) will return the number "10".
MID(text,start_num,num_chars)	This function returns a specific number of characters from a text string, starting at the position you specify and based on the number of characters you specify.	If cell A2 contains the string "purchase price", then =MID(A2,10,10) yields "price". It takes ten characters starting at the tenth position. If num_chars exceed the remaining string length, MID returns to the end of the string.
REPLACE(old_text, start_num, num_chars, new_text)	Replaces part of a text string, based on the number of characters you specify, with a different text string. Old_text is the original string, start_num is the position to start replacing text, num_chars is the number of characters to replace, and new_text is the new string to place in that position.	If cell A2 contains "2015", then =REPLACE(A2,3,2,"18") results in "2018" by starting at the third position and replacing two characters with "18".
RIGHT(text, [num_chars])	Returns the characters in a text string based on the number of characters you specify, starting from the far-right character position.	If cell A2 contains the string "item price", then =RIGHT(A2,5) will result in "price".

(Continued)

Function Name	Description	Example
SEARCH(find_text, within_text, [start_num])	Locates one text string within a second text string and returns the number of the starting position of the first text string from the starting character of the second text string. This function is not case sensitive.	If cell A2 contains the string "revenue", =SEARCH("e",A2,6) returns "7" as the position of the next "e" after the starting position of six characters. If the start_num argument value of 6 is omitted, the formula would return 2.
SUBSTITUTE(text, old_text, new_text, [instance_num]).	Similar to REPLACE. This function substitutes new_text for old_text in a text string. "Text" is the text string or the cell reference to text data.	If cell A2 contains "sales data", then =SUBSTITUTE (A2,"sales","cost") results in "cost data".

Concatenating Strings of Text

Concatenating data refers to combining or joining multiple strings of data to form a single string. In the current worksheet data example, the goal is to change the name order from the original version of last name, first name, and middle initial to a result of first name, middle initial, followed by last name. It would be useful to show it all together in a single field. The previous exercise separated the name data; all that is needed is to string it together in the desired order. There are a variety of ways to accomplish this in Excel. You can manually string together data using the ampersand (&), for instance, or you can use the CONCATENATE function to string together data to join into one cell.

CONCATENATE is a text function used to join up to 255 text strings into one text string. One of the advantages of using this function is that it allows the user to do some formatting of the data at the same time if needed, such as nesting the function in combination with the PROPER function to have the first character in each word capitalized.

In the data provided, the first name plus middle initial appears in column G, and the last name is stored in column F. In this exercise, you will join the data in columns G and F, using the ampersand, as it accomplishes the same thing as the CONCATENATE function with less typing.

 E09.14

To Concatenate Strings of Text

a. Click cell **H2**, then type **=**, click cell **G2**, type **&" "&**, click cell **F2**, and then press Enter.

b. Click cell **H2**, and then double-click the **AutoFill** handle to copy the formula down to H26. Resize the columns as needed to fit the contents. Cell H2 now displays "Rachel S. Anderson", combining the results of G2 and F2 with a space character between them.

> **Troubleshooting**
> Are spaces missing between the names in the final result? Check to see whether a space was typed between the double quotes in the formula. Recall that in addition to text from a cell reference, quotes can be used to string together additional characters — in this case, a space between the words.

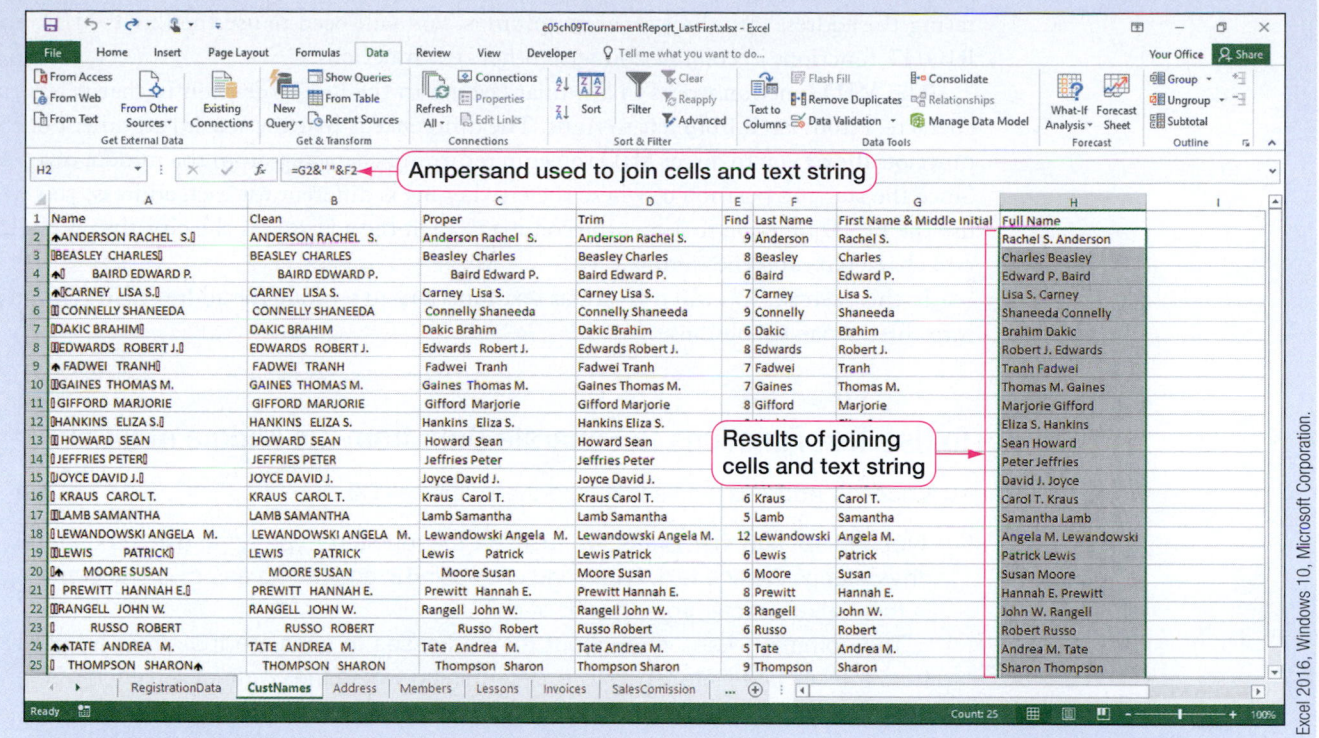

Figure 22 Using the ampersand to concatenate strings of text

c. **Save** 💾 the workbook.

REAL WORLD ADVICE | **Recognizing Data Patterns Is Important**

The secret to understanding how to cleanse your data is realizing that there are character patterns in the data. Delimiters such as commas and spaces in between words can become crucial signposts that the resourceful Excel user can exploit with text functions. When you see a character pattern in your data, you can use the FIND function to find just about anything, especially commas and spaces. Once you start looking for character patterns, you will be amazed at how many there are.

CONSIDER THIS | **Variations in Data Entry**

Given the sample name data in the CustNames worksheet exercises, what formula or formulas could be used to extract the middle initial data? What if some of the data contained a full middle name. What formula(s) could be used to take into account this variation in data?

Using Text Functions to Separate Data from the Middle of a Cell

On the Address worksheet, you have been provided with a list of addresses for members who have registered for an upcoming tournament. However, the addresses are all in one column, making it very difficult to conduct any analysis on where the members are located or to properly format the addresses for creating address labels for any upcoming mailings. Separating these addresses from a single address column into three final columns — Street Address, City, and State — will make it easier to conduct such analyses.

Examine the address in cell B2. Notice that there are three parts to the address: The street address is located in the left side of the cell, the city is located in the middle of the cell, and the state is located in the right side of the cell. To accomplish the task of separating the address into three separate columns, you will need to use the LEFT, MID, and RIGHT functions in conjunction with other text functions.

The **MID** function works in a similar fashion to the LEFT function in that it returns characters from a cell from left to right. The difference is that the second argument of the function allows you to direct MID to begin returning characters from the middle of a cell. Since the starting position of where the city begins is different for each address, you will use the FIND function to locate the comma (", ") in the address, as the city always begins two characters after the comma.

In this exercise, you will use various text functions to separate the addresses in column B into three separate columns.

 **E09.15**

To Use Text Functions to Separate Data from the Middle of a Cell

a. Click the **Address** worksheet, and then click cell **C2**.

b. Type **=FIND**, and then press Tab to insert the function. Type **","** to use the comma character as the find text, type **,** and click cell **B2**, and then press Enter. The comma is the 15th character from the left of cell B2.

   The comma is used throughout the addresses to separate the street address from the city and state. Therefore, determining where the comma is in each of the addresses will prove to be very useful.

c. Click cell **C2**, and then double-click the **AutoFill** handle to copy the formula down to C17.

d. Click cell **D2**, type **=LEN**, and then press Tab to insert the function. Click cell **B2**, and then press Enter.

   Determining the total length of the address will be useful in calculating how many characters to extract for the city part of the address.

e. Click cell **D2**, and then double-click the **AutoFill** handle to copy the formula down to D17.

f. Click cell **E2**, type **=LEFT**, and then press Tab to insert the function. Click cell **B2**, type **,** and click cell **C2**, type **-1**, and then press Enter.

   By subtracting one character from where the comma is positioned, the first 14 characters are extracted from the left.

g. Click cell **E2**, and then double-click the **AutoFill** handle to copy the formula down to E17.

h. Click cell **F2**, type **=MID**, and then press Tab to insert the function. Click cell **B2**, type **,** and click cell **C2**, and then type **+2,**. Click cell **D2**, type **-**, and then click cell **C2**. Type **-3**, and then press Enter.

   This extracts only the city from the middle of the address. The MID function begins extracting text in cell B2 at the 17th position. This position is used because the comma position in C2 is 15 and the city begins two characters after the comma. The third argument of the MID function dictates how many characters to extract from cell B2. Taking the length of B2 — 27 characters — and subtracting the number of characters up to and including the comma, 15, would result in "Santa Fe NM". Since you do not want to include the state abbreviation or the space after the city, you subtracted an additional three characters from the third argument.

i. Click cell **F2**, and then double-click the **AutoFill** handle to copy the formula down to F17. Resize the columns as needed to fit the contents.

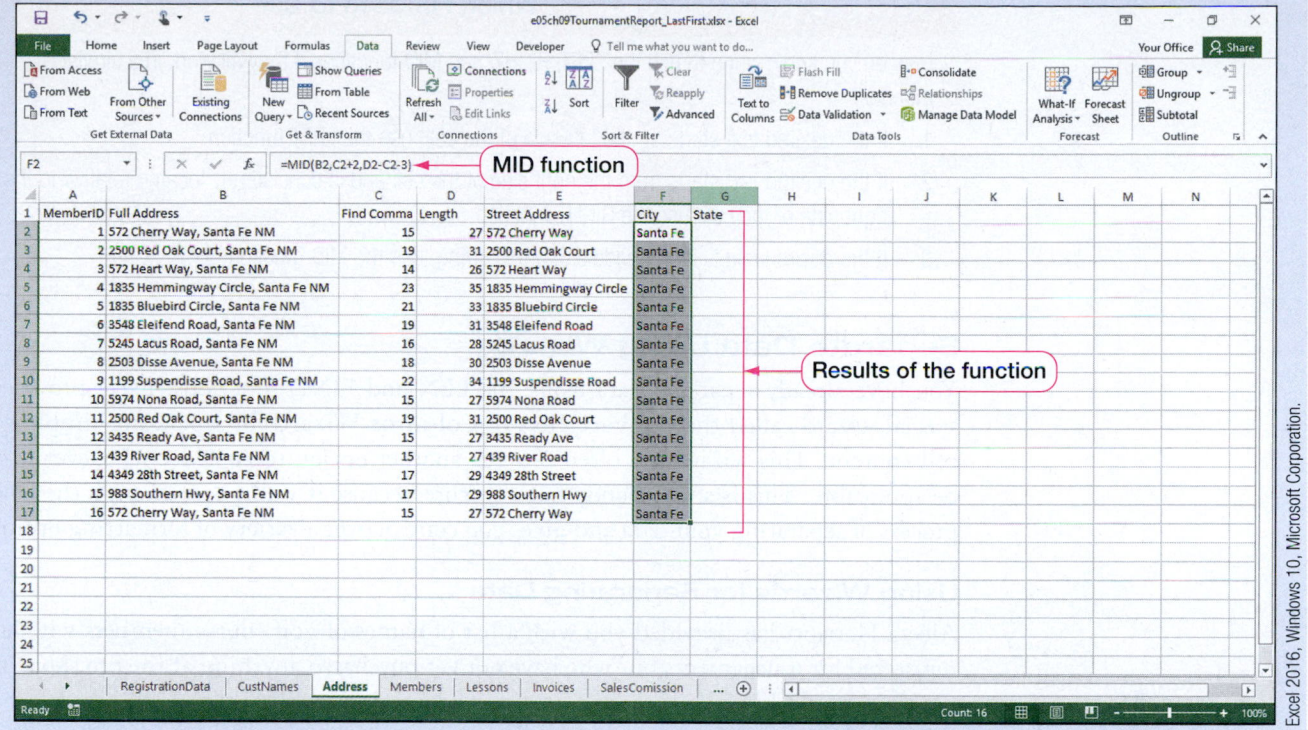

Figure 23   Using the MID function

> **j.** Click cell **G2**, type **=RIGHT**, and press Tab to insert the function. Click cell **B2**, type **,2**, and then press Enter.
>
> **k.** Click cell **G2**, and then double-click the **AutoFill** handle to copy the formula down to G17. This will extract the first two characters from the right of the text string in cell B2. Resize the column as needed to fit the contents.

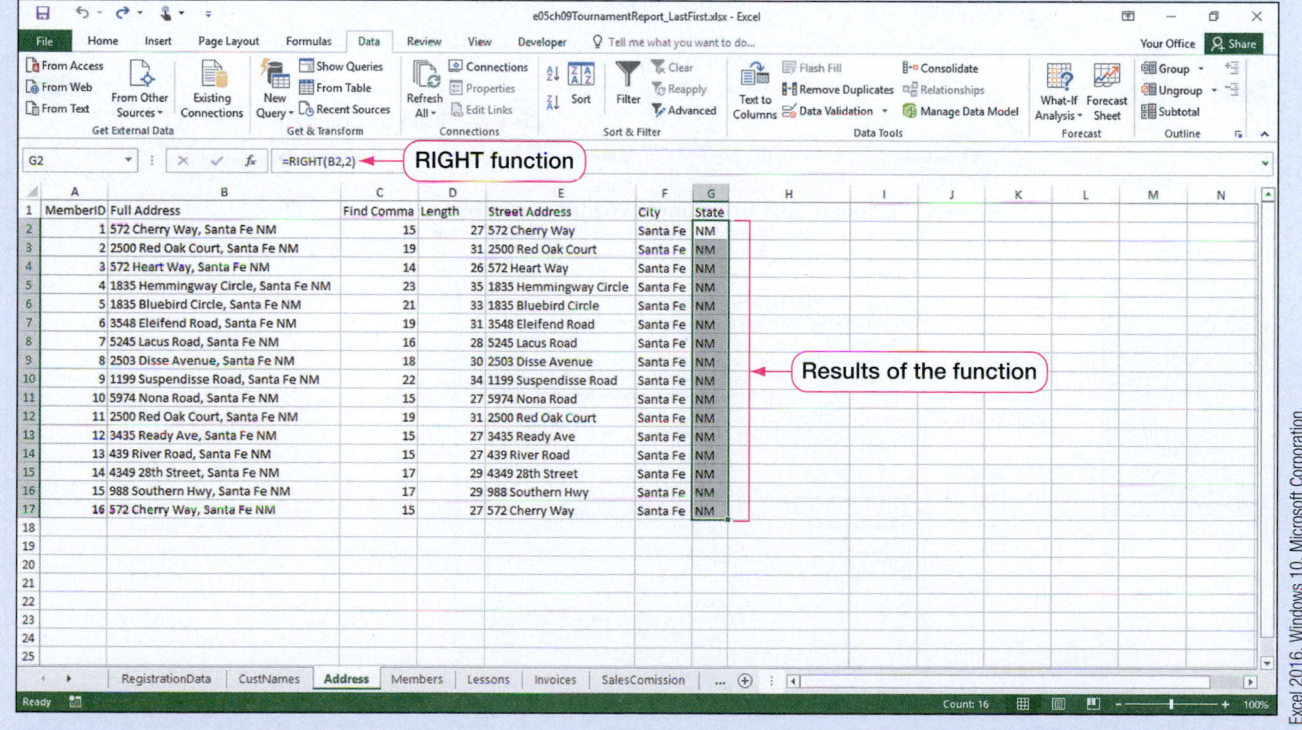

Figure 24   Results of the RIGHT function

> **l.** **Save** 💾 the workbook.

How do you know when to use the LEFT, RIGHT, and MID functions if they all work in a similar manner?

1. If the desired text starts on the left side of the cell, use the LEFT function.

2. If the desired text starts from the right side of the cell and is consistently located relative to the right side of the cell, use the RIGHT function.

3. If the desired text is in the middle of a text string, use the MID function.

Separate Data Using Wizards

You have already separated data using the LEN and FIND functions. Excel provides a special wizard called the **Convert Text to Columns Wizard** for separating simple data cell content. This wizard can often provide another option to consider whenever it can be applicable. This is a very handy Excel feature because it walks you through the whole process of separating your data and gives you control over a variety of formatting options.

Using Wizards for Separating Data

Aleeta Herriott has provided you with a list of names of golf course members who have registered for tournaments but who have not yet purchased anything at the pro shop. The pro shop would like to target them in a new promotion to offer them a 10% discount. In this exercise, you will separate the name data into two separate fields, using the Convert Text to Columns Wizard.

 E09.16

To Use Wizards for Separating Data

a. Click the **Members** worksheet, and then select cells **A2:A14**.

b. On the Data tab, in the Data Tools group, click **Text to Columns**.

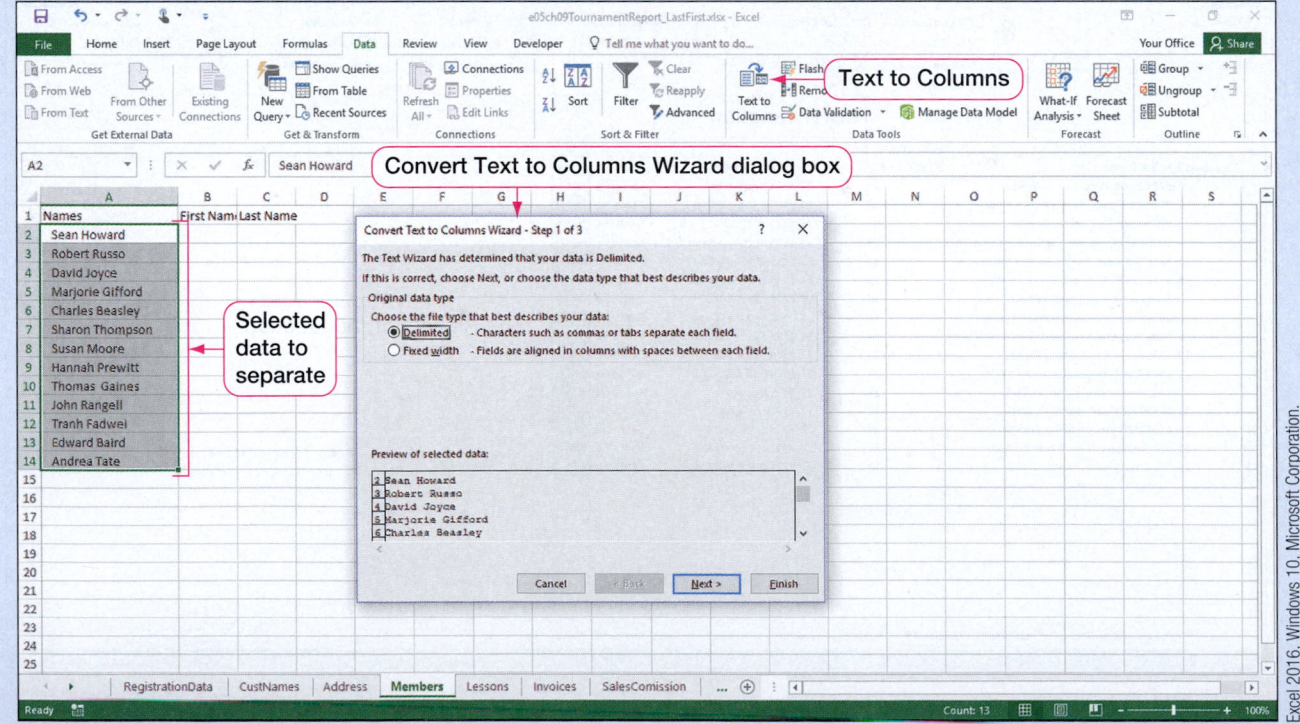

Figure 25 Convert Text to Columns Wizard

c. In the Convert Text to Columns Wizard, under Choose the file type that best describes your data, make sure **Delimited** is selected, and then click **Next**.

d. Under Delimiters, select the check box next to **Space**, click to uncheck the check box next to **Tab**, and then click **Next**.

e. Click in the **Destination** box, change the destination cell reference to $B$2, and then click **Finish**.

> ### Troubleshooting
> By default, the Convert Text to Columns Wizard will begin the output of the data in the first cell you selected. The result will be to paste the separated data over the original data. It is best practice to change the destination cell to begin to the right of your original data if possible.

f. Resize columns **B** and **C** as needed to fit the contents.

g. **Save** 🖫 the workbook.

REAL WORLD ADVICE   **Wizard Versus Text Functions Versus Flash Fill**

There are many tools in Excel to cleanse and reorganize data. The main goal is always to reach for the tool that fulfills the goal at hand in the most efficient manner. Now that you have seen how to separate data with text functions, Flash Fill, and the Convert Text to Columns Wizard, how do you know which one to choose over the others?

- The Convert Text to Columns Wizard is designed for simple cell content, so if you are separating text data rarely and the data fits the requirements of the wizard, the Convert Text to Columns Wizard will be the easiest and most efficient to use.

- If you will be converting data repetitively or the data consistently comes from an external source and needs to be cleaned up, text functions are the best option.

- Flash Fill works well with consistently organized data and is optimized for working on touch-enabled devices.

Removing Duplicates

It is easy to enter a customer contact more than once or to have multiple customer entries when merging customer data from multiple sources. This is one of the most common data entry errors. Even when steps are taken to minimize redundant data, there is a chance that duplicate entries will still result.

Excel provides an easy tool for removing duplicate entries: the **Remove Duplicates** button found on the Data tab in the Data Tools group. In the Remove Duplicates dialog box, you specify which columns you want the wizard to check. Excel searches whichever columns you have selected and prompts you to remove any duplicates that it finds. However, use this tool with caution, since it will not show what Excel is about to delete.

You have been asked to examine data that was manually entered concerning golf lessons attended by members of the golf club before a tournament in the past year. Since each member can attend only one lesson per day, any duplicate values should be removed. The record contains the member's last name, date of the lesson, and fee. In this exercise, you will use the Remove Duplicates tool to remove any duplicate entries on the Lessons worksheet.

 **E09.17**

To Remove Duplicates

a. Click the **Lessons** worksheet, and then select the data in cells **A2:C18**.

b. On the Data tab, in the Data Tools group, click **Remove Duplicates**.

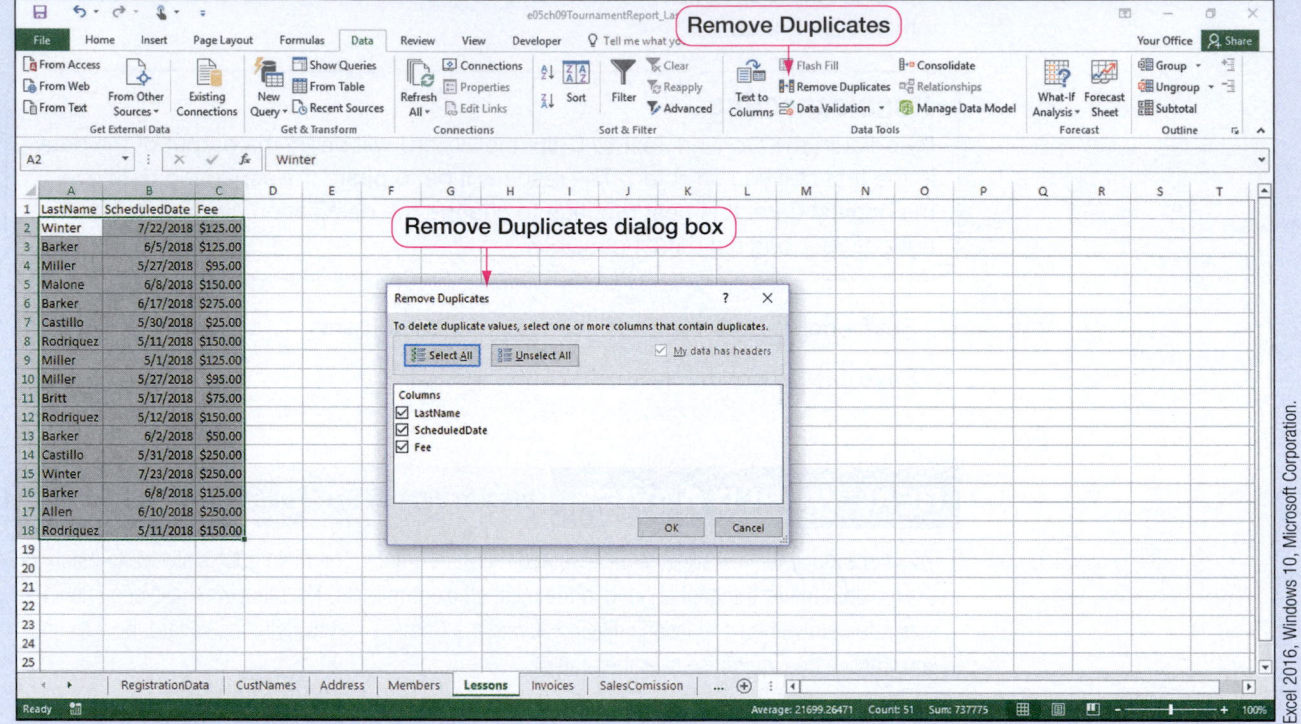

Figure 26 Remove Duplicates dialog box

c. Ensure that all three columns are selected to check for duplicates, and then click **OK**.

d. Excel returns a message saying 2 duplicate values found and removed; 15 unique values remain. Click **OK**.

e. Save 💾 the workbook.

REAL WORLD ADVICE | **Identifying Duplicate Data**

Identifying duplicate data can be a time-consuming and challenging task. While the best practice is to use a unique identifier or primary key for each record, duplicate data can still be created. Before removing data from a data set, be sure to thoroughly investigate the records to ensure that they are true duplicates.

Using Conditional Formatting to Identify Duplicates

In the previously discussed methods for removing duplicates, Excel automatically deletes the records once it finds them and you click OK, without specifying which records were deleted. If it is necessary to examine the records first, you can identify duplicates by using conditional formatting. Before Excel 2007, you had to write a complex logical test formula with conditional formatting to achieve the same result. Recent versions of Excel have made this task much easier to perform. With the Conditional Formatting feature, Excel has a special predefined rule for identifying duplicate values.

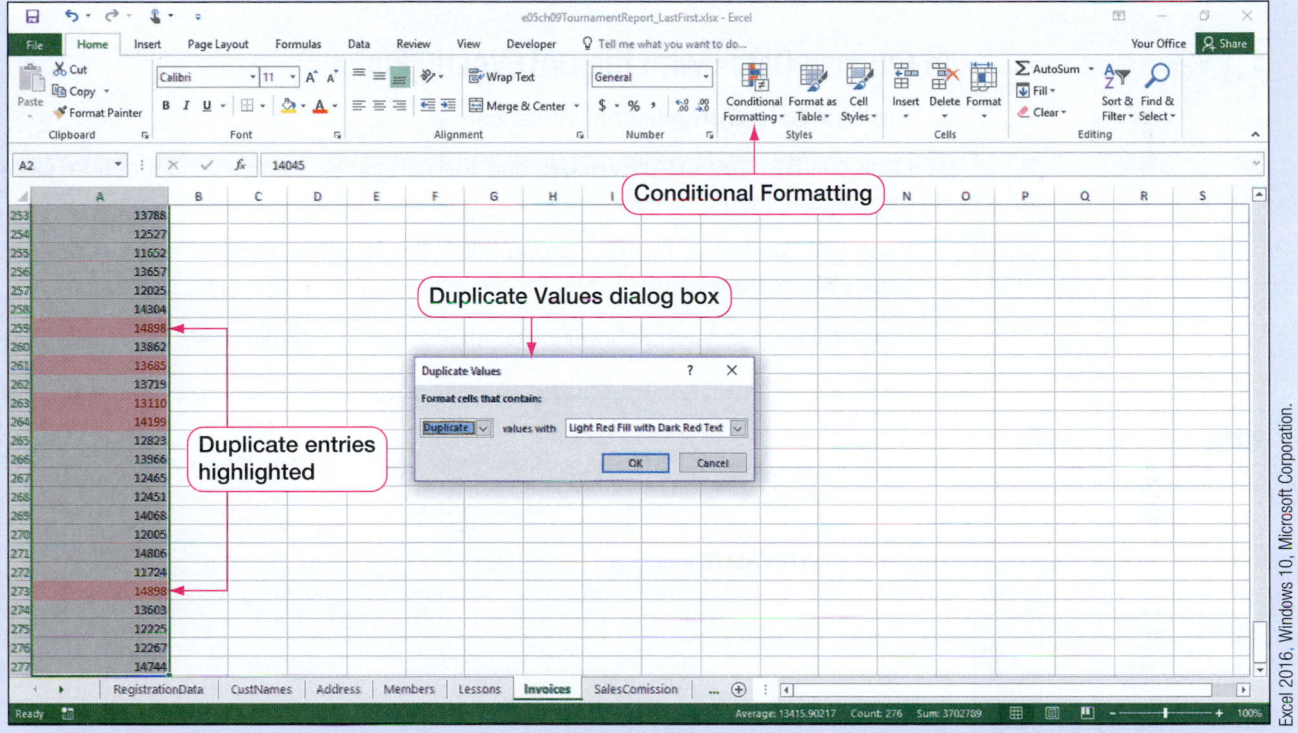

The accounts manager at the Red Bluff Golf Course & Pro Shop has asked you to go through a list of invoices for items related to several past tournaments to identify whether there are any duplicates among them. In this exercise, you will not be deleting any of the data; rather, you will simply highlight duplicate records for further investigation. In viewing the long list of numbers, it is apparent that the most efficient and simplest method would be to create a conditional formatting rule in Excel to highlight any duplicate invoices.

E09.18   To Use Conditional Formatting to Identify Duplicates

a. Click the **Invoices** worksheet, click cell **A2**, and then press Ctrl + Shift + ↓ to select cells A2:A277.

b. Click the **Home** tab, and in the Styles group, click **Conditional Formatting**.

c. In the gallery that appears, point to **Highlight Cells Rules**, and then select **Duplicate Values**.

Figure 27   Using Conditional Formatting to identify duplicates

d. Accept the default entries in the Duplicate Values dialog box, and click **OK**. The duplicate values are now highlighted.

e. Press Ctrl + Home to return to cell A1. In the Editing group, click **Sort & Filter**, and then click **Sort A to Z**. This will allow for easier viewing of the duplicate records.

f. **Save** the workbook.

Cleanse Date-Related Data

One of the biggest problems in combining data from a variety of sources is coming up with a standard date format. Some users include a full, four-digit year: others use two digits. Some include a zero with single-digit months; others do not. Furthermore, different countries order the date components completely differently.

Another problem with dates is that sometimes when you import web data into Excel or you paste it in as text from an external source, the default format for the dates is a text format. These text dates are usually left-aligned instead of right-aligned, and they may be marked with an error indicator icon (if error checking is turned on). This creates problems when the date field is used in other calculations, such as when you create a PivotTable and want to group the data by date.

Cleansing Dates with the DATEVALUE Function

The **DATEVALUE** function converts a date in a text format into a serial value. In Excel, a date is a number in which the value is calculated as the number of days since December 31, 1899. So January 1, 1900, is equivalent to a value of 1 in this system. Converting dates into serial values is what allows you to use dates in mathematical calculations.

You have been asked to convert the dates on a list of invoices related to purchases made for the next Seniors Golf tournament at the Red Bluff Golf Course & Pro Shop. In this exercise, you will cleanse these dates, which can then be used in PivotTables or other means of analysis.

 E09.19

To Cleanse Dates with the DATEVALUE Function

a. Click the **SalesCommission** worksheet.

b. Click cell **D2**, type =DATEVALUE, and then press Tab to insert the function. Click cell **B2**, and then press Enter.

c. Click cell **D2**. In the Number group, click the **Number Format** arrow, and then select **Short Date** as the format for the cell.

d. Double-click the **AutoFill** handle to copy the function down to D11.

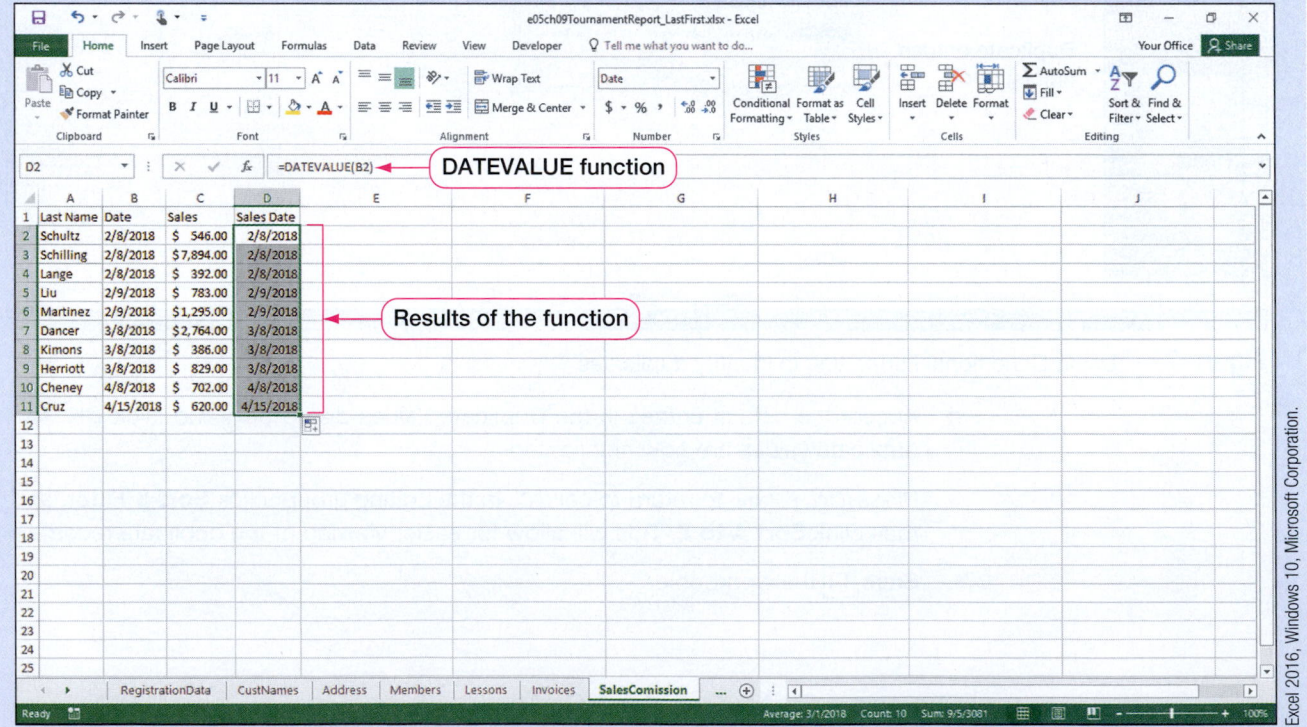

Figure 28   Using the DATEVALUE function

e. **Save** the workbook.

Reconstructing Dates Using Text to Columns

Because there are many different date formats, working with dates can be very tricky. For example, the standard European format for dates is DD/MM/YY, whereas in the United States, the standard is MM/DD/YY. Excel contains several date functions that make working with dates and converting dates much easier.

The date data from the Red Bluff Celebrity Pro-Am Tournament concerning purchases made at the pro shop before the 2018 tournament is in DD/MM/YYYY format. In this exercise, you will use the Convert Text to Columns Wizard to change the date format on a list of purchases.

E09.20

To Reconstruct Dates Using Text to Columns

a. Click the **Purchases** worksheet, and then select cells **B2:B11**.

b. Click the **Data** tab, and in the Data Tools group, click **Text to Columns**.

c. In the Convert Text to Columns Wizard, under Choose the file type that best describes your data, select **Fixed width**, and then click **Next**.

Troubleshooting

Before attempting to rearrange dates by using the LEFT, RIGHT, and MID text functions, keep in mind that Excel stores dates as a serial number, and it is the cell formatting that displays this serial number in a date format. The LEFT function extracts a specified number of characters from a text string starting from the far-left character. The RIGHT function does the same starting from the far-right character. And the MID function extracts characters starting in the middle of the text string. So applying the LEFT function to a date will return only the specified numbers beginning on the left of the serial number for that date. You can extract the day, month, and year from a date field by using Convert Text to Columns or applying the DAY, MONTH, YEAR functions.

d. There are no column breaks to add, remove, or move, so click **Next**.

e. Under Column data format, click **Date**, click the **Date** arrow, and then click **DMY**. Click the **Destination** box, and then adjust the cell reference by typing $C$2. Click **Finish**. Resize the columns if necessary to show all the dates.

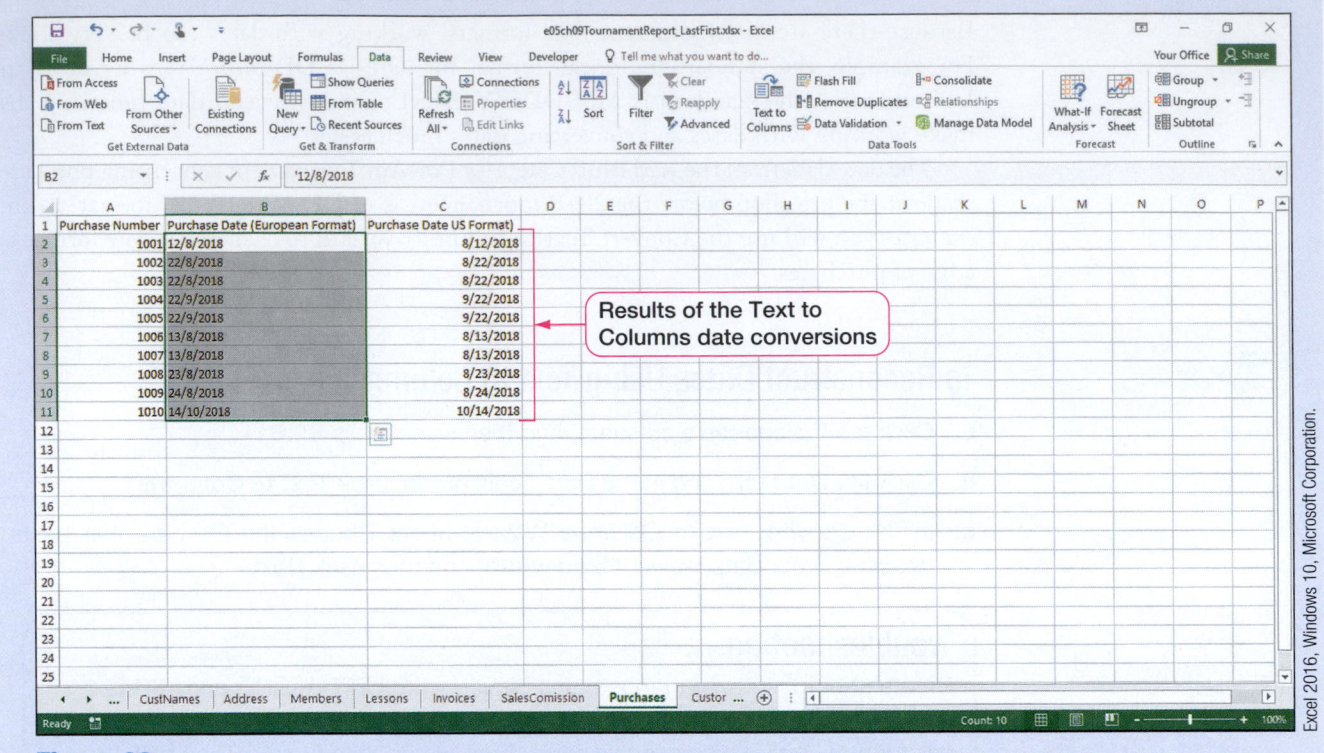

Figure 29 Dates in European format converted to U.S. format using Text to Columns

     f. Save 🖫 the workbook.

Creating Dates with Date Functions

Excel has many features that can help you to process date-related data. It might seem that working with dates in Excel is a confusing process. But any businessperson can tell you that doing calculations with dates and manipulating them is something that you are sure to encounter. Knowing how to apply some of the more sophisticated functions of Excel will increase your value to almost any company.

Aleeta Herriott has been so impressed with your work that she has asked for your help in sorting out some data from customer transactions that occurred just after the Red Bluff Celebrity Pro-Am tournament. The data has already been imported from the .csv file for a summary sales report and converted into an Excel format. But it still has some strange-looking date fields that are preventing Aleeta from running her own Excel formulas. When the raw data was first imported, it looked as if the source system put the name of the day (such as Tuesday) in front of the standard date format for the Ord_Date field. In addition, the standard date format of the data was imported into Excel as three separate fields with the headings Ord_Year, Ord_Day, and Ord_Month. Technically, there is nothing wrong with the data itself, but with several hundred thousand transactions in the report, it makes doing any date-related calculations challenging.

The **DATE** function returns the sequential serial number that represents a particular date. Making use of the DATE function allows a quick conversion of the data in the three separate fields, since you can find the serial date with the arguments =DATE(year, month, day).

QUICK REFERENCE	Common Date Functions in Excel
Function Name	**Description**
DATE(year, month, day)	Returns the sequential serial number that represents a particular date.
DATEVALUE(date_text)	Returns the serial number of the date represented by date_text. Use DATEVALUE to convert a date represented by text to a serial number.
DAY(serial_number)	Returns the day of the month from a date entry. The serial_number argument has to be a serial date or cell reference to a date formatted cell. The DATE function can be used to determine the serial number if needed.
MONTH(serial_number)	Returns the month (i.e., 1–12) of the date entry.
NETWORKDAYS(start_date, end_date, [holidays])	Returns the number of whole working days between two given dates.
WEEKDAY(serial_number, [return_type])	Returns the day of the week corresponding to a date (1–7). The optional return_type argument allows you to change how days are counted.
WORKDAY(start_date, days, [holidays])	Returns the corresponding date that is the number of days from the start_date, minus weekends and holidays. The start_date must be in serial or date format.
YEAR(serial_number)	Returns the year corresponding to a date. This works for years from 1900 to 9999.

In this exercise, you will use the DATE function to combine the separate date fields into one complete date.

 E09.21

To Create Dates with Date Functions

a. Click the **CustomerTransactions** worksheet, and then right-click the **column heading** for column E.

b. Click **Insert**. Click cell **E1**, type Complete_Date, and then press Enter. Resize column E to fit if necessary.

c. In cell E2 type =DATE, and then press Tab to insert the function. Click cell **B2** and type ,. Click cell **D2**, type , and click cell **C2**, and then press Enter.

d. Click cell **E2**. Click the **Home** tab, and in the Number group, click the **Number Format** arrow, and then select **Short Date** to format the value as a date. Double-click the **AutoFill** handle to copy the function down to E15.

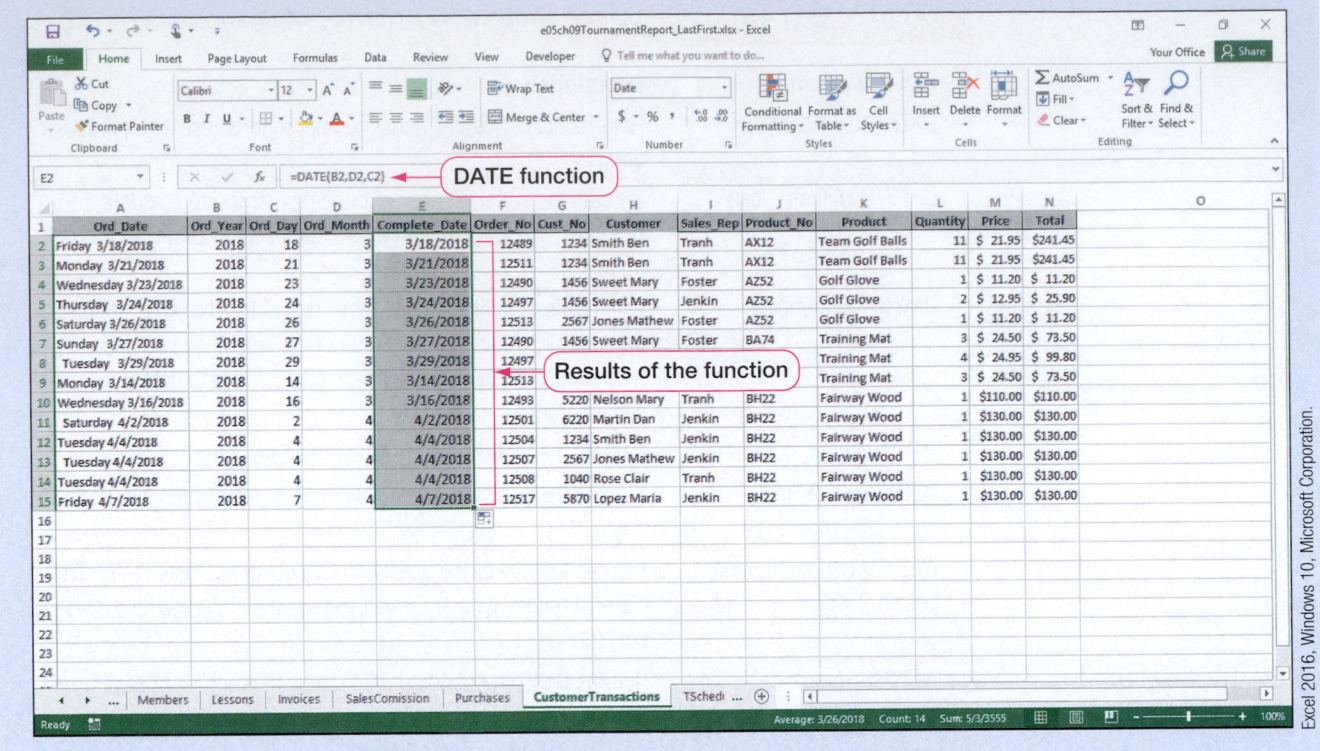

Figure 30 Using the DATE function

e. **Save** 🖫 the workbook.

Using the NETWORKDAYS and TEXT Functions

Because the Red Bluff Golf Course is famous for its competitive layout and challenging greens, it is often asked to host golf tournaments. It currently hosts several major and minor tournaments each year. The most popular event is the Senior Legends tournament, which occurs in December. Golf tournaments have to be scheduled years in advance, and members have to be alerted about them so that they know to expect times when the course will be unavailable to them. It is also important for the maintenance staff to schedule enough workdays to keep everything looking nice and for the inventory in the pro shop to be restocked in time for each event.

With this in mind, Barry Cheney, the Red Bluff Golf Course manager, has asked you to help him build a long-term tournament schedule report. In talking with him, you learned that he would really like to keep track of the number of working days he has between events so he can give members and staff plenty of notice before an event. With a little research, you discovered a function called **NETWORKDAYS**, which can be used to calculate the number of available work days between two given dates. Its syntax looks like this: =NETWORKDAYS(start_date, end_date, {holidays}).

The optional holidays argument at the end allows users to factor in how specific holidays might reduce the number of available work days. Additional research shows that the TEXT function can be used to display the name of the day by using the dddd format as one of the arguments. The **TEXT** function allows you to display numeric data as text in addition to using special formatting strings to display the text.

In this exercise, you will use the NETWORKDAYS and TEXT functions to help build the long-term tournament schedule report.

 **E09.22**

To Use the NETWORKDAYS and TEXT Functions

a. Click the **TSchedule** worksheet. Click cell **G5**.

b. Type **=NETWORKDAYS**, and press Tab to insert the function.

c. Click cell **F5**, type **,** and click cell **E6** to calculate the number of workdays between the end of one tournament and the beginning of the next, and then type **,**.

d. Click and drag cell **I5** down to cell **I12**. Press the F4 key to create an absolute cell reference to the range, and then press Enter.

e. Click cell **G5**, and then double-click the **AutoFill** handle to copy the function down to G9.

   Notice that cell G9 shows a negative number. This is because the formula in G9 does not refer to the correct start date for the next golf tournament.

f. To correct the error, click cell **G9**, and then click the **formula bar** to edit the E10 cell reference. Select the text **E10**, type **E13**, and then press Enter. The negative number should change to a positive 60.

g. Do the same for the 2019 Season tournament schedule. Click cell **G13**. Type **=NETWORKDAYS**, and press Tab to insert the function.

h. Click cell **F13**, type **,** click cell **E14**, and then type **,**.

i. Click and drag cell **J5** down to cell **J12**. Press the F4 key to create an absolute cell reference to the range, and then press Enter.

j. Click cell **G13**, and click and drag the **AutoFill** handle down to cell G16.

   Notice that you do not need to copy down to G17. For the 2019 season, the end date for the first 2020 event is unavailable. Therefore, you cannot calculate the available workdays between the 2019 Senior Legends event and the next event, since the schedule for 2020 is unknown at this time.

k. Click cell **H5**, type **=TEXT**, and then press Tab to insert the function. Click cell **E5**, type **,"dddd"**, and then press Enter.

l. Click cell **H5**, and click and drag the **AutoFill** down to cell H9. This allows you to determine the day of the week each event will start.

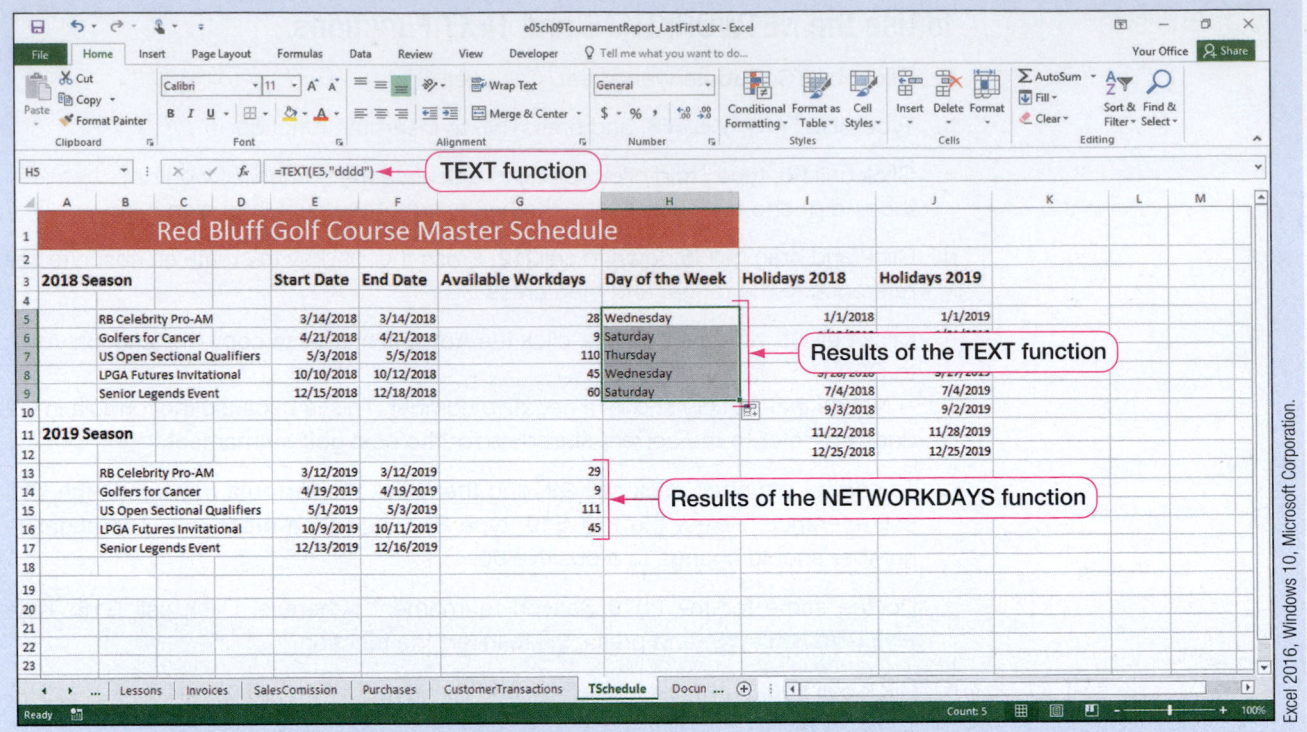

Figure 31 Results of the NETWORKDAYS and TEXT functions

m. Click cell **H5**, press Ctrl + C to copy the formula in H5. Select the range **H13:H17**, and press Ctrl + V to paste the formula into the range.

n. Complete the **Documentation** worksheet as directed by your instructor.

o. **Save** 🖫 the workbook, exit Excel, and then submit your file as directed by your instructor.

Concept Check

1. What is a web query? How is it used to import data into Excel? p. 492

2. What is a markup language? Give two examples, and describe how they are useful. p. 497

3. What are the benefits of importing data from an Access database into Excel? p. 505

4. How are character patterns in data used to help cleanse and manipulate data within a cell? p. 521

5. What does the Flash Fill feature do in Excel? How does Flash Fill handle text and numeric data differently? p. 510–512

6. What are Text functions? How are they used for cleansing data? p. 515–524

7. Why is it important to cleanse date-related data? p. 527–534

Key Terms

CLEAN 514
CONCATENATE 520
Convert Text to Columns Wizard 524
Data cleansing 510
Data verification 510
DATE 530
DATEVALUE 528
Delimiter 502
External data 491
FIND 515
Flash Fill 510
Foreign key 505
HTML 497

LEFT 515
LEN 517
LOWER 513
Markup language 497
Metadata 502
Microsoft Query 507
MID 522
NETWORKDAYS 532
Primary key 505
PROPER 513
Query 492
Relational database 505
Remove Duplicates 525
RIGHT 517

TEXT 532
Text data 502
Text file 502
Text functions 512
TRIM 513
UPPER 513
Web query 492
XML 497
XML element 497
XML map 497
XML schema 497

Visual Summary

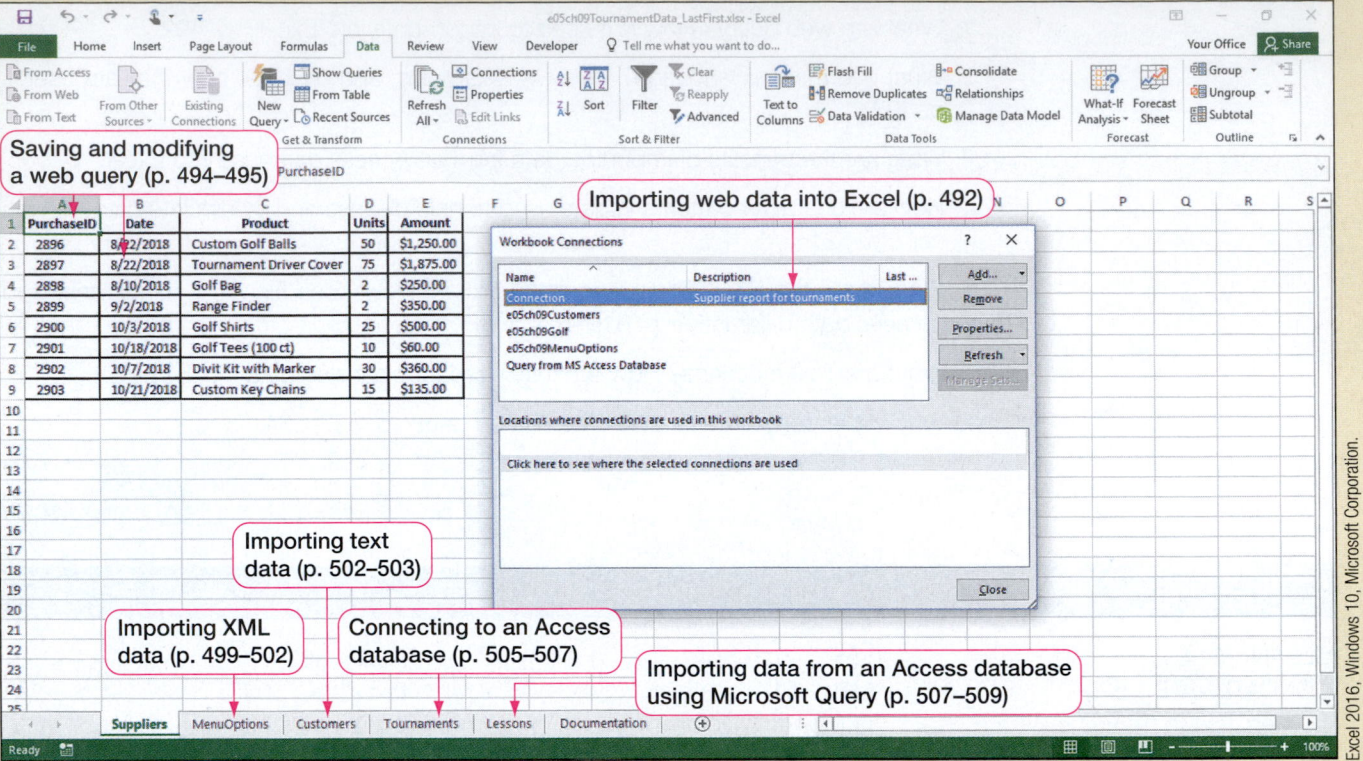

Figure 32

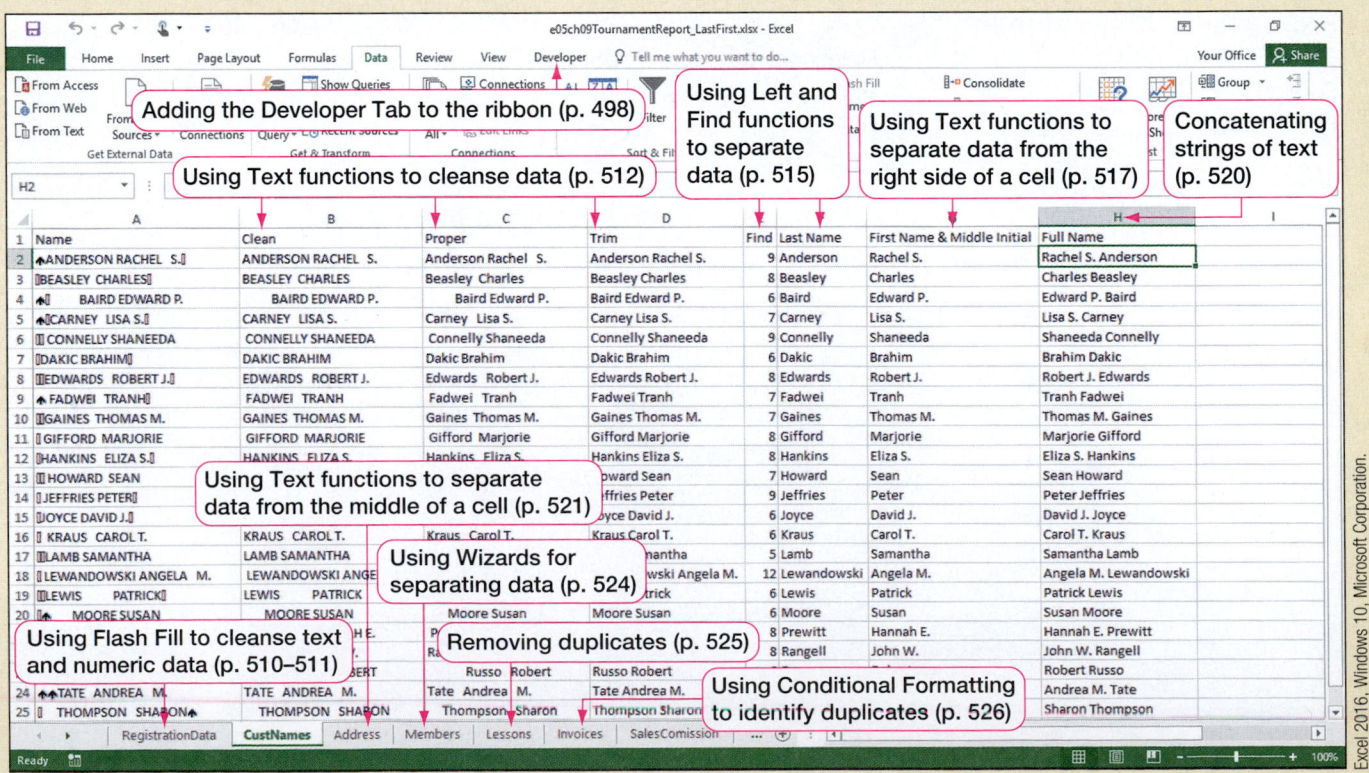

Figure 33

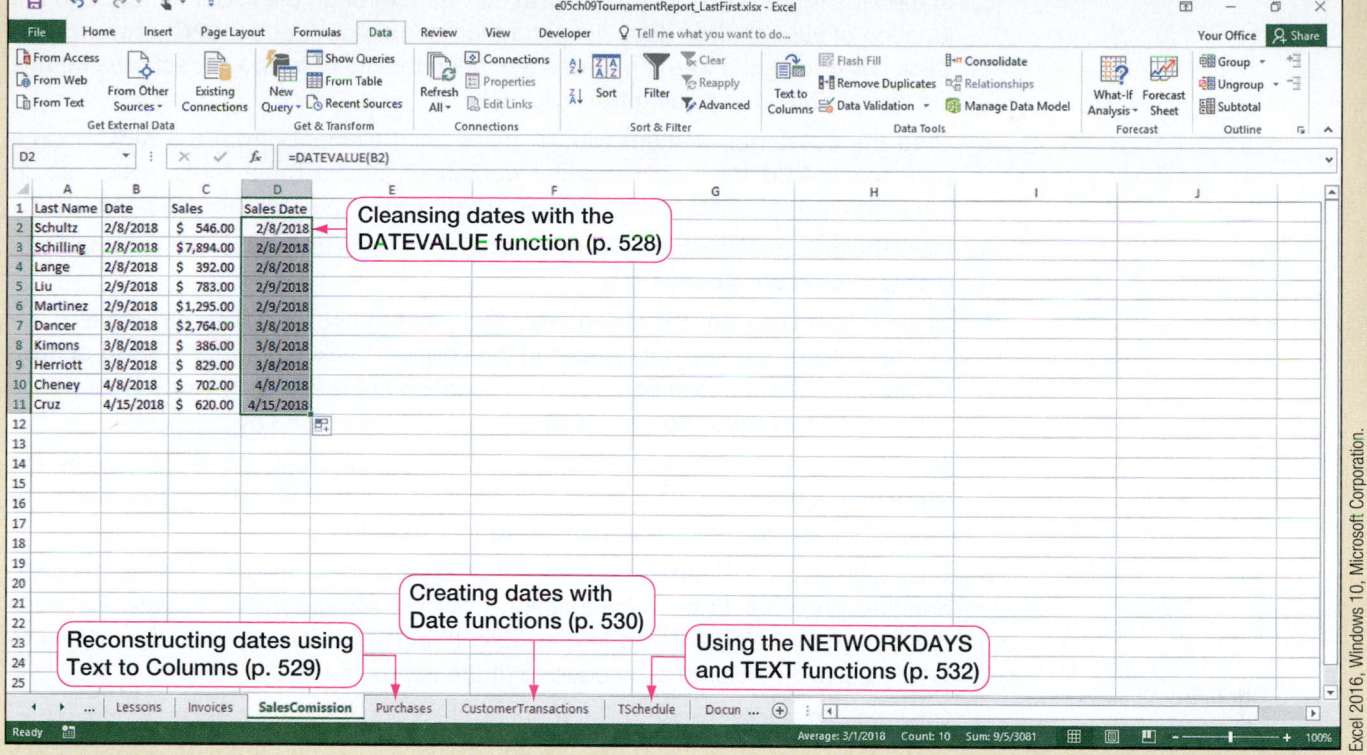

Figure 34

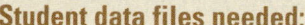

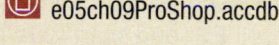

Practice 1

Student data files needed:

e05ch09Newsletter.xlsx

e05ch09Customer.xml

e05ch09ProShop.accdb

You will save your file as:

e05ch09Newsletter_LastFirst.xlsx

Sales & Marketing

Red Bluff Golf Course & Pro Shop Special Promotions Spreadsheets

The Red Bluff Golf Course & Pro Shop regularly runs special promotions to sell golf equipment and clothing. When customers visit the pro shop website, they can opt to receive electronic copies of the pro shop newsletter via e-mail. The website administrator then e-mails the pro shop an XML file containing the customer information at the end of every week. Customers who walk into the pro shop can also opt to receive the newsletter by writing their name and e-mail address on a sign-up sheet. At the end of each day, these names are entered into an Access database. You have been asked to take the XML file of the website customer data and integrate it with the customer data from the Access database. All that combined data then needs to be sorted and cleansed so it can be used to send out e-mail versions of the pro shop newsletter.

a. Open the Excel file, **e05ch09Newsletter**. Save it as **e05ch09Newsletter_LastFirst**, using your last and first name. If necessary, enable content.

b. Click the **Developer** tab, and in the XML group, click **Source**. In the bottom right corner of the window, click **XML Maps**.

c. In the XML Maps dialog box, click **Add**, navigate through the folder structure to the location of your student data files, and then double-click **e05ch09Customer.xml**. Click **OK** if you get a warning message stating that there is no XML schema for this file. In the XML Maps dialog box, click **OK**.

d. Drag the **customer** element with all of its child elements from the XML Source pane to cell **A1** of the WebNewsletter worksheet. On the Table Tools Design tab, in the External Table Data group, click **Refresh**. **Close** the XML Source pane.

e. Click the **InStoreNewsletter worksheet**. On the **Data** tab, in the Get External Data group, click **From Access**.

f. In the Select Data Source dialog box, navigate through the folder structure to the location of your student data files, and then double-click **e05ch09ProShop.accdb**. In the Import Data dialog box, verify the location in the **Existing worksheet** box is set to =$A$1 so the import starts at cell A1, and then click **OK**.

g. Select the cell range **A2:B9**, press Ctrl + C to copy the range. Click the **WebNewsletter** worksheet, click cell **A9**, and then press Ctrl + V to paste the range. Resize the columns as needed to fit the contents.

h. Click cell **C1**, type Cleansed Names, and then press Enter. In cell C2, type =CLEAN, and then press Tab to insert the function. Click cell **A2**, and then press Enter. Because the formula is being entered into an Excel Table, the formula is copied down to C16. Resize the column as needed to fit the contents.

i. Click cell **D1**, type Trimmed Names, and then press Enter. In cell D2, type =TRIM, and then press Tab to insert the function. Click cell **C2**, and then press Enter. Resize the column as needed to fit the contents.

j. Click cell **E1**, type Proper Names, and then press Enter. In cell E2, type =PROPER, and then press Tab to insert the function. Click cell **D2**, and then press Enter. Resize the column as needed to fit the contents.

k. Click cell **F1**, type Last Names, and then press Tab. In cell G1, type First Names, and then press Enter.

l. In cell F2, type =LEFT, and then press Tab to insert the function. Click cell **E2**, type ,FIND, and then press Tab to insert the function. Type ",", click cell **E2**, type)-1), and then press Enter. Resize the column as needed to fit the contents.

m. Click cell **G2**. You will use the RIGHT function to extract the first names from the names in column E. Type =RIGHT, and then press Tab to insert the function. Click cell **E2**, type ,LEN, and then press Tab to insert the function. Click cell **E2**, type)-FIND, and then press Tab to insert the function. Type " ", to use the space character as the find text, click cell **E2**, and then type)), and then press Enter. Resize the column as needed to fit the contents. The final formula should be =RIGHT([@[Proper Names]],LEN([@[Proper Names]])-FIND(" ",[@[Proper Names]])).

n. Click the **Documentation** worksheet. In cell A6, type in today's date. Click cell **B6**, and then type your name using the Firstname and Lastname format. Complete the remainder of the Documentation worksheet according to your instructor's direction.

o. Click **Save**, exit Excel, and then submit your file as directed by your instructor.

MyITLab®
Grader
Homework

Student data files needed:

 e05ch09SportsCustomers.xlsx

 e05ch09SportsCustomers.accdb

You will save your file as:

 e05ch09SportsCustomers_LastFirst.xlsx

Sports Store Customers

Sales &
Marketing

Joe Nelson has a small sports equipment store that has a growing list of customers. The different supervisors have been saving customer information in different formats. Joe would like to have all the data in an Excel spreadsheet. He has asked you to take on the task of getting the data together and putting them in the formats he would like for his planned marketing effort.

a. Open the Excel file, **e05ch09SportsCustomers**. Save it as e05ch09SportsCustomers_LastFirst, using your last and first name. If necessary, enable content.

b. Import the data from the query **qryCustomer** in the **e05ch09SportsCustomers.accdb** database into the **CustomerDatabase** worksheet in cell **A2**.

c. In cells **C2:I2**, type the following column headings: Clean Name, First Name, Last Name, Street Address, City, State, Full Name.

d. In cell **C3**, use the CLEAN and TRIM functions to remove any nonprintable characters and extra spaces from the name in column A. Resize the column as needed to fit the contents.

e. In cell **D3**, use the RIGHT, LEN, and FIND functions to extract the first name from column C. Use the PROPER function to ensure that all first names are in the appropriate case. Resize the column as needed to fit the contents.

f. In cell **E3**, use the LEFT and FIND function to extract the last name from column C. Use the PROPER function to ensure that all last names are in the appropriate case. Resize the column as needed to fit the contents.

g. In cell **F3**, use the LEFT and FIND function to extract the street address from column B. Use the PROPER function to ensure that all street names are in the appropriate case. Resize the column as needed to fit the contents.

h. In cell **G3**, use the MID, LEN, and FIND functions to extract the city name from the address in column B. Resize the column as needed to fit the contents.

i. In cell **H3**, use the RIGHT function to extract the state from the address in column B. Resize the column as needed to fit the contents.

j. In cell **I3**, use concatenation to put the customer first name and last name together with a space in between. Resize the column as needed to fit the contents.

k. **Save** the workbook, exit Excel, and then submit your file as directed by your instructor.

Student data files needed:

 e05ch09HOA.xlsx

e05ch09HOA_data.txt

You will save your file as:

 e05ch09HOA_LastFirst.xlsx

Finance & Accounting

Sales & Marketing

Investing in Homes

You volunteer for your homeowner association (HOA). The HOA has decided to invest in several stocks. To fund the investment, they are asking for donations from local businesses as a way to invest in the local community. The HOA officers have obtained a list of the businesses in the neighborhood and have asked you to create a spreadsheet with the list of names so they can send out a mailing. In addition, they have asked you to show them recent financial data related to the stocks in which they are investing.

a. Open the Excel file, **e05ch09HOA**. Save it as e05ch09HOA_LastFirst using your last and first name. If necessary, enable content.

b. Insert the file name in the **left section** of the footer on the **Businesses** worksheet.

c. Import the text file **e05ch09HOA_data.txt** into the Businesses worksheet, beginning in cell **A1**.

d. Use **Flash Fill** to cleanse the data in additional columns using the following guidelines.

- The names of the Customers should be arranged with the first name, a space, and then the last name.

- The phone number should be displayed in standard phone number format: (xxx) xxx-xxxx.

- The ZIP Code should be displayed with a hyphen between the first five digits and the last four digits.

e. Resize the columns as needed to fit the contents.

f. Delete any duplicate records, using the Remove Duplicates tool. A duplicate record is where all columns contain the same data.

g. The HOA has decided to invest in the following stocks: **KBH**, **HD**, and **AWI**. Import data related to these stocks on the appropriate stock worksheets, starting in cell A3. You may use the financial site of your choice, although you might find that http://finance.yahoo.com works best for web queries in Excel.

h. Resize the columns as needed to fit the contents on each worksheet.

i. Save the workbook, exit Excel, and then submit your file as directed by your instructor.

Additional Cases

Additional Workshop Cases are available on the companion website and in the instructor resources.

Microsoft Excel 2016

Chapter 10 | DATA TABLES, SCENARIO MANAGER, AND SOLVER

Production & Operations

Prepare Case

The Red Bluff Golf Course & Pro Shop Business Planning Analysis

Barry Cheney, the Golf Course Manager at the Red Bluff Golf Course & Pro Shop, has been considering expanding the clubhouse to accommodate a steady increase in business. This expansion could include more space for the pro shop and more guest accommodations. Barry will need to provide a detailed analysis of past sales along with sales forecasts to assure William Mattingly, the resort's CEO, that the money spent on the improvements and expansion will have positive financial benefits for Red Bluff. To increase management's understanding of the current capacities, Barry has collected data about traffic, sales, and product mix. He has asked you to analyze this data, using Excel's What-If Analysis tools.

Semmick Photo/Shutterstock

Student data file needed for this chapter:

 e05ch10ExpansionAnalysis.xlsx

You will save your file as:

 e05ch10ExpansionAnalysis_LastFirst.xlsx

Examining Cost-Volume-Profit Relationships

Managers need to analyze business data to help them plan and monitor the organization's day-to-day operations. **Cost-volume-profit (CVP) analysis** is the study of how cost and sales volume are related and the effect their relationship has on profit. Management relies on the accounting department to provide the data needed to perform CVP analysis. This data allows management not only to perform CVP analysis but also to examine operational risks as a suitable cost structure is chosen.

Consider the Red Bluff Golf Course & Pro Shop. Organizations such as this do not simply decide to renovate or expand operations on the basis of an impulse. Nor do they decide to acquire an existing business or open a new location that way. Managers spend a great deal of time analyzing past sales data along with projected future sales data to determine whether every strategy from beginning to end has the desired results in mind: increased profit or greater market share.

For example, if Red Bluff does expand or renovate its business, in what ways will it expand or renovate? Will the expansion include more space for the pro shop, an indoor golf simulator, or areas for guests to relax? Will it be for storing more of the retail products sold in the pro shop? Or will Red Bluff simply upgrade existing facilities? Management needs to know what the most popular services are before making any decisions about the types of areas to add. What about revenue? If a loan is taken out and Red Bluff's costs rise because of the interest on the loan, what sales volume or revenue does Red Bluff need to generate to cover the increased costs? CVP analysis is a way of evaluating the relationships among the fixed and variable costs, the sales volume — in terms of either units or dollars — and the profits. In this section, you will create a break-even analysis, work with conditional and custom formatting, use Goal Seek, and create data tables to analyze data.

Perform Break-Even Analysis

CVP analysis is used to help understand how changing volumes of sales or revenue affect profits. One of the main CVP analysis tools is break-even analysis, which can help managers understand the relationships among cost, volume, and profit. Managers can use **break-even analysis** to calculate the break-even point in sales volume or dollars, estimate profit or loss at any level of sales volume, and help in setting prices. The **break-even point** is the sales level at which revenue equals total costs; in other words, there is neither a profit nor a loss. Understanding how profit on an item or service is affected by other variables requires an analysis of the costs. This analysis helps to identify the items or services for which the profit changes as sales volume changes and those for which it does not.

When calculating the break-even point, you need to consider the fixed, variable, and mixed costs. **Fixed costs** are expenses that never change regardless of how much product is sold or how many services are rendered. For example, when the golf course is open for business, they have to pay management salaries, insurance, depreciation of building and equipment, and some other costs, regardless of how many customers they have during the day. **Variable costs**, by contrast, do change according to how many products are sold or services are rendered. For example, with every new golf course membership, Red Bluff provides three personalized golf balls to the new member. The cost of ordering the customized golf balls depends on how many memberships are sold. Thus, the cost of the supplies used varies depending on the services rendered. **Mixed costs** are costs that contain a variable component and a fixed component. Consider utilities, such as electricity and water. Utility companies charge a specific amount; electric companies charge per kilowatt-hour used, and water companies charge a base fee and then an additional amount per gallon used, but the bill will vary depending on the usage per billing cycle.

To determine the break-even point, the golf course needs to consider all costs before it can determine its profit. For example, consider the Red Bluff Golf Course & Pro Shop golf polo shirts. The manufacturer charges $22.79 — a variable cost — to produce one shirt. The total variable cost would be the variable cost per polo shirt multiplied by the number of polo shirts ordered. The manufacturer charges $15,000 per production run — a fixed cost — regardless of how many shirts are manufactured. This fee covers the costs that the manufacturer incurs to set up the production line. Red Bluff sells the golf polo shirts for $49.99 and would need to sell approximately 552 to break even. A graph displaying this analysis is shown in Figure 1.

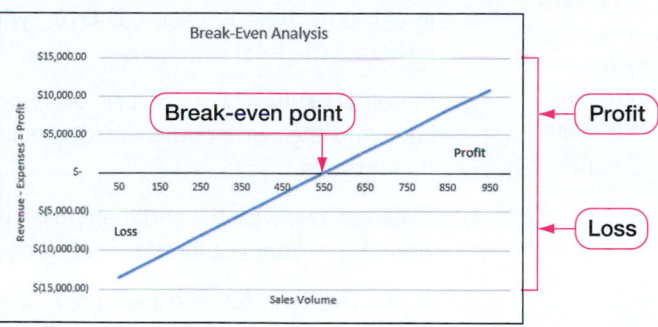

Figure 1 Break-even analysis chart

Opening the Starting File

Barry Cheney is considering raising the price of golf lessons. He has given you a workbook that includes information for some of the business activities, such as costs, prices, revenues, and profits, as provided by the accounting department. In this exercise, you will begin by opening the file.

E10.00

To Open the Starting File

a. Start **Excel**, click **Open Other Workbooks** in the left pane, and then double-click **This PC**. Navigate through the folder structure to the location of your student data files, and then double-click **e05ch10ExpansionAnalysis**. An Excel workbook opens that contains several worksheets containing information for a variety of business activities.

b. Click the **File** tab, click **Save As**, and then double-click **This PC**. In the **Save As** dialog box, navigate to the location where you are saving your project files, and then change the file name to **e05ch10ExpansionAnalysis_LastFirst**, using your last and first name. Click **Save**.

Performing a Break-Even Analysis

The Red Bluff Golf Course & Prop Shop offers golf lessons to its clients for a fee of $125.00 per lesson. The costs for each golf lesson comprises both fixed and variable costs. In this exercise, by conducting a break-even analysis, you will determine the minimum number of clients Red Bluffs needs to have signed up for golf lessons to offset the costs.

E10.01

SIDE NOTE
Pin the Ribbon
If your ribbon is collapsed, pin your ribbon open. Click the Home tab. In the lower right-hand corner of the ribbon, click Pin the Ribbon .

To Perform a Break-Even Analysis

a. If necessary, click the **Break-Even Analysis** worksheet. Click cell **D6**, type =, click cell **D4**, type *, and then click cell **D5**. Press Enter to calculate the gross revenue from golf lessons.

b. Click cell **D13**, type **=SUM**, and then press Tab to insert the function. Select cells **D9** through **D12**, and then press Enter to calculate the total fixed costs of providing golf lessons.

c. Click cell **D15**, type =, click cell **D6**, type *, and then click cell **C15**. Press Enter to calculate the total commission the golf instructors will earn.

d. In cell **D16**, type **=**, click cell **C16**, type *****, and then click cell **D4**. Press Enter to calculate the total cost of supplies.

e. In cell **D17**, type **=**, click cell **D15**, type **+**, and then click cell **D16**. Press Enter to calculate the total variable costs.

f. In cell **D18**, type **=**, click cell **D13**, type **+**, and then click cell **D17**. Press Enter to calculate the total expenses.

g. In cell **D19**, type **=**, click cell **D6**, type **-**, and then click cell **D18**. Press Enter to calculate the net income — how much profit the golf course will generate from golf lessons.

h. Click cell **D4**, type **50**, and then press Ctrl + Enter to try to find the break-even point. Notice that your net income is still negative (–$1,418.50).

i. In cell **D4**, type **60**, and then press Ctrl + Enter to try to find the break-even point. Notice that your net income is still negative (–$393.00). However, you are getting closer to finding the break-even point.

j. In cell **D4**, type **64**, and then press Ctrl + Enter. Notice that your net income finally has become positive: $17.20. Thus, Red Bluff would need 64 clients to sign up for golf lessons before it would make a profit. If more than 64 clients sign up for golf lessons, more profit will be generated.

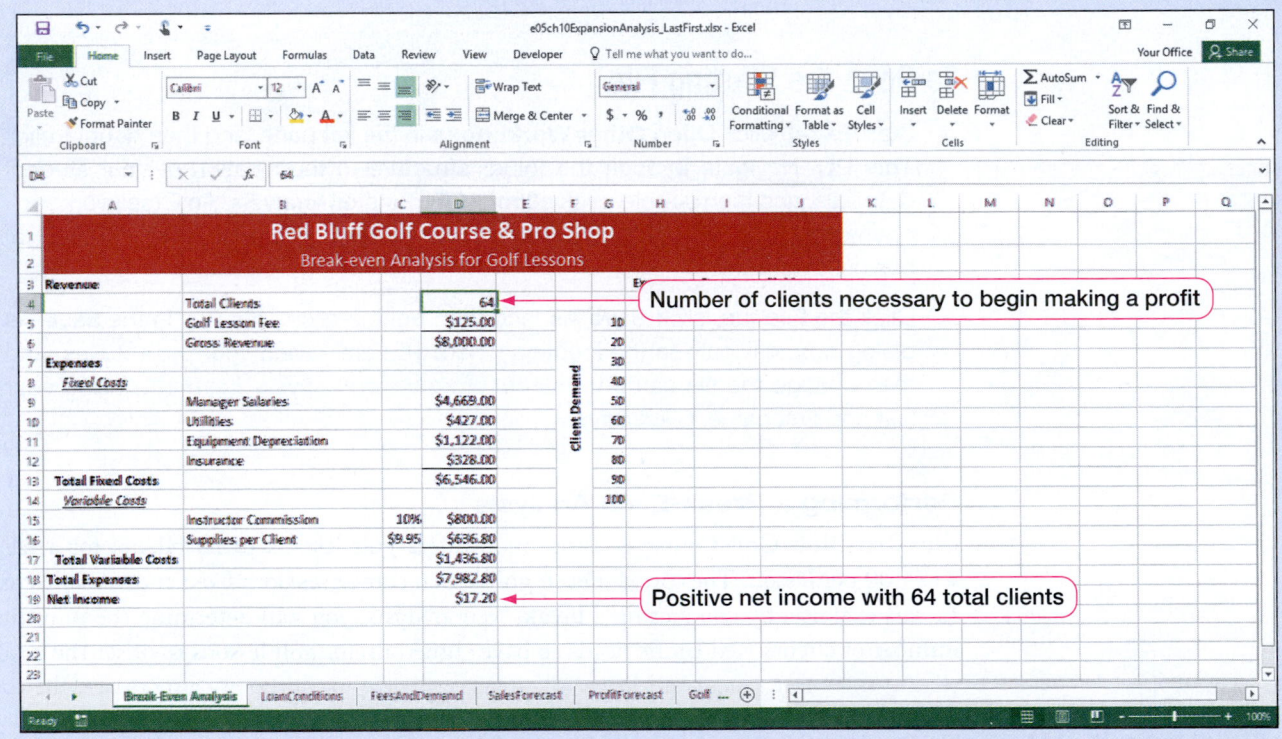

Figure 2 Working with a break-even analysis

Excel 2016, Windows 10, Microsoft Corporation.

k. Save 💾 the workbook.

SS **CONSIDER THIS** | **How Do You Contribute to Costs?**

Have you ever thought about the costs you add to or experience on a daily basis? Think about how the money you spend contributes to the business or organization you are paying. What about paying tuition? Buying lunch? Making a car payment? Paying student organization dues? Can you determine which of these would be fixed, variable, or mixed costs?

Using the Scroll Bar to Perform a Break-Even Analysis

Managers use break-even analysis to determine the minimum volume the business needs to make and sell if it is a manufacturer — or buy and sell if it is a retail business — to be sustainable. Once you know a variable cost per unit and total fixed costs, you can calculate the break-even point. By knowing the break-even point, you can set sales goals, prices, and employee hours. When you entered various numbers in the previous exercise, you were performing what-if analysis. **What-if analysis** is the use of several different values in one or more formulas to explore all the various results. These different values are called variables. A **variable** is a value that you can change to see how the change affects other values. Throughout your career, your day will consist of what-if questions. For example, "What if you sell more golf lessons at a lower price? Would you generate more net revenue than if you sold fewer at a higher price?"

REAL WORLD ADVICE | The Operative Word is "Tool"

The operative word in what-if analysis tools is "tools." It is important to understand that these tools help managers analyze data so the manager can make the best decision based on the information he or she has. Analyzing data is only one component of decision making. Managers make decisions through exploring different options as well as reviewing documents, personal knowledge, or business models to identify and solve problems and make decisions. These tools support organizational decision-making activities and are a method of analyzing and interpreting data.

Another way to determine the break-even point is by using a scroll bar. The **scroll bar** is a form control that allows you to change a number in a target cell location in single-unit increments. The scroll bar is a type of **scenario tool** because of the ability to calculate numerous outputs in other cells by referencing the target cell in formulas and functions. When you use scenario tools to aid in decision making, you are performing what-if analysis. For example, Red Bluff managers can use the scroll bar to change the number of clients and price of each golf lesson to determine when the business will meet and exceed its profit goal. This can be a challenge to determine whether you were to perform this analysis manually — by entering random numbers into cells — because it is extremely time consuming and you do not want users to make physical changes to your spreadsheet model. Additionally, in many cases, when the price increases, the total number of items that can be sold will decrease. In this example, the higher the price of a golf lesson, the fewer clients Red Bluff will have booking the service.

REAL WORLD ADVICE | The Scroll Bar Can Be Used with the VLOOKUP Function

If you are given a table of data, such as quantity and price information, you can use a VLOOKUP function to help connect values. For example, when the lesson fee is changed in cell D5, the VLOOKUP function will display a new value — Total Clients — in cell D4. When the values in cells D4 and D5 change, the results in Gross Revenue, Instructor Commission, Supplies per Client, Total Variable Costs, Total Expenses, and Net Income also change.

In this exercise, you will incorporate the scroll bar form control into the break-even analysis to make it easier to determine the number of clients necessary for Red Bluff to break even.

 E10.02

To Use the Scroll Bar to Perform a Break-Even Analysis

a. Click the **Developer** tab, and then, in the Controls group, click **Insert**.

b. Click **Scroll Bar (Form Control)** ⊟, and then draw the scroll bar in the area of cells **E4** through **E17**. Be careful not to select the ActiveX Scroll Bar from the Insert menu.

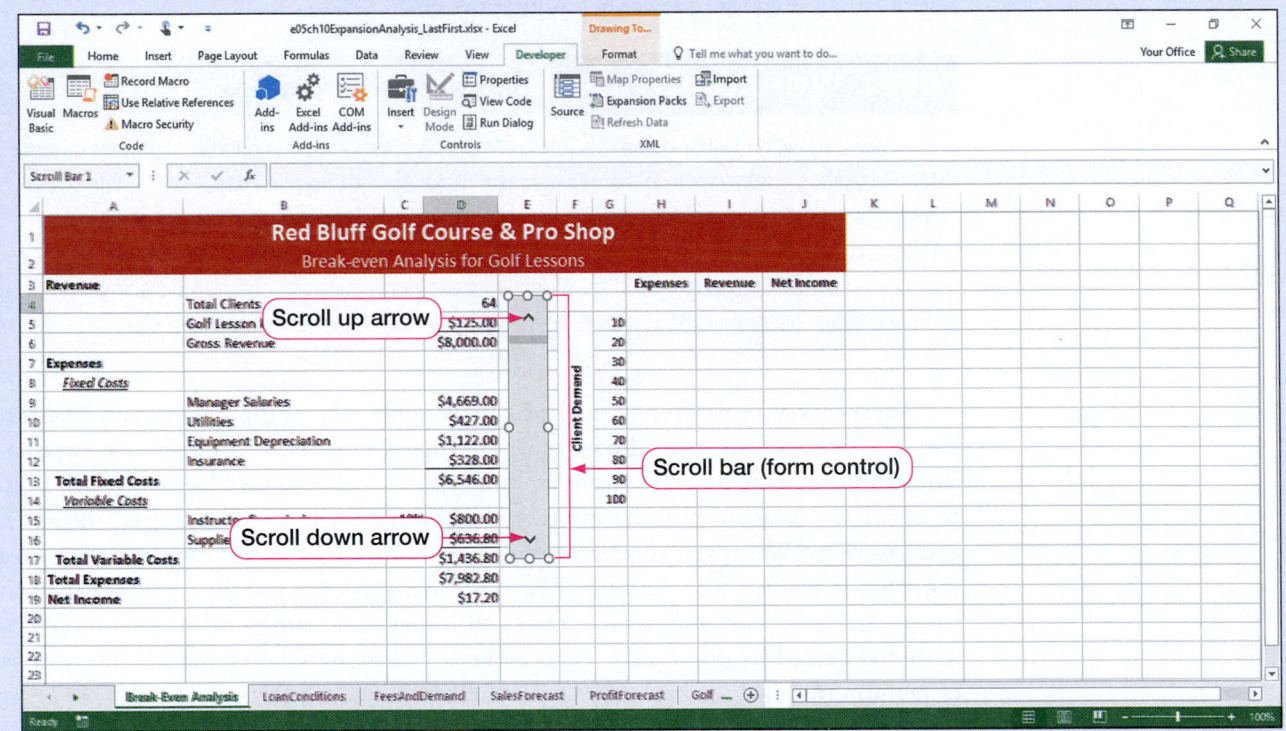

Figure 3 Break-even analysis using the scroll bar

Excel 2016, Windows 10, Microsoft Corporation.

c. On the Developer tab, in the Controls group, click **Properties**. In the Format Control dialog box, click the **Control** tab if necessary. Because you want to analyze the net income from 60 to 100 clients, you need to type the following criteria in the Format Control dialog box.

Current value: type **64**
Minimum value: type **60**
Maximum value: Leave at the default value of **100**
Incremental change: Leave at the default value of **1**
Page change: Leave at the default value of **10**
Cell link: click cell **D4**, moving the dialog box if necessary

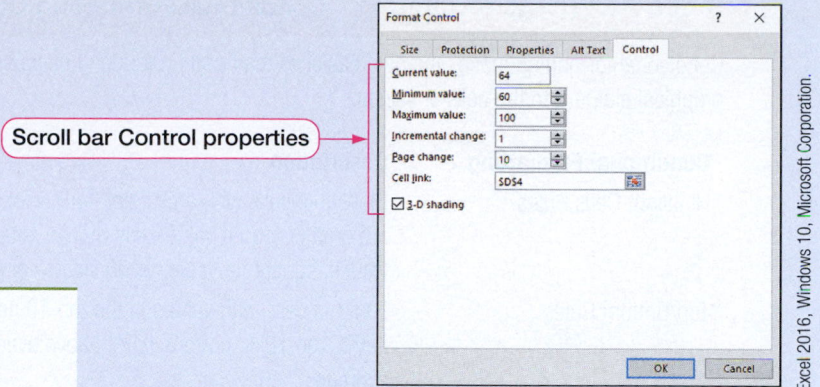

Scroll bar Control properties

Figure 4 Format Control dialog box

Excel 2016, Windows 10, Microsoft Corporation.

d. Click **OK**, click a cell away from the scroll bar to deactivate the scroll bar, and then click the **up** arrow on the scroll bar.

You will notice that the value decreases. Analyze the net income for 60 to 100 clients.

e. Scroll down to the maximum value of 100 by clicking the **down** arrow on the scroll bar.

Notice that with 100 clients, the golf course would make a profit of $3,709.

f. Scroll up until you have a net income that is at the break-even point. Notice that the golf course would have to service 64 clients to make a profit.

g. **Save** the workbook.

SS **CONSIDER THIS** | **How Would You Use the Scroll Bar?**

Using the scroll bar can be a quick and easy method to find the break-even point once the spreadsheet has been formulated. How could you find the break-even point if you wanted higher pricing? Would it be easier to type values into the price and clients cells? Would you rather change the data on the worksheet with a scroll bar? Which would be more efficient?

Using Conditional Formatting

When you format fonts, borders, alignment, fill colors, and so on, you are making the spreadsheet easier for you to use and read. The same is true of conditional formatting. **Conditional formatting** applies custom formatting to highlight or emphasize values that meet specific criteria, as seen in Table 1. This kind of formatting is called conditional because the formatting occurs when a particular condition is met. For example, a manager may want to highlight cells for employees who exceeded monthly sales quotas or products that are selling below cost.

Conditional formatting makes the data easier to read and understand because it adds a visual or graphical element to the cells or values.

Conditional Formatting	Description
Highlight Cells Rules	Highlights cells with a fill color, font color, or border if values are greater than a value, less than a value, between two values, equal to a value, or duplicate values
Top/Bottom Rules	Formats cells with values in the top 10 items, bottom 10 items, top 10%, bottom 10%, above average, or below average
Data Bars	Applies a color gradient or solid fill bar; the width of a solid fill bar symbolizes the current cell's value as compared to other cells' values
Color Scales	Formats different cells with different colors; one color is assigned to the lowest group of values, another color is assigned to the highest group of values, and gradient colors are assigned to other values
Icon Sets	Inserts an icon from the icon palette in each cell to point out values as compared to each other

In this exercise, you will use conditional formatting to highlight the Net Income value, in cell D19, in two different ways. One set of formatting will be applied if the net income results in a loss; another set of formatting will be applied if the net income results in a profit.

 E10.03

To Use Conditional Formatting

a. Click cell **D19**. Click the **Home** tab, and then, in the Styles group, click **Conditional Formatting**. Point to **Highlight Cells Rules**, and then click **Less Than** to open the Less Than dialog box.

b. In the Format cells that are LESS THAN box, type **0**. On the right side of the dialog box, click the **with** arrow, and then click to select the **Red Text** option, and then click **OK**.

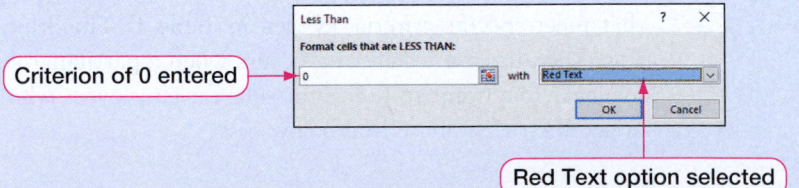

Criterion of 0 entered

Red Text option selected

Excel 2016, Windows 10, Microsoft Corporation.

Figure 5   Less Than dialog box

c. In the Styles group, click **Conditional Formatting**, and then point to **Highlight Cells Rules**, and then click **Greater Than** to open the Greater Than dialog box.

d. In the Format cells that are GREATER THAN box, type **0**. Click the **with** arrow on the right side of the dialog box, click to select the **Green Fill with Dark Green Text** option, and then click **OK**.

e. Click the **up** arrow on the scroll bar.

Notice that when the net income becomes a negative number, the font changes to red. This makes it easier for users to identify when the golf course has not reached the break-even point.

f. **Save** 💾 the workbook.

QUICK REFERENCE	Custom Formatting Can Be Created

Not only can you apply preset conditional formatting within Excel, but you can also create your own formatting properties for fill colors, font colors, border colors, and so on. There are three ways to create custom formatting in Excel. Begin each option by clicking the Conditional Formatting button.

1. Point to Highlight Cells Rules, and after selecting a rule, click the arrow to choose a color, and click Custom Format.

2. Click New Rule.

3. Click Manage Rules to open the Conditional Formatting Rules Manager dialog box. The color can be changed for an existing rule by choosing Edit Rule.

REAL WORLD ADVICE	How Much Is Too Much?

Have you ever seen a document or web page that is so busy with colors and graphics that it is too difficult to read? Where do you draw the line when using conditional formatting or custom formatting? Not only can too much formatting make worksheets difficult for your audience to read, but it can make the worksheets difficult for you to maintain. Although formatting gives you more control over styles and icons, improved data bars, and the ability to highlight specific items and display data bars for negative values to more accurately illustrate your data visuals, consider what the repercussions can be if you format too much. Think about someone who is visually impaired or color-blind. What is appealing to you may not be easy for someone else to read.

Analyze Variables in Formulas Through the Use of Data Tables

Excel contains three types of what-if analysis tools: Goal Seek, Data Tables, and Scenario Manager. A **data table** takes sets of input values, determines possible results, and displays all the results in one table on one worksheet. Because data tables focus on only one or two variables, the results are easy to read and share in tabular form. Although it is limited to only one or two variables, a data table can include as many different variable values as needed.

Using One-Variable Data Tables

A one-variable data table has input values that are listed either down a column, referred to as column-oriented, or across a row, referred to as row-oriented. A **one-variable data table** can help you analyze how different values of one variable in one or more formulas will change the results of those formulas. The formulas that are used in a one-variable data table must refer to only one input cell. For example, you can use a one-variable data table to see how different interest rates affect a monthly car payment by using the PMT function. In this case, the interest rate cell would be the input cell of the one-variable data table. The results display all possible interest rates provided in a data table after Excel performs a what-if analysis on these variables, as shown in Figure 6.

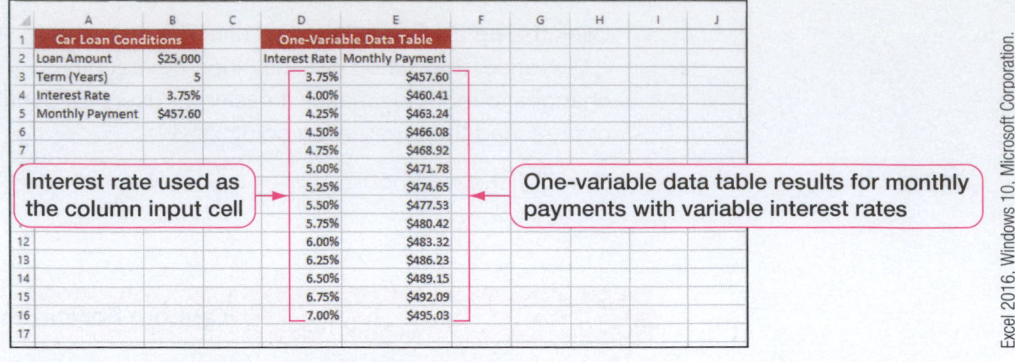

Figure 6   Analyzing data with a one-variable data table

In this exercise, you will help to create two one-variable data tables: one to determine how much the monthly payment on a loan would be based on varying interest rates, and the other to determine how the changes in client demand for golf lessons will affect the expenses, revenue, and net income. You will also apply some conditional formatting to add emphasis and increase the readability of the worksheets. Finally, you will build a traditional cost-volume-profit chart based on the one-variable data table that will further analyze the break-even point for golf lesson pricing.

 E10.04

To Use One-Variable Data Tables

a. Click the **LoanConditions** worksheet, click cell **D3**, type **4**, and then press Enter. Click in cell **D4**, type **5**, and then press Enter. Select the range **D3:D4**, and then drag the **AutoFill handle** down to cell D9. Click cell **E2**, type **=**, click cell **B6**, and then press Enter.

b. Right-click cell **E2**, and then select **Format Cells**. In the Format Cells dialog box, if necessary, click the **Number** tab. Under Category, click **Custom**, and then click the **Type** box. Delete any existing text, and then type **"Monthly Payment"** (including the quotation marks) to hide the results of the formula and display the typed text as a column heading. Click **OK**, and then select the range **D2:E9** to select the data for your data table.

c. Click the **Data** tab, and then, in the Forecast group, click **What-If Analysis**, and click **Data Table** to open the Data Table dialog box.

d. Click inside the Column input cell box, click cell **B4**, and then click **OK**. Notice that Excel calculated the monthly payment for each interest rate.

e. Select the range **E3:E9**. Click the **Home** tab, and then, in the Styles group, click **Conditional Formatting**. Point to **Data Bars**, and then, under Gradient Fill, select **Green Data Bar**.

SIDE NOTE
Using Cell B4 as the Column Input Cell
The interest rates being used are listed in a column. This is why you entered where the interest rate is in the model — cellB4 — into the column input cell box.

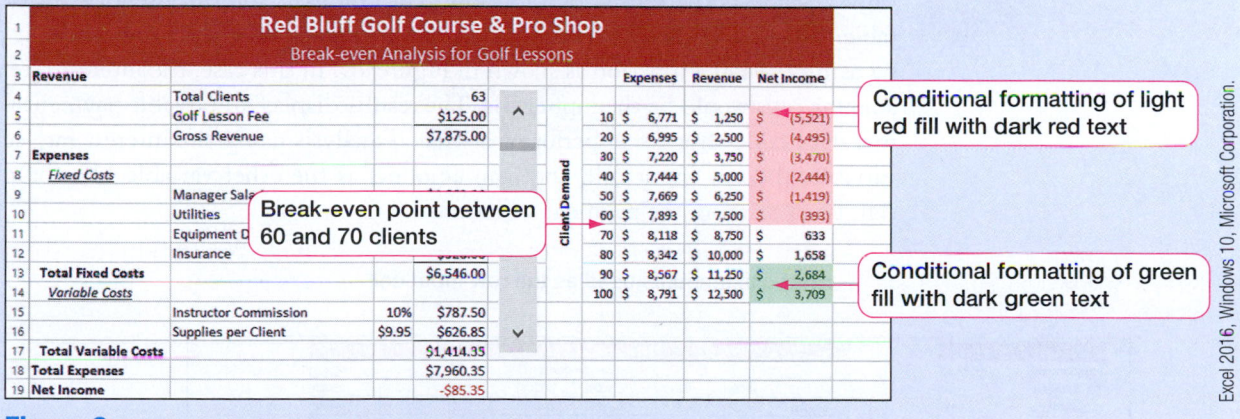

Figure 7   One-variable data table with conditional formatting

(Figure 7 annotations: "Gradient Fill Green Data Bar option applied"; "What-if analysis performed on variable interest rate"; Excel 2016, Windows 10, Microsoft Corporation.)

f.   Click the **Break-Even Analysis** worksheet, and then click cell **H4**. Type **=**, click cell **D18**, and then press Tab. In cell **I4**, type **=**, and then click cell **D6**, and press Tab. In cell **J4**, type **=**, click cell **D19**, and then press Enter.

SIDE NOTE

Hiding Formulas in Data Tables

Excel requires that at least one formula be referenced to create a data table. However, having the formulas visible does not add any value, so custom formatting is often used to hide them.

g.   Select the range **H4:J4**, right-click any of the selected cells, and then select **Format Cells**. On the Number tab, under Category, click **Custom**, and then click the **Type** box. Delete any existing text, and then type **;;;** to hide the results of the formulas. Click **OK**.

h.   Select the range **G4:J14** to select the data for your data table. Click the **Data** tab, and then, in the Forecast group, click **What-If Analysis**, and click **Data Table** to open the Data Table dialog box.

i.   Press Tab to move the insertion point to the Column input cell box, and then click cell **D4**, and click **OK**. Notice that Excel calculated the expenses, revenue, and profit on the basis of client demand.

j.   Select the range **J5:J14**. Click the **Home** tab, and then, in the Styles group, click **Conditional Formatting**. Point to **Highlight Cells Rules**, and then click **Less Than** to open the Less Than dialog box. In the Format cells that are LESS THAN box, type **0**, click the **with** arrow in the box to the right, and then, if necessary, click the **Light Red Fill with Dark Red Text** option. Click **OK**.

SIDE NOTE

Data Tables Automatically Update

If you change the formula used as a row or column input, the data table will be updated automatically as you update your data.

k.   Click **Conditional Formatting** again, and then point to **Highlight Cells Rules**, and click **Greater Than** to open the Greater Than dialog box. In the Format cells that are GREATER THAN, type **2000**, click the **with** arrow in the box to the right, and then click the **Green Fill with Dark Green Text** option. Click **OK**.

					Expenses	Revenue	Net Income
Red Bluff Golf Course & Pro Shop							
Break-even Analysis for Golf Lessons							
Revenue							
	Total Clients		63				
	Golf Lesson Fee		$125.00		10 $ 6,771	$ 1,250	$ (5,521)
	Gross Revenue		$7,875.00		20 $ 6,995	$ 2,500	$ (4,495)
Expenses					30 $ 7,220	$ 3,750	$ (3,470)
Fixed Costs					40 $ 7,444	$ 5,000	$ (2,444)
	Manager Sala				50 $ 7,669	$ 6,250	$ (1,419)
	Utilities				60 $ 7,893	$ 7,500	$ (393)
	Equipment D				70 $ 8,118	$ 8,750	$ 633
	Insurance				80 $ 8,342	$ 10,000	$ 1,658
Total Fixed Costs			$6,546.00		90 $ 8,567	$ 11,250	$ 2,684
Variable Costs					100 $ 8,791	$ 12,500	$ 3,709
	Instructor Commission	10%	$787.50				
	Supplies per Client	$9.95	$626.85				
Total Variable Costs			$1,414.35				
Total Expenses			$7,960.35				
Net Income			-$85.35				

(Figure 8 annotations: "Break-even point between 60 and 70 clients"; "Conditional formatting of light red fill with dark red text"; "Conditional formatting of green fill with dark green text"; "Client Demand" axis label; Excel 2016, Windows 10, Microsoft Corporation.)

Figure 8   One-variable data table of break-even analysis

l.   Select the range **G3:I3**, hold down Ctrl, and then select the range **G5:I14**. Click the **Insert** tab, and then, in the Charts group, click **Line**, and then select **Line** in the 2-D Line category. Click the **border edge** of the Line chart, and then drag to move it until the top left corner is in cell **F16**.

m.   Click **Chart Elements**, and then click the **arrow** to the right of Axis Titles, and click the check box for **Primary Horizontal**.

n. Click the **horizontal axis title** text box, and type Client Demand. Click the **Chart Title** text box, and type Cost-Volume-Profit.

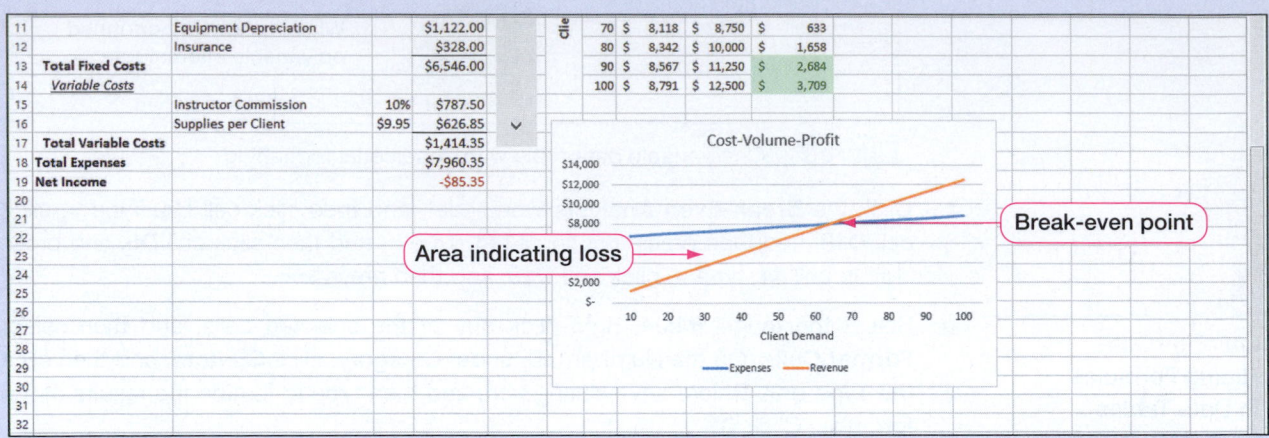

Figure 9 Traditional cost-volume-profit chart

Excel 2016, Windows 10, Microsoft Corporation.

o. Click any cell outside the chart to deselect it. Press Ctrl + Home to select cell A1.

p. **Save** 💾 the workbook.

SS **CONSIDER THIS** | **What Does the Chart Tell You?**

Have you ever heard that a picture is worth a thousand words? Look at the chart you just created. Can you tell where the break-even point is? Is it easier to look at the chart and tell instantly, or is it easier to look at the data table?

Using Two-Variable Data Tables

A two-variable data table has input values that are listed both down a column and across a row. A **two-variable data table** can help you analyze how changing the value of two variables affects the results of a formula. For example, you can use a two-variable data table to see how different interest rates and loan amounts affect a monthly car payment by using the PMT function as shown in Figure 10. In this case, the interest rate and loan amount cells would be the input cells. The results display all possible payment variations in a data table after Excel performs a what-if analysis using the interest rate cell as one variable, the row input cell, and loan amounts as the other variable, the column input cell, in calculating the payment variations.

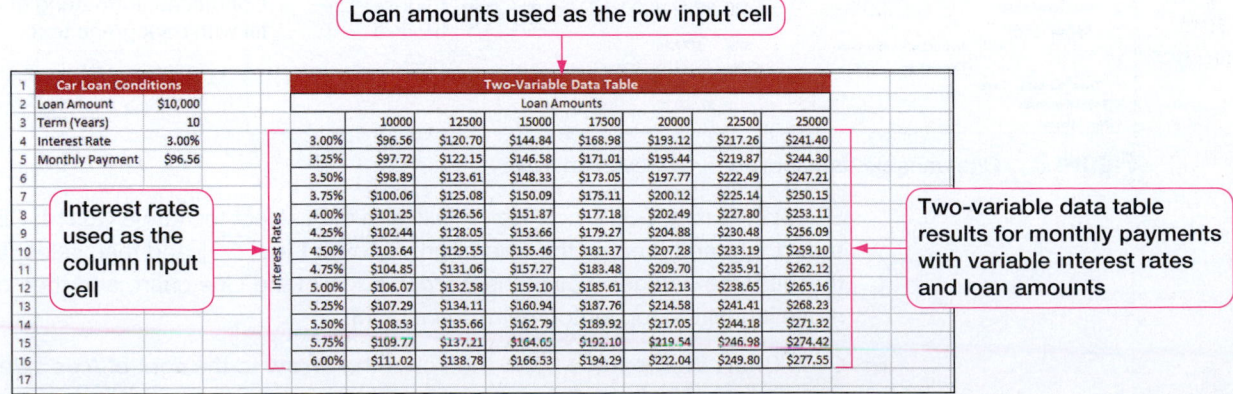

Figure 10 Two-variable data table for a car loan

Excel 2016, Windows 10, Microsoft Corporation.

A two-variable data table can be useful when you want to analyze the relationships among cost, sales volume, and profit. When doing so, you need to consider how demand affects the price of a product or service. The analyses you have performed thus far have assisted in determining the break-even point for products and services. Additionally, you have considered the quantity of products that may be sold or the number of clients that may be serviced. The bottom line is that these analyses have clearly indicated how this relationship between the price and revenue affects demand.

A product or service is **elastic** — or responsive to change — if a small change in price is accompanied by a large change in the quantity demanded. The opposite is also true. A product is **inelastic** — or not responsive to change — if a large change in price is accompanied by a small amount of change in demand. This effect is known as the price elasticity of demand and can be calculated by dividing the change in quantity demanded by the change in price. When you are calculating the elasticity as shown in Figure 11, some assumptions do need to be made about your business and how any changes in price will affect demand. The quotient is conveyed as an absolute value because it is assumed that demand will never increase when prices increase.

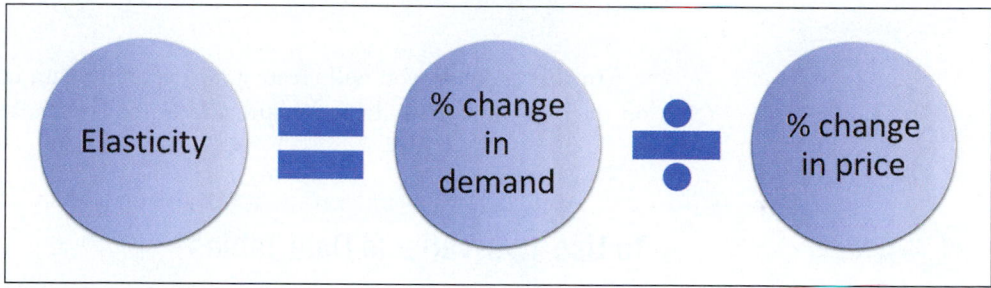

Figure 11   Elasticity formula

For example, the Red Bluff manager may assume that if he increases the price of golf lessons by 15%, demand will decrease by 20%. When calculating the elasticity, you are calculating the price elasticity of demand. Thus, if Barry wanted to calculate the elasticity of demand, the equation would be as shown in Figure 12.

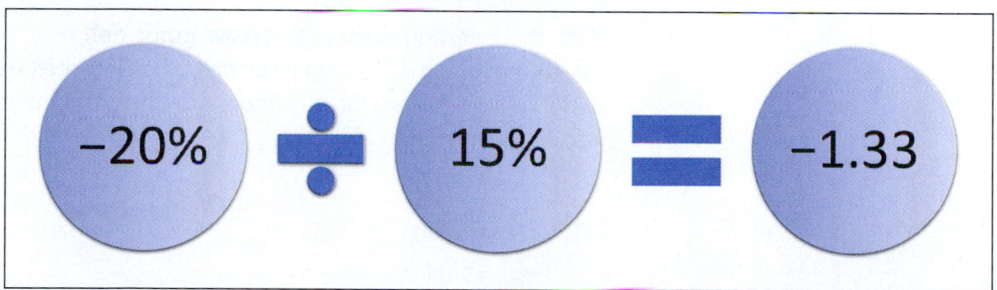

Figure 12   Elasticity calculation of price increase for golf lessons

In this formula, a decrease in demand of 20% divided by a 15% increase in price equals −1.33. Elasticity calculations can be evaluated as absolute values. Here, the elasticity value is 1.33. However, instead of having to calculate and interpret elasticity, you can use a two-way data table to view how the price of a product or service responds to change. In this exercise, you will create a two-variable data table to determine how much net income would be generated for golf lessons on the basis of varying prices and varying client demand.

REAL WORLD ADVICE	A Two-Variable Data Table Is Not Calculating Elasticity

The two-variable data table you are creating does not actually tell you about the elasticity of price versus demand. It calculates the outcomes of varying prices of golf lessons and client demand. In determining selling prices or financing a project, the risk is that the yield will not generate enough revenue to cover operating costs and to repay debt obligations. A two-variable data table gives you another way of assessing the risk associated with pricing a product or service at a certain level or anticipating a specific level of demand.

In this exercise, you will create a two-variable data table that will calculate revenue on the basis of various client demand and lesson fee scenarios.

 E10.05

To Use Two-Variable Data Tables

a. Click the **FeesAndDemand** worksheet, click cell **E3**, type **=**, then click cell **B7** to reference the Net Income formula that Excel will use to calculate your data table, and then press Enter.

b. Right-click cell **E3**, and then click **Format Cells**. On the Number tab, under Category, click **Custom**, click the **Type** box, delete any text, and then type **;;;** to use custom formatting to hide the formula results. Click **OK**.

c. Select the range **E3:L16** to select the data for your data table. Click the **Data** tab, and then, in the Forecast group, click **What-If Analysis**, and click **Data Table** to open the Data Table dialog box.

d. With the insertion point in the **Row input cell** box, click cell **B3**, and then press Tab to move to the Column input cell box. Click cell **B2**, and then click **OK**. Notice that Excel calculated the net income for the combination of client demand and golf lesson fees.

e. Select the range **F4:L16**, and then click the **Home** tab. In the Number group, click the **Number Format** arrow [General ▾], and then click **Currency**.

f. On the Home tab, in the Styles group, click **Conditional Formatting**, point to **Highlight Cells Rules**, and then click **Less Than** to open the Less Than dialog box. In the Format cells that are LESS THAN box, type **0**. If necessary, click the **with** arrow, click to select the **Light Red Fill with Dark Red Text** option, and then click **OK**.

g. Click **Conditional Formatting** again, and then point to **Highlight Cells Rules**, and then click **Greater Than** to open the Greater Than dialog box. In the Format cells that are GREATER THAN box, type **3500**, click the **with** arrow, click to select the **Green Fill with Dark Green Text** option, and then click **OK**. Press Ctrl + Home to select cell A1.

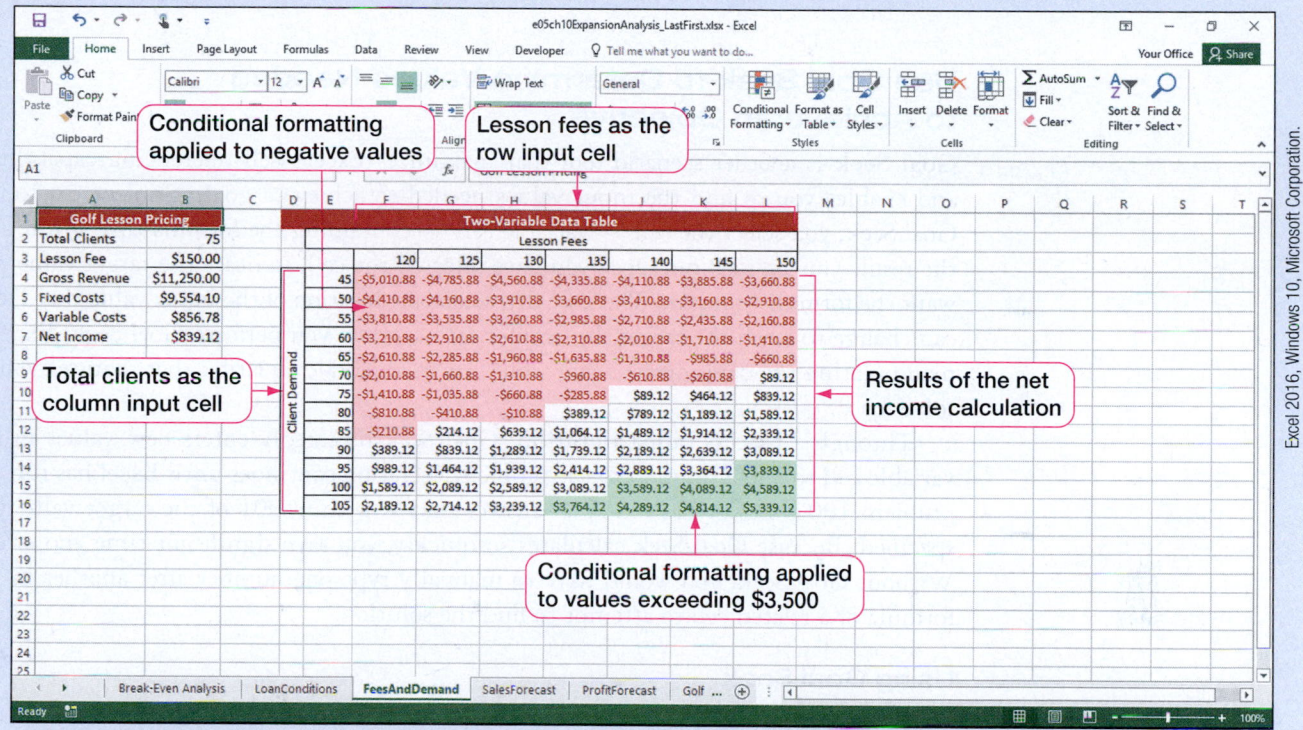

Figure 13 Two-variable data table of lesson fees and client demand

h. **Save** 🖫 the workbook.

| QUICK REFERENCE | Interpreting Elasticity |

Products and services are often evaluated by their elasticity. When interpreting elasticity, consider the following.

- Relatively elastic: If the elasticity is greater than 1, demand is very responsive to changes in price.

- Relatively inelastic: If the elasticity is less than 1, large changes in price will cause small changes in demand.

- Perfectly elastic: For high elasticity values, any change in price causes a vast change in demand.

- Perfectly inelastic: For elasticity values of zero, a change in price has no influence on demand.

- Unit elastic: For elasticity values of 1, any change in price results in an equal and opposite change in demand.

Use Goal Seek to Determine Values Needed to Achieve an Objective

Goal Seek is another scenario tool that maximizes Excel's cell-referencing capabilities and enables you to find the input values needed to achieve a goal or objective. To use Goal Seek, you select the cell — variable cell — containing the formula that will return the result you are seeking. Once you have selected the cell, indicate the target value you want the formula to return. Then, finally, select the location of the input value that Excel can change to reach the target. In simpler terms, when you perform Goal Seek, Excel is manipulating the data much as you would in an algebraic equation that requires you to solve for x.

Through a process called **iteration**, Goal Seek repeatedly enters new values in the variable cell to find a solution to the problem. Iteration continues until Excel has run the problem 100 times or has found an answer that is within .001 of the target value you specified. Because Goal Seek calculates so quickly, you save significant time and effort. Without Goal Seek, you would have to manually type one number after another in the formula or a related cell to attempt to find the solution.

Using Goal Seek

In this exercise, you will use Goal Seek to determine the number of boxes of golf balls and high-performance golf polo shirts Red Bluff needs to sell to meet its sales goals as well as the selling price of golf shorts and golf umbrellas required to meet its sales goals.

 E10.06

To Use Goal Seek

a. Click the **SalesForecast** worksheet, and then click cell **E5**.

b. Click the Data tab, and then, in the Forecast group, click **What-If Analysis**, and click **Goal Seek** to open the Goal Seek dialog box. Excel automatically selects the active cell as the Set cell value — in this case, cell E5.

Red Bluff wants to set a sales goal of $25,000 for stock golf balls. Because you know the selling price and target goal, you can calculate the quantity of boxes needed to sell to meet the sales goal.

c. Click the **To value** box, and then type 25000, press Tab to move to the By changing cell box, and then click cell **C5**.

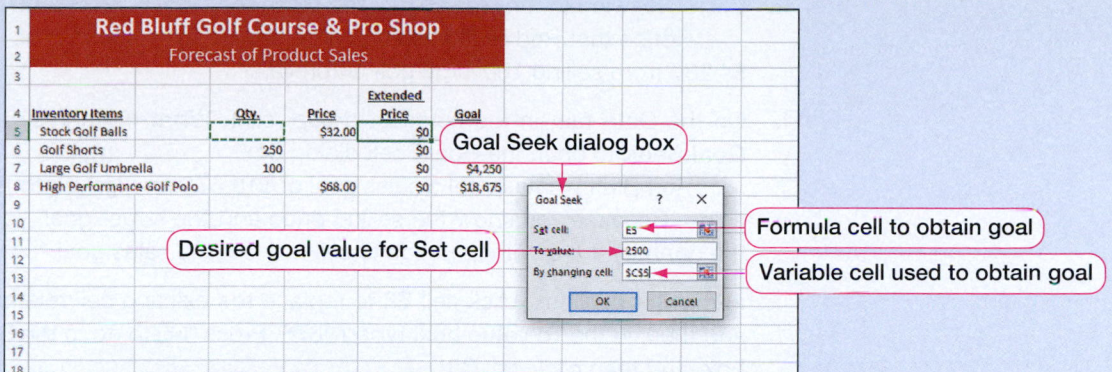

Figure 14 What-if analysis using Goal Seek

Excel 2016, Windows 10, Microsoft Corporation.

d. Click **OK** twice to run Goal Seek, and close the Goal Seek Status dialog box.

Notice that to reach its $25,000 sales goal for stock golf balls, Red Bluff would need to sell 781.25 packages of golf balls.

e. Click cell **C5**. Click the **Home** tab, and then, in the Number group, click the **Number Format** arrow General , click **Number**, and then click the **Decrease Decimal** button twice to format with no decimal places because the pro shop cannot sell part of a package of golf balls.

> ### Troubleshooting
>
> If Excel displays in the Goal Seek Status dialog box that it could not find a viable solution, click Cancel, and then ensure that you have entered the correct values in the Goal Seek dialog box. Some rules to keep in mind: Verify that the Set cell box contains a formula, the To value box contains the result desired for the formula, and the By changing cell box contains a reference to the cell that can be adjusted to achieve the goal.

f. Click the **Data** tab, and then, in the Forecast group, click **What-If Analysis**, and click **Goal Seek** to open the Goal Seek dialog box.

Red Bluff wants to set a sales goal of $12,500 for golf shorts. Because you know the quantity and target goal, you can calculate the price that must be charged to meet the sales goal.

g. In the **Set cell** box, replace the existing cell reference by clicking cell **E6**, press [Tab], and then, in the **To value** box, type **12500**. Press [Tab] to move to the By changing cell box, and then click cell **D6**.

h. Click **OK** twice to run Goal Seek, and close the Goal Seek Status dialog box.

Notice that Red Bluff should charge $50.00 to meet its sales revenue goal of $12,500 from selling 250 pairs of golf shorts.

i. On the Data tab, in the Forecast group, click **What-If Analysis**, and then click **Goal Seek** to open the Goal Seek dialog box.

Red Bluff wants to set a sales goal of $4,250 for large golf umbrellas. Because you know the quantity and target goal, you can calculate the price that must be charged to meet the sales goal.

j. In the **Set cell** box, click cell **E7** to replace the existing cell reference, press [Tab], and then, in the **To value** box, type **4250**. Press [Tab] to go to the By changing cell box, and then click cell **D7**.

k. Click **OK** twice to run Goal Seek, and close the Goal Seek Status dialog box.

Notice that Red Bluff should charge $42.50 to meet its sales revenue goal of $4,250 from selling 100 large golf umbrellas.

l. On the Data tab, in the Forecast group, click **What-If Analysis**, and then click **Goal Seek** to open the Goal Seek dialog box.

Red Bluff wants to set a sales goal of $18,675 for high-performance golf polo shirts. Because you know the selling price and the target goal, you can calculate the quantity the pro shop needs to sell to meet the sales goal.

m. In the **Set cell** box, click cell **E8** to replace the existing cell reference, press Tab, and then, in the **To value** box, type **18675**. Press Tab to go to the By changing cell box, and then click cell **C8**.

n. Click **OK** twice to run Goal Seek, and close the Goal Seek Status dialog box.

Notice that if 275 high-performance golf polo shirts are sold, the sales revenue goal of $18,675 will be met.

o. Click cell **C5**. Click the **Home** tab, and then, in the Clipboard group, click **Format Painter**, and select the cell range **C6:C8** to copy the Number format settings to these cells. Press Ctrl + Home to select cell A1.

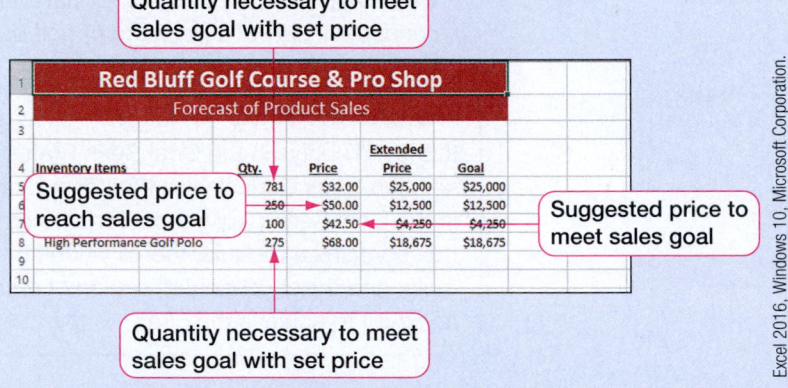

Figure 15   Results of Goal Seek analysis

p. **Save** 💾 the workbook. If you need to take a break before finishing this chapter, now is a good time.

QUICK REFERENCE	Changing Excel's Iteration Settings

Excel's default iteration settings can be changed by completing the following steps.

1. Start Excel, and then click the File tab.
2. Click Options.
3. Click Formulas in the left pane.
4. Under Calculation options, click Enable iterative calculation.
5. Select the Maximum Iterations and Maximum Change you would like Excel to perform.
6. Click OK.

Using the Scenario Manager

A **scenario** allows you to build a what-if analysis model that includes variable cells linked by one or more formulas or functions. By running the scenarios, you have the ability to compare multiple variables and their combined effects on the various calculated outcomes. Managers can use scenarios to view best-case, worst-case, and most likely scenarios in order to make decisions and solve problems. For example, the Red Bluff Golf Course & Pro Shop manager might want to compare best-case, most likely, and worst-case scenarios for sales based on sales volumes at the pro shop in a week.

Scenarios can be most beneficial because they can use multiple variables. Through the use of Goal Seek and data tables, you learned that you could use what-if analysis tools when you want to analyze the effects on various calculations when inputting one or two variables. Scenarios can evaluate one, two, or many variables. For example, the Red Bluff manager may want to view best-case, worst-case, and most likely scenarios of the pro shop's total net income based on variable costs, fixed costs, and gross revenue of both retail products and golf lessons. In this section, you will learn how to use the **Scenario Manager**, the third type of what-if analysis tool, to manage scenarios by adding, deleting, editing, and viewing scenarios and to create scenario reports.

Use the Scenario Manager to Create Scenarios

You can use scenarios to predict the outcome of different situations in your spreadsheet. Before creating a scenario, you need to design your worksheet to contain at least one formula or function. This formula or function will rely on other cells and can have different values inserted into it. The significant step in creating the various scenarios is identifying the various data cells whose values can differ in each scenario. You can then select these cells — known as **changing cells** — in the worksheet before you open the Scenario Manager dialog box. Once the Scenario Manager dialog box is open, you can enter and define the different scenarios. Each scenario includes a scenario name, input or changing cells, and the values for each input cell.

Designing a Scenario

Barry Cheney would like you to determine how much net income — profit — the Red Bluff Golf Course & Pro Shop is forecasted to generate on the basis of varying retail sales, revenue from services rendered, and variable costs. In this exercise, you will enter the formulas that will help to calculate each scenario.

 **E10.07**

To Design a Scenario

a. If you took a break, open the **e05chExpansionAnalysis** workbook.

b. Click the **ProfitForecast** worksheet.

c. Click cell **D6**, type **=SUM**, and then press Tab to insert the function. Select cells **D4:D5** to calculate the forecasted total or gross revenue, and then press Enter.

d. Click cell **D13**, type **=SUM**, and then press Tab to insert the function. Select cells **D9:D12** to calculate the total forecasted fixed costs, and then press Enter.

e. Click cell **D15**, type **=**, click cell **D6,** type *****, and then click cell **C15** to calculate the forecasted employee commissions. Press Enter.

f. In cell **D16**, type **=**, click cell **D13,** type **+**, and then click cell **D15** to calculate the forecasted total expenses. Press Enter.

g. In cell **D17**, type **=**, click cell **D6,** type **–**, and then click cell **D16** to calculate the forecasted net income. Press Enter.

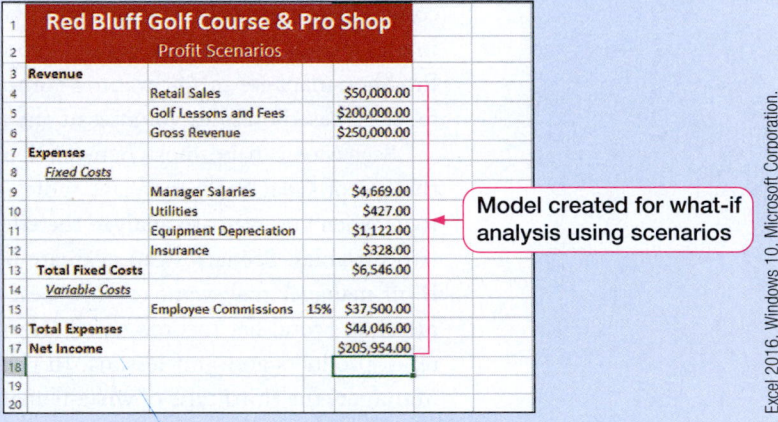

Figure 16   Forecasting model

h. Save 🖬 the workbook.

Adding, Deleting, and Editing Scenarios

Once you have identified the changing cells — which can be anywhere on your worksheet — you can then select these cells in the worksheet before you open the Scenario Manager dialog box, or you can enter the target cells directly into the Scenario Manager dialog box as well as entering and defining the different scenarios. Each scenario represents different what-if conditions to evaluate the spreadsheet model. Once scenarios have been added, they are stored under the name you assigned to them. The number of scenarios you can create is limitless. In this exercise, you will use the Scenario Manager to create various profit scenarios for the Red Bluff Golf Course & Pro Shop.

To Add, Delete, and Edit Scenarios

a. Click the **ProfitForecast** worksheet, and select the range **D4:D5**. These will be your changing cells.

b. Click the **Data** tab, and then, in the Forecast group, click **What-If Analysis**, and select **Scenario Manager** to open the Scenario Manager dialog box.

c. In the Scenario Manager dialog box, click **Add** to begin creating your first scenario. In the Add Scenario dialog box, type Most Likely Scenario in the Scenario name box.

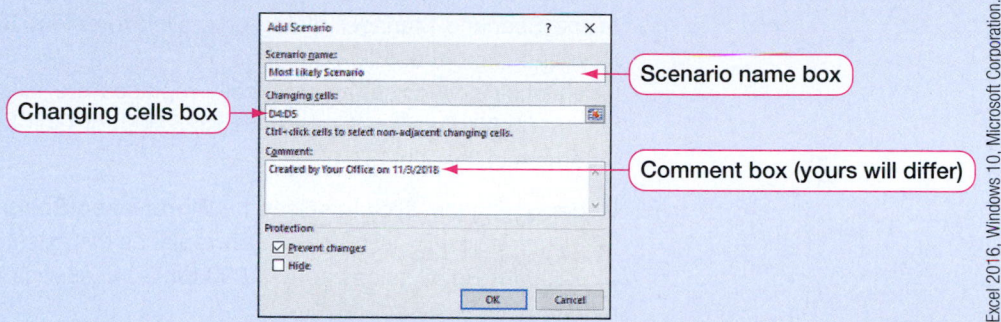

Figure 17 Add Scenario dialog box

d. Click **OK**. The values that are entered in cells D4 and D5 are the most likely scenario values. Click **OK**.

e. In the Scenario Manager dialog box, click **Add** to begin creating your second scenario. In the Add Scenario dialog box, type Best-case Scenario in the Scenario name box, and then click **OK**. The Scenario Values dialog box will open.

f. Barry Cheney believes that the best-case scenario would result in revenue of $100,000 in Retail sales and $325,000 in golf lessons and fees. Type 100000 in the $D$4 box, and then type 325000 in the $D$5 box.

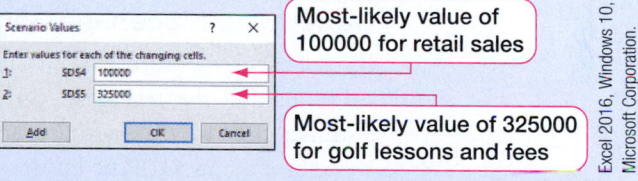

Figure 18 Scenario Values dialog box

g. Click **OK**, and then, in the Scenario Manager dialog box, click **Add**.

h. In the Add Scenario dialog box, type Worst-case Scenario in the Scenario name box, and then click **OK**. The Scenario Values dialog box will open.

i. Barry Cheney believes that the worst-case scenario would result in revenue of $25,000 in retail sales and $75,000 in golf lessons and fees. Type 25000 in the $D$4 box, type 75000 in the $D$5 box, and then click **OK**.

j. Because Barry has already created a forecast with the most likely scenario values entered, he decided that he does not need this scenario and e-mails you to let you know. In the Scenario Manager dialog box, under Scenarios, click to select **Most Likely Scenario**, and then click **Delete** to delete the most likely scenario.

k. Barry also informed you that the worst-case scenario would have retail sales forecasted at $20,000. In the Scenario Manager dialog box, under Scenarios, click to select **Worst-case Scenario**, click **Edit**, and in the Edit Scenario dialog box, click **OK**.

l. In the $D$4 box of the Scenario Values dialog box, change 25000 to 20000, and then click **OK**.

Viewing Scenarios

After you create the scenarios, you can view the results by using the Show button at the bottom of the Scenario Manager dialog box. This is helpful to double-check whether the values entered in each scenario are accurate. Excel will replace the existing values in your spreadsheet with those entered into each scenario. In this exercise, you will view the various scenarios created.

 **E10.09**

To View Scenarios

a. In the Scenario Manager dialog box, click to select **Best-case Scenario** under Scenarios, and then click **Show**.
Notice how Excel automatically replaces the existing values in D4 and D5 with $100,000 for Retail sales and $325,000 for Golf Lessons and Fees. The Net Income result is $354,704.

b. Under Scenarios, click to select the **Worst-case Scenario**, and then click **Show**.
Notice how Excel automatically replaces the existing values in D4 and D5 with $20,000 for Retail sales and $75,000 for Golf Lessons and Fees. The Net Income result is $74,204.

Create Scenario Reports

Although you can view your scenarios while the Scenario Manager dialog box is open, you will probably want to view them side by side to compare the results. Additionally, it is not possible to print and distribute the scenarios very easily this way. You can create a Scenario Summary report automatically by clicking the Summary button in the Scenario Manager dialog box. A **Scenario Summary report** lists the results of scenarios side by side, allowing the outcomes to be easily compared. The Summary button opens the Scenario Summary dialog box where you can choose the type of report you would like to create.

Generating a Scenario Summary Report

By selecting the Scenario Summary option, you can create a worksheet that includes subtotals and the results of the scenarios. In this exercise, you will create a Scenario Summary report so that Barry Cheney can view the current scenario modeled in the worksheet along with the best-case and most likely scenarios.

 **E10.10**

To Generate a Scenario Summary Report

a. In the Scenario Manager dialog box, click **Summary** to open the Scenario Summary dialog box.

b. Leave the Report type at the default selection of Scenario summary, verify the Result cell is **D17**, and then click **OK**. Notice that Excel adds a new worksheet named Scenario Summary to your workbook.

c. Format the Scenario Summary report so it is easier to read. Select cells **B6:C6**, click the **Home** tab, and then, in the Alignment group, click **Merge & Center**, and replace the **$D$4** text by typing Retail Sales. Press Enter.

d. Select cells **B7:C7**, click **Merge & Center**, and replace the **$D$5** text by typing Lessons and Fees. Press Enter. Adjust the width of column C so that the text can be read.

e. Select cells **B9:C9**. Click **Merge & Center**, and then replace the **$D$17** text by typing Net Income. Press Enter.

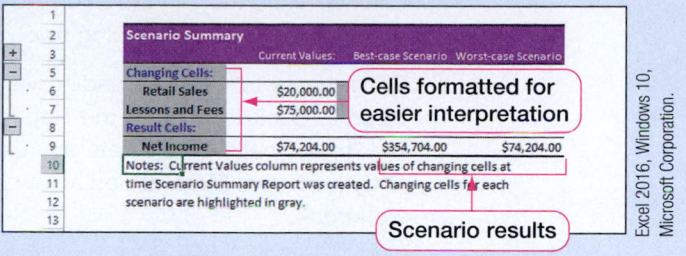

Figure 19 Scenario Summary report

f. **Save**  the workbook.

Generating a Scenario PivotTable Report

A scenario PivotTable report can also be created automatically by clicking the Summary button in the Scenario Manager dialog box. The Summary button opens the Scenario Summary dialog box, where you can choose the Scenario PivotTable report option. A **Scenario PivotTable report** summarizes the results of various scenarios side by side in a PivotTable format. In this exercise, you will create a Scenario PivotTable report that will allow management even more manipulation of data because of the two-dimensional view the report provides.

E10.11

To Generate a Scenario PivotTable Report

a. Click the **ProfitForecast** worksheet.

b. Click the **Data** tab, and then, in the Forecast group, click **What-If Analysis**, and click **Scenario Manager** to open the Scenario Manager dialog box.

c. In the Scenario Manager dialog box, click to select the **Best-case Scenario**, and then click **Edit**.

d. Barry Cheney wants to determine whether the Red Bluff Golf Course & Pro Shop can still be profitable if the employees earn different commissions based on sales. In the Edit Scenario dialog box, click the **Changing cells** box to place the insertion point after the range D4:D5, and then type **,C15**. Click **OK**.

e. In the Scenario Values dialog box, in the $C$15 box, verify that the value displays 0.15 to reflect the commission of 15%, and then click **OK**.

f. In the Scenario Manager dialog box, click to select **Worst-case Scenario**, and then click **Edit**.

g. In the Edit Scenario dialog box, click the **Changing cells** box to place the insertion point after the range D4:D5, and then type **,C15**. Click **OK**.

h. In the Scenario Values dialog box, click the row 3 **$C$15** box, delete the 0.15 value, type **0.075** to change the commission to 7.5%, and then click **OK**.

i. Barry also wants you to re-create the most likely scenario. In the Scenario Manager dialog box, click **Add**, type **Most Likely Scenario** in the Scenario name box, and then click **OK**. Your D4:D5, C15 changing cells will automatically be entered into the Changing cells box.

j. Type the following values for each changing cell in each box of the Scenario Values dialog box. Type **25000** in box 1, type **162500** in box 2, and type **0.10** in box 3.

k. Click **OK**, and then, in the Scenario Manager dialog box, click **Summary** to open the Scenario Summary dialog box.

l. Barry wants to view the ending values for gross revenue, commission, and net income. Click to change the Report type to **Scenario PivotTable report**, click the **Result cells** box, delete any existing text, type **D6,C15,D17**, and then click **OK**. Notice that Excel added a new worksheet named Scenario PivotTable to your workbook.

m. Format your PivotTable report to make it easier to read the data. Click cell **A1**, replace the existing text by typing Retail Sales and Golf Lessons and Fees, and then press Enter. Click the **Home** tab, and then, in the Cells group, click **Format**, and click **Column Width**. In the Column width box, set the width of column A to 34. Click **OK**.

n. In cell **A2**, type Scenario PivotTable Report, press Enter, select the range **A2:D2**, and then click **Merge & Center**. Click the **Bold** button, click the **Font Size** arrow, and then click **16**.

o. Click cell **A3**, type Scenarios, and then press Tab.

p. Add headings to your data. In cell **B3**, type Gross Revenue, and then press Tab. In cell **C3**, type Commission, and then press Tab. In cell **D3**, type Net Income, and then press Enter.

q. Select the range **B3:D3**, and then, in the Alignment group, click **Center**, and click **Format**. Click **Column Width**, and then, in the Column width box type 14, and click **OK**.

r. Select the range **B4:B6**, hold down Ctrl, select the range **D4:D6**, and then click the **Number Format** arrow, and click **Currency**. Click the **Decrease Decimal** button two times to format with no decimal places.

s. Select the range **C4:C6**, and then click the **Number Format** arrow, and click **Percentage**. Click the **Increase Decimal** button once to format with one decimal place, and then press Ctrl + Home to return to cell A1.

Scenario results in PivotTable format

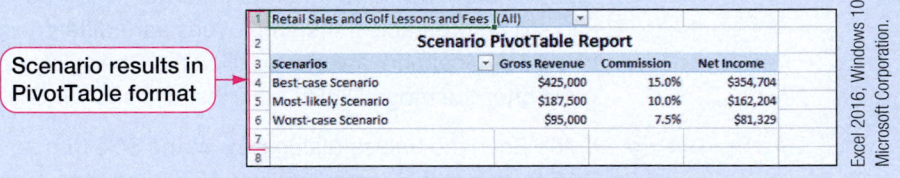

Figure 20   Scenario PivotTable report

t. **Save** the workbook. If you need to take a break before finishing this chapter, now is a good time.

Using Solver

An important item to note is that there is no true or right answer on whether, or how much, to raise prices. The answer depends in part on the businessperson's notion of how much demand he or she believes there is likely to be at the various prices and what that relationship is for that particular business. It may be risky to raise the price very high because a higher price will lower demand, which means that fewer units are likely to be sold at the higher price. However, if the demand stays the same or is higher than expected, the profit potential is also higher. This is when a tool such as Solver can help to give a businessperson enough information to make an educated decision.

Excel's **Solver** is an add-in that helps to optimize a problem by manipulating the values for several variables with constraints that you determine. A **constraint** is a rule you establish when formulating your Solver model. You can use Solver to find the highest, lowest, or exact value for a specific outcome by adjusting values for selected variables. Business managers can use Solver to minimize or maximize the output based on the constraints. For example, the golf course manager could use Solver to determine a sales strategy that will help the golf course maximize its profit, given a specific mix of services provided to clients. In this section, you will learn how to load the Solver add-in; find optimal solutions by setting objectives, changing variable cells, and defining constraints; generate a Solver answer report; and save and restore a Solver model.

Understand the Use of the Solver Add-In

Solver is one of many add-ins installed by default with Excel 2016. However, it is not attached to the ribbon by default. An **add-in** is an application with specific functionality geared toward accomplishing a specific goal. Because companies other than Microsoft develop the add-ins, they are not automatically activated when Excel is installed.

Loading the Solver Add-In

To use the Solver, you need to activate the add-in. This is a one-time setup task; once you have activated the Solver add-in, it will appear on the Data tab on the ribbon each time you launch Excel. In this exercise, you will load the Solver add-in.

 **E10.12**

To Load the Solver Add-In

a. If you took a break, open the **e05ch10ExpansionAnalysis** workbook.

b. Click the **File** tab, and then click **Options**, and click **Add-Ins**.

c. At the bottom of the View and manage Microsoft Office Add-ins pane, if necessary, click the **Manage** arrow, click **Excel Add-ins**, and then click **Go**.

d. In the Add-Ins dialog box, click the **Solver Add-in** check box, and then click **OK**.

e. To verify that the Solver add-in was added properly, click the **Data** tab, and then check to see that the Solver button is displayed in the Analyze group on the right side of the ribbon.

Solve Complex Problems Using Solver

The purpose of using Solver is to perform what-if analysis to solve more complex problems and to optimize the outcome. When you **optimize**, you are finding the best way to do something. For example, Barry Cheney may want to find the best product mix of the pro shop's retail products to maximize profitability. He could use Solver to find the values of certain cells in a spreadsheet that optimize — maximize or minimize — a certain objective. Thus, Solver helps to answer this type of optimization problem.

Before configuring the Solver constraints, you need to ensure that you create a spreadsheet model that can be used to manipulate the values for your variables. This involves creating a target cell, which defines the goal of your problem. For example, Barry may create a formula that calculates total revenue. Additionally, you need to select one or more variable cells that the Solver can change to reach the goal. You should evaluate your spreadsheet as you define your goal, identify one or more variables that can change in attaining the chosen goal, and then determine the limitations of the spreadsheet model. These variable cells are used to formulate the three Solver parameters: objective cell, changing cells, and constraints.

Your worksheet can also contain other values, formulas, and functions that use the target cell and the variable cells to reach the goal. For the Solver to work properly, the formula in the target cell must reference and depend on the variable cells for part of its calculation. If you do not construct your Solver model in this format, you will get an error message that states, "The Set Target Cell values do not converge."

REAL WORLD ADVICE	Solver Can Be Used for Many Analyses

The Excel Solver add-in can be a powerful tool for analyzing data. In many financial planning problems, an amount such as the unpaid balance on a loan or the amount saved in a retirement fund changes over time. Consider a situation in which a business borrows money. Because only the principal of the monthly payment reduces the unpaid loan balance, the business may want to determine how it can minimize the total interest paid on the loan if it pays more than the minimum payment each month.

Setting the Objective Cell and Variable Cells

The **objective cell** contains the formula that creates a value that you want to optimize — maximize, minimize, or set to a specific value. For example, the golf course manager may want to maximize the gross revenue of golf lessons by analyzing the number of customers per day in relation to the total number of instructors employed. The golf course manager would have to consider many factors; however, deciding the actual goal of using Solver is the first step in creating a Solver analysis.

Solver works with a group of cells, called variable cells, which take part in calculating the formulas in the objective and constraint cells. Solver adjusts the values in the variable cells to satisfy the limits on constraint cells and return the result you want for the objective cell.

The golf course manager wants you to find the total number of clients, the number of hours of lessons per day, and the number of instructors on duty needed to maximize net income. The worksheet you were given was previously set up with functions to calculate the net income.

 E10.13

To Set the Objective Cell and Variable Cells

a. Click the **GolfLessons** worksheet.

b. On the Data tab, in the Analyze group, click **Solver**.

c. Because Barry Cheney wants to maximize the net income, the cell that holds the net income will become the objective cell. In the Solver Parameters dialog box, click in the **Set Objective** box, and then click cell **D20**, moving the Solver Parameters dialog box if necessary.

d. Because you need to maximize the net income, set the objective to **Max**, which is Excel's default value.

e. Two variables that will have an effect on the net income are the total number of clients and the number of instructors on duty. Click in the **By Changing Variable Cells** box, and then select cells **D4:D5**.

Defining Constraints

Constraints are the rules or restrictions that your variable cells must follow when the Solver performs its analysis. For example, if Barry Cheney wants to maximize the net income on the basis of how many golf lessons are given per day, he would have to consider how many hours per day the course is open, how many instructors work per day, and how long it takes to give a lesson. In addition, the cost of supplies can vary depending on how many clients the instructors have. In this exercise, you will use the Solver Parameters dialog box to identify the various constraints in the model.

 **E10.14**

To Define Constraints

a. In the Solver Parameters dialog box, click **Add** to enter the first constraint. The Add Constraint dialog box will open.

b. The golf course can have no more than four instructors scheduled at any given time. On the **GolfLessons** worksheet, in the Add Constraint dialog box, in the Cell Reference box, click cell **D5**. If necessary, click the **arrow**, to select **<=** in the mathematical operands box, and then, in the Constraint box, type **4**.

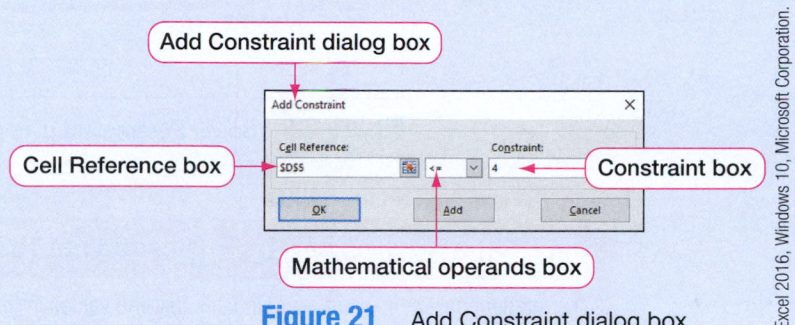

Figure 21   Add Constraint dialog box

c. Click **Add** to save the first constraint, and add another constraint.

d. Lessons can last from 45 minutes to 90 minutes each, and the golf course is open for 11 hours per day. This means that instructors can give anywhere from 7 to 14 lessons per day. Communicating this requires you to enter two constraints. In the Add Constraint dialog box, in the Cell Reference box, reference cell **D4**. Click the **arrow**, and select **>=** in the mathematical operands box, and then, in the Constraint box, type **7**.

e. Click **Add**, and then, in the Add Constraint dialog box, in the Cell Reference box, reference cell **D4**. Click the **arrow**, and select **<=** in the mathematical operands box if necessary, and then, in the Constraint box, type **14**.

f. In the Add Constraint dialog box, click **Add**. Because the instructors cannot service part of a client, you have to add a constraint to ensure that the value returned for cell D4 is a whole number. In the Add Constraint dialog box, in the Cell Reference box, reference cell **D4**. Click the **arrow**, and select **int** in the mathematical operands box. Excel will enter the word "integer" in the Constraint box. Click **Add**.

g. Because Red Bluff cannot have part of an instructor working, you have to add a constraint to ensure that the value returned for cell D5 is a whole number. In the Add Constraint dialog box, in the Cell Reference box, reference cell **D5**. Click the **arrow**, and select **int** in the mathematical operands box.

h. Click **OK**. Notice that the five constraints you entered appear under the Subject to the Constraints list of the Solver Parameters dialog box. Leave the Solver Parameters dialog box open for the next step.

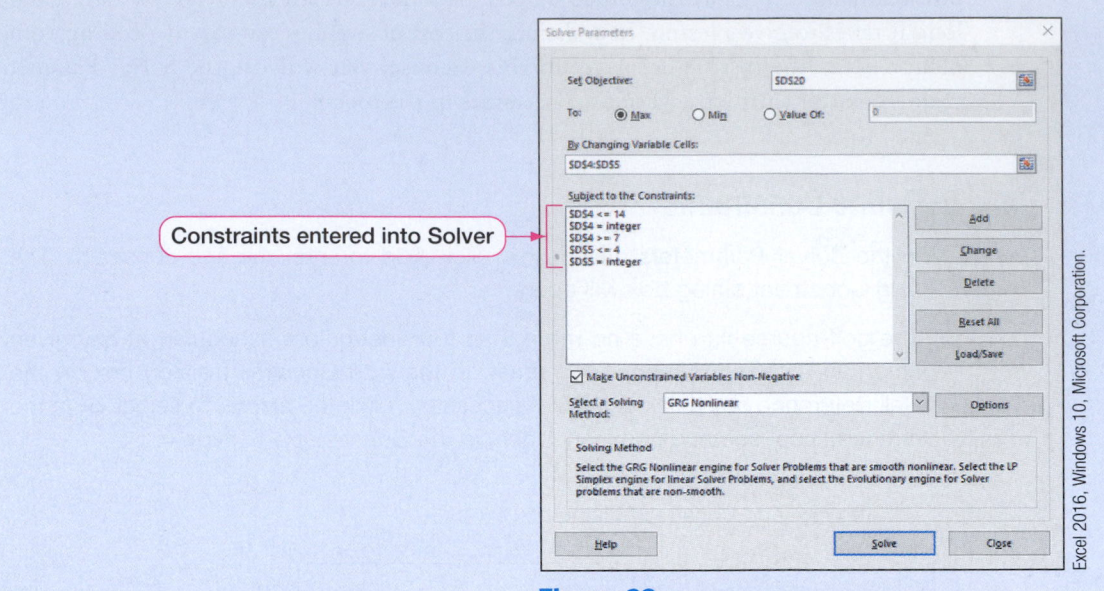

Constraints entered into Solver

Figure 22   Solver Parameters dialog box

QUICK REFERENCE	Constraints That Can Be Overlooked

The integer constraint — int — mandates that the values in the variable cells remain whole numbers. For example, the manufacturers of Red Bluff's retail products — such as golf balls and golf gloves — will not produce partial products. Thus, to guarantee that the variable cell values remain whole numbers, you need to create integer constraints for them.

The greater than or equal to zero constraint requires the variable cell values remain greater than or equal to zero when you run Solver. For example, the manufacturers of Red Bluff's retail products will not produce negative amounts of product. However, a negative value in a changing variable cell could possibly produce higher results in the objective cell. By default, the Make Unconstrained Variables Non-Negative check box is selected to guarantee that the variable cells remain greater than or equal to zero. If you want to let a variable cell be negative, you can uncheck the Make Unconstrained Variables Non-Negative check box and create a constraint that allows this to occur, such as D7>=−50.

One item to note: If Solver takes too long to solve, you can press $\boxed{\text{Esc}}$ to break Solver and stop running the analysis.

Selecting a Solving Method

Three solving methods are available within the Solver Parameters dialog box: Simplex LP, Evolutionary, and Generalized Reduced Gradient (GRG) Nonlinear. These solving methods relate to **linear programming** (LP), which is a mathematical method for determining how to attain the best outcome, such as the maximum profit or the lowest cost, in a given mathematical model, such as your spreadsheet, for a list of requirements — constraints — represented as linear relationships. Thus, linear programming is a specific case of mathematical programming and compares how the equation is displayed on a chart. When you run Solver, this mathematical programming is occurring behind the scenes.

The **Simplex LP method** is a linear model in which the variables are not raised to any powers and no transcendent functions — such as sine or cosine — are used. To use Simplex LP, your equations must not break the linearity. An in-depth discussion of algebraic linearity is beyond the scope of this chapter. However, in algebra, "linear" means that the slope-intercept equation for a line — $y = mx + b$ — is true. In linear programming, Excel plots all of the constraints as lines and finds the optimal result from the intersections of those lines. So formulas that function similar to the slope-intercept formula are linear. However, some functions and operators can potentially break linearity, such as MIN, MAX, IF, and DIVISION. If your formulas are linear, select the Simplex LP method because this method is the fastest and most reliable of the three methods. In fact, if you can purposefully design your models as linear, it is better.

For example, perhaps Barry Cheney wants you to use Solver to be able to determine what advertisements to purchase to maximize exposures yet stay under budget. In this case, you take the number of advertising units (the variable) and multiply it by the exposures per unit (a constant) and the cost (another constant) to get the amount of exposures and cost per advertisement type, such as television, Internet, and radio. Then you add all of those together and constrain it by the maximum amount you can spend, along with any other constraints. Then you optimize for maximum exposures. Notice that you multiplied the variable cells by a constant and then added them together, similar to the slope-intercept formula. Thus, if the constraints were plotted on a chart, the lines would be linear, as illustrated in Figure 23.

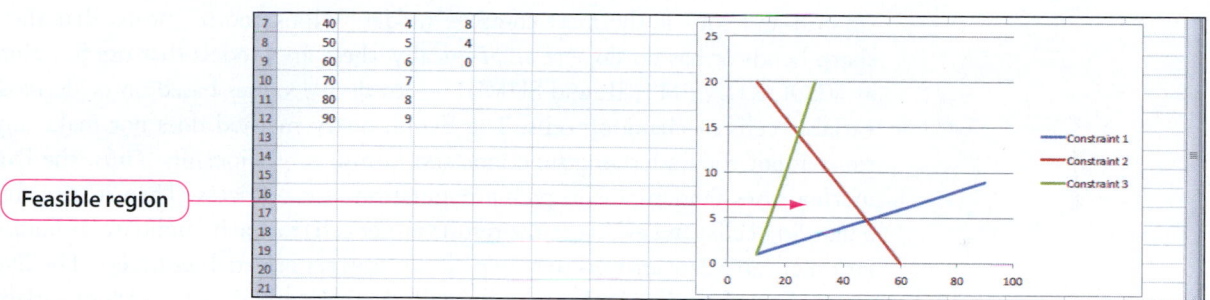

Figure 23   Linear chart with three linear constraints

The **GRG Nonlinear method** is used for more complex models that are nonlinear and smooth. It is also the default method that Excel's Solver uses. Smooth means that when the constraints are graphed, a curve of some kind exists: concave, convex, a wave, and so on. Generally, the model is smooth when it uses trigonometric functions or exponentials, multiplies the variables together, and so on. A nonlinear model is one in which just one of the constraint lines breaks the linearity of the model. You may have several constraints that are linear but one constraint line that breaks the linearity of the model, as shown in Figure 24.

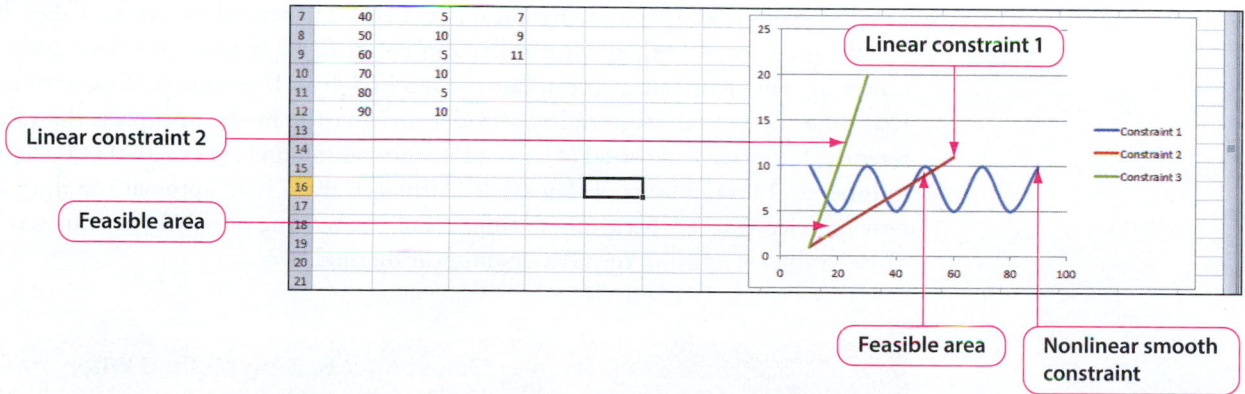

Figure 24   Nonlinear chart with two feasible areas

In the GRG Nonlinear method, Excel uses an iterative process and starting point. You tell Excel where to start, and it starts moving along the constraint lines — linear and nonlinear. The starting point is typically zero unless specific individualized business knowledge would indicate otherwise. As it moves along the graph lines, Excel is looking for peaks when maximizing and valleys when minimizing. When it finds a significant enough peak or valley, Excel finds an optimal answer. If you give Excel a different starting point, Excel may find a different locally optimal answer, particularly if a higher peak or a lower valley exists far away from the starting point that you used the first time. Thus, the GRG Nonlinear method is less reliable than the Simplex LP method. However, the Simplex LP method is limited in what can be modeled because linearity must be maintained.

There is a setting in GRG Nonlinear to help resolve this potential issue. You can take advantage of the Multistart method. This allows Excel to have multiple start points to compare all of the locally optimal answers. By way of this comparison, Excel can potentially find a probabilistically global optimal answer.

Finally, integer constraints break the linearity of a model even if you set it to use Simplex LP. Thus, integer constraints force GRG Nonlinear and a special branching method that takes longer. Also, if the model is actually linear, setting the method to GRG Nonlinear will force a linear model to be solved with GRG Nonlinear.

The **Evolutionary method** is used when a worksheet model is nonlinear and non-smooth and thus is the most complex model. "Nonsmooth" means that the line takes sharp bends or has no slope at all. Typically, these are models that use functions — such as VLOOKUP, PMT, IF, and SUMIF — to derive values based on or derived from the variable cells or changing cells. The Evolutionary method does not make any assumptions about the underlying functions and formulas relationship. Thus, the Evolutionary method uses randomness to pick a population of candidates. Then it uses the variables (changing cells) and evaluates the result (target cell) for each candidate. It holds the population of candidate answers to help pick the next set of variables to test. The Evolutionary method's name is inspired by nature itself. As the method picks random variables, it will use natural selection to reuse certain variables from the population that seem to yield better results. It will also use a crossover effect to combine variables from two known good answers in the population. Further, it will also randomly "mutate" to create new candidates for the population that may or may not be better than the other candidates.

This means that the Evolutionary method cannot guarantee the most optimal result but only the best result it found. Thus, every time you run the Evolutionary method, you might get a different answer. The Evolutionary method takes more processing power and time than the other methods. The only way the Evolutionary method knows when to stop is on the basis of the user-defined setting for length of time, number of iterations, or number of candidates. Therefore, the Evolutionary method is best only in situations that cannot be adequately modeled with an optimal answer method, that is, Simplex LP or GRG Nonlinear. Using the Evolutionary method is beyond the scope of this chapter.

With all three methods, scalability can be an issue. If there is a wide scale for the object or constraint values, it can cause issues in Solver. If you are dealing with numbers that differ by several magnitudes, consider revising the model to express the values differently. For example, instead of listing the number to purchase as 2,000,000, express the number as 2,000 in units of thousands. Although there is an automatic scaling setting, best practice is to uncheck this setting. As of the writing of this book, this setting can cause problems in using the GRG Nonlinear method.

QUICK REFERENCE	Selecting a Solving Method When You Are Not Sure Where to Begin

Start with Simplex LP. If your model is nonlinear, Solver will notify you. At that point, you can try the GRG Nonlinear model. If Solver still cannot seem to converge on — gather or develop — a solution, then try the Evolutionary model. One of these three models will eventually give you an optimal or good solution.

Generate and Interpret Solver Answer Reports

When you run Solver, an answer report is created in a new worksheet and named "Answer Report." Other items to be considered in producing a Solver Answer Report include the type of report you want to generate — Answer, Sensitivity, Limits, or Population — as well as deciding how you want your worksheet to look after you run the Solver. When the Evolutionary Solving method is used, the Population report is also available. If Solver finds an optimal solution and there are no integer constraints, two additional reports are available: the sensitivity report and the limits report.

Generating a Solver Answer Report

After you define the objective, variable cells, constraints, and solving method, you are ready to generate a Solver answer report. After you run Solver, you have several options before the report is generated. Once Solver displays a message that states it found a solution, you can choose the type of report that you want: Answer, Sensitivity, Limits, or Population. The **Solver Answer Report** lists the objective cell and the changing cells with their corresponding original and final values for the problem, input variables, and constraints. In addition, the formulas, binding status, and slacks are given for each constraint. The **Solver Sensitivity Report** provides information about how sensitive the solution is to small changes in the formula for the target cell. This report displays the shadow prices for the constraint — the amount the objective function value changes per unit change in the constraint. Because constraints are often determined by resources, a comparison of the shadow prices of each constraint provides valuable information about the most effective place to apply additional resources to achieve the best improvement. This report can be created only if your Excel model does not contain integer or Boolean — the values 0 and 1 — constraints. The **Solver Limits Report** displays the achieved optimal value and all the input variables of the model with the optimal values. Additionally, the report displays the upper and lower bounds for the optimal value. A variable cell could vary without changing the optimal solution. Finally, the **Solver Population Report** displays various statistical characteristics about the given model, such as how many variables and rows it contains.

You can also choose how you want your Excel model to behave, either restoring it to the original values or keeping the Solver solution. If you restore the original values, the original values that were entered into the variable cells before running Solver are restored. This can be helpful in case you have to run Solver again, because it keeps you from having to manually change the values back to what they were when you began. If you choose to keep the Solver solution, you will be able to see the final outcome on both the Answer Report and the Excel model. Regardless of which option you choose, you will still be able to run Solver over and over again as needed. In this exercise, you will generate a Solver Answer Report using the GRG Nonlinear method.

 **E10.15**

To Generate a Solver Answer Report

a. In the Solver Parameters dialog box, if necessary, click the Select a Solving Method **arrow**, and then click to select **GRG Nonlinear** solving method because the changing cells are being multiplied together.

b. Click **Options**, click the **All Methods** tab if necessary, and verify that the **Use Automatic Scaling** check box is unchecked.

c. Click the **GRG Nonlinear** tab. If necessary, click to check the **Use Multistart** check box, and then click to uncheck the **Require Bounds on Variables** check box. Click **OK**.

d. Click **Solve** at the bottom of the Solver Parameters dialog box.

e. In the Solver Results dialog box, verify that the **Keep Solver Solution** option is selected. This will display your optimal results on the spreadsheet as well as your report.

f. Under Reports, on the right side of the Solver Results dialog box, click to select **Answer**.

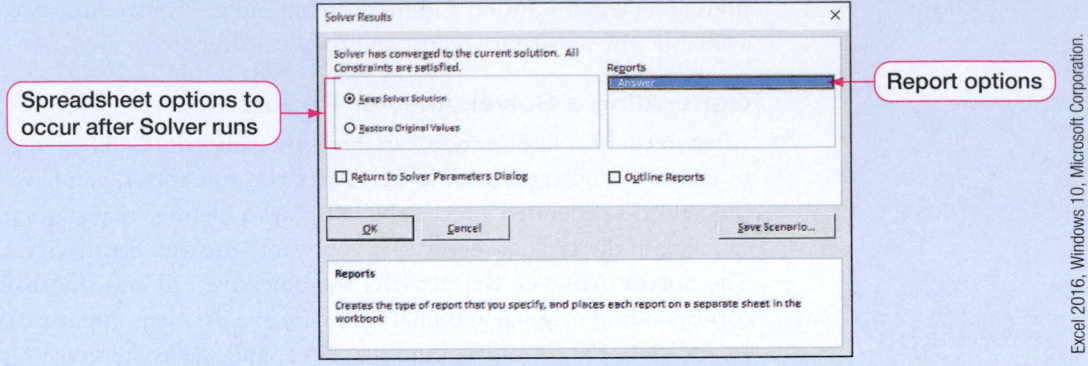

Figure 25 Solver Results dialog box

g. Click **OK**. Notice that a worksheet tab named Answer Report 1 now exists in the workbook.

h. Click the **Answer Report 1** worksheet, and then **Save** the workbook.

Interpreting a Solver Answer Report

The Solver answer report is divided into four sections: report details, objective cell information, variable cell information, and constraints information. The first three sections of the Answer Report you just created are shown in Figure 26. The report details section displays information about the Solver report: report type, filename, worksheet that contains the Excel model, and the date and time the report was created; Solver Engine details; and Solver Options that you set at the time you created the report.

The second section reports information about the objective cells: cell references; cell names; whether you searched for the minimum, maximum, or a specific value; and the original and final objective cell values. For example, in this model, you were trying to maximize the net income. Before Solver was run, the net income value was −$1,707.50; however, once Solver ran, the net income was maximized. The result indicated that the golf course could make $8,032.90 in profit.

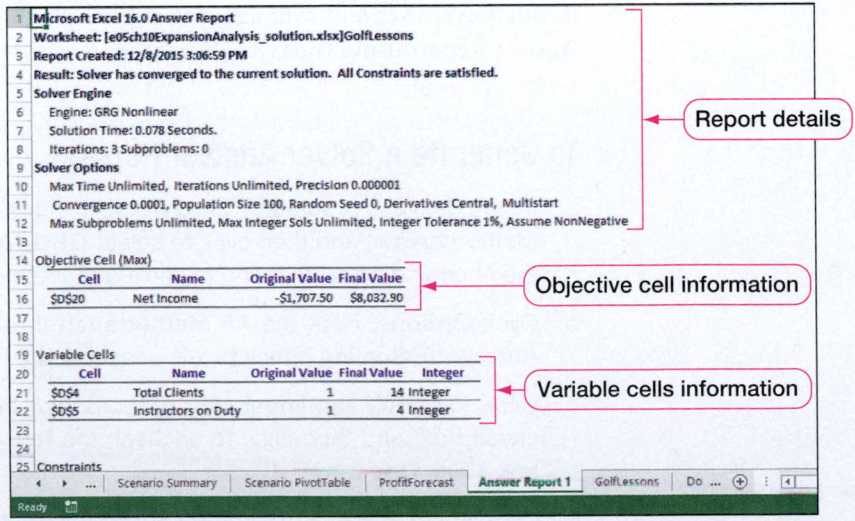

Figure 26 Solver Answer report

The third section displays information about the variable cells: cell references, variable cell names, original cell values, and final cell values. In your report, you can see that each of the four instructors can see 14 clients per day. This mix will create a profit of $8,032.90 per day.

The fourth section displays information about the constraints you entered — cell references, descriptions, new cell values, formulas, status, and slack — for each constraint. This section of the report can be seen in Figure 27. In your report, notice that the total clients slack is 7, the difference between the lower constraint of 7 and the upper constraint value of 14 for cell D4. A constraint is considered to be a **binding constraint** if changing it also changes the optimal solution. A less severe constraint that does not affect the optimal solution is known as a **nonbinding constraint**.

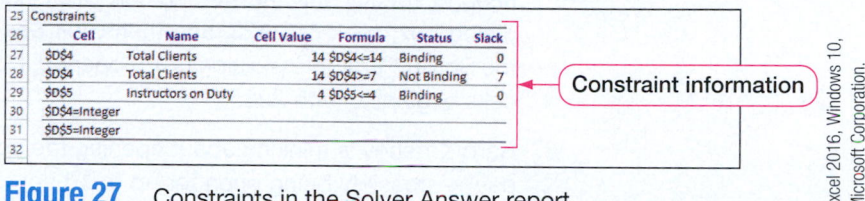

Figure 27   Constraints in the Solver Answer report

One point to note is that if you change your Excel model or Solver parameters, you must run Solver again to create an updated report. The names of new reports will be "Answer Report" followed by consecutive numbering: 1, 2, 3, and so on. Simply delete the reports you no longer need.

 CONSIDER THIS | **Why Is It Important to Know How to Read Solver Reports?**

You have spent a considerable amount of time creating your Solver answer report. Why do you think it is so important to be able to understand what the output data for the answer report is telling you? How would analyzing the data and interpreting the output affect management decisions? What factors would you consider when setting the variable constraints for any adjustments to the Solver model?

Saving and Restoring a Solver Model

When you save your workbook, the most recent Solver settings are automatically saved, even if you have multiple worksheets in which you created Solver parameters. For example, if you have made changes to your Solver constraints, the previous ones will not be saved. You can save your Solver settings as you work; that way, you can apply previous settings again in the future. By saving the Solver model, you save the objective cells, variable cells, and constraints, and Excel places this information in a few cells on the worksheet. Solver models can be easily saved and reloaded by clicking the Load/Save button in the Solver Parameters dialog box.

CONSIDER THIS | **How Could You Use Solver?**

Have you ever wondered what you need to get on your outstanding assignments and exams to earn a specific grade in a course? Or have you wondered how much of a salary increase you would need to budget for a specific purchase or how to meet certain goals for retirement? How could you configure Solver to determine the optimal solution? Which Solver model would you use to solve your problem? Which type of report would you choose?

In this exercise, you will learn to save and load solver models.

 **E10.16**

To Save and Restore a Solver Model

a. Click the **GolfLessons** worksheet. You will restore the original values in this worksheet. Click cell **D4**, type **1**, press Enter, then, in cell D5 type **1**, and press Enter. On the Data tab, in the Analyze group, click **Solver**.

b. In the Solver Parameters dialog box, click **Load/Save** to open the Load/Save Model dialog box.

c. Excel guides you through the process. Because you are saving this model, Excel prompts you to select a specific number of cells. In this case, Excel needs nine cells to write the objective cell, variable cell, and constraint data. However, you need to specify only the starting cell. Click inside the box in the Load/Save Model dialog box, click cell **A23**, and then click **Save**. Once the Sol model was saved, the Solver Parameters dialog box reopened. Notice how Solver placed data in nine cells beginning with A23.

d. Barry Cheney is thinking about opening the golf course for more hours during the day — possibly being open for up to 16 hours per day. In the Solver Parameters dialog box, under Subject to the Constraints, click to select **$D$4 <= 14** from the list of constraints, and then click **Change**.

e. In the Change Constraint dialog box, in the Constraint box, change the value of 14 to **25**. By adding additional hours and 15-minute lessons, additional clients can be served. Click **OK**.

f. If Barry extends the golf course operating hours, he will need to schedule more instructors each day. He knows that a minimum of four instructors will need to work; however, there could be up to seven scheduled in a given day. In the Solver Parameters dialog box, under Subject to the Constraints, click to select **$D$5 <= 4** from the list of constraints, and then click **Change**.

g. In the Change Constraint dialog box, click the **arrow**, and then click to select **>=** in the mathematical operands box. Click **OK**.

h. Click **Add** to add a new constraint that will limit the maximum number of instructors on duty to 7. In the Add Constraint dialog box, in the Cell Reference box, reference cell **D5**. If necessary, click the **arrow** and select **<=** in the mathematical operands box, and then, in the Constraint box, type **7**. Click **OK**.

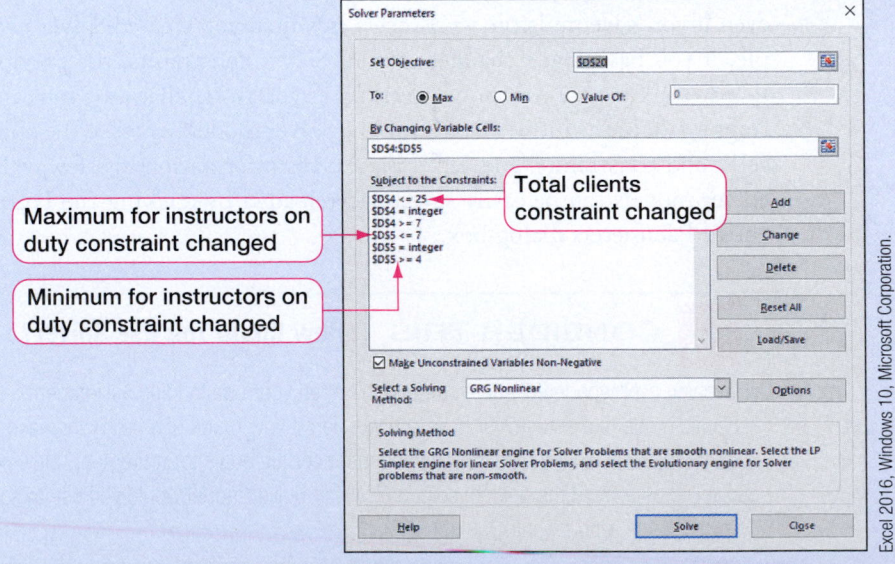

Figure 28 New model constraints loaded into the Solver Parameters dialog box

i. Click **Load/Save** to open the Load/Save Model dialog box, reference cell **B23** in the box, and then click **Save**.

j. In the Solver Parameters dialog box, click **Solve** to run Solver and open the Solver Results dialog box.

k. Click to select the **Restore Original Values** option, and then, on the right side of the Solver Results dialog box under Reports, click to select **Answer**.

   Click **OK**. Notice that a worksheet named Answer Report 2 now exists and that on the GolfLessons worksheet, the value of 1 was reset in cells D4 and D5.

l. Click the **Answer Report 2** worksheet. Notice that Red Bluff can maximize the instructors' schedule and realize a net income of $29,278.00 per day.

m. Complete the **Documentation** worksheet, **Save** the workbook, exit Excel, and then submit your file as directed by your instructor.

SS **CONSIDER THIS** | **What Does Answer Report 2 Tell You?**

Does it benefit the golf course management to stay open additional hours? How much more — if any — net income can the golf course generate on a daily basis? How many instructors will need to work each day? What else does the Solver answer report tell you?

QUICK REFERENCE | **Saving Solver Parameters**

You can save the last selections in the Solver Parameters dialog box with a worksheet by saving the workbook. Each worksheet in a workbook may have its own Solver selections, and all of them are saved. You can also define more than one problem for a worksheet by clicking Load/Save to save problems individually.

When you save a model, enter the reference for the first cell of a vertical range of empty cells in which you want to place the problem model. When you load a model, enter the reference for the entire range of cells that contains the problem model.

Concept Check

1. Why do managers use CVP analysis, and what does it help them learn about their business? p. 543

2. Discuss the difference between using a two-variable data table and calculating elasticity in analyzing costs. p. 549–554

3. Give three examples of how you could use Goal Seek. Describe how Goal Seek uses iteration to find the solution. p. 556

4. What are scenarios used for, and how can analyzing scenarios assist managers in decision making? p. 559

5. What are the two different types of Scenario Summary reports, and what are some ways in which they are useful? p. 562–563

6. What is Solver? What can Solver help managers determine? p. 564

7. What are the three main parameters needed to use Solver? Briefly define all three. p. 565–567

8. What does a Solver Answer report outline? Why is the option to Restore Original Values helpful? p. 571–573

Key Terms

Add-in   565
Binding constraint   573
Break-even analysis   542
Break-even point   542
Changing cell   559
Conditional formatting   547
Constraint   565
Cost-volume-profit (CVP)
   analysis   542
Data table   549
Elastic   553
Evolutionary method   570
Fixed cost   542

Goal Seek   556
GRG Nonlinear method   569
Inelastic   553
Iteration   556
Linear programming   568
Mixed cost   542
Nonbinding constraint   573
Objective cell   566
One-variable data table   549
Optimize   565
Scenario   559
Scenario Manager   559
Scenario PivotTable report   563

Scenario Summary report   562
Scenario tool   545
Scroll bar   545
Simplex LP method   568
Solver   565
Solver Answer Report   571
Solver Limits Report   571
Solver Population Report   571
Solver Sensitivity Report   571
Two-variable data table   552
Variable   545
Variable cost   542
What-if analysis   545

Visual Summary

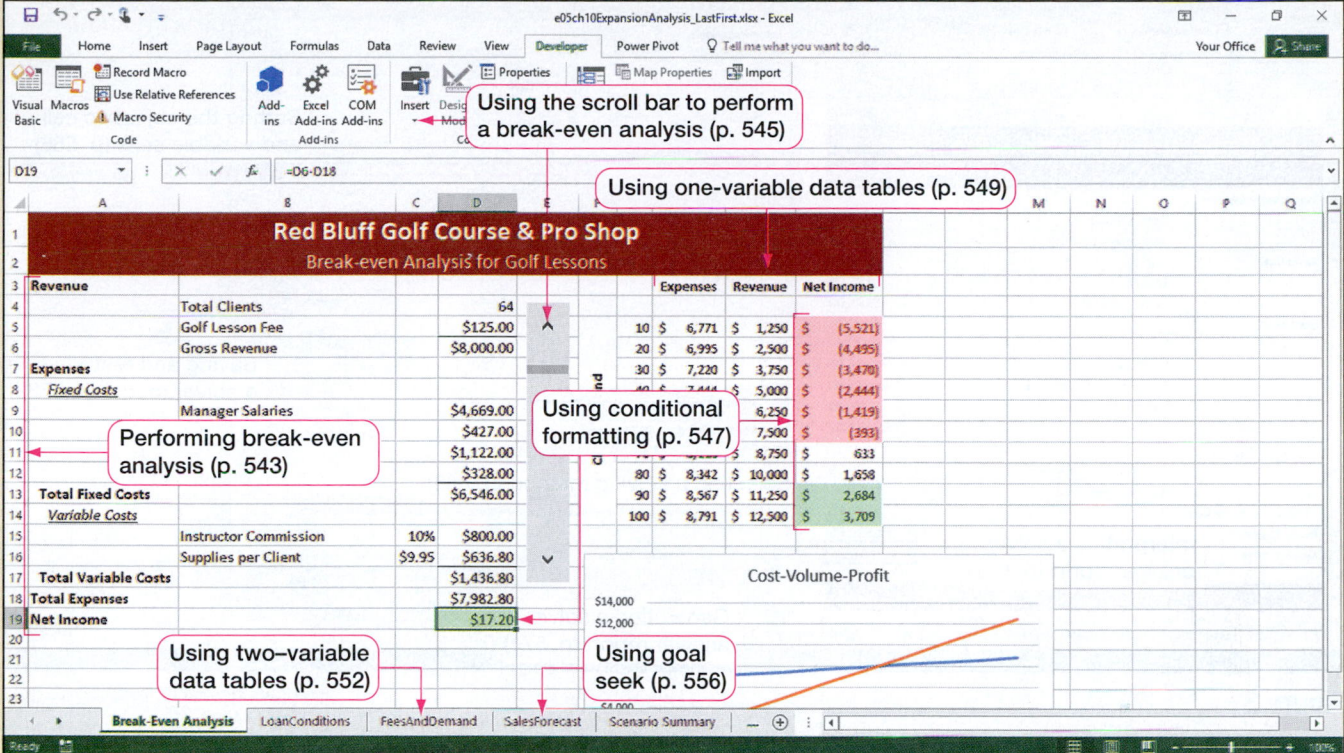

Using the scroll bar to perform a break-even analysis (p. 545)

Using one-variable data tables (p. 549)

Performing break-even analysis (p. 543)

Using conditional formatting (p. 547)

Using two–variable data tables (p. 552)

Using goal seek (p. 556)

Figure 29

Excel 2016, Windows 10, Microsoft Corporation.

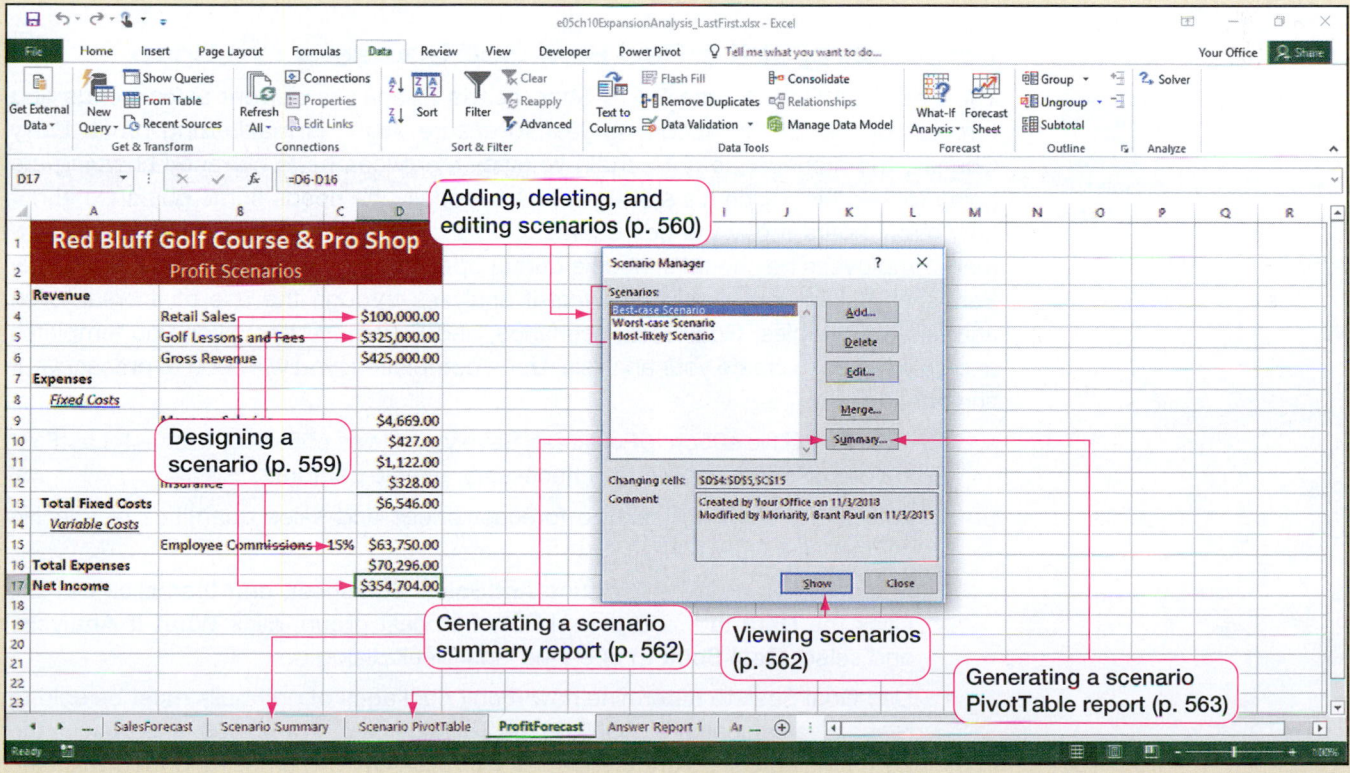

Adding, deleting, and editing scenarios (p. 560)

Designing a scenario (p. 559)

Generating a scenario summary report (p. 562)

Viewing scenarios (p. 562)

Generating a scenario PivotTable report (p. 563)

Figure 30

Excel 2016, Windows 10, Microsoft Corporation.

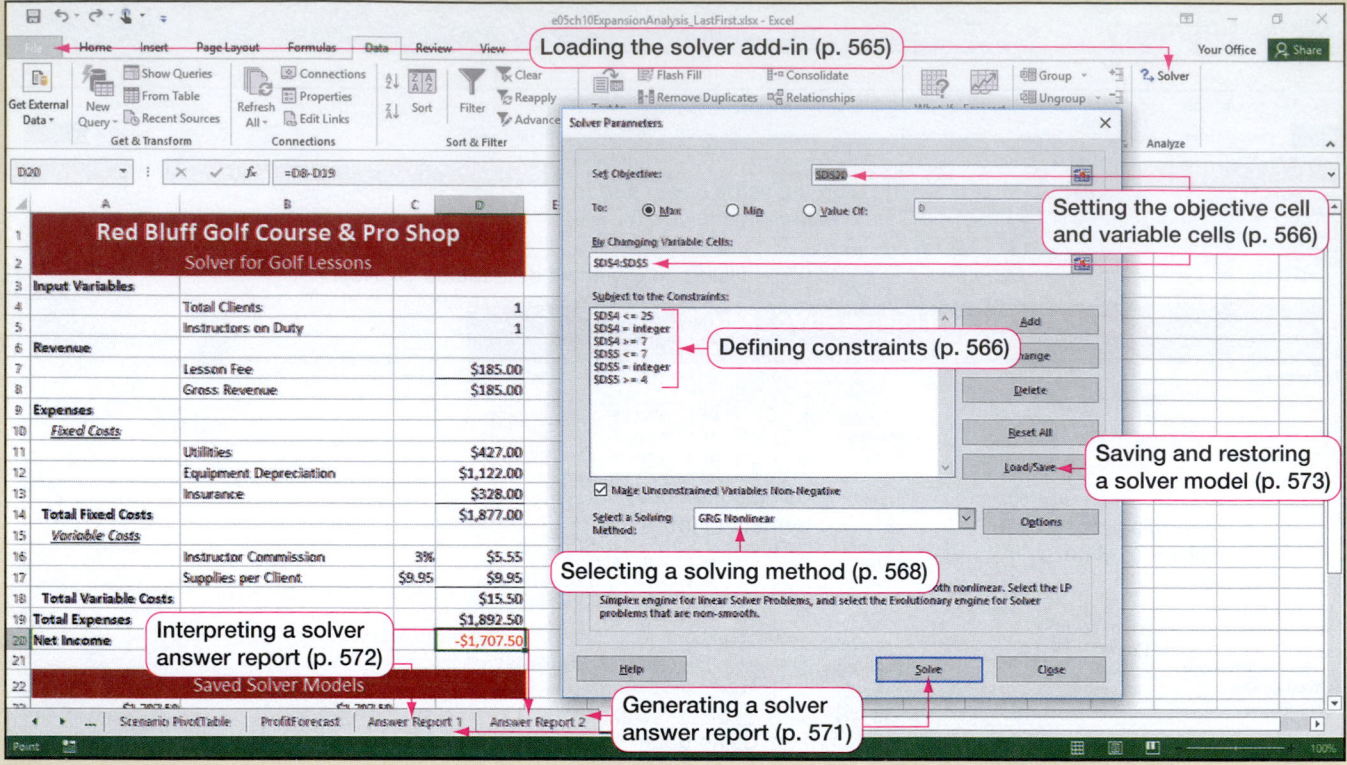

Figure 31

Excel 2016, Windows 10, Microsoft Corporation.

Practice 1

Student data file needed:	You will save your file as:
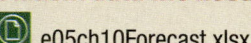 e05ch10Forecast.xlsx	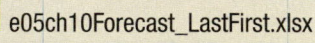 e05ch10Forecast_LastFirst.xlsx

Forecasting at the Red Bluff Golf Course & Pro Shop

Sales & Marketing

The Red Bluff Golf Course & Pro Shop needs to analyze current sales trends and forecast prices for the upcoming year to ensure that it is maximizing profit. Barry Cheney, the manager, is not certain whether the prices he is currently charging are going to help him reach his sales goals. Additionally, he needs some guidance about how many hours a day the golf course should be open for business as well as how many employees he should schedule during operating hours to maximize net income. Barry has asked you to perform what-if analyses through the use of a break-even analysis, data tables, Goal Seek, scenarios, and Solver. He has given you templates and data to use to create your analysis. Upon completion, you will need to present your findings to him.

a. Open the Excel file **e05ch10Forecast**. Save your file as **e05ch10Forecast_LastFirst** using your last and first name. If necessary, enable content.

b. Complete the following tasks to forecast prices and sales quantities of specific products, using Goal Seek.

- If necessary, click the **ProductsAndSales** worksheet, and then click cell **E5**. Click the **Data** tab, and then, in the Forecast group, click **What-If Analysis**, and select **Goal Seek** to open the Goal Seek dialog box.

- Use Goal Seek to determine how many packages of golf balls must be sold to reach a sales goal of $27,500. In the To value box, type **27500**, and then, in the By changing cell box reference cell **C5**. Click **OK** two times, and then open the Goal Seek dialog box again.

- Use Goal Seek to determine the selling price of golf umbrellas necessary to reach a sales goal of $9,000 if 250 are sold. In the Set cell box, reference cell **E6**; in the To value box, type 9000; and then, in the By changing cell box, reference cell **D6**. Click **OK** two times, and then open the **Goal Seek** dialog box again.

- Use Goal Seek to determine the number of graphite golf club sets that must be sold to reach a sales goal of $7,500. In the Set cell box, reference cell **E7**, and in the To value box, type 7500, and then, in the By changing cell box, reference cell **C7**. Click **OK** two times, and then open the Goal Seek dialog box again.

- Use Goal Seek to determine the number of platinum ladies golf sets that must be sold to reach a sales goal of $9,250. In the Set cell box, reference cell **E8**, and in the To value box type 9250, and then, in the By changing cell box, reference cell **C8**. Click **OK** two times, and then open the **Goal Seek** dialog box again.

- Use Goal Seek to determine the selling price of golf club cleaning kits necessary to reach a sales goal of $2,495 if 100 are sold. In the Set cell box, reference cell **E9**, and in the To value box, type 2495, and then, in the By changing cell box, reference cell **D9**. Click **OK** two times.

- Select cell range **D5:D9**. Click the **Home** tab, and then, in the Styles group, click **Conditional Formatting.** Point to **Highlight Cells Rules**, and then click **Greater Than**. In the Format cells that are GREATER THAN box, type 100. Click the **with** arrow, and then click **Custom Format**. Under Font style, click **Bold**, and then click **OK** two times to apply bold to the font of the product prices when the price is greater than $100. Press Ctrl + Home to select cell A1.

c. Complete the following tasks to forecast the best-case, worst-case, and most likely scenarios using Scenario Manager.

- Click the **MonthlyForecasting** worksheet. Click the **Data** tab, and then, in the Forecast group, click **What-If Analysis**, and then click **Scenario Manager** to open the Scenario Manager dialog box.

- Use Scenario Manager to configure the most likely scenario for this monthly forecast. Click **Add**, and then, in the Scenario name box, type Most Likely Scenario, and press Tab. In the Changing cells box, reference cells **D4:D5**, press and hold Ctrl, and then reference cell **C15**. The values that are currently on the spreadsheet are the values for the most likely scenario. Click **OK** two times.

- Use Scenario Manager to configure the worst-case scenario for this monthly forecast. Click **Add** to begin creating your second scenario, and in the Scenario name box, type Worst-case Scenario, and then click **OK**. In row 1, type 75000; in row 2, type 125000; in row 3, type 0.09; and then click **OK**.

- Use Scenario Manager to configure the best-case scenario. Click **Add** to begin creating your third scenario, and in the Scenario name box, type Best-case Scenario, and then click **OK**. In row 1, type 200000; in row 2, type 350000; in row 3, type 0.05; and then click **OK**.

- In the Scenario Manager dialog box, view each of your scenarios by clicking each scenario's name in the listing box, and then click **Show**. Click **Summary** to create a Scenario Summary report, if necessary, and in the Result cells box, reference cell **D18**, and then click **OK**.

- Click the **Scenario Summary** worksheet if necessary. To add headings to your data, delete the cell reference headings in cells **C6**, **C7**, **C8**, and **C10**. Click cell **B6**, type Retail sales, and then press Enter. In cell B7, type Equipment sales, and then press Enter. In cell B8, type Commission, and then press Enter. Click cell **B10**, type Net income, and then press Enter. If necessary, format the font as bold.

- Click the **MonthlyForecasting** worksheet. On the Data tab, in the Forecast group, click **What-If Analysis**, and click **Scenario Manager** to open the Scenario Manager dialog box, and then click **Summary**. Select the **Scenario PivotTable report** option. If necessary, in the Result cells box, reference cell **D18**, and then click **OK**.

- If necessary, click the **Scenario PivotTable** worksheet to format the report to make it easier to read. In cell **A1**, type Monthly Forecasting Solution, press Enter, and then set the width of column A to 27. In cell **A2**, type Scenario PivotTable Report, and press Enter, merge and center the range **A2:B2**, change the font size to **16** point, and then apply a **Bold** font style. In cell A3, type Scenarios. Press Tab, and then in cell B3, type Net Income, and press Enter. In the PivotTable Fields pane, in the Σ VALUES area, click **Net Income**, and then click **Value Field Settings**. Click **Number Format**, and in the Format Cells dialog box, click **Currency**, and then click **OK** twice. Resize the width of column B as needed.

d. Complete the following tasks to create a Solver answer report that determines the maximum net income that can be generated.

- Click the **NetIncomeForecast** worksheet, and then click the **Data** tab, and in the Analyze group, click **Solver**.

- In the Solver Parameters dialog box, in the Set Objective box, reference cell **D23**, and then, in the By Changing Variable Cells box, reference cells **D4:D5**. Click **Add** to begin entering your constraints.

- The pro shop can be open from 12 to 18 hours per day, depending on what Barry Cheney decides. In the Solver Parameters dialog box, click **Add** to add a constraint. In the Add Constraint dialog box, in the Cell Reference box, reference cell **D4**. Click the **arrow**, and select **>=** in the mathematical operands box, and then, in the Constraint box, type 12. Click **Add**, and then create a second constraint when the value in cell **D4** is <=18.

- Click **Add**. The pro shop can have three to seven employees working per day, depending on the day and time of year. Using the techniques you have practiced, create a constraint when the value in cell **D5** is >=3. Click **Add**, and then create another constraint when the value in cell **D5** is <=7.

- Click **Add**. The hours and employees must be integers. Using the techniques you have practiced, create a new constraint when the value in cell **D4** is an integer. Click **Add**, and then create another constraint when the value in cell **D5** is an integer. Click **OK**.

- To save your Solver model with the six constraints, click **Load/Save**, and in the Load/Save Model dialog box, reference cell **A25**, click **Save**, and then click **Solve** to run Solver. click **Restore Original Values**, click **Answer** under Reports, and then click **OK** to create a Solver answer report.

e. Complete the following tasks to create a two-variable data table with conditional formatting that will help to analyze the break-even point.

- Click the **GolfPricing** worksheet. The net income in cell D19 is the output cell that will be used in the data table to help determine the break-even point when the golf fee and total number of golfers vary. Click cell **G5**, and then type =, reference cell **D19**, and press Ctrl + Enter. To format cell G5 to hide the results of the function, right-click cell **G5**, and then click **Format Cells**.

- On the Number tab, click to select the **Custom** category, and then click inside the **Type** box. Delete any existing text, and then type ;;;. Click **OK**. Select the range **G5:R21** to select the data for your data table.

- On the Data tab, in the Forecast group, click **What-If Analysis**, and then click **Data Table** to open the Data Table dialog box. Reference cell **D5** in the Row input cell box, reference cell **D4** in the Column input cell box, and then click **OK**.

- Select the range **H6:R21**, and then format the cells as **Currency**. To view all the data, widen the columns if necessary.

- On the Home tab, in the Styles group, click **Conditional Formatting**. Point to **Highlight Cells Rules**, and then click **Less Than** to open the Less Than dialog box, and in the Format cells that are LESS THAN box, type 0. If necessary, click to select the **Light Red Fill with Dark Red Text** option, and then click **OK**.

- Click **Conditional Formatting** again, and then point to **Highlight Cells Rules**, and click **Greater Than** to open the Greater Than dialog box. In the Format cells that are GREATER THAN box, type 3500, and then click to select the **Green Fill with Dark Green Text** option, and click **OK**. Press Ctrl + Home.

f. Click the **Documentation** worksheet. In cell A6, type today's date. Click cell **B6**, and then type your name in the Firstname Lastname format. Complete the remainder of the **Documentation** worksheet according to your instructor's direction.

g. Click **Save**, exit Excel, and then submit your file as directed by your instructor.

Problem Solve 1

MyITLab® Grader

Homework

Student data file needed:

 e05ch10Schedule.xlsx

You will save your file as:

 e05ch10Schedule_LastFirst.xlsx

Scheduling Employees

Production & Operations

The Painted Paradise Resort & Spa is working on getting a handle on its expenditures on part-time labor. The management feels that there is some opportunity to improve scheduling to reduce costs in some areas. One area has the requirements that the schedules be five days a week with two days in a row off. With these constraints, they would like to build an optimal schedule (from a cost perspective). Management is also considering the impact of raises and potential benefits increases due to new regulations.

a. Open the Excel file, **e05ch10Schedule**. Save your file as e05ch10Schedule_LastFirst using your last and first name. If necessary, enable content.

b. The Schedule worksheet has the possible schedules each employee can work (rows 6–12). The 1s represent the days worked, and the 0s represent the days off (so each schedule has two days in a row off). The range D6:D12 contains the number of employees assigned to the schedule in the corresponding row. This range will need to be changed to fulfill the scheduling needs.

c. In cell **F14**, enter a formula that will calculate the total number of employees scheduled to work Sunday for all schedules A-G. Begin by multiplying the number of employees for schedule A, in cell D6, by the value representing whether or not employees are working that day in cell F6. Be sure to make the reference to cell D6 an absolute cell reference so that, when finished, the formula can be copied across the row. So far the result of the formula is 0 because schedule A has people scheduled off on Sunday. Next, add to the product, the number of employees scheduled to work Sunday for schedule B. Continue with the formula by adding a similar calculation for schedules C-G, making an absolute cell reference for each cell in column D.

d. Copy the formula over to **L14**.

e. In cell **D19**, calculate the total number of shifts scheduled, using the range F14:L14.

f. In cell **D21**, enter a formula that calculates the payroll for the week, which is the product of shifts scheduled and cost per employee per day.

g. Using Solver, minimize the Payroll/Week for the resort by determining the optimal number of employees to have assigned to each schedule. Remember these points as you complete the Solver Parameters dialog box.

- The number of people in the range F14:L14 must be greater than or equal to the demand (range F16:L16) so there are enough people working for that day's needs.

- The number of employees scheduled in D6:D12 must be greater than zero.

- Solve this model, using the Simplex LP method.

- Keep the Solver solution in the model.

- Create an Answer report.

h. In the Part-Time Expenses sheet, in cell **E8**, insert a formula to calculate the total annual part-time wage expense. The Benefit % is an estimate in the form of a percentage of total wages and needs to be added to the cost of wages based on the average part-time hours the average hourly rate.

i. Create nine scenarios based on the Part-Time Expenses. These scenarios are based on the possibilities management see for next year.

- The first three scenarios are based only on a variation in hours. The number given is the expected hours needed for next year. The actual hours may go as low as 90% of the 210,600 hours expected and as high as 110% of the 210,600 hours expected. Create three scenarios that show the effect of average, minimum, and maximum usage of hours on the Total PT Wage Expense. Use the 210,600 expected hours for the Avg scenario. Name the scenarios Avg Hours, Min Hours, and Max Hours.

- The next three scenarios are for the same three levels of hours usage but with a 3% increase in the wage rate. Name these three scenarios Avg Hours w/ Raises, Min Hours w/Raises, and Max Hours w/Raises.

- The last three scenarios are with the same three hours levels but with a 3% increase in wage rate and a Benefit % estimate of 32%. Name these three scenarios Avg Hours w/Raises&Benefits, Min Hours w/Raises&Benefits, and Max Hours w/Raises&Benefits.

j. Display the results of the nine scenarios created in the prior step by creating a scenario summary. Delete the row labels in **column C**. Replace the row labels by typing the following in the appropriate cell in **column B**: Part Time Hours, Part Time Wage, Part Time Benefits, and PT Wage Expense. Adjust the width of column B so that all labels are visible. The nine scenarios will display the data in a column for each scenario.

k. Save the workbook, exit Excel, and then submit your file as directed by your instructor.

Critical Thinking

Explain why you were able to use the Simplex LP method in the optimization model that you created. Briefly interpret each of the four sections in the Solver Answer report generated from the model.

Perform 1: Perform in Your Career

Student data file needed:

 e05ch10MobileApps.xlsx

You will save your file as:

 e05ch10MobileApps_LastFirst.xlsx

Mobile Applications

Accounting & Finance

You are investigating the possibility of developing applications (apps) for smartphones. After some research on the development process for mobile apps, you have determined that you can sell your app for $0.99 per download. You must pay a developer fee of $100 to sell your mobile app. When you sell your mobile app, the online store you are working with will charge you 30% per download, so your revenue on each download will be 70% of the selling price of the app. As part of this project, you will need to purchase a new laptop computer. A new laptop will cost $800. You will create a break-even model to investigate how many apps you will need to sell to make a profit on your new app. In addition to your new app, the company you work for has just finished developing three new apps that will be released in the coming weeks. They would like your help in forecasting sales given the selling price and sales goal of each new app.

a. Open the Excel file, **e05ch10MobileApps**. Save your file as e05ch10MobileApps_LastFirst using your last and first name. If necessary, enable content.

b. On the Break-EvenAnalysis worksheet, complete the following tasks to create your break-even analysis, using a scroll bar, and build a traditional cost-volume-profit chart from a one-variable data table that will help to analyze the break-even point.

   • In cell D7, calculate the gross revenue made from the number of apps sold in D4, the unit price in D5, and the percent per download in D6.

   • In cell D12, calculate the total fixed costs.

   • In cell D14, calculate the net income.

c. Insert a scroll bar in the area of cells E4 through E14. Format the scroll bar with the following criteria.

   • Current value: 1250

   • Minimum value: 1250

   • Maximum value: 1350

   • Incremental change: 10

   • Page change: Leave as the default value of 10

   • Cell link: D4

d. Using conditional formatting, highlight cell rules to format cell D14 so numbers that are less than zero display in light red fill with dark red text, and then scroll until you find the break-even point.

e. In cells G4:I4, create references to the Total Fixed Costs, Revenue, and Net Income from column D. Format the cells using semicolons (;) so that the results of the calculation are not visible in the worksheet.

f. Fill in the Total Fixed Costs, Revenue, and Net Income columns (range G5:I14), using a data table. Format the range as appropriate for the data.

g. Use conditional formatting to apply Green, Gradient Fill, Data Bars to the Net Income column of the data table.

h. Using the data table columns for Apps Sold, Total Fixed Costs, and Revenue, insert a line chart that displays the Total Fixed Costs and Revenue as series data and the Apps Sold as the Horizontal (Category) Axis. Delete the chart title if necessary. Move the chart so that the top left corner of the chart is aligned with the top left corner of F17.

i. On the **ForecastedSales** worksheet in cells D5:D7, calculate the extended price of the three new apps your company is going to release.

j. Using the extended price and the sales goal in cells E5:E7, use Goal Seek to find the quantity to sell in column B.

k. Save the workbook, exit Excel, and then submit your file as directed by your instructor.

Additional Cases

Additional Workshop Cases are available on the companion website and in the instructor resources.

Manipulating Data Sets for Decision Making

This business unit had two outcomes:

Learning Outcome 1:

Understand the benefits of analyzing data sets and learn techniques to import, organize, and clean data sets from a variety of sources.

Learning Outcome 2:

Utilize various forecasting and optimization tools, such as data tables, Scenario Manager, and Solver to support decision making.

In Business Unit 5 Capstone, students will demonstrate competence in these outcomes through a series of business problems at various levels from guided practice to problem solving an existing spreadsheet and performing to create new spreadsheets.

More Practice 1

Student data file needed:

 e05Indigo5.xlsx

You will save your file as:

 e05Indigo5_LastFirst.xlsx

Indigo5 Restaurant

Finance & Accounting

Production & Operations

Management at Indigo5, a five-star restaurant that caters to local patrons in addition to clients of the Painted Paradise Resort & Spa, has outsourced its data collection processes to a new firm in town. The data already collected, which is stored in the e05Indigo5 workbook, is not compatible in its current form with the database that Indigo5 now uses to store this data. You will need to use your knowledge of Excel functions to cleanse the data so it can be imported into the database.

Additionally, Indigo5's executive chef, Robin Sanchez, is regularly updating data in her database to make certain she has all the ingredients and recipes the kitchen needs to offer the high-quality food for which the restaurant is known. You have been asked to build a spreadsheet model that will assist managers in answering what-if questions about product pricing when Chef Sanchez wants to add a new menu item.

a. Open the Excel file, **e05Indigo5**. Save it as **e05Indigo5_LastFirst** using your last and first name. If necessary, enable content.

b. On the FoodCategories worksheet, separate the category number from the value in cell **A2** using Flash Fill. In cell **B2**, type **CAT01**, and then press Enter. In cell **B3**, type **CAT02**, and then press Enter.

c. Click the **Data** tab, and in the Data Tools group, click **Flash Fill** to complete the list of categories in column B.

d. Click cell **C2**. Separate the description of the category from the value in cell **A2** using Flash Fill. In cell **C2**, type **Appetizer**, and then press Enter. In cell **C3**, type **Fi**, and notice the suggestion Flash Fill provides. Press Enter to accept the suggestion, and complete the list of descriptions in column C.

e. Click the **Reviews** worksheet. You will need to convert the text in cell A2 to proper case. Click cell **E2**, type **=PROPER**, and then press Tab to insert the function. Click cell **A2**, and then press Enter to complete the formula. Double-click the **AutoFill** handle in cell **E2** to copy the formula down the column. If necessary, use AutoFit on the column so that all contents are displayed.

f. You will need to convert the numbers in cell B2 into an acceptable date format. Click cell **F2**, and complete the following.

- Type **=DATE** and then press ⟨Tab⟩ to insert the function.

- Type **LEFT** and then press ⟨Tab⟩ to insert the LEFT function.

  The LEFT function will be used to extract the four characters from the left side of cell B2 that represent the year.

- Click cell **B2**, type **,4,** then type **MID**, and press ⟨Tab⟩ to insert the MID function.

  The MID function will be used to extract the two characters in the middle of cell B2 that represent the month.

- Click cell **B2**, type **,5,2),RIGHT**, and then press ⟨Tab⟩ to insert the RIGHT function.

  The Right function will be used to extract the two characters from the right of cell B2 that represent the day.

- Click cell **B2**, type **,2))**, and then press ⟨Enter⟩ to end the nested function.

  The final formula should be **=DATE(LEFT(B2,4),MID(B2,5,2),RIGHT(B2,2))**.

- Double-click the **AutoFill** handle in cell F2 to copy the formula down the column. If necessary, use AutoFit on the column so that all contents are displayed.

g. Complete the following tasks to perform a break-even analysis for a new menu item. Fixed expenses have been spread evenly among all menu items.

- Click the **Break-even Analysis** worksheet. Click cell **D6**, type **=**, click cell **D4**, type *****, click cell **D5**, and then press ⟨Enter⟩ to calculate the gross revenue, that is, the amount of money generated from selling the new menu item.

- Click cell **D13**, type **=SUM**, and press ⟨Tab⟩ to insert the function. Select the cell range D9:D12, and then press ⟨Enter⟩ to calculate the total fixed costs. Click cell **D15**, type **=**, click cell **D4**, type *****, click cell **C15**, and then press ⟨Enter⟩ to calculate the total food cost based on how many items were sold.

- In cell **D16**, type **=**, click cell **D13**, type **+**, click cell **D15**, and then press ⟨Enter⟩ to calculate the total expenses. In cell **D17**, type **=**, click cell **D6**, type **-**, click cell **D16**, and then press ⟨Enter⟩ to calculate the net income, that is, how much profit the restaurant will generate from the new menu item.

- Apply conditional formatting to cell **D17** with the Custom Format option so numbers that are less than zero are displayed in red text and numbers that are greater than zero are displayed in green text, and then enter quantities in cell **D4** until you find the break-even point.

- Click cell **G4**, type **=**, click cell **D16**, and then press ⟨Tab⟩. In cell **H4**, type **=**, click cell **D6**, and then press ⟨Tab⟩. In cell **I4**, type **=**, click cell **D17**, and then press ⟨Enter⟩. Select cell range **G4:I4** to format with the formula results hidden. Right-click any of the cells in the selected cell range, and then click **Format Cells**. On the Number tab, select the **Custom** category, click in the **Type box**, remove any existing text, and then type **;;;**. Click **OK**.

- Select the cell range **F4:I18** for your data table. Click the **Data** tab, and in the Forecast group, click **What-If Analysis**. Click **Data Table** to open the Data Table dialog box. Press $$$Tab$$$ to move to the Column input cell box, reference cell **D4**, and then click **OK**.

- Select the cell range **I5:I18**, click the **Home** tab, and in the Styles group, click **Conditional Formatting**. Point to **Color Scales**, and then select **Green - White - Red Color Scale**.

- Select the cell range **G3:H3**, press and hold ⟨Ctrl⟩, and then select the cell range **G5:H18**. Click the **Insert** tab, and in the Charts group, click **Insert Line or Area Chart**, and then, in the 2-D Line category, click **Line**. Click the border edge of the chart, and then drag to reposition the top left corner into cell F20.

- Click the **Chart Tools Design** tab, and in the Data group, click **Select Data**, and then, under Horizontal (Category) Axis Labels, click **Edit**. With the insertion point in the Axis label range box, select the cell range **F5:F18**. Click **OK** two times.
- Click **Chart Elements**, click the **Axis Titles arrow**, and then select **Primary Horizontal**. Type Total Ordered, and then press Enter. Click the **Chart Title** box, type Break-Even Analysis, and then press Enter.
- Click an empty cell to deselect the chart.

h. Click the **Documentation** worksheet. Click cell **A8**, type today's date, click cell **B8**, and then type your name in the Firstname Lastname format.

i. Save the workbook, exit Excel, and then submit your file as directed by your instructor.

Problem Solve 1

Homework

Student data files needed:

 e05HotelFinancials.xlsx

e05HotelSales.accdb

You will save your file as:

e05HotelFinancials_LastFirst.xlsx

Finance & Accounting

Production & Operations

Financial Analysis for the Painted Paradise Resort & Spa

The hotel manager has asked for your help in conducting an analysis of sales for several of the room types offered at the Painted Paradise Resort & Spa. First you have been asked to conduct a sales forecast of three popular rooms. This information has been stored in an Access database and will need to be imported before any analysis can be completed. A list of potential customers from a new marketing campaign has also been included in the workbook you have been given. The data needs to be cleansed before it can be used. Finally, you have been asked to create three different sales scenarios for the hotel.

a. Open the Excel file **e05HotelFinancials**. Save your file as e05HotelFinancials_LastFirst using your last and first name.

b. Import the table **tblRoomTypes** from the e05HotelSales database. Place the imported data in cell **A3** on the **SalesForecast** worksheet as a Table.

c. In cell **D3**, type Quantity, and enter 1 as the quantity for each record that was imported.

d. In cell **E3** type Extended Price. In the cell range **E4:E6**, calculate the extended price for each room type by multiplying the room rate by the quantity.

e. In cell **F3**, type Goal, and in cells **F4** and **F5**, type 3000. In cell **F6**, type 8000.

f. Use Goal Seek to find the appropriate quantities of each room type in order for the extended price to meet the goals you typed in cell range F4:F6.

g. Format the cell range **D4:D6** as **General** with 0 decimal places.

h. Format the cell ranges **C4:C6** and **E4:F6** as Currency with 0 decimal places.

i. Adjust the column widths so that all data is visible.

j. On the **NewCustomers** worksheet, complete the following steps to cleanse the data in columns A through D.
- In cell **E2**, use the appropriate function to cleanse the nonprinting characters from cell **B2**. Copy the function down through cell **E11**.
- In cell **F2**, use the appropriate function to display the street address from **C2** in proper case. Copy the function down through cell **F11**.

- The data in the cell range **D2:D11** contains the customer's home city and state. The last two characters in each cell contain the state abbreviation. In cell **G2**, use the appropriate functions to display the only city from **D2**. Be certain to remove extra spaces from the city name. Copy the function down through cell **G11**.

- In cell **H2**, use the appropriate function to display only the state abbreviation from cell **D2**. Copy the function down through cell **H11**.

k. On the **Scenarios** worksheet, complete the following tasks to create a Scenario PivotTable Report.

- Use the Scenario Manager to add a **Most-likely scenario**. Use the cell range **D5:D7** as the Changing cells. The current values on the worksheet will be your Most-likely scenario values.

- Add a new scenario named **Best-case scenario**. In the Scenario Values dialog box, type **40** in **row 1**, type **65** in **row 2**, and type **80** in **row 3**.

- Add a new scenario named **Worst-case scenario**. In the Scenario Values dialog box, type **12** in **row 1**, type **24** in **row 2**, and type **50** in **row 3**.

- Create a Scenario PivotTable Report using cells **E8**, **C20**, and **C22** as your Result cells.

l. Complete the following tasks to format the report with appropriate headings and formatting.

- In cell **A1**, type **Room Reservations**.

- In cell **B3**, type **Gross Revenue**.

- In cell **C3**, type **Total Expenses**.

- In cell **D3**, type **Net Income**.

- Format the gross revenue, total expenses, and net income data as **Currency**, and **AutoFit** the widths of the columns as needed.

m. Save the workbook, exit Excel, and then submit your file as directed by your instructor.

Problem Solve 2

MyITLab® Grader
Homework

Student data files needed:

 e05ProductMix.xlsx

 e05SampleCustomers.txt

You will save your file as:

 e05ProductMix_LastFirst.xlsx

Product Mix Optimization

Production & Operations

3-D CustomAble Designs is a medical device company that utilizes 3-D printing technology to manufacture wheelchairs. They offer a standard model for the majority of their customer base but have recently starting implementing a design-your-own-chair service in which the chairs can be customized with some unique features and designs. You have been asked to use your knowledge of Excel to help them clean up some of their customer names that were corrupted when exported from their CRM system. You have also been asked to help with a Solver model that will help to determine the optimal mix of standard and custom wheelchairs necessary to maximize profit, given several labor and material constraints.

a. Open the Excel file **e05ProductMix**. Save your file as **e05ProductMix_LastFirst** using your last and first name.

b. Import the tab-delimited text file **e05SampleCustomers** into cell **A1** on the **RecentCustomers** worksheet.

c. In cell **C1**, type **CleanNames** as the column heading.

d. In the cell range **C2:C24**, insert a text function to clear any nonprinting characters and extra spaces from the names in column **A**.

e. In cell **D1**, type FirstName as the column heading.

f. In the cell range **D2:D24**, insert text functions to display only the first name from the right side of the clean names in column **C**. The names should be displayed in proper case.

g. In cell **E1**, type LastName as the column heading.

h. In the cell range **E2:E24**, insert text functions to display only the last name from the left side of the clean names in column **C**. The names should be displayed in proper case and not include any extra spaces.

i. Adjust the column widths so that all data are visible.

j. On the MaximizeProfits worksheet, complete the following so that a linear Solver model can be created.

- In cell **B18**, calculate the revenue of custom-designed wheelchairs, using the selling price in cell **E8** and the number of units produced in cell **B11**. Copy the formula over to cell **C18** to calculate the revenue from standard wheelchairs.

- In cell **B21**, calculate the costs of labor for custom-designed wheelchairs by multiplying the hourly rate in cell **B5** by the number of hours necessary to create a custom wheelchair in cell **E5** by the number of custom wheelchairs produced in cell **B11**. Use appropriate cell referencing so that the formula can be copied down to cell **B23** to calculate the costs of primary and additional materials for custom wheelchairs and can be copied over to calculate all costs for standard wheelchairs.

- In cell **B25**, calculate the profit of custom wheelchairs by subtracting the total costs from the revenue. Copy the formula over to cell **C25** to calculate the profit from standard wheelchairs.

- In cell **D18**, calculate the total revenue by adding the revenue from custom and standard wheelchairs. Copy and paste the formula into the cell range **D21:D23** and cell **D25**.

k. Create a Solver model, using the GRG Nonlinear method, by completing the following steps.

- Set the objective to maximize the total profit in cell **D25**.
- Set the changing cells to be the number of units to produce in the cell range **B11:C11**.
- Create a constraint that will ensure that the number of units to produce will be whole numbers.
- Create a constraint that will ensure that the number of units produced will not exceed the maximum expected demand in the cell range **B13:C13**.
- Create a constraint that will ensure that the used resources in the cell range **F12:F14** will not exceed the available resources in the cell range **H12:H14**.

l. Save the Solver model for use later, starting in cell **A28**.

m. Run Solver and create a Solver Answer Report.

n. Save the workbook, exit Excel, and then submit your file as directed by your instructor.

Critical Thinking

Discuss some reasons why the optimal product mix to maximize profits did not involve producing as many custom wheelchairs as the estimated maximum demand. Also, which constraint forced this model to use the GRG Nonlinear method instead of the Simplex LP method?

Perform 1: Perform in Your Life

Reception Budget What-if Analysis

Production & Operations

You are planning a wedding. Your fiancé has asked you to create an Excel workbook to ensure that the two of you do not go over budget. Your goal with this workbook is to determine what happens to your budget when the number of guests changes, when the cost of the meal goes up, and so on.

a. Open the Excel file **e05ReceptionBudget**. Save the file as e05ReceptionBudget_LastFirst using your last and first name.

b. Add a scroll bar to the Budget worksheet within the cell range E5:E25 that will allow you to determine what happens when the number of guests varies, using the following properties.

- Current and minimum value of 100
- Maximum value of 300
- Incremental and page change of 10
- Link the scrollbar to the appropriate cell

c. Given the current estimates on the worksheet, use the scroll bar to determine the maximum number of guests you can have at the reception without exceeding the amount available.

d. Create a two-variable data table that determines what happens to your budget if you add more people or the cost of the meal changes. You haven't decided on a caterer yet, but your current estimates are between $20 per person and $140 per person.

- Format the various budget remaining amounts in the data table appropriately.
- Add appropriate conditional formatting to the data table so that budgets with a positive value are highlighted in one way, those with negative values are highlighted in another way, and the break-even point is highlighted in a third way.

e. There is one break-even point, where the number of guests and the cost of the meal result in your budget having $0 remaining. Enter this information next to your two-variable data table in cells C29 and C30.

f. Use the Scenario manager to create two different scenarios, named appropriately, that will calculate the remaining budget with two different guest counts and cost per meal amounts.

g. Create a Scenario Summary Report to show your remaining budget with the two different scenarios created.

h. Insert a new worksheet, and change the name to **Bands**.

i. Import the **e05Bands** text file into the Bands worksheet. Separate data into separate columns. (**Company Name**, **Phone Number**, **Address**, **City**, **State** and **ZIP Code** are your column headers.)

- Create a new column, and use text formulas to concatenate the appropriate phone number formatting symbols to each phone number, e.g., (520) 345-3536.
- Create another new column, and use Flash Fill to insert a hyphen between the first five characters of the ZIP Code and the four-character extension.
- Adjust the column widths so that all data are visible.
- Use the Remove Duplicates tool to delete any duplicate data.

j. Save the workbook, exit Excel, and then submit your file as directed by your instructor.

Student data files needed:

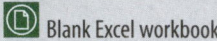 Blank Excel workbook

e05IncomeProjections.txt

You will save your file as:

 e05IncomeProjections_LastFirst.xlsx

Income Projections

Finance & Accounting

Production & Operations

An analyst recently helped your company to project its net income for the next several years on the basis of prior-year data. Unfortunately, the data was provided in a text file rather than an Excel workbook. This has made it very hard for your company to analyze the data. Your supervisor has asked you to convert the data into Excel and perform basic analysis on the data to present to the Planning Committee.

a. Start **Excel**, and then create a new blank workbook. Save the workbook as **e05IncomeProjections_LastFirst** using your last and first name.

b. Import the **e05IncomeProjections** text file onto a blank worksheet.

c. Format the worksheet as follows.

- Change the tab name to **BreakEven**.
- Insert a column between Column A and Column B. In the new Column B, insert a formula to correct the labels as appropriate. Hide Column A. (Hint: Use a Substitute or a Replace formula.)
- Add any rows as desired to make the data more visually appealing.
- Format as desired.

d. Replace numbers with formulas where appropriate.

e. Add a scroll bar to the worksheet. This will allow you to determine your operating profit as more units are sold. The scroll bar should be connected to the year 4 Units data. Your maximum plant capacity is 25,000 units. Use 500-unit increments.

f. Determine the Break-Even point for year 4, and enter the data in an appropriate location on the worksheet.

g. For the year 4 data, create a one-variable data table based on number of units to review the Revenue, Expenses, and Operating Profit. Use conditional formatting to highlight positive numbers and negative numbers in different ways. Apply appropriate formatting as desired.

h. Create a Cost Volume Profit Chart on a Chart Sheet. Ensure that all data and the sheet tab are labeled appropriately, and apply an appropriate chart style.

i. Insert a new worksheet, and change the name to **Solver**. Copy the data for the year 4 projection from the Break Even worksheet to the Solver worksheet.

j. Use Solver to create an Answer Report that shows the maximum operating profit possible by changing the number of units, the materials, labor, and variable overhead unit costs as well as meeting the following constraints.

- You cannot produce more than 25,000 units with your current equipment, and you can produce only whole units.
- The unit cost of materials can range from $15.20 to $17.60.
- The unit cost of labor can range from $23.75 to $27.50.
- The unit cost of variable overhead can range from $5.70 to $6.60.

k. Solve the model with the GRG Nonlinear method, and create an answer report.

l. Save your Solver model on the **Solver** worksheet for future use.

m. Save the workbook, exit Excel, and then submit your file as directed by your instructor.

Student data file needed:

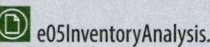 e05InventoryAnalysis.xlsx

You will save your file as:

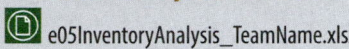 e05InventoryAnalysis_TeamName.xlsx

Production & Operations

The Other Bar and Grill Inventory Management

You are the bar manager at The Other Bar and Grill, a local restaurant that specializes in fresh-cooked meals for breakfast, lunch, and dinner. The general manager has given you an Excel workbook that contains data about the beverages offered and sold. You need to manage the inventory of beverage items to ensure that you have enough beverages for each day you are open for business and to determine pricing for special drink items.

Additionally, the database used for keeping track of inventory has been corrupted, causing some issues with the inventory data. You will need to use your knowledge of Excel to clean the inventory data.

a. Select one team member to set up the document by completing steps b–e.

b. Open your browser and navigate to https://www.onedrive.live.com, https://www.drive .google.com, or any other instructor-assigned location. Be sure all members of the team have an account on the chosen system.

c. Open the Excel file **e05InventoryAnalysis**. Save your file as e05InventoryAnalysis_TeamName using the name assigned to your team.

d. Create a new worksheet at the beginning of the workbook, and then rename Sheet1 as Contributors. List the names of the team members on the worksheet, and then add a heading above the name to read Team Members. Include any additional information on this worksheet required by your instructor.

e. Share the workbook with the other members of your team. Make sure each team member has the appropriate permission to edit the document.

f. On the DrinkForecast worksheet, complete the following tasks to forecast prices for drink specials.

• In the cell range **D5:D9**, type a formula that increases this year's quantity sold by 20%. Format the results appropriately.

• In the cell range **F5:F9**, type a formula that calculates the extended price for next year's forecast.

• The current prices are located in the cell range **E5:E9**. Use Goal Seek to determine new prices in the cell range E5:E9, based on the revenue goals for next year, located in the cell range **G5:G9**.

• Adjust the column widths so that all data are visible.

g. On the DrinkScenarios worksheet, complete the following tasks to create a Scenario summary report.

• In the cell range **E4:E8**, type a formula that calculates the extended price for next year's forecast. In cell **E9**, type a formula that calculates the gross revenue.

• In cell **E18**, type a formula that calculates the variable cost for all drinks sold.

• Open the Scenario Manager. Add a Worst-case scenario, and then use the Qty cells as the changing cells. The current values on the worksheet will be your Worst-case scenario values.

• Add a new scenario named Best-case scenario. Use the following values as your Scenario values.

Mojito: 175

Fuzzy Navel: 60

Strawberry Daiquiri: 45

Pina Colada: 30

The Other Special: 200

- Add a new scenario named Most-likely scenario. Use the following values as your Scenario values.

    Mojito: 150

    Fuzzy Navel: 45

    Strawberry Daiquiri: 30

    Pina Colada: 20

    The Other Special: 150

h. Create a Scenario summary report using the net income cell as your result cell. Format your report with the appropriate row headings, and then resize columns if necessary.

i. On the Inventory worksheet, complete the following steps to cleanse the data provided.

- Remove any duplicates that exist in the Inventory worksheet. Duplicate records occur where two or more rows are identical.

- The stock code should consist of all uppercase letters. Create a new column with the appropriate function to display the stock code correctly.

- Create a new column labeled ItemCode. Construct the item code by combining first the corrected stock code and then the item number.

- The data in the Category/Brand column has been corrupted the most. There are several spaces before and after the data that need to be removed. There are also symbols that need to be removed from the data. Additionally, the category and brand should be in two separate columns. Display the corrected values in their own columns labeled Category and Brand. The category data should be in proper case. Use as many columns to the right of the Inventory data as you need to accomplish these tasks.

- Use functions or Flash Fill to separate the units and measurement into two separate columns.

j. Save the workbook, exit Excel, and then submit your file as directed by your instructor.

Perform 4: How Others Perform

Student data files needed:

 e05OnlineOrderAnalysis.xlsx

 e05OnlineOrders.accdb

You will save your file as:

 e05OnlineOrderAnalysis_LastFirst.xlsx

Troubleshooting Online Orders

Finance & Accounting

The company you work for uses an online system to sell and ship its products to customers. It would like to begin analyzing this data, and management has compiled a subset of the data in an Access database. The company had a previous intern attempt an analysis, but he was not able to work well with the data in its current format. You have been asked to import the data into Excel and cleanse it for further analysis. Additionally, you have been asked to check the what-if analysis that was begun for the Exfoliator product the company sells. The intern attempted to build the what-if analysis, but your manager believes that some mistakes were made in the file.

a. Open the Excel file **e05OnlineOrderAnalysis**. Save your file as e05OnlineOrderAnalysis_LastFirst using your last and first name.

b. On the Transactions worksheet, import the qryTransactionDetails table from the e05OnlineOrders.accdb Access database file into cell **A1**. Complete the following steps to cleanse the data.

- The data in column B represents the transaction date but is stored as text. The data in column C represents the shipping date for the product but is also stored as text. Both columns are in the YYYYMMDD format. Use Text and Date functions to create two new columns, and convert the data into date formats that Excel will recognize.
- Using the two date columns created in the prior step, calculate the number of workdays between the date of the transaction and the shipping date. Your calculation should exclude weekends and any holidays. A listing of 2018 and 2019 holidays can be found in the Holidays worksheet.

c. On the Customers worksheet, import the tblCustomers table from the e05OnlineOrders.accdb database file into cell **A1**. Complete the following steps to cleanse the data.

- The previous intern had difficulty using text functions to cleanse the FullName field into FirstName and LastName fields. Use Flash Fill to cleanse the FullName field into these two new fields.
- Each U.S. ZIP Code should be a five-character code. Because some ZIP Codes begin with a zero, the leading zero gets removed when the ZIP Codes are imported into Excel. In a new column of data, use the Text function to correctly format the ZipCode field. (Hint: Try using "00000" as the format_text argument of the Text function.)

d. Complete the following tasks on the ExfoliatorAnalysis worksheet to correct the mistakes.

- Apply appropriate formatting to all numeric values.
- Check the series data for the chart to ensure that they are correct, and then correct them as needed.
- Check all existing formulas to ensure that they are correct, and then correct them as needed.
- In column I, ensure that the conditional formatting identifies values less than zero with a light red fill and dark red text while values greater than zero have a light green fill and dark green text.
- Ensure that the data table is set up correctly, including hiding any references to functions using custom formatting.

e. Save the workbook, exit Excel, and then submit your file as directed by your instructor.

Excel Business Unit 6

Building Financial and Statistical Models

Businesses are generating and consuming vast amounts of data. This data can be utilized to make informed business decisions. To accomplish this, the data can be analyzed by using a wide variety of tools in Excel. Functions in Excel can be used to calculate regular payments, interest rates, and the total interest and principal paid on a loan. Creating an amortization schedule will facilitate tracking of the interest and principal paid on a loan for each periodic payment. Bond and investments can also be analyzed by using Excel functions along with calculating the depreciation of assets. A statistical analysis can be completed in Excel by using functions or the Analysis ToolPak add-in. These tools can also be used to predict business outcomes, find relationships between data, and predict future values using a regression analysis.

Learning Outcome 1:

Using Excel financial functions, construct a loan analysis, calculate cumulative interest and principal, create an amortization schedule, analyze bonds and investments, and calculate depreciation of assets.

REAL WORLD SUCCESS

"As an intern in the accounting department of an electric engineering company, I was asked to transfer some accounting documents to an Excel workbook. During the process, I was able to identify an error in how the company calculated the depreciation of one of their assets."

- Emily, recent graduate

Learning Outcome 2:

Understand statistical language, understand the basic types of data, conduct a statistical analysis using Excel functions and the Analysis ToolPak, predict outcomes using probability distributions, use correlations and covariance to find relationships in data, and use regression analysis to predict future values.

REAL WORLD SUCCESS

"After graduation, I got a job at a small e-marketing firm. The managers were looking over some numbers to decide whether or not they should acquire a smaller company. They had decided to go with the acquisition until someone used statistics to analyze the distribution of the data. It turned out that a few outliers were skewing the numbers and it would have been a very bad decision to acquire the company. I never thought statistics had a place in business until I witnessed firsthand how just a few simple statistical methods can prevent bad decisions."

- James, recent graduate

Microsoft Excel 2016

Chapter 11 | LOAN AMORTIZATION, INVESTMENT ANALYSIS, AND ASSET DEPRECIATION

Prepare Case

Finance & Accounting

The Turquoise Oasis Spa Financial Analysis

Painted Paradise Golf Resort & Spa CEO William Mattingly recently announced that Genisys Corporation, a large technology company, will soon break ground on its new corporate headquarters about three miles from the resort. In addition, Genisys has proposed a partnership with the resort to provide lodging, recreation conferences, and other services to Genisys Corporation staff, executives, and VIP guests.

Turquoise Oasis managers Irene Kai and Meda Rodate believe that the new relationship with Genisys Corporation has the potential to double the spa's revenue. To handle the increased business, they plan several upgrades and improvements. The spa will have to handle more simultaneous clients while maintaining high-quality service.

The managers would like you to prepare an analysis of several options to finance these improvements and eventual expansion.

Subbotina Anna/Shutterstock

Student data file needed for this chapter:

 e06ch11Finance.xlsx

You will save your file as:

 e06ch11Finance_LastFirst.xlsx

Constructing a Loan Analysis

Businesses need to have a positive **cash flow** to survive. Cash flow is the movement of cash into and out of a business. The measurement of cash flow can be used to determine a company's value and financial situation. The statement of cash flow is particularly helpful in assessing a company's short-term viability, which includes its abilities to collect cash from customers and to pay bills. The longer a company stays profitable and the better it manages its cash flow, the better its viability. Once a company's value and financial situation have been determined, banks can use that information to determine the company's eligibility for business loans.

From a personal perspective, individuals deal with managing money on a regular basis. People need to understand not only how to successfully invest their money, but also how loans work — such as a car loan, a student loan, or a home loan, known as a mortgage. Personal finance is similar to managing an organization's cash flow except that it relates to the individual's or family's monetary choices. It addresses the ways in which individuals or families obtain, budget, save, and spend money, taking into account various economic risks and future life events, such as getting married or having a family.

An **economic risk** occurs when a chosen act or activity might not generate enough revenues to cover operating costs and repay debt obligations. This notion suggests that a choice has an effect on the outcome. Potential losses themselves may also be called risks. Almost any human endeavor, whether personal or professional, carries some type of risk, but some are more risky than others. For example, the Turquoise Oasis Spa may decide to obtain a bank loan to fund an expansion. Before the bank agrees to finance the loan, it will need to consider many factors, including the spa's cash flow and short-term viability. This will help the bank to determine the level of risk — whether the spa is likely to be able to repay the loan on time and in full.

Excel includes financial functions to use for business and personal analysis and financial management. It is important to understand the purpose and features of each function so you can apply them to a specific task or problem. These financial functions are designed to calculate the monthly payment and other components of a loan, determine the future value of an investment, compare and contrast different investment opportunities, and calculate the depreciation of assets over time. In the following section, you will conduct a loan analysis using the PMT, RATE, and NPER functions.

Construct a Loan Analysis with PMT, RATE, and NPER

Many businesses and individuals need to borrow money — it is a fact of life. If you need to apply for a loan, you will want to know the monthly payment, which depends on such factors as the loan terms: the principle amount, the interest rate, and the length of the loan. The type of loan that the Turquoise Oasis Spa is considering is an amortized loan. An amortized loan is a loan with scheduled periodic payments consisting of both principal and interest. This is different from other types of loans that have interest-only payment features and balloon payments.

Opening the Starting File

In this exercise, you will open an Excel workbook and begin conducting a loan analysis on four different loan options to fund the Turquoise Oasis Spa expansion.

E11.00

To Open the e06ch11Finance Workbook

a. Start **Excel**, click **Open Other Spreadsheets** in the left pane, and then double click **This PC**. Navigate through the folder structure to the location of your student data files, and then double-click **e06ch11Finance**.

b. Click the **File** tab, click **Save As**, and then double-click **This PC**. In the Save As dialog box, navigate to the location where you are saving your project files, and then change the file name to e06ch11Finance_LastFirst using your last and first name.

c. Click **Save**.

Using the PMT Function

The payment function, or **PMT function**, can be used to calculate a payment amount on the basis of constant payments and a constant interest rate. Payments on business loans, mortgages, car loans, or student loans can be calculated. For example, if the managers of the Turquoise Oasis Spa have determined that they need to borrow $200,000 to help fund the spa's expansion and the bank is charging 6.75% interest over a ten-year period, the managers can use the PMT function to determine what the monthly payment would be.

REAL WORLD ADVICE	Additional Costs of a Loan

The payment amount returned by the PMT function includes principal and interest but no taxes, reserve payments, private mortgage insurance, or fees that may be associated with the loan. Be sure to include other fees and charges when calculating your actual expenses associated with a loan. Additional costs can be quite substantial. If you fail to consider them, you may obtain a loan that you cannot afford.

To use the PMT function for the Turquoise Oasis Spa's loan, you have to understand the structure of the function and what each function argument is determining. The PMT function calculates payments for a loan for a fixed amount with a fixed interest rate and for a fixed period of time. The PMT function syntax uses five arguments. The first three are required, and the last two are optional: (1) interest rate per period (rate), (2) number of periods (nper), (3) present value (pv), (4) future value (fv), and (5) type (type). Notice that the optional arguments are represented by square brackets.

=PMT(rate, nper, pv, [fv], [type])

The **rate** argument is the periodic interest rate — the interest rate of the loan. For example, if the annual percentage rate (APR) is 12% and you make monthly payments, the periodic rate — the rate charged per period and in this case, per month — is 1%. This is calculated by dividing the APR by 12, the number of months in a year.

S S CONSIDER THIS	Determining the Per Period Rate of Interest

The key to determining the rate of interest per period is in the total number of payments and/or how frequently the payments are made each year. If they are monthly payments, then you need to divide the rate argument by 12. By what would you divide the rate if the payments were made quarterly? What if they were made yearly?

The **nper** argument is the total number of payments that will be made to pay the loan in full. The term of the loan is generally specified in years; however, payments are made several times a year. If the loan is for five years and you make 12 monthly payments, you would calculate the nper by multiplying the number of years by the number of payments in one year. Thus, five years times 12 monthly payments equals 60, which is the number to use in the formula.

The **pv** argument is the present value of the loan, also known as the principal when used in the PMT function. Usually, the loan amount is used as the present value. The PMT() function in Excel returns a negative number if all arguments are positive. This is due to the nature of cash flow. Whether the perspective is from the borrower or the lender determines whether the present value is entered as a positive or negative argument.

When viewed from the borrower's perspective, incoming cash flows are "positive," whereas outgoing flows are "negative." In calculating the loan from the borrower's perspective, the pv argument is positive because the borrower receives the cash — a cash inflow. Thus, the PMT function returns a negative amount because the borrower will pay that amount every period — a cash outflow.

In calculating a loan from the bank, or lender's, perspective, the pv argument is negative because the bank pays the money to the borrower — a cash outflow. Thus, the PMT function returns a positive amount because the bank will receive that payment every period — a cash inflow.

Best practice in calculating a loan payment or amortization is to do the calculations from the bank's perspective. Thus, to avoid receiving a negative answer, you can type a negative sign in front of the present value, ensuring a positive payment value. When you are working with financial functions, to avoid getting a wildly incorrect answer, it is important to keep in mind from whose perspective the problem is being calculated.

QUICK REFERENCE	Cash Flows

Cash Inflow: A lender or bank is receiving cash in a loan agreement.
Cash Outflow: A lender or bank is paying cash in a loan agreement.

The **fv** argument — future value of the loan — is the balance you want to reach after the last payment has been made. Consider any type of loan that you may have. The ultimate goal is to pay off the loan, meaning that the future value would be zero. If fv is omitted — because it is an optional argument — Excel assumes that the future value is zero.

CONSIDER THIS | Using the fv Argument

A business may lease office equipment and then make regular payments throughout the term of the lease. At the end of the lease, the business may have the option to purchase the equipment for a specific price, which is determined at the lease signing. The amount would be entered in the fv argument of the PMT function. What are some other uses of the fv argument?

The **type** argument indicates when the payments are due — at either the beginning (1) or the end (0) of a period, such as the end of a month, quarter, or year. If type is omitted (because it is an optional argument), Excel assumes that the value is 0, indicating an end of the period payment.

The Turquoise Oasis Spa can use the PMT function to calculate the monthly payment on Loan Option 1 for $200,000 at 6.75% annual interest rate over a ten-year period. Thus, the PMT function arguments would be as follows.

- Rate: 6.75% divided by 12 months = .5625%
- Nper: 10 years * 12 months = 120 months
- Pv: –$200,000 — Recall that this argument is negative because it represents an outflow of money.

Because the future value and type arguments are not given, you would end the PMT function after entering the present value and calculate the monthly payment as $2,296.48.

If you do not have a future value and the payment is made at the end of the period, you can stop at principal — the pv argument — and just type your ending parenthesis.

=PMT(.0675/12,10*12,-200000)

The amount of the payment can change depending on when the payment needs to be made — at either the beginning or the end of a period — because of how interest is calculated. If the payments are made at the beginning of a period, the total interest that will be paid on the loan is lower because the principal is being paid down faster. The **principal** is the unpaid balance amount of the loan. Because the future value is not given and you want to enter 1 in the type argument, you would type two commas after the present value argument to indicate that you want to skip the future value argument. The PMT function calculates the monthly payment as $2,283.64 and would be entered as follows.

=PMT(.0675/12,10*12,-200000,,1)

 CONSIDER THIS | **What-If Analysis for a Loan**

How could referencing cells with the loan terms allow you to perform what-if analysis? In **what-if analysis**, several different values are used in one or more formulas to explore all the various results. What if you decided that you could not afford the loan payments? How could you modify the interest rate, loan amount, and terms to find a payment that you can afford?

In this exercise, you will calculate a loan payment using the PMT() function. For determining cash flows, the calculations will be from the bank's perspective.

 E11.01

To Calculate Loan Payments Using the PMT Function

a. This workbook includes information for some of the financing options collected by the managers. Click the **LoanAnalysis1-3** worksheet. Click cell **B10**, and then examine the formula in the cell.

   The PV argument of the PMT() function is negative. This indicates that the calculation is from the bank's perspective. The bank will have to pay that amount at the beginning of the loan — a cash outflow.

b. Click cell **B11**, and then type **=PMT(** to begin the PMT function. Click cell **B7**, type **/**, and then click **B9** to calculate the rate argument. Because your payments will be monthly, you divided cell B7 by cell B9 to convert the annual interest rate into a monthly interest rate.

c. Type **,** to move to the nper argument.

d. Click cell **B8**, type *****, and then click cell **B9** to calculate the number of periods in the loan. Because the loan is for 10 years and each year will have 12 payments, there will be 10 × 12, or 120, payments.

e. Type **,** to move to the pv argument.

   Type **–** to indicate that the present value is negative, since this calculation is from the bank's perspective — a cash outflow. Click cell **B6** to select the beginning loan amount. Type **,,1)** to omit the fv argument and indicate that payments are due at the beginning of the period.

f. Press Enter.

   The completed function in cell B11 should appear as =PMT(B7/B9,B8*B9,-B6,,1). Notice that the difference between the periodic payment amounts in cells B10 and B11 depends on when the payment is made.

g. **Save** 🖫 the workbook.

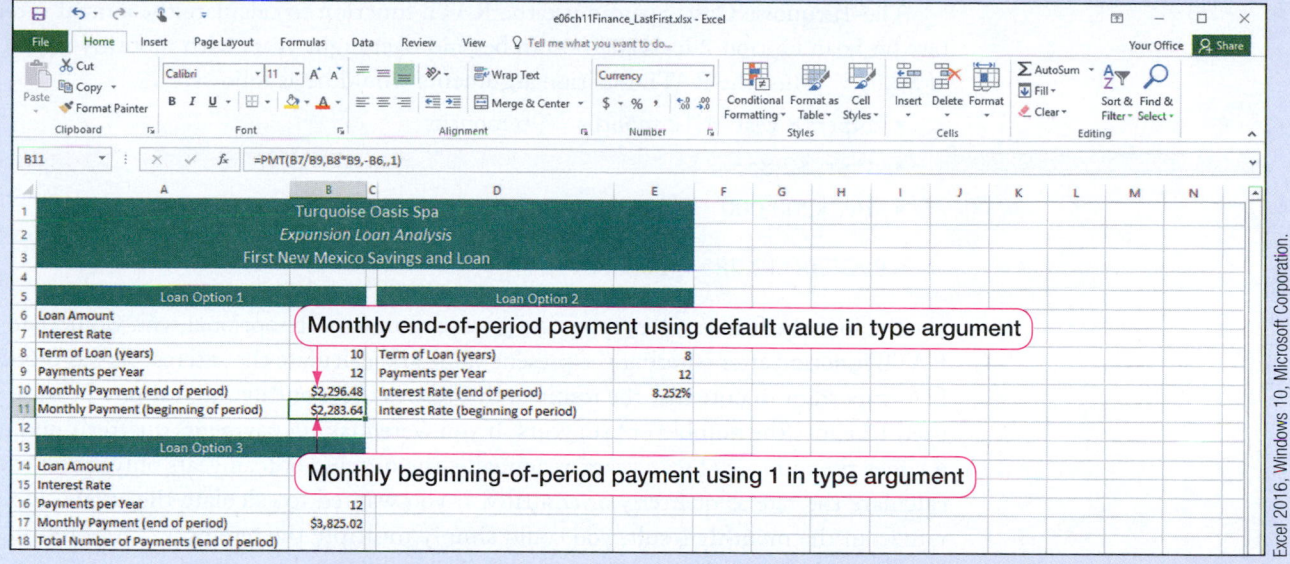

Figure 1 Loan analysis using the PMT function

QUICK REFERENCE	Understanding the PMT Function Syntax

The PMT function syntax has the following arguments.

Argument	Description
rate	The interest rate per period for the loan. Required.
nper	The total number of periods (payments) for the loan. Required.
pv	The present value, or the total amount that a series of future payments is worth now; also known as the loan amount. Required.
fv	The future value, or a cash balance you want to attain after the last payment has been made. If fv is omitted, it is assumed to be 0 (zero); that is, the future value of a loan is 0. Optional.
type	The number 0 (zero) or 1; indicates when payments are due. Optional.
	Set type equal to 0 — or omit — if payments are due at the end of the period.
	Set type equal to 1 if payments are due at the beginning of the period.

Using the RATE Function

The **RATE function** calculates the interest rate per period for an investment or loan, given that you know the present value of the loan, payment amount, and number of payment periods. This can be useful if you do not have all the information you need to calculate loan payments with the PMT function or you would like to verify the actual interest rate of the loan. The RATE function syntax uses six arguments. The first three are required, and the last three are optional: (1) number of periods (nper), (2) payment (pmt), (3) present value (pv), (4) future value (fv), (5) type (type), and (6) interest rate guess (guess).

=RATE(nper, pmt, pv, [fv], [type], [guess])

The **guess** argument is used when you want to guess what the interest rate will be. If nothing is entered, Excel assumes that the guess is 10%. If RATE does not calculate, or results in a #NUM! error, you can enter a guess value between 0 and 1.

The Turquoise Oasis Spa can use the RATE function to calculate the annual interest rate on Loan Option 2 for $200,000 to be paid over eight years with monthly payments of $2,853. Thus, the RATE function arguments would be as follows.

- Nper: 8 years * 12 months = 96 months
- Pmt: $2,853
- Pv: $200,000

=RATE(8*12,2853,-200000)

Because the future value, type, and guess arguments are optional, you would end the RATE function after entering the present value and calculate the interest rate as 0.688%. It is important to note that the result in this case is the monthly interest rate because you used 12 times the number of loan years. If you were making payments quarterly and used 4 times the number of loan years or annually, the number of loan years only, Excel would calculate the rate as quarterly or annually. If you wanted to calculate the annual interest rate from the monthly result, you could simply multiply the rate by 12. As a result, the bank would be charging the Turquoise Oasis Spa 8.252% annually.

=RATE(8*12,2853,-200000)*12

In this exercise, you will use the RATE function to calculate the interest rate for a loan for which the payment is due at the beginning of the period. For determining cash flows, the calculations will be from the bank's perspective.

 E11.02

To Calculate the Interest Rate of a Loan Using the RATE Function

a. Click cell **E10**, and notice that the RATE function has already been entered for the end of period Interest Rate. The RATE function returns 8.252%.

b. Click cell **E11**, and then type **=RATE(** to begin the RATE function.

c. Click cell **E8**, type *****, and then click cell **E9** to calculate the nper argument.

d. Type **,** to move to the pmt argument. Click cell **E7** to supply the monthly payment amount for the RATE function. Type **,** to move to the pv argument.

e. Type **−**, and then click cell **E6**. This will calculate the present value of the loan as negative for the RATE function, indicating that it is being calculated from the bank's perspective. The bank will have to pay that amount at the beginning of the loan — a cash outflow.

f. Type **,,1)***, and then click cell **E9** to calculate the annual interest rate for a loan where the payment is made at the beginning of the period. Press Enter.
   The completed function in cell E11 should appear as =RATE(E8*E9,E7,-E6,,1)*E9. Notice that the annual interest rate is 8.448% when the payment is made at the beginning of the period.

Troubleshooting

If the RATE function returns #NUM! instead of the expected interest rate, then check to make sure there is a negative sign before the pv argument. For the RATE function to work, either the pmt argument or the pv argument must be negative.

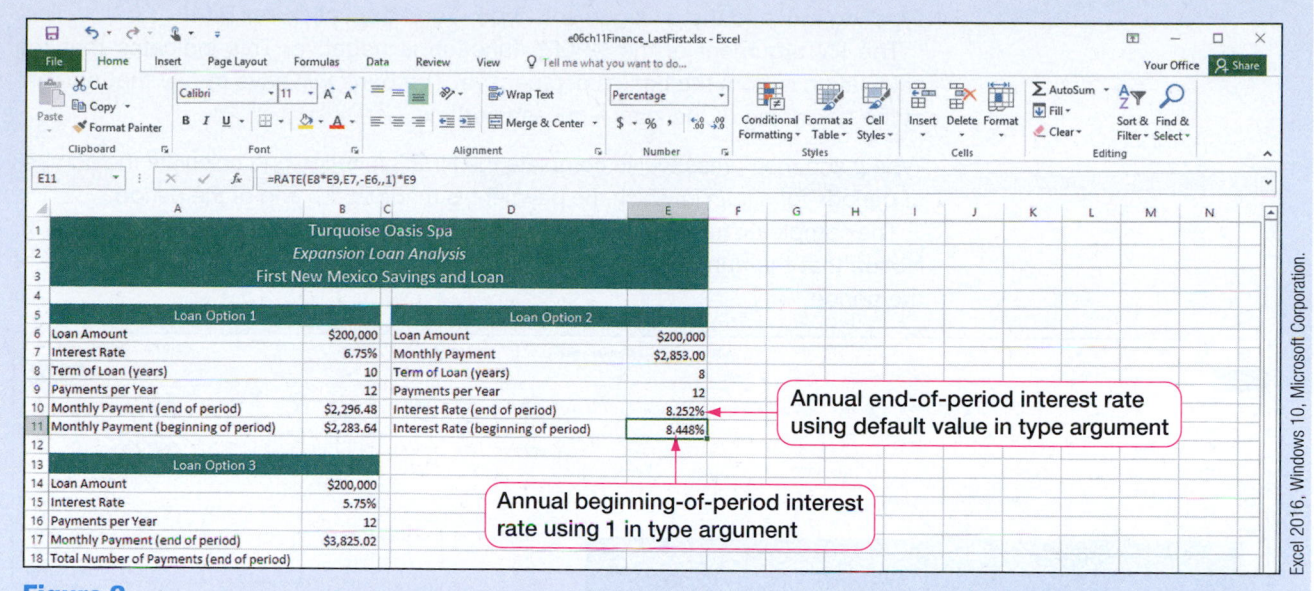

Figure 2 Loan analysis using the RATE function

g. **Save** 🖫 the workbook.

Using the NPER Function

The number of periods function, or **NPER function**, calculates the number of payment periods for an investment or loan if you know the loan amount, interest rate, and payment amount. The NPER function syntax uses five arguments. The first three are required, and the last two are optional: (1) rate (rate), (2) payment (pmt), (3) present value (pv), (4) future value (fv), and (5) type (type).

=NPER(rate, pmt, pv, [fv], [type])

The Turquoise Oasis Spa can use the NPER function to calculate the number of periods on Loan Option 3 for a $200,000 loan with an annual rate of 5.75% if the monthly payment is $3,825.02, paid at the end of the period. Thus, the NPER function arguments would be as follows.

- Rate: 5.75%
- Pmt: $3,825.02
- Pv: $200,000

=NPER(.0575/12, 3843.35, -200000)

In this exercise, because the future value and type arguments are optional, you will end the NPER function after entering the present value and calculate the number of periods as 60. For determining cash flows, the calculations will be from the bank's perspective.

 E11.03

To Calculate the Total Number of Periods Using the NPER Function

a. Click cell **B18**, and then type **=NPER(** to begin the NPER function.

b. Click cell **B15**, type **/**, and then click cell **B16** to calculate the monthly interest rate.

c. Type **,** to move to the pmt argument. Click cell **B17** to supply the monthly payment for the NPER function.

d. Type **,** to move to the pv argument. Type **-**, and then click cell **B14**.

The PV argument of the NPER() function is negative. This indicates that the calculation is from the bank's perspective. The bank will have to pay that amount at the beginning of the loan — a cash outflow.

e. Type **)**, and then press Enter to complete the NPER function and calculate the number of periods for a loan in which the payment is made at the end of the period.

The completed function in cell B18 should appear as =NPER(B15/B16,B17,-B14). Notice that the number of periods is 60 when the payment is made at the end of the period.

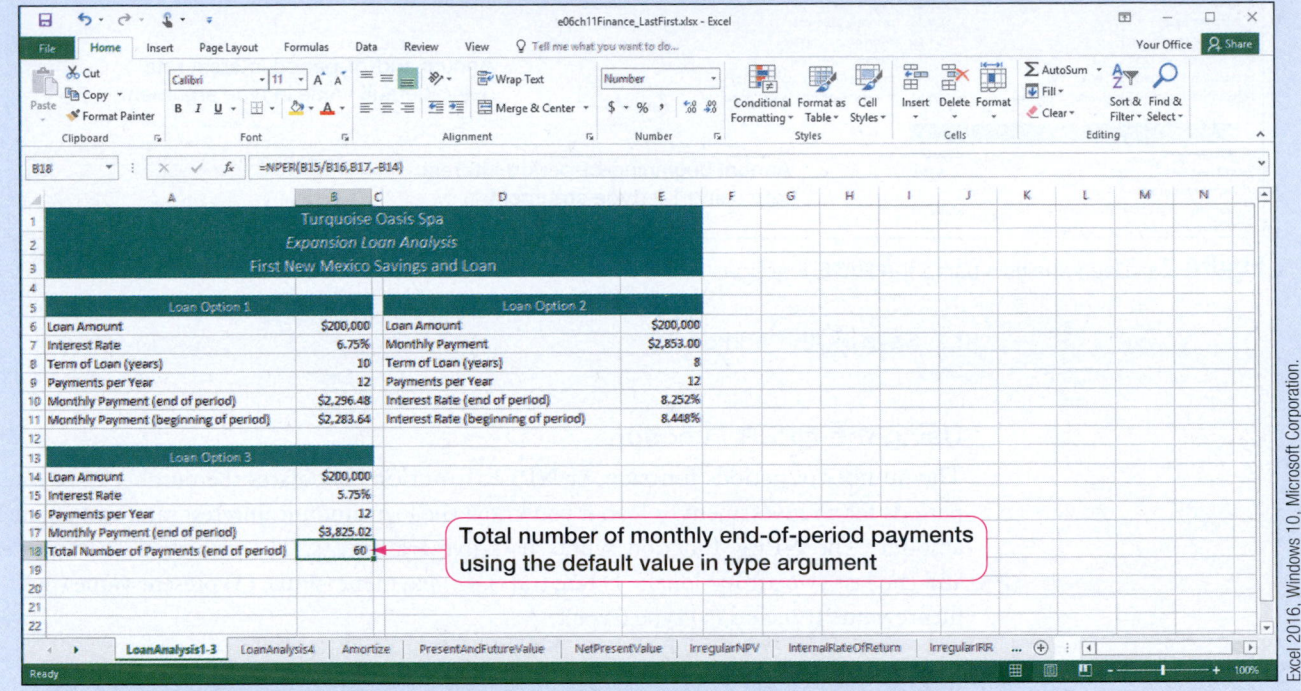

Figure 3 Loan analysis using the NPER function

f. **Save** 💾 the workbook.

Calculate Cumulative Interest and Principal Using CUMIPMT and CUMPRINC

Each loan payment in an amortized loan is made up of a principal amount and an interest amount. There are times when you will want to know the total interest or principal amount being paid over a particular time period. Consider a mortgage. If someone is paying on a mortgage, she can use the amount of interest paid throughout the year as a deduction on her federal income taxes. Thus, knowing the amount of cumulative interest paid can make it easier to complete this section on a tax return.

Using the CUMIPMT Function

The cumulative interest payment function, or **CUMIPMT function**, can be used to calculate the amount of interest paid over a specific number of periods, such as quarterly, annually, or for the whole term of the loan. Thus, if you do not want to calculate a running total of the interest paid, you can total the payments between two payment periods. The CUMIPMT function syntax uses six arguments, all of which are required: (1) rate (rate), (2) number of periods (nper), (3) present value (pv), (4) start period (start_period), (5) end period (end_period), and (6) type (type).

=CUMIPMT(rate, nper, pv, start_period, end_period, type)

The two new arguments are start_period and end_period; they indicate the period numbers during the life of the loan. Start_period defines the start of the payment period for the interval you want to sum. The end_period defines the end of the payment period.

The Turquoise Oasis Spa is also considering Loan Option 4 for $200,000 at an 8.25% annual interest rate for three years with payments of $18,550.84 made at the end of each quarter. They can use the CUMIPMT function to calculate the cumulative amount of interest payments for all three years or for each quarter. Thus, the CUMIPMT function arguments would be as follows.

- Rate: 8.25%
- Nper: 3 years * 4 quarters = 12 quarterly payments
- Pv: $200,000
- Start_period: 1
- End_period: 12
- Type: 0 — end of period payments

With this function, Excel does not allow you to place a negative sign in front of the pv argument. Thus, to display numbers from the bank's perspective, as a positive number, you can simply place a negative sign before the function name.

=-CUMIPMT(.0825/4, 3*4, 200000, 1, 12, 0)

In this exercise, you will use the CUMIPMT function to calculate the total and quarterly cumulative interest paid during a three-year loan. For determining cash flows, the calculations will be from the bank's perspective.

 **E11.04**

To Calculate Cumulative Interest Payments Using the CUMIPMT Function

a. Click the **LoanAnalysis4** worksheet.

b. Click cell **B13**, and type **=-CUMIPMT(** to begin the CUMIPMT function.

   The negative sign indicates that the CUMIPMT() function is from the bank's perspective. The bank will receive the interest payments on the loan — a cash inflow.

c. Click cell **B7**, type **/**, and then click cell **B9** to calculate the interest rate for the CUMIPMT function.

d. Type **,** to move to the nper argument. Click cell **B8**, type *****, and then click cell **B9** to calculate the number of periods.

e. Type **,** to move to the pv argument. Click cell **B6**, which contains the present value of the loan.

f. Type **,1** to move to the start_period argument and begin calculating interest in the first period.

g. Type **,12** to move to the end_period argument and stop calculating interest in the twelfth period. Type **,0)** to calculate the total cumulative interest payments for the life of the loan based on payments being made at the end of the period. Press Ctrl + Enter.

   The completed function in cell B13 should appear as =-CUMIPMT(B7/B9,B8*B9,B6,1,12,0). Notice that the cumulative interest is $27,815.02 when the payment is made at the end of the period.

h. Click cell **B17**, and type **=-CUMIPMT(** to begin the CUMIPMT function that will calculate the interest paid in the first quarterly payment. The negative sign indicates the CUMIPMT() function is from the bank's perspective. The bank will receive the quarterly interest payment on the loan — a cash inflow.

i. Click cell **B7**, and press F4 to lock the cell reference. Type **/**, click cell **B9**, and then press F4 to lock the cell reference. This calculates the rate for the CUMIPMT function and locks the cell references so that the formula can be copied down the column later.

j. Type **,** to move to the nper argument. Click cell **B8**, and press F4 to lock the cell reference. Type *****, click cell **B9**, and then press F4 to lock the cell reference. This calculates the number of periods for the CUMIPMT function and locks the cell references so that the formula can be copied down the column later.

k. Type **,** to move to the pv argument. Click cell **B6**, which contains the present value of the loan, and then press F4 to lock the cell reference.

l. Type **,** to move to the start_period argument. Click cell **A17**, which contains a 1, indicating the first quarterly payment. This cell reference will need to stay relative to the current cell when copied down the column.

m. Type **,** to move to the end_period argument. Click cell **A17**, which contains a 1, indicating the first quarterly payment. As the function is copied down the column, the CUMIPMT function will calculate the interest paid in each period.

n. Type **,0)** to move to the type argument and calculate the periodic interest for the first quarterly payment. Press Ctrl + Enter. The completed function in cell B17 should appear as =-CUMIPMT($B$7/$B$9,$B$8*$B$9,$B$6,A17,A17,0).

o. Double-click the **AutoFill** handle to copy the formula down to cell **B28**.

Notice that the amount of the cumulative interest payments decreases with each quarterly payment because the amount of principal is less after each quarterly payment.

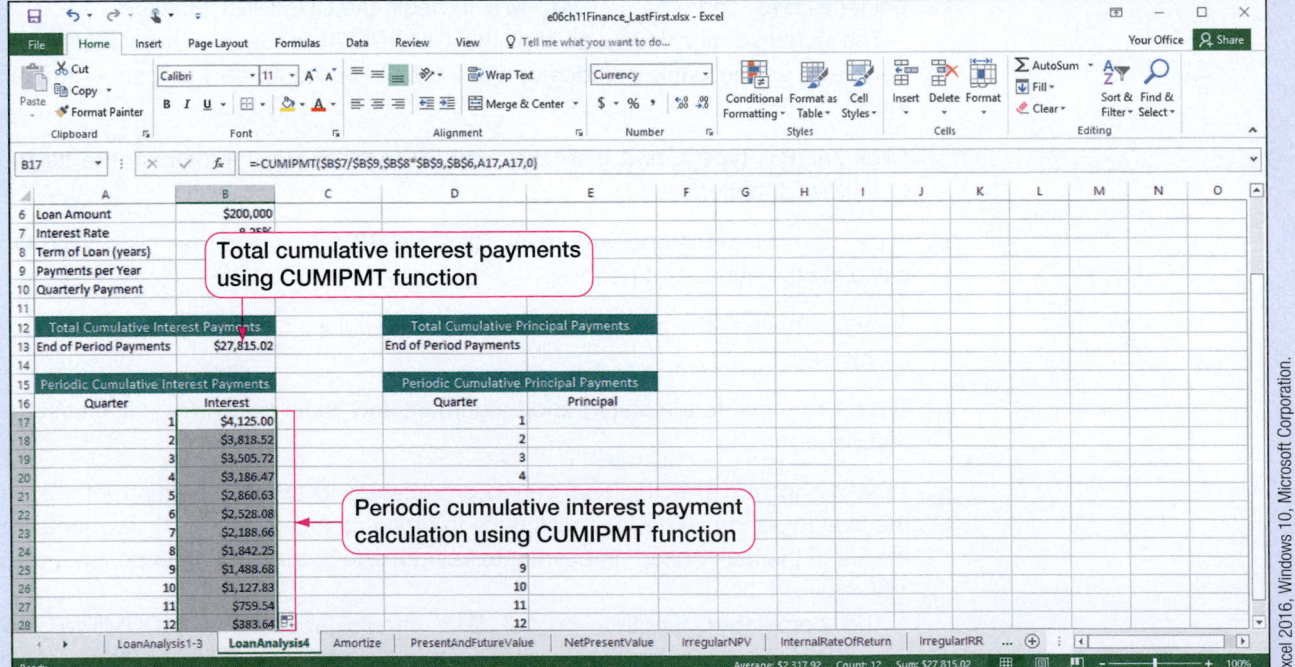

Figure 4 Loan analysis using the CUMIPMT function

p. **Save** 💾 the workbook.

Using the CUMPRINC Function

Similar to the CUMIPMT function, the cumulative principal function, or **CUMPRINC function**, can be used to calculate the amount of principal paid over a specific number of periods, such as quarterly or annually. Thus, if you do not want to calculate a running total of the principal paid, you can total the payments between two payment periods. The CUMPRINC function syntax uses the same six arguments that the CUMIPMT uses, all of which are required. As in using the CUMIPMT function, you cannot place a negative sign in front of the pv argument. To display numbers as a positive result, you can simply place a negative sign before the function name.

=-CUMPRINC(rate, nper, pv, start_period, end_period, type)

In this exercise, you will use the CUMPRINC function to find the total cumulative principal paid per year for the loan. For determining cash flows, the calculations will be from the bank's perspective.

 E11.05

To Calculate Cumulative Principal Payments Using the CUMPRINC Function

a. Click cell **E13**, and type **=-CUMPRINC(** to begin the CUMPRINC function.
   The negative sign indicates that the CUMPRINC() function is from the bank's perspective. The bank will receive the principle interest payment on the loan — a cash inflow.

b. Click cell **B7**, type **/**, and then click cell **B9** to calculate the quarterly interest rate.

c. Type **,** to move to the nper argument. Click cell **B8**, type *****, and then click cell **B9** to calculate the total number of payments.

d. Type **,** to move to the pv argument. Click cell **B6** to reference the loan amount.

e. Type **,** to move to the start_period argument. Type **1** to indicate that you want to calculate the cumulative principle paid, beginning in the first payment period. Type **,12** to move to the end_period argument and indicate that you want to stop calculating the cumulative principle paid in the twelfth period payment.

f. Type **,** to move to the type argument. Type **0)**, and press [Ctrl] + [Enter] to finish the function and calculate the total cumulative principal payments for the life of the loan based on payments being made at the end of the period. The completed function in cell E13 should appear as =-CUMPRINC(B7/B9,B8*B9,B6,1,12,0).

g. Click cell **E17**, and type **=-CUMPRINC(** to begin a CUMPRINC function that will calculate the cumulative principle paid each quarter of the loan period.
   The negative sign indicates the CUMPRINC() function is from the bank's perspective. The bank will receive the quarterly principle interest payment on the loan — a cash inflow.

h. Click cell **B7**, and press [F4] to lock the cell reference. Type **/**, click cell **B9**, and then press [F4].This calculates the rate for the CUMPRINC function and locks the cell references so that the formula can be copied down the column later.

i. Type **,** to move to the nper argument. Click cell **B8**, and then press [F4]. Type *****, click cell **B9**, and then press [F4] to calculate the number of payments and lock the cell references.

j. Type **,** to move to the pv argument. Click cell **B6**, and press [F4] to reference the current loan amount.

k. Type **,** to move to the start_period argument. Click cell **D17** to reference the first quarter as the starting period.

l. Type , to move to the end_period argument. Click cell **D17** to reference the first quarter as the ending period.

m. Type **,0)**, and press Ctrl + Enter to calculate the cumulative principal paid in the first quarterly payment. The completed function in cell E17 should appear as =-CUMPRINC($B$7/$B$9,$B$8*$B$9,$B$6,D17,D17,0).

n. Double-click the **AutoFill** handle to copy the formula down to cell **E28**.

Notice that the value of the cumulative principal payments increases with each quarterly payment. This is because with each payment, the principal gets smaller and therefore less per period interest is accruing on the amount and more of the payment goes toward paying off the principal.

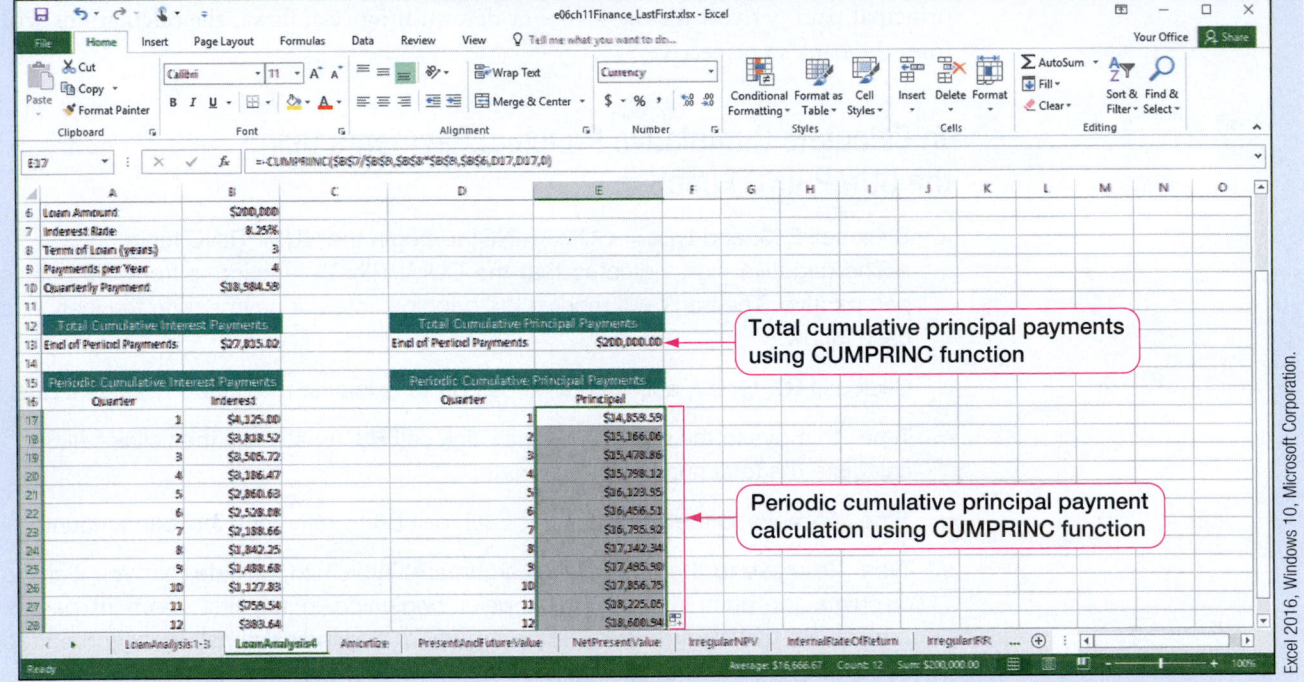

Figure 5   Loan analysis using the CUMPRINC function

o. **Save** 💾 the workbook.

Create an Amortization Schedule Using PPMT and IPMT

With the financial functions you have learned so far, you have some effective tools to help you make an informed decision about which loan option is best to finance the expansion project. Another tool that can help with the decision is an amortization table.

The term **amortize**, with respect to loan balances, refers to repaying the balance of a loan over a period of time in multiple installments — or payments. An **amortization schedule** is a table that calculates the interest and principal payments along with the remaining balance of the loan for each period. Similar to the CUMIPMT and CUMPRINC functions, which calculate the cumulative amount of interest and principal paid over a specified period of time, the IPMT and PPMT functions calculate the interest and principal portions that make up each periodic payment.

Using the PPMT and IPMT Functions

The principal payment function, or **PPMT function**, calculates how much of a specific periodic payment is going toward the principal amount of a loan. The PPMT function syntax uses six arguments. The first four are required, and the last two are optional:

(1) interest rate per period (rate), (2) period (per), (3) number of periods (nper), (4) present value (pv), (5) future value (fv), and (6) type (type).

The syntax of the PPMT function is very similar to that of the PMT function, with the addition of the period (per) argument. The **per** argument is a number that must be between 1 and nper and is the specific period for which a loan payment is being applied. As you make payments on an amortized loan, the amount you pay each period is the same, but how much of that payment is being applied toward the principal increases over time. The per argument is needed to keep track of each payment.

The interest payment function, or **IPMT function**, calculates how much of a specific periodic payment is going toward the interest that has accrued on the loan. The IPMT function syntax is the same as that of the PPMT function. When you begin making payments on an amortized loan, in the beginning, the majority of the amount being paid goes toward interest that has accrued on the remaining balance; this amount decreases over time as the principal is paid down.

Turquoise Oasis Spa could use an amortization table to analyze the loan options for additional improvements. For example, Irene Kai would like to borrow $25,000 for new equipment and to pay this loan off in one year. By creating an amortization table showing the date of each payment, she can see how much of each payment will be applied to the interest and to the principal as well as the balance of the loan. After creating the amortization table, she finds that the payment would be $2,160.29 per month, and the salon would end up paying $923.46 in interest over the life of the loan. In this section, you will create an amortization table to help Irene Kai analyze the repayment schedule to determine whether the payments are within the spa's budget.

REAL WORLD ADVICE — Things to Check in an Amortization Table

There are four things that you can check to ensure that you have accurately constructed your amortization table.

- The final remaining balance value in your table should be zero.

- A given periodic payment (PMT) will equal the sum of the interest payment (IPMT) and the principal payment (PPMT).

- The sum of the principal payments (PPMT) will always equal the loan amount. If you add interest, it will be the total amount paid over the course of the loan term in both interest and principal.

- All interest and principal paid should equal the sum of all the payments made.

You can check your calculations in one easy step. Highlight a range of cells, such as the IPMT and PPMT calculations for the first period, and Excel displays the Average, Count, and Sum for the selection in the status bar located at the bottom of the Excel window.

Creating an Amortization Schedule

When you create an amortization table, start with the simplest configuration. Initially, you should calculate the payment number, the payment amount, the interest and principal portions, and an ending balance for each payment. You can always add more details and complexity later. In this exercise, you will create an amortization table for the new equipment loan. The total number of payments is already calculated in cell G5 of the Amortize worksheet. For determining cash flows, the calculations will be from the bank's perspective.

To Create an Amortization Schedule

a. Click the **Amortize** worksheet.

b. Click cell **G6**, and then type **=PMT(** to begin the PMT function.

c. Click cell **C6** to reference the annual interest rate. Type **/**, and then click cell **C8** to reference the number of payments per year. This calculates the monthly interest for the PMT function.

d. Type **,** to move to the nper argument. Click cell **G5** to reference the number of payments.

e. Type **,-** to move to the pv argument. The calculations are from the bank's perspective. The bank will have to pay that amount at the beginning of the loan — a cash outflow.

f. Click cell **C5**, type **)**, and then press Ctrl + Enter to reference the loan amount and calculate the payments that will be made at the end of the period. The completed function in cell G6 should appear as =PMT(C6/C8,G5,-C5). Notice that the monthly payment will be $2,160.29.

g. Click cell **G7**, and then type **=**. Click cell **G5**, type *****, and then click cell **G6** to calculate the total amount that will be paid. Press Enter, and notice that the total amount that will be paid on the loan is $25,923.46.

h. In cell **G8** type **=**. Click cell **G7**, type **-**, and then click cell **C5** to calculate the total interest that will be paid on the loan. Press Ctrl + Enter, and notice that the total interest that will be paid on the loan is $923.46.

i. Click cell **C12**, type **=**, and then click cell **C5** to reference the beginning balance of the loan and begin creating your amortization schedule.

j. Press Tab, and type **=**. Click cell **G6**, press F4, and then press Ctrl + Enter to enter your payment. Double-click the **AutoFill** handle to copy the formula down to cell **D23**. The total in D24 should equal your results in cell G7.

k. Click cell **E12**, and then type **=IPMT(** to begin the IPMT function.

l. Click cell **C6**, and press F4 to reference the annual interest rate. Type **/**, click cell **C8**, and press F4 to reference the number of payments per year and calculate the monthly interest.

m. Type **,** to move to the per argument. Click cell **A12**, as this will be the first period of interest.

n. Type **,** to move to the nper argument. Click cell **G5**, and press F4 to reference the total number of payments.

o. Type **,** to move to the pv argument. Type **-**, click cell **C5**, and then press F4 to reference the loan amount. The PV argument of the IPMT() function is negative. This indicates that the calculation is from the bank's perspective. The bank will have to pay that amount at the beginning of the loan — a cash outflow.

p. Type **)**, and press Ctrl + Enter to complete the function and calculate how much of the monthly payment is being applied to the interest portion of the loan. The completed function in cell E12 should appear as =IPMT($C$6/$C$8,A12,$G$5,-$C$5). Double-click the **AutoFill** handle to copy the formula down to cell **E23**. The total in E24 should equal your results in cell G8.

q. Click cell **F12**, and then type **=PPMT(** to begin the PPMT function.

r. Click cell **C6**, and press F4 to reference the annual interest. Type **/**, click cell **C8**, and press F4 to reference the payments per year and calculate the monthly interest.

s. Type **,** to move to the per argument. Click cell **A12**, as this will be the first period of principal payments.

t. Type **,** to move to the nper argument. Click cell **G5**, and press F4 to reference the total number of payments.

u. Type **,** to move to the pv argument. Type **-**, click cell **C5**, and then press F4 to reference the loan amount.

The PV argument of the PPMT() function is negative. This indicates that the calculation is from the bank's perspective. The bank will have to pay that amount at the beginning of the loan — a cash outflow.

v. Type **)**, and press Ctrl + Enter to calculate how much of the monthly payment is being applied to the principal portion of the loan. The completed function in cell E12 should appear as =PPMT($C$6/$C$8,A12,$G$5,-$C$5). Double-click the **AutoFill** handle to copy the formula down to cell **F23**.

Notice how the principal portion of the payment increases as the loan is paid off, with $2,019.66 total principal being paid in the first payment and $2,148.20 total principal being paid in the last payment. The total principal in F24 should equal the loan amount in C5.

SIDE NOTE

Remaining Balance
Interest payments are the costs associated with the loan and are never deducted from the beginning balance.

w. Click cell **G12**, and then type **=**. Click cell **C12**, type **-**, and click cell **F12** to calculate the remaining balance after each payment by subtracting the principal payment from the beginning balance. Press Ctrl + Enter, and double-click the **AutoFill** handle to copy the formula down to cell **G23**. Note that the calculations will be negative until you fill in the beginning balance.

x. Your beginning balance for the next payment will be the same as the ending balance after the previous payment. Click cell **C13**, type **=**, and then click cell **G12** to calculate the beginning balance for the second period. Press Ctrl + Enter, and double-click the **AutoFill** handle to copy the formula down to cell **C23** to supply the beginning balance for the remaining periods.

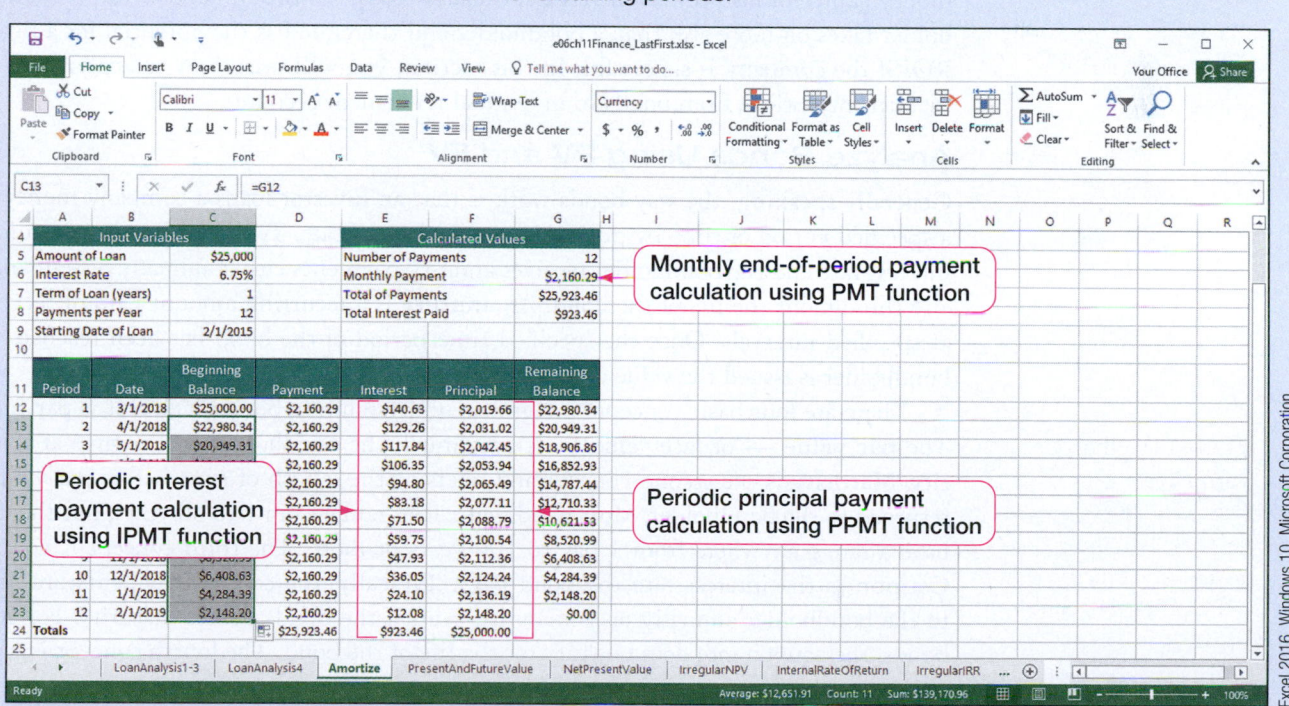

Figure 6 Amortization schedule

y. **Save** 🖫 the workbook. If you need to take a break before finishing this chapter, now is a good time.

Constructing a Financial Analysis of Investments

In addition to analyzing possible expansion finance options from a bank, managers at the Turquoise Oasis Spa would like to analyze some possible investment opportunities to help finance the expansion and generate revenue in the long term. Whether it is a business or an individual investing money, analyzing how the investments are performing is a critical part of the investment process. There are many methods by which money can be invested. Stocks and bonds are two examples of a category of investment called securities.

A **security** is a legal document that can be bought and sold and holds some financial value. Stocks are categorized as equity securities because the company gives partial ownership of its equity, defined as total assets minus total liabilities, by selling stock in the company. Bonds are categorized as debt securities because the company is indebted to the people who loan the company money through the purchase of bonds.

In terms of economic risk, a bond is typically considered less risky, in part because if a company fails, the debt owed to the bondholders are top priority and shareholders would lose any money invested in the company. A lower-risk investment can also mean a lower return on that investment. A **return on investment (ROI)** is the ratio of the amount of money gained or lost from an investment relative to the initial amount invested. A stockholder takes on more risk than a bondholder and therefore has the potential for a higher ROI if the company is successful. In this section, you will learn how to analyze various investment options from bonds to individual retirement accounts.

Analyze Bonds Using PV and FV

Generally speaking, the way bonds work is that an investor loans a company money for a specified period of time by purchasing a bond certificate. Typically, bonds have a fixed interest rate and the bondholder receives annuity payments either annually or semiannually throughout the life of the bond. An **annuity** is a recurring amount paid or received at specified intervals. Once the specified time period of the bond has been reached, the bondholder is issued the value of the bond.

There are four basic concepts integral to understanding bonds. The first is par value. The **par value** — or face value — is how much the bondholder will receive at maturity. **Maturity** is the second concept and refers to the length of time before par value is returned to the bondholder. Most bond maturities range from 1 to 30 years, but they can have a range anywhere from 1 day to 100 years or more. The third concept is coupon. **Coupon** is the interest rate the bond pays. Typically, the coupon payments are made to the bondholder annually or semiannually until the bond reaches maturity. For most bonds, the coupon rate does not vary for the life of the bond. The fourth concept is yield. In its most basic terms, **yield** is the amount of annual interest, expressed as a percentage of the par value, and determines how much investors will receive on their investment.

There are several different types of yield in referring to bonds. **Nominal yield** is the same as the coupon or interest rate. It is information provided when the bond is purchased and is considered the least helpful when it comes to analyzing the true value of a bond. **Current yield** considers the current market price of the bond, which may differ from the par value, and gives you a different yield rate on that basis. For example, consider the following: You purchase a bond with the following values on the open market for $800.

Par Value: $1,000

Coupon: 6% annually

Maturity: 1 year

If the bond's purchase price was the same as the par value, the nominal yield would be the same as the coupon of 6%, and you would have $1,060 ($1,000 * .06 = $60) at the end of the year when the bond reaches maturity. However, since the bond was purchased for $800, a more accurate yield calculation would be the current yield of 7.5% ($60/$800 = 7.5%). **Yield to maturity**, or YTM, is another yield calculation that takes into account the current market price and the time to maturity and assumes that coupon payments are reinvested at the bond's coupon rate. YTM is the most useful calculation in determining the value of a bond investment and the most difficult to calculate.

Using the PV Function

Regardless of how you decide to invest your money — whether you are saving for a home, college, or retirement — if you understand the basics of analyzing your investment portfolio, you will be able to assess its performance. One of the functions that can help you analyze an investment is the present value function, or PV function. The **PV function** is used to calculate the present or current value of a series of future payments on an investment. In other words, it calculates what the investment would be worth in today's dollars. It uses the same five arguments seen in other financial functions: (1) rate (rate), (2) number of periods (nper), (3) payment (pmt), (4) future value (fv), and (5) type (type). If you do not know the payment, you must enter the future value.

=PV(rate, nper, pmt, [fv], [type])

For example, if you were given the option of receiving $250,000 today or $300,000 seven years from now, which would you choose? Excel's PV function can help to determine the smarter choice. Assume that if you took the $250,000 today, you could invest that in a guaranteed risk-free bond at 3% yield rate for seven years. Using the PV function to calculate the present value of $300,000 with a discount rate of 3% for seven years, you see that the $300,000 seven years from now results in a lower present value — $243,927.45 — than $250,000 today.

=-PV(0.03,7,0,300000)

Turquoise Oasis Spa managers are considering a different option for financing part of the expansion: investing in a company bond with the following values.

Par value: $50,000

Maturity: 5 years

Coupon: 6%

YTM: 7.75%

The first step in determining whether or not this is a worthy investment is to calculate the present value of the investment. In this exercise, you will use the PV function to calculate the present value of the investment. For determining cash flows, the calculations will be from the bank's perspective.

 **E11.07**

To Calculate the Present Value of a Bond

a. If you took a break, open the e06ch11Finance_LastFirst workbook. Click the **PresentAndFutureValue** worksheet.

b. Click cell **B8**, type **=**, and then click cell **B6** to reference the Coupon Rate.

c. Type *****, click cell **B5**, then press ⌃Ctrl + ⏎Enter to reference the Par Value and calculate the coupon payment that will be paid to the bondholder one time a year for five years.

d. Click cell **B10**, and then type **=-PV(** to begin the PV function. The negative sign indicates that the PV() function is from the bank's perspective. The bank will receive the bond amount — a cash inflow.

e. Click cell **B9** to reference the yield to maturity rate.

f. Type **,** to move to the nper argument. Click cell **B7** to reference the maturity in years.

g. Type **,** to move to the pmt argument. Click cell **B8** to reference the annual coupon payment.

h. Type **,** to move to the fv argument. Click cell **B5**, type **)**, and press ⌃Ctrl + ⏎Enter to calculate the present value of the investment as a positive number. Notice that the present value of this particular bond is worth only $46,483.24, which is less than $50,000 and therefore not a good investment.

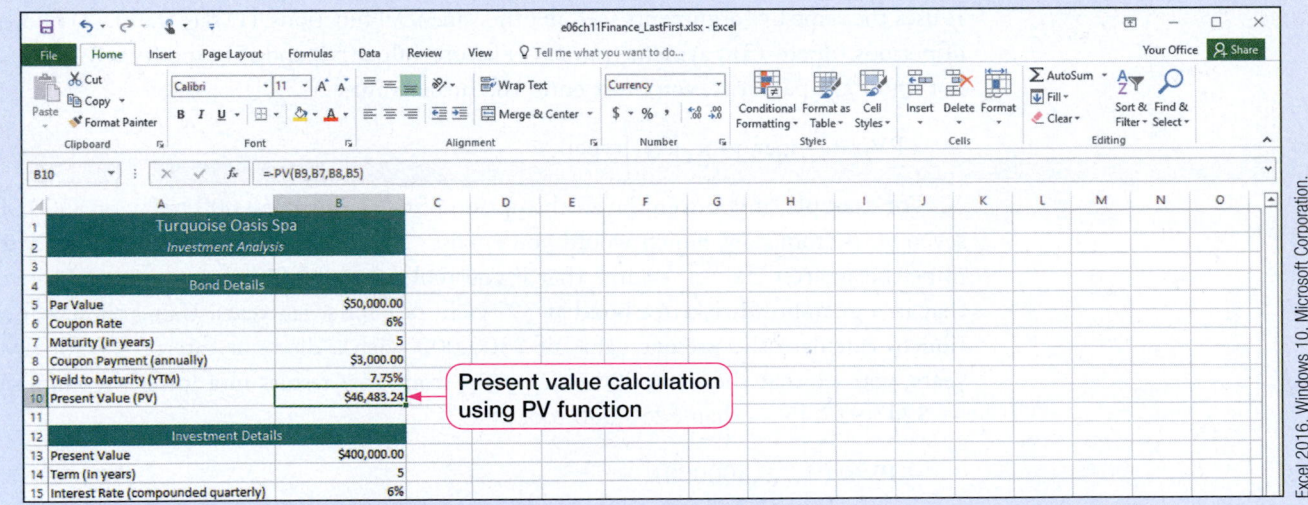

Present value calculation using PV function

Figure 7 Calculating the present value of a bond

i. **Save** 💾 the workbook.

Using the FV Function

The future value function, or **FV function**, is used to calculate the value of an investment with a fixed interest rate and term, as well as to calculate periodic payments over a specific period of time. The FV function syntax uses five arguments. The first three are required, and the last two are optional: (1) rate (rate), (2) number of periods (nper), (3) payment (pmt), (4) present value (pv), and (5) type (type). If you do not know the payment, you must enter the present value.

=FV(rate, nper, pmt, [pv], [type])

For example, you might decide to start saving for retirement and want to use the FV function to calculate how much money you would have by the age of 65. By using the FV function, you can determine how much your Individual Retirement Account (IRA) would be worth when you retire. If you contributed $2,500 per year to your IRA for 40 years — a total of $100,000 — with an interest rate of 8% annually, you would have nearly $650,000.

=FV(.08,40, -2500)

Turquoise Oasis Spa managers are considering investing money that would be provided by private investors. This would require them to wait for five years to allow the investment to grow. Payments and interest will be calculated quarterly. In this exercise, you will use the FV function to help the managers make their decision. For determining cash flows, the calculations will be from the bank's perspective.

To Calculate the Future Value of an Investment

a. Click cell **B16**. Type **=**, click cell **B13**, and then press Enter, to reference the present value, as the total investment will be a one time, lump-sum investment.

b. In cell B17, type **=FV(** to begin the FV function.

c. Click cell **B15**, and type **/4** to reference the interest rate and calculate the quarterly interest rate.

SIDE NOTE
Compound Interest
The interest rate must be divided by 4 and the term multiplied by 4 to account for the quarterly compounded interest.

d. Type **,** to move to the nper argument. Click cell **B14**, and type ***4** to reference the length of the term and calculate the number of periods.

e. Type **,** to move to the pmt argument. Type **0**, as there will be no payments.

f. Type **,** to move to the pv argument. Type **-**, and then click **B13** to reference the present value of the investment.
   The PV argument of the FV() function is negative. This indicates that the calculation is from the bank's perspective. The bank will have to pay that amount at the beginning of the investment — a cash outflow.

g. Type **)**, and press Enter to calculate the future value of this investment.

h. In cell B18, type **=**. Click cell **B17**, type **-**, and then click **B16** to calculate the total earned. Press Ctrl + Enter.
   Notice that the spa would earn $138,742 with this investment option.

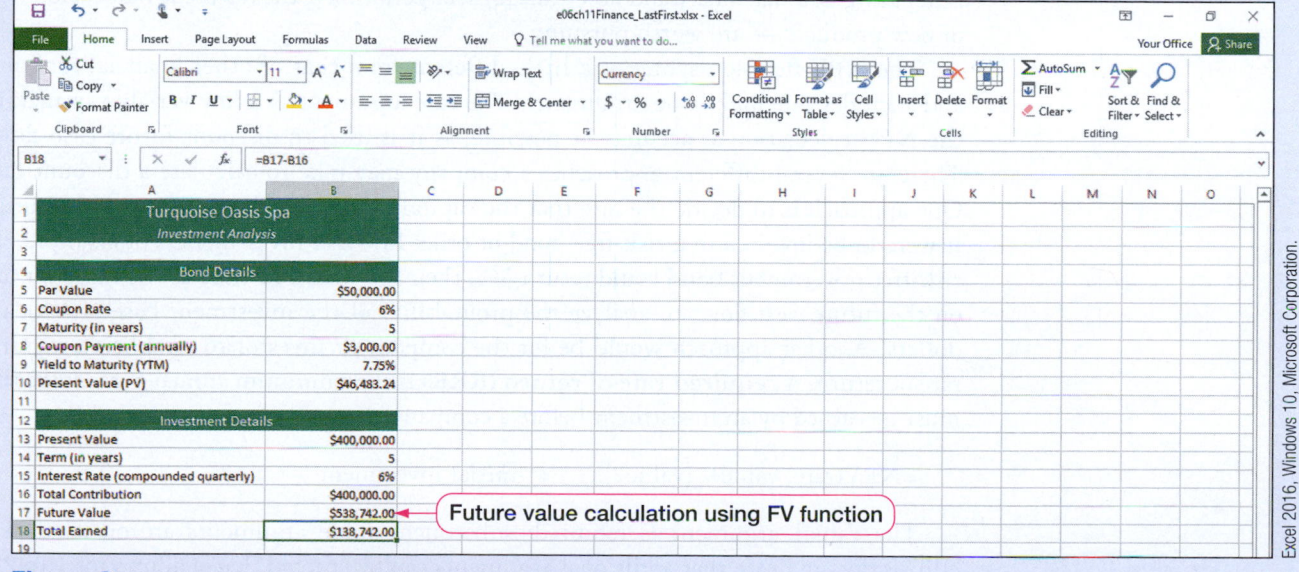

Figure 8   Calculating the future value of an investment

i. **Save** 💾 the workbook.

CONSIDER THIS | **Should Turquoise Oasis Spa Wait Until It Makes Money?**

Turquoise Oasis Spa could earn more than enough money to complete the upgrades and expansion if it accepted the money from the private investors and invested the money. Would this be a wise decision if it requires waiting five years to let the investment grow? What repercussions could the managers face if they do wait? Could it affect the amount of revenue that the spa will generate?

REAL WORLD ADVICE | **Making Assumptions with PV() and FV()**

The PV() and FV() functions do not take all factors into consideration. For example, inflation is not accounted for in the calculation. Further, the PV() and FV() functions rely on a guaranteed, constant rate. Many investments, such as investing in stocks, are not a simple or guaranteed rate. These functions will help you make more informed decisions. However, these functions do not take into account all variables.

Analyze Investments Using NPV, XNPV, IRR, and XIRR

Bond investments should be a part of any well-rounded investment portfolio. However, investors must also take into consideration other investment opportunities that may be higher risk but also offer a higher return. One method of analyzing various investment opportunities is to compare the projected future cash flow generated from the investment to that of a risk-free investment, such as a bond.

Using the NPV Function

The net present value function, or **NPV function**, is used to determine the value of an investment by analyzing a series of future incoming and outgoing cash flows that are expected to occur over the life of the investment. The function assumes that the cash flows occur at regular intervals, such as weekly, monthly, or quarterly. This function is used for capital budgeting and measures the surplus or deficit of cash flows in present value terms. **Capital budgeting** is the planning procedure used to evaluate whether an organization's long-term investment plans — such as acquiring a business or starting a new business, purchasing new machinery and new buildings, or performing the research and development of new products — are worth pursuing.

The NPV function syntax is a little different from that of other financial functions and includes rate and value arguments. The rate argument is a key variable in making the NPV calculation as accurate as possible, as it is used to discount future cash flows. There are several different approaches a company may take to calculate a discount rate. One approach is to decide the rate that the capital needed for the project could return if it were to be invested in a risk-free bond or other low-risk investment. For example, if a risk-free government bond could return 5%, then 5% would be used as the discount rate on the future cash flows to analyze the profitability of the investment based on today's dollars. Another approach would be for the company or investor to establish a required rate of return. A **required rate of return (RRR)** is the minimum annual percentage that must be earned by an investment before a company chooses to invest.

=NPV(rate, value1, [value2],…) + -initial investment

The value1 argument is required; subsequent value arguments are optional. The ellipsis dots indicate that additional arguments can be entered; Excel allows for 1 to 254 values to be entered. The NPV function uses the order of the value arguments to interpret the order of cash flows. Be sure to enter your values in the correct sequence, in which the value1 argument is the amount of estimated cash inflow for period 1 and not the initial amount of the investment in year 0. The initial investment amount must be subtracted outside of the NPV function to calculate the true net present value. Note that many times, the initial investment amount is recorded as a negative number. In that case, the initial investment would be added outside of the NPV function.

The managers at Turquoise Oasis Spa can use the NPV function to see whether it benefits them financially to invest in new equipment for the spa. Given an estimate of cash flows that would be generated with the new equipment and a discount rate based on a risk-free bond option, they can calculate whether the purchase of new equipment produces positive financial benefits. Suppose the spa invests $125,000 with a discount rate of 8% and the estimated cash inflows over the next three years were as follows.

> Year 1: $56,000.00
>
> Year 2: $45,000.00
>
> Year 3: $33,000.00

The net present value would result in a loss of −$8,371.44. Therefore, this would not be a good investment for Turquoise Oasis Spa, which could earn more money by investing in a risk-free bond. If the NPV results in a negative value, then the investment should be rejected. However, if the NPV results in a value greater than 0, then the investment should be considered.

=NPV(.08,56000,45000,33000) + -125000

Turquoise Oasis Spa managers are considering the equipment — such as massage tables, salon chairs, and sinks — that they want to purchase to complete the improvements and expansion. In this exercise, you will use estimated cash inflows as a result of the new equipment for use in your net present value analysis. The initial investment will be $125,000 with a discount rate of 2.56%. For determining cash flows, the calculations will be from the bank's perspective.

 E11.09

To Calculate the Net Present Value of an Investment

a. Click the **NetPresentValue** worksheet.

b. Click cell **B10**, type **=**, and then click cell **B6** to reference the initial investment amount, which will be the cash outflow for year 0. Press Ctrl + Enter.

c. Click cell **B15**, and then type **=NPV(** to begin the NPV function.

d. Click cell **B5** to reference the discount rate.

e. Type **,** to move to the value1 argument. Click cell **B11**, and drag to cell **B13** to select cells B11:B13, the cash flows for three years.

f. Type **)+**, and then click cell **B10** to end the NPV function and add the value of the initial investment. Press Ctrl + Enter to calculate the net present value of the investment. The complete function in B15 should appear as =NPV(B5,B11:B13)+B10.

   Notice that although the estimated cash inflows of the investment had not changed from the example above and what is contained in the worksheet, the result of the NPV function now yields a positive value of $2,973.76 versus −$8,371.44. This is due to the lower discount rate being a key factor in the calculation.

SIDE NOTE
Net Present Value
Any investment that yields a positive NPV should be considered. If the NPV is negative, it is not a good option.

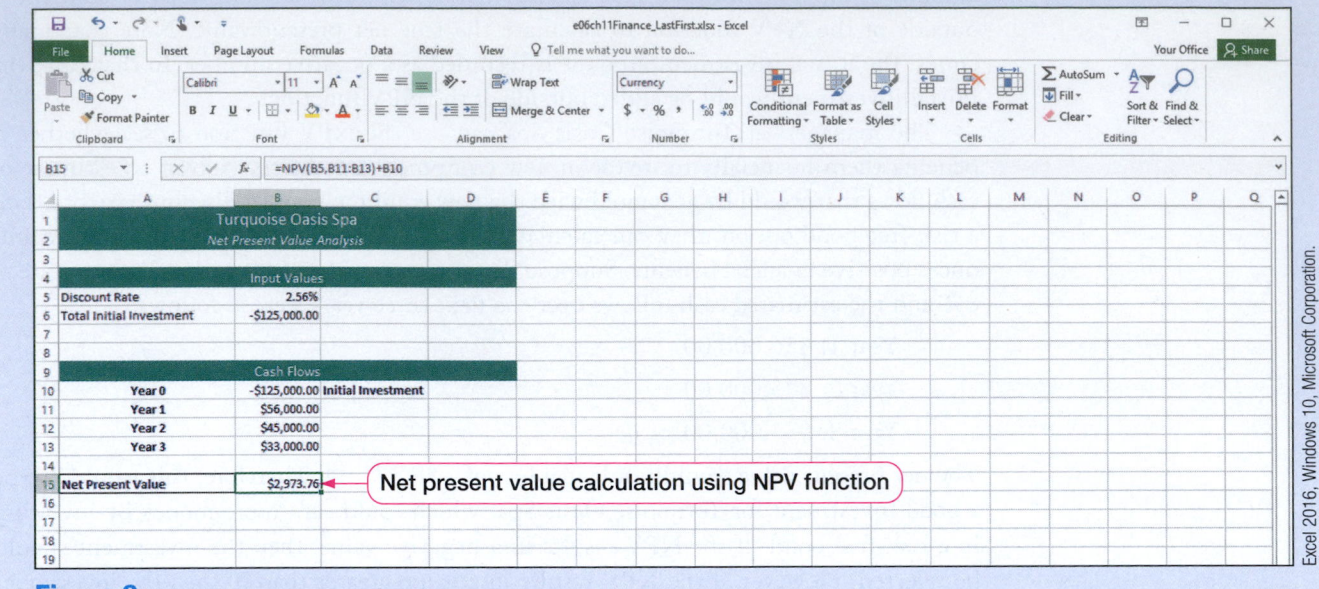

Figure 9 Net present value of an investment

g. **Save**  the workbook.

Using the XNPV Function

Similar to NPV, the irregular net present value function, or **XNPV function**, determines the value of an investment or business by analyzing an irregular time series of incoming and outgoing cash flows. The XNPV function syntax is a little different from that of the NPV function and includes rate, values, and dates arguments, all of which are required. The values argument corresponds to payments, and one of these values must be a negative value, which will most likely represent the initial loan disbursement. The dates argument corresponds with when the payments were made, including the date of the initial investment. All subsequent dates must be after the initial investment date, but they may be listed in any order.

=XNPV(rate, values, dates)

Turquoise Oasis Spa managers are considering another investment option that will require an initial investment amount of $125,000 with estimated cash inflows occurring irregularly over the next two years. In this exercise, you will use the XNPV function to calculate the net present value of the investment with a required return rate of 10%. For determining cash flows, the calculations will be from the bank's perspective.

> **E11.10**

To Calculate an Irregular Net Present Value of an Investment

a. Click the **IrregularNPV** worksheet.

b. Click cell **B20**, and then type **=XNPV(** to begin the XNPV function.

c. Click cell **B4** to reference the required rate of return.

d. Type **,** to move to the values argument. Click cell **B7**, and drag to select cell **B18** to reference the cash flows from 3/1/2018 to 3/1/2020.

e. Type **,** to move to the dates argument. Click cell **A7**, and drag to select cell **A18** to reference the dates of the cash flows.

f. Type **)**, and press Ctrl + Enter to complete the function and calculate the net present value of the investment based on the irregular cash flows. The complete function should appear as =XNPV(B4,B7:B18,A7:A18).

Notice that the net present value is –$355.61; therefore, it does not meet the required rate of return of 10%.

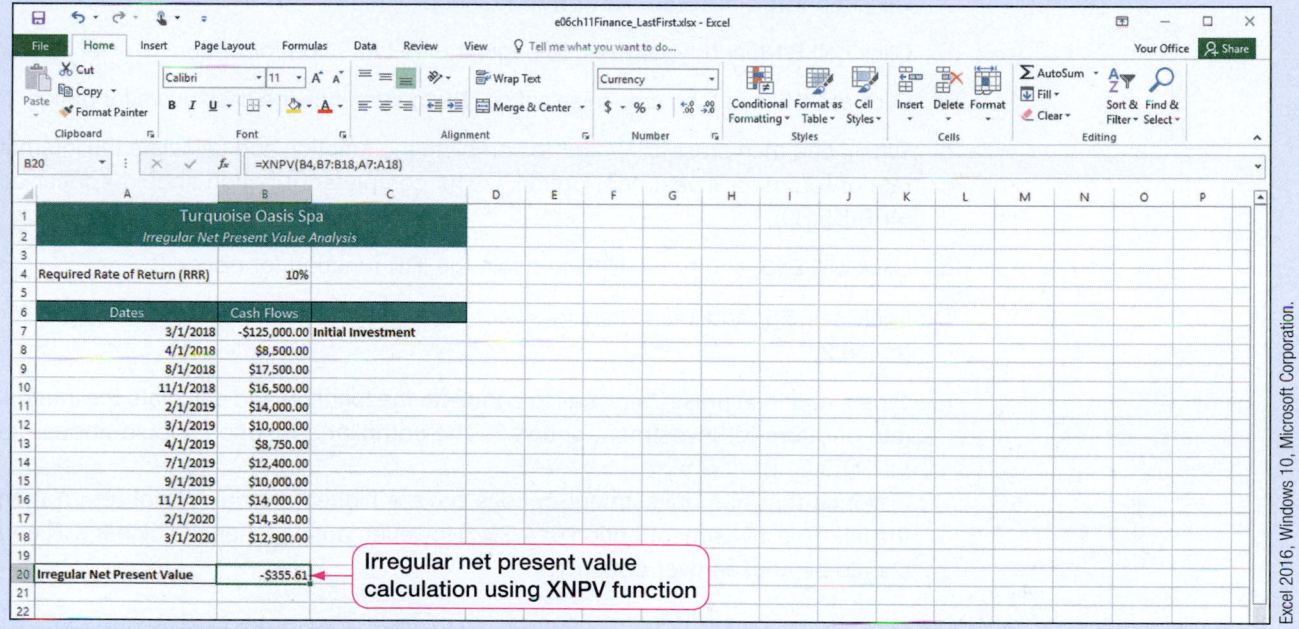

Figure 10   Irregular net present value of an investment

g. **Save** 💾 the workbook.

Using the IRR Function

The internal rate of return function, or **IRR function**, indicates the profitability of an investment and is commonly used in business to assist in choosing between investments. This function is generally used in capital budgeting to measure and compare how profitable a potential investment is. The IRR of an investment is the rate that makes the net present value of both positive and negative cash flows equal to zero. In other words, the IRR function determines the discount rate at which you would break even on an investment. If an investment's IRR is higher than an interest rate generated by a risk-free investment, such as a government bond, then the investment should be chosen. If you are comparing multiple investment options, the investment with the highest IRR would be considered the best and should be chosen first, assuming that all investments have the same amount of initial investment. The IRR function has two arguments, which you have seen in previous financial functions — values and guess — and returns a percentage.

=IRR (values, [guess])

Turquoise Oasis Spa can use the IRR function to see which investment would be the best option. For example, suppose option 1 requires an initial investment of $125,000 with yearly cash flows of $35,000 totaling $140,000 over a four-year period, while option 2 requires the same initial investment of $125,000 with yearly cash flows also totaling $140,000 but over a six-year period and with a majority of the investment's return occurring in the first two years. In this exercise, you will analyze the internal rate of return on each of these investments. Knowing that the current rate of a risk-free investment is 4.5%, management can make a more informed decision about which option is in the best financial interest of the company. For determining cash flows, the calculations will be from the bank's perspective.

 **E11.11**

To Calculate an Internal Rate of Return

a. Click the **InternalRateOfReturn** worksheet.

b. Click cell **B13**, and type **=IRR(** to begin the IRR function for option 1.

c. Click cell **B5**, and then drag to select cell **B9** to reference the cash flows for option 1.

d. Type **)**, and then press Ctrl + Enter to complete the function and calculate the internal rate of return for investment option 1. The completed function should appear as =IRR(B5:B9).

e. Click cell **E13**, and type **=IRR(** to begin the IRR function for option 2.

f. Click cell **E5**, and then drag to select cell **E11** to reference the cash flows for option 2.

g. Type **)**, and then press Ctrl + Enter to complete the function and calculate the internal rate of return for investment option 2. The completed function should appear as =IRR(E5:E11).

   Notice that both investment options have a higher internal rate of return than the risk-free investment option of 4.5%. However, option 2 has the higher IRR and should be chosen over option 1.

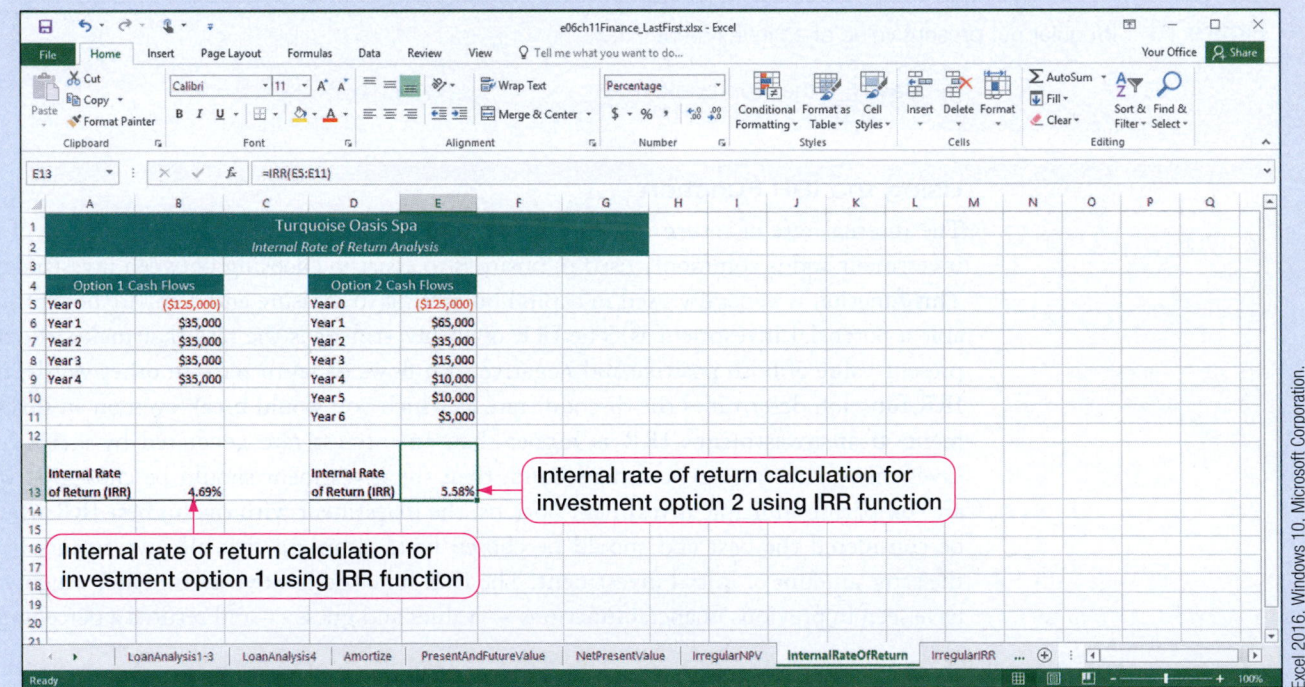

Figure 11   Comparing investments with the internal rate of return

h. **Save** 💾 the workbook.

CONSIDER THIS | **Making an Investment Decision**

At first glance, investment option 1 above may have seemed like the better choice, since the total return of $140,000 was realized in four years instead of six. However, the IRR function returns a higher rate of return for option 2. What do you think was the primary cause for the higher rate? Why?

Using the XIRR Function

Another way to analyze the rate of return is to use the irregular internal rate of return function, or XIRR function. The difference between the IRR function and the XIRR function is that the IRR function assumes that the cash flows are periodic, whereas the **XIRR function** analyzes a series of cash flows that are irregular or not periodic. The syntax of the XIRR function is similar to that of the IRR function with the addition of the dates argument. Additionally, as in the XNPV function, the series of values must contain at least one positive value and one negative value. The dates argument corresponds with when the payments were made, including the date of the initial investment. The first payment date indicates the beginning of the schedule of payments. All subsequent dates must be after the initial investment date, but they may be listed in any order.

=XIRR(values, dates, [guess])

Turquoise Oasis Spa managers are considering another investment option that will require an initial investment amount of $125,000 with estimated cash inflows occurring irregularly over the next two years. In this exercise, you will use the XIRR function to calculate the internal rate of return of the investment to determine whether or not it meets the 10% required rate of return. For determining cash flows, the calculations will be from the bank's perspective.

 **E11.12**

To Calculate an Irregular Internal Rate of Return

a. Click the **IrregularIRR** worksheet.

b. Click cell **B17**, and type **=XIRR(** to begin the XIRR function.

c. Click cell **B7**, and drag to select cell **B15** to reference the cash flows.

d. Type **,** to move to the dates argument. Click cell **A7**, and drag to select cell **A15** to reference the dates.

e. Type **)**, and then press Ctrl + Enter to complete the function and calculate the irregular internal rate of return. The completed function should appear as =XIRR(B7:B15,A7:A15).

Notice that this investment has an internal rate of return of 11.28% and meets the required rate of return of 10%.

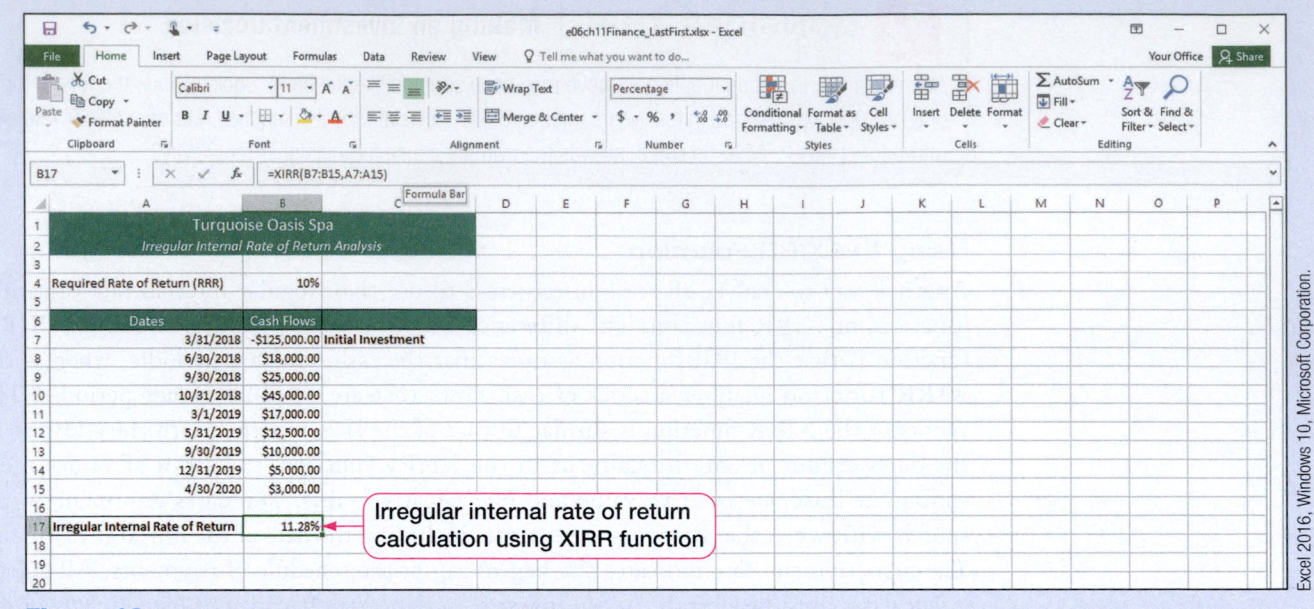

Figure 12 Irregular internal rate of return analysis

f. **Save** 💾 the workbook.

Calculating the Depreciating Value of Business Assets

Businesses are required, for tax and reporting purposes, to show that the original value of the property they purchase, such as buildings, vehicles, and equipment, is reduced — or depreciated — over time as the business "uses up" these assets. In this section, you will learn how to calculate the depreciation of assets, using three different approved methods.

QUICK REFERENCE	Methods of Depreciation

There are several accounting methods to depreciate an asset, and the IRS allows a business to choose whichever method is most advantageous as long as the same method is used throughout the life of the asset.

1. Straight-line depreciation (SLN) — The simplest and most commonly used method. Assumes that the value of the asset loses the same amount of value each year of its life.

2. Declining balance depreciation (DB) — Assumes that the value of an asset depreciates more in the first year than in the second year.

3. Double declining balance depreciation (DDB) — Requires that the straight-line depreciation method be used first to calculate the total percentage of the asset that is depreciated in the first year and doubles it. Each subsequent year of the asset's life, that same percentage is multiplied by the remaining balance to be depreciated.

Calculate the Depreciation of Assets Using the SLN, DB, and DDB Functions

As you learned, an amortization table can be used to analyze loan balances and repayments. A company can also use amortization tables to show the appropriate accounting or net book value of its tangible assets — such as machinery, equipment, buildings, vehicles, or property — for tax or reporting purposes. The **net book value** is equal to the original cost of the asset minus depreciation and amortization. To create an amortization table for asset depreciation, you would use functions that allow you to calculate the present value, future value, and depreciation of the asset over its useful life. When you depreciate the original cost of tangible assets, you first need to know the rules for depreciating the particular assets, because there are different rules for different types of assets. Depreciation represents a reduction in the amount of the original cost of a fixed asset that is used to reduce income as an expense for accounting and tax purposes. The idea is that because the item generates income over time, you should be able to deduct from that income the amount of the resource — or asset — used.

To calculate the depreciated value, you need to know the original cost of the asset, the asset's useful life, the asset's salvage value, and the rate at which the asset depreciates over time. The **salvage value** is what the asset is estimated to be worth at the end of its useful life. It is assumed that over time, these assets decline in value because of deterioration and obsolescence and therefore should be depreciated. Depreciation functions provide a method that matches the decline in value with the income that results from using the assets. In addition, you have to know what depreciation method the IRS expects you to apply to particular types of assets. The IRS, Generally Accepted Accounting Principles, and International Financial Reporting Standards all have specific requirements for depreciating assets and reporting depreciation based on the type of asset being depreciated.

To report the net book value of tangible assets, a depreciation schedule must be maintained. A **depreciation schedule** records the date when the asset was placed into service, a calculation for each year's depreciation, and the accumulated depreciation. An asset remains on the depreciation schedule until the asset becomes fully depreciated or is taken out of service — sold or discarded. Finally, the depreciation schedule should be evaluated annually to ensure accuracy. With a growing business and increased inventory, the Turquoise Oasis Spa must prepare a depreciation schedule for its tangible assets.

REAL WORLD ADVICE — Have You Thought About Depreciating Your Assets?

Have you ever run your own business? Maybe you owned a lawn mowing service. Suppose you purchased your own riding lawn mower. Come tax time, one method to reduce your taxes is by using depreciation. Rather than taking the full cost out in one year, you can take out a portion over several years. This is particularly useful for high-priced items.

Using the SLN Function

One way that you can calculate depreciation is using the straight-line depreciation function, or SLN function. The **SLN function** calculates the depreciation of an asset for a specified period using the fixed declining balance method. This means that the amount of money that is depreciated is the same for each year of the life of the asset. This is the easiest type of depreciation to calculate and is the depreciation method used by the majority of small businesses. The SLN function syntax uses three arguments, all of which are required: (1) initial cost of asset (cost), (2) salvage value (salvage), and (3) useful life (life) in numbers of years. The salvage value can be set to zero if that is what the expected salvage value is.

=SLN(cost, salvage, life)

Turquoise Oasis Spa managers need to track the tangible assets — such as massage tables, salon chairs, and sinks — that they previously purchased. In this exercise, you will create a straight-line depreciation table given the cost of the asset, salvage value, and useful life of the assets.

 **E11.13**

To Create a Straight-Line Depreciation Schedule

a. Click the **Depreciation** worksheet.

> ### Troubleshooting
>
> If you cannot see the Depreciation worksheet, you may need to click ⋯ to see additional worksheets.

b. Click cell **B8**, and type **=SLN(** to begin the SLN function.

c. Click cell **B3**, and press F4 to reference the cost of the assets and lock the cell reference so that the formula can be copied down the column later.

d. Type **,** to move to the salvage argument. Click cell **B4**, and press F4 to reference the salvage value of the assets.

e. Type **,** to move to the life argument. Click cell **B5**, and press F4 to reference the useful life of the assets.

f. Type **)**, press Ctrl + Enter, and then double-click the **AutoFill** handle to copy the function down to **B12**. The complete function should appear as =SLN($B$3,$B$4,$B$5).

g. Click cell **C8**, type **=**, and then click cell **B8** to reference the accumulated depreciation for the first year. Press Enter.

h. In cell **C9**, type **=**, and then click cell **C8** to reference the accumulated depreciation for the first year.

i. Type **+**, click cell **B9**, and then press Ctrl + Enter to reference the accumulated depreciation for year two. The completed formula should appear as =C8+B9. Double-click the **AutoFill** handle to copy the formula down to **C12**.

j. Click cell **D8**. Type **=**, click cell **B3**, and then press F4 to reference the cost of the assets and lock the cell reference so that the formula can be copied down the column later.

k. Type **–**, click cell **C8**, and press Ctrl + Enter to calculate the book value at the end of the first year. Double-click the **AutoFill** handle to copy the function down to **D12**.

   Notice that the book value at the end of year five is $1,750 — the same as the estimated salvage value.

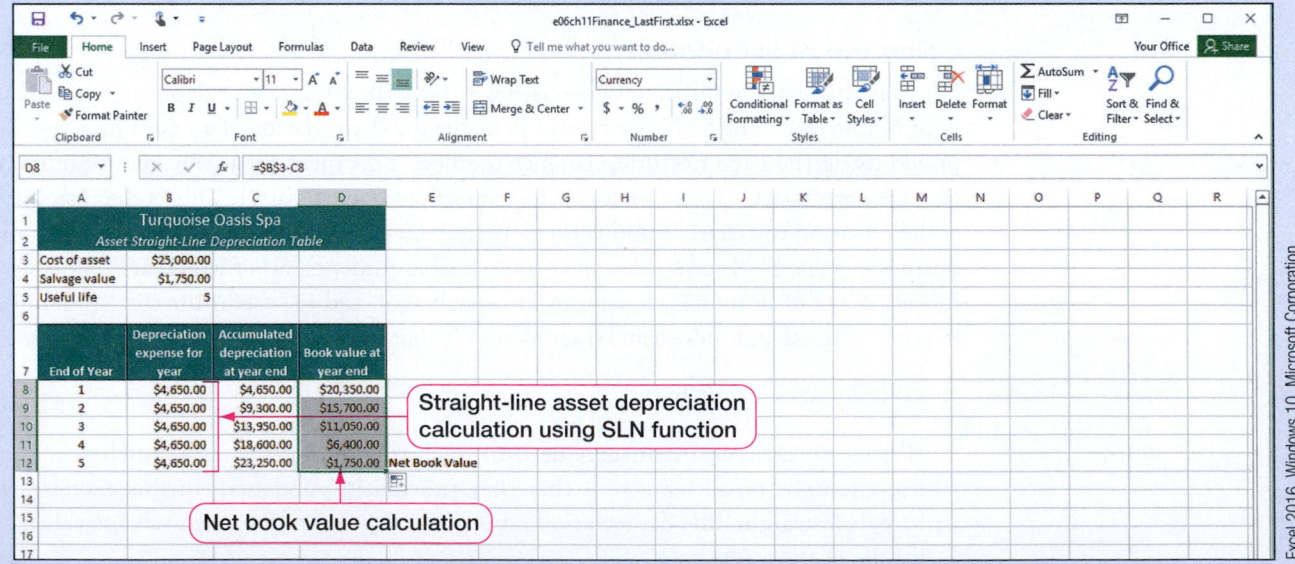

Figure 13   Straight-line asset depreciation table

l.   Save 🖫 the workbook.

Using the DB Function

Another way in which you can calculate depreciation is by using the declining balance function, or DB function. The **DB function** calculates the depreciation of an asset for a specified period using the fixed declining balance method. The difference between the DB function and the SLN function is that when you use the DB function, you can specify the period and month when the asset was placed into service. Thus, instead of spreading the cost of the asset evenly over its life, as you did with the SLN function, the DB function calculates the depreciation of the asset at an accelerated rate, which results in higher depreciation in earlier periods and progressively declining depreciation in each succeeding period. Because the month argument is optional, Excel assumes that the value is 12 if a value is omitted.

=DB(cost, salvage, life, period, [month])

In this exercise, you will calculate depreciation using the DB function.

 **E11.14**

To Create a Declining Balance Depreciation Schedule

a. Click the **Depreciation2** worksheet.

b. The equipment was placed into service at the beginning of May of the first year. Therefore, the period for the first year will be eight — May through December is eight months. Click cell **B8**, and then type **=DB(** to begin calculating the Declining Balance depreciation of the asset.

c. Click cell **B3**, and press F4 to reference the cost of the assets.

d. Type **,** to move to the salvage argument. Click cell **B4**, and press F4 to reference the salvage value of the assets.

e. Type **,** to move to the life argument. Click cell **B5**, and press F4 to reference the useful life of the assets.

f. Type **,** to move to the period argument. Click cell **A8** to reference the first period.

g. Type **,** to move to the month argument. Type **8)**, and press Ctrl + Enter to calculate the depreciation over an eight-month span. The completed function should appear as =DB($B$3,$B$4,$B$5,A8,8).

h. The equipment will be used from January to December for the remaining four time periods. Click the **Home** tab, and in the Clipboard group, click **Copy**. Click cell **B9**, and click **Paste**. Double-click to edit the cell, and delete the text **,8** from the end of the function, and then press Ctrl + Enter. The completed function should appear as =DB($B$3,$B$4,$B$5,A9).

i. Double-click the **AutoFill** handle to copy the function down to **B12**. Notice that the depreciation is declining as the periods increase with a depreciation value of $1,231.25 in year five.

Notice that the net book value of the asset at the end of its useful life is $5,190.56.

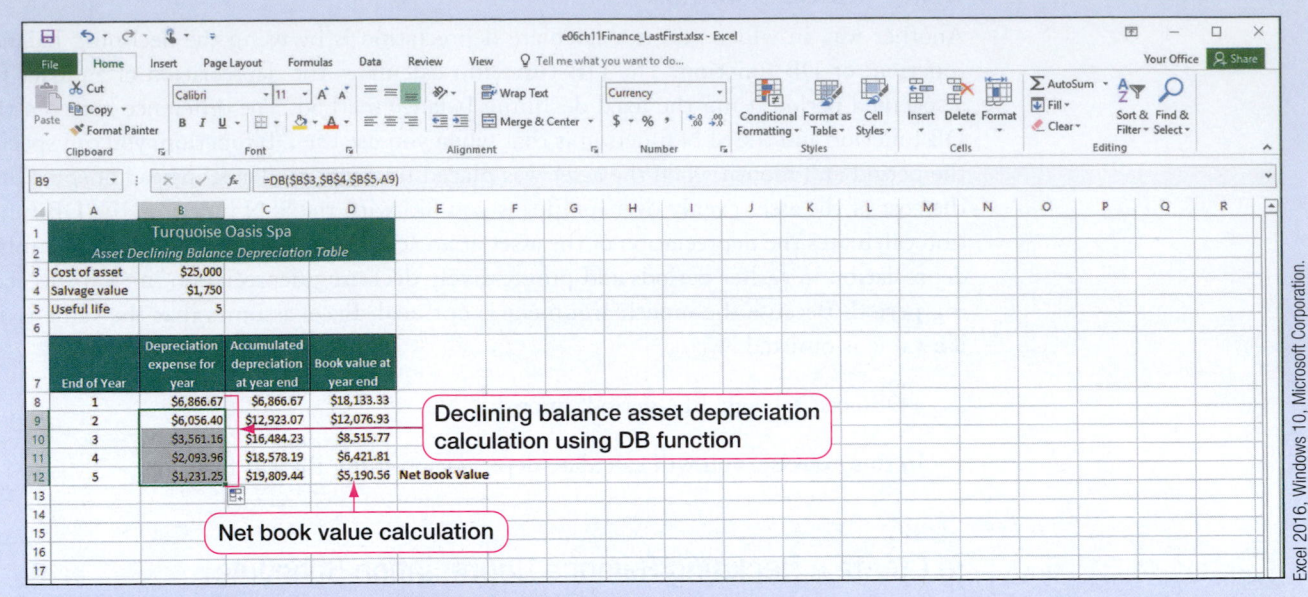

Figure 14 Declining balance asset depreciation table

j. **Save** 🖫 the workbook.

The declining balance method assumes that depreciation is more rapid earlier in the asset's life. Notice that the book value at year end in year five is greater than the salvage value. Remember that instead of spreading the cost of the asset evenly over its life, as you did with the SLN function, the DB function calculates the depreciation of the asset at an accelerated rate, which results in decreasing depreciation charges each succeeding period.

Using the DDB Function

Still another way in which you can calculate depreciation is by using the double declining balance function, or DDB function. The **DDB function** calculates the depreciation of an asset for a specified period using the double declining balance method. With the straight-line depreciation method, the useful life of the asset is divided into the total cost to arrive at an equal amount per year. The DDB function permits twice the straight-line annual percentage rate to be applied each year. For example, if you have a straight-line depreciation that is depreciating assets over a five-year period, the annual depreciation amount would be 20%. If the initial cost is $1,000, the depreciation would be 20% × $1,000 = $200 each year until the asset reaches a net book value of zero. With the double declining balance method, the depreciation amount would be 40% each year; 40% × $1,000 = $400 in the first year, 40% × $600 = $240 in the second year, and so on.

The DDB function syntax uses five arguments, four of which are required: (1) initial cost of asset (cost), (2) salvage value (salvage), (3) useful life (life), (4) period for which you want to calculate the depreciation (period), and (5) rate at which the balance declines (factor). The **factor** argument is optional; it is the rate at which the balance declines. If factor is omitted, Excel assumes the value to be 2 (the double declining balance method). The salvage value can be set to zero if that is what the expected salvage value is.

=DDB(cost, salvage, life, period, [factor])

In this exercise, you will calculate depreciation using the DDB function.

 **E11.15**

To Create a Double Declining Balance Depreciation Schedule

a. Click the **Depreciation3** worksheet.

b. Click cell **B8**, and type **=DDB(** to begin the DDB function.

c. Click cell **B3**, and press F4 to reference the cost of the assets and lock the cell reference so that the formula can be copied down the column later.

d. Type **,** to move to the salvage argument. Click cell **B4**, and press F4 to reference the salvage value of the assets.

e. Type **,** to move to the life argument. Click cell **B5**, and press F4 to reference the useful life of the assets.

f. Type **,** to move to the period argument. Click cell **A8** to reference the first period.

g. Type **)**, and press Ctrl + Enter to calculate the double declining balance depreciation of the asset, and then double-click the **AutoFill** handle to copy the function down to **B12**.

Notice that you would be able to deduct higher depreciation on your taxes. However, your net book value at the end of the five years would be less than it would be if you used the DB function.

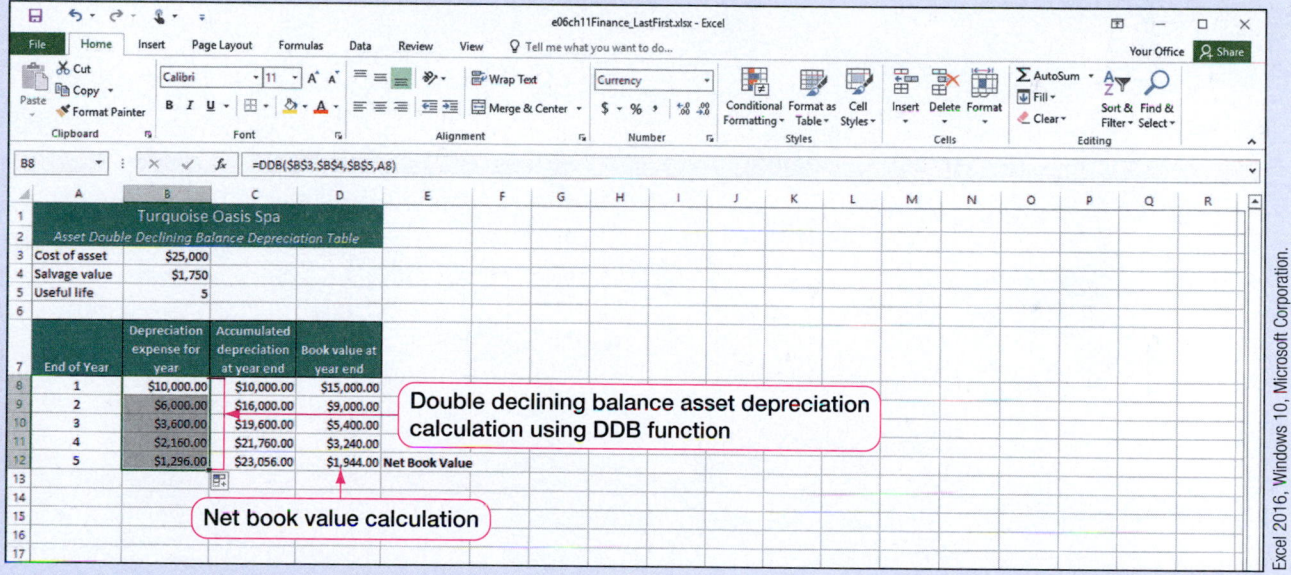

Figure 15   Double declining balance asset depreciation table

h. Insert the **file name** in the left custom footer section of the Header/Footer tab in the Page Setup dialog box on all worksheets in the workbook.

i. Complete the **Documentation** worksheet.

j. **Save** 💾 the workbook, exit Excel, and then submit your files as directed by your instructor.

Concept Check

1. What does the PMT function calculate? Describe the required arguments of the PMT function. p. 598

2. Explain the CUMIPMT function and its arguments. Why would it be beneficial to know the cumulative interest paid in a particular time period? p. 604

3. What is an amortization schedule, and what is its purpose? p. 608

4. How does estimating the present value of an investment lead to better financial decisions? p. 613

5. Discuss how the IRR and NPV functions can help in making informed financial decisions. p. 616–619

6. What are the differences between the three functions used to calculate asset depreciation discussed in this chapter? p. 622

Key Terms

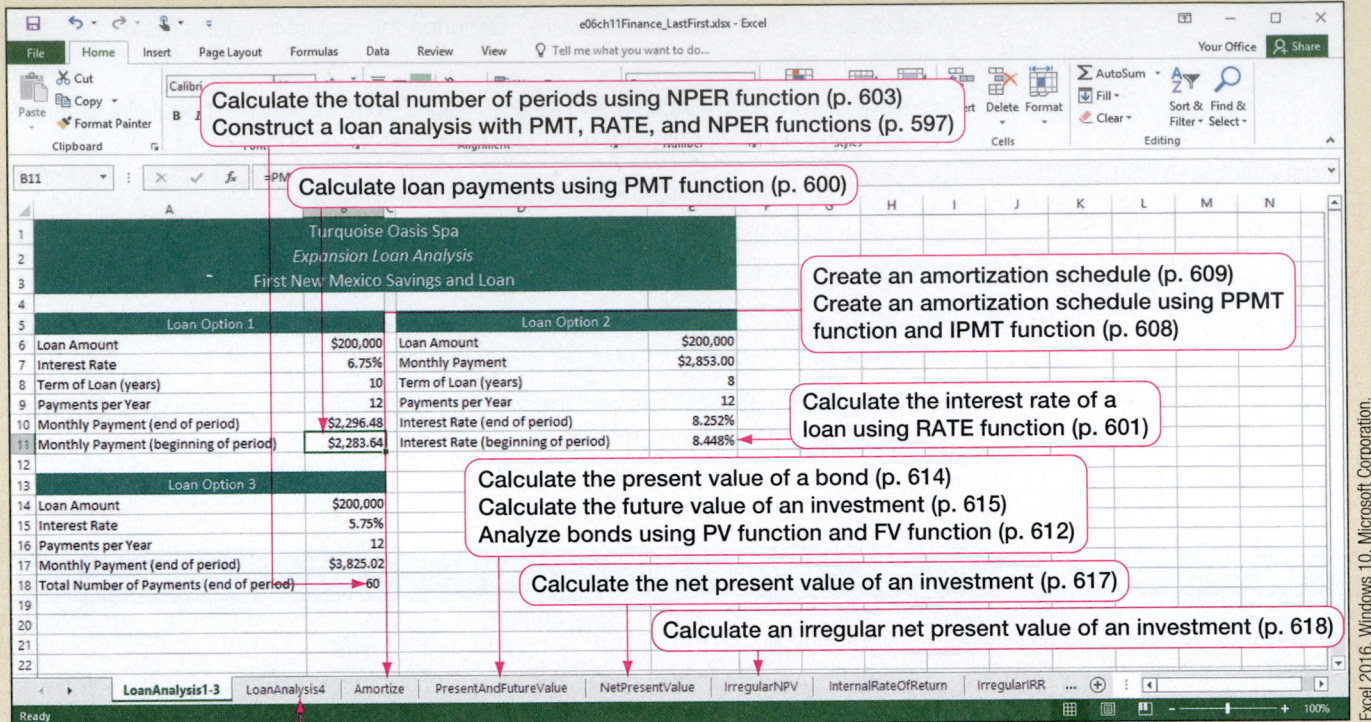

Figure 16

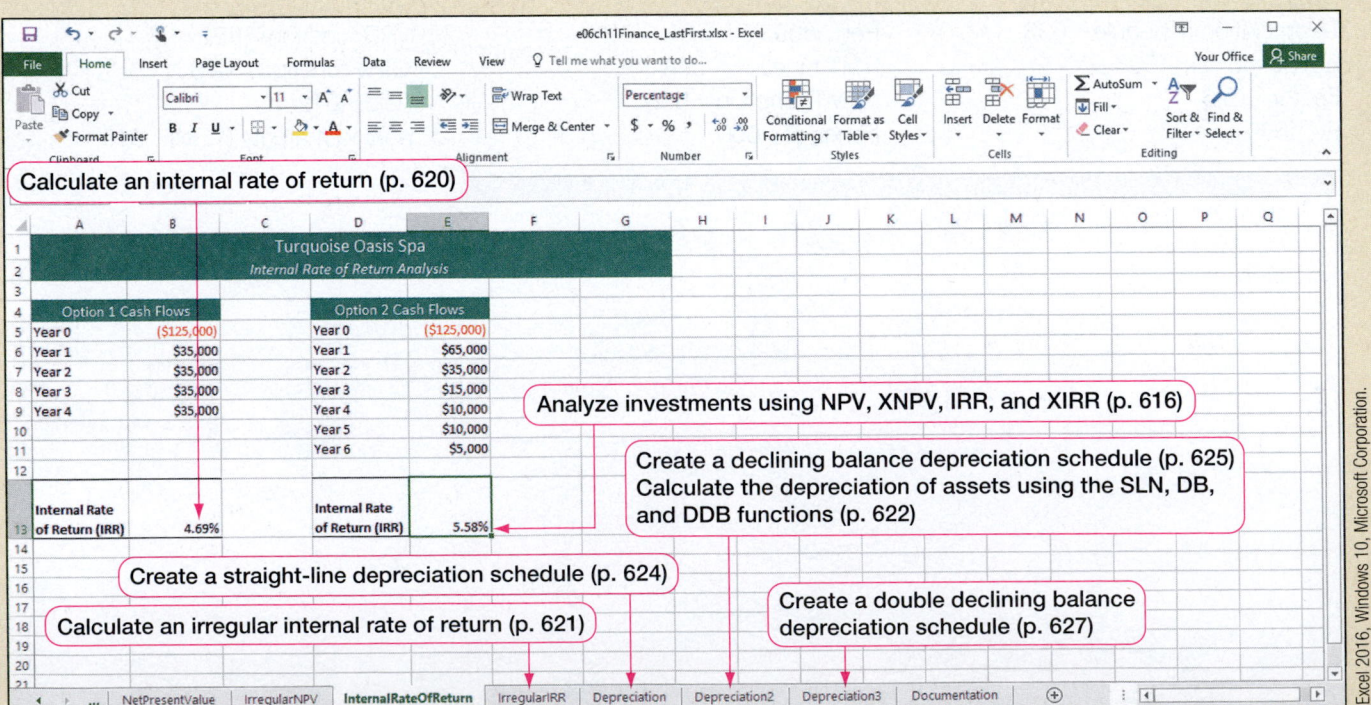

Figure 17

Student data file needed:

 e06ch11Equipment.xlsx

You will save your file as:

 e06ch11Equipment_LastFirst.xlsx

Loan Analysis and Depreciating Equipment at the Red Bluff Golf Course & Pro Shop

Finance & Accounting

The Red Bluff Golf Course & Pro Shop obtained a loan two years ago to purchase new golf carts for its members to use. Unfortunately, the manager, Barry Cheney, has not kept very good records for the loan or for depreciation of the golf carts. You have been asked to create a loan analysis and depreciation schedule. The Red Bluff Golf Course & Pro Shop has been making monthly payments, due at the end of the period, but it has not kept track of the actual loan — such as interest and principal. Additionally, depreciation has not been written off on yearly taxes. Mr. Cheney wants to begin writing off a portion of the cost of the golf carts this year, but he is not sure whether he should use a straight-line depreciation or declining balance method. You need to calculate both schedules and report your findings to him so he can get them approved by his accountant. Barry has given you templates to use to create your analysis. For determining cash flows, the calculations will be from the bank's perspective.

a. Open the Excel file, **e06ch11Equipment**. Save your file as e06ch11Equipment_ LastFirst using your last and first name.

b. On the Analysis worksheet tab, click cell **A10**, and then type =PMT(A6/D6,B6*D6,-C6) to calculate the monthly payment of the loan. Press Tab. The PV argument of the PMT() function is negative. This indicates that the calculation is from the bank's perspective. The bank will have to pay that amount at the beginning of the loan — a cash outflow.

c. In cell B10, type =IPMT(A6/D6,1,B6*D6,-C6) to calculate the interest portion of the monthly payment. Press Tab. The PV argument of the IPMT() function is negative. This indicates that the calculation is from the bank's perspective. The bank will have to pay that amount at the beginning of the loan — a cash outflow.

d. In cell C10, type =PPMT(A6/D6,1,B6*D6,-C6) to calculate the principal portion of the monthly payment. Press Tab. The PV argument of the PPMT() function is negative. This indicates that the calculation is from the bank's perspective. The bank will have to pay that amount at the beginning of the loan — a cash outflow.

e. In cell D10, type =-CUMIPMT(A6/D6,B6*D6,C6,1,12,0) to calculate how much interest was paid during the first year of the loan. Press Tab. The negative sign indicates that the CUMIPMT() function is from the bank's perspective. The bank will receive the principle interest payment on the loan — a cash inflow.

f. In cell E10, type =-CUMPRINC(A6/D6,B6*D6,C6,1,12,0) to calculate how much principal was paid during the first year of the loan, and then format the cell as **Currency**. Press Ctrl + Enter. The negative sign indicates that the CUMPRINC() function is from the bank's perspective. The bank will receive the principle interest payment on the loan — a cash inflow.

g. Click cell **B16**, and then type =IRR(B14:E14) to calculate the internal rate of return of the investment based on the expected cash flows in years 2018−2020. Press Ctrl + Enter.

h. Create a straight-line depreciation schedule by completing the following tasks.

- Click cell **H10**, type =SLN($G$6,$H$6,$I$6), press Ctrl + Enter, and then double-click the **AutoFill** handle to copy the function down to **H14**.

- Click cell **I10**, and then type =H10 to calculate the accumulated depreciation for the first year. Press Enter.

- In cell I11, type =I10+H11 to calculate the accumulated depreciation for year two, and then double-click the **AutoFill** handle to copy the function down to **I14**.

- Click cell **J10**, type =$G$6-I10 to calculate the book value at the end of year one by subtracting the accumulated depreciation at the end of year one from the initial cost. Press Ctrl + Enter, and then double-click the **AutoFill** handle to copy the function down to **J14**.

i. Create a declining balance depreciation schedule by completing the following tasks.

- Click cell **H17**, type =DB($G$6,$H$6,$I$6,G17), and then press Ctrl + Enter. Double-click the **AutoFill** handle to copy the function down to **H21**.

- Click cell **I17**, type =H17, and then press Enter to calculate the accumulated depreciation for the first year.

- In cell I18, type =I17+H18, and then press Ctrl + Enter to calculate the accumulated depreciation for year two. Double-click the **AutoFill** handle to copy the function down to **I21**.

- Click cell **J17**, type =$G$6-I17, and then press Ctrl + Enter to calculate the book value at the end of year one by subtracting the accumulated depreciation at the end of year one from the initial cost. Double-click the **AutoFill** handle to copy the function down to **J21**.

j. Create a double declining balance depreciation schedule by completing the following tasks.

- Click cell **H24**, type =DDB($G$6,$H$6,$I$6,G24), and then press Ctrl + Enter. Double-click the **AutoFill** handle to copy the function down to **H28**.

- Click cell **I24**, type =H24, and then press Enter to calculate the accumulated depreciation for the first year.

- In cell I25, type =I24+H25, and then press Ctrl + Enter to calculate the accumulated depreciation for year two. Double-click the **AutoFill** handle to copy the formula to **I28**.

- Click cell **J24**, type =$G$6-I24, and then press Ctrl + Enter to calculate the book value at the end of year one by subtracting the accumulated depreciation at the end of year one from the initial cost. Double-click the **AutoFill** handle to copy the function down to **J28**.

k. Click the **Documentation** worksheet. Click cell **A8**, and then type in today's date. Click cell **B8**, and then type in your first and last name. Complete the remainder of the **Documentation** worksheet according to your instructor's direction.

l. Save the workbook, exit Excel, and then submit your file as directed by your instructor.

Problem Solve 1

Homework

Student data file needed:

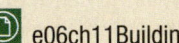 e06ch11Building.xlsx

You will save your file as:

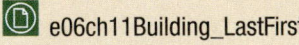 e06ch11Building_LastFirst.xlsx

Finance & Accounting

New Investment Analysis

Flanky's, a small manufacturer of custom clothing for dogs and cats, is considering the purchase of a new building as part of its long-term strategic plan. You have been asked to conduct an analysis on the loan as well as an investment analysis using the NPV function based on an estimated series of cash flows generated by the new building and a required rate of return of 18%. For determining cash flows, the calculations will be from the bank's perspective.

a. Open the Excel file **e06ch11Building**. Save your file as e06ch11Building_LastFirst using your last and first name.

b. Click the **BuildingAnalysis** worksheet, and in cell **C5**, calculate the amount to finance by subtracting the starting capital from the purchase price of the building.

c. In cell **C10**, calculate the end of period quarterly payment amount using the PMT function. Be sure the result is displayed as a positive number.

d. In cell **C11**, calculate the total cumulative interest that will be paid on the loan for all 28 end-of-the-period quarterly payments. Format as **Currency**. Be sure the result is displayed as a positive number.

e. In cell **C13**, calculate the total cost of the loan by adding the amount financed to the total cumulative interest.

f. In cell **F13**, calculate the net present value of the investment using the NPV function. If necessary, format cell F13 as **Currency** with **two** decimal places.

Critical Thinking
You have just calculated the net present value. What does the net present value tell in this instance, is this a good or a bad investment?

g. In cell **I7**, calculate the straight-line depreciation value of the building for year one, and copy the formula down though year 7.

h. In cells **J7:J13**, calculate the accumulated depreciation amount for each year.

i. In cells **K7:K13**, calculate the book value of the asset at the end of each year of its useful life.

j. In cell **I17**, calculate the declining balance depreciation value of the building for year one, and copy the formula down through year 7.

k. In cells **J17:J23**, calculate the accumulated depreciation amount for each year.

l. In cells **K17:K23**, calculate the book value of the asset at the end of each year of its useful life.

m. Select cells **I23:K23**, and in the Font group, click the **Border** arrow, then click **Thick Bottom Border**.

n. Complete the **Documentation** worksheet according to your instructor's direction.

o. Save the workbook, exit Excel, and then submit your file as directed by your instructor.

Perform 1: Perform in Your Life

Student data file needed:

e06ch11Home.xlsx

You will save your file as:

e06ch11Home_LastFirst.xlsx

Purchasing a Home

Finance & Accounting

You want to purchase a home in the future. You have decided to begin setting money aside each month toward your down payment. Your goal is to have 20% down when you are ready to purchase your home. To help determine how much you should put away and how long it will take, you have decided to create an Excel workbook to track your progress and help you visualize your success.

a. Open the Excel file, **e06ch11Home**. Save your file as e06ch11Home_LastFirst using your last and first name.

b. Create a blank worksheet, and rename the worksheet Home.

c. Enter the following data, and label appropriately.

 • Enter the amount you are planning to be able to pay for the home you want to purchase, $250,000.

 • Enter a formula to calculate the amount of down payment you will need, 20% of home purchase value.

 • Enter the amount of interest you will earn, 0.01%.

 • Enter the amount of money you are setting aside, $1,000/month.

d. Enter formulas to answer the questions below, labeled appropriately.

- How long would you need to put money aside to arrive at your 20% down payment?

- You want to buy a home within 2 years. In a blank cell, using the information above, calculate the amount you would need to set aside each month to accomplish this goal.

- You do not have enough money coming in to set this amount aside each month. Using the original information, what rate of interest would you need to earn to keep the monthly payments at $1,000?

- If you could set aside $1,500 at 2.45% interest, how much would you have set aside after 2 years?

e. You have decided that you will not be able to buy the home after 2 years unless you invest in low-risk bonds. You were able to find a short-term bond in which to invest. The par value is $10,000, the coupon rate is 5% annually, the maturity is 2 years, and the yield to maturity is 8%.

- Enter the data above in separate cells labeled appropriately.

- Create a formula to calculate the coupon payment and label.

- Determine the present value of the bond, and label appropriately.

f. You are not sure it's worth it to save the money. You decide to see what difference saving the money will mean as you make your future payments. Click on the **Amortization** worksheet. Complete the two amortization schedules using IPMT and PPMT functions.

g. To the right of your amortization schedules, calculate the total amount of savings due to the down payment.

- Below your amortization schedules, calculate the total payments made for each loan.

- Calculate the difference in the total payments made over the two schedules.

- From the result, subtract the original $50,000 deposit you made.

- Confirm the result of your calculation by calculating the total cumulative interest payments made for the life of the loan for each loan. Subtract the two calculated cumulative interest payments. The result should be the same as your calculation above. These calculations show the amount you have saved by having a down payment on your loan.

h. Format both worksheets to provide a professional appearance.

i. Save the workbook, exit Excel, and then submit your file as directed by your instructor.

Additional
Cases

Additional Workshop Cases are available on the companion website and in the instructor resources.

Microsoft Excel 2016

Chapter 12 | BUSINESS STATISTICS AND REGRESSION ANALYSIS

Prepare Case

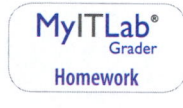

Sales & Marketing

The Turquoise Oasis Spa: Using Statistics in Decision Making

Like managers of other businesses, the managers at the Turquoise Oasis Spa face a lot of uncertainty in making decisions about the strategic direction of the company. Their current decision to fund an expansion of the spa comes with considerable uncertainty about how it will affect their future. Various statistical methods can be applied to business data to help make more informed decisions with more certainty about expected outcomes. Business statistics can be applied to many areas of a business, such as financial analysis, production, operations, and marketing. Thus, the uncertainty can be managed to some extent.

The managers of the Turquoise Oasis Spa would like you to use various statistical methods to analyze their business data to help them understand the data better so that they may make better-informed decisions.

Kaspars Grinvalds/Shutterstock

Student data file needed for this chapter:

 e06ch12Statistics.xlsx

You will save your file as:

 e06ch12Statistics_LastFirst.xlsx

Applying Basic Statistical Methods to Business

Businesses today collect large amounts of data about the everyday operations of the company, from prices of raw materials to the number of links clicked on the company website. With so much data so easily available, it is becoming increasingly important that people in business understand how to use that data to make good strategic decisions. Statistical methods can be used to analyze business data to support good decision making.

Statistics is the practice of collecting, analyzing, and interpreting data. There are two major branches of statistics: descriptive statistics and inferential statistics. **Descriptive statistics** is the process of deriving meaningful information from raw data. An example of the use of descriptive statistics would be to calculate the total revenue that a spa package generates over the course of a year.

Inferential statistics is the process of taking data from a sample of the population and making predictions about the entire population. An example of the use of inferential statistics would be to survey 100 random customers about their opinions on a new service being offered at the spa. Managers at the spa can use the results of that random sample to make assumptions about whether or not the new spa service would go over well. Inferential statistics relies heavily on laws of probability.

Probability is the likelihood that some event will occur based on what is already known. Statistics typically describe what has already happened, and probability describes what is likely to happen in the future. In this section, you learn some of the foundational terminology used in statistics and conduct basic statistical analyses using Excel to gain a better understanding of business data.

Understand the Language of Statistics

Businesses can use various statistical methods in many areas to get a better understanding of the organization. Statistics can be used to determine the effectiveness of advertising campaigns, to understand what factors contribute to the demand for your products, to spot seasonal trends in the sales of certain products, and much more.

Before you get too far into various statistical methods and how businesses can use them, you must understand some common statistical terms. Discussions of statistics constantly refer to data. **Data** is the values that describe an attribute of an object or an event. Almost anything can be considered data, from an employee's salary to the number of spa packages sold to the cost of the latest marketing campaign. A **data set** is a collection of related data consisting of observational units and variables. An **observational unit** is a person, object, or event about which data is collected. For example, in a data set consisting of gender, salary, and name of employees, the employees are the observational unit, and the variables are the gender, salary, and names.

Discussions of statistics often refer to populations and samples. In statistics, a **population** is defined as an entire collection of people, animals, plants, or whatever on which you may collect data. For the spa, a population could be the entire population of all guests who ever received spa services. However, by the time you collect the data for the entire population, the spa has likely had more customers, so you would have to collect more data, during which time there may be still more customers. Very rarely are statistics based on populations, as collecting all the data would be too costly and too time consuming. Instead, statistics focuses on samples. A **sample population** is a subset of a population. In particular, work with statistics relies heavily on random samples. A **random sample** is a subset of a population that has been selected by using methods in which each element of the population has an equal chance of being selected. The more random the sample, the more accurate the statistical analysis will be, in part because randomness eliminates bias.

Business professionals who use statistical analysis to support their decision making rely heavily on probability distributions. A **probability distribution** describes all the possible values and likelihoods that a given variable can be within a specific range. The probability distribution can be in the form of a graph, table, or formula. There are two general classifications of probability distributions: discrete probability distributions and continuous probability distributions. The classifications are determined on the basis of whether the probabilities are associated with discrete variables or continuous variables.

A **discrete variable** is a variable that can have only a finite number of values and all possible values are known. Examples of discrete variables in business are performance classifications of employees, the number of bars of soap in a box, and the number of different services a spa offers its customers. A **continuous variable** can contain an infinite number of different values within a range. Examples of continuous variables in business are the time between sales transactions, the weight of a package for shipping, and the amount of money a customer spends in any given visit.

Opening the Starting File

You will be using various statistical methods and analyses to better understand the products, revenue, sales volume, and customers of Turquoise Oasis Spa. You will also use various statistical functions to calculate the probability of meeting or exceeding various business goals and to discover relationships between variables that may be useful in making predictions. In this exercise, you will open the workbook containing the data you have been asked to analyze.

E12.00

To Get Started

a. Start **Excel**, click **Open Other Spreadsheets** in the left pane, and then double-click **This PC**. Navigate through the folder structure to the location of your student data files, and then double-click **e06ch12Statistics**.

b. Click the **File** tab, click **Save As**, and then double-click **This PC**. In the Save As dialog box, navigate to the location where you are saving your project files, and then change the file name to **e06ch12Statistics_LastFirst** using your last and first name. Click **Save**.

Understand the Basic Types of Data

Figure 1 illustrates the four basic levels of data used in statistics: nominal data, ordinal data, interval data, and ratio data. Each level adds to the next; thus, ordinal data is also nominal data, and so on. Having a strong understanding of these levels will help you to understand how to use various statistical functions and methods and how to interpret the results correctly.

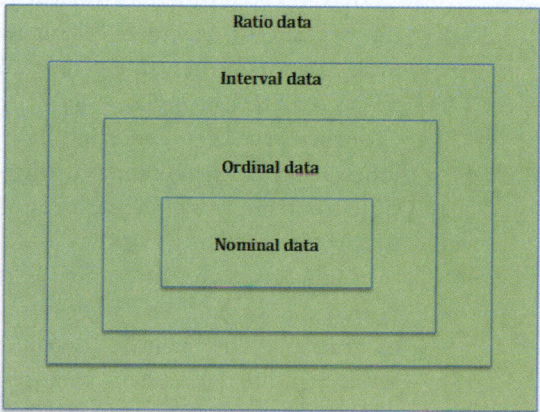

Figure 1 Four levels of data

Nominal data uses numbers for categorical or classification purposes only. Nominal variables are often used to categorize responses in a survey. For example, where respondents answer "Yes" or "No" to a specific question, nominal variables could be used to categorize the responses, such as 1 = Yes and 2 = No. It is also common to use nominal variables to categorize gender, such as 1 = Female and 2 = Male. It is important to note that some statistical functions, such as Average and Sum, would be meaningless to apply to nominal data.

Ordinal data uses numbers to rank data as first, second, third, and so on based on some scale. Ordinal data is useful in situations in which it is difficult to obtain accurate measurements. Some statistical analysis can be applied to ordinal data to derive additional meaning. For example, if a product is tested 100 times and the rate at which it fails is recorded on a scale of 1 to 10, then the average of all the product's failure rates on the scale could be useful. Ordinal data is more useful than nominal data in terms of what information can be derived, but having the actual time measurements of failure would be better.

Interval data measures the size of the difference between values. For example, with interval data, you know not only that one product test succeeded and one product test failed (nominal data) or that one product failed faster than another product (ordinal data), but also the difference in time intervals between when a product test failed and when a product test was successful.

Ratio data is similar to interval data except that the differences between the data can be quantified and proportions can be specified. For example, interval data may indicate that product 1 failed after 15 tests and product 2 failed after only five tests. Ratio data could state that product 1 passed three times as many tests as product 2 did.

Conduct Basic Statistical Analyses in Excel

Excel has many built-in functions that can be used to conduct basic statistical analysis on data. Knowledge of how to use even the most basic statistical functions can increase your understanding of the data and enable better decision making. In this section, you will assist the managers of the Turquoise Oasis Spa to better understand their data using basic statistical analysis.

Using the RAND Function to Generate a Random Sample

Randomness in selecting a sample from a population is crucial in conducting effective and accurate statistical analyses. The RAND function in Excel is one method that can help in creating a random sample. The function generates a random number between 0 and 1. The RAND function does not have any arguments.

RAND()

RAND is considered a volatile function because it generates a new number each time the worksheet is calculated. This means that every time any cell is edited or a new formula is created, the value generated by the RAND function will change. It is common practice to use Excel's Copy and Paste Values feature to prevent the values from changing once they have been generated. It is important to note that the values generated by this function are not truly random. Since an algorithm is used to generate the values, it is possible to predict what the next number generated will be; however, it is random enough to work in most situations.

Managers at the Turquoise Oasis Spa would like to select ten random customers who visited the spa on a given day to take part in a survey about new services that the spa is considering. They plan to use the results of the survey to make decisions about which services to offer. You have been provided with the customer IDs of 34 customers who visited the spa on May 11, 2017. In this exercise, you will use the RAND function to generate 34 random values. You will then use the random values to sort the customer IDs in a random order for selection.

 **E12.01**

To Create a Random Sample Using RAND()

SIDE NOTE
Pin the Ribbon
If your ribbon is collapsed, pin your ribbon open. Click the Home tab. In the lower right corner of the ribbon, click Pin the Ribbon ⊷.

SIDE NOTE
Random Sample
Because of the volatility of the RAND function, your results will be different from the image in Figure 2.

a. Click the **RandomSample** worksheet. Click cell **B3**, type **=RAND()**, and then press Ctrl + Enter to generate a random value between 0 and 1.

b. Use the **AutoFill** handle to copy the function down to cell **B36**.

c. Press Ctrl + C to copy the random values. On the Home tab, in the Clipboard group, click **Paste** 🗎, and then, in the Paste Values group, click **Values** 🗎 to replace the formula with its values.

d. Select the cell range **A2:B36**.

e. Click the **Data** tab, and in the Sort & Filter group, click **Sort**.

f. Click **My data has headers** if necessary. Click the **Sort by** arrow, and then select **RAND** as the column to use for the sort.

g. Click **OK**.

h. Select the cell range **A3:A12**.

i. Press Ctrl + C to copy.

j. Click cell **E3**, and then press Ctrl + V to paste the ten randomly selected customer IDs.

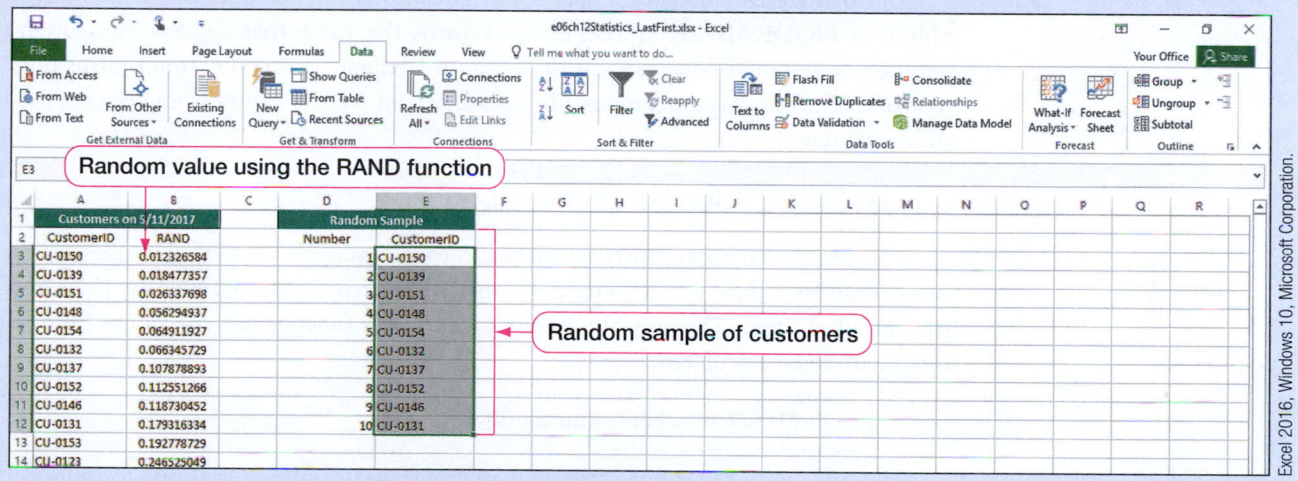

Figure 2   Creating a random sample with the RAND function

k. **Save** 🖫 the document.

Calculating the Mean, Median, and Mode of a Data Set

Three of the most basic descriptive statistics used are mean, median, and mode. Each of these calculations attempts to define the central tendency of a data set. The **central tendency** refers to the way in which data tends to cluster around some value. The **mean** is the average of all the variables in a sample, often referred to as the arithmetic mean. The **median** describes which value falls in the middle when all the values of the sample are sorted in ascending order. For example if there are seven variables, the median value is the fourth variable in the list, where there are three variables above and three variables below. If the total number of variables is even, then the median value is the mean of the two middle variables. The **mode** is the value that appears most often in a sample. Modes are useful only with discrete data that is sorted in either ascending or descending order. If there are multiple values in a data set that appear the same number of times, then the mode will be reported in Excel as the value that appears first: the lowest value if the values are sorted in ascending order or the highest value if the values are sorted in descending order.

<table>
<tr><td>QUICK REFERENCE</td><td>Calculating the Central Tendency of a Data Set</td></tr>
</table>

Mean, Median, and Mode

- Mean — The sum of all values in a data set divided by the total number of values
- Median — The middle value that separates the higher and lower halves of a data set
- Mode — The value that appears most often in a data set with discrete variables

To calculate the mean in Excel, the AVERAGE function is used. The only arguments inside the AVERAGE function are the values from which an average is to be calculated.

=AVERAGE(number1, [number2],…)

To calculate the median of a data set in Excel, the MEDIAN function is used. Again, the only arguments needed are the values from which the median value is to be calculated.

=MEDIAN(number1, [number2],…)

To calculate the mode of a data set in Excel, one of two functions is used: MODE. SNGL or MODE.MULT. MODE.SNGL returns the value that appears most often in a data set. If more than one variable occurs most frequently, this function returns only the first one. The only arguments used by this function are the values from which a mode is to be calculated.

=MODE.SNGL(number1, [number2],…)

MODE.MULT is an array function that returns a vertical array of the values that occur most often in a data set. If more than one value occurs most frequently, this function returns all of them. The only arguments used by this function are the values from which modes are to be calculated.

=MODE.MULT(number1, [number2],…)

The Turquoise Oasis Spa often sells its house brand of essential oils to independent massage therapists who practice in the area. Management would like to find out whether a random sample of orders placed over the past year has a central tendency. In this exercise, you will use the data provided to calculate the mean, median, and mode.

 E12.02

To Calculate the Mean, Median, and Mode of a Data Set

a. Click the **BasicStats** worksheet. On this worksheet, a random sample of 34 orders with the quantity of items sold in each order is provided.

b. Click cell **G2**, and then type **=AVERAGE(** to begin the AVERAGE function.

c. Click cell **C2**, and drag to select cell **C35**. Type **)**, and press Enter to calculate the mean of the number of units sold in the sample data set.

d. In cell **G3**, type **=MEDIAN(** to begin the MEDIAN function.

e. Click cell **C2**, and drag to select cell **C35**. Type **)**, and press Enter to calculate the median sales quantity value in the sample data set. Notice that since the number of values is an even number, the MEDIAN function returns the mean of the two middle values, which are 13 and 14.

f. In cell **G4**, type **=MODE.SNGL(** to begin the MODE function.

g. Click cell **C2**, and drag to select cell **C35**. Type **)**, and press Enter to calculate the most frequently occurring value in the sample data set.

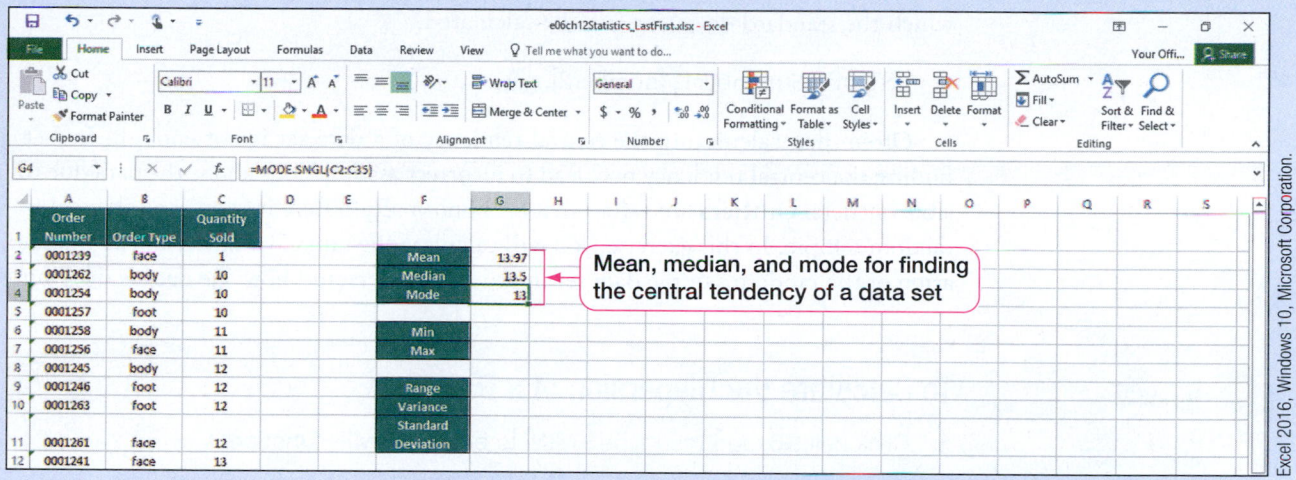

Figure 3 Calculating the mean, median, and mode of a data set

h. **Save** 💾 the document.

Calculating the Range, Variance, and Standard Deviation

Calculating the range, variance, and standard deviation of a data set is used to determine the dispersion of a data set. Knowing how a data set is dispersed can provide a better understanding of the data than the mean, median, and mode alone. For example, if a company lists its mean salary as $245,000, one might conclude that all salaries at the company are reasonably close to the mean. However, learning more about the dispersion of the salaries by calculating the range, variance, and standard deviation could reveal a much different picture of the salary distribution.

The **range** is the difference between the highest and lowest value in the data set. A range is the simplest method to calculate the dispersion of a data set and can provide a rough idea of how the data set is dispersed. However, a range can be misleading as a measure of spread if the data set consists of one excessively low value and/or one excessively high value. To calculate the range of a data set, the MIN and MAX functions are used. Subtracting the minimum value from the maximum value provides the range in a data set.

Variance is a calculation used in statistics to determine how far the data set varies from the mean. The higher the variance calculation, the more dispersed the data set. The smaller the variance, the more closely the data centers on the mean. Variance provides a more accurate picture of the dispersion of a data set than a range, but because of the way it is calculated, the value is not in the same units as the mean.

To calculate the variance of a data set in Excel, one of two functions is used: VAR.S or VAR.P. VAR.S is used to calculate the variance of a sample data set, and VAR.P is used to calculate the variance of a data set consisting of an entire population. Since most statistical analyses are based on random samples, VAR.S is used more often. The only arguments required are the values from which the variance is to be calculated.

=VAR.S(number1, [number2],…)

The **standard deviation** is the most commonly used method for determining the average spread of a data set from the mean. Mathematically, the standard deviation is calculated by taking the square root of the variance. It is most useful because its value is in the same units as the median and therefore is easiest to interpret.

To calculate the standard deviation of a data set in Excel, one of two functions is used: STDEV.S or STDEV.P. STDEV.S is used to calculate the standard deviation of a sample set of data, and STDEV.P is used to calculate the standard deviation of a data set consisting of an entire population. Again, since most statistical analyses are based on random samples, STDEV.S is used most often. The only arguments required are the values from which the standard deviation is to be calculated.

=STDEV.S(number1, [number2],…)

Often, just calculating the central tendency of a data set is not enough. In fact, just finding the central tendency may lead to incorrect assumptions about the data due to possible outliers. **Outliers** are values that are abnormally different from the other values in a random sample. In this exercise, you will calculate the range, variance, and standard deviation of the random sample data set in order to understand how the data is distributed.

 **E12.03**

To Calculate the Dispersion of a Data Set

a. Click cell **G6**, and then type **=MIN(** to begin the MIN function.

b. Click cell **C2**, and drag to select cell **C35**. Type **)**, and press Enter to calculate the minimum value in the sample.

c. In cell **G7**, type **=MAX(** to begin the MAX function.

d. Click cell **C2**, and drag to select cell **C35**. Type **)**, and press Enter to calculate the maximum value in the sample.

e. Click cell **G9**. Type **=**, click cell **G7**, and then type **-**. Click cell **G6**, and press Enter to calculate the range of values in the sample.

f. In cell **G10**, type **=VAR.S(** to begin the VAR.S function.

g. Click cell **C2**, and drag to select cell **C35**. Type **)**, and press Enter to calculate the variance of the sample.

h. In cell **G11**, type **=STDEV.S(** to begin the STDEV.S function.

i. Click cell **C2**, and drag to select cell **C35**. Type **)**, and press Ctrl + Enter to calculate the standard deviation of the sample.

   Notice that the standard deviation is quite small, at only 3.79, indicating that the sales values stay somewhat close to the mean.

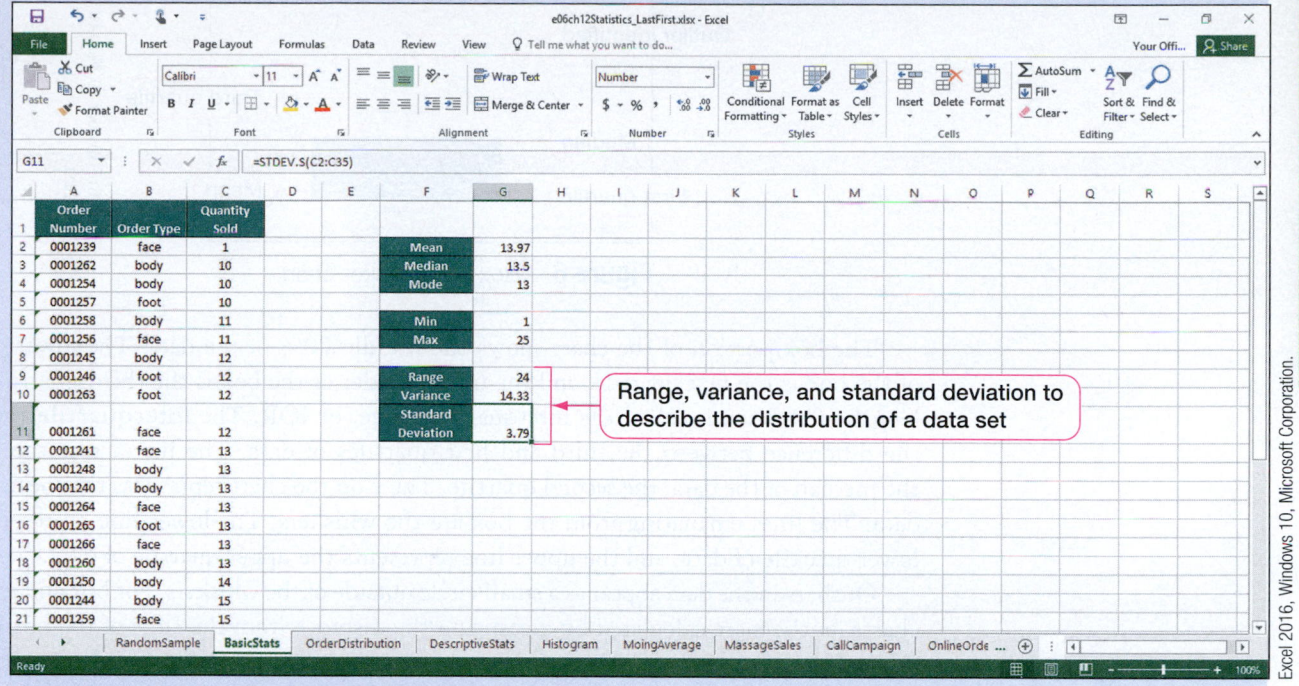

Figure 4 Calculating the dispersion of a data set

    j. Save ⊟ the document.

Visualize Outliers With a Box and Whisker Chart

As was previously mentioned, outliers are data that are abnormally different from other values in the data set. Defining outliers can be accomplished in many ways. The key to understanding outliers in your data is to determine where outliers are in relation to the rest of your data. A box and whisker chart, a new chart type available in Excel 2016, provides an efficient method of visualizing the distribution of your data and highlights outliers as part of the chart. Box and whisker charts visually represent several key statistical measures. First, they show the median and the mean of the data in relation to the distribution of the data. Next, they graphically represent the first and third quartiles of the data.

    A **quartile** is a descriptive statistic that divides data into four equal groups, or quartiles. Each quartile consists of 25% of the data. The first quartile splits the lower quarter of the data from the upper three quarters of the data. The second quartile is equal to the median of the data and splits the data into equal halves. The third quartile splits the lower three quarters of the data from the upper quarter of the data. Figure 5 shows a graphical representation of quartile data.

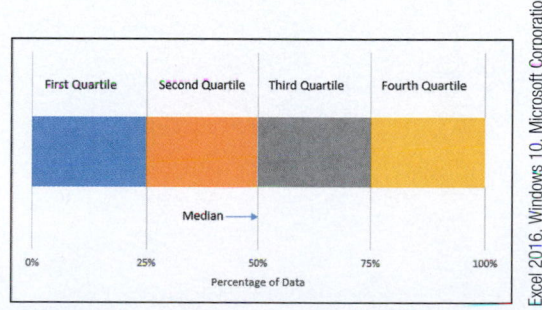

Figure 5 Distribution of data represented with quartiles

    Last, box and whisker charts display outliers in the data. Figure 6 shows a box and whisker chart.

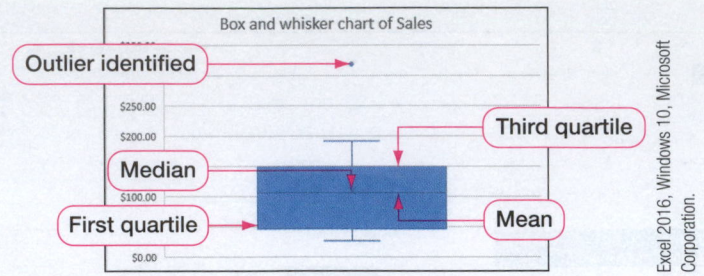

Figure 6 Box and whisker chart

The box portion of the chart shows the middle 50% of the data. The lower border of the box is the first quartile, and the upper border of the box is the third quartile. The length of the box is called the interquartile range, or IQR. The **interquartile range** is the difference between the third and first quartiles of data. The line across the box is the median of the data, the second quartile. The x on the chart represents the mean of the data. The lines emanating from the box are the whiskers. The lower line represents the lower quartile of data, and the upper line represents the upper quartile of data.

Outliers in the data appear as a small circle outside of the whiskers. For box and whisker charts, outliers are calculated by measuring the distance from the edge of the box on the chart. If a data point is 1.5 times the interquartile range above the third quartile, it is considered an outlier. Likewise, if a data point is 1.5 times the interquartile range below the first quartile, it is considered an outlier.

In this exercise, you will visualize the distribution of the quantities sold in the random sample of data for which you previously calculated statistics.

 **E12.04**

To Create a Box and Whisker Chart

a. Select the cell range **B1:C35**, click the **Insert** tab, and in the Charts group, click **Insert Statistic Chart** ![icon].

b. Select **Box and Whisker**.

   A box and whisker chart is inserted into the worksheet. Notice the outliers for the face box and whisker, indicating that the orders consisting of 1 and 25 products are abnormal in comparison to the rest of the data.

c. Double-click the **Chart Title**, and delete the text. Type Distribution of Orders.

d. Move the chart so that it covers the cell range **I2:P15**, and click outside of the chart to deselect it.

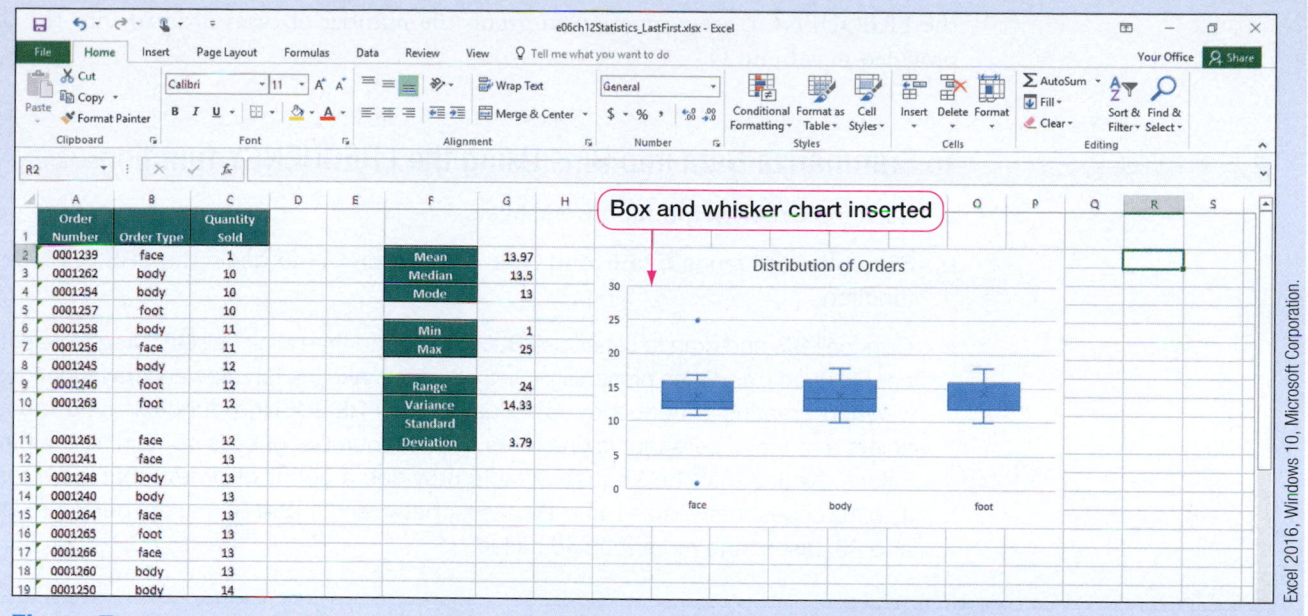

Figure 7   Box and whisker chart of quantities ordered

    e. **Save** 💾 the document.

Creating a Frequency Distribution Using the FREQUENCY Function

Businesses often have to work with data sets that contain thousands of records or more. In working with large data sets, it can be useful to group the data into bins. **Bins** are the intervals into which you want to group your data. For example, the Turquoise Oasis Spa places orders for cases of bath salts through a wholesaler. To summarize several orders worth of data, it may prove beneficial to determine how many orders of bath salts were for 1 to 10 cases, for 11 and 20 cases, for 21 to 30 cases, for 31 to 40 cases, and for more than 40 cases.

The FREQUENCY function in Excel is an array function that creates a frequency distribution that calculates how often values occur within a bin. An **array function** is a function that can perform multiple calculations on one or more items in an array. Array functions look different from other functions because curly brackets { } are required for the function to calculate correctly.

The FREQUENCY function uses two arguments: (1) Data_array; and (2) Bins_array.

    {=FREQUENCY(Data_array, Bins_array)}

The Data_array argument is an array of or a reference to a set of values from which you want to count the number of times a particular range of values occurs. Blank cells and cells that contain text are ignored in this argument.

The Bins_array argument is an array or reference to the upper values of the intervals you want to group the values in the Data_array argument into.

The FREQUENCY function always returns one additional value than there are bins referenced in the Bins_array argument. For example, if there are four bins consisting of 10, 20, 30, and 40, the function will return five values, including a count of values in the Data_array argument that are equal to more than 40, that is, counts of $1 \leq 10$, $11 \leq 20$, $21 \leq 30$, $31 \leq 40$, and > 40.

Since the FREQUENCY function is an array function, once it has been typed into a cell, you must press [Ctrl] + [Shift] + [Enter] instead of just [Enter] for it to calculate properly. Array functions are often referred to as "CSE" functions because of the keys pressed to create the functions.

You have been given a random sample of 29 orders. In this exercise, you will use the FREQUENCY array function to group the number of cases ordered into the bins provided in column D.

 **E12.05**

To Summarize Data into Bins Using the FREQUENCY function

a. Click the **OrderDistribution** worksheet.

b. Select the cell range **E2:E6**, and type **=FREQUENCY(** to begin the FREQUENCY function.

c. Click cell **B2**, and drag to select cell **B30**. Type **,** and then click cell **D2.** Drag to select cell **D5**, type **)**, and then press Ctrl + Shift + Enter to make the function an array function.

   When creating a frequency table using the FREQUENCY function, you must select a range of cells that is one more than the number of cells containing the bin values. Notice that the frequency table provides a count of orders that were for 1 to 10 cases, between 11 and 20 cases, between 21 and 30 cases, between 31 and 40 cases, and more than 40 cases.

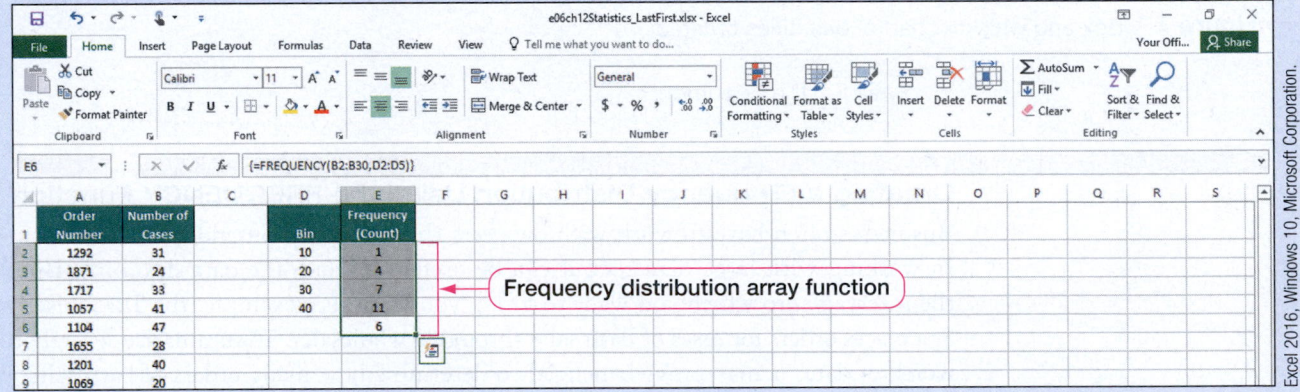

Figure 8   Summarizing data into bins with the FREQUENCY function

d. Click cell **D6**, and then type **More** as the label for the number of orders with more than 40 items.

> ### Troubleshooting
> If the FREQUENCY function is not returning expected results, be sure there are curly brackets surrounding the function. This indicates that it is an array function. {=FREQUENCY(B2:B30, D2:D5)}. If there are no curly brackets, then you must delete the functions and start over with step b.

e. **Save** 🖫 the document.

Generate Descriptive Statistics and Other Analyses Using the Analysis ToolPak

The Analysis ToolPak allows you to conduct a variety of statistical analyses with ease. For example, instead of typing out individual functions to calculate the mean, median, mode, variance, and standard deviation, you can generate all of those and more using the Analysis ToolPak. As of the date of this publication, the Analysis ToolPak is available in Excel with Office 365 for Macs.

Adding the Analysis ToolPak

Depending on the options that were selected when Excel was installed, the Analysis TookPak may or may not be available by default in Excel. In this exercise, you will manually install the Analysis ToolPak add-in.

 **E12.06**

To Add the Analysis ToolPak Add-In

a. Click the **File** tab, click **Options**, and then click **Add–Ins**.

b. At the bottom of the Excel Options dialog box, ensure that **Excel Add-ins** is selected in the Manage box, and then click **Go**.

c. In the Add-Ins dialog box, click the **Analysis ToolPak** check box, and then click **OK**.

d. Click the **Data** tab, and in the Analyze group, verify that the Data Analysis tool is now available.

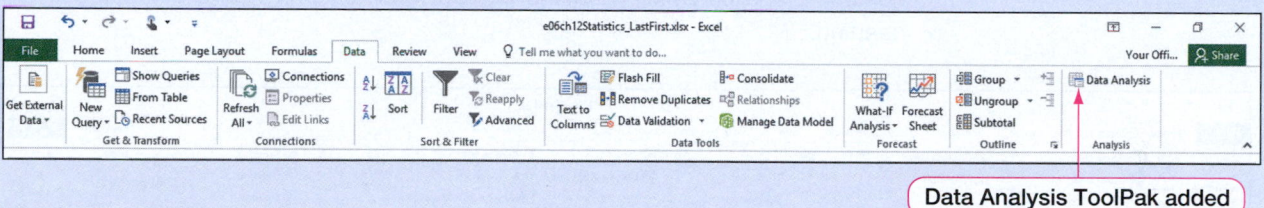

Data Analysis ToolPak added

Figure 9 Data Analysis button added to the Data tab

Excel 2016, Windows 10, Microsoft Corporation.

e. **Save** the document.

Generating Descriptive Statistics

Many of the statistical analyses that you have employed with Excel functions and more can be automatically generated by using the Analysis ToolPak's Descriptive Statistics tool.

The managers of the Turquoise Oasis Spa have provided you with a sample set of data containing monthly revenue amounts for the last year. In this exercise, you will generate descriptive statistics on the sample data set to gain a better understanding of the data.

 **E12.07**

To Generate Descriptive Statistics Using the Analysis ToolPak

a. Click the **DescriptiveStats** worksheet.

b. On the **Data** tab, in the Analyze group, click **Data Analysis**.

c. Select **Descriptive Statistics** from the Data Analysis dialog box, and then click **OK**.

d. Inside the Descriptive Statistics dialog box, click the **Input Range** box, and then select the cell range **B1:B13**.

e. Next to Grouped By, be sure that **Columns** is selected.

f. Click the **Labels in First Row** check box, indicating that the first row contains the Sales Revenue label.

g. Under Output options, click **Output Range**, click the **Output Range** box, and then click cell **E1**.

h. Click the **Summary statistics** check box, and then click **OK**.

Notice that many of the basic statistical calculations are generated automatically, including mean, median, mode, range, variance, and standard deviation. Notice that the value for the mode of the data is #N/A because there is no value in the data that occurs more than once.

i. Resize columns **E** and **F** to fit the contents by double-clicking the line between column E and column F and the line between column F and column G in the heading.

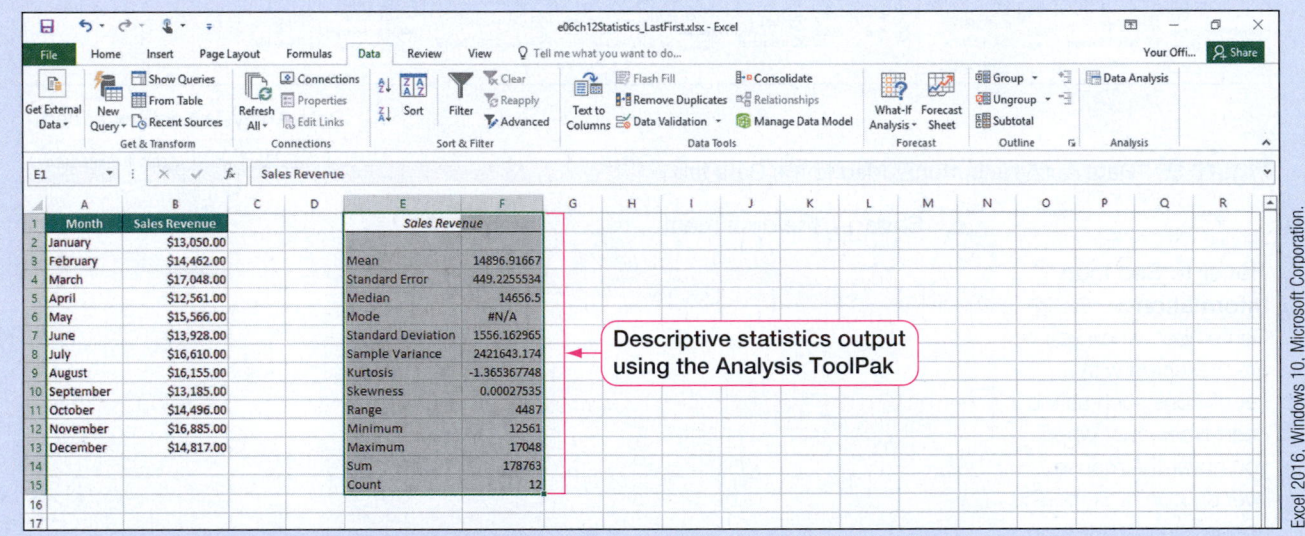

Figure 10 Descriptive statistics output

j. **Save** the document.

The results of the descriptive statistics output show that the spa's monthly revenues were relatively steady throughout the year with a standard deviation of approximately 1,556.

QUICK REFERENCE | Descriptive Statistics

Below is a list of statistical functions and descriptions that are generated by the Descriptive Statistics tool in the Analysis ToolPak.

Statistical Function	Description
Mean	The average of the variables in the sample
Standard error	Used to determine how accurate the sample mean predicts the population mean by dividing the standard deviation by the square root of the sample size
Median	The middle value(s) when all the values of the sample are sorted in ascending order
Mode	The value that appears most often in a sample. If there is no mode, then #N/A will appear
Standard deviation	The most commonly used method for determining the average spread of a data set from the mean
Sample variance	A measure of how far the data in the sample are spread from the mean
Kurtosis	Characterizes the peakedness or flatness of a distribution compared to the normal distribution
Skewness	Characterizes the degree of asymmetry of a distribution around its mean
Range	The difference between the largest and smallest values in the sample
Minimum	The smallest value in the sample
Maximum	The largest value in the sample
Sum	The sum of all values in the sample
Count	The count of all values in the sample

Using a Histogram to Visualize Data in Bins

Earlier, you created a frequency distribution using the FREQUENCY array function in Excel. Frequency distributions can be visualized by using a histogram. A **histogram** is a statistical graph that summarizes the distribution of data and how the data fits into defined bins. In prior versions of Excel, histograms were created with the Analysis ToolPak or by using carefully crafted column charts. Excel 2016 has introduced histograms as a default chart type. On the Histogram worksheet tab, sample data from 30 customers is provided, along with the number of items each of these customers has purchased over the course of one year. In this exercise, you will create a histogram to visualize the distribution of data.

 E12.08

To Create a Histogram

a. Click the **Histogram** worksheet.

b. Select the cell range **A1:B31**, click the **Insert** tab, and in the Charts group, click **Insert Statistic Chart** .

c. Select **Histogram**.

A histogram is placed into the chart. By default, a histogram may not be formatted in a way that is descriptive of the data.

d. Double-click the **horizontal axis** to open the Format Axis pane. Click the **Bin Width** option button, and in the text box clear the default text, type **10**, and then press Enter. This will divide the data into six bins. Each bin contains data points over a ten-point interval. For example, the first bin contains data points from 21 to 30.

e. Double-click the **Chart Title** box. Delete the default text, type Histogram of Items Purchased, and then click outside of the chart to deselect it.

f. **Close** ☒ the Format Axis pane, and move the histogram chart so that it is within the range **E4:K18**.

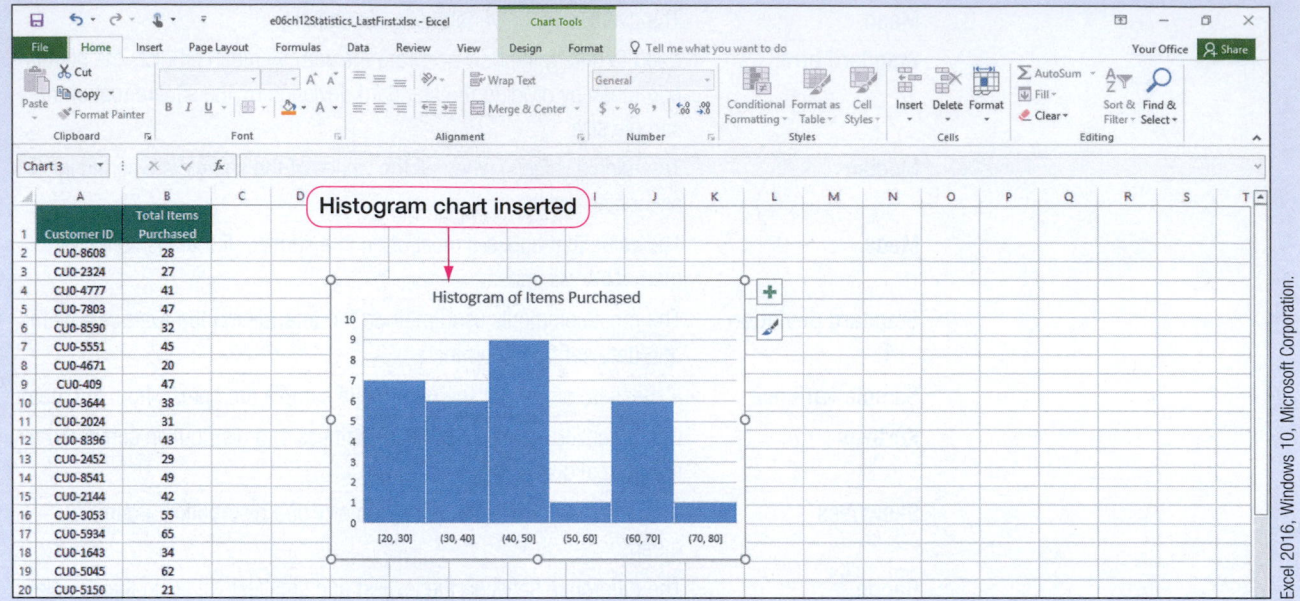

Figure 11 Histogram of items purchased

g. **Save** 🖫 the document.

REAL WORLD ADVICE	Creating Bin Values

Although Excel automatically generates bin values, you may want to define your own bin ranges depending on the amount of data you have sampled. There are several common methods of calculating the number and width of bins in data. You can also use the Underflow and Overflow bin options for extreme data points in your sample.

Calculating a Moving Average

A useful calculation for businesses that want to track sales over time, for example, is called a moving average. A **moving average** calculates the average of values over time on the basis of specified intervals. For example, a business may wish to see the average sales for every three months in a given year. Moving averages can be useful in spotting trends over a period of time by smoothing out any fluctuations that may occur during each consecutive interval. Moving average data can be used to create charts that show whether the value is trending upward or downward.

You have been provided with monthly sales data for the past year. In this exercise, you will calculate a moving average for every three months to determine whether there is an upward or downward trend over the course of the year.

To Calculate a Moving Average Using the Analysis ToolPak

a. Click the **MovingAverage** worksheet.

b. On the **Data** tab, in the Analyze group, click **Data Analysis**.

c. In the list of Analysis Tools, select **Moving Average**, and then click **OK**.

d. Click the **Input Range** box, and then select the cell range **B2:B13**.

e. Click the **Interval box**, and type **3** to set the interval for every three months.

f. Click the **Output Range** box, and then click cell **C2**.

g. Click the **Chart Output** check box to include a chart, and then click **OK**.

h. Edit the chart title to read Moving Sales Average, edit the horizontal axis label to read Months, and then edit the vertical axis label to read Sales. Click outside the chart to deselect it.

Notice the difference between the Actual and Forecast lines included in the chart. This indicates that despite the fluctuations in monthly sales, the overall trend is fairly flat with neither an upward nor a downward trend.

SIDE NOTE
Expecting #N/A Values

The moving average for the first two months returns #N/A. This is due to the interval's being set to 3.

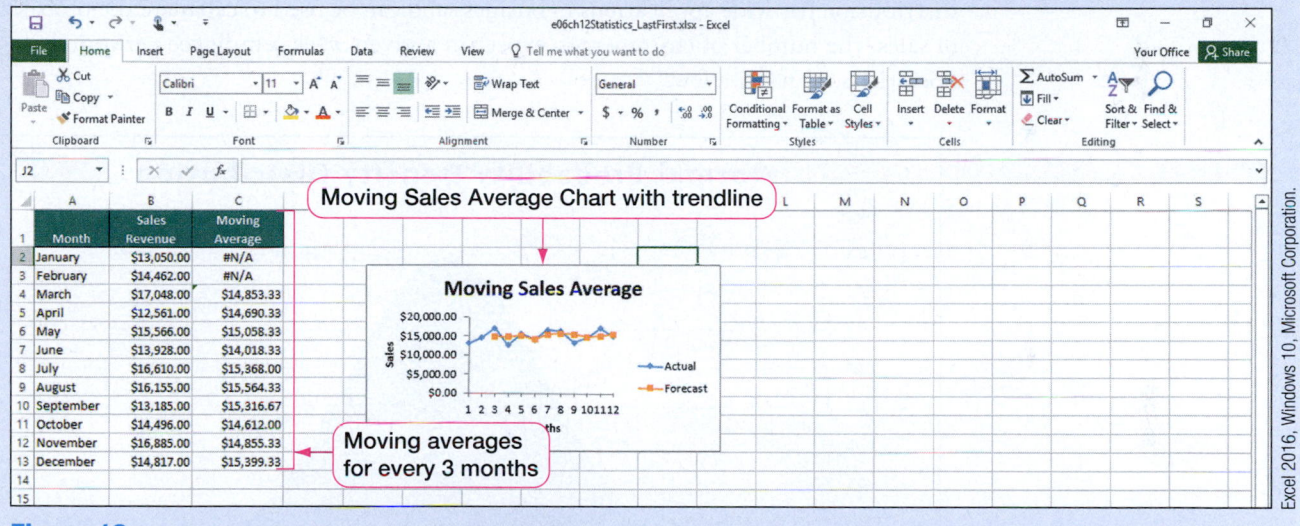

Figure 12 Calculating a three-month moving average

i. **Save** the document. If you need to take a break before finishing this chapter, now is a good time.

SS CONSIDER THIS | Selecting Appropriate Intervals

In calculating a moving average, it is important that the interval chosen is appropriate for the data. What interval would be appropriate for a call center that makes thousands of calls in a day? For a small business that makes an average of ten outside sales a day?

Applying Probability Distributions to Business

All businesses operate on a large amount of uncertainty. Small businesses such as the Turquoise Oasis Spa tend to experience more volatility than large organizations and can therefore benefit greatly from using probability distributions to estimate future outcomes and events. Probability distributions are useful in predicting demand for products and services, successful marketing campaigns, effectiveness of advertising, and much more.

In this section, you will use several different probability distributions to predict various aspects of the business. You will use the normal, binomial, exponential, Poisson, and hypergeometric distributions.

Predict Business Outcomes Using Probability Distribution Functions

Excel offers many probability distribution functions with wide applications across many different industries of business, science, engineering, and mathematics. The probability distribution functions most commonly used in business are NORM.DIST, BINOM.DIST, EXPON.DIST, POISSON.DIST, and HYPGEOM.DIST. In this section, you will assist the managers at the Turquoise Oasis Spa in predicting various business outcomes, using these probability distribution functions.

Using the NORM.DIST Function

A **normal distribution** is one of the most important distributions in statistics. When charted, as pictured in Figure 13, it takes on the shape of a bell and is often referred to as the "bell-shaped curve," where 68% of all values occur within one standard deviation from the mean, 95.45% of values fall within two standard deviations from the mean, and 99.8% of values fall within three standard deviations from the mean. The normal distribution has wide applications in business and can be used to calculate the probability of sales, the number of customers to expect in a given week, employee performance, and operations, to name a few.

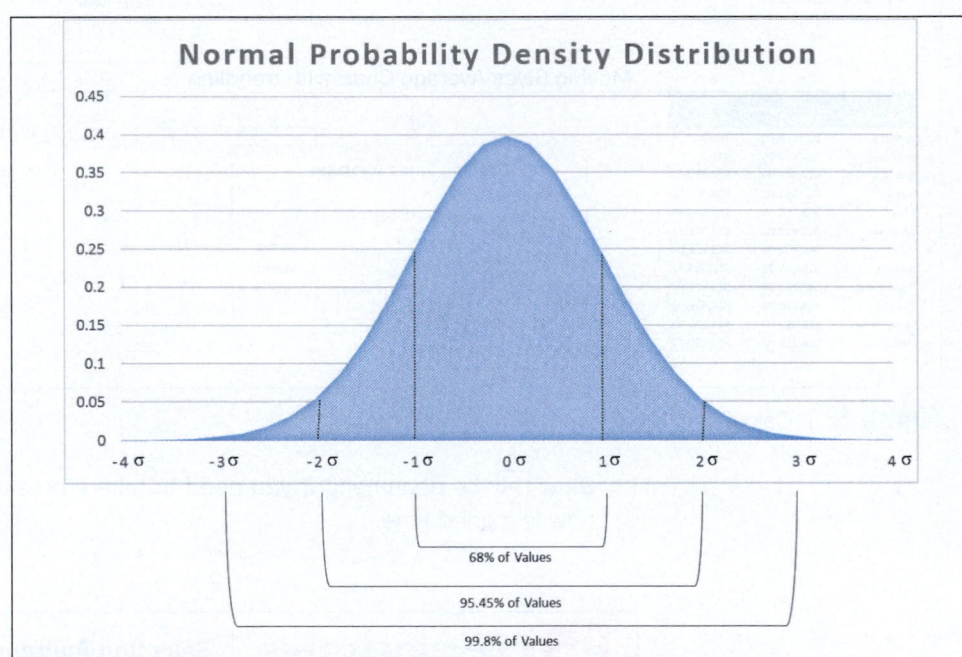

Figure 13   Normal probability density distribution

QUICK REFERENCE	Normal Distribution

- Many economic, social, and natural events follow the normal distribution.
- 68% of values will fall within one standard deviation from the mean.
- 95.45% of values will fall within two standard deviations from the mean.
- 99.8% of values will fall within three standard deviations from the mean.

The NORM.DIST function can be used to calculate the probability of an event occurring by using the mean and standard deviation of a continuous variable data set, assuming that the data follows a normal distribution. The NORM.DIST function uses four arguments: (1) x, (2) mean, (3) standard_dev, and (4) cumulative.

=NORM.DIST(x, mean, standard_dev, cumulative)

- The x argument is the value for which you want to calculate the probability of occurrence.
- The mean argument is the average value in the data set.
- The standard_dev argument is the standard deviation of the data set.
- The cumulative argument accepts either a TRUE or a FALSE value. If TRUE, the result will be the probability of a value being less than or equal to the value of the x argument, known as the **cumulative distribution function**. If FALSE, the result will be the probability of a value being equal to the value of the x argument, known as the **probability density function**.

Statistically, the probability of a specific x value for continuous data is 0, but the FALSE argument can be used to create a probability distribution of the data set.

Managers at the spa want to know how likely it is that they will exceed their goal of selling 30 massages over the course of the next week. You have been given data of weekly massage sales for the past seven weeks to use in your calculation. In this exercise, you will use the NORM.DIST function to calculate the probability of various sales levels in the data.

 E12.10

To Calculate Probability of Sales Using NORM.DIST

a. If you took a break, open the **e06ch12Statistics** workbook. Click the **MassageSales** worksheet.

b. Click cell **E1**, and then type =AVERAGE(to begin the AVERAGE function.

c. Click cell **B3**, drag to select cell **B9**, type), and then press Enter to calculate the mean for the weekly massage sales quantities.

d. In cell **E2**, type =STDEV.S(to begin the STDEV.S function.

e. Click cell **B3**, drag to select cell **B9**, type), and then press Ctrl + Enter to calculate the standard deviation of the sample of weekly massage sales volume.

f. Click cell **E4**, type 30, and then press Enter as the desired minimum sales goal in week 8.

g. In cell **E5**, type =1-NORM.DIST(to begin the NORM.DIST function. By default, the NORM.DIST function returns the probability of a value being less than or equal to the x value. Therefore, if the desired probability is for a value greater than the x value, you have to subtract the result from 1.

h. Click cell **E4**, and then type , to move to the mean argument.

i. Click cell **E1**, and then type , to move to the standard_dev argument.

j. Click cell **E2**, and then type , to move to the cumulative argument.

k. Type TRUE), and press Ctrl + Enter to calculate the probability of selling more than 30 massages in week 8.

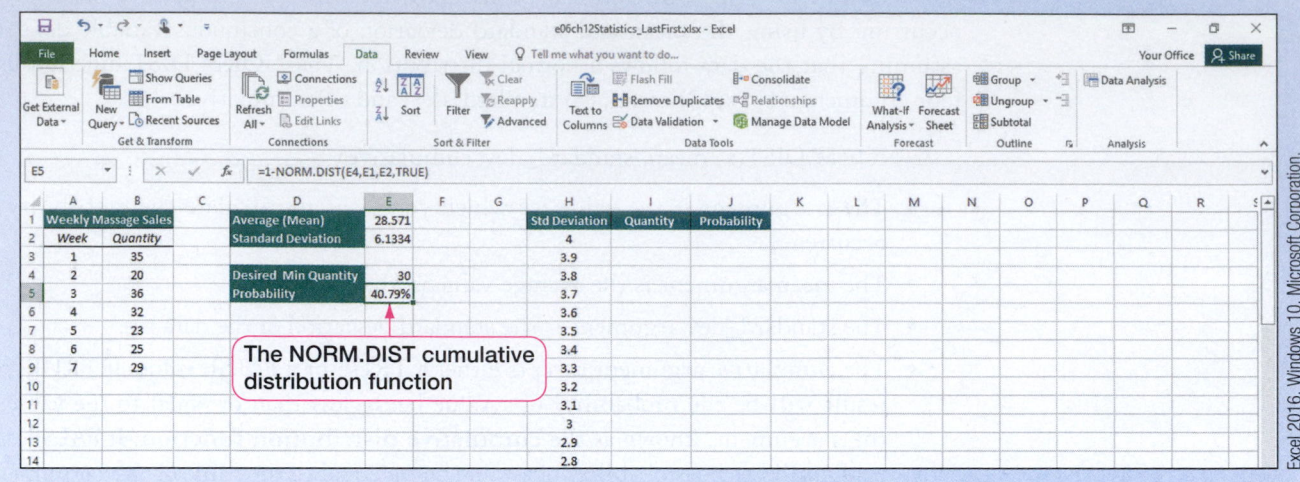

Figure 14 Probability of breaking a sales goal using the NORM.DIST function

 l. **Save** 💾 the document.

Charting a Normal Distribution

Visualizing the normal distribution of the weekly massage sales can help the managers of the spa to understand what the expectations should be for future weeks. In this exercise, you will create a chart that visualizes the normal distribution by first calculating the probability of values occurring within four standard deviations of the mean, both positive and negative.

 **E12.11**

To Visualize a Normal Distribution with a Scatter Chart

a. On the MassageSales worksheet, click cell **I2**.

b. Type **=** and click cell **H2**. Type *****, click cell **E2**, and then press F4 to lock the reference so that the formula can be copied down the column.

c. Type **+**, click cell **E1**, and then press F4. Press Ctrl + Enter to calculate what the quantity of massages sold would be if the unit quantity were equal to four standard deviations above the mean.

d. Use the **AutoFill** handle to copy the formula down to **I82** (four standard deviations below the mean).

e. Click cell **J2**, and then type **=NORM.DIST(** to begin the NORM.DIST function.

f. Click cell **I2**, and then type **,** to move to the mean argument.

g. Click cell **E1**, press F4, and then type **,** to move to the standard_dev argument.

h. Click cell **E2**, press F4, and then type **,** to move to the cumulative argument.

i. Type **FALSE)**, and then press Ctrl + Enter to calculate the probability that the spa will sell a number of massages that are exactly four standard deviations above the mean in a given week.

j. Use the **AutoFill** handle to copy the formula down to **J82**.

k. Select the cell range **I2:J82**, and then click the **Insert** tab. In the Charts group, click the **Insert Scatter (X, Y) or Bubble Chart** 📊 button, and then select the **Scatter with Smooth Lines** chart.

l. Move the chart to within the cell range **A11:F23**.

m. Click the **Chart Title** text box, and then type **Weekly Sales Distribution**.

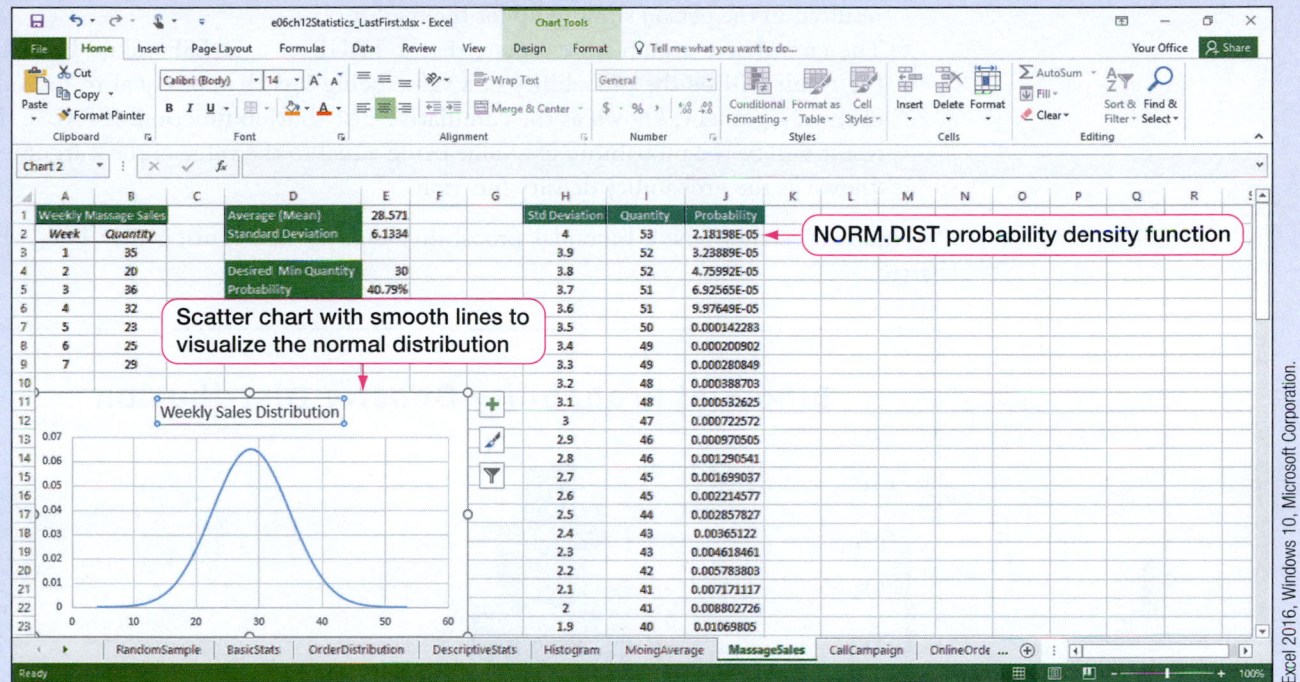

Figure 15 Visualizing the normal distribution with a scatter chart

n. **Save** 💾 the document.

Using the BINOM.DIST Function

The spa initiated a phone campaign to get current and former customers to subscribe to its health and beauty magazine. After 30 phone calls, there was a 35% success rate of converting a prospective customer, or lead, to a paid subscriber. Statistical analysis could be applied to this data to calculate the probability of successfully converting 0 leads, 1 lead, 2 leads, and so on. The binomial distribution can do just that. The binomial distribution is a very common probability distribution that has many applications in business. The **binomial distribution** is a discrete probability distribution that is used to model the number of successful trials based on the total number of trials and the rate of success.

The BINOM.DIST function uses four arguments: (1) number_s, (2) trials, (3) probability_s, and (4) cumulative.

=BINOM.DIST(number_s, trials, probability_s, cumulative)

- The number_s argument is the number of successes for which you want to calculate the probability of occurrence.

- The trials argument is the number of independent trials that have taken place. For the spa, it is the number of subscription phone calls placed.
- The probability_s argument is the probability of success for each trial. This is based on the data previously collected, in which 35% of the phone calls placed resulted in the person signing up for the mailing list.
- The cumulative argument accepts either a TRUE or a FALSE value. If TRUE, the result will be the probability of a value being less than or equal to the value of the x argument, known as the cumulative distribution function. If FALSE, the result will be the probability of a value being equal to the value of the x argument, known as the probability density function.

Figure 16 shows how a binomial probability density distribution may look when charted.

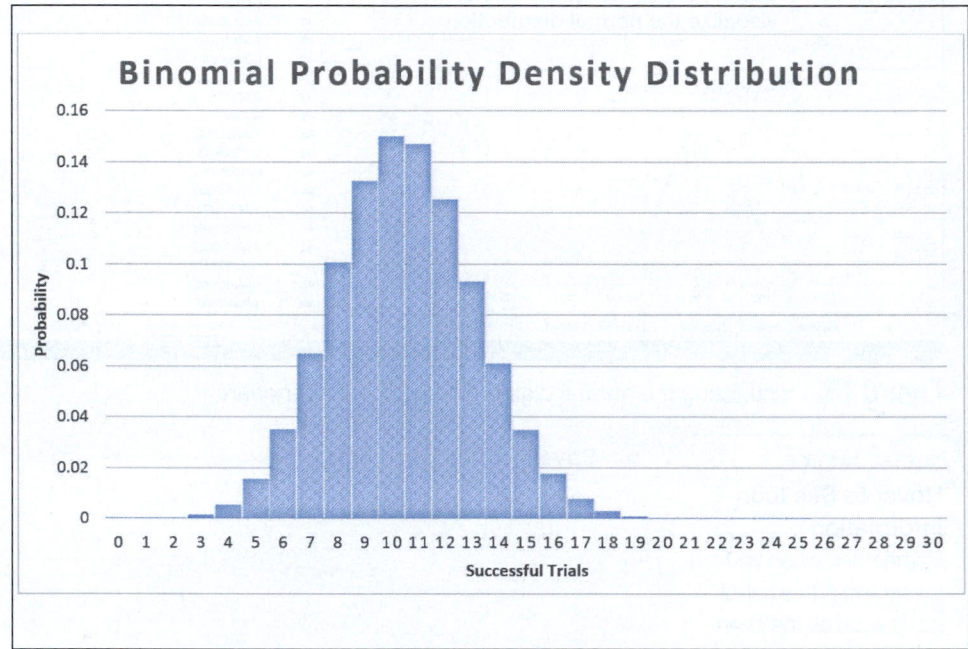

Figure 16   Binomial probability density distribution

In this exercise, you will use the BINOMIAL.DIST function to calculate the probability of success during a phone campaign, given a sample size of 30 and a 35% success rate.

 **E12.12**

To Calculate the Probability of Success Using BINOM.DIST

a. Click the **CallCampaign** worksheet.

b. Click cell **B5**, and type =BINOM.DIST(to begin the BINOM.DIST function.

c. Click cell **A5**, and then type **,** to move to the trials argument.

d. Click cell **B1**, press F4, and then type **,** to move to the probability_s argument.

e. Click cell **B2**, press F4, and then type **,** to move to the cumulative argument.

f. Type FALSE), and press Ctrl + Enter to calculate the probability that exactly 0 out of 30 calls will result in a successful sign-up.

g. Use the **AutoFill** handle to copy the formula down to **B35**.

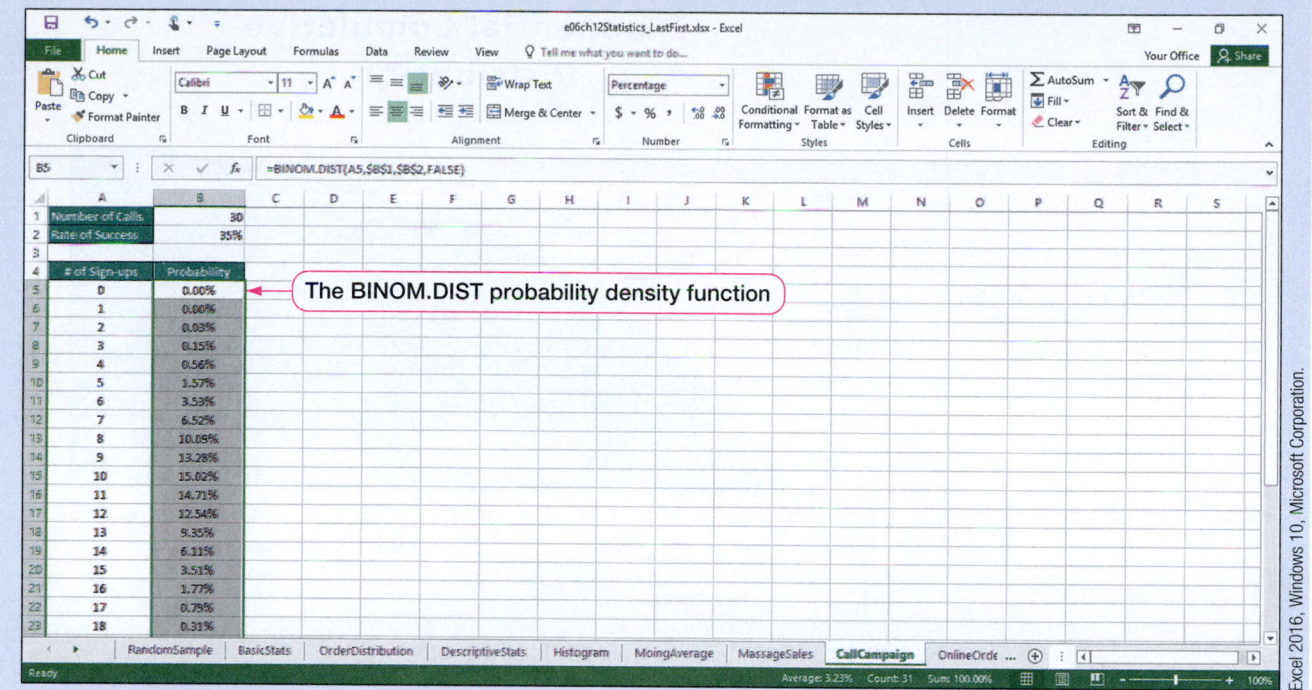

Figure 17 Probability of success using the BINOM.DIST function

    h. Save 🖫 the document.

Notice that the most likely number of successful sign-ups is ten out of every 30 phone calls, at 15.02%. Managers at the spa can use this information as a way to set expectations for each phone representative. If a representative is able to consistently outperform the most likely number of sign-ups, then perhaps a best practice can be established to increase the overall rate of success.

Using the EXPON.DIST Function

Managers at the Turquoise Oasis Spa have been tracking how frequently online sales of their spa products have been occurring. They would like to estimate when the next ten online orders will occur. The exponential distribution can do just that. The **exponential distribution** is a continuous probability function that models the times between events. The EXPON.DIST function uses three arguments: (1) x, (2) lambda, and (3) cumulative.

    =EXPON.DIST(x, lambda, cumulative)

- The x argument is the value representing the number of events for which you want to calculate the probability of occurrence.

- The lambda argument is the inverse of the mean and is calculated by dividing 1 by the mean value.

- The cumulative argument accepts either a TRUE or a FALSE value. If TRUE, the result will be the probability of a value being less than or equal to the value of the x argument, known as the cumulative distribution function. If FALSE, the result will be the probability of a value being equal to the value of the x argument, known as the probability density function.

Figure 18 shows how an exponential cumulative distribution may look when charted.

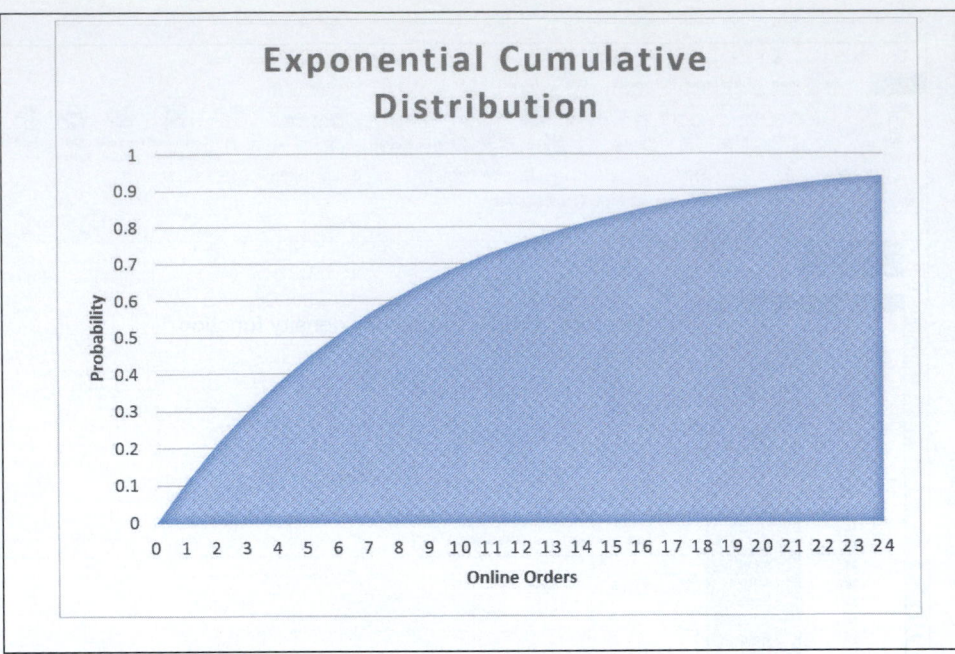

Figure 18 Exponential cumulative distribution

In this exercise, you will use the EXPON.DIST function to calculate the probability of a sale.

 E12.13

To Calculate the Probability of When a Sale Will Occur Using EXPON.DIST

a. Click the **OnlineOrders** worksheet.

b. Click cell **A2**, and then type **=EXPON.DIST(** to begin the EXPON.DIST function.

c. Type **B2,** to move to the lambda argument.

d. Type **1/**, click cell **D2**, and then press [F4]. Type **,** to move to the cumulative argument.

e. Type **TRUE)**, and press [Ctrl] + [Enter] to calculate the probability of an online sale taking place in 1 hour or less. The final function should appear as =EXPON. DIST(B2,1/$D$2,TRUE).

f. Use the **AutoFill** handle to copy the function to **A25**.

Notice the various probabilities for sales taking place within the next 1 to 24 hours. Since TRUE was used for the cumulative argument, each of the probabilities is for less than or equal to the x value.

g. Click cell **F3**, and then type **=IFERROR(VLOOKUP(RAND(),**

h. Click cell **A2**, drag to select cell **B25**, and press [F4]. Type **,** to move to the col_index_num argument.

i. Type **2,TRUE),1)** to complete the formula. The final formula should appear as =IFERROR(VLOOKUP(RAND(),$A$2:$B$25,2,TRUE),1).

This formula uses the VLOOKUP function to look up a random probability value generated by the RAND function. Where an approximate match is found, it returns the number of hour(s) when a sale will occur from column B. The IFERROR function is necessary because if the random variable generated is less than the probability of a sale occurring in 1 hour or less, the result would be an error and should be 1.

j. Use the **AutoFill** handle to copy the formula to **F12** to estimate when the next ten online orders will be placed.

k. Click cell **H2**, and type **=**. Click cell **A11**, type **-**, and then click cell **A6**. Press [Ctrl] + [Enter] to calculate the probability of an online sale occurring within the next 5 to 10 hours by subtracting the probability of an online sale occurring within 5 hours from the probability of one occurring within 10 hours or less.

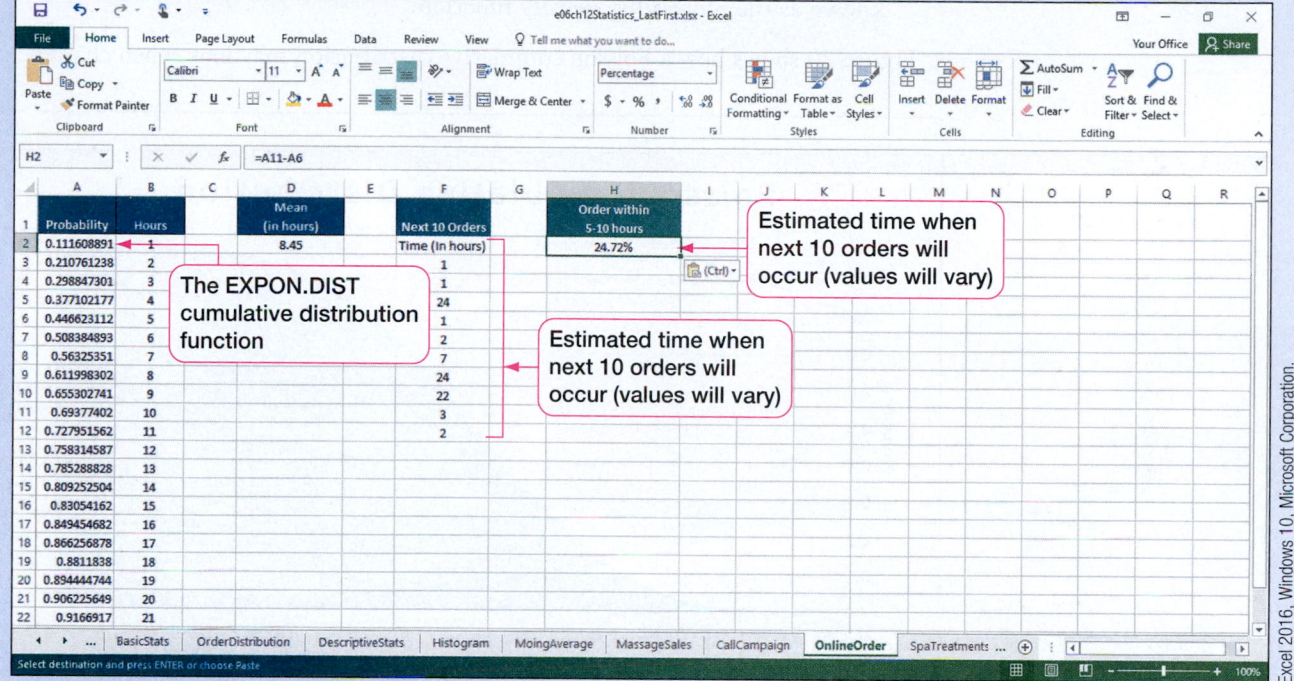

Figure 19 Predicting the time of online sales using EXPON.DIST

l. **Save** 🖫 the document.

Managers could use this statistical model to ensure that the technology used to support online sales can support the number of online sales expected to occur throughout the day.

REAL WORLD ADVICE | **Continually Monitoring Statistics**

These important statistics should be tracked continually and consistently. As the company grows, you may find that the average time between orders will decrease and additional employees and/or web and database servers may be required to process the orders.

Using the POISSON.DIST Function

Managers at the Turquoise Oasis Spa have provided three weeks of spa services sales data and are interested in predicting the number of spa services that will be sold over the next seven days. The Poisson distribution can do just that. The **Poisson distribution** is a discrete probability function that has wide business applications. It is used most often to predict demand for a product or service.

The Poisson distribution calculates the probability that a specified number of events will occur based on the mean of the data set. The POISSON.DIST function uses three arguments: (1) x, (2) mean, and (3) cumulative.

=POISSON.DIST(x, mean, cumulative)

- The x argument is the value representing the number of events for which you want to calculate the probability of occurrence.
- The mean argument is the value representing the mean of the data set.
- The cumulative argument accepts either a TRUE or a FALSE value. If TRUE, the result will be the probability of a value being less than or equal to the value of the x argument, known as the cumulative distribution function. If FALSE, the result will be the probability of a value being equal to the value of the x argument, known as the probability density function.

Figure 20 shows how a Poisson cumulative distribution may look when charted.

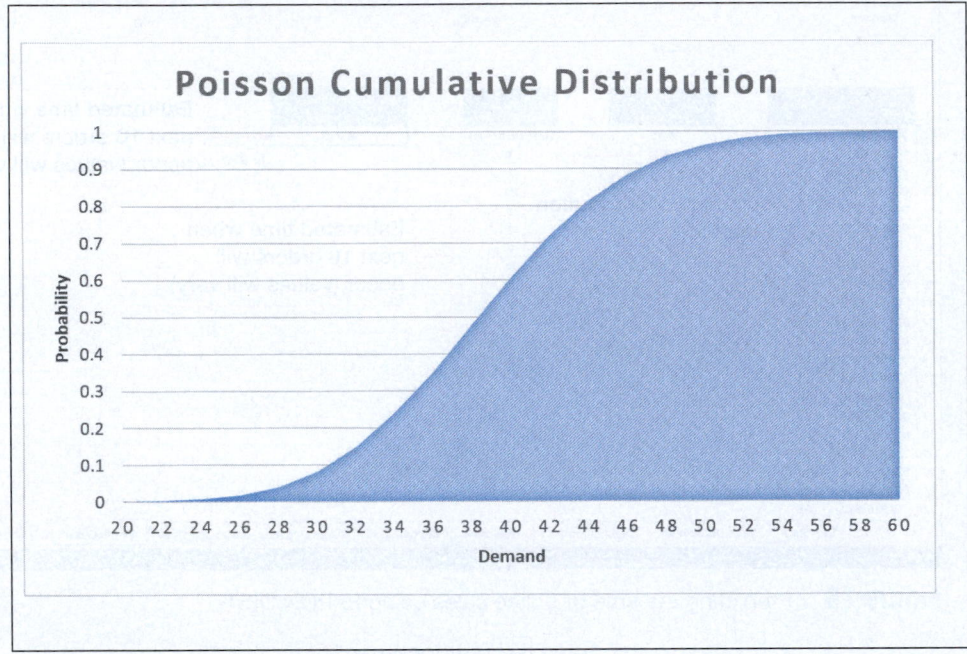

Figure 20   Poisson cumulative distribution

In this exercise, you will use the POISSON.DIST function to predict the number of orders that will be placed in the next week.

 E12.14

To Predict the Number of Orders Placed in the Next Week Using POISSON.DIST

a. Click the **SpaTreatments** worksheet.

b. Click cell **D2**, and then type **=POISSON.DIST(** to begin the POISSON.DIST function.

c. Click cell **E2**, and then type **,** to move to the mean argument.

d. Click cell **B25**, press [F4], and then type **,** to move to the cumulative argument.

e. Type **TRUE)**, and then press [Ctrl] + [Enter] to calculate the probability of selling 20 or fewer spa treatments. The completed function should appear as =POISSON.DIST(E2,$B$25,TRUE).

f. Use the **AutoFill** handle to copy the function down to **D22** (60 or fewer).

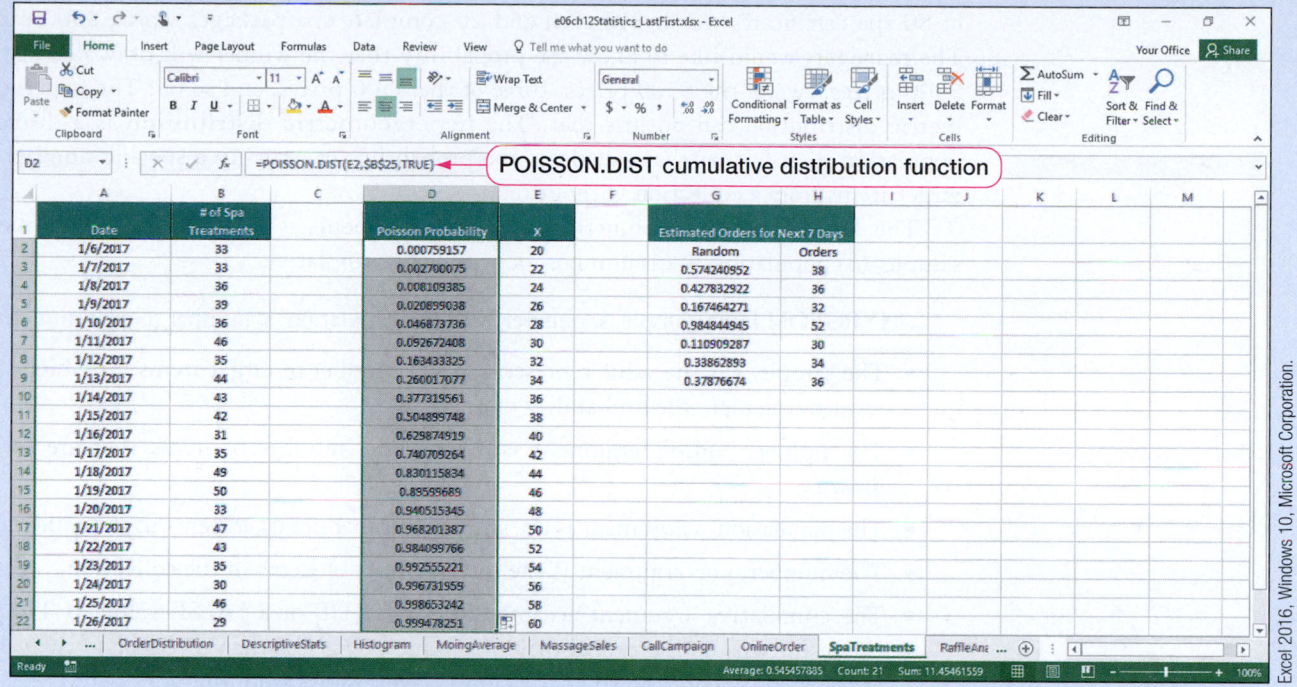

Figure 21 Using the POISSON.DIST function

SIDE NOTE
Random Probabilities
Because of the volatility of the RAND function, your results will be different from the image in Figure 21.

g. Click cell **G3**, type **=RAND()**, and then press Ctrl + Enter to generate a random decimal between 0 and 1. This will serve as a random probability to aid in estimating the orders for the next week.

h. Use the **AutoFill** handle to copy the function down to **G9**.

i. With the cell range **G3:G9** selected, on the Home tab, in the Clipboard group, click **Copy**. Click the **Paste** button arrow, and then, under the **Paste Values** heading, click **Values** to replace the volatile RAND function with the values it generated.

j. Click cell **H3**. Type **=VLOOKUP(**, click cell **G3**, and type **,** to move to the table array argument.

k. Click cell **D2**, drag to select cell **E22**, and then press F4.

l. Type **,2,TRUE)**, and then press Ctrl + Enter to complete the function.

m. Use the **AutoFill** handle to copy the function down to **H9**.

   Notice that the VLOOKUP function uses the randomly generated probability value as the lookup value in the function. It then looks for an approximate match in the Poisson Probability column and returns the corresponding number of spa treatment orders in the same row. Managers at the Turquoise Oasis Spa now have an estimated number of spa treatments for the next seven days.

n. **Save** the document.

Managers at the spa can use this statistical model to assist in scheduling massage therapists for the week to be sure they have enough therapists available to meet the likely demand.

Using the HYPGEOM.DIST Function

Managers at the Turquoise Oasis Spa are planning to have a grand reopening once the expansion is complete. To help generate buzz about the event, they will be giving away raffle tickets to customers who use the spa services throughout the month of June. The winner will be allowed to draw ten envelopes from a barrel of 100 envelopes consisting of 80 spa certificates worth $50 each and 20 complete spa packages worth $500 each. The managers would like to know the probability that the winner will draw one of the $500 prizes, two of the $500 prizes, three of the $500 prizes, and so on. The hypergeometric distribution can do just that. The **hypergeometric distribution** is a discrete population distribution that calculates the probability of drawing a specific number of target items from a collection without replacement.

The HYPGEOM.DIST function uses five arguments: (1) sample_s, (2) number_sample, (3) population_s, (4) number_pop, and (5) cumulative.

=HYPGEOM.DIST(sample_s, number_sample, population_s, number_pop, cumulative)

- The sample_s is the value representing the number of target items for which you want to calculate the probability of occurrence.
- The number_sample argument is the specific number of items that are to be drawn.
- The population_s argument is the specific number of target items in the collection.
- The number_pop argument is the total number of items in the collection.
- The cumulative argument accepts either a TRUE or a FALSE value. If TRUE, the result will be the probability of a value being less than or equal to the value of the x argument, known as the cumulative distribution function. If FALSE, the result will be the probability of a value being equal to the value of the x argument, known as the probability density function.

Figure 22 shows how a hypergeometric probability density distribution may look when charted.

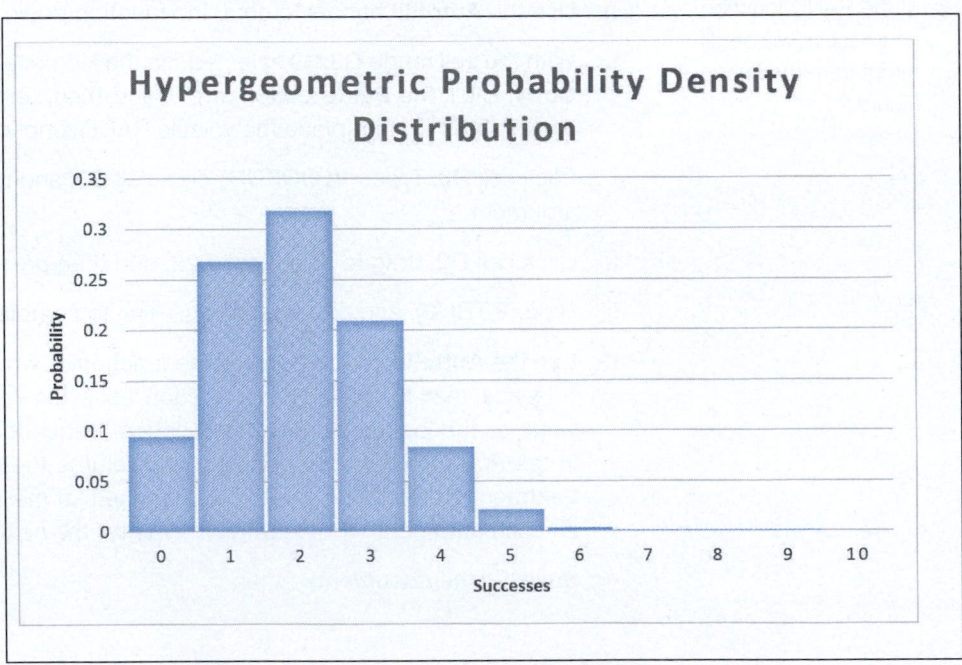

Figure 22   Hypergeometric probability density distribution

In this exercise, you will use the HYPGEOM.DIST function to calculate the probability of someone winning the spa's contest.

 **E12.15**

To Calculate the Probability of Drawing the Top Prize Using HYPGEOM.DIST

a. Click the **RaffleAnalysis** worksheet.

b. Click cell **E2**, and then type **=HYPGEOM.DIST(** to begin the HYPGEOM.DIST function.

c. Click cell **A2**, and then type **,** to move to the number_sample argument.

d. Click cell **B2**, and then type **,** to move to the population_s argument.

e. Click cell **C2**, and then type **,** to move to the number_pop argument.

f. Click cell **D2**, and then type **,** to move to the cumulative argument.

g. Type **FALSE)**, and then press Ctrl + Enter to calculate the probability of the winner drawing exactly 0 top prize envelopes. The completed function should appear as =HYPGEOM.DIST(A2,B2,C2,D2,FALSE). Use the **AutoFill** handle to copy the formula down to **E12** (exactly ten top prize envelopes).

h. Click cell **F2**. Type **=(**, click in cell **A2**, and type ***500)** to calculate the cost of a customer drawing the top prize.

i. Type **+(**, click cell **B2**, type **-**, and click cell **A2**, to calculate the number of envelopes left to draw.

j. Type **)*50**, and press Ctrl + Enter to calculate the total cash value of envelopes drawn if 0 are top prizes. The completed formula should appear as =(A2*500)+(B2-A2)*50. Use the **AutoFill** handle to copy the formula down to **F12**.

k. Click cell **G2**, and then type **=**. Click cell **E2**, type *****, click cell **F2**, and then press Ctrl + Enter to calculate the expected value of the drawing based on the probability of drawing 0 top prize envelopes and the total cash value of ten $50 envelopes. Use the **AutoFill** handle to copy the formula to **G12**. The total expected value of the ten envelopes drawn by the winner should equal $1,400.00.

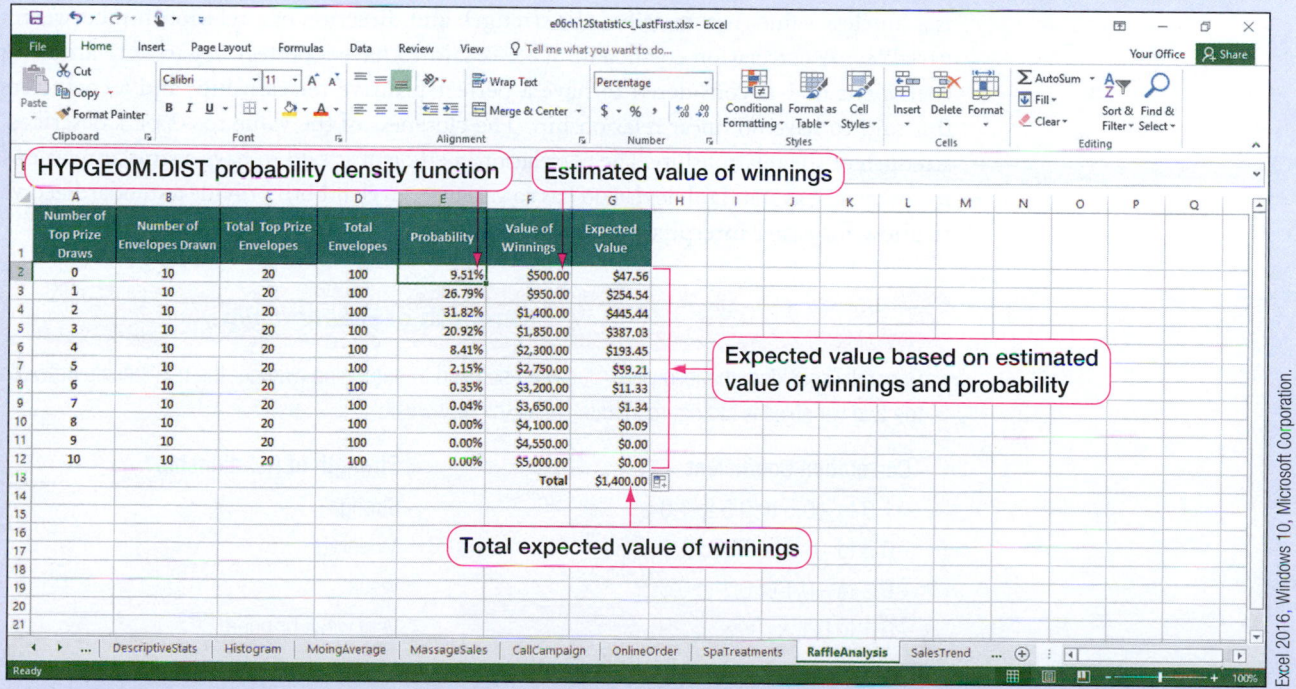

Figure 23 Calculating the probability of drawing the top prize using the HYPGEOM.DIST function

l. **Save** 💾 the document. If you need to take a break before finishing this chapter, now is a good time.

Raffles and contests like this can raise awareness of a company's existence and services offered, increasing customer traffic. It is important for management to be able to estimate the total costs of the contest winnings in case the winner is extremely lucky and beats the odds.

Finding Relationships in Data

So far, you have learned the benefits of basic statistical analysis in gaining a better understanding of data as well as the benefits of probability distributions in predicting the likelihood that certain events will occur. Identifying relationships in data can help you to answer these questions: Did the most recent marketing campaign increase sales? Do the age and gender of your customers have anything to do with how much money they spend? To understand how to answer these and similar questions and then move to predicting outcomes, you need to understand the concepts of correlation and regression.

In this section, you will learn to identify relationships in your data using covariance and correlation functions as well as regression analysis to identify trends, relationships between variables, and make predictions.

Find Relationships in Data Using COVARIANCE.S and CORREL

Managers at the Turquoise Oasis Spa are interested in knowing whether there is a relationship between the age of their clients and the amount of money the clients spend. The covariance and correlation formulas are used to describe linear relationships between data. **Covariance** is a formula that can calculate the relationship between two variables, such as age and dollars spent, as well as the direction of the relationship. If one variable increases and the other variable also increases, then the relationship is considered positive. If one variable increases and the other variable decreases, then the relationship is considered negative.

The correlation formula produces a value between −1 and 1 that is called the correlation coefficient. The **correlation coefficient** is represented by the letter "r" in statistics and is a unitless value that describes the strength and direction of a relationship between two variables. A correlation coefficient of −1 is said to have a perfect negative relationship, a coefficient of 1 is considered to have a perfect positive relationship, and a coefficient of 0 is said to have no linear relationship. The closeness of the value to −1 or 1 describes the strength of the relationship. The correlation coefficient is said to have a similar relationship to covariance as standard deviation has to variance, in that both provide a standardized value to allow for easier interpretation of the data.

QUICK REFERENCE	Strength of Relationship

Generally speaking, the following values can be used to determine whether the relationship between the two variables is strong, moderate, weak, or very weak.

Correlation Coefficient	Strength of Relationship
−1.0 to −0.5 or 0.5 to 1.0	Strong
−0.5 to −0.3 or 0.3 to 0.5	Moderate
−0.3 to −0.1 or 0.1 to 0.3	Weak
−0.1 to 0.1	Very weak or none

Correlation Does Not Equal Causation

A correlation coefficient of .889 tells you only that there is a strong positive relationship between the two variables. It does not mean that an increase in one variable actually causes the other variable to increase. Be sure to keep in mind that correlation does not imply causation.

Using the COVARIANCE.S Function

To calculate the covariance in Excel, one of two functions is used: COVARIANCE.S or COVARIANCE.P. COVARIANCE.S is used to determine a relationship between two variables in a sample; COVARIANCE.P is used to determine a relationship between two variables in an entire population. You will use COVARIANCE.S, since you are dealing with sample sets of data. The only arguments are the arrays of cells that contain the two variables.

=COVARIANCE.S(array1, array2)

The value that the COVARIANCE.S function returns can be difficult to interpret at times because it is not standardized. A covariance of 7, for example, can be interpreted as a positive relationship, but the strength of that positive relationship can only be said to be weaker than it would be if the number had been 10.

Managers at the spa assume that, to a certain extent, the age of a client may be related to how much money the client spends at the spa. For example, someone who is 40 years old could spend more money than someone who is 20 years old. In this exercise, you have been given a random sample of sales data along with the ages of the customers to use Excel to determine whether or not there is a relationship between age and revenue and the strength of that relationship.

 E12.16

To Determine the Relationship Between Two Variables Using COVARIANCE.S

a. If you took a break, open the **e06ch12Statistics** workbook. Click the **SalesTrend** worksheet.

b. Click cell **D2**, and then type =COVARIANCE.S(to begin the COVARIANCE.S function.

c. Click cell **A2**, drag to select cell **A37**, and then type , to move to the array2 argument.

d. Click cell **B2**, and drag to select cell **B37**. Type), and then press [Ctrl] + [Enter] to calculate the covariance between age and sales at the Turquoise Oasis Spa.

   Notice that the COVARIANCE.S function returns 390.8442, indicating a relationship between age and sales amount. The relationship is positive in that as the age of the customer increases, so does the amount of money they spend at the spa.

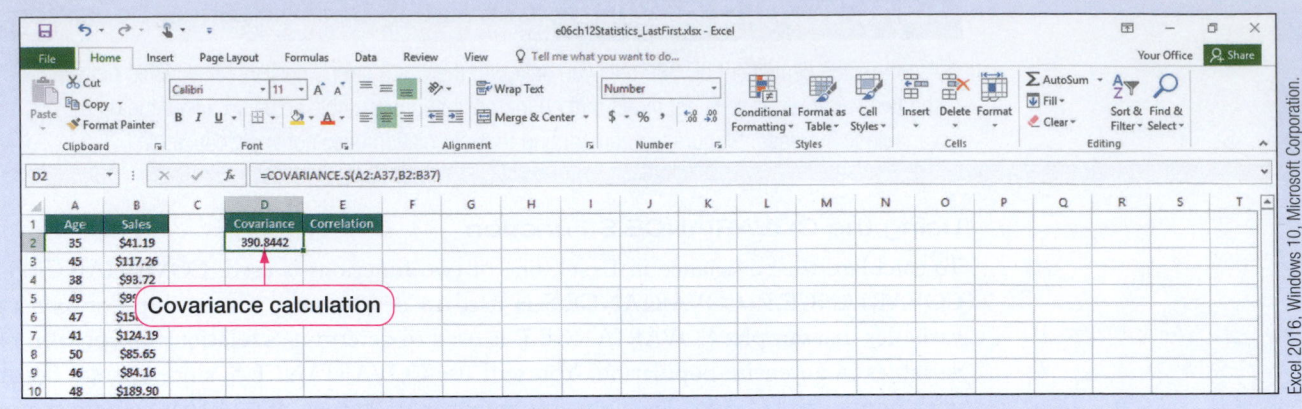

Figure 24 Determining the relationships between two variables using the COVARIANCE.S function

e. **Save** 💾 the document.

Using the CORREL Function

To calculate the correlation coefficient between two variables in Excel, the CORREL function is used. The only arguments are the arrays of cells that contain the two variables.

=CORREL(array1, array2)

In this exercise, you will use the CORREL function to calculate the correlation coefficient of the age of customers and the amount they have spent at the spa.

 **E12.17**

To Calculate a Correlation Coefficient Using CORREL

a. On the SalesTrend worksheet, click cell **E2**.

b. Type **=CORREL(** to begin the CORREL function.

c. Click cell **A2**, drag to select cell **A37**, and then type **,** to move to the array2 argument.

d. Click cell **B2**, drag to select cell **B37**, and then type **)**. Press Ctrl + Enter to calculate the correlation coefficient between age and sales.

Notice that the correlation coefficient is approximately .65, indicating a strong positive correlation between age and sales.

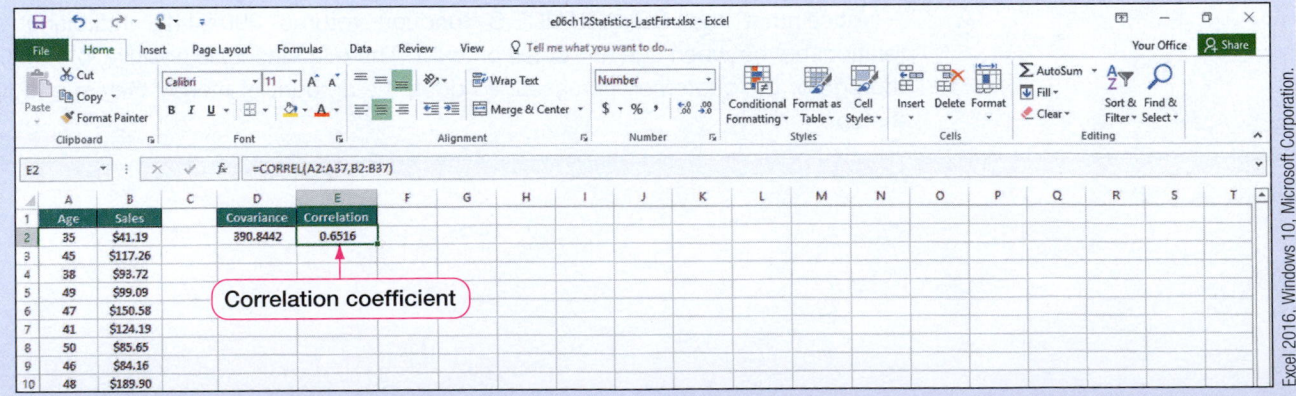

Figure 25 Calculating a correlation coefficient using the CORREL function

e. **Save** 💾 the document.

Visualizing Relationships with a Scatter Chart

Correlation coefficient values are easy to interpret, but it is often more powerful to create a chart that illustrates that relationship visually. In this exercise, you will visualize a correlation using a scatter chart.

 **E12.18**

To Visualize Relationships Between Two Variables Using a Scatter Chart

a. On the SalesTrend worksheet, select the cell range **A1:B37**.

b. Click the **Quick Analysis** tool 📊 at the bottom of the range selection, click **Charts**, and then click **Scatter**.

c. Click the **Chart Elements** button ➕ next to the chart, and then click the **Axis Titles** and **Trendline** check boxes.

d. Click the **Vertical Axis** Title text box, delete the **Axis Title** text, and then type Sales Revenue.

e. Click the **Horizontal Axis** Title text box, delete the **Axis Title** text, and then type Age.

f. Edit the chart title to read Sales-Age Correlation.

g. Move the scatter chart into the cell range **D4:J17**.

Notice that the trendline with its upward slope also indicates a strong positive relationship between the age of the clients of the spa and the amount of money spent.

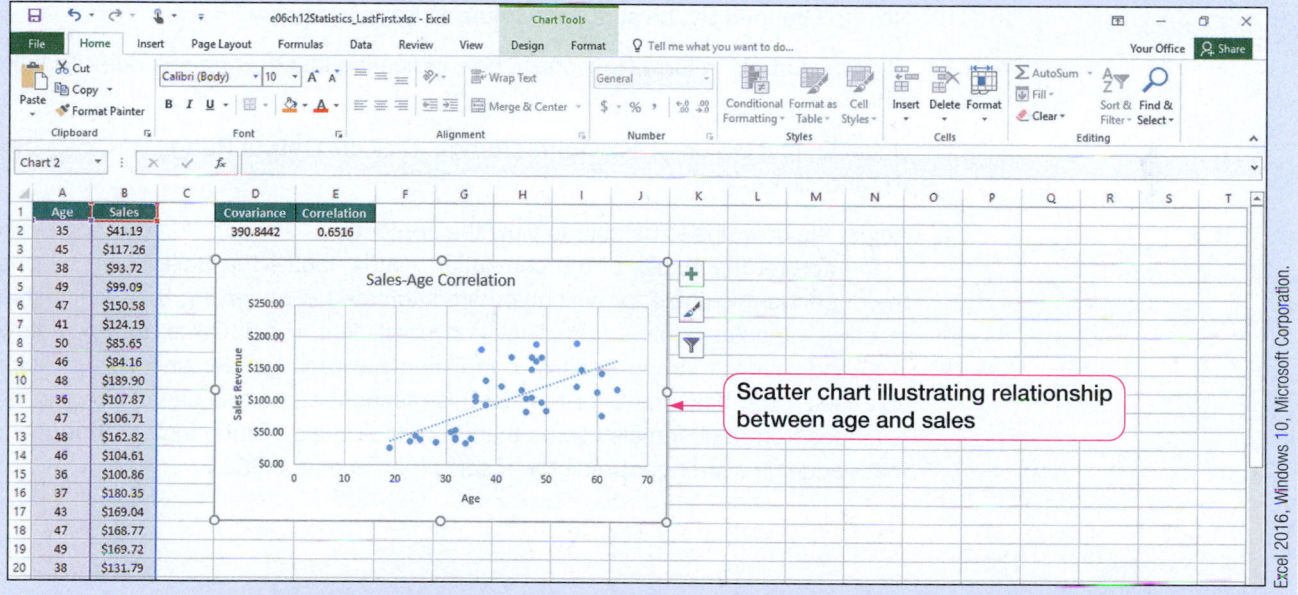

Figure 26   Scatter chart with a trendline

h. **Save** 💾 the document.

Determine Relationships Between Multiple Variables Using a Correlation Matrix

Calculating the correlation coefficient using the CORREL function is useful to determine the type and strength of a relationship between two variables. However, in business, there may be several independent variables that affect a dependent variable. For example, age of customers may not be the only variable that has a relationship with revenue; gender and income could also be factors.

Using the Analysis ToolPak to Create a Correlation Matrix

To calculate the correlation coefficients of several different variables, the Analysis ToolPak offers a method to create a correlation matrix. In this exercise, you create a correlation matrix of three different variables. You have been given a random sample of customer data with age and gender along with the amount of money spent on a given visit to the spa. Since gender is listed as either male or female in the data set provided, you must first convert it to numerical nominal data using an IF function.

 E12.19

To Create a Correlation Matrix Using the Analysis ToolPak

a. Click the **CorrelationMatrix** worksheet.

b. Click cell **B2**, and then type **=IF(** to begin an IF function.

c. Click cell **A2**, type **="Male",1,2)**, and then press ⎡Ctrl⎤ + ⎡Enter⎤ to create nominal data that can be used in the correlation calculation for gender, where male = 1 and female = 2.

d. Use the **AutoFill** handle to copy the formula to **B37**.

e. Click the **Data** tab, and then click **Data Analysis**.

f. In the list of Analysis tools, select **Correlation**, and then click **OK**.

g. Click the **Input Range** box, and then select the cell range **B1:D37**.

h. Next to Grouped By, be sure that **Columns** is selected.

i. Click the **Labels in First Row** check box, indicating that the first row does contain labels.

j. Under Output options, click **Output Range**, click the **Output Range** box, click cell **F1**, and click **OK**.

k. Adjust the columns to be able to view the contents.

   To interpret the results of the correlation matrix, locate the Sales row. Sales is the dependent variable for which you are interested in observing the relationship to other variables. Notice the correlation coefficient in cell G4 is approximately .746, indicating a strong positive correlation between gender and sales. Since you used 1 for male and 2 for female, this means that the spa can expect higher revenues from their female clients than from their male clients. In fact, it appears that gender is a stronger predictor of sales than age, at 0.652.

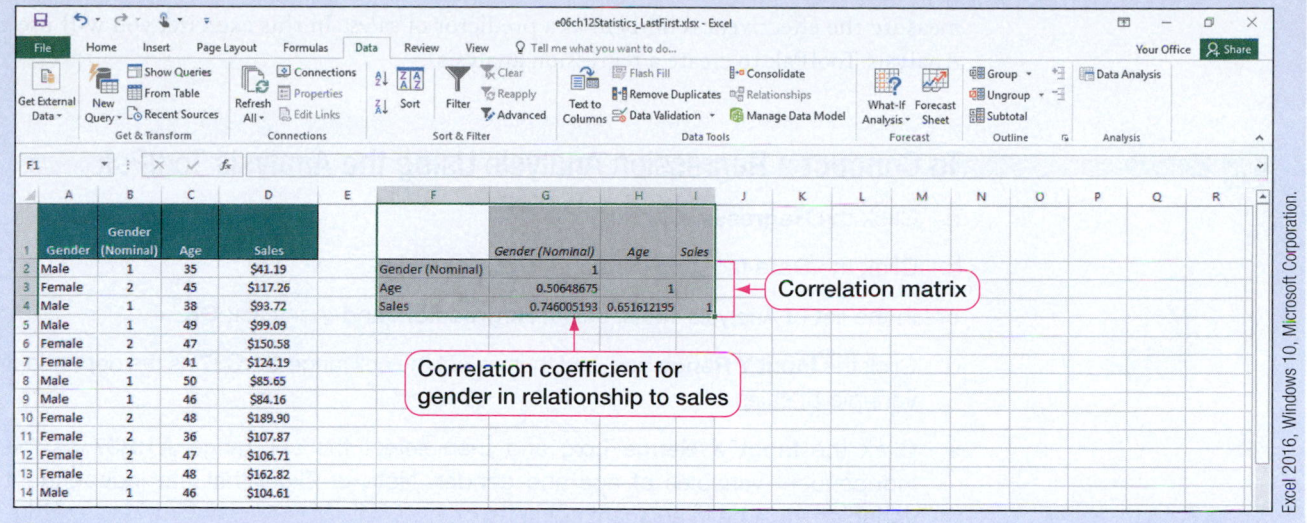

Figure 27 Correlation matrix showing the relationship between multiple variables

SIDE NOTE

Hover to See Icon Information

Remember, when you are presented with a set of icons such as the chart types, that when you hover the mouse over an icon, a ScreenTip appears to offer descriptive information.

I. **Save** the document.

CONSIDER THIS | **Direction of Relationship**

In the example above, you attributed the value of 1 for male and 2 for female. The result of the correlation matrix indicated a strong positive relationship between gender and sales. What would happen to the direction of the relationship between gender and sales if you attributed the value of 1 to female and 2 for male?

Use Regression Analysis to Predict Future Values

The next step in statistical analysis is to put your assumptions to the test and determine whether the relationships between the data are strong enough to make predictions about future events. **Regression analysis** is a method used to predict future values by analyzing the relationships between two or more variables. You will examine the relationship between age and gender of your clients and sales a bit further to determine whether the combination of age and gender is a good predictor of revenue.

Creating a Regression Analysis Using the Analysis ToolPak

Excel's Analysis ToolPak provides an easy way to conduct a regression analysis on two or more variables. One distinction between the variables that must be made up front is which variable is the dependent variable and which is the independent variable. In this scenario, the sales are the dependent variable because sales are what you want to be able to predict. Age and gender become the independent variables, and you want to be able to measure the effectiveness of them as a predictor of sales. In this exercise, you will use the Analysis ToolPak to create a regression analysis.

 **E12.20**

To Conduct a Regression Analysis Using the Analysis ToolPak

a. Click the **Regression** worksheet.

b. Click the **Data** tab, and then click **Data Analysis**.

c. In the list of Analysis Tools, select **Regression**, and then click **OK**.

d. Click the **Input Y Range** box, and then select the cell range **C1:C37** as the dependent variable of sales.

e. Click the **Input X Range** box, and then select the cell range **A1:B37** as the independent variables of age and gender. Note in Excel that the independent variables must be in adjacent columns.

f. Click the **Labels** check box to indicate that the label fields were included in the selection.

g. Under Output options, click **Output Range**.

h. Click the **Output Range** box, click cell **E10**, and then click **OK**.

i. Adjust the columns as necessary so that all values are visible in the SUMMARY OUTPUT.

The summary output produced by the Regression tool includes a lot of information. However, the key to its interpretation is in three values.

- R-squared
- Intercept coefficient
- Age coefficient

The **R-squared** value, in cell F14 of the SUMMARY OUTPUT, was calculated by squaring the correlation coefficient, labeled as Multiple R in the output. This provides a more conservative estimate of the independent variable's ability to predict the value of the dependent variable.

As you can see, the R-squared value is approximately 0.657, or 65.7%. This can be interpreted as age and gender accounting for 65.7% of the sales revenue generated by a customer.

The **intercept coefficient** value, in cell F26 of the SUMMARY OUTPUT, is the value at which a regression line will cross the y-axis and is used in the slope intercept formula to predict values.

The intercept coefficient value is approximately −46.7.

The regression equation includes the intercept coefficient value (approximately −46.7), along with the age coefficient and gender coefficient to predict the value of the dependent variable. The age coefficient in cell F27 is approximately 1.59, and the gender coefficient in cell F28 is approximately 56.26.

The resulting regression equation in the context of age, gender, and sales is as follows.

Sales (Y) = (age * 1.59) + (gender * 56.26) + −46.7

In this exercise, you will create regression equations for several combinations of age and genders.

 E12.21

To Use the Regression Equation to Predict Values

a. Click cell **G3**, and type **=(** to begin constructing the regression equation.

b. Click cell **E3**, type *****, click cell **F27**, and press F4 .

c. Type **)+(**, click cell **F3**, and type *****. Click cell **F28**, press F4 , and type **)+**.

d. Click cell **F26**, press F4 , and then press Ctrl + Enter to complete the regression equation to predict the sales revenue generated by a client who is 45 years of age and female.

e. Use the **AutoFill** handle to copy the formula to **G6**.

Notice that the sales revenue estimate based on age is closer to some of the actual values near the same age and gender but farther away on others. This is because, as the R-squared value indicates, age and gender account for only 65.7% of the revenue. Other variables also have an effect on revenue, such as income levels, time of visit, and perhaps even weather.

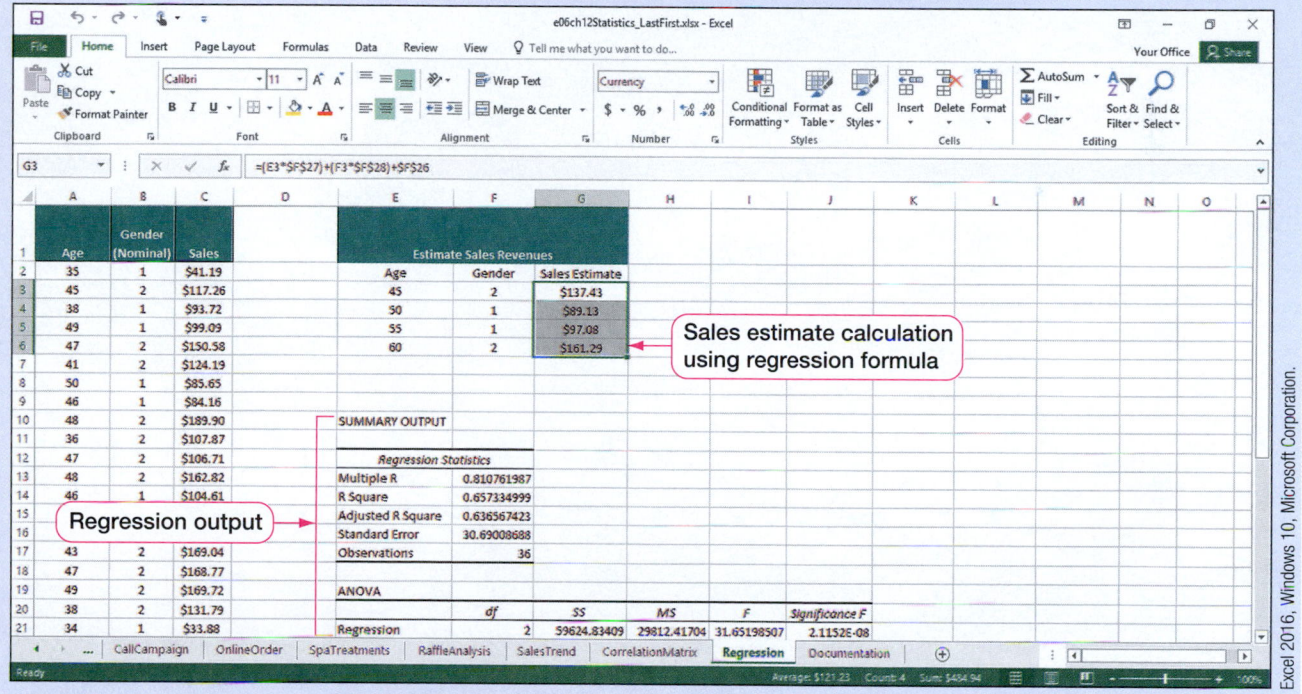

Figure 28 Regression analysis and predicted sales values

f. Complete the Documentation worksheet.

g. **Save** 🖫 the workbook, exit Excel, and then submit your file as directed by your instructor.

You could improve the accuracy of this statistical model by collecting additional customer data and running the regression analysis with other independent variables. Additional or alternative independent variables could increase the R-squared value, possibly indicating a more accurate predictor(s) of sales revenue.

Generally, the overall model is considered statistically significant in predicting the dependent variable if the Significance F value (in cell J21) is less than 0.05. Each independent variable is considered statistically significant if its p-value (cells I27 and I28) is less than 0.05.

Concept Check

1. Discuss the difference between population and sample data. Which one is used more often in statistics? Why? p. 636

2. Describe the four types of data used in statistics. What is an example of each type? p. 637

3. Discuss how calculating the range, variance, and standard deviation of a data set can help to spot differences in two data sets with the same mean. p. 641

4. What is a histogram, and how is it beneficial for understanding data? p. 649

5. What are two probability distributions used in business? What is one practical application for each? p. 652

6. What are covariance and correlation, and what can they tell you about data? p. 664

7. What can be learned from a correlation matrix? p. 668

8. What is the R-squared value, and how is it related to the correlation coefficient? p. 670

Key Terms

Visual Summary

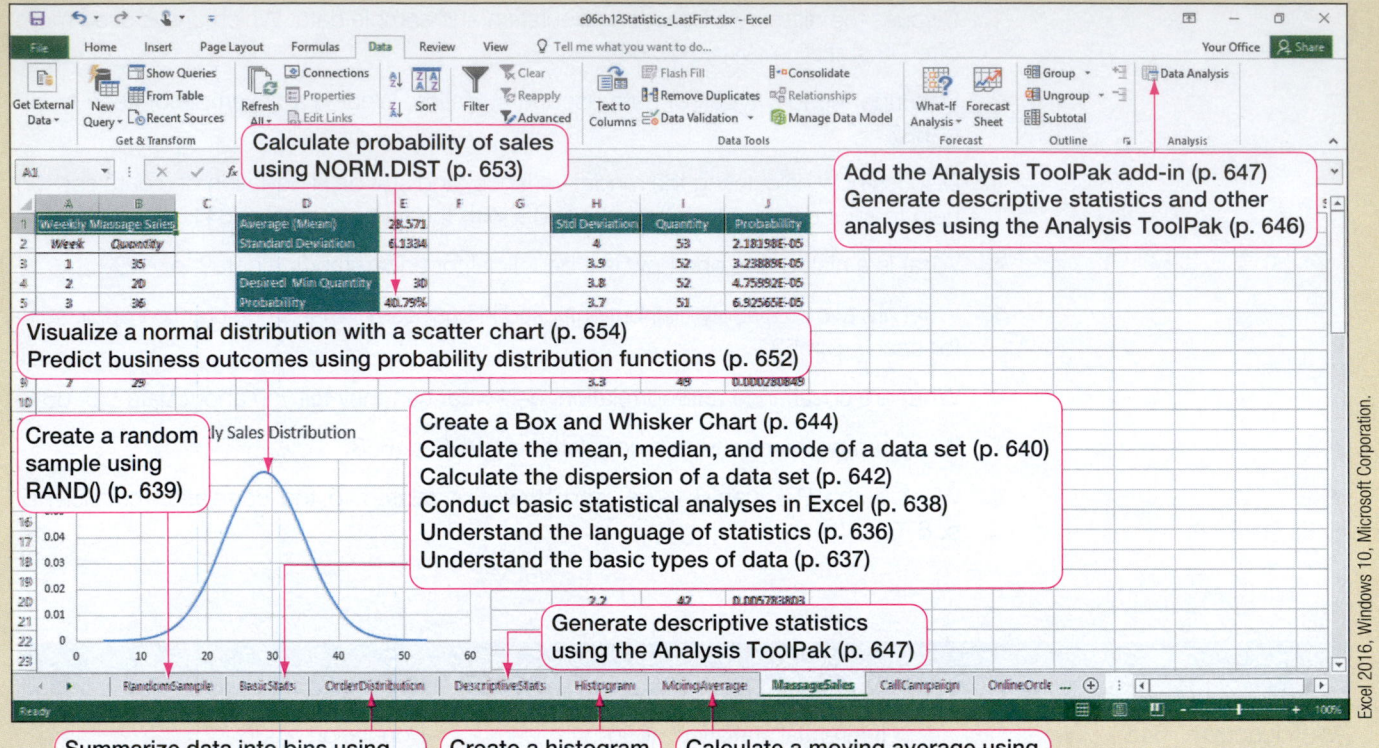

Calculate probability of sales using NORM.DIST (p. 653)

Add the Analysis ToolPak add-in (p. 647)
Generate descriptive statistics and other analyses using the Analysis ToolPak (p. 646)

Visualize a normal distribution with a scatter chart (p. 654)
Predict business outcomes using probability distribution functions (p. 652)

Create a random sample using RAND() (p. 639)

Create a Box and Whisker Chart (p. 644)
Calculate the mean, median, and mode of a data set (p. 640)
Calculate the dispersion of a data set (p. 642)
Conduct basic statistical analyses in Excel (p. 638)
Understand the language of statistics (p. 636)
Understand the basic types of data (p. 637)

Generate descriptive statistics using the Analysis ToolPak (p. 647)

Summarize data into bins using the FREQUENCY function (p. 646)

Create a histogram (p. 649)

Calculate a moving average using the Analysis ToolPak (p. 651)

Excel 2016, Windows 10, Microsoft Corporation.

Figure 29

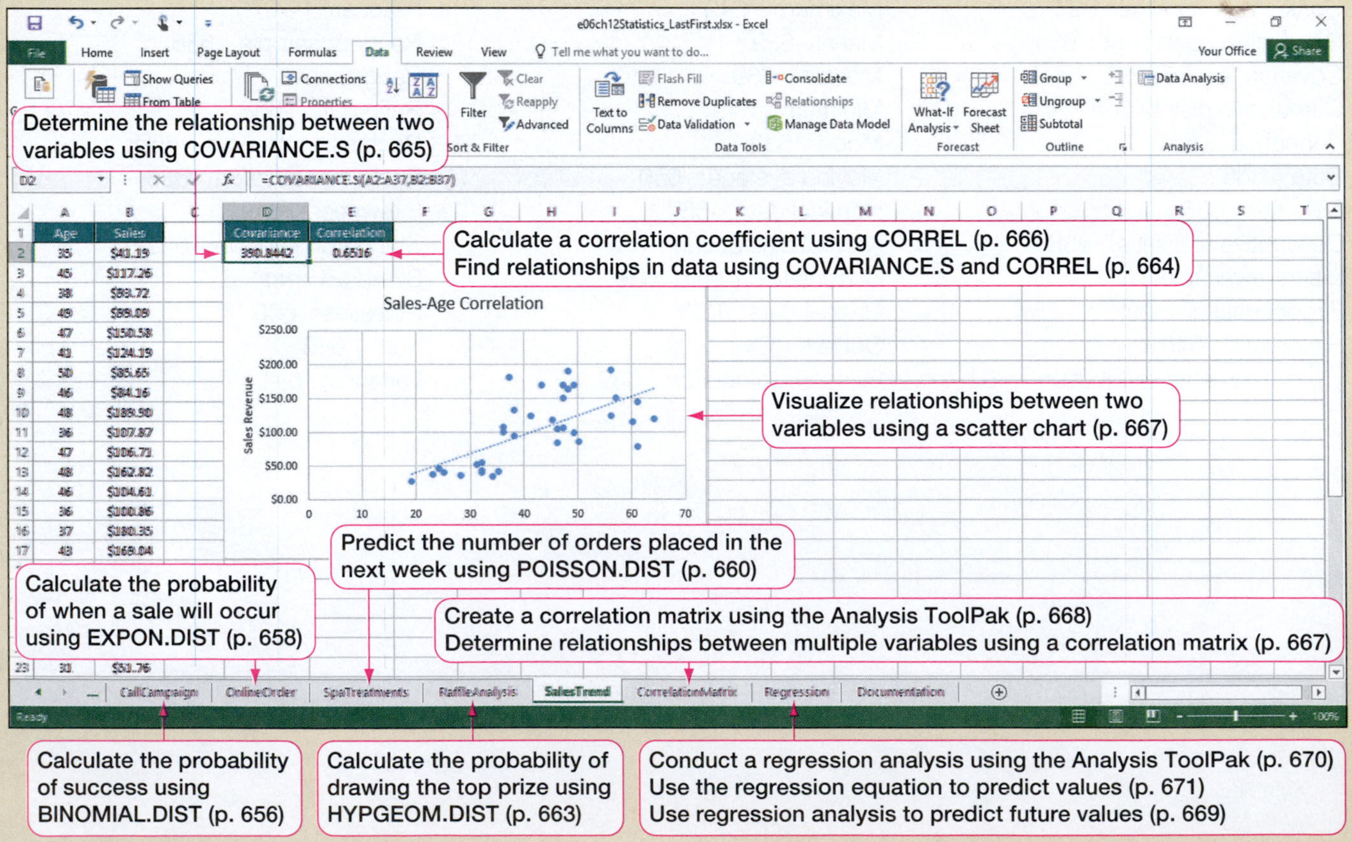

Determine the relationship between two variables using COVARIANCE.S (p. 665)

Calculate a correlation coefficient using CORREL (p. 666)
Find relationships in data using COVARIANCE.S and CORREL (p. 664)

Visualize relationships between two variables using a scatter chart (p. 667)

Predict the number of orders placed in the next week using POISSON.DIST (p. 660)

Calculate the probability of when a sale will occur using EXPON.DIST (p. 658)

Create a correlation matrix using the Analysis ToolPak (p. 668)
Determine relationships between multiple variables using a correlation matrix (p. 667)

Calculate the probability of success using BINOMIAL.DIST (p. 656)

Calculate the probability of drawing the top prize using HYPGEOM.DIST (p. 663)

Conduct a regression analysis using the Analysis ToolPak (p. 670)
Use the regression equation to predict values (p. 671)
Use regression analysis to predict future values (p. 669)

Excel 2016, Windows 10, Microsoft Corporation.

Figure 30

Student data file needed:

 e06ch12Sales.xlsx

You will save your file as:

 e06ch12Sales_LastFirst.xlsx

Statistical Analysis of Sales Data

Sales & Marketing

Angela is the president of PetInk, a company that specializes in memorializing pets in charcoal drawings. Her company has been extremely successful in selling charcoal sketches along with pet supplies and grooming services. She has collected data for four regions within theUnited States over the past year and has realized the need for analyzing her sales data. You will create a workbook that includes statistical analyses so she can better understand her business, such as predicting sales and the probability of reaching the forecasted sales figures.

a. Open the Excel file, **e06ch12Sales**. Save your file as e06ch12Sales_LastFirst using your last and first name.

b. Click the **Sales Data** worksheet, click cell **K2**, and then type =AVERAGE(E3:E962) to calculate the mean sales revenue. Press Enter.

c. Click cell **K3**, and then type =STDEV.S(E3:E962) to calculate the standard deviation. Press Enter.

d. Click cell **K4**, and then type =COVARIANCE.S(E3:E962,F3:F962) to calculate the covariance between the monthly sales and the number of items sold. Press Enter.

e. Click cell **K5**, type =CORREL(E3:E962,F3:F962) to calculate the correlation coefficient that describes the type and strength of the relationships between the two variables. Press Enter.

f. Create a box and whisker chart that displays the sales revenue. Select the cell range **E3:E962**. Click the **Insert** tab, in the Charts group, click **Insert Statistic Chart**, and click **Box and Whisker**.

g. Reposition the chart to fit within the cell range **J7:M20**. Change the Chart Title to Revenue. Click the **Chart Elements** button, click **Axes**, and then click **Primary Horizontal**.

h. Create a histogram that displays the sales volume. Select the cell range **F3:F962**. Click the **Insert** tab, in the Charts group, click **Insert Statistic Chart**, and then click **Histogram**.

i. Reposition the chart to fit within the cell range **J22:M35**. Change the Chart Title to Sales Volume.

j. Click outside the chart area, click the **Data** tab, and then, in the Analyze group, click **Data Analysis**. In the Data Analysis dialog box, select **Regression**, and then click **OK**.

k. Click the **Input Y Range** box, and then select the cell range **F2:F962**. Click **the Input X Range** box, and then select the cell range **E2:E962**. Click the **Labels** check box. Click **Output Range**, click the **Output Range** box, click cell **N2**, and then click **OK**. Adjust the columns as necessary so all the data from the Summary Output can be viewed.

   Notice that in the box and whisker chart, there are several data points with large revenue values. The correlation indicates a moderate correlation. The model would not be considered statistically significant, as the Significance F value is greater than 0.05.

l. Click the **Store Successes** worksheet. In cell **B1**, type 80 as the number of company stores. Press Enter. In cell **B2**, type .22 as the success rate of total stores meeting the sales forecast. Press Enter.

m. In cell **B5**, type =BINOM.DIST(A5,$B$1,$B$2, FALSE) to calculate the probability of there being exactly 0 successes using the binomial distribution function. Use the **AutoFill** handle to copy the function to **B45**.

n. Click the **Documentation** worksheet. Click cell A6, and then type in today's date. Click cell **B6**, and then type in your first and last name. Complete the remainder of the **Documentation** worksheet according to your instructor's direction.

o. Save the workbook, exit Excel, and then submit your file as directed by your instructor.

Problem Solve 1

Student data file needed:

 e06ch12Coffee.xlsx

You will save your file as:

e06ch12Coffee_LastFirst.xlsx

Sales Volume Analysis

Sales & Marketing

Coffee House Blues is a local coffee shop that offers tasty coffee beverages and live blues and blues-inspired music. You have been asked to conduct some statistical analysis on the shop's sales volume data. Coffee House Blues is also in the middle of promoting an upcoming blues festival and would like you to calculate the probabilities of selling specific numbers of tickets.

a. Open the Excel file **e06ch12Coffee**. Save your file as e06ch12Coffee_LastFirst using your last and first name.

b. Click the **SalesVolume** worksheet tab. In cell **G1**, calculate the mean of the sales volume. In cell **G2**, calculate the sample standard deviation.

c. In cell **B2**, calculate the probability of selling the exact number of products calculated in cell **A2**, using the normal distribution function and the mean and sample standard deviation calculated in the prior step. Use the **AutoFill** handle to copy the formula to **B82**.

d. Create a scatter chart with smooth lines to graph the distribution of sales volume and probabilities.

e. Give the chart the title of Sales Volume Distribution.

f. Reposition the chart within the cell range **E4:K18**.

g. Click the **Tickets** worksheet. In cell **B1**, type 50 as the number of people contacted in the trial.

h. In cell **B2**, type .2 as the success rate of selling tickets to the festival. Format the cell as **Percentage**.

i. In cell **B5**, calculate the probability of there being exactly 0 successes using the binomial distribution function. Format the cell as **Percentage** with **3** decimal places.

j. Use the **AutoFill** handle to copy the function to **B55**.

k. Complete the **Documentation** worksheet according to your instructor's direction.

l. Save the workbook, exit Excel, and then submit your file as directed by your instructor.

Student data file needed:

e06ch12Thick.xlsx

You will save your file as:

e06ch12Thick_LastFirst.xlsx

Production & Operations

Errors, Errors and More Errors

You work for a coating company that applies film to glass. The film applied to the glass has a specific thickness it must achieve. In the past, your company has experienced quality issues that have resulted in higher costs, lower revenue, and dissatisfied customers. As a result, your company is considering the purchase of a new machine to improve the quality. The vendor of the machine has graciously allowed your company a trial use of the machine to ensure that you can obtain the necessary quality. Twenty-five units have been run through the machine, and the thickness of the film has been measured. Your boss has asked you to perform a statistical analysis on the data to determine whether the company should purchase the machine. The results have been input into a workbook.

a. Start Excel, and then open the **e06ch12Thick** workbook. Save it as e06ch12Thick_LastFirst.

b. On the Thickness worksheet, the cell range B4:B28 contains the results of the 25 tests in micrometers. Use the Analysis ToolPak add-in to insert Descriptive Statistics starting in cell D3.

c. Enter the desired thickness of 542 micrometers, and calculate the probability of obtaining a film that is exactly that thickness in cells H3 and H4 respectively.

d. Create 11 bins between 541.5 and 542.5 in increments of .1 to use in the CSE formula FREQUENCY. Place your column headings in G6 and G7 with the Bins and FREQUENCY functions beneath.

e. Create a Histogram chart. Accept the default number of bins, and label the chart appropriately. Place the chart to the right of your Bins and FREQUENCY functions.

f. Create a Moving Average Chart, available in the Analysis ToolPak. The interval should be 2. Place the data and accompanying chart below your Descriptive Statistics.

g. Create a box and whisker chart to visualize any outliers in the data. Label the chart appropriately, and remove the primary horizontal axes. Place the chart to the right of your Histogram.

h. Create a Binomial Distribution using 15 trials and the probability of success of 75%. Place this data to the right of your Moving Average chart.

i. Given that the film must be 542 +/− 0.2 micrometers thick, should your company purchase the machine? Enter your decision in cell B2 (Yes or No).

j. Format the worksheet appropriately.

k. Complete the **Documentation** worksheet according to your instructor's direction.

l. Click Save, close Excel, and then submit your file as directed by your instructor.

Additional Cases

Additional Workshop Cases are available on the companion website and in the instructor resources.

Building Financial and Statistical Models

This business unit had two outcomes:

Learning Outcome 1:

Using Excel financial functions, construct a loan analysis, calculate cumulative interest and principal, create an amortization schedule, analyze bonds and investments, and calculate depreciation of assets.

Learning Outcome 2:

Understand statistical language, understand the basic types of data, conduct a statistical analysis using Excel functions and the Analysis ToolPak, predict outcomes using probability distributions, use correlations and covariance to find relationships in data, and use regression analysis to predict future values.

In Business Unit 6 Capstone, students will demonstrate competence in these outcomes through a series of business problems at various levels from guided practice to problem solving an existing spreadsheet and performing to create new spreadsheets.

More Practice 1

Student data file needed:

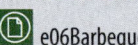 e06Barbeque.xlsx

You will save your file as:

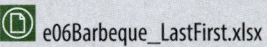 e06Barbeque_LastFirst.xlsx

Borrowing Money for a New Business

Finance & Accounting

You have been complimented many times on your cooking ability, and people love your barbeque. In the past, you have catered events out of your home. You would like to purchase a food truck and begin to sell your barbeque and other specialties to local customers. To apply for a business loan, you need to set up a model that will help you analyze the loan you need to move forward with your plan. You will develop a spreadsheet model to help determine how much of a loan you can afford. You also want to analyze last year's sales data using statistical functions and calculate the depreciation of assets.

a. Start **Excel**, click **Open Other Workbooks** in the left pane, and then double-click **This PC**. Navigate through the folder structure to the location of your student data files, and then double-click **e06Barbeque**. A workbook opens displaying investment options for the business.

b. Click the **File** tab, click **Save As**, and then double-click **This PC**. In the **Save As** dialog box, navigate to the location where you are saving your project files, and then change the filename to **e06Barbeque_LastFirst** using your last and first name. Click **Save**.

c. Click the **Loan Amortize** worksheet, and then complete the following tasks to calculate the number of loan payments, the end of the period payments, the total to be paid, and the total interest to be paid.

- Click cell **G5**, type **=C7*C8**, and then press Enter.
- In cell **G6**, type **=PMT(C6/C8,G5,-C5)**, and then press Enter.
- In cell **G7**, type **=G6*G5**, and then press Enter.
- In cell **G8**, type **=G7-C5**, and then press Enter.

d. Complete the following tasks to construct an amortization schedule in the cell range C12:G35.

- Click cell **C12**, type **=C5**, and then press Tab.
- In cell **D12**, type **=$G$6**, and then press Tab.

- In cell **E12**, type =IPMT($C$6/12,A12,$G$5,-$C$5), and then press Tab.
- In cell **F12**, type =PPMT($C$6/$C$8,A12,$G$5,-$C$5), and then press Tab.
- In cell **G12**, type =C12-F12, and then press Enter.
- Click cell **C13**, type =G12, and then press Ctrl + Enter. Use the **AutoFill** handle to copy the formula down to cell **C35**.
- Select range **D12:G12**. Use the **AutoFill** handle to copy the formula down to range **D13:G35**.

e. Create formulas to calculate the cumulative interest and cumulative principal.

- Click cell **I12**, type =-CUMIPMT($C$6/$C$8,$G$5,$C$5,$A$12,A12,0), and then press Ctrl + Enter. Use the **Autofill** handle to copy the formula down to cell **I35**.
- Click cell **J12**, type =-CUMPRINC($C$6/$C$8,$G$5,$C$5,$A$12,A12,0), and then press Ctrl + Enter. Use the **Autofill** handle to copy the formula down to cell **J35**.

f. Click the **Depreciation** worksheet. Click cell **B16**, type =IRR(B14:E14), and then press Enter to calculate the internal rate of return.

g. Complete the following tasks to calculate the straight-line depreciation schedule of the equipment.

- Click cell **H10**, type =SLN($G$6,$H$6,$I$6), and then press Ctrl + Enter. Use the **Autofill** handle to copy the formula down to cell **H14**.
- Click cell **I10**, type =H10, and then press Enter. In cell **I11**, type =I10+H11, and then press Ctrl + Enter. Use the **Autofill** handle to copy the formula down to cell **I14**.
- Click cell **J10**, type =$G$6-I10, and then press Ctrl + Enter. Use the **Autofill** handle to copy the formula down to cell **J14**.

h. Complete the following tasks to calculate the declining balance depreciation schedule.

- Click cell **H17**, type =DB($G$6,$H$6,$I$6,G17), and then press Ctrl + Enter. Use the **Autofill** handle to copy the formula down to cell **H21**.
- Click cell **I17**, type =H17, and then press Enter. In cell **I18**, type =I17+H18, and then press Ctrl + Enter. Use the **Autofill** handle to copy the formula down to cell **I21**.
- Click cell **J17**, type =$G$6-I17, and then press Ctrl + Enter. Use the **Autofill** handle to copy the formula down to cell **J21**.

i. Complete the following tasks to calculate the double declining balance depreciation schedule.

- Click cell **H24**, type =DDB($G$6,$H$6,$I$6,G24), and then press Ctrl + Enter. Use the **Autofill** handle to copy the formula down to cell **H28**.
- Click cell **I24**, type =H24, and then press Enter. In cell **I25**, type =I24+H25, and then press Ctrl + Enter. Use the **Autofill** handle to copy the formula down to cell **I28**.
- Click cell **J24**, type =$G$6-I24, and then press Ctrl + Enter. Use the **Autofill** handle to copy the formula down to cell **J28**.

j. Click the **Statistical Analysis** worksheet. Complete the following tasks to create descriptive statistics from the 2017 sales data.

- Click the **Data** tab, and then, in the Analyze group, click **Data Analysis**. In the Data Analysis dialog box, select **Descriptive Statistics**, and then click **OK**.
- In the **Input Range** box, type $B$3:$B$15, verify that **Columns** is selected as the Grouped by option, and then check the **Labels in First Row** check box.
- Click **Output Range**, and in the **Output Range** box, type $D$4, and then check the **Summary statistics** check box. Click **OK**.

k. Click cell **H13**, and then type =1-NORM.DIST(H12,E6,E10,TRUE) to calculate the probability of selling 300 racks of ribs in week eight.

l. Click cell **K4**, type =J4*$E$10+$E$6 to calculate what the sales revenue would be if it were equal to four standard deviations above the mean, and then press [Ctrl] + [Enter]. Use the **AutoFill** handle to copy the formula down to **K84** (four standard deviations below the mean).

m. Click cell **L4**, type =NORM.DIST(K4,$E$6,$E$10,FALSE) to calculate the probability that the sales revenue will be exactly four standard deviations above the mean in a given week, and then press [Ctrl] + [Enter]. Use the **AutoFill** handle to copy the formula down to **L84** (four standard deviations below the mean).

n. Select cells **K4:L84**, and then click the **Insert** tab. In the Charts group, click **Insert Scatter (X, Y)**, and then select the **Scatter with Smooth Lines** chart. Move the chart so the top left corner is in the top left corner of cell **A22**. Resize the chart so the bottom right corner is in the bottom right corner of cell **H39**. Click the **Chart Title** text box, and then replace Chart Title with **Weekly Sales Revenue**.

o. Complete the **Documentation** worksheet according to your instructor's direction.

p. Click **Save**, exit Excel, and then submit your file as directed by your instructor.

Problem Solve 1

MyITLab® Grader
Homework

Student data file needed:
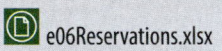 e06Reservations.xlsx

You will save your file as:
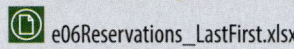 e06Reservations_LastFirst.xlsx

Hotel Reservations Analysis and Predictions

Sales & Marketing

The majority of reservations for the hotel at the Painted Paradise Resort & Spa are made online. On average an online reservation is placed every 17.9 minutes. You have been asked to use the exponential probability distribution function to estimate when the next online reservations will take place. You will also calculate a moving average of weekly revenues and use the Poisson probability distribution to estimate the number of reservations over the next five days.

a. Open the Excel file **e06Reservations**. Save your file as **e06Reservations_LastFirst** using your last and first name.

b. Click the **OnlineReservations** worksheet, and create a statistical model that will estimate when the next ten online reservations will occur, as well as the probability of an online reservation occurring within 12—20 minutes.

   • In cell **A5**, use the Exponential probability distribution function to calculate the probability that the next online reservation will be made within two minutes. Use the **AutoFill** handle to copy the function down to cell **A34**.

   • In cell **D3**, create a formula that will estimate when the next ten online reservations will take place, using a random variable. Use the **AutoFill** handle to copy the function down to cell **D12**. If the formula results in an error, the value **2** should be displayed.

   • In cell **F2**, create a formula that will calculate the probability of the next online reservation occurring within 12—20 minutes.

c. On the **ReservationRevenue** worksheet, create a moving average and a statistical model that will estimate the number of room reservations each day for the next five days.

   • In cells **C2:C13**, use the Analysis ToolPak to create a Moving Average for every three weeks. Include a chart with the output. Position the chart so that the upper left corner begins in cell **A15**.

   • Create a statistical model using the Poisson distribution function. In cell **F25**, calculate the mean number of reservations.

- In cell **H2**, use the Poisson probability distribution function to calculate the probability of 50 or fewer reservations. Use the **AutoFill** handle to copy the function down to **H22**.
- In cells **K3:K7**, use the RAND function to create random variables. Copy and Paste Values so that the random variables do not change every time the worksheet is calculated.
- In cells **L3:L7**, create a formula that will estimate the number of reservations that will take place over the next five days. If the formula results in an error, the value **50** should be displayed.

d. Complete the **Documentation** worksheet according to your instructor's direction.

e. Save the workbook, exit Excel, and then submit your file as directed by your instructor.

Problem Solve 2

MyITLab®
Grader
Homework

Student data file needed: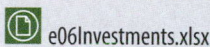
e06Investments.xlsx

You will save your file as: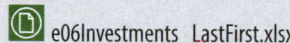
e06Investments_LastFirst.xlsx

Investment Analysis

Production & Operations

You have been asked to analyze some investments for the company you work for. The first is a bond analysis in which you are given the par value, coupon rate, maturity, and yield to maturity for two different bonds to consider. For each bond, you will calculate the present value to determine which investment is better. Next you will analyze the historical performance of two stocks to compare for investing.

a. Open the Excel file **e06Investments**. Save your file as e06Investments_LastFirst using your last and first name.

b. On the **Bond Analysis** worksheet, use the values provided to calculate the coupon payment for each bond in cells B5 and C5.

c. In cell **B7**, calculate the present value of the first bond, using the data provided and the coupon payment.

d. In cell **C7**, calculate the present value of the second bond, using the data provided and the coupon payment.

e. Add formatting to the worksheet to provide a professional appearance.

f. The **Historical Performance** worksheet contains closing stock prices for two stocks in the cell ranges **B2:B37** and **C2:C37**. Calculate the mean, median, sample standard deviation, min, max, and range for each of the closing stock prices. Place the calculations for Stock #1 in the cell range F2:F7 and the calculations for Stock #2 in the cell range G2:G7. Format the calculations appropriately.

g. Create two histograms to further explore the distribution of the closing prices for each stock. Place the first histogram approximately in the cell range **E9:K22**. Place the second histogram in the cell range **M9:S22**.

h. Change the title of the first histogram to Stock #1 Closing Prices. Change the title of the second histogram to Stock #2 Closing Prices.

i. Complete the **Documentation** worksheet according to your instructor's direction.

j. Save the workbook, exit Excel, and then submit your file as directed by your instructor.

Critical Thinking

Considering the present values you calculated for each of the bonds on the Bond Analysis worksheet, which bond would you choose? Examining the stock data further, what differences exist in the stock performances? What other types of charts would be appropriate for examining the data provided?

Student data file needed:

 Blank Excel workbook

You will save your file as:

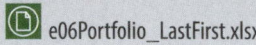 e06Portfolio_LastFirst.xlsx

Personal Investment Analysis

Finance & Accounting

Financial decisions are a part of our lives, and knowing how to properly analyze investment options is crucial to making good investment decisions. In this exercise, you will analyze two different investment options.

a. Start **Excel**, and then create a new workbook. Save the file as **e06Portfolio_LastFirst** using your last and first name.

b. Rename the Sheet1 worksheet to **Option1**.

c. Set up the worksheet to calculate the irregular net present value of an investment by using the following information.

- Initial investment amount: **$7,500.00**
- Discount rate of **3.5%**
- Expected incoming cash flows are to occur on the following dates:

Dates	Cash Flows
1/1/2018	−$7,500.00
2/15/2018	$1,750.00
4/15/2018	$1,500.00
8/20/2018	$2,350.00
10/20/2018	$1,900.00
12/20/2018	$850.00

- Format all cash flow values as **Currency**.

d. Add a new worksheet to the right of Option1, and name it **Option2**.

e. Set up the worksheet to calculate the present value of an investment bond, using the following information.

- Par Value: **$7,500.00**
- Coupon Rate: **7%**
- Maturity: **3** years
- YTM: **5.2%**

f. Calculate the annual coupon payment.

g. Calculate the present value of the bond. Be sure the function returns a positive value.

h. Format all cells with appropriate formatting.

i. Add a new worksheet to the right of Option2, and name it **Option3**.

j. Set up the worksheet to calculate the internal rate of return of an investment, using the following expected future cash flows.

Year	Cash Flow
0	−$7,500.00
1	$4,950.00
2	$2,450.00
3	$1,750.00

k. Calculate the internal rate of return based on the series of expected cash flows.

l. Add formatting to each worksheet to give the file a professional appearance.

m. Insert the **file name** in the left custom footer section of the Header/Footer tab in the Page Setup dialog box on all worksheets in the workbook.

n. Save the workbook, exit Excel, and then submit your file as directed by your instructor.

Perform 2: Perform in Your Career

Student data file needed:

 e06Buy.xlsx

You will save your file as:

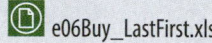 e06Buy_LastFirst.xlsx

Do We Need to Buy?

Production & Operations

You work for a motherboard manufacturing company in the Quality Assurance department. In your job, you are responsible for testing the motherboards to ensure that the proper voltage is getting to all components. On the basis of recent test results, you believe your company may need to consider purchasing a new solder wave board. Because these machines usually cost millions of dollars, you want to ensure that you have all your data validated and verified before you bring your findings to management. A failure rate greater than 2% is considered abnormal. Your immediate supervisor has begun a workbook with the most recent findings, which you will use to complete your analysis.

a. Open the Excel file **e06Buy**. Save the file as **e06Buy_LastFirst** using your last and first name.

b. On the **Volts** worksheet, use the Analysis ToolPak add-in to generate Descriptive Statistics concerning the volt data in column B. Place the output in cell **D4**. Autofit the contents of the columns to see all of the data.

c. Insert the CSE formula **FREQUENCY**, using the Bin array in the cell range **G6:G16**.

d. Create a box and whisker chart of the Volts data, and place the chart so that the upper left corner starts in cell **J5**. Delete the horizontal axis label, and provide an appropriate chart title.

e. Create a Moving Average Chart, available in the Analysis ToolPak. The interval should be **2**.

f. Move or adjust the chart (s) and data to improve the appearance of your worksheet.

g. The box and whisker chart identifies an outlier in your data. In which batch did the outlier appear? Place your answer in cell **B2**.

h. On the **Analysis** worksheet, calculate the monthly payments on the two loans in the worksheet. The first loan is for the repair of the machine; the second loan is for the purchase of a new one.

i. Complete the two partial amortization schedules, using IPMT and PPMT functions.

j. At the top of each amortization schedule, calculate the total interest and principal paid.

k. Complete the **Documentation** worksheet according to your instructor's direction.

l. Save the workbook, exit Excel, and then submit your file as directed by your instructor.

Student data file needed:

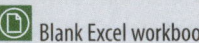 Blank Excel workbook

You will save your file as:

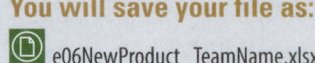 e06NewProduct_TeamName.xlsx

New Product Investment

Finance &
Accounting

You and a team of three to five other students have been presented with an investment opportunity. You need to conduct some statistical analysis on this new product investment opportunity. You will use the normal probability distribution to analyze the possible rates of return. You will also use the binomial probability distribution to analyze the number of successful trials one can expect from the product.

a. Select one team member to set up the database by completing steps b–d.

b. Open your browser, and navigate to https://www.onedrive.live.com, https://www.drive.google.com, or any other instructor-assigned location. Be sure all members of the team have an account on the chosen system, such as a Microsoft or Google account.

c. Create a new spreadsheet document, and name it **e06NewProduct_TeamName** using the name assigned to your team.

d. Rename Sheet1 as **Contributors**. List the names of the team members on the worksheet, and then add a heading above the names to read **Team Members**. Include any additional information on this worksheet as required by your instructor.

e. Share the spreadsheet with the other members of your team. Make sure each team member has the appropriate permission to edit the document.

f. Create a new worksheet entitled **ProductInvestment**. Set up the worksheet to create a normal probability distribution table, using the following information.

- Mean rate of return is **12.8%**.
- Standard deviation of the rate of return is **3.85%**.
- Create column headings for **Standard Deviations**, **ROR**, and **Probability**.
- Under the **Standard Deviations** heading, create a column of values ranging from **4** to **−4** in increments of .1.
- Under the **ROR** heading, calculate the value of ROR if it were to be four standard deviations from the mean, and then use **AutoFill** to copy the formula down the column.
- Under the **Probability** heading, calculate the probability that the ROR is exactly four standard deviations from the mean, and then use **AutoFill** to copy the function down the column.

g. Create a scatter chart with Smooth Lines to visualize the normal distribution.

- Give the chart a title of **ROR Probability Distribution**.
- Adjust the horizontal axis to have a minimum value of **−10%** and a maximum value of **30%**.
- Change the Label Position of the vertical axis to **Low**.
- Position the chart near the top of your probability distribution table.

h. Create a new worksheet entitled **ProductTesting**. The manufacturers of the new product claim that the product's battery will last for 12 hours 90% of the time. Set up the worksheet to calculate the probability of successful trials based on the following information.

- Number of Trials: **130**
- Success Rate: **85%**

- Calculate the probability of exactly 90 successful trials.
- Calculate the probability of no more than 100 successful trials.
- Calculate the probability of more than 110 successful trials.

i. Insert the **file name** in the left custom footer section of the Header/Footer tab in the Page Setup dialog box on all worksheets in the workbook. In a custom header section, include the **names** of the students in your team. Spread the names evenly across each of the three header sections: left section, center section, and right section.

j. Save the workbook, exit Excel, and then submit your file as directed by your instructor.

Perform 4: How Others Perform

Student data file needed:

e06Decisions.xlsx

You will save your file as: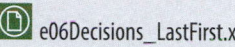

e06Decisions_LastFirst.xlsx

Analysis to Support Decision Making

Sales & Marketing

Finance & Accounting

Robert Smith, owner of a small but growing clothing store, is looking for ways to fund an expansion. He had an intern attempt to conduct some analysis on a possible loan and other investments, but Robert suspects that the analysis is not accurate, and he does not want to make any decisions until he is sure he can trust the analysis. The intern also attempted to conduct some statistical analysis on the business. Examine the worksheet, and correct any mistakes in the formulas and functions.

a. Start **Excel**, and then open the file **e06Decisions**. Save your file as e06Decisions_LastFirst using your last and first name.

b. On the **LoanAnalysis** worksheet, you will find a number of visible errors in the loan analysis conducted by the intern.
- Examine the function in cell **B6**. The RATE function is returning a #NUM! error message instead of the APR. Correct the formula, and then make sure it returns the correct APR according to the loan information in the cells above. Each loan payment is to be made at the beginning of the period.
- Examine the principal and interest payment formulas in the cell range **C11:D11**. The sum of those two calculations does not equal the monthly payment in cell B2. Correct both formulas so they equal the monthly payment, and then use **AutoFill** to copy the formulas down to the end of the amortization schedule.

c. Click the **Investments** worksheet tab. On this worksheet, you will find errors in various formulas and functions that cause the investment analysis to lead to bad decisions.
- Examine the formula in cell **B5** that is calculating the coupon payment. Make the necessary correction so the coupon payment is calculated correctly.
- Examine the PV function in cell **B7** for errors. The function is missing a cell reference for one of the arguments. Make the necessary corrections.
- Examine the NPV function in cell **E13** for errors. Make the necessary corrections to ensure that the Net Present Value is being calculated correctly.

d. Click the **Stats** worksheet. On this worksheet, you will find errors in various statistical functions.
- Examine the function in cell **B7**. This function should calculate the probability of earning no more than $13,000 in sales revenue. Examine the function, and then make the appropriate changes.
- Examine the function in cell **B8**. This function should calculate the probability of earning more than $12,500 in sales revenue. Examine the function, and then make the appropriate changes.

- Examine the function in cell **D6**. This function should calculate the probability of the next customer entering the store within the next five minutes. Examine the function, and then make the appropriate changes. Use **AutoFill** to copy the function down to cell **D17**.
- Examine the function in cell **L3**. The function in the cell range L3:L9 should calculate the frequency of values based on the data in the cell range I3:I17 and the bins in the cell range K3:K8. The function is an array function but has been created incorrectly. Examine the function, and then make the appropriate changes.
- Complete the **Documentation** worksheet according to your instructor's direction.

e. Save the workbook, exit Excel, and then submit the file as directed by your instructor.

Excel Business Unit 7

Enabling Decisions with Data Visualization and VBA

Business must make decisions quickly and accurately to maintain a competitive advantage in the global market. They can use digital dashboards to make sense of the vast amounts of data they are collecting. Features in Excel such as Power Pivot, Power View, form controls, and Visual Basic for Applications can create powerful dashboards that can be used to quickly gain information and knowledge from data. Power Pivot can connect data from various sources and visualize the data with PivotTables and PivotCharts. Power View can create sophisticated interactive visualizations. Form controls can enhance the usability and control data input on a worksheet. Finally, Visual Basic for Applications can provide powerful enhancements for dashboards. When combined, these tools can create powerful for decision making applications.

Learning Outcome 1:

Understand the basics of designing a dashboard, develop familiarity with the data model in Excel, develop data models using Power Pivot and create PivotTables and PivotCharts using Power Pivot, incorporate Office Add-ins in a dashboard, use Power View to generate reports, and prepare a dashboard for production.

REAL WORLD SUCCESS

"Over the summer, I worked as a consultant for a small clothing store in the Midwest. The management there was just starting to realize the benefits of making data-driven decisions. They used Excel for various accounting tasks but never really thought of it as a way to analyze large amounts of data. I was able to use the PowerPivot feature in Excel to build a data model that allowed for easy analysis of millions of records from multiple sources and create a simple dashboard to track various metrics. As a result, that company is making progress toward its goal of expanding its store locations."

- Lupe, recent graduate

Learning Outcome 2:

Use form controls to enhance spreadsheets, understand the components of VBA, improve the readability of VBA, use VBA to create custom functions and use loops in a Sub procedure, troubleshoot VBA, assign VBA procedures to events, and secure a workbook.

REAL WORLD SUCCESS

"I interned for an auto parts manufacturing plant last summer and was asked to assist with a data cleansing project. The person working on the project had spent hours cleaning the data and was not getting very far. I was able to use a little bit of VBA to loop through thousands of rows in a matter of minutes."

- Francis, recent graduate

Microsoft Excel 2016

Chapter 13 | THE EXCEL DATA MODEL AND BUSINESS INTELLIGENCE

Prepare Case

Sales & Marketing

The Red Bluff Golf Course & Pro Shop Dashboards, KPIs, and Data Visualizations

Management at the Red Bluff Golf Course & Pro Shop has been collecting data on the business for the past three years. The managers are looking for ways to create visualizations of their data to help make important strategic decisions about the future of the company and to solicit private investments in Red Bluff. You have been given access to a sample set of sales data from 2015-2017 and have been asked to conduct further analysis, create some useful visualizations of the data, and put together a dashboard of charts and tools for management to easily see the business from multiple perspectives. You will use the business intelligence features in Excel 2016 that are scalable for use with millions of records.

Lichtmeister/Shutterstock

Student data files needed for this chapter:

 e07ch13Sales.accdb

 e07ch13Analytics.xlsx

You will save your file as:

 e07ch13Analytics_LastFirst.xlsx

Exploring the Importance of Business Intelligence

Business intelligence is not just a buzzword. **Business intelligence (BI)** refers to a variety of software applications that are used to analyze an organization's data to provide management with the tools necessary to improve decision making, cut costs, and identify new opportunities. The role of BI has increased over the last decade because the amount of data being collected by businesses continues to grow at a rapid rate.

This increasing dependence on BI has manifested itself in many forms in the business community over the past few years. The most recent trend, which shows no signs of slowing, is the desire for digital dashboards. **Digital dashboards** are mechanisms that deliver BI in graphical form. Dashboards provide management with a big picture view of the business, usually from multiple perspectives using various charts and other graphical representations. There are many factors that are driving businesses to use the power of dashboards. Figure 1 shows the top pressures that are driving these dashboard initiatives according to Aberdeen Group, Inc., a provider of research to help organizations and individuals make better business decisions. In this section, you will learn about the dashboard design concepts, explore the Excel data model, conduct some analysis, and build a dashboard.

BUSINESS DRIVERS FOR DASHBOARD INITIATIVES	
Alignment of strategy and activities	27%
Improved timeliness and accuracy of business decisions	30%
The need for one view of the business date	33%
The need for data-driven decisions	37%
The need to gain visibility into key business processes	43%

Aberdeen Group

Source: Aberdeen Group, 2009

Figure 1 Top pressures driving dashboard initiatives

 CONSIDER THIS | Decisions, Decisions, Decisions . . .

A typical manager engages in over 300 different tasks and decisions each day. These often involve interacting with many different people, using a variety of different channels and technologies. The number of channels and technologies a manager must master is growing. Do you think technology increases, decreases, or holds steady the volume and speed of decision making today?

Understand the Basics of Dashboard Design

Dashboards are becoming more and more important today as a tool for helping managers run their businesses. Dashboards are no longer just for executives and are being integrated at all levels of the business and in many different industries. You will likely encounter them in other classes as you discuss management techniques such as Balanced Scorecards and Six Sigma. Both of these management initiatives involve generating key performance indicators and dashboard reports for all levels of the organization. Using dashboards, everyone from the CEO to the delivery truck driver can have a personalized view of information to see quickly and easily how well they are performing.

How a dashboard is designed has just as much of an impact on its effectiveness as does the data displayed. Think of the dashboard in a car. The gauges and layout of the dashboard are designed to help the driver make better decisions and interpret important things such as relative speed, gas consumption, and critical malfunctions in a very immediate and effective way. The driver has to monitor the situation constantly and make crucial decisions about what to do with the car. An effective dashboard supports effective decision making.

This analogy holds true for the "driver" of a company. A manager must be able to quickly review and monitor the current health of the company and make decisions in a timely manner to correct problems. A dashboard can be a huge help to a manager because it is specifically organized to provide relevant alerts and monitor the business as a whole. Typically, dashboards are oriented around specific business activities, such as sales analysis, cash flow, employee productivity, and customer service. Some typical features of a dashboard might include the following.

- A visually oriented single-screen user interface that is intuitive and easy to navigate
- Interactive controls that allow the user to customize the data display
- Integration of multiple types of data from a variety of sources
- Data that is updated frequently so it reflects the current situation
- Information oriented toward a specific problem or decision
- A layout that does not require a lot of training to use effectively

In Excel, dashboard components typically consist of tables, PivotTables, PivotCharts, conditional formatting, and other features. There are also some basic design concepts that you need to take into consideration when creating a dashboard.

Keeping It Simple

Adding more and more data and charts to a dashboard can be tempting. However, you must always keep in mind the basic principle: When it comes to dashboards, less is more. If users cannot easily interpret your dashboard, then you may have made it too complicated. An overly complicated dashboard is not usable as a management tool. Remember that one of the primary goals is to help the user navigate and interpret a large quantity of data at a glance.

Making Sure It Is Well Defined

Stay focused on a specific business problem. A company can track product sales, employee productivity, customer complaints, revenue, portfolio value, machine defects, and so on. However, doing all of these in the same dashboard is ill advised. As a general rule, the more defined you can make your theme, the more useful your users will find the dashboard.

Knowing Your Users

Not all users are alike. They can have different decision-making styles. You can increase the success of your dashboard by taking personal preferences into account whenever possible. You should interview the main users of the dashboard to see what they would find most useful. The earlier you can let them see your dashboard design, the fewer headaches you will have later in the project. Changes are easier to make early in development than they will be when you are almost done.

Defining Crucial KPIs

A **key performance indicator (KPI)** is a quantifiable measure that helps managers to define progress toward both short-term and long-term goals. Some KPIs are year-to-date (YTD) sales growth, customer satisfaction, call resolution rates, and percent of market share, as shown in the Quick Reference table. In fact, every functional area of business has its own set of commonly used KPIs. Often, many firms in the same industry will all focus on similar KPIs because they are so critical to the nature of their business — for example, profit margin.

QUICK REFERENCE	Commonly Used Business KPIs

Business Area	KPI
Accounting	• Gross profit • Operating margin • Cumulative annual growth rate • ROI (Return on investment) • Cost of goods sold
Finance/Accounting	• Gross yield • Price-to-earnings ratio (P/E) • Earnings before interest, taxes, depreciation, and amortization (EBITDA) • Earnings per share (EPS) • Budget ratio
Marketing/Sales	• Market share by segment • Customer churn rate (rate of growth or decline of customers) • Customer lifetime value • Cost per lead • Productivity by channel
Personnel	• Productivity ratios • Turnover rates • % overtime • Employee satisfaction rates • % absenteeism
Operations	• Out of stock % • Defect rate • Production cycle time • On-time delivery • % downtime
Customer Service	• Customer satisfaction • First call resolution rate • Average wait time • % of dropped calls • Time per call
IT	• Access speed • Site click-through • System availability • Service satisfaction levels • Project success rates

Using Strategic Placement

A good dashboard should help to summarize complex data so users can interpret the information at a glance. The dashboard needs to make it as easy as possible for users to read and understand the data. The layout of the dashboard can have a big impact on its usability. Figure 2 illustrates the particular regions of a screen to which a user's eyes tend to pay attention, according to research conducted by the Poynter Institute.

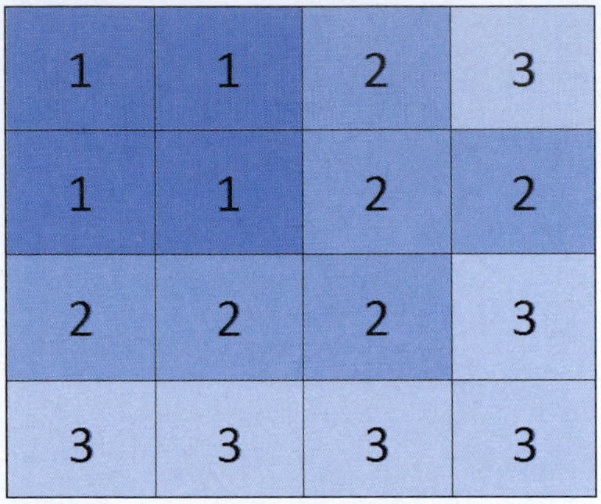

1	1	2	3
1	1	2	2
2	2	2	3
3	3	3	3

Figure 2 Design layout priority zones

Regions with the number 1 appear to have prominence over the other regions. This means that the eyes tend to spend more time in that part of the screen than in others. This research can be useful in strategically placing components of a dashboard to maximize its effectiveness.

Designing with White Space

Empty space on the screen that gives the eyes a place to rest is called **white space**. White space helps to keep a design simple, accessible, and visually pleasing to users. It is not necessarily white, just devoid of content. There is no rule for how much white space to include in your design. Generally speaking, you should include more white space than you initially think is necessary. However, including too much white space may mean that you are wasting valuable screen space. Including the right amount of white space can give an elegant feel to your dashboard and make it easier for the user to read.

Opening the Starting File

You will use various tools to create data visualizations using Office Add-ins, create and modify a data model in Excel using Power Pivot, conduct some analysis, and create a dashboard using Excel's Power View. In this exercise, you will open the starting file.

E13.00

To Open a Workbook

a. Start **Excel**, click **Open Other Workbooks** in the left pane, and then double-click **This PC**. Navigate through the folder structure to the location of your student data files, and then double-click **e07ch13Analytics**. A workbook opens to which you will add dashboards.

b. Click the **File** tab, click **Save As**, and then double-click **This PC**. In the **Save As** dialog box, navigate to the location where you are saving your project files, and then save the file as e07ch13Analytics_LastFirst using your last and first name.

c. Click **Save**.

Following are several commercially available products that exist to make it easy to create complex dashboards.

- Cognos
- Hyperion
- Dundas
- Corda
- SQL Server Analysis Services
- Oracle Business Intelligence

While these programs may be powerful and effective, they all suffer from two significant drawbacks. First, they require a software purchase; although some tools are nominally "free," the free or trial versions may have limited functionality and/or may not be legal to use for your company. Second, off-the-shelf software nearly always requires that its users have that particular software installed on their computers.

There are many benefits to using Microsoft Excel to create digital dashboards.

- Minimal costs — Not every business is a multibillion-dollar business that can afford to purchase top-of-the-line BI software, but most businesses use Microsoft Office. Leveraging the capabilities of Microsoft Excel is a very cost-effective solution without compromising too much on usability and functionality.

- Broad familiarity — From the entry-level sales representative to the CEO, familiarity with Excel is widespread. People who have some experience with Excel will spend less time learning how to use the dashboard and more time getting value from what is displayed than would be necessary with the other products.

- Flexibility — With the appropriate know-how, Excel can be much more flexible in the variety of analytics it can provide in a dashboard than many off-the-shelf solutions. Such features as PivotTables, AutoFilters, Form controls, and Power View allow you to create mechanisms that allow the audience multiple perspectives of the data.

- Rapid development — Having the capability to create your own reporting mechanisms in Excel can reduce your reliance on the IT department's resources. With Excel, not only can you develop reporting mechanisms faster, but you can also have the flexibility to adapt more quickly to changing requirements.

REAL WORLD ADVICE — **Dashboard Design and the Systems Development Life Cycle**

Creating dashboards requires far more preparation than a standard Excel model does. It requires closer communication with business leaders, stricter data modeling techniques, and following certain best practices. The systems development life cycle (SDLC) provides a structure for managing complex IT projects. One of the SDLC models is broken into six stages: analyze, design, develop, implement, test, and maintain. Following this SDLC model can provide the necessary guidance for creating an effective dashboard.

Explore the New Data Model

You can create many different types of models using Excel. For example, a financial model can be useful in evaluating loans or investments, a statistical model can be useful in predicting demand for a particular product, and a Solver model can be used to determine the optimal number of workers to hire to maximize profits. Excel 2016 provides the ability to create a data model. A **data model** is a collection of tables and their relationships that reflect the real-world relationships between business functions and processes — for example, how products relate to inventory and sales or how customers relate to revenues and sales volume. This feature allows your analysis to integrate data from multiple tables, effectively creating a relational data source inside Excel.

Relational data is a topic traditionally reserved for databases such as Microsoft Access; however, with this new functionality in Excel, you need to have a basic understanding of relational data. **Relational data** is data about a particular person, place, or event that is stored in multiple tables. For example, the data about employees is stored in an employee table, and data about the products that the company sells is stored in a products table. These two tables are related through the transactions that take place when the employees sell the products. Most organizations store their data in a relational database to ensure that their data is secure, accurate, and consistent. Before Excel 2013, it was very complicated and time consuming to integrate relational data into an analysis.

Data can be added to the data model from a variety of sources. Data from two or more tables imported from an external data source such as an Access database or SQL Server are automatically added to the data model. Data in a text file, in a range of cells, organized into tables, or in a SharePoint list can also be added to the data model by using the Power Pivot COM Add-in.

Importing Data with Power Query

Power Query is a powerful business intelligence tool that is used to discover data, connect it to your workbook, and transform the data into a more useful state. Previously available as a separate download, Power Query is now installed by default with Excel 2016. Power Query allows for data connections from the Internet via URLs, from a variety of stand-alone files, from a wide array of database connections, from SharePoint lists, and from Microsoft's Azure service. There are advanced features available for Power Query with a Power BI Subscription for Office 365. These features include the ability to share queries and view usage analytics on shared queries.

The benefit of using a tool such as Power Query is that it not only imports your data, but also can clean and transform the data before the data is imported into a worksheet. An added benefit is that the steps used to clean and transform the data can be stored as part of the data query and are then applied when a data connection is refreshed.

The database you have been given contains a list of employees in the table tblEmployees. The last names of the employees have been typed in as all lowercase text. Additionally, the hire date field contains a date-time stamp. For the purposes of this analysis, the time portion of the field needs to be removed. In this exercise, you will import the data with Power Query and transform the last name and hire date fields.

 E13.01

To Import Data into Excel Using Power Query

a. Click the **Data** tab, and then, in the Get & Transform group, click **New Query**.

b. Point to **From Database**, and then select **From Microsoft Access Database**.

c. Browse to your student data files, select **e07ch13Sales**, and then click **Import**. The Power Query Navigator window will now show a list of all tables in the database.

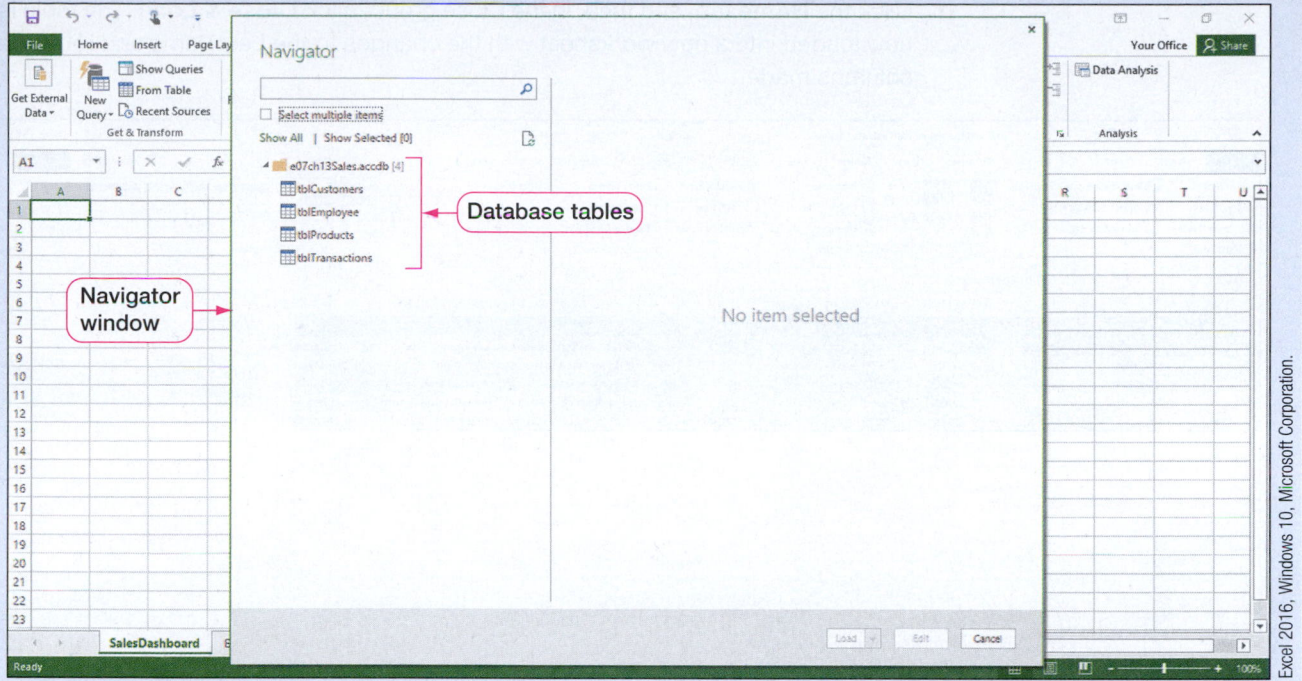

Figure 3 The Navigator window

SIDE NOTE

Applied Steps

Each step in the import process is listed in the Applied Steps portion of the Query Settings and will be executed on the data when the connection is refreshed.

---

d. Click the **tblEmployee** table, and then click **Edit**. This will open the Query Editor.

e. Click the **LastName** column. Click the **Transform** tab, and in the Text Column group, click **Format**, and then click **Capitalize Each Word**.

   Notice that the column now contains last names in the proper case, with the first letter of each work capitalized.

f. Click the **HireDate** column. On the Transform tab, in the Date & Time Column group, click **Date**, and then click **Date Only**.

   Notice that the time portion of the column has been removed. The data can now be loaded into Excel.

g. Click the **Home** tab, and then, in the Close group, click **Close & Load**. The table is now loaded into a new worksheet with the changes to the LastName and HireDate columns made.

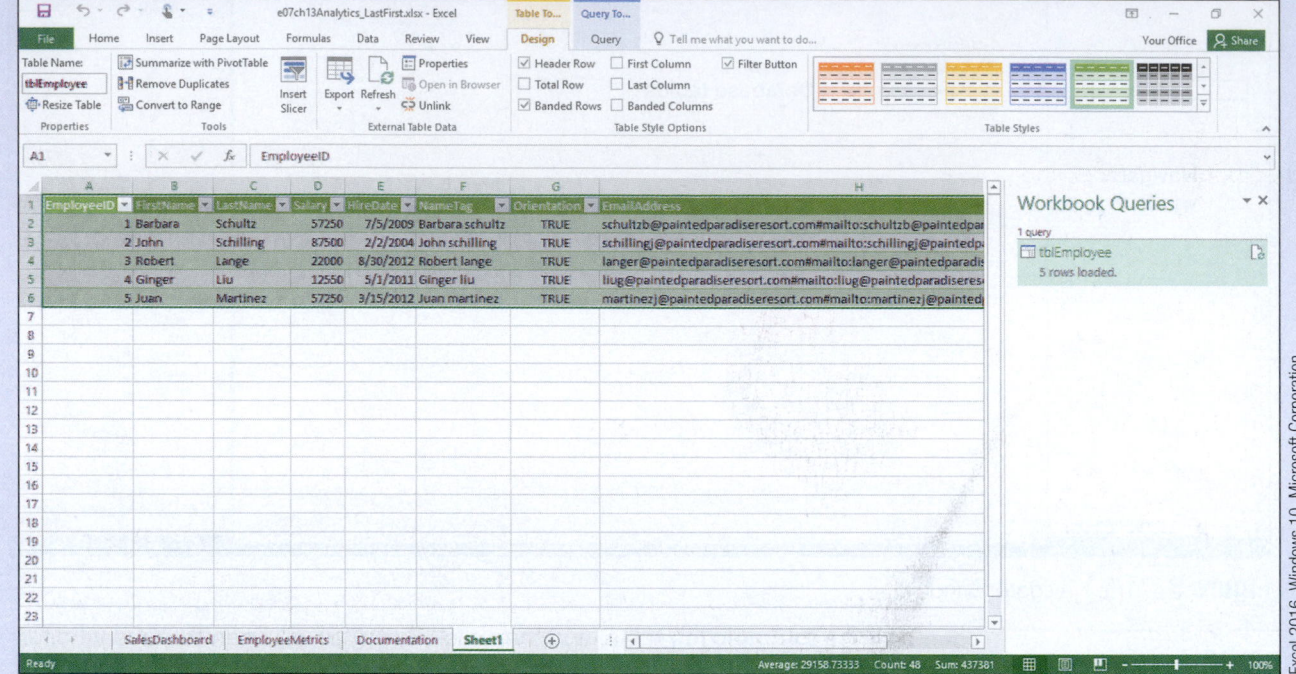

Figure 4   tblEmployee table loaded into Excel

h. Click any **blank cell** to deselect the table. Rename the worksheet **Employees**. **Close** ☒ the Workbook Queries pane.

i. **Save** 🖫 the document.

Building a Data Model Using an Access Database

Many organizations store data inside a relational database such as MySQL or Oracle or in a database management system such as Microsoft Access. Earlier versions of Excel have allowed for data connections from external sources, but Excel now has the ability to maintain the relationships between multiple tables. The e07ch13Sales database contains some sample sales data from Red Bluff Golf Course & Pro Shop that will form the foundation of your analysis. In this exercise, you will connect to the database and import all the tables into your workbook.

 **E13.02**

To Create a Data Connection to an Access Database

a. Click the **Data** tab and then, in the **Get External Data** group, click **From Access**.

b. Browse to your student data files, select **e07ch13Sales**, and then click **Open**.

c. In the Select Table dialog box, click **Enable selection of multiple tables**.

d. Click the check boxes to select the **tblCustomers**, **tblProducts**, and **tblTransactions** tables in the database.

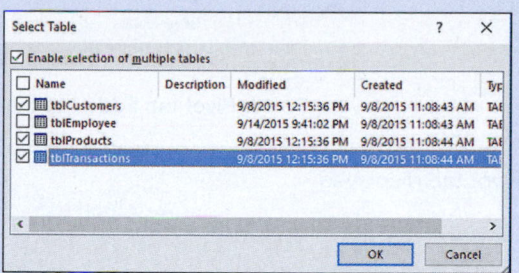

Figure 5 Select Table dialog box

Excel 2016, Windows 10, Microsoft Corporation.

e. Click **OK**. In the Import Data dialog box, click to select **Only Create Connection**. Notice that the **Add this data to the Data Model** check box is selected by default.

f. Click **OK**.

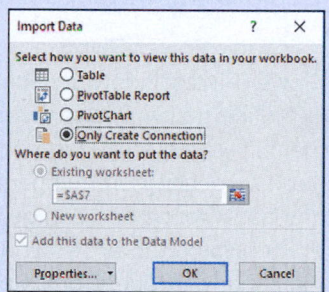

Figure 6 Import Data dialog box

Excel 2016, Windows 10, Microsoft Corporation.

g. **Save** 🖫 the document.

Exploring the Power Pivot Window

Now that you have imported relational data into the Excel workbook, a data model exists. As was stated previously, this makes it easy to integrate data from multiple tables in your analysis. To view and edit the data model, you must enable the Data Analysis add-ins. These include Power Pivot, Power View, and Power Map. In this exercise, you will enable the Data Analysis add-ins to view the data model that you created in the previous exercise. The Data Analysis add-ins are only available Office 365 ProPlus and Enterprise subscriptions. These add-ins are not included in Home and Student subscription versions of Office 365.

 **E13.03**

To Enable the Data Analysis Add-ins

a. Click the **File** tab, click **Options**, and then click **Advanced**. At the bottom of the Excel Options dialog box, in the Data group, select the **Enable Data Analysis add-ins: Power Pivot, Power View, and Power Map** check box.

> **Troubleshooting:**
> The Data Analysis add-ins are only available in Office 365 ProPlus and Enterprise subscriptions. If you do not have an option to Enable Data Analysis add-ins check your subscription type of Office.

b. Click **OK**.
Notice that the Power Pivot tab that has been added to the ribbon.

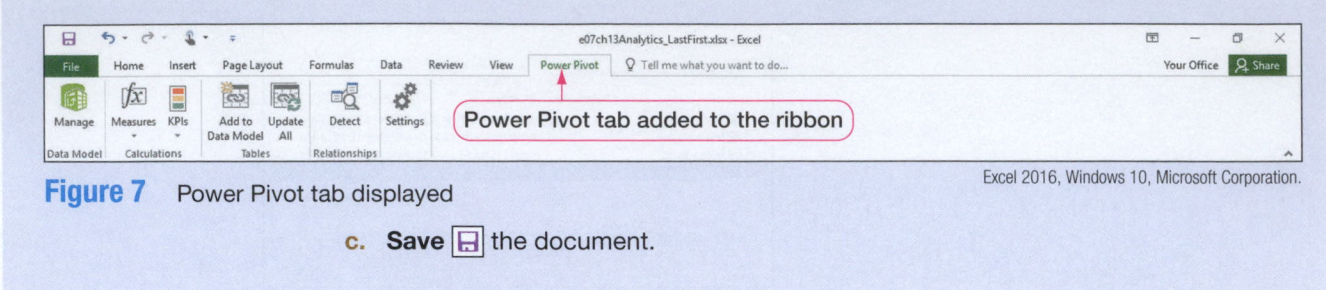

Figure 7 Power Pivot tab displayed

Power Pivot tab added to the ribbon

Excel 2016, Windows 10, Microsoft Corporation.

   c. Save 🖫 the document.

The Power Pivot Add-in is now installed. In this exercise, you will explore the Power Pivot window.

 **E13.04**

To Explore the Power Pivot Window

a. Click the **Power Pivot** tab, in the Data Model group, click **Manage** to open the Power Pivot window. If necessary, maximize the Power Pivot window.

Notice that a Power Pivot window opens separately from the workbook. The default view of the data model resembles a traditional Excel workbook, with each table appearing on a separate worksheet. The Excel workbook remains open in the background and can be easily viewed by closing the Power Pivot window.

The Home tab allows you to perform a variety of tasks, including adding new data from a variety of data sources; refreshing your data model to sync with changes made in the source data; creating PivotTables and PivotCharts; formatting, sorting, and filtering data; creating simple calculations and KPIs; and changing views.

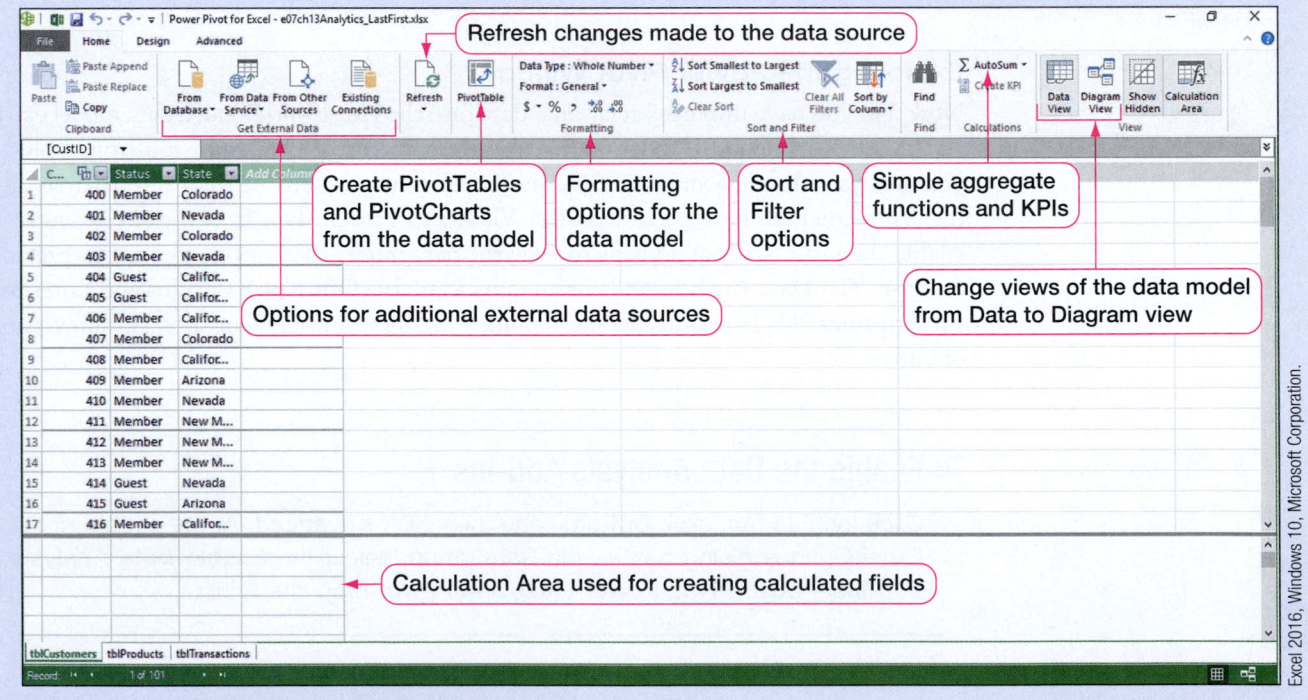

Figure 8 Power Pivot window Home tab

b. Click the **Design** tab.

The Design tab allows the ability to modify table properties, create more complex calculated fields, create and edit relationships between worksheets, and more.

Create and manage relationships in the data model

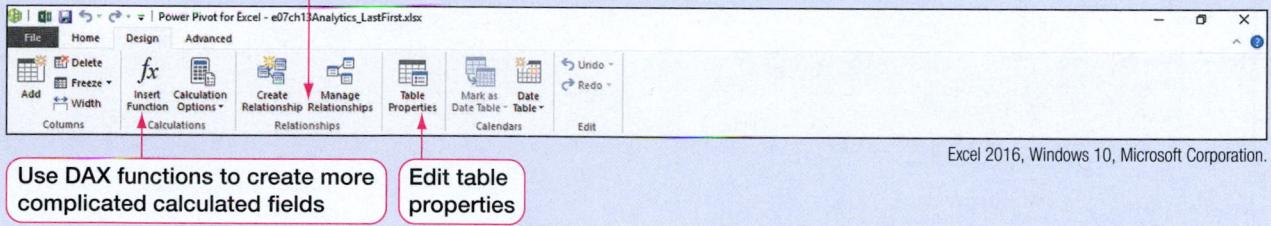

Use DAX functions to create more complicated calculated fields

Edit table properties

Excel 2016, Windows 10, Microsoft Corporation.

Figure 9 Power Pivot window Design tab

c. Click the **Advanced** tab.

The Advanced tab includes options that go beyond the scope of this book but include changing and managing different data perspectives for a particular user group or business scenario and allowing for easier navigation of very large data sets.

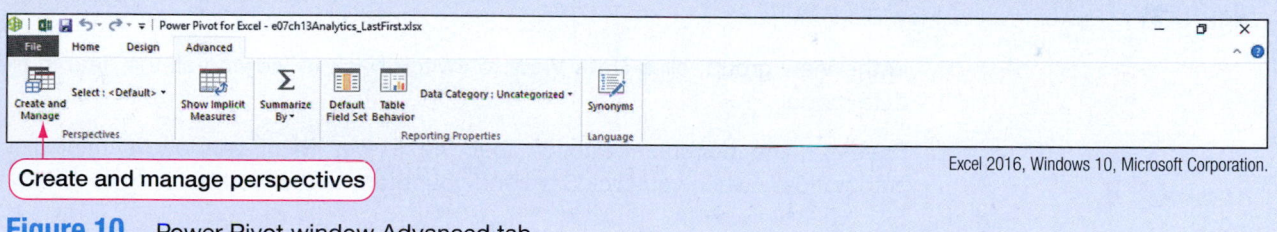

Create and manage perspectives

Excel 2016, Windows 10, Microsoft Corporation.

Figure 10 Power Pivot window Advanced tab

Now that you have an idea of what options are available on each of the tabs on the ribbon of the Power Pivot window, you can explore existing relationships in the data with Power Pivot. In this exercise, you will switch views in Power Pivot to visualize the database relationships from the database file.

 E13.05

To View Relationships in Power Pivot

a. In the Power Pivot window, click the **Home** tab, and in the View group, click **Diagram View** to see the current relationships in the data model.

b. If necessary, to view all relationships, click **Fit to Screen** ⊞ on the zoom bar. The relationships that are already established were imported from the Access database when the data connection was made.

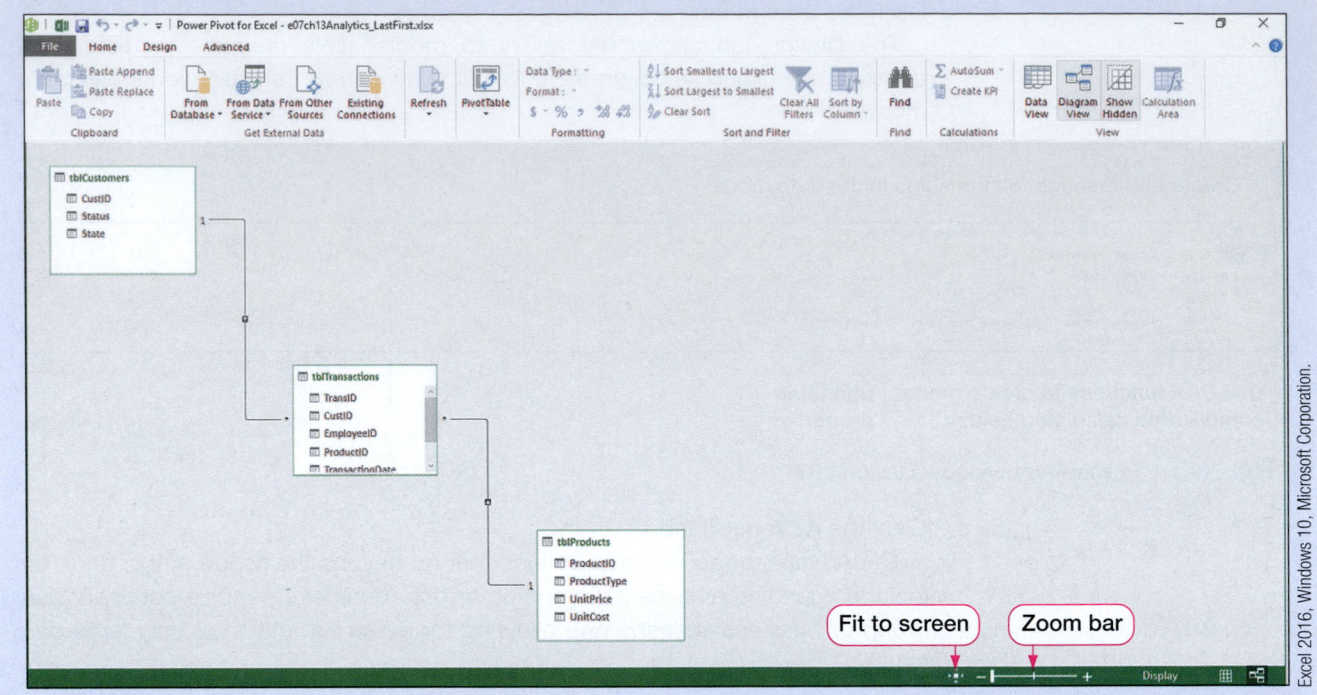

Figure 11 Power Pivot window Diagram View

c. In the View group, click **Data View** to switch back to viewing all the data in the data model.

d. **Save** 💾 the document. Notice that the Power Pivot window is minimized automatically when you click Save and you return to the workbook.

Adding a Table to the Data Model

Comprehensive data analysis often requires data from different sources. A human resources database might keep track of employees who have attended a required training session, and a separate sales database might keep track of online sales and in-person sales. Often, additional data may need to be incorporated into the data model to make it easier to conduct certain analyses. For example, in a previous exercise, you imported the tblEmployee table into the Employees worksheet. This data needs to be related to the rest of the Access tables for the data model to be complete. In this exercise, you will add this table to the data model and establish a relationship with the tblTransactions table to be used in future analyses.

 E13.06

To Add an Excel Table to the Data Model

a. Click the **Employees** worksheet if necessary, and then click anywhere in the Excel table.

b. Click the **Power Pivot** tab, and then, in the Tables group, click **Add to Data Model**.
   The Power Pivot window opens, and you see the data from the tblEmployee table added to a worksheet labeled tblEmployee.

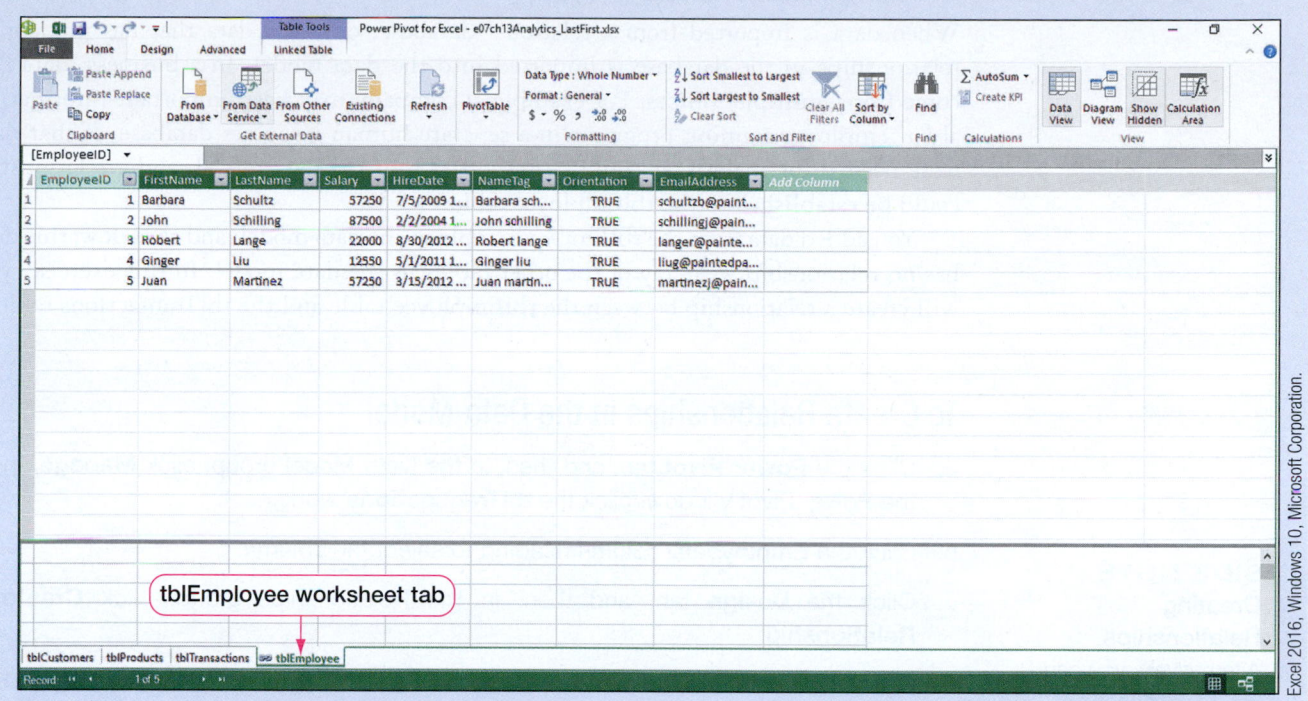

Figure 12 tblEmployee added to the data model

c. **Save** 💾 the document.

Create Advanced Data Models Using Power Pivot

Power Pivot and Excel not only give you the ability to conduct analyses on data from multiple sources, but also allow you to do more advanced data modeling in Power Pivot. Power Pivot allows you to create calculated columns and calculated fields and to establish KPIs all within Excel; these can then be used in PivotTables, PivotCharts, and other analysis tools. The data provided in the e07ch13Sales database did not include all the data needed for the various analyses. The managers of the Red Bluff Golf Course & Pro Shop would like you to create additional columns that calculate the revenue, costs, and profit earned from each transaction as well as calculated fields that calculate the total profit earned. You will then use those calculations to create KPIs that will measure each employee's effectiveness in terms of meeting monthly and yearly profit goals.

REAL WORLD ADVICE	Connecting to Large Data Sets Using the Microsoft Azure Marketplace

The Microsoft Azure Marketplace is a cloud computing platform that offers a variety of features and services to individuals and businesses. One of the many services it provides is access to very large data sets for use in analysis. There are several data sets available for free, and they can be accessed in the Power Pivot window. Click the Home tab, and in the Get External Data group, click From Data Service, and then click From Microsoft Azure Marketplace. There are a variety of categories based on type of data and price. Having access to large data sets allows you to explore all the analysis tools available in Excel.

Creating Relationships in the Data Model

When data is imported from a relational database, only the data that has predefined relationships in the database is imported into the data model. In a business, data can come from multiple sources. For example, a company may keep important information about employee training programs in a separate human resources database. If that data were needed for analysis, it could be imported into the data model, and a relationship could be established to the tblEmployee table.

You added data from the tblEmployee table to the data model, and as of now, this data has no relationship with any of the other tables in the data model. In this exercise, you will create a relationship between the tblEmployee table and the tblTransactions table.

 E13.07

To Create Relationships in the Data Model

a. Click the **Power Pivot** tab, and then, in the Data Model group, click **Manage**. In the Power Pivot window, click the **tblTransactions** worksheet.

b. Click the **EmployeeID** column heading to select the column.

c. Click the **Design** tab, and then, in the Relationships group, click **Create Relationship**.

d. Confirm that **tblTransactions** is selected in the Table 1 list and that **EmployeeID** is selected in the Columns list.

e. Select **tblEmployee** from the Table 2 list, and then select **EmployeeID** from the Columns list.

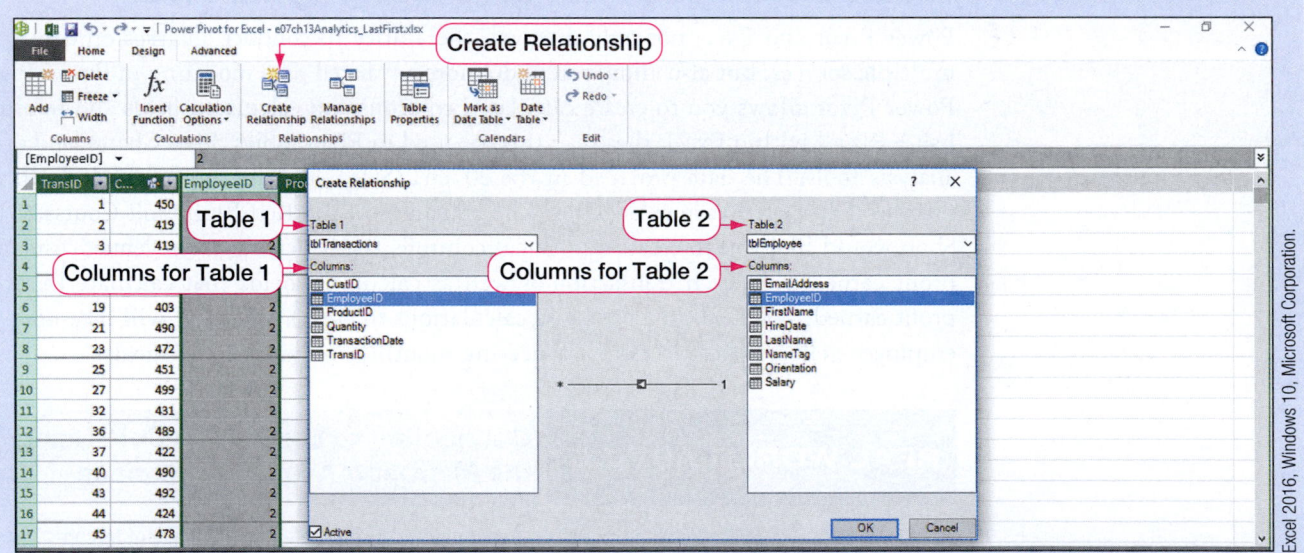

Figure 13 Create Relationship dialog box

f. Click **OK**.

g. Click the **Home** tab, and then, in the View group, click **Diagram View** to see the new relationship.

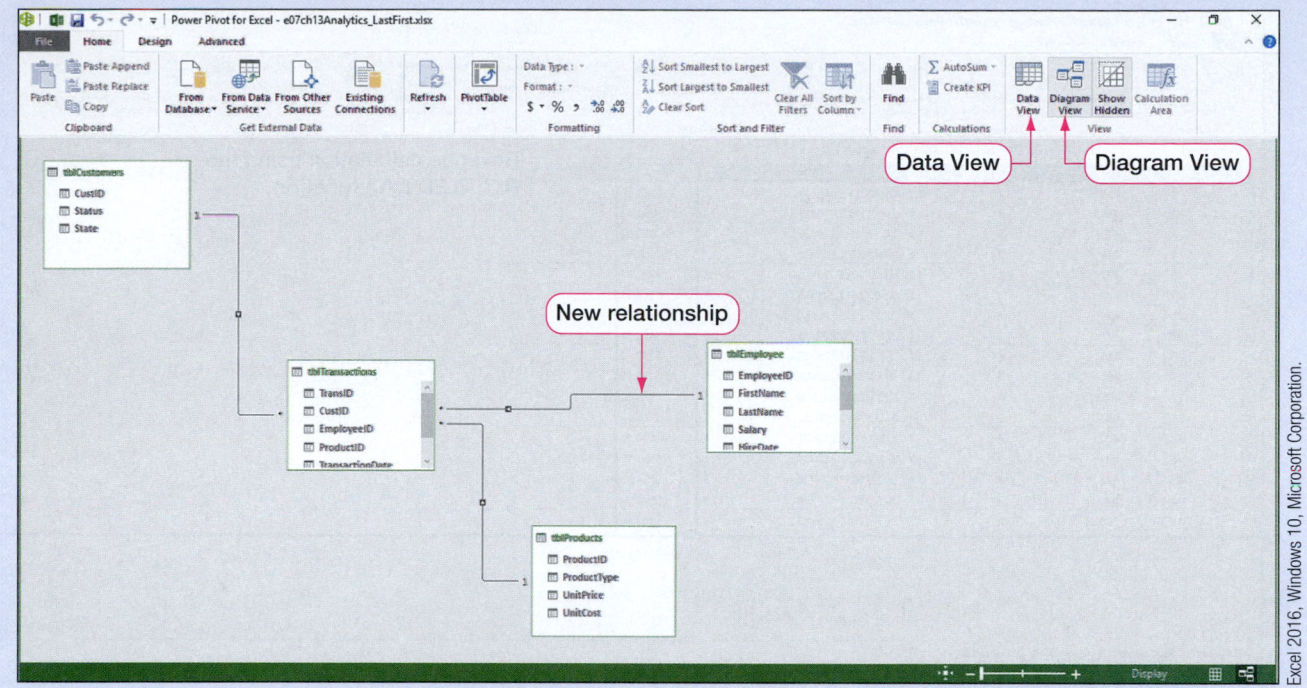

Figure 14 Diagram view with new relationship

Excel 2016, Windows 10, Microsoft Corporation.

h. Click the **Home** tab, and then, in the View group, click **Data View** to return to the Data view of the Power Pivot window.

i. **Save** 🖫 the document.

Adding Calculated Columns in Power Pivot

A calculated column is created inside the Power Pivot window and is based on data that is already a part of the data model. The data imported from the Access database included the quantity of items sold in each transaction along with the cost of the product and the selling price. However, these values exist in different tables. The managers at the Red Bluff Golf Course & Pro Shop would like you to include revenue, costs, and profit in future analyses.

In this exercise, you will create calculated columns for revenue, costs, and profit in the tblTransactions table. To accomplish this, you will use a category of functions called Data Analysis eXpressions (DAX). A DAX function called RELATED is used exclusively inside the Power Pivot window and belongs to, and essentially works the same as, a LOOKUP function. It uses the relationships established in the data model to retrieve a value from a related table to be used in a calculation in another table.

 **E13.08**

To Create a Calculated Column

a. Click the **Power Pivot** tab, and then, in the Data Model group, click **Manage**.

b. On the tblTransactions worksheet, double-click the **Add Column** column heading, type Revenue as the new column heading, and then press Enter.

c. With the Revenue column selected, type =RELATED(tblProducts[UnitPrice])*[Quantity], and then press Enter. The RELATED function uses the relationship established in the data model to retrieve the UnitPrice value from the tblProducts table for the appropriate item purchased in a particular transaction. The unit price multiplied by the quantity gives you the revenue generated from that transaction.

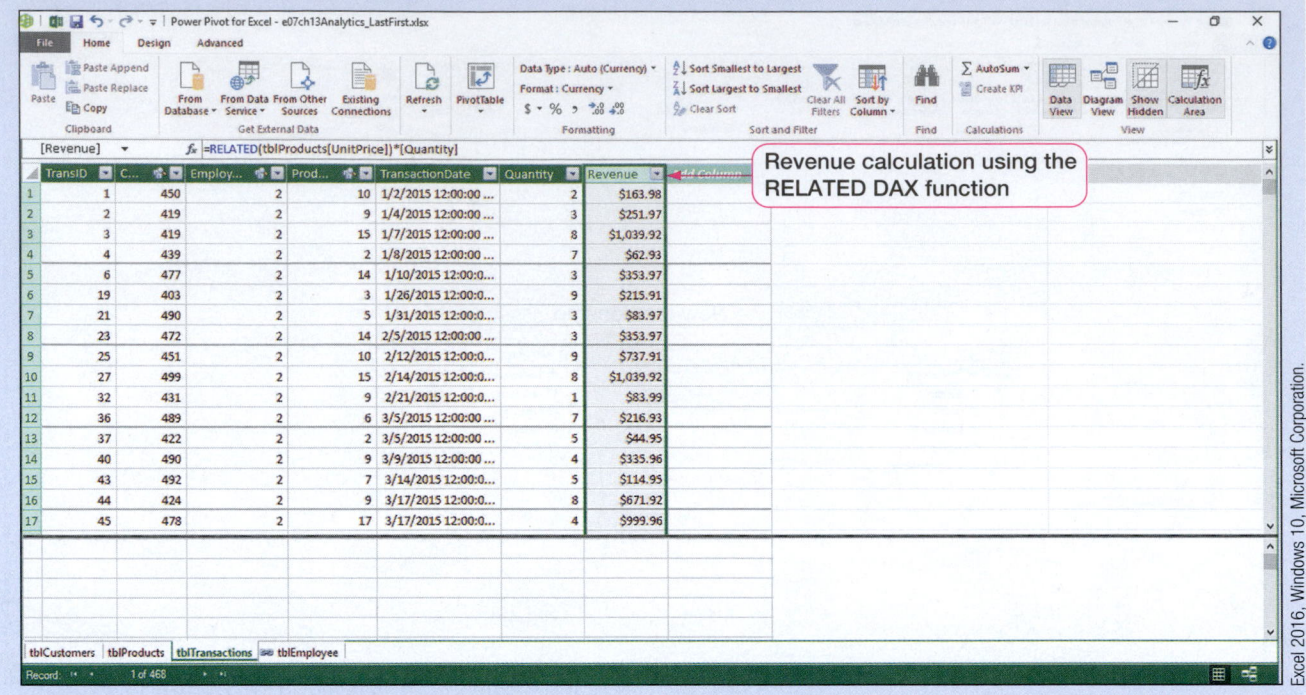

Figure 15 Calculated column of revenue

d. Double-click the next **Add Column** column heading, type Costs as the name for a second calculated column, and then press Enter.

e. With the Costs column selected, type =RELATED(tblProducts[UnitCost])*[Quantity], and then press Enter to calculate the costs associated with each transaction.

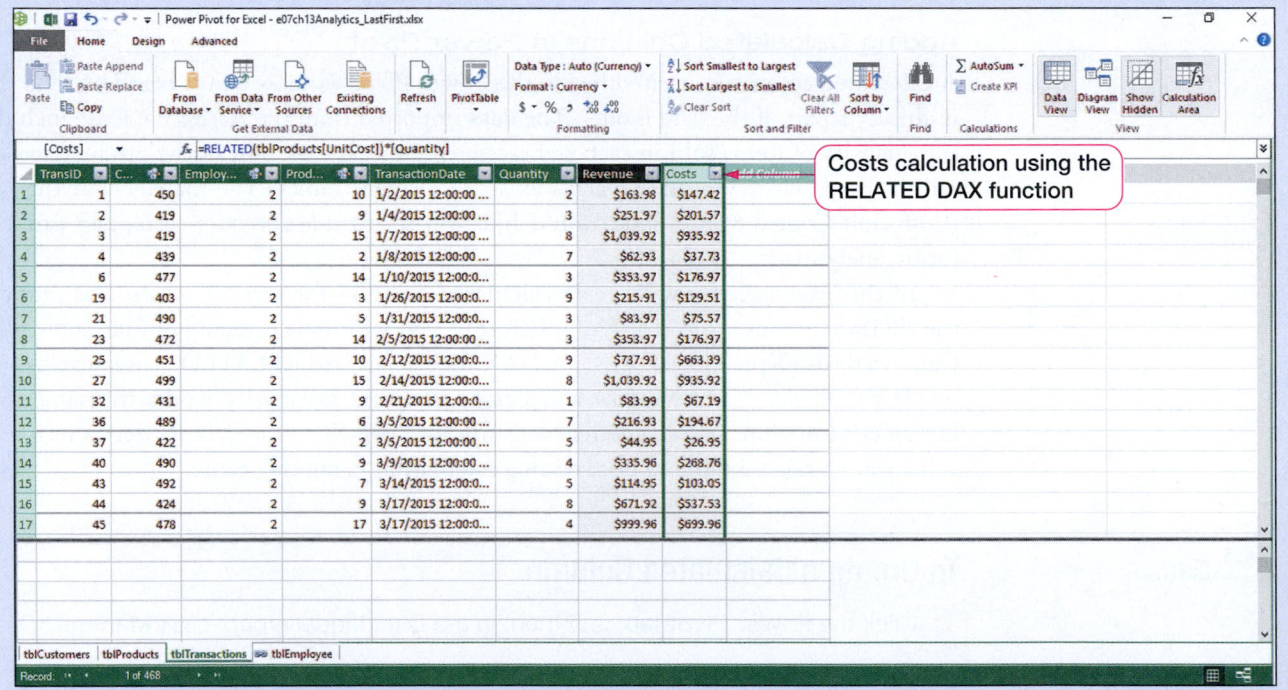

Figure 16 Calculated column of costs

f. Double-click the next **Add Column** column heading, type Profit as the name for a third calculated column, and then press Enter.

g. With the Profit column selected, type =[Revenue]-[Costs] to calculate the profit generated from each transaction, and then press Enter.

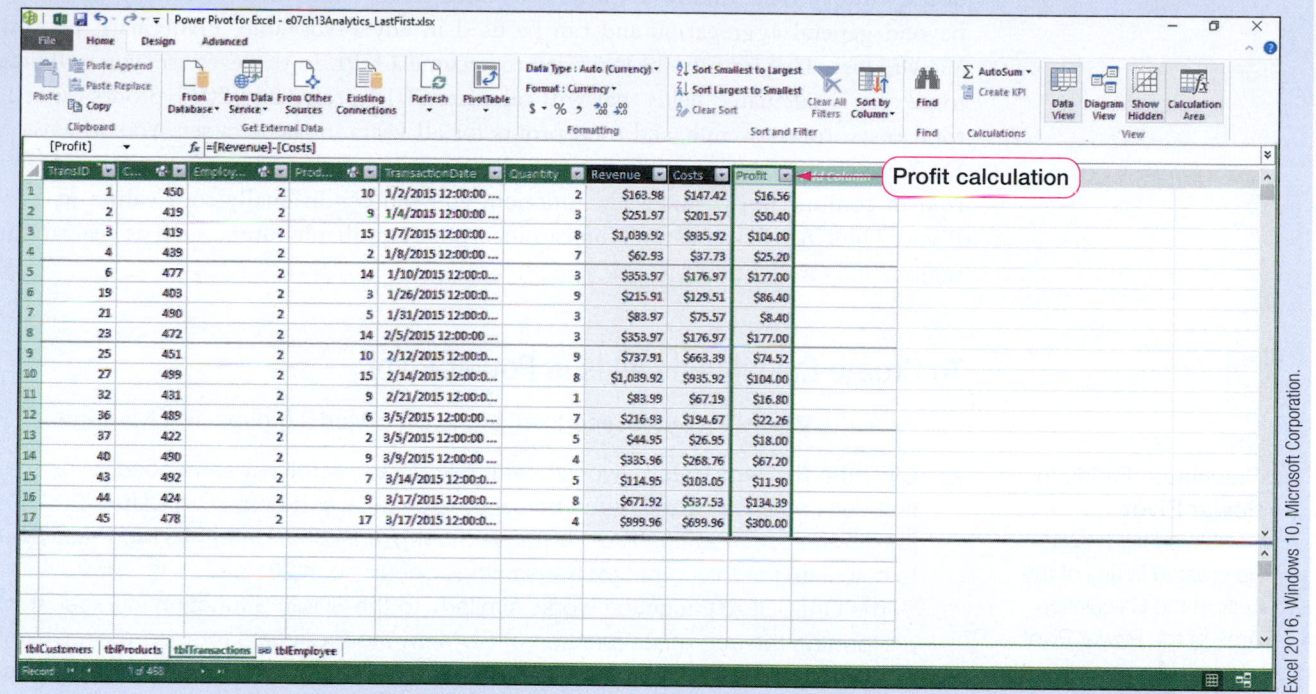

Figure 17 Calculated column for profit

h. **Save** 🖫 the document.

QUICK REFERENCE	DAX Functions

There are many DAX functions available for use in Power Pivot. Many of the functions have the same names and functionality as regular Excel functions with which you are already familiar but have been modified to use DAX data types and work with tables and columns. Below are the various categories of DAX functions.

- Date and Time
- Mathematical and Trigonometric
- Statistical
- Text
- Logical
- Filter
- Information
- Parent/Child

Adding Calculated Fields in Power Pivot

A calculated column and a calculated field are similar in that both are based on a formula or aggregate function; they differ on the basis of how they are used in analysis. In a PivotTable, for example, a calculated column would most likely be placed in a column or row, whereas a calculated field would most likely be placed in the Values area. There are two types of calculated fields, referred to as measures in earlier versions of Power Pivot: implicit and explicit. An **implicit calculated field** is created when you drag a field such as Sales or Quantity Sold into the Values area of a PivotTable. The calculation takes place, but a new calculated field is not being created. Implicit calculated fields can use only standard aggregated functions such as AVERAGE, SUM, COUNT, and MAX. An **explicit calculated field** is created when a formula is typed in the Calculation Area of the Power Pivot window. Explicit calculated fields can use a wide variety of functions beyond general aggregation and can be used in any PivotTable, PivotChart, or Power View report. They can also be extended to become a KPI. In this exercise, you will create five explicit calculated fields that will calculate 2016 profits and 2017 profits as well as total costs, total revenue, and total profits for all years in the data set. You will use the DAX function, CALCULATE, to filter the data by year. Using the CALCULATE function in conjunction with a SUM function, you can conditionally sum values in Power Pivot. The CALCULATE function can incorporate multiple filters, such as year, month, region, and employee ID.

 **E13.09**

To Create Calculated Fields in Power Pivot

a. Click the **Power Pivot** tab, and then, in the Data Model group, click **Manage**.

b. Click the **tblTransactions** worksheet if necessary, scroll left as needed, click the first cell in the Calculation Area below EmployeeID, and type =CALCULATE(SUM (tblTransactions[Profit]),YEAR(tblTransactions[TransactionDate])=2016). Press Enter to calculate the total profit for transactions occurring in 2016.

The CALCULATE function works similarly to the SUMIFS function in Excel. It is performing the aggregate function of SUM on the Profit field for records in which the year of the TransactionDate is equal to 2016. The YEAR function extracts 2016 from the TransactionDate field for filtering.

> **Troubleshooting**
>
> If the Calculation Area is not visible in the Power Pivot window, on the Home tab, in the View group, click Calculation Area.

c. Change the default name of **Measure 1** to 2016 Profit.

d. On the Home tab, in the Formatting group, click the **Format** arrow, and then select **Currency**.

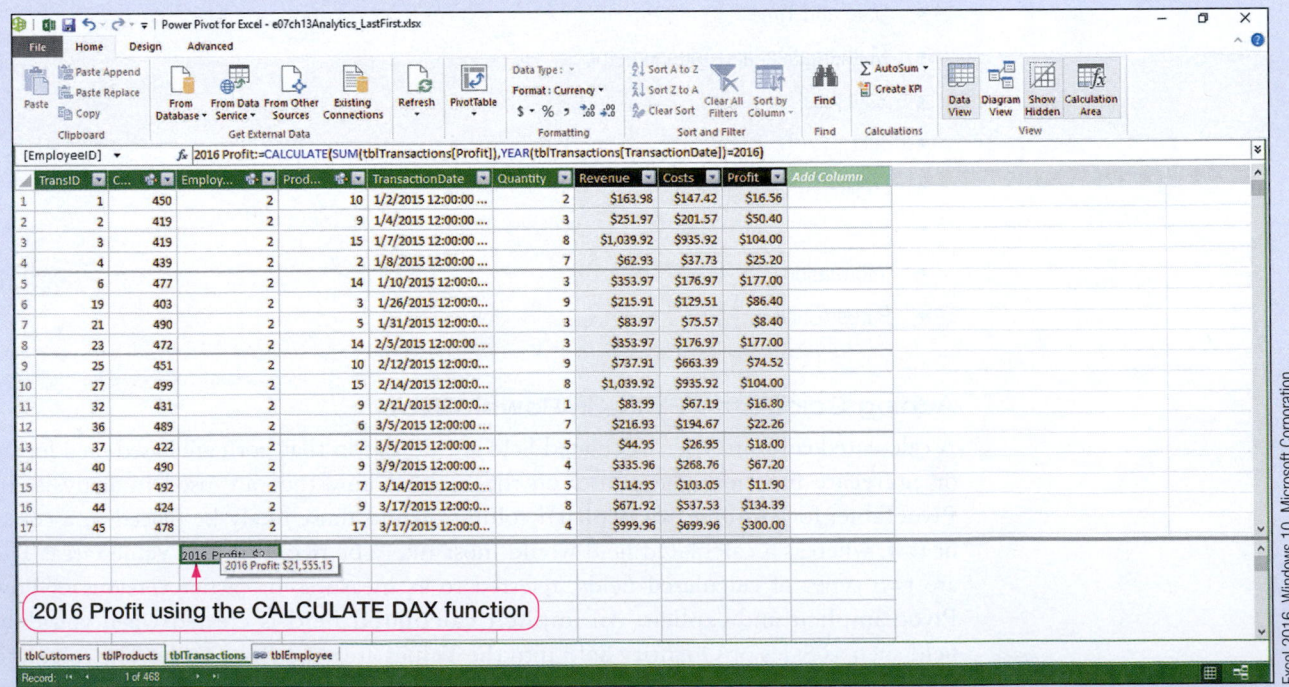

Figure 18 Calculated field for 2016 profit using CALCULATE

SIDE NOTE

Viewing the Results of the Calculated Field

The results of the calculated field can be viewed by expanding the width of the cell or by pointing to the calculation.

e. Click the **cell to the right** in the Calculation Area under the ProductID column to create a second calculated field, type **=CALCULATE(SUM(tblTransactions[Profit]), YEAR(tblTransactions[TransactionDate])=2017)**, and then press Enter. This will calculate the total profit for transactions occurring in 2017.

f. Change the default name of **Measure 1** to 2017 Profit.

g. On the Home tab, in the Formatting group, click the **Format** arrow, and then select **Currency**.

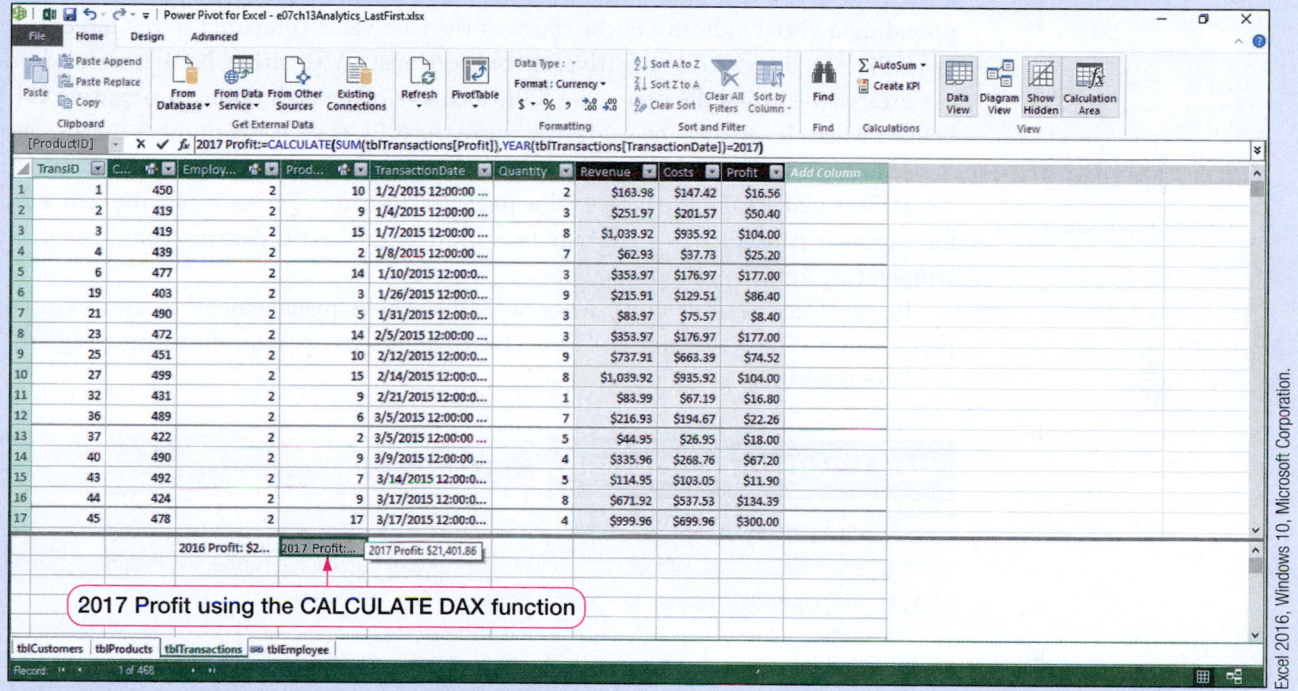

Figure 19 Calculated field for 2017 profit using CALCULATE

h. Click the **Revenue** column heading to select the Revenue column. On the Home tab, in the Calculations group, click **AutoSum** to calculate the total revenue for all transactions in the data set. AutoSum uses the Sum function to add up all the values in the column and places a new calculated field in the Calculation Area below the column, titled Sum of Revenue.

i. Click the **Costs** column heading to select the Costs column, and then click **AutoSum** to calculate total costs for all transactions in the data set.

j. Click the **Profit** column heading to select the Profit column, and then click **AutoSum** to calculate the total profits for all transactions in the data set.

k. **Save** the document.

QUICK REFERENCE	Naming Calculated Fields

There are a few things to consider in naming your calculated fields.

- Choose names that easily identify the calculations they will perform, as they will be visible in all PivotTable and PivotChart field lists.
- Each calculated field should be given a unique name within a table.
- Avoid names that have already been given to calculated columns within the same workbook.

Defining a Key Performance Indicator

Calculated fields can be extended to become KPIs. The managers of the Red Bluff Golf Course & Pro Shop would like you to create some KPIs that will measure employee performance. A KPI in Power Pivot includes the following: base value, target value, and status thresholds. A **base value** is a calculated field that resolves to a value. A base value, for example, can be the calculated field created as an aggregate of 2017 Profit. A **target value** can be either another calculated field that resolves to a value or an absolute value. A target value, for example, can be the aggregate of 2016 Profit or a monthly sales goal that every employee should meet. Finally, a **status threshold** is defined by the range between a high value and low value. In Excel, the status threshold is displayed with a graphic providing a visual indicator of the status of the base value compared to the target value.

KPIs can be positive, negative, or bidirectional. A **positive KPI** is defined when the greater the value, the better the KPI, such as a company's profit. A **negative KPI** is defined when the greater the value, the worse the KPI, such as the number of sick days in a specific time period. A **bidirectional KPI** is defined when the value becomes worse the farther it deviates from the target value in either direction. For example, the temperature for storing a particular product may be a bidirectional KPI; damage could occur if the temperature gets too cold or too hot.

In this exercise, you will define a KPI to help management measure employee performance. The KPI will measure each employee's monthly profit earnings against an absolute target value of $4,000.

REAL WORLD ADVICE | **KPIs Without Power Pivot**

KPIs were a part of business long before Power Pivot became available. If your company is using a previous version of Excel without Power Pivot, you can use Conditional Formatting Icon Sets instead to indicate proximity to various KPI goals.

 E13.10

To Create a KPI with an Absolute Target Value

a. Click the **Power Pivot** tab, and then, in the Data Model group, click **Manage**.

b. On the tblTransactions worksheet, in the Calculation Area, click the **Sum of Profit** calculated field.

c. Click the **Home** tab, and then, in the Calculations group, click **Create KPI**.

d. In the Key Performance Indicator (KPI) dialog box, confirm that **Sum of Profit** is selected as the KPI base field (value).

e. Under Define target value, click in the **Absolute value** box, and then type **4000**.

f. Under Define status thresholds, click and slide the low value threshold — on the left side of the box — to **2800**. Click and slide the high value — on the right side of the box — to **3800**.

g. Under Select icon style, ensure that the first icon style is selected. When you are creating KPIs in Excel, only the first icon style can be displayed in PivotTables. The other icon style options are useful in displaying KPI status symbols in a Power View report.

SIDE NOTE
Define Status Thresholds
The low and high threshold values can also be typed directly into the boxes attached to the sliders.

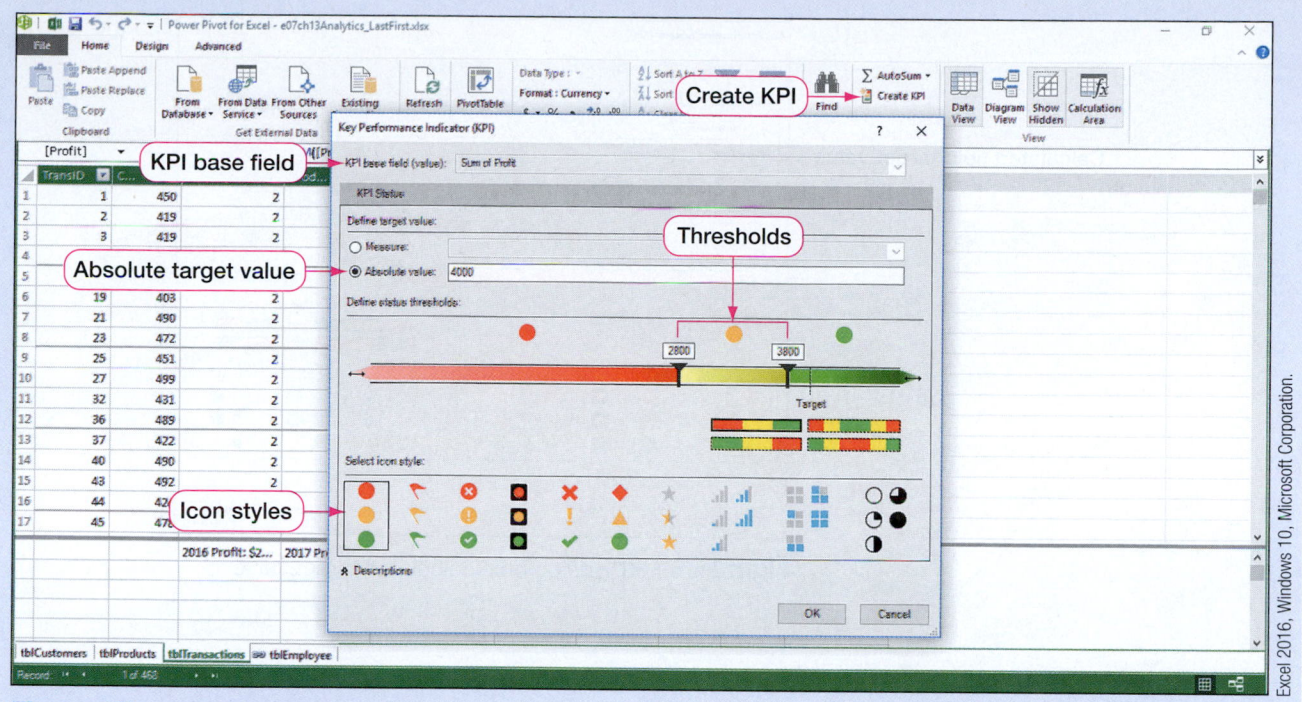

Figure 20 KPI dialog box: absolute target value

h. Click **OK**. Notice that the KPI indicator is now to the right of the calculated field.

i. **Save** the document.

Create a KPI Using a Calculated Target Value

The KPI for profit was created by using an absolute value. This value will not change until the KPI itself is edited. To create a more dynamic measure, KPIs can be created by using calculations in the data model. In this exercise, you will create a KPI with a calculated field as the target value. The KPI will measure each employee's 2017 profit earnings against his or her 2016 profit earnings.

 **E13.11**

To Create a KPI with a Calculated Target Value

a. Click the **Power Pivot** tab, and then, in the Data Model group, click **Manage**.

b. On the tblTransactions worksheet, in the Calculation Area, click the **2017 Profit** calculated field.

c. Click the **Home** tab, and then, in the Calculations group, click **Create KPI**.

d. In the Key Performance Indicator (KPI) dialog box, confirm that **2017 Profit** is selected as the KPI base field (value).

e. Under Define target value, click the Measure drop-down, and then select **2016 Profit**.

f. Under Define status thresholds, click and slide the high threshold value to **105%** and the low value to **80%**.

g. Under Select icon style, ensure that the first icon style is selected.

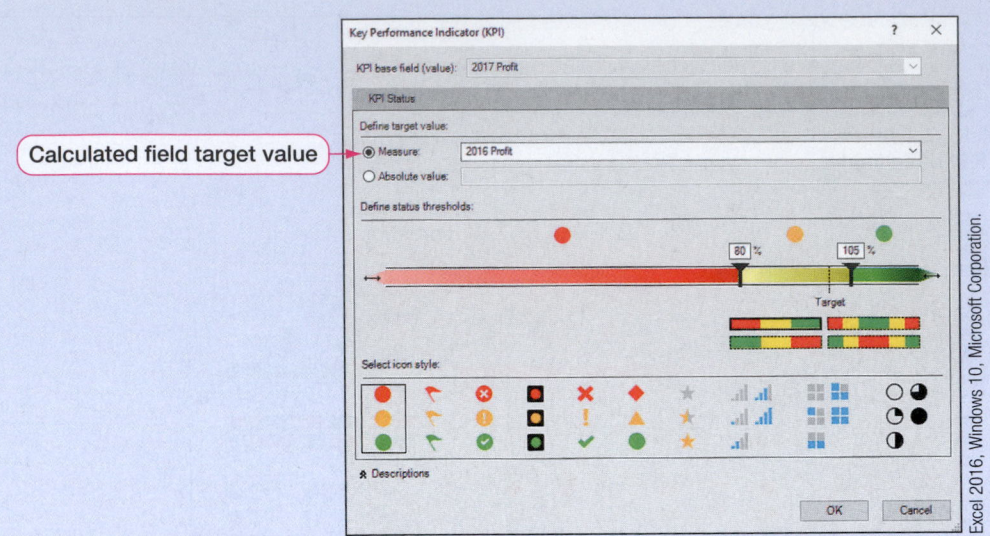

Calculated field target value

Figure 21 KPI dialog box: calculated target value

h. Click **OK**.

i. Save  the document.

Create PivotTables and PivotCharts with Power Pivot

PivotTables and PivotCharts are a major component in any dashboard, and with Excel 2016, they can be created with data from multiple sources without any additional software or add-ins as long as the data is relational data. Having Power Pivot installed gives you more options than a traditional PivotTable offers. Not only can you create a single PivotTable or PivotChart on a worksheet with Power Pivot, but you can also create a PivotTable and PivotChart on the same worksheet as well as two PivotCharts arranged vertically or horizontally or four PivotCharts on the same worksheet. The managers of the Red Bluff Golf Course & Pro Shop want to get a better understanding of the sales data over the past three years. You have been asked to create a simple dashboard consisting of four PivotCharts and slicers to be able to easily view different aspects of the sales data. **Slicers** are visual controls that allow you to quickly and easily filter your data in an interactive way. They can be used to replace the filter icons in PivotCharts. Slicers are not compatible with versions of Excel before 2010.

Creating a Simple Sales Dashboard with PivotCharts

The Power Pivot window has options to create multiple PivotCharts on the same worksheet using data from all connected data sources. This can be an easy way to create a simple dashboard for management to get a better picture of how things in a particular business area are going. In this exercise, you will create dashboard consisting of four PivotCharts.

E13.12

To Use Power Pivot to Create Four PivotCharts

a. Click the **Power Pivot** tab, and then, in the Data Model group, click **Manage**.

b. In the Power Pivot window, click the **Home** tab if necessary. Click the **PivotTable** arrow.
   Notice the various options for creating combinations of PivotTables and PivotCharts.

c. Select **Four Charts** from the menu.

d. In the Create Four PivotCharts dialog box, click **Existing Worksheet**, click the **Collapse Dialog** button 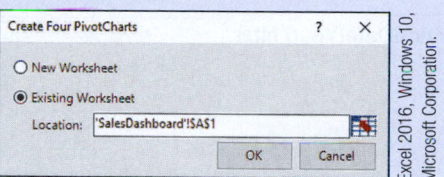, and then click the **SalesDashboard** worksheet.

e. Click cell **A1**, and then, in the Range Selection dialog box, click **OK**.

Figure 22   Create Four PivotCharts dialog box

f. Click **OK** again to create the layout for four PivotCharts.

g. Complete the following tasks to create a PivotChart comparing the 2015 costs and the 2015 revenue by month.

> **SIDE NOTE**
> **AXIS (CATEGORIES)**
> Fields placed in the AXIS (CATEGORIES) make up the horizontal axis (*x*-axis) of the PivotChart.

- If necessary, click **Chart 1**. In the PivotChart Fields pane, click **tblTransactions** to view the available fields, and then drag the **TransactionDate** field to the **AXIS (CATEGORIES)** area at the bottom of the PivotChart Fields pane.

    Notice that the TransactionDate field is automatically grouped into Year, Quarter, and Month in addition to showing the individual dates.

- Drag the grouping for **TransactionDate(Year)** to the **FILTERS** area.

- Remove the grouping for **TransactionDate(Quarter)** by dragging the field out of the AXIS (CATEGORIES) area and into the worksheet.

- Remove the **TransactionsDate** field by dragging the field out of the AXIS (CATEGORIES) area and into the worksheet.

- If necessary, expand **tblTransactions**. Select the **Revenue** field to add it to the **VALUES** area.

- Select the **Costs** field to add it to **the VALUES** area.

- On the chart click the **TransactionDate(Year)** filter, expand the options, and then select **2015**. Click **OK**.

- Right-click the **chart object** that was just created, and then select **Change Chart Type**. In the Change Chart Type dialog box, click **Combo**. In the Choose the chart type and axis for your data series area, for the Sum of Revenue series, click the **Chart Type** arrow, and select **Line**.

- Click **OK**.

- This combo chart allows you to easily compare the costs and revenue from each month.

- Click the **Analyze** tab, and then, in the PivotChart group, in the **Chart Name** box, type Sales-Costs-2015, and press Enter to name the chart.

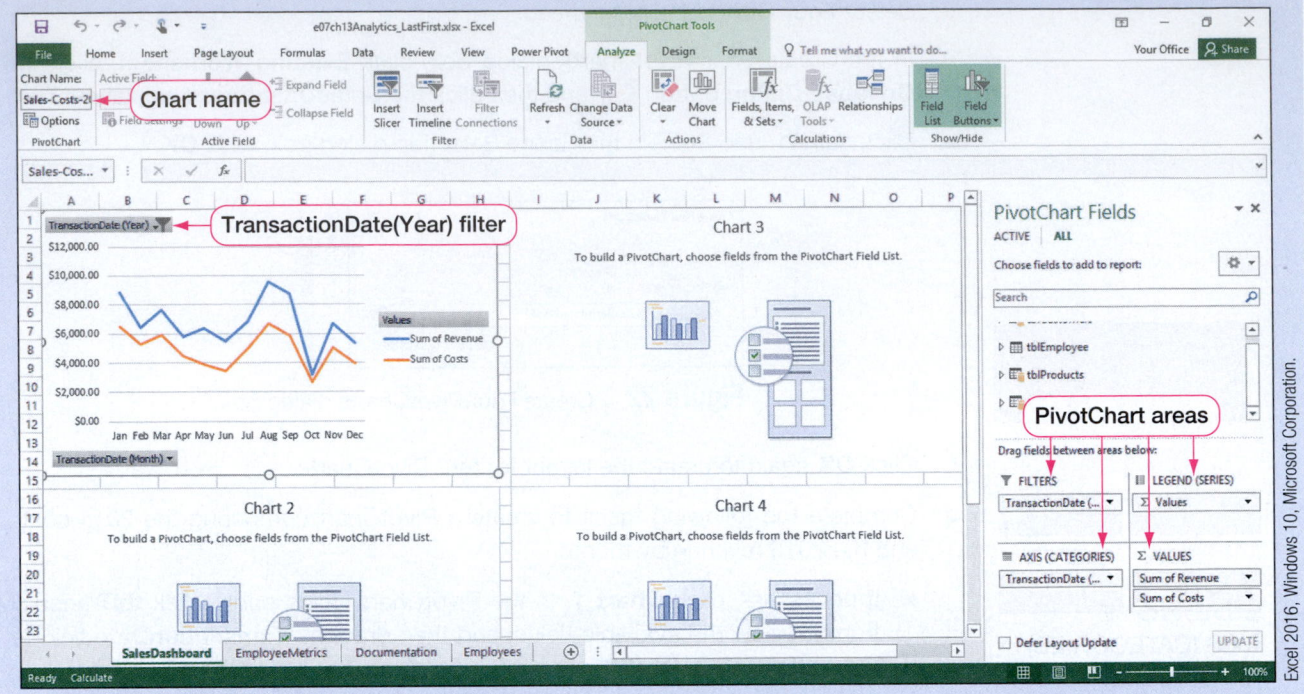

Figure 23 Combo chart for Sales-Costs-2015

h. Click **Chart 2**, and then complete the following tasks to create a PivotChart comparing the 2016 costs and the 2016 revenue by month.

- If necessary, in the PivotChart Fields pane, click **ALL** under the PivotChart Fields heading to view all available tables in the data model. Click **tblTransactions** to view the available fields, and then drag the **TransactionDate(Month)** field to the AXIS (CATEGORIES) area.

- Drag the **TransactionDate(Year)** field into the FILTERS area.

- Click to select the **Revenue** check box, and then click to select the **Costs** check box to add the fields to the VALUES area.

- On the chart, click the **TransactionDate(Year)** filter, expand the options, and then select **2016**. Click **OK**.

- Right-click the chart, and then select **Change Chart Type**.

- In the Change Chart Type dialog box, click **Combo**, and change the Chart Type of the Sum of Revenue to **Line**. Click **OK**.

- On the **Analyze** tab, in the PivotChart group, click the Chart Name box, and then type Sales-Costs-2016 to name the chart.

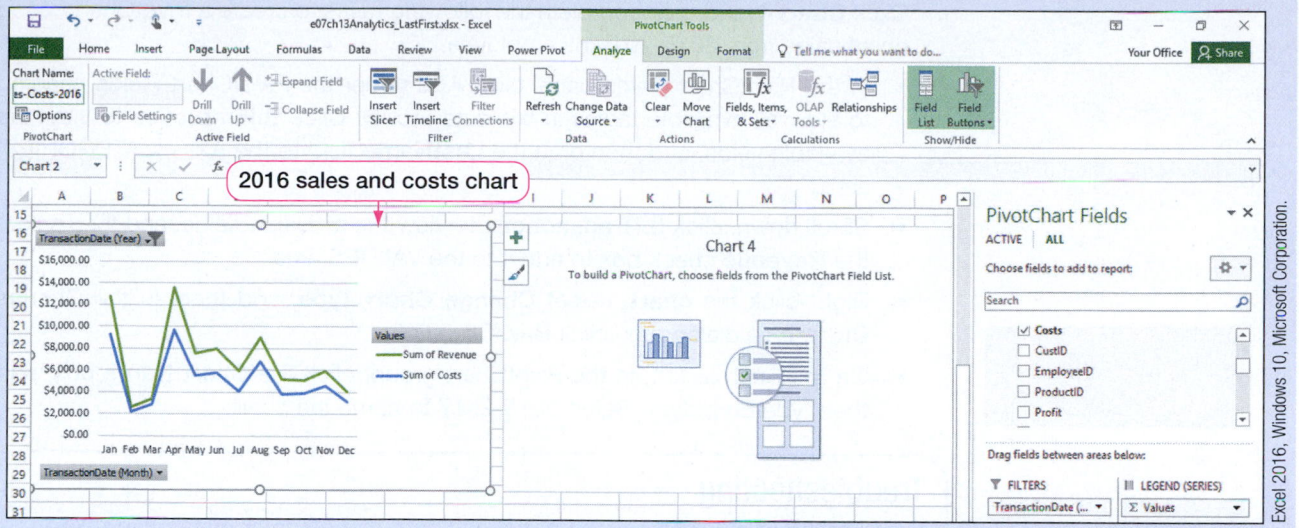

Figure 24 Combo chart for Sales-Costs-2016

i. Click **Chart 3**, and then complete the following tasks to create a PivotChart comparing the 2017 costs and the 2017 revenue by month.

- If necessary, in the PivotChart Fields pane, click **ALL** under the PivotChart Fields heading to view all available tables in the data model. Click **tblTransactions**, and then drag the **TransactionDate(Month)** field to the AXIS (CATEGORIES) area.

- Drag the **TransactionDate(Year)** field into the FILTERS area.

- Click to select the **Revenue** check box, and then select the **Costs** check box to add them to the VALUES area.

- On the chart click the **TransactionDate(Year)** filter, expand the options, and then select **2017**. Click **OK**.

- Right-click the **chart**, and then select **Change Chart Type**.

- In the Change Chart Type dialog box, click **Combo**, and change the Chart Type of the Sum of Revenue to **Line**. Click **OK**.

- On the Analyze tab, in the PivotChart group, click the **Chart Name** box, and then type Sales-Costs-2017 to name the chart.

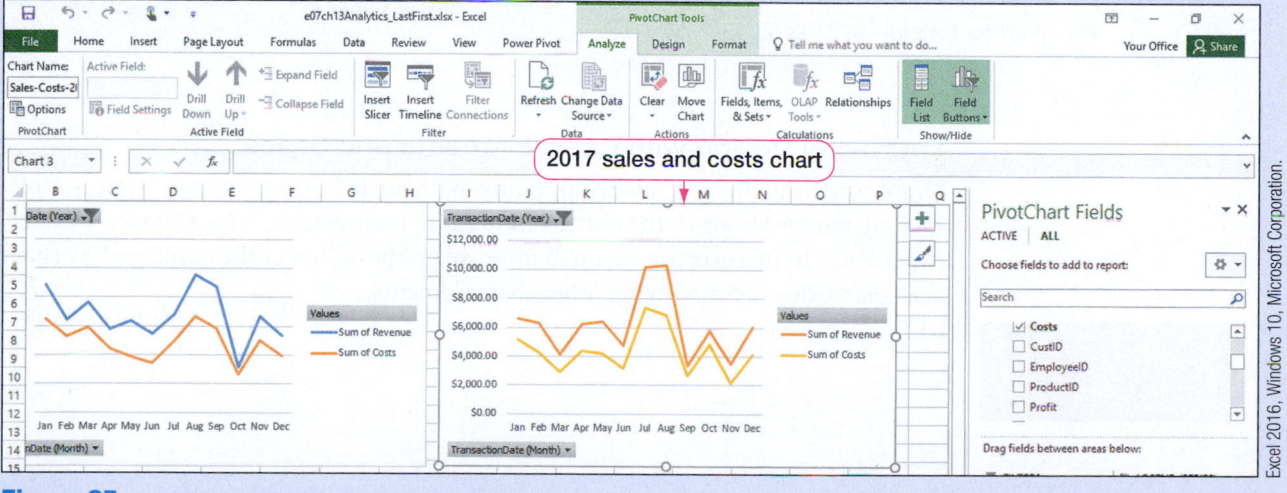

Figure 25 Combo chart for Sales-Costs-2017

j. Click **Chart 4**, and then complete the following tasks to create a PivotChart based on all sales from 2015-2017 by employee.

- In the PivotChart Fields pane, click **ALL** under the PivotChart Fields heading to view all available tables in the data model. Click **tblEmployee** to view the available fields, and then drag the **LastName** field to the AXIS (CATEGORIES) area.

- Scroll down, click **tblTransactions** to view the available fields, and then select the **Revenue** check box to add it to the VALUES area.

- Right-click the **chart**, select **Change Chart Type**, and then, in the Change Chart Type dialog box, click **Bar**. Click **OK**.

- On the Analyze tab, in the PivotChart group, click the **Chart Name** box, and then type **Employee-Sales-2015-2017** to name the chart.

> **Troubleshooting**
>
> Some of the axis values on the charts may be out of place or overlapping. You will improve on the formatting of the charts in the next exercise.

k. Save 🖫 the document.

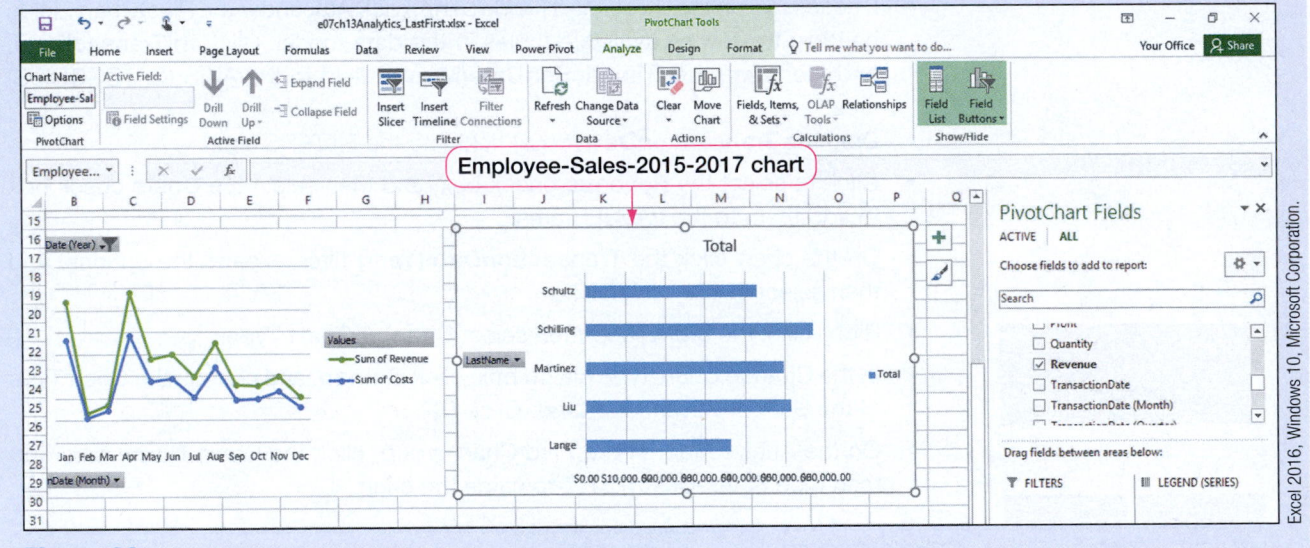

Figure 26 Bar chart for Employee-Sales-2015-2017

Improving Design with Chart Elements and Styles

Dashboards should be visually appealing without being distracting. Some simple and modest modifications to the charts can increase their readability and create a better user experience. In this exercise, you will improve on the design of the dashboard by changing the chart titles and modifying other chart elements.

 **E13.13**

To Improve Dashboard Design

a. Click the **Sales-Costs-2015** chart, and then complete the following tasks.

- Click **Chart Elements** ➕ next to the chart, and then click to select **Chart Title** to add a chart title above the chart.

- Edit **Chart Title** to read 2015 Sales and Costs.

- Click **Chart Styles** 🖌 next to the chart, and then select **Style 3** from the Style list. Click **Chart Styles** 🖌 to close the Chart Styles gallery.

- Click the Analyze tab if necessary, and then in the Show/Hide group, click **Field Buttons** to hide the filters on the PivotChart.

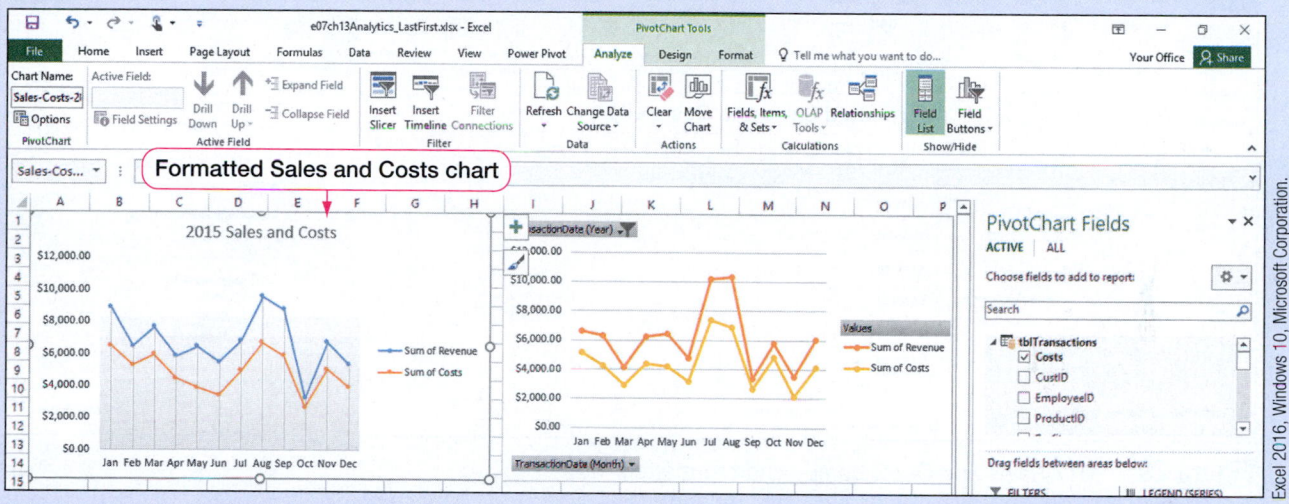

Figure 27   2015 Sales and Costs combo chart formatted

b. Click the **Sales-Costs-2016** chart, and then complete the following tasks.

- Click **Chart Elements** ➕, and then click **Chart Title** to add a chart title above the chart.

- Edit **Chart Title** to read 2016 Sales and Costs.

- Click **Chart Styles** 🖌, and then select **Style 3** from the Style list. Click **Chart Styles** 🖌 to close the Chart Styles gallery.

- Click the Analyze tab if necessary, and then, in the Show/Hide group, click **Field Buttons** to hide the filters on the PivotChart.

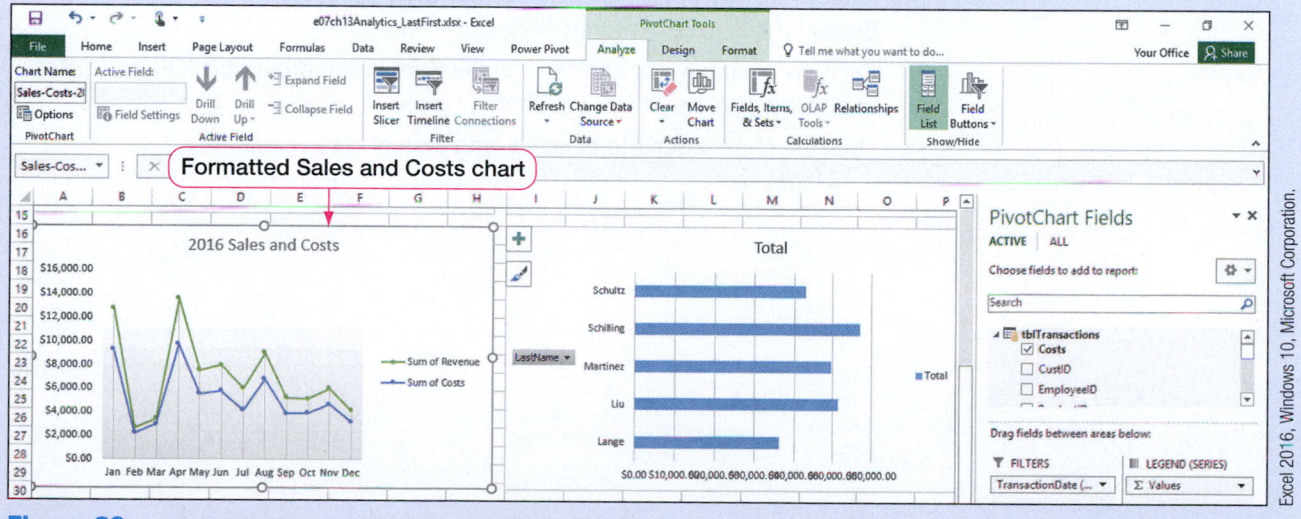

Figure 28   2016 Sales and Costs combo chart formatted

c. Click the **Sales-Costs-2017** chart, and complete the following tasks.

- Click **Chart Elements** ⊞, and then click **Chart Title** to add a chart title above the chart.

- Edit **Chart Title** to read 2017 Sales and Costs.

- Click **Chart Styles** 🖌, and then select **Style 3** from the Style list. Click **Chart Styles** 🖌 to close the Chart Styles gallery.

- Click the Analyze tab, if necessary, and then, in the Show/Hide group, click **Field Buttons** to hide the filters on the PivotChart.

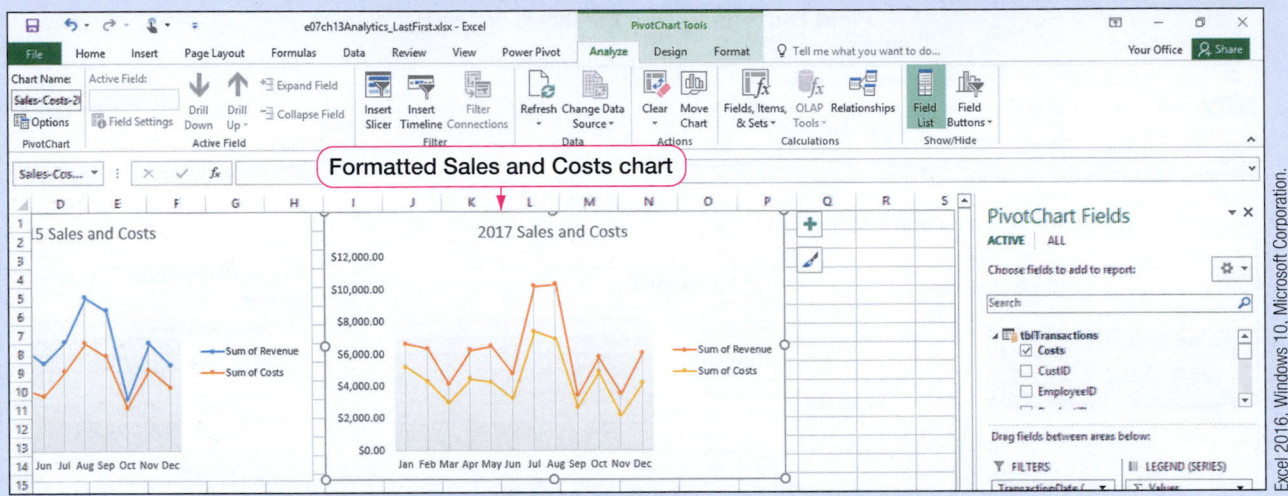

Figure 29   2017 Sales and Costs combo chart formatted

d. Click the **Employee-Sales-2015-2017** chart, and then complete the following tasks.

- Edit **Chart Title** to read 2015-2017 Sales by Employee.

- Click the **Format** tab, and then, in the Current Selection group, select **Horizontal (Value) Axis** from the Chart Elements menu. Click **Format Selection**.

- In the Format Axis pane, expand the **Number** section, select **Currency** from the Category list, change the **Decimal places** to 0, and **Close** ☒ the Format Axis pane.

- Click **Chart Styles** 🖌, and then select **Style 3** from the Style list. Click **Chart Styles** 🖌 to close the Chart Styles gallery.

- Click the **Analyze** tab, and then, in the Show/Hide group, click **Field Buttons** to hide the filters on the PivotChart.

- Click the chart legend to select it, and then press Delete.

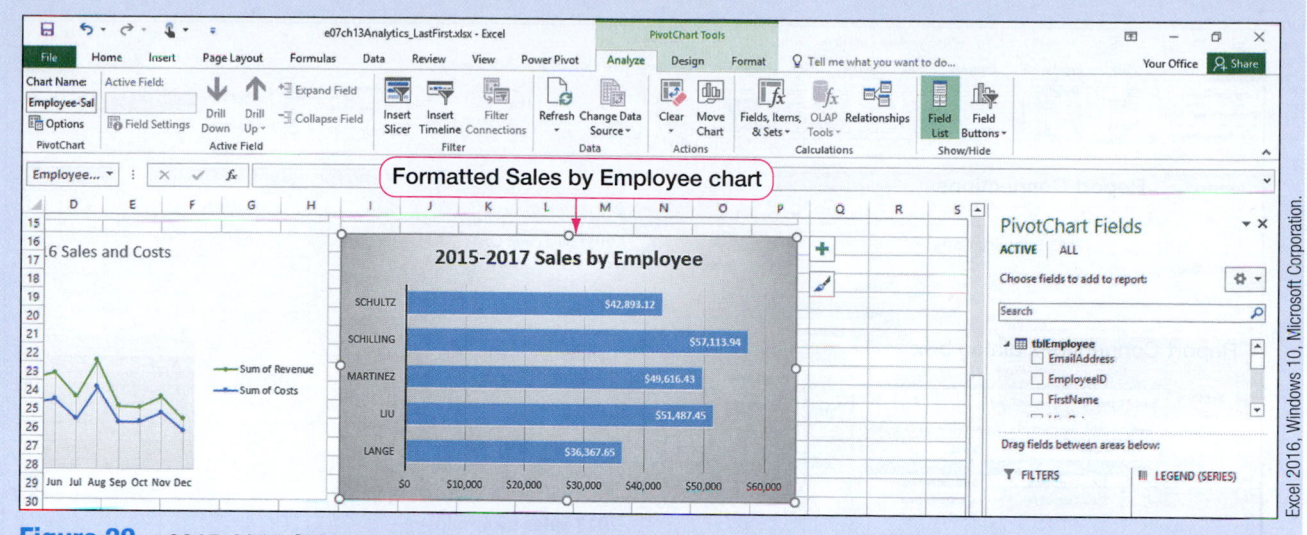

Figure 30 2015-2017 Sales by Employee bar chart formatted

    e. Save 🖫 the document.

Enhancing a Dashboard with Slicers

The current dashboard with four pivot charts lacks an easy and efficient way to filter the sales data to see the data from different perspectives. For example, the managers at the Red Bluff Golf Course & Pro Shop would like to be able to see the sales and costs for particular product categories or type of guest or even by employee. In this exercise, you will be adding slicers to the dashboard.

 **E13.14**

To Add Slicers

a. Click the **SalesDashboard** worksheet if necessary, and then click the **2015 Sales and Costs** chart.

b. Click the Analyze tab if necessary, and then, in the Filter group, click **Insert Slicer**.

c. In the Insert Slicers dialog box, click the **All** tab.

d. Scroll to the **tblCustomers** table, and if necessary, expand to view the table fields. Click to select the **Status** check box.

e. Scroll to the **tblEmployee** table, and if necessary, expand to view the table fields. Click to select the **LastName** check box.

f. Scroll to the **tblProducts** table, and if necessary, expand to view the table fields. Click to select the **ProductType** check box.

g. Click **OK** to create a slicer for each of the checked boxes.

h. If necessary, click the **ProductType** slicer to select it. On the Options tab, in the Slicer group, click **Report Connections**.

i. In the Report Connections dialog box, confirm that **Sales-Costs-2015** is checked, and then click **Sales-Costs-2016**, **Sales-Costs-2017**, and **Employee-Sales-2015-2017** to connect the **ProductType** slicer to all the charts.

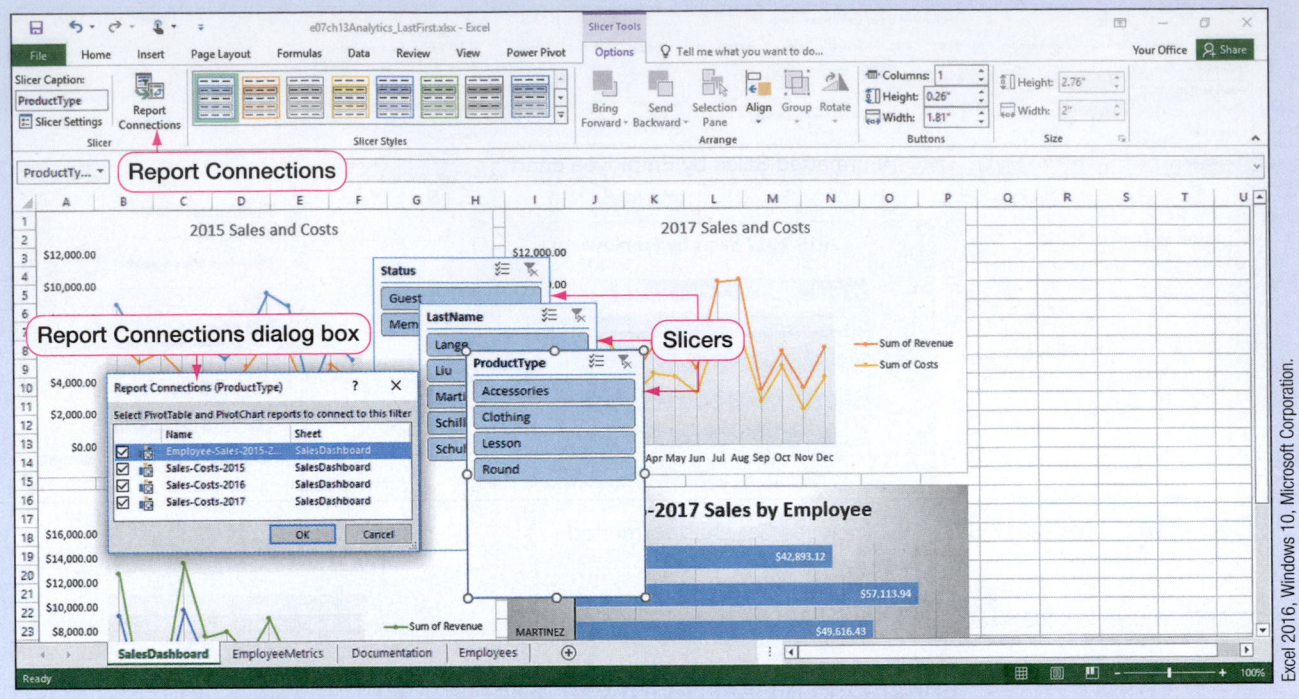

Figure 31 Report Connections (ProductType) dialog box

j. Click **OK**.

k. Repeat steps h - j for the LastName and Status slicers.

l. Reposition the right side of the **2017 Sales and Costs** and **2015-2017 Sales by Employee** charts at the right edge of column **S** to make room for the slicers.

m. Reposition and resize the **slicers** to fit between the charts within columns I through K.

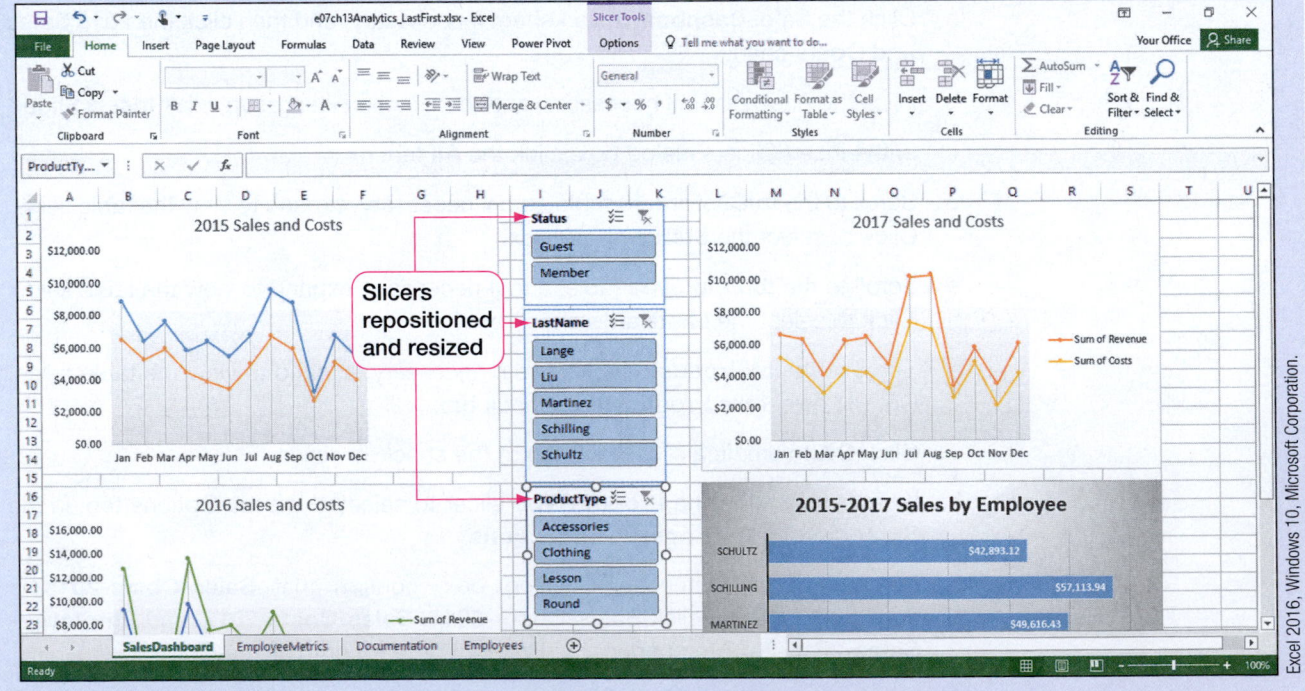

Figure 32 SalesDashboard with Status, LastName, and ProductType slicers

n. Click the **2015-2017 Sales by Employee** chart, click the **Analyze** tab, and then, in the Filter group, click **Insert Timeline**.

o. Click to select the tblTransactions field **TransactionDate**, and then click **OK** to add a timeline slicer to the dashboard.

p. Resize and reposition the **slicer** to the right of the 2015-2017 Sales by Employee bar chart.

Notice that the Sales Dashboard now has easy and effective ways to filter the data displayed in the charts. Multiple fields can be used simultaneously to filter the data by holding Ctrl while clicking each field.

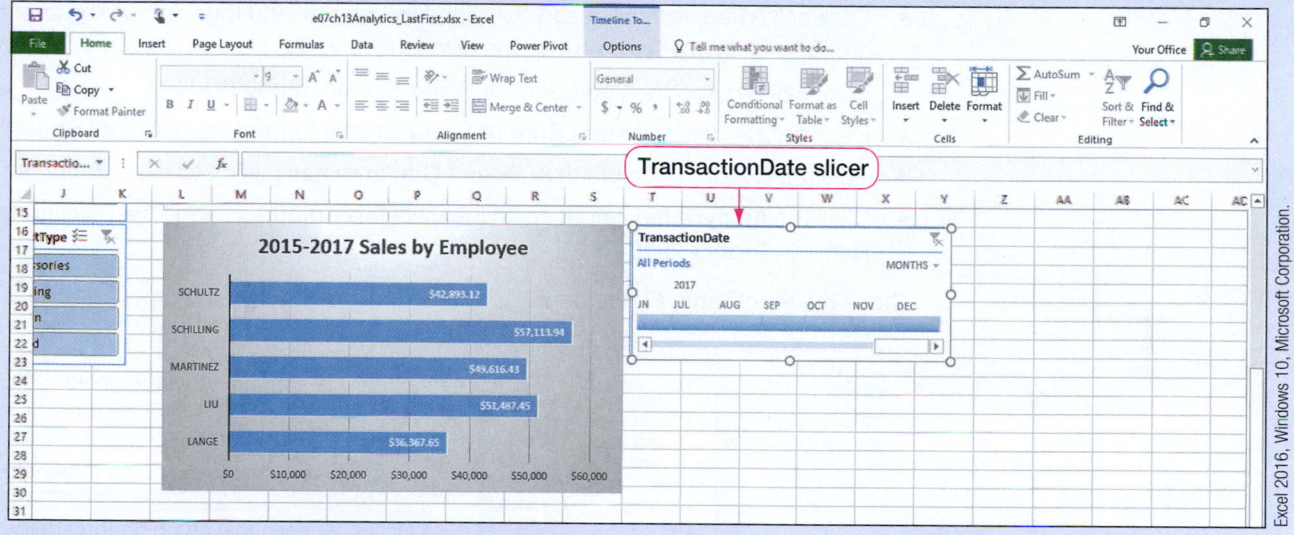

Figure 33 SalesDashboard with timeline slicer

q. **Save**  the document.

Incorporating KPIs into a Dashboard

In earlier exercises, you created two KPIs. One KPI measures profit earnings to an absolute target value of $4,000, and the other compares 2017 profit earnings against 2016 profit earnings. These KPIs can be incorporated into PivotTables with additional values and/or filters.

In this exercise, you will create another dashboard displaying the profit goal KPI and additional analysis.

E13.15

To Incorporate the Yearly Profit Goal KPI into a Dashboard

a. Click the **EmployeeMetrics** worksheet, and then click cell **A1**. Click the **Insert** tab, and then, in the Tables group, click **PivotTable** to create a PivotTable.

b. In the Create PivotTable dialog box, select **Use an external data source**, and then click **Choose Connection**.

c. In the Existing Connections dialog box, confirm that **e07ch13Sales** is selected under Connections in this Workbook, and then click **Open**.

d. In the Existing Worksheet field, confirm that **EmployeeMetrics!$A$1** is the Location, and then click **OK**.

e. In the PivotTable Fields pane, click **ALL**. Click to expand the **tblEmployee** table, and then drag the **LastName** field to the ROWS area.

f. Scroll down to **tblTransactions**, and then drag the **TransactionDate (Year)** field to the ROWS area, below LastName.

g. Click to select **Profit**, and add the field to the VALUES area. If necessary, click to expand the tblTransactions table. Click the **Sum of Profit** KPI to expand it, and then select **Status** to add the KPI status threshold symbols to the PivotTable.

Notice that both Lange and Schilling fell below the bottom threshold value of $2,800 in one of the years.

h. Make the following changes to the PivotTable.

- Click cell **A1**, and then edit **Row Labels** to read Employee by Year.
- Click cell **A1** again if necessary. Click the **Home** tab, and then, in the Alignment group, click **Wrap Text** to wrap the new label in cell A1.
- Click cell **B1**, and then edit **Sum of Profit** to read Yearly Profit.
- Click cell **C1**, and then edit **Sum of Profit Status** to read $4,000 Goal Status.
- Adjust the width of columns **A**, **B**, and **C** to automatically fit to their contents.
- Click the **Analyze** tab, and then, in the PivotTable group, change the PivotTable Name to Profits-2015-2017.

j. Close the **PivotTable Fields** pane.

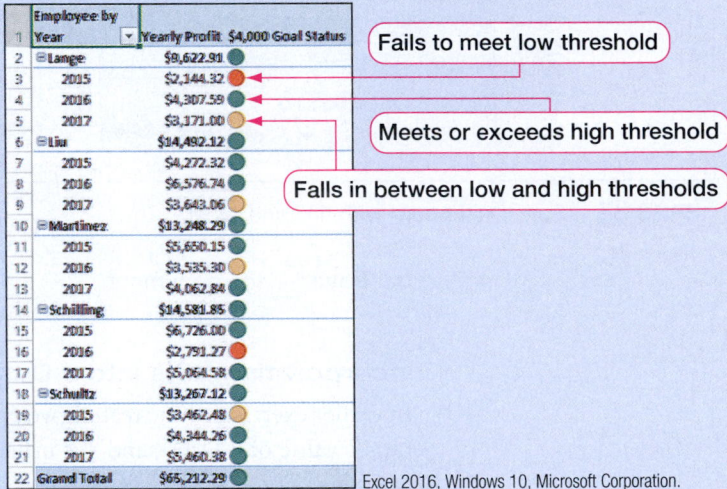

Excel 2016, Windows 10, Microsoft Corporation.

Figure 34 Yearly Profit KPI in a PivotTable

j. Save  the document.

Incorporating KPI Values and Status Fields into a PivotTable

The status field of a KPI from the data model displays icons in the PivotTable. The value calculated by the KPI can also be displayed in a PivotTable, using the status field of the KPI. You have been asked to create a PivotTable that uses the 2017 profit KPI to measure employee performance. In this exercise, you will incorporate the KPI in a PivotTable that displays employees 2017 profits.

E13.16

To Incorporate the 2017 Profit KPI into a Dashboard

a. Click the **EmployeeMetrics** worksheet, and then click cell **A24**.

b. Click the **Insert** tab, and then, in the Tables group, click **PivotTable**.

c. In the Create PivotTable dialog box, click **Use an external data source**, and then click **Choose Connection**.

d. In the Existing Connections dialog box, confirm that **e07ch13Sales** is selected under Connections in this Workbook, and then click **Open**.

e. In the Existing Worksheet field, confirm that **EmployeeMetrics!$A$24** is the Location, and then click **OK**.

f. In the PivotTable Fields pane, click **ALL**. Click to expand **tblEmployee**, and then drag the **LastName** field to the ROWS area.

g. Scroll down and click to expand **tblTransactions**, expand the **2017 Profit KPI**, and then click **Value (2017 Profit)** to add the calculated field to the VALUES area.

h. Click **Status** to add the KPI status threshold symbols to the PivotTable.

Notice that employees Lang and Liu fell below the lowest threshold of 80% of 2016 profits and the remaining three employees met or exceeded the highest threshold value of 105% of 2016 profits. The total profits for 2017 fell within 80% and 105% of the 2016 profits.

i. Make the following changes to the PivotTable.

- Click cell **A24**, and then edit **Row Labels** to read Employees.
- Click cell **C24**, and then edit **2017 Profit Status** to read % of 2016 Goal.
- Adjust the width of columns **A**, **B**, and **C** to automatically fit to their contents.
- Click the **Analyze** tab, and then, in the PivotTable group, change the PivotTable Name to Profits-2017.

j. **Close** the PivotTable Fields pane.

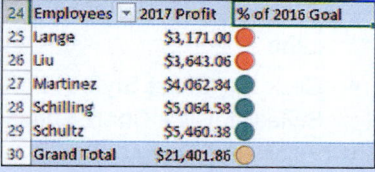

Excel 2016, Windows 10, Microsoft Corporation.

Figure 35   2017 Profit KPI in a PivotTable

k. **Save** the document.

Incorporating KPIs into PivotCharts

In previous exercises, you added KPIs into PivotTables for analysis on a dashboard. KPIs can also be incorporated into PivotCharts created from the data model. In this exercise, you will incorporate the Sum of Profit KPI into a chart to add a visualization that shows how each employee's yearly profits compare to the goal.

 E13.17

To Incorporate the KPI Goal into a Combo Chart

a. Click the **EmployeeMetrics** worksheet, and then click cell **D1**. Click the **Insert** tab, and then, in the Charts group, click **PivotChart**.

b. In the Create PivotChart dialog box, click **Use an external data source**, and then click **Choose Connection**.

c. In the Existing Connections dialog box, confirm that **e07ch13Sales** is selected under Connections in this Workbook, and then click **Open**.

d. In the Existing Worksheet field, confirm that **EmployeeSalesMetrics!$D$1** is the Location, and then click **OK**.

e. On the Analyze tab, in the Show group, click **Field List**. In the PivotChart Fields pane, click **ALL**. Click to expand **tblEmployee**, and then drag the **LastName** field to the AXIS (CATEGORIES) area.

f. Scroll down, click **tblTransactions**, and then drag the **TransactionDate (Year)** field to the AXIS (CATEGORIES) area below LastName.

g. Click **Profit** to add the calculated field to the VALUES area.

h. Click the **Sum of Profit KPI** to expand it, and then click **Goal** to add the KPI target value to the VALUES area.

i. Right-click the **chart object**, and then select **Change Chart Type**.

j. In the Change Chart Type dialog box, click **Combo**.
Notice the line chart in which the yearly profit goal of $4,000 appears as a line across the chart.

k. Click **OK**.

l. Make the following changes to the chart:

- Click **Chart Elements** ⊞, and then click **Chart Title** to add a chart title above the chart.

- Edit **Chart Title** to read 2015-2017 Profit Goals.

- Click the **Format** tab, and then, in the Current Selection group, select **Series "Sum of Profit"** from the Chart Elements list.

- In the Current Selection group, click **Format Selection**. In the Format Data Series pane, adjust the Gap Width to **100%**. **Close** ☒ the Format Data Series pane.

- Click the **Chart Styles** ✏ next to the chart, and then select **Style 8** from the Style list. Click **Chart Styles** ✏ to close the gallery.

- Click the **Analyze** tab, and then, in the PivotChart group, edit Chart Name to read Profit-2015-2017.

- On the Analyze tab, in the Show/Hide group, click **Field Buttons** to hide all filters.

- Reposition the chart to fit within the cell range **D4:K18**.

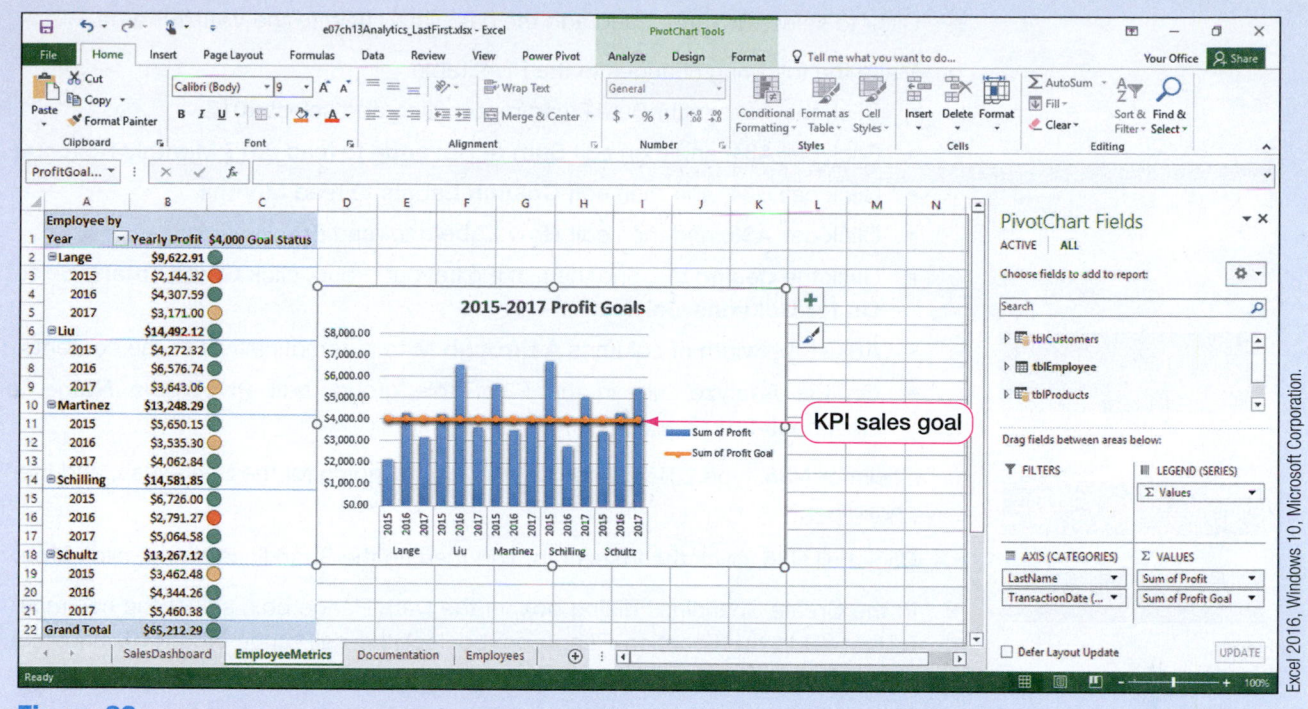

Figure 36 KPI goal added to combo chart

m. **Save**  the document.

Creating PivotTables with Sparklines

Another common method of representing data graphically for dashboards created in Excel is to use Sparklines. **Sparklines** are miniature charts that provide a way to graphically summarize a row or column of data in a single cell. There are three different types of Sparklines: line, column, and win/loss. The managers of the Red Bluff Golf Course & Pro Shop feel that they would benefit from comparing trends in sales revenue from each sales representative. In this exercise, you will create a PivotTable and add Sparklines that illustrate the trend over each month of 2017 for each sales representative.

E13.18

To Add Sparklines to a PivotTable

a. Click the **EmployeeMetrics** worksheet, and then click cell **A34**. Click the **Insert** tab, and then, in the Tables group, click **PivotTable** to insert another PivotTable into the Dashboard.

b. In the Create PivotTable dialog box, click **Use an external data source**, and then click **Choose Connection**.

c. In the Existing Connections dialog box, confirm that **e07ch13Sales** is selected under Connections in this Workbook, and then click **Open**.

d. In the Existing Worksheet field, confirm that **EmployeeMetrics!$A$34** is the Location, and then click **OK**.

e. In the PivotTable Fields pane, click **ALL**. Click to expand **tblEmployee**, and then drag the **LastName** field to the ROWS area.

f. Scroll down, click **tblTransactions**, drag **TransactionDate (Year)** to the FILTERS area, and then drag the **TransactionDate (Month)** field to the COLUMNS area.

g. Click to select **Revenue**, and add the calculated field to the VALUES area.

h. Make the following changes to the PivotTable.

- Click the TransactionDate (Year) report filter, and select **2017**.
- Click cell **A34**, and then edit **Sum of Revenue** to read 2017 Monthly Revenue.
- Click cell **B34**, and then edit **Column Labels** to read Months.
- Click cell **A35**, and then edit **Row Labels** to read Employees.
- Click the **Design** tab, and then, in the Layout group, click **Grand Totals**. Select **On for Columns Only**.
- Adjust the width of columns **A through M** to automatically fit to the contents.
- On the **Analyze** tab, in the PivotTable group, edit **PivotTable Name** to Revenues-2017Trends.

i. Click cell **N35**, type 2017 Trends as a column heading for the Sparklines, and then press ⏎.

j. Click cell **N36**. Click the **Insert** tab, and then, in the Sparklines group, click **Line**.

k. In the Create Sparklines dialog box, in the Data Range box, select the cell range **B36:M40**. In the Location Range box, select the cell range **N36:N40**, and then click **OK**.

l. Click the **Design** tab, and then, in the Show group, select the check boxes for **High Point** and **Low Point** to highlight the lowest and highest monthly profits for each employee.

m. Select the cell range **M34:M35**. Click the **Home** tab, and then, in the Clipboard group, click **Format Painter** ✎ to copy the formatting of the selected cells. Select the cell range **N34:N35** to paste the formatting to the selected cells.

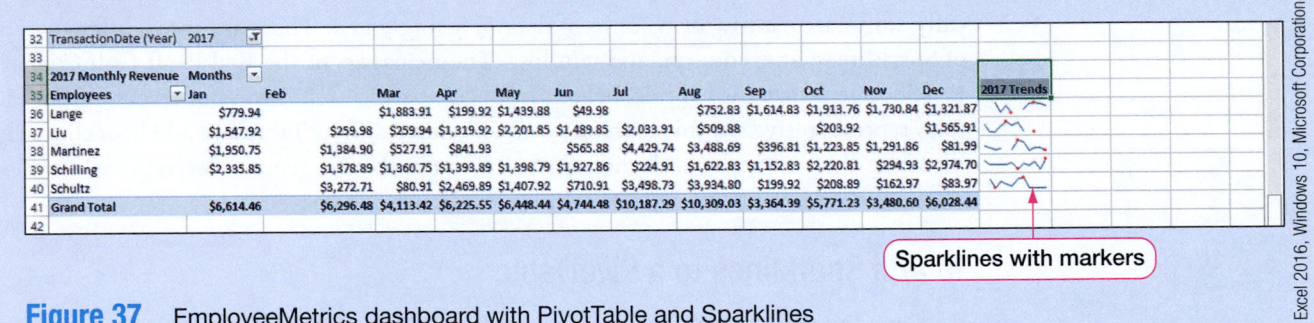

Figure 37 EmployeeMetrics dashboard with PivotTable and Sparklines

n. **Save** 💾 the document.

Use Office Add-ins for Office for Data Visualizations

In Office 2013, Microsoft introduced apps for Office. Now called Office Add-ins, these apps are created on a platform that allows app developers to create new and engaging consumer and enterprise experiences within the Office applications, such as Word, Excel, and Outlook. An **Office Add-in** is essentially a web page that is hosted inside an Office application. These Add-ins can be used to extend the functionality of the application. For example, Bing Maps has an app for Office that displays demographic data on a map to create stunning data visualizations. Other Add-ins for Excel provide advanced analytic capabilities or data visualizations.

Incorporating Bing Maps Visualization

Red Bluff Golf Course & Pro Shop tracks some demographic information about its customers, including their home states. In this exercise, you will incorporate state and revenue data from the data model and chart it by using the Bing Maps app from the Office Store.

 E13.19

To Use the Bing Maps App for Office

a. Click the **EmployeeMetrics** worksheet, and then click cell **L1**. Click the **Insert** tab, and then, in the Tables group, click **PivotTable** to insert another PivotTable into the dashboard.

b. In the Create PivotTable dialog box, click **Use an external data source**, and then click **Choose Connection**.

c. In the Existing Connections dialog box, confirm that **e07ch13Sales** is selected under Connections in this Workbook, and then click **Open**.

d. In the Existing Worksheet field, confirm that **EmployeeMetrics!$L$1** is the Location, and then click **OK**.

e. In the PivotTable Fields list, scroll down to **tblCustomers**, and then drag the **State** field to the ROWS area.

f. Scroll down to **tblTransctions**, drag **TransactionDate (Year)** to the COLUMNS area, and then select **Revenue** to add it to the VALUES area.

g. Make the following changes to the PivotTable.

- Click cell **L1**, and then edit **Sum of Revenue** to read Total Revenue.

- Click cell **L2**, and then edit **Row Labels** to read State.

- Click cell **M1**, and then edit **Column Labels** to read Year.

- Click the **Design** tab, and then, in the Layout group, click **Grand Totals**. Select **Off for Rows and Columns**.

- Click the **Analyze** tab, and then, in the PivotTable group, change the PivotTable Name to YearlyRevenuesByState.

h. Click the **Insert** tab, and then, in the Add-ins group, click the **Bing Maps App** . If necessary, click **Trust this add-in**.

SIDE NOTE
More Add-ins
Clicking the Store icon will open a window that will allow you to explore additional Add-ins for Excel.

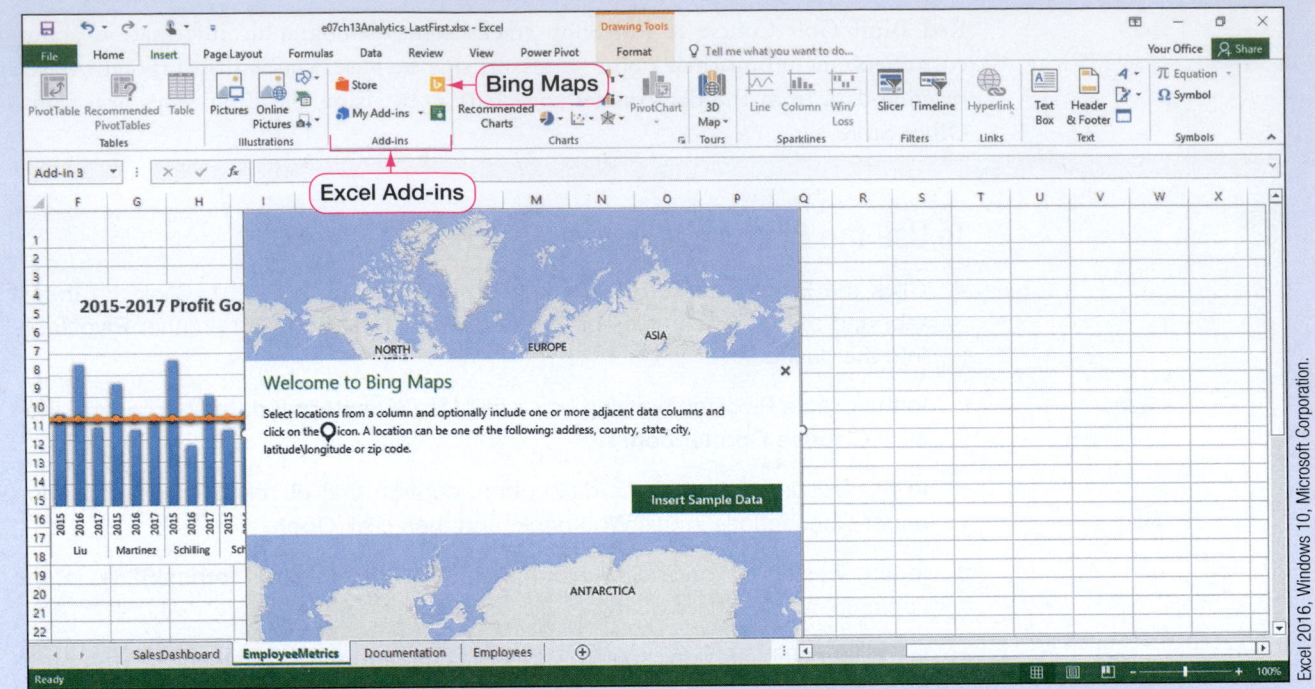

Figure 38 Bing Maps app added

Troubleshooting

If you are not already logged in to your Microsoft account, you will be prompted to sign in before the app can be installed.

i. Resize the map, and then reposition it so that it fits below the YearlyRevenuesByState PivotTable. The map should fit within the cell range **L8:O27**.

j. Select the data in the cell range **L2:O7**, and then, on the Bing Map, click the **Show Locations** {} icon.
   Notice the zoom in, zoom out, and pan navigation buttons at the top of the map. Explore the controls. Also explore the Filter ▼ and Settings ⚙ features.

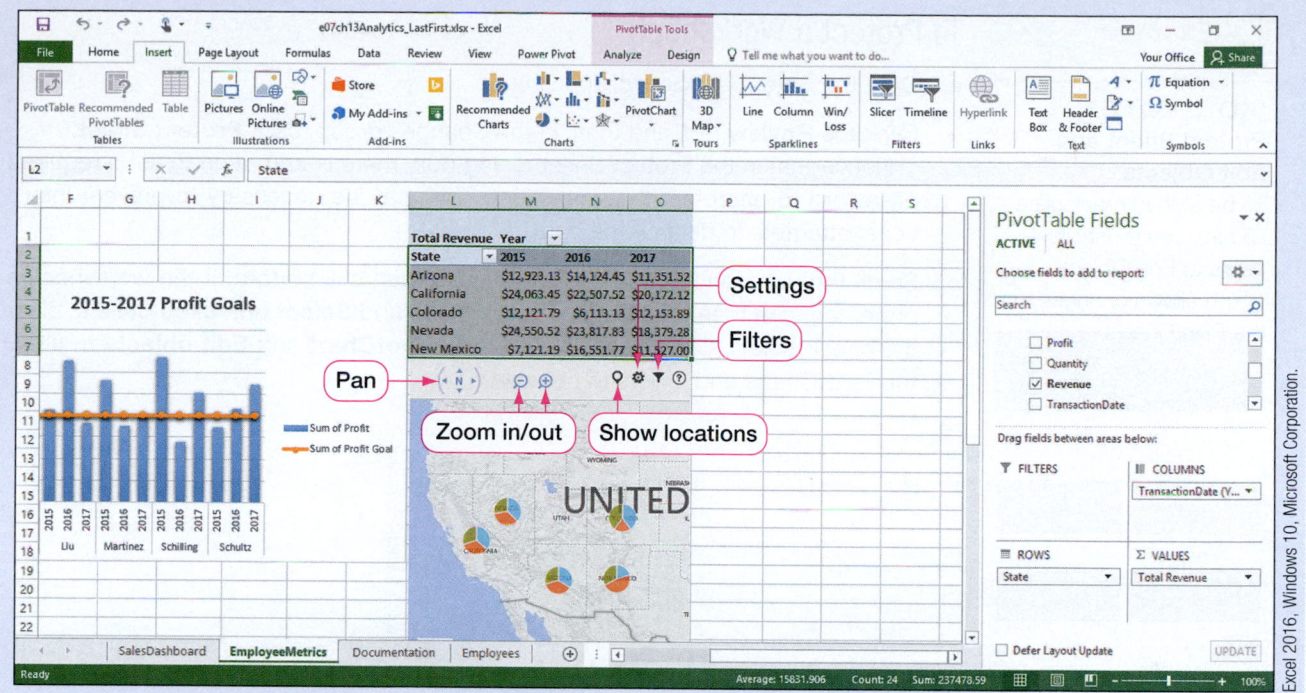

Figure 39 Revenues by state added to Bing Map

SIDE NOTE
Bing Maps Refresh
It may be necessary to refresh the Bing Map App when a file is first opened, as it may show a default map view.

k. **Save** 🖫 the document.

Prepare a Dashboard for Production

Once a dashboard has been designed to meet the business requirements, there are several steps you need to take to get it ready for use. This process may include protecting various worksheets and cells from accidental mistakes, hiding various elements from the user that are not necessary for the dashboard, and making some simple design modifications to enhance the user experience.

Protecting Excel Worksheets

Because dashboards are designed for the specific needs of end users, it is important to ensure that once the dashboard contains all the required data, certain protections are in place to avoid accidental deletion of various objects or incorrect modifications. The managers at the Red Bluff Golf Course & Pro Shop who will be benefiting from these dashboards are not as comfortable with Excel as you are, and they do not want to accidentally delete data or otherwise compromise the data. In this exercise, you will protect the important elements of the workbook.

 **E**13.20

To Protect a Worksheet

SIDE NOTE
Protect Sheet and Edit Objects
To be able to manipulate Slicers, you must allow users to Edit Objects, which allows changes to the PivotCharts.

a. Click the **SalesDashboard** worksheet.

b. Click the **Review** tab, and then, in the Changes group, click **Protect Sheet**.
   Notice that in the Protect Sheet dialog box, there is an option to set a required password to unprotect the worksheet. This may be necessary to prevent intentional attempts to destroy the data.

c. Scroll through options of actions that users can still perform if the worksheet is protected, and then click **Select locked cells** and **Select unlocked cells** to clear the check boxes. Click **Use PivotTable & PivotChart** and **Edit objects** to allow the PivotCharts and slicers to be used.

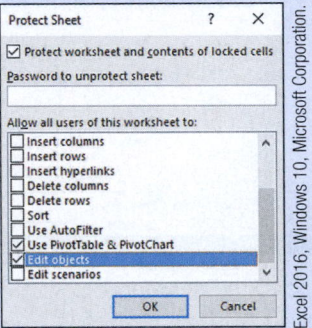

Figure 40 Protect Sheet dialog box

d. Click **OK**. With the sheet protected, no cells can be selected, no additional data can be added to the worksheet, and no columns or rows be inserted or deleted.

e. Click the **EmployeeMetrics** worksheet.
   Before protecting the worksheet, make sure that all columns have been adjusted to automatically fit to their contents.

f. Click the **Review** tab, and then, in the Changes group, click **Protect Sheet**.

g. Scroll through the options of actions that users can still perform if the worksheet is protected, and then click **Select locked cells** and **Select unlocked cells** to clear the check boxes. Click **Use PivotTable & PivotChart** to allow for the PivotTable filters to be used.

h. Click **OK**.

i. **Save** the document.

Sₛ **CONSIDER THIS** | **Using Excel Web Add-ins**

Excel Web Add-ins encourage and facilitate sharing and collaboration. However, the Excel Web App does not support all the features available in the full desktop version of Excel, such as Protect Sheets. What other things should you take into consideration, depending on how you expect users to access your Excel workbook?

Hiding Unnecessary Screen Elements

Many of the interactive elements of Microsoft Excel can be hidden from users. Normally, controls such as the ribbon and scroll bars are useful and necessary parts of working with Excel. However, when a dashboard is presented to a user, it is preferable to hide any unnecessary objects that may distract the user from the dashboard's content. In this exercise, you will hide screen elements from the dashboard.

 **E13.21**

To Hide Screen Elements

a. Click the **View** tab.

b. In the Show group, click the **Gridlines** and **Headings** check boxes to deselect them.

c. Right-click the **Employees** worksheet, and then select **Hide** to hide the worksheet from view.

d. Press ⌃Ctrl + F1 to minimize the ribbon and maximize dashboard space. If necessary, click the EmployeeMetrics worksheet.

SIDE NOTE
Toggle the Ribbon
You can expand and collapse the ribbon by pressing ⌃Ctrl + F1.

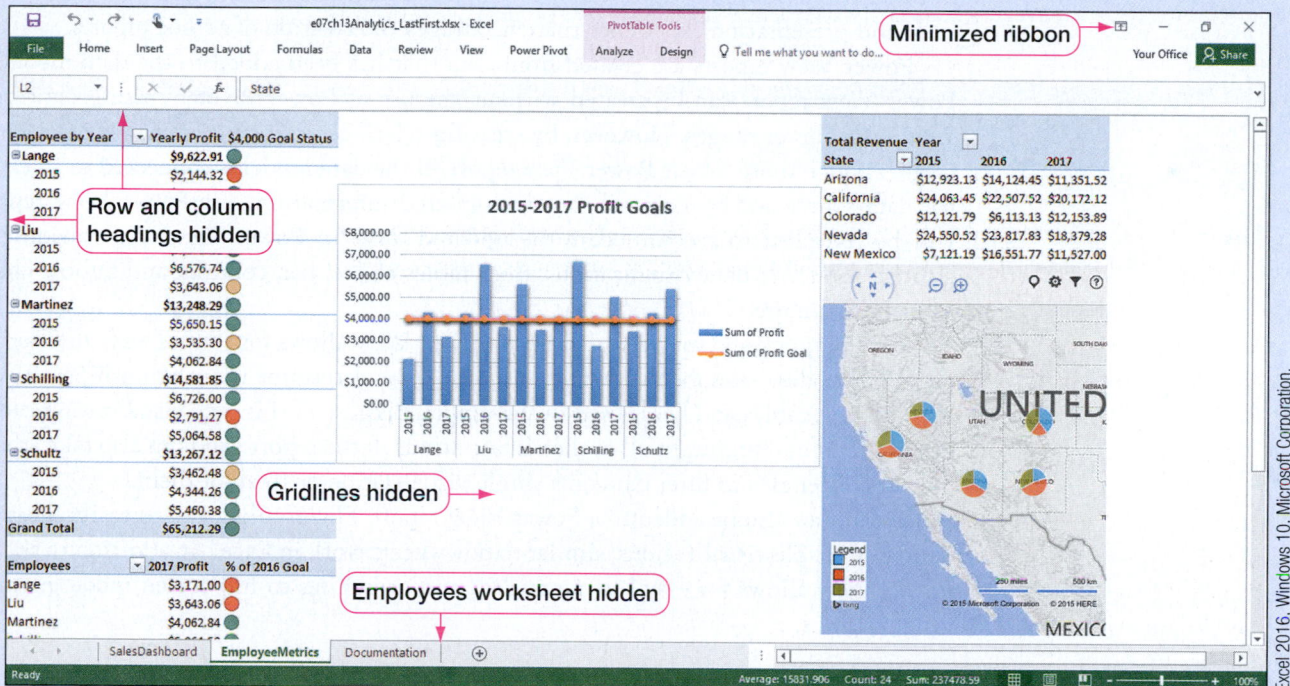

Figure 41 EmployeeMetrics dashboard with elements hidden

e. **Save** 💾 the document. If you need to take a break before finishing this chapter, now is a good time.

REAL WORLD ADVICE | **Hiding Screen Elements**

You may be tempted to hide the Vertical and Horizontal scrollbars under Display options for this workbook if all of the elements fit on your screen. However, consider the various screen sizes that may be used to view the data. Smaller screens and those with lower resolutions may not be able to view all the data if those screen elements are hidden.

Exploring the Benefits of Personalize Business Intelligence

Dashboards are great for people who know exactly what questions they have and what answers they want to derive from the data. However, it is often necessary to view data from multiple perspectives first, to gain a better understanding of the data, before those questions can be known. Microsoft knows that being able to quickly analyze large amounts of data is extremely important for business intelligence. This is why Power Pivot was integrated in Excel, beginning with Excel 2013. Microsoft also understands the benefits of being able to quickly analyze that data visually, which is where Power View comes in.

Power View, combined with Power Pivot in Excel, provides all the BI tools necessary to lead to better decision making. In this section, you will explore the Power View tool and create a report for the managers of the Red Bluff Golf Course & Pro Shop that demonstrates some of the key features.

Generate Visual Reports with Power View

Power View in Excel offers powerful data visualization tools that were once available only in third-party BI applications. **Power View** is an interactive data visualization, exploration, and presentation experience that encourages the creation of ad hoc reports.

Power View reports are created from data that has been added to the data model. A Power View report can be created without the use of Power Pivot by using data from separate tables or ranges. However, by creating relationships using Power Pivot, you can create a much more robust Power View report. If the data model is connected to an external data source and that source contains updated information, any Power View reports will be refreshed to accommodate the updated data. In Power View, you can quickly create a variety of data visualizations, from tables to pie, bar, column, and bubble charts to maps and more.

Beyond quick and easy visualizations, Power View allows for several ways to filter the data. Power View uses metadata in the data model to determine the relationships between the different tables and fields used in the report. Because of this, one visualization can be used to filter and highlight all of the visualizations in the report. You can also take advantage of a filter area to filter data on a single visualization or to all of them.

Slicers can also be added to a Power View report. Slicers allow you to easily filter the data in multiple visualizations, similar to how slicers work in Excel. In addition to slicers, Power View allows for easy sorting of data and switching to full-screen mode for some visualizations.

Installing the Silverlight Plug-in

Excel's Power View requires that Microsoft's Silverlight be installed. **Silverlight** is a powerful tool for creating interactive user experiences. It is a free plug-in powered by the .NET framework and is compatible with multiple browsers, devices, applications, and operating systems.

 E13.22

To Install Microsoft Silverlight

a. If you took a break, open the **e07ch13Analytics** workbook and, if needed, click the **EmployeeMetrics** worksheet.

b. Open your browser, and navigate to http://www.microsoft.com/silverlight/.

c. Click **DOWNLOAD NOW** to begin the download and installation process of the latest version of Silverlight.

d. Follow the prompts to download and install Silverlight, and then close your browser.

Inserting a Power View Report Sheet

The Power View report sheet has a fixed size, unlike other worksheets in Excel. There are no scroll bars, and the report sheet may remind you of a PowerPoint slide. When you first insert a Power View report sheet, three panes are visible: the Design pane, the Filters pane, and the Power View Fields pane. Before any data is added to the Power View report, the options available on the Power View tab on the ribbon are limited to a few, such as Undo and Redo, setting a theme, adding a picture or image, refreshing the data, and creating and editing relationships in the data model. Additional contextual tabs will become available once you begin creating the report. In this exercise, you will insert a new Power View report sheet into the workbook and explore the layout.

 E13.23

To Insert a Power View Report Sheet

a. Press Ctrl + F1 to expand the ribbon if necessary. Click the **File** tab, and then click **Options**.

b. Click **Customize Ribbon**, and then click the **Choose commands from** arrow, and select **Commands Not in the Ribbon**.

c. Scroll until you see **Insert a Power View Report**, and click to select it.

d. Under the Main Tabs list, click **Insert**, and then click **New Group**. Click **Rename**, and type Reports. Click **OK**.

e. Click **Add**.

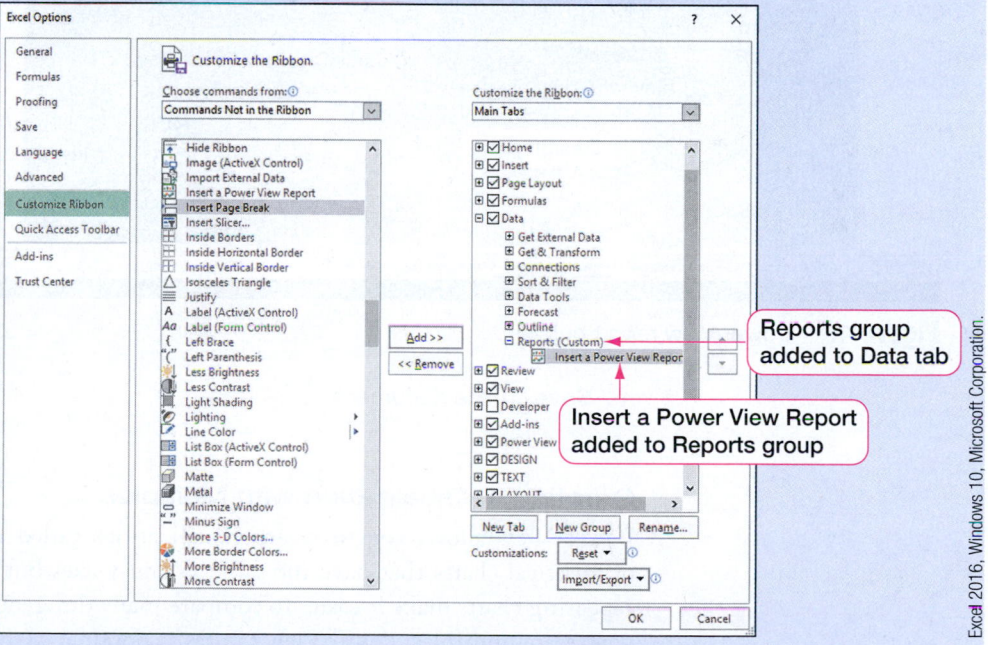

Figure 42 Customizing the ribbon to add Power View

f. Click **OK**.

A new group will now appear in the Insert tab on the far right of the screen containing the Power View icon.

> ## Troubleshooting
>
> If you do not have Silverlight installed, you will be prompted to install it before you can continue. If necessary, click Install Silverlight, and follow the prompts. Once it has been installed, click Reload.

g. Click the **Insert** tab, and in the Reports group, click **Power View**. Right-click the **Power View1** worksheet, and then select **Rename**.

h. Type InteractiveReport as the worksheet name, and then press Enter.

i. Examine the various components that make up the Power View report builder.

j. Click the **Click here to add a title** text, and type Red Bluff Golf Course & Pro Shop Sales Report.

k. Click the **Power View** tab, and then, in the Themes group, click **Themes**. Select **Hardcover** in the seventh row of the fourth column to add a theme to the Power View Report.

l. In the Themes group, click **Background**, and then select **Dark1 Vertical Gradient**.

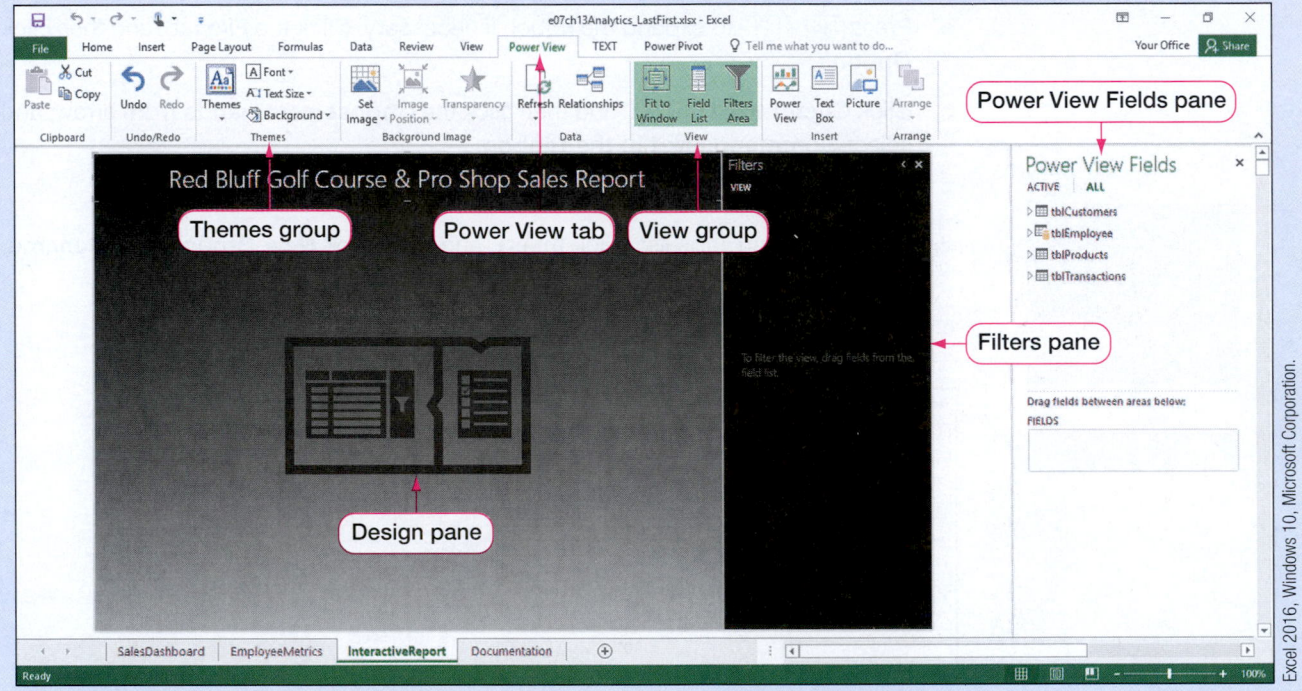

Figure 43 Power View report builder

m. **Save** 💾 the document.

Creating a Visualization with Multiples

Power View allows you to create visualizations called multiples. **Multiples** are series of identical charts that have the same x- and y-axes but contain different values. These repeating charts make it easier to compare many different values at the same time. When you create multiples, Power View creates a container with one chart for each of the values. For example, if you have a column chart of monthly sales, you could add a year field to the multiples field and have one column chart for each year. There are two different types of multiples: vertical multiples and horizontal multiples. **Vertical multiples** will expand across the width of the container and wrap down the container in the available space. If not all multiples fit in the available space, a vertical scroll bar is also added. **Horizontal multiples** expand across the available space in the container, and if additional space is needed, a horizontal scroll bar is added.

In this exercise, you will create a clustered column chart with horizontal multiples to display the monthly sales from year to year.

 **E13.24**

To Create Multiples

a. On the **InteractiveReport** worksheet, scroll through the Power View Fields pane, and then expand **tblTransactions** to view available fields.

b. Select **TransactionDate (Month)** and **Σ Revenue**. Notice that once data has been added to the Design pane, the DESIGN tab appears on the ribbon.

c. On the DESIGN tab, in the Switch Visualization group, click **Column Chart**, and then select **Clustered Column**. Notice that in the Power View Fields pane, the choices have changed to accommodate the options for a clustered column chart.

d. In the Power View Fields pane, click the **TransactionDate (Year)** arrow, and select **Add as Horizontal Multiples**.

e. In the Design pane, drag the **edge** of the clustered column chart to the right so that all three charts are visible.

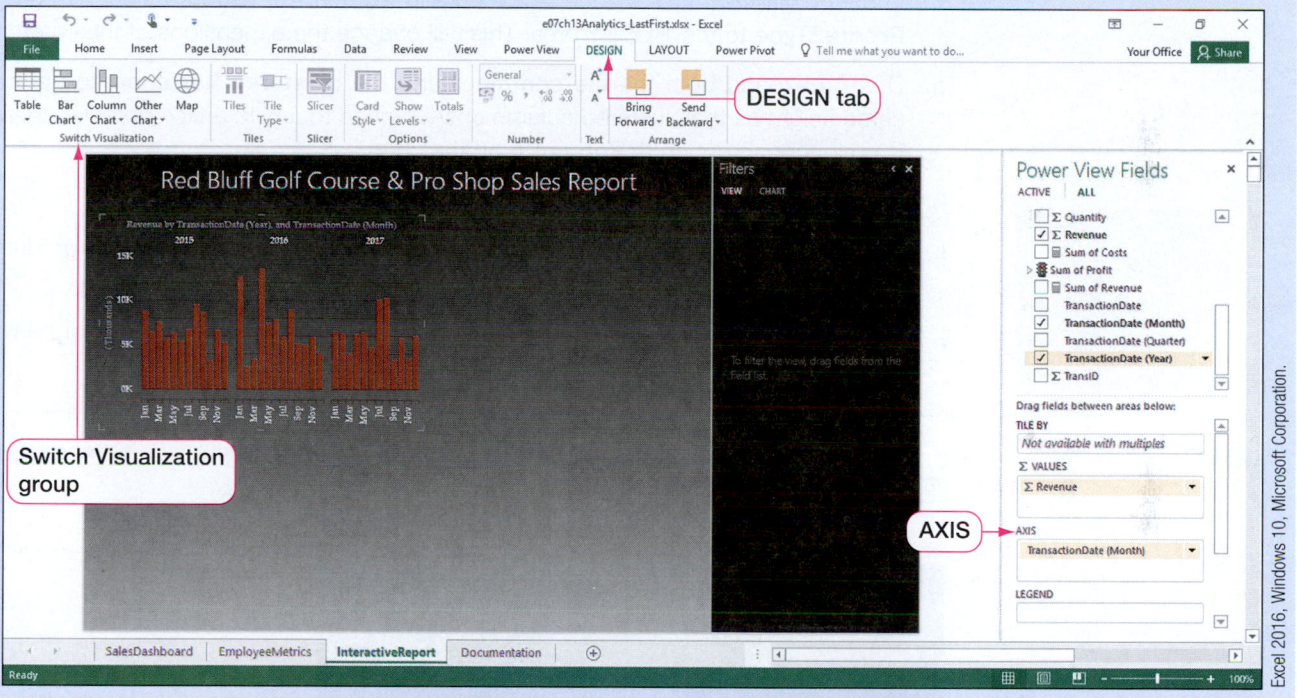

Figure 44 Horizontal Multiples visualization

f. Point to the chart, and click the **Pop out** {} icon in the top right corner of the chart to see the chart in full-screen view.

g. Click the **Pop in** {} icon to return the chart to its previous size.

h. **Save** 🖫 the document.

Creating a Visualization with Tiles

Multiples are a great way to see all the charts at one time. However, that may not always be the most effective way to analyze data. Power View offers a visualization feature called tiles. **Tiles** provide a dynamic navigation strip that allows you to navigate through a series of charts on the basis of a particular value, such as a chart visualizing sales by employee with tiles for each product category. This allows the user to quickly see data from a specific product category with the click of a tile.

In this exercise, you will create a bar chart visualization that will compare total sales for each employee with tiles on the basis of product type.

 **E13.25**

To Create a Bar Chart with Tiles

a. Click the **Power View** tab, and then, in the View group, click **Field List**, if necessary, to display the Power View Fields pane. Click an empty area of the Design pane to deselect the chart.

b. In the Power View Fields pane, expand **tblEmployee**, and then select **LastName**. Notice that a new table is being created to the right of the chart.

c. In the Power View Fields pane, scroll down to **tblTransactions**, and then select **Σ Revenue**.

d. On the **DESIGN** tab, in the Switch Visualization group, click **Bar Chart**. Select **Clustered Bar**.

e. In the Design pane, expand the size of the clustered bar chart so all values are visible.

f. In the Power View Fields pane, scroll up and expand **tblProducts**, and then drag **ProductType** to the TILE BY area. This will change the dimensions of the chart.

g. Drag to expand both the **tile container** and the **clustered bar chart** to be the same height as the clustered column chart. Notice that with a tile container, there is no longer an option to **Pop out** {} on the chart.

h. **Close** the Filters pane and the Power View Fields pane.

i. Click on the various tiles to see how the employee sales compare for other product types.

j. Explore the ability to filter all visualizations by clicking the bar for the last name **Lange** on the Revenue by LastName bar chart.

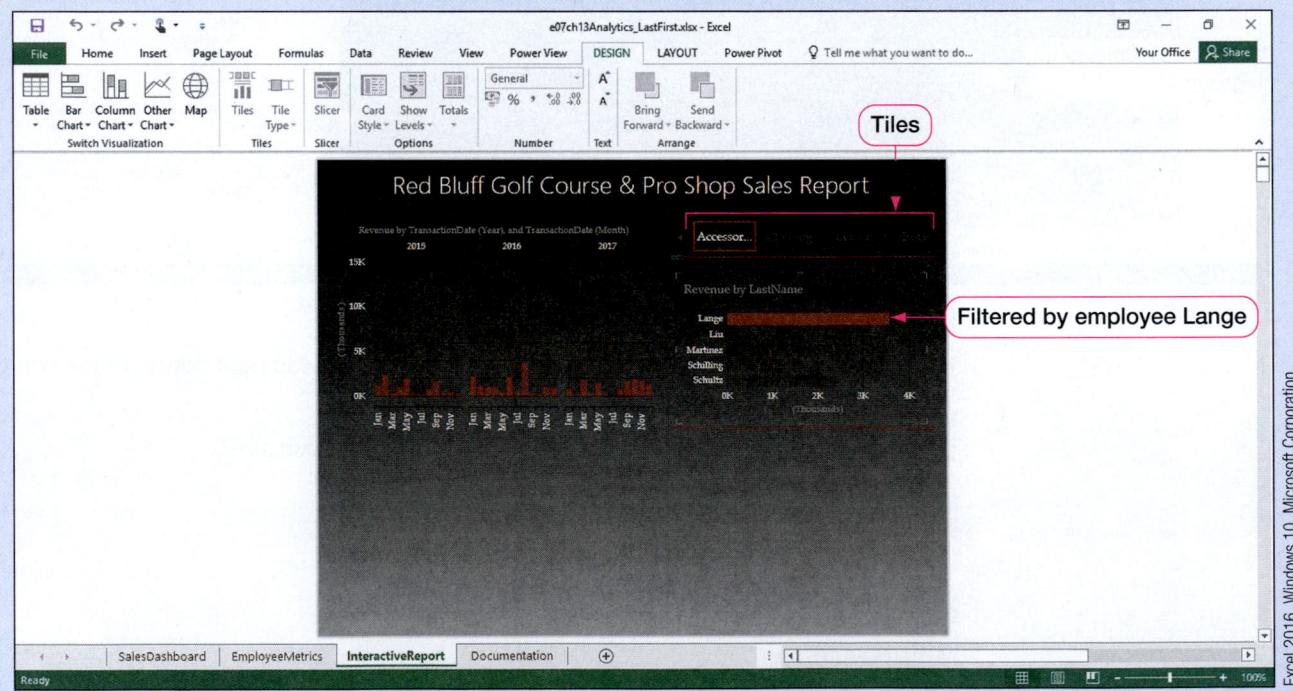

Figure 45 Power View report filtered by employee Lange

k. Click anywhere inside the chart container, but not on a bar, to remove the filter.

l. **Save** 💾 the document.

Creating a Map Visualization in Power View

The Bing Maps app is one way to create data visualizations that illustrate data with a geographic element. However, the Bing Maps app has limited interactive capabilities. Beyond zooming and panning around, there is no interaction. Excel's Power View report includes a map visualization that can be used with filters or slicers or even to filter other charts in the report. In this exercise, you will create a map visualization to add to the Power View report.

 **E13.26**

To Create a Map Visualization in Power View

a. Click an empty area below the **clustered column chart**.

b. Click the **Power View** tab, and then, in the View group, click **Field List** to display the Power View Fields pane. In the Power View Fields pane, expand tblCustomers if necessary, and then click to select **State**. Expand tblTransactions if necessary, select **TransactionDate (Year)**, and then select **Σ Revenue**.

c. On the **DESIGN** tab, in the Switch Visualization group, click **Map**. If necessary, click **Enable Content** in the Privacy Warning bar.

d. If necessary, drag the **Map** under the clustered column chart. Drag the **right-middle sizing handle** to the right to expand the width of the Map visualization. Click **Zoom Out** 🔍 so that the following states are visible: California, Nevada, Arizona, Colorado, and New Mexico.

e. On the Map visualization, on the legend, click **2015** to filter all other visualizations to show only 2015 revenue.

f. **Close** the Power View Fields pane.

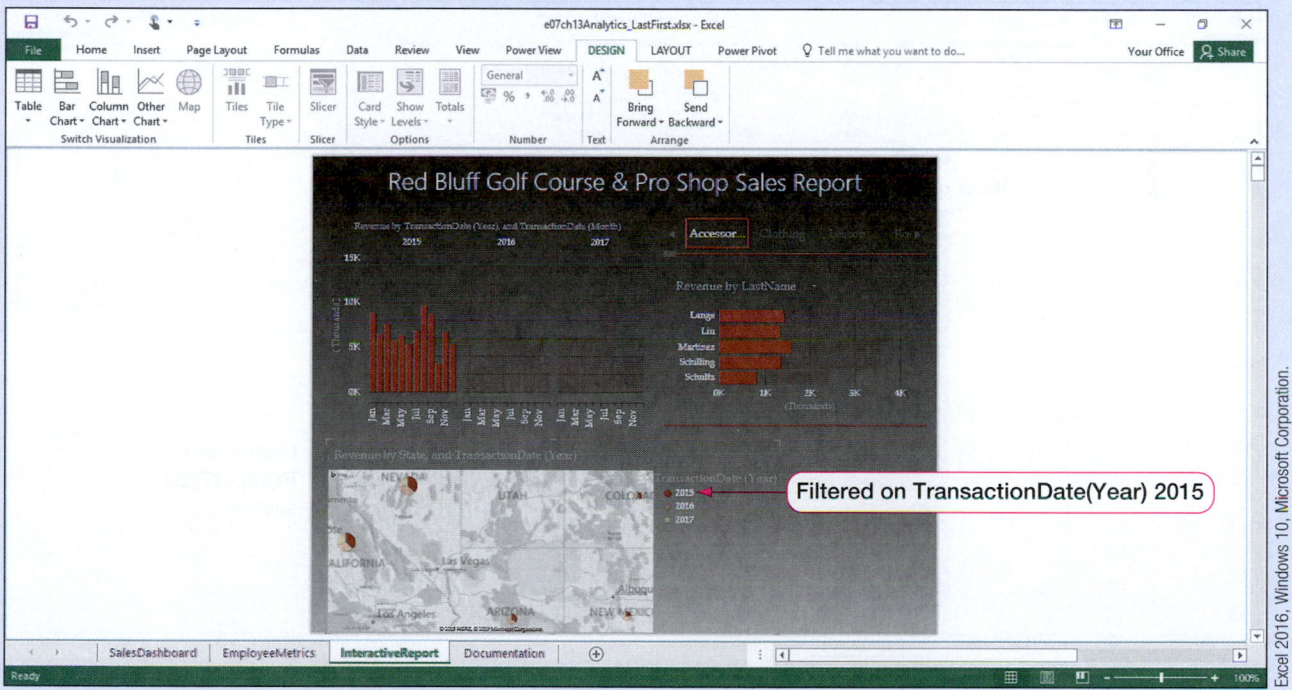

Figure 46 Power View report filtered to TransactionDate (Year) 2015

g. Click just below the **TransactionDate (Year)** legend to clear the 2015 filter.

h. **Save** 💾 the document.

Adding Slicers to a Power View Report

Slicers in a Power View report work just as they do in an Excel worksheet, allowing an easy way to filter data and charts with the click of the button. As you have already seen, the Power View report makes it easy to filter data from other data visualizations. However, it is often useful to add slicers for data that is not necessarily a part of any of the visualizations. In this exercise, you will add Status and ProductType slicers to the report that will allow the managers of the Red Bluff Golf Course & Pro Shop to see the revenue for members and guests as well as any particular product type.

E13.27 To Add Slicers to a Power View Report

a. Click the **Power View** tab, and in the View group, click **Field List** to view the Power View Fields pane. Click an empty area of the Design pane to the right of the map.

b. Expand tblCustomers if necessary, and then click to select **Status**.

c. On the **DESIGN** tab, in the Slicer group, click **Slicer** to create a slicer from the Status field.

d. Adjust the height of the Status slicer by dragging the **bottom middle sizing handle** up to just below **Member**.

e. Click an empty area below the **Status** slicer. Expand tblProducts if necessary, and then click **ProductType**.

f. On the DESIGN tab, in the Slicer group, click **Slicer** to create a slicer from the ProductType field.

g. Drag the **ProductType** slicer below the Status slicer. Adjust the size appropriately.

h. Use the slicers to filter the report to show only revenue from **Members** and **Clothing**.

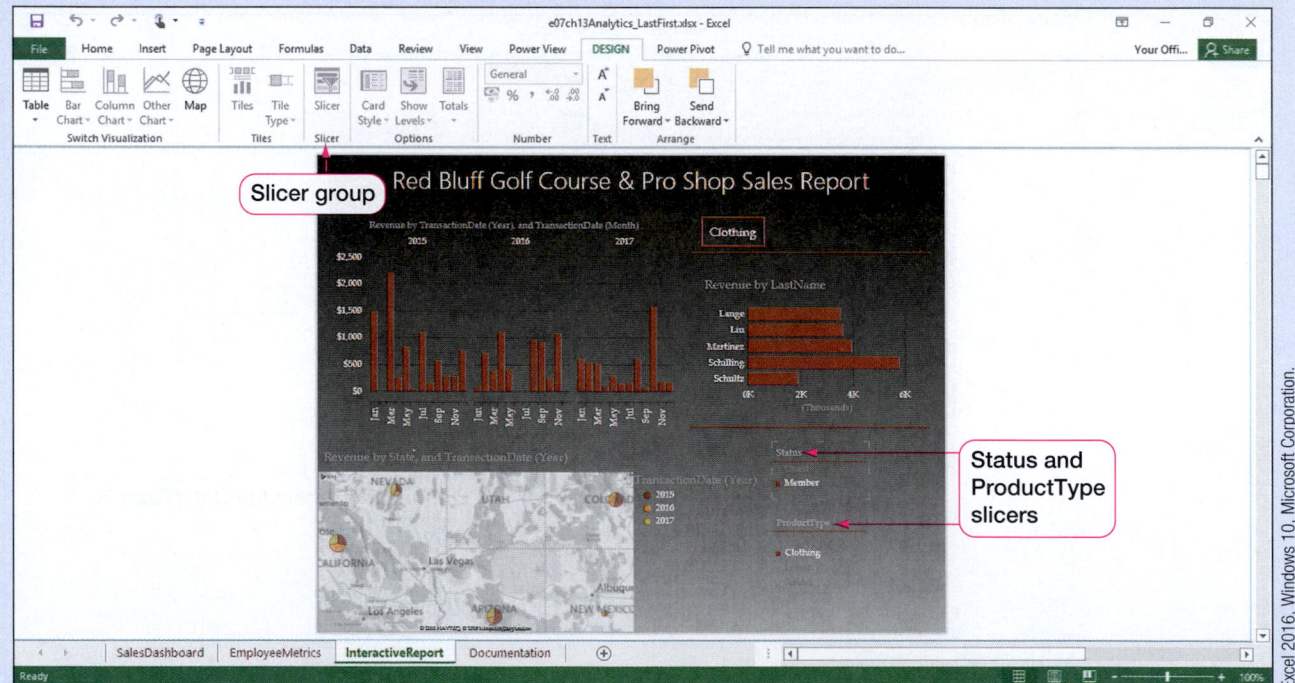

Figure 47 Slicers added to Power View report

i. **Close** the Power View Fields pane.

j. Click **Clear Filter** on the Status and ProductType slicers.

k. Complete the **Documentation** worksheet.

l. **Save** the document, exit Excel, and then submit your files as directed by your instructor.

Concept Check

1. What are some basic design concepts to consider when you are creating a digital dashboard? p. 689

2. Describe the data model, and explain how it can improve data analysis. p. 693

3. Discuss some of the advanced data modeling techniques made possible with Power Pivot. p. 701

4. Describe how Power Pivot can be used to create a simple dashboard, and discuss a few simple ways to enhance the value of a dashboard. p. 710

5. What are Office Add-ins, and what are some benefits of using them? p. 724

6. What are some recommended changes to prepare a dashboard for production, and why are they recommended? p. 727

7. What are the benefits of a Power View report, and how is it different from a dashboard? p. 730

Key Terms

Base value   708
Bidirectional KPI   708
Business intelligence (BI)   689
Data model   693
Digital dashboard   689
Explicit calculated field   705
Horizontal multiples   732
Implicit calculated field   705

Key performance indicator (KPI)   690
Multiples   732
Negative KPI   708
Office Add-ins   724
Positive KPI   708
Power Query   694
Power View   730
Relational data   694

Silverlight   730
Slicer   710
Sparkline   723
Status threshold   708
Target value   708
Tiles   733
Vertical multiples   732
White space   692

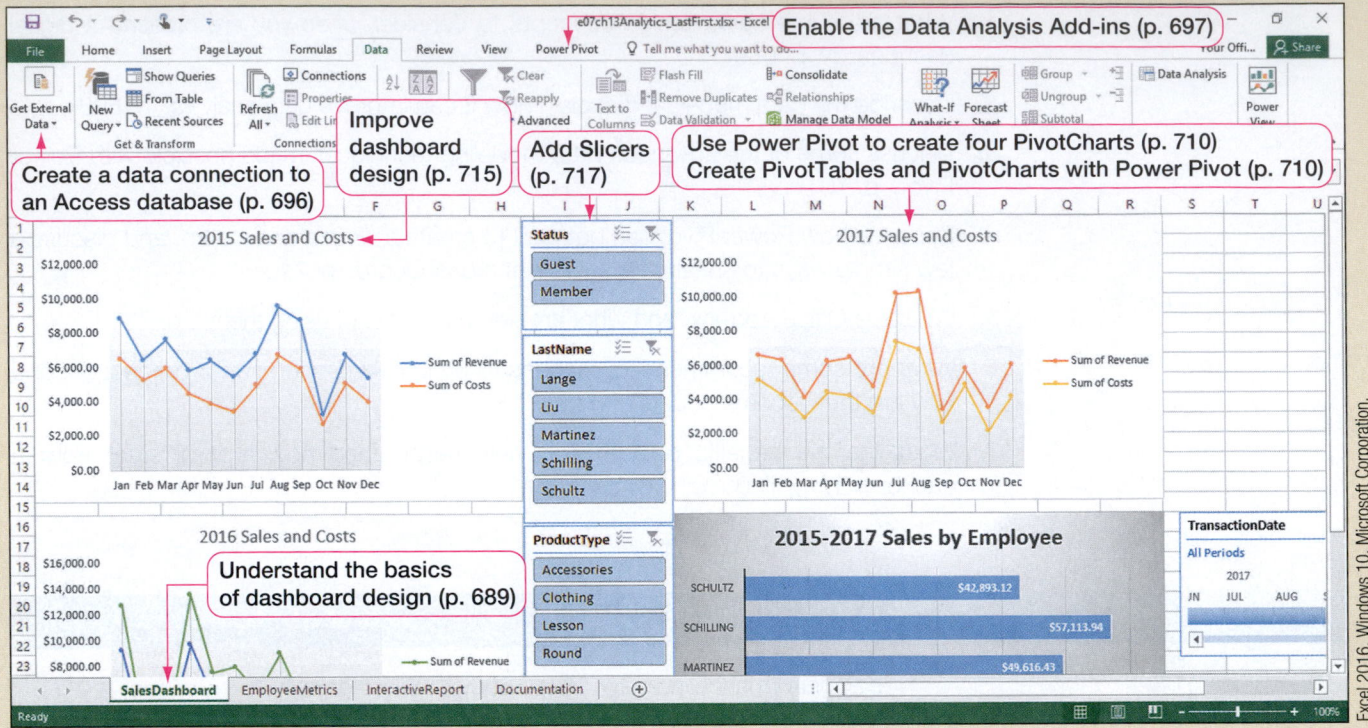

Figure 48

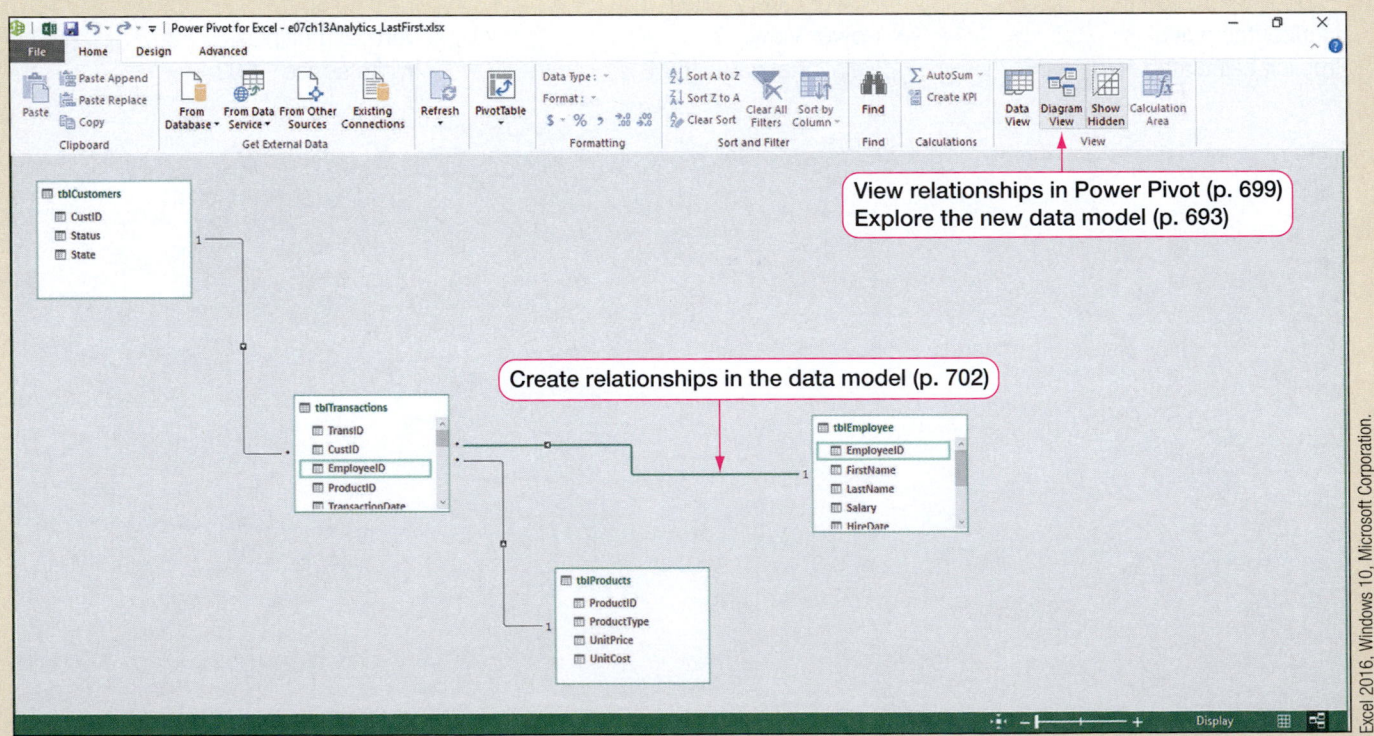

Figure 49

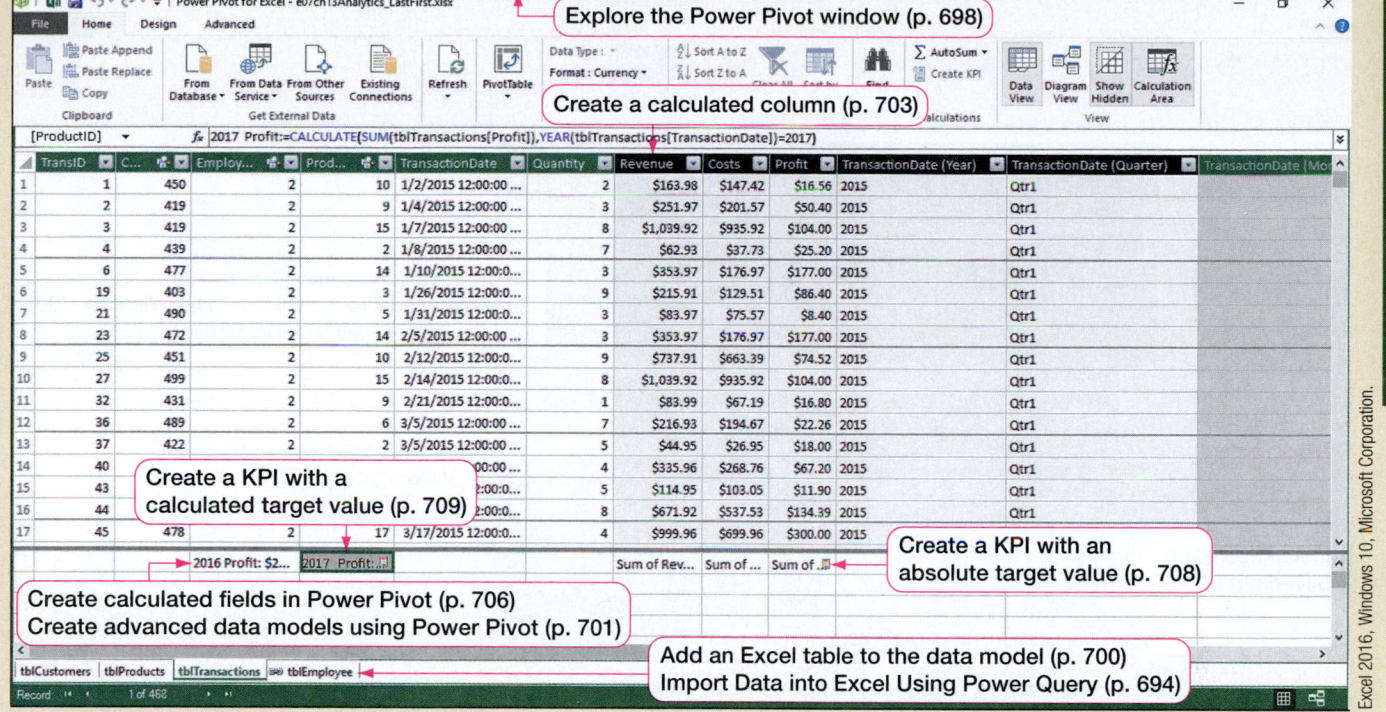

Figure 50

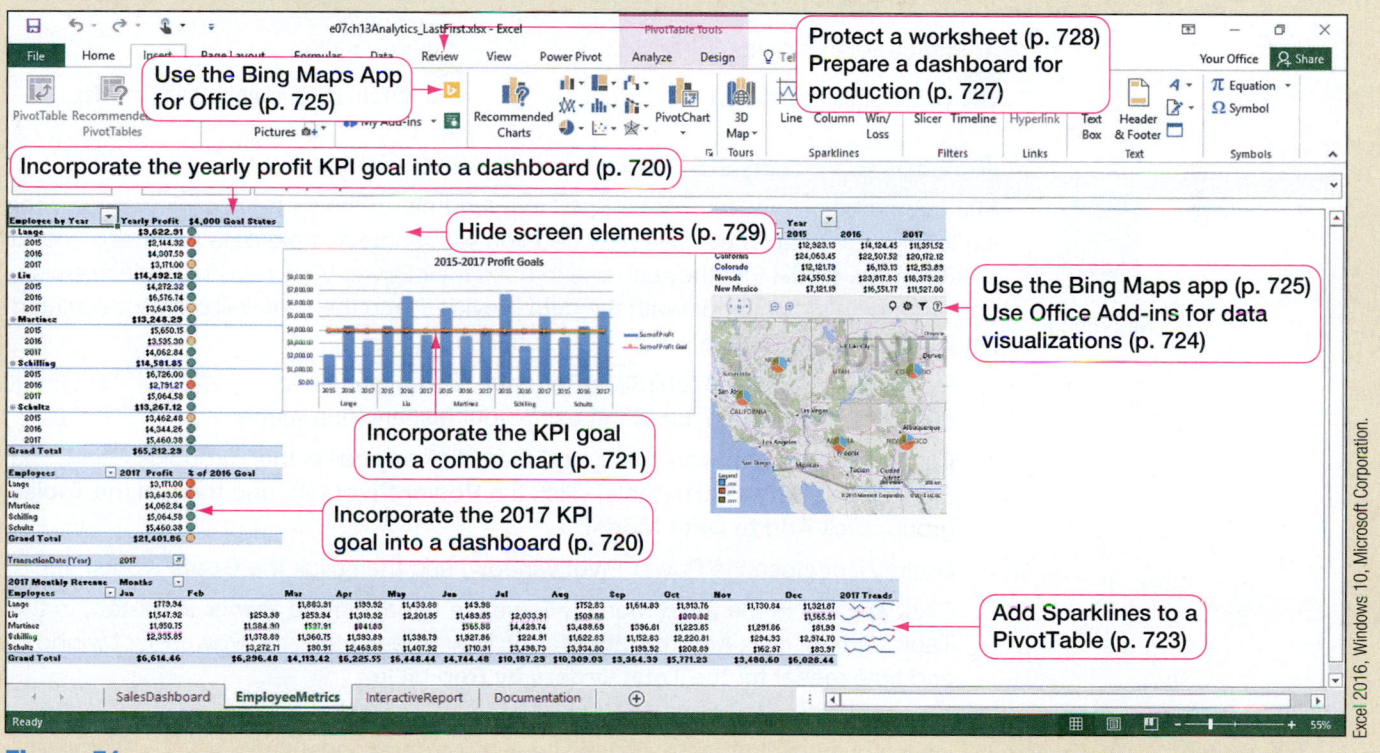

Figure 51

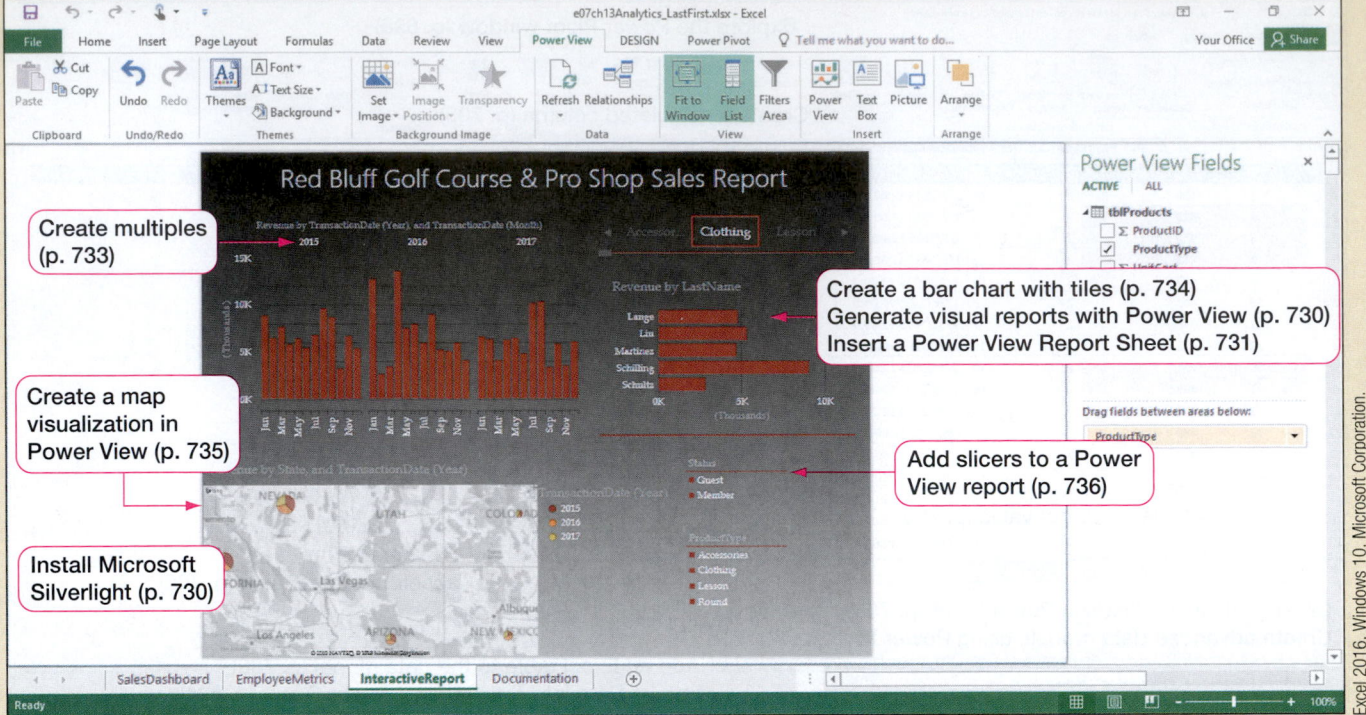

Figure 52

Create multiples (p. 733)

Create a map visualization in Power View (p. 735)

Install Microsoft Silverlight (p. 730)

Create a bar chart with tiles (p. 734)
Generate visual reports with Power View (p. 730)
Insert a Power View Report Sheet (p. 731)

Add slicers to a Power View report (p. 736)

Excel 2016, Windows 10, Microsoft Corporation.

Practice 1

Student data file needed:

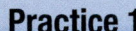 e07ch13SpaRevenue.xlsx

You will save your file as:

e07ch13SpaRevenue_LastFirst.xlsx

Advanced Analysis at the Turquoise Oasis Spa

Sales & Marketing

Managers at the Turquoise Oasis Spa have read about the benefits of Power View for exploring their data. They have provided you with some sample data and need you to create a data model that they can use to build their Power View report. In this exercise, you will create a data model with the data provided, and then you will create calculated fields, calculated columns, KPIs, and relationships.

a. Open the Excel file **e07ch13SpaRevenue**. Save your file as **e07ch13SpaRevenue_LastFirst** using your last and first name.

b. Click the **SalesData** worksheet, and then click any cell in the Turquoise Oasis Spa Sample Sales 2014-2016 table. Click the **Power Pivot** tab, and then, in the Tables group, click **Add to Data Model**.

c. Minimize or close the Power Pivot window, and then click the **Goals** worksheet.

d. Click any cell in the 2016 Monthly Revenue table. On the Power Pivot tab, in the Tables group, click **Add to Data Model**. Minimize or close the PowerPivot window, and then repeat for the **Total Orders by Rep** table.

e. On the Power Pivot tab, in the Data Model group, click **Manage**, and make the following changes to the **SpaSales** sheet in the data model.

- Double-click the **Add Column** column heading, type Revenue, and then press [Enter]. Type =[UnitPrice]*[QuantitySold], and then press [Enter]. Click the **Home** tab, and then, in the Formatting group, click the **Format** arrow, and then select **Currency**.

- Double-click the **Add Column** column heading, type Costs, and then press [Enter]. Type =[UnitCost]*[QuantitySold], and then press [Enter]. On the Home tab, in the Formatting group, click the **Format** arrow, and then select **Currency**.

- Double-click the **Add Column** column heading, type **Profit**, and then press Enter. Type **=[Revenue]-[Costs]**, and then press Enter. On the Home tab, in the Formatting group, click the **Format** arrow, and then select **Currency**.

f. Click the **RevGoals2016** worksheet, and then make the following changes to the RevGoals2016 worksheet in the data model.

- Select the **MonthlySalesActual** column. On the Home tab, in the Formatting group, click **Format** arrow, and then select **Currency**.

- Select the **MonthlySalesGoal** column. On the Home tab, in the Formatting group, click **Format** arrow, and then select **Currency**.

- Select both the **MonthlySalesActual** and **MonthlySalesGoal** columns, and then, in the Calculations group, click **AutoSum** to create two calculated fields in the Calculation Area: Sum of MonthlySalesActual and Sum of MonthlySalesGoal.

- In the Calculation Area, click the **Sum of MonthlySalesActual** calculated field, and then, in the Calculations group, click **Create KPI**.

- Under Define target value, in the Measure box, select **Sum of MonthlySalesGoal**.

- Under **Define status thresholds**, click and slide the low value threshold to **75%** and the high value threshold to **100%**.

- Under **Select icon style**, select the flags icon set (the second option from the left).

- Click **OK**.

g. Create a relationship in the data model between the SpaSales table and the OrdersByRep table by completing the following tasks.

- Click the **OrdersByRep** worksheet in the Power Pivot window, and then select the **SalesRep** column.

- Click the **Design** tab, and then, in the Relationships group, click **Create Relationship**.

- In the Table 2 box, select **SpaSales**.

- Select **SalesRep** in the Columns field, and then click **OK**.

- Click **Save** to return to the workbook.

h. Click the **Documentation** worksheet. Click cell **A6,** and then type in today's date. Click cell **B6**, and then type in your first and last name. Complete the remainder of the **Documentation** worksheet according to your instructor's direction.

i. Save the workbook, exit Excel, and then submit the file as directed by your instructor.

Problem Solve 1

MyITLab®
Grader
Homework

Student data file needed:
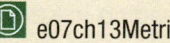 e07ch13Metrics.xlsx

You will save your file as:
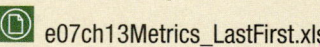 e07ch13Metrics_LastFirst.xlsx

Milligan's Boutiques

Sales & Marketing

Tammy Milligan owns a chain of small boutique stores in Ohio, Michigan, Illinois, and Indiana. She is a big believer in the benefits of BI for measuring progress and making strategic decisions. She has provided you with some sample sales data and would like you to create a dashboard that will give her an overview of how her business is doing. In this exercise, you will build a data model based on the sample data and create a dashboard, complete with KPIs and a map that shows which states are generating the most orders.

a. Open the Excel file **e07ch13Metrics**. Save your file as **e07ch13Metrics_LastFirst** using your last and first name.

b. On the **SalesData** worksheet, add each of the three tables to the data model.

c. Edit the data model by completing the following tasks on the SalesData2016 worksheet.

- Format the PurchaseDate field as ***3/14/2001**.
- Format the Price field as **Currency**.
- Create a calculated column entitled Revenue, and type =[Price]*[Quantity] to calculate the revenue generated from each sale.
- Format Revenue as **Currency**.
- Create a calculated field for the sum of revenue.
- Create a KPI that measures the Sum of Revenue value against the absolute value of $500.00. Maintain the default thresholds of 200 and 400, and select the first set of icon styles.
- Create a relationship between SalesData2016 and VolumeByEmp, using the EmployeeID field.

d. Refer to Figure 53 and the following steps to create a dashboard for Milligan's Boutique. In the Power Pivot window, create a **Chart and Table (Horizontal)** combination on the **MetricsDashboard** worksheet in cell **B2**, and complete the following.

e. Format the PivotChart by completing the following.

- Drag the **LastName** field from VolumeByEmp to the AXIS (CATEGORIES) area.
- Drag the **Category** field from SalesData2016 to the LEGEND (SERIES) area.
- Drag the **Quantity** field from SalesData2016 to the VALUES area to calculate the sum of quantity sold.
- Change the chart type to a **Stacked Column** chart.
- Apply **Style 9** to the PivotChart.
- Add a Chart Title that reads Category Volume by Employee.
- Add a Primary Vertical Axis title that reads Sales Volume.
- Hide all field buttons.
- Add a Timeline slicer connected to the PivotChart and positioned below the chart. Apply the TimelineStyle Light 6 to the slicer.

f. Format the PivotTable by completing the following.

- Drag the **LastName** field from VolumeByEmp to the ROWS area.
- Drag the **Sum of Revenue Value** field from SalesData2016 to the VALUES area.
- Drag the **Sum of Revenue KPI Status** field to the VALUES area.
- Name the PivotTable EmployeeRevGoals.
- Rename the **Row Labels** heading in J2 as Employees.
- Rename the **Sum of Revenue** heading in K2 as 2016 Revenue.
- Rename the **Sum of Revenue Status** heading in L2 as $500 Goal Status. If necessary, resize the column to fit the text.
- Apply the PivotTable Style, **Pivot Style Medium 14** to the PivotTable.

g. In the Power Pivot window, create a PivotTable on the Metrics Dashboard worksheet in cell **B25**, and complete the following.

- Drag the **State** field from OrdersByState to the ROWS area and the **Orders** field to the VALUES area.
- Rename the Row Labels heading in **B25** as State, and rename the Sum of Orders heading in **C25** as Total Orders.
- Apply the PivotTable Style, **Pivot Style Medium 14** to the PivotTable.
- Name the PivotTable OrdersByState.

h. Insert the Bing Maps App for Office to the MetricsDashboard worksheet, and complete the following.

- Use the data in the OrdersByState PivotTable to generate circles onto the map.
- Change the pin color to be **Window Green**.
- Position the map within the cell range **E25:J39**.

i. Prepare the dashboard for production by completing the following.

- Hide the SalesData worksheet
- Hide the column and row headings as well as the gridlines from the Metrics Dashboard worksheet.
- Protect the worksheet, allowing only **Use PivotTable & PivotChart** and **Edit objects**.
- Minimize the ribbon.

j. Complete the Documentation worksheet according to your instructor's direction.

k. Save the workbook, exit Excel, and then submit the file as directed by your instructor.

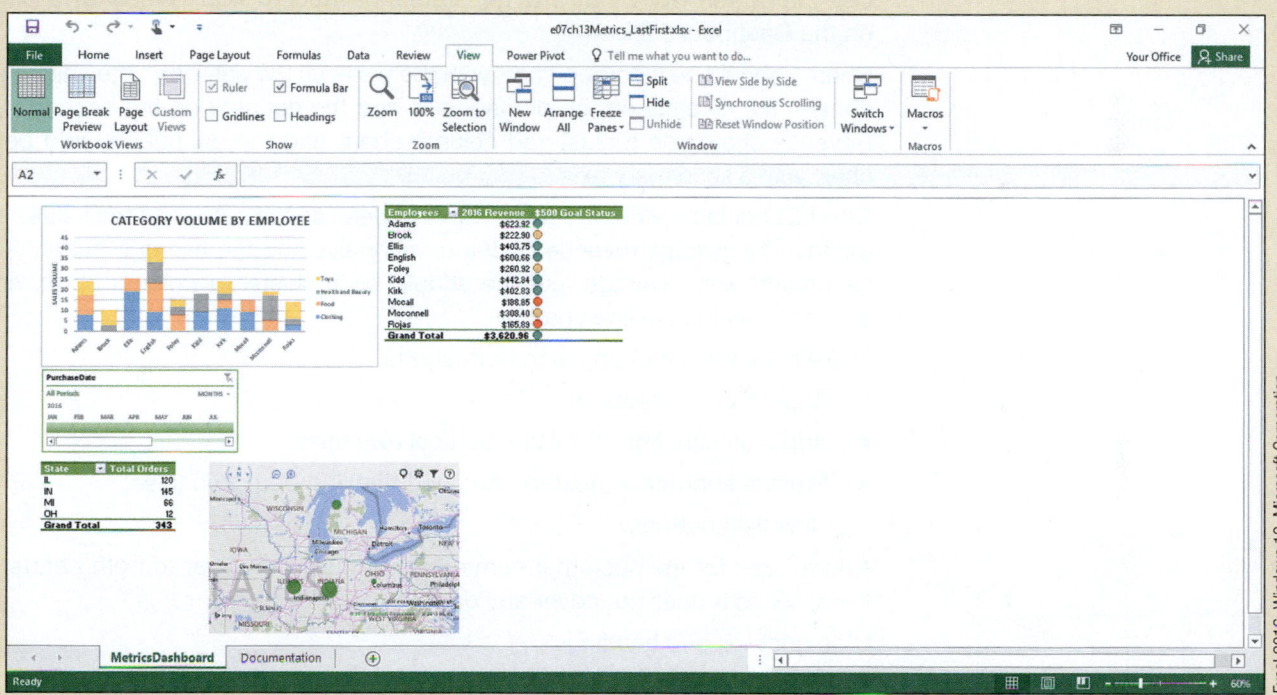

Figure 53 Metrics dashboard

Perform 1: Perform in Your Career

Student data files needed:

 Blank Excel Workbook

e07ch13Dashboard_data.txt

You will save your file as:

e07ch13Dashboard_LastFirst.xlsx

Visualizing Customers

Your boss has asked you to create a dashboard to review the sales for October 2018. He would like to see the sales by week and the average sales by week in dollars and quantity. He would like to see whether there is any correlation between the amount and the quantity sold in a week.

Information Technology

a. Start Excel, and then create a new blank workbook. Save the workbook as 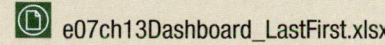 e07ch13Dashboard_LastFirst using your last and first name.

b. Rename Sheet1 as Dashboard.

c. Import the data from the tab-delimited text file **e07ch13Dashboard_data.txt**.

- In the first step of the Text Import Wizard, be sure to indicate that your data contains headers.
- Add this data to the data model, and create only a connection to the data file.

d. Make the following changes to the data in the Power Pivot window.

- Format the **Date** field as ***3/14/2001**.
- Format the **Qty** field as **Whole Number**.
- Format the **Unit Price** as **Currency**.
- Add a calculated column named **Revenue** that multiplies the Qty and Unit Price. Format the column as **Currency**.
- Add a calculated column named **Week** to determine the week number. Use the **WEEKNUM** formula with the Date field as the argument.
- Add a total to the Qty column and the Revenue column.

e. Use the PowerPivot window to generate a dashboard with **Two Charts (Vertical)** on the **Dashboard** sheet.

f. Chart 1 should be a combo chart with the week as the category; the values should contain the revenue on the primary axis and the quantity on the secondary axis. Revenue should be a clustered column chart, and the quantity should be a line chart with a secondary axis.

g. Chart 2 should be a combo chart with the week as the category; the values should contain the average revenue on the primary axis and the average quantity on the secondary axis. Average revenue should be a clustered column chart, and the quantity should be a line chart.

h. Make the following changes to both charts.

- Apply **Quick Layout 3**.
- Add a primary horizontal and vertical axis titles.
- Provide appropriate text for the chart title and both axis titles.
- Hide field buttons.

i. Add a slicer for the customer name, and connect the slicer to both charts. Move the slicer so it does not cover any data.

j. Hide gridlines and headings.

k. Format the workbook to print on one page.

l. Protect the worksheet, allowing the options to Use PivotTable & PivotChart and to Edit objects.

m. Save the workbook, close Excel, and then submit the file as directed by your instructor.

Additional
Cases

Additional Workshop Cases are available on the companion website and in the instructor resources.

Microsoft Excel 2016

Sales & Marketing

OBJECTIVES

1. Enhance spreadsheets with form controls p. 746

2. Understand the components of VBA p. 752

3. Create custom functions with VBA p. 757

4. Improve readability of VBA with formatting and structure p. 759

5. Troubleshoot VBA p. 762

6. Create and use loops in VBA p. 763

7. Assign VBA procedures to events p. 767

8. Protect and secure a workbook p. 772

Prepare Case

The Red Bluff Golf Course & Pro Shop Spreadsheet Enhancement with Form Controls and VBA

Managers at the Red Bluff Golf Course & Pro Shop have been using dashboards to keep track of sales from golf lessons, clothing, accessories, and so on. You have been given access to a workbook with a sample dashboard and Power View report based on the sales from 2013 to 2015. You have been asked to use some of the developer tools — including form controls and VBA — to enhance the dashboard and Power View report, provide more security, and add new functionality.

OZaiachin/Shutterstock

Student data file needed for this chapter:

 e07ch14Dashboards.xlsx

You will save your files as:

 e07ch14Dashboards_LastFirst.xlsm

 e07ch14DebugVBA_LastFirst.txt

 e07ch14Module1_LastFirst.txt

Enhancing the Readability and Interactivity of Dashboards

A **digital dashboard** is a tool that delivers business intelligence in graphical form. Dashboards provide management with a big picture view of the business, usually from multiple perspectives using various charts and other graphical representations. Simple dashboards may consist of a few charts that represent sales data over a particular period of time or from various perspectives, such as product category or department. Dashboards are typically designed to encourage interaction with the user. Slicers are one way to encourage interaction. **Slicers** are visual controls that allow you to quickly and easily filter your data in an interactive way. If you are interested in knowing how to create dashboards in Excel, please refer to Chapter 13 of the Excel Comprehensive book. In this section, you will use form controls to encourage more interaction with dashboards and create dynamic labels to increase the readability of a dashboard.

Enhance Spreadsheets with Form Controls

Form controls have many uses in Excel. A **form control** is an object that can be placed into an Excel worksheet, providing the functionality to interact with your models. Form controls can be used to help users select data by providing menus, lists, spinners, and scroll bars. In the context of dashboards, form controls can provide a simple way to interact with your analysis in a way that is backwards compatible with earlier versions of Excel.

Opening the Starting File

You have been given access to a workbook that is connected to the Red Bluff Golf Course & Pro Shop sales database with an existing dashboard and Power View report. You will use a variety of developer tools to enhance the functionality of the dashboard and Power View report. Some of the changes you will make to the workbook require it to be saved as a macro-enabled workbook. In this exercise, you will open the starting file and save it as a Macro-Enabled Workbook.

E14.00

To Open the a Workbook and Save It As a Macro-Enabled Workbook

a. Start **Excel**, click Open Other Documents in the left pane, and then double-click **This PC**. Navigate through the folder structure to the location of your student data files, and then double-click **e07ch14Dashboards**.

b. Click the **File** tab, and click **Save As**. Click **Browse**, click the **Save as type** arrow, and then select **Excel Macro-Enabled Workbook (*.xlsm)**. Navigate to the location where you are saving your project files, and then change the filename to e07ch14Dashboards_LastFirst using your last and first name. Click **Save**.

Troubleshooting

The files for this chapter must be open with macros enabled. You may have opened the file from a trusted location as seen in Chapter 8. If you are not using a trusted location you can enable macros by clicking the File tab, Options, Trust Center, Trust Center Settings, Macros Settings, and Enable All Macros.

Adding the Developer Tab

Form controls in Excel are located on the Developer tab of the ribbon. In this exercise, you will add the Developer tab to the ribbon.

E14.01

SIDE NOTE
Pin the Ribbon
If your ribbon is collapsed, pin your ribbon open. Click the Home tab. In the lower right corner of the ribbon, click Pin the Ribbon ⊞.

To Add the Developer Tab

a. Click the **File** tab, and then click **Options**.

b. In the Excel Options dialog box, in the left pane, click **Customize Ribbon**.

c. In the Main Tabs list, click the **Developer** check box.

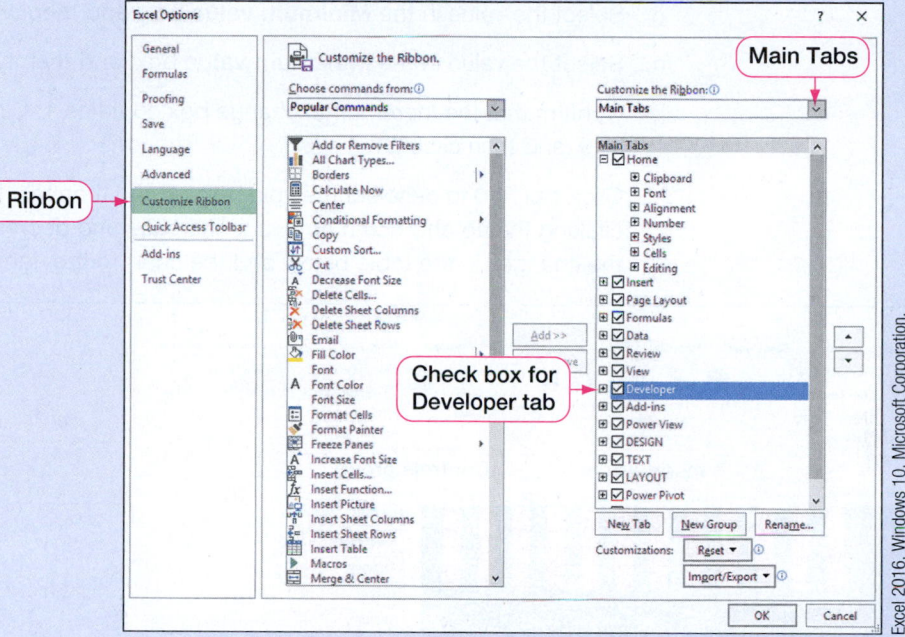

Figure 1 Excel Options dialog box

d. Click **OK**.

Adding a Spin Button

Spin buttons and scroll bars can enhance a user's experience with a dashboard. A **spin button**, also referred to as a spinner, is a form control that is linked to a specific cell. As the up and down arrows on the button are clicked, the value in the linked cell increases and decreases accordingly. In this exercise, you will create a simple spin button to provide the user with an easy way of increasing and decreasing the year of the sales data.

E14.02

To Add a Spin Button

a. Click the **RevenueDashboard** worksheet. This worksheet consists of a simple dashboard with charts, tables, slicers, and sparklines.

b. Click cell **A19**. Click the **Developer** tab, and then, in the Controls group, click the **Insert** arrow.

c. Under Form Controls, click **Spin Button (Form Control)** ⊡.

d. To insert the Spin Button, drag **a vertical rectangle** in cell **A19** to the right of the year value.

e. Right-click the **spin** button, and then select **Format Control**.

f. In the Format Control dialog box, on the Control tab, select the value in the **Current value** box, and then type 2013.

g. Select the value in the **Minimum value** box, and then type **2013**.

h. Select the value in the **Maximum value** box, and then type **2015**.

i. Confirm that the Incremental change box contains **1**. Click the **Cell link** box, click **A19**, and then click **OK**.

j. Click cell **A19** to deselect the spin button, and then test the added functionality by clicking the up and down arrows to increase and decrease the year, and observe the changes in the table below and the chart to the right.

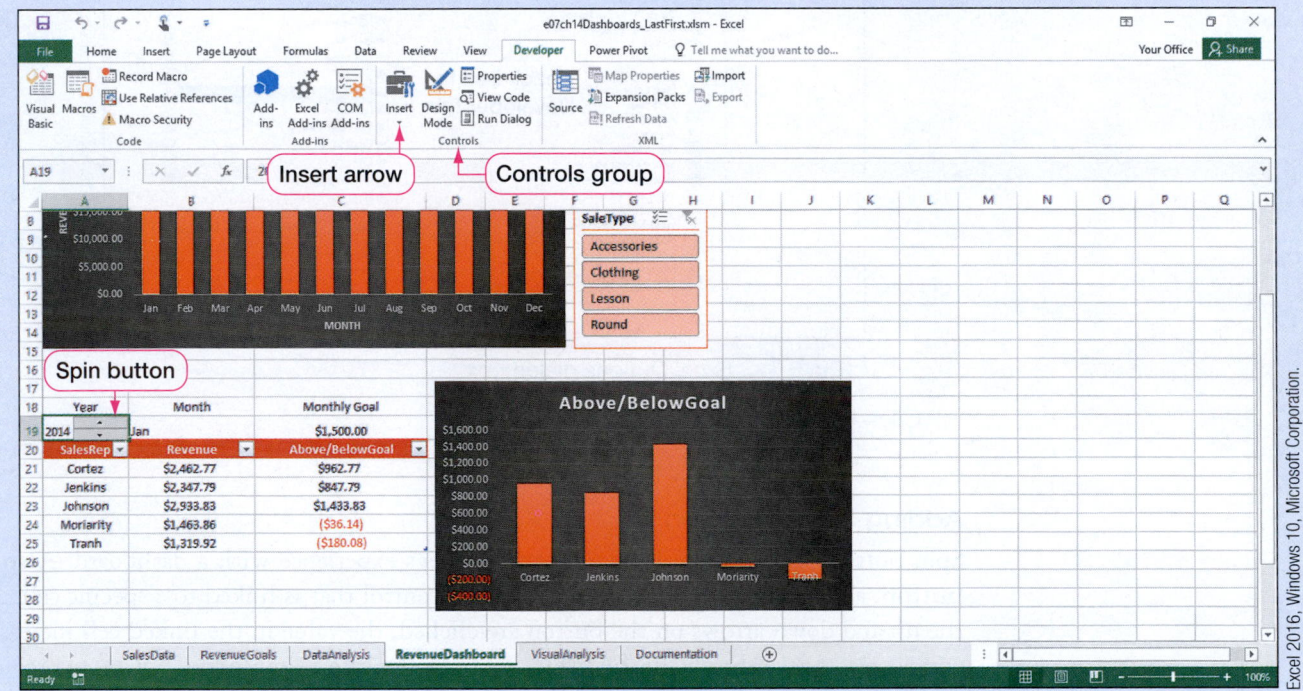

Figure 2   Spin button added

k. **Save** 🖬 the workbook.

Creating a Lookup Table to Use with Form Controls

Some form controls, such as the scroll bar, require some additional work to create the values that will be used by the object. Creating a lookup table and using the VLOOKUP function is a common approach to linking values to various form controls. In this exercise, you will create a lookup table for months to use with a scroll bar control.

E14.03 To Create a Lookup Table

a. Click the **DataAnalysis** worksheet.

b. Click cell **E1**, type **1**, and then press [Tab]. Type **Jan**, and press [Enter].

c. In cell **E2**, type **2**, and then press [Tab]. Type **Feb**, and press [Ctrl] + [Enter].

d. Select the cell range **E1:F2**. Click the **AutoFill** handle, and drag to the cell range **E12:F12** to create a listing of months from Jan to Dec.

e. Select the cell range **E1:F12**. Click inside the **Name** box, type **Month_Range**, and then press [Enter] to create a named range for the lookup table.

f. Click the **RevenueDashboard** worksheet, click cell **B17**, and then type **1**. This value will be used as the lookup value in the VLOOKUP function to retrieve the appropriate month from the Month_Range named range.

g. Click cell **B19**, select **the text**, and then type the following function: **=VLOOKUP(B17, Month_Range, 2, False)**.

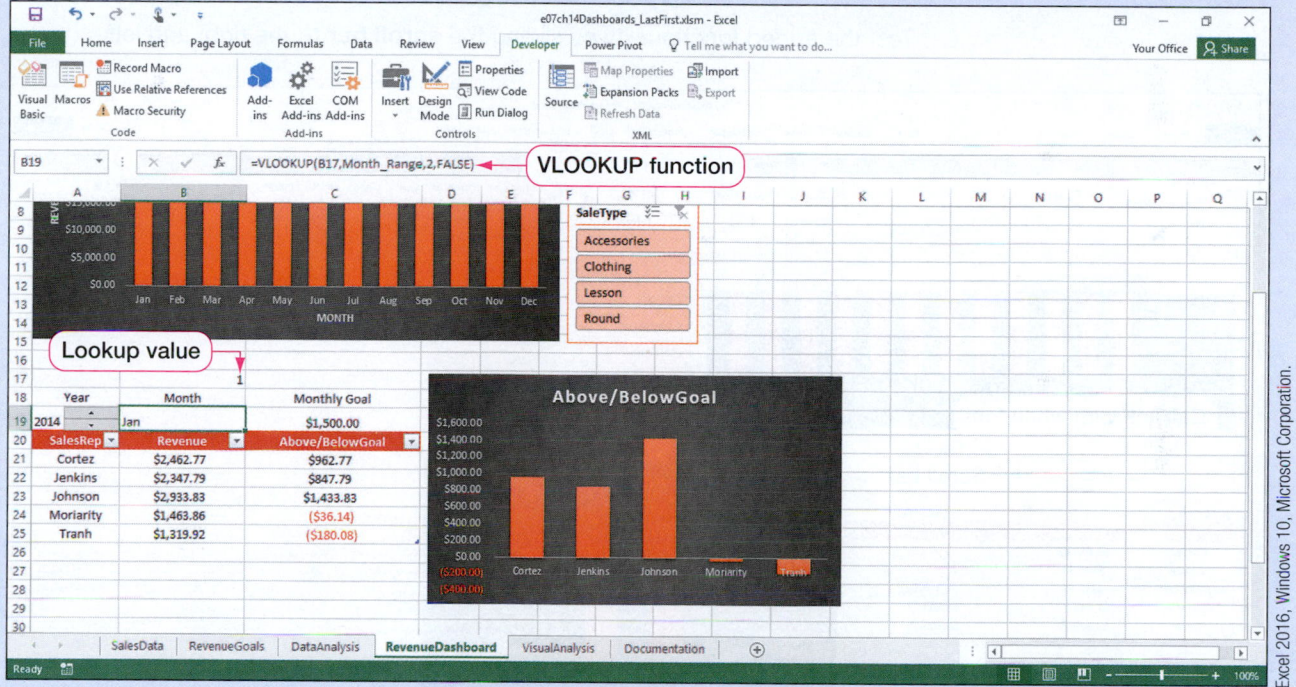

Figure 3 VLOOKUP function added

h. **Save** the workbook.

Adding a Scroll Bar

Now that you have created a lookup table with the appropriate values and have added the VLOOKUP function to cell B19, you will add the scroll bar form control. A **scroll bar** has a function very similar to that of the spin button. However, with a scroll bar, the value of the linked cell is increased or decreased by sliding the scroll bar to the left or right. In this exercise, you will create a scroll bar so that the user can easily scroll through different months.

 **E14.04**

To Add a Scroll Bar

a. If necessary, click the **Developer** tab, and then, in the Controls group, click the **Insert** arrow. Under Form Controls, select **Scroll Bar (Form Control)** .

b. Drag a **horizontal rectangle** inside cell **B19** to the right of the value.

c. Right-click the **scroll bar**, and then select **Format Control**.

d. In the Format Control dialog box, on the Control tab, select the value in the **Current value** box, and then type **1**.

e. Select the value in the **Minimum value** box, and then type **1**.

f. Select the value in the **Maximum value** box, and then type **12**. Leave the existing values in the Incremental change and Page change boxes.

g. Click the **Cell link** box, click cell **B17**, and then click **OK**.

h. Click cell **B17**, and then change the font color to white so that it is not visible in the model.

i. Test the added functionality by sliding the **scroll bar** to the right and left.

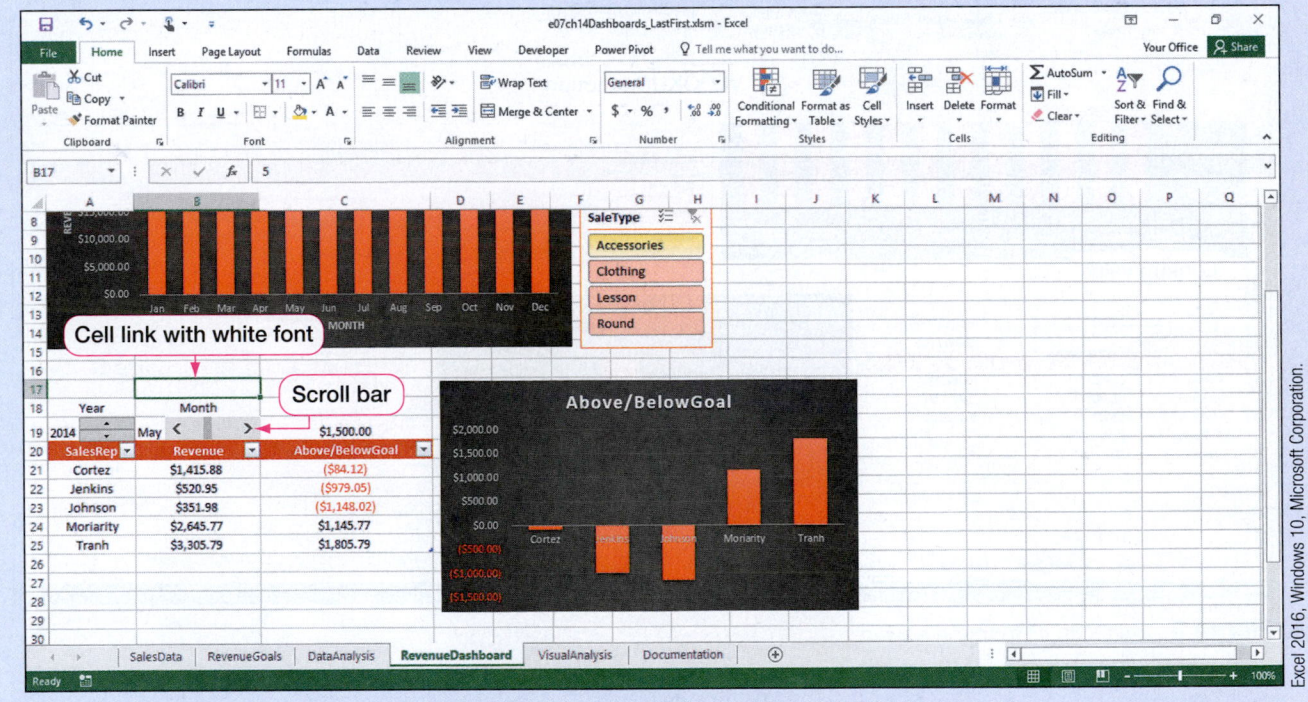

Figure 4 Scroll bar added

j. **Save** the workbook

Creating Dynamic Labels

Labels are critical to dashboard design and can add clarity to the graphics being displayed. Dynamic labels offer additional clarity in PivotCharts by displaying the year and/or month that is being displayed when filtered. In this exercise, you will create dynamic labels on the Sales Revenue chart.

 **E14.05**

To Create Dynamic Labels

a. Click the **Insert** tab, and then, in the Text group, click **Text Box**.

b. Drag to create a box in the top left corner of the **Sales Revenue column chart**.

c. Click the **formula bar**. Type **=**, click the **DataAnalysis** worksheet, and then click cell **B1**. Press [Enter].

> ### Troubleshooting
>
> If you did not click the formula bar before typing =, then the cell reference will not work. Just delete the typed =, click the formula bar, and type = again.

d. On the **Home** tab, in the Font group, increase the font size to **14**. Click the **Fill Color** arrow, and then select **No Fill** to remove the default white fill.

e. Click the **Font Color** arrow, and then select **White, Background 1**.

f. Click the **Drawing Tools Format** tab, and then, in the Shape Styles group, click the **Shape Outline** arrow. Select **No Outline**.

g. Test the functionality of the dynamic label by clicking on different years in the **Year** slicer. If necessary, adjust the size of the text box to accommodate the value.

 You will now add another dynamic label for the SaleType.

h. Click the **Insert** tab, and then, in the Text group, click **Text Box**.

i. Drag to create a box in the top right corner of the **Sales Revenue column chart**.

j. Click the **formula bar**. Type **=**, click the **DataAnalysis** worksheet, and then click cell **B2**. Press [Enter].

k. On the Home tab, in the Font group, increase the font size to **14**. Click the **Fill Color** arrow, and then select **No Fill** to remove the default white fill.

l. Click the **Font Color** arrow, and then select **White, Background 1**.

m. Click the **Drawing Tools Format** tab, and then, in the Shape Styles group, click the **Shape Outline** arrow. Select **No Outline**.

n. Click **Accessories** in the SaleType slicer, and then adjust the size of the box to accommodate the value.

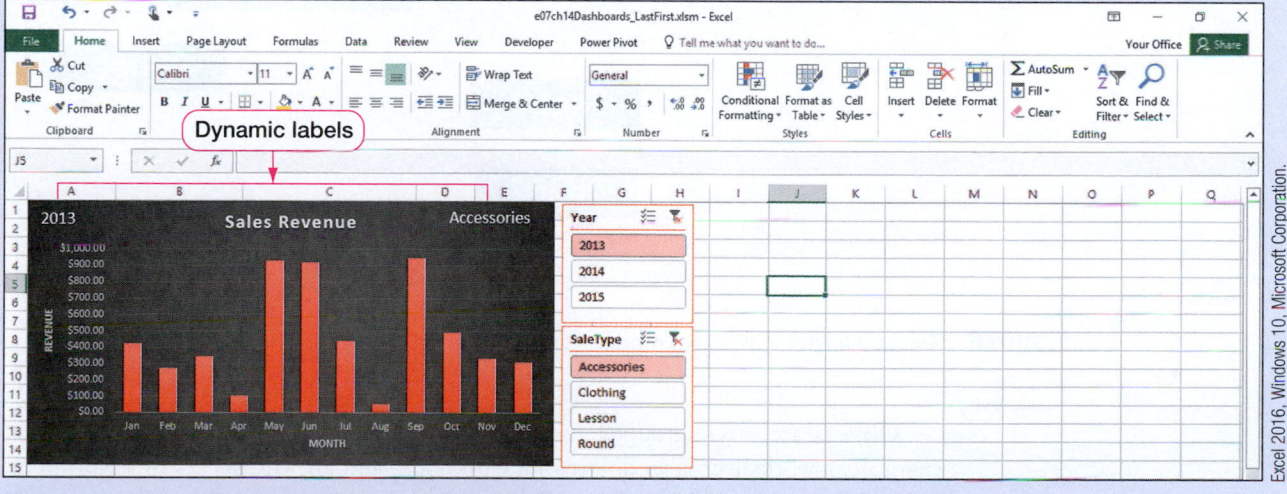

Figure 5 Dynamic labels added

o. Click **Save**. If you need to take a break before finishing this chapter, now is a good time.

Leveraging the Power of Visual Basic for Applications (VBA)

VBA (Visual Basic for Applications) is a powerful programming language that is part of most Microsoft Office applications: Word, Access, Excel, and PowerPoint. VBA allows a user to implement a wide variety of enhancements to any of these applications. VBA is particularly valuable in automating repetitive tasks; in that way, it is similar to macros, but it provides additional tools that can enhance the functionality and usability of an Excel application. VBA is considered a very basic form of object-oriented programming. **Object-oriented programming (OOP)** uses a hierarchy of objects — also called classes — as the focus of the programming. VBA manipulates objects by using the methods and properties associated with them. In this section, you will explore the various components of VBA and create simple procedures that will enhance an Excel workbook and provide additional security to protect the data.

Understand the Components of VBA

The key to using VBA effectively to enhance your dashboard or any other Excel application is to understand Excel's object model. An **object model** is a hierarchical collection of objects, consisting of properties, methods, and events that can be manipulated by using VBA. Excel is made up of several dozen objects. **Objects** are combinations of data and code that are treated as a single unit including workbooks, worksheets, charts, and PivotTables — and even Excel itself is an object. Objects can also serve as containers for other objects. For example, Excel is an object called an application. This application object contains workbook objects, workbook objects contain worksheet objects, and worksheet objects contain cell range objects. Figure 6 shows a partial object model for Excel.

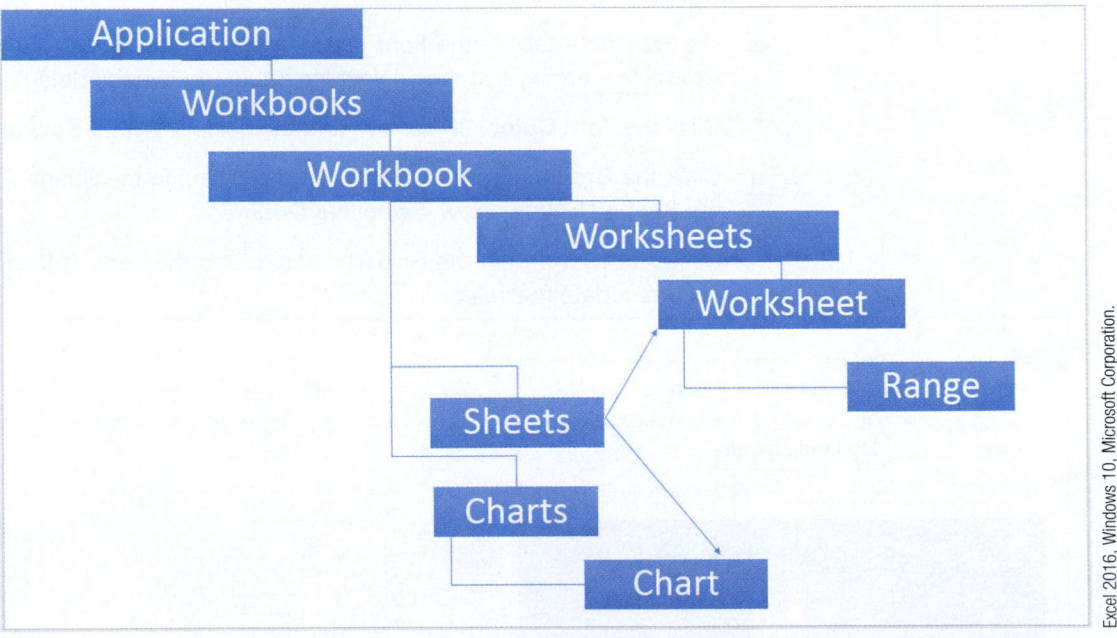

Excel 2016, Windows 10, Microsoft Corporation.

Figure 6   Partial hierarchical object model

Objects are often grouped together into what are called **object collections**. For example, a worksheet is an object in a workbook, and all worksheets in a workbook collectively are also an object. A particular object can be referenced inside a collection by referring to the object collection and then the name or number that represents that specific member of that collection. For example Sheets("Sheet2") is a reference to a worksheet with the name Sheet2 that is a member of the Sheets object collection.

QUICK REFERENCE	Object Collections
Object Collection	**Description**
Workbooks("Book1")	Refers to a workbook named Book1
Sheets("Sheet1")	Refers to a worksheet named Sheet1
Range("A2:C23")	Refers to the range of cells A2:C23
Charts(2)	Refers to the second chart in a workbook
ChartObjects(3)	Refers to the third embedded chart in a worksheet
Windows(3)	Refers to the third open Excel workbook window

When you refer to a particular object using VBA, the objects need to be referred to in their hierarchical structure. For example, to refer to cell A1 in a specific worksheet, you would need the following code.

Application.Workbook(workbookname.xlsx).Sheets("Sheet1").Range("A1")

The periods between each object are referred to as separators. **Separators** indicate the distinction between the object container and the member of that container.

Having to type the entire hierarchy each time a particular object is used can be tedious. Therefore, VBA provides special object names that can be used to refer to specific objects. For example, ActiveCell refers to the specific cell that is currently selected in the workbook.

QUICK REFERENCE	VBA Special Object Names
Property	**Description**
ActiveCell	The currently selected cell in the workbook
ActiveChart	The active chart sheet or chart contained in a ChartObject on a worksheet. This property is Nothing if a chart is not active.
ActiveSheet	The active worksheet
ActiveWindow	The active window
Selection	The selected object. It could refer to a range object, shape, chart, and so on.
ThisWorkbook	The workbook object that contains the VBA procedure being executed. This object may or may not be the same as the ActiveWorkbook object.

Every Excel object has properties. **Properties** are attributes of an object that can be referred to or manipulated by using VBA. For example, the cell range object has properties such as value and address.

QUICK REFERENCE	Properties of Common Objects	
Object	**Property**	**Description**
Workbooks	Name	The name of the workbook
	Path	The directory in which the workbook resides
	Saved	Whether or not the workbook has been saved
	HasPassword	Whether or not the workbook has a password
Worksheets	Name	The name of the worksheet
	Visible	Whether or not the worksheet is visible

Object	Property	Description
Range	Address	The cell reference of the range
	Comment	A comment attached to the cell
	Formula	The formula entered in the cell
	Value	The value entered in the cell
Chart	ChartTitle	The text of the chart's title
	ChartType	The type of chart: bar, column, line
	HasLegend	Whether or not the chart has a legend

An object's properties can be easily modified with a simple expression: Object.Property = expression. For example, to rename a worksheet that is currently selected, using VBA you would type the following expression: ActiveSheet.Name = "NewSheetName".

Excel objects also have methods. A **method** is an action Excel performs on an object. For example, one of the methods for a Range object is ClearContents. When this method is called, values would be cleared from the range. The basic syntax required to call an object's method is as follows:

ObjectName.Method

For example, to clear the values in the cell range A1:A5, you would type the following.

Range("A1:A5").ClearContents

QUICK REFERENCE | Common Methods and Descriptions

Object	Method	Description
Workbooks	Close	Closes the workbook
	Protect	Protects the workbook
	SaveAs	Saves the workbook with a specified file name
Worksheets	Delete	Deletes the worksheet
	Select	Selects and displays the worksheet
Range	Clear	Clears all content in the range
	Copy	Copies the values in the range to the Clipboard
	Merge	Merges the cells in the range
Chart	Copy	Copies the chart to the Clipboard
	Select	Selects the chart
	Delete	Deletes the chart
Worksheets	Select	Selects all the worksheets in the workbook
Charts	Select	Selects all chart sheets in the workbook

Methods often have parameters that must be included to use the method on the object. A **parameter** is a special kind of variable used to refer to one of the pieces of data provided in a method. For example, the Workbook object has a SaveAs method that requires the file name as a parameter. Most methods contain required and optional parameters. The basic syntax for providing parameters in a method is as follows:

object.method parameter1: = value, parameter2:= value2

For example,

ActiveWorkbook.SaveAs Filename:="NewWorkbookName", FileFormat:=52

saves the active workbook as NewWorkbookName.xlsm.

QUICK REFERENCE	Common FileFormat Values
FileFormat Value	**File Extension**
51	.xlsx
52	.xlsm
6	.csv
−4158	.txt

Exploring the Visual Basic Editor

The **Visual Basic Editor (VBE)** is the tool built into Microsoft Office that is used for creating and editing VBA. At the top of the VBE screen is the title of the workbook that is currently open and being edited. Directly under the application title are the File menu and Standard toolbars, which are visible by default. On the left side of the Visual Basic Editor is the Project Explorer. The **Project Explorer window** contains a hierarchical list of all the objects in open workbooks, including macros, modules, and worksheets. VBA in an Excel workbook can be contained either in a specific worksheet, in the specific workbook, or within a module. Below the Project Explorer window is the Properties window. The **Properties window** contains a list of all the properties of a selected object such as name, size, and color. Depending on your system settings, the Properties window may not be displayed by default when the VBE is opened. The larger window on the right of the Visual Basic Editor is the Code window. The **Code window** is where all the VBA code is typed and where VBA generated by a recorded macro can be viewed and edited. In this exercise, you will explore the VBE and insert a new module.

 E14.06

To Explore the VBE

a. If you took a break, open the **e07ch14Dashboards** workbook and, if needed, navigate to the **RevenueDashboard** worksheet. Click the **Developer** tab, and in the Code group, click **Visual Basic**. If necessary, **Maximize** the window.

b. If the AnalysisToolPak Add-in is installed in Excel, you will see an open Code window with FUNCRES.XLAM in the title bar. **Close** this window if necessary.

c. Click **Insert**, and then select **Module**.
   Notice the Project Explorer window, Properties window, and Code window.

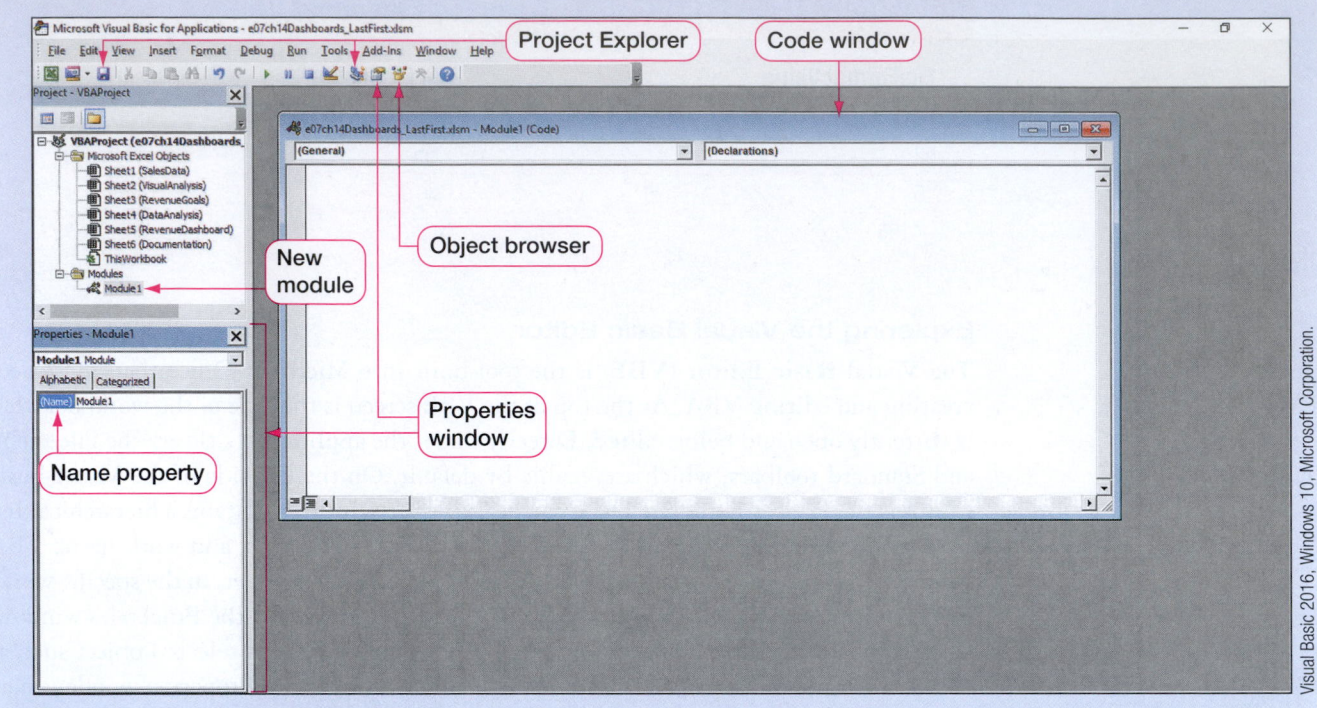

Figure 7 The Visual Basic Editor

d. In the Properties window, click inside the **Name** box. Replace the Module1 text with **e07ch14Module1_LastFirst** using your last and first name.

A **module** is simply a container for code. The two primary types of procedures that are supported by VBA are Sub procedures and function procedures. A **Sub procedure** performs an action on your project or workbook, such as renaming a worksheet or clearing filtered values from PivotTables. A **function procedure** is a group of VBA statements that perform a calculation and return a single value. Function procedures are often used to create custom functions that can be entered in worksheet cells. You can have zero or hundreds of Sub procedures and functions written within a single module. Modules are most often used to store any public procedures that are not driven by events such as the opening of a workbook. If a Sub procedure is to run when a workbook opens or a worksheet becomes active, then it is typically stored in the workbook or worksheet object to take advantage of the Procedure menu at the top of the Code window.

CONSIDER THIS | **Public Versus Private Sub Procedures**

There are public and private Sub procedures. By default, Excel makes all Sub procedures public, which means that they are available to be accessed in the Macro window. If a Sub procedure is private, then the code is viewable only inside the VBE. What are some advantages and disadvantages of creating public and private Sub procedures?

Create Custom Functions with VBA

Function procedures can provide custom calculations that are used frequently in a business and are not part of the extensive functions available in Excel. These custom functions do not have to be complicated, but they can be created to ensure consistency in calculations.

To create a function procedure, you must first declare that it is a function and then provide the function with a name and an opening parenthesis. After the opening parenthesis, you must provide a name for the value or values that the function needs to perform its calculation and declare the data type(s) that Excel should expect from the value(s). A closing parenthesis is required to end the function.

Function Commission (salesTotal As Currency)

The next line of code is where the calculation of the function is defined. Simply type the FunctionName, declared in the first line, an equal sign, followed by the ValueName, defined in the first line, and then the calculation you would like the function to perform.

Commission = salesTotal * .15

In this example, the function Commission would be calculated by multiplying the value supplied by the user by .15. The value supplied by the user could be a number typed into the function or a cell reference.

Creating a Function Procedure

In this exercise, you will create a custom function that will take the total sales value and multiply it by 15% to calculate the total commission paid.

 **E14.07**

SIDE NOTE

Capitalization

Capitalization is important in programming. Once a procedure has been named or a variable has been declared, the VBE will autocorrect for capitalization.

To Create a Function Procedure

a. Click inside the **Code window**, declare a function procedure by typing Function COMMISSION(salesTotal As Currency), and then press Enter.

    The Function key word is what tells Excel that you are creating a function procedure. COMMISSION is the name given to the function. The value that the function will use in its calculation is named salesTotal and will be a Currency data type.

b. Type the comment 'This function will multiply the total sales amount by 15%, and then press Enter.

c. Type COMMISSION = salesTotal * 0.15, and then press Enter.

    Note that COMMISSION is the name of the function and is required for the function procedure to return a value.

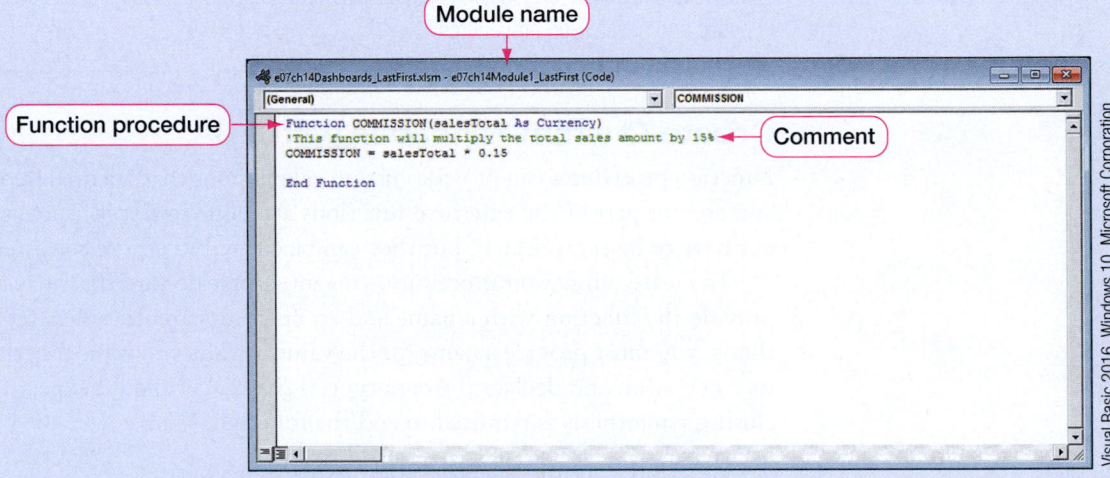

Figure 8   COMMISSION function procedure

d. Save 🖫 the workbook

Using a Custom Function

Now that you have created a new function in the VBE, it can be used in any worksheet in the workbook. In this exercise, you will use the newly created function in the RevenueDashboard worksheet.

 **E14.08**

To Use a Custom Function

a. Press [Alt] + [F11] to switch to the workbook.

b. On the RevenueDashboard worksheet, click cell **A27**, type Total Sales, and then press [Tab].

c. In cell **B27**, type =SUM(RevenueGoals[Revenue]) to sum the values of the Revenue column in the RevenueGoals table. Press [Ctrl] + [Enter].

d. Format cell B27 as **Currency**.

e. Click cell **A28**, type Commission, and then press [Tab].

f. Click cell **B28**, and then type =COMMISSION(B27) to use the COMMISSION function. Press [Ctrl] + [Enter].

g. Format cell B28 as **Currency**.

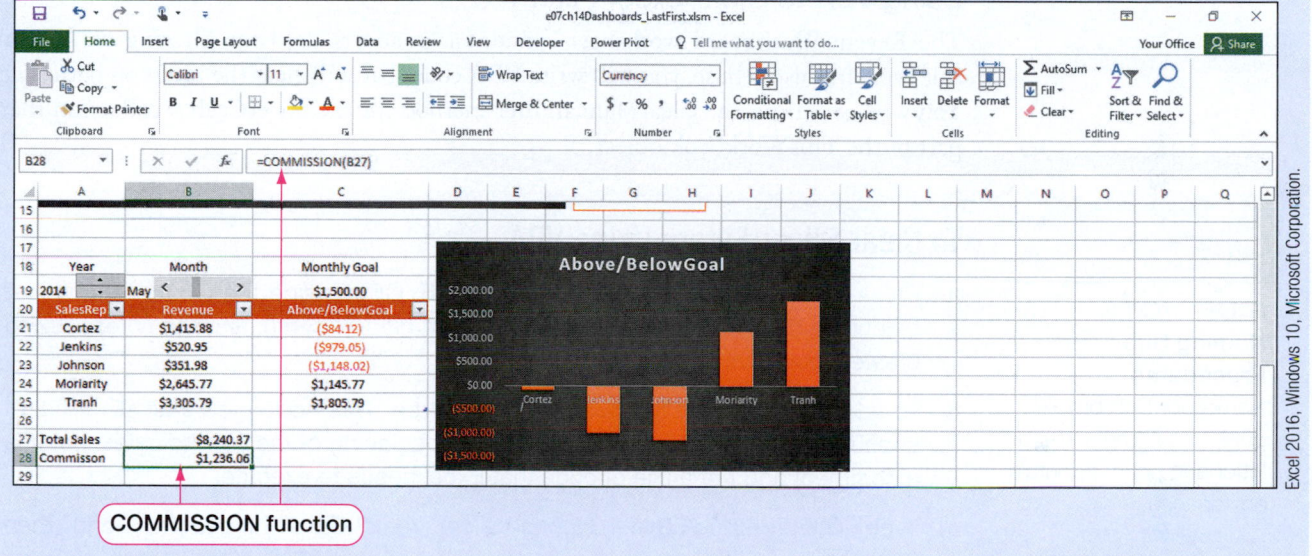

COMMISSION function

Figure 9 COMMISSION function used

h. **Save** 🖫 the workbook.

Improve Readability of VBA with Formatting and Structure

An important aspect of writing VBA is making sure the code is easy to read so that you and others can interpret what is happening. This means frequently using indentation, comments, and line breaks. This is especially true in working with more complex code.

You need to take extra steps to keep the code legible and to document what steps you are taking and why. This will make it easier on you and others who may need to edit, analyze, or troubleshoot the code. One of these extra steps will be using [Tab] to create indentations in the code.

Commenting code in VBA is an excellent way of explaining the purpose and intention of a procedure. This way, you can add straightforward documentation about what the procedure is doing and what steps to take next. If you are developing more complicated procedures, you might want to leave yourself notes about what still needs to be completed or what statements are not working as expected. Adding comments in the Code window is as simple as typing an apostrophe. The (') symbol tells the VBE to ignore any text following the apostrophe on a line of the code.

Also, the VBE interprets code on a line-by-line basis, which means that if you type part of a statement on a line and press [Enter] before the end of the statement, it will create a syntax error. So lengthy statements may become difficult to read, because without pressing [Enter], the lines of code will extend continuously to the right. However, placing a space followed by an underscore character at the end of the first line of code and pressing [Enter] will break the code to a second line. This tells the VBE that the two lines of code should be treated as one.

REAL WORLD ADVICE | **Using the Macro Recorder to Learn VBA**

An easy way to gain a better understanding of how VBA works is to use the Macro Recorder to generate VBA code for actions you want to complete. See Chapter 8 for information about recording macros. The code that is generated can be useful in identifying the key elements of the language and how the objects, properties, methods, and events work together to accomplish specific tasks.

Using VBA to Clear Slicer Filters

The RevenueDashboard worksheet contains two slicers used for filtering on Year and SaleType. In this exercise, you will write VBA code that will clear the filters on both slicers. You will be calling the ClearManualFilter method for the SlicerCaches collection that is part of the ThisWorkbook object.

 **E14.09**

SIDE NOTE
Naming Sub Procedures
Names for Sub procedures must begin with a letter and cannot contain any spaces.

SIDE NOTE
View the Object Browser
Press [F2] in the VBE to display the Object Browser, which shows properties, methods, and events for an object.

To Clear Slicer Filters Using VBA

a. Press [Alt] + [F11] to switch back to the VBE. Click inside the Code window just below the End Function statement, type Sub clearSlicers(), and then press [Enter] to create a new Sub procedure.

b. To add a comment to the Sub procedure, type 'This code clears all slicer filters specified. Press [Enter]. The (') symbol at the beginning of the line indicates that it is a comment and not a line of code that Excel needs to execute.

c. Type ThisWorkbook.SlicerCaches("Slicer_Year").ClearManualFilter, and then press [Enter].

d. Type ThisWorkbook.SlicerCaches("Slicer_SaleType").ClearManualFilter, and then press [Enter].

clearSlicers Sub procedure

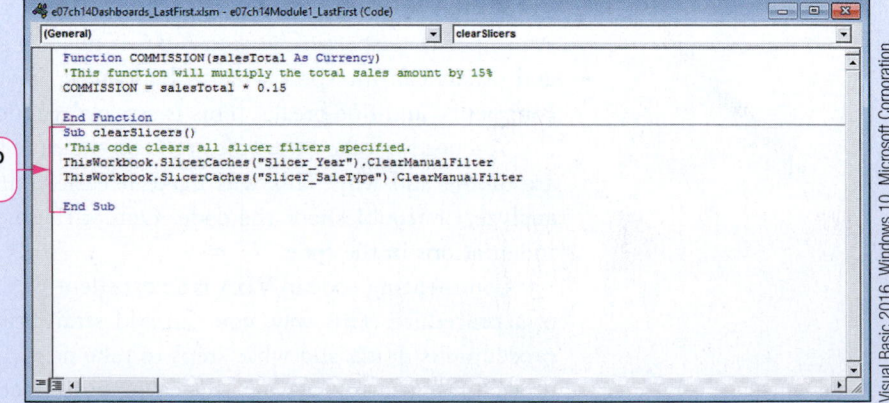

Figure 10 clearSlicers Sub procedure

e. Click **Save** 🖫.

f. To test the VBA code, press Alt + F11 to toggle back to the workbook. Click **2013** on the Year slicer, and click **Accessories** on the SaleType slicer.

g. Press Alt + F11 again to toggle back to the editor. Press F5 to run the clearSlicers Sub procedure.

h. Press Alt + F11 again to toggle back to the workbook, and observe all the slicer filters have now been cleared.

i. **Save** 🖫 the workbook.

Assigning VBA Code to a Button Control

The clearSlicers Sub procedure is not very useful without giving the user a way of running the code from the dashboard. Sub procedures can be added to command buttons for easy access. In this exercise, you will add a command button to the RevenueDashboard that runs the clearSlicers Sub procedure.

 E14.10

To Assign a Sub Procedure to a Button Control

a. Click the **Developer** tab, and then, in the Controls group, click the **Insert** arrow. Under Form Controls, select **Button (Form Control)** ▭.

b. Drag to create a **rectangular button** to the right of the **Year** slicer, within the cell range **L1:M2**.

c. In the Assign Macro dialog box, select **clearSlicers**, and then click **OK**.

d. Right-click the **button** form control, and then select **Edit Text**. Delete the existing button text, and then type Clear Slicers. Click outside the button to confirm the change.

e. To test the functionality of the new button, apply some filters using the slicers, and then click the **Clear Slicers** button to clear them.

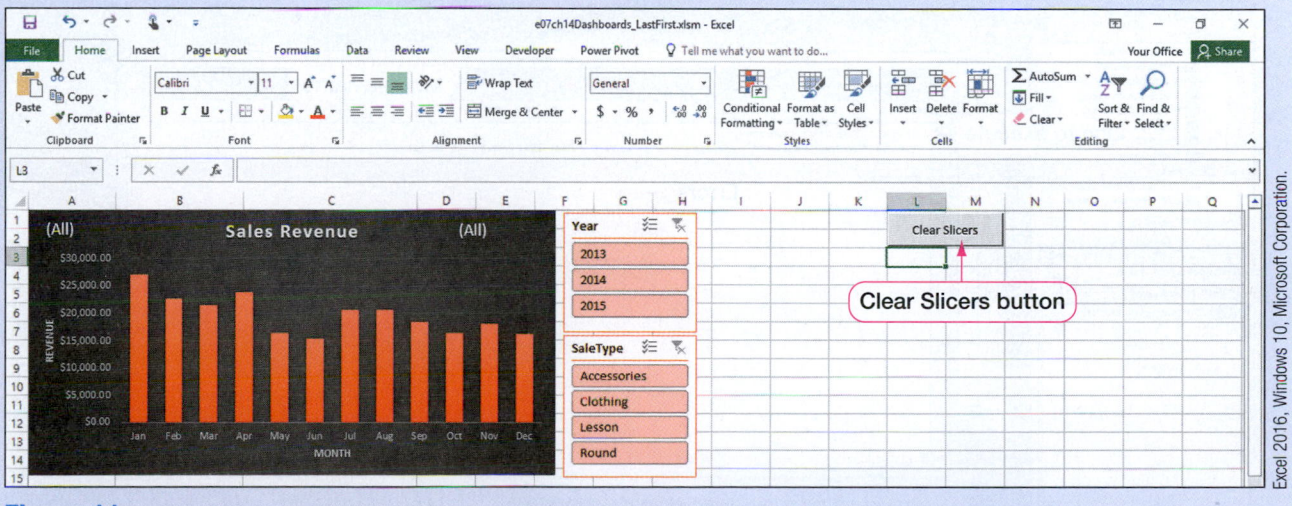

Figure 11 Clear Slicers button

f. **Save** 🖫 the workbook.

Troubleshoot VBA

You may have encountered some errors when you attempted to write VBA code. Some of the errors may have been caused by pressing [Enter] to break up a line of code without inserting a space and an underscore or by some other syntax error. With those types of errors, the VBA code cannot be executed until the problem is corrected. The other common VBA error is called a run-time error. A **run-time error** occurs when the code is executed, displaying a description of the error. The VBE includes a tool called the debugger to help troubleshoot run-time errors. When the debugger is used, the code is executed one line at a time to make it easy to identify the exact point where the run-time error occurs.

Debug VBA

In this exercise, you will create a new module and enter a simple Sub procedure. The Sub procedure will contain a fairly obvious error to help you learn how to use the VBE debugger.

 **E14.11**

To Debug VBA

a. Press [Alt] + [F11] to switch to the VBE. Click **Insert**, and then select **Module**.

b. In the Properties window, select the text in the **Name** property, type **e07ch14DebugVBA_LastFirst** using your last and first name, and then press [Enter]. Click in the **Code Window**.

c. Any spelling errors in this code are intentional for the purposes of this exercise. Please type this code exactly as follows.

- Private Sub troubleShoot () and then press [Enter].
- Sheets("RevenuDashboard").Range("A16"). Valu = "Red Bluff Monthly Revenue" and then press [Enter].

d. Press [F8] to enter debug mode. Notice that the first line of code is highlighted in yellow.

> **SIDE NOTE**
> **Debug Mode**
> You can also enter debugging mode by clicking the Debug menu and then selecting Step Into.

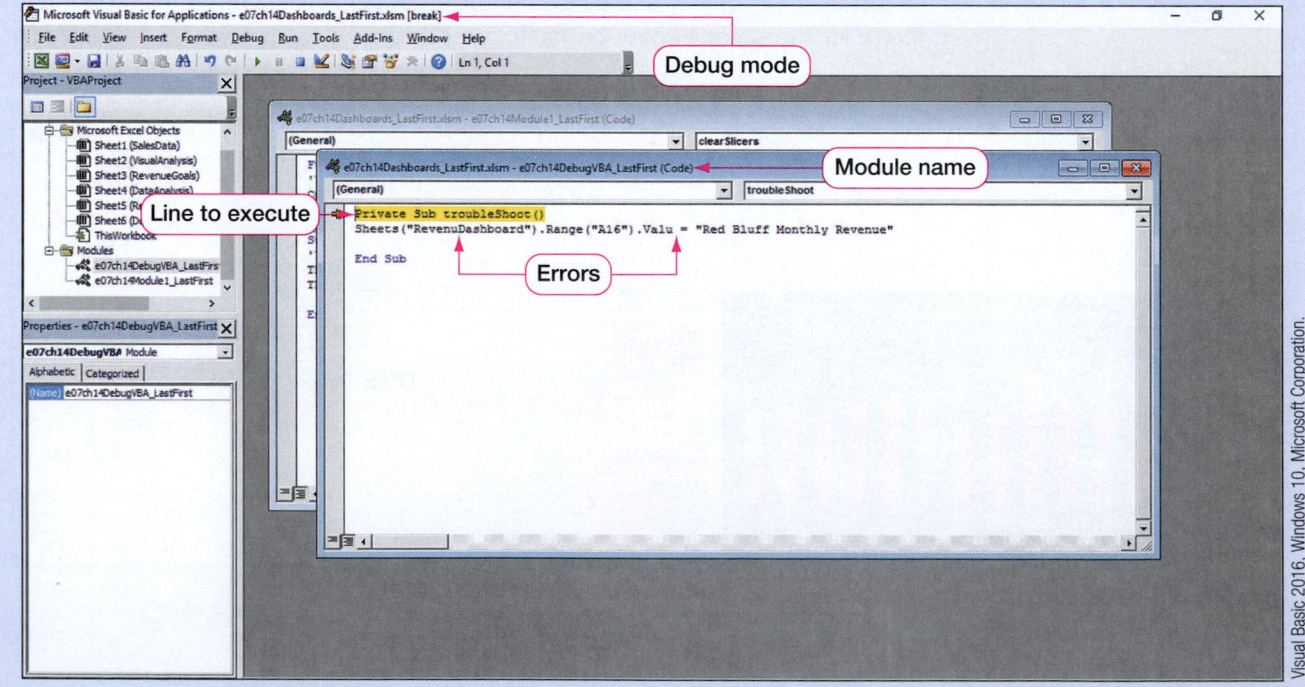

Figure 12 VBA debug mode

Visual Basic 2016, Windows 10, Microsoft Corporation.

e. Press F8 again to execute that line of code. No warnings or errors are displayed, and the next line of code is now highlighted.

f. Press F8 again to execute the second line of code. A run-time error is displayed, stating Subscript out of range.

    This error can occur for a variety of reasons, but a very common one is when the code refers to an object that does not exist in the workbook. In this case, the name of the sheet is misspelled.

g. Click **Debug**, and then correct the spelling of the sheet name to RevenueDashboard. Press F8 to execute the second line again.

h. Another error message is displayed, indicating that the object does not support this property or method. Click **Debug**, and then notice that the Value property is misspelled as **Valu**. Correct the spelling of the Valu property to Value. Press F8 to execute the second line again.

i. The second line of code executes without any additional errors, and the first line of code in e07ch14Module1_LastFirst is highlighted. Press F8 to exit debugging mode.

j. Press Alt + F11 to switch back to the workbook. Notice that the text has been added to cell A16.

k. **Save** 🖫 the workbook.

Create and Use Loops in VBA

The clearSlicers Sub procedure created earlier to automatically clear the filters from the Years and SaleType slicers was effective, but if more slicers are added to the dashboard, the procedure has to be modified to include the additional slicers. A more effective use of the VBA code would be to use what is called a loop. A **loop** is used to execute a series of statements multiple times. The number of times the code is executed can be determined by a specified number until a condition is true or false, or the code can continue to execute however many objects there are in a collection. There are essentially two categories of loops: Do loops and For…Next loops.

QUICK REFERENCE		Types of Loops in VBA
Loop Type		**Description**
Do Loop	**Do…While loop**	Loops while a specified condition is true
	Do…Until loop	Loops until a specified condition is true
For…Next loop	**For loop**	Loops until a specified number of loops have been completed
	For…Each loop	Loops through an object collection or an array

The appropriate loop type needed to be able to clear the filters for all slicers in a workbook is the For…Next loop. The syntax of the For…Next loop is as follows.

For Each element In group

code to execute

Next element

In the context of using the For…Each loop to loop through a collection of objects, the element is the object, and the group is the collection of those objects. In the syntax of the For…Each loop, the data type of the element and group must be the same. This often requires that in the VBA code, before the loop begins, variables be declared with a data type specified.

Declaring a Variable

A **variable** is space in a computer's memory that is given a name and is used to store a value of a specified data type. To create a variable, the space needs to be allocated in the computer's memory. This is known as dimensioning a variable. VBA abbreviates this as Dim, and it is a required command before a variable can be created.

The syntax for declaring a variable and assigning a data type to it is as follows.

Sub procedureName ()

Dim variableName As DataType

End Sub

You can also declare multiple variables and assign them all a data type at one time by using the following syntax.

Sub procedureName ()

Dim variable1 As DataType1, variable2 As DataType2, variable3 As DataType3

End Sub

There are several data types in VBA; the most common ones are Currency, String, Single, Double, Boolean, and Variant.

In this exercise, you will begin working toward creating a For…Each loop that will clear the filters on any number of slicers that may be added to the RevenueDashboard worksheet. First, you will need to declare a variable to use within the For…Each loop.

 **E14.12**

To Declare a Variable

a. Press [Alt] + [F11] to switch to the VBE.

b. Click the **e07ch14Module1_LastFirst** Code window, click just below the End Sub statement of the clearSlicers procedure, and then press [Enter].

c. Create a new Sub procedure by typing Sub slicerLoop (), and then press [Enter].

d. Type the following comment: 'This code will loop through all slicers in the workbook and clear the filters. Press [Enter].

e. Declare a variable of the SlicerCache type by typing Dim slicers As SlicerCache, and then press [Enter] twice to make the code easier to read. Now that you have created a variable of the type SlicerCache, you are now ready to begin the For…Each loop.

Creating a For…Each Loop

In this exercise, you will create the VBA code to loop through all of the SlicerCache objects in the collection of SlicerCaches in the ThisWorkbook object.

 **E14.13**

To Create a For…Each Loop

a. Begin the loop by typing For Each slicers In ThisWorkbook.SlicerCaches, and then press [Enter] twice.

   This line of code is what begins the loop. Excel will go through each of the slicerCache objects in the collection of SlicerCaches and perform the next line of code.

b. Create the code to execute by typing slicers.ClearManualFilter, and then press [Enter] twice.

c. End the loop by typing Next slicers, and then press [Enter].

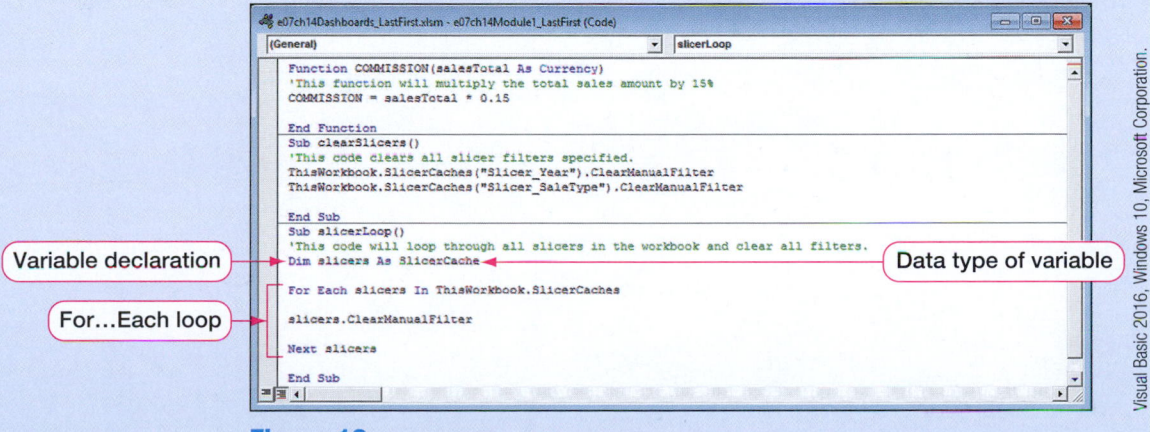

Figure 13 slicerLoop Sub procedure

d. **Save** 💾 the workbook.

Adding Slicers to Test Loop Effectiveness

Now that you have created a For...Each loop to accommodate the addition of more slicers on the RevenueDashboard worksheet, you can add new slicers and keep the functionality of the Clear Slicers button. In this exercise, you will add two additional slicers, filter the chart using all four slicers, and run the loop by clicking the Clear Slicers button.

 E14.14

To Test Effectiveness of the For ... Each Loop

a. Press [Alt] + [F11] to switch to the RevenueDashboard worksheet, and then click the **Sales Revenue** column chart.

b. Click the **Analyze** tab, and then, in the Filter group, click **Insert Slicer**.

c. Check the boxes for **SalesRep** and **Status**, and then click **OK**.

d. If necessary, click the **Status** slicer, and then resize it to be 1" in height and 1.5" in width. Click the **Options** tab, and then, in the Slicer Styles group, select **Slicer Style Dark 3** from the Dark category.

e. Click the **SalesRep** slicer, and then resize it to be 2" in height and 1.5" in width. Click the **Options** tab, and then, in the Slicer Styles group, select **Slicer Style Dark 3** from the Dark category.

f. Reposition the **Status** and **SalesRep** slicers to the right of the Year and SaleType slicers. Position the SalesRep slicer above the Status slicer. If necessary, right-click the **Clear Slicers** button, and then drag to the right to make room for the slicers.

g. Select the **Year** and **SaleType** slicers. On the Options tab, in the Slicer Styles group, select **Slicer Style Dark 3** from the Dark category.

h. Use each of the four slicers to filter the Sales Revenue column chart, and then click the **Clear Slicers** button. Notice that since the Clear Slicers button is still assigned to the clearSlicers procedure, the additional slicers are not affected by the code.

i. Right-click the **Clear Slicers** form control button, and then select **Assign Macro**.

j. Select **slicerLoop** to change the macro assigned to the button, and then click **OK**.

k. Click **any cell** to deselect the Clear Slicers button.

l. Click the **Clear Slicers** button to confirm that the code now affects all slicers and that there are no errors.

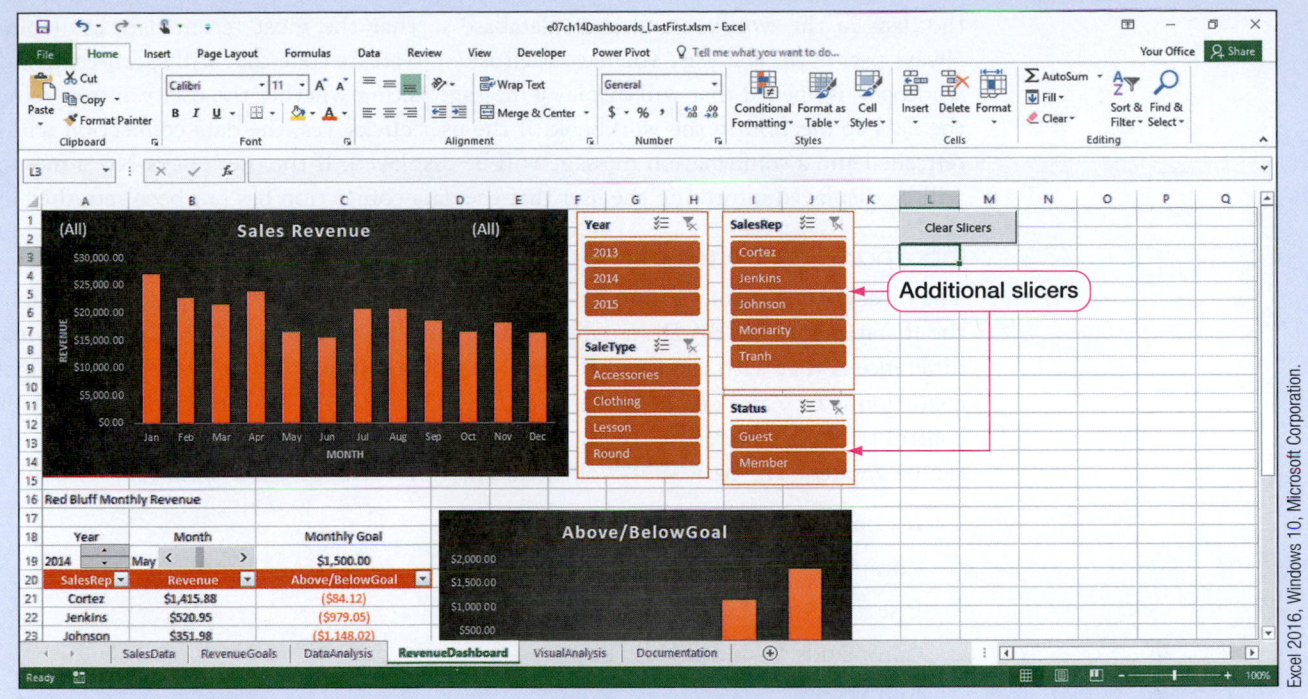

Figure 14 Additional slicers added

    m. Save 🖫 the workbook.

Assign VBA Procedures to Events

VBA code can be executed by a variety of methods, most commonly by assigning the code to a button or by setting up the code to execute when an event occurs. An **event** is an action initiated either by a user or by VBA code. An example of an event at the application level would be when a user creates a new workbook; an event at the workbook level would be when a user opens or closes a workbook.

QUICK REFERENCE		Common Events
Object	**Event**	**Description**
Application	SheetCalculate	Detects when formulas in any worksheet have been recalculated
	NewWorkbook	Detects when a user creates a new workbook
	WorkbookBeforeClose	Occurs after a user closes a workbook but before Excel actually closes it
Workbook	Open	Detects when a workbook is opened
	BeforeClose	Runs specified code before a workbook closes
	BeforeSave	Occurs after a user has clicked Save but before Excel actually saves the file
Worksheet	Activate	Detects when a specified worksheet is activated
	Deactivate	Detects when a specified worksheet is no longer the active sheet
	Change	Detects when any cell in a specified worksheet is changed

If the managers like the enhancements you make to the workbook, they will connect the data in the workbook to their database so that the most recent data available is always part of the analysis. You have been asked to create code that will execute when the workbook is opened that will display a message asking whether the user wants to refresh the data connection in the workbook. If the user clicks Yes, the data connection will be refreshed and a confirmation message will be displayed. If the user clicks No, a message will be displayed informing the user that the data connection has not been refreshed.

Incorporating Conditional Statements into VBA

The most basic method of running VBA commands in response to a specific condition is the If statement. A VBA IF statement is very similar to the Excel IF function. The main difference is that with the Excel IF function, you are limited to only one outcome if the condition is true and one outcome if the condition is false. With the VBA If-Then-Else control structure, there is virtually no limit to the number of commands and logic that can be applied. The basic syntax of the If-Then-Else structure is as follows.

> If Condition Then
>
> Commands if condition is true
>
> Else
>
> Commands if condition is false
>
> End If

The condition portion of the structure is an expression that is resolved to either true or false. If it is true, then the first set of commands is run; otherwise, the second set of commands is run. In this next exercise, you will create an If-Then-Else statement in which the condition is to check how the user responds to a message box asking whether or not to refresh the data connection. The commands will make use of message boxes. A **message box** is a dialog box object that is created by using the MsgBox command. The message box is used to display an informative message to the user and includes buttons the user can interact with. The MsgBox syntax is as follows:

> MsgBox("Message Text", Buttons, "Message Title")

The only required argument in the MsgBox is the Message text or Prompt argument.

In this exercise, you will incorporate an IF statement into a Sub procedure. This exercise requires a more complicated procedure; therefore, you will be including comments and adding extra white space to make the code easier to read and understand.

 **E14.15**

To Incorporate Conditional Statements

a. Press `Alt` + `F11` to switch to the VBE.

b. Click the **Code window**, and click just below the End Sub statement of the slicerLoop procedure, and then press `Enter`.

c. Create a new procedure by typing Sub refreshData(), and then press `Enter`.

d. Type the following comment: 'This line of code will display a message box to the user. Press `Enter` twice.

e. To create a message box, type dataConnection = MsgBox("Would you like to refresh the data connection?", vbQuestion + vbYesNo, "Data Connection"). Press `Enter` twice.

   The message box will display a question mark and Yes/No buttons because you typed vbQuestion + vbYesNo for the buttons argument of the message box.

This line of code creates a message box with the message text, a question style with Yes and No buttons, and a title of Data Connection. The user's response of Yes or No will be stored in the dataConnection variable.

f. Type the following comment, using multiple lines.

'This If statement will refresh the data connection and display a confirmation message 'if the user clicks Yes to the message box. If the user clicks no, another message box 'will be displayed informing the user that the data connection was not refreshed.

g. Press Enter twice, and then begin the If statement by typing If dataConnection = vbYes Then. Press Enter twice. This line of code will check the value of the message box, and if the user clicks the Yes button, it will execute the next block of code.

h. Type   ThisWorkbook.Connections("ThisWorkbookDataModel").Refresh,   and then press Enter twice. This line of code, when executed, will refresh the dashboard with any changes made to the data model. This will be useful once the dashboard is connected to the sales database.

i. To create a confirmation message box, type MsgBox ("The data connection has been refreshed."). Press Enter twice, type Else to begin the Else statement, and then press Enter twice.

j. To create a message box if the user clicks No, type MsgBox ("The data connection has not been refreshed."). Press Enter twice.

k. To end the If statement, type End If, and then press Enter.

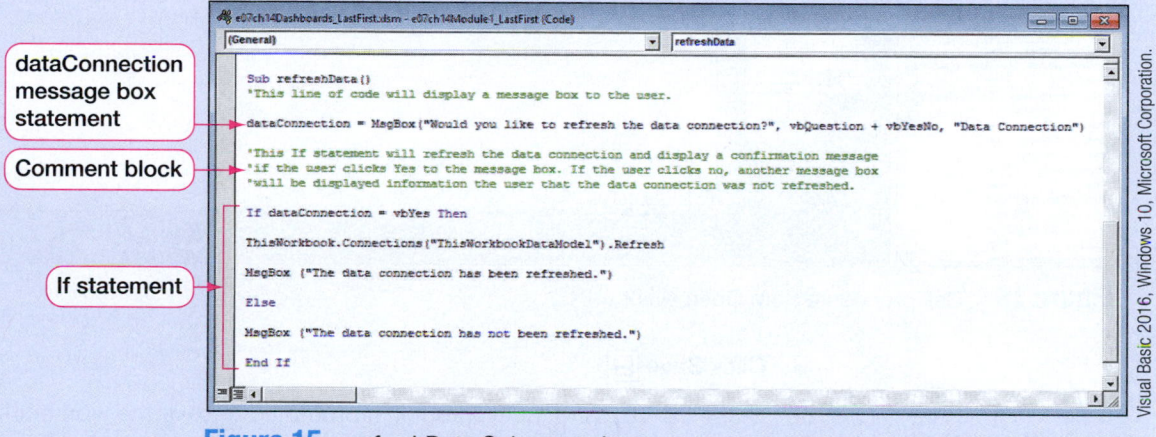

Figure 15   refreshData Sub procedure

l. **Save** 💾 the workbook.

Assigning a VBA Procedure to the Open Event

The refreshData Sub procedure is not complete. It should run every time the workbook is opened. By using the Call statement, a Sub procedure can be run from within another Sub procedure. In this exercise, you will call the procedure to execute when the workbook opens, using the Open event in the ThisWorkbook object.

 **E14.16**

SIDE NOTE
Using the Object and Procedure Lists
Alternatively, you can select Workbook from the Object list at the top of the Code window and select Open from the Procedure list.

To Assign a VBA Procedure to the Open Event

a. If necessary, press Alt + F11 to switch to the VBE, and in the Project Explorer window, double-click the **ThisWorkbook** object to open the Code window for ThisWorkbook.

b. To create a new private Sub procedure for the Open event, type Private Sub Workbook_Open(), and then press Enter.

c. To call the refreshData procedure, type Call refreshData, and then press Enter.

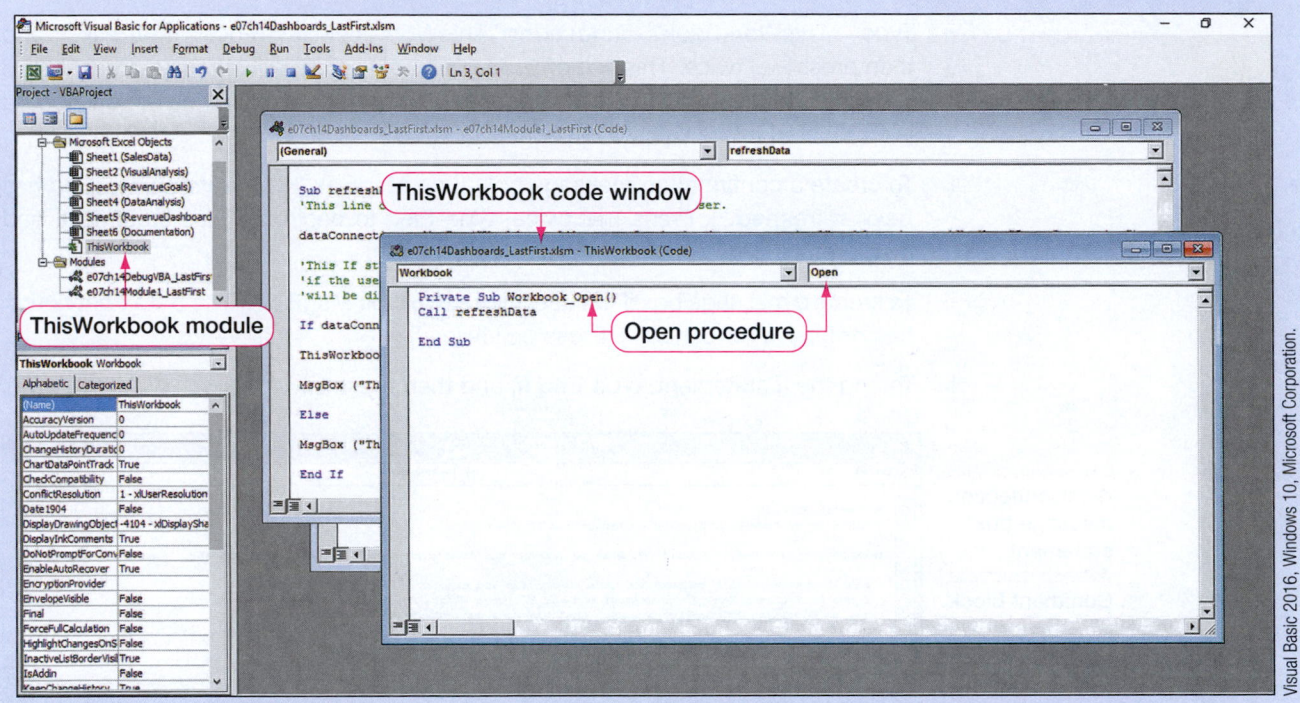

Figure 16   Call procedure from Open event

d. Click **Save** 💾.

e. Close the VBE and the workbook. If prompted to save the workbook, click **Save**.

f. Test the **procedure** by opening the workbook again. Notice the Data Connection message box.

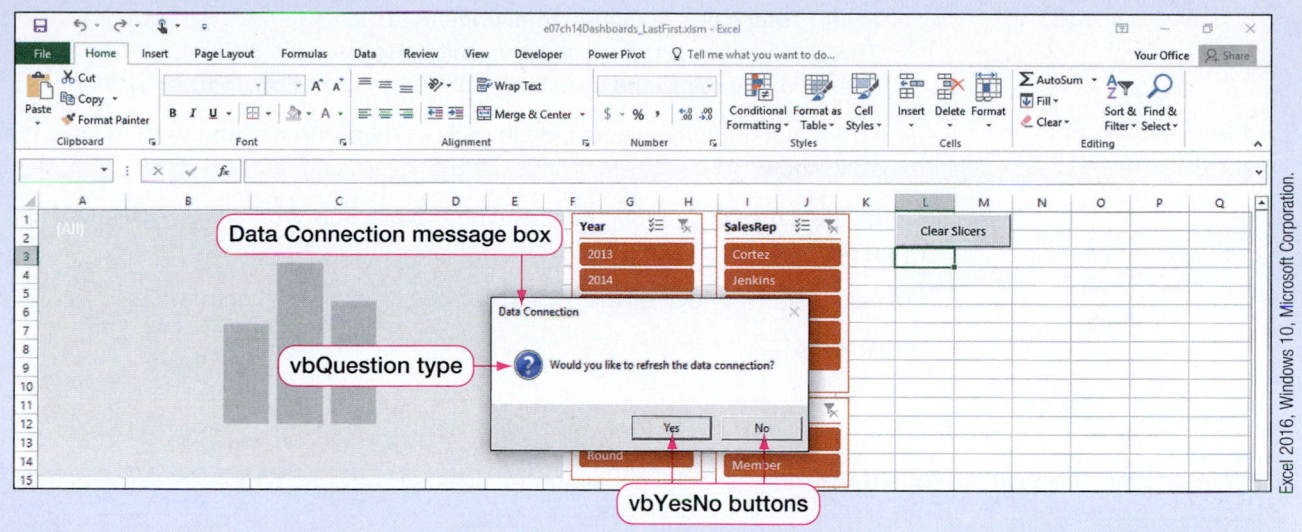

Figure 17 Data Connection message box

g. Click **Yes**, and then click **OK**.

Assigning a VBA Procedure to the Activate Event

The e07ch14Dashboards_LastFirst workbook contains a Power View report located on the VisualAnalysis worksheet. **Power View** is an interactive data visualization, exploration, and presentation experience that encourages the creation of beautiful ad hoc reports. New employees may not be familiar with Power View or the information contained within the report. In this exercise, you will create a procedure that will display a message box providing the user with some definitions of the data used in the report. This message box will include line breaks to make its content easier to read and concatenation symbols to allow the code to be broken up into multiple lines. You will use the character code Chr(13) to indicate a carriage return and an ampersand (&) to concatenate text in the prompt argument. The message box will open automatically when the VisualAnalysis worksheet is activated.

 **E14.17**

SIDE NOTE
Power View Availability
Remember that Power View is available only in Office 365 ProPlus and Enterprise editions of Excel.

To Assign a VBA Procedure to the Activate Event

a. Press [Alt] + [F11] to switch to the VBE. Click the **e07ch14Module1_LastFirst** code window, and click just below the End Sub statement of the refreshData procedure, and then press [Enter].

b. To create a new Sub procedure, type Sub powerView () and then press [Enter].

c. Type the following comment block:

'This procedure displays a message box providing definitions for data used in the report.

'It will be assigned to the Activate event of the VisualAnalysis worksheet.

Press [Enter] twice.

d. In this step, press [Enter] after each underscore character. To create the message box, type Description = MsgBox("This report is designed to provide you with an interactive visual summary of the sales data. " & _

"Some of the data is described below." & Chr(13) & Chr(13) & _

"TotalSales: Total sales revenue of items sold." & Chr(13) & _

"TotalCosts: Total costs of items sold." & Chr(13) & _

"Profit: Total sales revenue - total unit costs." & _

"This does not account for any non-unit based costs." & Chr(13) & Chr(13) & _

"Feel free to explore the visualizations.", vbInformation, "Power View")

e. In the Project Explorer window, double-click **Sheet2(VisualAnalysis)** to view the Code window.

f. To create a new private Sub routine, type Private Sub Worksheet_Activate(), and then press Enter.

g. To call the powerView routine, type Call powerView, and then press Enter.

h. Click **Save** 💾.

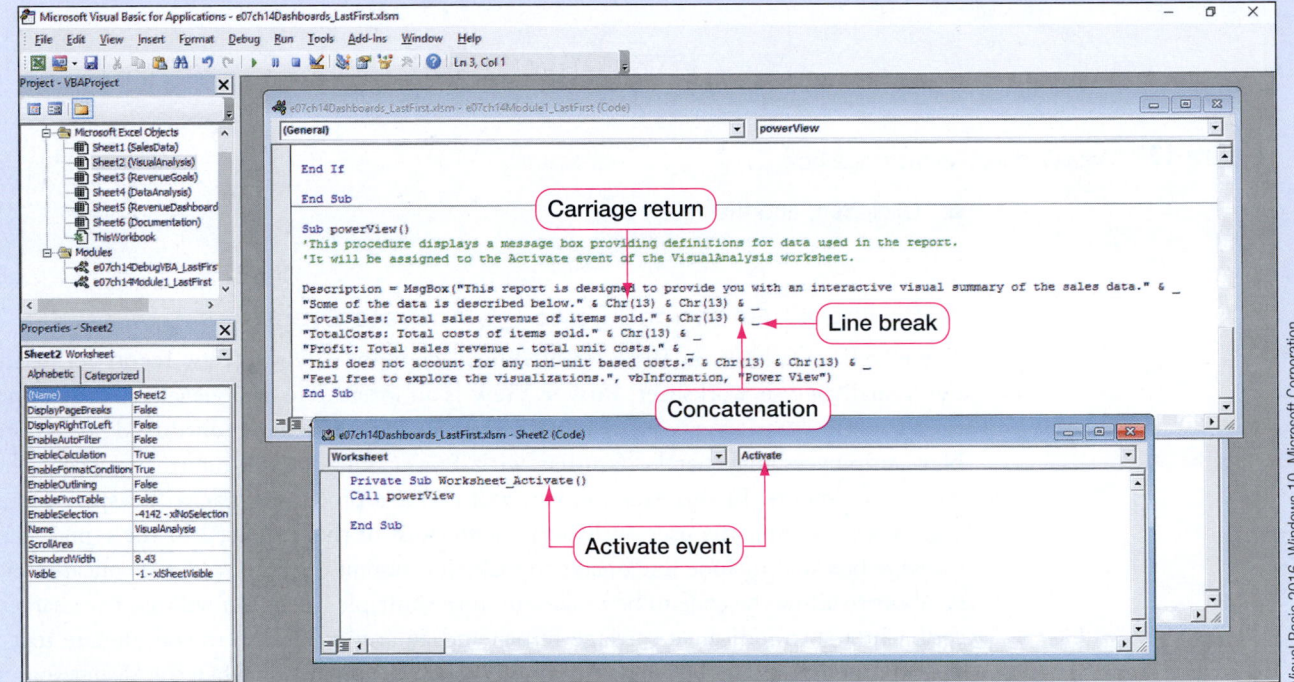

Figure 18 powerView Sub procedure on Active event

i. Press Alt + F11 to switch back to the workbook, and then click the **VisualAnalysis** worksheet to see the message. Click **OK** to close the message box. The visualization is then generated.

Protect and Secure a Workbook

The managers at the Red Bluff Golf Course & Pro Shop who will benefit from Excel dashboards and Power View reports have varying competencies when it comes to using Excel. You do not want to risk giving an Excel novice access to the worksheets that contain the raw data where he or she could potentially damage or delete the data.

Protecting worksheets from intentional or unintentional modification can be done by simply hiding the worksheets in the Excel workbook. However, those worksheets can easily be made visible with a right-click or through the Options menu under the File tab. VBA provides a more secure method of hiding worksheets by using the xlVeryHidden property.

Using the xlVeryHidden Property

In this exercise, you will use xlVeryHidden and assign it to the Visible property of the Sheet object to hide specific worksheets in the workbook. The sheets that are hidden by assigning this to the Visible property cannot be made visible without altering the VBA code.

 E14.18

To Make Sheets Very Hidden

a. Click the **SalesData** worksheet. Press Alt + F11 to switch to the VBE.

b. Click the **e07ch14Module1_LastFirst** code window, click just below the End Sub statement of the powerView procedure, and then press Enter.

c. To create a Sub procedure, type Sub hideSheets(), and then press Enter.

d. To add the following comment, type 'This procedure will make the SalesData, RevenueGoals, and DataAnalysis worksheets hidden. Press Enter twice.

e. To hide the SalesData worksheet, type Sheets("SalesData").Visible = xlVeryHidden, and then press Enter.

f. To hide the RevenueGoals worksheet, type Sheets("RevenueGoals").Visible = xlVeryHidden, and then press Enter.

g. To hide the DataAnalysis worksheet, type Sheets("DataAnalysis").Visible = xlVeryHidden, and then press Enter.

hideSheets procedure →

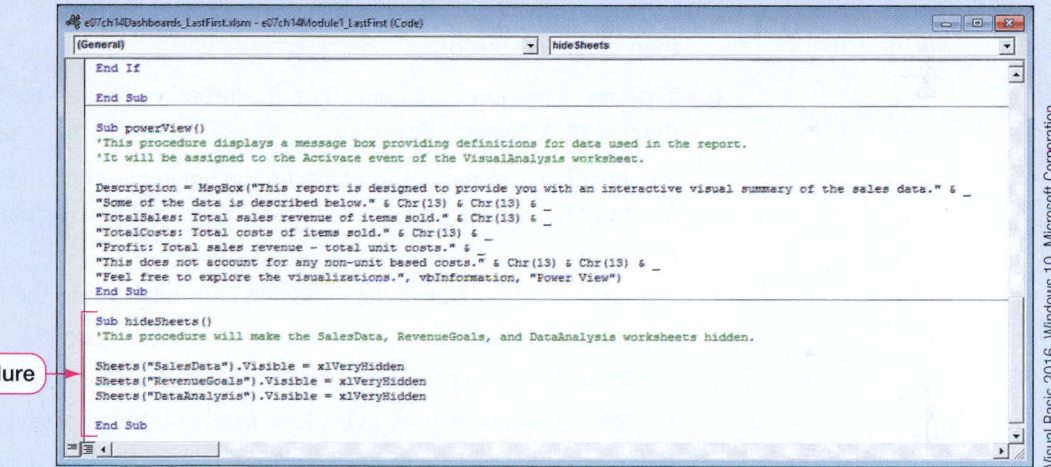

Figure 19 hideSheets Sub procedure

h. Click **Save** 🖫.

i. Press F5 to run the procedure. Press Alt + F11 to switch back to the workbook, and then observe that the three worksheets are no longer visible.

Providing Access to Hidden Worksheets

Some managers may need to access the raw data in a workbook and should not be required to know VBA to be able to unhide those worksheets. In this exercise, you will create a procedure that, upon execution, will prompt the user for a password to make the hidden sheets visible. This will require the use of an input box. An **input box** is an effective way of using VBA code to increase the interactivity of a dashboard by prompting the user for information and storing that information in a variable to be used later.

 **E14.19**

To Provide Access to Hidden Sheets

a. Press [Alt] + [F11] to switch back to the VBE.

b. Click the **e07ch14Module1_LastFirst** code window just below the End Sub statement of the hideSheets procedure, and then press [Enter].

c. To create a new Sub procedure, type Sub showSheets (), and then press [Enter].

d. Type the following comment block.

'This procedure will prompt the user for a password if they wish to view 'the hidden worksheets. If the password is correct, the sheets will 'be made visible. Press [Enter] twice.

e. To declare a new variable to store the password, type Dim password as String, and then press [Enter].

f. To provide the password variable with the password, type password = "Show Sheets", and then press [Enter].

g. To create a variable to store the password response of the user, type access = InputBox("Enter the password to view hidden sheets:", "Show Sheets"), and then press [Enter] twice.

h. Type the following comment: 'The If statement makes the sheets visible if the password is correct. Press [Enter].

i. To begin the If statement to compare the value stored in the access variable from the Input Box to the password variable, type If access = password Then, and then press [Enter].

j. Make the sheets visible if the condition is true by typing the following.

- Sheets("SalesData").Visible = True, and then press [Enter].
- Sheets("RevenueGoals").Visible = True, and then press [Enter].
- Sheets("DataAnalysis").Visible = True, and then press [Enter].

k. Type Else to begin the code if the condition is false, and then press [Enter].

l. To create a message box that informs the user of an invalid password, type invalid = MsgBox("The password is invalid", vbCritical, "Invalid Password"), and then press [Enter].

m. End the If statement by typing End If, and then press [Enter].

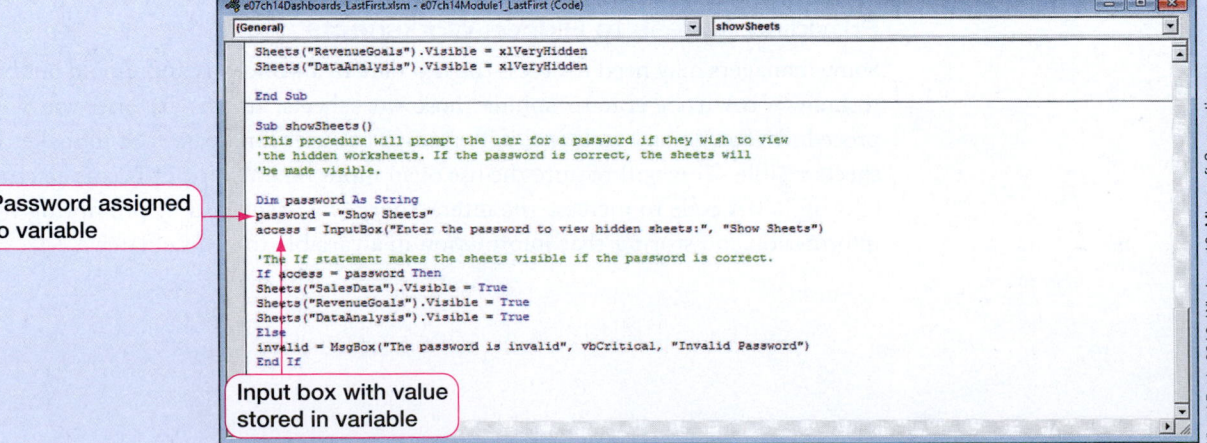

Password assigned to variable

Input box with value stored in variable

Visual Basic 2016, Windows 10, Microsoft Corporation.

Figure 20 showSheets Sub procedure

n. Click **Save** 🖫. Press [Alt] + [F11] to switch back to the workbook.

o. Click the **RevenueDashboard** worksheet tab if necessary. Assign the showSheets macro to a button on the RevenueDashboard worksheet by completing the following tasks.

- Click the **Developer** tab, and then, in the Controls group, click the Insert arrow. Under Form Controls, select **Button (Form Control)** ▭.

- Drag a **rectangular button** within the range **L6:M8**.

- In the Assign Macro dialog box, select **showSheets**, and then click **OK**.

- Select the **button text**, type View Hidden Sheets, and then click any cell to deselect the button.

- Click the **View Hidden Sheets** button, type Show Sheets as the password, and then click **OK**. Confirm that the three sheets are now visible.

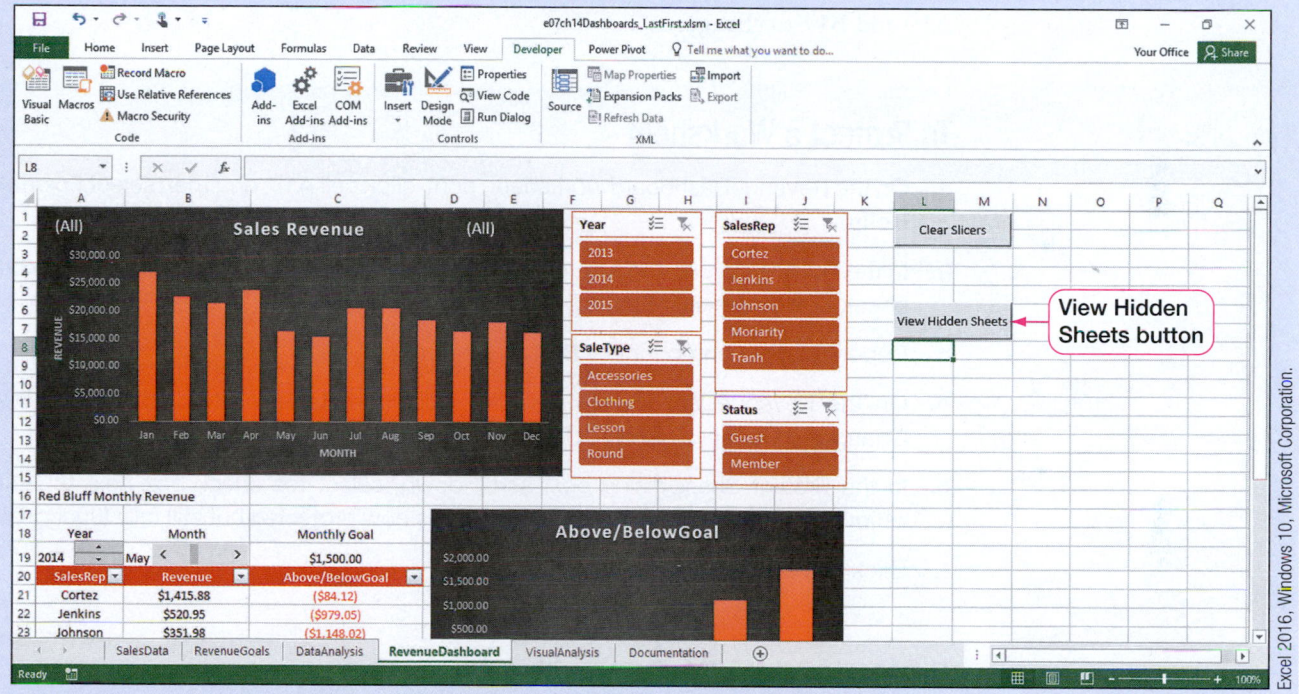

Figure 21   View Hidden Sheets button

p. Click **Save** 🖫.

Assigning a Procedure to the BeforeClose Event

Now that the hidden sheets are visible, you will need to run the hideSheets procedure again so that no unauthorized person can access the sheets. In this exercise, you will call the hideSheets procedure to execute when the BeforeClose event occurs.

 **E14.20**

To Call a Procedure on the BeforeClose Event

a. Press [Alt] + [F11] to switch to the VBE.

b. In the Project Explorer window, double-click **ThisWorkbook** to open the Code window.

c. Click the **Procedures** arrow, scroll up, and then select **BeforeClose**. A new Private Sub procedure is created on the BeforeClose event that will execute before Excel closes the workbook but after the user has clicked Close.

d. To call the hideSheets procedure, type **Call hideSheets**, and then press (Enter).

e. Click **Save** 🔲. **Close** ☒ the **VBE**, and then **Close** ☒ the **workbook**.

f. Open the **e07ch14Dashboards_LastFirst workbook**, and, if necessary, click **Enable Content**. Click **No** when prompted to refresh the data connection, click **OK**, and then verify that the three worksheets are now hidden.

Protecting a Worksheet

The RevenueDashboard worksheet is now in its final state and needs to be protected to prevent unintentional changes. Before the worksheet is protected, you need to ensure that the cells that must be allowed to be changed to use the dashboard are not locked. Cells A19 and B17 need to be allowed to change, as they are linked to the spin button and the slider. In this exercise, you will protect the RevenueDashboard worksheet and allow cells A19 and B17 to change.

 E14.21

To Protect a Worksheet

a. On the RevenueDashboard worksheet, right-click cell **A19**, and then select **Format Cells**.

b. In the Format Cells dialog box, click the **Protection** tab, and then click the **Locked** check box to deselect Locked. Click **OK**.

c. Repeat steps a and b for cell **B17**.

d. On the RevenueDashboard worksheet, click the **Review** tab, and then, in the Changes group, click **Protect Sheet**.

e. In the Protect Sheet dialog box, scroll down, select the check box next to **Edit objects**, and then click **OK**. The worksheet is now protected but still fully functional.

f. Click **Save** 🔲.

Protecting the VBA Code with a Password

Protecting the VBA code with a password ensures that no unauthorized person will access the code. It is considered best practice to export any VBA modules as text files before protecting them with a password. Thus, if the password is lost or the workbook becomes corrupt, you will have a copy of the VBA code. In this exercise, you will export the VBA modules and then protect the VBA with a password.

 E14.22

To Protect the VBA Code with a Password

a. Press (Alt) + (F11) to switch to the VBE.

b. In the Project Explorer window, if necessary, click to expand VBAProject (e07ch-14Dashboards_LastFirst.xlsm). Right-click **e07ch14Module1_LastFirst**, and then select **Export File**. Navigate to where you are saving your student files, click the **Save as type** arrow, and then select **All Files**. Click inside the **File name** box, edit the **.bas** extension to **.txt** and then click **Save**.

c. Right-click **e07ch14DebugVBA_LastFirst**, and then select **Export File**. Click the **Save as type** arrow, and then select **All Files**. Click inside the **File name** box, edit the **.bas** extension to **.txt**, and then click **Save**.

d. On the menu click **Tools**, and then select **VBAProject Properties**.

e. Click the **Protection** tab, and then, in the Lock project area, select the **Lock project for viewing** check box.

f. Click the **Password** field, and then type C22!twb.

g. Click the **Confirm password** field, and then type C22!twb again.

h. Click **OK**.

i. **Close** ☒ the **VBE**, and then click **Save** 🔲. The password will not take effect until the workbook is closed. Close the workbook.

j. Open the **e07ch14Dashboards_LastFirst** workbook. Click **No** to the Data Connection prompt, and then click **OK**. Press ⟮Alt⟯ + ⟮F11⟯ to switch to the VBE.

k. If necessary, click **View**, and then click **Project Explorer** to view the Project Explorer window. Double-click **VBA Project (e07ch14Dashboards_LastFirst.xlsm)**. Type C22!twb in the VBAProject Password dialog box, and then click **OK**. If necessary, click to expand **VBAProject (e07ch14Dashboards_LastFirst.xlsm)** to view the modules.

l. Click **Save** 🔲. Press ⟮Alt⟯ + ⟮F11⟯ to switch to the workbook.

m. Complete the Documentation worksheet, and then submit your file as directed by your instructor.

Concept Check

1. What are form controls, and how can they be used to enhance interactivity with a dashboard? p. 746

2. Describe the object model in Excel. p. 752

3. What are function procedures, and how can organizations use them? p. 756

4. What are some common practices that can help to improve the readability and understanding of VBA code? p. 759

5. Describe the purpose of debug mode in the VBE and why it is useful. p. 762

6. List the categories of loops used in VBA, and describe each type of loop. p. 763

7. Describe three scenarios in which assigning a VBA procedure to an event would enhance the workbook. p. 767

8. What can be done to ensure that unauthorized changes are not made to a workbook? p. 772

Key Terms

Code window   755
Digital dashboard   746
Do…Until loop   763
Do…While loop   763
Event   767
For loop   763
For…Each loop   763
Form control   746
Function procedure   756
Input box   773
Loop   763
Message box   768

Method   754
Module   756
Object collection   752
Object model   752
Object-oriented programming
   (OOP)   752
Objects   752
Parameter   754
Power View   771
Project Explorer window   755
Properties   753
Properties window   755

Run-time error   762
Scroll bar   749
Separators   753
Slicer   746
Spin button   747
Sub procedure   756
Variable   764
VBA (Visual Basic for
   Applications)   752
Visual Basic Editor (VBE)   755

Visual Summary

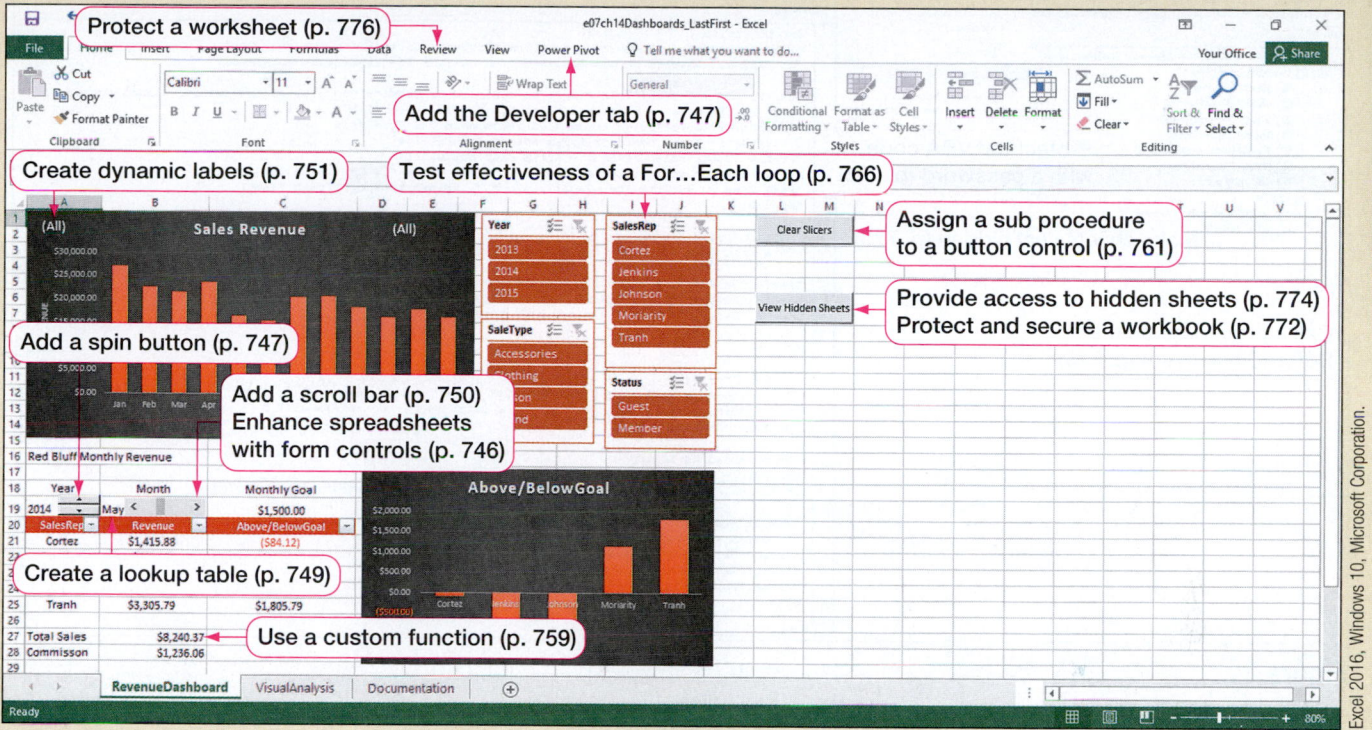

Protect a worksheet (p. 776)

Add the Developer tab (p. 747)

Create dynamic labels (p. 751)

Test effectiveness of a For...Each loop (p. 766)

Assign a sub procedure to a button control (p. 761)

Add a spin button (p. 747)

Provide access to hidden sheets (p. 774)
Protect and secure a workbook (p. 772)

Add a scroll bar (p. 750)
Enhance spreadsheets with form controls (p. 746)

Create a lookup table (p. 749)

Use a custom function (p. 759)

Figure 22

Excel 2016, Windows 10, Microsoft Corporation.

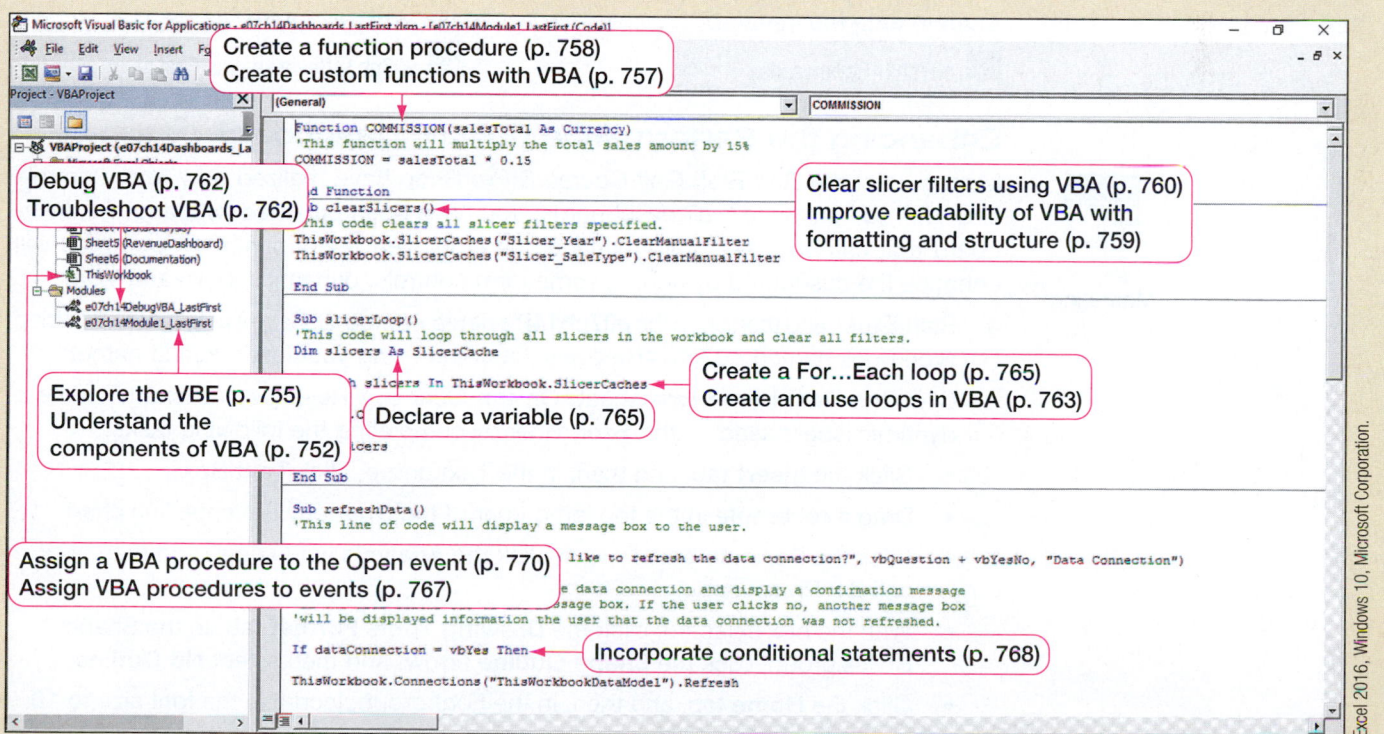

Create a function procedure (p. 758)
Create custom functions with VBA (p. 757)

Debug VBA (p. 762)
Troubleshoot VBA (p. 762)

Clear slicer filters using VBA (p. 760)
Improve readability of VBA with formatting and structure (p. 759)

Explore the VBE (p. 755)
Understand the components of VBA (p. 752)

Create a For...Each loop (p. 765)
Create and use loops in VBA (p. 763)

Declare a variable (p. 765)

Assign a VBA procedure to the Open event (p. 770)
Assign VBA procedures to events (p. 767)

Incorporate conditional statements (p. 768)

Figure 23

Excel 2016, Windows 10, Microsoft Corporation.

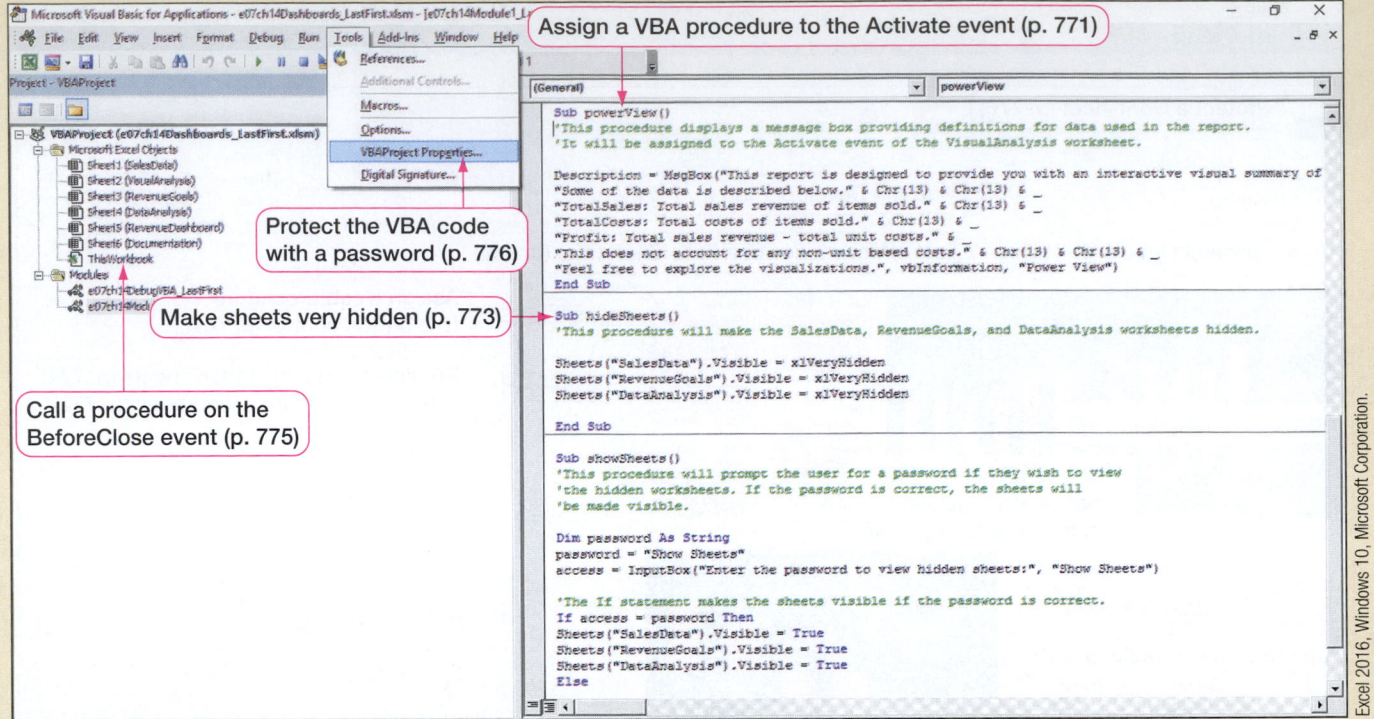

Figure 24

Student data file needed:

 e07ch14Reviews.xlsx

You will save your file as:

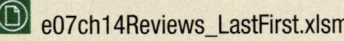 e07ch14Reviews_LastFirst.xlsm

Enhancing the Performance Review Dashboard

Sales & Marketing

Managers at the Red Bluff Golf Course & Pro Shop have realized how form controls and VBA can enhance their dashboards. You have been provided with another dashboard that can be used to aid managers in employee performance reviews. You will enhance the dashboard by adding some form controls, dynamic labels, and VBA.

a. Start **Excel**, and then open the **e07ch14Reviews** workbook. Save it as a Macro-Enabled Workbook named e07ch14Reviews_LastFirst using your last and first name.

b. Click the **Dashboard** worksheet. On the Quarterly Revenue line chart, create a dynamic label based on the **Year** slicer by completing the following tasks:

- Click the **Insert** tab, and then, in the Text group, click **Text Box**.

- Drag a **rectangle** in the top left corner of the Quarterly Revenue line chart.

- Click the **Formula bar**. Type **=**, click the **Analysis** worksheet, and then click cell **B1**. Press Enter.

- With the box selected, click the **Drawing Tools Format** tab. In the Shape Styles group, click the **Shape Outline** arrow, and then select **No Outline**.

- Click the **Home** tab, and then, in the Font group, increase the font size to 16.

- Adjust the size of the box as necessary to accommodate the font size.

c. Repeat step b to add a dynamic label in the top left corner of the Revenue and Costs combo column chart and the Total Revenue pie chart. Use cell **B14** from the **Analysis** worksheet for this step.

d. Add a spin button form control to cell I23 by completing the following tasks:

- Click the **Developer** tab, and then, in the Controls group, click the **Insert** arrow. Select **Spin Button (Form Control)**.
- Drag the small square **Spin** button in the cell range **I22:I23** to the right of the year label and year number.
- Right-click the **Spin** button, and then click **Format Control**.
- Type 2013 in the Current and Minimum value fields.
- Type 2015 in the Maximum value field.
- Click the **Cell link** field, click cell **I23**, and then click **OK**.

e. Create a lookup table to be used with a scroll bar form control by completing the following tasks.

- Click the **Analysis** worksheet. Click cell **I1**, type Value, and then, in the cell range **I2:I5**, type the values 1, 2, 3, and 4.
- Click cell **J1**, type Quarter and then, in the cell range **J2:J5** type the values Q1, Q2, Q3, and Q4.
- Select **I1:J5**, click the **Name** box, and then type Quarters to give the range of cells a name.

f. On the Dashboard worksheet, add a scroll bar to the right of Q1 in cell **J23** by completing the following tasks.

- Click the **Dashboard** worksheet, click cell **J21**, and then type the number 1 to be used as the lookup value.
- Click cell **J23**, and then type =VLOOKUP(J21,Quarters,2,FALSE).
- On the Developer tab, in the Controls group, click the **Insert** arrow, and then select the **Scroll Bar (Form Control)**.
- Drag a **horizontal rectangle** in cell **J23** to the right of the Q1 text.
- Right-click the **Scroll Bar**, and then select **Format Control**.
- Type 1 in the Current value and Minimum value fields.
- Type 4 in the Maximum value field.
- Click the **Cell link** field, click cell **J21**, and then click **OK**.
- Click cell **J21**, click the **Home** tab, and then in the Font group, change the font color to **White, Background 1**.

g. Create a VBA Sub procedure that will clear filters in all slicers in the workbook, even if more slicers are added, by completing the following tasks.

- Press Alt + F11 to switch to the VBE, click **Insert**, and then select **Module**.
- In the Properties window, click the **Name** field, and then type ReviewModule_LastFirst using your last and first name.
- Click the **Code window**, type Sub clearSlicers (), and then press Enter.
- Type the following comment: 'This code will loop through all the slicers in the workbook and clear all filters. Press Enter twice.
- Type Dim allSlicers As SlicerCache to declare a variable with a data type of Slicer Cache, and then press Enter twice.
- Type For Each allSlicers In ThisWorkbook.SlicerCaches, and then press Enter twice.
- Type allSlicers.ClearManualFilter, and then press Enter twice.
- Type Next allSlicers, and then press Enter.

h. On the Dashboard worksheet, assign the Sub procedure to a Button form control by competing the following tasks.

- Press Alt + F11 to switch to the workbook.

- On the Developer tab, in the Controls group, click the **Insert** arrow, and then select **Button (Form Control)**.
- Drag a **button** within the cell range **J1:K3**. In the Assign Macro dialog box, select **clearSlicers**, and then click **OK**.
- Edit the button text to Clear Slicers, and then, if necessary, adjust the size of the button so that all text is visible.

i. Add the **SalesRep** slicer to the dashboard by completing the following tasks.
- Click the **Quarterly Revenue** line chart.
- Click the **Analyze** tab, and then, in the Filter group, click **Insert Slicer**.
- Click the **SalesRep** check box, and then click **OK**.
- Resize the **SalesRep** slicer to be 1.5" in width and 2" in height.
- Reposition the **SalesRep** slicer to fit within the cell range **J5:K14**, in between the Year and SaleType slicers and the pie chart.
- Click the **Options** tab, and then, in the Slicer Styles group, select **Slicer Style Dark 6**.
- On the **Options** tab, click **Report Connections**, click the **PivotTable2** check box, and then click **OK**.

j. Click the **Documentation** worksheet. Click cell **A6**, and then type in today's date. Click cell **B6**, and then type your first and last name. Complete the remainder of the **Documentation** worksheet according to your instructor's direction.

k. Click **Save**, close Excel, and then submit your file as directed by your instructor.

Problem Solve 1

Student data file needed:

 e07ch14Goals.xlsm

You will save your file as:

 e07ch14Goals_LastFirst.xlsm

Goals and Results

Sales & Marketing

You recently started a new job. Your predecessor began a file to track the sales by year, by quarter, and by sales representative. The dashboard is supposed to calculate the commission payout based on a changing percentage for a month/year. You have been asked to complete this dashboard.

a. Open the **Excel** workbook **e07ch14Goals**. Save your file as e07ch14Goals_LastFirst using your last and first name.

b. On the **Lookups** worksheet, create a list of month numbers and month names.

c. On the **Dashboard** worksheet, above the Goals table in cell **B22**, create a lookup formula that will return the month name based on the month number entered in cell E22.

d. Add a Spin Button to cell **A22** to change the year. It should allow the years to change between 2017, 2018, and 2019.

e. Add a Scroll Bar across cells B22 and C22 that changes the month name. It should be linked to the month number in cell **E22**. As the user changes the month, the name displayed should be updated accordingly. Change the appropriate properties of the control so that only the months January through December can be selected.

f. Create a Clustered Column chart based on the data in the Goals table that shows sales representatives who are above/below goal. Position the chart so that it covers the highlighted month number cell.

g. Use **Chart Style 4** for the chart so it is consistent with the other chart on the worksheet.

h. Add slicers to the Sales by Quarter chart for **Year** and **Rep**. Format and size appropriately in the white space next to the Chart.

i. Create two dynamic labels for the Sales by Quarter chart. Add two text boxes to the chart; one text box should be linked to the pivot field **Year**, and the other should be linked to the pivot field **Rep**. The PivotTable for both fields is located on the Analysis worksheet.

j. Create a macro to clear the two slicers. Use a For...Each loop to account for additional slicers being added to the workbook.

k. Review the Commission macro. There is an error in the macro, and it will not run. Correct the macro.

l. Add comments to the Commission macro so future users will know what each step of the macro does.

m. Run the macro with a commission rate of 20%.

n. Insert a Button on the Dashboard worksheet that will run the macro to clear the slicers. Place the button to the right of the Sales by Quarter chart. Edit the text of the Button to Clear Slicers.

o. Insert a Button that will run the Commission macro. Place the button to the right of the Total Sales calculation in B28. Edit the text of the Button to Calculate Commission.

p. Hide Gridlines and Row and Column Headers.

q. Complete the **Documentation** worksheet according to your instructor's direction.

r. Click **Save**, close Excel, and then submit your file as directed by your instructor.

Critical Thinking

A common step in creating Dashboards is to use the Protect Worksheet feature found on the Review tab. Given the Dashboard built in this exercise, what problems might be associated with protecting the Dashboard worksheet? How could these issues be corrected to provide full functionality of the Dashboard and still protect the worksheet?

Perform 1: Perform in Your Life

Student data file needed:
 Blank Excel workbook

You will save your file as:
 e07ch14Expenses_LastFirst.xlsm

Personal Expenses Dashboard

Finance & Accounting

Keeping track of personal expenses is the first step to becoming financially independent. If you can keep track of what you spend your money on, then you may be able to find areas where you can save money to afford a car payment or start paying back any student loans. In this exercise, you will create a few simple charts on a dashboard based on data that you will provide. You will then enhance the dashboard by adding form controls and VBA.

a. Start **Excel**, create a new blank workbook, and then save it as a Macro-Enabled Workbook with the name e07ch14Expenses_LastFirst using your last and first name.

b. Rename Sheet1 to ExpenseData. Use this worksheet to make a table of expenses. Be sure to make a note of the date, a description of the expense, the amount of the expense, and the category to which the expense belongs. Some examples of categories may be Food, School, Entertainment, Rent, ATM withdrawal, and the like. If you have a bank account, you may be able to export a file of expenses from the bank's website.

c. Create two additional worksheets in the workbook, and then rename one Analysis and the other Dashboard.

d. You will use the Analysis worksheet to create any lookup tables necessary for use with form controls such as scroll bars or spin buttons or PivotTables.

e. Create two charts and one table on the Dashboard worksheet based on the data on the ExpenseData and/or Analysis worksheets. One of the charts should be created from the data in the Excel table.

f. Add two slicers to the Dashboard worksheet that will allow you to filter the data in the chart.

g. Create a table on the Dashboard worksheet showing expense data from different days or months by category. Add one form control, either a spin button or scroll bar, to change the day or months.

h. Create a VBA module named ExpenseModule_LastFirst using your last and first name.

i. Create a VBA Sub procedure that will loop through all slicers and clear the filters, and then assign that Sub procedure to a form control button on the Dashboard worksheet.

j. Insert the **file name** in the left custom footer section of the Header/Footer tab in the Page Setup dialog box on all worksheets in the workbook.

k. Click **Save**, close Excel, and then submit your file as directed by your instructor.

Additional
Cases

Additional Chapter Cases are available on the companion website and in the instructor resources.

Enabling Decisions with **Data Visualization and VBA**

This business unit had two outcomes:

Learning Outcome 1:

Understand the basics of designing a dashboard, develop familiarity with the data model in Excel, develop data models using Power Pivot and create PivotTables and PivotCharts using Power Pivot, incorporate Office Add-ins in a dashboard, use Power View to generate reports, and prepare a dashboard for production.

Learning Outcome 2:

Use form controls to enhance spreadsheets, understand the components of VBA, improve the readability of VBA, use VBA to create custom functions and use loops in a Sub procedure, troubleshoot VBA, assign VBA procedures to events, and secure a workbook.

In Business Unit 7 Capstone, students will demonstrate competence in these outcomes through a series of business problems at various levels from guided practice to problem solving an existing workbook and performing to create new workbooks.

More Practice 1

Student data files needed:

 e07Indigo5.accdb

 e07Metrics.xlsx

You will save your file as:

 e07Metrics_LastFirst.xlsm

Restaurant Metrics

Sales & Marketing

Robin Sanchez, owner and chef of the Indigo5 restaurant, would like to start paying closer attention to the sales data in order to make strategic decisions about the future of the restaurant. Robin has provided you with a small sample of sales data from 2015-2016 in an Access database. You have been asked to import the data into the Excel data model, conduct some analysis, create a simple dashboard, and then enhance it with some simple VBA.

a. Start **Excel**, click **Open Other Workbooks** in the left pane, and then double-click **This PC**. Navigate through the folder structure to the location of your student data files, and then double-click **e07Metrics**. A workbook opens displaying a blank worksheet.

b. Click the **File** tab, click **Save As**, and then double-click **This PC**. In the **Save As** dialog box, navigate to the location where you are saving your project files, and then, in the **Save as type** box, select **Excel Macro-Enabled Workbook**. Change the filename to e07Metrics_LastFirst using your last and first name. Click **Save**.

c. Import the Employees table to the workbook, and transform the FirstName and HireDate fields.

- Click the **Data** tab. In the Get & Transform group, click **New Query**.
- Point to **From Database**, and then select **From Microsoft Access Database**.
- Browse to your student data files, select **e07Indigo5**, and then click **Import**.
- Click the **Employees** table, and then click **Edit**.
- Click the **FirstName** column. Click the **Transform** tab, and in the Text Column group, click **Format**, and then select **Capitalize Each Word**.
- Click the **HireDate** column. On the Transform tab, in the Date & Time Column group, click **Date**, and then select **Date Only**.
- Click the **Home** tab, and in the Close group, click **Close & Load**.

- Rename the worksheet Employees.
- Close the **Workbook Queries** pane.

d. On the **SalesDashboard** worksheet, import the data from the e07Indigo5 database into the Excel data model by completing the following.

- Click the **Data** tab, and then, in the Get External Data group, click **From Access**.
- Browse to your student data files, select **e07Indigo5**, and then click **Open**.
- In the Select Table dialog box, select **Enable selection of multiple tables**.
- Click the **ProductCategories** and **Transactions** check boxes to select the tables in the database, and then click **OK**.
- In the Import Data dialog box, click the **Only Create Connection** option, and then click **OK**.

e. On the **Employees** worksheet, click anywhere in the table. Click the **Power Pivot** tab, and then, in the Tables group, click **Add to Data Model**. If the Power Pivot tab is not visible, you will need to install the Add-in as explained in Chapter 13.

f. Enhance the data model by completing the following.

- In the Power Pivot window, click the **Design** tab, and then, in the Relationships group, click **Create Relationship**.
- In the Create Relationship dialog box, **Employees** should be selected as the Table 1 value and **ServerID** as the Columns value. Select **Transactions** from the Table 2 list, select **ServerID** from the Columns list, and then click **OK**.
- Click the **Transactions** worksheet, and then click the **TransDate** column heading. Click the **Home** tab, and then, in the Formatting group, click the **Format** arrow. Select *3/14/2001.
- Double-click the next **Add Column** column heading, and then type EstimatedRevenue. Press Enter, and then type =RELATED(ProductCategories[AvgPrice])*[Qty]. Press Enter.

g. To create a calculated field just below the ServerID column, click in the Calculation Area, and then type 2016Revenue:=CALCULATE(sum(Transactions[EstimatedRevenue]),YEAR (Transactions[TransDate])=2016). On the Home tab, in the Formatting group, click the **Format** arrow, and then select **Currency**.

h. To create another calculated field just below the CategoryCode column, click in the Calculation Area, and then, type 2017Revenue:=CALCULATE(sum(Transactions[Estimate dRevenue]), YEAR(Transactions[TransDate])=2017). On the Home tab, in the Formatting group, click the **Format** arrow, and then select **Currency**.

i. Create a new KPI for Sales Revenue by completing the following.

- Click the **2017Revenue** calculation. Click the **Home** tab, and then, in the Calculation group, click **Create KPI**.
- In the Create KPI dialog box, under Define target value, in the Measure box, select **2016Revenue** from the calculated field Measure list.
- Adjust the status thresholds to be a low of 90% and a high of 105%.
- Click **OK**.

j. Create a simple dashboard by completing the following.

- On the **Home** tab, click the **PivotTable** arrow, and then select **Chart and Table (Horizontal)**.
- In the Create PivotChart and PivotTable (Horizontal) dialog box, click **Existing Worksheet**, click the **Range Selection** button, and then click the **SalesDashboard** worksheet. Click cell **A1**.
- Click **OK**, and then click **OK** again.

k. Create a PivotChart by completing the following.

- In the PivotChart Fields pane, expand **Transactions**, and then drag **EstimatedRevenue** into the VALUES.

- Expand **ProductCategories**, and then drag **CategoryDescr** into the Axis (CATEGORIES) area.

l. Improve the design of the PivotChart by completing the following.
- Click the **Design** tab, and in the Chart Styles group, click **More**, and then select **Style 6**.
- Edit the Chart Title text to be Indigo5 Revenue.
- Click the chart **legend**, and press Delete.
- Click the **Analyze** tab, and then, in the Show/Hide group, click the **Field Buttons** icon to remove the filter buttons from the PivotChart.

m. Create a PivotTable by completing the following.
- Click the **PivotTable1** placeholder, and then, in the PivotTable Fields pane, expand **Employees**. Drag **FirstName** into the ROWS area.
- Expand **Transactions**, expand **2017Revenue**, and then drag **Value (2017Revenue)** into the VALUES area. Drag **Status** into the VALUES area.

n. Add slicers to the PivotChart by completing the following.
- On the **Analyze** tab, in the Filter group, click **Insert Slicer**.
- In the Insert Slicers dialog box, click the **All** tab, and then click the check box for **CategoryDescr**. Click **OK**.
- With the CategoryDescr slicer still selected, on the Options tab, in the Slicer group, click **Report Connections**.
- If necessary, click the check box for **PivotTable1**, and then click **OK**.
- Click the **Indigo5 Revenue** chart. On the Analyze tab, in the Filter group, click **Insert Timeline**. Click check box for **TransDate**, and then click **OK**.

o. Modify the slicers by completing the following.
- Select the **CategoryDescr** slicer. On the Options tab, in the Slicer Styles group, select **Slicer Style Other 2**.
- On the Options tab, in the Buttons group, click in the **Columns** box, and change the value to 2.
- On the Options tab, in the Size group, click the **Width** box, and change the value to 2.2. Reposition the slicer so that the top left corner of the slicer is positioned in cell **J9**.
- Click the **TransDate** timeline slicer. On the Options tab, in the Timeline Styles group, select **Timeline Style Light 5**.
- In the timeline slicer, click the **MONTHS** arrow, and select **YEARS**. On the Options tab, in the Size group, click the **Width** box, and change the value to 1.5.
- Reposition the slicer to fit within the range **B16:D22**.

p. Create a VBA Sub procedure using a For...Each loop to clear all slicers by completing the following.
- Press Alt + F11 to switch to the VBE.
- Click **Insert**, and then select **Module**.
- In the Properties Window, select the text in the **Name** property, and then type Indigo5VBA_LastFirst using your last and first name.
- Click the **Code Window**, type Sub clearSlicers (), and then press Enter.
- To add a comment to the procedure, type 'Procedure clears all slicers in workbook using a For Each loop. Press Enter twice.
- To declare a variable with a data type of SlicerCache, type Dim slicers as SlicerCache, and then press Enter.
- To create a For…Each loop, type For Each slicers in ThisWorkbook.SlicerCaches, and then press Enter. Type slicers.ClearAllFilters, and then press Enter. Type Next slicers, and then press Enter twice.
- Press Alt + F11 to switch to the workbook.

q. Add a button to the dashboard to clear all slicers. Click the Developer tab, and then, in the Controls group, click the **Insert** arrow. Click **Button (Form Control)**, and drag to create a rectangular button within the cell range **F16:G17**. In the Assign Macro dialog box, click **clearSlicers** and click **OK**.

r. Right-click the **button** form control, and then click **Edit Text**. Delete the existing button text, and then type Clear Slicers. Click outside the button to confirm the change.

s. Click the **Documentation** worksheet. Click cell **A6**, and then type in today's date. Click cell **B6**, and then type in your first and last name. Complete the remainder of the Documentation worksheet according to your instructor's direction.

t. Save the workbook, exit Excel, and then submit your file as directed by your instructor.

Problem Solve 1

MyITLab®
Grader
Homework

Student data files needed:

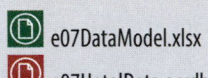 e07DataModel.xlsx

e07HotelData.accdb

You will save your file as:

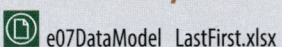 e07DataModel_LastFirst.xlsx

Advanced Data Modeling and Power View Report for the Hotel

Sales & Marketing

Managers at the Painted Paradise Resort & Spa hotel keep track of reservations in a database and would like to be able to view the data differently. You have been asked to create a data model in Excel based on the data in the database file provided. You will then create a Power View report so that the managers can view the reservation data with charts and visualizations.

a. Open the Excel file **e07DataModel**. Save your file as e07DataModel_LastFirst using your last and first name.

b. Create a connection to the **e07HotelData** database located with your student files using the Data tab.
   • Click any cell outside of the existing tables on the **HumanResources** worksheet.
   • Select all tables in the database.
   • Create only a connection to the data.

c. Add the tables on the **HumanResources** worksheet to the data model.
   • reate a relationship between the HumanResources data and the JobCodes data using the JobID fields.

d. On the **Reservations** worksheet, in the Power Pivot window, format the **CheckInDate** and **CheckOutDate** fields as ***3/14/2001**.

e. Create a new calculated column on the Reservations worksheet to the right of the DiscountID column.
   • Name the calculated column AmountDue.
   • Calculate the amount due after the discount has been applied to the SubTotal, for example, SubTotal * (1- Discount). Use the RELATED DAX function to retrieve the appropriate Discount amount from the DiscountTypes data.

f. Create a new calculated field on the Reservations worksheet just below the ResYear column.
   • Name the calculated field 2017Revenue.
   • Use the CALCULATE function to sum the AmountDue column for reservations that took place in 2017.
   • Format as **Currency**.

g. Create a new calculated field on the Reservations worksheet just below the 2014Revenue calculated field.

- Name the calculated field 2018Revenue.
- Use the CALCULATE function to sum the AmountDue column for reservations that took place in 2018.
- Format as **Currency**.

h. Create a KPI based on the following information.

- Use the 2018Revenue calculated field as the base field (value).
- Use the 2017Revenue calculated field as the Measure.
- Set the minimum status threshold to 80%.
- Set the maximum status threshold to 105%.
- Select the flags icon style, located second from the left.

i. Close the Power Pivot Window, and click in a blank cell. Insert a Power View worksheet to the right of the HumanResources worksheet.

- Rename the Power View1 worksheet HotelReport.
- Apply the **Flow** theme (located in the seventh row of the first column).
- Apply the **Dark2 Solid** Background.
- Add a title of 2017-2018 Reservations Report.

j. Create a pie chart that illustrates the amount of revenue generated from each room type.

- Use the RoomType field in the Rooms data and the AmountDue from the Reservations data.
- Create Horizontal Multiples, using the ResYear field in the Reservations data.
- Adjust the width of the pie chart so that it extends half of the width of the Design pane. Place the pie chart in the top left portion of the Design pane.

k. Create a map visualization that illustrates the number of reservations made from each state.

- Use the GuestState field from the Guests data and the ID field from the Reservations data.
- Summarize the ID field by using Count (Distinct).
- Use the ResYear field from the Reservations Data as the COLOR.
- Adjust the size of the map visualization to fill the remaining portion of the top right side of the Design pane, to the right of the pie chart.

l. Create a table that illustrates the monthly revenue generated in 2018 along with the KPI flag status icon.

- Use the ResMonth field from the Reservations data.
- Use the 2018Revenue Value and Status from the Reservations KPI data.
- Place the table under the pie chart in the bottom left portion of the Design Pane.

m. Create a clustered bar chart that illustrates the amount revenue generated for each discount type.

- Use the Description field from the DiscountType data.
- Use the AmountDue field from the Reservations data.
- Create a tile by using the ResYear field from the Reservations data.
- On the Layout tab, in the Synchronize group, click the **Axes** arrow, and select **Horizontal Axis the Same Across All Tiles**.
- Place the clustered bar chart under the map visualization in the bottom right portion of the Design pane.
- Close the Power View Fields pane and the Filters Area.

n. Complete the **Documentation** worksheet according to your instructor's direction.

o. Click **Save**, exit Excel, and then submit your file as directed by your instructor.

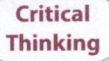
Critical Thinking

Revisit the Power View report constructed in this exercise. What changes could be made to the report to increase its analysis capabilities? Consider the table containing the revenue generated by month that contains the KPI status. If this were converted into a chart, what would be the best choice of chart types, and how would the KPI be best visualized?

Problem Solve 2

Student data file needed:

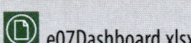
e07Dashboard.xlsx

You will save your file as:

e07Dashboard_LastFirst.xlsm

e07HotelVBA_LastFirst.txt

Production & Operations

Enhancing the Hotel Dashboard with VBA

The managers at the Painted Paradise Resort & Spa hotel use a dashboard to keep track of their top guests at the hotel and to track revenues by room type. You have been asked to enhance the dashboard and make it more secure by adding dynamic labels to the charts and using VBA.

a. Open the Excel file **e07Dashboard**. Save your file as a Macro-Enabled Workbook with the name e07Dashboard_LastFirst using your last and first name.

b. Click the Dashboard worksheet, and create dynamic labels for Year and Quarter on the Top Guests by Nights Stayed clustered column chart.
- Use cell B1 on the Analysis worksheet as the value for the Year dynamic label. Place it in the top left corner of the chart, and increase the font size to 16.
- Use cell B2 on the Analysis worksheet as the value for the Quarter dynamic label. Place it in the top right corner of the chart, and increase the font size to 16.

c. Create a Quarter dynamic label on the 2018 Revenue & Goal combo chart.
- Use cell B2 on the Analysis worksheet as the value for the Quarter dynamic label. Place it in the top right corner of the chart, increase the font size to 16, and remove the outline.

d. Insert a new VBA module in the VBE with the name e07HotelVBA_LastFirst using your last and first name.

e. Create a new Sub procedure that will loop through all the slicers on the Dashboard worksheet and clear the filters.
- Name the Sub procedure clearSlicers.
- Use the name slicers as your variable of the data type **SlicerCache**.
- Create a For…Each loop to loop through each of the slicers in the ThisWorkbook. SlicerCaches collection.
- Create an extra space in between lines of code to make it easier to read.

f. Add a Button (Form Control) onto the Dashboard worksheet within the cell range G2:G3. Assign the clearSlicers Sub procedure to the button, and edit the button text to be Clear Slicers.

g. Create a new Sub procedure in the e07HotelVBA_LastFirst module that will use the xlVeryHidden method to hide the Data and Analysis worksheets. Name the Sub procedure hideSheets.

h. Assign the hideSheets Sub procedure to the BeforeClose event in the ThisWorkbook Code window.

i. Create a new Sub procedure in the e07HotelVBA_LastFirst module that will display an input box requesting a password in order to unhide the Data and Analysis worksheets.

- Name the Sub procedure showSheets.
- Name the variable to store the password psw, and set the data type to String.
- Assign the value Password1234 to the psw variable.
- Create an input box. You will store the response of the input box in a variable named access. Type Enter the password to view the worksheets as the prompt. Type Show All Sheets as the title.
- Insert an If statement that checks whether the value stored in the **psw** variable is equal to the value stored in the **access** variable.
- If the two values are equal, change the visible property of the Data and Analysis worksheets to True.
- If the two values are not equal, display a message box with the Invalid Password as the prompt.

j. Add a Button (Form Control) onto the Dashboard worksheet within the cell range G7:G8. Assign the showSheets Sub procedure to the button, and edit the button text to be Show Sheets.

k. Export the e07HotelVBA_LastFirst module as a .txt file with the same name.

l. Complete the **Documentation** worksheet according to your instructor's direction.

m. Click **Save**, exit Excel, and then submit your files as directed by your instructor.

Perform 1: Perform in Your Life

Student data file needed:

 Blank Excel workbook

 e07Stock.txt

You will save your file as:

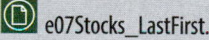 e07Stocks_LastFirst.xlsm

Master Trader

Finance & Accounting

You have invested in several stocks and want to review how well your investments have done. You believe this will be easier to review if you can visually represent the data, so you have decided to create a dashboard to showcase your results.

a. Start **Excel**, and then create a new workbook. Save the file as e07Stocks_LastFirst using your last and first name.

b. Rename Sheet1 as Dashboard.

c. Import the data from the tab-delimited text file named **e07Stock.txt**.

- Be sure to indicate that your data contains headers in the first step of the Text Import Wizard.
- Add this data to the data model, and create only a connection to the data file.

d. Make the following changes to the data in the PowerPivot window.

- Format the **Date** field as ***3/14/2001**.
- Format the **Open**, **High**, **Low** and **Closing** fields as **Currency**.
- Add a calculated column called **Change** that subtracts the Open value from the Closing value, and format the column as **Decimal Number**.

e. Use the PowerPivot window to generate a dashboard with **Two Charts (Horizontal)** on the Dashboard worksheet.

f. Chart 1 should be a Clustered Bar chart with the Stock as the Filter and the Date as the Category; the Values should contain the Average Open and Closing amounts.

g. Chart 2 should be a Combo chart with the Stock as the filter and the Date as the Category; Values should contain the Average High on the Primary Axis and the Average Change on the Secondary Axis. Both variables should be Line charts.

h. Make the following changes to chart 1.
- Add a chart title.
- Remove the legend.
- Apply Style 12.
- Remove the field buttons from the chart.

i. Make the following changes to chart 2.
- Add a chart title.
- Apply Style 8.
- Apply Quick Layout 3.
- Move the legend to the bottom of the chart.
- Remove the field buttons from the chart.

j. Add a Slicer for the Stock, and connect the slicer to both charts.

k. Create a Sub procedure that will clear the Stock slicer.

l. Add a button to the Dashboard worksheet to run the macro.

m. Hide Gridlines and Headings.

n. Insert the **filename** in the left custom footer section of the Header/Footer tab in the Page Setup dialog box on all worksheets in the workbook.

o. Protect the worksheet allowing on the options to Use PivotTable & PivotChart and to Edit Objects.

p. Click **Save**, exit Excel, and then submit your file as directed by your instructor.

Perform 2: Perform in Your Career

Student data file needed:

 e07Online.xlsx

You will save your file as:

 e07Online_LastFirst.xlsm

Managing Online Goals

Production & Operations

You are in charge of managing five employees at a computer recycling company. Your company has created an online portal your customers can use to contact you when it is time for a pickup, rather than calling a customer service agent directly. The system has been designed to randomly select the next employee in a grouping. Because there are goals your employees need to meet, you want to analyze the data from the last year to ensure that workloads are being distributed as evenly as possible.

a. Open the Excel file **e07Online**. Save your file as a **Macro-Enabled Workbook** with the name e07Online_LastFirst using your last and first name.

b. Add each of the four tables on the Data worksheet to the Data Model in PowerPivot.

c. Add the following relationships in PowerPivot.
- Between the SalesData table, Customer field and the Customers table, ID field.
- Between the SalesData table, Employee field and the Employees table, Code field.
- Between the SalesData table, Month field and the Months table, Month Number field.

d. Create a new column on the Months tab named MonthSort. Construct the field to display the month number, a hyphen, and the month name. January should display as "01-January".

e. In Power Pivot, on the SalesData tab, format the Amount column as **Currency**.

f. Add a calculated field that calculates the sum of the Amount column.

g. Create a KPI with the sum of the Amount column as the base field and an absolute value of $100,000 as the target value. Adjust the thresholds to be 25,000 and 85,000. Use the default icon style option.

h. Create a simple Dashboard on a new worksheet, using **Chart and Table (Horizontal)**.

i. Rename the new worksheet Dashboard.

j. Add another PivotChart from Power Pivot to the Dashboard worksheet below the existing PivotChart.

k. Create and format the two charts and PivotTable using the following steps.
- The first chart should show the Sales by Employee for October, November, and December. Use the MonthSort field to properly sort the months. Place the legend at the bottom of the chart.
- The second chart should show Sales by Month. Use the MonthSort field to properly sort the months. Remove the chart legend.
- For each chart, hide the field buttons and add a chart title.
- Your PivotTable should show the Employee Name, the value of the employee's KPI, and the Status.

l. Add a slicer for the Customer name that is connected to both PivotCharts. Place the slicer in the cell range J11:K19.

m. Create a Sub procedure that will clear the slicer.

n. Add a button to the Dashboard worksheet to run the macro. Place the button under the slicer.

o. Protect the worksheet, allowing the options to Use PivotTable & PivotChart and to Edit objects.

p. Hide Gridlines and Headings on the **Dashboard** worksheet.

q. Complete the **Documentation** worksheet according to your instructor's direction.

r. Click **Save**, exit Excel, and then submit the file as directed by your instructor.

Perform 3: Perform in Your Team

Student data file needed:

 e07Analysis.xlsx

You will save your files as:

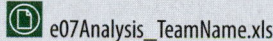 e07Analysis_TeamName.xlsx

Team Analysis

Sales & Marketing

A local department store would like to reap the benefits of using data analysis to make strategic decisions about the future of the business. You will collaborate with a team of three to five other students to develop a data model in Excel and use it to create a simple dashboard.

a. Select one team member to set up the database by completing steps b-e.

b. Start Excel, and then open the **e07Analysis** workbook located with your student files.

c. Save the workbook as **e07Analysis_TeamName** using the team name assigned to your team by your instructor.

d. Open your browser and navigate to https://www.onedrive.live.com, https://www.drive .google.com, or any other instructor-assigned location. Be sure all members of the team have an account on the chosen site, such as a Microsoft or Google account.

e. Upload the **e07Analysis_TeamName** workbook to your account, and then share it with your team members, ensuring that each member has permission to edit the document.

f. Examine the steps below and meet with your team members to discuss who should take on which tasks. Some steps will need to be done before others can be completed.

g. Create a new table on the Data worksheet named **MonthSort** with the following data.

Order	Month
'01	Jan
'02	Feb
'03	Mar
'04	Apr
'05	May
'06	Jun
'07	Jul
'08	Aug
'09	Sep
'10	Oct
'11	Nov
'12	Dec

h. Add each of the **tables** on the Data worksheet to the data model.

i. Establish the appropriate **relationships** between the tables based on common fields.

j. Format the **fields** in the PowerPivot window appropriately.

k. On the **Transactions** tab, create a calculated column for Revenue using the Transactions and Products data, and then format it as **Currency**.

l. On the **MonthSort** tab, create a calculated column for **MonthOrder**, using the appropriate functions and the MonthSort data to concatenate the Order, a "-", and the Month.

m. On the **Transactions** tab, create a calculated field for 2015 Total Revenue, using the appropriate DAX function, and then format it as **Currency**.

n. On the **Transactions** tab, create a calculated field for 2016 Total Revenue, using the appropriate DAX function, and then format it as **Currency**.

o. Create one more **calculated field** of your choosing, and then format it appropriately.

p. Create two KPIs of your choosing, one with an absolute value as the target value and one with a calculated field as the target value.

q. Create a dashboard on the Dashboard worksheet, using data from the data model. At a minimum, the dashboard must include the following items.
- Add two **PivotCharts**, one of which displays the KPI goal in a combo chart.
- Add one **PivotTable** that displays the other KPI status value.
- Add two **slicers** that are connected to either both PivotCharts or one PivotChart and the PivotTable.
- Format all of the items to create a professional-looking dashboard.

r. Complete the **Documentation** worksheet according to your instructor's direction. At a minimum, include enough detail to identify which parts of the worksheets or workbook each team member completed.

s. In a custom header section for all worksheets, include the **names** of the students in your team. Spread the names evenly across each of the three header sections: left section, center section, and right section.

t. Click **Save**, exit Excel, and then submit your file as directed by your instructor.

Perform 4: How Others Perform

Student data file needed:

 e07Retail.xlsm

You will save your files as:

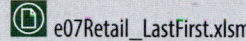 e07Retail_LastFirst.xlsm

Dashboard Errors

Sales & Marketing

Peter Shaw, a manager at Goods & Stuff, a small retail store in the Midwest, attempted to create a dashboard to keep track of sales. The dashboard is not working as expected, and he is getting error messages when he tries to run some VBA code. In this exercise, you will examine the dashboard and then make the necessary changes.

a. Start Excel, and then open **e07Retail**. Save your file as e07Retail_LastFirst using your last and first name.

b. Explore the elements on the Dashboard worksheet. Notice that the slicer is not working and that when you use the spin button and scroll bar, an error message appears.

c. Unprotect the worksheet, and then unlock the cells linked to the form controls.

d. Use the **Month** slicer, and notice that the label on the Revenue by Category Pie chart does not change.

e. Modify the value in the box on the pie chart to be a dynamic label for Month, using the appropriate field on the Analysis worksheet.

f. Protect the worksheet, ensuring that the slicer object can still be used.

g. Click the **Show All Sheets** button, and then use the Debug mode to locate and fix the error in the showSheets Sub procedure.

h. Save and close the workbook, and you will notice another VBA error message. Enter Debug mode, and then locate and fix the method causing the error.

i. Save and close the workbook.

j. Open the workbook again, click the **Show All Sheets** button, and then type Password as the password to show all sheets.

k. Click **Save**, exit Excel, and then submit your file as directed by your instructor.

Appendix

Microsoft Office Specialist Excel 2016 (Core)			
Chapter	**MOS Obj #**	**Objective**	**Your Office Heading**
1.		**Create and Manage Worksheets and Workbooks**	
	1.1	**Create Worksheets and Workbooks**	
Chapter 1	1.1.1	Create a Workbook	Creating a New Workbook
Chapter 9 & Online	1.1.2	Import Data from a Delimited Text File	Importing Text Files (Ch9) & Importing a .txt File (Online)
Chapter 1	1.1.3	Add a Worksheet to An Existing Workbook	Deleting, Inserting, Renaming, and Coloring Worksheet Tabs
Chapter 1	1.1.4	Copy and Move a Worksheet	Moving or Copying a Worksheet
	1.2	**Navigate in Worksheets and Workbooks**	
Online	1.2.1	Search for Data Within a Workbook	Finding and Replacing Data
Chapter 1	1.2.2	Navigate to a Named Cell, Range, or Workbook Element	Navigating Between Worksheets
Chapter 8	1.2.3	Insert and Remove Hyperlinks	Navigating with Hyperlinks
	1.3	**Format Worksheets and Workbooks**	
Chapter 1	1.3.1	Change Worksheet Tab Color	Deleting, Inserting, Renaming, and Coloring Worksheet Tabs
Chapter 1	1.3.2	Rename a Worksheet	Deleting, Inserting, Renaming, and Coloring Worksheet Tabs
Chapter 1	1.3.3	Change Worksheet Order	Moving or Copying a Worksheet
Chapter 1	1.3.4	Modify Page Setup	Changing Page Orientation and Print Range
Chapter 1	1.3.5	Insert and Delete Columns or Rows	Inserting and Deleting Columns or Rows
Chapter 2	1.3.6	Change Workbook Themes	Changing Themes
Chapter 1	1.3.7	Adjust Row Height and Column Width	Adjusting Column Width and Row Height
Chapter 1	1.3.8	Insert Headers and Footers	Adding Headers and Footers
	1.4	**Customize Options and Views for Worksheets and Workbooks**	
Chapter 8	1.4.1	Hide or Unhide Worksheets	Hiding Worksheets
Chapter 2	1.4.2	Hide or Unhide Columns and Rows	Hiding Worksheet Rows
Online	1.4.3	Customize the Quick Access Toolbar	Customizing the Quick Access Toolbar
Chapter 1	1.4.4	Change Workbook Views	Using Worksheet Views
Online	1.4.5	Change Window Views	Changing Window Views
Online	1.4.6	Modify Document Properties	Modifying Document Properties
Chapter 2	1.4.7	Change Magnification by Using Zoom Tools	Showing Functions and Formulas
Chapter 2	1.4.8	Display Formulas	Showing Functions and Formulas
	1.5	**Configure Worksheets and Workbooks for Distribution**	
Chapter 1	1.5.1	Set a Print Area	Changing Page Orientation and Print Range
Chapter 1	1.5.2	Save Workbooks in Alternative File Formats	Exporting a Workbook to PDF
Chapter 1	1.5.3	Print All or Part of a Workbook	Using Print Preview and Printer Selection
Chapter 1	1.5.4	Set Print Scaling	Changing Page Margins and Scaling
Chapter 1	1.5.5	Display Repeating Row and Column Titles on Multipage Worksheets	Using Print Titles

Microsoft Office Specialist Excel 2016 (Core)

Chapter	MOS Obj #	Objective	Your Office Heading
Online	1.5.6	Inspect a Workbook for Hidden Properties or Personal Information	
Online	1.5.7	Inspect a Workbook for Accessibility Issues	
Online	1.5.8	Inspect a Workbook for Compatibility Issues	
2.		**Manage Data Cells and Ranges**	
	2.1	**Insert Data in Cells and Ranges**	
Chapter 1	2.1.1	Replace Data	Dragging and Dropping & Modifying Cell Information
Chapter 1	2.1.2	Cut, Copy, or Paste Data	Cutting, Copying, and Pasting
Chapter 2	2.1.3	Paste Data by Using Special Paste Options	Using Paste Options/Paste Special
Chapter 1	2.1.4	Fill Cells by Using Auto Fill	Using Series (AutoFill)
Chapter 1	2.1.5	Insert and Delete Cells	Inserting and Deleting Cells, Clearing Cells, and Cell Ranges
	2.2	**Format Cells and Ranges**	
Chapter 1	2.2.1	Merge Cells	Merging and Centering Versus Centering Across
Chapter 2	2.2.2	Modify Cell Alignment and Indentation	Aligning Cell Content
Chapter 2	2.2.3	Format Cells by Using Format Painter	Copying Formats
Chapter 1	2.2.4	Wrap Text Within Cells	Wrapping Text and Line Breaks
Chapter 2	2.2.5	Apply Number Formats	Number Formatting
Chapter 2	2.2.6	Apply Cell Formats	Number Formatting
Chapter 2	2.2.7	Apply Cell Styles	Using Built-In Cell Styles
	2.3	**Summarize and Organize Data**	
Chapter 4	2.3.1	Insert Sparklines	Exploring Sparklines
Online	2.3.2	Outline Data	Creating Outlines & Collapse Groups of Data in Outlines
Chapter 2	2.3.3	Insert Subtotals	Using Tables and the Total Row
Chapter 2	2.3.4	Apply Conditional Formatting	Highlighting Values in a Range with Conditional Formatting
3.		**Create Tables**	
	3.1	**Create and Manage Tables**	
Chapter 2	3.1.1	Create An Excel Table from a Cell Range	Applying Table Styles
Chapter 2	3.1.2	Convert a Table to a Cell Range	Applying Table Styles
Chapter 6	3.1.3	Add or Remove Table Rows and Columns	Creating a Structured Reference in a Table
	3.2	**Manage Table Styles and Options**	
Chapter 2	3.2.1	Apply Styles to Tables	Applying Table Styles
Chapter 2	3.2.2	Configure Table Style Options	Applying Table Styles
Chapter 2	3.2.3	Insert Total Rows	Using Tables and the Total Row
	3.3	**Filter and Sort a Table**	
Chapter 2	3.3.1	Filter Records	Using Tables and the Total Row
Online	3.3.2	Sort Data by Multiple Columns	Sorting Data on Multiple Columns
Chapter 2	3.3.3	Change Sort Order	Applying Table Styles
Chapter 9	3.3.4	Remove Duplicate Records	Removing Duplicates & Using Conditional Formatting to Identify Duplicates

Microsoft Office Specialist Excel 2016 (Core)

Chapter	MOS Obj #	Objective	Your Office Heading
4.	**Perform Operations with Formulas and Functions**		
	4.1	**Summarize Data by Using Functions**	
Chapter 3	4.1.1	Insert References	Using Relative Cell Referencing & Using Absolute Cell Referencing & Using Mixed Cell Referencing
Chapter 2	4.1.2	Perform Calculations by Using the SUM Function	Using the SUM Function by Selecting Destination Cells
Chapter 2	4.1.3	Perform Calculations by Using MIN and MAX Functions	Using MIN and MAX
Chapter 2	4.1.4	Perform Calculations by Using the COUNT Function	Using COUNT and AVERAGE
Chapter 2	4.1.5	Perform Calculations by Using the AVERAGE Function	Using COUNT and AVERAGE
	4.2	**Perform Conditional Operations by Using Functions**	
Chapter 3	4.2.1	Perform Logical Operations by Using the IF Function	Using Logical Functions
Chapter 5	4.2.2	Perform Logical Operations by Using the SUMIF Function	Using the SUMIF Function
Chapter 5	4.2.3	Perform Logical Operations by Using the AVERAGEIF Function	Using the AVERAGEIF Function
Chapter 5	4.2.4	Perform Statistical Operations by Using the COUNTIF Function	Using the COUNTSUMIF Function
	4.3	**Format and Modify Text by Using Functions**	
Chapter 3	4.3.1	Format Text by Using RIGHT, LEFT, and MID Functions	Using Text Functions
Chapter 3	4.3.2	Format Text by Using UPPER, LOWER, and PROPER Functions	Using Text Functions
Chapter 3	4.3.3	Format Text by Using the CONCATENATE Function	Using Text Functions
5.	**Create Charts and Objects**		
	5.1	**Create Charts**	
Chapter 4	5.1.1	Create a New Chart	Creating Charts in an Existing Worksheet
Online	5.1.2	Add Additional Data Series	Add a Data Series to a Chart
Chapter 4	5.1.3	Switch Between Rows and Columns in Source Data	Correcting a Confusing Chart
Chapter 4	5.1.4	Analyze Data by Using Quick Analysis	Creating Pie Charts
	5.2	**Format Charts**	
Chapter 4	5.2.1	Resize Charts	Modifying a Chart's Position Properties
Chapter 4	5.2.2	Add and Modify Chart Elements	Modifying an Existing Chart
Chapter 4	5.2.3	Apply Chart Layouts and Styles	Creating Charts in an Existing Worksheet & Changing the Data and Appearance of a Chart
Chapter 4	5.2.4	Move Charts to a Chart Sheet	Placing Charts on a Chart Sheet
	5.3	**Insert and Format Objects**	
Chapter 4	5.3.1	Insert Text Boxes and Shapes	Inserting Objects
Chapter 2	5.3.2	Insert Images	Inserting a Picture
Chapter 4 & Online	5.3.3	Modify Object Properties	Changing the Data and Appearance of a Chart (Ch4), Adding Color to Chart Objects (Ch4), & Changing Border Properties of an Object (Online)
Online	5.3.4	Add Alternative Text to Objects for Accessibility	Adding Alternative Text to Objects for Accessibility

Microsoft Office Specialist Excel 2016 (Expert)

Chapter	MOS Obj #	Objective	Your Office Heading
1.		**Manage Workbook Options and Settings**	
	1.1	**Manage Workbooks**	
Chapter 7	1.1.1	Save a Workbook as a Template	Creating a Template from a Workbook
Online	1.1.2	Copy Macros Between Workbooks	Copying Macros Between Workbooks
Chapter 7	1.1.3	Reference Data in Another Workbook	Linking Workbooks
Chapter 6	1.1.4	Reference Data by Using Structured References	Creating a Structured Reference in a Table
Chapter 14	1.1.5	Enable Macros in a Workbook	Opening the Starting File
Chapter 8	1.1.6	Display Hidden Ribbon Tabs	Adding the Developer Tab to the Ribbon
	1.2	**Manage Workbook Review**	
Chapter 7	1.2.1	Restrict Editing	Keeping Track of Changes
Chapter 8	1.2.2	Protect a Worksheet	Unlocking Cells
Chapter 7 & Online	1.2.3	Configure Formula Calculation Options	Linking Workbooks (Ch7) & Modifying Calculation Options (Online)
Chapter 8	1.2.4	Protect Workbook Structure	Protecting Workbook Structure
Online	1.2.5	Manage Workbook Versions	Managing Workbook Versions
Chapter 8	1.2.6	Encrypt a Workbook with a Password	Encrypting a Workbook
2.		**Apply Custom Data Formats and Layouts**	
	2.1	**Apply Custom Data Formats and Validation**	
Online	2.1.1	Create Custom Number Formats	Creating Custom Number Formats
Online	2.1.2	Populate Cells by Using Advanced Fill Series Options	Populating Cells by Using Advanced Fill Series Options
Chapter 8	2.1.3	Configure Data Validation	Setting Up a List Validation & throughout the chapter
	2.2	**Apply Advanced Conditional Formatting and Filtering**	
Chapter 2	2.2.1	Create Custom Conditional Formatting Rules	Using Conditional Formatting to Assist Decision Making & throughout the book
Chapter 2	2.2.2	Create Conditional Formatting Rules That Use Formulas	Using Conditional Formatting to Assess Benchmarks Using Font Formatting
Chapter 2	2.2.3	Manage Conditional Formatting Rules	Removing Conditional Formatting
	2.3	**Create and Modify Custom Workbook Elements**	
Online	2.3.1	Create Custom Color Formats	Creating Custom Color Formats
Online	2.3.2	Create and Modify Cell Styles	Creating and Modifying Cell Styles
Chapter 7	2.3.3	Create and Modify Custom Themes	Creating a Template from a Workbook
Chapter 8	2.3.4	Create and Modify Simple Macros	Creating an Absolute Macro Reference & Working with Relative Macro References
Chapter 8	2.3.5	Insert and Configure Form Controls	Adding a Macro to a Button
	2.4	**Prepare a Workbook for Internationalization**	
Online	2.4.1	Display Data in Multiple International Formats	Displaying Data in Multiple International Formats
Online	2.4.2	Apply International Currency Formats	Applying International Currency Formats
Online	2.4.3	Manage Multiple Options for +Body and +Heading Fonts	Managing Multiple Options for +Body and +Heading Fonts

Microsoft Office Specialist Excel 2016 (Expert)

Chapter	MOS Obj #	Objective	Your Office Heading
3.	**Create Advanced Formulas**		
	3.1	**Apply Functions in Formulas**	
Chapter 5	3.1.1	Perform Logical Operations by Using AND, OR, and NOT Functions	Integrate Conjunction Functions into IF Statements
Chapter 5	3.1.2	Perform Logical Operations by Using Nested Functions	Combining an AND Function in an OR Function
Chapter 5	3.1.3	Perform Statistical Operations by Using SUMIFS, AVERAGEIFS, and COUNTIFS Functions	Using the SUMIFS Function, Using the AVERAGEIFS Function, & Using the COUNTIFS Function
	3.2	**Look Up Data by Using Functions**	
Chapter 3 & Chapter 5	3.2.1	Look Up Data by Using the VLOOKUP Function	Using LOOKUP and Reference Functions (Ch3) & Explore LOOKUP Functions (Ch5)
Chapter 5	3.2.2	Look Up Data by Using the HLOOKUP Function	Using the HLOOKUP Function
Chapter 5	3.2.3	Look Up Data by Using the MATCH Function	Using the MATCH Function
Chapter 5	3.2.4	Look Up Data by Using the INDEX Function	Using the INDEX Function
	3.3	**Apply Advanced Date and Time Functions**	
Chapter 3	3.3.1	Reference the Date and Time by Using the NOW and TODAY Functions	Using Date and Time Functions
Chapter 9	3.3.2	Serialize Numbers by Using Date and Time Functions	Creating Dates with Date Functions
	3.4	**Perform Data Analysis and Business Intelligence**	
Chapter 9 & Chapter 13	3.4.1	Import, Transform, Combine, Display, and Connect to Data	Importing Data from an Access Database Using Microsoft Query (Ch9) & Importing Data with Power Query (Ch13)
Chapter 7	3.4.2	Consolidate Data	Consolidating Data by Position & Consolidating Data by Category
Chapter 10	3.4.3	Perform What-If Analysis by Using Goal Seek and Scenario Manager	Using Goal Seek & Using Scenario Manager
Online	3.4.4	Use Cube Functions to Get Data out of the Excel Data Model	Using Cube Functions to get Data out of the Excel Data Model
Chapter 11	3.4.5	Calculate Data by Using Financial Functions	Constructing a Financial Analysis of Investments
	3.5	**Troubleshoot Formulas**	
Chapter 8	3.5.1	Trace Precedence and Dependence	Finding and Correcting Circular References
Chapter 8	3.5.2	Monitor Cells and Formulas by Using the Watch Window	Opening and Using the Watch Window
Online	3.5.3	Validate Formulas by Using Error Checking Rules	Validating Formulas by Using Error Checking Rules
Chapter 8	3.5.4	Evaluate Formulas	Using the Evaluate Formula Tool
	3.6	**Define Named Ranges and Objects**	
Chapter 3	3.6.1	Name Cells	Creating Named Ranges Using the Name Box
Chapter 3	3.6.2	Name Data Ranges	Creating Named Ranges Using the Name Box
Chapter 6	3.6.3	Name Tables	Creating a Data Table in Excel
Chapter 3	3.6.4	Manage Named Ranges and Objects	Modifying Named Ranges

Microsoft Office Specialist Excel 2016 (Expert)			
Chapter	**MOS Obj #**	**Objective**	**Your Office Heading**
4.		**Create Advanced Charts and Tables**	
	4.1	**Create Advanced Charts**	
Chapter 4	4.1.1	Add Trendlines to Charts	Analyzing with Trendlines
Chapter 4	4.1.2	Create Dual-Axis Charts	Creating Combination Charts
Online	4.1.3	Save a Chart as a Template	Saving a Chart as a Template
	4.2	**Create and Manage PivotTables**	
Chapter 6	4.2.1	Create PivotTables	Creating PivotTables
Chapter 6	4.2.2	Modify Field Selections and Options	Building a PivotTable
Chapter 6 & Online	4.2.3	Create Slicers	Adding a Slicer to the PivotTable & Adding a Timeline Slicer (Online)
Chapter 6	4.2.4	Group PivotTable Data	Building a Pivot Table
Online	4.2.5	Reference Data in a PivotTable by Using the GETPIVOTDATA Function	Reference Data in a PivotTable Using the GETPIVOTDATA Function
Chapter 6	4.2.6	Add Calculated Fields	Configuring PivotTable Options
Chapter 6	4.2.7	Format Data	Configuring PivotTable Options
	4.3	**Create and Manage PivotCharts**	
Chapter 6	4.3.1	Create PivotCharts	Adding a PivotChart
Chapter 6	4.3.2	Manipulate Options in Existing PivotCharts	Adding a PivotChart
Chapter 6	4.3.3	Apply Styles to PivotCharts	Adding a PivotChart
Online	4.3.4	Drill Down into PivotChart Details	Drilling Down into PivotChart Details

Glossary

3-D formula a formula that references the same cell or range of cells across multiple worksheets in a workbook.

3-D named range a named range that references the same cell or range of cells across multiple worksheets in a workbook.

3-D reference allows formulas and functions to use data from cells and cell ranges across worksheets.

A1 reference method this refers to the way cell references are written. If letters appear for the column headings, the reference style for Excel is currently A1. In this mode, cells are referenced using a letter for the column and a number for the row.

A

ABS function a function that returns the absolute value of a number, that is, the number without its negative sign.

Absolute cell reference the exact address of a cell when both the column and the row need to remain constant regardless of the position of the cell when the formula is copied to other cells.

Absolute macro reference a reference in a macro that affects the same cells every time the macro is run.

Active cell the cell that is the recipient of an action, such as a click, calculation, typing, or paste; identified by the thick green border. Only the active cell can have data entered into it.

Active worksheet the worksheet that is visible in the Excel application window. The active worksheet tab has a white background with bold letters and a thick bottom border.

Add-in an application with specific functionality geared toward accomplishing a specific goal.

Add-ins for Office enhancements for the features in Office that can be installed from the Microsoft Store.

Advanced Filter a way to filter data in which the filtering criteria are set up on the spreadsheet. The filtering criteria must be set up as rows above the data table with field headings that are identical to the data set; criteria can be set up in one or more cells below the field names.

Aggregate to consolidate or summarize data. Functions such as SUM, COUNT, and AVERAGE aggregate an entire set of data.

Amortization schedule a table that calculates the interest and principal payments along with the remaining balance of the loan for each period.

Amortize pay off the balance of a loan over a period of time in multiple installments or payments.

AND function a function that returns TRUE if all logical tests supplied are true; otherwise, it returns FALSE.

Annuity a recurring amount paid or received at specified intervals.

Any value validation a type of data validation that utilizes the input message as a means to communicate rules for entering data in a cell.

Application Start screen the first screen that is seen when a program is opened but an existing program file is not open.

In this screen, you can select a blank document, workbook, presentation, database, or one of many application-specific templates.

Area chart a chart that emphasizes the magnitude of change over time and depicts trends.

Argument variables or values a function requires in order to calculate a solution. A value passed to a function, either as a constant or a variable.

Array function a function that can perform multiple calculations on one or more items in an array. Array functions look different from other functions because curly brackets { } are required for the function to calculate correctly.

AutoFill a feature that copies information from one cell or a series in adjacent cells into adjacent cells in the direction in which the fill handle is dragged.

AutoRecovery a feature that will attempt to recover any changes made to a document since your last save if something goes wrong.

AVERAGE function a function that returns an average or mean from a specified range of cells.

AVERAGEIF function a function that averages the cells that meet the specified criteria.

AVERAGEIFS function a function that averages a range of data, selecting data to average based on the criteria specified.

B

Banding alternating the background color of rows and/or columns to assist in tracking information.

Bar chart a chart that displays data horizontally and is used for comparison among individual items.

Base value a calculated field that resolves to a value as part of a KPI.

Bidirectional KPI a KPI in which the value becomes worse the farther it deviates from the target value in either direction, such as the temperature for storing a particular product; damage could occur if the temperature gets too cold or too hot.

Binding constraint a constraint is binding if changing it also changes the optimal solution.

Binomial distribution a discrete probability distribution that is used to model the number of successful trials based on the total number of trials and the rate of success.

Bins intervals in which you want to group your data.

Bootcamp Mac software that allows the user to decide which operating system Mac, operating system or Windows, to run.

Break-even analysis used to calculate the break-even point in sales volume or dollars, estimate profit or loss at any level of sales volume, and help in setting prices.

Break-even point the sales level at which revenue equals total costs; at the break-even point, there is neither a profit nor a loss.

Built-in cell style predefined and named combination of cell and content formatting properties.

Built-in function a function included in Excel that can be categorized as financial, statistical, mathematical, date and time, text, or so on.

Bullet a symbol that appears before each item to create a list of items, or identifies a summary point.

Business intelligence (BI) a variety of software applications that are used to analyze an organization's data to provide management with the tools necessary to improve decision making, cut costs, and identify new opportunities.

C

Capital budgeting the planning procedure used to evaluate whether an organization's long-term investments are worth pursuing.

Cash flow The movement of cash into and out of a business.

Cell alignment allows cell content to be left-aligned, centered, and right-aligned on the horizontal axis, as well as top-aligned, middle-aligned, and bottom-aligned on the vertical axis.

Cell range the cells in the worksheet that have been selected.

Cell reference a reference to a particular cell or cell range within a formula or function instead of a value.

Cell the intersection of a row and a column in a table or worksheet.

Central tendency the way in which data tends to cluster around some value.

Change history information that is maintained about all changes made to a shared workbook in past editing sessions.

Changing cell the cell or cells used to identify the various data cells whose values can differ in each scenario.

Chart sheet a special worksheet that is dedicated to displaying chart objects.

Circular reference an error in a worksheet indicating a single formula that references itself or multiple formulas that reference each other.

CLEAN a text function that removes any nonprinting characters from a text string

Cleansing text removing unwanted chartacters, rearranging data in a cell or correcting erroneous data.

Clipboard a temporary storage location where information that was cut or copied is stored until you paste, move, or clear the information.

Close the command to close an Office file without exiting the associated program.

Cloud computing computing resources, either hardware or software, being used by another computer over a network. Files that are stored in a remote location can be stored, accessed, and edited.

Code window the window where VBA code is typed and where VBA that is generated by a recorded macro can be viewed and edited.

Codification scheme a set of rules that combine data values in specific formats and locations to generate a new data value.

Codified data value value created by following a system of rules in which the position of information is tied to its context.

Collaboration allows workbooks to be shared among different users and then merged together for a final product.

Column a vertical set of cells that encompasses all the rows in a worksheet.

Column chart a chart that is used to compare data across categories and show change, sometimes over time.

Combination chart a chart that displays two different types of data by using multiple chart types in a single chart object.

Comment a text box, similar to a sticky note, that is attached to a cell in a worksheet in which you can enter notes or give instructions.

Compare and Merge Workbooks the command that will compare the changes made in each shared workbook and then provide the option to update the workbook with those changes.

Competitive advantage a strategic advantage that a business has over its competition. Attaining a competitive advantage strengthens a business and positions it better within the business environment.

Complex function a function that combines multiple functions within a formula.

CONCATENATE a text function that is used to join up to 255 text strings into one text string.

Conditional aggregate function a function that consolidates or summarizes a subset of data that has been filtered based upon one or more criteria.

Conditional formatting allows the specification of rules that apply formatting to cells, appointments, contacts, or tasks as determined by the rule outcome. Also applies custom formatting to highlight or emphasize values that meet specific criteria. It is called "conditional" because the formatting occurs when a particular condition is met.

Conditional math function a function that will calculate only when a specified condition is met.

Consolidate by category aggregates data in cells with matching row and/or column labels. Data does not need to be in the same relative position to create a summary sheet.

Consolidate by position aggregates data in the same position in multiple worksheets. A summary sheet can be created but only when the source worksheets have an identical structure.

Constant a number that does not change.

Constraint a rule that you establish when formulating your Solver model.

Contextual tabs a ribbon tab that contains commands related to selected objects so you can manipulate, edit, and format the objects. This ribbon tab does not appear unless the object is selected.

Contiguous cell range a range consisting of multiple selected cells, all of which are directly adjacent to at least one other cell in the selected range.

Continuous variable can contain an infinite number of different values within a range.

Convert Text to Columns Wizard a special wizard that is used for separating simple data in Excel.

Convert to Range an option used to convert a data table back to a range of data; the formatting remains, but the functionality of tables, such as adding new columns or rows, will no longer automatically be added or updated to the named ranges, and formulas would need to be manually copied down a column.

Correlation coefficient a unitless value that describes the strength and direction of a relationship between two variables. A correlation coefficient of −1 is said to have a perfect negative relationship; a coefficient of 1 is considered to have a perfect positive relationship; a coefficient of 0 is said to have no relationship. The closeness of the value to −1 or 1 describes the strength of the relationship.

Cost-volume-profit (CVP) analysis the study of how cost and volume are related and the effect their relationship has on profit.

COUNT function a function that returns the number of cells in a range of cells that contain numeric data.

Count   the count of all values in a sample.

COUNTA function   a function that returns the number of cells within a range that contain any type of data.

COUNTIF function   a function that counts the number of cells that meet a specified criteria.

COUNTIFS function   a function that allows for multiple criteria in multiple ranges to be evaluated and counted.

Coupon   the interest rate that a bond pays.

Covariance   a formula that can calculate the relationship between two variables, such as age and dollars spent, as well as the direction of the relationship. If one variable increases and the other variable also increases, then the relationship is considered positive. If one variable increases and the other variable decreases, then the relationship is considered negative.

CUMIPMT function   a function used to calculate the amount of interest paid over a specific number of periods, such as quarterly or annually.

Cumulative distribution function   the probability of a value being less than or equal to the value of x.

Current yield   Considers the current market price of a bond, which may differ from the par value, and gives a different yield rate on that basis.

Custom validation   a more complex type of data validation that allows the user to apply multiple criteria simultaneously by using formulas.

D

Data bar   graphical display of data that is overlaid on the data in the cells of the worksheet.

Data cleansing   the process of fixing obvious errors in the data and converting the data into a useful format.

Data model   a collection of tables and their relationships that reflect the real-world relationships between business functions and processes.

Data point   an individual piece of data being charted.

Data series   a group of related data values to be charted.

Data set   a collection of related data consisting of observational units and variables. Also, organized data; includes fields and data that have context and meaning.

Data table   a what-if analysis tool that takes sets of input values, determines possible results, and displays all the results in one table on one worksheet.

Data validation   a process of using rules that determine what can and cannot be entered in specific cells.

Data verification   the process of validating that the data is correct and accurate.

Data visualization   the graphical presentation of data with a focus on qualitative understanding.

Data   the values that describe an attribute of an object or an event.

Date and time functions   functions that are used for entering the current day and time into a worksheet as well as for calculating the intervals between dates.

Date data   data recognized by Excel as a date; takes the form of a serial number, with the number 1 representing January 1, 1900.

Date validation   a type of data validation that specifies that only a date can be entered into a cell.

DATE   a function that returns the sequential serial number that represents a particular date.

DATEDIF function   a function that enables you to calculate the time between two dates.

DATEVALUE   a function that converts a date in a text format into a serial number.

DB function   a function used to calculate the depreciation of an asset for a specified period using the fixed declining balance method.

DDB function   a function used to calculate the depreciation of an asset for a specified period using the double declining balance method.

Decimal validation   a type of data validation that restricts users to enter only data that contains digits and allows decimal places.

Decision tree   a diagramming tool that allows you to break down potential decisions in a logical, structured format.

Default   a setting that is automatically in place unless you specify otherwise.

Delimiter   a way of indicating the beginning and end of a text data segment.

Dependent cell   a cell whose value depends on the value in the active cell for its result.

Depreciation schedule   records the date when the asset was placed into service, a calculation for each year's depreciation, and the accumulated depreciation.

Descriptive statistics   the process of deriving meaningful information from raw data.

Destination cell   the cell that received the result of an operation such as Paste or an AutoSum function.

Developer tab   a tab that is not visible by default on the ribbon that contains the buttons needed to create, edit, and run macros.

Dialog box   a user window that provides more options or settings beyond those provided on the ribbon.

Dialog Box launcher   an icon in a group that opens a corresponding dialog box or task pane.

Digital dashboard   a mechanism that delivers business intelligence in graphical form. Dashboards provide management with a big picture view of the business, usually from multiple perspectives, using various charts and other graphical representations.

Discrete variable   a variable that can have only a finite number of values and all possible values are known.

Do...Until loop   loops through code until a specified condition is true.

Do...While loop   loops through code while a specified condition is true.

Document   a letter, memo, report, brochure, resume, or flyer.

Double prime symbol   straight quotation marks that are used in functions and formulas to let Excel know that the element is a text string and not a numeric value, cell reference, or named range.

Drilling down   a method for accessing the detailed records used in a PivotTable to get to the aggregated data.

DSUM function   a database function that is ideal for setting up a criteria range and then calculating the sum based on the filters within that criteria range.

E

Economic risk   the risk that a chosen act or activity will not generate sufficient revenues to cover operating costs and to repay debt obligations.

Elastic   Responsive to change; a small change in price is accompanied by a large change in the quantity demanded.

Embedded chart   an object located on the same worksheet with the data.

Encryption a method of protecting a workbook by assigning a password that unscrambles the code once it has been opened.

Error Alert a message that informs a user when entered data violates validation constraints.

Evaluate Formula a tool that breaks down a formula into its individual pieces and evaluates each part separately so you can see how the formula works.

Event an action initiated either by a user or by VBA code.

Evolutionary method the method used when a worksheet model is nonlinear and nonsmooth and typically uses functions such as VLOOKUP, PMT, and IF to derive values based on or derived from the variable cells or changing cells.

Excel database a way of storing data in Excel that is made up of records (rows) and fields (columns).

Explicit calculated field a field that is created when a formula is typed in the Calculation Area of the Power Pivot window. Explicit calculated fields can use a wide variety of functions beyond general aggregation and can be used in any PivotTable, PivotChart, or Power View report. They can also be extended to become a KPI.

Exponential distribution a continuous probability distribution that is used to model the time in between events.

External data any data not stored locally or not in an Excel format (.xls or .xlsx).

F

Factor an argument for the rate at which the balance declines. If factor is omitted, Excel assumes the value to be 2.

Field a specific piece of information that is stored in every record and, when formatted, appears as a column in a database table. An item of information in a worksheet column that is associated with something of interest.

File extension three or four characters after the file name that is preceded by a period and that is used by the Windows operating system to determine which programs should be used to open a file.

File path the physical location of the file starting with a letter that represents the drive and separates folders with a "\".

Fill Across Worksheets a command that can be used to copy cell contents, formats, or both contents and formats to worksheets in a group.

Fill color the background color of a cell.

Filtering a process of hiding records that do not meet specified criteria in a data set.

Financial functions functions that are used for common financial calculations such as interest rates, payments, and analyzing loans.

FIND a text function that locates one text string within a second text string and returns the number of the starting position of the first text string from the left of the second text string.

FIND function a function that searches for a specified string of text in a larger string of text and returns the position number where the specified text begins.

Fixed cost an expense that never changes regardless of how much product is sold or how many services are rendered.

Flash Fill recognizes patterns in data as you type and automatically fills in values for text and numeric data.

Font a style of displaying characters, numbers, punctuation, and special characters. Also the way letters in words look, including the size, weight, and style.

For loop loops through code until a specified number of loops have been completed.

For…Each loop loops through an object collection or an array.

Foreign key a shared field that is not a primary key but serves as a link to a table in which the same field is a primary key of the other table.

Form control an object that can be placed into an Excel worksheet, providing the functionality to interact with your models.

Format Painter a tool that allows you to copy a format and apply it to other selections.

Formula performs a mathematical calculation (or calculations) using information in the active worksheet and other worksheets to calculate new values; it can contain cell references, constants, functions, and mathematical operators.

Function a built-in formula that performs operations against data based on a set of inputs, such as the SUM or AVERAGE function. Some functions, called null functions, do not require arguments.

Function Arguments a dialog box that provides additional information and previews the results of a function being constructed.

Function procedure a group of VBA statements that performs calculations and returns a single value.

Fv an argument used for the future value of the loan—the balance you reach after the last payment has been made.

FV function a function used to calculate the value of an investment with a fixed interest rate, term, and periodic payment over a specific period of time.

G

Gallery a set of menu options that appear when you click the arrow next to a button.

Goal Seek a scenario tool that maximizes Excel's cell-referencing capabilities and enables you to find the input values needed to achieve a goal or objective.

Graphical format the presentation of information in charts, graphs, and pictures.

GRG Nonlinear method a method used when the worksheet model is nonlinear and smooth; it is the default method that Excel's Solver uses. A nonlinear model is one in which just one of the constraint lines breaks the linearity of the model. You may have several constraints that are linear, but one constraint line that curves breaks the linearity of the model.

Gridlines the vertical and horizontal lines on a worksheet that help define a cell's boundaries.

Group a collection of records along with some introductory and summary information about the records. A logical grouping of commands on the ribbon.

Grouping selecting multiple worksheets at a time.

Grouping variable a field within a data set that could be used to categorize or group for the purpose of comparison.

Guess an argument used when you want to guess what the interest rate will be. If nothing is entered, Excel assumes that the guess is 10 percent.

H

Help a window opened via the Help button or the F1 key.

Histogram a statistical graph that summarizes the distribution of data and how the data fits into defined bins.

HLOOKUP function a function that helps to retrieve values located in another location and is used when your comparison values are located in a row horizontally.

Horizontal multiples multiples that expand across the available space in the container, and if additional space is needed, a horizontal scroll bar is added.

HTML short for Hypertext Markup Language, the language that defines how web page content is displayed in a browser.

Hypergeometric distribution a discrete population distribution that calculates the probability of drawing a specific number of target items from a collection.

Hyperlink a link that opens another page or file when you click on it. In Excel, a hyperlink can open a worksheet, another workbook, a file, a picture, an e-mail address, a photo, a web page, or another program.

I

IF function a function that returns one of two values depending on whether the supplied logical test being evaluated is true or false.

IFERROR function a function used for detecting an error and displaying something more user-friendly than the error message.

Implicit calculated field a field that is created when you drag a field such as Sales or Quantity Sold into the Values area of a PivotTable. The calculation takes place, but a new calculated field is not being created. Implicit calculated fields can use only standard aggregated functions such as AVERAGE, SUM, COUNT, MAX, etc.

INDEX function works in conjunction with the MATCH function; returns the value of an element in a table or array selected by the row and column number indexes and has two argument lists to select.

INDIRECT function a function that can change a text string within a cell to a cell reference.

Inelastic Not responsive to change; a large change in price is accompanied by a small amount of change in demand.

Inferential statistics the process of taking data from a sample of the population and making predictions about the entire population.

Information data that has context, meaning, and relevance and therefore is valuable to the user.

Input box an effective way of using VBA code to increase the interactivity of a dashboard by prompting the user for information and storing that information in a variable to be used later.

Input message the message that appears when a user makes a validated cell active and prompts a user before data is entered with information about data constraints.

INT function rounds down any decimal values to the nearest whole integer.

Intercept coefficient part of a regression analysis; the value at which a regression line will cross the y-axis.

Interquartile range the difference between the third and first quartiles of data.

Interval data measures the size of the difference between values.

IPMT function a financial function that calculates how much of a specific periodic payment is going toward the interest that has accrued on the loan.

IRR function a function used to indicate the profitability of an investment. It is commonly used in business in choosing between investments.

Iteration a process that repeatedly enters new values in the variable cell or cells to find a solution to the problem.

K

Key performance indicator (KPI) a quantifiable measure that helps managers define progress toward both short-term and long-term goals.

Keyboard shortcut keyboard equivalents for software commands that allow you to keep your hands on the keyboard instead of reaching for the mouse to perform actions.

KeyTips a form of keyboard shortcut. Pressing the Alt button will display KeyTips (or keyboard shortcuts) for items on the Ribbon and the Quick Access Toolbar.

Kurtosis characterizes the peakedness or flatness of a distribution compared to the normal distribution.

L

Landscape orientation for page layout and printing purposes, landscape indicates that the page is wider than it is tall.

LEFT a text function that returns the characters in a text string on the basis of the number of characters you specify, starting from the left side of the string.

LEFT function returns the characters in a text string based on the number of characters you specify, starting with the far left character in the string.

Legend an index within a chart that provides information about the data.

LEN a text function that calculates the length of a specified string by returning the total number of characters in a string.

Line chart a chart that is used to convey change in data over a period of time; good for showing trends.

Linear programming a mathematical method for determining how to attain the best outcome in a given mathematical model.

List validation a type of data validation that presents the user with a list of data values from which the user can choose.

Live Preview a feature that shows the results that would occur in your file if you were to click that particular option.

Local templates templates that are stored in the default Templates folder on your hard drive.

Logical function a function that returns a result, or output, based on evaluating whether a logical test is true or false.

Logical operator used to create logical tests and includes <, >, <=, >=, and <>.

Logical test an equation with comparison operators that can be evaluated as either true or false. Also known as a logical expression.

Lookup and reference functions functions that look up matching values in a table of data.

Loop Used in VBA to execute a series of statements multiple times.

LOWER A text function that converts all uppercase characters in a text string to lowercase.

M

Macro a group of programmed instructions in Excel that automate tasks and play them back when the macro is run.

Markup language a programming language that uses special sequences of characters or "markup" indicators called "tags" inserted in the document to indicate how the document should look when it is displayed or printed.

MATCH function a function that looks for a value within a range and returns the position of that value within the range.

Mathematical operator parentheses ( ), exponentiation ^, division /, multiplication *, addition +, or subtraction −.

Maturity the length of time before par value is returned to the bondholder.

MAX function a function that examines all numeric values in a specified range and returns the maximum value.

Maximize the button located in the top right corner of the title bar that enlarges a window to its maximum size, which offers the largest workspace.

Maximum the largest value in the sample.

Mean the average of all the variables in a sample, often referred to as the arithmetic mean.

Median describes which value falls in the middle when all the values of the sample are sorted in ascending order.

MEDIAN function a function used to measure the central tendency or the location of the middle of a set of data.

Merge & Center a feature that combines selected cells into a single cell and then centers the text within that single cell.

Message box a dialog box object created in VBA and used to display informative messages to the user that includes buttons the user can interact with.

Metadata data about data. It describes the content and context of the data.

Method an action that Excel performs with an object.

Microsoft Query a special tool to help users import individual data fields into their Excel applications and keep the worksheet data synchronized with the data in the external sources.

MID a text function that returns a specific number of characters from the middle of a text string, starting at the position you specify, based on the number of characters you specify.

MIN function a function that examines all numeric values in a specified range and returns the minimum value.

Mini toolbar a toolbar that appears after text has been selected and that contains buttons for the most commonly used formatting commands, such as font, font size, font color, center alignment, indents, bold, italic, and underline.

Minimize the button that reduces a window to a taskbar button.

Minimum the smallest value in the sample.

Mixed cell reference using a combination of absolute cell referencing and relative cell referencing for a cell address within a formula by preceding either the column letter or the row value with a dollar sign to "lock" as absolute while leaving the other portion of the cell address as a relative reference.

Mixed cost a cost that contains a variable component and a fixed component.

Mode the value that appears most often in a sample.

MODE function a function that returns the most frequently occurring value in a range of data.

MODE.MULT function a function that returns the most frequently occurring values in a range of data.

MODE.SNGL function a function that returns the most frequently occurring value in a range of data.

Module a container for VBA code.

Most Recently Used list a list maintained by Office of your most recently modified files: documents, spreadsheets, databases, and presentations.

Moving average calculates the average of values over time, based on specified intervals.

Multiples a series of identical charts that have the same x- and y-axes but contain different values.

N

Name Manager used to create, edit, delete, or troubleshoot named ranges in a workbook.

Named range a cell or group of cells that have been given a name, other than the default column and row cell address reference, that can then be used within a formula or function.

Negative KPI a KPI in which the greater the value, the worse the KPI, such as the number of sick days in a specific time period.

Nested IF function a function that uses IF functions as arguments within another IF function and increases the number of logical outcomes that can be expressed.

Net book value the original cost of an asset minus depreciation and amortization.

NETWORKDAYS a function that calculates the number of available work days between two given dates and will omit holidays if provided.

Nominal data uses numbers for categorical or classification purposes only.

Nominal yield information provided when a bond is purchased; considered the least helpful when it comes to analyzing the true value of a bond.

Nonbinding constraint a less severe constraint that does not affect the optimum solution.

Noncontiguous cell range a range consisting of multiple selected cells, at least one of which is not directly adjacent to at least one other cell in the selected range.

Normal distribution one of the most important distributions in statistics. When charted, it takes on the shape of a bell and is often referred to as the "bell-shaped curve," in which 98% of all values occur within three standard deviations from the mean.

Normal view the default view of PowerPoint that displays the Left hand pane (thumbnails) and the Slide pane work area.

NOT function a function that is used when there are many options that fit the desired criteria and only one option that does not fit the criteria.

NOW function a function used to display the current date and time in a cell.

Nper an argument used for the total number of payments that will be made to pay the loan in full.

NPER function a function used to calculate the number of payment periods for an investment or loan if you know the loan amount, interest rate, and payment amount.

NPV function a function used to determine the value of an investment by analyzing a series of future incoming and outgoing cash flows expected to occur over the life of the investment.

Numeric data data that contains only the digits 0-9 and possibly a period (.) for a decimal place and/or a hyphen to indicate negativity.

O

Object collection a group of objects that are also considered objects themselves, such as sheets and workbooks.

Object model a hierarchical collection of objects, consisting of properties, methods, and events that can be manipulated by using VBA.

Object-oriented programming (OOP) uses a hierarchy of objects, also called classes, as the focus of the programming.

Objective cell a cell that contains the formula that creates a value that you want to optimize: maximize, minimize, or set to a specific value.

Objects combinations of data and code that are treated as a single unit, including workbooks, worksheets, charts, PivotTables, and even Excel itself.

Observational unit a person, object, or event about which data is collected.

Office Add-in essentially a web page that is hosted inside an Office application and can be used to extend the functionality of the application.

Office Background an artistic design displayed in the upper right in the title bar of Office.

Office Backstage a feature that provides access to the file-level commands, such as saving a file, creating a new file, opening an existing file, printing a file, and closing a file, as well as program options and account settings.

Office Theme a color scheme used by Office.

One-variable data table a data table that can help you analyze how different values of one variable in one or more formulas will change the results of those formulas.

OneDrive an online cloud computing technology provided by Microsoft and integrated with Office 2016 that offers a certain amount of free collaborative storage space.

Online templates templates that are stored online and downloaded to your hard drive.

Optimize to find the best way to do something.

OR function a function that returns TRUE if any one logical test supplied is true; otherwise, it returns FALSE.

Order of operations the order in which Excel processes calculations in a formula that contains more than one operator.

Ordinal data uses numbers to rank data as first, second, third, and so on based on some scale.

Outliers values that are abnormally different from the other values in a random sample.

P

Page Break Preview a view that does not show page margins, headers, or footers, but allows you to manually adjust the location of page breaks.

Page Layout view a view that shows page margins, print headers and footers, and page breaks.

Pane a smaller window that often appears to the side of the program window and offers options or helps you to navigate through completing a task or feature.

Par value how much the bondholder will receive at maturity.

Parameter a term generally used to describe a value included for calculation or comparison purposes that is stored in a single location (a worksheet cell, for example) so that it can be used many times but be edited in a single location. Also, a special kind of variable used in VBA to refer to one of the pieces of data provided in a method.

Per an argument that is represented as a number that must be between 1 and nper and is the specific period for which a loan payment is being applied.

Pie chart a chart that displays a comparison of each value to a total.

PivotChart a built-in analysis tool that allows for graphical representations of a PivotTable.

PivotTable an interactive table that extracts, organizes, and summarizes source data.

PMT function a function used to calculate a payment amount based on constant payments and a constant interest rate.

Poisson distribution a discrete probability function that has wide business applications. It is used most often to predict demand for a product or service.

Population any entire collection of people, animals, plants, or other items on which you may collect data.

Portable Document Format (PDF) a file type that preserves most formatting attributes of a source document regardless of the software in which the document was created.

Portrait orientation for page layout and printing purposes, portrait indicates the page is taller than it is wide.

Positive KPI a KPI in which the greater the value, the better the KPI, such as a company's profit.

Power Query a business intelligence tool that is used to discover data, connect it to your workbook, and transform the data into a more useful state.

Power View an interactive data visualization, exploration, and presentation experience that encourages the creation of ad hoc reports.

PPMT function a financial function that calculates how much of a specific periodic payment is going toward the principal amount of a loan.

Precedent cell a cell that supplies a value to the formula in the active cell.

Presentation an oral performance aid that uses slides or stand-alone silent presentation, such as that at a kiosk.

Primary key a field that functions as an identifier for each row or record.

Principal the unpaid balance amount of a loan.

Print Preview backstage view of how a document, workbook, presentation, table, or other object will appear when printed.

Probability the likelihood that some event will occur based on what is already known.

Probability density function the probability of a value being equal to the value of x.

Probability distribution describes all the possible values and likelihoods that a given variable can be within a specific range; can be in the form of a graph, table, or formula.

Project Explorer window a window that contains a hierarchical list of all the objects available in open workbooks including macros, modules, and worksheets.

PROPER a text function that will capitalize only the first letter of each word in the text string while changing the other characters to lowercase.

Properties attributes of an object that can be referred to or manipulated by using VBA.

Properties window a window that contains a list of all the properties of a selected object, such as name, size, and color.

Protected View a view of the file in which the contents can be seen and read but cannot be edited, saved, or printed until editing is enabled. By default, Office will open files from e-mail or a web browser in this view.

Pseudo code the rough draft of a formula or code. It is intended to help you understand the logic and determine the structure of a problem before you develop the actual formula.

Pv the present value of an investment or loan.

PV function a function used to calculate the present or current value of a series of future payments on an investment.

Q

Quartile a descriptive statistic that divides data into four equal groups.

Query a question that you would ask a database.

Quick Access Toolbar located at the top left of the Office window, it can be customized to display commonly used buttons.

Quick Analysis a contextual tool that appears when you select data in a worksheet and offers single-click access to formatting, charts, PivotTables, and Sparklines.

R

R-squared part of a regression analysis; calculated by squaring the correlation coefficient. This provides a more conservative estimate of the independent variable's ability to predict the value of the dependent variable.

R1C1 reference style this refers to the way cell references are written. If numbers appear for the column headings, the reference style for Excel is currently R1C1.

Random sample a subset of a population that has been selected by using unpredictable methods in which each element of the population has an equal chance of being selected.

Range a group of cells in a worksheet that have been selected or highlighted; performed commands will affect the entire range. Also, the difference between the highest and lowest value in the data set.

Rate an argument in several financial functions that notes the periodic interest rate — the interest rate of the loan. Also, the periodic interest rate used for calculating interest accrued.

RATE function a function used to calculate the interest rate for an investment or loan, given that you know the loan or present value, payment, and number of payment periods.

Ratio data similar to interval data except that the differences between the data can be quantified and proportions can be specified.

Raw data elements or raw facts numeric or text that may or may not have meaning or relevance.

Recommended Charts a feature that quickly analyzes a selection in a worksheet and recommends chart types that best fit your data.

Record all of the categories of data that pertain to one person, place, thing, event, or idea and that are formatted as a row in a worksheet or database table.

Regression analysis a method used to predict future values by analyzing the relationships between two or more variables.

Relational data data about a particular person, place, or event that is stored in multiple tables.

Relational database a collection of tables linked together by shared fields. Each table consists of rows and columns, each row being uniquely identified by a primary key field.

Relative cell reference default cell reference in a formula to a cell address position that will automatically adjust when the formula is copied or extended to other cells; the cell being referenced changes relative to the placement of the formula.

Relative macro reference a reference in a macro that identifies cells relative to the location of the active cell when the macro was recorded.

Remove Duplicates a tool in Excel for removing duplicate entries in data.

Required rate of return (RRR) the minimum annual percentage that an investment must earn before a company chooses to invest.

Restore Down a button that, when a window is at its maximum size, will restore the window to a previous, smaller size. When a window is in the Restore Down mode, this button expands the window to its full size.

Return on investment (ROI) the ratio of the amount of money gained or lost from an investment relative to the initial amount invested.

Ribbon the row of tabs with buttons across the top of the application where you will find most of the commands for the application. The ribbon differs from program to program, but each program has two tabs in common: the File tab and the Home tab.

Ribbon Display options three options for ribbon display: Auto-Hide Ribbon, Display Tabs, and Display Tabs and Command.

RIGHT a text function that returns the characters in a text string on the basis of the number of characters you specify, starting from the far-right character position.

Roaming settings a group of settings that offer synced user-specific data that affect the Office experience

ROUND function a function that is used to round a number to a specific number of digits.

Row a horizontal set of cells that encompasses all the columns in a worksheet.

Run-time error occurs when VBA code is executed, displaying a description of the error.

S

Salvage value what an asset is estimated to be worth at the end of its useful life.

Sample population a subset of a population.

Sample variance a measure of how far the data in the sample are spread from the mean.

Scatter chart a chart that shows the relationship between numeric variables.

Scenario Manager allows you to manage scenarios by adding, deleting, editing, and viewing scenarios and to create scenario reports.

Scenario PivotTable report summarizes the results of various scenarios side by side in a PivotTable format.

Scenario Summary report lists the results of scenarios side by side, allowing the outcomes to be easily compared.

Scenario allows you to build a what-if analysis model that includes variable cells linked by one or more formulas or functions.

Scenario tool a tool that enables a user to calculate numerous outputs in other cells by referencing the target cell in formulas and functions.

ScreenTip a small box that provides a name or other information about the object to which you are pointing.

Scroll bar a form control that is linked to a specific cell. As the scroll bar slides left to right or up and down, the value in the linked cell increases or decreases accordingly. Also, a form control used in what-if analyses that allows you to change a number in a target cell location in single-unit increments.

Security a legal document that can be bought and sold and holds some financial value.

Separators indicate the distinction between the object container and the member of that container.

Shortcut menu a list of context-sensitive commands related to a selection that appears when you right-click.

Silverlight a powerful tool for creating interactive user experiences. It is a free plug-in powered by the .NET framework and is compatible with multiple browsers, devices, applications, and operating systems.

Simplex LP method a linear model in which the variables are not raised to any powers and no transcendent functions such as sine or cosine are used. A linear model can be charted as straight lines.

Skewness characterization of the degree of asymmetry of a distribution around its mean.

Slicer a visual control that allows you to quickly and easily filter your data in an interactive way; can replace filter icons in PivotCharts.

SLN function a function used to calculate the depreciation of an asset for a specified period using the fixed declining balance method.

Solver an add-in that helps to optimize a problem by manipulating the values for several variables with constraints that you determine.

Solver Answer report a report that lists the target cell and the changing cells with their corresponding original and final values for the problem, input variables, and constraints. In addition, the formulas, binding status, and slacks are given for each constraint.

Solver Limits Report a report that displays the achieved optimal value and all the input variables of the model with the optimal values. Additionally, the report displays the upper and lower bounds for the optimal value.

Solver Population Report a report that displays various statistical characteristics about the given model, such as how many variables and rows it contains.

Solver Sensitivity Report a report that provides information about how sensitive the solution is to small changes in the formula for the target cell. This report displays the shadow prices for the constraint — the amount that the objective function value changes per unit change in the constraint. This report can be created only if your Excel model does not contain integer or **Boolean** — the values 0 and 1 — constraints.

Source cell(s) the cell(s) that contain the data supplied to a function.

Sparkline a miniature chart embedded into cells on a spreadsheet, providing a way to graphically summarize a row or column of data in a single cell.

Spin button a form control that is linked to a specific cell. As the up and down arrows on the button are clicked, the value in the linked cell increases and decreases accordingly.

Spreadsheet a two-dimensional grid that can be used to model quantitative data and perform accurate and rapid calculations with results ranging from simple budgets to financial and statistical analyses.

Standard deviation the most commonly used method for determining the average spread of a data set from the mean. Mathematically, the standard deviation is calculated by taking the square root of the variance.

Standard error used to determine how accurately the sample mean predicts the population mean by dividing the standard deviation by the square root of the sample size.

Standard filter displays the values in the field that can be toggled on and off through the use of check boxes.

Static data data that has been manually calculated and then typed into a worksheet.

Statistics the practice of collecting, analyzing, and interpreting data.

Status threshold defined by the range between a high value and a low value as part of a KPI.

Structured reference a formula that refers to table columns by names that were generated when the table was created.

Sub procedure a VBA procedure that performs an action on your project or workbook.

SUBTOTAL Function a function that will only run calculations on the data that is in the subset when a filter is applied. Also, a function that can return any of 11 different values including all of the AutoSum functions, the product, standard deviation, and variance.

Sum the sum of all values in the sample.

SUM function a function that adds all of the numeric information in a specified range, list of numbers, list of cells, or any combination.

SUMIF function a function that sums a number of cells that meet a specified criteria.

SUMIFS function a function that sums a range of data, selecting data to total based on the criteria specified.

Summary variable data that is not categorical in nature and can be aggregated by summing, counting, or averaging.

Syntax the structure and order of the function and the arguments needed for Excel to run a function.

T

Table an organized grid of information, arranged in rows and columns.

Table style a predefined set of formatting properties that determine the appearance of a table.

Tabular format the presentation of information such as text and numbers in tables.

Target value a value that can be either another calculated field that resolves to a value or an absolute value as part of a KPI.

Tell me what you want to do a help tool in the title bar of Office applications that can launch commands in addition to accessing traditional help.

Template a workbook that provides a starting point for building other similar workbooks.

Text data can contain any combination of printable characters, including letters, numbers, and special characters available on any standard keyboard.

TEXT a text function that allows you to display numeric data as text in addition to using special formatting strings to display the text.

Text file a simple container of text data that is structured by the use of delimiters.

Text function a function that manages, manipulates, and formats text data.

Text length validation a type of data validation used to limit the number of characters that can be entered into a cell.

Text-to-speech an Excel feature that reads the values of text back to you. Headphones or speakers are required for this feature to work properly.

Theme a set of design elements such as fonts, styles, colors, and effects associated with a theme name that enables you to create professional, color-coordinated documents quickly.

Tiles a dynamic navigation strip in Power View allowing you to navigate through a series of charts on the basis of a particular value.

Time data data recognized by Excel as representing time; represented as a decimal value, where .1 is 144 minutes, .01 is 14.4 minutes, and so on.

Time validation a type of data validation that specifies that only time values can be entered into a cell.

TODAY function a function that is used to return the current date into a cell.

Toggle button a type of button that turns the feature on with one click and turns the feature off with a second click.

Touch mode applies to touch screen devices; the ribbon and shortcut menus are enlarged to make selecting commands with your fingertip easier.

Trace dependents a tool that automatically draws arrows from the active cell to its dependent cells.

Trace precedents a tool that automatically draws arrows from the precedent cells to the active cell.

Trendline a line that uses current data to show a trend or general direction of the data.

TRIM a text function that removes all spaces from text except for single spaces between words. Use TRIM on text that you have received from another application that may have irregular spacing.

Trusted Location a folder that has been identified in the Microsoft Office Trust Center as a safe location from which to open files that contain active code, including macros.

Two-variable data table a data table that can help you to analyze how changing the value of two variables affects the results of a formula.

Type an argument to indicate when the payments are due either at the beginning (1) or the end of a period (0). If type is omitted (because it is an optional argument), Excel assumes that the value is zero.

U

UPPER a text function that converts all characters in a string to uppercase.

USB drive a small and portable storage device, popular for moving files back and forth between a lab, office, and/or home computer.

V

Validation criteria constraints that limit what users are allowed to enter into a particular cell.

Variable a value stored in a cell and used in a formula or function. The value can be changed to see how the change affects other values. Also, space in a computer's memory that is given a name and is used to store a value of a specified data type.

Variable cost a cost that changes on the basis of how many products are sold or services are rendered.

Variance a calculation used in statistics to determine how far the data set varies from the mean.

VBA (Visual Basic for Applications) a powerful programming language that is part of most Microsoft Office products that users can use to implement a wide variety of enhancements to Microsoft Office applications.

Vertical multiples multiples that expand across the width of the container and wrap down the container in the available space. If not all multiples fit in the available space, a vertical scroll bar is also added.

Virtualization software that mimics Windows in order to run Office on a Mac.

Visual Basic Editor (VBE) the tool built into Microsoft Office that is used for creating and editing VBA.

Visual Basic for Applications (VBA) a computer programming language that is part of most Microsoft Office products that users can use to implement a wide variety of enhancements to Microsoft Office applications.

VLOOKUP function a function that matches a provided value in a table of data and returns a value from a subsequent column. It also helps to retrieve values located in another location and is used when your comparison values are located in a column vertically to the left of the data you want to find.

W

Watch Window an Excel feature that makes it possible to monitor cells the user considers important in a separate window.

Web query a method for importing data into a spreadsheet directly from a web page.

What-if analysis an analysis that changes values in a spreadsheet to explore all the various results.

White space space in a document or worksheet that does not contain data of any kind, allowing the user's eyes to rest.

Whole number validation a type of data validation which requires that only integer (whole number) values can be entered in a cell.

Workbook an Excel file that contains one or more worksheets.

Worksheet each instance of a spreadsheet; a grid of columns and rows in which data is entered.

X

XIRR function a function used to analyze a series of cash flows that are irregular or not periodic.

XML an acronym for Extensible Markup Language, which allows users to define their own tags in order to define the content of the document. Used for web documents and transmitting data between systems.

XML element includes the start and stop tags and everything in between them.

XML map the same as an XML schema in that it describes the structure of an XML document. Excel either creates an XML map on the basis of an existing schema or creates a default map.

XML schema describes the structure of an XML document in terms of what XML elements it will contain and their sequence.

XNPV function a function to determine the value of an investment or business by analyzing an irregular time series of incoming and outgoing cash flows.

Y

Yield The amount of annual interest, expressed as a percentage of the par value; determines how much investors will receive on their investment.

Yield to maturity (YTM) a yield calculation that takes into account the current market price and the time to maturity and assumes that coupon payments are reinvested at the bond's coupon rate.

Index

H

Headers, worksheets, 92–93
Help, **37**, 37–39
Hiding rows, 141–142
    filtering and, 344
Histograms, **649**, 649–650
HLOOKUP function, 301, **305**, 305–307, 305 (fig.)
Horizontal multiples, **732**, 733 (fig.)
HTML, **497**
Hypergeometric distribution, **662**, 662 (fig.)
Hyperlinks, **456**, 456–457
HYPGEOM.DIST function, 661–663

I

Icon sets, 137–139
IFERROR function, 313–316, **314**
IF function, **198**, 198 (table), 199–200, 200 (fig.),
        201 (table), **272**
    conjunction functions, 283–290
    creating, 273–275
    decision trees, 273, 282, 282 (fig.)
    nested, 277–283
    using, 272–277
    using elements in, 275–277
Images
    inserting, 33, 34
    resizing, 33, 34
    in worksheets, 119
Implicit calculated field, **705**
INDEX function, 307–312, **309**
INDIRECT function, **312**, 312–313
Inelastic, **553**
Inferential statistics, **636**
InfoPath, 2
Information, **328**
Input box, **773**
Input Message, **438**
Intercept coefficient value, **670**
Interest rate
    calculating with RATE, 601–603
    coupon, 612
    guessing, 602
    for PMT, 598
Internal rate of return, 619–620. *See also* IRR function
International Financial Reporting Standards, 623
Interquartile range, **644**
Interval data, **638**
INT function, **180**, 180 (table), 181–182
Investments
    bond analysis, 612–615
    irregular net present value, 618–619
    net present value analysis, 616–618
iPad, 2
IPMT function, **609**
Irregular internal rate of return, 621–622. *See also* XIRR function
Irregular net present value, 618–619. *See also* XNPV function
IRR function, **619**, 620
IRS, 622, 623
Iteration, **556**

K

Keyboard shortcuts, **17**, **57**
    copy and paste, 21–22, 65

cut, 65
    saving files, 19, 29
    undo and redo, 22
    worksheet navigation, 57–58
    zooming, scrolling, and navigating with, 16–18
Key performance indicators (KPIs), 690, 691
    defining, 708–709
    incorporating into dashboards, 719–720
    in PivotCharts, 721–723
    in PivotTables, 720–721
KeyTips, **17**
KPIs. *See* Key performance indicators
Kurtosis, **649**

L

Labels
    axes, 216, 228, 229, 229 (fig.)
    data, 230–231, 231 (fig.)
    dates on, 362
    dynamic, 750–751
    row labels from fields, 353
Landscape orientation, **94**
Left-aligned, 62
LEFT function, **189**, 189 (table), 190–191, **515**, 516,
        517 (fig.)
Legends, 230–231, 230 (fig.), 231 (fig.)
LEN function, **517**, 518 (fig.)
Linear forecast trendline, 234
Linear programming (LP), **568**
Linear trendline, 234
Line breaks, 63–64
Line charts, **220**, 220–221, 221 (fig.), 225
LinkedIn, 8
Links
    relative, 407
    to source data, 402–405
    between workbooks, 407–409
Lists, Most Recently Used, 14
List validation, **438**, 438–439
Live Preview, **26**
Loan analysis, 597–611
    additional costs, 598
    payment calculation, 600–601
    PMT function for, 598–601
    what-if analysis, 600
Local templates, **417**, 418–419
Logical functions, **197**, 197–200, 198 (table), 201 (table), **269**,
        269–290
    database functions, 298–301
    data retrieval, 308–313
    error handling in, 313–316
Logical operators, **269**, 269 (table)
Logical test, **269**
Logical truth tables
    AND, 284 (table)
    OR function, 285 (table)
Lookup and reference functions, **193**, 193–194, 193 (table)
LOOKUP functions, 301–307
Lookup tables, 748–749
Loops, **763**, 763–767
LOWER function, **513**
LP. *See* Linear programming
Lync. *See* Microsoft Skype

M

Macro buttons, 452–454
Macro Recorder, 760
Macros, **449**
   absolute references, 450–451
   adding to buttons, 452–454
   locations for storing, 449, 449 (table)
   modifying, 454–455
   relative references, 452
Macs, 3
Map visualizations, 735
Margins, 93–94
Mark as Final, 468–469
Markup languages, **497**
MATCH function, 307–309, **308**
Mathematical operators, **132**, 133 (table)
Math functions, 180–182, 180 (table)
   conditional, 296–298
Maturity, **612**
MAX function, 125, **128**, 128–129
Maximize, **6** (table)
Maximum, **649**
Mean, **639**, 640–641, **649**
Median, **639**, 640–641, **649**
MEDIAN function, **184**, 184 (table)
Merge & Center, **71**, 72
Merging cells, 71–72
Merging workbooks, 413–414
Message box, **768**
Metadata, **502**
Method, **754**
Microsoft Access, 2. *See also* Access
Microsoft account, 3
   Backstage and, 8
Microsoft Azure Marketplace, 701
Microsoft Excel, 2. *See also* Excel
Microsoft Office
   interface, 2–29
   programs in, 2
   sharing files between versions, 15
   versions, 2–3
Microsoft Office ProPlus, 2
Microsoft Office Trust Center, 449
Microsoft OneNote, 2
Microsoft Outlook, 2
Microsoft PowerPoint, 2. *See also* PowerPoint
Microsoft Power Query, 492
Microsoft Publisher, 2
Microsoft Query, **507**, 507–509
Microsoft Silverlight, 730
Microsoft Skype, 2
Microsoft Surface, 31
Microsoft Word, 2. *See also* Word
   opening, 3–5
MID function, **522**, 523 (fig.)
MIN function, 125, **128**, 128–129
Minimize, **6** (table)
Minimum, **649**
Mini toolbar, **35**, 36
Misleading charts, 215
Mixed cell reference, **165**, 169–172, 170 (fig.)
Mixed costs, **542**

Mode, **639**, 640–641, **649**
MODE function, **184**
MODE.MULT function, **184**
MODE.SNGL function, **184**, 184 (table)
Module, **756**
Most Recently Used list (MRU), **14**
Moving average, **650**, 651
Moving cells, 68
MRU. *See* Most Recently Used list
MRU Templates, 15
Multiples, **732**, 733

N

Name Box, 173, 174
Named ranges, **165**, 173–178
   3-D, 396
   creating from selections, 176, 177
   creating with Name Box, 173, 174
   in formulas, 176, 177
   modifying, 174, 175
   naming conventions, 173
   spanning multiple worksheets, 396
   using, 175–176
   when to use, 178
Name Manager, **174**, 175, 175 (fig.)
Naming files, 12
Navigation
   changing tools, 465
   keyboard shortcuts, 16–18
   workbooks, 55–59, 455–461
   worksheets, 56–59
Navigation pane, 23
Negative KPI, **708**
Nested IF function, **277**, 277–283
   conjunction functions, 283–290
   decision tree, 282, 282 (fig.)
Net book value, **622**, 626
Net present value, 616–618. *See also* NPV function
NETWORKDAYS function, **532**, 532–534
Nominal data, **637**
Nominal yield, **612**
Nonbinding constraint, **573**
Noncontiguous cell range, **65**, 67, 67 (fig.)
Nonprintable characters, 514
Normal distribution, **652**, 652 (fig.)
   charting, 654–655
Normal view, **86**
NORM.DIST function, 652–654
NOT function, **283**
   within IF functions, 286
NOW function, **186**, 186 (table), 187
Nper, **598**
NPER function, **603**, 604
NPV function, **616**
Number Format Dialog Box Launcher, 32–33
Number formatting, 105–107, 106 (table)
   accounting *versus* currency, 108
   with Dialog Box Launcher, 32–33
   formulas and, 276
   negative values, 108
Numeric data, **62**

Print Preview, **89**, 89–90
Print range, 94–95
Print titles, 91
Private data, 495
Probability, **636**
   using BINOM.DIST for, 656–657
   using EXPON.DIST for, 658–659
   using NORM.DIST, 653–654
Probability density function, **653**
Probability distribution, **636**, 651
   functions for, 652–664
Project Explorer, **755**
PROPER function, **513**, 520
Properties, **753**
   chart position, 217–218
   xlVeryHidden, 772–773
Properties window, **755**
Protected View, **15**
Protecting worksheets, 461–469, 776
   for dashboards in production, 727–728
Pseudo code, **287**
Pv, **599**
PV function, **613**, 613–614, 616

Q

Quartile, **643**
Query, **492**
   web, 492–496
Quick Access Toolbar, **18**
   customizing, 7
   keyboard shortcuts and, 17
   KeyTips for, 17
   saving file with, 18, 19
   undo and redo buttons, 22, 23
Quick Analysis tool, **215**, 239, 240
Quick Save, 55

R

R1RC reference style, **312**, 313
RAND function, 638–639
Random sample, **636**
Range, **641**, **649**
Rate, **598**
RATE function, **601**, 601–603
Ratio data, **638**
Raw data, **328**
Reading Mode, 15
Recommended Charts, **216**
Records, **53**
Redo, 22–23
References
   3-D, 395–397
   absolute macro, 450–451
   relative macro, 452
   templates and, 422
Regression analysis, **669**, 669–672
Regression equation, 670, 671
RELATED function, 703
Relational data, **694**
Relational database, **2**, **505**
Relationships
   in data model, 702–703
   viewing with Power Pivot, 699–700

Relative addressing, 132–133
Relative cell reference, 132–133, **165**, 166–168, 168 (fig.)
Relative links, 407
Relative macro references, **452**
Remove Duplicates button, **525**, 526
Replacing text, 23, 24
Required rate of return (RRR), **616**
Residuals, 672
Resizing
   charts, 217, 219
   images, 33, 34
Restore Down, **6** (table)
Return on investment (ROI), **612**
Ribbon, **5**
   Access, 5 (fig.)
   adding Developer tab to, 450, 498, 499, 746–747
   buttons, 6 (fig.)
   common interfaces, 8
   Excel, 5 (fig.)
   Font group, 24, 25
   Office 2016, 5–6
   pinning open, 6–7
   PowerPoint, 5 (fig.)
   running macros from, 453
   tabs, 6
   Word, 5 (fig.)
Ribbon Display Options, **6** (table)
Ribbon groups, 6
Right-aligned, 62
RIGHT function, **517**, 518 (fig.)
Roaming settings, **14**
ROI. *See* Return on investment
Rotating text, 112
Rotation of charts, 237
ROUNDDOWN function, 180, 180 (table)
ROUND function, **180**, 180 (table), 183
ROUNDUP function, 180, 180 (table)
Row labels
   choosing fields for, 353
   dates on, 362
Rows, **53**
   adjusting height, 75–76, 78
   AutoFit for height, 76, 77
   banded, 333 (fig.), 334
   deleting, 73–75
   hiding, 141–142
   hiding headings, 459–460
   inserting, 73–75
   selecting, 73
   total, 129–131
RRR. *See* Required rate of return
R-squared value, **670**
Run-time error, **762**

S

Salvage value, **623**, 626
Sample population, **636**
Sample variance, **649**
Scaling, 93–94
Scatter charts, **222**, 222–223, 223 (fig.), 225, 654–655
   relationship visualization with, 667

changing styles, 331
creating, 330–331
data extraction from, 340
lookup, 748–749
naming, 331
PivotTable from, 348–350
Table styles, **121**, 121–123
Table Tools Design tab, 129, 130 (fig.)
Tabular format, **105**
Target value, **708**
absolute, 708–709
calculated, 709–710
Taskbar, starting Word, 4
Tax rates, 332
Tell me what you want to do box, **27**, 28–29
Templates, **417**
creating from workbook, 420–421
external references and, 422
MRU, 15
online, 419–420
using existing, 418–420
Terms of service, 11
Text
aligning in cells, 111
in charts, 235, 236, 236 (fig.)
cleansing, 189
copying and pasting, 20, 21–22
date data reconstruction from, 529–530
entering, 20, 21–22
finding and replacing, 23, 24
rotating, 112
selecting, 21, 25
wrapping, in cells, 63–64, 64 (fig.)
Text data, **62**, **502**
Text files, **502**, 502–504
formats, 503 (table)
TEXT function, **532**, 532–534
Text functions, 188–192, **189**, **512**
data cleansing with, 512–518, 521–523
wizards and Flash Fill *versus*, 525
Text Import Wizard, 503
Text length validation, **442**, 442–443
Text-to-speech, 445–448, **446**
Themes, **123**
workbook, 123–124
Tiled view option, 406, 406 (fig.), 407 (fig.)
Tiles, **733**, 734
Time
decimal portions of days, 110
formatting, 109–110
Time data, **62**
Time validation, 441, **441**
TODAY function, 178, **186**, 186 (table), 187
Toggle buttons, **24**
Total row, 129–131
Touch mode, **59**
Touch Mode button, 6–7
Touch screens, Excel 2016, 59
Trace dependents, **432**, 432–433
Trace precedents, **432**, 432–433
Trendlines, **232**, 233, 233 (fig.)
exponential, 234
Trends, 234

Trig functions, 180–181
TRIM function, **513**
Troubleshooting
formulas, 135
functions, 201–203
VBA, 135
Trusted Location, **449**, 450
Two-period moving average trendline, 234
Two-variable data tables, **552**, 552–555
Type, **599**

U

Undo, 22–23
Ungrouping, 387, 389
UPPER function, **513**
USB drive, **10**

V

Validation criteria, **437**
Variable cells, 566
Variable costs, **542**
Variables, **545**, **764**
continuous, 637
declaring in VBA, 764–765
discrete, 637
grouping, 350
summary, 350
Variance, **641**
covariance, 664
sample, 649
VBA. *See* Visual Basic for Applications
VBE. *See* Visual Basic Editor
Vertical multiples, **732**
Virtualization, **3**
Visual Basic Editor (VBE), **755**, 755–756
Visual Basic for Applications (VBA), **449**, **752**
for button controls, 761
components of, 752–754
conditional statements in, 768–769
custom functions, 757–759
data types, 764
formatting code, 759–760
loops, 763–767
modifying macros with, 454–455
procedure assignment to events, 769–772
protecting code with password, 776–777
slicer filters and, 760–761
special object names, 753
troubleshooting and debugging, 762–763
variable declaration, 764–765
VLOOKUP function, **193**, 193 (table), 301, **302**
with approximate match, 302–303
with exact match, 303–305, 304 (fig.)
form controls and, 748–749
scroll bar with, 545
using, 193–195

W

Watch Window, **435**, 436–437
Web queries, **492**
importing data with, 492–493
modifying, 494–495
saving, 495–496